Business Executive's Handbook

Business Executive's Handbook

Edited by

STANLEY M. BROWN

Associate Editors

LILLIAN DORIS
EDITH J. FRIEDMAN
JOHN D. SMYERS
BERTRAND R. CANFIELD

Revised by

LILLIAN DORIS

FOURTH EDITION

New York
PRENTICE-HALL, INC.
1953

L. C. Cat. Card No. 53-8347

PRINTED IN THE UNITED STATES OF AMERICA

Preface

The *Business Executive's Handbook* is designed to provide, within the covers of one handy volume, direct and practical answers to the business man's questions and problems.

The information contained in the Handbook is specific and to the point. Forms, tables, short cuts, listings of facts, ideas, outlines of procedures—these will save the business man time, trouble, and expense. Whether the problem to be dealt with relates to *Selling, Advertising, Credit, Insurance, Direct Mail*—to mention only a few of the subjects included—the Handbook supplies reliable information in concise form.

This fourth edition is a complete revision, printed from entirely new type, just like a brand-new book. The sections have been rearranged into more compact units and presented in related groupings. Most of the sections have been expanded to bring in new ideas, procedures, and practices, and all of the tabular matter and statistics have been brought up to date. New subjects of interest to the business man have been added. Thus, two completely new sections, one on *Employee Benefit Plans* and one on *Raising Capital to Finance Current Needs,* have been included. Two new subsections —*What Every Business Man Should Know About Accounting* and *How to Use Accounting Results for Executive Control*—have been added to accounting material previously covered.

We are grateful to the scores of people who reviewed the parts of the book that describe the practices of their companies, and repeat our acknowledgment to the hundreds of business men throughout the country who contributed generously of their time and experience in the preparation of the original edition and previous revisions.

STANLEY M. BROWN
LILLIAN DORIS

Contents

(A detailed table of contents will be found at the beginning of each section.)

SECTION I

Successful Selling By Direct Mail

I. HOW TO SELL BY DIRECT MAIL

2. TESTING DIRECT-MAIL ADVERTISING

3. COPY WRITING FOR DIRECT-MAIL SELLING

4. COST OF DIRECT-MAIL SELLING

5. SUCCESSFUL DIRECT-MAIL IDEAS

6. HOW TO GET AND BUILD MAILING LISTS

7. HOW TO WRITE SALES LETTERS

8. SALES LETTER CAMPAIGNS

9. DEVICES THAT MAKE SALES LETTERS WORK

SECTION I

Successful Selling by Direct Mail

1. HOW TO SELL BY DIRECT MAIL

What products can be sold by mail. Sooner or later in the life of most business concerns, the question arises as to the advisability of using the mails for direct sales—that is, for soliciting actual orders as distinguished from using the mail to influence a sale that will be closed later by a salesman. If a product can be sold at all, it can be sold by mail. However, this fact is of academic interest only, inasmuch as businessmen are primarily interested in profitable methods of selling their products.

Judging by the type of product that has been sold profitably by mail, without the aid of a salesman, it can be concluded that products or services with the following characteristics are suitable for profitable mail-order sales:

1. The product or service has a high degree of uniqueness in that it is totally different from others or stands alone in some respect. Thus a product that could easily be picked up at any corner store would be difficult to sell by mail; whereas a proposition such as the Book-of-the-Month Club plan of selling books would, because of its high degree of uniqueness, make a good mail-order proposition. It does not follow, however, that everyday products cannot be sold by mail. The tremendous success of the Green Brothers, of Denver, Colorado, in selling quality food products by mail shows that a product which is ordinarily purchasable at any store can, through uniqueness of quality, combined with uniqueness of packaging, be profitably sold by mail.

2. The sales appeal is not so limited that lists of prospects to be solicited by mail cannot be compiled.

3. The product or service has a definite price and can be sold on open account, cash with order, C.O.D., by free trial, or on approval.

4. The product or service to be sold lends itself to easy description.

5. The price is not too low to absorb the cost of the mail-order campaign and delivery. Products that cost the consumer less than $2 or $3 generally are not suitable for mail-order sale. (See pages 32 *et seq.* for cost of direct-mail selling.)

6. The price is not so high that the prospect will refuse to make the expenditure without seeing what he is getting. Thus, houses, high-priced cars, certain machinery, and the like, are not suitable mail-order items.

Plans for direct-mail selling. One of three plans can be chosen for direct-mail selling: the continuous plan, the wear-out plan, or the campaign plan. The plan that should be selected depends upon the price of the product, whether it is an established or new product, whether it is used continuously, the size of the market, and similar factors.

Under the *continuous* plan, advertisements are mailed throughout the year without any particular continuity of message. Such plans are adopted particularly by retailers offering different products from time to time, or advertisers who, like parts dealers, have definite, comparatively small lists of customers, and who sell products that are used constantly.

The *wear-out* plan is used in the sale of a single product that can be sold to a number of lists. The advertiser mails to one list and continues his periodic mailings until the returns from any one list are insufficient to pay for the mailings. He has then "worn-out" the list, and turns to another to repeat the process.

The *campaign* plan comprises a number of related mailings all directed toward a final climactic mailing. Taken separately, they may only describe a feature of the product; taken together, the mailings tell the entire story. Advertisers with complicated products will usually prefer the campaign plan.

Steps in planning direct-mail selling. Each of the following steps must be considered in planning the direct-mail campaign:

1. Know and use the facts concerning the market for the product or service.
2. Select the lists.
3. Plan the advertising budget to be spent on direct mail.
4. Time the direct advertising to the individual marketing problem.

5. Select the basic theme for the promotional activity.
6. Decide upon the form of piece that will best present the message.
7. Prepare the advertising piece.
8. Test the proposed mailing and, if results warrant continuation, proceed with the entire mailing.

Each of these items is discussed below.

Know and use facts. In some phases of selling and advertising it is exceedingly important that the merchandiser discover the character of individuals and groups composing the market before a campaign is undertaken. In the field of direct-mail selling, however, a detailed investigation in advance is not absolutely essential. The reason for this difference is the fact that, at a comparatively low cost, a test mailing can be made, and the profitability of the venture proved. Similarly, while other types of marketing may require a thorough analysis of competitors' activities to discover strong and weak points in their products, in direct-mail selling the advertiser's general knowledge of his competitors' products is ordinarily sufficient to help him develop a distinctive basic selling idea for his product. His direct-mail tests will tell him whether the selling idea he has chosen to talk about in his letter is the correct one.

Once direct-mail selling has proved a profitable method of distributing a company's product, very little special study in the form of market surveys is necessary, provided, of course, that there is an alertness to the ever-changing moods and habits of buyers, and that testing is made a prerequisite of every large mailing.

Select the lists. The choice of lists is the most important factor in direct mail. The most expertly conceived and elaborately prepared direct-mail campaign will fail if the lists are not good, while even a poorly executed campaign may bring results if the lists are excellent.

The subject of the mailing list is too important for brief treatment. It is therefore given separate treatment, beginning at page 49.

Plan the advertising budget for direct mail. The usual methods of budgeting expenditures for space and other advertising are discussed on page 152. In the direct-mail field the only sound approach to the question of how much to spend on advertising is, first, to have a thorough knowledge of the costs, and, second, to test constantly. The mail-order seller must have known facts regarding the results of his advertising. He buys, with a given advertisement or series of advertisements, a certain number of direct sales or direct sales leads. Thus there is a direct relation between the cost and the results obtained. While this cost is not constant, the advertiser can, over a period of time, find upper and lower limits between which he may expect to find his selling cost. He will then appropriate for advertising an amount set by multiplying the number of sales he believes necessary by the cost per sale—usually taking the upper figure.

Time the direct-mail advertising. Proper timing of the promotion effort is essential to obtaining the best results from direct-mail advertising. Such factors as seasonal variations of the particular business, customers' buying habits, and the like, must be considered. Notice how the intensive campaign of the Southern States Iron Roofing Co., described on page 104, was planned to reach the prospects at the most favorable time. It is interesting to observe that, in the original tests made before the most favorable buying period, the letter that was selected to be used in this campaign pulled 11 per cent inquiries. When it was mailed to the entire list four months later, at the most favorable time, the response was 14 per cent.

Aside from timing in relation to individual marketing problems, timing in relation to general marketing problems must be considered. Experience has proved that mailings should not be undertaken in times of national crisis, such as a stock crash or a declaration of war, when the public is absorbed in a presidential election, before a holiday, and immediately before or after important income tax payment dates.

Select the basic theme for the promotional activity. Some appeal must be selected to form the major theme of the advertisement. To arrive at the appeal, or theme, it is necessary to study: (1) the product itself, (2) the ways it has been or can be used, and (3) the users of the product. From the following examples of themes that have been used in successful direct-mail campaigns, it is evident that, in arriving at the theme, the creators of the advertising matter in each case had analyzed carefully each of the three basic sources and had selected one that had a basic appeal and was capable of effective copy and art treatment.

Purpose	*Theme and Execution*
Selling wire fences	Your local dealer can give you a good tip. Acting on knowledge gained from a survey of the agricultural market, to the effect that farmers rely upon the advice of local dealers, Republic Steel Corporation built a campaign around the theme of taking a tip from a dealer. The direct-mail piece was a four-page broadside, carrying on the address side a photograph of the local dealer, with a caption, "Take a tip from (and the name of the dealer)." The first spread was a letter to the prospect signed by the dealer; the inside contained illustrations covering features of the product and a build-up for the dealer. The free offer of a booklet was used to bring the prospect to the dealer's store.
Selling advertising space in low-priced popular magazines	The magazines appeal to the average woman and therefore are a good advertising medium. A booklet, prepared by Fawcett Publications, Inc., told the story of "Myrtle," the average woman. The booklet, when folded, resembled a woman's handbag.
Selling accounting machines	Leading companies are using National machines. The National Cash Register Company used this testimonial theme, carrying the heading "Does it with Nationals." A series of folders, each one playing up the name of a well-known company that does its work with National machines, was sent to businessmen.
Selling fire insurance	The company is an old, established one whose prestige and reputation assure excellent service. Three letters offering a booklet entitled "You're in Good Company" were prepared by the Merrimack Mutual Fire Insurance Company and distributed to prospects by its agents.

Decide upon the form of advertising. In deciding upon the form that the direct-mail advertising will take to express the theme selected and carry the message effectively, the advertiser has a number of types upon which to draw. Broadly classified, they are: (1) letters, (2) cards, (3) leaflets, (4) folders, (5) broadsides, (6) booklets, (7) self-mailers, (8) brochures, (9) catalogues, (10) house organs, and (11) novelties.

Any one of these forms may be used also for the *follow-up*—the advertisement that is sent in response to an inquiry. Depending on the circumstances, a single piece (a letter), or a whole series of mailings may be used to give the desired information. Each form presents its particular problem of mailing, as well as of the reply form to be used with it. The various forms are discussed briefly below.

In addition to deciding upon the form the advertising piece shall take, the direct-mail advertiser must also decide whether a premium shall be offered as an inducement to the prospective customer.

The sales letter. Letters, of course, are the most common direct-mail medium because they come closest to personal selling. If the purpose of the mailing is to get immediate orders or inquiries, letters are generally used. The subject of "How to Write Sales Letters" is treated fully in a separate section, beginning at page 58.

In the preparation of letters for large-quantity distribution, one of the following processes may be used: (1) multigraph, (2) multilith, (3) super-process, (4) printing, or (5) automatic typewriter.

Multigraphing. Multigraphing is one of the common forms of producing letters for direct mail. In this process the letters are set in type similar to that used by a typewriter, and placed on a circular drum. The drum rotates and prints through a ribbon. The final effect is much like typewriting. Up to 6,000 copies can be produced per hour. Facsimile typewritten letters may be personalized on a typewriter, by the use of a matching ribbon, or may be filled in on the addressing machine. See also page 408.

Multilith—offset printing. The photo-offset process has come into prominence in recent years as a method of preparing direct-mail letters. For a description of this process, see page 212. Up to 5,800 reproductions can be made per hour. Fill-ins can be made as in the case of multigraphing.

Super-process—flat-bed process. The super-process, or flat-bed process, is produced on a flat-bed press through a ribbon with typewriter type. It produces a personalized letter at from one-third to one-half less cost than the automatic typewriter (Hooven or Autotypist), and at from 10 per cent to 20 per cent more cost than by multigraph. The type simulates typewriter type exactly. Certain of the characters are deliberately uneven, and the periods punch through the paper exactly as with the typewriter. The fill-in is done on a typewriter having the same type and ribbon as the letter. While automatic typewriting requires first-class postage, multigraph, multilith, and flat-bed letters may be mailed at the third-class letter rates. See page 501.

Printing. Some firms selling by direct mail have their letters printed. This method has the advantage of lower cost, inasmuch as the letterhead may be printed at the same time as the body of the letter. In the long run, a considerable saving may be effected, but it is generally agreed that for best results the processed letter (multigraph, multilith, super-process) is advisable.

Automatic typewriter. The Hooven, Autotypist, Robotyper, and Flexowriter methods use automatic typewriters. For a description of the process, see page 409. Letters produced in this way are original typewritten letters with perfect fill-ins. The process is much slower and more costly than any of the other methods of duplication mentioned. As indicated above, such letters must be mailed at the first-class letter rate.

Personalizing the direct-mail sales letter. The object of personalizing sales letters is not to delude the reader into believing that the letter was produced solely for him, but rather to get the attention of the reader. These methods have been used successfully to personalize sales letters:

1. Fill-in of salutation on the typewriter or by stencils.
2. Insertion of the reader's name in the body of the letter. This step has been done perfectly by letter-service organizations, in processed letters.
3. Brush-scripting of the name of the prospect at the top of the letter, as in the illustration on page 125.

Four-page letters. The direct-mail advertiser who wishes to send a long message, without at the same time using enclosures such as folders, leaflets, circulars, and the like, may find the four-page letter suitable for the purpose.

The first page is usually devoted to the letter, which is no different from the single-sheet letter except that there must be some tie-up between the letter and the inside pages. The copy and illustrations on the inside pages of the four-page letter generally contain the material that is to convince the reader and arouse in him the desire to do what the advertiser wants him to do. The fourth page of the letter may be blank, may be of the same nature as the second and third page, or may form the address section of a self-mailer. For organizations engaging in a considerable amount of institutional advertising—real estate companies, for example—the fourth page may be used for institutional advertising; that is, to keep the name of the advertiser before the public, to make known the qualities of the firm and the service offered by it, and the like.

Postal cards and mailing cards. The government postal card, carrying a message that is flashed to the prospect, has proved a useful medium, especially for retailers. Postal cards have been used extensively by local merchants to announce weekly sales and specials, seasonal items, new departments or services, and to keep the name of the firm before its customers. The wholesaler has also used postal cards for somewhat similar purposes. Private mailing cards have also been used to introduce more elaborate mailing pieces and to vary a campaign composed of more detailed selling messages. Copy and illustrations can be handled effectively even by smaller advertisers if they are equipped with proper machines for card reproduction. To be effective, solid type should be avoided on cards. Simple illustrations that catch the eye, headlines that tie in with the copy, and short sentences help to get the card read.

For postal information as to government cards and private mailing cards, see pages 511-513.

Leaflets. Any small-sized sheet, printed on one or both sides, and folded, is a leaflet. When used in direct-mail advertising, it must be designed to fit the size of the envelope into which it is to go. Because the leaflet is small, it must overcome the disadvantage of size by excellence of copy, good typography, and attractive layout. The leaflet, if used to supplement a letter, should support the sales message. Thus, a leaflet designed to supplement a letter offering the sale of stores and a garage was made up as follows: page 1, an attractive heading and indication of the nature of the property; page 2, a map showing the exact location of the property; page 3, text showing the details of location, the reasons why the location is desirable, and other information as to size, construction, heating, rents obtainable, and the prospect for increase in value; and page 4, institutional copy.

The leaflet is used frequently in direct-mail advertising for announcements of special events. It is particularly suitable in selling an inexpensive item, since its cost is not great. Furthermore, it can be inserted easily in an envelope.

Folders. A folder is larger than a leaflet, printed usually on heavier stock, and folded more than once. Because of the variety of sizes that the folder may take, it can be used separately or as an envelope enclosure to supplement a letter. A complete story may be told in a folder. The reader should be able to open the folder naturally and follow the illustrations and copy without trouble. Three thoughts should be kept in mind in deciding upon the size of the folder and the arrangement of its folds: (1) keep the idea simple; (2) select a size that cuts economically from a standard-size sheet; and (3) consider the envelope into which it is to go.

Broadsides. An enlarged folder, about 19 × 25 inches in size or larger, is often called a "broadside." Usually it is designed as a self-mailing piece.

The broadside is used to give a smashing impression of a single idea or to tell a lengthy story in picture or type. Because of the variety of folds that are possible, and the combination of color and illustration that may be used, the broadside possesses a high degree of adaptability and variability. To carry out its purpose of a smashing impression, its text must be concise, its illustrations simple, and its copy not crowded. The broadside, nevertheless, must tell a complete sales story. It must attract the prospect's attention to the outside and maintain the interest with each step of the unfolding process.

It is necessary to keep in mind that the broadside must be suitable for the mailbag. If, when folded, the broadside is larger than the general run of mail, it may be delivered torn, folded again in half, or curled up. The following sizes are best suited for mailing: 9½ × 6¼ inches, or 9½ × 4⅙ inches, folded from a sheet 19 × 25 inches or 25 × 38 inches; or 8 × 5½ inches, folded from a sheet 22 × 32 inches.

Booklets. A booklet is a small book whose pages are in multiples of four to permit binding as a book by stitching, stapling, or glue. The term, however, has been applied to a multitude of different kinds of advertising pieces from a small bound insert to a large handbook. The booklet is used to elaborate and impress a point that requires considerable space for its presentation. It tells a complete story of the product or service.

Booklets have been used for the following purposes:

1. As an aid to salesmen.
2. To create inquiries.
3. To answer inquiries.
4. To instruct customers on the use of a product.
5. For trade and consumer sales promotion.
6. To promote group interests.
7. General propaganda.

The size, kind of paper, quality of cover, and extent to which color and illustration will be employed vary with the purpose of the booklet and the amount of money available for its production. The person planning the booklet should keep in mind that too large a booklet may be wasteful; one that is too small may not offer enough information; one with too much copy may discourage the reader; and one with too many pictures may be interesting but, because of lack of copy, not persuasive enough to bring results.

Self-mailers. A self-mailer is prepared for mailing with a portion of the first page given over to the address. The mailing piece is held together at the open fold by a seal or a cancelled postage stamp. Leaflets, folders, broadsides, and booklets may take the form of a self-mailer. In designing self-mailers, care must be used to see that the two sides of the folder—that is, the address side and the back—are kept absolutely distinct to avoid confusion. The outside of the self-mailer must pique the prospect's curiosity so that he will break the seal and open the folder. An illustration and a tie-in phrase or a single word, or a photograph, will lead the prospect to open the folder. Testimonials, a list of the uses of the product, or directions for use, as, for example, recipes, frequently fill the back of the self-mailer. These mailing pieces may also carry enclosures, which should be fastened to the folder with a paster, not a stapler.

Brochures. Beautiful, de luxe booklets, prepared at considerable cost, are generally termed *brochures*. They are commonly used whenever it is necessary to make an impression on the reader. Business houses, advertising agencies, investment dealers, and others use them as a sort of window-dressing device.

Catalogues. Catalogues that are designed to sell products to wholesalers, retailers, or consumers make buying possible without a personal inspection of the goods. Along with the description of the merchandise, there are usually an illustration and text presentation of the benefits of the product, data on various methods of using the product, and convincing copy on consumer satisfaction that the product offers through its quality, construction, and the like. Thus the catalogue not only lists, describes, and illustrates the merchandise offered, but does a selling job as well. The catalogue may or may not show the price. Frequently prices are offered in a separate listing. To meet the problem of changes in items, prices, and other data that are included in the catalogue, some firms prefer to prepare less elaborate catalogues and issue them more frequently.

If the company has a diversified line of products, it may handle the catalogue problem in one of the following ways:

1. Issue a wide range of separate catalogues.
2. Issue departmentalized or sectionalized catalogues.
3. Provide loose-leaf catalogues with supplements showing changes.
4. Prepare a portfolio consisting of a folder or envelope in which loose sheets are conveniently filed.

Where catalogues are prepared at infrequent intervals, bulletins are generally issued from time to time to keep the catalogue up to date.

The catalogue may serve to aid the company's salesmen, develop inquiries and convert them into sales, sell special groups or interests, and sell the consumer direct.

House organs. A house organ is a publication issued periodically by a firm for the purpose of maintaining contacts, creating goodwill, and establishing a favorable attitude toward the organization so that the reader will give preference to the firm when he is in need of its product or service. It is not designed to obtain direct, immediate action.

House organs fall into four main types:

1. Sales department house organs. These are prepared essentially for the salesmen. Information and ideas for increasing sales are passed on to the sales force through the house organ.
2. Dealer house organs. These aim at developing goodwill among dealers and maintaining communication between the manufacturer and the dealer.
3. Buyer house organs. These are designed to create a favorable attitude toward the house and to increase the use of its products.
4. Employee house organs. These are prepared to promote goodwill within the organization.

Dealer house organs and buyer house organs offer the advertiser an opportunity to aid the sale of goods by building goodwill among sales outlets and by passing on to the buyer information that will help keep him satisfied with his purchase and content to repeat or replace it in the future.

Novelties. In the field of direct advertising, novel forms are constantly being introduced. The pop-up, animated cards and models are only a few of the novelties that have been used.

The most common advertising novelties are the blotter and the calendar. Wherever possible, the advertising blotter should carry a message that will be remembered. Timely features increase the value of the blotter, for they give the advertiser an added excuse for mailing his sales message to his prospect. A calendar is often used, most commonly a one-month calendar plate, printed as part of the advertisement. As an envelope stuffer, a blotter travels "postage free," because the stamp that carries a letter or bill is usually sufficient for the blotter as well.

Calendar advertising is institutional advertising, and its purpose is to make the advertiser's name familiar to buyers. Proper presentation of calendars is highly important, because the manner of giving often determines whether the calendar will be hung in a prominent position or stowed away out of sight.

Premiums. Almost all people are interested in receiving something for nothing. That is why direct-mail advertisers make lavish use of premiums, spending millions of dollars a year on them. Advertisers play upon the human trait of wanting something for nothing almost to the extent that they play upon the prospect's inherent curiosity. When premiums are offered in combination with the sale of an item, the customer is usually permitted to keep the premium even though he returns the item. These premiums should tie in closely with the product being offered for sale. Otherwise, a prospect who has no interest in the product might place an order only to get the premium, with no thought of keeping the product.

Premiums add considerably to the cost of direct-mail selling. A test, therefore, should be conducted to compare the pull of the product when offered with a premium with its pull when offered without a premium. Unless the test clearly indicates that the number of sales resulting from the premium offer more than justifies the additional expense, the premium should not be offered. It is frequently possible to cut the expense by reducing the cost of the premium without diminishing its appeal. For example, the pull of a 50-page premium booklet is substantially as strong as the pull of a 100-page booklet because the appeal is in the subject matter, not the size, of the booklet.

Reply forms. The selection of a reply form must be made in all cases where the objective of the mailing is to obtain orders or inquiries, or ascertain in some measure the success of the mailing. Here is a list of the ways in which the reply can be facilitated:

1. Enclose a separate business reply card.
2. Attach the business reply card to the booklet, folder, or mailing piece with a seal, or by means of slits like a picture in a photograph album.
3. Provide for a tear-off reply card on the letterhead, folder, or other mailing piece.
4. Use a business reply envelope.
5. Provide a card, coupon, blank, or order form to be returned in a business reply envelope.
6. Use a combination letter and return envelope, especially for letters requesting a remittance with order. Usually the combination letter and envelope is a patented device in which the letter and envelope are one piece, with the place at which the envelope is to be torn off indicated by markings.

The return card must tell the entire story of its purpose so that, if it becomes separated from the enclosure, it will be clearly understood. It should be attractive and simple, with plenty of room for signature and address.

The envelope. Without losing sight of the postal regulations with regard to envelopes, it is possible to make the envelope help in the selling job. A few examples will illustrate how this can be done. Nunn-Busch Shoe Company of Milwaukee used a cellophane envelope to enclose a four-color-process promotion broadside. While permitting full visibility of the enclosure, the envelope added to the general appearance and interest value of the broadside. Special permission to use this type of envelope had to be secured from Washington, D. C.

The National Sportsman, Inc., Boston publisher of sporting magazines, tested a plain envelope against one in which the entire back of the envelope was covered with an attractive photograph of a lake-and-woods scene printed in cool green. The pictured envelope pulled 3.386 per cent cash orders for subscriptions, while the plain envelope brought 2.976 per cent. The larger returns more than paid for the cost of the envelopes.

The Book-of-the-Month Club found that on a mailing to teachers the response was doubled, and on a mailing to golfers the response was almost trebled, by writing the prospect's name in brush script across the outside of the envelope.

Some advertisers have made third-class mail pay well by making type talk on the envelope. With an interesting flash or message on the envelope, they attract the attention of the reader and arouse his curiosity as to the contents of the envelope. Others have used a mailing with an outside window envelope to increase results. The enclosure, of course, contains the name of the person to whom it is addressed, and this fill-in, showing through the window, is what attracts the attention of the recipient. The letter, of course, must hold the attention once it has been attracted.

Where successive mailings are to be made, attention must be paid to varying the style of the envelope in order to give each mailing distinction, and to prevent prospects from recognizing the sender of the material before he opens the envelope. Variety can be achieved by changing the color, shape, style, arrangement of name and return address, or by using a different flash or message.

Letterheads. If successive letters are to be sent to the same list, variety in the use of letterheads is as essential as variety in the use of envelopes. Changes in color, style, and size of the letterhead increase the likelihood that the copy will be read. Many firms experienced in direct-mail advertising find that occasionally it is worth while to dispense with the letterhead entirely; instead, they place the company name and address at the bottom of the letter, starting the letter with the selling message, with a flash, or with an illustration that ties up with the message.

Preparing the advertising piece. After the form that the advertising piece will take has been selected, the actual preparation is begun. The steps in putting together the direct-mail advertisement vary, of course, with the working processes of the individual, and with the facilities available in the advertising department. The usual steps are:

1. Make a trial dummy of the booklet, leaflet, or whatever form the advertisement is to take, mapping out the illustrations and indicating the headlines. In this step consideration should be given to the size of the mailing piece, its mailing weight, and the cost of mailing. For economy, the size of the sheet used should be standard or of a size that will cut from a standard sheet without waste. For information as to mailing methods and costs, see the "Postal Guide" at pages 485 et seq. For information as to paper stocks, see page 238.
2. Determine the size and face of type that will be used and the kind of illustration.
3. Select the paper stock suitable for the job.
4. Have the illustrations made.
5. Write the copy to fit the space.
6. Have plates made of the illustrations, if necessary.
7. Have type set for copy.
8. When proof of copy is returned, make paste-up dummy, allowing space for illustrations.
9. Submit dummy and corrected proof of copy to the printer for final revised proof.
10. Correct the page proofs and O.K. for printing.

This sketchy outline of the procedure for getting together the direct-mail advertisement makes the process appear considerably simpler than it is. The self-question chart on direct advertising, given below, gives a clearer idea of the many points that must receive attention in the preparation of direct-mail advertising.

SELF-QUESTION CHART ON DIRECT ADVERTISING *

What factors determine the selection of this medium?
- What is the main purpose of the advertising effort?
- Can direct advertising best accomplish this purpose?

What factors determine the form of the piece?
- How much material must be presented?
- Are illustrations and type matter relatively equal in sales importance? Is message mainly attention-getting, or mainly informative?
- What kind of illustration best fits the purpose?
- What kind of art work do the illustrative needs suggest?
- What general form of piece will best present the message? (Leaflet, stuffer, package insert, blotter, calendar, circular, illustrated letter, booklet, book, catalogue, broadside?)

What factors determine production?
- What kind of engraving and printing do illustrations require? (Letterpress, lithography, gravure, collotype, etc.) Is color a major factor?
- What kind of paper does reproduction require? Is mailing weight important?
- Is length of run suitable for economical use of printing process chosen?
- What sheet or page size will cut to advantage from standard-size stock?
- Will this cut of stock provide press sheets of proper size?
- Will stock fold the required number of times without cracking?
- Has grain direction been checked with direction of main folds?
- Has number of folds been checked against weight of stock?
- Is stock heavy enough to require scoring?
- If piece is to be machine-folded, has dummy been checked with printer or binder to avoid waste of paper in imposition, and to allow possible economies in binding?
- Is stock available in duplicate lots if needed?
- Is piece a self-mailer? If not, will it fit standard-size envelope?
- If a self-mailer, is sufficient space left for address?

---

* Excerpt from a larger chart in *The Technique of Advertising Production*, by Thomas Blaine Stanley, Prentice-Hall, Inc., New York.

Has complete dummy, including envelope, if any, been checked for mailing weight? (Allow for ink, stamps, stickers, etc.)

Layout and general factors

If folder, circular, or broadside, have folds been planned to open consecutively with progress of message, and without obliging reader to turn piece in his hands as he reads?

Does the effort to achieve novelty and interest sacrifice legibility or ease of reading in any way? (Monotony in type treatment, and in size and shape of illustrations should be avoided, but not at the expense of a clear presentation of the message.)

Has care been taken to harmonize line and halftone illustrations appearing on the same page? (Tint blocks under line cuts, or line borders around halftones, will help to pull the two together. As a rule, the halftones should dominate such a combination showing.)

Is it possible to use a folding scheme in which one piece of display does double duty (*i.e.*, is seen on both of two spreads as they are opened consecutively)? Watch stock envelope size when planning unusual folds, and remember that grain of paper should run with major folds.

Is each pair of facing pages or set of facing areas designed as a unit?

If color is used, has piece been planned for maximum effect? Does color as planned accomplish more than merely attract attention?

Has proposed color treatment been considered from the point of view of appropriate suggestion (of qualities such as warmth, coolness, purity, etc.)?

Do important cost or time factors tend to change any decision suggested above?

Testimonials. The sincere testimonial of a user or an expert has a powerful pull in direct-mail selling. Testimonials are often secured without actual solicitation in the following ways:

1. Letters that build goodwill lead the user to express his appreciation of the product. A friendly letter written to a customer on any occasion may bring an acknowledgment that expresses appreciation of the product.

2. A letter that invites criticism may be answered with an expression of the merits of the product. The president of LaSalle Extension University writes each student a congratulatory letter at the end of his training and asks for criticisms and suggestions for improving the training. The letter brings many fine testimonials.

3. A company salesman always numbers among his customers

personal friends who will give him a testimonial letter in reciprocation of the salesman's cooperation.

4. A letter written to obtain information and orders may solicit comments. The American Bandage Corporation sent out 2,000 letters of this type and enclosed the following reply card:

I'M A GOOD SPORT—MR. BURKET:
HERE IS YOUR INFORMATION—

______ "a.b.c. GAUZEBAND" is satisfactory

______ We are sending an order today

______ We have on hand stock to last about ____________ days

Other comments: __________________

____

The last line secured 44 testimonials—more than 2 per cent of the whole list and more than 10 per cent of the replies.

Permission to publish a testimonial. It is always advisable to secure permission to publish a testimonial, whether or not it is legally necessary to have the sender's permission. The person who goes to the trouble to write a testimonial letter is usually willing to grant permission for its publication. A simple, straightforward request will get the desired permission.

Effective use of testimonials. There are various ways in which testimonials may be used effectively. Among the possibilities are the following:

1. Use excerpts of the testimonial in sales letters.
2. Reproduce testimonial letters separately as full-sized letters.
3. Reproduce two or more testimonials on one page in a smaller size than the originals. It is not advisable to put many on a page because if the type size is reduced too much the testimonials will be difficult to read.
4. Reproduce each testimonial separately in the form of a miniature letter.
5. Quote parts of a large number of testimonials in a circular.
6. Use a portrait of the endorser next to each testimonial. This is more effective in letters to dealers than to consumers.

2. TESTING DIRECT-MAIL ADVERTISING

Importance of testing direct-mail advertising. The key to success in direct-mail advertising is careful testing and careful checking of results of tests. By experience with small mailings, it is possible to determine in advance whether the complete mailing will be successful and to eliminate guesswork. So important is this step in direct-mail advertising that some large companies have set up a direct-mail laboratory for the purpose of testing and recording results of each proposed mailing.

The value of testing will stand or fall on these "musts": (1) The names chosen must be a fair sample of the list. (2) The mailings to be compared must be identical except for the point being tested. (3) Accurate records of replies must be kept. (4) The mailing or condition of mailing must not be altered once a test has proved satisfactory.

What shall be tested. Many advertisers test to determine only the value of several different mailing pieces. On the other hand, some large advertisers test to determine every possible element of the mailing. An exhaustive list of tests that have been made by direct-mail advertisers cannot be given because the number of variables that can be tested is countless. The following list, however, gives a clear picture of the kinds of tests frequently made.

LIST OF COMMON TESTS OF DIRECT-MAIL ADVERTISING

Proposition

Type of proposition
Unit of sale most suitable
Selling price
Terms of payment
Shall a premium be offered?

Mailing List

Responsiveness of different types of lists
Areas that can be circularized profitably

Timing

Frequent *vs.* infrequent mailings
Interval between mailings
Time of year, month, or day in which to mail to particular groups or localities

Type of Mailing Piece

Letters, broadsides, booklets, folders tested against each other
Various combinations of mailing pieces
A cheaper mailing piece *vs.* a more expensive one
Printed announcements *vs.* Government post cards

Letters

Different appeals
Automatic typewritten letters *vs.* processed letters
Personalized *vs.* nonpersonalized
Letters with fill-in *vs.* those without fill-in
Multigraphed fill-in *vs.* automatic typewritten
Two-page *vs.* both sides on one letterhead
One color *vs.* two colors
Style and size of letterheads
Engraved stationery and high-grade stock *vs.* less expensive grades

Enclosures

Number of enclosures
Types of enclosures
Inclusion of a "pass-along" card for a friend
One-color *vs.* two-color enclosures
Methods of affixing enclosures
Addition of card for another product

Envelopes

Color of envelope
Flash on the envelope
Hand-addressed *vs.* type-addressed *vs.* stencil-addressed
Style and size of envelope
Window envelopes *vs.* addressed envelopes
Testimonials on back of envelope

Stamps

Metered postal indicia *vs.* precanceled stamps
Commemorative *vs.* ordinary stamps
Stamped *vs.* metered postage
First-class *vs.* third-class postage

Reply Forms

Business reply cards *vs.* business reply envelopes
Business reply card *vs.* plain reply card
One-color *vs.* two-color reply card
Filled-in reply card *vs.* plain reply card
Air-mail business reply envelope *vs.* regular business reply envelope
Unstamped business reply card *vs.* stamped reply card *vs.* stamped, addressed envelope

Color of reply form
Tab on reply card
Order form as part of mailing piece *vs.* separate card order form

Results of tests. The National Research Bureau has compiled a chart (see Figure 1) of the overall results from testing hundreds of direct-mail pieces. However, companies that test constantly find that many of the results do not hold for all of the company's products, and the results at one time might not be the same as at another. For this reason, constant testing and retesting are essential.

How large a test shall be made. No hard-and-fast rules can be set as to how large a mailing should be used to test the list, the mailing piece, or any other variable. A good deal depends upon the type of list, the price of the product, the purpose of the test, and the quota necessary to make the mailing profitable. In figuring how much to mail on any test, it is advisable to think, not in terms of number of pieces mailed, but in terms of the quota set. Thus, if a mailing of 1,000 letters required a quota of 5 orders to prove it profitable, it would be unwise to make two tests of 1,000 each to determine which of two letters pulled better, because the results from the two tests would not be sufficiently different to warrant drawing any positive conclusion. If one mailing brought 7 orders and the other 5 orders, it is entirely possible that the extra 2 orders could be attributed to special cases that did not at all represent the rest of the list. If the test were increased in size, say to 5,000, and one letter brought 35 orders and the other 20 orders, there would be no doubt as to which was the better letter.

In some lines, especially if the product is low in price, a fair test of a 10,000 list is 1,000, provided the 1,000 names are geographically representative.

Testing the variables. Only one variable should be tested at a time, and care should be taken to eliminate all extraneous factors that might influence the returns. It would be fatal to the value of the test to change any detail of the mailing other than the item that is to be tested. Of course, several tests can be made at the same time, covering different variables. Thus, simultaneously with the test as to appeal, another split mailing can be made to test the reply form. The mailings testing the appeal would be identical with each

Reliable Direct Mail Data

This chart presents a composite picture of direct mail findings of The National Research Bureau. The data presented, is a compilation of overall results from testing hundreds of direct mail pieces.

The basic findings tally with those of most direct mail users. There will be some variance, but by and large, these basic principles, applied consistently, will produce better than average results.

Form of Mailing
- The letter ranks first in importance.
- The most effective mailing unit consists of an outside envelope, a letter, circular, reply form, and business reply form.

Color
- Two color letters outpull one color letters.
- An order form printed in colored ink on colored stock outpulls an order form printed in black ink on white stock
- A two colored circular proves more effective than a one colored circular.
- Colored inks on an envelope corner card will generally do better than black ink.
- Colored inks, to be effective, must be used in correct proportions -- the predominant color being used sparingly
- Color is totally ineffective unless used with proper discretion -- color can attract or repel.

Outside Envelopes
- Illustrated envelopes increase returns if properly tied into the direct mail offer.
- Variety in types and sizes of envelopes pays in a series of mailings

Reply Envelopes
- A reply envelope increase responses to a questionnaire mailing
- A reply envelope produces a higher percentage of cash-with-order returns
- A reply envelope increases responses to a collection letter

Letters
- Form letters using indented paragraphs will outpull those in which indented paragraphs are not used.
- A two page letter run on two separate sheets of paper will ordinarily outpull a letter run on both sides of one sheet.
- A separate letter with a circular will generally do better than a combination letter and circular
- A form letter with an effective running headline will ordinarily do as well as a filled-in letter
- Underscoring pertinent sentences and phrases usually increases results slightly.
- A time limit for replying, where practical, usually increases returns.
- A two page letter ordinarily outpulls a one page letter.
- The offer of a premium or special inducement ordinarily increases returns.
- Authentic testimonials in a sales letter increase the pull.

Reply Cards
- An air-mail reply card will outpull a standard reply card if there is a logical reason for speed in replying.
- Postage-free business reply cards will bring more responses than the type to which the prospect must affix a postage stamp.
- Reply cards with postage stamps affixed will not ordinarily increase the response sufficiently to warrant the additional cost over standard business reply cards.
- Reply cards with "guarantee stubs" attached will ordinarily increase response over reply cards not bearing stubs.
- Reply cards with an illustration of the product or service being offered will ordinarily do better than those without an illustration.

Postage
- Third class mail ordinarily pulls as well as first class mail.
- Postage meter pulls better than postage stamps
- A "designed printed permit" does as well as a postage meter.
- Air mail postage seldom warrants the extra cost over first class postage.

Follow-ups
- A well organized follow-up campaign consists of five letters.
- The average direct mail promotion campaign is spaced over a 12 month period with one mailing every thirty days.
- A teaser campaign, to be effective, must consist of a series of follow-ups, released in rapid succession. The time-lag should not exceed two weeks between mailings
- A direct sales letter that produces a satisfactory number of orders on the first mailing can be repeated 30 days later and produce an additional satisfactory return.

Letterheads
- Specially designed letterheads, tailored to fit the sales message, will often outpull a standard letterhead.
- Change-of-pace in letterhead appearance will increase response in a series of mailings.
- A 20# stock is usually satisfactory for sales letters Special mailings to professional groups often warrant a quality bond stock.
- Two color letterheads are usually more effective than one color letterheads

Mailing Lists
- A company's own customer list is its best prospect list.
- A list of known mail order buyers will ordinarily outpull a compiled list.
- Lists bearing names of individuals will outpull lists with firm names only
- Mailing lists should be "cleaned" twice a year, on the average.
- Telephone directories, used without discrimination, usually represent the poorest mailing lists.
- A prospect list compiled with the assistance of salesmen often proves to be a "cream" list.

Circulars
- A circular that deals specifically with the offer contained in the letter will prove more effective than a circular of an institutional nature
- The cost of a full-color circular is warranted in the sale of food and home furnishings by mail.
- A circular usually proves ineffective in the sale of news magazines and news services.
- A type-set circular will outpull a type-written circular.
- A reply coupon on a circular usually increases returns.

Addressing
- Hand-written addressing reduces returns.
- Label addressing is not as effective as typewritten or stencil addressing.
- A "clean" stencil address is usually just as effective as type-written address
- Envelopes addressed to an individual in conjunction with a company are less likely to be opened by a mail clerk,

The NATIONAL RESEARCH BUREAU, INC., 415 N. Dearborn St., Chicago 10, Illinois

Figure 1. Direct Mail Data.

other except for the appeal; the mailings testing the reply form would be identical with each other except for the reply form.

If several lists are to be used in a mailing, more than one list should be used in testing a variable. The size of the list will, of course, influence the number of different tests that will be made. On a mailing list of 1,000, for example, it is hardly likely that more than one variable can be tested.

In order to be able to check results from comparative tests, the reply form must be so keyed that, when returns come in, they can be credited to the proper mailing. The most common method of keying is to use different key numbers on the reply cards, each representing a unit of the mailing, or different colored reply cards.

Mechanics of the test. If a specific test is being made to determine whether or not the campaign, complete in all its details, will bring a sufficient number of returns to indicate success of the entire mailing, the procedure is very simple. A certain percentage of the list to be used is circularized, and the returns are checked and tabulated.

If a comparative test is to be made to determine the relative value of one method or detail against another of the same general type, the procedure is more complicated. For instance, let us suppose that two entirely different folders, one elaborate and the other inexpensive, have been written, and that it is necessary to determine which will prove more profitable. Here is the procedure that is followed:

1. Determine a quota for each piece on the basis of the number of returns that must be received to make the mailing profitable.
2. Address all the envelopes to be used in both tests.
3. Alternate these envelopes into two groups.
4. Stuff, stamp, and seal each group, one with the first mailing, the other with the alternate.
5. Deliver both to the post office at the same time.

In this way all extraneous factors have been eliminated. Letters go out on the same day to the same territory, to the same quality names. Of course, they are keyed differently to make it possible to credit the correct mailing.

Recording results of direct-mail tests. A record of each mailing should be kept not only as a guide to the results of the particular

SCHEDULING INSTRUCTIONS (T)

CARD OR SLIP KEY		FOLD NO.	ISSUED BY				
MAILING PIECE	KEYS	PAGES	MULTI.	PRINTED NEW	PRINTED STOCK	FILLED IN	OUTSIDE
LETTER							
OUTLINE PAGES							
CIRCULAR							
BRIEF							
BOOKLET							

RETURN		FILL IN	TYPED	STENCIL	MULTI.	PRINTED	PERMIT	GOV'T	PRIVATE
CARD	SLIP								
RETURN ENVELOPE NUMBER									STAMPED

ADDRESSING		POSTAGE		OUTGOING ENVELOPE NUMBER
ENVELOPES		1c METER		CHECKING AS SHOWN BELOW
SLIPS		BULK		ENVELOPE SLUG:
CARDS		OUTSIDE		
LETTERS		OTHER		

LIST

ARTICLE				
SCHEDULE OF		QUOTA–M.	QUOTA–TOT. SCH'D	NO. SCHEDULED
DATE MAILED	PRICE $	COST–M.	QUOTA–TOT. M'L'D	NO. MAILED
EXTRA COPIES	NO.	TO COLL. BOOK:		
WITH WORKSHEET		TO FOREIGN:		
TO PHAX (EXCEPT CARDS)				
TO OTHER DEP'T				
CHARGE – ADV.:				
WORK DONE	BY		DATE	AMOUNT
ADDRESSED				
FILLED IN				
ADDRESSED ENTIRE LIST		NUMBER KILLED		
FIRST NAME ADDRESSED				
			PAGE NO.	
LAST NAME ADDRESSED				
			PAGE NO.	
FIRST NAME ADDRESSED				
			PAGE NO.	
LAST NAME ADDRESSED				
			PAGE NO.	

8.51F7 12-51 2M

Figure 2a. Advertising Department Mail Order Record.

FREE INQUIRIES		BILL ORDERS			15 DAYS ORDERS (D)*			3 MONTHS ORDERS (C)**			RETURNS	
WEEK ENDING	NO.	WK. END.	NO.	AMOUNT	WK. END.	NO.	AMOUNT	WK. END.	NO.	AMOUNT	MONTH	NUMBER
				$			$			$		

*(D)=DUPLICATES, FOR SERVICE AND MAIL ORDER DEPTS.

**(C) BAD CREDITS, FOR SERVICE AND MAIL ORDER DEPTS.

Figure 2b. Record of Results of Mailing.
(*Reverse side of Figure 2a.*)

test but for future use. Figure 2a illustrates a record that is kept of each mailing—test as well as complete mailings. A record of the results is kept on the reverse side (Figure 2b).

If the article is sold on approval, a record is kept of the articles returned on the orders resulting from the test mailings as well as from the final mailings. The invoice returned with the article bears the key number of the mailing. These invoices are tabulated each week and the total is entered in the column provided for this purpose on the record card (Figure 2b).

3. COPYWRITING FOR DIRECT-MAIL SELLING

Definition of copy. Copy is the written selling-message of an advertisement, including mailing pieces and sales letters. Copy embodies the planning behind the advertisement, and involves layout and production as well. (See *Preparing the advertising piece*, page 19.) To be successful, copy must interest the reader. He must think it was written only for him; it must appeal to him. Experience shows that the appeal to self-interest is the most effective. These appeals are basic: desire for social recognition, for romance, for long life, to make money, to save money, to save time, to save energy, to obtain comfort.

The headline sets the tone of the copy. Copy is usually divided into the following progressive parts: the headline, amplification of the headline, explanation and proof of claims, advantages, and closing. The headline will set the tone of the copy. It may (1) be newsy: "New diesel tractors now in four sizes"; (2) contain advice and promise: "The Easy Way to Wax Floors," or "Your summer trips can be more fun"; (3) be dramatic: "Caught by rising tide in shark-filled waters"; (4) be provocative and surprising: "Which are worse—blowouts or skids"; (5) be selective: "For the one man in seven who shaves every day"; (6) command: "Use an Evinrude and get more fish." The body of the copy will follow the headline. Unusual claims may be proved by reports of special tests, tests the readers can make, trial offers, guaranty, samples, and testimonials.

Fundamental principles of direct-mail copy writing. Application of the following fundamental principles increases the pull of direct-mail copy:

1. Think as the prospect thinks. If you think the way the prospect thinks, you are going to write to him just the way he thinks and he will then behave the way you want him to behave. The ability to put yourself in the prospect's place is the secret of success in copy writing as well as in personal selling.

2. Use the word *new*, either directly or indirectly, whenever you reasonably and honestly can. The word *new*, or any connotation of the word, is a magic sales word.

3. Emphasize the positive. Anything you say, say in a positive way instead of a negative way.

4. Attract attention. How you attract attention is very important. Talk about something the prospect is interested in, not about something you are interested in.

Distinguishing features of mail-order advertising. Mail-order copy is the one form of copy that contains all the points of copy writing. These are its distinguishing features: (1) Usually has very strong news and promise headlines and uses subcaptions liberally; (2) presents descriptions and merits intensely, in as many different ways as space permits; (3) gives strong proof of claim; (4) gives precise descriptions to facilitate ordering; (5) stresses urgency of ordering at this time (sometimes offers bonus for prompt ordering); (6) gives very clear instruction for ordering.

Readability test. The text of the copy should be specific, concise, and vivid. Here is one readability test: (1) Did you use familiar words? (2) Are your sentences short? (3) Have you varied the sentence structure to relieve monotony? (4) Are the paragraphs short and unified? (5) Does everything contribute to the main idea? (6) Have you made the argument simple enough for the reader to remember the main points?

Final check of copy. As a final check, the copy should be examined for these points: (1) Is it interesting to the reader? (2) Is it clear? (3) Is anything in it likely to be misunderstood? (4) Is the most important point given the most prominence? (5) Is it adequate? (6) Is it accurate? (7) Can the story be told in fewer words? (8) Does it make the reader want to buy the product advertised?

4. COST OF DIRECT-MAIL SELLING

High cost of direct-mail selling. It is, of course, impossible to give an exact figure for the cost of selling by mail, but contrary to the general belief, the cost is high. The preparation and mailing of an ordinary one-page letter, with a one-page enclosure, multilithed in two colors, cost $45 to $50 per 1,000. The cost of a more elaborate mailing is proportionately higher. At present high production costs, you must be able to absorb a selling cost of approximately 40 per cent to sell profitably by direct mail, assuming you have normal manufacturing costs and overhead.

Finding costs. Estimate of costs will determine the appropriation for direct-mail advertising. But, before direct-mail costs can be estimated, certain points must be considered: the percentage of sales to allow for selling costs (advertising plus mailing), and the amount of business expected from a mailing. For articles costing less than $10, orders amounting to 4 per cent of the mailing are considered excellent; 2 per cent for a new product is considered optimistic. The following example shows how to figure an appropriation:

Article sells for $4.50.
Allowable selling cost is 33⅓ or $1.50.
Your list has 25,000 names.
You expect a 3 per cent return, or 750 orders.
At $1.50 each, the selling cost on the 750 orders equals $1,125.
Hence, you can spend 4½ cents each for a simple mailing piece ($1,125 ÷ 25,000).

Items that affect cost. Some or all of the following items enter into the cost of each mailing:

1. *Postage.* The cost of regular third-class metered or bulk mail per 1,000 is fixed. Mailings of other classes are mailed at the actual postage rate.

2. *Addressing.* The cost of stencilling and addressing envelopes is fixed. When outside lists are rented, the cost is the actual rental charge.

3. *Fill-ins.* A three- or four-line fill-in costs about $1 more per 1,000 than a one-line fill-in. Pen and ink fill-ins are slightly more expensive than typed or stencilled ones.

4. *Envelopes, outgoing and reply.* The size and stock of the envelopes determine their cost. Slugging adds to the cost.

5. *Paper.* Colored paper is slightly more expensive than white. Coated paper is considerably more expensive than bond paper.

6. *Printed reply cards.* The size of the card and the stock affect the cost. Two-color cards are more expensive than one-color cards.

7. *Printed order forms.*

8. *Circulars.* The size, number of colors, whether printed on one or both sides, and the stock affect the cost of the circular.

9. *Multigraphing.* The cost depends on the size of the copy. Multigraphing in red and black is no more expensive than multigraphing in black only.

10. *Multilithing.* A two-color multilith job costs more than a one-color job.

11. *Collating and mailing.* Each operation necessary to collate and mail adds to the cost. These operations include collating, folding, nesting, inserting, sealing and metering, tieing, sorting, and making delivery to the post office. The more enclosures, the higher the cost.

Although the creative and overhead costs are not included in the cost of a specific mailing, they affect decisively the cost of direct-mail selling. The salaries of the head of the department, his assistants, copywriters, and clerks are included in the cost of delivering the finished product. The department must also bear its share of the overhead. These costs thus affect the number of orders necessary to make direct-mail selling profitable.

Cost per order. The cost per order pulled by the mailing, rather than the cost per mailing, is the important consideration. The

Cost of Mailing 1,000 Letters	*Orders Received (Percentage and Number of Items)*	*Mailing Cost per Order*	*Cost of Delivering Product ($1 per Item)*	*Gross Sales ($5 per Item)*	*Loss*	*Profit*
$50.00	1% (10)	$5.00	$10.00	$50.00	$10.00	
$50.00	1½% (15)	$3.33	$15.00	$75.00		$10.00
$50.00	2% (20)	$2.50	$20.00	$100.00		$30.00
$50.00	2½% (25)	$2.00	$25.00	$125.00		$50.00

preceding table shows the cost per order of an item that costs $1 and sells for $5, and the profit on a mailing of 1,000, based on varying returns. The table also demonstrates that there is little chance of making a reasonable profit on items selling for less than $2.50. These figures do not take into consideration returns and credit losses.

How to arrive at a quota. For a mailing to be profitable, it must pull a certain number of orders per thousand. That number is the quota. To arrive at a quota, the following formula is used:

$$\frac{\text{Cost of the Mailing}}{\text{Selling Cost per Unit}} = \text{Quota}$$

To find the selling cost per unit, start with the selling price and subtract all non-selling costs plus the required profit on the unit. For example, suppose the selling price of the product is $6, the manufacturing cost is $1.80, the overhead is $1.20, and the required profit on the item is $.60. The selling cost would be $6 minus $3.60, or $2.40. If the cost of the mailing were $60, the quota would be $60 divided by $2.40, or 25. If the product is sold on approval, and an allowance of 15% of sales must be made for returns of the product, the quota would be increased by 15% of 25, or 4, and the gross quota would be 29.

In a business that sells many products, the advertising department might not know the manufacturing cost, overhead, and profit per item. In that case, management might supply the advertising department with a figure that represents the selling cost per item. Thus, if manufacturing costs were 30%, overhead 20%, and the desired profit 10%, the cost of selling would be 40% (100% − 60%). The figure management would arrive at to be used in the formula would be the reciprocal of 40% or 2½. The formula would then be expressed as follows:

$$\frac{2\tfrac{1}{2} \times \$60}{\$6} = 25 \text{ quota}$$

How cooperation with the printer can cut costs. Close cooperation with the printer can sometimes reduce the cost of a mailing. The printer can analyze a layout and tell whether or not it can be executed without waste. Frequently a few minor changes in the planning will eliminate waste and substantially reduce the cost. Too often, however, the printer is not consulted until it is too late to make the change.

How multigraph slugs cut envelope cost. Losses due to excessive estimates of the quantity of envelopes to be printed for a direct-mail effort can be eliminated by multigraphing the exact quantity of envelopes. A company that does a large volume of direct-mail advertising, using a great variety of corner cards and slogans on its envelopes, ran into losses because more envelopes would be printed with a particular corner card than could be used. The surplusage occurred, in many cases, because a particular mailing piece had stopped "pulling." The company now prints corner cards on its envelopes on the multigraph, using metal slugs prepared by an outside firm. By printing its own envelopes, the company can prepare the exact quantity for a particular mailing and rerun when necessary. Besides eliminating the loss due to wastage, it also saves time by avoiding outside printer's delays.

The plan is also applicable to postal indicia.

How repeat sales affect direct-mail costs. If you are selling a product that will give you a steady repeat business, you probably can afford a higher sales cost than the normal 40 per cent. Repeat orders provide a substantial profit beyond the cost of the first sale. Firms selling seeds by mail exemplify businesses that are able to pay heavily for their first sale. To cite one example, W. Atlee Burpee considers an approximate cost of 30 cents per inquiry from magazine advertising, which is followed up by mail, a good investment even though *no* money is made on a customer during the first year. In the industrial field it cost $1 to obtain a $2.25 trial order from industrial concerns, but repeat orders filled through the mail cost only 37 cents each, and the average repeat order amounts to $12.

Each advertiser can determine the proper rate of follow-up for his own business by testing. Robert Stone, in *Profitable Direct Mail Methods*, published by Prentice-Hall, Inc., says that before making the test the advertiser must have these facts before him:

1. The natural rate of use or consumption for the commodity being sold.

2. The average number of annual purchases made by the average customer for his industry.

3. The average unit of sale.
4. Maximum annual potential sales that can be expected from a customer.

5. SUCCESSFUL DIRECT-MAIL IDEAS

An entire campaign features "Promotional Preview." Donahue Sales Corporation promotes the sale of Talon zippers in a direct-mail campaign featuring a promotional package. "Promotional Preview" is a continuing direct-by-mail service to the notions merchandising and buying personnel. Each mailing consists of an attractive cover with an inside pocket for inserts. The pocket avoids loss in handling and permits easy removal of the individual inserts. The format of each issue is basically unchanged except for color. The cover is made of heavy stock and is attractively designed, featuring a zipper and the trademark "Talon." When folded, the cover is 14½ × 11 inches.

Individual inserts report on advance styles in color and fabric that directly affect the merchandising of zippers. The pockets also contain copies of consumer advertising on Talon zippers appearing in fashion magazines and pattern fashion books. The department store buyer thus sees how the manufacturer is promoting Talon zippers to the consumer. Two Order Blanks, in duplicate, are inserted in the pocket. One is the blank regularly used to order staple zipper items. Sometimes a special order blank is included to stimulate immediate orders.

"Promotional Preview" is mailed third or fourth class, depending on the weight of the issue, in a sealed envelope with a stiffener. The envelopes are individually addressed where possible. A slug informs the recipient that the envelope contains the latest issue of "Promotional Preview." The mailing schedule is one month in advance of the date when buying activities of particular events begin.

From an initial distribution of 1,200 copies, "Promotional Preview" is now mailed to a carefully selected list of 2,700 recipients. The mailing list is continually "tailored." From each issue, the more pertinent leaflets are sent with a covering letter as a continuing service to 4,000 smaller retailers.

A novelty campaign increases sales. Foote & Jenks, who sell vanilla to ice cream manufacturers, concentrate on the spectacular in mailings. During a year's campaign, which won a Direct-Mail Advertising Association award, the firm sent out mailings at intervals of three weeks to 3,500 prospects. Every mailing was a novelty, with a slogan tieing it in with a bid for business. On the theory that it is human nature to be inquisitive, Foote & Jenks send all mailings out in provocative containers—cardboard boxes, tubes, and the like—instead of envelopes.

One of the most spectacular mailings was a huge menu resembling that of a *de luxe* restaurant. It was labeled "Café de Vanille," and offered a menu of the finest vanillas under "Specialties of the House." A table d'hôte menu and Budget Selections offered the economy vanillas. A folder on which a plastic knife was attached to an illustration of a plate of vanilla ice cream, said, "Our Bid for a Slice of your Vanilla Business." A plastic hook, attached to a folder, had a sign hung on it, which read: "Our Bid Hangs on this Hook." A swatch of wool with a Hart Schaffner & Marx label was attached to a folder, which compared Foote & Jenks products with Hart Schaffner & Marx tailoring: "The material is the same—but the excellence of the finished product is the result of the maker's skill. So it is with vanilla. Like Hart Schaffner & Marx . . . we take pride in our work." A tiny bottle of real vanilla, a miniature pickaxe, and a tape measure were among the other novelty mailings. The firm's sales have risen 800 per cent since it emphasized spectacular techniques. It writes and prepares its own mailings.

Campaign stressing engineering evidence boosts sales of staple item 65 per cent. A 65 per cent increase in sales of a staple mechanical item that possessed no particular novelty appeal was achieved by the Wayne Pump Company of Fort Wayne, Indiana, in a campaign of four monthly mailings.

To increase the sale of Wayne Foot Valves, the campaign was directed to 4,000 large oil companies and jobbers. The valve had been marketed for eight years and was developed to eliminate the troubles caused by competitive valves. The campaign was theretofore built around this theme, showing how the use of the valve would increase customer satisfaction with Wayne pumps and reduce the number of service calls.

In each mailing the customer was asked to write for a sample valve on approval. This sample was not given away but was billed subject to return. A further description of the four mailings follows.

Comparison with competitive products. Since the mailings were directed to men with engineering knowledge, the first mailing consisted entirely of an engineering test showing performance comparisons between Wayne valves, and other leading makes, labeled A, B, etc.

Protective and quality features stressed in 2nd and 3rd mailings. In the second mailing, a folder pointed out how a valve which did not contain the Wayne construction features could be ruined in installation. It also showed how rough treatment in installation could not harm Wayne valves. This idea was carried further in the third mailing folder. Titled "It Floats," the folder added further engineering evidence that would lead the engineer to investigate Wayne valves.

Price mentioned in last mailing. In the last mailing a folder, titled "Give those fine new pumps protection," contained a summation of the entire campaign and a final appeal for action. The price was mentioned in this last piece as a clinching argument for immediate adoption of Wayne Foot Valves.

The total cost of the campaign, including postage and mailing, was approximately $1,250. The 65 per cent increase in sales due to the campaign proved a profitable return.

One-week blotter campaign builds restaurant trade. Given a product or a service that will, of itself, bring customers back in repeat trade, a good advertising campaign to draw the first customers may be sufficient to build up a permanent trade without any further advertising. Such was the experience of a Philadelphia cafeteria, which solved the problem of drawing customers for the first time by distributing, for one week, menus printed on blotters. The plan worked so well that no advertising has been needed since, because the excellent food did the work of bringing the customers back again.

The advertising attack was simple. A good grade of uncoated white (suggestive of cleanliness) blotting paper was selected and cut to menu size. An attractive menu was printed on the blotter by a company with experience in this line of work. As soon as business houses opened Monday morning, a crew of four telegraph messengers was employed to distribute 1,500 menus, one for each desk in the locality. This was repeated for the rest of the week, until distribution had been made in one block in each direction from the cafeteria. By Friday, the cafeteria had a waiting line during the noon hours, and the trade has since been of a repeat variety.

The explanation is apparently simple. Businessmen were loath to throw out a perfectly good blotter, and as a result they were faced all morning with an attractive, tempting menu. Appetite appeal did the rest.

Good copy boosts business to dealers 35 per cent. Many wholesalers might take a tip from A. Bohrer, Inc., New York City, and advertise directly to dealers much as dealers do to consumers.

Bohrer, a fruit and vegetable wholesaler, periodically sends to prospective dealers an inexpensive 6¼ x 9 inch leaflet emphasizing one or another of its products—but only one in each leaflet. The secret of success (35 per cent increase in business in one year and 25 per cent more customers) is simply good copy. Here are samples:

Bohrer's Orange Aid!

If your customers dote on sweet and tangy orange juice . . . if you want minimum skin and maximum juice . . .

. . . talk to Bohrer's about oranges! Bohrer's can give you orange aid . . . (yes, and lemon aid) . . . that will mean more profit to you . . .

* * *

Don't Whip Bohrer's Potatoes!

Boil them . . . French-fry them . . . Lyonnaise them . . . but please . . . oh, please! don't whip them!

We love our potatoes . . . because they are the best money can buy. Specially selected . . . and superbly graded.

Of course, if you must serve them mashed . . . or whipped . . . we will have to say okay. But kindly whip them gently . . . because we're so fond of them. Thank you.

* * *

We Have Never Been Hit With A Ripe Tomato!

Nobody has ever thrown a ripe tomato at anyone in Bohrer's . . .

But Bohrer's have tomatoes that are hits!

How Limericks helped dealers sell underwear.* A combination cartoon and Limerick promoted sales of Jockey Underwear for Coopers, Inc., Kenosha, Wisconsin. Post cards were furnished to dealers at prices starting at $3.50 for 600 cards. The back of each

* *The Reporter of Direct Mail Advertising.*

card carried a selling message and the dealer imprint. During the spring months, dealers bought 694,000 cards and reported an enthusiastic response from customers.

Thirty Limericks were included in each series used by Coopers, and the series were changed each Spring and Fall. Each Limerick and its accompanying cartoon were printed in black and white on colored stock. One of the cards showed a jovial gentleman eating an ice cream cone. The Limerick read:

A weather forecaster named Hawes
Lost his job at the bureau because
Jockey Longs kept him cozy
And so while it froze, he
Predicted warm days without pause.

Humorous educational booklet promotes sales of quality merchandise. Odd and interesting facts about its products, in an attention-getting booklet, promotes goodwill and stimulates sales for S. Stroock & Co., Inc., New York clothing manufacturer. Use of humorous cartoons and verses promotes the sales of its quality, high-priced merchandise. They can be readily used in space ads, letters and mailing cards. The idea is open to many applications.

The booklet is distributed by S. Stroock & Co., Inc. to department store executives, men's and women's wear buyers, specialty shops, garment manufacturers, and readers of institutional advertisements. It is a 24-page, 8 x 5½ inch booklet entitled "Stroock's Animal Kingdom" and shows through humorous verses and Thurber-like drawings the history and habitats of unusual animals whose fur is used in Stroock garments. The animals described in the booklet are the vicuna, kashmir goat, camel, llama, alpaca, misti, huarizo, suri, guanaco, and angora goat. Each verse occupies a two-page spread headed by a humorous drawing of the animal and illustrated by smaller drawings on the opposite page.

The verses, in addition to describing the animals, bring out the feature qualities of their fur and mention the care taken by Stroock in selection and manufacture. This is well illustrated in the following excerpt from the poem describing the llama.

They breed from Peru to Bolivia's Crest
And you can't pack them singly (that's not a jest).
They'll rebel and repel every effort you make
Until six are lined up for the trip that you take.

Stroock imports the down and weaves it like magic
Into a warm and luxurious fabric—
Even men make the most of its warmth and its beauty
And they buy it in coats both for style and for duty.
Like Vicuna and Camel it gives insulation.
For long wear choose Stroock Llama—the coating sensation.

Change to humorous direct mail pays.* Long users of conservative, serious, and technical mailing pieces, the Barrett Bindery Co., Chicago, Ill., decided to switch to direct mail in a lighter, humorous vein, with profitable results.

It switched to a series of humorous monthly desk calendars that featured the "Busy Barretts" in cartoon sketches. They are shown each month as comic little people performing various plant operations. The calendars are about seven inches high, on thick white cardboard.

For instance, one mailing, which promoted gummed seals, showed five Barretts busily working on seals. One doughty workman, on a ladder, squirts water on the labels; another Barrett, well entangled with tape wound around him, applies paste to the labels with a large brush; another examines the seals with a magnifying glass. A two-inch calendar is printed near the cartoon, and below is a concise advertising message. A different colored ink is used each month.

The company has found its switch to the humorous-type piece beneficial in terms of results. It is a change that might profitably be followed by other users of the more conservative, straightforward type of mailing pieces.

Montage of newspaper headlines drives home sales message.† An effective mailing piece that reproduced newspaper headlines of winter storms served as a reminder of bad-weather conditions and drove home the selling features of a heating apparatus. By collecting newspaper items or headlines pertinent to particular products or services others may easily adapt the same idea.

As an opening gun for selling stokers and other heating equipment in the South, C. A. McDade & Sons, Montgomery, Ala., sent to prospects a folder which served as a reminder that the past winter had been the coldest in 40 years. Headed "Remember Last Winter," the front cover of the folder showed a montage of weather

* *Geyer's Topics.*
† *Domestic Engineering.*

news from the front pages of various newspapers. Some of the headlines were as follows: "Below-Zero Wave Sweeps In On City," "Bitter Cold Grips D. C. And Sweeps Nation," "Atlanta Digs Out of Record Snow as Force of 800 Works on Streets," etc. Contents of the folder reminded prospects that it was best to prepare in advance for such unexpected weather conditions by immediately installing adequate heating equipment.

Informal memo calls attention to mailing enclosure. Short, informal memos enclosed with mailing pieces provide a saving in paper and catch the reader's attention more dramatically than the conventional letter of transmittal.

Attached to an advertising folder sent to prospects by Eastern Air Lines, Inc., New York City, was a 4 x 5 inch "memo" sheet signed by the vice-president of the company. Copy in typewriter type read as follows:

I believe you'll enjoy reading the enclosed folder—but you'll also find in it something more than enjoyment. Because it tells the story of "two little buyers"—one who used Eastern Air Lines, one who didn't—and what happened to some very bright ideas they had. One of these buyers could be you.

So take a minute to read the story, won't you? Because if you're not flying regularly to market with Eastern Air Lines, this message may point the way to extra benefits for yourself and for the store.

Empty gift boxes stimulate Christmas coat sales.* A Christmas promotion idea, easily adaptable by retailers, consisted of sending empty boxes in gift wrappings to representative businessmen. Cownie Furs, Inc., furrier in Des Moines, Iowa, wrapped three hundred coat boxes bearing the firm name and tied them with blue and silver ribbon. These were delivered to businessmen throughout the city by the firm's truck driver. Enclosed in the box was a letter which read in part:

Dear ————:

Disappointed to find this box empty?

Don't let that "certain one" be disappointed even more on Christmas. This box filled with Cownie Furs will make you an outstanding success as a Santa Claus.

Our gifts range from fur pups at . . . cents, fur mitts at . . . . ., fur

* *Dry Goods Journal.*

muffs from . . . and fur hats as low as . . . . ., up to a fur jacket, or scarf, or a full-length fur coat from . . . . to as high as you want to go.

The boxes brought in numbers of telegrams and special delivery letters showing that the cleverness of the idea was appreciated.

Tested direct-mail ideas for Christmas.* The following direct-mail ideas used by three department stores were directly responsible for booming Christmas sales to out-of-town customers. A representative gift catalog or circular mailed early and accompanied by a letter emphasizing the comfort and convenience of shopping by mail should also prove profitable.

In place of a catalog, Wolf & Dessauer Co., Ft. Wayne, Ind. sent out a 11 x 10 inch holiday folder with a red cover containing a cut-out candle decoration. The center spread was devoted to a color illustration of the outside of the store building decorated for Christmas, and captioned "The Great Christmas Shop of All Northern Indiana." At either side, according to floor location, was a listing of the various items carried by the store. On the page facing the inside back cover, the customer's attention was directed to a bright green booklet placed in a pocket cut into the inside back of the double cover. This was entitled "Christmas Shopping Guide and Memorandum" and contained a suggested list of gifts for men, women, young men, boys, children aged two to six, girls aged seven to fourteen, baby, the home, and the boys in the camps. Opposite each listing was a blank page where the customer could make notes. No prices or detailed descriptions were included.

Benjamin's, Salisbury, Md. sent all customers a "Boxful of Christmas Ideas" which accomplished the same purpose as a circular or catalog. A lightweight cardboard box measuring 7¼ x 4 x 1½ inch contained forty separate sheets featuring gift items selected from various departments of the store. Each sheet was illustrated by a pen sketch or actual photograph, and variety was introduced by using black and a roto brown ink.

Concentrating on business from men, Davidson Bros. Co. Inc., Sioux City, Iowa, sent a letter over the signature of Miss Kay Stephen, gift secretary, to a selected list of some 200 names, offering her services as gift counsellor and personal shopper. The response to this letter was extremely gratifying. The same store sent out a

* *Dry Goods Journal.*

mimeographed list of gift suggestions in the shape of a Christmas tree, with each item separated by leaders or dots. The base of the "tree" was formed by the slogan, "The Gift Store, Davidson Brothers Company."

Simple mailing pieces increase telephone sales 40 per cent. A 40 per cent increase in telephone sales resulted from the use of simple mailing pieces by Robert H. Bryson, a Montreal drugstore. The mailings, which can be easily adapted by any retail store or small business firm equipped to handle telephone sales, also increased the average size of such orders by 80 per cent.

Twelve mailing pieces were sent to a list of 2,000 customers over a nine-month period. Many of the pieces were one-fold cards measuring 6 x 4 inch in folded form (see Figure 3). Opened up, the cards had a short message tying in with the illustration on the face of the card and followed by a list of special bargains. For instance, the card shown in Figure 3, titled "A Good Rule," had the following copy:

The rule we use in measuring success, is not our sixty years in business—not the amount of sales—but the number of customers we satisfy.

Telephone orders from our Customers are steadily increasing—Proof of the confidence they have in our ability to serve them reliably, promptly, and economically. Always telephone us for your requirements, and as an added inducement, we offer these attractive values.

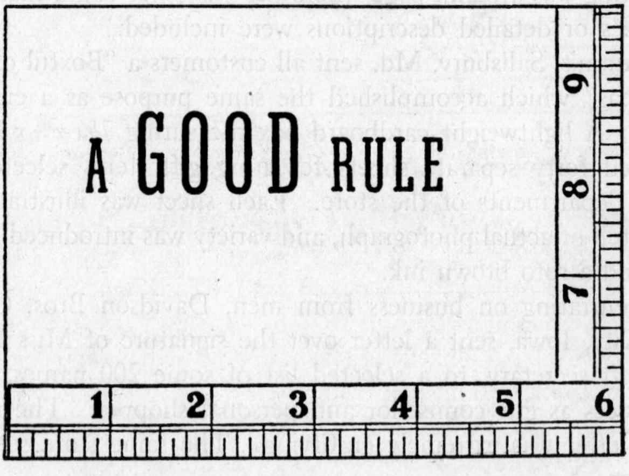

Figure 3. Mailing Card That Increased Telephone Sales.

This is followed by a list of special offers. This same folder was also sent out with a six-inch ruler attached to the front cover.

The card showing the location of the store (Figure 4) carried a similar theme in the copy:

> In addition to serving so many Customers residing in St. Andrew and St. George Wards, every day we receive a great many telephone orders from residents of Westmount, Notre Dame de Grace, Hampstead and Montreal West.
>
> We want our customers to telephone us, so whenever you are in need of anything, no matter how small it may be—don't hesitate to telephone MArquette 2391.
>
> We hope these items may be the means of having you telephone us today.

This was followed by a list of specials.

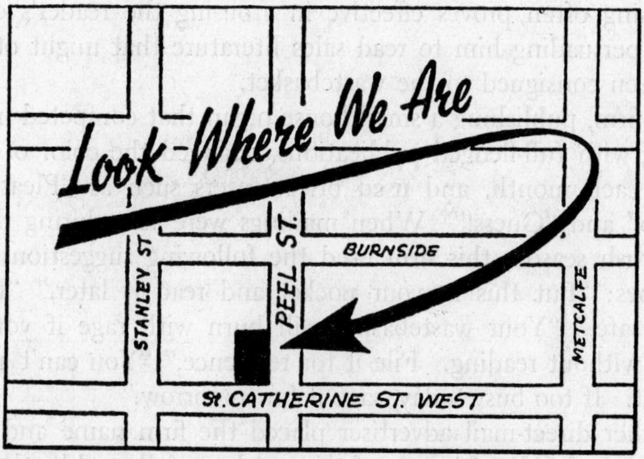

Figure 4. Another Mailing Card That Increased Telephone Sales.

Pre-test offer of new product brings results. A pre-test offer of a new product opened 2,320 new accounts in a mailing of 87,317 letters for The American Bandage Corp. of Chicago. The company directed its campaign to industrial concerns only, for the purpose of introducing "a.b.c. Gauzeband," a new type of bandage that adheres to itself but not to skin, hair or clothes.

Letters sent to prospects offered a dozen rolls of bandage to be used for 10 days under actual working conditions without any obligation to pay. After the trial period, if the product proved satisfactory, the prospect returned the shipping memo to the manufacturer and was billed for the merchandise shipped. If the merchandise had not proved satisfactory, the unused portion was returned to the manufacturer and no charge was made for the quantity used.

All letters were accompanied by reply cards and descriptive literature. One of these pamphlets contained an attention-getting idea that can easily be adapted by other companies. The red cover was captioned: "Here's News!" Below this was reproduced part of a newspaper clipping headlined: "New Discovery Cuts First Aid Costs. Satisfies employees; pays big dividends." Below this was printed in white: "Read The Inside Story . . ." The pamphlet itself described various features, uses and users of the product.

Envelope teasers catch attention and arouse curiosity.* The use of a flash or teaser message on envelopes containing direct-mail advertising often proves effective in arousing the reader's curiosity and in persuading him to read sales literature that might otherwise have been consigned to the wastebasket.

One firm, publishing a small house organ that competed in reader interest with full-fledged publications, changed the color of the envelope each month, and used brief teasers such as "Please Open Me Up" and "Guess!" When mailings were sent during the prospects' rush season, this firm used the following suggestions on the envelopes: "Put this in your pocket and read it later," "Put this in the safe," "Your wastebasket will burn with rage if you throw this in without reading. File it for reference," "You can't afford to dump it. If too busy today, save it for tomorrow."

Another direct-mail advertiser placed the firm name and address at the upper left-hand corner of the envelope, followed by the words: "Present the Golden Dozen." Inside the envelope was a folder which described and illustrated twelve outstanding values.

A folder offering some seasonal special of interest to women was contained in an envelope which showed a line cut of a smartly dressed young woman. The picture caption, "Fortunate, indeed, is the woman who has waited until now," persuaded the average recipient to open the envelope.

A small-town advertiser ran the following copy on an envelope: "Did you Know . . . That you are regarded as a child or moron

* *Member's Bulletin,* D.M.M.A. Inc.

by some of the 'big shots' who write books, movie hits, and advertising?" The envelope contained a single sheet of paper headed: "Children Under 13 Should Not Try to Read This Ad." Copy went on to describe ads that are insults to reader intelligence, and contrasted them with his own policy of telling the intelligent truth about his wares.

Reply cards attract prospect's attention. Edward Stern & Company, Inc., inserted a reply card with a perforated stub in its 9 x 11½ inch, six-page illustrated booklet (Figure 5). When the booklet is first opened, the stub is visible immediately, thus calling attention to the reply card. The stub bears the following imprint on each side: "For a demonstration of STERN LETTERPRESS fill in

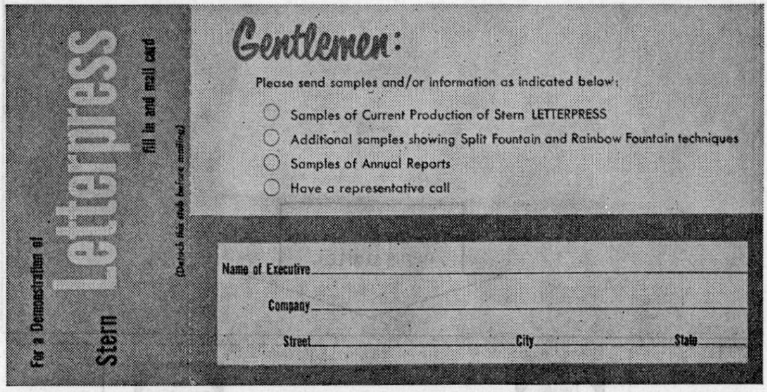

Figure 5. Reply Card Inserted in Booklet.

and mail card. Detach this stub before mailing." Each issue of "Printact," which is the house organ, encloses a reply card for a demonstration of a Stern product.

Foote & Jenks used a double reply card, titled, "Hot as a firecracker," to which a tiny firecracker was attached with Scotch tape. The inside of the card contained a printed message that ended, "From now on . . . your orders will be marked 'Hot as a Firecracker.' "

The Lederle Laboratories Division of American Cyanamid Company uses an intriguing device for a reply card. Lederle sends monthly newsletters to doctors and dentists. The newsletters have a cardboard backing, which, when folded, forms a cover for mailing the newsletter. The edges of the cover are held together by a flap attached to the back edge of the cover by perforations and inserted in a slit on the front of the cover (see Figure 6). This flap is a reply card, the reply address being printed on the inside of the card. Each reply card is a request for a sample of a specific Lederle product. The device makes it impossible for the recipient to overlook or misplace the reply card because it is an integral part of the newsletter.

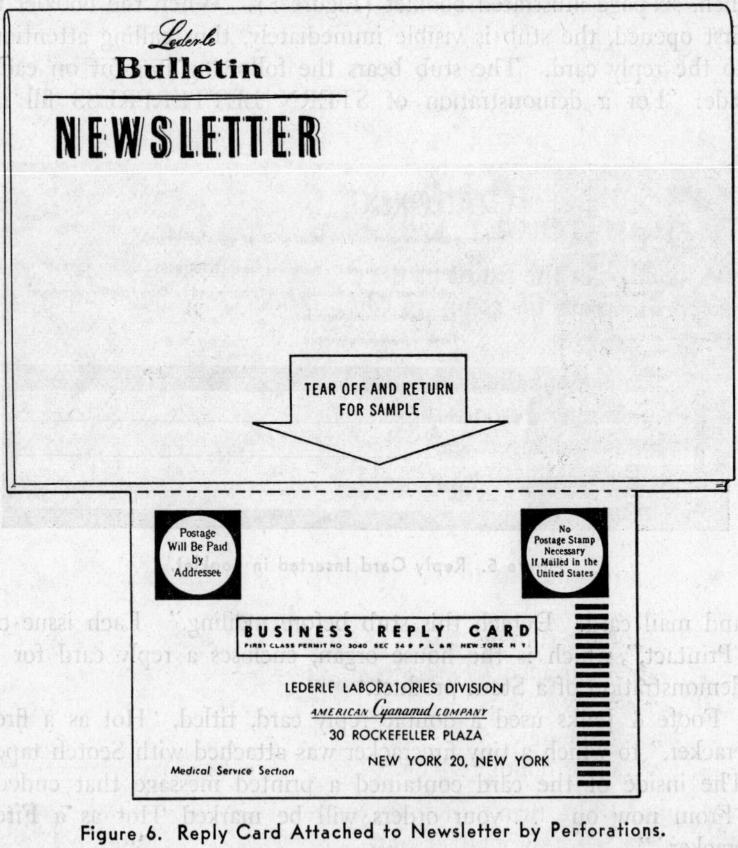

Figure 6. Reply Card Attached to Newsletter by Perforations.

Map give-aways promote public relations and attract prospects. A map of local territory proved a popular give-away folder for a Virginia secretarial school, and can be easily adapted as a mailing piece by retailers, insurance companies, laundries, garages, hotels, and others.

A map of Arlington, Virginia, occupied the middle spread of a one-fold, 7 x 9¾ inch give-away designed by the Arlington Institute to publicize the school facilities and to attract new students. Distributed to local residents and transients, local stores and bus terminals, the cover of the folder was headed "New Map of Arlington County Showing New Streets and Bus Lines." A picture of the institute occupied the middle of the cover, followed by the name and address of the school. The back cover of the folder was headed: "Additional copies of this map may be secured FREE in:" This was followed by brief ads of shops and bus terminals who were distributing the folder. The only sales "plug" contained in the give-away was the spotting of Arlington Institute on the map, and a promotion message on the back cover.

6. HOW TO GET AND BUILD MAILING LISTS

Where to get the list of prospects. The sources of prospect lists are too numerous for complete enumeration. The most important include:

1. Customers of the firm.
2. Names rented from other firms.
3. Names exchanged with other firms.
4. Names supplied by list brokers.
5. Directories.
6. Rating books.
7. Membership lists from organizations.
8. Public records.
9. Lists built through space or radio advertising.
10. Names supplied by satisfied customers and prospects.
11. Salesmen's reports.
12. Press clippings.
13. Special list-building plans.

Names of the firm's own customers as a mailing list source. One of the most profitable sources for a good mailing list is the company's own records. Active customers, inactive customers, cash customers, C.O.D. purchasers may all be good prospects for further sales. In a department store, for example, a direct-mail piece on hosiery can be sent to buyers of women's shoes. To use another example, a firm selling roofing material and paint uses its list of satisfied buyers of roofing material as prospects for paint sales.

Names rented from other firms. Most firms selling by mail are glad to rent their lists of prospects or customers to noncompeting firms. For example, many magazines will be glad to rent the names of their expired subscribers. Book publishers will often rent the names of those who have not recently purchased. Direct-mail sellers of general merchandise often allow noncompeting firms to mail to their names. The rentor agrees with the list owner to test a certain number of names, usually 1,000 or 2,000, at a normal renting rate of about $15 per thousand. If the test proves successful, mailings are made to the entire list. Either of two procedures may be followed:

1. The rentor sends empty envelopes to the list owner, who addresses and returns them with the understanding that the rentor will mail the envelopes and not make a list of the names.

2. The rentor delivers stuffed, sealed envelopes to the list owner for addressing and mailing, together with a check to cover the cost of postage. The list owner addresses the envelopes, meters, and sorts if necessary, and delivers them to the post office. Post-office receipts give proof of mailing.

A large percentage of direct-mail sellers rely heavily on the lists of others to bring them their business. Lists of buyers of any one item are usually good direct-mail prospects for other items and are well worth the rental charge involved.

Names exchanged with other firms. Exchanges of lists are generally made between noncompetitive firms whose lists are more or less similar from the standpoint of type of prospect. For example, a book publisher might exchange lists with a publisher of a magazine, or with a publisher of an entirely different type of book. The procedure is similar to that outlined in the preceding paragraph, except that in place of a rental fee for the list, each firm addresses from its own list an equivalent amount of mailing matter delivered by the other for addressing. As in the case of rented lists, tests are usually made before large lists are exchanged.

Names supplied by list brokers. The function of the list broker is to suggest mailing lists of prospects for anyone interested in using the mails for advertising. List brokers are found in every important city. They sometimes operate in connection with firms offering letter services, such as multigraphing, processing, addressing, and mailing. The broker may arrange for the rental of lists from other firms.

To obtain best results in dealing with a list broker, the most successful plan is to call him in and explain the entire plan of sales. He will know what good prospect lists are available and how much they will cost. More than one broker can be consulted, if desired.

Brokers work on a percentage basis, usually 20 per cent, which is paid by the list owner. Each broker has a few lists that he handles on an exclusive basis—that is, other brokers cannot handle except through him—and many other lists which are open to all brokers.

The advantage of working with a broker is that he has accumulated a great deal of information about various lists and can recommend those which have the best chance of bringing back a profit. He will know which lists are doing well for other houses, and which are not. He may discourage the use of a particular list and suggest new lists about which the mailer might not otherwise know. Experienced direct mailers avail themselves of the services of brokers constantly; new firms in direct mail would do well to lean heavily on the judgment of the better known brokers.

Directories. Hundreds of directories are published each year, many of which can be profitably utilized by firms selling by mail. The great advantage of these directories, of course, is that they are comparatively inexpensive. For instance, Polk's Bankers Encyclopædia, which contains a list of all the banks in the country, together with all the important executives of those banks, can be had for about $20. Martindale-Hubbell Law Directory, containing the names and addresses of over 160,000 attorneys, can be had for about $39. Obviously, if such lists can be used, they are much cheaper to obtain than rented lists.

The objection to the use of such directories is that, because of frequent usage, the names are not so responsive as are those on rented lists. Hence, it is necessary to analyze these directory lists carefully and to select the names that seem most logical. For example, it is possible to secure at a low price a book containing the names of many thousand corporation directors; but few direct-mail firms can mail profitably to the entire list. As an illustration, it might happen that directors who are treasurers of corporations would be better prospects than those who are presidents; or that directors who are secretaries might buy more willingly than those who are treasurers. Where lists are large enough, it is worth while to study them to determine whether or not there is some logical breakdown that would make at least part of the list pay.

The most common directories are trade directories, telephone directories, street directories, city directories, blue books and credit-rating books.

Membership lists from organizations. Membership lists of clubs, social organizations, lodges, trade associations, professional groups, labor unions, and other organizations make good mailing lists for some types of propositions. The roster of membership is usually obtained from the secretary or president upon tactful request and satisfactory explanation of the use to which it is to be put. Sometimes some inducement must be offered for the use of the list.

A list of trade and commercial associations with the names and addresses of the secretaries is published annually by the United States Department of Commerce.

Using public records for mailing lists. Public records frequently make excellent mailing lists. These are obtainable from national sources and county, state, and municipal records. Thus, voting and tax lists, marriage licenses, building permits, automobile licenses, and the like, supply valuable names. Inquiry at the place in which the public record is filed should be made to determine whether the names may be copied from the source, or whether a list can be secured upon application. Sometimes a nominal fee is charged for the list.

Lists built through space or radio advertising. Some direct-mail firms obtain most efficient results from leads obtained from space advertising or through radio advertising. To build a list rapidly, the most successful procedure is to offer a premium, such as a booklet, an article of merchandise, or some other item.

The greatest advantage of building a list through advertising is that it is an exclusive list; no one other than the advertiser has access to it. It is also a selective list. The disadvantage is that such lists are expensive to build.

It is not unusual, for instance, for a list of names compiled from magazine advertising to cost 50 cents a name. Obviously, business obtained from these names must be substantially greater than that obtained from rented or directory lists before there will be any profit on the investment.

To eliminate curiosity seekers from the list a small charge may be made for the premium offered.

Names supplied by satisfied customers and prospects. Customers and other prospects may be willing to supply names of friends, relatives, or acquaintances who might be interested in the proposition. The following practices have been found useful in building mailing lists with the aid of satisfied customers:

1. Send letters to all customers at one time asking them to suggest names of friends who might be interested in the product or service. Supply a form for listing the names.
2. Send a letter, or a series of letters, to each new customer within a reasonable period after he has made his first purchase, and in the letter, or in one of the series, ask for a list of names.
3. Offer a premium in return for the favor of submitting names. If salesmen are used, they can deliver the premium.
4. Ask for a list of names and offer a substantial reward if actual sales are made to any of the prospects. For example, a profit-sharing plan was used by a fuel- and oil-burner dealer to get prospects' names from customers. Each customer for whom a job had been installed received an impressive folder, the cover of which resembled a bond. Upon opening the document, the customer found ten perforated coupons with ruled lines for the names and addresses of suggested prospects. If a sale were made within three months to one of the names filed the customer was given five dollars.
5. If distribution is through a dealer, wholesaler, or jobber, and names of customers are sought, enclose a return post card in the package, and offer a premium if the card is returned by the customer.

Building a list through salesmen. Various methods have been used to secure the co-operation of the sales force in building up a list of names that are good mail-order prospects. Among these are:

1. Have salesmen send in daily, weekly, or monthly reports of prospects upon whom they have called.

2. Supply salesmen with report forms, cards, or other equipment that simplifies the process of noting names of prospects.

3. Require salesmen to submit certain information about the prospect in addition to his name and address, to permit proper classification of the prospect.

4. Place a limit on the number of names to be submitted. This tactic assures a better grade of names.

5. Set up rules that must be met before names can be considered acceptable prospects.

6. Offer incentives to arouse interest in suggesting live-prospect names.

7. Educate salesmen in the importance of mailing-list work, and show them by means of booklets, sales meetings, and bulletins how to gather names of prospects.

Lists built through clippings. The list that is compiled by making press clippings of direct leads for sales is likely to be up to date and correct. For example, clippings of marriages may form the basis of circularization for furniture sales, and news items of fires may create a list of prospects for fireproof roofing. The clippings can be secured at a low cost from firms offering newspaper-clipping services. Careful instruction should be given as to the clippings desired and the areas to be covered.

Special list-building plans. Any number of miscellaneous ways can be mentioned for collecting names of prospects. For example, retail stores frequently undertake to build their lists through special services. The personal shopping bureau may keep a list of names of shoppers assisted; a special boys' broadcast as a store-promotion stunt may yield the names of all persons attending the broadcast and furnish an excellent list of prospects for junior clothing. One department store builds a mailing list by having a birthday registration book in the children's department. An inexpensive present is sent to each child on its birthday. This prompts customers to register their children and to notify the store of changed addresses.

Contests are a common method of building mailing lists. Employee contests with prizes offered for the person submitting the largest number of names resulting in sales have helped to build good lists. Contests in which the public participates is another popular method, for the names and addresses of those who take part in the contest can thus be secured.

Checking names before adding to list. Some companies enhance the quality of their mailing lists and thus increase the percentage of returns from each mailing by checking all names before adding them to the list. The trouble and expense of this preliminary check are considered worth while if frequent and expensive mailings are made from the list. The checking is usually done by the sales or credit department.

How to keep mailing lists. Any organization that has invested time and money in building up mailing lists will want to keep a careful file of them. Since lists may be kept in the form of cards, a directory, a book, a printed list taken from a book, typewritten sheets, or in the form in which it is received from various sources, some system must be devised for locating the lists as they are needed. File boxes, drawers, and bookcases are generally used for housing the lists. In addition, a card record is made up for each individual list, indexed by field, subject, or title. A record of the number of times the list is used may be made directly on the index card.

The list of prospects, if made on 3 x 5 inch cards or stencils, should be grouped geographically by city or town and state, in alphabetical order. The names in each group should also be alphabetical, preferably with the last name first. This arrangement facilitates the weeding out of "undeliverables."

A number of concerns using stencils report that if a list is to be used ten to twelve times a year, it is more economical to have a stencil made for each name, to be used in addressing, than to have the list addressed by typewriter or by hand each time.

Increasing the effectiveness of the mailing list. If the mailing lists are broken down after use to segregate the names of those who have responded from those who have remained inactive, the effectiveness of the lists is increased.

Lists of individuals must be watched for errors in the spelling of names, incorrect addresses, wrong titles, and other mistakes. Corrections should be made, and names of persons who have moved and left no address or who have died should be removed. Lists of firm names must be watched for similar errors. Changes in names of buyers, managers, presidents, secretaries, and other officers must be noted, and the names of bankrupt firms must be removed.

Keeping a list up to date requires not only constant vigilance to insure that the details are accurate but also breakdown of the list into special classifications that suit the purposes of the firm. Such classifications may be: (1) sources of the list; (2) type of list; (3) frequency of purchase; (4) profession of prospect; (5) volume of purchases; and the like.

Care must be exercised in deciding whether names should be removed entirely from the mailing list into an inactive list because no response has been received after repeated mailings. Such factors as the profit on a sale, repeat possibilities, and any other items showing how much can be spent on mailing to a prospect before it becomes unprofitable to do so must guide the firm in segregating inactive names from his lists.

Occasional checking of mailing lists by salesmen and dealers in particular territories may help to keep the list correct. An established procedure in the organization for getting information from various company departments to the mailing department, as to changes in names, addresses, and closings of accounts, will facilitate keeping the list correct.

The checkup mailing. The mailing list should be cleaned out at regular intervals to remove the names of persons not receiving the mail. To accomplish this step the statement "Return Postage Guaranteed" is included on the envelope under the sender's return address, in the upper left-hand corner of the envelope. All envelopes carrying this statement which cannot be delivered are returned to the sender (unless the Form 3547 statement is used), with the reasons for nondelivery.

When a list is several years old, it is usually worth while to obtain forwarding addresses of prospects. To secure such addresses, there can be printed or rubberstamped on the lower left-hand portion of the envelope or wrappper used to send third- or fourth-class mail: "If addressee has removed and new address is known, notify sender on Form 3547, postage for which is guaranteed." The post office will destroy the mail not delivered but will send a card with the new address. There is a charge for each card.

Keeping a personal mailing list up to date. When mailings are addressed to personnel instead of to the firm, a check of changes in names should be made at intervals. To verify the accuracy of the 5,000 retailers' names on the list, Durene Association of America sent the following letter to personnel managers of 701 department stores. It drew an immediate response of 84.5 per cent from these stores.

To The Personnel Manager

Dear Sir:

Please do us the favor of having one of your people check the enclosed list of executives, making necessary deletions and additions.

Your co-operation will enable us to provide full courtesy and ensure safe delivery of informative mailings concerning the consumer advantages of the merchandise from your regular resources which is made of Durene yarn.

A stamped addressed envelope is provided for return of the corrected list.

I shall much appreciate your help.

A. C. Layton Newsom
EXECUTIVE SECRETARY

ACLN:ch
ENC.

Other ways of cleaning out a list. Various other methods can be used for bringing a mailing list up to date. One way is to make a free offer in a letter that is sent to the entire list. This method was used, for example, by a printer who sent a mailing piece in the form of a French folder, on the back of which was an inspirational poem. Beneath the verse was a notice to the effect that copies of the poem printed on good stock and suitable for framing would be supplied to the reader without charge. Over 50 per cent of the firms on the mailing list responded to this offer.

It is sometimes profitable to clean out the entire list by frankly asking the prospect to make corrections and to indicate any suggestions he has with regard to his listing. *Parents' Magazine* checked its mailing list with a frank, inexpensive mailing piece sent to a list of 9,300 space buyers. The mailing piece consisted of a large envelope enclosing a Reply-O Form (see page 122) monarch-size letter. Three words, "Keep It Clean," comprised the only copy that appeared on the envelope, other than the third-class indicia, the return postage guaranty, and the return address. The letter repeated the envelope copy on the letterhead with the question mark "Keep It Clean?" and then said:

We're trying to—our complimentary mailing list, that is. So—you will be a good fellow—and slide the card—out of the pocket—on the back of this sheet—and let us know—whether you've moved—died—changed your name—gotten a better job—or anything else—that may have happened to you—that makes our present stencil—incorrect . . .

This plan brought 46.1 per cent returns.

Master control system keeps mailing lists in order. Users of direct mail might benefit from the neat master customer control card system developed by the Broadway Department Store, Los Angeles, Calif.

The store's card system is primarily for mailings to increase buying by charge customers, but it can be used as easily for lists compiled from cash or C.O.D. customers to whom deliveries have been made. The system classifies purchasers according to the type of goods they have purchased—"shoe" purchasers, "dress" purchasers, "hat" purchasers, and the like.

Periodically, mailings are sent to the shoe purchasers telling them of sales of hats, dresses, coats, etc.; to hat purchasers telling them of sales of shoes, dresses, coats, and so forth. Of course, mailings about shoe bargains are not sent to the recent shoe purchasers, nor mailings about hat bargains to recent hat purchasers. By informing customers of other goods available, which they have not already purchased, the company secures a gratifying response. Results vary from 5 to 25 per cent. Mailings range from 2 to 10,000.

7. HOW TO WRITE SALES LETTERS

The uninvited guest. What is the person whose name is on your mailing list likely to be doing at the time your sales letter reaches him? The executive may be dictating a letter, figuring out estimates, interviewing a salesman, or talking over the telephone. The retailer may be serving a customer, taking stock, considering a new proposition, making up his books, or planning a sale. The housewife may be preparing breakfast, washing dishes or clothes, sweeping, cleaning carpets, or hanging pictures. Each of these and the many other persons you are seeking to address may be doing one or another of a thousand things at the moment your sales letter is delivered. You have no way of knowing what their activities are, what their thoughts are; but you may be certain that they are doing and thinking something. No one is just waiting for your letter to arrive.

What this means for the sales letter writer is largely a matter of viewpoint. To one the situation may seem to be bristling with obstacles, like a barbed-wire section of No Man's Land. To another it may be alive with opportunities.

No one is just waiting for your letter to arrive. But the opportunities in the situation arise from the fact that everyone is waiting for something—waiting in the sense of working toward, aiming at, or hoping for it. To the executive it may be a method of reducing costs; to the retailer a means of increasing sales; to the housewife a new way of lessening the drudgery of her daily routine. Then, into the mind of the name on your mailing list, preoccupied as it is with such problems, hopes, ambitions, and fears, walks the uninvited guest—your sales letter.

No uninvited guest is at once welcomed with open arms. He has to make his way in the face of indifference and suspicion. So also does your sales letter.

The reader is constantly thinking of himself, is mulling over in his conscious or subconscious mind ways and means of achieving certain things that mean a great deal to him. If the sales letter tries merely to distract his attention by clamoring about itself and about what it wants, there is a conflict of which the reader can readily rid himself by simply reaching toward the wastebasket. If, however, the letter talks about the reader—tells the executive that it can show him a method of reducing his costs, or the retailer a means of increasing his sales, or the housewife a new way of lessening the drudgery of her work—the *me* interest is stirred, and the reader is prepared to "listen."

What is it that makes a letter sell? The letter wants and asks the reader to do something—to "mail the enclosed card today," to "ride in the new Standard," to "examine this book for five days without obligation." The reader, however, already has his own wants. He is not interested in what you are wanting and asking him to do. He is not interested, that is, until you show him that what you are wanting and asking him to do is so closely connected with what he himself wants, that by doing as you ask he will be taking a step nearer one of his own hopes and desires or a step further away from an old fear or anxiety. In a word, the letter that sells is the letter that succeeds in tying up what it has to offer with the reader's wants.

Know your reader; know your product. To tie up what you have to offer with the reader's wants, study your reader and study your product—imaginatively. By putting yourself in the reader's place, find out what his interests are. Then study your product to discover how it can be made to tie up with those interests. Above all, cultivate the habit of visualizing clearly and simply. Eliminate from your mind the preconceived notions as to human nature and the technical knowledge of your product that prevent you from seeing the wood for the trees.

The ingredients of the successful sales letter. For the successful sales letter there can be no formula. Sales letter writing places a premium upon originality—upon keeping one step ahead of the times. What pulls today because it is new, is old tomorrow and has to be thrown into the discard. If, however, a formula were to be stated, the ingredients of the successful sales letter might be listed as follows:

1. *The opening*—which gains the reader's attention by tying in with his thoughts and emotions concerning himself, thus exciting his curiosity and tempting him to read further.
2. *The explanation or description*—which pictures for the reader the main features of your product or service.
3. *The motive*—which creates in the reader the *want* for what you are selling by describing what your product or service will do for him; how it will contribute to his pleasure, comfort, security, or gain.
4. *The evidence*—which establishes in the reader's mind conviction as to the truth of your statements and the value of your product to him.
5. *The penalty or inducement*—which gets the reader to act at once.
6. *The close*—which tells the reader exactly what to do, how to do it, and makes action easy.

These are the essential ingredients. The method of their combination, however, varies when different hands do the mixing.

Getting the reader's interest in the opening. The opening must flag the reader's attention. It can do this best by speaking to him of himself—his problems, hopes, ambitions, and fears. Then, his interest excited, the reader is led into a description of the product or service offered and is made to want it and to act in order to get it, *for what it will do for him.* Notice how the following openings tie up with the particular reader's wants.

TO AN EXECUTIVE

Dear Mr. Simpson:

Do you ship by Parcel Post?

If you do, you can't afford to miss knowing about a new and very efficient method of handling C.O.D. and insured shipments. It will speed up your shipments—and cut your labor and error costs by 30%.

This remarkable and simple system is fully described and illustrated in a little booklet entitled, "If You Ship by Parcel Post." . . . .

TO A RETAILER

Dear Mr. Beckman:

Do the companies that furnish you with the fountain pens you now sell ever think about your turnover problems?

For example, how often does their advertising demand that you handle a new color?

Here's Sheaffer's way—our new Grey Pearl, one of the most beautiful colors we've ever introduced, was announced to our dealers nearly four months ago. Shipment of this color wasn't promised until October, and we won't begin to advertise it until June of next year.

What does it mean?

It means that Sheaffer dealers are given an opportunity to move out the oldest color in their stock to prepare for the new color, which will be shown to customers

only when the dealers are ready for it.

The selfish way is suddenly to flood the country with advertising. . . . .

TO A DOCTOR

Dear Doctor Blake:

Doctor, what shall I do for my cold?

At this season of the year your patients ask you that troublesome question many times.

The local symptoms of colds in the head are quickly relieved by the use of EfeDroN Hart Nasal Jelly.

EfeDroN promptly relieves the nasal congestion by contracting capillaries, reducing turbinates, and diminishing hyperemia. It quickly opens the nasal air passages..........

TO A YOUNG MAN

Dear Mr. Williams:

Step into your employer's office tomorrow and demand a 100 per cent increase in your salary. Will you get it?

Could you step out to some other firm and get a job paying twice your present salary? Probably not, or you would do it, of course.

Yet this is exactly what LaSalle-trained men are doing every day..........

TO A WHITE-COLLAR WORKER

Dear Mr. Burnett:

On pay day—does your money go around? Or does it fail to stop all the gaps made by last month's bills?

Just yesterday we helped a family solve a problem that threatened to cause the head of the house to lose his job. It was the same old story—pay reduced, and unexpected extra expenses had thrown the family budget out of gear. Creditors were pressing. Bills had to be paid to save his credit—and to save his job.

This problem was solved through our Personal Loan Department..........

TO A MOTHER

Dear Mrs. Ferguson:

After baby's food and baby's clothes, the most important thing you have to decide upon is the little cart baby is going to ride in—is going to be seen in—is going to be admired in.

Never a child came into the world but was worthy of as good a cart..........

TO A FARMER

Dear Mr. Jensen:

You're interested in better hay? You want to increase the value of your hay crop, and at the same time put up that crop with less expense?

The John Deere Way of Making Hay will do both these things. The method is built around the John Deere-Dain System Rake. Do not confuse this rake with the common side-delivery rake. It is different, because it has—

curved teeth
inclined front frame
wheels of adjustable width

—all of which are absolutely necessary to make a light, fluffy windrow. It is a left-hand rake.........

Whether you are selling a fountain pen or an automobile, a lipstick or a piece of real estate, the principle is the same. Discover what the reader is most interested in, and play to that interest as a baseball pitcher pitches to the batter's weakness. Forget yourself, and tell the reader what your product or service *will do for him.*

Tell a story to get interest. One of the fundamental interests of all human nature is the interest in a story. The most sophisticated person can be attracted by an anecdote or a short narrative. The story should have a close application to the subject and purpose of the letter and, of course, should be very skillfully written.

Example of story beginning. The following paragraphs illustrate a story opening that immediately enlists the interest of the reader. The letter begins with a narrative that is full of warm human interest. In the very first sentence it begins to sell fish. The first paragraph leads the reader on to the next. Notice how its third paragraph starts with a query, often an effective device for waking up the reader when the letter comes to a point where the indifferent reader is likely to doze. Paragraph four introduces the offer in a pleasantly offhand manner: "You won't mind, will you, if I ship some of my fish direct to your home?" The clauses, "It won't cost you anything unless . . ." and "Try the fish at my expense, and judge for yourself whether . . ." are effective in the direct-mail selling of many products.

Dear Friend:

Way back in 1623, a small group of Pilgrims gathered in their small fish huts to name this fishing port Gloucester. They were a hardy lot of folks, living mostly on game and salt water fish. They built small boats and braved the treacherous waters off Gloucester to get fish for their families. In those times women folks helped too—for every hand meant more food for the cold winter months to come.

I remember, as a small boy, my father telling me about being lashed to the mainmast in a stiff blow, when his father's schooner was half buried in the plunging sea. It was a hard life. But still, Gloucester boys follow it year after year. It's in our blood. It's our way of Livin'. Nature has located us close to the richest waters there are.

Have you ever wondered why Gloucester is one of the greatest fishing ports in the world? You see, we have many varieties of delicious fish landed here daily. More good fish come right in here to Gloucester than any other port in the world. That's why you can never say you've tasted fish at its perfect prime unless you get it direct from Gloucester.

So you won't mind, will you, if I ship some of my fish direct to your home? It won't cost you anything, unless you feel like keeping it. All I ask is that you try the fish at my expense, and judge for yourself whether it isn't exactly what you have always wanted.

This letter of the Frank E. Davis Fish Company contained five more paragraphs and an enclosure.

Using news as an attention-getter. News in a sales letter will usually supply the attention value necessary to enlist and carry the reader's interest, but it should always lead to and tie up with the selling message. Here are two letters that make good use of the news opening.

Dear Sir:

Last week the XYZ Company checked over its stock of our ice-cream cans, and sent us 500 cans for re-tinning. They feel that putting their cans in condition now will save them money next spring and summer. They know that in the busy season, no one has time to wait for a can to be re-tinned—it is quicker and easier to order a new one.

Of course, you know we make more money by selling you new cans than by re-tinning your old ones. But we want to be selling you cans a good many years, and we know that if we can save you money on your annual expenditure for cans, you are going to think mighty well of us and of our cans.

Now, won't you please go over your stock and send us every one of our cans you have that needs re-tinning? You know our charge for this re-tinning is only one-fourth the price of a new can.

And if you don't use our cans, you may feel that our low re-tinning charge is another good reason for using our cans next year.

Dear Sir:

We all sympathize with our neighbor, Mr. J. P. Jones, whose home burned to the ground last Thursday.

And we all hope we shall never have a similar disaster affect our own homes. There is one sure way to eliminate this ever-present menace of Fire. That's to be certain the roof, where most residential fires start, is of fire-resistant material.

Flintkote Mineral Surfaced Shingles give you this fire resistance. Every package carries the approved label of the Fire Underwriters' Laboratory. Insurance companies recognize, in most communities, the fire-safety of Flintkote Mineral Surfaced Roofs by giving lower insurance rates.

Let us talk with you about your home. Give us a ring today . . . we shall be pleased to call at your convenience.

Cordially yours,

Stunt letters to get attention. Stunts are used in letter writing to get attention. They have been used in sales letters, promotion letters, and collection letters principally. If the stunt meets the following tests, the letter may be effective:

1. Is it in good taste? You can't risk offending the reader.
2. Does it tie up with the subject of the letter?
3. Is it original? You don't want the reader to say "old stuff" and stop there.
4. Does its cleverness distract from the message? A stunt may be so clever that the reader forgets about what he is being asked to do.

Example of stunt letter that meets the tests. The following letter gets right down to brass tacks with its stunt. The two brass-headed paper staples inserted on the first line cannot offend anyone, and cannot hurt anyone. The stunt is original in its approach and is not so clever that the reader forgets what the writer wants.

Mr. Tag Buyer:

Getting down to brass tacks . . . . [Here the two brass heads appeared] . . . . it's your tag business we're after.

Will you meet us half way and let us show you what we can offer on your tag requirements?

It won't take but a few minutes of time to take samples of your tags, mark on them the quantities that you buy, drop them in the postage prepaid envelope attached—and mail.

Will you do it? You can bet the favor will be most welcome and that prices and samples will reach you by return mail.

Thanks a lot.

Yours very truly,

WURZBURG BROTHERS

We are ready to supply all sizes of good tags . . . plain . . . printed . . . numbered . . . perforated . . . scored . . . all weight stocks . . . metal eyelets . . . plain eyelets . . . with deadlocks, wires or strings . . . in gangs . . . in fact almost any type of tag you want.

A stunt opening that worked. The stunt used in the following letter not only attracted attention but tied up immediately with the quality of the product that was offered. The letter, sent to 300 carefully selected prospects, brought 40 replies and resulted in sales of 56 units.

You can really
treat 'em rough!

(Here was attached a pearl)

(Here was a drawing of a hammer, poised ready to strike the pearl)

HoTaY Pearls will take an awful beating. Even hammering doesn't faze them. Not that you are likely to hammer your necklace, but this shows you that they are all that I claim.

HoTaY Pearls are not the ordinary simulated pearls. Their beauty is inherent. They are to all intents unbreakable. They will not scale or crack. They will wear and wear and WEAR and retain their original luster.

I'll send you postpaid a graduated necklace 18 inches long with a non-tarnish safety clasp of white metal in an attractive box for only $3.00. These are identical with those I formerly sold at $10.00 and up.

This chance comes to you just when you are beginning to think of the perplexing Christmas problem. Then there are birthdays to remember all through the year—graduation presents for next spring or maybe a really different and breath-taking bridge prize.

This 18 inch graduated necklace will nestle alluringly at your throat. It is the season's most popular length. The beads are perfectly matched and evenly graduated to the size knowing buyers are choosing. At only $3.00 it is a real bargain.

Those who bought HoTaY Pearls years ago still prize and praise them and ask for more. Those in the business have valued them at much more than the price I charge.

I haven't a great many, so it's best to act without delay. Mail the convenient card TODAY, so that you'll not be disappointed.

Very truly yours,
J. D. Oakley

Story opening combined with stunt. A mail advertising agency reported unusually good results from the following letter, which combines a story opening with a stunt. An opened oyster was faintly imprinted at the top of the sheet. Half an imitation pearl was tipped in at the correct spot in the outline of the oyster. The regular letterhead form appeared at the bottom of the sheet, while the statement "You Have to Open Oysters to Get Pearls" headed the top of the sheet. The pearl, of course, provided the lead for the story that follows.

Mr. Jones:

In the South Sea Islands deep-chested natives dive time after time, bringing up great handfuls of oysters in the hope that some of them may contain pearls.

There is no way of telling which oysters *do* bear pearls, and the oysters themselves are strangely reticent about the whole matter. A diver may work for hours without acquiring more than the basis for a stew. But the law of averages dictates that every so often he *will* find a pearl . . . and the more oysters he brings up the more pearls he will find.

Your business, like ours, is based on that old law of averages.

Your oysters are your prospects; your pearls, the orders you sell. Not all of those prospects can be sold, but the law of averages says that if you call on enough of them . . . tell enough of them your story . . . keep the mailman placing your literature on their desks . . . you will get the orders you need to keep growing and prospering. And if you concentrate on a list of *known* prospects, you are bound to increase the number of orders you get from the calls you make.

Before you start your Fall selling, it will pay you to scrutinize your lists of prospects carefully . . . make sure that you have enough "oysters" to keep the pearls rolling in during the months ahead. If your lists are old or incomplete, we can supply you with new ones that are up-to-the-minute in the information they contain and double-checked for accuracy.

Our list service covers more than 8,000 local and national markets. A copy of our 19— list catalog, giving estimated counts and prices of these markets, is yours for the asking. It doesn't cost you a penny to call AT 4457, or to drop the enclosed card in the mail, but it may pave the way to more sales and more profitable sales in the future. Call us, or use the postage-free card, today.

Yours very truly,

BURGESS-BECKWITH, INC.

Gadgets and stunts. A broadcasting company has made effective use of gadgets attached to colored cards to call attention to the selling message on the cards. For example, a red card measuring 7½″ × 5″ has a tiny hatchet slipped into an opening on the card, with the following heading and message:

WHY NOT BURY THE HATCHET?

Are you at war with that vicious monster, Increasing Selling Costs? If so, there's probably nothing you'd like better than to bury the hatchet.

Retailers, wholesalers, service organizations—large and small alike—

have found that KSO-KRNT advertising keeps their selling costs down and sales up. Call 3-2111 today and ask a KSO-KRNT representative to show you "case histories" of Des Moines advertisers who are selling more economically on KSO or KRNT.

Iowa Broadcasting Company
Craig Lawrence
Commercial Manager

Tests to apply to an opening. Don't be satisfied with an opening until you have tested it with the following questions:

1. Is it timorous? An opening that is lacking in vitality or is hackneyed will not impress the reader. Avoid such weak expressions as, "It gives us pleasure to inform you"; "You will be interested to know that"; "I am offering something that may interest you."

2. Is it negative? An opening that contains an unpleasant suggestion or an apology does not attract the reader. For example, avoid suggesting trouble, or that you are taking the reader's valuable time. Of course, if the principal purpose of the article is to protect the reader from trouble or disagreeable experience, the negative suggestion may be effective.

3. Is it relevant? If the opening is not relevant, no matter how interesting and clever it is, it will fail in its purpose of holding the reader's attention. The opening must tie up with the sales message of the letter.

4. Is it indirect and vague? A colorless generalization cannot excite the curiosity of the reader and make him feel inclined to read further. If the opening seems vague, make it direct and specific and notice how it gains strength. For example, compare the following openings:

Vague: It does not cost much to run an Electrolux.

Specific: A few pennies a day—25 to 70 cents a week—that is all it costs to run an Electrolux.

5. Is it too smart? Mere smartness will deprive the letter of character and may offend the reader. The following is effective as an attention-getter, but so is stepping on a person's toes.

I hope I am wrong
in addressing you as
Dear Ostrich:
But you should not avoid facing facts, etc.

Create desire for the product. After favorable attention has been obtained, the next step is to create a desire in the reader for the product that is offered. To achieve this end, the reader should be told what your product or service will do for him. The central selling point should be selected and fitted to a need or desire of the prospect. The prospect must be made aware of that need or desire by appeal to his intellect or his emotions. *Appeal to emotions* is the more important of the two in a sales letter. Fundamentally, people act on the rather simple notion of desiring to have pleasant things and to avoid unpleasant things. This does not mean that the writer of a sales letter can afford to neglect to give facts and logical arguments that will convince the reader of the superiority of the product in satisfying his needs. It merely means that in the appeal to reason the importance of emotional appeal should not be overlooked.

A letter that disguises the appeal to reason. As an illustration of the above principle, take the case of an automobile agency trying to interest a banker in the purchase of a low-priced car. A low-priced car? A banker? Impossible, you may say, to make any contact with an individual of this class—a man whose everyday experience teaches him to think slowly and cautiously and to act only after careful check and double-check—impossible to make contact with this man by any means other than mere cold logic and reasoning. But consider how persuasively the emotional appeal is put forward in the following letter:

Dear Mr. Spencer:

At a meeting of bankers at the Missouri Athletic Club last month, there was only one bank president who did not own a Ford.

He asked the others,

> "Why do you fellows ride around in Fords when you can afford the best?"

One answer was,

> "I made my money through sound investments and careful management, and there is more value dollar for dollar in a Ford than in any other car made."

Another answer was,

> "In the first place, my investment is very small. I can afford to let my car stand on the street in all kinds of weather, can park it in a small space, and then at the end of the year can trade it in and get greater value in proportion than with any other car I ever owned."

We offer the best investment in the automotive world.

Come in and see us. Our showrooms are attractively arranged for your comfort. You are under no obligation to buy.

Sincerely yours,

This letter is a skillful sales message, for two reasons. First, it opens by speaking to the banker of himself and his own interests—"At a meeting of bankers . . ."—and thus stimulates him to read further. Second, although at first glance it may appear to be an appeal to reason, on closer analysis it shows itself to be really an emotional appeal cleverly disguised. It addresses itself to the emotion to which, above all others, a banker would probably be most susceptible—the desire to make even his minor purchases sound and dividend-paying investments. Furthermore, it conveys its message the more effectively by refraining from arguments regarding body style, gasoline consumption, easy-riding qualities, etc., etc., and, instead, merely quoting the opinions of those to whom a banker would be most willing to listen—his own colleagues. If the emotional appeal can be used to sell a low-priced automobile to a banker, it can be adapted even more readily to other products and to other classes of people.

What emotions can you appeal to? The emotional appeals are numerous, but basically they simmer down to these six: love, duty, pride, gain, self-indulgence, and self-preservation or fear. These are also the primary buying motives.

In a sales letter, the more motives you can appeal to, the more effective may be your sales letter. Thus, if you are attempting to interest a married man in the purchase of insurance, you can appeal to some or all of the following emotions: (1) his *love* for his wife and family; (2) his sense of *duty* in providing for his dependents; (3) his *pride* in meeting his responsibilities; (4) his sense of *gain* in purchasing a form of insurance that is an investment as well as a protection; and (5) his *fear* either that his dependents will be left destitute in the event of his death or that he will be without a source of income in his old age.

Determining which emotion to appeal to. Determining which emotion or emotions to stir is, once again, a matter of knowing your reader, knowing your product, and tying a Gordian knot between the two. If you are selling a business magazine to an executive, you may stress gain (the magazine will prove a valuable source of new ideas), and/or fear (by not subscribing the executive may miss something and, as a result, may fall behind in the competitive race).

In selling to a retailer you may choose to play up to his pride in the quality of the merchandise that he sells; his sense of gain if price is a feature of your product; or his fear that, if he fails to stock your goods, he may lose business to those of his competitors who do.

In selling furniture to a housewife you may aim to stir her pride in her home; cosmetics, her personal pride or vanity; a luxury, her self-indulgence; a baby carriage, her love for her child.

If you are to make your reader *want* your product for what it will do for him and *act* in order to get it (and not merely eye it from afar with mild approval), it is to the appropriate emotion or buying motive in him that your sales letter must be addressed. After you have stirred in the reader the feeling of wanting what you have to offer, it is a relatively easy matter to prove to him that he should have it.

The following sales letters, each of proved effectiveness in its particular field, illustrate how in actual practice the emotional appeal has been used in the selling of different types of goods and services to various classes of people.

"Make-and-save-money" appeal—specimen letter. The most powerful sales letters are those that offer the recipient the probability of making money, or of saving it. The following letter is in the "make-and-save-money" class:

Dear Sir:

If we offered you one hundred dollars a month, would you accept it? Besides saving you that much money monthly, the following offer simplifies the buying and cutting of your trimmings.

To make pockets for the normal monthly output of one thousand dozen suits requires one thousand ninety-one yards of "Indian Head" or "Fruit of the Loom" muslin, the price of either of which is eighteen cents a yard. The thousand dozen pockets cost you—not including the cost of laying out and cutting—$196.38.

We can supply you with seven by eight pockets (the standard size), at ten cents a dozen, or one hundred dollars for the thousand dozen—a genuine saving to you of about one hundred dollars a month.

In addition to this saving, you have the benefit of another service. In order to get the advantageous price of eighteen cents a yard on the muslin, you have to buy at least a case of it. From us you can buy just as much as you need. Our large stock and quick delivery enable you to receive your goods just a few hours after the order reaches us.

The pockets are neatly wrapped in packages of fifty dozen, each of which contains ten folds of five dozen. This arrangement enables you to give your contractor just the number he needs. Our cutting machine not only insures neat and clean cutting, but also makes the pockets perfect in size and shape.

You cannot afford to neglect this opportunity. The more quickly you act, the sooner your saving begins.

We shall gladly send you a fifty-dozen package on approval if you mail the enclosed card immediately.

Yours truly,

Durability is a strong appeal. If durability of your product is the selling point that will stimulate the buyer, the following letter may be adapted.

Dear Mr. Bascom:

Getting 58 years of average service out of a McCormick-Deering Ball-Bearing separator in about 4 years is unusual—but read the letter from Anton J. Johnson, Manager, Macomb Dairy Company, Macomb, Illinois.

> "Our No. 6 McCormick-Deering cream separator, purchased from you in December, 19—, is still in daily service. A conservative estimate of the amount of milk put through this separator in four years is 425,000 gallons. At 60 degrees Fahrenheit our butterfat loss is less than 1/100 of 1 per cent. The remarkable thing, however, is that without special attention this separator has never been out of service a single day in four years. If this separator ever wears out (which seems doubtful) we certainly would put in another McCormick-Deering."

With an average production of 5,188 pounds of milk per cow, per year, it would take 12 cows a total of 58 years to produce 425,000 gallons of milk. In other words, Mr. Johnson's McCormick-Deering cream separator has done in four years the work that would be required in 58 years on a 12-cow dairy farm. Space does not permit us to list all the many desirable features of this cream separator, but the enclosed folder includes practical information that will be of special interest.

Farming today and in the future holds the greatest promise for the man who takes advantage of every possible means of lowering his production costs. The McCormick-Deering line of farm operating equipment offers many opportunities for reducing crop production costs. In addition, it presents possibilities for making the difficult farm tasks easier and speeding up the seasonal operations that frequently have an influence on crop yield and quality, thus bringing proportionately greater returns from both equipment and labor.

There is no expense involved in becoming posted on what is latest and best in equipment. You can do this at "Farm Machine Headquarters" —the above-named McCormick-Deering dealer's store. You and your family are always welcome. You can secure practical information and see the machines best adapted to your needs. Make it a point to come in and get better acquainted and look over the facilities available for McCormick-Deering service.

Very truly yours,

A letter appealing to love, self-preservation, maternal instinct, and thrift. The following letter deals with opening a bank account for a baby:

Dear Baby:

We have just learned of your arrival in our city and want to congratulate you—and mother and daddy and everybody—on the happy event.

For a little while you will not bother your head about the big world outside. You'll just delight in mother's smile, and learn to wiggle your toes and with great frequency ask as best you can with a limited vocabulary, "When do I eat?"

But it is not far, my dear, from the cradle to college, from swaddling clothes to wedding gown; today's babe is tomorrow's bride. Now, mother will stand watch over you while a doting dad fights life's battles the harder on your account. But after a while you, too, will be grown up—a beautiful American girl, ready to step into a home of your own.

Wouldn't it be a fine thing for you to begin to build a bank account now? Then, by the time you are big, it, too, will have grown until you will have enough money to do any number of things—to pay your way through college—to buy that lovely trousseau—to buy for yourself the many, many pretty things that mother, perhaps, longed for.

We like the plan so well that we have already placed a dollar in a brand-new bank account for you. If daddy or mother will put a dollar with the one we have given you and will add another each month, your bank account will grow so fast that by the time you are a grown-up lady you'll have a lot of money.

Tell daddy or mother to come in soon and sign a signature card so that they can take care of your account for you until you are big enough to come to the bank yourself.

Affectionately yours,

A letter appealing to desire for knowledge and self-esteem. A magazine for the general public is offered in the following letter:

Dear Mr. Owens:

If you think the world is larger than your parish, this letter has reached the right man.

If you would keep up with the newest plays in Paris, the literary gossip of London, the talk of the Continent. . . .

If you want to know the difference between rumor and fact about Russia and Germany, the truth about France and England. . . .

If you care for news from China and Japan, from India and the Argentine. . . .

If, in short, you want to talk intelligently or to listen with discretion. . . .

Then, here is the magazine for you.

From every large city in every civilized country the leading newspapers and magazines come to the offices of the *LIVING AGE*. There the editors select, translate, and reprint the finest material they can find—political articles, short stories, poems, and book reviews.

With the *LIVING AGE* on your table, you will keep up to the mark on foreign affairs every week in the year.

Here we wish to make only one point more—that it is of an extremely practical nature.

At the bottom of this page there is a coupon. It quotes you the generous rate of *Three Months for One Dollar*—the regular price is *Six Dollars* a year. Fill out and send it to us with your remittance, and you will find yourself looking at the world with a more understanding, a more interested eye.

Sincerely yours,

A letter appealing to beauty, exclusiveness, pleasure, and pride.

A SAGA IN WOOL *

A short time ago, in one of the locked rooms of the Metropolitan Museum, I saw a rug, and I want to tell you about it.

It was an old rug, of a motif that predates Christianity; an example of a handicraft born before history and which lives on, owing nothing to modern science or invention.

This rug had been cast over a group of chairs, obscuring them under its negligent folds.

Within the room there was a stillness, faintly accented by the staccato voice of a distant Elevated. Outside, just beyond the huge expanse of plate-glass window, a gusty wind had arisen and was chasing rubbish up and down the street.

I straddled a chair, folded my arms on its back, and stared at the rug. It was at one and the same time the most subdued and the most vivid object I had ever beheld. The longer I looked, the more did I wish to

* Reproduced by permission of Mr. Jules Livingston, of the Livingston Company, Binghamton, N. Y.

look. Here was the immortal germ of artistic creation, woven by mortal and unknowing hands—the sole perpetuation of a vision, dreamed long ago and far away.

I gave myself up unconsciously to a long journey. I saw a blistered hillside; against it the sunbaked wall of a flat-roofed hut; and against the wall, beneath a crude scaffold, a rude loom. Below, a rough roller; above it, a dull cotton warp, golden brown by reason of the dazzling glare, and suggesting a foundation as basic as the earth itself. High up, the balls of yarn, a rare gaudy blob here and there, but most of them soft as the blossoms in a rose garden.

Most fascinating of all to my gaze, however, were the thin-fingered hands that plied against the cumbersome skeleton.

I saw no bodies, only hands. I saw these hands change from youth to old age; one moment smooth with the oil of youth, and next wrinkled and dry in old age—changing hands, but always the same rug, making light of a lifetime though itself not yet completely born.

With the passing of a decade, the weft shot from left to right; another ten years of brown-fingered painting of still music on a harp, and back went the weft, locking beauty in its cage. And always, just beneath the level of the hands, the pattern developed resplendently, until finally this vibrant, enduring fabric—with its strange power of remaining unsullied, of smiling across the centuries—was completed.

Pressed by lips, knees, and feet, long since decayed, familiar of shrine and prayer, of castle and orgy; background for the changing web of soiled humanity; victim of the mart, bought and sold, sold and bought—and yet retaining within itself that indestructible essence of purity which dwells forever within the trampled soul of beauty.

How many rugs of this kind are there in existence today? Not very many to be sure—that is, if one demands AGE as well as enduring beauty. But there ARE hundreds of masterpieces today possessing all the subtle charm, romance, beauty, and that indefinable something we in the Oriental Rug business call "soul."

Yes, we have them right here in Binghamton.

If you demand something MORE than just so many square feet of floor covering, come over to Clinton Street and see these creations of the weavers' art. Look at them. Look through them and see the artist's soul caught up in a web of wool.

You will not be importuned to buy, but should you perchance be interested in possessing one or more of them for your very own, you will find the prices most reasonable.

We consider it a pleasure to display these treasures, and we hope you will come.

Sincerely yours,

Seasonal appeal—specimen letter. Sales letters can often be advantageously based on a seasonal appeal—spring, summer, fall, winter, and most of the holidays. Here is a before-Christmas successful letter that was sent to silver-fox ranchers:

Mr. E. S. Carson
McCammon, Idaho.

The Mrs. expects something.

You know how the fair sex are on Christmas. So give her, with all your love. . . .

A beautiful silver-fox scarf. One of your own fox skins can be transformed into a lovely neckpiece. That's a gift that continues to give pleasure for many years.

Such a gift bears eloquent evidence that you still care. Pays an appreciative tribute to heaven's best gift to any man—a good wife.

Let us convert one of your fox skins into an Elliott custom scarf. In style, workmanship and wear, an Elliott custom scarf has every refinement of a Fifth Avenue creation.

How much does it cost? You'll be pleased when you hear it—only $14. Surely that's cheap for the smile in her eyes on Christmas morn when she says: "It's perfectly gorgeous—you *are* a dear!"

Obey that good impulse. Send on one of your best pelts immediately. It's the human thing to do.

Yours—for a real Christmas for her,

Exclusiveness appeal helps sell quality product. What made the following letter that was sent to 140 grocers bring 12 per cent returns—17 orders within 2 days, with more orders following? First, attention is gained by placing the recipient in an exclusive group. Second, the benefit for the buyer is clearly shown. Third, confidence in the product is established by the guaranty. Fourth, protection of the buyer is offered in refusing to sell to price cutters. Fifth, action is stimulated in the closing and facilitated by an enclosed reply card. Note also the short paragraphs that make the letter easy to read.

We understand you are among the "400" of the highest class establishments in the United States serving a clientele that appreciates the *superlative* in foods.

Being not only up to the minute but ahead of it, you have heard of Those Green Bros. Denver Pascal Celery, The World's Finest—unequalled anywhere at any price—Nutty, Crisp, Sweet, Delicious, Waxy white.

When you buy our Pascal celery—three of us have a treat coming, you, your customer, and ourselves. Your high class trade will be delighted to know that they can get our *Pascal, The National Delicacy* from you regularly.

You take no chances. We guarantee perfect delivery by fast railway express.

Our Pascal is so popular that many thousands of individuals in every state in the Union have ordered it as Thanksgiving, Christmas and good-will gifts—costing $1.70 per DeLuxe Box of 12 stalks. Our celery has a National reputation; you can reap the benefits, charging a price that will show you from 50% to 75% profit, and your customers will want it. You get the benefit of our wholesale price, because we can eliminate the cost of the individual DeLuxe Gift Box and "fixings."

We don't sell to price cutters. Please read the enclosed circular. Our price to you, delivered to your door—

Pascalettes (celery hearts), 4 to 6 stalks to bunch, per bunch.......

Country Club Brand, 12 stalks to bunch, per bunch...............

Shouldn't you start *right now* by writing an initial order on the enclosed postpaid card? Then, after you receive the trial shipment, place a standing order to arrive certain days of EVERY WEEK.

As Go Getters and "Profit Makers," do it now.

Ac-celery-atingly yours,

THOSE GREEN BROTHERS

Appeal to reader's vanity useful in subscription letter. Attention-getting approaches are particularly effective when tied in closely with the subject matter of the letter. In the following example, a medical publisher appeals directly to personal vanity and professional pride. The ingenious first sentences impel further reading.

Dear Doctor:

Will you sit on a jury?

As a dermatologist, you naturally are a good judge of literature on the venereal infections. Will you examine the AMERICAN JOURNAL OF SYPHILIS, GONORRHEA AND VENEREAL DISEASES and give us your opinion of its worth to the average dermatologist?

Your examination of the Journal may help us solve a perplexing problem—how to find those dermatologists who want to keep themselves fully informed on venerology—and it may reveal to you an unsuspected source of great assistance in meeting some of your difficulties.

We don't know the answer to our difficulty—but we suspect it is simply to acquaint the non-subscribing dermatologists with the Journal. We, therefore, are considering sending the Journal on a free trial basis to a representative group—a jury—of them. And we should like you to be one of that jury!

Here's what we propose: To send the Journal to you for three months at our expense. We won't ask you to pay a penny for it—not even for postage! Our only request will be that you read it and analyze its worth to you.

We should desire you to judge the Journal as a juror—and bring in your verdict in the same manner! If your decision is that you cannot use the Journal—simply write us a note requesting us to stop sending it —if you like it and want us to continue it, you need do nothing further. We will then enter a subscription for you for a full year—we will not count the three months—and we will bill you at the regular rate of $7.50.

You can't lose—you will be doing us a favor—and you may gain immeasurably! Accept our invitation, on the form below, today!

Cordially yours,

Yes, I will serve on the jury! I will consider the Journal on your offer. At the expiration of the trial period, enter my subscription for one year at $7.50 unless I request service of the Journal discontinued.

Dr. ....

DS-55 Street & Number City & State

Convince the reader that your product meets his needs or desires. You have secured the reader's attention with a good beginning and have made him aware of his need or desire for the product. Your next job is to convince him that your statements are true and that the product meets his needs or desires.

The methods by which you can carry conviction are illustrated in the following pages. These methods are:

1. *Guaranty of the product.* To be convincing, a guaranty must be expressed in simple language and with few, if any, reservations.

2. *Trial use or free examination.* This is an old stand-by and will always be one of the most effective forms of evidence. It appeals to the reader's common sense—seeing is believing—and to his cautious desire to avoid taking any risks or spending any money until he has had the opportunity to "show himself." Readers of sales letters, in fact, have become so accustomed to being offered free trial or examination of certain articles—books, for example—that in many cases they will not respond to a letter which does not contain such an offer.

3. *Samples.* The sample method is convenient for a wide variety of products—soap, tooth paste, perfume, hair tonic, shaving cream, cosmetics, breakfast foods, coffee, milk chocolate, wall plaster and wallpaper, paints and varnishes, beaver board, and so forth.

4. *Tests.* Tests as a form of evidence may be of two kinds: (a) tests that you, the seller, have made; and (b) tests that the reader can conduct himself.

5. *Facts and figures.* Facts and figures must be specific and must

be presented in a form that will enable the reader readily to grasp their significance. For the general public, dramatization and graphic description are the best media; the reader can then visualize the data as a part of the story.

6. *Testimonials*. The reader is more likely to accept statements from a third person than from you. While it is true that in these days many people have come to feel, as far as testimonials are concerned, that "the devil can cite Scripture for his purpose," nevertheless there probably never will be a time when a letter with testimonials will not be stronger than one without. Outwardly the reader may scoff, but inwardly he is impressed in spite of himself. For this reason it is usually advisable to include testimonials either in the body of the letter or in the enclosures.

Example of letter carrying conviction. Almost every paragraph of the following letter selling a cockroach powder carries a conviction that is contagious.

Dear Mr. Ashton:

Every cockroach on your premises
is there with your full permission.

I will undertake to prove this to you—if you will give two minutes to the reading of this letter.

I will rid your premises of every last trace of roaches without one penny of your money being produced. I mean every syllable of that statement. I can't make it too strong. So, I am going to repeat it and emphasize it.

Tell me how many floors or rooms you have, and what size they are.

I'll send you enough of MURRAY'S ROACH DOOM to exterminate every roach. And they'll stay exterminated for one year by Shrewsbury clock—one year.

Now let me tell you what MURRAY'S ROACH DOOM is.

It's a powder that isn't poisonous. It is practically odorless.

It is distributed, first, by means of the Murray powder "Gun," which a ten-year-old child can use. Get it where the roaches are. Then the fun begins.

Roaches can't keep away from this powder. They love it. But the minute they touch it they actually go crazy. They race through every nook and cranny of their hiding places. They carry it with them. They distribute it where no human agency could reach. The young roaches, which very rarely appear in public, come in contact with it, and they're gone.

The strength of MURRAY'S ROACH DOOM doesn't abate for one

year. As the eggs, which are deposited in the runway, hatch out, the young encounter the powder. And they're gone.

And I prove all these things to you by standing behind my 24-year guarantee of "No riddance—no pay."

You send me no money until the roaches are gone.

I'm even enclosing a Special Trial Offer slip which lets you in on a special price when you do remit—because you will . . . . . it never misses.

If you can name any fairer offer than that I'll gladly sign it—but, remember, you're responsible for the presence of roaches on your premises after this.

Very sincerely yours,

The letter is the proof. A letter-service concern sold its direct-mail service through the sales letter that is reproduced in Figure 7. The attractive appearance, the perfect matching of the fill-ins, and the clever use of testimonials—all were proof of the quality of the service the concern was prepared to offer.

Trial offer brings in accounts. The following letter, sent to several manufacturers of men's shirts, was directly responsible for three excellent accounts that buy several thousand dollars' worth of the firm's pins a year. The letter carries conviction through its offer to send a quantity of the pins, without charge, to the prospect.

Mr. Anthony Jones, please

Why have so many firms like yours switched to De Long Shirt Pins?

Because they have found, most of them by testing the pins before adopting them, that De Long Shirt Pins are the best kind for their purpose.

Would you care to test these distinctive pins? It's easy to do so—and it costs you nothing. Simply tell us which of the accompanying sizes is best suited to your needs and we'll send you a pound gratis. Ask one of your star operators to put them to a thorough test.

She'll like them because, thanks to their extra large, slightly dome-shaped, smooth heads, they won't irritate her fingers. Operators can pin garments with them hour after hour without suffering finger irritation.

As they have strong, smooth, needle-sharp points, De Long Shirt Pins glide smoothly through thick fabrics, and they don't make ugly marks on fine fabrics like silk.

Made of solid brass wire, *they never rust*. You'll agree that such pins are preferable to quick-rusting steel or adamantine pins which, by making unsightly rust spots on garments, cause no end of headaches, customer dissatisfaction and unnecessary expense.

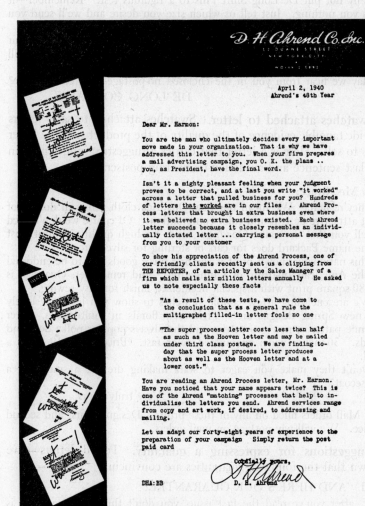

D. H. Ahrend Co. Inc.
52 DUANE STREET
NEW YORK CITY
WORTH 2-5892

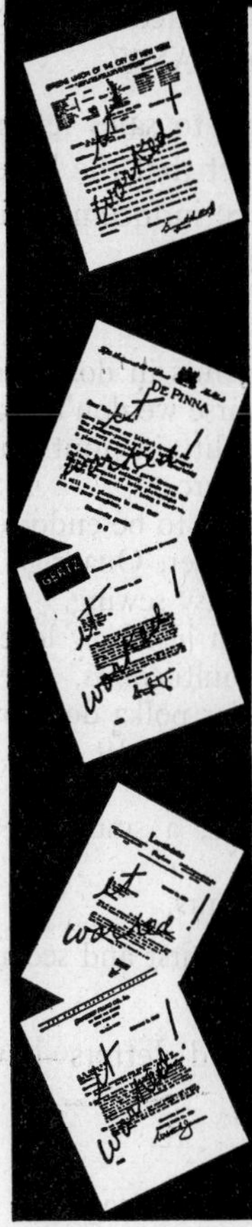

April 2, 1940
Ahrend's 48th Year

Dear Mr. Harmon:

You are the man who ultimately decides every important move made in your organization. That is why we have addressed this letter to you. When your firm prepares a mail advertising campaign, you O. K. the plans .. you, as President, have the final word.

Isn't it a mighty pleasant feeling when your judgment proves to be correct, and at last you write "it worked" across a letter that pulled business for you? Hundreds of letters that worked are in our files . Ahrend Process letters that brought in extra business even where it was believed no extra business existed. Each Ahrend letter succeeds because it closely resembles an individually dictated letter ... carrying a personal message from you to your customer

To show his appreciation of the Ahrend Process, one of our friendly clients recently sent us a clipping from THE REPORTER, of an article by the Sales Manager of a firm which mails six million letters annually He asked us to note especially these facts

> "As a result of these tests, we have come to the conclusion that as a general rule the multigraphed filled-in letter fools no one
>
> "The super process letter costs less than half as much as the Hooven letter and may be mailed under third class postage. We are finding today that the super process letter produces about as well as the Hooven letter and at a lower cost."

You are reading an Ahrend Process letter, Mr. Harmon. Have you noticed that your name appears twice? This is one of the Ahrend "matching" processes that help to individualize the letters you send. Ahrend services range from copy and art work, if desired, to addressing and mailing.

Let us adapt our forty-eight years of experience to the preparation of your campaign Simply return the post paid card

Cordially yours,

D. H. Ahrend

DHA:BB

Figure 7. The Letter Is the Proof.

(On the original the black border was a royal blue. "It worked" appeared in red.)

Why not put De Long Shirt Pins to a rigorous test? Remember—it costs you nothing. Just tell us which size you desire and we'll send you a pound—about 4500 pins—without charge.

If you agree, as so many others do, that they are the best pins for your purpose, we'll gladly quote prices—prices which we're confident will please you.

May we hear from you in the enclosed no-postage-required envelope?

DE LONG COMPANY

Swatches attached to letter. Swatches attached to sales letters provide tangible evidence of the quality of the product that the letter aims to sell. Here is a letter that carries a suggestive inducement in the last sentence and an action-motivating postscript.

Dear Mrs. Bruce:

They're here! We mean our new Quadriga cloth prints in dozens of most attractive designs and color combinations. Of course we don't need to tell you that the name Quadriga stands for high quality in prints just as the name Packard does for cars or sterling for silverware.

This nationally known print is the first piece goods line to be endorsed by the American Institute of Laundering. And remember, Quadriga is the 80-square print with a special needleized finish for easy sewing.

We are enclosing a few sample swatches to show you just how lovely the new Spring designs are. Vivid new florals in multi-colors, clever juvenile patterns, new geometrics and the always popular polka dots and plaids. 36-inches wide; guaranteed color fast. Priced only 19 cents a yard.

Don't they make you eager to start making dresses, a smock or a housecoat?

Very truly yours,

P.S. Mail orders filled on any of these prints. Designate first and second choice. We will pay postage on mail orders.

Suggestions for expressing a guaranty. Tested letters have shown that the following guaranties are convincing:

(1) AND HERE'S OUR GUARANTEE:

If, after you've read the first issue, you don't think the magazine is the most exciting, entertaining and VALUABLE you ever saw—or if you don't think you're getting back HUNDREDS OF DOLLARS worth of value for the one dollar you are spending—just drop us a line. WE'LL LET YOU KEEP THE COPY WE SENT YOU WITHOUT CHARGE. AND WE'LL CANCEL THE BILL ALTOGETHER—OR, IF YOU'VE ALREADY SENT US YOUR DOLLAR, WE'LL SEND IT BACK TO YOU AT ONCE—NO QUESTIONS ASKED!

Repeated as follows in a P.S.

MONEY BACK GUARANTEE. We'll send your dollar back at once and you can keep the issue we sent, if you are not 100% satisfied with YOUR LIFE.

(2) All SHEAFFER pens are guaranteed for life, and the SHEAFFER LIFETIME is guaranteed unconditionally against everything except loss, for the life of the owner.

(3) In fairness to yourself—check the above questions before you buy. Only FRIGIDAIRE answers all of them in the way you want them answered. And only FRIGIDAIRE is backed by a three-year General Motors guarantee.

(4) The moment this booklet reaches you, turn to the back cover and read carefully the remarkable PAPEC guarantee, which has been printed for years and which no other cutter has been able to meet.

How to offer trial use or free examination. When you have reached that part of the sales letter in which you are ready to offer the product for trial or for free examination, compare your paragraphs with the following for strength, directness, and tone.

(1) I am enclosing a postage paid card, marked for my attention. As soon as you return it, I will arrange to have a machine delivered to you so you can try it, and if you don't believe it will save you time and money, I will take it back—NO OBLIGATION ON YOUR PART AT ALL. Just use the card. Put it in the mail tonight with your name and date you want to try the machine.

(2) The book costs $4. And remember, after you have looked it over you are free to return it within five days—if you can part with it! Under these conditions, since you risk nothing, isn't it just good business to at least *see* the book, and then decide? The enclosed card brings it to you.

(3) The enclosed card requires not even a stamp to bring you a LONGWEAR GLADSTONE BAG, postpaid and free of charge. Compare it with any fine bag. Keep it for a week. Take it on a trip. Then. . .

If you are convinced that there are more miles of travel-satisfaction per dollar in the LONGWEAR than in any other bag you've ever seen, mail your check for $14.85. Otherwise, return the bag at my expense.

(4) Simply fill out the enclosed FREE EXAMINATION CARD. Mail it (no postage necessary), and I'll ship you one of these beautiful Bathroom Showers for you to look at and examine and use. Then, at the end of five days, if you don't think it's worth $12.95 instead of the $7.95 I am asking for it. . . . if you feel that you can part with it . . . return it at my expense. But if you like it—and I know you will—just keep it and send me only $7.95.

How to make the reader ask for a sample. Is your offer of a sample inviting? That is the test after you have written the paragraph. The following paragraphs show by example how to make the offer of a sample irresistible:

(1) We want you to try HEINZ RICE FLAKES at our expense. So we'll send you a generous free trial package—enough for three delicious servings—free. Just fill in your name and address on the enclosed card, and drop it in the mail—no postage required.

(2) Let us send you samples of these sturdy, laboratory-proved COLUMBIAN CLASP envelopes for your heavier-than-letter mail. Just fill in and return the enclosed card—no stamp required—and the samples will come to you by return mail.

(3) This sample of INGRAM'S SHAVING CREAM brings you seven of the *coolest* shaves you've ever had in your life!

INGRAM'S is the first shaving cream primarily planned to take the nicking sting out of the morning shave and to leave a clear cheek and a cool skin when the job is finished. Its three special ingredients cool and soothe your face the moment you put on the lather.

You'll find that INGRAM lather is luxurious and extra-heavy—and that it lies close to the bristles and retains its moisture and thus keeps the skin surface wet. You can shave closer, or more often, without discomfort.

A week from today, after you've enjoyed seven cool INGRAM shaves, get the economical regular size of INGRAM'S—more than enough for 100 shaves. It's waiting for you at the nearest drug store now.

Examples of paragraphs asking the reader to make a test. The directions given to the reader for making the test must be simple, clear, and explicit to insure favorable results. The following illustrations are suggestive of ways to express the invitation to try the test:

(1) Try this dissolving test. Put one of the new curly IVORY FLAKES in your hand. Pour a teaspoonful of warm water over it. Then another. Notice how the flake melts away first at the curly edges—then completely! In the wash basin, one swish dissolves the new IVORY FLAKES instantly, even in lukewarm water—they can't flatten down on the fabric. No danger of soap spots.

(2) Here is the way to put SUNBRITE double-action to a real test. Cut an onion with a knife. Wash the knife in soapsuds. Then cut a lemon. The knife *looks* clean! But the onion odor still persists. Now sprinkle the knife with SUNBRITE CLEANSER. Rub, rinse, and dry. Not a trace of onion remains. That's the way double-action SUNBRITE ALWAYS WORKS.

(3) Will you try this experiment?

Ask your jeweler to show you a perfect deep-sea pearl. Put the enclosed DELTAH manufactured pearl alongside it. Then try to tell them apart!

The jeweler can do it—with the aid of his magnifying glass. But neither you nor any other person not an expert in precious stones can distinguish the natural from the manufactured pearl.

In luster, in weight, in iridescence, in color, the little pearl we are sending you will measure up to all the requirements of the genuine deep-sea pearl. Step on it! It will stand the weight of an ordinary-size man. Boil it in hot water! It will come out lustrous, with the soft opalescence that only a pearl can give. Weigh it! You will find it heavy, firm, indistinguishable in any way from the natural pearl, except to the expert with his magnifying glass.

An example of effective use of a test to convince. If the seller has tested his product and wishes the reader to know about that test, the description of the test must be interesting as well as convincing. Notice how in the following example the narrative form of telling about the test keeps the reader interested and at the same time brings out the merit of the product:

Behind the footlights of Boston's Jordan Hall, four famed performers awaited the curtain . . . four famous radio sets, hidden by a silken screen . . . ready for the tone-test.

And just beyond the orchestra pit—what an audience! Fifty-four members of the noted New England Conservatory of Music. *Teachers* of music—connoisseurs of tone—ready to listen.

The master of ceremonies was talking, "Each set will perform anonymously. Not by name, but by number. And to insure fairness, five senior classmen from the Massachusetts Institute of Technology will handle the sets."

Half an hour later a GENERAL ELECTRIC RADIO—known only as "Number 3"—had sung its way to a new tone triumph! Pitted against three *higher-priced* sets, it won the *best tone* vote of Boston's best-trained ears. Won *three times* as many votes as all the other radios combined . . . 41 out of 54 votes!

In some instances it may be better to present the material showing the tests made by the manufacturer in an illustrated enclosure.

Examples of facts and figures to convince the reader. To be convincing, the facts and figures must be verifiable. Notice how the following examples present verifiable facts:

(1) Fabrication economies possible with EVERDUR not only absorbed the difference in the cost between the two metals, but, in addition, provided an average saving in the cost of the finished bolts of 14.75 per cent for a thousand pieces.

(2) For with one motion, Addressograph does the work of 50 to 100 motions—10 to 50 times faster—and absolutely without error.

(3) Detroit's large department stores just recently made 672 sales from 2 small advertisements in the *Free Press*. One advertisement of 143 lines, single column, featuring a $1.95 dress, produced 511 customers. The other advertisement of 165 lines, single column, featuring a suit at $16.50, produced 161 customers. Here is a high rate of production . . . low cost of selling . . . $3,652.95 worth of sales from 308 lines.

Good selling knows neither seasons nor "situations." Here is proof . . . outstanding . . . that business is being done in Detroit . . . that *Free Press* readers have the dollars and are spending them with those advertisers who make a bid for their business.

How to write the testimonial paragraphs. If testimonials are to be mentioned in the letter, they must be brief. The following short paragraphs can be adapted easily to any product:

(1) Over in Springfield, Ohio, the Armstrong Manufacturing Company has been making tubs and pails for 15 years. They used to make them from galvanized steel, but last year they changed to ARMCO INGOT IRON.

Why? Let Mr. Armstrong tell you in his own words:

> "We now use ARMCO INGOT IRON GALVANIZED SHEETS after having given them a thorough test to determine the workability and welding qualities of the metal. The iron forms easily, and the coating does not peel. Our loss, caused by the poor working qualities of steel, has decreased 10% since we changed to ARMCO. In addition, our tubs and pails find a more ready market, because ARMCO is so well and favorably known."

You, too, will find that the use of ARMCO will reduce your costs and at the same time increase your sales.

(2) The other day someone asked Judge Ben Lindsay, of Juvenile Court fame, if he wouldn't name his favorite O. Henry story.

> "My favorite O. Henry story," said the judge, "is *all of them.* No writer ever had greater knowledge of human nature, and the charm of his stories makes it possible to read them over and over again."

Have you got your set yet? Almost everybody else in this country seems to have. More than four million volumes of these inimitable stories have been sold to American readers in the past few years.

Getting the reader to "act now." In the opening of your sales letter you have excited the reader's interest. With this interest as a basis you have proceeded to build up, by imaginative word-pictures or vital language, a description of what your product or service will do for the reader. You have cited facts and figures, tests, testimonials, or some other form of evidence. The reader now wants your product; and he is convinced of its value to him. But how are you to overcome his natural human tendency to procrastinate—to put off until "tomorrow" what you want him to do today?

The answer is, by imposing a penalty upon delay. Hold out an inducement to immediate action—perhaps a premium of some sort. Or, impress upon the reader the fact that circumstances over which you have no control have compelled you to limit the quantity of the goods that you are selling or the period over which you can sell them at their present price.

This idea has been applied in a great variety of ways to different types of goods and services. In the sale of books there is the "free volume as a premium," the "damaged book sale," the low price that can be given only for a short period because of "rapidly rising production costs." In the sale of magazines there is the "special introductory offer for new subscribers." In the sale of insurance there is the offer of a premium in the shape of a diary, a fountain pen, a wallet, and so forth, only a limited number of which are available for distribution. In the sale of jewelry and other merchandise, the "gift certificate that is worth $5 to you if you buy before March 1" has proved effective, as has the "special birthday-dividend check which can be cashed with us only if it is mailed on or before midnight October 31."

These are only a few examples from among many, but they serve to illustrate the point. To interest the reader, to make him want your goods, to convince him of their worth—these are essentials of sales letter writing. In themselves, however, they are not sufficient to induce the reader to "act and act now." To get him to do this you have to stir in him a definite fear of the consequences of delay on his part. Moreover, you have to give him a reasonable and specific explanation of the facts of the situation, so that he will know in his own mind that you are not bluffing but mean exactly what you say—that if he fails to act at once, he will miss an opportunity that may never return.

Make it easy for the reader to "act now." Again, getting immediate action depends a good deal upon your ingenuity in *making action easy*. This may involve temporarily catering to the reader's weakness for putting things off. You need not try to get him to decide upon your main proposition immediately—he would probably balk at that. Besides, you can afford to bide your time. Instead, lead him off on the right foot by merely asking him to take the first and minor step—to mail your card for further particulars, for a free trial or examination of the goods, for a sample, for a salesman's call. Then, after he has taken this first step, it should not be difficult to keep him from turning back. Be sure, however, that you make plain exactly what you want him to do. Leave as little as possible to his own decision or volition. Do not offer him a choice of alternatives. Make the action to be taken clear, simple, and "without obligation."

Example of "limited-time" offer to get immediate action. The entire letter reproduced below stimulates the reader to action. It contains an inducement to immediate action and shows how easy it is to obtain the product offered. Furthermore, its tone is adapted to people who are likely to want to understand accounting.

Dear Sir:

May we send you, with our compliments, HOW TO UNDERSTAND ACCOUNTING, by H. C. Greer?

Will you accept with our compliments, in return for doing us a small favor, a copy of H. C. Greer's HOW TO UNDERSTAND ACCOUNTING—a new, 250-page book which every man in business ought to have?

The favor is simple, and may in itself be highly profitable to you. Briefly, we want you to make a test for us.

In the COMPLETE ACCOUNTING COURSE described in the enclosed circular, we have something which we do not hesitate to call one of the outstanding developments of the day in accounting training. So marked are its advantages that we feel that, if once the material can be placed in the right hands, further urging on our part will be unnecessary.

This course has been developed by Northwestern University and is now used. . . .

And now here is the courtesy we should like you to render: Will you look through this course, go over some of the lectures, putting the material to any test you desire, and see if this isn't just the training you want to make the plans you have made for your business future come true?

If you will do this, we will include with your course, without charge, a copy of HOW TO UNDERSTAND ACCOUNTING. But whether or not you keep the course, *this book is yours in return for your courtesy.*

Just fill in and mail the attached reply card, and both the COMPLETE ACCOUNTING COURSE and the book HOW TO UNDERSTAND ACCOUNTING will come to you immediately. Then, after you have examined the course, if for any reason whatever you decide that it isn't exactly the thing to help you get ahead, merely send it back at our expense—and keep the book HOW TO UNDERSTAND ACCOUNTING.

But we must have your reply at once. THIS OFFER IS GOOD FOR A LIMITED TIME ONLY. So fill in and mail the reply card *now.*

Very truly yours,

Immediate action urged because low price is experimental. Here is a letter that overcomes the reader's tendency to put off action by showing him that it is to his advantage to act now. The device used is to fix a new low price and to try it out for a month. The reductions in prices are explained by the seller's desire to make more sales.

Dear Sir:

I want to introduce to you, as an experienced traveler, a Gladstone Bag so handsome that you will be proud to carry it into the most exclusive hotel lobby.

I want to send you this fine bag entirely at my own expense—and you're to be under no obligation whatever.

I want to give you just a hint about the many features of this Gladstone that will appeal to you—and tell you how I can make a very low price this month to a selected group of men.

My LONGWEAR Gladstone Bag is genuine. . . .

You'll Like the Bag—You'll Marvel at My Low Price

I've studied the luggage business for a long time. I've actually sold a *half million* of my bags. And, as the largest distributor of luggage in the world, I can afford to sell for less.

Just a short time ago I sold my genuine Cowhide Gladstones for $19.85 each—and *that* was a bargain! Thousands of discriminating travelers bought them, many saying the bags were worth $30. I dropped the price to $17.50—and sold *more* bags—then to $16.50.

There's one further tumble—$14.85—and that I can justify only if it will boost my sales way up. I think it will—but I'm going to find out this month by trying this price to a selected group of men. So $14.85 is my price to you *if you act promptly.*

Buy or not—but at least *see* this great bag free!

The enclosed card requires not even a stamp to bring you a LONGWEAR Gladstone Bag, postpaid and free of charge. Compare it with *any* fine bag. Keep it a week. Take it on a trip. Then. . . .

If you are convinced that there are more miles of travel-satisfaction in the LONGWEAR than in *any* other bag you've ever seen, mail your check for my low price. Otherwise, return the bag *at my expense.*

But remember, this is an experiment to see if the $14.85 price will sell more bags. So, if you're thinking of getting a bag—even a little bit—you'll want to hurry your card along.

Cordially yours,

Examples of closings that stimulate action. The examples of complete letters given in this section contain suggestions for strong closings that make action easy. Below are several more examples taken from letters that have worked.

(1) Don't let the heating plant dominate your home life. Find out now—before another day has passed—how little it really costs to enjoy Oil-O-Matic heat without work or worry. Telephone today for a FREE Heating Survey. This will prove an accurate estimate of how much Oil-O-Matic heating will cost in your home. Installed in your present heating plant in but a few hours' time. Act now while present prices are in effect.

(2) This offer expires on December 1. If you are not prepared to order at once on the inclosed order blank, send me the attached post card, and I shall reserve a set for you for ten days.

(3) Five cents a week is the average cost to you for an intelligent view of Public Affairs if you take advantage of our special introductory offer of $1.00 for twenty issues. This offer is good for ten days. Write your name and address on the enclosed postage paid card and mail it now. We will bill you later.

(4) RIGHT NOW, not later, is the time for you to begin to watch sub-surface Washington developments, so that you may know what is in prospect, and be prepared to shift your plans and operations as the necessity arises. Use the enclosed order card to start the Letters coming to you AT ONCE.

(5) BUT LET ME WARN YOU . . . this offer is such a sensational bargain that it has never been offered to anyone before. We will never offer it to anyone again, and it is only open for a limited time. You can cash this special birthday-dividend check with us only if it is mailed on or before midnight, October 31, 19. . .

. . . so don't delay. All you have to do now is to pick up your pen and endorse the check on the back. Then mail it today in the postage paid envelope. NOTHING ELSE. We'll do the rest.

How to write to special classes of buyers. A sales letter to a special class of buyers is constructed in the same way as any other sales letter. That is, it must attract favorable attention, create desire, carry conviction, and stimulate to action. The fundamental appeals mentioned on page 70 apply to sales letters to a special class of buyers as strongly as they do to sales letters generally. However, the structure, substance, and appeals must be adjusted to the class of buyers. In the following paragraphs selected letters are presented that are addressed to particular classes of buyers. These letters have proved successful because they recognize the habits, tastes, desires, and needs of the class in question.

Hints that help sell dealers by mail. A sales letter must take into account the following characteristics of this group of buyers:

1. The dealer's principal concern is to make profits and turn the product over quickly.
2. He is attracted by offers of help and service. The assistance may be in the form of aids in advertising, form letters that can be sent to his prospects, aids in window displays, offers of more customers, selling tools, instruction manuals for sales clerks, and the like.
3. The dealer wants convincing proof that the product will sell readily and that sales will be profitable. Offers of samples, trial orders, and enclosures of folders and booklets help to get the order.
4. The dealer, as a businessman, requires a short letter, written in crisp, colloquial language, and one that is attractive, colorful, and businesslike.

A sales letter to dealers that stresses the profit possibilities. The following letter to clothing dealers stresses the money-making appeal and strongly urges the dealer to inspect the line with no obligations to buy:

Dear Mr. Smith:

If yours is the problem of getting more customers into your store, we know that we can interest you.

We are after more business and want part of yours by deserving it.

Frankly, the "Club Clothes" line is a profit-maker and in its price ranges it is second to none, for it compares on every point of fabric, tailoring, and style with the more costly nationally advertised makes. Repeat orders prove our profit claims, and today over 1,400 shrewd, progressive retailers throughout the country favor and feature "Club Clothes."

Why not let us prove what we say? Let us send you, for your examination, a set of suits which we wholesale at $19.50 to retail at $30, or a group at $22 retailing at $35.

The mere effort of returning the post card will bring these suits to you without the slightest obligation. Look them over carefully, giving them the most critical inspection, and we feel certain that you will quickly see the turnover and profit possibilities of the line.

Drop the card in the mail today.

Very truly yours,

What to remember in writing to executives. In writing to executives it is necessary to keep in mind the following characteristics of this group:

1. An executive is usually busy. However, this does not mean, as many people believe, that letters to executives must be limited to less than a page in length. A number of companies, including successful mail-order houses, have used letters as long as seven pages, with good results. Of course, the long letter must use devices for making the letter physically easy to read that may not be necessary in a short one. Such devices as frequent and interesting captions, different colored inks, illustrations, examples, and tabulations help to break up the letter.

2. He is on the lookout for ideas and products that will increase profits, promote efficiency, cut costs, and build goodwill. He must be shown with convincing evidence that the product has merit and that the price is fair. Facts, figures, and testimonials are effective.

3. He reads quickly. Present the letter in language that is easy to read. Clarity and language that appeal to the imagination are much more important than superficial dignity and restraint in the letter.

Successful letters to executives. The two letters reproduced below together brought the TelAutograph Corporation over 36 per cent response, much of which can be attributed to the high degree of personalization, proper attention to the mechanics of fill-in matter, prompt follow-up, and attention to the interests of executives. The first letter drew a 25 per cent response—for the most part requests for the folders offered via an enclosed requisition form. The first line of the fourth paragraph was filled in with the reader's name and reference to his specific products, such as "Mr. Jones, other manufacturers of equipment such as yours have." . . . The second letter was sent out three weeks later to those who did not reply to the first. This follow-up letter drew a 15 per cent response. Enclosure of the requisition form, printed on a different color paper, enabled the sender to distinguish replies to the follow-up letter from belated replies to the first letter.

ORIGINAL MAILING PIECE

We have just completed a job for you. We are now ready to submit in folder form the results of our experience in working with basic systems and procedures of a sizeable cross section of manufacturing companies. We invite you to accept copies without charge and without feeling obligated in any way.

These folders will prove valuable to you as a check on your own plant's operations. They offer you a means of comparing your own systems with those of other plants. You'll find much helpful information in them that may enable you to cut corners in time and cost.

Our facts are based on actual in-the-plant surveys made by specially trained engineers—aided in many companies by executives like yourself. They represent our experience in a cross section of plants, both small and large, differing widely in physical layouts, nature of products and in volume of business.

Mr. Jones, other manufacturers of equipment such as yours have basically similar procedures. Of course, they vary in terminology and in scope for different types of business and for different plant sizes—simple in small plants and complex in large ones.

We present six basic systems: SALES ORDER . . . PRODUCTION PLANNING AND SCHEDULING . . . INSPECTION AND QUALITY CONTROL . . . WAREHOUSING AND SHIPPING . . . JOB COST ANALYSIS . . . OFFICE RECORDS-CREDITS-AND-CASHIERING. Each of these systems is discussed fully in an easy-to-read, graphically illustrated four-page folder. Three such folders are now ready to be placed in your hands:

SALES ORDER—Answers such questions as: What is the crucial test of an efficient sales order procedure? What are other companies doing to keep their hard-won customers from slipping through their fingers—by insuring fast, errorless service on orders . . . avoiding slip-ups on delivery promises . . . handling unexpected delays and order changes easily and quickly.

PRODUCTION PLANNING AND SCHEDULING—Gives you a quick picture of a typical planning and scheduling system. Tells how companies have developed systems that enable them to plan production on quick-turnover basis . . . how they get action on schedule changes instantly . . . stop production on not-so-urgent stock items . . . make way for rush orders . . . and keep inventories at a minimum. Discusses management's problem of correlating the responsibilities of the production and sales departments.

INSPECTION AND QUALITY CONTROL—Shows what other companies are doing to reduce their scrap losses, lower salvaging costs, hold down "off-standard" products, or "seconds," and eliminate production hold-ups due to late reports from laboratories. Cites specific examples in six different types of industries.

Experiences summarized in folder form, analyzing the last three of the six procedures, are now "in work." These will be available to you in a short time. All have this single purpose—to help executives like yourself compare their present mode of operation with systems now in use in other companies.

Since we are sending these folders without charge or obligation, it occurs to us that you may want copies sent to several of your department heads or systems men—in addition to your own copies. Please feel free to requisition as many as you need.

To avoid unnecessary delays in getting them to you, we are enclosing a convenient requisition form. Please check which of the folders you desire for yourself, and which ones we should send to other men in your company. Slip this form into the stamped envelope attached and drop it into your out-going mail.

Cordially yours,

W. F. Vieh

President

FOLLOW-UP LETTER

A short time ago I wrote you in regard to several new folders we've prepared for free distribution to the management of a cross section of manufacturing companies. As mentioned in my previous letter, these folders summarize our company's experience during many years past in working with basic manufacturing systems and procedures.

I firmly believe that you'll find these folders, as described in the leaflet enclosed, of great value. Each one presents a system common to your plant, to ours, and to the majority of all plants.

These folders not only offer you a means of comparing your own operating procedures with those in other plants, but included in each folder is a considerable amount of helpful information designed to help you cut corners in time and cost in your operations.

Since I wrote you, we've received requests from many hundreds of executives like yourself, manifesting great interest in our presentation of systems. We've supplied these men with copies, as well as their various department heads and systems men.

May I repeat my invitation to you to obtain copies of these folders. They will be sent you without charge or obligation. We want you to feel perfectly free to request as many copies as you need—for yourself and for other men in your company responsible for basic operations.

A requisition form and stamped addressed envelope are enclosed for your convenience in requesting copies. Please check which of the folders you desire and which ones we should send to other men in your company. It'll be a pleasure to see that they're sent without delay.

Very truly yours,
W. F. Vieh
President

Hints on writing to men consumers. In writing to a businessman concerning an article or service for use in his business, the hints given in the preceding paragraphs on writing to executives should be considered. In writing to men consumers about an article or service for personal or domestic use, the following points should be remembered:

1. Men look upon expenditures as investments. A purchase of a home is an investment in comfort and security; a purchase of a radio is an investment in wholesome recreation; a purchase of good clothes is an investment in appearance.

2. They want to be shown why the product offered should be given preference. Therefore the reason-why appeal should be used.

3. They respond to the following appeals: ambition and desire for success, power, responsibility, recognition or honor, and greater income.

A good letter to men consumers.

Dear Mr. Smith:

When you build your home, it will pay you to remember that cheap materials are not necessarily economical materials. Low first cost seldom buys durability, but often leads to expensive upkeep or replacement.

This is particularly true when metals that rust are used for service where water and moisture are encountered. Anaconda metals cannot rust and are by far the most economical to use. Copper sheet metal work, brass pipe plumbing, copper or Everdur hot water tanks, bronze screens, and solid brass or bronze hardware pay for their slightly higher first cost many times over by the repair and replacement expense they save.

The attached sheet points out those instances in which economy dictates the use of rust-proof metals. For further information, send the enclosed card for the booklet described at the left.

Very truly yours,
THE AMERICAN BRASS COMPANY

What to stress in letters to women. The following summary of the characteristics of women in the home will aid the letter writer in striking the correct tone and appeal of a sales letter to that class of buyers.

1. Women respond to descriptions that envision satisfaction from the use of the article. Sell them "dreams of leisure hours, of rest, and of happy, contented homes, and simplified housework," says Marion Hertha Clarke.

2. They are not impressed by technical descriptions of the construction of the product.

3. They want to receive good value for their money. They are practical as well as visionary.

4. They are influenced by the physical make-up of the copy. It should be attractive and personal. Social stationery may be more effective than the usual business sheet.

5. The dominant appeals are: mother love, instinct for the beautiful, thrift, and the instinct to save labor.

Other helpful hints in preparing direct mail for women are contained in the following summary of a survey made by Miss Helen Slator, Director of the Consumer Division of Francis H. Leggett & Co., New York: *

(1) Women are fundamentally curious. They do not throw direct mail away. They want to find out what is in it.

(2) The morning mail seems to get the best reaction from most women. Women are more relaxed after getting the family off to work or to school, and can read the morning mail with fewer interruptions.

(3) Each woman who reads direct mail wants to know that *she is important*. Make her think you are talking to her as an individual.

(4) Women like "gilding the lily." They like to have appeals "dressed up."

(5) Women are confused by complex ideas. Make your presentations simple. Avoid wild colors, trick folds, die-cuts.

(6) Women like an unselfish approach to a sales explanation. That is, women want to know what the product will do for them, not why the manufacturer wants to sell it.

(7) Women are fundamentally honest and can understand or see through dishonesty or "white lies" better than men. So make your direct mail truthful.

---

* The Reporter of Direct Mail Advertising, Oct. 1940, p. 8.

(8) Women object to the words that men ad-writers put into hypothetical conversations.

Example of sales letter to women. The following letter was sent out by a firm of New York resident buyers:

My dear Mrs. Babthorne:

Have you ever had some friend in the dress business take you around to a manufacturer's, and let you pick the exact model you wanted, at the wholesale price?

Remember what a bargain it was—how far below the regular retail store figure it was priced?

Well, that is the service we offer you on all your dresses and coats. We do not take you to one manufacturer. We bring the best from the stocks of a hundred manufacturers here, for you to choose from, at wholesale prices.

Now, here is the point. As resident buyers for a number of out-of-town stores, we are making the rounds of the manufacturers every day. You know yourself what bargains you can pick up even in the stores just by shopping around. Imagine, then, what we can do when we are daily shopping among the manufacturers themselves. Whenever they bring out some "Special," or whenever they have only a few of a style left, or whenever they finish copying their designer's model gowns, we get them.

At such a time the manufacturers, who cannot afford to bother with such small lots, are willing to let us have them at our own price. The result is that we can offer you many of the season's loveliest and most distinctive models, in all sizes, in the most fashionable colors and materials, at actually less than their regular wholesale prices.

Come and see for yourself. It costs nothing to be shown. And if you can save half on all your dresses, you wish to know it. Be sure to look here before you buy your next dress.

Sincerely yours,

How to write to business women. The habits and needs of the business woman are different in some respects from those of women in the home. A letter to business women should take into account the following characteristics:

1. The business woman is in the habit of receiving business letters. The letter should therefore be businesslike in appearance. Ordinary business letterheads may be more suitable than social stationery.

2. She has learned how to be efficient and practical and looks for efficiency and practicality in the products offered her.

3. She remains ever the woman, and therefore the appeals mentioned on page 96 apply.

A good letter to business women. The following letter, which was written on a business letterhead, appeals to the business woman's desire to appear energetic and pleasant and to her need to be comfortable. It also takes into account her taste for attractive clothes.

My dear Miss Jones:

Wouldn't you say that of the three or four top requisites for any woman's business success the one about second on the list is:

"Boundless energy and a pleasant face, free from nervous frowns." Wrong, uncomfortable shoes can affect everything from her posture to the expression in her face as well as the state of mind and nerves at the end of her busy day.

Some women seem to swing along so buoyantly—yet are always in the lead with the newest, daintiest, most frivolous new shoe fashions. They know that glorious extra support doesn't have to mean extra weight in shoes—when they walk on weightless Rhythm Treads.

You can prove all this for yourself in less time than it takes to put on your lipstick. Visit Stern Brothers third floor Shoe Salon—they have the exclusive on Rhythm Steps for New York City. Try on any of their gorgeous new spring Rhythm Step styles—then take three steps. You'll notice the difference quickly, we think—for so many women have.

Now is the ideal time to make this 3 Step Test. Stern's glorious new array of Rhythm Step styles is so complete you can easily find the perfect footwear companions to the newest fashions in your wardrobe—and with that extra comfort too, which is so important to the business girl.

We promise you—there's a real walking thrill waiting for you—in the newest, smartest Rhythm Step shoes.

Cordially yours,

Making a letter to professional people effective. Among the professionals are lawyers, doctors, dentists, teachers, ministers, musicians, artists, actors, writers, and architects. They have in common the following characteristics that must be considered in writing sales letters to them:

1. Professionals are accustomed to weighing evidence and arriving at conclusions independently. The letter should therefore be phrased in a manner that seems to allow full independence of decision.

2. They are accustomed to dealing with individuals and being

treated with great respect. The letter, to receive attention, must appear absolutely individual. Care must therefore be taken in making fill-ins match. The tone of the letter should be dignified and seldom familiar. The language should be conventionally correct.

3. The letter should be confined to one page in length. Enclosures can be used to convey the evidence.

4. Professionals possess an instinct for orderliness and beauty. The appeal to this quality may be used if combined with substantiated facts. If the article or service offered is designed to satisfy professional needs, the professional appeal can be used; if intended for personal needs, the appeal is the same as that of letters addressed to educated and cultured people in general.

A letter using the professional appeal. Here we have a letter to architects reminding them of a certain product and the readiness of the company to be of service. The letter is really a sales-promotion letter. Notice its dignity, briefness, and tone.

Dear Sir:

Many architects are already familiar with the Westinghouse Magnalux lighting unit from experience. However, because it is such a popular unit and because it has so many fine points, I am reminding you about it by means of the enclosed descriptive sheet.

But, as you know, differing requirements of application, style, and price call for different units to meet those conditions. Westinghouse has a wide variety of lighting units to meet every sort of need.

The services of lighting specialists, who devote their full time to application and layout, are available to you for whatever assistance you may feel they can give you on your lighting jobs—at no cost or obligation, of course.

Whenever you want complete information on our units, or want the help of a lighting specialist, let me know. I'll see that you get it.

Yours very truly,

How to write a sales letter to farmers. Before you can write effectively to farmers, you must know the general characteristics of this class of buyers and adapt your letter to their traits. Whatever the product, the following characteristics of the reader cannot be lost sight of:

1. The farmer is concerned with utility and must have complete facts. He cannot be sold with generalizations; he is quick to detect

insincere statements. Price, quality, and service are important considerations.

2. He has more time, except during the planting and harvesting seasons, than city dwellers to spend on his mail. Therefore letters can be two pages long and can contain numerous enclosures.

3. He is not impressed with fancy language. Nor is it necessary to try to use the farmer's language. The risk of making the letter sound artificial and forced is too great. Simple, standard English is the best.

4. Guaranties and free trials convince the farmer, as do testimonials, carefully substantiated facts, and figures.

Example of letter to farmers. The J. I. Case Company letter entitled "A Story of Lower Farm Power Costs," reproduced in Figure 8, dramatizes the reduction in power costs made possible by the tractor. The letter was printed on buff paper. Requests for catalogues showed that the letter was effective.

The letters used by the Southern State Roofing Co. in its direct-mail campaign, described on pages 104-120, are excellent examples of letters to farmers. They illustrate perfectly the four principles of writing to farmers, listed above.

Where to mention price in a sales letter. The traditional treatment of price in a sales letter is to have it follow the sales talk. However, the price can appear in any part of the letter if it is handled properly. In the letter on page 123 it is referred to in the first paragraph; in the letter on page 66 it is mentioned in the third paragraph; in the letter on page 74 it appears at the end.

Hints for proper handling of price. The following hints for proper handling of price have been offered by experienced sales letter writers:

1. Don't appear to apologize for the price. Avoid getting into the frame of mind where you think your price is high, and you will avoid unconsciously apologizing for the price.

2. Don't use such expressions as "and the price is amazingly little," or, "the price is only $350," to minimize the price.

3. Give the price the appearance of being small by presenting it in understandable terms of how little it is for the value received, as, for example, the price per day if the item is a service for a year; the

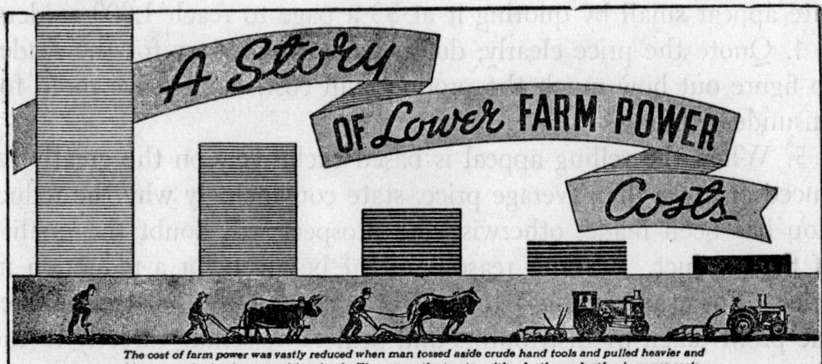
A Story
OF Lower FARM POWER
Costs

The cost of farm power was vastly reduced when man tossed aside crude hand tools and pulled heavier and bigger capacity implements with animals. Then came the tractor with a further reduction in power costs.

PRESENT day improvements in tractors are almost as striking in reduction of power costs as the change from hand tools to animals. For example -- a new Case tractor as compared with one of fifteen to twenty years ago of equal power costs half as much, weighs half as much, costs less than half as much to operate, is vastly easier to operate, and travels many times faster All this means a great reduction in power costs and a greater opportunity for profit from the farm business

Your problem today is a matter of selecting the right tractor and using it to best advantage I hope, therefore, for your own best interests that you will read carefully the booklet enclosed. Written largely by present Case users, it gives

FORTY REASONS WHY CASE POWER IS THE LOWEST COST FARM POWER

Inquire about the performance of Case tractors near you. Ask about fuels burned and the amount consumed, ask about wearing qualities, repairs, and other upkeep expense, ask about ease of starting and steering under load ask about the resale value of used Case tractors, and you'll be surprised After four to five years of hard use Case tractors are selling for two-thirds the original purchase price People are just beginning to learn of the performance and long life built into them

Detailed catalogs tell just why Case tractors burn a variety of fuels from gasoline to furnace oil economically, require but little upkeep expense, reduce farm power costs and are the choice of discriminating buyers. These catalogs can be secured free of charge and without obligation. The enclosed card is for your convenience Merely sign and drop in your mail box

Yours for a larger farm income
thru lower power costs,

J I CASE COMPANY,

J. F. Arvie

Branch Manager

J. I. CASE COMPANY
444-454 N. Front Street
COLUMBUS, OHIO

Figure 8. A Letter That Dramatizes Reduction in Farm Power Costs.

cost per year if the product has a long life, and the like. The advertising salesmen of the *Saturday Evening Post* make the $8,000 page rate appear small by quoting it at $3 a page to reach 1,000 readers.

4. Quote the price clearly; don't make it necessary for the reader to figure out how much the product will cost; don't leave room for misunderstanding.

5. When the selling appeal is based exclusively on the greatly reduced or lower-than-average price, state convincingly why the reduction has been made; otherwise the prospect will doubt the quality of the product. Various reasons might be given for a reduction in price. For example, the letter might state that the seller eliminates the profit taken by distributors and dealers by selling directly to the consumer, or by selling only for cash.

8. SALES LETTER CAMPAIGNS

Follow-up letters break down sales resistance. When a sale depends upon the cumulative effect of repeated arguments and appeals, or the presentation of new ones, follow-up letters help to increase orders. By a repetition of appeals and a variety of arguments, a series of sales letters tends to break down sales resistance and build up the desire to buy. This is a task that a single sales letter might not be able to accomplish.

Three types of follow-up letters are used: (1) the campaign series, (2) the wear-out series, (3) the continuous series.

How to determine length of campaign series. A campaign series must be planned in advance. Six major factors help to determine the number of letters and enclosures, the length of each letter, and the time interval between letters. They are:

1. *The cost of the campaign.* Printing, paper, and mailing costs must be predetermined.

2. *The article or service to be sold.* If the price is high or the article is new, a long series might be required to develop confidence or wear down resistance.

3. *The price of the article or service.* The higher the price, the greater the sales resistance. This in turn influences the number of letters necessary in a series.

4. *Margin of profit.* It is important to know in advance if the margin of profit justifies the campaign.

5. *The type of prospect.* The prospect's age, intelligence, education, wealth, occupation, gullibility, or skepticism help to determine the number of units and the length of the series.

6. *Ultimate purpose of the campaign.* If the purpose is to introduce a new product, the series should be long enough to educate the prospect and create desire. If the purpose is to prepare for a salesman's call, a few one-page letters might arouse sufficient interest and curiosity to accomplish this purpose. If the purpose is to stimulate inquiries, then each letter should be written with this aim in view.

In a follow-up campaign, each letter is definitely related to the others in the series. Taken in its entirety, a series should perform the same functions as are found in a single sales letter—namely, attract attention, create interest and desire, stimulate conviction, and induce action. Letter No. 3 in a series, for instance, presupposes letters No. 1 and No. 2, and paves the way for subsequent letters.

Test mailing list with wear-out series. The wear-out series is used principally to test the effectiveness of a mailing list. The length and number of letters in a series are not planned in advance, and subsequent letters are not sent out until returns from the previous mailing have been checked—and then only to those prospects who did not respond. Although all letters are prepared to sell the same product or service, each letter is separate and distinct from preceding or following letters.

Use continuous follow-up series to keep product or service before public. The continuous follow-up series is sent out at intervals year after year and is intended to keep a product or service before the buying public. This system does not restrict itself to the sale of one article or service; each unit is distinct from others in the series. A department store used the following series in which most of the mailing pieces were in the form of printed circulars:

January ..... Announcement of after-Christmas sales and reductions in all departments.
February .... Announcement of fashion show and sale of famous-make shoes.
March ..... Three printed folders showing spring merchandise for Easter wear.

April .... Letter announcing new credit plan for customers.
May .... Sale of women's spring coats and men's suits.
June .... Folders for bridal gowns and trousseaus; folder of summer camp equipment.
July .... Announcement of special purchases in misses' dresses for week end of July 4.
August ..... Folders on August furniture sales and household furnishings.
September .. Announcement of back-to-school sales and fall millinery.
October .... Letter advertising wraps and evening gowns for the social season.
November .. Announcement and booklets of Christmas sales throughout the store.
December .. Special letter to persons who have bought books, announcing a book-of-the-month club, and soliciting membership.

Example of intensive campaign follow-up. The following campaign letters used by Southern States Iron Roofing Co. illustrate a campaign by a company that has found direct mail the most effective medium for reaching its rather scattered market. The campaign was planned to cover the first half of a year. Its purpose was simple: to secure orders for steel roofing from farm owners. It had a secondary purpose of establishing a favorable impression for the company and its products in the mind of the Southern farmer, whether or not he bought immediately. The campaign consisted of two parts: (1) A mailing to a large list for inquiries (this was a one-shot effort); and (2) a concentrated follow-up of the inquiries from this big mailing.

For the first part, the company used two lists, one of farm owners and the other of former buyers. The list of farm property owners was compiled from the tax records of individual counties. The list to which the campaign was directed consisted of 479,232 farm owners throughout an eleven-state territory. The list of former buyers consisted of 26,921 names. Inquiries from either list received practically the same set of follow-up letters. The schedule of mailing follows:

Quantity	*Title*	*Date*
506,153	(1) Original mailing for inquiry	January 7 to 21
71,757	(2) Answer to inquiry	As inquiries were received
72,321	(3) 1st follow-up	February 12
75,841	(4) 2nd follow-up	March 15
77,126	(5) 3rd follow-up	April 17

The third follow-up letter contained a card on which the inquirer could request further information about a "Summer Special" combination offer on roofing and paint. The middle of April generally marks the end of the company's good season as farmers swing into their summer work. Rather than mail to the complete list of inquirers all through the summer, the list was cut down materially by asking for the second inquiry; then only those who showed their interest were sent the second set of follow-up letters. The following schedule was used for those who responded to the third follow-up:

Quantity	*Title*	*Date*
3,721	(6) Answer to inquiry	As cards were received
3,853	(7) 1st follow-up to that	May 13
3,919	(8) 2nd follow-up to that	June 5

The series of eight letters are reproduced with an explanatory comment preceding each letter.

LETTER 1

(Soliciting inquiries for "Roofing Book." Enclosure: Card)

For the 4:32 mail train

Will you accept a valuable Book FREE?

In a few days I am going to send you an interesting Book that shows how to SAVE MONEY on Roofing. I'll tell you more about this in just a minute—but first, listen to an interesting story.

T. C. Kormat needed a Roof. He got one from a small Roofing Company (which has since gone out of business).

Ed Wilson also needed a Roof. He ordered an EVERWEAR Roof direct from the Southern States Iron Roofing Company.

Less than five years later Kormat had to do the whole job over again because the Roof he bought didn't last.

But Ed Wilson, who ordered the Genuine EVERWEAR Roof, still has it on his building. It looks just as good as it did when he put it on 18 years ago. Ed Wilson made a mighty wise deal when he got that EVERWEAR Roof.

By now you are probably wondering who I am and how I happened to write to you. My name is Charlie Foster. I am General Manager of the Southern States Iron Roofing Company, one of the oldest and best known Steel Roofing Manufacturers in the country. We manufacture Genuine EVERWEAR Roofing. I'm not bragging when I say that but I will admit that I'm mighty proud of the Roofing we make.

For over a quarter of a century now we've been making Zinc Galvanized Steel Roofs for all types of buildings—Steel Roofs *that have to be good* because they have the fine character and reputation of this Company built right into them——Steel Roofs that have covered more than a half million buildings in the South and SAVED MONEY for the owners.

Of course, I don't know whether you need any Roofing right now for any of your buildings or not, but I do want you to know more about EVERWEAR so that you can SAVE MONEY when you do need to cover some of your buildings.

EVERWEAR Roofing is made of PRIME, Full-weight, Grade "A" Steel, heavily coated on both sides with Galvanizing that is 98 and 44 1/100% Pure Zinc. And Zinc, as you know, is the best metallic coating for the rust-proofing of Steel. Therefore, EVERWEAR gives you long-lasting, water-tight Roofs for your home, barns, and other buildings—Roofs that SAVE YOU MONEY in the long run. It is Fire-proof, Lightning-proof, Rust-resisting. That's the kind of Roofing you want on your buildings, isn't it?

I'd like to go on and on—telling you more about EVERWEAR Guaranteed Roofing but this letter just isn't big enough. That's why I want to send you the Book I told you about in the first part of this letter. It tells you the whole story about Genuine EVERWEAR Roofing.

This book contains much valuable Roofing information. It shows pictures and descriptions of the many styles of Genuine EVERWEAR Roofing. Also letters from folks who have SAVED MONEY by using it on their buildings. The Book shows how you, too, can SAVE MONEY by ordering DIRECT-FROM-THE-FACTORY——and keeping all the extra profits right in your own pocket.

It shows the same kinds of Roofing that Mr. Phillips, Mr. Merdith, and Mr. Brantley have on their buildings. And,—

Mr. Phillips ordered his EVERWEAR Roofing TEN YEARS ago. Mr. Merdith got his FIFTEEN YEARS ago. Mr. Brantley put on his first EVERWEAR Roof about TWENTY YEARS ago. And they all say, "*It's fine Roofing, it hasn't leaked a drop.*"

These folks are just a few of the many thousands who have SAVED MONEY and have gotten better Roofs by using EVERWEAR. Let me prove that we can do the same for you. You be the judge as to whether or not you think EVERWEAR Roofing can save you money and also give you a better Roof. Just read our Book—see our LOW PRICES for this high grade Roofing—and then decide for yourself.

I've got your Roofing Book all packed up—ready to go. But I want to make sure that it's going to reach you PERSONALLY.

Therefore, to make absolutely sure that I've got your address right—and that you will get this Book without delay—just fill out the enclosed card and drop it in the mail. No postage is necessary—I take care of that when your card gets here.

Sincerely yours,

Charlie Foster

CF:AFT

P.S. When you order Roofing from us we pay all the Freight Charges.

LETTER 2

(Answers to inquiries. Built around the "Roofing Book" (catalogue) that the prospect wrote for. On the envelope the company emphasizes that this is something the prospect has asked for. The letter plays up interesting points in the catalogue and tries to sell the prospect on the company and its roofing. A special effort is made to persuade the prospect to write about his roofing problems or to ask for quotations. Correspondence is invited by enclosing a "letter sheet" on which the prospect can write about his roofing needs. The mailing carries all the information necessary for ordering: specifications of roofing, prices, order blank, reply envelope.)

Serving the Roofing Needs
of the South for 26 Years

From the
ROOFING HEADQUARTERS
of the South!

. . . Here's the Roofing Book you asked for.

When you have looked this over, you will see why 569,700 wise property owners have ordered EVERWEAR Galvanized "PRIME" Steel Roofing from us during the past twenty-six years. Some of your very own neighbors probably have EVERWEAR Roofing on their homes or other buildings; and they can tell you better than I can what satisfactory roofing it is.

But I'm not going to take up your time, telling you why over half-a-million well-informed property owners think EVERWEAR Roofing is so good. You are much more interested in what EVERWEAR Roofing will do for you when it's on your own buildings—how strong and tough it is—how it will keep out rain and moisture—how it is fireproof—lightning-proof—will not curl, crack, or dry out, and how it will increase the value of your property.

You're interested in the low price and the fact that you don't have to paint this roofing every year to make it last. These are the things you are interested in—so that's what I want to tell you about:

—EVERWEAR ROOFING IS PRICED VERY LOW. Our roofing is priced low because we manufacture it in large quantities, and sell it direct to you. Look at the low prices in the Roofing Book I am sending you. You don't have to add any freight to these prices. *We pay all the freight charges right to you.*

—LASTS MUCH LONGER than ordinary roofing. When you put Genuine EVERWEAR Roofing on your home or other buildings you KNOW IT is there to stay for many, many years. Because it is made of "PRIME" steel, galvanized on both sides with a heavy coating that is 98 and 44/100% pure zinc. And zinc is one of the most rust-resisting metals known. This is why genuine EVERWEAR Roofing will last so much longer than ordinary light-weight galvanized roofing. In fact your EVERWEAR Roof should last as long as the building you put it on.

—EVERWEAR Steel Roofing is GUARANTEED. Every sheet of galvanized steel used in making Genuine EVERWEAR Roofing is marked "PRIME" before it leaves the steel mill. We insist that every sheet be marked "PRIME" so that we can guarantee the roofing to you. You may examine your roofing before accepting it. If you find that it is not as represented by us, or if you are not satisfied with it in every way, just send it right back to us, and we will pay the freight both ways. And of course, we will return all your money to you. You will not be out of pocket a single penny.

You Get These Patented End-Lock Cleats . . . FREE
(U.S. Patent Office Number 1880318)

You'll find the patented End-Lock Cleats, which we give you FREE with your order for Lock-Tight, Improved 5 V-Crimp, and Seal-Tight Roofing, are fully described in your EVERWEAR Roofing Book. Property owners find these patented cleats very valuable for holding down the end of the sheets where they lap.

There is a special EVERWEAR Galvanized Steel Roofing and Siding for every purpose. When looking through your Book, notice that you can now get DRAIN-type roofing as low as corrugated. See the safety drain in the Seal-Tight sheets. And see the tall sharp V-Crimps and wide gutter space in the Improved EVERWEAR 5 V-Crimp Roofing. And, above all, be sure to read—and study—the page on Genuine EVERWEAR Lock-Tight Roofing.

Notice how the side edges "lock-tight" together and form a water-tight seam, and how all the nail-heads are covered with the solid sheet of steel. Having all the nail-heads covered, this way, saves you a lot of time and trouble—and money, too. The sun can't draw out the nails. You won't have to go up on your roof every few years "to tighten the nails."

Now just in case you want to hear what some of the property owners who use our roofing have to say about it, here are just a few of their letters:

"I'm well pleased with my roofing. My fire insurance agent changed (lowered) the rate, without my saying anything about it. I hope to send you another order this year."

C. H. Arendall,
Adamsville, Tenn.

"Your (EVERWEAR) Roof is the best I know of. Every sheet cut square made to fit. I got my first roofing from you

7 years ago, it still looks like new; and 4 years ago I got some more. My father uses your Lock-tight and he's well pleased with it."

Erwin L. Carmley,
Brewton, Ala.

"I received the roofing OK, in good condition. I saved at least $27 on my order. When I need some more roofing I'm going to order from you."

B. T. Meetze,
Lexington, S. C.

These good folks and a half-a-million others are enjoying the money-saving and trouble-free service of EVERWEAR Roofing and Siding. You, too, can save money and end your roofing troubles by ordering your roofing direct from our factory.

It is very easy to order from us at our low, freight-paid prices. Read how easy it is on page 16 of our Roofing Book. Ordering by mail from us is just as simple as driving up to our factory and picking out what you want. Here's all you do. . . .

. . . . Just look through the EVERWEAR Roofing Book and select the kind of roofing you want. Then measure your building (see page 16 of the book), fill out the order blank for what you want, and mail it to us in the enclosed envelope that needs no stamp.

Or, if you don't want to bother with figuring how much roofing you'll need, just put the measurements of your building on the enclosed Correspondence Sheet and send us these measurements. We'll give you, absolutely FREE, an estimate of just what your roofing will cost.

Send your order or the measurements of your building. Get the roofing and siding that you've been wanting. Don't let your buildings deteriorate. Don't put up with leaks and unsafe roofs. Protect your home, your family and property during storms of all kinds. And don't delay. There's nothing to be gained by waiting, as the freight-paid prices of EVERWEAR Roofing are now very low.

Sincerely yours,
Charlie Foster

CF:AFV

P.S. Guaranteed EVERWEAR Galvanized Steel Shingles come in 7 different styles and 4 beautiful colors. Write for FREE Shingle Book showing styles and colors.

LETTER 3

(First follow-up. A price hook with a time limit features this letter. It also contains all the essential information for ordering.

Letterhead showed someone speaking into a microphone, and carried this message: Flash! Here are more roofing savings for property owners who act now. New . . . Lower Prices on EVERWEAR Roofing. Company's name and address were at the bottom of the letterhead.)

This Offer Good Until March 2

February 12, 19. .

"Now I can save you still
more money on your roofing. . . ."

EVERWEAR Roofing is already priced so low that only once in a blue moon am I able to write you a letter like this. However, this is an emergency, so we must tell you that . . .

. . . . for a limited time we are slashing prices on
all styles of EVERWEAR Roofing and Shingles.

This reduction will be in effect from February 12 to March 2. During that time you can get any quantity of genuine EVERWEAR Roofing and Siding at 16¢ a square below our regular prices. Steel shingles are 20¢ a square lower. The price list I am enclosing gives you the new, reduced prices, which may save you as much as several dollars on your order. Compare the reduced prices on this list with the prices in the Roofing Book we sent you not long ago, and see just what you save.

This offer applies only to orders mailed before Midnight, March 2. You would be wise to send your order at once to get the advantage of these low prices.

The Facts Behind This Unusual Offer

You may wonder what emergency would cause us to cut the already-low price of EVERWEAR Roofing. Well, the emergency was caused by the long cold spell throughout the Southern States during January. Remember those freezing days? You did not feel much like working outside and neither did the other property owners who ordinarily would have bought and applied roofing in January. They put off ordering until the end of the cold spell.

That left us in a "hole" because most of the steel we had planned to make into roofing and ship during January is still sitting in our factories. That would be all right except for the fact that 'way last fall we placed orders for 153 carloads of steel to be delivered now. The steel mills are starting to ship these orders, and we have no room to pile the steel.

When I called the managers together the other day, they said, "Charlie, we either have to rent additional warehouse space or sell a lot of roofing in a hurry. We must make room for the big lots of steel that are coming in now. The railroad is already starting to run the cars on our sidings."

Well, rather than pay out rent for storage space, we decided to pass this money along to our customers by temporarily reducing our prices. Naturally we would rather let you pocket an extra saving than let the storage man pocket rent money. Either way costs us money, but the first way saves for you, so of course that is what we want to do.

Why This Offer Must End March 2

Although we would like to continue this price reduction after March 2, it must end on that date. All possible space in our factories has to be cleared by then to make room for the shipments from the steel mills. This chance to save extra dollars on the roofing you need will not last long, so why not order today.

The price list I have enclosed gives all prices and other information necessary for ordering. Once you have figured out how much roofing or shingles you need, you can sit down in an easy chair and fill out the order form. We even pay the postage on the enclosed reply envelope.

SEND NO MONEY—unless you want to

We are glad to ship your roofing without a penny's deposit. When it arrives at the freight station, you may examine it to make sure it is just as good as we say it is. If you think it is not, just tell the freight agent to ship it right back at our expense. It will not cost you a penny. If you like it—and I believe you will—you can keep it and just pay the freight agent the reduced price that appears on the price list I'm sending with this letter. You don't have to pay him for the freight because we pay that.

We are not asking you to buy anything you don't see first. EVER-WEAR Roofing must satisfy you, or you do not have to accept it. It is just like having our store right in your town, except that we offer you anything in our complete stock at direct-from-factory prices rather than high local prices.

Take advantage now of these "February Sale" bargains. Prices may not be as low as this again for a long time. Make out your order and mail it today.

Hurriedly,

Charlie Foster
General Manager

P.S.—Even if you do not want your roofing or shingles shipped yet, you still can take advantage of these low prices. Fill out your order and send it NOW—no deposit necessary. Add a note saying that you do not want the roofing to reach you until . . . (and fill in the date). We allow you to reserve roofing for shipment at "February Sale" prices as far ahead as March 31. The only requirement is that you mail your order by Midnight, March 2, and that shipment is made not later than March 31, 19. .

LETTER 4

(Second follow-up. This was the most effective single piece used in the campaign. The certificate was filled in with the prospect's name. The two-page letter was run on the front and back of the letterhead. The envelope flash, the cover of the folder, and the first paragraph of the letter all emphasized the idea of the certificate and its value. The mailing contains all necessary information for ordering.)

This offer good
only until April 13, 19—

Now—save 50¢ a square on
guaranteed EVERWEAR Lock-Tight Roofing . . .

Your name on the enclosed certificate makes it possible for you to save as much as \$8.00 or \$10.00 on your next roof . . . IF YOU ACT NOW.

> Until April 13, this certificate entitles you to a special allowance of 50¢ a square on EVERWEAR Lock-Tight Roofing . . . the roofing that covers every nail head with a solid sheet of steel. Until that same date, it also entitles you to an allowance of 24¢ a square on EVERWEAR Seal-Tight Roofing.

This special offer is being made only to a selected group of property owners—to just 7 out of every 100 Southern Farm owners. We make it at this time not because we expect to make money on any roofing we sell at such a reduction but because experience has proved that one new EVERWEAR Lock-Tight Roof leads to another . . . particularly when the first one is used by one of the respected and well-known members of a community.

For example, when you put a Lock-Tight Roof on your house, folks are bound to notice it and ask your opinion of it. They may even come by to examine the heavy "PRIME" sheets and the sturdy locks that snap the sheets together. And we are so confident that you are going to be satisfied with your Lock-Tight Roof and give it a boost with many of your neighbors, that we are glad even to lose money to get you to send in your order for Lock-Tight Roofing at this time.

Of course, whether we lose money is our worry; most important to you is the fact that by using your certificate and ordering now you can get premium Lock-Tight Roofing for only 39¢ more per square than 5 V-Crimp . . . as little as \$3.90 more on an order for ten squares.

Extra Saving with Lock-Tight Roofing, Too

That 50¢ a square you save by ordering Lock-Tight Roofing now is just the beginning of your savings, for Lock-Tight is built to give you more years of fire-proof, leak-proof protection than any other sheet roofing.

You know from experience that most roofing troubles start right around the nail hole. A tiny drop of water leaks in; the decking beneath rots; the nail pulls loose; . . . and pretty soon this all adds up to trouble and expense for you. Well, Sir, Lock-Tight Roofing rules out all this trouble right from the start because on a Lock-Tight Roof *every nail head is covered with a solid sheet of steel.* This keeps the nail head bone-dry even in a driving rain.

Lock-Tight gives you extra protection at the three other vital spots on a roof—as the folder I am enclosing explains. This extra protection naturally adds years of life to each Lock-Tight Roof. When you divide the cost of roofing by the number of years you can expect it to last, you will almost certainly find that Lock-Tight is far less expensive than any other roofing.

Remember that the price of Lock-Tight even before this 50¢ special reduction was already the rock-bottom factory price, freight-paid to you. The additional reduction means that this is an opportunity that comes only once in ten years—an opportunity you should not pass up if you plan to buy roofing this year.

FREE Roofing Estimate Service

Without charge or obligation to you, we are glad to estimate just how much roofing you need and tell you in advance what it will cost, right to the penny. In order to get this free service, all you have to do is fill in the dimensions of your roof on the back of the sheet I have enclosed for you to use in writing me. I'll have one of our roofing experts figure your entire job and rush the figures right back to you.

How to Get Your Discount

Because we are not making this offer to everyone, we have registered the certificate in your name. It must be used only by you, and before April 13, 19. . , in order to get this discount.

The folder that I am enclosing gives you the regular and also the reduced prices that you may have by using this certificate. It also gives you the facts about various styles of EVERWEAR Roofing. Select your roofing from it, and then use the enclosed order blank to mail your order before the deadline, April 13. Be sure to enclose your price reduction certificate with your order so that we will know you are entitled to the special discount.

I'll count on hearing from you in the next few days.

Expectantly,
Charlie Foster

CF:AKX

P.S.—In case you need some corrugated galvanized steel and have misplaced your Roofing Book, you can also figure the corrugated price by using the 5 V-Crimp price given in the enclosed folder. Subtract 7¢

from the 5-V price for 1¼ inch corrugated; subtract 12¢ from the 5-V price for 2½-inch corrugated.

LETTER 5

(Third follow-up. This letter asks for a second inquiry. The purpose was to cut down the mailing list drastically, since, by the middle of April, Southern farmers are exceedingly busy with their crops. The letter and card enclosed offer a substantial saving, but by experience the company knows that any farmer who takes time at this busy season of the year to fill out an inquiry card is a "hot" prospect and deserves concentrated attention for the next month or so. The letter also provides a way of bringing the company's paint line, which sells later in the spring, to the attention of prospects.)

Rush message—Mail at once

Read how this "Summer Special"
slashes 40¢ a square off price
of your EVERWEAR Roofing . . .

You certainly will not want to miss an opportunity like this, so mail the enclosed card at once for complete details of the "Summer Special" by which you save 40¢ a square on EVERWEAR Steel Roofing and Shingles—a saving that amounts to about 10% on most styles.

Here, in brief, is the plan that enables you to make such a saving:

> For every gallon of "Southern States" Guaranteed Paint that you buy, we allow you a reduction of 40¢ on the price of one square of roofing—any style or weight.

Take Time Now to Order—and Save Plenty

Since you probably will need paint and roofing before long, you naturally would be wise to buy them both at the best possible price. For that reason, this "Summer Sale" reduction (which lasts only to June 30) is your opportunity. You can make a saving by placing your order for roofing and paint at once—a saving that more than repays the small time and effort required for this. Even if you do not plan to use them at once, you can afford to order at this money-saving price and store them until you are ready to use.

Are We Foolish to Make Such an Offer?

We might seem foolish to some folks when we make a reduction now on roofing that probably will be bought anyway at full prices in the fall—but we do not think we are. You see, if people do not complete their roofing in early spring, they ordinarily put it off until fall, even though leaks threaten to ruin much of their property. They lose, of course, but so do we because our business falls off during the summer and we are faced with the necessity of either letting some of our loyal workers go—which we certainly don't intend to do—or carrying more men on our pay roll than we actually need in the slack season.

By making you an offer so attractive that it would be worth acting upon even in the middle of spring planting, we hope to keep our factories humming and our men at work. Will you help us by figuring your paint and roofing needs for the next six months and ordering at today's low prices? You will be helping yourself too, because every gallon of paint ordered means 40¢ saving on a square of EVERWEAR Roofing or Shingles.

New Free Book Tells How to Cut Property Upkeep Cost

Now, I know that up to date I have not told you about our line of "Southern States" Paint—so rather than just say that its quality is as high as our roofing in every way, I am going to send you a new book (coming from the printer in the next day or two) that is packed with facts about "Southern State" Paint.

From this book you can find out for yourself about the unusual spreading and lasting qualities of our paint. In addition it has many suggestions for lengthening the life of your buildings and farm equipment. Likewise it has money-saving ideas for the practical painter: how to make paint go further and cover better, how to prepare a surface for painting, how to make brushes last longer, what paint to use for each surface, etc.

As I said, I have a copy of this book for you, but first I would like to be sure you want it. Will you put your OK on the enclosed card and return it to me? The book will reach you within a few days then.

The same card will bring you the complete story about our amazing "Summer Special," together with a new roofing price list showing the regular prices on EVERWEAR Guaranteed Steel Roofing—prices that are 16¢ a square lower than they were in January. Thus the card brings you all the information you need for taking advantage of our "Summer Special."

Don't Miss This—Mail Your Card *Today*

Mailing a little card that requires no postage is a pretty easy way to save 40¢ a square on your roofing—why not sign that card right this minute while you have it in hand. There is no obligation, and it can save you plenty.

Expectantly,
Charlie Foster
General Manager

CF:ALM

P.S.—I know you will be interested in the recent results of 153 laboratory tests on our roofing at Pittsburgh Testing Laboratory, Pittsburgh,

Pa. Scientists found that the weight of the protective zinc coating on EVERWEAR Sheets averaged 32% heavier than United States Government requirements for standard roofing. Because even a small increase in the weight of the zinc coating substantially lengthens the life of the roofing, EVERWEAR Roofing may last 64% longer than sheets which would pass Government standards as "good" roofing . . . and that is something to consider in buying your next roofing!

LETTER 6

(Answer to inquiry—second series. The letter makes a combination offer of roofing and paint. The letterhead was varied to emphasize paint.)

For the 4:32 mail train

How to save 40¢ a square
on steel roofing . . .

Enclosed with this letter is the paint book I promised to send you, together with a roofing price sheet and full information about our special "Summer Sale" offer. This unusual offer enables you to save 40¢ a square on roofing if you purchase your paint needs at the same time. I am mighty glad to be able to make such a money-saving offer to you, because my business grows only if I can save money for Southern property owners who are building or repairing.

Briefly, the offer is this: For each gallon of paint that you purchase you are entitled to one square of roofing at a 40¢ reduction from our already-low, freight-paid prices. The enclosed folder gives you the details.

Understand, please, that the roofing and paint on which this special offer is made are our full-quality, first-line products—the same ones that we sell every day at full price. We make such a reduction only because we want to encourage you to buy your roofing and paint now, rather than waiting until fall. That way—although we may lose money—we can keep our factories busy and our men at their places throughout the summer, which is usually our dull season.

Figure What You Save

These prices make it worth while for you to buy now, even if you have to store your paint and roofing for a while before you have time to use them. The money you save more than repays the slight inconvenience. For example, on an order for 14 squares of roofing you save $5.60 if you buy paint at the same time. That's worth saving!

If you have absolutely no use for paint at this time, there is certain to be one or more of your neighbors who can use paint. By combining your roofing order with a neighbor's paint order you can still take advantage of this reduction.

To make it easy to order, we have prepared a combination roofing-and-paint order form and enclosed it with this letter. It has a blank for ordering paint and a blank for ordering roofing. These are on opposite pages, facing each other. Just fill in each one, and then for each gallon of paint ordered, deduct 40¢ from the price of a square of roofing.

We are always glad to hear from our friends like yourself, so be sure to write us if there is any way we can help you select the proper roofing or paint.

Cordially yours,
Charlie Foster
General Manager

CF:ALT

P.S.—Our Estimate service is FREE. Just send us the measurements of your building and we will figure, without charge or obligation, the paint and roofing you need and the total price.

LETTER 7

(First follow-up. Second series. Again it was necessary for the mailing to carry prices on both paint and roofing and a combination order blank. The letter and folder were built around new laboratory tests that established the high quality of EVERWEAR Roofing.)

Spring Bargain Season
19..

Here is what thrifty buyers
do when they want to be sure
of getting their money's worth . . .

They ask: "How does this product you are offering me compare with the requirements of the United States Government's Bureau of Standards?"

Through the years they have come to know that "Bureau of Standards requirements" spell quality, whether they are buying sewing machines or bath tubs, motor oil or steel roofing. The Bureau is Uncle Sam's checking laboratory. It sets up certain standards of performance and excellence that all products purchased by the Government must meet. Because the Government is so careful in its purchases, practical farmers and other businessmen figure that when they demand the same standards as the Government, they are sure to get full value and satisfactory merchandise.

Facts about Government Standards for Galvanized Roofing

The U. S. Bureau of Standards rates galvanized steel roofing by the thickness of its protective coating of zinc galvanizing; the thicker the coating, they have learned, the longer a sheet will last. Moreover, a small increase in the weight of the coating means a much greater increase in the life of the roofing.

In view oı these facts, I know you will be interested in tests we had made recently on EVERWEAR Roofing sheets by an independent steel laboratory, the Pittsburgh Testing Laboratory, in Pittsburgh, Pa. They made a total of 153 tests, and found that EVERWEAR's zinc coating averaged 32% heavier than U. S. Government standards for "good" roofing.

What This Means to You

This means that you can buy—at regular prices—a roofing that is 32% better than Government standards. And because just a small increase in the weight of the zinc coating adds greatly to the life of the roofing—roofing experts indicate that such roofing with 32% heavier coating should last 64% or more longer than roofing that just meets Government standards.

Therefore, though you pay no more for the heavier-coated EVERWEAR Roofing it should give you 64% more trouble-free storm-proof service.

You can sit at home in your easy chair and order EVERWEAR Roofing by mail, direct-from-the-factory. The enclosed order blank shows you how to figure the roofing you need; and the price sheet shows you the details of each kind of roofing as well as the low, factory prices at which you can purchase now.

Our estimate service is free, if you would like to have us figure your roofing needs for you. Just send the dimensions of your roof to our experts and tell them what style of EVERWEAR Roofing you want. They figure just how much you need and tell you to the penny the freight-paid price on it.

Extra Saving on EVERWEAR Now

Right now our Summer Special on EVERWEAR Roofing and "Southern States" Paint gives you an opportunity to get this heavier-coated roofing at an unusual saving . . .

For every gallon of "Southern States" Paint or Varnish
that you buy, you are entitled to a reduction of 40¢
on one square of EVERWEAR Roofing.

Figure what this means to you: for example, on an order for only ten gallons of paint and ten squares of roofing, you save $4.00—a remarkable saving on paint and roofing that are already offered at bargain prices.

The enclosed combination order blank has space for ordering paint and roofing together, and it also gives you more detailed information about this "Summer Special." The price sheets on paint and roofing give you the information you need in choosing these products.

You need not send cash or check with your order. Order now, while the order blank and envelope are at hand. Then pay your freight agent only after you have examined and approved your paint and roofing.

This offer is good for a limited time only, so better act at once.

Cordially,

Charlie Foster
General Manager

CF:AMD

P.S.—If you have no need for both paint and roofing at this time, please do not hesitate to order just the one product you do need. The enclosed price sheets give the correct prices to use in ordering either paint or roofing by themselves, and you may use the enclosed order blank to return your order for fast service.

LETTER 8

(Second follow-up. Second series. In this letter roofing is ignored completely, and a paint special is concentrated upon. This is the last letter of the follow-up campaign.)

Next week I am sending you
a full gallon of paint FREE
to try at my expense . . .

Will you fill in (on the slip I am enclosing) the grade and color of house paint that you want? Then I can send you by return freight a full gallon of "Southern States" paint absolutely free.

The idea is that you agree to take this free gallon of paint and try it on your home or outbuilding—you to be the sole judge of whether it is the best paint you ever bought at its price. The only requirement is that, at the time I send you the free gallon, you place a tentative order for at least five more gallons of the same grade paint. By the time you have used up that first trial gallon, I feel you will agree with thousands of other Southern property owners that "Southern States" is the most paint for the money on the market today. If you don't, then just return the remaining five gallons to us at our expense . . . and without obligation to you in any way.

How can you lose on this offer?

We give you the first gallon free so that you can find out about our paint without risking one penny of your own. The decision is entirely up to you. If you say, "No, I don't like your paint," we take back the remaining five gallons and instantly refund any freight or money you have paid. If you do like the paint—and we believe you will—the first extra gallon is still yours FREE, and you can finish your painting with the remaining five gallons . . . and pay us just the low, freight-paid price on them.

By taking advantage of this offer, you get six gallons of paint at our usual price for five. For example, if you order "Southern States" First-Quality House Paint, we would send you one gallon free and then five at the regular price of $2.40 per gallon: a total of only $12 for six gallons or at the amazingly low price of $2 per gallon for what is practically the finest house paint made—a paint that few local dealers can begin to equal at less than $3.50 a gallon.

You don't have to take our word for how good our paints are: we are giving you the opportunity to try them without risking a cent. You may choose a free trial gallon of any of these four grades:

"Southern States" First-Quality House Paint ..	$2.40 per gal.
"Economy" House Paint	1.65 per gal.
Mildew-Resisting Paste Paint	3.34 per gal.
Barn & Roof Paint	1.40 per gal.

You will find these listed on the enclosed price sheet, together with a complete description and all colors. You may order several different colors if you want, rather than have all six gallons one color.

You won't have to bother about thinner either. You always get a gallon of turpentine FREE with every five gallons of "Southern States" paint. The turpentine will be sent right along with your paint.

How to get your free trial gallon—*Be sure to read this.*

You may give us the information about the trial gallon you want in the space provided on the pink request slip. Then attach this slip to a tentative order (on the regular paint order blank) for five gallons more to be shipped at the same time that we send the test gallon. You can either send payment for the five gallons with your order, or else we are glad to ship them to you C. O. D. In either case, at any time after you have tested the first gallon and decide that you do not want to keep the other five, your money is subject to instant refund.

Since we pay the freight on all orders for five gallons or more, there will be no freight charges for you to pay.

This opportunity to test "Southern States" paint at our expense is good only until June 30, so fill out the request and mail it today. The paint is all ready to ship to you. All I need is your "OK."

Expectantly,
Charlie Foster

CF:AML

P.S.—Whether you keep or return the five gallons, the one FREE gallon is yours without obligation. There are no "strings" to our offer.

9. DEVICES THAT MAKE SALES LETTERS WORK

Devices that make sales letters work. A good sales letter can be made a better sales letter if it is combined with a device for getting attention and action. In the following paragraphs examples are given of devices that have given sales letters a special pulling power.

Extra-size letter. The following letter took the form of a self-mailing folder measuring 13½ × 20 inches when open. It was folded in half from left to right and then three times to measure 4½ × 10 inches when folded for mailing. An attractive illustration on the address side suggested that the reader open the folder. When the folder was opened, there appeared these words in a design that suggested speed: "There's a big letter for you inside." Then appeared the following letter in enormous typewriter type, on an enlarged J. I. Case Company letterhead. The number of cards received and the number of farmers who visited Case dealers to see the mower and other hay tools were evidence that the mailing piece was effective.

Hay Time Is
No Play Time

When it's time to make hay there's no time to waste with machinery that breaks down or gives trouble in the field. Maybe there's corn to be laid by, grain harvest coming on, perhaps something else—but there's always something to make haying a rush season job.

And it's no time to make your horses pull a hard-running mower. After the long, hard grind of spring work they are in no shape to worry along under a load of neck weight and side draft. It's hot, sultry weather, and you need to keep them in good condition for harvest.

Maybe you can afford hours of wasted labor—possibly your horses can stand the risk of sore necks—but nobody can afford to take chances on a hay crop. Don't blame the weather entirely for sun-bleach, rain-damage, leaf-loss, and the other things that make the difference between hay worth a good price on the market or in your own mangers, and the other kind—at which both buyers and "bossies" turn up their noses.

With exceedingly few exceptions you can beat the weather and escape most of these losses if you use a modern method of hay making and have machinery you can depend on to get every job done right on time. For the cutting operation you can't beat the Case Hi-Lift Oil Bath Mower described in the enclosed folder. The difference in quality and value of hay on only ten acres might easily pay for it in a single year. But this is a mower that will give you years of good service. It is light-running and has easy adjustments for maintaining a clean cut and minimizing the replacement of working parts.

Don't wait until the last minute—see this great mower now at your Case dealer.

At the same time get full information on Case sulky and side delivery rakes as well as the new Case combination cylinder and push bar hay loader with tight bottom—the loader that has the best features of both types, and saves a lot of loose leaves. Learn all about the pick-up method of baling hay or straw that puts it in the bale with less labor than to put it in a stack. Just check the enclosed card, sign and drop it in the mail.

Very truly yours,

Form letter personalized by photos. What better way to get "in step" with the reader at the outset than to let him come face to face with his own photograph? By using the pictures of hotel executives published in a trade journal, an Indiana furniture firm constructed a novel letter to be sent to the person photographed. A form letter on the subject of hotel chairs was prepared, and the picture of the executive was cut out and pasted at the top of the letterhead. Alongside the picture, the following copy was typewritten:

GOOD MORNING
You look to me like a man
who would appreciate
GOOD HOTEL CHAIRS

An additional copy of the hotel publication was secured, and a similar cutout was pasted on the envelope next to the name and address.

The envelope and letter succeeded in securing eye attention from the reader, and the envelope had a better chance of getting past the mail clerk and into the hands of the executive.

Devices to facilitate action by the reader. The fact that it contains a device to make it easy for the reader to act is one of the reasons for the success of the letter reproduced in Figure 9. An application is attached to the letter; the need for an envelope is eliminated; and the directions for forwarding are simple. Notice the following about the letter:

(1) The evidence of confidence in what is offered. "Don't send any money. See the policy first and, if you're satisfied, then just mail your check for $3.65."

(2) The stimulation to one specific action at the close.

Reply-O-Letter makes it easy for the reader to act. The Reply-O-Letter is a patented device used by the Reply-O-Products Corporation, New York, in the letter service that it supplies. The

N M EBY PRESIDENT
E O KUNAU, VICE PRESIDENT
L WIEBELER TREASURER

Policy Holders from Coast to Coast
ESTABLISHED 1927

J W WALKER VICE PRESIDENT
M H GREGORY, SECRETARY
A B MAHON ASS'T TREASURER

POSTAL LIFE INSURANCE & CASUALTY COMPANY

4727 WYANDOTTE STREET
KANSAS CITY, MO.

Dear Friend:

We have just put a NEW accident policy on the market that COSTS ONLY ONE CENT A DAY!

This policy will pay you up to $100.00 a month for a period of TWENTY-FOUR MONTHS if you are disabled.

It has a special HOSPITAL BENEFIT which pays in addition as much as $50.00 a month for TWO MONTHS for hospital care in accidental injury.

It pays up to $1,000.00 to your beneficiary if you are killed! And it covers accidents such as happen every day--accidents due to riding in or driving automobiles, house trailers, trucks, taxicabs or buses (including school or chartered buses); being struck by vehicles on any public street, road or highway; accidents while operating or riding in trains, street cars, elevators, mail, express or baggage cars; accidents while riding as a fare-paying passenger on a regularly scheduled airplane.

It also covers being injured or killed by lightning, tornadoes, hurricanes; by the collapse of the outer walls of a building or the burning of any church, theater, library, school or public building and numerous other accidents. This new policy covers farm implement, wagon, and tractor accidents--being kicked by a horse or mule, or gored by a bull or cow--and accidents while riding a bicycle.

As an emergency benefit, the company will pay all expenses up to $100.00 of putting you in touch with friends or relatives if you are injured

A medical benefit of $20.00 is provided in case of minor injuries--this benefit alone is nearly six times the amount of the yearly premium.

Think of all this protection for only $3.65 a year! You do not have to be killed to secure the indemnity, but if you are killed, it pays for that too. So you have protection whether you live or die.

More than A QUARTER MILLION people have already bought Postal accident policies. Men, women and children are eligible. No medical examination is required, and it does not matter how many other policies you have.

Just fill in and return application today! Don't send any money. See the policy first and if you're satisfied, then just mail your check for $3.65.

The policy will be sent directly to you and no salesman will call.

Sincerely yours,

J. W. Walker

Vice President

JWW:A
27

REFERENCES: TRADERS GATE CITY NATIONAL BANK · PLAZA BANK OF COMMERCE · FIRST NATIONAL BANK

OVER ONE-HALF MILLION DOLLARS PAID IN CLAIMS

COPYRIGHT 1939

NO ENVELOPE NECESSARY
JUST—FOLD, SEAL AND MAIL

APPLICATION

This Policy Is Issued to Men, Women and Children. To Avoid Any Errors Please Print All Information.

Please send me one of your NEW, IMPROVED accident policies for FREE EXAMINATION, without obligation. If I decide to keep the policy I will send you a check for $3.65 to cover the first year's premium. I certify that I am in sound condition mentally and physically and that the following answers are true and correct.

Full Name ______________________
PRINT NAME IN FULL

Address ______________________
STREET NO OR R. F. D.

____
CITY STATE

Sex ______ Age ______ Birth Date: Month ______ Day ______ Year ______

Occupation ______________________

Print below name, address and relation of person to whom you want insurance paid in case you are killed.

Beneficiary ______________________
NAME RELATIONSHIP

Address ______________________

If you want additional applications for friends or relatives, check here (______).

Figure 9. A Sales Letter That Has Met All Tests.

reply card is slipped into a pocket attached to the letter. The card serves as the inside address on the letter and makes it unnecessary for the person to whom it is addressed to write his name and address on the card. It also enables the sender to check the exact number of replies to a letter sent out with the reply card. Companies which have used the Reply-O-Letter have indicated that it has helped to increase the percentage of returns and has also cut operating costs by reducing the motions required to complete a campaign.

Personalization and showmanship important. By catching the eye and persuading attention through personalization, the following letter (Figure 10) produced excellent results for Mailings, Incorporated, a direct-mail service. The prospect's name was written across the top, brush-scripted in gold paint. An Aspirin tablet was attached on the left. Here was showmanship and personalization of a high order.

Tie-up with premium. Using a rabbit's foot charm as a premium in a direct-mail campaign to sell accident policies required a letter that brought both the superstition and the premium to the attention of the prospect. A provocative opening question and a closing reference to the premium, in the Maryland Casualty Company letter reproduced below, shows a simple but effective tie-in. A common-sense appeal, supported by facts, is used.

My dear Mr. Hunt:

Would you trust to luck to protect you against accidents, Mr. Hunt?

Even a good luck charm will not prevent them. It is an established fact that one person in twenty-seven will be seriously injured this year. You may be that one.

If you are, your income is more needed than ever. Your home expenses must go on and in addition there are hospital, doctors' and nurses' bills. Accident Insurance guarantees you a weekly income while you are disabled, plus payment of hospital, doctors' and nurses' bills up to the amount specified in the policy. You can relax from worry.

Invest in an accident policy. Then, if you are injured, you will be lucky. One of our agents, Mr. Robert L. Ward, Parker Building, Bridgeville, will call on you within a few days. Incidentally, he has a rabbit's foot charm for you.

Yours very truly,

Rabbit's Foot Accident — Vice-President

Mr. Fraser

Does your D. M. give you a headache?

Here's relief:

No --- not Aspirin --- but experience!

Patent medicines, panaceas and poultices have their place --- but, they try to correct, they don't prevent.

If you're displeased with your Direct Mail results --- perhaps we can be the Doctor.

We can apply "preventative medicine" or give your direct mail a tonic stimulant. Experience in creating and producing millions of mailing pieces (5,000,000 for the Book-of-the-Month Club alone) has taught us what to do and what not to do.

Most doctors charge a fee for consultation. We run a Clinic --- diagnose your case and prescribe copy and ideas without charge.

If you should retain us for treatment, you will receive the skilled services of a Specialist at the modest fee of a General Practitioner.

There's a Prescription card enclosed that's already filled in with your name. It will bring a Specialist and Case Histories of remarkable cures.

Professionally yours,

Lewis Kleid

LK:G LEWIS KLEID, President

Mailings incorporated 25 WEST 45th STREET • NEW YORK CITY

Figure 10. Showmanship in a Personalized Sales Letter.

MUTUAL BROADCASTING SYSTEM

NEW YORK OFFICES ★ 1440 BROADWAY

Sept. 11, 1940

Mr. Robert Bruce
Prentice-Hall, Inc.
New York City

Dear Mr. Bruce:

Recently, in a booklet of school-pad proportions,* complete with pencil, we pointed out that Mutual's new Volume Plan stands ready to save you 20 - 30% of your network time cost.

Attached here, is a story of a different color -- a fact, not a forecast. A story of what leading advertisers are actually doing about Mutual's new Volume Plan.

It is the story of three of the latest clients to sign Mutual volume contracts.

And by the way, isn't this a three-fold answer to the armchair critics who confide, "Certainly it's a marvelous value, but can Mutual clear time?"

Sincerely,

Robert A. Schmid

Robert A. Schmid
Director of Advertising

RAS:LP

*If by any chance you failed to receive your copy of "Air-rithmetic", or would find another helpful, we would be glad to send one of our limited supply on its way.

Figure 11. Novel Presentation of Testimonials.

Novel presentation of testimonials. Miniature testimonial letters were inserted in the sales letter of the Mutual Broadcasting System shown on page 126. The miniatures were kept in place by means of a pocket placed in back of the letterhead. The reproductions were graduated in length so that each letterhead would show. (See Figure 11.) The shortest measured 2½ inches; the longest, 3½ inches. A black arrow above the date pointed to the insertion. The letter merely calls attention to "what leading advertisers are actually doing about Mutual's new Volume Plan."

How to get the most out of successful sales letters. A letter that has brought results can be used again and again. It should not be discarded until it ceases to work.

A successful letter can even be repeated as a follow-up. Variations can be added to get attention. The following devices have been used successfully on repeat letters:

1. Reproduce the letter on a different colored paper with the word C O P Y in red ink across its face and a brief note in red ink in the upper right-hand corner. One firm added the following note:

> "91 Arizona employers accepted the offer made in my letter of July 5.
> "With the thought that the original may not have reached you, I am sending this duplicate.
> "I hope you, too, will want to take advantage of this special offer.
>
> D.A.L."

2. Use the same letter with a handwritten and initialed sentence at the top of the page, such as: "Did you overlook this letter mailed to you recently? D.A.L."

SECTION 2

Profitable Advertising

Pretesting by the Consumer-Jury Method

6. HOW TO DESIGN AND REGISTER A TRADE-MARK

7. COPYRIGHT PROCEDURE

8. PRINTING AND TYPOGRAPHY

9. GLOSSARY OF ADVERTISING PROCEDURE

SECTION 2

Profitable Advertising*

1. WHAT ADVERTISING CAN DO SUCCESSFULLY

What is advertising? Advertising is not necessarily what you see or hear. That advertisement in a national magazine or newspaper, that program you hear over the air—that is not "advertising"; that is merely a part of advertising.

Advertising is not a "thing apart." It is not divorced from the rest of business. In fact, it cannot be successful unless and until it is part and parcel of business.

There is only one way to obtain an accurate answer to the question, What is advertising? and that is, to study a list of the functions of a large advertising and sales-promotion department.

Functions of an advertising department. If you could sit down with the executive in charge of such a department, in the offices of a company spending several million dollars annually in advertising, and ask him, What does your department do? here is how he would answer that question. "First," he would say, "with regard to strictly advertising functions, this is what we do:

ADVERTISING DUTIES

Preparation of the advertising budget
Supervision of the preparation and purchase of space in

Newspapers	Car cards
Magazines	Posters
Radio	Theater programs
Television	Directories
Business papers	Outdoor advertising
Industrial publications	Window displays
Farm papers	Counter displays
Religious papers	Novelties
Class journals	Booklets

* Acknowledgment is made to Albert Frank-Guenther Law, Inc., Advertising, for assistance in revising this Section.

Supervision of the preparation of cards and labels
Preparation of catalogues
Preparation of package inserts
Preparation of motion pictures (including talking pictures when used for consumer advertising)
Preparation of consumer samples
Supervision of copy testing
Preparation of consumer house organs
Supervision of improvements of packages, labels, tags, display cartons
Supervision of trade-mark design
Purchase of paper, artwork, engravings, mats, electros, and other material used in advertising (except where agency does such detail and advertising department approves)
Preparation and maintenance of files of advertising material, scrapbooks of same, etc.
Analysis and study of competitive advertising
Wrapping and distributing advertising material
Contact with the advertising agency
Preparation and maintenance of mailing lists (which apply to advertising work as distinguished from mailing lists prepared and maintained by the sales-promotion department)
Purchase of office supplies and fixtures for advertising department (except where purchasing department does this)
Advertising accounting work (in addition to work carried on by regular accounting department)
Co-operation with engineering and/or production department in developments that will affect advertising
Sales-convention work to explain reasons for and values of advertising and to present advertising plans (as distinguished from more detailed convention work often carried on by the sales-promotion department)
Preparation of advertising exhibits for sales conventions
Development and preparation of advertising portfolios for salesmen (except where these are almost entirely made up of promotion-department material)
Preparation of advertising material directed at company's personnel
Sales-analysis work to determine where best to carry on special advertising effort
Analysis of dealer and distributor media advertising (sometimes in co-operation with sales-promotion department)
Individual dealer and distributor correspondence on advertising matters
Co-operation in preparing annual report (where company makes report something more than a balance sheet)
Co-operation with other departments on public-relations work
Choice and purchase of consumer premiums
Representing the company in associations or other organizations devoted to advertising

Supervision of our co-operation with testing bureaus where results of work are used for advertising purposes
Preparation of purchase and display signs on the factory or office building
Checking and maintaining record of advertising returns"

"Then," he would continue, "with respect to so-called 'sales-promotion functions,' which are part and parcel of advertising, this is what we do:

SALES PROMOTION DUTIES

Preparation of direct mail done by dealers and distributors
- Preparation and/or checking of lists for dealers or distributors
- Preparation of folders or pamphlets to accompany monthly statements sent out by dealers
- Preparation of folders or pamphlets for counter distribution
- Preparation of complete mail campaigns
- Preparation of new customer letters
- Preparation of lost customer letters

Planning and supervision of motion pictures (for dealer or distributor effect)
Preparation of permanent display stands (as opposed to perishable display material)
Preparation of dealer identification signs
Co-operation in the issuance of house magazines:

A. Internal
   1. Sales
   2. Employee
B. External
   1. Dealer

Purchase of paper, artwork, engravings, mats, electros, and other materials used in sales promotion
Preparation of dealer samples
Preparation and maintenance of files and scrapbooks, etc., of promotion material
Sales-promotion accounting work (in addition to work done by accounting department)
Purchase of office supplies and fixtures for sales-promotion department (except where purchasing department does this)
Maintenance of mailing lists (which apply to promotion work)
Preparation of sales-promotion budget
Exchange of experiences within far-flung parts of large organizations
Co-operation with engineering and/or production departments in developments that will affect promotion duties
Experimental sales work. This means actual selling in the field to test the effects of certain promotion plans

Handling of sales-training courses (under supervision of sales department) for
- Company salesmen
- Distributors' salesmen

Sales training in the field (where not done by representatives of sales department)
Co-operation with sales department in following through individual dealer inquiries
Sales correspondence (where not handled by sales department)
Keeping of sales records (where not handled by sales department)
Development of salesmen's portfolios (except where these are largely advertising)
Development of visual sales presentations
Preparation of sales bulletins (where this is not done by an assistant sales manager)
Preparation of salesmen's sample case (where not done by sales department)
Development of salesmen's display material
Working with sales department to prepare material for sales conventions (except advertising exhibits)
Salesmen and dealer training
- Programming of meetings instructing in product and how to sell

Informing salesmen of new equipment, new product, etc. (where not done by sales department)
Securing data by which sales quotas can be assigned
Special-analysis work of customer problems too complicated for individual salesmen to handle
Co-ordination of programs and itineraries of traveling representatives from home office to branches so there will be no overlapping or backtracking of effort
Contacting of dealers in matters other than sales
Contacting of distributors in matters other than sales
Dealer and distributor adjustments (where not handled by sales department)
Planning distributor and dealer contests
Educational work among dealers' salespeople
Working with dealers on customer-control systems
Arrangement for distribution of films among dealers and distributors
Individual dealer and distributor correspondence dealing with promotional matters
Analysis of dealer and distributor direct-mail advertising
Liaison work for distributors and their dealers—as between licensees and dealers
Guidance of trade relations through
- Education
- Trade associations

Meetings
Product information
Preparation and supervision of product exhibits in trade meetings
Preparation and supervision of product exhibits in dealers' stores
Planning and supervision of demonstrations (except salesmen's demonstrations)
Helping dealer with his advertising budget
Sales research
Analysis to determine new product needs
Sales analysis to determine where best to carry out promotion effort
Analysis of accounts, new and lost, to determine promotion effort
Development of sales-facilitating services, such as time-payment plans
Maintenance of unit sales records for individual products
Corresponding with home-demonstration agents and home-economics teachers
Planning and supervision of exhibition of product in branch houses
Preparation of material for trade shows
Handling of trade-show space where sales department does not take over function
Contact with competitors
Study and analysis of competitive products from the standpoint of product improvement
Contact with trade associations whose members sell company's products"

"And then," he would conclude, "there are some functions that we are sometimes called upon to do which may not be strictly advertising or sales promotion—but nobody else is equipped to do these things, so we undertake to do them. They include:

BORDERLINE DUTIES

Production of direct-mail material (other than that used by dealers)
Creation and design of letterheads, billheads, shipping labels
Supervision of the preparation and distribution of traveling window displays
Preparation of instruction sheets and manuals to insure proper use of products
Preparation and supervision of factory outside display signs
Distribution of display material
Supervision of design and purchase of salesmen's automobiles where these are used for advertising purposes
Co-operation with window display services
Distribution of circulars and pamphlets to the consumer
Distribution of circulars and pamphlets to the trade
Supervision of premium distribution
Gathering of photographic evidence of use of product

Gathering of testimonial data
Supervision of printing plant, duplicating department
Institutional publicity
Gaining publicity for the firm for new products
Market research
Complete cataloguing of product
Clearing house for leads from distributors or dealers
Following through with dealers' inquiries developing from advertising and promotion effort
Co-ordinating sales and advertising activities
Maintaining file of historical material of company's activities
Preparation of salesmen's catalogue
Preparation, supervision, and distribution of special exhibits for schools and colleges"

Who advertises. No more than 1,000 companies in this country spend in excess of $50,000 annually in so-called commissionable advertising—that is, advertising in magazines, newspapers, radio, trade papers, farm papers, etc. But there are over 13,500 advertisers listed in the advertising directory. The remaining 12,500 advertisers, therefore, are comparatively small advertisers. Consequently, when you think of advertising, think of it, not as practiced by the 1,000 large advertisers of this country but as practiced by the 12,500 smaller advertisers.

Think of a typical hardware store. What percentage of the items carried do you suppose are actually *demanded* by brand name by the majority of customers who make purchases? Ask yourself that question with regard to department stores. Picture the thousands of items stocked by a typical department store and then realize the tiny percentage *demanded* by brand name.

Copy, art, radio technique, media—all are of paramount importance. But they can rarely carry the entire burden of making the merchandise move into consumption. They should seldom be asked to carry that terrific load. Advertising should and must be merchandised if the utmost is to be squeezed out of the advertising investment.

Facts for smaller advertisers. In looking at the overwhelming majority of advertisers, those whose total advertising appropriations are less than $100,000 annually, these facts are revealed:

First, these advertisers spend sufficient money for actual consumer advertising to cover the country only thinly. Second, with this thin coverage, these advertisers can usually hope to create, through their own advertising, only a sporadic consumer *demand*. Third, their advertising can, and should, create consumer *interest*. Fourth, their advertising can, and should, create a measurable degree of consumer acceptance.

Now, when we view the results of the consumer advertising of the large majority of our advertisers in this light, some further facts promptly become clear. These may be summarized as follows: First, consumer *interest* is a passive quality. It means little to the advertiser unless and until it is cultivated—developed. Second, consumer *acceptance* is also a passive quality. It, too, is of little importance as an asset unless and until it is cultivated—developed. Third, both consumer *interest* and consumer *acceptance* are actually consumer *demand* in the incipient stage. The breath of life must be pumped into them. They must be vitalized—energized.

Developing demand for an advertiser's product. These additional facts are of importance to the advertiser on the question of developing demand for a product. First, consumer interest and consumer acceptance ripen most quickly into consumer demand in the retail store. The retailer is the modern magician who, practically with the wave of a wand, can turn the consumer interest and consumer acceptance developed by the manufacturer's advertising into consumer demand. Second, the retailer can also nurse along the actual consumer demand created by the manufacturer, play along with it, build it up. Third, the retailer has a consumer demand of his own. Very often his own consumer demand is stronger than the consumer demand possessed by most of the brands that he stocks. This is particularly true of department stores. The large department stores in many cities spend more money advertising specific items in their areas than do the manufacturers of these items. They have a powerful consumer demand. The retailer can take his consumer demand and turn it over to the manufacturer.

But will the retailer wave that magic wand over the manufacturer's consumer interest and consumer acceptance? Will the retailer nurse along the manufacturer's actual consumer demand? Will the retailer turn over his own consumer demand to the manufacturer? No, he will not, if he is ignored in the manufacturer's planning.

First and foremost, then, throw overboard the delusion that irresistible consumer demand is created by small consumer-advertising appropriations. Second, *merchandise the manufacturer's consumer advertising to and through the trade.*

The distributor, in the final analysis, holds the key to success in consumer advertising in so far as the majority of advertisers are concerned. If he is roused to enthusiasm about the manufacturer's advertising, if he is not merely told to tie up but is shown how to tie up, then the manufacturer gets the bonus on his advertising appropriation to which he is justly entitled.

Tools for merchandising the advertising. Here is a list of the tools available to the advertising man who wants to do a thorough job of merchandising the advertising:

Related selling in retail stores
Case histories
Store histories demonstrations
Circularizing dealers' prospects
Bill inserts for stores
New shipping cartons for trade shipments
Direct-mail campaign to dealers
Advertising allowances
Profit-sharing plan for distributors
Helping dealer sell right product (like device for measuring gloves, etc.)
Bulletins for dealers on various subjects (telephone selling, collection letters, etc.)
Mailing lists of jobbers' salesmen and retail salespeople (home addresses)
Tags on merchandise (to help salespeople do more effective selling job)
Co-operative merchandising with a noncompetitive manufacturer
Securing interest of wives, mothers, etc. of dealers, salespeople, manufacturers' salesmen
Bringing back lost customers (both lost accounts to the manufacturer and lost customers to the dealer)
Store-wide promotions—promotions in more than one department—interdepartment merchandising
Plans for tying up with special events—new events, holidays, etc.
Finding changes in consumer habits (rug sizes have not kept pace with changes in room design)
Clinics for dealers and salespeople
Merchandising manual for retailer
Helping retailers sell outside the store
Deals—free deals, etc.
Premiums for dealers
Mat service
Promotion kits for dealers
Motion pictures for distributors
Counter catalogue
Manual for dealer and salespeople
House magazine for dealers
Dealer contest
Accounting system for retailers
Trade paper advertising
Handling inquiries received from the advertising
Reports from salesmen
Portfolio for manufacturers' salesmen

Bulletins for manufacturers' salesmen
Contest for manufacturers' salesmen
Quota system for distributors
Sales manual
Special merchandise arrangements
Special tables or sections for stores
Window display contest; interior display contests
Routing exclusive window displays from one dealer to another
General helps for salespeople
Jobbers' salesmen contests
Consumer contest
Promotional calendar
Style promotions
Special "weeks"
Anniversary promotions
Sampling
Guaranty
Installing department in stores
Exhibition and demonstration trucks and trailers
Model stock plans
Development of new uses
Giant blow-ups
Counter cabinets
Use of demonstrators
Window displays
Interior displays
Counter demonstration devices
Itinerant displays
Assortment packages
Improved method of packing
New convenience of the container
New use of the package
New size (larger or smaller) for container
New labels for container
New color scheme for container
New general design of container
New construction of container
Cross advertising on package
Double-use containers
Improved package design
Package inserts
Tested sales sentences
Clubs for salespeople
Correspondence course for salespeople
Instruction manual for salespeople
Manual for jobbers' salesmen
Quotas for jobbers' salesmen
Dealers' salesmen contests
Fashion show
Tests of brand pulling power
Factory showrooms (model store at factory, etc.)
Advertising novelties and specialties —calendars, etc.
Exclusive agency plan
Miniature models for demonstration purposes, etc.
Trial offers
Dramatic demonstration ideas for products
Trade-ins
Installment selling
Consignment selling
Exhibit at shows, fairs, etc.

Many of these tools may not fit into the tool chests of most advertising men. Nevertheless, each and every one is part and parcel of the big job of merchandising the advertising. It will pay any advertising man to check this list periodically and determine what he is not doing that he should do—and what he is doing that can be done better. It is in this kind of soil that advertising functions most effectively. It is when these things are done that we have fewer so-called advertising failures.

2. MAKING THE BEST USE OF AN ADVERTISING AGENCY

Choosing an advertising agency. The choice of an advertising agency should be the subject of careful investigation and consideration. At the present time there are in the United States approximately 3,500 concerns that call themselves advertising agencies. However, although these concerns do business under the same general title, there is considerable variation in the nature of the services that they perform. The success of the advertising will depend to a large extent upon the success in choosing the agency best fitted to handle any particular advertising situation.

What points to investigate in choosing an advertising agency. The best basis upon which an advertiser can select an advertising agency is *facts*—as to the agency's experience, its record of past success, and the like. The following paragraphs discuss a number of specific points that might be investigated. The points are listed on page 141.

1. *History of agency's chief executives.* The success of an advertising agency, even more than that of most other businesses, depends upon the experience and ability of its chief executives. The advertiser should inquire who are the agency's chief executives and, particularly, what has been their sales, general business, and advertising experience. The advertiser himself suffers from the handicap of specialization in his chosen field. One of the reasons for placing advertising in the hands of an agency is to benefit from the agency's broad knowledge of selling methods and market conditions. Can the agency demonstrate, by pointing to what it has done for other clients, that it does possess a broad knowledge of modern selling methods and the vision to apply them effectively to a particular situation?

2. *Who will handle account.* The advertiser may inquire beforehand who is to handle his account—that is, who in the agency is to plan the expenditure of his appropriation. Since the relation between an advertiser and his agency is an intimate one, much depends upon the personal factor. Is the individual in the agency who is to handle the account acceptable to the advertiser on grounds of personality, as well as on grounds of ability and experience?

1. List the names of your agency's chief executives.
   (*a*) State briefly the sales, general business, and advertising experience of the executives listed above.
   (*b*) Are the above executives active in the conduct of the agency's business?
2. Which member of your agency would handle our account?
3. How many accounts are you now handling?
4. Give the names of the accounts that you are now handling. State how long you have handled each.
   (*a*) Give such facts and figures as are not confidential to show how you have contributed to the sales of the companies whose accounts you have handled.
   (*b*) What merchandising plans have you originated for your clients?
   (*c*) List the names of accounts that you have gained during the past two years.
   (*d*) List the names of accounts that you have lost during the past two years.
5. Outline briefly your experience in and knowledge of our line of business.
6. By which associations are you recognized?
7. On what basis of compensation would you handle our account?

Points to Investigate in Choosing an Advertising Agency.

3. *Number of accounts that agency handles.* This factor is likely to bring up, in the advertiser's mind, the question of large versus small agencies. Some advertisers feel that if they select a large agency, or an agency that has several very large accounts, their own advertising will not receive proper attention if their appropriation is relatively small. On the other hand, the criticism is sometimes made that many of the smaller agencies are one-man businesses and cannot give adequate service. The question is one on which no general statement can be made. However, if the advertiser's appropriation is relatively small, and he is doubtful that his account should be given to a large agency, he can ask the agency to give him the names of companies whose advertising it has handled on appropriations comparable to his, and can then get in touch with those companies to ascertain whether their experience with the agency has been satisfactory.

4. *Names of accounts now on agency's books.* The advertiser

may ask the agency to list the names of its leading accounts, and to state how long it has handled each account. Can the agency give evidence that it has originated merchandising plans for its clients, or has its work been chiefly the "placing" of advertising?

Also to be considered are the names of accounts that the agency has gained during the preceding, say, two years, and the names of accounts lost during that period. A high turnover of accounts is an unfavorable factor.

The advertiser may write to the companies whose names have been given, requesting a statement as to their experience with the agency.

5. *Agency's knowledge of advertiser's line of business.* This is one point to which the advertiser is likely to give too much weight. Unless the advertiser's line is especially difficult, the question may not be important, and too much emphasis should not be placed on it. One of the objects of retaining an agency is to benefit from an outside, fresh viewpoint and insight.

6. *Completeness of recognition.* Recognition means that the agency is granted commissions by the media in which the advertising is placed. There are various media associations that grant recognition to agencies:

A.N.P.A.	American Newspaper Publisher's Association.
A.B.P.	Associated Business Papers
P.P.A.	Periodical Publishers' Association.
A.P.A.	Agricultural Publishers' Association.

Recognition from an association is generally honored by the members of the association. However, recognition by an association is not binding upon the members, and some media act independently of their association in investigating and recognizing agencies; for example, the Curtis Publishing Company grants its own recogniton. Further, an agency that is not recognized by a national association may be recognized by a local association or by individual media. Some publications do not grant commissions to agencies, and hence do not recognize them; this is true of a number of trade papers, which feel that a general agency cannot serve the interests of clients in their specialized field, and maintain their own "service departments" to service the advertising in their publications.

The system of agency recognition arose from the necessity, on the part of advertising media, of having information as to the financial standing and integrity of agencies from whom the media were accepting advertising. Essentially, recognition has two implications:

(*a*) That the agency has met certain requirements established by the media. In this sense recognition is a recommendation by the association to its members that the agency is a good credit risk, that it conducts its business on a legitimate basis, and that the media are warranted in accepting the agency's advertising.

(*b*) That the agency is active in the field in which it has obtained recognition. An agency cannot obtain recognition from an association merely by meeting the association's requirements as to financial strength, business methods, and so on. The agency must be actively engaged in placing advertising in, for example, business papers, or newspapers, before the association representing the media in one of these fields will grant the agency recognition.

The chief requirements for recognition are the following:

(*a*) *Financial strength.* Since the agency is often solely liable to the media for the payment of bills covering the advertising that it has placed for its clients, the associations naturally inquire carefully into the financial strength of an agency before granting recognition.

(*b*) *Constructive service to clients.* Before recognition is granted, the agency must satisfy the associations that it has had adequate experience in the practice of advertising and that it is performing a constructive service for its clients.

(*c*) *Sound business methods.* An agency may not make indirect or secret rebates to clients of a portion of the commissions allowed by the media.

From the advertiser's standpoint recognition is important because an agency that lacks recognition may have difficulty in securing credit from the media, and possibly the advertiser may be asked to guarantee payment. Moreover, the agency is likely to be prejudiced in favor of the media in the field in which it has obtained recognition.

7. *Method of compensation proposed.* A number of methods of compensation, each of which has its advantages and disadvantages, are in common use. These are discussed on page 148, *et seq.*

Some agencies, a small percentage of the total number, solicit accounts on a price basis, offering special inducements and indirect rebates of various kinds. The practice is contrary to the standards of the American Association of Advertising Agencies, which require an agency to conform to its agreements with media and to retain the full amount of compensation granted by media owners without direct or indirect rebating.

The seven points discussed above outline the scope of the investigation that an advertiser may make before he chooses an agency. It will be noted that one question that is *not* asked is how the agency will handle the advertising if it secures the advertiser's business. This is a question that advertisers frequently ask agencies, and sometimes, in response to it, agencies prepare advertising plans for the prospective client. In many cases they will prepare complete advertisements, with copy and illustrations. A few large agencies, however, will not do this. The large majority will if the account is worth while.

Scope of agency service. Originally advertising agencies were little more than brokerage or commission houses, selling space in media. However, these pioneer agencies early found that it was to their advantage to contribute to making the space that they sold productive for the advertiser, and accordingly they broadened their function to include the writing of the advertising. Later there were further developments, until at the present time the term "advertising agency" no longer truly describes the services that an agency makes available to its clients. Agencies now commonly act as marketing counselors; in many cases they are practically partners in the business, in everything but name.

The chief services of the present-day agency are as follows: *

1. *Analysis of the product.* The agency usually makes a thorough study and analysis of the product before any advertising is prepared. In other words, from the intermediate ground that it occupies between the advertiser on the one hand and the public on the other, the agency reviews the advertiser's proposition. What are the distinctive features of the product? In design, is it what the public wants? Would changes in design widen the appeal and increase sales? Is the packaging effective? Is the product priced right? How does it compare with competitive products? That this analysis of the product is worth while from the advertiser's standpoint has been

* Developed from an outline of agency services prepared by the American Association of Advertising Agencies.

demonstrated many times. Agencies have contributed suggestions on product design, packaging, pricing, and other problems, which have proved invaluable to their clients. For example, the agency handling the Bon Ami account recommended that Bon Ami be made up in a new package, which could be left in the bathroom. Similarly, a number of ideas suggested by another agency were incorporated in a model of the Buick car. Continuous advice on problems connected with the product itself is one of the newer features of agency service.

2. *Analysis of the market.* This involves a study of the product's present and potential markets. What are the product's principal markets at the present time? Are there potential markets as yet untapped? Where are they? In which markets is competition most acute? How do consumers react to the product? Those who buy—why do they buy, and how often? Can new uses be found for the product that would result in more frequent buying? Those who do not buy—why do they not buy? Do they prefer competing products? If so, why—style, packaging, price? These are examples of questions which the advertising agency, because of its familiarity with selling methods and markets, is peculiarly fitted to answer from experience or to develop by research.

3. *Analysis of present sales structure.* What is the advertiser's present sales and distribution setup? Is it producing results? Are relations with dealers satisfactory? Are selling costs in line? Possibly the advertiser should add new channels of distribution or eliminate some of those now in use? Questions such as these fall within the province of the advertising agency's work.

4. *Formulation of definite plan.* On the basis of the facts obtained from its analysis of the product, the market, and the present sales structure, the agency will probably recommend a definite plan. It is worth noting, however, that this "definite plan" may or may *not* be that the client undertake an advertising campaign. Although any agency is likely to be prejudiced in favor of advertising as a means of developing a business, the right kind of agency will not advise a client to advertise unless it is satisfied that advertising will produce results. An agency cannot afford to be associated with a failure, since its reputation is built upon its record in increasing sales. It may be that modification of the product will be necessary before advertising is undertaken. Possibly the time is not propitious for an advertising campaign in the client's line of business. Consideration

Advertising

Determining basic copy appeal	Production
Copy research	Traffic control
Copy testing	Advertising economies
Copy writing	Advertising checking
Copy supervision	Art policies
Space-buying policies	Radio

Merchandising the Advertising

Retail promotion program	Getting jobber's salesman's co-operation
Dealer-help program	Traveling among jobbers and jobbers' salesmen
Window displays	Traveling among retailers
Interior displays	Advertising portfolios
Counter merchandising units	Contest for distributors
Education of salespeople	Retail mats
House magazine for dealer	Films—reprints of ads—etc.
House magazine for salespeople	
Seasonal drives by retailer	
Getting jobber co-operation	

Tying up Advertising with Sales Organization

Sales portfolios	Distribution of jobber material through salesmen
Bulletins to salesmen	Advertising training for salesmen
Distribution of dealer material through salesmen	Checking advertising appeals with salesmen
Traveling with salesmen	Getting advertising information from sales force
Maintaining salesmen's interest and enthusiasm	Study of salesmen's reports
Sales conventions	Promotion ideas for salesmen to pass on to distributors
Sales manuals	
Contests for salesmen	
Advertising portfolios	

General Sales Promotion

Catalogue	Demonstration devices
Price lists	Flow of letters, bulletins, etc., to trade
Trade shows	Follow-up of advertising inquiries
Trade conventions	Special plans for local areas
Sampling	Special emergency plans
Premiums	

Merchandise

Styling and designing	Pricing
Size or quantity units	General study of merchandise
Development of special features	Market research
Trade names and trade-marks	New uses
Packages	New markets
Shipping cartons	

General Policies

Trade discounts	Organization of sales force
Public relations	Compensation of sales force
Employee relations	Distribution policies
Distribution channels	Manufacturing policies
Elimination of, or additions to, line	

Miscellaneous

Publicity	Work with stockholders

Functions Performed by Advertising Agencies.

of all the factors involved may make it advisable for the client to spend only a small sum on advertising at the present moment, later gradually increasing his appropriation. The right kind of agency can be relied upon for a frank statement of the facts and for a reasonable appraisal of future prospects.

If, however, the agency believes that an advertising campaign can successfully be inaugurated, the definite plan may comprise recommendations as to the market to which the campaign should be directed, the media to be used (newspapers, class magazines, trade publications, radio, outdoor, car cards, and the like), the features of the product that are to be emphasized, and the nature of the appeals that the advertising is to contain.

5. *Execution of plan.* Execution of the plan includes:

(*a*) Writing, designing, and illustrating advertisements, or other appropriate forms of the message.

(*b*) Contracting for the space or other means of advertising.

(*c*) Proper incorporation of the message in mechanical form, and forwarding of the message with instructions for the fulfilment of the contract.

(*d*) Preparation of catalogues, trade literature, dealer broadsides and portfolios, dealer displays, direct-mail literature, and so forth.

(*e*) Preparation of material for salesmen, such as sales kits.

(*f*) Checking and verifying of insertions, display, or other means used.

(*g*) Auditing, billing, and paying for the service, space, and preparation.

How to work with an advertising agency. The function of the advertising agency may be said to be twofold:

1. To interpret the advertiser to the public.
2. To interpret the public to the advertiser.

For best success, the advertiser and his agency should work in close collaboration.

Two mistakes that advertisers frequently make in working with agencies are:

1. Having given their account to the agency and determined the appropriation, they sit back and expect the agency to do the rest.

They adopt the attitude, "Here's what I want to spend; now you go ahead and get the results." This attitude is a handicap to the agency, which definitely needs the advertiser's co-operation. A free exchange of viewpoints, ideas, and experience is to the benefit of both parties concerned.

2. At the opposite extreme is the advertiser who handicaps his agency by undue interference, and particularly by trying to force onto the agency his own personal preferences and prejudices or those of other executives of the company (not to mention his wife).

It is often difficult for the advertiser to appreciate the agency's viewpoint. However, bringing a different, fresh viewpoint to the advertiser's business is one of the chief services that an agency can perform. Perhaps the best procedure is for the advertiser to give the agency a free hand in formulating its plans for the advertising; then, to examine these plans closely, question thoroughly, and require the agency to justify whatever appears doubtful—but give it the opportunity to so justify itself.

Some additional "don'ts" are:

1. Don't regard your advertising merely as a plaything; it is an expensive toy.

2. Don't place undue faith in advertising "company tradition," "company name," or "established reputation." What the public wants is a better article at a lower price.

3. Don't begin by telling your agency "exactly what kind of advertising I want." Give the agency an opportunity to determine what kind of advertising you need.

4. Don't be impatient if, after your advertising appears, results in accordance with your expectations are not immediately forthcoming. Although there have been cases of instantaneous success, as a rule it takes time to make an impression—time, and persistent advertising.

Three plans of agency compensation.* The media bill the agency, and the agency, in turn, bills the advertiser. A recognized agency receives a commission from the various media in which the advertising is placed. The rate is fixed by the individual medium, but it is usually 15 per cent of the card rate. In addition, an extra 2

* From Otto Kleppner, *Advertising Procedure*, 4th ed. New York: Prentice-Hall, Inc., 1950.

per cent cash discount is often allowed on the net payment made by the agency (2 per cent on 85 per cent). Many publications, however, allow no extra discount for cash and require that the agency pay by a fixed date to obtain the agency commission.

The following are the three plans of agency compensation in most common use:

1. *Straight commission plan.* Under the straight commission plan the agency accepts as payment for its services the commission granted by the media upon the client's advertising. The client merely pays the card rates.

EXAMPLE

For space costing $3,000 the publisher bills the agency	$3,000.00	
Less 15%	450.00	
Net	$2,550.00	
Discount for cash, 2% on net	51.00	
Agency pays publisher		$2,499.00
Agency bills client	$3,000.00	
Cash discount if client pays promptly	51.00	
Client pays agency		$2,949.00

In connection with the cash discount, it should be noted that the client receives only 2 per cent on the net (or 2 per cent on 85 per cent), and that he does not receive 2 per cent on the gross. It is held that the agency commission, like a professional service bill, is not subject to cash discount.

Art work, engraving, typographical setups, and so forth, are usually billed to the client at cost plus an amount which will yield the agency 15 per cent of the total charge.

EXAMPLE

Art work	$450.00	
Plates	180.00	
Typographical composition	45.00	
	$675.00	
Plus agency service	119.12	
Charge to client for mechanical costs		$794.12

The same arrangement is followed in the purchase of radio time; the agency receives a commission, ordinarily 15 per cent, from the broadcasting station on the cost of the time. The cost of talent and incidents of broadcasting is usually non-commissionable. The better agencies make a service charge, usually on the basis as previously described for mechanical charges.

2. *15 per cent,* less commissions plan.* Another method used by a number of agencies is that of charging for their services a flat fee representing usually 15 per cent of the card rates (and of expenditures for art work or mechanical charges), crediting the client with whatever commissions and discounts they receive.

EXAMPLE

There is spent in		
Publication A	$10,000.00	
Publication B	20,000.00	
Publication C	2,000.00	
There is also spent		
Art work	500.00	
Type setup and plates	145.00	
Total expenditure	$32,645.00	
Assume that agency commissions on publications A and B were 13% each, and 2% for cash on net amount, and assume that publication C granted no commission to agencies; the total commission and discounts would be		$ 4,422.00
which would be credited to the advertiser.		
Agency fee for its services is †	5,072.64	
The advertiser would actually be debited	$37,717.64	
and credited	4,422.00	
leaving his total bill		$33,295.64

It will be noted that this plan does not result in a saving to the advertiser. In the example the total fee to the agency is $5,072.64, while the total of commissions and discounts is $4,422; $5,072.64 — $4,422 = $650.64. Of this, $113.82 represents the fee on art work and type setup and plates, leaving $536.82 as the amount that the

* This is advertising parlance, but, as has been pointed out previously, the practice today is to add an amount that will yield the agency 15 per cent of the total charge.

† The agency fee is arrived at by ascertaining the *net* space costs (card rates less whatever commission is allowed) and adding thereto an amount which will yield 15 per cent of the total charge. Service fee on art and mechanical charges figured in the manner previously described.

advertiser has to pay in excess of what he would have had to pay under the straight-commission plan. In fact, the 15-per-cent-less-commissions plan cannot result in a saving to the advertiser, since, if the agency's fee amounted to less than the total of commissions and discounts, the plan would, in effect, be a concealed means of rebating and would therefore be illegitimate. The advantage to the advertiser in the 15-per-cent-less-commissions plan is that the danger that the agency will be biased toward the media from which it receives the largest commissions is removed. It is immaterial to the agency whether a certain piece of its client's advertising is placed in a publication that allows no commission to agencies, or in one that grants 15 per cent; the agency's fee is the same in either case. Accordingly, the 15-per-cent-less-commissions plan is suitable for use when the agency has to do considerable work among media where the amount of commissions varies, or some grant a commission and others do not. Another advantage is the comparative simplicity of its bookkeeping.

3. *Retainer plus commissions plan.* The chief value of an agency to a client may consist in its research, its counsel, and its ideas, though little publication advertising is used. A "retainer-plus-commissions" plan has been introduced to provide for this situation and offers a method that is rapidly coming into wide acceptance. By this plan the agency is assured a definite income of, say, $15,000 for the year. Toward this amount the agency will credit whatever commissions it receives. The client pays a monthly retainer that is to make up for the difference between the income from commissions and the set fee. If the commissions exceed the fee, the client need pay no retainer, and the agency continues on its straight-commission basis.

EXAMPLE 1

Retainer fee set for the year	$15,000.00
Commissions from publications amount to . .	11,500.00
Client credited with this sum.	

EXAMPLE 2

Retainer fee set for the year	$15,000.00
Commissions from publications amount to . .	15,500.00
Client need pay no further retainer, but only the card-rate cost of the space used.	

The agency is not allowed to rebate its commissions, and accordingly cannot agree to a flat fee that represents less than the commissions from the media.

The retainer-plus-commissions plan provides a solution to the paradoxical situation whereby an agency serves one master but apparently receives its payment from another. The retainer plan, as its name implies, retains the agency to serve the client without preference toward any form of media. Further, there is no incentive to rush the client into advertising.

Agreement with the advertising agency. It is highly advisable today for an agency and client to agree in advance on the terms of their relationship and to include such terms in a formal instrument, frequently a contract. Such a contract may take various forms, and most agencies have standard contracts that can be adapted to fit the requirements of a particular situation. In the case of smaller accounts, a letter may be sufficient. In order to avoid any possibility of later misunderstandings, any agency-client agreement should include: the effective date of the relationship and the method by which the agreement may be cancelled; the routine for approval of expenditures, billing, and payment for space and time; how the agency is to be reimbursed when media do not allow full commission; the care of client property; cancellation of work in progress; the procedure governing short rates, refunds, and cash discounts; charges for materials and services purchased; and the fees to be charged, if any.

3. FIXING THE ADVERTISING APPROPRIATION

Three methods in common use. Three methods of determining the advertising appropriation are in common use:

1. Percentage-of-sales method.
2. Unit-of-sales method.
3. Market-survey method.

Each of these has its advantages and disadvantages for particular businesses. The first two recommend themselves to many advertisers by the fact that they are relatively easy to use. The third is less easy but more thorough; the market-survey method is being increasingly used.

Percentage-of-sales method. This method consists of setting aside for advertising a fixed percentage of some figure related to sales volume. The figure may be:

1. Percentage of gross or net sales for a preceding period.
2. Percentage of average of gross or net sales for several periods in the past.
3. Percentage of estimated gross or net sales for a future period.
4. Percentage of average of gross or net sales for one or more periods in the past and estimated sales for one or more periods in the future.

The figure most generally taken by advertisers using the percentage-of-sales method is a percentage of estimated sales for a future period (a year, a half year, or a quarter). Many advertisers who formerly allocated to advertising a percentage of sales for a period in the past, or a percentage of average sales for several periods in the past, have changed their ground. Their reasoning is that past sales are not a good index to the amount that should be spent for future advertising. They are prepared to back up their analysis of the market for their product with an advertising expenditure in proportion to the sales volume that they aim to achieve.

Other advertisers, who wish to be more conservative and to offset any undue optimism as to the future, use a combination figure representing a percentage of average sales for a certain period in the past and estimated sales for a certain period in the future.

A variation of the percentage-of-sales method is to use a percentage of profits instead of a percentage of sales. The objection to this plan is that profits are dependent upon operating efficiency and many other factors, and the advertising appropriation should not be affected by these.

How the percentage is determined. There is no formula for determining the percentage figure to be used in the percentage-of-sales method. The figure varies in different industries, and also with companies in the same industry, from 1 per cent to as high as 30 per cent of gross sales. In many cases the figure is based upon the average figure for the industry as a whole, or upon figures used by other companies in the same line. In the final analysis, the advertiser has to decide the percentage in the light of his individual circumstances. A company recently formed might feel that 25 per cent was not too high, while one that has been established for a number of years might spend 5 per cent. The matter is one of judgment for each particular business.

Advantages and disadvantages of percentage-of-sales method. The chief advantages of the percentage-of-sales method are two:

1. It is easy to use.
2. It relates advertising expenditure to sales volume. That is, the amount spent for advertising is made dependent upon the volume of sales—usually upon the estimated volume of sales for a future period. To base advertising expenditure upon sales volume is, in general, a logical procedure.

As against the above, two important disadvantages of this method are:

1. Where, as is often the case, the percentage figure is based upon the figure for the industry as a whole or upon figures used by other companies in the same line, the method is liable to become one of just keeping up, proportionately to sales, with competitors' advertising. Competitors may be wasteful in spending money on advertising or may have overlooked opportunities that increased advertising would turn into sales. The advertiser has to be careful that he is not allowing himself to be led by the blind.
2. Although the percentage-of-sales method does relate advertising expenditure to sales volume, this relation is often approximate and indefinite. For example, assume that sales for the coming year are estimated at $1,000,000. It is decided to appropriate 5 per cent of this figure, or $50,000, for advertising. This amount appears and is considered "adequate." However, whether $50,000 is the amount actually required (neither too much nor too little) to enable advertising to play its part in the $1,000,000 sales program may not be known. In this respect the percentage-of-sales method does not compare favorably with the market-survey method, under which a reasonable sales objective for the given period is first decided; then the job that advertising is to do is determined; and finally an amount is appropriated for advertising that will be sufficient for advertising's part in the sales program.

Unit-of-sales method. This method consists of allocating to advertising a fixed sum per unit of sales. Production costs are known;

selling costs are known from past experience; an estimate of sales for a future period—say, one year—is made. A certain sum per unit of anticipated sales is then appropriated for advertising. Thus, an automobile manufacturer might estimate his sales for the coming year at 400,000 cars and set aside for advertising $5 per car. His total appropriation would then be $\$5 \times 400{,}000$, or $2,000,000.

Advantages and disadvantages of unit-of-sales method. Some of the advantages of this method are:

1. If the sum per unit is not arrived at by guesswork, but is the sum which, judged by past experience, will be necessary to move each unit through the market, this method definitely relates advertising expenditure to sales volume, and is reliable and at the same time easy to use. It is particularly convenient for companies selling specialty goods, such as automobiles, refrigerators, oil burners, washing machines, and so forth.

2. The unit-of-sales method can readily be applied to co-operative advertising by a manufacturer and his dealers. The manufacturer allocates to advertising a fixed sum per unit of anticipated sales and also assesses the dealer a fixed sum. The dealer's assessment is commonly charged to the dealer on his invoice and is usually included in the list price to the dealer, not billed as a separate item. The majority of automobile manufacturers operate on this plan.

3. The unit-of-sales method has also been successfully used by co-operative associations of manufacturers, fruit growers, and so forth. For example, co-operative organizations of fruit growers have determined the advertising appropriation for the industry by assessing against each member a certain number of cents per case.

The chief limitation of the unit-of-sales method is the difficulty of applying it in many lines of business. For example, the method can hardly be used by a company selling style merchandise, or, in general, by a company selling in irregular markets.

Market-survey method. This method is being increasingly favored. Stated in its simplest terms, it consists of determining, for a certain future period, the job that advertising is to do as a part of the sales program, and then appropriating whatever amount will be necessary to enable advertising to do that job. In fixing the advertising appropriation by the market-survey method, the advertiser asks himself three general questions:

1. What is the sales objective to be for the next six months, the next year, or longer?

2. What part is advertising to play in the plan to reach that objective; what is to be advertising's job?

3. How much money will advertising require to do its job?

Different companies follow different procedures in answering these three questions. Some depend chiefly upon information obtained from past experience, and from sales managers, salesmen, dealers, and similar sources. Other companies inquire exhaustively into market conditions and potentialities. The procedure in such cases may be briefly outlined as follows:

1. The total market is divided into merchandising and trading areas, or spheres of sales influence. The idea here is that division of the total market into sections facilitates analysis and, in the end, the direction of selling effort to those sections which the analysis shows have not been fully exploited or which are likely to prove most profitable.

2. With the trading areas determined and mapped, the next step is to make an analysis of each area. Factors entering into the analysis are:

(*a*) Past sales record of each area. This record should cover several years, so that the trend of sales in the area will be apparent.

(*b*) Buying power index for each area. This index should be made as simple as possible. The object should be to include only factors that will affect sales of the advertiser's own product. For example, a company selling an electric refrigerator would be interested chiefly in the number of wired homes, income tax returns, bank deposits, and similar data.

(*c*) Index figure indicating the relative cost of selling in each area. This figure can be obtained from past sales records. The object of including it is to avoid overspending in areas where the cost of selling is high.

3. On the basis of the past sales record, buying power index, and index of relative cost of selling, a sales quota for each area is set.

4. The advertising appropriation for each trading area is determined in the light of the facts obtained from the above analysis.

Advantages and disadvantages of market-survey method. The chief point in favor of the market-survey method is that it represents an attempt to substitute for guesswork a method of determining the advertising appropriation which is founded on known facts. It defines the job that advertising is to do, and then allocates the amount necessary for that job. The market-survey method is, indeed, more than just a means of deciding how much to spend for advertising. It is a thorough review of the company's marketing and selling system, of which advertising is one part, and points the way to a planned program.

The chief objection to the market-survey method is the work and expense that it entails. Furthermore, unforeseen changes may upset the most careful calculations. Nevertheless, if applied with common sense, it will clarify advertising and selling policies to a marked degree.

What to charge to advertising costs. After the advertising budget has been determined, the question of what is properly chargeable to advertising arises. The following list of items is recognized as properly chargeable to the advertising appropriation:

Space:

Cartons and labels (when used exclusively for advertising purposes, such as in window displays)

Package inserts (when used as advertising and not just as direction sheets)

Paid advertising in all recognized media, including:

Newspapers	Theater programs
Periodicals	Outdoor advertising
Business papers	Window displays
Technical journals	Counter displays
Farm papers	Store signs
Religious papers	Novelties
Class journals	Booklets
Car cards	Directories
Catalogues	Direct advertising
Slides	Reprints of advertisements used in mail or for display
Export advertising	Radio
Dealer helps	Television
Posters	

House magazines to dealers or consumers

Motion pictures (including talking pictures) when used for advertising

All other printed and lithographed material used directly for advertising purposes

Administration:

Salaries of advertising department executives and employees
Office supplies and fixtures used solely by advertising department
Commissions and fees to advertising agencies, special writers, or advisers
Expenses incurred by salesmen working for advertising department
Traveling expenses of department employees engaged in departmental business
(Note: In some companies these go into special "Administration" account)

Mechanical:

Art work
Typography
Engraving
Mats
Electros
Photographs
Etc.

Miscellaneous:

Transportation of advertising material (to include postage and other carrying charges)
Fees to window display installation services
Other miscellaneous expenses connected with items on the above list

The guardian of the advertising budget must be on constant guard against the following improper advertising charges:

Free goods
Picnic and bazaar programs
Charitable, religious, and fraternal donations
Other expenses for "goodwill" purposes
Cartons
Labels
House magazines going to factory employees
Bonuses to trade
Special rebates
Salesmen's samples (including photographs used in lieu of samples)
Welfare activities among employees
Recreational activities such as baseball teams, etc.
Instruction sheets
Packages
Press agency
Stationery used outside advertising department
Price lists
Salesmen's calling cards
Motion pictures for sales use only
Membership in trade associations
Entertaining customers or prospects
Annual reports
Showrooms
Demonstration stores
Sales convention expenses
Sales expenses at conventions
Cost of salesmen's automobiles
"Special editions" which approach advertisers on "goodwill" basis

Because advertising, like sales work, is, admittedly, far from being a scientific procedure, there are some advertising charges that may or may not be proper advertising expenses. Circumstances will indicate what the decision should be. These charges include:

Samples
Demonstrations
Fairs
Canvassing
Rent
Telephone and other overhead expenses, apportioned to advertising department
House magazines going to salesmen
Membership in associations or other organizations devoted to advertising
Testing bureaus
Advertising portfolios for salesmen
Contributions to special advertising funds of trade associations
Display signs on the factory or office building
Light
Heat
Depreciation of equipment used by advertising department
Advertising automobiles
Premiums
Salesmen's catalogues
Research and market investigations
Advertising allowances to trade for co-operative effort

4. SELECTING THE RIGHT ADVERTISING MEDIA

Principal media. The principal media available for advertising by advertisers with merchandise to be sold to the general public include:

1. Newspapers.
2. Magazines.
3. Radio.
4. Television.
5. Farm papers.
6. Direct mail.

This group accounts for over 75 per cent of the total sum spent in so-called consumer advertising. Other media that account for a smaller volume include:

1. Outdoor advertising.
2. Car cards.
3. Premiums.
4. Advertising specialties.
5. Trade papers.

Selecting the right media. One question frequently asked in connection with these media is: Which one is best? Only one answer can be made to that question—namely: It all depends.

No one medium is best for everybody. In fact, there is no one medium that is necessarily best for any specific advertiser. That is why we see some advertisers putting the lion's share of their budget into radio one year, into magazines the next year, and perhaps into newspapers the third year.

Undoubtedly, certain sets of circumstances exist that definitely indicate the advisability of using one or the other of these media to the exclusion of all the others. Other sets of circumstances occur that sometimes definitely point to a certain combination of these media. But, more often, two advertising experts might make radically different media suggestions to the same advertiser—and both might be right! Advertising is far from being a science. Until it does become a science—if it ever does—the selection of media will be most often a matter of opinion, backed up by experience; scientific selection of media is only rarely possible.

Suppose, therefore, we scan quickly the major values offered by each of the principal media, bearing in mind that none of these major values may be the exclusive property of any one of the media. For example, the magazines might be pointed to as the medium to use for broad national coverage. However, if that is done, the newspapers will promptly point out that some highly successful national campaigns have been run exclusively in newspapers, and, of course, the radio people will make the same assertion. Therefore, while we will endeavor to assign certain specific points of merit to each of the media, it must be remembered that, actually, there is no such sharp cleavage between them.

Magazines. Magazines tend to classify themselves upon bases of frequency of issue, type of editorial content, sex of reader, economic status of reader, and so on. There are women's magazines, fiction magazines, weekly and monthly magazines, so-called class magazines like *Harper's*, and others. Magazines at one time were looked upon as *the* national advertising media. However, newspapers began to challenge that claim, and, of course, radio has certainly challenged the leadership of magazines. In general, however, it may be said that magazines and radio offer an excellent advertising "buy" to the company with a broad national distribution. The distribution phase is important because magazine circulation is apt to be scattered over the entire country, and if distribution does not follow the advertising, there is considerable waste.

Virtually all advertising media have made dollar gains each year during the post war period, as evidenced by the fact that the total dollar volume of advertising almost doubled from 1946 to 1951. Magazines have taken part in this year-by-year increase along with the other media. From a relative high for the years 1944–1946, however, their percentage share of the total advertising volume has decreased slightly each year for the past five years. This may be due, in part, to the growth of television, though the latter has not been a dominant medium for a sufficient time to make any generalization on the matter. Many magazines of various types will continue, nevertheless, to be vitally important vehicles for a large number of advertisers. Actually hundreds of trade names that are household words today became part of our everyday language almost entirely through the power of magazine advertising.

The long life and leisurely reading enjoyed by most magazines is an exceptional advantage. Few magazines are purchased and discarded within a day; an average might be a life of a week for the weekly magazines and a month for the monthly publications.

Newspapers. No other nation has as many newspapers as the United States. Without a doubt, the newspapers represent the voice of the people. There is scarcely a home in the country that cannot be reached with some regularity through a daily, semi-weekly, or weekly newspaper. Nearly 1,800 daily and over 10,000 weekly newspapers are published in the United States.

Newspapers carried national advertising almost before magazines came into existence. They are, today, the backbone of the majority of the advertising programs of manufacturers. The basic reason for this fact is that, actually, of our several hundred thousand manufacturers, only a comparative handful have national distribution—or sufficient national distribution to justify national magazine advertising. However, of manufacturers with sectional, or state, or even merely trading-area distribution, there is no end. These manufacturers usually find that newspapers enable them to buy circulation that matches their distribution—and circulation that outruns distribution is usually either complete waste or rather expensive circulation.

In 1951 there were 1,292 companies (excluding retailers) who spent $25,000 or more in newspaper advertising. This advertising covered a total of 3,136 products. In brief, newspapers constitute the most widely used media for manufacturers. They enable an advertiser to put his advertising pressure precisely where and when he feels it should be put. Schedules can be changed quickly—in 24 hours when necessary. They make it possible for an advertiser to start in a small way, and expand gradually. They enable him to run a campaign quickly in a territory that needs bolstering.

As advertising has become more and more a business policy planned with all of the timeliness and swiftness of action of a military campaign, newspapers have become more popular as an advertising medium. Successful advertising demands elasticity, mobility, and change of pace. Newspapers make all of this feasible.

Radio and television. At the end of 1951, there were 42,800,000 homes with radio sets. Of these, 26,600,000 had more than one set. In addition, some 25,850,000 automobiles had radios. Radio as an advertising medium enjoyed a rapid rise which has only been overshadowed by the more spectacular growth of television. Like anything that has enjoyed a mushroom growth, radio has had millions in advertising money wasted on it; it has also created millions in sales for advertisers. Hundreds of advertisers exist whose entire business has been built by radio advertising. Some former magazine advertisers now put practically all of their consumer advertising appropriations into radio; the same is true of some newspaper advertisers. By and large, radio has created more advertising than it has siphoned off from other advertising media.

Television advertising has been called the "ultimate in advertising technique" because it combines all the known advantages of sight and sound. As an advertising medium it combines the demonstration advantages of motion pictures with the home coverage of other media. Its growth from the relative infancy period of one million sets in 1948 to twenty million by the end of 1952 has been one of the miracles of the Post World War II era.

Through demonstration techniques on television, small one-man organizations have become medium-sized corporations in twelve months!

Television costs whereby sponsors spend as much as $100,000 for a single one-hour program have been a major problem to the television industry in attracting a wider diversification of advertising. The obvious appeal of television created a mad rush to the medium by a host of advertisers, many of whom either were not adaptable to video or misused it with resultant colossal waste of their advertising dollars. During 1953, the construction of more stations in more markets introduced a competitive element with resultant leveling off of costs.

Purposes accomplished by radio and television advertising. Advertisers have used radio and television successfully to accomplish the following purposes. In nearly all cases merchandising and promotional tie-ins have also been employed.

1. Introduce a new product.
2. Demonstrate product or service (television).
3. Remedy seasonal drop of sales volume.
4. Establish product name in mind of the consumer.
5. Familiarize consumers with new and varied uses of a product.
6. Dramatize special features of a product or service.
7. Reach specific audiences—for example, children, housewives.
8. Build mailing lists.
9. Boost holiday "specials."
10. Educate the public to quality of product.
11. Promote public confidence in service or product.
12. Gain additional retail outlets.
13. Encourage retailers to push a product.
14. Build industrial morale.
15. Maintain top prices in a price-cutting market.
16. Force retailers to stock product despite small margin of profit.

Types of successful radio and television programs. The following list cites the different types of radio and television programs that have met with success. In many cases a program may consist of combined elements such as a musical program combining music with dramatic skits, a news program interspersed with music and educational talks, or a studio contest combined with popular music.

AMUSEMENT PROGRAMS

Drama	*Music*	*Audience Participation*
Complete plays	Popular	Studio contests
Variety shows	Classical	Listener contests
Skits	Backgrounds	Games
Serial	Interludes	Personal experiences
		Quiz

"SERVICE" PROGRAMS

News	*Sports*	*Educational*	*Public Service*
News flashes	Game results	Music	Employment service
Commentators	Game descriptions	Literature	Safety program
	Sport comments	Interviews	Personal advice
		Talks	Political speeches
			Institutional
			Weather reports

Major values offered by radio. Radio offers equal opportunities to the small and to the large advertiser. Through spot broadcasting, through programs having as many as a dozen different sponsors, advertisers with actually tiny budgets have "gone on the air" and put their message over. Television spots with carefully conceived use of animation, live action, and demonstration produced on film, or participation in live programs have been most successful.

Spot broadcasting may be defined as local radio or television advertising, although there are advertisers who use as many as 300 or 400 stations simultaneously in a radio spot campaign. Because all such broadcasting originates from the studios of the stations selected, the use of electrical transcriptions, or recordings, has become an economic necessity in most of these programs. A program is selected, rehearsed, and recorded in some metropolitan center convenient to talent and production experts, and individual discs are shipped to the stations carrying the campaign. Special equipment "feeds" the record into the station's transmitter, and a local announcer takes care of the commercials. The whole procedure may be compared to the shipment of plates and mats to local newspaper offices for simultaneous insertion in a dealer-advertising campaign. Television spots produced on film follow the same general procedure as radio, except that a greater variety of techniques is used in this medium, which combines both sight and sound.

The wide use of recorded or filmed material in spot broadcasting does not mean that facilities for local live talent shows have been neglected. Many stations are prepared to work with their local clients in the production of programs, and the larger stations maintain very complete production units and talent staffs.

Radio and television are, essentially, entertainment. To that extent, they are somewhat of a gamble, just as is a show on Broadway or a Hollywood movie. However, smart advertisers are, more and more, buying proved and tested programs. This is as true of the small advertiser as it is of the large.

Farm papers. Few publications get a closer and more appreciative reading than the well-established farm paper. If ever a publication is read "like a bible," that publication is the successful farm paper. What is more, it is apt to be the "bible" for the entire farm family.

Farm papers divide naturally into two groups, national and state. National farm papers have a national circulation; state farm papers usually confine their circulation to a single state. The farm papers have survived every advertising vicissitude. At the bottom of the 1933 depression they stood up better than did most advertising media. They offer a highly valuable shortcut to the great farm market. Actually, they have as competing advertising media only the radio and the semiweekly and weekly newspaper. They always succeed in putting up a good fight against the rural newspaper. The radio, however, it becoming increasingly important as a competitor. More and more advertisers are finding it advisable to supplement their farm paper advertising with radio to strengthen certain sales territories.

Direct mail. Direct mail is not always looked upon as a consumer-advertising medium. It is used to such a large extent, however, in conjunction with the other advertising media that it certainly warrants mention here. It must be remembered that a great many advertisers, whether they use magazines, newspapers, radio, or farm papers, offer a booklet, a leaflet, a premium, or an advertising novelty. When these inquiries come to the advertiser, they become part of a direct-mail follow-up. Most advertising budgets make a fairly liberal allowance for consumer direct-mail work. For a complete discussion of direct-mail advertising, see page 5 *et seq*.

Outdoor advertising. The two principal forms of outdoor advertising are posters and paint. Posters are sold in the standard twenty-four-sheet size and smaller three-sheet panels. Paint is standardized to some extent, but the size of the display is flexible.

The panels for twenty-four-sheet posters are of two kinds: illuminated and non-illuminated. The illuminated panels cost from about \$35 to \$60 per month, and the non-illuminated panels range from about \$12.50 to \$22 per month.

Ordinarily, posters are available for a minimum period of one month and in quantities based upon a 100-showing for each city. The 100-showing in a market corresponds to the number of posters, determined by the plant operators on the basis of population and extent of street pattern, required to cover the market's principal streets. The intensity of the coverage afforded by this basic showing is taken to be the normal degree for the market. For partial coverage, 75-, 50-, and 25-showings are usually available, which consist respectively of three-quarter, one-half, and one-quarter of the number of posters in the 100-showing.

Each plant operator has only a limited number of panels in each city, thus permitting only a certain number of 100-showings in any one month. Posters are ordinarily contracted for well in advance, and since the war, most of the plants in the better areas have been completely sold out. It is usually advisable, therefore, to plan poster advertising well ahead of the time of appearance.

Outdoor advertising has a complete geographical selectivity. It may be used to cover a single city or state, or the entire country. This medium has considerable flexibility within a given market. It offers full color and a dominating size, which is frequently of importance to smaller advertisers who may be out-advertised in number of impressions, but among posters, at least, cannot be out-advertised in the size of the individual panel or the colors appearing on it.

Painted bulletins are generally purchased on a twelve-month or a thirty-six-month contract. They may be selected individually, and the price of each is often subject to individual negotiations. The more expensive and elaborate painted bulletins are located within the city limits on heavy traffic arteries. They are sometimes located at eye level or may be elevated and visible from a great distance. Highway bulletins situated out on the open road are more frequently sold at a standard price and are less expensive than artery locations.

Many of the most important advertising agencies use the National Outdoor Advertising Bureau, Inc., a cooperative organization, for the purpose of servicing their outdoor advertising campaigns.

Car cards. Car cards appearing in streetcars, subways, elevated trains, busses, and even taxicabs, are sold very much as are twenty-four sheet posters—by towns and on the basis of full, half, or quarter service. For reminder advertising, and as part of an advertising campaign in which other media are used, they serve an excellent purpose.

Premiums. While it may not be absolutely correct to classify premiums as an advertising medium, they are used in many instances as such. For this reason they bear discussion here.

Premiums are used for the following purposes:

1. To help introduce new products.
2. To help increase the unit of sale.
3. To help consumers use the product correctly.
4. To encourage more frequent use of the product.
5. To win the interest of children.
6. To check radio programs.
7. As prizes in contests.

Premiums are offered in the following ways:

1. In a package—as some of the cereal manufacturers do.
2. Through a coupon—as some of the soapmakers do.
3. As a combination sale—where a manufacturer offers his regular item and a premium in combination.
4. Through the consumer returning a stipulated number of box tops or bottle tops.

Premiums are of all types, ranging from seeds, miniature posters and stamps to coffee makers, lamps, silverware, and every other conceivable item.

Millions of dollars are spent annually in this country on premiums, and the premium business has grown as a result. Procter & Gamble distributed premiums valued at over $1,000,000 in the course of a single year.

Advertising specialties. Some times there is difficulty in differentiating between an advertising specialty and a premium. In general, an advertising specialty is an article that is usually given without cost and always without condition of sale of other goods. It always bears the name of the company that gives it away. The simplest kind of advertising specialty is a pencil, with the name of the giver on it. Knives, watch fobs, desk calendars, desk weights, blotters, wall calendars—all of these are advertising specialties. Many of these specialties have an amazingly long life. They build a tremendous amount of goodwill and have a great advertising value.

Trade papers. Trade papers are magazines or newspapers devoted editorially to business or the professions. A tremendous number of them are published. Since every industry has its own particular features, and the structure within each field is peculiar to it, trade papers are difficult to classify. They do, however, fall into two broad classifications: horizontal media and vertical media.

Horizontal media appeal to a common interest of many industries and, therefore, circulate among many industries. Broad examples in this class are *National's Business* and *Business Week,* which treat business generally and are of interest to everyone connected with business. Other more specific examples would be *Purchasing News, Printers' Ink, Sales Management, Factory Management and Maintenance,* and others.

Each of the vertical papers deal with a single industry or a single phase of one industry. Some examples of this group are *Oil and Gas Journal, Hotel Management, American Druggist,* and *Modern Brewery Age.*

Trade papers can also be generally classified into business papers and professional or technical papers. The former are concerned with phases of business that follow production—namely, transportation, distribution, advertising, selling, credit, auditing, and so forth. The professional or technical papers cover production problems addressed to engineers, chemists, and technicians, and are likely to be highly technical. In addtiion, there are many publications that appeal to the professions—medicine, engineering, architecture, and so forth, and the numerous phases and shades of interests within each profession.

5. TESTING YOUR ADVERTISING

Can an advertiser forecast the results of his advertising? The great question which every advertiser asks himself is: How can I tell whether the money that I am about to spend on advertising will produce the hoped-for results? In general, there are two ways in which an advertiser can answer this question for himself.

1. In determining whether the advertising that he proposes to launch will produce results, he can rely on his own judgment, supplemented by the knowledge and accumulated experience of his advertising agency.

2. He can pretest his advertising. That is, he can experiment and test on a small scale before advertising on a large scale and can then base his large-scale advertising on the results that he obtains from his tests.

Advertiser's personal judgment not reliable. With regard to the first of the above methods—the advertiser's relying on his personal judgment—it is a curious fact that, although ninety-nine out of a hundred businessmen will hesitate to pass on a question relating to finance or production, few will hesitate to state definitely that such-and-such is a good or a bad piece of advertising and will support their statements with arguments that seem to them entirely convincing. Yet the most positive opinions have been proved again and again, when checked by actual results, to be wrong, and very far wrong. If this seems an exaggeration, refer to the two advertisements reproduced in Figure 12. One of these advertisements produced a greater number of inquiries than the other. Which one was it? Even if you are successful in choosing which one interested the most men, the fact that the handkerchief advertisement outpulled the cold cream advertisement by 50 per cent will cause you to question whether, after all, you can depend on yourself to judge advertising and be sure that you are right. And you must be sure that you are right before you begin to plan the expenditure of your own advertising appropriation.

The advertising agency, because of its specialized knowledge and accumulated experience, is undoubtedly a better judge of effective advertising than the advertiser himself. However, tests have shown that advertising men are far from infallible.

What pretesting aims to do. The fact that tests have shown that advertisers and advertising men are not reliable judges as to which advertisements will produce results is not entirely surprising. Personal prejudices are one factor. Close contact with the product, and remoteness from the public, is perhaps another factor. Still a third is the "professional viewpoint," which causes an advertiser or advertising man to judge advertisements in accordance with stand-

From Kleppner, "Advertising Procedure." New York: Prentice-Hall, Inc.

Figure 12. The Test Ads That Launched Kleenex Tissues for Handkerchiefs.

The newspaper advertisements above were run to test the comparative interest of women in the use of Kleenex Tissues for handkerchiefs in contrast to their use for removing cold cream—the chief advertisement outpulled the cold cream advertisement by 50 per cent. As a result, Kleenex Cleansing Tissues became Kleenex Disposable Tissues, and later Kleenex Tissues, reflecting ards other than the simple, practical standards of the consumer. Many other explanations of the unreliability of personal judgment could be found, but what is of chief importance is the fact that, whatever the explanation, personal judgment and experience cannot be depended upon to any great extent.

Pretesting attempts to eliminate mere opinion, prejudice, and theory in the planning of an advertising campaign. It aims to subject the ingredients of the campaign to tests on a small scale—tests conducted on the same public that is to read the final advertising and ultimately purchase the product—with the object of discovering which ingredients will have the desired effect and produce the desired results.

There are a number of methods of pretesting. These are described in the following pages.

Pretesting by the Sales-Area Method

What the sales-area method is. The so-called sales-area test may be illustrated by the following hypothetical case. The product to be advertised is a toilet soap. Analysis of the product and of the market suggests that a number of different advertising appeals are possible. For example, one appeal might be the purity appeal; this particular soap has been shown by chemical analysis to be purer than any other soap in its price class. Another approach might be the beauty appeal; buy this soap to protect and beautify your complexion. A third appeal might be semihumorous. A fourth possibility might be an appeal to fear; a poor complexion is a social handicap. The advertiser himself may favor one type of advertising; his advertising manager another; his agency perhaps a third. The fundamental question is: Which of these various appeals is the best; which will produce the greatest public response and hence the greatest sales results? Before launching his advertising and spending his appropriation, the advertiser wishes to be able to answer this question with a degree of certainty. He decides to conduct a sales-area test.

Procedure in the sales-area test. To conduct his sales-area test the advertiser proceeds as follows:

1. He selects sales areas in various sections of the country.
2. In each of these areas he chooses one or more cities to serve as "test" cities.

3. In the same areas he chooses one or more cities to serve as "control" cities.

4. In the control cities he continues to run the advertising that he has previously been using; or, in the event that he has not been advertising, he withholds his advertising from the control cities.

5. In the test cities he substitutes for the old advertising the new advertising that he proposes to use subsequently on a large scale.

6. A careful check is kept of sales in the control and test cities (the old *versus* the new advertising), and on the basis of the results obtained, the advertiser decides whether the new advertising will be successful.

To continue the hypothetical case mentioned above, assume that the advertiser wishes to test the purity appeal against the fear appeal. Assume, further, that he chooses a certain section as one of his sales areas; that City *A* and City *B* are to be the test cities in this area; and that City *X* is to be the control city in this area. Then, in City *A* the purity appeal is run; in City *B* the fear appeal is run; and in City *X* the previous campaign is continued. A careful tabulation of sales in the three cities is made.

Suppose that analysis of the results obtained from the test in this particular area reveals the following facts:

1. In City *X*, the control city, sales are slipping. This may suggest that the effect of the advertising campaign that is now being used is probably waning.
2. In City *A* the purity appeal stimulated an increase of 6.5 per cent in dollar sales.
3. In City *B* the fear appeal stimulated an increase of 16.5 per cent in dollar sales.

In this particular area, therefore, the fear appeal is considerably more effective than either the present campaign or the purity appeal. If results from tests in other sales areas were similar, the advertiser would undoubtedly choose the fear appeal in preference to the purity appeal as his next large-scale campaign, with reasonable assurance that he was making no mistake.

Safeguards to observe in sales-area testing. From the above description of the procedure followed in pretesting by the sales-area method, it is apparent that there is danger of the results being distorted unless the greatest care is exercised. There are many variables that have to be taken into account; for example, the closing down of a large factory in either the control city or one of the test cities would probably affect the tests. If the results of a sales-area test are to be reliable, as many of the variables as possible must be controlled or eliminated. The following are a number of practical safeguards derived from the experience of companies that have used the sales-area test.

1. *Factors to consider in choosing sales areas.* A single sales area, no matter how large, cannot be depended upon to give reliable results. Not less than three areas, but preferably five, should probably be used. Moreover, the sales areas chosen should, as far as possible, be typical of larger territories, and in the aggregate should be typical of the total territory in which the product is sold.

2. *Factors to consider in choosing test and control cities.* The following are the most important factors:

(*a*) The test and control cities should be as nearly comparable as possible.

(*b*) Small cities are of little value for testing purposes; 30,000 population may be taken as the minimum.

(*c*) A growing, progressive city is more suitable than a city whose population is standing still or declining.

(*d*) Each of the cities should be an independent market; that is, the bulk of the purchasing by consumers should be done within the city itself, and not to any great extent in neighboring cities.

(*e*) Cities that have a number of different sources of income are preferable to cities depending to a great degree on a single industry. The purchasing power of a city that is dependent upon a single industry follows the curve of current conditions in that industry.

(*f*) The dealer setup in each city should be equal. Avoid cities in which one dealer, or a chain organization, dominates the market.

(*g*) As a final check, it is advisable to obtain first-hand information as to current business conditions in each of the cities under consideration. Cities in which abnormal conditions prevail (owing to closing down of a plant, strikes, and the like) can then be eliminated from the list.

3. *Check of sales for period preceding tests.* In order that the

effect of the advertising which is being tested can be accurately measured, it is necessary that sales in the test and control cities be checked for a period preceding the tests; sales during the testing period and during the period preceding the tests are then compared. How long should the preliminary checking period be? In deciding this it must be remembered that sales of the same product, in the same city, and without any material change in business conditions, fluctuate greatly from week to week. In some of the tests that have been conducted, the preliminary checking period has varied from two weeks to three months. Two weeks is entirely too short a period to take account of sales fluctuations. Four or six weeks would appear to be the minimum, and a longer period is advisable if the expense involved is not prohibitive.

4. *How long should the test period be?* The answer to this question depends to a certain extent upon the type of product that is being advertised. Some products are purchased frequently; others only at intervals. The advertising must be given time to produce results. Four or six weeks is the minimum for a product that is bought frequently. Hurrying the tests will produce misleading results. The longer the period in which the advertising is tested, the more likely it is that variables tending to distort the results will be eliminated.

5. *How should sales in the test and control cities be checked?* Companies that have used the sales-area test have found it advisable actually to check the sales themselves, through weekly or semiweekly calls at the stores, rather than rely on the dealers to furnish reports. It is not necessary, however, to check sales in all the stores in the test and control cities. It is usually true that a percentage of the stores in any city do most of the business; small stores may safely be ignored for testing purposes.

6. *Should the sales check be of jobbing sales or retail sales?* Sometimes a check of jobbing sales is used instead of a check of retail sales. There are advantages and disadvantages in this method. Some of the advantages are:

(*a*) A check of jobbing sales reduces to a minimum the expense involved in the collection of sales data.

(*b*) The advertising tests can be started immediately, without a preliminary checking period, since figures on past sales to jobbers are usually readily available. When retail sales are checked, it is necessary to delay the tests of the advertising while sales data for the preliminary checking period are being collected.

Some of the disadvantages of checking jobbing sales instead of retail sales are:

(*a*) It is necessary to use larger sales areas, and this increases the cost of the advertising during the test period.

(*b*) The test period has to be longer, because of the "lag" between retail sales and jobbing sales.

(*c*) Jobbing sales are a less direct check on the effects of the advertising than retail sales.

The majority of companies conducting sales-area tests favor a check of retail sales rather than jobbing sales.

7. *Sales conditions uniform in all test and control cities.* It is important that sales conditions be kept as uniform as possible in all the test and control cities. During the testing period there should be no extra sales effort on the part of dealers, the sales force, or newspapers that perform merchandising services for the advertiser. If dealers and salesmen push sales with more than usual enthusiasm during the testing period, then the tests are not tests strictly of the advertising. When tests are being conduced, it is a good plan to keep the program confidential until it is under way, and then not to encourage dealers and salesmen to be unduly aggressive.

Advantages and disadvantages of sales-area method. In comparison with other methods of pretesting, the sales-area method has a number of advantages, as well as certain disadvantages. The following are some of the disadvantages:

1. The sales-area method involves considerable expense. The check of sales during the perliminary checking period and during the testing period is expensive. So also is the actual running of the advertisements in the test cities for periods that may extend from four weeks to three months.

2. The sales-area method requires time. Taking into account the preliminary checking period and the testing period itself, dependable results can hardly be obtained in less than three months as a minimum. To lessen this difficulty, however, there is the possibility of

running test campaigns concurrently with the regular campaign; that is, while a campaign is being run on a national scale, certain cities are segregated, and future campaigns are tested in those cities. This is the procedure followed by a number of companies using the sales-area test. Some of these companies have had as many as four or six campaigns under test at the same time that another campaign was being used nationally. The test campaign that proves to be most effective is then chosen as the next national campaign.

3. By its nature, the sales-area test can be applied only through local media—chiefly newspapers. It cannot be used in national magazines.

4. The practical problems involved in applying the principles of the sales-area test may in some cases be hard to solve. There are numerous factors that may affect the results of the tests, and these factors are often not subject to the advertiser's control. The sales-area method of testing must therefore be applied with the utmost vigilance, and the results very carefully interpreted in the light of the total situation.

As against the above, the following are some of the advantages of the sales-area method:

1. The sales-area plan is the only method of pretesting that is a direct check upon sales. Under other methods the effect of the advertising upon sales is usually estimated by indirect means.

2. Although the sales-area method is expensive and takes time, if a large sum of money is to be spent on the final advertising campaign, the expenditure involved in pretesting is justifiable. A large advertiser who does not test merely because of the expense may be open to the criticism that he is penny wise and pound foolish.

3. If a sales-area test is planned and executed carefully, the results are dependable. The experience of advertisers who have used the sales-area test would appear to confirm this. Among these advertisers are the following: Pepsodent, Listerine, Ambrosia, Campbell's Soup, Fleischmann's Yeast.

Pretesting by the Inquiries Method

What the inquiries method is. As its name suggests, the inquiries method is a system of testing advertisements by a count of the inquiries that different advertisements pull. The system is comparable to the methods used by mail-order advertisers. Mail-order advertisers generally "key" all their advertisements, usually through the use of key numbers on coupons; the key number is different on each advertisement. A record is kept of the number of inquiries pulled by each advertisement and of the inquiries that resulted in sales. Analysis of his records enables the mail-order advertiser to know, with regard to each advertisement that he runs, the following facts:

1. Number of inquiries that the advertisement pulled.
2. Number of these inquiries that were consummated as sales.
3. Cost per sales.

Through this system of coupons, inquiries, and tabulations of cost per sale, the mail-order advertiser obtains definite answers to his problems. For example, there may be doubt as to whether Publication *A* is better for advertising purposes than Publication *B*. The mail-order advertiser can run test advertisements in both publications (exactly the same advertisement being used in each); his results may show that the cost per sale in Publication A is 85 cents, while the cost per sale in Publication *B* is 57 cents; on the basis of these results the advertiser would choose Publication *B* for regular use. The inquiries system of testing so-called "general" advertising is an attempt to apply mail-order testing methods to general advertising, with a view to building up for the general advertiser as solid a foundation of facts and figures as that enjoyed by the mail-order advertiser.

Procedure in the inquiries test. One of the chief differences between the sales-area method and the inquiries method is that the sales-area method tests the complete campaign (in a limited area), whereas the inquiries method is often used to test the various elements in the campaign, for the purpose of determining the most productive combination of those elements. Assume that an advertiser wishes to pretest by the inquiries method a campaign that he has formulated. His procedure is roughly as follows:

1. Certain media are chosen for purposes of the tests.
2. In the test media the advertiser runs his campaign and keeps a record of the inquiries produced. To stimulate inquiries, an offer

—commonly in the form of a coupon—is placed on each advertisement. (See Figure 13 and the explanation of it on this page.)

3. The various elements in the campaign are tested, only one particular being changed at a time. For example, the advertising as first run may bear a certain type of headline. It is desired to test another type of headline. Then the advertisement is run again, with only the headline changed, under exactly similar conditions—in the same media, in the same size, in the same position, with the same offer, and so forth. A count of the inquiries produced indicates which is the more effective type of headline. The other elements that it is desired to test are changed one at a time; and, when the tests are concluded, the advertiser can tell from his count of inquiries which is the most productive combination of the various elements that his advertising is to contain.

The following are a few of the points that may be tested as described above, by a count of inquiries:

1. Which media are most effective? Within limits, a count of inquiries is a useful guide for the advertiser in his selecton of media.
2. What size of space is most productive—full pages, half pages, quarter pages, or smaller?
3. Are preferred positions in publications worth the extra cost?
4. Is color worth the extra cost?

Explanation of Figure 13.

(1) Common form of offer of booklet, without coupon. Instructions simple. Product pictured.
(2) Common form of coupon for free booklet.
(3) Free offer; literature pictured. Small charge to cover mailing costs for distant residents secures interest only of those who are prospects.
(4) Common form of coupon where several products are sold and information on each is handled in separate literature. Enables classification of mailing list.
(5) Method of developing trial orders. Limitation of time of offer stirs reader to prompt action.
(6) Attention of certain class of prospects called to free offer of sample. Absence of coupon reduces number of non-prospect inquiries.
(7) Charge of 10 cents eliminates those who make practice of clipping coupons. Check list helps classify prospects.
(8) Hidden offer of a sample cuts down number of inquiries from coupon clippers. Inquiries show actual reading of ad. Expectation of automatic repeat sales makes offer possible.
(9) Simple effort to get inquiries.

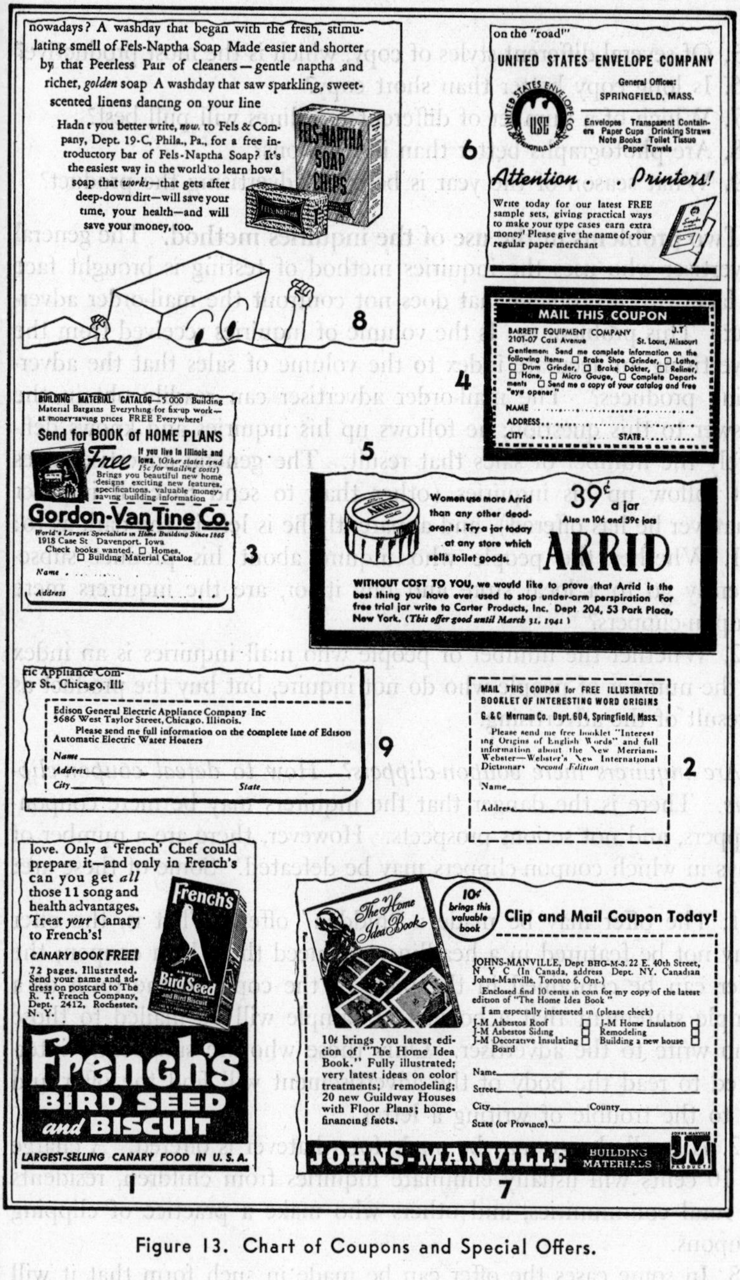

nowadays? A washday that began with the fresh, stimulating smell of Fels-Naptha Soap Made easier and shorter by that Peerless Pair of cleaners—gentle naptha and richer, golden soap A washday that saw sparkling, sweet-scented linens dancing on your line
Hadn't you better write, now, to Fels & Company, Dept. 19-C, Phila., Pa., for a free introductory bar of Fels-Naptha Soap? It's the easiest way in the world to learn how a soap that works—that gets after deep-down dirt—will save your time, your health—and will save your money, too.
FELS-NAPTHA SOAP CHIPS
8
on the "road!"
UNITED STATES ENVELOPE COMPANY
General Offices: SPRINGFIELD, MASS.
Envelopes Transparent Containers Paper Cups Drinking Straws Note Books Toilet Tissue Paper Towels
6
Attention . . Printers!
Write today for our latest FREE sample sets, giving practical ways to make your type cases earn extra money! Please give the name of your regular paper merchant
MAIL THIS COUPON
BARRETT EQUIPMENT COMPANY J.T
2101-07 Cass Avenue St. Louis, Missouri
Gentlemen: Send me complete information on the following items: ☐ Brake Shoe Grinder, ☐ Lathe, ☐ Drum Grinder, ☐ Brake Dokter, ☐ Reliner, ☐ Hone, ☐ Micro Gauge, ☐ Complete Departments ☐ Send me a copy of your catalog and free "eye opener"
NAME
ADDRESS
CITY STATE
4
BUILDING MATERIAL CATALOG—5 000 Building Material Bargains Everything for fix-up work—at money-saving prices FREE Everywhere!
Send for BOOK of HOME PLANS
Free If you live in Illinois and Iowa. (Other states send 15c for mailing costs) Brings you beautiful new home designs exciting new features, specifications, valuable money-saving building information
Gordon-Van Tine Co.
World's Largest Specialists in Home Building Since 1865
1918 Case St Davenport, Iowa
Check books wanted. ☐ Homes. ☐ Building Material Catalog
Name
Address
3
5
Women use more Arrid than any other deodorant. Try a jar today at any store which sells toilet goods.
39¢ a jar
Also in 10¢ and 59¢ jars
ARRID
WITHOUT COST TO YOU, we would like to prove that Arrid is the best thing you have ever used to stop under-arm perspiration For free trial jar write to Carter Products, Inc. Dept 204, 53 Park Place, New York. (This offer good until March 31, 1941)
ric Appliance Com-
or St., Chicago, Ill.
Edison General Electric Appliance Company Inc
5686 West Taylor Street, Chicago, Illinois.
Please send me full information on the complete line of Edison Automatic Electric Water Heaters
Name
Address
City State
9
MAIL THIS COUPON for FREE ILLUSTRATED BOOKLET OF INTERESTING WORD ORIGINS
G. & C. Merriam Co. Dept. 604, Springfield, Mass.
Please send me free booklet "Interesting Origins of English Words" and full information about the New Merriam-Webster—Webster's New International Dictionary Second Edition
Name
Address
2
love. Only a 'French' Chef could prepare it—and only in French's can you get all those 11 song and health advantages. Treat your Canary to French's!
CANARY BOOK FREE!
72 pages. Illustrated. Send your name and address on postcard to The R. T. French Company, Dept. 2412, Rochester, N.Y.
French's Bird Seed
French's BIRD SEED and BISCUIT
LARGEST-SELLING CANARY FOOD IN U. S. A.
1
10¢ brings this valuable book
Clip and Mail Coupon Today!
The Home Idea Book
JOHNS-MANVILLE, Dept BHG-M-3, 22 E. 40th Street, N Y C (In Canada, address Dept. NY. Canadian Johns-Manville, Toronto 6, Ont.)
Enclosed find 10 cents in coin for my copy of the latest edition of "The Home Idea Book"
I am especially interested in (please check)
J-M Asbestos Roof ☐ J-M Home Insulation ☐
J-M Asbestos Siding ☐ Remodeling ☐
J-M Decorative Insulating Board ☐ Building a new house ☐
Name
Street
City County
State (or Province)
10¢ brings you latest edition of "The Home Idea Book." Fully illustrated; very latest ideas on color treatments; remodeling; 20 new Guildway Houses with Floor Plans; home-financing facts.
JOHNS-MANVILLE BUILDING MATERIALS
7

Figure 13. Chart of Coupons and Special Offers.

5. Of several different styles of copy, which is the most productive?
6. Is long copy better than short copy?
7. Which of a number of different headlines will pull best?
8. Are photographs better than illustrations?
9. What season of the year is best for advertising the product?

Two problems in the use of the inquiries method. The general advertiser who uses the inquiries method of testing is brought face to face with a problem that does not confront the mail-order advertiser. This problem is: Is the volume of inquiries received from the advertising an accurate index to the volume of sales that the advertising produces? The mail-order advertiser can readily obtain the answer to this question; he follows up his inquiries and knows definitely the number of sales that result. The general advertiser does not follow up his inquiries (other than to send to each inquirer whatever he has offered), and apparently he is left in the dark as to:

1. Whether the people who inquire about his product subsequently go to a local store and buy it; or, are the inquirers mere coupon-clippers?
2. Whether the number of people who mail inquiries is an index to the number of people who do not inquire, but buy the product as a result of the advertising.

Are inquirers mere coupon-clippers? How to defeat coupon-clippers. There is the danger that the inquirers may be mere coupon-clippers, and not serious prospects. However, there are a number of ways in which coupon-clippers may be defeated. Some of these are:

1. The offer may be made a "hidden" offer. That is, the offer may not be featured in a headline, nor need there be a coupon; the offer can be contained in the body of the copy, in the form of a simple statement that a booklet or sample will be mailed to those who write to the advertiser. Only those who are sufficiently interested to read the body of the advertisement will find the offer and go to the trouble of writing a letter.
2. A small charge may be made for whatever is offered. A charge of 10 cents will usually eliminate inquiries from children, residents in rural communities, and others who make a practice of clipping coupons.
3. In some cases the offer can be made in such form that it will

interest only those who are prospects for the advertised product. For example, if a manufacturer of pipe tobacco offered a free ash tray to inquirers, he would doubtless receive thousands of worthless inquiries—from women, cigarette and cigar smokers, and others. If, on the other hand, he offered a pipe reamer, the bulk of his inquiries would come from men who were pipe smokers and potential users of his product.

4. The offer may be conditioned upon the inquirer's mailing to the advertiser a carton or some other evidence of the fact that he has purchased the product.

By testing from time to time, there can also be determined the number of inquirers who subsequently become purchasers and the percentage of coupon-clippers among the inquirers. One method is to use anonymous follow-ups. These follow-ups consist of cards on which a number of products are listed, the name of the advertiser's product being among them; the people receiving the cards are asked merely to check off the products that they have recently purchased. The cards do not bear the name of the advertiser, but of a dummy "research bureau."

Is volume of inquiries an index to volume of sales? A number of studies have been made of the reliability of inquiries as a criterion of sales. Dr. Daniel Starch conducted an "Analysis of Five Million Inquiries" produced by 3,500 advertisements of 163 advertisers over a period of 12 years. Doctor Starch's conclusion was that sales figures roughly parallel volume of inquiries. Other investigators have reached the same conclusion. However, fundamentally the answer to the question as to whether volume of inquiries is an index to volume of sales depends upon the manner in which the inquiries method is used. Carelessly applied, it may produce misleading results; adequately safeguarded, its dependability is correspondingly increased.

Safeguards to observe in testing by the inquiries method. The following are the chief safeguards:

1. *Do not force inquiries.* It would obviously be easy to obtain a very large number of inquiries if the offer were featured in the advertisement and dominated everything else. The offer should be simple and businesslike; also, if at all possible, the offer should be of

such a nature that it will interest only those who are potential users of the advertised product.

2. *Test only one particular at a time.* This is a fundamental principle of testing by the inquiries method. If it is desired to test the effectiveness of two different types of headlines, then everything other than the headlines must remain the same. If the value of preferred position in a publication is to be tested, the advertisement in the preferred position must be exactly the same as that in the nonpreferred position. If two different offers are to be tested, then except for the change in the offers the advertisements must be alike to the minutest detail. The reason for the principle that only one particular should be tested at a time is apparent; if, for example, both headline and offer were changed, it would be difficult to determine which of the two changes produced the variation in results.

3. *Rely only on comparative count of inquiries.* The number of inquiries obtained from a single advertisement has little meaning. There must be some standard with which the results can be compared. This standard is the number of inquiries received from one or more other advertisements run under exactly similar conditions. If, for example, Advertisement *A* pulls 5,000 inquiries, this by itself has little significance. If, however, Advertisement *B* is run under exactly the same conditions and pulls 8,000 inquiries, it is reasonable to conclude that Advertisement *B* is a better sales instrument than Advertisement A; if, further, the only difference between the two is in the headlines, then the results indicate that the type of headline used in Advertisement *B* is more effective than that used in Advertisement A.

In addition to the three safeguards mentioned above, other safeguards will suggest themselves as necessary in particular cases. The inquiries methods cannot be applied automatically or with mathematical precision. It needs the support of strong common sense. For example, an advertiser running copy in an expensive magazine, such as *Town & Country*, would doubtless receive poor returns if he used a coupon, for the reason that people would not wish to mutilate an expensive and beautifully printed magazine; if it was desired to key the advertisement, a hidden offer or a simple request that readers write to the advertiser would be more logical. Similarly, if an advertiser intends to use a coupon, it may be advisable for him not to place his advertisement on the back cover of certain serious magazines of which many readers keep files; readers would not wish to cut the back cover of a magazine of this type.

Pretesting by the Consumer-Jury Method

Procedure in the consumer-jury test. In general, the consumer-jury test consists of submitting to a "jury of consumers" specimens of the advertising that it is proposed to use. The jury is asked to rank the various pieces of advertising in the order of their effectiveness. The advertising chosen by the majority is run in the campaign.

In practice, the methods followed by advertisers in applying the consumer-jury test differ considerably in detail. For example:

1. In some cases the advertising submitted to the jury is in final form; that is, the headlines and copy are set in type, the illustrations made, and so forth, and what the jury sees are final proofs showing the advertisements as they would actually appear in publications. In other cases the advertising submitted to the jury is in rough-draft form, with the headlines and layout merely sketched in. The latter method is the more economical.

2. Occasionally, when the advertisements that are under test are given to the jury, the jury is required not to analyze them but merely to give an answer to some such question as: "Which of these advertisements would be most likely to make you want to buy the product?" On the other hand, some advertisers have required the jury to analyze the advertisements, and to rate them for attention value and appeal, or for attention value, headline, and text.

3. Some advertisers mail the advertisements to the members of the jury, the arrangement being that the members of the jury will receive a small gift in return for their services. Other advertisers prefer to send out investigators to interview the members of the jury and obtain their reactions at first hand.

Safeguards to observe in using the consumer-jury test. The following are the chief safeguards:

1. The persons chosen for the jury should be typical prospects for the product. If, for example, the product to be advertised is a baby food, as far as possible the jury should be comprised of women who have babies.

2. The number of persons tested should be adequate. Tests on a small number may produce misleading results. A jury of two hundred persons may be regarded as a safe minimum.

Advantages and disadvantages of the consumer-jury test. The criticism most frequently made of the consumer-jury test is that it requires the jury to express a conscious reaction to the advertisements, whereas under actual conditions the reaction of the consumer to the advertisements that he sees is largely subconscious. Critics of the consumer-jury test say that no one can tell, merely by looking at two or more advertisements, which would have the greatest effect upon him if read in a publication. There is also the difficulty of getting the jury to be strictly honest. For example, if two advertisements for the same product are submitted to a jury, and one features low price while the other features the established reputation of the manufacturer, doubtless quite a number of the jury will *vote* for the reputation appeal, whereas in "real life" it would be the price appeal that would stimulate them to *buy*.

Various means have been used to overcome the difficulties outlined above. One advertiser tested his advertisements by direct mail. The advertisements were set up in exactly the form in which they would appear in publications. Then the last few lines of each advertisement, in which the reader was urged to call at his local store and purchase the product, were removed; in their place was inserted a hidden free offer—a sample of the product would be sent to inquirers. The advertisements under test were mailed to a split list; included in each envelope was a card bearing only the advertiser's name and address and, on the reverse side, three blank lines on which the inquirer could write his name and address. The product was not mentioned on the cards, and no effort was made to direct attention to the free offer. A count of the inquiries received indicated which was the strongest advertisement.

Another advertiser, who was employing field investigators to test two different types of advertising, used a simple trick to obtain frank and unartificial responses from the people who were interviewed. An investigator would call on an individual, and say that he wished to obtain an opinion regarding a new kind of advertising that his company was thinking of using. Then, reaching into his briefcase, he would pretend that he could not find what he was looking for, but, drawing out two advertisements, would say: "Oh, incidentally, while I'm looking for the new advertising, would you mind taking a look at these two ads?" A moment later he would produce a new set of advertisements and discuss these with the person being interviewed. When the interview was concluded, the investigator would ask: "By the way, you remember the two advertisements that I showed you first? Can you describe them for me?" The advertisements first shown were, of course, the advertisements under test, and the individual's ability to describe one or the other more fully and completely indicated which had made the greater impression upon him.

Mention has been made of some of the disadvantages of the consumer-jury tests. However, this method of testing also has important advantages. Chief among these is the fact that it involves no great expenditure of time and money, and that it is comparatively easy to use. An advertiser who cannot afford to test by the sales-area method or by the inquiries method will find the consumer-jury method of considerable value.

6. HOW TO DESIGN AND REGISTER A TRADE-MARK

Adapted from Kleppner, "Advertising Procedure." New York: Prentice-Hall, Inc.

New Trade-Mark Act. A new Trade-Mark Act, commonly referred to as the Lanham Trade-Mark Act, went into effect on July 5, 1947. Streamlined to conform to present day business needs, it affects, in one way or another, every trade-mark owner or prospective owner. The act codifies all existing laws on trade-marks, formerly contained in many different statutes with conflicting court interpretations. It also makes many changes in the rules that formerly governed the design and protection of trade-marks.

First let us discuss what the law says, and then apply the provisions to the practical problems of designing a trade-mark.

What registration of a trade-mark means. Registration of a trade-mark is not obligatory, for a trade-mark rightfully belongs to the first person who has used it. Furthermore, Federal registration applies only to the use of trade-marks in interstate and foreign commerce. State registration may still be sought in one or more states for protection in intrastate commerce. However, the new Federal law offers wider protection than the former statutes and makes application under the state registration laws less necessary.

Registration does not automatically protect the owner from litigation. Once the trade-mark has been registered, the Patent Office is empowered to refuse the registration of infringing ideas, but the owner himself has to bring suit actually to restrain the use by another who has unlawfully apppropriated his trade-mark.

Advantages of registration on the Principal Register. All trade-marks that are registrable under the act may be registered on the Principal Register. The supplemental Register is described on page 192.

Registration on the Principal Register gives a trade-mark these advantages:

1. It is constructive notice of the registrant's claim to ownership of the mark.

2. It is *prima facie* evidence of the registrant's exclusive right to use the registered mark in commerce on the goods or services specified in the certificate of registration, subject to any conditions or limitations stated therein. This does not preclude an opposing party from proving any legal or equitable defense or defect which might have been asserted if the mark had not been registered.

3. The owner may obtain an incontestable right to use the trade-mark. See page 189.

4. It provides a record that others can consult before adopting a trade-mark to make sure they are not unwittingly infringing upon an existing trade-mark, or adopting a trade-mark too similar to another mark previously used for a similar product.

5. It gives Federal courts jurisdiction in infringement actions.

6. Domestic registration is necessary before a trade-mark can be registered in certain foreign countries.

7. The owner of a registered trade-mark can secure an automatic embargo at the customs of any foreign goods entering this country that infringe on that trade-mark.

8. The award of damages for infringement is not limited to actual injury but may in the discretion of the court be increased to three

times the amount of actual damages. The treble damages are not regarded as a penalty but as compensation.

What marks are registrable? The law permits registration of three types of marks.

1. Marks distinguishing goods.
2. Marks distinguishing service. For example, a symbol to distinguish the services rendered by a telephone company, a hotel, a restaurant; a distinctive feature of a radio program; a character name in any service, or a title or slogan.
3. Collective and certification marks. A "certification" mark is one used on products of persons other than the owner of the mark to certify the origin, material, quality, or standard of goods, or that work was done by union labor. The "seal of approval" of Good Housekeeping is one illustration. A "collective" mark refers to a trade-mark or service mark designating membership in a co-operative, association, or other collective group or organization.

The "must-nots" of trade-mark law. To be protected, the mark

1. Must not be immoral, deceptive, or scandalous.
2. Must not disparage or falsely suggest a connection with persons, living or dead, institutions, beliefs, or national symbols, or bring them into contempt or disrepute.
3. Must not contain the flag or coat of arms of the United States, any state, municipality, or foreign nation.
4. Must not use a name, portrait, or signature of a living person, except by his written consent.
5. Must not use the name, signature, or portrait of a deceased President of the United States during the life of his widow, except by her written consent.
6. Must not resemble a trade-mark previously registered or used by another and not abandoned, if its use is likely to cause confusion or mistake or to deceive purchasers. But see page 189 for concurrent registrations.
7. Must not be merely descriptive or deceptively misdescriptive.
8. When applied to the goods, must not be primarily geographically descriptive or deceptively misdescriptive of them, except as indications of regional origin in a collective or certification mark.
9. Must not be primarily merely a surname.

A mark can be registered even though it is merely descriptive, or geographically descriptive, or is primarily a surname *if it has become distinctive of the applicant's goods in commerce.* Five years of exclusive and continuous use prior to filing application may be accepted by the Commissioner as *prima facie* evidence that the mark has become distinctive. A mark that is unregistrable because of the prohibitions enumerated in 1 through 6 above can never become registrable as distinctive.

Notice of registration. Registration of a mark on the Principal Register is constructive notice of the registrant's claim of ownership thereof. Nevertheless, the owner of a mark must give notice that his mark is registered by displaying with the mark as used the words "Registered in U. S. Patent Office" or "Reg. U. S. Pat. Off." or the letter "R" enclosed within a circle, thus ®. (See also Figure 14.)

THERMOS
TRADE-MARK REG. U. S. PAT. OFF.

TEXTRON
REG. U. S. PAT. OFF.

SANFORIZED
TRADE ® MARK

MOJUD®

*BAND-AID is the Reg. Trade-mark of Johnson & Johnson for its adhesive bandage.

Figure 14. How to Show That a Trade-Mark Is Registered.

From Kleppner, "Advertising Procedure." New York: Prentice-Hall, Inc.

The top four examples show how to designate that a trade-mark has been registered, as specified by statute. The Band-Aid statement illustrates another effective way. "Registered" may be spelled out as well as abbreviated.

Duration of a registered mark; affidavit of use. A registered trade-mark is good for twenty years. However, during the sixth year the owner must file an affidavit in the Patent Office showing that the mark is still in use or showing that its nonuse is due to special circumstances which excuse the nonuse and is not due to any intention to abandon the mark. Each registration may be renewed after twenty years' use for another twenty-year period.

Use by related companies. A holding, parent, or controlled corporation can use a trade-mark owned by a subsidiary, and vice versa.

Conflicting trade-marks. Can a mark that is registered as a trade-mark for one product be used for an entirely different class of goods? The law says "Yes," by permitting the "concurrent" registration of the same or similar marks by more than one user entitled to its use, if such concurrent use will not result in confusion, mistake, or deception of purchasers. The Commissioner can grant a concurrent registration only if both marks were used concurrently prior to the application date of any registrant. Also, the grant of concurrent registration must contain conditions and limitations on the mode or place of use of the goods, which the equities between the owners dictate.

Assignment of trade-marks. An owner of a trade-mark can assign it with the goodwill of the business in which the trade-mark is used, or with that part of the goodwill of the business connected with the use of the mark. The assignment must be recorded in the Patent Office. The assigned registration can be canceled if the mark is being used so as to misrepresent the source of the goods or services in connection with which the mark is used.

Incontestability of trade-marks. No one can contest an owner's use of a trade-mark after it has been in continuous use for five consecutive years, if the following conditions are met:

1. There has been no final decision adverse to the registrant's claim of ownership, or his right to register the mark or to keep it on the register.
2. There is no dispute pending in the Patent Office or in a court.
3. The owner has filed the required affidavit mentioned at the top of this page.

4. The mark is not the common descriptive name of any article or substance, patented or otherwise.

5. There is no right to cancel as shown under 2 of the following paragraph.

6. The registration on the Principal Register does not infringe a valid right acquired under the law of any state or territory by use of a mark or trade-name from a date prior to the date of the publication of the registered mark.

Cancellation of registrations. Anyone who believes he will be damaged by a mark's registration may apply for cancellation:

1. Within five years from date of registration under the new Act or publication of marks registered under old Acts; or

2. At any time if:

(*a*) The mark becomes the common descriptive name of an article or substance on which the patent has expired, or has been abandoned;

(*b*) The registration was obtained fraudulently;

(*c*) The registration was obtained contrary to certain prohibitory provisions of the law;

(*d*) The mark has been assigned and is being used by the assignee to misrepresent;

(*e*) The registrant does not properly control the use of the mark.

The Federal Trade Commission may apply to cancel registration on any grounds under 2.

Item 2 (*a*) has great significance to advertisers. The names of a number of formerly patented products are no longer protected. Examples are *Singer* for sewing machines, *Stillson* for wrenches, *Shredded Wheat*, *Linoleum*, and *Aspirin*. Other advertisers have lost their trade-mark rights because the trade-mark is so commonly used as the name for a class of products that the public regards it as descriptive of the *class* rather than as the identifying mark of *one product* in that class. *Cellophane* was originally the trade-mark of the DuPont Company, but is now used by anyone making that type of product. But only DuPont can call its product *DuPont Cellophane*. Many large advertisers campaign continually to prevent people from using the trade-mark of their product to apply to a whole class of goods.

Remedies. Trade-mark owners may institute civil actions whenever an infringing mark is likely to cause confusion or deceive buyers about the origin of goods or services. Also, the printing of labels, signs, wrappers, receptacles, advertisements, and similar materials bearing imitations or counterfeits of a registered mark, and intended to be used with the sale in commerce of such goods or services, is an actionable offense. However, in the latter case, the trade-mark owner is not entitled to recover profits or damages from innocent infringers. Furthermore, the issue or periodical containing infringing matter cannot be stopped if to do so would delay the normal delivery of the issue.

Protecting foreign trade-marks in the U. S. and U. S. trade-marks abroad. The new Act specifically shows how the United States will protect the trade-marks of foreign owners who are domiciled or have businesses in the countries which offer protection to owners of trade-marks registered in the United States. Such protection by foreign countries may come through treaties between the United States and a foreign country relating to trade-marks or trade names, conventions to which the United States and other countries have become parties, and laws of foreign countries affording protection to citizens of the United States. Thus, United States protection to foreign owners and foreign protection to American owners of trade-marks is a reciprocal matter.

The law outlines specifically what the foreign owner must do to obtain protection of his trade-mark in the United States. So far as the protection in foreign countries of marks registered in the United States is concerned, the law merely states that citizens or residents of the United States shall have the same benefits as are accorded to foreign owners entitled to protection in the United States. The United States owner of a trade-mark must still register separately in each country of the world where he thinks protection is desirable.

Many countries permit the registration of a vast array of marks and names that are not eligible for registration on the Principal Register in the United States. However, many countries also require that an outside concern must first register its trade-mark device in its own country. What is the American owner of a trade-mark to do if he can't register his trade-mark because it failed to meet the requirements of the Principal Register in the United States? To meet this situation, a Supplemental Register is established on which one can register virtually any mark not registrable on the Principal Register, provided the mark is capable of distinguishing one person's products from those of another without confusion—for example, by means of descriptive words, surnames, slogans, appearance of goods or package, and the like.

For domestic purposes, registration on the Supplemental Register is *not* equivalent to registration on the Principal Register, nor is it a substitute for it. The Supplemental Register does not provide a side door for giving domestic protection to ideas that do not qualify for the Principal Register. Registering a mark on the Supplemental Register does, however, place a mark on a public record that may be consulted by others who may be thinking of using a similar trade-mark, to avoid unintentional confusion.

The owner of any trade-marked product which shows signs of developing into national prominence will find it most advisable to protect that trade-mark properly in all foreign countries in which he may some day do business. If he does not do so at the outset, he may find an unpleasant surprise awaiting him when he tries to do it later. Most other countries, particularly those in Latin America, have an entirely different concept of property rights in trade-marks. The owner of the trade-mark is the man who *registers it first*, regardless of whether he originated the trade-mark or has even used it. As a result, piracy of American trade-marks is common abroad. Such experiences have been very costly for American advertisers and emphasize the importance of securing full legal protection before advertising extensively.

The Canadian trade-mark law. The Canadian law differs essentially from the present United States law in the following respects: (1) The first one to use a trade-mark becomes its owner, *provided that he applies for registration within six months;* in the United States, registration is entirely optional. (2) The Canadian act divides marks into "word marks" and "design marks"; each is considered separately and must be registered separately. In the United States they are considered together and can be registered at one time. (3) A trade-mark cannot consist of a corporation or personal name, although a trade-mark may be registered if it is the chief part of the corporate name of the applicant. For example, *Coca-Cola* might be registered by the Coca-Cola Company.

Effect of Food, Drug and Cosmetic Act on trade-marks. Under the Federal Food, Drug and Cosmetic Act a drug product may not be designated by a name which includes or suggests the name of one or more *but not all* active ingredients. This rule is actually applying to drug products the principle that a trade-mark must not be deceptive either in its implication or in its substance.

Designing a trade-mark. We have considered up to this point the legal background of trade-marks in order that the ideas we offer as trade-marks may be legally valid. We now probe into the elements of creating a trade-mark that will be effective from the advertising point of view. A word of caution should first be given, however. *The services of an attorney should be secured in any contemplated action before the proposed trade-mark is used in any way whatsoever; certainly before any money is spent in printing or packaging.*

Forms of trade-marks. The forms of trade-marks in most frequent use and that would be acceptable for registration under the new law may be grouped into these classifications:

1. *Dictionary words*

   Flit *(insecticide)*
   Sunbeam *(toaster)*
   Ivory *(soap)*
   Spry *(shortening)*
   Caterpillar *(tractors)*
   Old Gold *(cigarettes)*

2. *Coined or invented words*

   Spam *(meat)*
   Alemite *(lubricant)*
   Kleenex *(tissue)*
   Duco *(paint)*
   Teel *(dentifrice)*
   Kodak *(camera)*

3. *Foreign words*

   Bon Ami *(soap)*
   La Favorita *(cigar)*

4. *Personal names (actual, fictitional, historical, mythological)*

   Chesterfield *(cigarettes)*
   Prince Albert *(tobacco)*
   Robert Burns *(cigars)*
   Lincoln *(car)*
   Venus *(pencils)*
   Hercules *(explosives)*

5. *Geographical names*

Paris *(garters)*	Kalamazoo *(parchment)*
Waterbury *(clocks)*	Pittsburgh *(paints)*

6. *Initials and numbers*

R.C.A. *(radio, television)*	4711 *(perfume)*
A.C. *(spark plugs)*	7-20-4 *(cigars)*
Z.B.T. *(talcum powder)*	A-1 *(sauce)*

7. Portraits, designs, symbols, usually used in connection with one of the foregoing.

8. Novel uses of color.

A single trade-mark may embody several of the foregoing elements, as a picture and a coined word, a symbol and a syllable, or a personal name plus a coined word. The use of a word for a trade-mark generally gives the owner the right to alternative ways of expressing the idea—with a picture or symbol. They may be used separately, together, or interchangeably. (For example, the word *Gargoyle,* a trade-mark for oil, may appear in print, but the idea can also be expressed by a picture of a gargoyle.) It is an advantage to have a trade-mark word that can be illustrated, so that the idea can be expressed both verbally and visually.

Dictionary words. Dictionary words are those which are found in the dictionary but which are used in the trade-mark in an *arbitrary, suggestive, or fanciful manner*—such as *Spry, Sunbeam, Old Gold.* The chief element to consider in choosing a dictionary word is that it be one that is not ordinarily used in describing that type of product.

If the question, "Is the term 'descriptive' of the product or merely 'suggestive' of it?" arises, that is a danger sign which the advertising man should heed. The warning cannot be repeated too often that it is inexcusable for a person creating a trade-mark to cause trouble by arguing too close to the letter of the law and by not respecting its spirit.

Coined or invented words. Coined words (*Linit, Graftex, Duco*) are one of the best forms of trade-mark to protect. The courts have held: "When a person forms a new word to designate an article made by him, which has never been used before, he may obtain such a right to that name as to entitle him to the sole use of it as against others who attempt to use it for the sale of similar articles." The possible disadvantage of coined words is first, that it is difficult to create a word that is distinctive and practical; and second, that it places on the advertiser the complete burden of explaining what the product is.

The misspelling or hyphenating of a word (Yung-felo instead of Young Fellow, Heldryte for Held Right, Neva Wet for Never Wet) gives it no rights that a phonetic pronunciation or correct spelling of the word would not have. This does not make a coined or nondescriptive word out of one which would otherwise be descriptive.

Foreign words. A foreign word is treated just as the English translation of that word. *Le Bon* was held ineligible for use as a trade-mark for baking powder because its English translation is *good,* and *good* is regarded as a descriptive term.

Personal names. A personal name as applied to a product may serve as a trade-mark, provided: it has already been in use and serves to distinguish the particular product; or it is written in a distinctive way; or it is not merely primarily a surname. We have therefore old and well-known names serving as trade-marks in cases such as Sherwin-Williams for paints, Elizabeth Arden for cosmetics, McKesson & Robbins for drugs.

Names chosen for trade-marks should be as simple to pronounce and as easy to use as a coined word. The name itself should be sufficiently uncommon to be distinguishable from others. It is difficult to protect a proper name against others having the same name, particularly for a comparative newcomer upon the advertising scene whose product shows high promise of success and which will most likely invite imitators.

Geographical names. Place names are no longer a good source of ideas for new trade-marks, even though many famed trade-marks are geographical names: *Nashua* Blankets, *Palm Beach* Cloth, *Elgin* Watchs, *Kalamazoo* Stoves. They came into being when the law on trade-marks was less strict. The law does not now look with favor on permitting one man to use a city, town, or regional name exclusively in connection with his products, when others making similar goods in that area may have the same desire and right to use it for their products.

Initials and numbers. Initials and numbers are the most difficult type of ideas to establish as trade-marks; they are the hardest for people to remember and the easiest to imitate. Numbers usually lack visual value and number trade-marks are confusingly alike.

Portraits, designs, symbols. A portrait of a person is legally acceptable as a trade-mark. Anyone may use the portrait of a deceased person (provided it is not already being used on a similar product). Portraits of living people may be used only with their consent. From the advertising standpoint, portraits are not highly effective as trade-marks. Most portraits look very much alike when reduced to the small size that may be required for trade-mark purposes. They are not easily reproduced. The style of picture they represent may go out of fashion quickly. The whiskers of the Smith Brothers may have helped make their portraits a valuable trade-mark (as has the fortune spent in the advertising of them), but other successful examples are few.

A trade-mark must not include the flag or any insignia of the United States, or of any state or municipality, or of any foreign country. It must not be the insignia of the Red Cross or of any organization that has adopted and publicly used an emblem. (The only exception to this is the right of firms who used a red cross on their products prior to the incorporation of the American National Red Cross in 1904.) The trade-mark must not be immoral, deceptive, scandalous, or against public policy.

Color and other devices. The color or appearance of goods is not a valid trade-mark. The law does not wish to give a monopoly of a color to any one person, since the number of colors is limited. A match company was unable to protect the color of its match heads as a trade-mark; a soap manufacturer the color of his soap; a bottle maker the color of his bottles; and a tire manufacturer the color of his tires. It is a well-settled rule that there can be no trade-mark in the mere form, size, or color of the package containing a product. But color may constitute a valid trade-mark when impressed in a particular design.

For example, a red strip across a shovel has been used as a trade-mark as has been a colored strand in a wire. The use of color is valid in these instances because it is used in a limited way, and is not the basic over-all color of the product. From the advertising viewpoint, the use of color has many drawbacks, chief of which is the fact that it may be hard to show the trade-mark in publication advertisements.

How to create a trade-mark. A trade-mark needs to be distinctive so that it may overcome confusion with competing articles, help the reader recollect the advertised brand when he thinks of buying the product, and assist him to recall previous advertisements whenever he sees or hears the trade-mark.

The trade-mark should be simple. It should require no explanation. If a design is used, it should have one distinguishing feature easy to remember and to put into words.

If a picture is adopted, it should be one that will not soon become obsolete. No element that the normal progress of time and custom may make obsolete should be introduced in a new trade-mark. If pictures of people are to be used, beware of the changes that take place in the style of hairdressing and of clothing.

In the designing of a trade-mark, cognizance must also be taken of the method whereby it is to be reproduced. Automobiles usually carry their trade-marks on their radiators and on the hubs of their wheels. Simple, open-faced designs are here particularly necessary. For jewelry, a trade-mark even more simple is required to permit of reduction in size. For most package goods, a trade-mark with its width three-fifths its height will be found adaptable to the container and to advertisements alike.

The use of broadcasting influences the choice of a trade-mark. A word that can be dramatized, or a name that suggests a radio personality, is preferable to a colorless combination of words or numbers or syllables or designs.

Copy demands of a trade-mark word. The suitability of a word for use as a trade-mark can well be decided by good copy sense. The word should be as adaptable as some of the patented reading lamps, which can be hung, clamped, or stuck anywhere and still give forth their light.

The following qualifications help a trade-mark in its work. A single trade-mark may not embody all of these virtues, but it may at least strive to achieve them. Words chosen for trade-mark purposes should be:

1. *Simple and crisp.* Such words are typified by *Crisco, Ritz, Sanka, Lux, Zonite, Mazda.*

2. *Easy to say, spell, and recognize.* What is the average reader to do with names such as *Hexylresorcinol, Houdailles, Hyomei, Telekathoras, Glycothymoline, Sempre Giovine?* Advertisers of products with such names may find it necessary to run an explanatory line spelling the name phonetically. This is one of the two ways out of the difficulty. The other way is to change the name before the product is advertised. Trade-marks must be easy for people to recognize when they hear them over the radio, and easy to spell. Lehn & Fink, makers of Pebeco, have received mail calling their produce *Pebigle, Pedalgo, Pebisco, Publico.*

3. *Pronounceable in one way only.* Is *Olivilo* to be pronounced "Ah-leev-eye-lo," or "Olive-eelo;" *Pall Mall,* "Pawl Mawl" or "Pal Mal"? The public's pronunciation may be corrected by a simple expedient, such as was used by the Standard Oil Company. Their name, Socony, was mispronounced "sock-ohnee" and "soak-ohnee." The desired pronunciation was So-co′-ny, which they impressed by printing their name SoCOny and So*co*ny. But new trade-marks should be so created that they do not need such assistance. It is also well to guard against the selection of a word that can be punned, or unpleasantly rhymed, or mispronounced by competitors' salesmen.

4. *Distinctive.* A great fault of many new trade-marks is that they are commonplace. One directory of commercial names lists *National* 95 times; *Champion,* 122; *Star,* 134; *Ideal,* 142; *Universal,* 149; and *Standard,* 184. What claim to individuality could any new trade-mark make if it consisted of, or included, one of these terms?

5. *Suggestive of the product.* The trade-mark must not describe the product literally, but it can suggest the nature, use, action, or quality of an article; for example, *Rinso* Soap, *Caterpillar* Tractors, *Zerone* Anti-freeze, *Sunkist* Oranges. In contrast, *Electrolux* is a poor name for a *gas* refrigerator being sold in competition with *electric* refrigerators. (Servel, Inc., makers of Electrolux refrigerators, recognizing that fact, have changed the emphasis from *Electrolux* Refrigerators to *Servel* Gas Refrigerators.)

As previously indicated, the word must not be deceptively misdescriptive.

7. COPYRIGHT PROCEDURE

Outline of copyright procedure. Copyright procedure is relatively simple. The three requirements to be met are:

1. Published works that are copyrighted must bear the copyright notice.
2. Application for registration of a copyright claim should be made to the Register of Copyrights, Library of Congress, Washington 25, D. C., on a form supplied by the Register of Copyrights. A different form is used for each class of copyrightable material. To obtain the proper application form for the class of material that it is desired to copyright, write to the Register of Copyrights. When the application for registration of copyright is filed, it should be accompanied by the stipulated fee, which in most cases is $4.
3. A number of copies of the work should be deposited with the Register of Copyrights, at the time the application is made. The number of copies required to be deposited is usually two, although in some cases only one copy is required.

Classification of copyrightable material. Under the United States Copyright Law, copyrightable material is classified as:

1. Books, including composite and cyclopedic works, directories, gazetteers, and other compilations. The term "book" includes pamphlets, leaflets, or single pages.
2. Periodicals, including newspapers.
3. Lectures, sermons, addresses, prepared for oral delivery.
4. Dramatic or dramatico-musical compositions.
5. Musical compositions.
6. Maps.
7. Works of art; models or designs for works of art.
8. Reproductions of a work of art.
9. Drawings or plastic works of a scientific or technical character.
10. Photographs.
11. Prints and pictorial illustrations, including prints or labels used for articles of merchandise.
12. Motion-picture photoplays.
13. Motion pictures other than photoplays.

Requirements of Copyright Office governing works reproduced in copies for sale or public distribution. The following are the requirements of the Copyright Office governing this type of copyrightable material:

1. *Publish work with copyright notice.* In connection with the copyright notice, the following rules should be observed:

(*a*) *Form of copyright notice.* The usual form of copyright notice, and one that complies with the copyright law, is:

COPYRIGHT 19— BY
PRENTICE-HALL, INC.

Although the above form is sufficient to satisfy the requirements of the copyright law, it is often advisable to add, underneath the copyright notice, a statement such as the following:

ALL RIGHTS RESERVED. NO PART OF THIS WORK MAY BE REPRODUCED IN ANY FORM, BY MIMEOGRAPH OR ANY OTHER MEANS, WITHOUT PERMISSION IN WRITING FROM THE COPYRIGHT PROPRIETOR.

A statement such as that given above is a specific warning to the public, which is generally not aware of the necessity for obtaining written permission to use copyrighted material.

(*b*) *Special form of copyright notice permitted in certain cases.* In the case of works (6)-(11), specified in the classification list above, the copyright notice may consist of the symbol ©, accompanied by the initials, monogram, mark, or symbol of the copyright proprietor. However, the name of the copyright proprietor must appear on some accessible part of the copies.

(*c*) *Place where copyright notice should appear.* In a book or other printed publication, the copyright notice should be placed on the title page or on the back of the title page. In a periodical the notice should appear either on the title page or on the first page of text of each separate number, or under the title heading. In a musical work the copyright notice should be placed either on the title page or on the first page of music.

(*d*) *Use of fictitious name in copyright notice undesirable.* The name of the copyright owner given in the notice should be the real name of a living person, or his trade name if he always uses one, or the name of the firm or corporation owning the copyright, and no other. The use of a fictitious or pen name is not prohibited and might suffice in certain cases but is not desirable.

2. *Deposit copies of the work with Register of Copyrights.* In connection with the deposit of copies, the following information will be useful:

(*a*) *Number of copies to be deposited.* Immediately after publication, generally, two copies of the work should be sent to the Register of Copyrights, Library of Congress, Washington 25, D. C. However, if the work is by a foreign author, and has been published abroad in a foreign language, only one copy is required to be deposited with the Register of Copyrights. For a work published abroad in English, only one copy need be deposited to secure temporary (*ad interim*) copyright protection. In the case of a contribution to a periodical, one complete copy of the periodical containing the contribution should be deposited. The form of application for each different class of copyrightable material states the number of copies required to be deposited.

(*b*) *Affidavit required in certain cases.* In the case of books published in the United States, the application for copyright is required to be accompanied by an affidavit of manufacture. A different form of application is used for each class of copyrightable material; if an affidavit is necessary, provision is made for it in the application form.

(*c*) *Free mailing privilege.* The copies of works sent to be registered for copyright may be mailed to the Copyright Office free, if directly delivered for that purpose to the postmaster. The Copyright Office does not furnish franking labels, and the copies cannot be mailed by deposit in a street mail box; they must be taken to the post office and delivered to the postal authorities; a receipt may be obtained upon request.

Requirements of Copyright Office governing works not reproduced in copies for sale or public distribution. Copyright may be secured on certain classes of works, copies of which are not produced for sale or public distribution:

1. *Lectures and oral addresses, dramatic or musical compositions.* One complete manuscript or typewritten copy of the work should be deposited with the Register of Copyrights.

2. *Photographs.* In the case of photographs reproduced in copies for sale or otherwise published, one photographic print should be deposited.

3. *Works of art.* This includes paintings, drawings, sculpture, models or designs for works of art, and drawings or plastic works of a scientific or technical character. One photograph or other identifying reproduction of the work should be deposited.

4. *Motion-picture photoplays.* A title and description, together with one print taken from each scene or act, should be deposited.

5. *Motion pictures other than photoplays.* A title and description, together with not less than two prints taken from different sections of a complete motion picture, should be deposited.

In the case of each of the works listed above, if they are subsequently reproduced in copies for sale or distribution, a second deposit, application for registration, and the payment of a second fee must be made.

Term of copyright in the United States. The original term of copyright in the United States is 28 years. Within one year prior to the expiration of the original term, the copyright may be renewed for an additional 28 years. The total of 56 years (original term plus renewal term) is the longest possible period for which a work can be copyrighted in the United States.

Copyright fees. The following are the fees required by the Register of Copyrights:

For registration of a claim to copyright in any published or unpublished work (except a print or label used for article of manufacture), including certificate	$4.00
For registration of a claim to copyright in a print or label used for article of manufacture, including certificate	6.00
For recording the renewal of copyright, including certificate	2.00
For every additional certificate of registration	1.00
For certifying a copy of an application for registration of copyright, and for all other certifications	2.00
For recording every assignment, agreement, power of attorney, or other paper not exceeding six pages	3.00

(For each additional page or less, 50 cents; for each title over one in the paper recorded, 50 cents additional)

For recording each notice of use containing not more than five titles 2.00
(For each additional title, 50 cents)

For each hour of time consumed in searching Copyright Office records, indexes, or deposits, or services rendered in connection therewith 3.00

Remittances should be made by money order or bank draft, payable to the Register of Copyrights, Library of Congress, Washington 25, D. C. Checks may not be accepted by the Register in payment of copyright fees unless certified.

Copyright on a new edition of a copyrighted work. If a work which has previously been copyrighted is reissued with changes or revisions, application should be made, on a special form available from the Register of Copyrights, for copyright protection on the new material contained in the work. A mere reprinting of a work previously copyrighted needs no additional protection and cannot be recopyrighted, but if substantial changes have been made, these changes should be protected by an application form with two copies of the revised edition and the required fee. The application should include a brief statement of the new material on which copyright is claimed, and the title and author of the original edition if different from the title and author of the revised edition. The fee is the same as that for registration of an original edition ($4, except for a commercial print or label, where it is $6).

Copyright on an unpublished manuscript. Copyright may be obtained on a manuscript or typewritten copy of a dramatic composition, a musical composition, or a lecture, sermon, or address prepared for oral delivery. However, text matter in general is classified under the broad category of "book," and is not copyrightable until *after* it has been printed and *published* with the copyright notice. Hence, the answer to the question "Can a manuscript be copyrighted before publication?" is "No—unless the manuscript is a dramatic composition, a musical composition, or a lecture, sermon, or address prepared for oral delivery." Prior to publication literary manuscripts are protected under the common law without the need for observing any formalities, provided authorship and date of creation are established.

Quotations from a copyrighted work. The utmost caution should be observed in the quotation or use of copyrighted material in a new work. It is not generally understood that quotation from or use of material from a copyrighted work can be made only upon written permission of the copyright owner. Suit for damages, and enforced withdrawal of the infringing work from circulation, may be the penalty for infringement of copyright. Publishers require the author of a manuscript to obtain written permission to quote from another work. Quotations from publications of the Government and other official bodies can be made without permission, unless the publication contains material otherwise copyrighted. In all cases where quotations are made, the following information should be cited:

1. Name of the author.
2. Title of the work from which the quotation is made.
3. Name of the publisher, and the city of publication.
4. Date of publication.

It may also be advisable to include the copyright notice that appears upon the work from which the quotation is taken.

Copyright on prints and labels. Prints and labels published in connection with the sale or advertisement of articles of merchandise may be copyrighted for 28 years, with the privilege of renewal for an additional 28 years. Promptly after publication with the copyright notice, two copies should be sent to the Register of Copyrights, together with application Form KK and the registration fee of $6. In the case of prints published as advertisements in periodicals, send either two copies of the periodical or one copy of the periodical with one tear sheet or proof copy of the print. If a print or label is first published without the copyright notice, it cannot subsequently be copyrighted.

Prints and labels include advertisements in words, pictures, or design, or a combination thereof, that constitute original artistic or literary composition. No registration can be made in the Copyright Office if the *only* distinctive element is one of the following: a trade name, a business slogan, a well-known symbol or standard printer's ornamentation, typography or coloring, or a mere listing of the contents of the article of merchandise. Prints or labels that have been registered and later revised are registrable only if the revisions are in themselves copyright matter or so alter the composition as to make it a new work.

The Copyright Office will not register a print or label that is no more than trade-mark subject matter, which can only be registered at the Patent Office, but will register a claim in a print or label that contains copyrightable matter even though it also includes a trademark. However, it should be clearly understood that copyright registration does not give the claimant rights available only by trade-mark registration at the Patent Office.

Copyright in Great Britain. The term of a British copyright (except in the case of photographs and sound records) is the life of the author, plus 50 years from the date of his death. In the event that the work is that of joint authors, the copyright is in force for the life of the one who dies first and either another 50 years or the life of the one who dies last, whichever period is the longer. The term of copyright for photographs and sound records is 50 years from the date on which the original negative or the original plate was made.

Registration of copyright is not required in Great Britain. The British Copyright Act provides that copyright shall subsist:

1. In the case of a published work, if it was first published within such parts of the British Dominions to which the Act applies.
2. In the case of an unpublished work, if the author was, at the date of the making of the work, a British subject or a resident within the British Dominions.

If a work is published in Great Britain, the only formal requirement that has to be met is delivery of a copy of the work, within one month after publication, to the Library of the British Museum and, on demand (with some exceptions) to the Bodleian Library at Oxford, the University Public Library at Cambridge, the Library of the Faculty of Advocates at Edinburgh, the Library of Trinity College, Dublin, and the Welsh National University Library at Aberystwyth.

The absence of a copyright notice in a work published in Great Britain does not mean that the work is not copyrighted. The copyright notice is not required under the British Copyright Act.

HOW TO PROTECT IDEAS LEGALLY IN THE UNITED STATES

From Kleppner, "Advertising Procedure." New York: Prentice-Hall, Inc.

IDEA	SPECIAL METHOD OF PROTECTION	REQUIREMENTS FOR THIS PROTECTION	DURATION	REMARKS
	Regarding the Product and the Business			
1. PRODUCT (construction or composition)	Patent from Patent Office, Washington, D. C.	Must be a new invention of an art, machine, manufacture, composition of matter, or else a new and useful improvement in one.	17 years, not renewable.	The idea becomes public property when patent expires.
2. PRODUCT (appearance)	Design Patent from Patent Office.	Must be new, ornamental, and original.	3½, 7, or 14 years at option when patent is issued. Not renewable.	1. Idea becomes public property when patent expires. 2. Refers to design or appearance, not to construction or composition of product.
3. TRADE-MARK; SERVICE MARK; CERTIFICATION MARK (certifying origin, quality, etc.); COLLECTIVE MARK (showing membership in group)	Registration with Patent Office. (Trade-marks can be registered also in individual states.)	1. Must not resemble another mark, if confusion will arise. 2. Must not be primarily merely a surname. 3. Must not be merely descriptive or deceptively misdescriptive. See p. 187 for 8 more must-nots.	Perpetual if used. Registration, 20 years. Renewable for similar periods upon expiration.	1. A word may be a trade-mark. 2. A registered trade-mark may become incontestable after 5 years of undisputed use. 3. Registration is constructive notice of a claim of ownership. 4. The phrase "Reg. U.S. Pat. Off." or ® should appear.

4. TRADE NAME (name that applies to a business as a whole, and not to an individual product)	First user can restrain infringer in court on grounds of unfair competition.	Unfair practice involving use of trade name.	As long as name is used.	A trade-mark is not a trade name. "Wheaties" is a trade-mark; "General Mills" is a trade name, protected differently.
5. PERSONAL NAME	See Trade-Mark.			1. Poor trade-mark. 2. Can't be registered as trade-mark if primarily merely a surname. 3. Can't adopt name of living person without consent. 4. Name of deceased President requires widow's consent.
6. PACKAGE CONSTRUCTION	Patent.	See requirements for patenting Product (No. 1 above).	17 years, not renewable.	
7. PACKAGE DESIGN	1. Design patent. 2. Registration as trade-mark (sometimes possible). 3. Infringers can be restrained in court on grounds of unfair competition.	See requirements under Product (appearance) (No. 2 above).	3½, 7, or 14 years at option when patent is issued. Not renewable.	1. If a design of the package meets all the requirements of a trade-mark, it may be registered as a trade-mark. 2. If people, deceived by purposeful similarity in appearance between two products, buy the infringer's product thinking they are buying the original, this provides basis for court action . . . whether or not package design has been patented or registered.

HOW TO PROTECT IDEAS LEGALLY IN THE UNITED STATES—*Continued*

Idea	Special Method of Protection	Requirements for this Protection	Duration	Remarks
8. Package Insert (leaflet wrapped with product, but not attached to it)	Copyright.	See Copyright, at end of table.		Write to Register of Copyrights for application form.
9. Label	"	1. Must be an artistic or intellectual creation. 2. Must be attached to product or its container. 3. Must be descriptive of product. 4. For other requirements see Copyright, at end of table.	28 years, renewable once.	1. A label to be coypyrightable must be descriptive. 2. Must be attached to product.
10. Title of Periodical (as "The Saturday Evening Post")	Registration (as a trade-mark).	Title of the periodical is really its identifying device and is regarded as its trade-mark. See Trade-Mark (No. 3).	See Trade-Mark (No. 3 above).	
11. Title of Single Book (as novel or text book)	No special form of protection. Might be protected in court on grounds of unfair competition.			

	Regarding the Advertisement			
12. Publication Advertisements (as a whole)	Copyright.	See Copyright, at end of table.		Write to Register of Copyrights for application form.
13. Car Cards	"	"		Write to Register of Copyrights for application form.
14. Outdoor Posters	"	"		
15. Direct Mail (subject matter)	"	"		Write to Register of Copyrights for application form.
16. Direct Mail (special construction)	Patent.	See patent requirements under Product No. 1 above.	17 years, not renewable.	
17. Radio and Television Programs	Copyright.	See Copyright, at end of table.		Write to Register of Copyrights for application forms.
18. Title of Radio and Television Programs	Service mark may be a title. (See No. 3.)			
19. Slogan	A slogan cannot be copyrighted or registered.			
20. Illustrations	Copyright.	"		Write to Register of Copyrights for application form.
21. Copy	"	"		Write to Register of Copyrights for application form.
22. Radio—Television (commercial)	"	"		Write to Register of Copyrights for application form.

HOW TO PROTECT IDEAS LEGALLY IN THE UNITED STATES—*Concluded*

Idea	Special Method of Protection	Requirements for this Protection	Duration	Remarks
23. Merchandising idea, selling plan, advertising idea	No special way to protect such ideas in the abstract.			If the idea is sufficiently concrete, it may provide the basis of a contract with someone to pay for it *if it is original.*
24. Physical Material and forms for use in such plans as in No. 23 above	Copyright possible. Patent possible.	See Copyright, at end of table. See requirements for patenting under No. 1 above.		
25. Color	An advertiser cannot reserve the exclusive right to use a particular color, but he may register as his trademark an arbitrary combination of colors used with his label.			An advertiser may restrain another from imitating the color scheme, package design or label arrangement so as to be mistaken for his, on the ground of unfair competition.

COPYRIGHT	APPLICATION FORMS
1. Must be an artistic or intellectual creation. 2. In case of booklet, book, dramatic and musical composition, copyright notice *must* appear on title page or page following, and must read Copyright (or Copr.) 19.. by .... 3. In case of photographs and illustrations, or other works of art which may be defaced by above copyright notice, it may be abbreviated as follows, provided somewhere on print name appears in full: © (initials). 4. Duration, 28 years; renewable once. For Further Information Regarding trade-marks and patents, write Commissioner of Patents, Washington 25, D. C. Regarding copyrights, write to Register of Copyrights, Washington 25, D. C.	Write to Register of Copyrights for forms as follows: Class A — Books. Class B — Periodicals, newspapers (Form B) Class C — Lectures, addresses, for oral delivery Class D — Dramatic or dramatic-musical compositions Class E — Musical compositions. Class F — Maps. Class G — Works of art or their designs. Class H — Reproductions of works of art. Class I — Drawings of technical character Class J — Photographs. Class K — Prints and pictorial illustrations (Form K). Prints or labels used for merchandise (Form KK). Class L — Motion picture photoplays. Class M — Other motion pictures.

From Kleppner, "Advertising Procedure." New York: Prentice-Hall, Inc.

8. PRINTING AND TYPOGRAPHY

Printing processes. Of the three types of printing processes, (1) letterpress, (2) intaglio, and (3) lithography, the first two are most commonly used for advertising purposes.

Letterpress covers all types of printing from raised surfaces in which the type or design stands out in relief and comes in direct contact with the paper. In the intaglio process the printing surface is depressed, or etched, thus producing a raised impression on the paper. A common use of the intaglio process is in the printing of "engraved" visiting cards. Rotogravure is a form of intaglio printing in which the plate etching is done by a photochemical process.

Lithographic printing, sometimes called planographic printing, is printing from a plane surface, one which is neither intaglio nor relief. This type of process has three broad classifications: direct lithography, offset lithography, and photo-offset lithography. In *direct* lithography, the printing plate or surface comes in direct contact with the paper. In *offset*, or indirect, lithography, the printing plate or surface transfers its impression to an intermediary rubber roller, which in turn prints on the paper. *Photo offset* is merely an elaboration of this latter method, employing a photographic negative in preparing the printing plate.

Another process of photolithography is called *photolith*. It is used for reproducing short runs (small quantities) of simple black-and-white copy, including testimonial letters, sales bulletins, and pages for a sales manual. The process is inexpensive in small quantities and it is fast; but it does not reproduce photographic subjects sharply.

Because of the increased use of photo offset in recent years in the advertising field, the advantages and uses of this method are described more fully below.

Advantages of photo offset. The following advantages of the photo-offset process show why this method of printing has replaced letterpress work to a considerable extent in the advertising field:

1. Saves typesetting costs. Photo offset permits high-speed quantity reproduction of copy without the typesetting costs incurred by letterpress printing.

2. Saves storage space. Photo-offset plates do not require much storage room. It is standard practice among lithographers to keep plates for one year, particularly if these plates have half tones. Negatives are kept indefinitely.

3. Saves engraving costs. In the photo-offset process, screening is necessary only for half tones. Black-and-white drawings or illustrations are pasted on the copy page and photographed, without necessitating the extra time and expense of making engravings or line cuts.

4. Permits use of fancy-finish papers. Rippled, pebble stock, and other fancy-finish papers that are impractical in letterpress printing because the type impression does not fill in the paper crevices can be offset with perfect results. The rubber blanket of the offset press fills in the paper crevices and leaves a clean-cut type impression.

5. Permits enlargement or reduction of all sorts of copy, including type. Photo offset permits effects that could not be obtained without exorbitant expense by other printing processes. Copy can be reduced to miniature size and still be legible. An advertising agency reverses this process for an eye-catching sales letter. The typewritten letter is "blown up" to giant size and sent to prospects.

6. Permits tone and shade control of half tones. The offset process permits a control of printing shade and tone that is not possible in letterpress. Such control is particularly effective in the offset printing of half tones.

Uses of photo offset. The photo-offset process has become popular principally because of its expense-saving features and its adaptability to the forms of advertising used by large and small concerns. Broadsides, testimonials, letters, labels, package inserts, post cards, folders, and other types of mailing pieces have been printed effectively and cheaply by photo offset. By this process magazine and newspaper advertisements can be reproduced in direct-mail pieces such as folders and broadsides. Bulletins for salesmen, distributors, or consumers can be turned out in quantity inexpensively by this method.

Preparation of copy for photo offset. The one point to bear in mind when preparing copy that is to be photo offset is to lay it out *exactly* as it is to appear in the finished piece. If the copy is composed of previously printed illustrations and printed type matter (proofs or clipped pages), the copy can be mounted in exact proportion and printed in its original size or reduced or enlarged. If the illustrations are in varying colors or require reduction or enlargement, separate negatives will be required. In such a case the layout should indicate the exact size and position of the illustrations.

If typewritten copy is to be photographed, clean copy from a black ribbon will serve. However, it may be advisable to use a special carbon-paper ribbon in an electric typewriter, which provides an evenness in the weight of each stroke. If the copy is written in this manner on a sheet of paper backed up by a sheet of carbon paper, with the carbon side facing the back side of the sheet, the copy will have the greater density desirable for photographing.

How to plan a printing job. The businessman whose printing requirements are too small or too occasional to necessitate the employment of an advertising manager or an agency to handle the work will save time, money, and energy if he outlines the problem of buying printing as follows:

1. Determines what the printed job is to accomplish.
2. Determines the form it is to take.
3. Prepares the copy and artwork.

Step number one is the crystallization of the idea that a piece of printing is to fulfill a definite need, accomplish a definite purpose, or do a certain job better than anything else can do it. At this stage only the rough idea of the finished job is known.

Step number two requires an expert knowledge of printing—its possibilities and its limitations—or expert advice. This is the stage at which the format is decided; the stage at which the type, illustrations, colors, size, shape, paper, binding, and other details are settled. All this work should be done with the co-operation of the printer. A mistake too often made by the inexperienced is that of neglecting to call in the printer until after much of the work is done. Only the buyer who is thoroughly familiar with printing—who knows the printer's processes and tools—can eliminate this consultation with the printer or defer it until a later time.

The third and final step is the preparation of the copy and art work. This should always be the last step. The specifications of the finished job are now known, and the copy can be written to fit the allotted space, and the proper illustrations correctly made. To write the copy before knowing where it is to go often means rewriting, padding, or cutting, or changing the layout, to the detriment of the job in general. If the illustrations are prematurely made, they may fit haphazardly into the final plan, or new illustrations or alterations in the old ones may be necessary.

The new printing buyer who has never before dealt with printers may wonder about the choice of a printer to do the work. For the first job, the best choice is a printer of sound reputation for good work and service to the customer. Succeeding jobs may be taken to the same printer if he proves satisfactory, or the buyer may take his work to several printers and obtain competitive bids. He should be sure that where prices vary, the results will be the same. Giving business to a printer whose chief virtue is low prices is a questionable economy, since cheap printing is usually money wasted; good printing is not necessarily expensive printing, but poor printing is expensive at any price.

How type is set. The buyer of printing, and particularly the occasional buyer, ordinarily need not concern himself with the technical aspects of printing; such, for example, as the way in which the type is set in the printer's plant, the kind of machines used and the method of their operation, and so forth. However, the following very brief statement of how type is set may assist the new printing buyer to understand the printer's end of the work and some of the terms that he may use when talking to the customer.

Type used in printed matter is principally of two kinds:

1. Foundry type. 2. Machine type.

Foundry type is set by hand, in single letters, and is redistributed after the job is printed, to be used again. Display faces are commonly set in foundry type; for example, the headlines in advertisements, set in large type, are commonly foundry type. The body matter in expensive advertising pieces is also sometimes set in foundry type. Hand setting, it is usually considered, has finer points than machine setting; it is, however, considerably more expensive.

Machine type is cast by a machine and is re-melted after the job is done. Machine type is of two kinds:

1. Single types. 2. Slugs.

The monotype casts and sets single letters that are very similar to foundry type. Monotype is generally used in advertising pieces, where the columns of body matter are of irregular widths.

The linotype (or the intertype, a machine almost identical to the linotype) casts a line of type at a time, on a single slug. Linotype is generally used for extensive pieces of copy; a booklet, for example, would ordinarily be set on the linotype.

The monotype and the linotype are both operated from keyboards, roughly similar ot the keyboard on a typewriter.

Another machine, the typograph, is sometimes used. This machine, which may be used to set display faces, is not operated from a keyboard, but is manually operated.

Choosing a type face. Pages 216-220 illustrate some of the better known type faces. The characteristics of each are described briefly

This type is CASLON

THIS PARAGRAPH IS SET IN CASLON. An old proverb of typography is, "When in doubt, use Caslon." Caslon is warm and sympathetic, yet impersonal. It is one of the most serviceable of all types, one of the most easily read, and one of the most widely used. There are a number of varieties of Caslon; this is Caslon Old Style. *Caslon Old Style italic is illustrated by this sentence.*

This type is KENNERLEY

THIS PARAGRAPH IS SET IN KENNERLEY. Kennerley, like the Caslon Old Style face illustrated above, combines beauty of form with a high degree of legibility. And legibility is, of course, the primary consideration in the choice of a type face. Printed matter has but one function: it is meant to be read. *Kennerley italic is illustrated by this sentence.*

This type is GARAMOND

THIS PARAGRAPH IS SET IN GARAMOND. Garamond is one of the most useful and beautiful of type faces, and is one of the faces most frequently used by advertisers. Its grace and beauty make it suitable for use where the beauty of the product itself is one of the points featured in the advertisement. *Garamond italic also has a good appearance; the italic is illustrated by this sentence.*

This type is CLOISTER

THIS PARAGRAPH IS SET IN CLOISTER. As will be seen from this paragraph, Cloister sets a slightly darker page than either Caslon or Garamond. Cloister is a good type for the body matter of advertisements, and it also gives excellent results when used for display; its appearance in display may be judged from the line set in 24 point. *Cloister italic is illustrated by this sentence.*

This type is BODONI

THIS PARAGRAPH IS SET IN BODONI. The types previously illustrated — Caslon, Kennerley, Garamond, and Cloister — are all so-called Old Style faces. Bodoni is a so-called Modern face. Old Style types can be distinguished by their slanting serifs (serifs are the little bars or finishing strokes at the tops and bottoms of letters) and by their slight contrast between light and heavy strokes. Modern type faces have greater contrast between light and heavy strokes, and have precise but graceful lines. Bodoni comes in a number of varieties; this is Bodoni Book. The headline is set in Bodoni Bold. *Bodoni italic is illustrated by this sentence.*

This type is CENTURY

THIS PARAGRAPH IS SET IN CENTURY. Century, like Bodoni, is a Modern type face. It is not an especially good looking face, particularly in the larger sizes, but its legibility in the smaller sizes is to be recommended. Where it is necessary to fit a large message into a comparatively small space, Century is a good choice. *Century italic is illustrated by this sentence.*

This type is SCOTCH

THIS PARAGRAPH IS SET IN SCOTCH ROMAN. Scotch Roman may be considered a Modern face, although it has certain of the characteristics of Old Style faces. While it is not especially beautiful, Scotch Roman is a very legible, useful face for both display and text purposes. Its appearance in display may be judged from the line set in 24 point. *Scotch Roman italic is illustrated by this sentence.*

This type is FUTURA

THIS PARAGRAPH IS SET IN FUTURA. Futura is an example of a so-called Sans Serif face. Sans Serif faces have straight lines, with no contrast between light and heavy strokes, and they have no serifs. Sans Serif faces are popular because they strike a modern note. Futura may be used as either a body or a display type. However, although it is a good looking type, it is not very easily read, and hence should not be used except where only a few lines have to be set. Futura comes in a number of weights; this is Futura Medium. *Futura italic is illustrated by this sentence.*

This type is KABEL

THIS PARAGRAPH IS SET IN KABEL. Kabel, like the Futura type illustrated above, is a Sans Serif face. It has the modern styling of a streamlined automobile. As in the case of other Sans Serif faces, Kabel should be used sparingly. Kabel comes in a number of weights; this is Kabel light. *Kabel italic is illustrated by this sentence.*

This type is GIRDER

THIS PARAGRAPH IS SET IN GIRDER. Girder is an example of a so-called Square Serif face. Square Serif faces have simple, square serifs of the same weight as the type lines. Square Serif faces, like Sans Serif faces, create a modern atmosphere. Girder comes in a number of weights; this is Girder light.

beneath the illustrations. Each face is illustrated in two sizes, 24 point and 12 point leaded (see page 224). The number and variety of type faces seem endless and the novice is at a loss to know which type to choose for his particular work, but the illustrations in the preceding pages will dispel some of the mysteries associated with type faces and their uses.

The type faces illustrated in the preceding pages are only a few of the almost innumerable varieties available. However, the business-man who is not an expert in typography will do well to restrict his choice to one or other of the faces shown; he can then be reasonably sure that the results obtained will be satisfactory. Only the expert should attempt the striking or unusual.

The types shown are illustrated in only two sizes, but it should not be forgotten that a wide range of sizes is available (as illustrated in Figure 15). Also type of the same face and size can be set in capitals, in capitals and small capitals, in italic, and so on. Some of these variations are illustrated in Figure 16 on page 223.

THIS LINE IS SET IN CAPITALS (OR CAPS)

THIS LINE IS SET IN CAPS AND SMALL CAPS

THIS LINE IS SET IN SMALL CAPS

This Line is Set in Caps and Lower Case

this line is set in lower case

This line is set in italic

This line is set in boldface

Capitals are well suited to short headlines, but not to lines of body type. THIS SENTENCE IS AN ILLUSTRATION OF THE DIFFICULTY FOUND IN READING PRINTED MATTER THAT IS SET COMPLETELY IN CAPS; THE LINES OF TYPE ARE TOO EVEN, AND THERE IS TOO LITTLE TO CATCH THE EYE. In contrast, it is at once apparent that this sentence, set in lower case, is much easier to read.

Caps and small caps are suitable chiefly for subheadings; they are not sufficiently striking to serve as headlines. Italic type is graceful, but it, too, is not easily read; it is best to use italic sparingly. Boldface may be used for headlines or, when emphasis is desired, for short paragraphs of text matter or even for complete advertisements.

How type is measured. Type matter has its own peculiar system of measurement. Until recent times type sizes were known by names. Now a standard system, known as the point system, is used. There are approximately 72 points to the inch, and all type sizes are given in points. Sizes from 72 point down to 4 point are available; some of the more commonly used sizes are illustrated in Figure 15. Figure 16 shows the basic resemblance in the various members of a type "family."

Although the size of the type itself is indicated in points, the dimensions of the space which the type is to occupy (the length of the lines and the depth of the space) are not indicated in points but in

THE SIZE of

48 point

THE SIZE of ty

42 point

THE SIZE of type

36 point

THE SIZE of type

30 point

THE SIZE of type

24 point

THE SIZE of type

18 point

THE SIZE of type

14 point

THE SIZE of type

12 point

THE SIZE of type

10 point

THE SIZE of type

8 point

Figure 15. Common Type Sizes (Caslon Old Style).

From Kleppner, "Advertising Procedure." New York: Prentice-Hall, Inc.

A FAMILY OF TYPE

Caslon Old Style

A FAMILY OF TYPE

Caslon Old Style italic

A FAMILY OF TYPE

Caslon Bold

A FAMILY OF TYPE

Caslon Bold italic

A FAMILY OF TYPE

Caslon Condensed

A FAMILY OF TYPE

Caslon Shaded

a family of type

Caslon Old Style

a family of type

Caslon Old Style italic

a family of type

Caslon Bold

a family of type

Caslon Bold italic

a family of type

Caslon Condensed

a family of type

Caslon Shaded

Figure 16. A Family of Type.

From Kleppner, "Advertising Procedure." New York: Prentice-Hall, Inc.

picas. The pica (or pica em, as it is sometimes called) is $\frac{1}{6}$ of an inch, or 12 points. For example, this book is set 25×42 picas; that is, the pages are 25 picas wide and 42 picas deep. Since a pica is one-sixth of an inch, a page 25×42 picas is $4\frac{1}{6}$ inches wide and 7 inches deep.

In newspaper advertising still a third term, the agate line, is used. The agate line always means $\frac{1}{14}$ of an inch deep and one column wide. There are 14 agate lines in every inch of space, measured from the top of the page to the bottom, regardless of the number of printed lines actually set up within that space.

To summarize: there are 72 points to the inch, 6 picas to the inch, 14 agate lines to the inch.

Use of leading. By leading is meant space between the lines of type. If type is set without any space between the lines, it is said to be set solid. For the sake of appearance and legibility, it is generally advisable to insert space between the lines. The printer does this by inserting so-called leads, which are thin strips of metal separating the lines of type. Leading is specified in points. Figure 17 is an illus-

Leaded 1 point:

The citizen is inevitably nation-conscious nowadays, inevitably conscious, too, of the reaction of foreign and international events upon his purse and his larder, his home and his employment. Man is more and more identified with his country and its fortunes. Is there then a philosophy of international life in which patriotism—this identification of the man with his country—has its part?

Leaded 2 points:

The citizen is inevitably nation-conscious nowadays, inevitably conscious, too, of the reaction of foreign and international events upon his purse and his larder, his home and his employment. Man is more and more identified with his country and its fortunes. Is there then a philosophy of international life in which patriotism—this identification of the man with his country—has its part?

Figure 17. A Piece of Copy Leaded 1 Point, and the Same Piece of Copy Leaded 2 Points.

tration of the difference in appearance and legibility between a paragraph set leaded 1 point and a paragraph of the same type leaded 2 points (the type used is Electra, the face in which this book is set. The body type of this book is leaded 2 points).

The amount of lead that should be used depends upon a number of factors, such as the type face in which the copy is to be set, the size of type to be used, and the length of the lines. In general, small faces need less lead than large ones; light faces need less lead than heavy ones; and short lines need less lead than long ones. On the bottom of this page two tables are given that will be useful in this connection.

The first shows column widths for easy reading, and the second the amount of lead that it is advisable to use with various sizes of body types.

COLUMN WIDTHS FOR EASY READING

Size of Type	*Column Width, in Picas*
6	8 to 10
7	8 " 12
8	9 " 13
9	10 " 14
10	13 " 16
11	13 " 18
12	14 " 21
14	18 " 24
18	20 " 34

AMOUNT OF LEAD TO USE BETWEEN LINES OF BODY TYPE FOR EASY READING

Size of Type	*Minimum Lead*	*Maximum Lead*
6	Solid	1 Pt.
7	Solid	1 "
8	Solid	2 "
9	1 Pt.	2 "
10	1 "	4 "
11	1 "	4 "
12	2 "	6 "
14	3 "	8 "
18	4 "	8 "

Preparing copy for the printer. In the printing business the material that the printer is to set in type is referred to as the "copy." The copy sent to the printer should be carefully prepared. If the copy is "dirty"—if, for example, part is typewritten and part handwritten, or if the copy is interlined with changes, or if, in general, it is difficult to follow—the printer will take this into account in figuring his price for the job. Clean, neat copy, therefore, results in a saving to the customer.

All copy should be typewritten. Be sure, also, that your copy is correct. The printer makes a separate charge for all changes made on the proofs. Hence it pays to spend time in revising the copy before it is sent to the printer, rather than to rewrite it on the proofs.

Detailed specifications should always accompany the copy. The printer will want to know the dimensions (width and depth), the type face to be used, the type size, the leading, and any other details that may be required in a particular case. It often pays to prepare a layout, or sketch, for the printer; the layout will indicate exactly how the customer wants the finished job to appear.

Computation of space and copy-fitting. One of the necessary steps in the preparation of a piece of advertising for the printer is the computation of the space that a particular piece of copy will occupy, or the fitting of the copy to the amount of space available in the layout.

If the customer has consulted his printer early in the procedure, the layout and specifications are known before the copy is written; the type face and size are determined, and the problem is one of knowing how much copy to write. If the customer has already written his copy and does not want to change it, the problem is one of knowing how much space the copy will fill if it is set in a certain face and size, or of knowing what face and size to use in order to have the copy fit a certain area.

Copy fitting by word count. Given a certain amount of space and the size of type that is to be used, the approximate number of words can be found by the following method.

1. Reduce the dimensions of the space to points by multiplying the number of inches by 72 or the number of picas by 12. Thus, a space 4 inches, or 24 picas wide, is 288 points in width ($4 \times 72 =$

288, or $24 \times 12 = 288$). If the depth of the space is 6 inches, or 36 picas, the space is 432 points deep ($6 \times 72 = 432$, or $36 \times 12 = 432$).

2. The next step is to calculate the number of ems * of type in the space which, in step (1), was determined to be 288 points wide and 432 points deep. This is done by dividing the number of points in the width by the size of the type in points, dividing the number of points in the depth by the size of the type in points, and then multiplying the two figures obtained; the result is the number of ems of type in the space. Thus:

If the type to be used is 10 point:

$$288 \div 10 = 28.8, \text{ length}$$
$$432 \div 10 = 43.2, \text{ depth}$$
$$28.8 \times 43.2 = 1244.16, \text{ ems of type}$$

If the type to be used is 11 point:

$$288 \div 11 = 26.1, \text{ length}$$
$$432 \div 11 = 39.2, \text{ depth}$$
$$26.1 \times 39.2 = 1023.12, \text{ ems of type}$$

If the type to be used is 12 point:

$$288 \div 12 = 24, \text{ length}$$
$$432 \div 12 = 36, \text{ depth}$$
$$24 \times 36 = 864, \text{ ems of type}$$

If the type to be used is 14 point:

$$288 \div 14 = 20.5, \text{ length}$$
$$432 \div 14 = 30.8, \text{ depth}$$
$$20.5 \times 30.8 = 631.40, \text{ ems of type}$$

3. For convenient figuring, the average word is taken to be 3 ems in length. To complete the computation and find the number of words that will fill the given space, divide the number of ems in the space by 3:

In 10 point, $1244.16 \div 3 = 414.72$ words will fill the space
11 " $1023.12 \div 3 = 341$ " " " " "
12 " $864 \div 3 = 288$ " " " " "
14 " $631.4 \div 3 = 210.4$ " " " " "

The above computations are for type that is set *solid*—that is, with-

* The *em* is approximately the space occupied by the capital M in the size of type used.

out any extra space between the lines of type. When type is leaded, the space computation must take the leading into consideration. The leading has the effect of increasing the depth of the lines of type, but does not increase the width. Thus, if the type to be used is 12 point, and it is to be leaded 2 points, for the width the 12 point computation is used, but for the depth the type is considered to be 14 points. For example, assume that a space 4 inches (or 24 picas) wide, and 6 inches (or 36 picas) deep, is to be set in 12 point type leaded 2 points; then the number of words in the space is calculated as follows.

$$4 \text{ inches (or 24 picas)} = 288 \text{ points}$$
$$288 \div 12 = 24, \text{ width}$$
$$6 \text{ inches (or 36 picas)} = 432 \text{ points}$$
$$432 \div 14 = 30.8, \text{ depth}$$
$$24 \times 30.8 = 739.2, \text{ ems of type}$$
$$739.2 \div 3 = 246.4, \text{ words in space}$$

For the convenience of their customers, many printers prepare tables showing the number of words of type per square inch. Such a table is illustrated below. The figures are, of course, only approximate, and apply to the average type face.

To illustrate the use of the table, assume that a space 4 inches by 6 inches is to be set in 12 point type, solid. In this space there are $4 \times 6 = 24$ square inches. According to the table, there are 12 words to the square inch in 12 point type set solid; then the number of words that will fit the space is $24 \times 12 = 288$. According to the table, there are 11 words to the square inch in 12 point type leaded 2 points; hence, if the space 4 inches by 6 inches were to be set in 12 point type leaded 2 points, there would be $24 \times 11 = 264$ words.

NUMBER OF WORDS OF TYPE PER SQUARE INCH

Size of Type	*Set Solid*	*Leaded Two Points*
5	69	49
5½	55	45
6	48	37
7	36	27
8	30	23
9	25	20
10	20	15
11	15	12
12	12	11
14	10	9

Some printers go further, and, when preparing tables for the use of their customers, take into consideration the fact that the number of words per square inch varies with different type faces. The table given on this page is a portion of a table used by one printer to show the number of words per square inch for some of the more commonly used type faces.

NUMBER OF WORDS PER SQUARE INCH FOR VARIOUS TYPES

	6 Point	*8 Point*	*10 Point*	*12 Point*	*14 Point*
Bodoni	52	29	19	15	11
Bodoni Bold	48	26	17	13	10
Bookman	43	27	17	12	9
Caslon No. 471	53	36	23	15	11
Caslon No. 540	58	32	21	14	10
Cloister Old Style	53	32	22	15	13
Cloister Bold	45	30	20	14	11
Futura Light	—	32	22	15	12
Futura Medium	—	31	19	14	12
Futura Bold	—	28	17	11	8
Garamond Old Style	50	32	21	16	12
Garamond Bold	44	28	18	14	10

Copy fitting by character count. Word-count methods of copy fitting are not always accurate enough for careful work. Where exactness is necessary, the character-count method is preferable. As an illustration of the character-count method, assume that a space 3 inches by 4 inches is to be set in 11 point Caslon No. 540, leaded 1 point. How many lines of typewritten copy will be required to fill the space? The calculation is made as follows:

1. The printer will supply the customer with specimens of type faces, and, after the face to be used has been chosen, the customer can determine the average number of characters to an inch by counting the characters per inch in the specimen of the type chosen. The number of characters per linear inch for 11 point Caslon No. 540 is found to be 15; the number of characters in a line 3 inches long is, therefore, $15 \times 3 = 45$.

2. The next step is to find the number of lines in the depth. Since the type is 11 point leaded 1 and there are 72 points to the inch, there will be 6 lines in one inch and 24 lines in the space 4 inches deep $[(72 \div 12) \times 4 = 24]$.

3. The number of characters in the space 3 inches by 4 inches is now found by multiplying the number of characters per line by the number of lines; $45 \times 24 = 1080$.

4. A typewriter with pica type types 10 characters to an inch; a typewriter with elite type types 12 characters to an inch. Suppose that the typewriter has elite type, and that it is set to type lines 5 inches in length. Then the number of typewriter characters per line is $12 \times 5 = 60$.

5. The number of characters of 11 point Caslon No. 540 leaded 1 in the space 3 inches by 4 inches was found to be 1080. The number of typewriter characters per line was found to be 60. The number of typewriter lines, each 5 inches in length, which will be required to fill the space 3 inches by 4 inches is found by dividing 1080 by 60 ($1080 \div 60 = 18$). Hence the copywriter should write 18 lines of copy, 5 inches in length, to fill the space on the layout.

Many printers provide their customers with character-count tables, showing the number of characters per linear inch for various type faces. The following is a portion of a table of this kind.

CHARACTERS PER LINEAR INCH

	Size of Type				
Type Face	*10*	*11*	*12*	*14*	*18*
Bodoni	16	15	14	13	10
Caslon No. 540	16	15	13	10	9
Scotch Roman	17	16	13	11	8
Century	14	13	12	11	10
Cloister	20	18	17	16	12
Garamond	18	17	16	14	11

Always use the tables provided by the printer who is to do the work. If your printer has no such tables, reliable tables can be obtained from the Mergenthaler Linotype Company, Brooklyn, New York; the Intertype Corporation, Brooklyn, New York, or the Lanston Monotype Machine Company, Philadelphia, Pennsylvania.

Proofreader's marks. After the printer has set the copy, he submits a proof to the customer. Since the printer is not responsible for errors in the finished job unless they have been marked on the proof, the customer should read the proof with the utmost care. For convenience, a standard set of proofreader's marks is used to indicate the changes to be made; these marks are illustrated in Figures 18 and 19 on pages 232 and 233.

Illustrations. Illustrations are of two kinds: half tones and line cuts. The half tone is used to reproduce photographs and drawings that have gradations in tone between black and white. The half tone breaks the illustration into small dots, known as the screen, which by their comparative size render all the intermediate tones. Half tones can be made in many screens—that is, with various numbers of dots to a given area. The finer the screen, the more dots, and the truer the reproduction. Before you have your half tones made, it is wise to consult your engraver. He will advise you what screen to use in order to obtain the best possible results on your paper; the proper screen to use is determined by the paper to be used.

Line cuts reproduce only black lines. They are used for simple illustrations that have no intermediate shadings. However, a semblance of shades or tones can be introduced into line cuts by mechanical processes, such as the Ben Day, which adds patterns of dots or cross-hatchings to indicate the various gradations.

There are many variations of line cuts and half tones, each suited to certain kinds of jobs; nearly all are adaptable to color work. It is also possible to make combination plates—half tones and line cuts together. A number of different types of illustrations are shown in Figures 20-27, pages 234-237.

Paper. The small or occasional buyer of printing will seldom be confronted with the necessity of buying paper. The printer can recommend the proper paper to use and can secure it for the customer. Paper may be roughly divided into three classifications:

1. Writing. 2. Book. 3. Cover.

The chart on pages 238-241 summarizes much useful information with regard to each of these three types of paper.

Jobs are usually printed on large sheets, which are cut to the proper size after printing. Since paper comes in standard sizes, most of which are kept in stock by large paper houses, certain sizes for the finished job are more economical than others, as there is less waste in the cutting. Here, again, the advice of the printer is valuable. The tables on page 242 give recommended paper sizes for booklets and catalogues and recommended paper sizes for unstitched circulars.

∧	Make correction indicated in margin.
Stet	Retain crossed-out word or letter; let it stand.
• • • • Stet	Retain words under which dots appear; write "Stet" in margin.
×	Appears battered; examine.
═	Straighten lines.
√√√	Unevenly spaced; correct spacing.
//	Line up; i.e., make lines even with other matter.
run in	Make no break in the reading; no ¶
no ¶	No paragraph; sometimes written "run in."
out see copy	Here is an omission; see copy.
¶	Make a paragraph here.
tr	Transpose words or letters as indicated.
₰	Take out matter indicated; dele.
₰̂	Take out character indicated and close up.
¢	Line drawn through a cap means lower case.
6	Upside down; reverse.
⁐	Close up; no space.
#	Insert a space here.
⊥	Push down this space.
□	Indent line one em.
[	Move this to the left.
]	Move this to the right.

⌐¬	Raise to proper position.
└┘	Lower to proper position.
////	Hair space letters.
W.f.	Wrong font; change to proper font.
Qu?	Is this right?
l.c.	Put in lower case (small letters).
s.c.	Put in small capitals.
Caps	Put in capitals.
C+s.c.	Put in caps and small caps.
rom.	Change to Roman.
ital.	Change to Italic.
≡	Under letter or word means caps.
=	Under letter or word, small caps.
—	Under letter or word means Italic.
∿∿	Under letter or word. bold face.
,/	Insert comma.
;/	Insert semicolon.
:/	Insert colon.
⊙	Insert period.
/?/	Insert interrogation mark.
(!)	Insert exclamation mark.
/=/	Insert hyphen.
’∨	Insert apostrophe.
“∨ ”∨	Insert quotation marks.
∨	Insert superior letter or figure.
∧	Insert inferior letter or figure.
[/]	Insert brackets.
(/)	Insert parenthesis.
1/m	One-em dash.
2/m	Two-em parallel dash.

Figure 18. Proofreader's Marks.

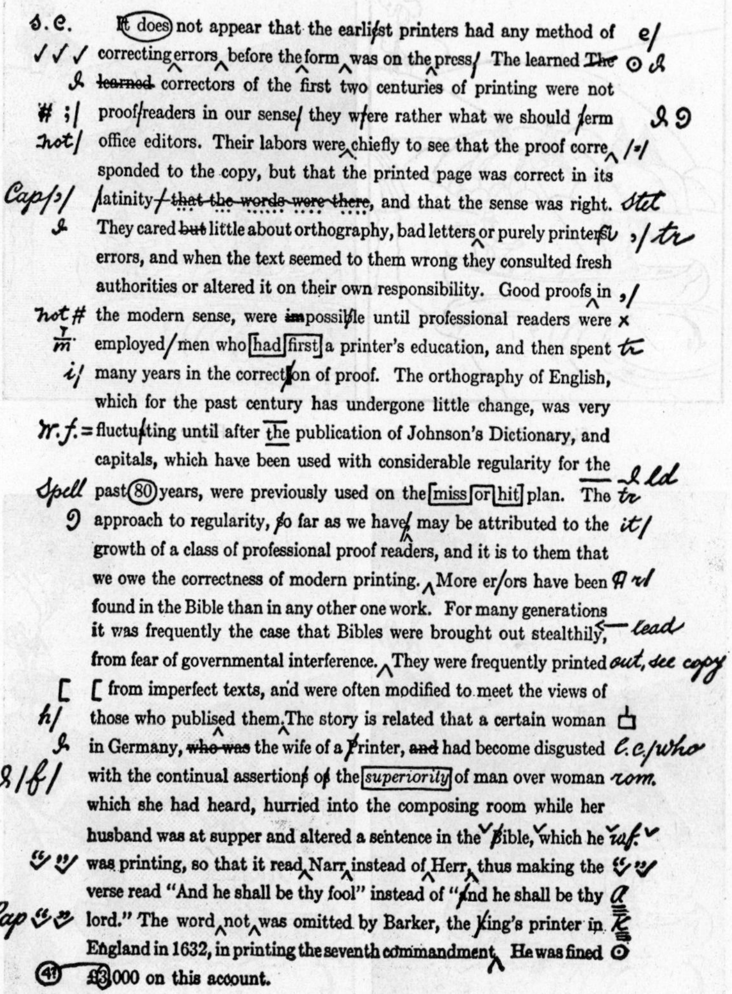

It does not appear that the earliest printers had any method of correcting errors before the form was on the press. The learned The learned correctors of the first two centuries of printing were not proof readers in our sense they were rather what we should term office editors. Their labors were chiefly to see that the proof corre sponded to the copy, but that the printed page was correct in its latinity that the words were there, and that the sense was right. They cared but little about orthography, bad letters or purely printers errors, and when the text seemed to them wrong they consulted fresh authorities or altered it on their own responsibility. Good proofs in the modern sense, were impossible until professional readers were employed men who had first a printer's education, and then spent many years in the correction of proof. The orthography of English, which for the past century has undergone little change, was very fluctuating until after the publication of Johnson's Dictionary, and capitals, which have been used with considerable regularity for the past 80 years, were previously used on the miss or hit plan. The approach to regularity, so far as we have may be attributed to the growth of a class of professional proof readers, and it is to them that we owe the correctness of modern printing. More errors have been found in the Bible than in any other one work. For many generations it was frequently the case that Bibles were brought out stealthily, from fear of governmental interference. They were frequently printed [from imperfect texts, and were often modified to meet the views of those who publised them.The story is related that a certain woman in Germany, who was the wife of a Printer, and had become disgusted with the continual assertions of the superiority of man over woman which she had heard, hurried into the composing room while her husband was at supper and altered a sentence in the Bible, which he was printing, so that it read Narr instead of Herr, thus making the verse read "And he shall be thy fool" instead of "and he shall be thy lord." The word not was omitted by Barker, the king's printer in England in 1632, in printing the seventh commandment He was fined £3,000 on this account.

Figure 19. A Piece of Corrected Proof.

Figure 20.

Figure 21.

Figure 22.

Figure 23.

Figure 20: Line Plate. The line plate (or line cut, as it is frequently called) is the simplest form of photoengraving. Note that there are no gradations of tone between black and white; shading can be suggested only by lines of various weights and by areas of solid black. A line plate cannot be made from a photograph, a painting, or a wash drawing; it can be made only from a drawing that consists of lines and of areas of solid black. The drawing from which this line plate was made was a pen-and-ink sketch. A line plate is the least expensive form of photoengraving and can be printed on even the roughest papers with good results.

Figure 21: Line Plate With Ben Day. The Ben Day process, named after the man who perfected it, adds life and sparkle to a line plate, and gives it some of the gradations of shading found in a half tone. Ben Day is available in various "screens"; a pattern book may be obtained from your engraver. In the line plate shown in Figure 21, five screens have been used; close study of the picture will reveal where the different screens were "laid on." Ben Day is a hand operation, and hence is expensive. Compare the line plate with Ben Day with the line plate illustrated in Figure 20 and with the square-finish half tone illustrated in Figure 22.

Figure 22: Square-Finish Half Tone. There are various kinds of half tones. The simplest is the so-called square-finish half tone. The term "square-finish" does not refer to the shape of the picture or to the shape of the plate, for a picture which is oval or circular may be reproduced as a square-finish half tone. The term refers to any half tone on which the screen covers the entire area. A square-finish half tone is the least expensive type. Comparison of Figure 22 with Figure 20 shows the obvious difference between a half tone and a line plate. The half tone has subtle gradations of shading between the black and white areas.

Figure 23: Half Tone Showing Screens. The term "screen" refers to the fact that when the picture is being photographed, a screen is placed in the camera in front of the plate. Screens are known by numbers; those most commonly used are 55, 60, 65, 85, 100, 110, 120, 133, 150. In Figure 23 three screens are illustrated; namely, 85, 55, and 110. The fineness of the screen affects the fidelity of the results obtained. The proper screen to use depends upon the quality of the paper on which the half tone is to be printed. Smooth-finish paper can "take" a fine-screened half tone; the coarser grades of paper require coarse-screened half tones.

Figure 24.

Figure 25.

Figure 26.

Figure 27.

Figure 24: Vignette Half Tone. The so-called vignette half tone, illustrated in Figure 24, shows the object against a background that fades away with soft, cloudlike effect. Vignette half tones can be used very effectively in advertisements or advertising literature, but paper of good quality, and first-class presswork, are required. On paper of the coarser grades, a vignette half tone tends to smudge rather than fade. Thus, a vignette half tone can seldom be employed in a newspaper; it can be used, however, in a magazine that is printed on good paper stock. A vignette half tone costs approximately 50 per cent more than a square-finish half tone.

Figure 25: Silhouette Half Tone. In the square-finish half tone illustrated in Figure 22, the screen covers the entire area of the picture. There are times, however, when a screen over the background is not desired. When all that is wanted is the object, a silhouette half tone (sometimes called an outline-finish half tone) may be ordered. In Figure 25, everything but the subject is cut away, and hence the background is pure white. A silhouette half tone has more character than a square-finish half tone; the objects silhouetted stand out clearly on the page. A silhouette half tone costs about 50 per cent more than a square-finish half tone.

Figure 26: Highlight Half Tone. A highlight half tone (also sometimes called a drop-out half tone) is one in which certain areas of the picture are highlighted or cut away. In the highlight half tone illustrated in Figure 26, the area around the fish is highlighted; so also is the fisherman's white shirt and a part of the sky in the background. When the half tone is made, the white areas in the original illustration are covered by the screen; the screen covering the areas that are to be highlighted is then tooled out by hand, and the areas so tooled are pure white. A highlight half tone is approximately three times as expensive as a square-finish half tone.

Figure 27: Surprint. It may be desired to combine a half tone and a line plate in a single engraving. This can be done in either of two ways. In a surprint, the line plate material (Fishing in Canada) is made to appear superimposed upon the half tone picture. In a so-called combination plate (see Figure 23) the line plate and the half tone adjoin each other. These figures could have been made square half tones, but the screen would then have covered the entire area, and the printed material would have been less legible. There is a slight extra charge for a surprint; a combination plate costs about twice as much as a square-finish half tone.

COMPARISON CHART OF PAPER STOCKS

including only the better known writing, book, and cover papers

Paper	Specification	Description	Photo-Engraving Recommended	Comments
WRITING Basic size: 17 x 22	Flat Writing.	This is the paper used in the making of inexpensive school writing tablets and notebooks. Better grades of it are used in correspondence stationery.	A. Line plates.	I. Not used extensively for advertising purposes. II. As the quality of a Flat Writing stock becomes better, it moves into the class of Bonds.
	Bonds.	Most letters received in the business office are on this stock. Its grades vary from that in which wood pulp and sulphite are used, to the better qualities made of linen rags. The weight in most common use is 20 lbs. (17 x 22-20).	A. Line plates. B. 100-screen halftones. C. Highlight halftones.	I. Bonds provide a large variety of tints. II. Some come in finishes such as "crash," simulating the cloth; also glazed. Most bonds come in a plain unglazed finish. III. Engraving plates for use on bonds should be etched deep.
	Ledger.	A very fine quality sheet of writing paper, used mostly for documents and accounting work. Has a tough, sturdy body, and a surface finish which has been plated (compressed between sheets of metal).	A. Line plates. B. 100-screen halftones.	I. Comes mostly in white and buff.

	LEDGER (*Cont.*)	Is heavier, as a class, than bonds; also more expensive. In its lighter weights it is also used for executive stationery.		
BOOK Basic size: 25 x 38	Newsstock.	Received its name from its use for newspapers. The least expensive of book papers and sometimes considered as a class by itself. Has a thin, porous body and a rough surface.	A. Line plates. B. 65-screen halftones, tooled well. C. Quarter tones.	I. Comes mostly in white (which varies in its tones). II. Qualities vary. Finish does not have to be specified.
	Antique.	A book paper whose body is of higher quality and heavier weight than that of news, but that likewise has a rough, uneven surface.	A. Line plates only.	I. Limited range of colors. II. Has a number of different finishes, as *eggshell, antique wove, antique laid.*
(*Cont.*)	Machine Finish. (M. F.)	The least expensive of the book papers which can take half tones dependably well. Represents an additional process through which antique paper goes. The stock is "sized," or immersed in chemicals, which fill up the pores, making the paper less absorbent. It is then "calendered" or ironed, the surface obtaining the smooth finish which permits the use of half tone. Sometimes known as "S. & C." (Sized and Calendered.)	A. 120-screen halftones.	I. Moderate range of colors. II. A very utilitarian paper. permits reproduction of wash drawings and photographs. Creases well. Especially good for booklets and catalogues to be issued in quantity.

COMPARISON CHART OF PAPER STOCKS—*Continued*

including only the better known writing, book, and cover papers

PAPER	SPECIFICATION	DESCRIPTION	PHOTO-ENGRAVING RECOMMENDED	COMMENTS
BOOK (*Cont.*)	English Finish.	A grade smoother than Machine Finish, but not as high as the one next described. For most purposes in which a halftone is to be used, this offers a serviceable, attractive stock.	A. 120-screen halftones	I. Moderate range of colors. II. Folds well. Can withstand fingering and usage. Good for leaflets and booklets, house organs, and moderately high-class catalogues.
	Sized and Super ("S.&.S.C."). Calendered	This is a machine-finished paper which has been "sized," like Machine Finish and English Finish, but that has been given an additional ironing. The surface is consequently glossy.	A. 133-screen halftones	I. Moderate range of colors. II. Folds well. Suited for uses similar to those of English Finish, when a more attractive effect is sought.
	Enamel Coated ("Coated").	The smoothest of book papers. This is a machine-finish paper that has been given a coating of clay and glue, then passed through the calender rolls at high speed. The result is a hard surface, dull, or glossy. Is brittle. Does not fold well. Otherwise shows reproductions to very best advantage.	A. 133, 150-screen halftones. Can take vignette finish.	I. Most expensive of the book papers. Looks good. Good for extra fine work. Cannot stand much fingering and usage.

COVER Basic size: 20 x 26	Antique.	This cover has a rough-surfaced finish. Antique cover is usually rougher than antique book.	A. Line plates.	I. Broad range of finishes, including *ripple linen, crash,* and many fancy-finish patterns. II. Good for folders, and for booklet covers.
	Plated.	The surface has been pressed, as in ledgers.	A. 120-screen halftones.	I. Good for booklet covers.
	Enamel Coated ("Coated").	A cover stock that has been given a treatment similar to book coated stock.	A. 133, 150, 175-screen halftones.	I. The acme of cover stocks in appearance.

From Kleppner, "Advertising Procedure." New York: Prentice-Hall, Inc.

RECOMMENDED PAPER SIZES FOR BOOKLETS AND CATALOGUES

This Page Size	In the Following Number of Pages	Cuts Economically Out of These Sheet Sizes
3 × 6	4, 8, 16, 24, 48	25 × 38—38 × 50
4 × 9	4, 6, 8, 16, 24, 48	25 × 38—38 × 50
4½ × 6	4, 8, 16, 32, 64	25 × 38—38 × 50
6 × 9⅛	4, 8, 16, 32	25 × 38—38 × 50
9¼ × 12⅛	4, 8, 16, 32	25 × 38—38 × 50
3½ × 6⅜	4, 8, 16, 24, 48	30½ × 41—41 × 61
5 × 7¼	4, 8, 16, 32, 64	30½ × 41—41 × 61
7⅜ × 9⅞	4, 8, 16, 32	30½ × 41—41 × 61
10 × 14⅞	4, 8, 16	30½ × 41—41 × 61
3¾ × 5⅛	4, 8, 16, 32, 64	32 × 44—44 × 64
3¾ × 6⅞	4, 8, 16, 24, 48	32 × 44—44 × 64
5¼ × 7⅝	4, 8, 16, 32, 64	32 × 44—44 × 64
7½ × 10⅝	4, 8, 16, 32	32 × 44—44 × 64
10¾ × 15⅝	4, 8, 16	32 × 44—44 × 64

RECOMMENDED PAPER SIZES FOR UNSTITCHED CIRCULARS

This Page Size	In the Following Number of Pages	Cuts Economically Out of These Sheet Sizes
3⅛ × 6¼	4, 6, 8, 12, 16, 24	25 × 38—38 × 50
4⅛ × 9½	4, 6, 12, 16, 24	25 × 38—38 × 50
4¾ × 6¼	4, 8, 16, 32	25 × 38—38 × 50
6¼ × 9½	4, 8, 16, 32	25 × 38—38 × 50
9½ × 12½	4, 8, 16, 32	25 × 38—38 × 50
3¾ × 6¾	4, 6, 8, 12, 16, 24	30½ × 41—41 × 61
5⅛ × 7⅝	4, 8, 16, 32	30½ × 41—41 × 61
7⅝ × 10¼	4, 8, 16, 32	30½ × 41—41 × 61
10¼ × 15 ¼	4, 8, 16	30½ × 41—41 × 61
4 × 5½	4, 8, 16	32 × 44—44 × 64
4 × 7¼	4, 8, 16, 24	32 × 44—44 × 64
5½ × 8	4, 8, 16, 32	32 × 44—44 × 64
8 × 11	4, 8, 16, 32	32 × 44—44 × 64
11 × 16	4, 8, 16	32 × 44—44 × 64

9. GLOSSARY OF ADVERTISING PROCEDURE

From Kleppner, "Advertising Procedure." New York: Prentice-Hall, Inc.

The following is a list of selected advertising terms with definitions drawn from authoritative sources or based upon general acceptance. In many instances this glossary does not confine itself to a definition of a term, but indicates the practices connected with it as well.

A.A.A.A. The 4 As. American Association of Advertising Agencies. The national organization of advertising agencies.

A.A.W. The Advertising Association of the West. An organization of West Coast advertising groups.

A.B.C. Audit Bureau of Circulations. The organization sponsored by publishers, agencies, and advertisers for securing accurate circulation statements.

A.B.P. Associated Business Publications, an organization of trade, industrial and professional papers.

A.C.A. American Communications Association.

Account executive. That member of an advertising agency staff who directs the handling of a client's advertising. He serves as the liaison man between the agency and the advertiser—one of the highest positions in an agency. Known also as *contact man.*

Acetate. Incorrect name for cellulose-nitrate for a radio recording disc.

Across the board. Scheduling a radio or television program at the same time on at least five consecutive weekdays, usually starting Monday.

Adjacencies. The programs on the same radio or television station immediately preceding and following the one under consideration.

Ad lib. To extemporize lines not written into the script, or music not in the musical score. Music or lines so delivered.

Advertising agency. A professional organization rendering advertising service to two or more clients.

Advertising Council. The joint body of the A.A.A.A. and the A.N.A., through which public-service projects are developed and channeled to advertisers for their support.

Advertising Research Foundation. A joint body created by the A.A.A.A. and the A.N.A., devoted to media research.

A.F.A. Advertising Federation of America, a federation of member divisions representing different advertising activities.

Affiliate. An independent radio station that carries programs provided by a network.

A.F.M. American Federation of Musicians.

A.F.R.A. American Federation of Radio Artists.

Agate line. A unit measurement of publication advertising space, one column wide (no matter what the column width) and one-fourteenth of an inch deep.

Agent. (1) Same as advertising agency. (2) A representative of radio performers or commercial artists who makes business contracts for them with advertisers or advertising agencies.

Aided-recall method. A method used in testing memory of advertisements. Some clue, such as the campaign theme, is given that may assist in recalling the brand name.

Allocation. The assignment of frequency and power made by the Federal Communications Commission to a broadcasting station.

Amplitude Modulation (A.M.). The method of transmitting sound by varying the *size* of the electro-magnetic wave, in contrast to varying its *frequency* (F.M.). Also called *Standard Broadcasting.*

A.N.A. Association of National Advertisers.

Animation. Can refer to animated cartoons or to animated objects, like packages or marionettes. May be limited animation on silent films only, or regular animation with a sound track, a costly process.

Announcement. A short advertising message in a radio or television broadcast; a brief commercial. *Straight announcement*, usually about 100 words, runs about one minute; *spot announcement*, about 50 to 75 words; *station break*, 20- to 30-word statements in the pause between programs; *cut in*, usually a local announcement inserted into a network program; *participating* announcement, usually 100 to 150 words incorporated into a local entertainment or informative program containing announcements of other participating advertisers.

Announcer. The member of a radio or television station staff assigned the duty of introducing and describing program features to the radio audience.

A.N.P.A. American Newspaper Publishers' Association, the major trade association of daily and Sunday newspaper publishers.

Antique-finish paper. Book or cover paper that has a rough, uneven surface. It can reproduce illustrations from line plates but not from half tones.

Appeal. Asking the prospect for a decision in favor of the advertiser's product or service; usually by a plea to a desire that will be satisfied by the benefit bestowed by the advertised product or service.

Applause mail. Letters of comment or appreciation received by radio stations or sponsors from the listening audience; fan mail.

Area sampling. See *sampling.*

A.S.C.A.P. American Society of Composers, Authors, and Publishers. An organization that protects the copyrights of its members and collects royalties in their behalf.

Ascending letters. Those with a stroke or line going higher than the body of the letter—*b, d, f, h, k, l,* and *t*—and all capitals. The *descending* letters are *g, j, p, q,* and *y.*

Aspect ratio. The numerical ratio of the television frame width to the frame height, 4:3.

Association test. A method of measuring the degree to which people are familiar with brand names. A commodity is mentioned, and respondents are asked to tell which brand name comes to mind first. Can also be conducted for trade-mark design, slogan, package, layout.

Audience composition. The number and kinds of people listening to a radio or television program, classified by their age, sex, income, and the like.

Audience flow. The statistical composition of the total audience of a specific radio program showing: the fractions of the whole (a) "inherited" from the same station's previous program, (b) transferred from another station, and (c) tuned in for the first time.

Audience participation show. A radio program in which the studio audience takes part—especially quiz shows and the like.

Audience turnover. The total number of different listeners to a given radio or television program over a specific number of consecutive broadcasts; or the rate at which a program increases its audience of different listeners over a given span of performances.

Audimeter. An electromechanical device patented by Nielsen attached to home radio receivers that records set operation and station tuning; its records supply the data for the Nielsen Radio Index.

Audition. A tryout of artists or musicians or programs under broadcasting conditions.

Author's corrections, author's alterations. (Abbreviated *a.a.*) Alterations or changes made in proofs (called *author's proofs*) not due to printer's errors and so chargeable to whoever is paying for composition. Unnecessary expense for this item can be reduced by careful editing of copy before it is sent to the printer.

Background. A broadcasting sound effect, musical or otherwise, used behind the dialogue or other program elements for realistic or emotional effect.

Backing up. Printing the second side of a sheet as a separate process. In fine printing it is necessary for the ink to dry on one side of the sheet before the other side is printed.

Balance. The placing of instruments, voices, or sound effects in relation to each other and to the microphone to produce the best tonal or dramatic effect.

Balloons. A visualizing device with the words of a person pictured coming right from his mouth; borrowed from the newspaper comic pages.

Balopticon (balops). A type of television animation made possible through the use of a Balopticon machine.

Basic network. The minimum grouping of stations for which an advertiser must contract in order to use the facilities of a radio or television network.

Basic weight. The weight of a ream of paper if cut to the standard or basic size for that class of paper. The basic sizes are: writing papers, 17 × 22 inches; book papers, 25 × 38 inches; cover stocks, 20 × 26 inches.

Batter. Type injured or broken in a form or the damaged part of a printing plate.

Bearers. (1) Excess metal left on an engraving to protect and strengthen it during the process of electrotyping. (2) strips of metal placed at the sides of a type form for protection during electrotyping.

Bed. The part of a printing press upon which the type or form is placed.

Ben Day process. The process invented by Benjamin Day whereby an engraver can produce mechanically a great variety of shaded tints and mottled effects in line plates.

Billboard. (1) A poster panel for outdoor advertising. (2) The announcement at the beginning of a broadcast which lists the people starred or featured.

Billboard commercial. A television commercial that appears briefly before a television viewer in the form of a poster.

Billing. (1) Amount of business done by an advertising agency. (2) Name credit of talent on the air in order of importance.

Bit. A small part in a dramatic program is a *bit* part, and the performer who plays it is a *bit* player.

Bite. The depth of the etch attained in engraving by each separate application of the etching acid.

Bleeding. Printed matter trimmed so that the type or plates run over the edges of a sheet and the illustration as printed has no margin but runs to the edge of the paper.

Block. (1) A set of consecutive time periods on the air; or a strip of the same time on several days. (2) Wood or metal base on which the printing plate is mounted. (3) British term for photoengraving or electrotype.

Blow-up. Photo enlargement of written, printed, or pictorial materials, as of a publication advertisement to be used as a poster or transmitted through television.

Blueprint. A quick, low-price photographic print, in white on a dark blue background that enables the advertiser to prepare a type layout while the engraving is still being made.

B.M.B. Broadcasting Measuring Bureau, cooperative organization to measure audiences of radio stations and networks.

B.M.I. Broadcast Music, Inc. Chief function: to provide music to radio and television shows with minimum royalty fees, if any.

Body type. The type commonly used for reading matter, as distinguished from *display* type used in the headlines of advertisements. Usually type 14 points in size, or smaller.

Bogus work. Newspaper or other compositors' resetting of advertisements for which the publication has received complete mats or plates; required by union contracts. The resetting is not used.

Boiler plate. Pages in stereotype supplied by news agencies or other syndicates to country weeklies to cut their costs of composition. Also called *patent insides.* These pages often include news and advertisements. Boiler plate originally meant any thin metal sheet.

Boldface type. A heavy line type, for example, the headings in these definitions.

Bond paper. The writing paper most frequently used in commercial correspondence, originally a durable quality used for printing bonds and other securities. The weight in most extensive use for letterheads is 20 lb. (17 × 22-20).

Book paper. A paper used in printing books, as well as for lightweight leaflets and folders, distinguished from *writing papers* and *cover stocks.* Basic size, 25 × 38.

Box-top offers. An invitation to the consumer to get a gift or premium by sending in the label or box top from a package of the product (with or without an additional payment).

Brand. A product sold under a trade-mark, grade-mark, or quality mark.

Brand name. The spoken trade-mark, a part of a trade-mark, in contrast to the pictorial mark; a trade-mark word.

Bridge. Music or sound effect cue linking two scenes in a radio show.

Brightness control. Control knob on the television receiver that varies the amount of illumination of the reproduced image.

Broadcast spectrum. That part of the range of frequencies of electromagnetic waves assigned to broadcasting stations.

Brochure. A fancy booklet or monograph.

Bugs. Cause of trouble in broadcasting equipment that is working imperfectly.

Bulldog edition. That edition of a morning paper that is printed early the preceding evening and sent to out-of-town readers on the night trains. If an advertiser does not get his copy in early, he misses this edition.

Burnishing (engraving). The mechanical act of making the dark areas in a half tone appear still darker. It is accomplished by smoothing over the dots in a half tone with a tool which causes those dots to spread and fill up the areas between them.

Buying space. Buying the right to insert an advertisement in a given medium, such as a periodical, a program, or an outdoor sign; *buying time* is the corresponding term for purchase of radio or television broadcast privilege.

Bye-bye. The radio script line beginning: "We now leave our studio . . ."; or "We now take you to . . ."; "We return you to . . ."; and the like.

Calendered paper. A paper with a smooth, burnished surface, secured by passing the paper between heavy rolls, called calenders.

Call letters. The combination of letters assigned by the Federal Communications Commission to a broadcasting or other radio station, which serves as its official designation and establishes its identity, as WJZ, WOR, KGN.

Camera light. Pilot light on television cameras indicating which camera is on the air.

Camera lucida. Familiarly *lucy.* An optical device having a prism that enables the eye to bring an original to be copied into focus with the drawing paper on which it is to be copied. A phantom image of both in one plane permits tracing the image in different scale for reduction or enlargement.

Caption. The heading of a chapter, section, or page; the descriptive matter accompanying an illustration.

Carbro. A photographic process for color printing on paper from separation negatives. Prints on yellow, red, and blue sensitized *car*bon tissue are made by contact with special *bro*mide prints from the separation negative. (Hence the name *carbro.*) After development the three separate color prints are transferred in register to a permanent support.

Casting off. Estimating the amount of space a piece of copy will occupy when set in type of a given size.

C.C.A. Controlled Circulation Audit. The organized official statement of circulations of publications (usually trade papers) that are given away, in contrast to publications with paid circulations that qualify under the Audit Bureau of Circulations.

Centering control. The knob on a television receiver for properly framing the picture on the television screen.

Center spread. The space occupied by an advertisement on the two facing center pages of a publication. The two pages will always be a continuous sheet, so that printing is better and reading is easier than on other kinds of double-page spreads. Often it is possible to print such an advertisement without losing the space usually taken up by the center margins or gutters.

Chain. (1) A group of advertising agencies that cooperate, although they are owned individually. (2) A group of retail outlets with the same ownership, management, and business policy. (3) A regularly established system of radio stations interconnected by high-grade wire telephone circuits over which program features are distributed for simultaneous broadcasting through the associated stations. (4) A network of television stations.

Channel. A band of radio frequencies assigned to a given radio or television station.

Chase. The iron or steel frame in which the type is locked up for the press or to make plates.

Checking copy. A copy of a publication sent to an advertiser or to his agency so that he may see that his advertisement appears as specified.

Class A rates. Rates for the most costly radio or television time, usually between 6 P.M. and 11 P.M., are called Class A rates; the next most costly are Class B, and so on. Each station sets its own rules for rate classification.

Clear. To obtain legal permission from responsible sources to use a photograph or quotation in an advertisement or to use a certain musical selection in a broadcast. To *clear time* is to arrange with a station to provide time for a commercial program.

Clear-channel station. A radio station that is allowed the maximum power is given a channel on the frequency band all to itself, with possibly one or two sectional or local stations far removed from it, so as not to interfere. (See *Local-channel station; Regional-channel station.*)

Closing date; closing hour. (1) The day or hour when all copy and plates must be in the publisher's hands if the advertisement is to appear in a given issue. The closing time is specified by the publisher. If proof is to be seen, all material has to be in when *first forms close*. (2) The last hour or day that a radio program or announcement may be submitted for approval to a station or network management to be included in the station's schedule.

Clubbing offer. An arrangement whereby subscriptions to two or more different publications are offered at a reduced combination price. Considered in judging the character of the circulation of a publication.

Coarse-screen half tone. A half tone with a comparatively low, or coarse, screen; usually 60, 65, or 85 lines to the inch.

Coated paper. A paper to which a coating has been applied, giving it a smooth, hard finish, suitable for the reproduction of fine half tones.

Coaxial cable (television). A special metallic cable size for transmitting the visible part of a telecast.

Coined word. An original and arbitrary combination of syllables forming a word for which the advertiser prescribes the meaning. Extensively used for trade-marks, as *Kodak, Gro-Pup, Zerone, Ami-dent.*

Color proof. Combined impressions from separate color plates.

Column-inch. A unit of measure in a periodical one inch deep and one column wide, whatever the width of the column.

Combination plate. A half tone and line plate in one engraving.

Combination rate. (1) A special space rate for two papers, such as a morning paper and an evening paper, owned by the same publisher. Applies also to any other special rate granted in connection with two or more periodicals. A *forced* combination is the rate for two or more papers in which space cannot be bought separately—with no rate but the combination rate. (2) The rate paid for a combination plate.

Comic strip. A series of cartoon or caricature drawings.

"Coming up." The cue given by the director or engineer of a program warning the cast that in 10 seconds the program will go on the air.

Commercial program. A sponsored program from which radio broadcasting stations derive revenue on the basis of the time consumed in broadcasting it.

Competitive stage. The advertising stage a product reaches when its general usefulness is recognized, but its individual superiority over similar brands has to be established in order that it shall secure the preference. (Compare *Pioneering stage; Retentive stage.* See *Spiral.*)

Composition. Typesetting.

Comprehensive. A layout accurate for size, color scheme, and other necessary details.

Consumer advertising. Advertising directed to those people who will personally use the product, in contrast to trade advertising, industrial advertising, professional advertising.

Consumer goods. Products that directly satisfy human wants or desires, like food and clothing; also products sold to an individual or family for use without further processing; as distinct from *industrial goods.*

Continuity. A written radio script including spoken lines and cues for musical numbers used by artists and directors in rehearsing and presenting radio features.

Continuous tone. Shading in a negative that is not formed by screen dots.

Contract year. The period of time, in space contracts, running for one year beginning with the insertion of the first advertisement under that contract. It is usually specified that the first advertisement shall appear within thirty days of the signing of the contract.

Convenience goods. Those consumer goods that are bought frequently at near-by (convenient) outlets without comparing prices, styles, qualities; as distinct from *shopping goods.*

Conversion table. Table showing what the equivalent weight of paper stock of a given size would be if the sheet were cut to another size.

Cooperative advertising. (1) Joint promotion through a trade association for firms in a single industry. (2) Joint promotion of a national advertiser (manufacturer) and local retail outlet in behalf of the manufacturer's product on sale in the retail store.

Cooperative program. A radio network program sponsored in each station area by a local advertiser who usually pays for the time at local rates and shares the cost of talent pro rata.

Copy. (1) The text of an advertisement. (2) Matter for a compositor to set. (3) Illustrations for an engraver to reproduce. (4) Any material to be used in the production of a publication.

Copy approach. The method of opening the text of an advertisement.

Copyholder. An assistant who reads copy aloud to the proofreader (word for word, capitals, initials, and punctuation marks), who reads and corrects the proof itself.

Copyright. Legal protection afforded an original intellectual effort. Application blanks are procurable from the Copyright Office, Library of Congress, Washington, D. C.

Copy writer. A person who creates the text of advertisements and often the idea to be visualized as well.

Cover. The front cover of a publication is known as the *first cover;* the inside of the front cover is the *second cover;* the inside of the back cover is the *third cover;* the outside of the back cover is the *fourth cover.* Extra rates are charged for cover positions.

Coverage. (1) The portion of an area, community, or group reached by an advertising medium. (2) The area in which a radio station or network of stations *can* be heard according to engineering standards; or the portion of the area that the station or network reaches most effectively.

Cover stock. A paper made of heavy, strong fiber; used for folders and for booklet covers. Some cover stocks run into the low weights of paper known as *book paper,* but most cover stocks are heavier. Basic size 20 × 26 in.

Crash finish. A surface design on paper, simulating the appearance of rough cloth.

Cream plan. The tactics of directing the advertising to the most potential class of buyers first, then to the next best market, and so on, "taking the cream off first." Used in selling specialties. (Compare *Zone plan; National plan.*)

Cropping. Trimming part of an illustration to enable the reproduction to fit into a specific space. Cropping is done either to eliminate nonessenti background in an illustration or t change the proportions of the illustra tion to the desired length and widt

CU. Close-up (in television).

Cue. (1) The closing words of a radi actor's speech and a signal for an other actor to enter. (2) A soun musical or otherwise, or a manua signal calling for action or proceedin (3) A phrase designating the transfe of the point of program origin; or, a in the case of network identifications a line such as, "This is the Columbi Broadcasting System," "This is th National Broadcasting Company," "This is the Mutual Broadcastin System," as a signal to radio and tele phone operators for switching chan nels.

Cue sheet. An orderly tabulation o radio program routine containing al cues.

Cut. A photoengraving, electrotype, o stereotype; derived from the term *woodcut.* In England called a *block.*

Cut. (1) To stop transmission or any part of the radio or television program abruptly, either by stopping performers or by use of an electrical switch on the control board. (2) The deletion of program material to fit a prescribed period of time.

Cut-out. A window or store counter sign with a design literally cut out of it.

Cylinder press. A press with a rotating cylinder under which a flat bed containing type or plates slides forward and backward. Used for large-quantity work, or for advertisements of large size.

Dead metal. Excess metal left on an engraved plate for protection during electrotyping. Such metal portions are sometimes called bearers.

ealer imprint. The name and address of the dealer, printed or pasted on an advertisement of a national advertiser. In the planning of direct mail, space is frequently left for the dealer imprint.

ecalcomania. A transparent gelatinous film bearing an advertisement, which may be gummed onto the dealer's window. Also known as *transparency*.

eckle edge. The untrimmed ragged edge of a sheet of paper.

efinition. Clean-cut radio and television transmission and reception.

elete. "Omit." Used in proofreading.

epth of columns. The dimension of a column space measured from top of the page to the bottom, in agate lines, or in inches.

Die-cut. An odd-shaped paper or cardboard for a direct-mail piece or for display purposes, cut with a special knife-edge die.

Direct advertising. Any form of advertising reproduced in quantity by or for the advertiser and issued by him or under his direction directly to definite and specific prospects by means of the mails, canvassers, salesmen, dealers, or otherwise—as through letters, leaflets, folders, or booklets.

Direct half tone. A superior type of half tone made by photographing an object itself instead of a picture of it.

Direct-mail advertising. That form of direct advertising sent through the mails.

Director. (1) The person who writes or rewrites, then casts and rehearses, a radio program, and directs the actual air performance. (2) Head of an agency art department or of a manufacturer's advertising department.

Direct process. In two-, three-, and four-color process work, color separation and screen negative made simultaneously on the same photographic plate.

Direct-view receiver. A type of television receiver in which the picture is viewed directly on the face of the cathode-ray tube.

Disc. Electrical recording on an 8-to-10-inch platter for use in broadcasting.

Disc jockey. The master of ceremonies of a radio program of transcribed music (records).

Display. Attention-attracting quality. (1) *Display type* uses sizes larger than 14 point. Italics, boldface, and sometimes capitals are used for display; so are hand-drawn letters and script. (2) *Display advertisements* are set in different type sizes and styles, with varying line widths, various leading between lines, considerable white space, and sometimes illustrations. Newspaper space rates distinguish between *display* and *undisplay*, the latter being set in one size type. *Display* space in newspapers usually is not sold in units of less than 14 column lines; there is no such minimum requirement for *undisplay* classified advertisements. A *display order* from a department store to a newspaper requires the newspaper to set up an advertisement according to layout and instructions furnished and to supply the store with proofs; sometimes called a *wait order*, since it does not authorize insertion of the advertisement. (3) *Window display, interior display*, and *counter display* are different methods of advertising by showing the actual goods to be promoted. *Open* display puts the goods where they can be actually handled and examined by the customer; *closed display* has the goods in cases and under glass. (See *Traveling display*.)

Dissolve. The overlapping of an image produced by one camera over that of another, and the gradual elimination of the first image.

Dolly. A mobile truck on which the television or moving-picture camera is mounted.

Double-decker. Outdoor advertising that stands erected one above another.

Double-leaded. See *Leading.*

Double-page spread or double truck. Two facing pages; called a center spread if the pages are in the center of a publication.

"Down-and-under." A direction given to a musician or sound effects man playing solo in a broadcast to quiet down from his present playing level to play under the lines of dialogue that follow.

Drop-out half tone. See *Half tone.*

Dry-brush drawing. A drawing made with a brush using ink or paint extra thick and dry.

Dubbing. Recording made by re-recording from one or more records.

Dubbing in. The addition of one television film to another; as, for example, the part containing the advertiser's commercial to the part that carries the straight entertainment.

Dummy. (1) Blank sheets of paper cut and folded to the size of a proposed leaflet, folder, booklet, or book, to indicate weight, shape, size, and general appearance. On the pages of the dummy the layouts can be drawn. Useful in designing direct-mail advertisements. A dummy may also be made from the proof furnished by the printer. (2) An empty package or carton, used for display purposes.

Duotone. An ink that on drying gives the printed page the appearance of having been printed in two colors.

Duplicate plates. Photoengravings made from the same negative as an original plate.

Ears of newspaper. The boxes or announcements at the top of the front page, alongside the name of the paper, in the upper right- and left-hand corners. Sold for advertising space by some papers.

Electrical transcription. A form of high-fidelity recording made especially for broadcasting and allied purposes; its surface noise is very low.

Electric spectaculars. Outdoor advertisements in which electric lights are used to form the words and design. Not to be confused with illuminated *posters* or illuminated *painted bulletins.* Space on electric spectaculars is sold by the individual stand.

Electrotype. A metal facsimile of another plate made by the electrotype process. When several identical plates of a reproduction are required one original can be made, and electrotypes can be made from that. Electrotypes cost less than original plates. They are made from a wax mold unless otherwise specified; a lead mold is more costly. Sometimes faced with steel for long runs.

Em. The square of a body of any given type face, the letter *M* being as wide as it is high. Usually short for *pica em.*

Enameled paper; enamel-coated stock. A book or cover paper that can take the highest-screen half tone. It is covered with a coating of china clay and a binder, then ironed under high-speed rollers. This gives it a hard, smooth finish too brittle to fold well. Made also in dull and semidull finish.

English finish (E.F.). A hard, even, and unpolished finish applied to book papers.

Engraving. Cutting a design (picture or type) in hard metal. The printing plate thus made now usually has a raised (not incised) surface. The impression from such a plate also is called an engraving.

Equivalent weight of paper. The weight of a given paper stock in terms of its basic weight.

Ethical advertising. (1) Advertising that comports with the standard of equitable, fair, and honest content. (2) Advertising of a preparation addressed to physicians only, in contrast to advertising a similar product addressed to the general public.

Extended covers. A cover that is slightly wider and longer than the pages of a paper-bound booklet or catalogue; one that extends or hangs over the inside pages. Also called *overhang* and *overlap*. (See *Trimmed flush*.)

Face. (1) The printing surface of type or a plate. (2) The style of type.

Facing text matter. The position of an advertisement in a periodical opposite reading matter.

Facsimile broadcasting. A process of transmitting and receiving by radio such graphic material as pictures and printed matter.

Fade. To diminish or increase the volume of sound on a radio broadcast. *Cross-fading* is gradually increasing volume of sound from one source while gradually decreasing the volume of sound from another source—*fading in* one sound while *fading out* the other. In television, *fading in* is the gradual appearance of the screen image brightening from black to full visibility.

Fading. The variation in the intensity of a radio or television signal received over a great distance, arising from transmission conditions.

Fading area. The area in which a broadcasting station suffers from the widest variations in fading, usually extending from fifty to seventy-five miles beyond the transmitter to points three or four hundred miles distant.

Family of type. Type faces related in design, as Caslon Bold, Caslon Old Style, Caslon Bold Italics, Caslon Old Style Italics.

Fanfare. A few bars of music (usually trumpets) to herald an entrance or announcement in broadcasting.

F.C.C. Federal Communications Commission, the Federal authority empowered to license radio stations and to assign wave lengths to stations "in the public interest."

Field intensity contour map. A map upon which field intensities delivered by a broadcasting station are plotted, with points receiving equal levels of significant values joined by a continuous line.

Field intensity measurement. The measurement of a signal delivered at a point of reception by a radio transmitter in units of voltage per meter of effective antenna height, usually in terms of microvolts or millivolts per meter.

15 and 2. The terms on which recognized advertising agents secure space from the publishers: 15 per cent commission from publishers on the gross amount of space used, plus 2 per cent (for the client) on the net for cash payment.

Fill-in. (1) The salutation and any other data to be inserted in the individual letters after they have been printed. (2) The blurring of an illustration due to the closeness of the lines or dots in the plate or to heavy inking.

Film rush. A print quickly made for inspection of a television film that has just been taken, to see if it is necessary to retake any part of the picture while the actors are still available and while the props are still in place.

Film transmission. The transmission of the sound and picture of motion picture film by television.

Firm order. A definite order for space (especially in magazines) that is not cancellable after a given date known as a firm order *date*. The firm order date is the latest date at which the advertisement can be cancelled.

Flat-bed. A printing press (for letterpress printing) containing a flat metal bed on which forms of type and plates are locked for printing.

Flat proofs. Ordinary rough proofs, or *stone* proofs, taken of type when it is on the compositor's workbench, in contrast to *press proofs* made after the type has been carefully adjusted to give the best possible impression.

Flat rate. A uniform charge for space in a medium, without regard to the amount of space used or the frequency of insertion. When *flat rates* do not prevail, *time discounts* or *quantity discounts* are offered.

F.M. or frequency modulation. A method of broadcasting to provide reception comparatively free of interference day and night to a service area apparently limited to about twice the radius to the horizon from the transmitter. It permits a large number of stations to use a wave length.

Following, next to, reading matter. The specification of a position for an advertisement to appear in a publication. Also known as *full position*. This *preferred position* usually costs more than *run-of-paper* position.

"Follow style." Instruction to compositor to set copy in accordance with a previous advertisement or proof.

Font. An assortment of type in one siz and face, including numerals, punc tuation marks, and all letters and sym bols in proper proportions.

Font, wrong. See *Wrong font*.

Foreign advertising. (1) Newspape advertising paid for directly or ind rectly by a manufacturer or nationa distributor (usually nonresident), a contrasted with *local advertising* which is paid for by the local retailer at a lower rate. Also known as *na tional advertising*. (2) Advertising in another country.

Foreign-language advertising. Do mestic advertising printed in a lan guage other than English.

Form. (1) Pages of type locked in plac in a strong, rectangular iron frame known as a *chase*. Usually holds 1, 2 4, 8, 16, 32, or 64 pages (hence it is uneconomical to print booklets with 10, 12, 20, 26, or 50 pages). (2) The general style of a book, as op posed to its subject.

Format. The size, shape, style, and ap pearance of a book or publication.

Forms close. The date on which all copy and plates for a periodical advertisement must be in.

Foundry proofs. The proofs of a typographical setup just before the material is sent to the foundry for electrotyping; identified by the heavy funeral-black border (foundry rules).

4 As. American Association of Advertising Agencies (A.A.A.A.).

Four-color process. The photoengraving process for reproducing color illustrations by a set of plates, one of which prints all the yellows, another the blues, a third the reds, the fourth the blacks (sequence variable). The plates are referred to as *process plates*.

Free lance. An independent artist or copy writer who takes individual assignments from different accounts, but is not otherwise in their employ, or associated with any of them.

Frequency. The number of alternations per second that a transmitter radiates. Frequency is measured in kilocycles or *thousands* of alternations per second.

Frequency Modulation (F.M.). The method of transmitting sound by varying the *frequency* of the electromagnetic wave, in contrast to varying its *size* (A.M., amplitude modulation).

F.T.C. Federal Trade Commission.

Full position. A special preferred position of an advertisement in a newspaper: Either (1) the advertisement both follows a column or columns of the news reading matter and is completely flanked by reading matter as well, or else (2) the advertisement is at the top of the page and alongside reading matter.

Full showing. In car cards, one card in each car of a line, or of the city, in which space is bought. In an outdoor poster schedule, a 100-intensity showing.

Furniture. Pieces of wood and metal designed to fill blank spaces between pages and around type forms when locked in a chase. Sizes are usually multiples of 12-point or pica.

Galley proofs. Proofs on sheets usually 20 to 22 inches long, printed from type as it stands in *galley trays* before the type is made up into pages.

Gang. A group of plates, type pages, or the like arranged in a form for printing with a single impression; a sheet thus printed. In photoengraving, a group of repeated originals set up or negatives stripped in for multiple reproduction—especially for labels or folding boxes.

Ghost. An unwanted image appearing in a television picture; for example, as a result of signal reflection.

Ghosted view. An illustration giving an X-ray view of a subject.

Grain. In machine-made paper the direction of the fibers, making the paper stronger across the grain and easier to fold with the grain.

Gutter. The space composed of the two inside margins of facing printed pages.

Group discount. A special discount in radio station rates for the simultaneous use of a group of stations.

Hairline. A fine or delicate line in type, rule, or engraving; any type character that is very light throughout, or the lighter parts of modern types with serifs.

Half showing. One half of a full showing of car cards; a 50-intensity showing of outdoor posters or panels.

Half tone. A photoengraving plate, photographed through a glass screen (in the camera) that serves to break up the reproduction of the subject into dots and thus makes possible the printing of half tone values, as of photographs. Screens vary from 45 to 300 lines to the inch. The most common are 120- and 133-line screens for use in magazines; 65- to 85-line screens for use in newspapers. *Square* half tone—one in which the corners are square and which has an all-over screen; *Silhouette* or *outline* half tone—one in which a part of the background is removed; *Vignette* half tone—one in which background fades away at the edges; *Surprint*—a plate in which a line-plate negative is surprinted *over* a half-tone negative, or vice versa; a *Combination* plate—one in which line-plate negative is adjacent to (but not upon) half-tone negative; *Highlight* or *drop-out* half tone—one in which dots are removed from various areas to get greater contrast.

Hand composition. Type set up by hand, as distinguished from type set up by machine. (Compare *Linotype composition; Monotype composition.*)

Hand lettering. Lettering that is drawn by hand, as distinguished from type that is regularly set.

Hand tooling. Handwork on an engraving or plate to improve its reproducing qualities, charged for by the hour. Unless the plate is a *highlight half tone,* hand tooling is needed to secure pure white in a half tone.

Haphazard sampling. See *Sampling.*

Head. Display caption to summarize contents and get attention. *Center* heads are centered on type matter; *side* heads, at the beginning of a paragraph; *box* heads, enclosed by rules; *cut-in* heads, in an indention of the text.

Head-on position. An outdoor advertising stand that directly faces traffic on a highway.

"Hold." Instruction indicating what part of copy is to be reproduced; warning to stop after some preliminary operation as "Send blueprint and hold"; instruction to keep in type matter that is set up but not to be used immediately.

Hooperating. A term for a radio program's audience-rating as determined by C. E. Hooper, Inc., quantitative audience-measurement service.

House organ. A publication issued periodically by a firm to further its own interests, inviting attention on the strength of its editorial content. Also known as *company magazine* and *company newspaper.*

Iconoscope. The special television camera that picks up the image to be sent.

Identification. The radio voice that periodically tells (in the "pause for station identification") what station is broadcasting—as: "This is Station WCBS, New York," or "This is CBS . . . the Columbia Broadcasting System."

Impose. To place in order on a flat surface (an *imposing stone* or *table*) type matter, cuts, et cetera, and to lock them up in a chase.

Inch. The unit of advertising measurement, a space one inch deep and one column wide, a *column inch.*

Individual location. The location of an outdoor advertisement in which there is but a single panel, and not several adjacent ones.

Industrial goods. Commodities (raw materials, machines, et cetera) destined for use in producing other goods; also called *producer goods;* distinct from *consumer goods.*

Inherited audience. The portion of a radio program's audience that listened to the preceding program on the same station.

Insertion order. Instructions from an advertiser authorizing a publisher to print an advertisement of specified size on a given date at an agreed rate; accompanied or followed by the copy for the advertisement.

Inserts. (1) In letters or packages, an enclosure usually in the form of a little slip bearing an advertisement. (2) In periodicals, a page printed by the advertiser, or for him, and forwarded to the publisher, who binds it up in the publication. Usually in colors and on heavier stock (if the publisher permits).

Intaglio printing. Printing from a depressed surface, such as from the copper plate or steel plate that produces *engraved* calling cards and announcements. *Rotogravure* is a form of intaglio printing. Compare *Letterpress printing* and *Lithographic printing.*

Interference. The reception of an undesired radio or television program or extraneous electrical noise simultaneously with a desired program.

Island position. Position in a newspaper entirely surrounded by reading matter. Not generally procurable.

Job ticket. A sheet or an envelope that accompanies a printing job through the various departments, bearing all the instructions and all records showing the progress of the work.

Judgment sampling. See *Sampling.*

Justification of type. Arranging type so that it appears in even-length lines, with its letters properly spaced.

"Keep standing." Instructions to printer to hold type for further instructions after it has been used on a job. Where it may be necessary to hold type for any length of time, it is better to have an electrotype of the set-up made.

Kennelly-Heaviside layer. A canopy or layer that forms at night in the upper atmosphere, against which A.M. radio signals are reflected back to earth. Television waves penetrate the Kennelly-Heaviside layer and do not reflect back.

Keying an advertisement. Giving an advertisement a code number or letter so that when people respond, the source of the inquiry can be traced. The key may be a variation in the address, or a letter or number printed in the corner of a return coupon.

Key plate. The plate in color process with which all other plates must register.

Key station. The point at which a radio network's principal programs originate. There may be several.

Kinescope. The television picture tube in which electrical impulses are translated into picture elements at the receiver. The face of the tube is commonly called *the television screen.*

Kinescope recording. A motion picture film of a television program direct from the face or screen of the Kinescope receiver tube.

Known-probability sampling. See *Sampling.*

Kodachrome. A one-exposure color-photographic process yielding color transparencies without visible color grains or screens and requiring no color registration of elements.

Kraft. A strong paper used for making tension envelopes, wrappers for mailing magazines, and the like.

Laid paper. Paper showing a regular water-marked pattern, usually of parallel lines.

Lanham Act. The Federal Trade-Mark Act of 1946, supplanting the previous Federal trade-mark acts.

Layout. A working drawing showing how an advertisement is to look. A *printer's layout* is a set of instructions accompanying a piece of copy showing how it is to be set up.

l.c. Lower-case letters.

Leaders. A line of dots or dashes used to guide the eye across the page, thus: . . . .

Leading (pronounced **ledding**). The insertion of metal strips (known as *leads*) between lines of type, causing greater space to appear between these lines. The usual size is 2 points. Leaded type requires more room than type that is not leaded but set *solid.*

Ledger papers. A high-grade writing paper of tough body and smooth, plated surface. Used for accounting work and for documents.

Legend. The title or description under an illustration. Sometimes called cut-line.

Letterpress printing. Printing from a raised or relief surface, like a rubber stamp or metal type. Most advertisements are printed by the letterpress method. Exceptions are *lithography* (and *offset*); *intaglio* (and *rotogravure*).

Limited time station. A radio station that is assigned a channel for broadcasting for a specified time only, sharing its channel with other stations at different times.

Linage. The total number of lines of space occupied by one advertisement or a series of advertisements.

Line. A unit for measuring space one-fourteenth of a column-inch.

Line drawing. A drawing made with brush, pen, pencil, or crayon, with such shading as occurs produced by variations in size and spacing of lines, not by tone.

Line plate. A photoengraving made without the use of a screen from a drawing composed of lines or masses, which can print on any quality stock.

Linotype composition. Mechanical type setting by molding a line of type at a time. The Linotype machine is operated by a keyboard resembling that of a typewriter. (Compare *Hand composition; Monotype composition.*)

Lip-synchronization (lip-sync). The method in television of having the voice of the performer recorded as he speaks. Requires more rehearsal and equipment and costs more than narration.

Lithographic printing. The process of printing from a flat surface, usually a stone, on which the design has been drawn. Invented in 1796 by Alois Senefelder of Munich. Used for color work of large quantities, such as labels and package inserts. (See *Offset printing.* Compare *Intaglio printing* and *Letterpress printing.*)

Live. A broadcast by actual musicians and speakers, in contrast to a transcribed or recorded broadcast, and used to mean the opposite of *dead.*

Local advertising. Newspaper advertising paid for by the local retailer at a *local* or lower rate than that charged the *national advertiser.*

Local-channel station. A radio station that is allowed just enough power to be heard near its point of transmission and is assigned a channel on the air wave set aside for local-channel stations. (Compare *Regional-channel station; Clear-channel station.*)

Locking up. Tightening up the type matter put into a chase preparatory to going to press.

Log. A record of every minute of radio broadcasting, including all errors. An accurate journal required by law.

Logotype, or logo. Two or more letters, or a whole word, or distinctive setting of a name, cast on one body.

Lower case (l.c.). The small letters in the alphabet, such as those in which this is printed, as distinguished from *UPPER CASE OR CAPITAL LETTERS.* Named from the lower case of the printer's type cabinet in which this type was formerly kept.

Machine-finish (M.F.) paper. The cheapest of book papers that take half tones well. A paper which has had its pores filled ("sized") but which is not ironed. Thus it possesses a moderately smooth surface. Smoother than *antique,* but not so smooth as *English-finish* or *sized and supercalendered paper.*

Mail-order advertising. That method of selling whereby the complete sales transaction is negotiated through advertising and the mails, and without the aid of a salesman. Not to be confused with *direct-mail advertising.*

Make good. A free re-run of an advertisement in which there has been a serious error in reproduction or transmission.

Make-ready. The process of adjusting the form of type or the plates for the press to insure good printing. A preliminary proof of the form on the press is inspected for those letters or plates that appear lighter than the rest of the material. *Overlays* and *underlays* of paper are inserted under the printing surfaces to secure the uniform pressure necessary to obtain even effects. The skill and care in this work represent one of the hidden elements that serve to make a good printing job.

Make-up of a page. The general appearance of a page; the arrangement in which the editorial matter and advertising material are to appear.

Marketing. Those business activities that aid the movement of goods and services from production to consumption.

Matrix; "mat." (1) A mold of paper pulp, or similar substance, made by pressing a sheet of it into the type setup or engraving plate. Molten lead is poured into it, forming a replica of the original plate known as a *stereotype.* (2) The brass molds used in the Linotype.

Mat shot. A motion picture within the main television picture—as a boy swinging a bat in a picture frame being held by another.

Matter. Composed type, often referred to as: (1) *dead matter*—of no further use; (2) *leaded matter*—having extra spacing between lines; (3) *live matter*—to be used again; (4) *solid matter*—lines set close to each other; (5) *standing matter*—held for future use.

M.C. Master of Ceremonies.

Medium. (1) The vehicle that carries the advertisement, as newspaper, magazine, letter, car card, radio, television, and so on. (2) The tool and method used by an artist in drawing illustrations, as pen and ink, pencil, wash, or crayon.

Megacycle (radio). 1,000 kilocycles. For example, 50,000 kilocycles = 50 megacycles.

M.F. Machine-finish paper.

Microphone. An instrument for converting sound-wave impulses into corresponding electrical impulses, used in broadcasting for "picking up" programs from studios and other points.

Milline rate. A unit for measuring the rate of advertising space in relation to circulation; the cost of having one agate line appear before one million readers. Calculated thus:

$$\text{Milline rate} = \frac{\text{Actual line rate} \times 1{,}000{,}000}{\text{Circulation}}$$

Modern type. See *Old style type.*

Modulation. The process of combining or impressing the sound, program, or audio-frequency energy upon the carrier of a broadcasting station.

Moiré. A pattern formed by two or more conflicting screens, or screen angles, as in making a half tone from another half tone or from a steel engraving. It resembles the watered silk fabric, called moiré (French, *watered*).

Monitor. A loudspeaker and its associated amplifier used in the control room to listen to the radio program being transmitted, and to stand vigil on a program as it is broadcast to see what is said and done and what the program sounds like.

Monotype composition. Type set by a machine in which the individual letters are separately molded and automatically assembled into lines, as distinguished from *Hand composition* and *Linotype composition*.

Month preceding. *First month preceding* publication means that the closing date falls on the given day during the month that immediately precedes the publication date of a periodical. "Closing date is the 5th of the first month preceding" means that the forms of the March issue, for example, close February 5. *Second month preceding* would mean that forms close January 5; *third month preceding*, December 5.

Mortise. An opening cut through a plate, block, or base, to permit insertion of other matter, usually type.

National advertising. (1) The advertising of any trade-marked product that potentially could be sold by dealers throughout the nation. (2) The advertising of a manufacturer or producer in contrast to the local advertising of a retailer. (3) Any advertising appearing in a medium with nationwide circulation.

National brand. A manufacturer's or producer's brand that has wide distribution through many outlets; distinct from a private brand.

National plan. The tactics in advertising campaigns of trying to get all the business that can be secured all over the country at one time. When rightfully used, it is the outgrowth of numerous *Zone plans*. Compare *Cream plan*.

Natural fold. That method of folding a direct advertisement whereby the continuity of the copy is preserved a the advertisement is opened.

Network. A permanent setup intercon necting broadcasting stations for the purpose of distributing radio or tele vision programs for simultaneous broadcasting by such stations.

Next to reading matter (n.r.). The position of an advertisement immedi ately adjacent to editorial or news matter in a publication.

Nielsen food-drug service. A dealer panel reporting flow of goods by type and brand in food and drug stores.

Nielsen Radio Index. A reporting service for broadcasters and advertisers based on the use of the Audimeter. Operated by the A. C. Nielsen Co., this service regularly reports program ratings, trends, and the amount and distribution of radio listening by periods of the day.

Off-screen announcer. The effect of having the voice of an unseen speaker on a television commercial.

Offset. (1) The method of lithographic printing whereby the impression is not transferred directly to the paper, but to a rubber blanket and then to the sheet. Gives a softer effect than direct lithography. Makes possible the use of rough-surfaced stock in the reproduction of lithographic illustration. (2) The blotting of a wet or freshly printed sheet against an accompanying sheet. Can be prevented by slip-sheeting. Antique paper absorbs the ink and prevents offsetting.

Old English. A style of black-letter or text type, now little used except in logotypes of trade names or names of newspapers.

Old style type (o.s.). Originally the face of Roman type with slight difference in weight between its different strokes, as contrasted with *modern type*, which has sharp contrast and accents in its strokes. Its serifs for the most part are oblique; modern serifs are usually horizontal or vertical.

100-intensity showing. A standard showing of outdoor panels, enough to provide even and thorough coverage. The number of panels varies with each city. Also known as a 100-showing.

One-time rate. The rate paid by an advertiser who uses less space than that necessary to earn a time or rate discount, when such discounts are offered. Same as *transient rate.*

One-way screen. A half tone with the screen in one direction only; it does not have the cross-section that gives the dot effect. Good for odd effects. Makes tooling difficult.

Opticals. The visual effects that are put on a television film in a laboratory, in contrast to those that are included as part of the original photograph.

Order-of-merit method. Testing a piece of copy or an illustration, advertisement, trade-mark, design, or package, giving first place to the one with the highest vote, and rating the others in order of their votes.

Originate. (1) To send a broadcast from a specific location. (2) To create a radio program.

O.S. Old style type.

Overlapping circulation. The extent to which two or more media duplicate one another in reaching the same prospect. Sometimes this is a desirable feature, providing an immediate cumulative effect.

Overrun. The number of pieces of matter printed in excess of the specified quantity. According to the trade custom, an advertiser agrees to accept an overrun of no more than 10 per cent at pro rata cost.

P.; pp. Page; pages.

Package. A special radio or television program or series of programs, bought by an advertiser (usually for a lump sum), that includes all components all ready to broadcast with the addition of the advertiser's commercial.

Page proof. A proof of type matter and plates arranged by pages, as they are finally to appear. Usually is made ("pulled") after *galley proof* has been shown and corrections are made.

Panel. (1) A permanent board or jury maintained by an advertiser, agency, or medium to secure comparable data on product acceptance, use, and the like. *Consumer* panels report purchases of food, drugs, et cetera. In *dealer* panels representatives of a research organization check stocks of certain stores to determine relative flow of goods. (2) The part of an outdoor sign board on which posters are pasted.

Participating program, or show. A radio or television show in which a number of advertisers can have their products featured or mentioned. Also see *Audience participation show.*

Pattern plate. (1) An electrotype of extra heavy shell used for molding in large quantities to save wear on the original plate or type. (2) An original to be used for the same purpose.

Photoengraving. (1) An etched, relief printing plate made by a photomechanical process—as a half tone or line cut. (2) A print from such a plate. (3) The process of producing the plate.

Pica; pica-em. The unit for measuring width in printing. There are 6 picas to the inch. Derived from *pica,* the old name of 12-pt. type (⅙ inch high), and the letter M of that series, whose width likewise is ⅙ inch. A page of type 25 picas wide is 4⅙ inches wide (25 ÷ 6 = 4⅙).

Picture resolution. The clarity with which the television image appears on the television screen.

Pi or pied type. A type setup that has become disarranged.

Pioneering stage. The advertising stage of a product in which the need for such product is not recognized and must be established, or when the need has been established but the success of a commodity in filling those requirements has to be evidenced. See *Competitive stage; Retentive stage; Spiral.*

Plant owner. In outdoor advertising, the person who arranges to lease, erect, and maintain the outdoor sign and to sell the advertising space on it.

Plate. Any piece of metal, electrotype or stereotype, including type matter, line engraving, or half tone (or any two or all of these) from which impressions are made by a printing operation. The contents may be a page unit or an advertisement or other unit.

Plated stock. Paper with a high gloss and a hard, smooth surface, secured by being pressed between polished metal sheets.

Platen. The part of a printing press that holds the paper and presses it against the type or plate.

Playback. The playing of a recording for audition purposes.

Point; pt. (1) The unit of measurement of type, about 1/72 inch in depth. Type is specified by its point size, as 8 pt., 12 pt., 24 pt., 48 pt. (2) The unit for measuring thickness of paper, one-thousandth of an inch.

Poll. An enumeration of a sample (see *Sampling*) to get data that may be projected for the whole market. *Pantry polls,* conducted by the *Milwaukee Journal* and other newspapers take inventories on foods, toilet articles, et cetera, on consumers' shelves to analyze brand preferences, frequency of purchase, and the like. *Presidential preference polls* attempt to forecast the results of presidential elections by gathering data on political preferences in representative areas.

Poster. An outdoor advertising sheet or series of sheets.

Poster panel. A standard surface on which outdoor posters are placed. The posting surface is of sheet metal. An ornamental molding of standard green forms the frame. The standard poster panel is 12 feet high by 25 feet in length (outside dimensions).

Poster plant. The organization that provides the actual outdoor advertising service.

Poster showing. The unit of sale for poster service. The number of panels in a showing varies from city to city.

P.P.A. Periodical Publishers' Association, a group of magazine publishers that recommends agency recognition. For newspaper recognition, see A.N.P.A.

Precision sampling. See *Sampling.*

Pre-date. In larger cities, a newspaper issue that comes out the night before the date it carries, or a section of the Sunday issue published and mailed out during the week preceding the Sunday date.

Preferred position. A special desired position in a magazine or newspaper for which the advertiser must pay a premium. Otherwise the advertisement appears in a *run-of-paper* position, that is, wherever the publisher chooses to place it.

Primary service area. The area to which a radio broadcasting station delivers a high level of signal of unfailing steadiness and of sufficient volume to override the existing noise levels both day and night at all seasons of the year. The limits of the primary service area as determined by field-intensity measurements are usually considered to be the 5-millivolt-per-meter contour.

Principal Register. The main register for recording trade-marks, service marks, collective marks, and certification marks under the Lanham Federal Trade-Mark Act. (See *Supplementary Register.*)

Printers' Ink Model Statute. The act directed at fraudulent advertising, prepared and sponsored by *Printers' Ink*, the advertising journal.

Private brand. A wholesaler's or retailer's product labeled and sold under his own trade-mark in his territory, in contrast to the *national* or nationally advertised brand.

Process plates. Photoengraving plates for printing two, three, or four colors, one over the other, to produce the final desired effect.

Process printing. Letterpress color printing in which one color is printed over the other by means of a set of process plates.

Producer. (1) One who originates and presents a radio program. (2) The individual or the broadcasting company that offers a program for observation or consideration, or who brings a performance before the public.

Production. (1) The conversion of an advertising idea into an advertisement, mainly by a printing process. (2) The building, organization, and presentation of a radio or television program.

Production department. (1) The department of an advertising agency responsible for the mechanical production of an advertisement, dealing with printers and engravers. In some agencies it includes the copy and art departments. (2) The department responsible for the proper broadcasting of a radio program.

Production director. Individual in charge of a radio studio program.

Program following. The radio program that follows a given program. Important in deciding upon the desirability of the station and hour.

Program opposite. The radio programs that are running over other stations at the same time as the given program and broadcasting to the same territory; the competition for the radio audience that a program experiences.

Program preceding. The radio program that is on directly before a given program. A good "program preceding" enhances the desirability of the time on the air.

Progressive proofs. A set of photoengraving proofs in color, in which: the yellow plate is printed on one sheet and the red on another; the yellow and red are then combined; next the blue is printed and a yellow-red-blue combination made. Then the black alone is printed, and finally all colors are combined. The sequence varies. In this way the printer matches up his inks when printing color plates.

Projection. The application to an entire market of data (quantitative, usually in percentage form) derived from a representative sample.

Proof. (1) An inked impression of composed type or of a plate for inspection or for filing. (2) In engraving and etching, an impression taken to show the condition of the illustration at any stage of the work. Taking a proof is *pulling a proof*.

Publisher's statement. The statement of circulation issued by a publisher.

Quads. Blank pieces of metal (not type-high) used by the printer to justify (or fill out) lines where the amount of type does not do so.

Quarter showing. One fourth of a *full* showing in car cards or outdoor advertising.

Quarter tones, or double-process tones. A development of the half-tone plate for use in reproducing illustrations on newspaper and other rough stock; made in a coarse screen by a process that retains more detail than the ordinary coarse-screen half tone.

Quota. A set goal for sales or other effort (including *sampling*), in terms of dollars, sales units, or a percentage of the total goal. See *Sampling.*

Railroad showing. An outdoor advertisement conspicuously placed so that it can be seen by passengers on trains.

Randomization. In consumer reaserch a method of securing random (unbiased) selection of respondents. See *Sampling.*

Rate card. A card giving the space rates of a publication and data on mechanical requirements and closing dates.

Rate-holder. The minimum-sized advertisement that must appear during a given period if an advertiser is to secure a certain time or quantity discount. It holds a lower rate for an advertiser.

Reading notices. Advertisements in newspapers set up in a type similar to that of the editorial matter. Must be followed by "Adv." Charged for at rates higher than those for regular ads. Many publications will not accept them.

Ream. In publishing and advertising, 500 sheets of paper (not 480). Thousand-sheet counts have been introduced.

Rebroadcast. A radio program repeated at a later hour to reach the parts of the country in a different time belt.

Recognized agency. An advertising agency recognized by the various publishers or their associations and granted a commission for the space it sells to advertisers. The commission is usually *15 and 2,* 15 per cent on the gross with 2 per cent on the net for cash—the 2 per cent going to the advertiser, not to the agency.

Recorded program. Any radio program consisting of phonograph records or electrical transcriptions and not depending upon the presence of artists in the studio at the time of the actual broadcast.

Regional-channel station. A radio station that is allowed more power than a local station but less than a clear-channel station. It is assigned a place on the frequency band set aside for regional channel stations. (See *Local channel and Clear channel.*)

Register. Perfect correspondence in printing; of facing pages when top lines are even; of color printing, when there is correct superimposition of each plate so that the colors mix properly.

Registering trade-mark. In the United States, the act of recording a trade-mark with the Commissioner of Patents.

Register marks. Cross lines placed on a copy to appear in the margin of all negatives as a guide to perfect register.

Release. A statement by a person photographed authorizing the advertiser to use that photograph. In the case of minors, the guardian's release is necessary.

Relief printing. Printing in which the design reproduced is raised slightly above the surrounding, nonprinting areas. Letterpress is a form of relief printing contrasted with *Intaglio printing* and *Lithography*.

Remote control. The operation of broadcasting a program from a point removed from the regular studios of the station.

Remote pickup. A broadcast originating outside the studio, as from a hotel ballroom, football field, or the like.

Representation. Space (or time) salesman or sales organiaztion, usually independent of the medium owner. A station representative may sell time for several stations.

Repro proofs, or reproduction proofs. Exceptionally clean and sharp proofs from type for use as copy for reproduction.

Respondent. One who answers a questionnaire or is interviewed in a research study.

Retentive stage. The third stage of a product, reached when its general usefulness is everywhere known, its individual qualities thoroughly appreciated, when it is satisfied to retain its patronage merely on the strength of its past reputation. (See *Pioneering stage; Competitive stage; Spiral.*)

Retouching. The process of correcting or improving art work, especially photographs.

Reversed plate. (1) A line-plate engraving in which whites come out black, and vice versa. (2) An engraving in which right and left, as they appear in the illustration, are transposed.

Roman type. (1) Originally, type of the Italian and Roman school of design, as distinguished from the blackface Old English style. Old style and modern are the two branches of the Roman family. (2) Type faces that are not italics are called roman.

R.O.P. Run-of-paper position; any location in a publication convenient to publisher.

Rotary press. A press possessing no flat bed, but printing entirely with the movement of cylinders.

Rotation. Repeating a series of advertisements by beginning again with No. 1 after all have been run.

Rotogravure. The method of *intaglio printing* in which the impression is produced by cylinder plates chemically etched and affixed to rollers of a rotary press; useful in large runs of pictorial effects.

Rough. The first pencil draft of an illustration executed in crude style, submitted to the advertiser for O.K. before it is finished.

Routing out. Tooling out dead metal on an engraving plate.

R.P.M. Revolutions per minute, speed at which a radio transcription or phonograph record is played. Most transcriptions run 33⅓ r.p.m.; most phonograph records, 78 r.p.m.

Rule. A strip of type-high metal (usually brass) with a line or lines on its face, used in tabular composition vertically (column rule) or to set off matter horizontally (cut-off rule).

Run of paper. See *r.o.p.*

Saddle stitching. Binding a booklet by stitching it with wire through the center, passing through the fold in the center pages and the backbone. Enables the booklet to lie flat. When a booklet is too thick for this method, *side stitching* is used.

Sales promotion. (1) Those sales activities that supplement both personal selling and marketing, co-ordinate the two, and help to make them effective;

for example, displays. (2) More loosely, the combination of personal selling, advertising, and all supplementary selling activities.

Sales-promotion department. The liaison department between the sales department and the advertising department which investigates new markets, inquiries resulting from advertisements, and follows up salesmen's visits with proper letters and literature.

Sampling. (1) The method of introducing and promoting merchandise by distributing, free or at a reduced price, miniature or full-size trial packages of the product. (2) Studying the characteristics, attitudes, buying habits, et cetera, of a selected part of an entire market that is truly representative in order to apply to the entire market the data secured from the miniature part. *Haphazard* sampling (also called *accidental* or opportunistic) takes respondents wherever they are found—the quickest, least scientific method. *Quota* sampling leaves the actual choice of respondents to the investigator (and for this reason is called a *judgment* sample), specifying that such and such proportions of the total response be in certain strata (economic, educational, vocational, sex, marital condition). Any example based on such strata specification is a *stratified* sampling. *Randomization*—the means of securing a *random* sample—selects the respondents by mathematical tests that assure an equal chance of being selected to each respondent of the total being studied. *Precision* sampling and *known-probability* sampling are almost synonymous with random sampling. *Area* sampling is stratified random sampling, with different areas scientifically selected to represent the different strata or cells that make up the whole body to be studied. *Systematic* sampling is a less exact sort of random sampling, in which the prescribed respondents are chosen by taking every tenth, twentieth (or some other designated how-many-th) of the total number to be studied—such as interviewing the twentieth family in every street. So sampling may be classified as *controlled* and *uncontrolled* (or *judgment*) sampling.

S.C. (1) Single column. (2) Small caps.

Scale rate. In photoengraving, the standard cost rate.

Scaling down. Reducing illustrations to the size desired.

Scanning. The television process of changing a light image into an electrical signal, or vice versa.

Score. To crease cards or thick sheets of paper so that they can be folded.

Script show. A serial radio program, usually 15 minutes, on the air three or five times a week at the same hour and station; a television serial.

Secondary service area. The area beyond the primary service area where a broadcasting station delivers a steady signal of sufficient intensity to be a regular program service of loudspeaker volume by both day and night and at all seasons of the year.

Segue. (Pronounced segway; Italian, "it follows.") The transition from one musical theme to another without a break or announcement.

Self-mailer. A direct-mail advertisement folder, booklet, or book that requires no envelope for mailing.

Separation, color. Isolation on separate negatives by the use of color filters (or by applying acid-resisting paint to the plate) of the parts of an illustration to be printed in the given colors.

Service the script. To cast, rehearse, and present the material set down in the manuscript for a radio program.

Shallow half tone. An inferior half tone in which the dots have not been deeply etched so that the detail of the illustration is lost. When half tones have been overdeveloped, they may have their dots undermined.

Sheet. The old unit of poster size, 26 × 39 inches. The standard-size poster is called a 24-sheet.

Shopping goods. Products that the consumer buys infrequently and usually in an outlet not a neighborhood store, and that are selected after comparing price, style, and quality of different items—for example, jewelry, apparel, millinery, and furniture; distinct from *convenience goods.*

Short rate. The difference between the low contract rate for a planned advertising campaign and the higher rate actually earned on space or time used that is less than that contracted for.

Shoulder. The space between the upper or lower extremes of a type letter and the edge of the body on which it is mounted. The shoulder does not print. The type size, as given in points, includes the shoulder, thus accounting for the fact that a 36-point type letter, for example, does not appear exactly ½-inch in height.

Side stitching. The method of wire-stitching from one side of a booklet to the other. Wiring can be seen on front cover and on back. Used in thick booklet work. Pages do not lie flat. See *Saddle stitching.*

Signature. (1) The name of an advertiser. (2) The musical number or sound effect that regularly identifies a radio program. (3) A sheet folded ready for stitching in a book, usually sixteen pages, but with thin paper thirty-two pages; a mark, letter, or number is placed at the bottom of the first page of every group of sixteen or thirty-two pages to serve as a guide in folding.

Silhouette half tone. One in which all background is eliminated, the product alone appearing. Also known as *Outline half tone.*

Silk screen. A method of printing posters by forcing ink (or inks) through the meshes of a silk cloth that has the design to be reproduced imposed on it.

Sized and supercalendered paper (s. and s. c.). Machine-finish book paper that has been given extra ironings to insure a smooth surface. Takes half tones very well.

Sized paper. Paper that has received a chemical bath to make it less porous. Paper sized once and ironed (calendered) is known as *machine-finish.* If it is again ironed, it becomes *sized and supercalendered (s and s. c.).*

Slip-sheeting. Placing a sheet of paper (tissue or cheap porous stock) between the sheets of a printing job to prevent them from offsetting or smudging as they come from the press.

Slug. Notation placed on copy to identify it temporarily, and not to be reproduced in final printing.

Small caps (abbreviated *s.c.* or *sm. caps*). Letters shaped like upper case (capitals) but about two-thirds their size—nearly the size of lower-case letters. In body text small caps (with initial caps) look better than all caps for single words, phrases, or sentences. THIS SENTENCE IS SET WITH A REGULAR CAPITAL LETTER AT THE BEGINNING, THE REST IN SMALL CAPS.

Sniping. The mounting of an outdoor advertisement wherever space and opportunity permit, as against rocks, barrels, fences, and the like. Organized advertising is opposed to this.

Sound effects. Various devices or recordings used in radio to produce lifelike imitations of sound, such as walking up stairs, ocean waves, phone bells, and auto horns.

Space buyer. The officer of an advertising agency responsible for the selection of printed media for the agency's clients.

Space discount. A discount given by a publisher for the linage an advertiser uses. Compare *Time discount*.

Space schedule. A schedule showing the media in which an advertisement is to appear, the dates on which it is to appear, its exact size, and the cost.

Special representative. An individual or organization that represents a certain publisher in selling space outside the city of publication. The same special representative may serve two or more publishers of different cities. Also known as *foreign representative*.

Spectacular. A large electric sign, usually with motion and changing lights.

Spiral. The advertising evolution through which a product passes in its acceptance by the public. The stages are the *pioneering*, the *competitive*, and the *retentive*.

Split channel. Two or more radio network sections working simultaneously with different programs.

Split run. A method of testing the relative value of two advertisements by running each in one-half of all copies of a newspaper or magazine issue.

Sponsor. The firm or individual that pays for talent and broadcasting station time for a radio or television feature; the advertiser on the air.

Spot broadcast. A radio program issued directly from a station in behalf of a national advertiser, in contrast to a *network* broadcast, which is broadcast over a series of connected stations; or a *local* broadcast, which is a program sent out by a local advertiser over a station in his city.

Spread. (1) Two facing pages, a double-page advertisement. (2) Type matter set full measure across a page, not in columns. (3) Stretching any part of a broadcast to fill the full allotted time of the program.

Stage. See *Spiral*.

Staggered schedule. A schedule of space to be used in two or more periodicals, arranged so that the insertions alternate.

"Stand by." Cue that the radio program is about to go on the air.

Station announcement. The announcement made to identify a radio transmitter.

Station break. The interval of time between two radio programs, usually on the hour, half-hour, or quarter hour, used for the station identification required by the FCC; and the announcement broadcast during that interval.

Station director. The radio executive in charge of the operation and management of a broadcasting station.

Steel-die embossing. Printing from steel dies engraved by the *intaglio process*, the sharp, raised outlines being produced by stamping over a counter die. Used for monograms, crests, stationery, and similar social and business purposes.

Stereotype. A plate cast by pouring molten metal into a matrix. One of the least expensive forms of duplicate plates. Lacks the strength and sharpness of detail of an electrotype.

Newspapers are printed from stereotypes. Should not be used in magazine advertisements.

Stet. A proofreader's term—"Let it stand as is; disregard change specified." A dotted line is placed underneath the letter or words to which the instructions apply.

Stock cut. An electro of an engraving, ornament or other design kept in stock by dealers, furnished by typefounders, electrotypers and engraving houses, and costing less than original engravings.

Stone. Printer's stand or table with flat, smooth top (formerly of stone) for composing type.

Stone proof. See *Flat proofs.*

Storecasting. The broadcasting of radio programs and commercials in stores; usually supermarkets.

Story board. The former in which the television film commercial is planned, including pictures, action, and narrative.

Studio. A room especially adpated by suitable acoustic treatment and by the installation of microphones and associated equipment, signaling lights, and other essentials to the presentation and picking up of sound programs for broadcasting purposes.

Substance No. (Usually followed by a figure, as *Substance No. 16, Substance No. 20, Substance No. 24.*) In specifying paper stock, the equivalent weight of a given paper in the standard size.

Superimposition. Showing a trademark or package in television right over live action at a moment when the excitement in the action has subsided, as at time out in a game.

Supplementary Register. A record of trade-marks that do not qualify under the Principal Register, useful chiefly for export advertising purposes.

Surprint. (1) A photoengraving in which a line-plate effect appears over the face of a half tone, or vice versa. (2) Printing over the face of an advertisement already printed.

Sustaining program. Entertainment or educational feature performed at the expense of a broadcasting station or network; in contrast to a *commercial program,* for which an advertiser pays.

T. Time, or times, as 1-t, 5-t, the frequency with which an advertisement is to appear.

T.A.B. Traffic Audit Bureau.

Tear sheets. Copies of advertisements torn from newspapers.

Telecast. A sound and pictorial image that has been sent by television.

Television. The method of broadcasting both sound and pictorial effects.

T.F. (1) Till-forbid. (2) To fill. (3) Copy is to follow.

TV. Television.

Till-forbid; run T.F. Instructions to publisher meaning: "Continue running this advertisement until instructions are issued to the contrary."

Time buyer. The member of an advertising agency responsible for making the proper selection of radio coverage for the agency's clients, corresponding to the space buyer for advertisements in publications.

Time discount. A discount given to an advertiser for the frequency or regularity with which he inserts his advertisements. Distinguished from *quality discount,* for amount of space used.

Tint block. Usually a solid piece of zinc, used to print a light shade of ink for a background.

To fill (T.F.). Instructions to printer meaning: "Set this copy in the size necessary to fill the specified space indicated in the layout."

Tr. Transpose type as indicated, a proofreader's abbreviation.

Trade advertising. Advertising directed to the wholesale or retail merchants or sales agencies through whom the product is sold.

Trade-mark. Any device or word that identifies the origin of a product, telling who made it or who sold it. Not to be confused with *trade name*.

Trade name. A name under which a business is conducted; applies to a business as a whole, not to a product.

Traffic Audit Bureau (T.A.B.). An organization designed to investigate how many people pass and may see a given outdoor sign, to establish a method of evaluating traffic and measuring a market.

Traffic department. The department in an advertising agency responsible for the prompt execution of the work in the respective departments and for turning over the complete material for shipment to the forwarding department on schedule time. When one person handles this work, he is called an *accelerator*.

Transcription. See *Electrical transcription*.

Transcription program library. A collection of transcription records from which the radio advertiser may draw. Stations subscribe to various transcription libraries, and the advertiser need merely find out to which library a station subscribes and specify which numbers from the library service he wishes.

Transient rate. Same as *one-time rate* in buying space.

Transit radio. The broadcasting of radio programs and commercials in buses.

Transparency. Same as *decalcomania*.

Traveling display. An exhibit prepared by a manufacturer of a product and loaned by him to each of several dealers in rotation. Usually based on the product and prepared in such a way as to be of educational or dramatizing value.

Trimmed flush. A booklet or book trimmed after the cover is on, the cover thus being cut flush with the leaves. Compare with *Extended covers*.

25 X 38—80. Read *twenty-five, thirty-eight, eighty*. The method of expressing paper weight, meaning that a ream of paper 25 × 38 inches in size weighs 80 lbs. Similarly, 25 × 38—60, 25 × 38—70, 25 × 38—120, 17 × 22—16, 17 × 22—24, 20 × 26—80, 38 × 50—140.

Type face. The design and style of a type letter. Type faces are usually named after men, as, Caslon, Della Robbia, Jensen, Goudy. In machine composition, the faces are known also by code numbers.

Type page. The area of a page that type can occupy; the total area of a page less the margins.

Up. Number of times a cut or page is duplicated in a form; one page two "up" is a two-page form; four pages two "up" is an eight-page form.

Video. Currents or equipment for transmitting television pictures (from Latin meaning *see*); television, as contrasted with audio or radio.

Vignette. A half tone in which the edges (or parts of them) are shaded off gradually to very light gray.

Visual show. A radio program presented before a studio audience.

"Wait order." Instructions to a periodical to set up an advertisement and hold it for an insertion order.

Warm-up. The 3- or 5-minute period immediately preceding a broadcast in which the announcer or star puts the studio audience in a receptive mood by amiably introducing the cast of the program, or discussing its problems.

Wash drawing. A brush-work illustration, usually made with diluted India ink or water color so that, in addition to its black and white, it has varying shades of gray, like a photograph. Half tones, not line plates, are made from wash drawings. Wash drawings are extensively used to picture merchandise, as they can emphasize details better than photographs.

Wax engraving. The process of coating a plate with wax upon which the design is drawn, photographed, or impressed, and which is then cut through to the metal base. Used in making maps.

Wax-mold electrotype. An electrotype made from an impression taken in a sheet of wax; less expensive than lead mold. See *Electrotype*.

Wet printing. Color printing on specially designed high-speed presses with one color following another in immediate succession before the ink from any plate has time to dry.

W.F. See *Wrong font*.

Window envelope. A mailing envelope with a transparent panel, permitting the address on the enclosure to serve as a mailing address as well.

Wire circuits. A metallic conducting path connecting for communication purposes two or more points, such as broadcast transmitter, broadcasting studios, and remote sources of programs.

Woodcuts. Wooden printing blocks the design of which is carved by hand; in common use before photoengraving.

Work-and-turn. Printing all the pages in a signature from one form and then turning the paper and printing on the second side, making two copies or signatures when cut.

Wove Paper. Paper having a very faint, cloth-like appearance when held to the light.

Wrong font (w.f.). Letter from one series mixed with those from another series, or font. See if you can pick out the wrong font in this sentence.

Zinc etching. A photoengraving in zinc. Term is usually applied to line plates.

Zone plan. The tactics in an advertising campaign of concentrating on a certain limited geographical area rather than trying to cover the entire country at once, as in the *national plan*, or picking the choice prospects from different parts of the country at the same time, as in the *cream plan*.

Zooming. The effect in television of having a title or trade-mark grow bigger on the screen, like the locomotive of a train rushing right at you.

SECTION 3

Sales Management

1. DETERMINING SALES TERRITORIES

2. SALES QUOTAS

3. RECRUITING AND SELECTING SALESMEN

4. EQUIPPING SALESMEN

5. TRAINING SALESMEN

6. METHODS OF COMPENSATING SALESMEN

7. CONTRACTS FOR SALE OF MERCHANDISE

8. CONTRACTS APPOINTING SALES AGENTS

9. CONTRACTS EMPLOYING SALESMEN

10. FOREIGN TRADE TERMS OF SALE

SECTION 3

Sales Management

1. DETERMINING SALES TERRITORIES

What is a sales territory? A sales territory is the geographical area in which a salesman's activities are conducted. Most wholesale salesmen are confined to the territory to which they are assigned, whereas salesmen selling direct to consumers are often not restricted to definite territories but are permitted to sell wherever they wish. Frequently no territories are assigned to commission salesmen or to those engaged in the introduction of new products when the market is undeveloped or when the goods are highly competitive specialties or intangibles.

Certain functional types of salesmen, such as missionary salesmen engaged in sales promotional work, or specialty salesmen concentrating on the introduction of a new item or on reviving the sale of an inactive product, are usually not assigned a territory of their own but are transferred from territory to territory as the need for their specialized service demands.

Occasionally salesmen are assigned to a definite territory but given freedom to operate wherever they wish, subject to certain restrictions. In such cases a salesman is generally held responsible for production in his assigned territory, receives credit for all sales in his territory, and has referred to him all inquiries that originate in his territory. However, sales may be made to prospects or customers outside of a salesman's assigned territory through a mutual understanding with all salesmen in the organization to the effect that compensation for sales made outside of an assigned territory shall be divided with the salesmen in whose territory the sale is made. Commission salesmen "split" their commissions on such extraterritorial sales. Salesmen who are paid a bonus receive corresponding adjustments in quota.

Definite territories may be assigned to wholesale distributors and retail dealers as well as individual salesmen, and similar protection plans are devised to give the distributors protection within their territories. Moreover, there appears to be a trend toward the establishment of definite territorial assignments for both salesmen and wholesale and retail outlets.

Why establish sales territories? Sales territories are established for the following reasons:

1. To fix definite responsibility on salesmen for desired performance.
2. To save a salesman's time.
3. To insure maximum service to customers.
4. To make comparisons between the performance of salesmen in various territories.
5. To avoid conflicts between salesmen and overlapping of sales efforts.
6. To equalize more nearly the opportunities for all salesmen.
7. To adapt the personality of the salesman to the prevailing type of buyer in a territory.
8. To facilitate control and operation of salesmen by the management.
9. To effect reductions in traveling expenses.
10. To avoid aimless traveling and needless backtracking by salesmen.
11. To insure a salesman ample sales opportunities.
12. To prevent a salesman from having more work than he can do efficiently.
13. To insure adequate coverage of the potential market.
14. To meet competition more effectively.

Why salesmen are not restricted to territories. Salesmen are not restricted to territories for the following reasons:

1. Sales territories are difficult to establish fairly.
2. Some salesmen may operate more effectively when they are not restricted to a definite area.
3. Some salesmen prefer to operate where they can get the best results, irrespective of territory.
4. Territory reductions arouse resentment on the part of salesmen and create dissatisfaction.

5. The security of territorial protection is not conducive to maximum activity on the part of some salesmen.

Establishing basic sales territories. The first step in a scientific determination of a sales territory is to consider the market potential and the number of salesmen needed in the distribution of the product. This insures each salesman in the organization equal opportunities from the standpoint of potential sales.

Use of indexes. To determine the potential for each territory, a market index or indexes relating to the product or service being sold is first selected. Some factors to be considered in selecting a market index are: the price of the product; whether it is a luxury or a necessity; and whether it is an industrial or individual consumption item. For such lines as refrigerators, washing machines, ranges, and other products where industry sales figures are available by states, the industry figures may form the base of the index. In addition to the current sales index, other indexes measuring potential consumption should be selected. In the case of products for individual consumption, the factors of population, buying power, standards of living, and distributive outlets should be considered and indexes relating to these factors employed.

The consumption factor of population may be expressed by the following specific indexes: foreign-born population, colored population, literate population, native whites, families, rural population, urban population, adult population, dwellings, and so forth.

The basic consumption factor of buying power may be expressed by any one or several of the following indexes: income tax returns, value of farm crops, value of livestock, individual bank deposits, check transactions, per capita wholesale and retail sales, automobile ownership, and so forth.

The factor of standards of living may be expressed by the following indexes: telephones, wired homes, radio ownership, life insurance sales, magazine circulation, and so on.

Indexes of distributive outlets include: number of wholesalers and retailers in the case of companies distributing through middlemen.

These market indexes may be weighted according to their relative importance in respect to the potential of the market being measured.

Using indexes in determination of a basic sales territory. The next step in using a market index or indexes in the determination of a sales territory is to convert the index figures selected, which may be available in county, city, state or trading area units, to a percentage of the United States total of the index factors. For example, a manufacturer of agricultural implements selects the market index "rural population" for determining the potential of a basic sales territory. By consulting the latest United States census, the percentage of the total national rural population for each county and state can readily be determined and used as the index of potential for each county and state in the country. Other index factors may be combined with "rural population" to obtain a combined index and each factor may be weighted according to its relative importance.

Determination of number of salesmen needed according to potential market. After the potential of each county, state, or trading area in the country has been determined, the total number of customers and prospects to be contacted by salesmen is ascertained for each area.

The call frequency of the salesman as affected by the frequency of purchase, density of the market, extent of sales development, competition, and cost of coverage should next be determined. In some cases, salesmen must call daily; in others, monthly, and in selling many products an annual visit is sufficient.

By dividing the total number of customers and prospects in the United States by the number of contacts a salesman can make in a year, the number of salesmen needed to cover the national market is ascertained.

Allotment of potential market to salesmen. When the number of salesmen required to cover the national market potential has been decided upon, the national sales potential is divided into as many potentially equal sales territories as there are customers and prospects and salesmen needed to develop them. If one hundred salesmen are needed to develop the country, each salesman is assigned one per cent of the national potential, comprising all or a part of one or more counties, cities, states, or trading area units expressed in percentile of the national total of the index selected to express potential sales.

For example, the national manufacturer of agricultural implements has 500,000 selected farmer customers and prospects in the United States. Assuming that a salesman can contact four farmers a day while working 250 days a year, he can make a total of 1,000 contacts annually. On a call frequency of once a year, the number of salesmen needed to cover the country in this case is the 500,000 contacts divided by 1,000 contacts per man, or 500 salesmen. The basic potential territory of each salesman would be one five-hundredth of the national rural population expressed in all or part of one or more counties.

If a limited number of salesmen is needed, the state unit may be the minimum unit for basic territory establishment. In sales organizations cultivating the country more intensively the county unit may serve as a basis. Salesmen of consumer goods sold through wholesale and retail outlets may have territories established on the "trading-area"-unit basis.

Adjusted basic sales territories. After sales territories based on market potential, number of prospects, and number of accounts a salesman can handle have been established, it is necessary to adjust these basic territories to conform to purely local conditions, taking into consideration transportation facilities, competition, existing demand, extent of sales development, cost of coverage, method of distribution, economic conditions, type of product, ability of the salesman assigned to the area, and other factors affecting the ability of the company to attain its share of the potential volume of sales in the area. Basic sales territories in practically all cases must be adjusted to take into consideration these factors.

Adjustment to method of travel. Basic sales territories must be reshaped to conform to the transportation lines and method of travel used by the salesmen in covering the areas. When a salesman travels by automobile, the territory may conform to highway lines. When railroads are used, a territory must necessarily be shaped by the prevailing lines of railroads. A careful study should be made of all train, trolley, air, bus, boat, and automobiles routes in shaping the sales territory for most economical and efficient coverage.

Adjustment to competition. The amount and character of competition are important factors to be considered in expanding or contracting a basic sales territory. If competition is localized and intense within a basic sales territory, the size of the area may be restricted to permit more frequent coverage and to meet existing competition more effectively. When competition is limited, the basic territory may be expanded, since frequent coverage to meet competition is not necessary.

If, on the other hand, competition is so firmly entrenched in a sales territory that there is little likelihood that a salesman can secure a profitable volume, the basic area may be expanded to enable the salesman to obtain a profitable volume, or the salesman may be withdrawn from the territory, and it may be turned over to a broker or sold direct by mail.

Adjustment to existing demand. The existing demand for a product or service has a direct bearing on the adjustments that must be made in the size of a basic territory. If a strong demand exists for an item, selling progress is slow, and the basic sales territory may be restricted to insure thorough coverage. If, however, a new product is being introduced for which there is little existing demand, the basic territory may be expanded to enable the salesman to secure a profitable volume of sales.

Adjustment for extent of sales development. If the policy of a company favors intensive distribution, basic sales territories will be restricted to permit thorough coverage. If, on the other hand, a policy of broad, national distribution is pursued, expanded, basic territories must result.

Adjustment for profitable operation. The size of a sales territory must be regulated by the cost of travel in relation to the sales volume that may be secured therein. If, for example, the maximum ratio of direct selling expense to expected sales is 3 per cent, and anticipated sales are $100,000, the cost of covering the area must not exceed $3,000. Accordingly, the basic territory must be adjusted in area to permit coverage for this figure.

Adjustment for method of distribution. If a product is sold through wholesale outlets exclusively, the basic territory may be larger than would be the case if the product were sold direct to the consumer. Salesmen calling on retail grocers should have smaller territories than men calling on retail hardware outlets.

Adjustment for type of product. Basic territories for salesmen of repeat essentials may be relatively small in comparison with those of salesmen of novelties or luxuries.

Adjustment for ability of salesmen. The basic territory of an able salesman may be expanded, while the territory of a mediocre salesman may have to be contracted. A new and inexperienced salesman may require a more limited area than a more experienced man.

Adjustment for individual factors. The basic territories of salesmen with family responsibilities may be so arranged as to enable these men to live at home. Other salesmen who prefer continuous travel may be assigned to larger areas where more travel is involved. Some salesmen are more successful with intensive cultivation of their territories, and these men should be assigned restricted areas.

All of these factors should be taken into consideration in expanding or contracting basic sales territories so that each territory may be adjusted in area to afford maximum sales and profits.

Sources of sales-territory data. In determining basic sales territories and adjusting them to the various factors affecting the sales potential of an individual concern, there is a wealth of information available. Valuble information is published by the U. S. Census Bureau, the U. S. Bureau of Foreign and Domestic Commerce, and other Government bureaus, as well as various trade associations, state governments, colleges and universities, and commercial organizations. Publications of the Bureau of Foreign and Domestic Commerce of the U. S. Department of Commerce are excellent sources of territory information. The census of distribution made by the U. S. Census Bureau is an accurate source of market data available for the establishment of sales territories.

In addition to these sources, the following publishing organizations provide excellent territory information: Sales Management, Incorporated, New York City; Hearst Magazines, Inc., New York City; Curtis Publishing Company, Philadelphia; The Crowell Publishing Company, New York City; Printers' Ink Publications, New York City; and Industrial Marketing, Chicago.

Allocating sales territories. A sales territory may be allocated along political lines as state, county, township, city, or ward; or by transportation lines or buying habits that take no cognizance of political boundaries. Salesmen of consumer goods distributed through wholesale and retail outlets should have territories allocated by trading-area lines rather than by political boundaries. The same is true of wholesale and retail distributors of consumer goods. A salesman of industrial goods, insurance, securities, and other products or services not distributed through retail or wholesale outlets may have territories allocated by county lines.

Reallocating sales territories. Sales territories must be examined at least annually and adjustments made in the size of the area to meet shifting demand, competition, and economic conditions affecting the potential of the area; to equalize the opportunities of all salesmen; and to secure a fair ratio of expense to the sales volume.

There is an urgent need in many sales organizations for consolidating or reducing the area of sales territories and for insuring thorough cultivation at a savings in time and expense. Restricted territories result in better service to customers, more frequent contacts, more new prospects, lower freight costs, and greater sales volume and profits than larger territories. When the factual evidence of market potential and sales volume is compared in a sales territory, both management and salesmen are usually quick to concede that the area can be reduced with a saving in expense and an increase in efficiency and profit.

2. SALES QUOTAS

What is a sales quota? A sales quota answers the question "What sales should I expect to secure?" From the management standpoint, it is the proportional part or share of the total sales volume that may be expected from a given market. In other words, it is a goal of sales accomplishment, a task, objective, or standard that a sales organization strives to attain.

There are four distinct types of sales quotas, the most common of which is the estimated volume of sales that a company expects to secure within a definite period of time. As sales volume is one of the most important as well as the most conveniently computed factors of sales accomplishment, a majority of quotas are of this type. The estimate may be expressed in terms of dollars and cents or in units such as pounds, cases, gallons, and so forth.

The growing interest in profitable sales is contributing to an increasing use of "profit quotas," which are established to estimate the profit expectancy from a given territory. Profit quotas may be expressed in percentages of gross profit sought from the sale of single items or groups of items in given markets.

The necessity of curtailing sales expense has resulted in the establishment of "expense quotas" in some sales organizations. The maximum expense that may be expected from operations in a given market is established, and expenses are controlled by this standard. A large industrial manufacturer established an expense quota of ½ of 1 per cent of total net sales in small, thickly settled territories and 4 per cent of total net sales in large, thinly settled territories.

To encourage performance of specific sales operations, "activity quotas" are established on "number of calls," "number of interviews," "number of prospects secured," "number of service calls," "number of new customers," and so forth, which may be expected from a given territory in a specified time. Quotas may be set for such activity as "hours spent in the field daily," "miles traveled by automobile," "miles walked," and so on.

Division of sales quotas. Sales quotas are prepared for wholesale and retail salesmen, retail dealers, wholesale distributors, branches or sales divisions, as well as for individual products, groups of products, and types of customers.

While quotas for salesmen are the most common, many organizations also establish quotas for retail dealers and wholesale distributors as the basis of evaluation of distributor and dealer activities.

Product quotas are established for individual products and principal-product lines in order to obtain better co-ordination of production and sales, to insure that each product or product line will receive its share of sales efforts, and to enable the distribution of advertising for each product more equitably.

To provide for seasonal variations and to set the incentive closer to the salesman or distributor, quotas are usually broken down into quarterly, monthly, or weekly periods. Variables in seasonal activity and territorial conditions can thus be reflected in these breakdowns.

Advantages of sales quotas. Organizations using sales quotas find that they have the following advantages:

1. Permit measurement of sales ability.
2. Aid in co-ordinatnig production and sales.
3. Serve as a basis for sales compensation.
4. Set definite goal for accomplishment.

5. Enable comparisons between salesmen, distributors, retailers, branches, and so on.
6. Provide incentive.
7. Serve as the basis for sales budgets.
8. Enable the proper distribution of advertising, sales promotion effort, warehouse stocks, and manpower.
9. Increase the efficiency of the distributing system.

Weaknesses of sales quotas. The limitations of sales quotas are as follows:

1. Arbitrary establishment without taking into consideration enough factors to insure an accurate estimate of expected sales volume.
2. Arbitrary increases in quotas at periodic intervals without sufficient consideration of the factors involved.
3. Complex statistical methods for establishing quotas that are not understood by the salesman and arouse suspicion as to their accuracy.
4. Time and expense involved in making necessary research to establish a quota accurately.
5. Inadequate rewards for attainment of quotas.
6. Failure to consider the human element, especially the particular ability of the salesman or the distributor, and to secure his co-operation.

Essentials of a good quota. A good sales quota should have the following characteristics:

1. It should be attainable; that is, it should not be set so high that it is impossible of accomplishment. When a quota is set too high, the salesman or the dealer either loses interest or forces his efforts and creates ill will.
2. Simplicity is fundamental to a good sales quota. Complicated methods of determining a quota not only involve time and expense but create misunderstanding and arouse suspicion on the part of salesmen and dealers who are not clear as to the method used in arriving at the quota.
3. The views of salesmen, sales executives, and distributors should be considered in the establishment of a sales quota to insure their co-operation in attaining the goal set.

4. Flexibility is an important consideration in adjusting a quota according to variable seasonal and economic conditions. It is a mistake to establsh a quota and disregard those influences which are constantly affecting the possibility of attainment. Accordingly, some sales organizations make monthly or quarterly adjustments in quotas to keep them in line with changing conditions.

5. Incentives should be provided for stimulating the salesmen to meet their quotas. While it might be said that no special incentive should be necesary, the actual purpose of the quota is to encourage greater effort, and without an incentive it may fail of its purpose. That is why many firms offer salaried and commission men cash bonuses for making their quotas, and why some companies pay higher rates of commission to those making their quotas and still higher rates to those exceeding their quotas.

Bases for sales quotas. Several factors must be taken into consideration in establishing a fair sales-volume quota: (a) past sales; (b) market potential; (c) estimates of salesmen and distributors; (d) manufacturing output; (e) advertising and sales promotion effort; (f) selling cost; (g) product improvements; (h) prices; (i) business conditions; (j) competition; and (k) particular ability of the salesmen or distributors. All of these factors must be weighted and considered carefully in arriving at a fair sales-volume quota. Each factor is discussed briefly below.

1. *Past sales.* The initial basis for a sales-volume quota is past sales performance. The past year's sales, as well as an average for several years preceding, should be considered in establishing a trend of sales. Sales alone, however, are not a measure of the sales potential of a salesman or a dealer in most cases. Sales volume should not be used exclusively as a basis for a quota. However, sales volume in past years is a definite and important factor in establishing the quota formula and provides a conservative basis for quota estimates.

2. *Market potential.* No sound sales-volume quota can be established without a knowledge of the potential market. The market potential is most conveniently measured by selecting one or more market indexes. Some sales organizations use as many as nineteen separate factors in measuring market potential. However, for the

sake of economy and to avoid complication, a simple index is recommended.

As in the establishment of sales territories, the market indexes of people and homes, purchasing power, standards of living, and distributive outlets may be used with varying weights according to the type of commodity under consideration.

The index of people and homes may be expressed by one or more of the following: population, total families, dwellings, literate native white population, colored population, and so on.

The standards-of-living index may be expressed by: automobile registrations, telephones, electric domestic customers, radio ownership, and so forth.

The buying-power index may be expressed by: bank deposits, income tax returns, check transactions, per capita sales, and so on.

The distributive-outlet index may be expressed by number of consumers, manufacturers, and retail and wholesale outlets.

In establishing sales quotas for industrial products, the following market indexes may be used: value of manufactured products, number of manufacturers, number of industrial power consumers, and so forth.

An example of the use of market indexes in establishing sales quotas is the method employed by a large electric appliance manufacturer. An index of purchasing power for electric refrigerators is compiled by states and counties by:

(a) Tabulating refrigerator sales for a period of years, converted into percentage of the national total.
(b) Selecting the most typical percentage for each state, allowing for trend.
(c) Establishing the relationship of sales by states to the industry sales percentage.
(d) Adjusting the state index by a climatic factor that is necessary to bring the index into line with actual sales.
(e) Applying the climatic adjustment factor to county figures.
(f) Using the adjusted county index to break down the industry state-sales percentage; index would be used without this step for those products whose sales are not reported by states.
(g) Regrouping final county index figures according to distributor's territory.

This index is considered, along with past sales performance, in preparing distributors' quotas, with the index given a weighting of one to two thirds.

The average annual sales of distributors are also converted to a percentage of the United States total and compared with the index.

National advertisers frequently use the combined circulation figures of the magazines in which their advertising appears as an index of market potential.

A large automobile tire manufacturer uses automobile registration figures as an index in establishing sales-volume quotas; a manufacturer of domestic sheeting uses department-store sales volume as an index in establishing quotas.

3. *Estimates of distributors and salesmen.* The psychological value of asking salesmen or distributors for estimates of future sales volume is constructive, since they will accept quotas more readily when they have a part in their determination. The value of these estimates is dependent largely on the type of salesman and the product being sold. Intelligent salesmen or high-grade distributors frequently can make very accurate estimates of future sales volume.

4. *Manufacturing output.* This factor should also be considered in establishing a sales-volume quota, and the point of profitable production should be kept in mind in determining the quota figure.

5. *Advertising and sales-promotion effort.* The extent of advertising and sales-promotion effort has a direct bearing on the attainment of a sales-volume quota, and the amount to be invested in advertising should be compared with previous investments in determining the quota figure. An increase in advertising and sales-promotion effort should be paralleled by an increase in the sales-quota figure.

6. *Selling cost.* The cost of selling a given volume should be considered in establishing a sales-volume quota. To absorb the expense of salesman's compensation and travel as well as promotion, a territory must produce a certain volume of business. Accordingly, the profitable minimum volume of sales that must be secured to cover costs is a factor in determining a volume quota.

7. *Product improvements.* This factor has a definite bearing on sales-volume quotas. The introduction of a new product or an improvement in an old product should make it possible for a sales-

man or a distributor to attain a greater volume of sales, and the quota must be adjusted upward accordingly.

8. *Prices.* "Price policy" is an important factor in the establishment of sales quotas. A sharp reduction in price, for example, may result in a salesman's or a distributor's obtaining a considerably greater volume of sales with no additional effort. In a period of rising prices, however, sales may be curtailed, and quotas should be reduced.

9. *Business conditions.* Economic conditions have an important bearing on the sales-quota figure. In periods of improved business, quotas may be higher, whereas in periods of depression, economic conditions call for a reduction in quota figures.

10. *Competition.* The character and strength of competition have a bearing on the establishment of sales quotas. The amount of the potential sales available is reduced in proportion to the strength of competition. Accordingly, the competitive situation in each area must be carefully examined.

11. *Sales ability.* The ability, attitude, and experience of the salesman are important factors in determining whether or not he can attain the quota figure. The human factor cannot be overlooked in determining sales quotas. If a salesman does not have the ability to attain the potential determined by market analysis and consideration of other factors, the quota figure must be reduced to come within reach of his ability.

Securing acceptance of quotas by salesmen. A sales-volume quota is of little value unless salesmen, dealers, or distributors concerned are convinced of the fairness of the quota and accept it as a reasonable expectation of sales, possible of attainment. Accordingly, those concerned in attaining the quota should be consulted in its preparation. In one large electrical-equipment sales organization individual salesmen are required to estimate their sales volume; these estimates are checked by branch managers, who in turn forward them to district managers; the latter forward their sales estimates for their respective territories to the home office, where the total of these field estimates are combined to form a national quota. In each step of the process, the factors of past sales, selling costs, product improvement, business conditions, competition, advertising and sales promotion effort, and the ability of the salesman are considered.

After the sales or distributing organization is convinced of the fairness of the quota, the quota objectives should be kept before them by frequent reports on quota performance and personal conferences. Charts or graphs illustrating the progress of each distributor, dealer, or salesman in the attainment of quotas are effective aids in insuring quota performance.

3. RECRUITING AND SELECTING SALESMEN

The recruiting problem. Recruiting is a continuous problem in most sales organizations because of resignations, retirements, disabilities, replacements, transfers, and deaths. In the sale of luxuries, specialties, and intangibles, recruiting is more difficult than in staple lines, and few salesmen volunteer for work in these fields. Accordingly, it is necessary for management to "sell the job" to men who can qualify for selling life insurance, securities, home appliances, and similar luxury or intangibles lines. On the other hand, many small sectional or local sales organizations distributing staple or industrial products have low personnel turnover and no recruiting problem.

In large as well as small organizations distributing all types of products, a periodic review of sales personnel is desirable. Personnel requirements should be anticipated, and necessary changes planned at least a year in advance.

A large manufacturer of electrical apparatus requires each of its sales departments annually to budget its probable requirements for salesmen for the ensuing year by quarters. In this way the company is able to recruit and select competent men and train them properly for the openings that may develop. Instead of waiting until a demand for salesmen suddenly presents itself before seeking men to fill the opening, good management plans in advance for future personnel.

The recruiting process. The process of recruiting salesmen is analogous to selling. The sales manager must locate prospective salesmen; he must learn as much as possible about their personal history and circumstances; he must present his proposal to them, convince them of the opportunities in the sales work, and then follow up to make sure that everything is done to help the recruit succeed in his new work.

Determining type of salesman wanted. The first step in the recruiting process is to arrive at a definite understanding as to the type of man best qualified to perform the sales job. Obviously, the type of salesman will vary widely with the type of product or service to be sold, class of buyer, demand for the product, and nature of the sales job.

The method of determining the type of salesman qualified to perform a specific sales job is to prepare a job analysis describing the duties to be performed by the salesman, together with the difficulties likely to be encountered in the work. Such a duty and difficulty analysis discloses the specific requirements of the job, together with personal characteristics necessary to perform the duties and surmount the difficulties. A list of duties and difficulties may be readily prepared by consulting sales supervisors and salesmen and drawing on the experience of the management. Opposite the duties and difficulties may be listed the obvious personal qualities needed, such as technical ability, college education, appearance, tact, initiative, analytical ability, age, nationality, physique, and so on.

The apparatus salesmen of a large electrical equipment manufacturer must possess the following personal qualities to perform the duties and meet the difficulties in their specific work: (1) technical ability and general intelligence; (2) business sense; (3) energy or willingness to work; (4) personality; (5) appearance; (6) leadership or ability to organize, supervise, and inspire others; (7) character and loyalty.

In addition to such personal traits, other factors, including age, education, marital status, previous experience, membership in organizations, and savings, should also be considered, since these relate to the duties to be performed and the difficulties to be encountered in the specific sales job.

Analysis of the personal qualifications and characteristics of the present salesmen in a sales organization will serve to reveal the personal characteristics desirable for selling a specific product or service. For example, if the successful salesmen in an organization at the period when they were inducted into the business were under thirty years of age, college graduate, single, and without previous selling experience, it might be assumed that these characteristics were desirable for men who were to be engaged for selling the product in question.

Likewise, a study of the characteristics of successful salesmen of competitors in the same industry might also reveal traits identified with success in selling that type of product. An analysis of the membership of the life insurance "Million-Dollar Round Table," composed of million-dollar producers, revealed that 32 per cent of the group were formerly salesmen, 29 per cent business executives, and 21 per cent professional men. This study shows that over 80 per cent of the successful salesmen in this group came from three sources.

Establishing standard personal qualifications. By studying the duties and difficulties of a specific sales job, the type of product or service to be sold, the class of buyer, and by analyzing the characteristics of present salesmen in the organization as well as successful salesmen in the business as a whole, a standard of personal qualifications may be readily established and used as a basis for future selection. Many sales managers have a general conception of the type of man desired, but few have reduced to writing the exact qualifications necessary for success in selling a specific product or service.

When several functional types of salesmen are employed in an organization, separate standard characteristics should be established for each type. A junior salesman may require certain personal characteristics not demanded by the work of a missionary salesman. An export salesman may need far more knowledge, experience, and education than a domestic senior salesman. A sales engineer may need considerable technical education and mechanical aptitudes.

Sources of salesmen. When the type of salesman wanted has been determined, and standard qualifications for the sales job have been established, the sources from which such men may be selected are next explored.

The sources of present successful salesmen in the organization should first be considered. Analysis of the employment records of salesmen currently connected with the organization will reveal those sources from which the outstanding salesmen have been obtained in the past.

Likewise, analysis of the major sources from which salesmen for the entire industry are obtained will indicate likely sources of recruits. Through trade associations, industry magazines, by exchange of information with co-operative competitors, the most likely sources of salesmen can be identified. An industry study made for the life insurance business revealed that there are the following four major sources of prospective agents:

1. From those personally known to the sales manager.
2. From centers of influence or nominators. Recruits secured through these two sources averaged $11,500 production in their first month under contract.
3. From the present agency force.
4. Through direct mail advertising.

Recruits from group 3 averaged $7,500 production during their first month, while recruits from group 4 averaged only $1,500. As compared with the average length of time needed to complete negotiations with recruits from sources 3 and 4, approximately six times as long is required to induct into the business recruits from sources 1 and 2. This type of industry experience is invaluable to a sales manager in determining the most likely sources of salesmen for his organization.

Other sources of salesmen. Following is a summary of the possible sources of prospective salesmen.

1. *Company rotation training.* A growing number of companies, large as well as small, are using rotation training as a source of salesmen. Selected groups of young men are trained by rotating them for a year or more in various departments of an organization, during which time their work is carefully observed and rated. At the completion of the training, a decision is made as to the acceptability of the trainee for sales work.

A progressive manufacturer of drug specialties recruits annually twenty-five selected college graduates; they are paid a salary plus expenses while they are in training. The candidates spend four weeks in the New York office of the company, followed by fourteen months of sales experience in the field. At the end of that time, men who have proved their ability as salesmen are retained by the company, while those who are not selected are given a cash graduation present, and an effort is made to place them in other organizations. During the training period, company officials lecture to the trainees on such subjects as business organization and practices, current business problems, principles of salesmanship, food and drug legislation, fair trade, export advertising and merchandising, sales promotion, and similar subjects.

2. *Hiring from within.* The current trend is toward the employment of salesmen from within an organization before any search is made outside. Men recruited from the office or factory are familiar with company policies and products and are loyal. Moreover, the management has had an opportunity to observe them closely and judge their abilities. A meat-packing company with 3,000 employees follows a firm policy of exhausting all possibilities among plant employees before looking elsewhere for salesmen.

3. *Through present salesmen.* New salesmen may be recommended by experienced, successful men now representing the company. In their dealings with customers, salesmen have an opportunity to become acquainted with promising sales material. Wholesale salesmen have an opportunity to observe salespeople in retail stores, many of whom are possible candidates for wholesale-selling work. Through his acquaintance with such retail salespeople, a manufacturer's salesman is in a position to observe their industry, courtesy, and other qualifications.

The sales manager of a large paint manufacturer says: "We get good leads on new men from our own good salesmen. Poor salesmen, on the other hand, rarely produce good sales candidates."

4. *Through present customers.* Customers who are favorably disposed toward a product and organization are frequently in a position to recommend likely salesmen. Nominating letters may be sent to selected lists of customers asking them for names of prospective salesmen. Life insurance agency managers and other specialty sales executives send out a continuous series of nominating letters to policyholders and customers. Purchasing agents who have frequent contact with salesmen are usually qualified to recommend candidates for sales positions.

5. *Advertising.* Periodical advertising in the classified and display sections of daily newspapers and business magazines is a commonly used source of salesmen. However, exaggeration and misrepresentation by advertisers have in large part discredited classified advertising as a source of salesmen. Direct-mail advertising to selected occupational groups and recommended prospects is often an effective source. Advertising in business magazines is selective in coverage

and normally produces a higher-grade candidate than newspaper advertising.

6. *Schools and colleges.* The alumni placement services of colleges, particularly those offering business administration courses, provide a source of experienced salesmen with academic training. Men who are completing their college work are being sought intensively by many progressive sales organizations operating training schools. One large floor covering organization that recruits annually twenty-five men for sales-training classes interviews some 2,000 candidates at forty-three universities each year.

7. *Hiring from competitors.* Fewer sales organizations are hiring from competitors than in the past. It is difficult to transfer a salesman successfully from one company to another in the same competitive field. Men hired from competitors are frequently independent in attitude, difficult to control, and demanding.

8. *Voluntary applicants.* Occasionally, voluntary applicants provide a favorable but limited source of candidates. Naturally, in periods of depression, the volume of voluntary applicants increases. This source must be considered supplementary rather than basic.

9. *Employment agencies.* While some employment agencies list salesmen, they are usually more concerned with placing clerical workers and are little interested in placing salesmen on commission. The specialized sales employment agencies, however, recommend higher type sales personnel. These agencies are more familiar with the qualifications demanded in salesmen and are a more reliable source of sales material.

Selecting salesmen. When a candidate for sales work has been discovered in one of the sources previously described, the next and more difficult problem is to determine his fitness for the sales work under consideration. The process of measuring or testing sales applicants is receiving more attention today than ever before. Effective manpower is the fundamental of every successful sales force. High turnover of salesmen and the expense of recruiting, selection, and training emphasize the importance of a sound selection system.

Process of selection. The process of selection requires two basic steps. The first step is to consider the personal qualifications required for the sales job. These qualifications may be determined as discussed previously by a job analysis; consultation of the personal-history records of present successful and unsuccessful salesmen in the organization; and consideration of the type of product, class of trade, prevailing demand, and price. These factors will determine the specific personal qualifications sought in an applicant as indicated by his age, education, number of dependents, previous experience, health, previous income, and other considerations. A standard of qualifications for each of these personal-history factors should be established before applicants are selected.

When the personal requirements for a specific sales job have been determined, the next step is to establish a system for comparing the qualifications of candidates for sales work with the standard qualifications established. The system may be compared to a yardstick or tape in making linear measurements. The elements of a good selection system are:

1. Application forms.
2. Letters of reference from previous employers.
3. Personal interviews.
4. Intelligence and aptitude tests.
5. Physical examinations.
6. Field observations.

Application forms. When an applicant applies for sales work, he is usually given a preliminary application blank calling for basic information relative to his age, education, previous experience, dependents, previous income, and number of previous employers. Later, at a second interview, he is asked for additional information on a long form listing factors considered significant by the employer in respect to the personal qualifications necessary to perform the sales work successfully.

A long form of application suitable for employment of salesmen is illustrated on pages 296 and 297, Figures 28a-b.

In a number of companies the information supplied by the applicant on the application form is scored by giving a numerical value to each personal history factor listed on the form. Critical scores obtained from actual production records of present salesmen in the organization are used to evaluate the personal history score of the applicant. By starting with a preliminary application form

NY 626-48282-10M-3-30

....
(Name of Company)

APPLICATION FOR POSITION

(Must be in applicant's own Handwriting)

City.. Date..........................

Name...
(First Name) (Middle Name) (Last Name)

Present address ....
(Street and Number) (City) (State) (Telephone)

Permanent address...
(Street and Number) (City) (State) (Telephone)

Do you live with parents.................. Board.................. Rent or own home.............. Rent per month..................

Age.............. Height.............. Weight.............. Present condition of health..........................

Physical defects...

How much time have you lost through illness in last two years..

Married or single......................... Number of children......................... Other dependents..........................

Name of Person to be notified in case of Emergency:

....
(Name) (Street and Number) (City) (State) (Telephone)

From what grade of schools did you graduate and when..

Other educational work...

....

Name and address of present or last employer (state which)..

.... How long there.................... Salary....................

Nature of duties with above...

....

Name and address of last three employers, length of time with each and reason for leaving:

....

....

....

Character references...
(Name) (Street & Number) (City) (State)

....
(Name) (Street & Number) (City) (State)

....
(Name) (Street & Number) (City) (State)

Starting salary expected.............................. Signature..

(OVER)

Figure 28a. Application for Position.

THESE ADDITIONAL QUESTIONS ARE TO BE ANSWERED BY APPLICANTS FOR A POSITION ON SALES FORCE
(Salesman, Distributor, Demonstrator, etc.)

Do you own real estate: .... Value .... Incumbrance ....

Do you own stock or bonds: .... Value .... Incumbrance ....

Do you own a car: .... Make ....

Do you carry liability Insurance: .... Amount ....

Have you any loans or debts: .... How much past due: ....

Particulars of same: ....

Have you any other income besides what you will receive from us: .... Amount $ ....

What insurance do you carry: Life $ .... Health $ .... Accident $ ....

Have you ever been employed by us before: .... In what capacity and where: ....

Have you any relatives in our employ: ....

Name of personal acquaintances in our employ: ....

In what territories have you had more than six month's experience: ....

....

With what territories are you most familiar: ....

What territory do you prefer: ....

What classes of trade have you sold: ....

What experience have you had in our line: ....

Have you ever been bonded, and for what amount: ....

Has bond ever been refused: ....

Can you give a surety bond (at our expense): ....

Does last or any previous employer claim any unpaid balance against you: ....

Applicant hereby consents to immediate dismissal if at any time hereafter

(*a*) *Applicant's bond be cancelled by Surety for any reason.*

(*b*) *It becomes apparent that applicant has made false, evasive, or incomplete answer in application for Surety bond, to any questions therein, and more particularly to the following: "18—Have you ever been discharged from any position? Give particulars"; "19—Have you ever been in arrears or default in your present, or any previous employment? Give full particulars"; "20—Do you owe any present or past Employer anything? If so, to whom, how much, on what account, how secured and when due."*

....

Signature of Applicant.

APPLICANTS FOR SALES FORCE POSITIONS MUST FURNISH POST CARD SIZE BUST PHOTOGRAPH

Figure 28b. Application for Position—Reverse Side of Figure 28a.

undesirable applicants are quickly eliminated, and time of interviewers is conserved.

Personal interviews. Applicants for sales work are universally required to be interviewed by one or more sales executives for the purpose of determining whether the candidate's qualifications fit him for the sales job and to enable the employer to present the job to the applicant. While many experienced sales executives pride themselves on their ability to select salesmen solely by personal interview, personal judgment has been proved to be an ineffective method of evaluating an applicant's likelihood of success in the sales organization. Opinions of interviewers are usually subjective, colored by personal experiences, and often unreliable. Nevertheless, with all their limitations, personal interviews remain one of the fundamental methods of ascertaining the intangible personal characteristics of an applicant which reveal his fitness for sales work.

In an effort to make personal interviews more valid, an interview judgment-rating form, on which interviewers check their impressions, provides a guide for each interviewer, prevents hasty opinions, and enables comparison of the views of several interviewers. A form of judgment chart is given in Figure 29, on page 299. Some sales executives prefer to interview an applicant in his own home, at a club, or in an informal social setting. In a large electrical equipment manufacturing organization, selected applicants are taken in groups of ten to attend a luncheon with the general sales executives, where each candidate is required to give a short talk about himself and tell specifically why he is interested in becoming a salesman for the company. After the luncheon, the sales executives carefully rate each of the applicants and decide which ones may be qualified for sales work.

Many companies are using as an interviewers' guide a "patterned interview," listing significant questions to be asked by the interviewer.

A telephone check or personal interview of previous employers is desirable as a means of verifying the information obtained during the personal interview.

References. A form is frequently sent to previous employers of a sales applicant to verify questions of fact regarding dates of previous employment and amount of income received. An example

J U D G M E N T ** C H A R T

Interviewed by.......... Name........................

Date........ ....

* * * * * * * * * * * * *

The prospective salesman should be judged on the qualities set out below. First, in reaching a judgment on a quality, mark, in the blank space following each of the questions, an "N" indicating negative and a "Y" indicating affirmative, or with a "?" if you are undecided. These questions, while not an exclusive list of points involved in each quality, will give you an indication of the elements to be considered in evaluating that particular quality. Then, indicate your opinion on each quality by making a check (✓) on the line, just where you think it ought to be. For example, if, in item 1, you think the prospective salesman is a little lower than "good", but not quite low enough to be recorded as "Fair" put the check mark on the line somewhere between 75 and 50.

oooooooooooooooooooooooooooo

	Excellent	Good	Fair	Poor

APPEARANCE 100_____75_____50_____25_____
Facial expression pleasing?___Erect carriage?___Clothes neat?___Hands and nails clean?___Physique impressive?___Inspires confidence?___Awkward?___ Sits erect in chair?___

MANNER 100_____75_____50_____25_____
Courteous?___Smoked uninvited?___Friendly?___Agreeable?___Polite?___ Over-familiar?___Breezy?___Grouchy?___Optimistic?___Rough?___Enthusiastic?___ Objective minded?___Tactful?___

PHYSICAL CONDITION- 100_____75_____50_____25_____
Would be willing to have exam by our doctor?___Nervous?___Eyes bright?___ Skin clear?___Exercises?___Recent serious ailments or conditions?___

VOICE-LANGUAGE 100_____75_____50_____25_____
Any foreign accent?___Sectional accent?___Speech peculiarities?___Talks too loud-too low?___Enunciates clearly?___Mumbles words?___Good vocabulary?___ Mistakes in grammar?___

DETERMINATION-COURAGE- 100_____75_____50_____25_____
Any athletic record?___Likes tough job?___Strong reaction to adverse comment on his selling ability?___Insists on consideration for job?___Confident he could sell product?___Easily discouraged about opportunity?___Annoyed by interruption?___

LOYALTY-COOPERATIVENESS- 100_____75_____50_____25_____
Mentions former employers favorably?___Complains of former superior?___ Complains of "raw deal"?___Would accept suggestions?___

HONESTY-RELIABILITY- 100_____75_____50_____25_____
Willing to be bonded?___Looks you in the eye?___Hesitant about any of past record?___Any discrepancies in experiences?___Previous positions of responsibility?___Boastful?___Sincere?___

IMAGINATION-RESOURCEFULNESS- 100_____75_____50_____25_____
Sells himself effectively?___Started and carried through any projects?___ Full of ideas?___Good Sales talk about previous items sold?___Good talk on hypothetical sales problem?___ Has checked company and products?___

INTELLIGENCE 100_____75_____50_____25_____
Good scholastic record?___Quick reaction to explanation of our Products? Slow in giving answers?___Open-minded?___Tolerant?___

KNOWLEDGE OF CURRENT AFFAIRS- 100_____75_____50_____25_____
Interested in political & economic problems?___Understands functions of Congress and Courts?___Reads something besides newspapers?___Familiar with names in public affairs?___

INDUSTRY 100_____75_____50_____25_____
Easy going attitude?___Hard worker in previous job?___Ambitious?___Worked while in school?___

METHODICAL 100_____75_____50_____25_____
Jumps at conclusions?___Kept records in former job?___Keeps personal record?___ Good attitude towards daily reports?___Explains ideas clearly?___Thrifty?___ Even tempered?___

PARTICIPATION IN INTERVIEW- 100_____75_____50_____25_____
Talked too much?___Organized answers to questions?___Volunteers information?___ Merely answers questions?___

REMARKS ----

Figure 29. Judgment Chart.

of such a form is the four-page folder reproduced on pages 301-303 (Figures 30a-b-c-d.) Aside from questions of fact, little worthwhile information is ordinarily obtained when the opinion of the previous employer is sought on questions of the applicant's habits, industry, conduct, and ability.

Intelligence and aptitude tests. No single selection device has aroused more interest in recent years than aptitude and intelligence tests. Although tests have demonstrated their value in a few sales organizations, a majority are in the experimental stage, and little evidence has been produced to reveal their value in the selection of salesmen. Many sales executives are vainly seeking for general aptitude tests which will enable them to predict the future sales success of a candidate for sales work. So far, no such test has been devised. Intelligence tests of mental alertness, personality, and the like, are in no sense a measure of proficiency in selling.

A large electrical equipment manufacturer uses the following intelligence and aptitude tests in selecting salesmen: Army, Alpha and Beta Tests; the Inglis Vocabulary Test; the McQuarrie Test for Mechanical Ability; The Vocational Interest Blank for Men by E. K. Strong, Jr.; and the Personality Inventory by R. G. Bernreuter. This company is developing a procedure to help establish the reliability of these tests.

A test of selling aptitudes for a specific sales job must take into consideration the duties and difficulties involved in the specific work, and some companies are developing their own aptitude tests along these lines.

Sales managers, with the assistance of sales testing consultants, are experimenting with different types of tests and making comparisons between the scores that new salesmen receive at the time they are employed and their subsequent success as measured by sales volume, new accounts, and so forth. These tests are also being evaluated by personal ratings of the salesmen's records, made by their supervisor and other sales executives. Tests are of little value until the meaning of the test scores in terms of probability of success in selling is determined.

Physical examinations. Good health has such a direct bearing on the personal appearance, mental attitude, and industry of a

Dear Sir:

Mr. is being considered as a sales representative of this Agency. Your opinion of his fitness for our business will assist us in deciding whether or not he is likely to succeed as a life insurance salesman.

For your convenience we have arranged page 3 so that you can indicate your opinion by entering a few check marks.

We want to be fair to Mr. as well as to our Agency and Company. It would be unjust to him and disadvantageous to us to appoint him if he is not suited to our business. In order that his qualifications may be properly appraised, we hope you will give page 3 your prompt and thoughtful attention.

Yours very truly,

Figure 30a. First page of four-page reference letter.

WE REQUIRE
OF THOSE WHO REPRESENT US:

1. A record of success in previous work
2. A record of industry.
3. Happy home life
4. Self-reliance
5. Physical energy—endurance
6. Demonstrated ability to manage own affairs
7. Ambition to get ahead
8. Mental alertness
9. Eagerness to render social service
10. Loyalty

Probably no one life insurance salesman could possess all these qualifications. He should, however, possess a goodly number of them. Many of the others may be cultivated.

Figure 30b. Page 2 of four-page reference letter.

Your answer to each question may be indicated by a cross (X) placed in the proper brackets. If the applicant has not been in your employ, please answer only questions 5 to 9 inclusive.

1. Mr. .... states that he was in your employ as ....
Does this correspond with your record? Yes ( ) No ( )

2. He states that he left because ....
....
Is this an adequate statement? Yes ( ) No ( )

3. Were you personally acquainted with him and his work?
Yes ( ) No ( )

4. Was he always honest in financial dealings? Yes ( ) No ( )

	Exceptional	Very Good	Satisfactory	Poor	Very Poor
5. How do you rate his *personal habits* and and *conduct?*	( )	( )	( )	( )	( )
6. How do you rate his *industry?*	( )	( )	( )	( )	( )
7. How do you rate his *determination* in spite of difficulties?	( )	( )	( )	( )	( )
8. How do you rate his fitness for a *selling position?*	( )	( )	( )	( )	( )
9. How do you rate his ability to direct his own work?	( )	( )	( )	( )	( )

10. Would you be willing to re-employ him? Yes ( ) No ( )

We shall appreciate any additional information that may assist us in judging the applicant's fitness for the position.

Signature ....

Figure 30c. Page 3 of four-page reference letter.

> Please give any further information which you feel might affect the applicant's success as an insurance salesman. This information will be held in strict confidence.

Figure 30d. Page 4 of four-page reference letter.

salesman that physical examinations are universally given by all progressive companies in qualifying candidates for sales work. In some types of selling, unusual demands on the physical fitness of a salesman call for rigid physical qualifications.

Observation on the job. When candidates for sales work are observed selling in the field, an opportunity is afforded to check their qualifications on the job before they are contracted.

Summary of selection methods. A sound selection procedure includes several of the selection devices previously described. Each method of selection should be tested in the light of experience by comparing the performance of the salesman selected with the ratings and evaluations made by the sales executives who interviewed him at the time of his selection. Continuous experimentation with various selection devices is necessary to insure an effective selection system.

4. EQUIPPING SALESMEN

Need for sales equipment. An increasing number of sales organizations are aiding salesmen to improve their effectiveness by providing them with tested selling tools to save the salesmen's time; gain the attention of the buyer; make multiple selling appeals to the sight, touch, taste, and hearing of the buyer; keep salesman and prospect on a direct line of thought; avoid interruptions and distractions during sales presentations; provide salesmen with an abundance of selling points; enable salesmen to tell a complete story; increase the salesman's confidence; dramatize the sales presentation; and save the buyer's time.

Qualities of good sales equipment. Well-planned salesmen's equipment should meet the five following requirements:

1. It should be related to the product or service being offered. Trick attention-getters not relevant to the salesman's presentation

simply serve to distract the prospect and confuse the presentation.

2. Equipment should be designed to permit a prospect to participate in its use, thereby experiencing for himself the advantages illustrated by the equipment, and, at the same time, satisfying the human instinct to touch and handle the novel and ingenious.

3. Equipment should be light in weight and not bulky to permit easy handling and encourage use by the salesmen. Much interesting and convincing equipment is not used because of its large size.

4. Attractiveness in appearance and design is fundamental to good sales equipment. The quality of the product or service being offered by the salesman is reflected in the appearance of the sales equipment.

5. Novelty in conception to attract attention and arouse interest is characteristic of good sales equipment.

Types of selling equipment. The type of selling equipment required by a salesman depends upon the nature of the product, type of prospect or customer, method of travel, number of salesmen employed, and custom in the trade. Salesmen of technical products are equipped with engineering data, mechanical-performance figures, cost information, blueprints, illustrations of installations, and facts for technically trained buyers. Consumer goods salesmen, on the other hand, carry equipment to illustrate design, beauty, appearance, ease of operation, comfort, and similar consumer appeals.

The objective of salesmen's equipment is to provide the average salesman with information and devices to enable him to tell a better sales story, to add printed weight to his statements, to save time, to hold attention, and to create a more lasting impression of the product or service on prospects.

The most important types of salesmen's equipment are:

1. Samples of the product being sold by the salesman.
2. Various types of miniature models, including working models, nonoperating models, cross-section models, and toy models.
3. Portfolios, including loose-leaf, pyramid-easel, accordion-fold, and zipper, in standard 8½ × 11 inch and miniature sizes.
4. Motion-picture projectors and sound and silent motion pictures in 16-mm. width.
5. Sound and silent slide films and projectors.
6. Demonstrating devices.

7. Charts and diagrams.
8. Advertising materials, including booklets, folders, broadsides, proofs of publication advertisements, business cards.
9. Sales and sample cases.
10. Sales manuals.
11. Service and engineering manuals, catalogues, price lists, and policy books.
12. Automotive trailers.

Applications of selling equipment. The various types of selling equipment mentioned above have been applied to aiding salesmen in: locating prospects; securing interviews; staging interviews; opening interviews; and demonstrating, presenting, and closing sales. In addition, this equipment is used in training salesmen and facilitating the operation and control of salesmen in the field. Examples of the use of various types of sales equipment in locating prospects and making presentations follow.

Equipment to locate prospects. A large manufacturer of oil-burner and domestic stoker equipment equips dealer salesmen with sound-slide films and sound-slide projectors featuring the benefits of the product. The films are shown by the salesmen to their friends, neighbors, and acquaintances, who are asked for the names of any of their friends who might enjoy seeing the pictures. As a result of these showings, live prospects are uncovered. In one two-week period one salesman made sixty-one showings, uncovered eighteen prospects, and closed five sales for an average return of $2.20 per showing.

Equipment to secure interviews. Salesmen may be provided with special equipment to enable them to secure interviews with prospects. One automobile manufacturer supplied retail salesmen with miniature models of passenger cars, suitable as paperweights or toys for children. Salesmen offered these models to prospects in return for an opportunity to present the features of the car. The Fuller Brush Company has for a long time been offering through its salesmen gift brushes as inducements to prospects to grant interviews to salesmen. Other novelty equipment, including memorandum books, ash trays, mechanical pencils, and business cards, are furnished salesmen to aid them in securing interviews.

Staging interviews. Salesmen who are confronted with the problem of finding a suitable place to conduct interviews and demonstrations with prospects are equipped with automobile sales trailers fitted up as salesrooms, which are driven to a consumer's home or a dealer's place of business. Faced with the difficulty of getting the prospect to come to the showroom, salesmen with trailers overcome this problem by bringing the showroom to the prospect. The advantages of sales trailers are: (1) interruptions are prevented; (2) the novelty of a trailer presentation is impressive; (3) a full line of samples and sales equipment is available; (4) longer and more complete presentations are possible; and (5) actual demonstrations with the product are possible. On the other hand, trailers are difficult to park and operate in congested areas, while the initial investment and cost of operation are high.

Opening interviews. Salesmen are provided with various types of equipment to use in opening sales interviews. Portable, record-playing radios were used by salesmen of a large meat packer to play to retail merchants a five-minute recording of the company's radio broadcast. An optical equipment maker aided salesmen in opening interviews by providing them with a small paper box bearing the question, "Would you swap one of yours for this?" When the prospect opened the box, he found a glass eye.

Demonstrating equipment. Many companies equip their salesmen with unique demonstrating devices to enable them to present outstanding features of their products in dramatic and novel ways. A motor truck maker has equipped salesmen with miniature truck models with removable power units to demonstrate how easily power units can be removed from the trucks.

Presentation equipment. To aid salesmen in making more effective sales presentations, various types of equipment have been devised. The most common type is a presentation portfolio in which sales points are arranged in logical order and illustrated with charts, photographs, or cartoons, accompanied by brief explanations. Included in presentation portfolios are testimonial letters, illustrations of product installations, names of users, clippings, diagrams of construction features, and advertising, all or a part of which may be referred to by a salesman in making his presentation.

Advertising portfolios containing proofs of advertisements, schedules of insertion, circulation coverage, and testimonials of effectiveness are also supplied to salesmen to aid them in presenting their advertising story.

Sound motion-picture and slide-film projectors and films are standard sales equipment in many organizations for selling both consumers and dealers.

Charts and diagrams are effective sales tools. An appliance manufacturer devised a large chart, or "visualizer," mounted on the product, featuring principal selling points with novel demonstrating devices attached for use by retail salesmen in making sales presentations.

Closing equipment. While much of the previously described sales equipment contributes to closing a sale, special equipment for this purpose has been designed in a number of companies. A large stationery supply house has equipped its salesmen with novelty order books, 2 × 2 feet in size, as a suggestion to customers and a reminder to salesmen that the mission of the salesman is to secure orders. An automobile manufacturer equipped retail salesmen with a "closing stone," a gilt pocket piece, to remind them to ask for an order.

Training equipment. Equipment for training manufacturers', distributors', and dealers' salesmen consists of sales manuals, policy books, catalogues, specification sheets, engineering and service manuals, sound and silent motion pictures, and slide films. Some of this equipment is carried regularly by a salesman for ready reference as a source of answers to objections and technical information.

Many manufacturers train dealer salesmen with sound slide films and records issued periodically throughout the year. A large electrical appliance manufacturer furnishes the following equipment to retail dealers: twelve slide films and records, sound slide film projector, film and record-carrying case, and twelve dozen film pamphlets. The dealer shares with the manufacturer in the cost of this training equipment. Similar training equipment is provided by other large manufacturers.

Operating equipment. To facilitate the operation and control of salesmen in the field, a variety of forms are provided for reporting on calls, interviews, sales, lost orders, missionary work, adjustments, credits, and traveling expenses. Figures 31, 32, 33a and 33b (pages 308-311) illustrate typical sales reports that are included in a sales-

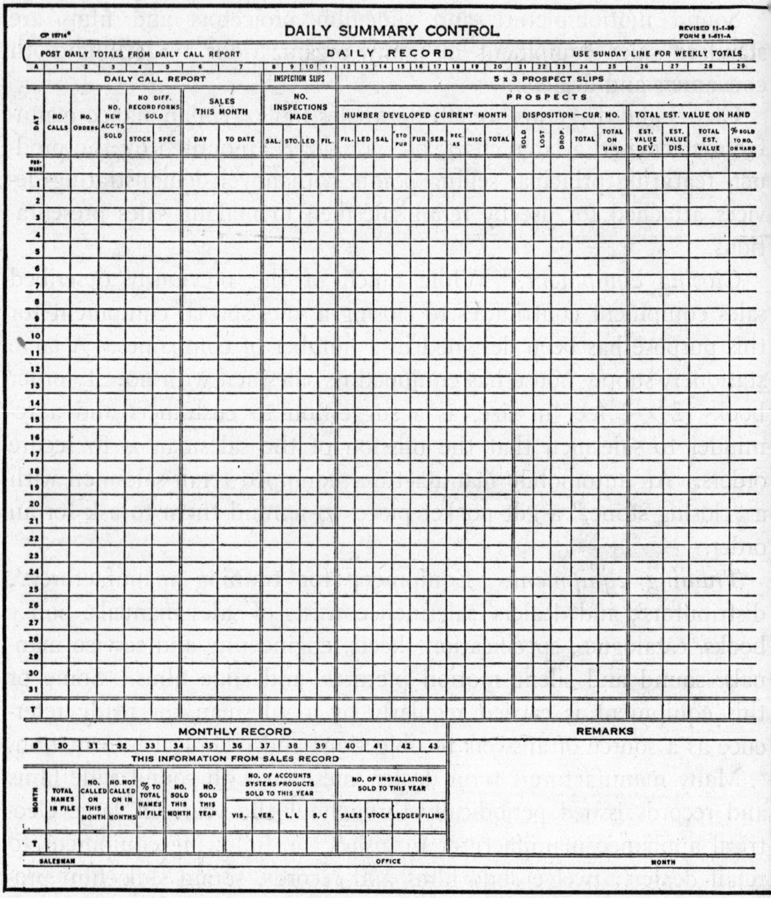

CP 19714*

DAILY SUMMARY CONTROL

REVISED 11-1-39
FORM S 1-611-A

POST DAILY TOTALS FROM DAILY CALL REPORT — DAILY RECORD — USE SUNDAY LINE FOR WEEKLY TOTALS

A 1 2 3 4 5 6 7 8 9 10 11 12 13 14 15 16 17 18 19 20 21 22 23 24 25 26 27 28 29

DAY | DAILY CALL REPORT: NO. CALLS; NO. ORDERS; NO. NEW ACC'TS SOLD; NO. DIFF. RECORD FORMS SOLD (STOCK, SPEC); SALES THIS MONTH (DAY, TO DATE) | INSPECTION SLIPS: NO. INSPECTIONS MADE (SAL., STO., LED, FIL.) | 5 x 3 PROSPECT SLIPS: PROSPECTS — NUMBER DEVELOPED CURRENT MONTH (FIL., LED, SAL, STO PUR, FUR, SER., REC. AS, MISC, TOTAL); DISPOSITION—CUR. MO. (SOLD, LOST, DROP., TOTAL, TOTAL ON HAND); TOTAL EST. VALUE ON HAND (EST. VALUE DEV., EST. VALUE DIS., TOTAL EST. VALUE, % SOLD TO NO. ON HAND)

FOR-WARD
1 2 3 4 5 6 7 8 9 10 11 12 13 14 15 16 17 18 19 20 21 22 23 24 25 26 27 28 29 30 31
T

MONTHLY RECORD — REMARKS

B 30 31 32 33 34 35 36 37 38 39 40 41 42 43

THIS INFORMATION FROM SALES RECORD

MONTH | TOTAL NAMES IN FILE | NO. CALLED ON THIS MONTH | NO. NOT CALLED ON IN 6 MONTHS | % TO TOTAL NAMES IN FILE | NO. SOLD THIS MONTH | NO. SOLD THIS YEAR | NO. OF ACCOUNTS SYSTEMS PRODUCTS SOLD TO THIS YEAR (VIS., VER., L. L, S. C) | NO. OF INSTALLATIONS SOLD TO THIS YEAR (SALES, STOCK, LEDGER, FILING)

T

SALESMAN — OFFICE — MONTH

Figure 31. Daily Summary Control.

A daily summary report of individual salesman's activities, showing amount and type of activity as well as results.

N. Y. 631-51871-50M-6-30.

This list must be mailed to your District and Territory Sales Manager not later than Saturday P. M. giving routing for the following week

Salesman's Advance Route List

Name ____________________

Permanent Address ____________________

For the week ending Saturday, ____________, 19__, and Sunday following.

	CITY	STATE	Name Hotel or Care General Delivery
Sunday			
Monday			
Tuesday			
Wednesday			
Thursday			
Friday			
Saturday			
Sunday			
	FOLLOWING WEEK		
Monday			
Tuesday			

Figure 32. Route List.

A simple form of planning sheet giving a salesman's itinerary for the next succeeding period.

Form 42

TO BE FILLED IN BY BRANCH	AMOUNT	TOTALS
SALARY		
EXPENSE		
LESS E. B. A.		
STOCK		
NET AMT PAID	CHECK NO	

Salesman's Weekly Report

BRANCH

WEEK ENDING ________________ 19 ____

NAME ________________________ HDQTRS. ________________

CLASS ________________________

TERRITORY ____________________

NUMBER OF DAYS WORKED	NUMBER OF CALLS	NUMBER OF ORDERS

ENTER DATES BELOW	RAILROAD AND INTERURBAN FROM	TO	R. R. FARE	AUTO EXPENSE	TOWN AND NAME OF HOTEL	HOTEL EXPENSE	SLEEPER	OTHER EXPENSE	TOTAL EXPENSE
SUN					B D S L				
MON					B D S L				
TUES					B D S L				
WED					B D S L				
THURS					B D S L				
FRI					B D S L				
SAT					B D S L				
	TIME CARD RECEIVED	TOTALS							
	SAMPLE REPORT RECEIVED					TOTAL EXPENSE FOR WEEK (EXCEPT SALARY)			

EXTS. O. K. ____________ APPROVED ____________ APPROVED ____________ APPROVED ____________ PAY ____________ (OVER)

TERRITORY MGR

Printed in U. S. A.

Figure 33a. Salesman's Weekly Expense Report.

A weekly report giving details of expenditures.

Report of Expenses

INSTRUCTIONS

Expense accounts must be mailed at end of each week. The week's expenses will commence with breakfast Sunday and end with lodging Saturday, making the full week.

Under the head "R. R. & Interurban" enter names of towns to and from which each trip is made and amount of fare.

Railroad fares incurred on your own account or on trips outside of your own territory are not chargeable in the expense account.

Foot each of the five columns, show the TOTAL expense on the BOTTOM RIGHT hand line.

Each charge must be itemized, stating what it is for, and only such charges as are deemed reasonable and necessary will be allowed.

We do not pay for chair car or other transportation extras, except straight sleeping car rate for night trips.

All auto livery or sample charges must be accompanied by a receipt.

Automobiles, livery are not to be used as a convenience and are to be employed only when it will enable you to accomplish in one day that which without auto would require two or more days.

Salary or expenses will not be paid when salesmen are not working because of illness or other reasons.

No allowance will be made for incidental expenses unless previously arranged.

We do not honor drafts or send money by telegraph.

We pay legitimate traveling expenses necessarily incurred in the transaction of our business (such as hotel bills—for lodging and meals only—railroad fares and postage) at exactly the prices paid by our salesmen. We do not pay laundry, barber or any personal expense. Any overcharge or manipulation of expense items is dishonest and will not be tolerated.

Charge only such hotel bills as are incurred when working territory outside of your home city or "headquarters town," as hotel expenses incurred while you are at home or in "headquarters town" are not chargeable to us.

The above instructions must be strictly observed and daily and weekly reports agree exactly or expense accounts will be subject to deduction.

Checks will not be mailed until new time card and all reports are received.

Totals on reverse side of this sheet represent actual expense incurred.

Signature

Where shall we send check?

Town --

Care of --

Figure 33b. Reverse Side of Figure 33a.

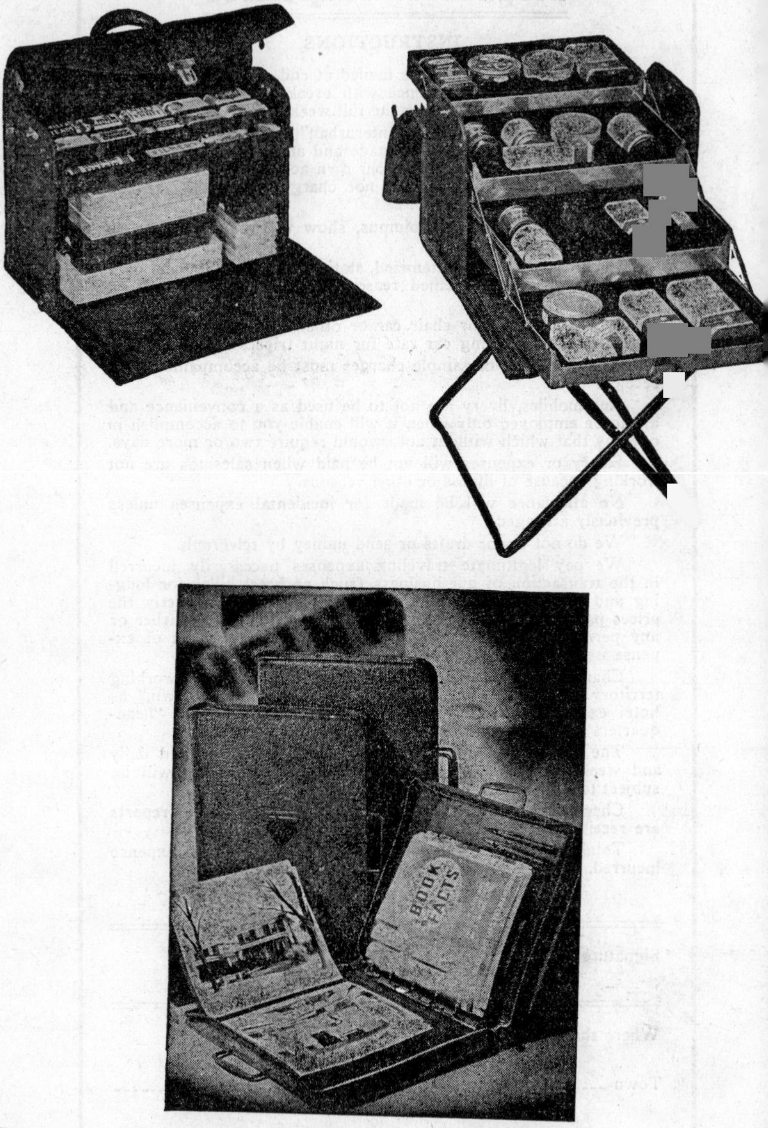

Figure 34. Various Types of Sales Kits. At the lower right is a portable Illustravox Sound Slide Film Projector used by manufacturers', wholesalers', and

retailers' salesmen for making visual presentations to consumers. The recorded sales talk is synchronized with the illustration projected on the screen.

man's equipment. Order books, price lists, and specification forms are also included in a salesman's equipment.

Equipment cases and kits. For convenience in carrying and protection, all of the aforementioned equipment is packed in sample cases or sales kits. The sales kits should be designed to insure the safety of their contents; to be readily accessible; to display the product to its best advantage; and to provide for convenient arrangement. A sales kit should be shaped for ease in handling and storage; light in weight to encourage its use; of good external appearance to create a favorable impression on prospects and customers; and so arranged internally as to permit individual items to be shown without unpacking.

Sales kits may be made to order to suit the requirements of an individual organization, or standard cases may be purchased that fit the equipment needs of many concerns. A periodic review of salesmen's cases to insure their good appearance and completeness is desirable. A few examples of sales kits are illustrated on pages 312 and 313.

Getting salesmen to use equipment. Some salesmen feel that sales equipment arouses resistance of prospects, is not needed in many interviews, is undignified to carry, and wastes energy. For these reasons, much helpful sales equipment is not used by salesmen, and the management is confronted with the problem of selling its value to the salesmen themselves.

To overcome these objections, first, the equipment should be well designed, convenient to carry, light in weight, attractive in appearance, novel in conception, and kept up to date. Second, new equipment should be tested by one or two salesmen in a small area to discover its weaknesses and correct them before the equipment is given to the entire sales force. Third, after the equipment has been tested, it should be sold to the sales organization at sales meetings to arouse mass enthusiasm. Definite examples of the use of the equipment in the field should be discussed, the proper use demonstrated, and results of effective use cited. Fourth, some concerns charge salesmen for equipment to insure that it will be properly handled and used. This charge may be rebated after a certain volume of merchandise has been sold or when the equipment is retired. Fifth, by following through on equipment to prospects, some companies insure that it will be used. One industrial manufacturer gets salesmen to use presentation equipment by writing prospects that a salesman will call and use the equipment in his presentation. Salesmen are given a copy of the letter to prospects as a reminder to use the equipment in their presentations.

5. TRAINING SALESMEN

Why train salesmen? Growing competition and declining profit margins are creating a greater need for trained salesmen and emphasizing management's responsibility for developing sales personnel. Heretofore sales training has been considered a "fair-weather" activity, a luxury to be indulged in during periods of prosperity only, to be treated as an unnecessary overhead expense, and to be eliminated in periods of depression. Effective man power is the major problem of sales management, and sound training is a fundamental step in insuring sales effectiveness.

A constructive sales-training program makes possible the following accomplishments:

1. Increases sales.
2. Reduces selling costs.
3. Attracts a high type of salesman to the organization.
4. Results in better service to customers.
5. Safeguards the company's investment in new salesmen.
6. Reduces the number of salesmen by developing the ability of the individual.
7. Meets increasing competition and growing sales resistance.
8. Reduces the turnover of salesmen by making them more productive.
9. Shortens the time necessary to place a new salesman on a profitable producing basis.
10. Simplifies supervision and control of salesmen.
11. Insures satisfaction of customers through proper representation of product or service.
12. Stimulates salesmen through exchange of selling methods.
13. Provides sales-executive material.

Comparison of the work of trained with untrained salesmen shows 10 to 15 per cent greater sales by trained men.

Who should be trained? The problem of sales training from a manufacturer's standpoint involves six classes of personnel: (1) apprentices, (2) new experienced salesmen, (3) present salesmen, (4) sales supervisors, (5) field sales-management executives, including branch managers, division managers, and district managers, (6) distributor's and dealer's salesmen.

Training apprentices. Both large and small sales organizations are establishing training courses for young men starting out in business. From these training groups men with selling aptitude are selected for sales work. Typical of such programs is the Student Engineers' Course of an electric equipment manufacturer, from which men are selected for the Sales Engineers' Course. Men who have satisfactorily completed this course go into the General Office Sales Department and from there into field sales work.

A building material producer offers a similar apprentice program. College graduates are recruited annually and trained for a period of approximately nine months in company history, organization, manufacturing facilities, and financial position; following this, in the engineering, research, production, advertising, credit, traffic, legal, accounting, and claims departments. This training is supplemented by required outside reading and actual field experience in retail stores.

Training new experienced salesmen. Irrespective of previous sales experience, salesmen who are beginning work with a sales organization require training to acquaint them with new products, policies, selling problems, difficulties, and duties. Salesmen who are new in an organization are receptive to sales training, and practically all companies today give some degree of training to new salesmen.

Training present salesmen. Training a senior salesman who has been with an organization for some time is the most difficult sales-training problem. Many older men are not receptive to new ideas, consider that they know all that should be known about their work, are set in their ways, are too proud to admit lack of knowledge, and resent sales training as a childish activity. However, senior salesmen require periodic retraining as their information becomes outdated and as new products and policies create new selling problems. Training for senior salesmen, however, must be emoved from the academic and must be "sugar-coated" with practical material. The group conference discussion method is the most uitable for older experienced men.

Training sales supervisors. The burden of field sales training falls on the sales suprvisor in charge of a group of six to ten men in the field. For this reason, special courses have been established in a number of companies to train supervisors in the best method of training salesmen under their supervision. Since retraining or continuation training is usually a responsibility of supervisors, the training of these men is very important. Supervisors become part of the sales-training staff in many organizations and should be instructed in the best techniques for carrying on field training.

Training field sales-management executives. In some organizations, branch managers are responsible for field supervision of salesmen in their territories and function as field trainers of salesmen for continuation and retraining of senior salesmen in the field. Some companies conduct special sales-training courses at the home office for branch managers, district managers, and division managers to train them in developing the men in their charge.

Training wholesale and retail dealers and their sales managers. Manufacturers distributing through wholesale and retail outlets also assume responsibility for training wholesale and retail dealers and their sales managers. The objective of a dealers' training program is to train the dealer so that he will be able to train his own salesmen. A large electric appliance manufacturer trains retail sales managers with a series of sound slide films entitled "Selecting Salesmen," "Supervising Salesmen," and "Holding Sales Meetings."

Training wholesale and retail salesmen. Large manufacturer sales organizations train wholesale and retail salesmen employed by dealers and distributors. Because of the large number of salesmen of this class, many of these training programs consist of correspondence courses.

Subject matter of training. The subject matter of a sales-training program depends upon the duties of the salesmen and the difficulties encountered in selling the specific product or service.

A job analysis should be made to determine the duties of the salesmen and indicate the information that they must receive through training to enable them to perform these duties efficiently. In addition, a difficulty analysis should be made of the obstacles encountered by the salesmen in carrying out their work. The usual weaknesses of salesmen are in personality, knowledge, working system, and selling technique. A training course should present material to aid a salesman in correcting these difficulties.

The choice of subject matter depends upon the duties and difficulties of the salesmen to be trained and usually includes information on:

1. The product.
2. The market.
3. The company history and organization.
4. Advertising and sales promotion.
5. Policies on credit, service, adjustments, prices, and delivery.
6. Duties of salesmen.
7. Difficulties, and how to meet them.
8. Sales methods, involving locating prospects, planning presentations, conducting interviews, demonstrating, answering objections, and closing.
9. Systematizing, time control, and work organization.
10. Servicing customers.
11. Sales equipment.
12. Sales territories.

Tools for sales training. After subject matter has been obtained based on the duty and difficulty analysis of the work of the salesmen, this material must be arranged in convenient form to impart to the salesmen. Training information is presented in the form of sales manuals, motion-picture films, slide films, charts, problems, bulletins, house organs, playlets, and dialogues.

The sales manual is the basic training tool. It is usually a loose-leaf, 8½ × 11 inch binder, containing all of the essential information presented in the sales-training course. The material in the manual may be issued to salesmen serially and inserted in the loose-leaf binder as the course develops. Sometimes pocket-sized manuals or handbooks, each dealing with a specific subject in the training course, are printed and distributed to salesmen for study.

Sound slide films and records are the basis of many manufacturers' sales-training programs for their own salesmen as well as for the salesmen of distributors and dealers. A large carpet manufacturer uses two technicolor sound slide films, "Craftsmanship" and "Sale-ing Orders," to train retail rug salesmen.

Sound motion pictures are being used in increasing numbers in training manufacturers' as well as distributors' and retailers' salesmen.

Phonographic recordings of salesmen's presentations for analysis and discussion are being made by progressive sales organizations as a part of their training program.

Supplementing these basic sales-training tools are charts to visualize sales points, the sales process, and organization for group instruction. Other supplementary tools are problems or cases taken from field sales experience of the salesmen being trained to serve as a basis for group discussions. Bulletins, house organs, outlines, and dramatizations also have a part in the modern sales-training program.

Sales-training meetings. Sales-training meetings should be planned in advance, and consideration should be given to the following important features:

1. The subject of a sales-training meeting should be timely and significant, not a discussion of petty grievances and routine matters, but the solution of the principal selling problems encountered in the field. The introduction of a new product, the inauguration of a new feature, a new sales policy, a tested method of meeting competition, a better way of overcoming common objections, a more effective use of time—all these are important subjects to be considered at a training meeting. Each meeting should concern itself with only one subject to insure thorough treatment. Salesmen may be invited to suggest a subject, or the management may select the subject.

2. Treatment of the subject should next be planned in detail. A sound slide film or motion picture featuring the subject may be shown to the group. One of the salesmen may be called upon for a brief discussion of the topic. A question-and-answer treatment may be used, or a demonstration by two salesmen, one posing as a prospect, may be arranged. An outside speaker or a customer

may be invited to talk. A dramatic sketch may be staged by sales-office employees. A problem may be distributed in advance of the meeting for group discussion.

3. An outline and timetable of the program of the meeting is next prepared to provide a proper time for announcements, presentations, intermission for refreshments, and a closing summary. A training meeting should start and stop on time, and move briskly according to schedule, but not too rapidly for the group to absorb the material presented.

4. Build up the meeting by creating anticipation with preliminary announcements to the salesmen. Urge the men to come prepared to make suggestions or participate in discussion of the subject of the meeting.

5. Control the meeting by adhering closely to the time schedule, keeping discussion on the subject, silencing the talkative member of the group, avoiding criticism, sidetracking embarrassing complaints, encouraging participation by all, and avoiding competition with the speaker by excluding distracting charts, papers, and samples.

6. Provide for the comfort of those attending with plenty of light, fresh air, and ventilation. A "no-smoking" rule creates a better atmosphere.

Types of sales training. Sales training may be classified according to method as individual, group or conference, field or job, and correspondence. The most common method of sales training is by group conferences at which lectures, round-table discussions, playlets, or dialogues are presented. This type of training is the least expensive, quickest, and most effective way of getting across information on the product; product applications; company policies on credits, collections and adjustments; advertising and sales promotion; company history and organization; routine duties; and sales techniques. Successful group training depends upon adequate preparation by the trainer and trainees, a favorable time and a comfortable place for the meeting, control of participants in the discussion, participation by the trainees, and, in conclusion, summarization of the information developed at the meeting.

Group training alone, however, is inadequate to develop salesmen. It is lacking in realism, is impersonal, and gives little opportunity to acquire skills vital to a salesman's effectiveness.

Individual training is the most important type of sales training because it takes into account the strength and weakness of an individual salesman and gives the trainer an opportunity to adjust his instruction to the individual need for knowledge or skill in selling. Since this type of training is expensive and slow, it is often neglected in the training process. Through individual conferences following field observation of a salesman's methods, a trainer can point out the specific difficulties of a salesman and advise him how to improve his technique.

Field training or coaching on the job is a form of individual instruction. Selling is a complicated skill that cannot be learned from books and may only be acquired slowly by field experience. Field sales experience without supervision or correction, however, often serves merely to fix imperfection. Accordingly, field coaching or training on the job is necessary to point out a salesman's strength and weakness. A tried field-training formula is the "D. O. C. method," or demonstration, observation, and correction by the trainer. By repeating this formula for several days with a skilled trainer, a salesman learns by actually doing much faster than he would by reading, listening, or watching in group conferences. While information may be acquired and the acquisition of selling skill speeded up by individual study, lectures, and group conferences, coaching on the job is vital to a sound training program.

Some companies have adapted the principles of the "Job Instruction Training" used by the War Manpower Commission during World War II to the field training of salesmen.

Sales training by correspondence is a common and inexpensive method of developing salesmen. It provides information but gives no opportunity to develop skill, establish correct work habits, and improve methods by actually doing the job under proper supervision.

Where to conduct training. Group or conference training may be conducted at the home office, branches, or at hotels in selected cities throughout the sales territory. Home-office training is generally practiced by small organizations training a limited number of salesmen, as well as by manufacturers of technical products that can be discussed most effectively at the home office or factory.

Individual or field training is conducted in the salesman's territory in combination with group training in the branch office. Companies with large sales organizations often use this type of training, thus saving the expense of bringing the salesmen into the home office for training, and making it possible for the salesmen to become producers at the earliest possible time.

After a salesman has received preliminary training in a branch office and in the field, he may be brought into the home office for advanced training in the product, product applications, and company policies.

Sources of training material. The primary source of sales-training material is found in the duties of salesmen and the difficulties encountered by them in the field. Training material coming from this source is looked upon by the salesmen as practical, and it has a realistic value not found in "desk-made" training courses. While the time and expense involved in duty and difficulty analysis are considerable, this is an unparalleled source of training data.

Trade associations have developed sales-training material that can be adapted to the use of individual sales organizations in their field.

Textbooks in salesmanship are a source of excellent ideas that may be incorporated in a sales organization's training program. *Salesmanship, Practices and Problems,* Second Edition, by B. R. Canfield (McGraw-Hill, 1950), describes the twenty principal problems encountered by salesmen of various types of goods and services and suggests successful methods of solving these problems. These methods may be applied in training salesmen of any type of product or service.

6. METHODS OF COMPENSATING SALESMEN

Aims of a compensation plan. A successful compensation plan for salesmen is one that secures the highest volume of sales, pushes the sale of the most profitable items, offers the salesmen an incentive to work harder, and at the same time permits sales to be made at a cost that returns a good profit to the employer. A plan that attains these ends necessarily recognizes the needs and problems of the salesmen. The objectives of a successful plan are as follows:

For the Company

(1) Stimulate salesmen to increase sales.
(2) Encourage loyalty to the firm.
(3) Promote co-operation of salesmen with each other and with the firm.
(4) Discourage overselling.
(5) Encourage salesmen to push high-profit items.
(6) Eliminate requests for special consideration and favors.
(7) Provide reasonable profit over sales expense.
(8) Provide control over salesmen's activities.

For the Salesman

(1) Increase their earnings in proportion to their sales accomplishments.
(2) Afford a reasonable payment for services.
(3) Pay for time spent in missionary work.
(4) Provide living wage during training.
(5) Promote pride in company.
(6) Provide security.
(7) Provide for retirement.
(8) Provide for seasonal slumps.
(9) Compare favorably to wage scales in similar lines.

Factors in the choice of a plan. The factors that determine the choice of a compensation plan are:

1. The cash resources of the company.

2. The speed with which business can be closed in the field. The compensation plan for salesmen who are required to do considerable missionary work will be different from that in a field where little creative selling is required of the salesmen because of an established demand for the product created by advertising.

3. The policies of competitors.

4. The type of product. A product that requires extraordinary sales ability may call for a different plan of compensation from one that can be sold by men of average ability. Certain products, for instance, require specialized or technical knowledge on the part of salesmen, such as in the case of machinery parts, and so forth; others, such as staple products, require merely good selling ability. Both fields should be compensated accordingly.

5. The market for the product. Products sold in a narrow market, such as those appealing to limited groups of customers, require one type of compensation plan, while products sold to broad classes of customers may call for an altogether different plan.

6. The method of distribution. If the product is sold to dealers, distributors, wholesalers, and others who in turn sell to consumers, sales are frequently made automatically. The compensation plan will take this factor into account. On the other hand, if creative

selling is called for, as in the case of products sold directly by th manufacturer to the consumer, another type of compensation migh apply.

7. The advertising policies of the company. Well-advertisec products may require very little creative selling on the part of th salesman, while products that are not well known may call for a greater degree of sales ability. The compensation plan should take care of the salesman who has to spend part of his time creating a demand for the product.

8. The ability of the salesman. Obviously, certain selling jobs call for greater ability than others. Salesmen of outstanding ability who are accustomed to earning large salaries and enjoying a high standard of living prefer compensation plans that offer payment in direct proportion to the volume of sales made. On the other hand, some salesmen who have not proved themselves good earners may not be content to accept employment on a commission basis.

9. The variety of products making up the line. A man selling a variety of products may more easily maintain or increase his wage level than a man selling one product. This factor may affect the type of compensation.

10. Price of product and margin of profit. High-priced items are often more difficult to sell than low-priced items, and the salesman should be compensated accordingly. Also, the margin of profit dictated by such factors as cost, demand, established trade practices, and so on, may enter into the determination of the method of compensation.

Testing the compensation plan. To inaugurate a compensation plan and put it into operation are not enough. The plan should be tested from time to time to detect hidden weaknesses, and steps should be taken to eliminate them. The following questions will help employers test the compensation plan:

1. Are the aims of the plan and their relative weight clearly defined? The plan should bring out the relative importance of increasing sales, getting new business, promoting goodwill, doing missionary work, reducing sales expense, selling specific items, and so on.

2. Is the relationship of compensation costs to profits fair?

3. Do the results show the plan to be successful? The conclu-

.ve test is the results obtained. Records must be maintained that /ill disclose whether the salesmen are doing missionary work, /hether they are developing new accounts, whether they are push-ng only certain items, and whether they are doing all parts of heir selling job.

4. Are most of the salesmen satisfied with the plan? It is wise o consider the opinions of the salesmen in regard to the compen-ation plan, for in consulting the salesmen an opportunity is of-ered to promote loyalty and enthusiasm toward the company, as vell as to disclose weaknesses in the compensation plan.

5. Is the plan flexible? The plan should be sufficiently flexible :o provide for additional compensation for men with unusual ability.

Types of plans. The two basic plans for compensating sales-men are (1) salary, and (2) commission. The type and size of the company and individual trade and market problems make it ex-pedient in many cases to use a variation or combination of these plans. Some of these plans will be discussed later.

Salary compensation. Under this plan a certain sum is paid to the salesmen each week regardless of the amount of sales made. The salary method of compensation is usually employed when considerable missionary work is required, when the efforts of several salesmen are necessary to complete a sale, or when it is desired to help salesmen maintain a living wage during training periods and seasonal slumps. Firms engaging in the type of business that has little yearly sales fluctuation and can therefore forecast their sales volume fairly accurately often pay salesmen on a flat-salary basis. Sales executives are usually paid a straight salary. The advantages and disadvantages of the salary plan to the company and to the salesman are as follows:

ADVANTAGES

For the Company

(1) Bookkeeping is simplified.
(2) A fixed cash responsibility is undertaken.
(3) Better control of men is obtained.
(4) Men are easily recruited.

For the Salesman

(1) Personal security is afforded.
(2) Home office control develops desirable habits of work.
(3) Income can be budgeted.
(4) Compensates for missionary work that may not result immediately in sales.

(5) Overselling of customers is prevented.
(6) Salesmen's time can be arranged for nonselling activities.
(7) Loyalty of salesmen to the company is promoted.
(8) Co-operation among salesmen is encouraged.
(9) The transfer of salesmen from one territory to another is facilitated.

(5) Management takes risk fo time invested in selling.
(6) Wage level during trainin periods and seasonal slumps i maintained.
(7) Changes in business condi tions are not immediately re flected in lower salaries.

Disadvantages

For the Company

(1) It does not set a definite ratio of cost to sales.
(2) Incentives for greater sales efforts are lacking.
(3) A lower type of sales personnel is attracted.
(4) It is difficult to adjust to declining business activity.
(5) Salesmen demand periodical increases.
(6) Responsibility is on the management to make a good selection of men.
(7) Salaries must be paid to salesmen before they prove their ability.

For the Salesman

(1) Incentives are limited.
(2) Income is limited.
(3) Improvement in business is not immediately reflected in high earnings.
(4) Does not reward superior sales efforts.

Commission compensation. A commission is a percentage payment on sales. Compensation of salesmen working on a straight commission therefore fluctuates in direct relation to their sales accomplishments. Thus commission compensation may be considered the most direct form of payment for sales effort.

The commission plan is usually applied to the sale of specialties of fairly high price that have a broad market, such as automobiles, life insurance, office equipment, and so on. It is also commonly used in house-to-house or direct-to-the-customer selling, or where a high level of selling ability is required. The advantages and disadvantages of this plan, to company and salesmen, are as follows:

Advantages

For the Company

(1) The company with limited capital can obtain a selling staff.
(2) The plan immediately reflects the salesman's ability.
(3) The ratio of costs to sales is known immediately.
(4) More aggressive salesmen are attracted.
(5) The plan provides the incentive of higher earnings for greater sales effort.
(6) Sales costs are automatically reduced when sales decline.

For the Salesman

(1) Larger income is possible, and the incentive is greater.
(2) Greater independence is afforded.
(3) Co-operation with other salesmen is unnecessary.
(4) Sales efforts do not help to pay other salesmen who produce less.
(5) During periods of business prosperity earnings are rapidly increased.

Disadvantages

For the Company

(1) More bookkeeping is involved.
(2) The control of men is weakened.
(3) The employment problem is greater because many men prefer straight salaries.
(4) Salesmen's morale may be impaired if their earnings decline during business slumps.
(5) Customers are exposed to overselling.
(6) Missionary work is discouraged.
(7) Salesmen are inclined to concentrate on live prospects, to neglect profitable items that are hard to sell, and to spend little time in originating new business.
(8) Co-operation with other salesmen is reduced.

For the Salesman

(1) Irregularity of income lessens security.
(2) Little assistance is offered by the home office.
(3) During business depressions income falls rapidly.

When prices are unstable, the straight-salary plan and the straight-commission plan are usually unsatisfactory. For example, commission rates may prove too high for the changing price level, and employers may find themselves burdened with excessive selling expenses. On the other hand, salesmen earning a straight salary during a period of rising prices may find their earnings out of line with the earnings of salesmen on a commission basis. Frequently companies change their methods of payment to meet changing conditions.

Variations of the commission compensation plan. The straight-commission plan discussed in the preceding paragraphs makes no allowances for such factors as volume, difference in salability of items, differences of profitability of items to the company, or other factors. The following variations of the straight-commission plan make allowances for such differences:

1. Commission rate varying for individual items. In order to stimulate salesmen to push profitable items that are hard to sell, a higher rate of commission is given as an incentive. Items that are easy to sell and have a wide demand carry a lower rate of commission.
2. Sliding scale of commissions. Salesmen are paid a certain percentage up to a certain volume of business, after which the rate is increased or decreased progressively as sales grow in volume.
3. Group commissions. Various products are classified into groups, and rates of commission are set up for each group.

Drawing account. This plan is actually a variation of the straight-commission plan and consists of an advance loan on a salesman's anticipated commission paid at regular intervals like a salary. The amount of the drawing account is generally determined by the expected sales based upon experience. For example, a company may give a salesman 10 per cent commission and $40 per week drawing account, based on the experience that a salesman selling that particular product will earn at least $40 per week commission. If a new product upon which no sales data exist is being sold, the amount of the drawing account is determined upon the company's anticipated sales based upon market research.

If the salesman has exceptional ability, his commission compensation will produce earnings over the drawing account, and these earnings will go to his credit. If, for any reason, the commission earnings fall below the drawings in any set period, this deficit is regarded as the salesman's indebtedness to the company. Such overdrafts are generally handled in the following ways:

1. A deduction is made from commission earnings in periods when such earnings are higher than normal.
2. A limit is placed on the total amount of overdrafts, and the salesmen are allowed to "pay back" a small percentage weekly. When the limit is reached, the drawing account is discontinued until the indebtedness has been paid in full.
3. The amount of the drawing account is reduced until the overdraft has been cleared.
4. Excess commission is set up as a reserve against overdrafts. The balance is paid to salesmen at the end of the year.
5. Salesmen are requested to sign one-year notes for overdrafts over a specified amount.
6. Overdrafts are written off at the end of the year so that salesmen may not feel too discouraged by accumulation of debts.
7. The overdraft accumulation is split 50-50 with the salesmen at the end of the year.

In all cases salesmen who consistently run up overdrafts must be carefully watched. With some salesmen the situation indicates that the commission or compensation plan needs adjustment. With others, the situation indicates poor planning or poor salesmanship and may necessitate replacement of the men. The advantages and disadvantages of drawing accounts are as follows:

Advantages

For the Company

(1) Exercises some control over the salesmen.
(2) Adds to incentives of the commission plan.
(3) Keeps salesmen satisfied during training periods and seasonal slumps.
(4) Provides an incentive to keep sales up to normal expectancy.
(5) Attracts more salesmen, thus permitting the company to have a wider selection of new men.

For the Salesman

(1) Assures a steady income despite slump periods.
(2) Permits budgeting.
(3) Indicates company interest and co-operation.

DISADVANTAGES

For the Company

(1) Salesmen may leave with a deficit.
(2) Collection of overdrafts may cause ill feeling between management and salesmen.
(3) Involves considerable bookkeeping.
(4) Overdrafts cause mental handicap which interferes with the salesmen's production.
(5) May involve heavy losses, particularly when conditions bring sales below normal expectancy.
(6) Discourages missionary work, and may influence salesmen to earn no more than the minimum.

For the Salesman

(1) Puts salesmen in debt to the company.
(2) Requires a set volume of sales
(3) Makes salesmen depend on the company's own estimation of possible sales.

The bonus plan. A bonus is a special reward for effort resulting in increased sales or reduced expenses beyond a set goal or quota. The bonus is usually arranged on a percentage basis, although in some cases it may consist of a flat-cash award. It is always used in conjunction with some other form of compensation.

To illustrate the operation of a simple bonus plan, a company paying 10 per cent commission to its salesmen sets a monthly quota of $5,000 sales, and offers a 5 per cent bonus for sales exceeding this quota. A salesman bringing in orders totaling $7,000 for the month would obtain $700 commission plus 5 per cent of the $2,000 overage, or $100.

In the sale of low-priced items, staple merchandise, and consumer goods where the co-operative effort of salesmen is not a factor in the success of a sale, it is customary to give individual bonuses based upon the performances of the individual salesmen. In such cases the quotas are often based upon past performances of the individual salesmen or upon the sales expectancy in the particular territories covered by the salesmen. One advantage of the individual bonus is that the salesman is actually competing with himself and therefore does not feel that less energetic salesmen may reap the rewards of his labors.

Where teamwork of salesmen is an important merchandising

factor, such as in the sale of high-priced items, machinery and industrial goods, and particularly where the sales force is divided into districts under the control of district sales managers, group bonuses are generally paid. While group bonuses do stimulate co-operativeness of salesmen, they often permit the lazy or inefficient salesman to benefit by the labors of the more active members of his group.

Described below are several common types of bonus plans in which either the quota arrangement or the method of applying the bonus has been adapted to meet specific needs.

1. The bonus based upon a quota of sales. A quota based upon previous sales volumes for a particular period is established, and a bonus is offered for certain percentages obtained over this quota. For example, if a company's sales for a previous year totaled $100,000, it might offer a 2 per cent bonus for a 10 per cent increase of the sales volume, a 5 per cent bonus for a 20 per cent increase, and so on.

2. The bonus based upon a quota of individual product sales. Where it is desired to push special items such as high-priced or slow-moving merchandise, a sales quota for the specific item is established, and a bonus is offered on sales exceeding this quota.

3. The bonus based on lower selling-cost quota. Where it is desired to reduce traveling expenses, a quota based upon sales expenses is established, and a bonus is offered for reducing expenses below this quota. One disadvantage of this plan is that it tends to reduce sales activity.

4. The profit-sharing bonus. This plan offers as a bonus a percentage of the company's yearly profits. To avoid misunderstandings with the salesmen, this plan should clarify the basis for arriving at profits. Generally, such a plan is complicated to operate and often causes salesmen dissatisfaction in lean years, when profits are small, and company dissatisfaction when earnings are high.

5. The bonus based on sales activities. Where it is desired to stimulate missionary work, a bonus may be offered for interviewing a certain number of prospects, arranging a certain number of store displays, and so forth. In such a plan the bonus is often a flat-cash award.

6. The sliding-scale bonus. There are two common forms of sliding-scale bonuses. One plan is the establishment of a flat re-

ward for attaining a quota and the offering of a bonus equal to the percentage attained of that quota. For example, if a bonus of $500 is offered for attaining a $10,000 sales quota, and a salesman succeeds only in selling $5,000 within the quota period, he would receive 50 per cent of the award, or $250. Another plan increases the bonus according to a fixed scale. For instance, a company may offer 5 per cent of the first $5,000 sales, 7 per cent of the second $5,000, and 10 per cent on anything over this amount.

The advantages and disadvantages of bonus plans are as follows:

ADVANTAGES

For the Company

(1) Offers an additional incentive for better co-operation of salesmen.
(2) Is sufficiently flexible to serve specific needs, such as the pushing of special items, reducing costs, and so on.
(3) Can be adjusted to suit conditions without interfering with the regular method of compensation.
(4) Creates a more satisfied group of salesmen by giving an opportunity to save, thus reducing turnover of the sales organization.
(5) Builds morale.

For the Salesman

(1) Permits increase in income in addition to the regular compensation plan.
(2) Indicates co-operation and interest of the management.
(3) Rewards unusual sales efforts.

DISADVANTAGES

For the Company

(1) May encourage salesmen (in the case of group bonuses) to be lazy.
(2) Causes disputes over quota arrangements.
(3) May involve excessive selling expense when prices are going up.

For the Salesman

(1) If quotas are unfair, salesmen must pay for the management's mistake.
(2) May be used as an excuse for reduction of regular compensation.
(3) May stress the sale of hard-to-sell items.
(4) Too sporadic, and often requires long periods of waiting before payment is made.

The point system. The point system is a flexible means of measuring payment to salesmen for the performance of specific selling tasks, and for penalizing them for things the company does not want done. In its simplest form the plan consists of evaluating by points the sale of each of a number of products sold by a company, assigning the lowest number of points (usually 1 point) to the product easiest to sell, and then grading the other products and points accordingly. The point might represent a single item, a quantity such as a ton or case, or dollar sales. The points are given dollar values, and salesmen are paid on the basis of the number of points accumulated by each salesman.

The point system my also be used in evaluating specific jobs, such as interviewing new prospects, reducing expenses, increasing the number of daily calls, and so on. Points may be deducted for the neglect of these duties or for certain acts such as causing complaints from customers, and the like. In determining the number of points to be assigned to each duty, it is customary to assign the lowest number of points to the work with the least resistance, such as the turning in of daily reports.

Compensation may be based entirely upon the point system or upon a point system in conjunction with a salary. In the latter case the amount paid over salary would be based upon the number of points accumulated. One method of operating this plan is to give each salesman a point handicap based upon his salary, the lowest salaried man having the lowest handicap. For example, a man receiving $25 per week may be required to reach a mark of 1,000 points, thereafter receiving the dollar value of the points. A $50-per-week man would be required to reach a mark of 2,000 points, and so on.

Some companies change the point value of product sales according to the months in which sales are easier or harder, thus leveling the compensation of salesmen over slump periods.

The advantages and disadvantages of the point system are as follows:

ADVANTAGES

For the Company	*For the Salesman*
(1) Gives strict control over salesmen's activities.	(1) Provides a direct reward for a good selling job.

(2) Can be adapted to any selling situation.
(3) Provides an incentive to perform difficult or onerous selling tasks.
(4) Provides an accurate measure of sales ability.

(2) Provides for seasonal slumps.

DISADVANTAGES

For the Company

(1) May require excessive amount of record keeping.
(2) Salesmen dispute point values or penalty scores.

For the Salesman

(1) Overemphasis on missionary work.
(2) Overemphasis on hard-to-sell items.
(3) Must accept company's evaluation of points and penalties.

Use of the point system in a sliding-scale bonus plan. The sliding-scale principle explained on page 328 can be used effectively with the point system in stimulating salesmen to make greater efforts than seems justified by the flat-bonus plan. For example, a large midwestern food company paying salesmen salary plus expenses plus a flat bonus based on points found that salesmen were satisfied to reach a certain income level and did not have sufficient incentive to make greater sales efforts beyond that level. By giving scaled values to the points, the company gave the salesmen an opportunity to work into new brackets of business that offered bigger rates of compensation.

In the flat-bonus plan the point quota was established by the dollar cost of each man to the company. When the salesman reached the number of points equal to his salary and expenses, he went on bonus and was paid at the rate of 50 cents flat per point sold. Thus, a man being paid $200 salary and $150 expenses was set a quota of 350 points. If he earned 400 points, he would receive as an income $350 salary and expenses, plus $25 for the 50 extra points.

In the accelerated bonus plan, instead of starting this man on a 350-point basic starting point and paying him a flat 50 cents per point, the following scale of bonus payments was applied:

300 points to 349 points	25 cents per point basis
350 points to 399 points	50 cents per point basis
400 points to 449 points	75 cents per point basis
450 points and up	$1 per point basis

Thus, if a salesman earned 400 points, he would receive $350 salary and expenses plus a bonus of $37.50 (representing 50 points at 25 cents per point or $12.50 plus 50 points at 50 cents or $25).

Variations and combinations of basic compensation plans. Many combinations and variations of the basic compensation plans described above have been used effectively in meeting the specific needs of companies. In fact, some companies employ several types of compensation plans within the organization. The choice of the proper plan depends upon such factors as the type and size of the company, the type of product, sales objectives, personnel, and so forth. A few of these combinations will be discussed in detail; others listed are self-explanatory.

1. Salary and commission. Firms paying a flat salary plus a commission on all sales over a certain amount are able to exercise more control over their men than if they paid on the straight-commission basis. Moreover, they can make the plan more attractive to salesmen than the straight-salary plan. This plan assists salesmen during slump seasons and encourages them to do missionary work. One firm using this plan paid new salesmen a low salary plus a flat one third of the regular salesmen's commission, thus inducing the salesmen to go on the more desirable straight-commission basis.

Sometimes the commission is based on all sales made by a particular group of people. This plan is especially suitable where salespeople's efforts overlap, and where co-operation is desirable.

2. Salary, expenses, and commission. This is a slight variation of the above plan and is particularly useful where traveling expenses are a considerable item. The percentage commission paid in this plan is usually relatively small.

3. Salary plus commission plus bonus. This plan is often applied where large territories are to be covered. The salary is usually based upon the expense of covering the territory. Bonus is paid above a specified weekly or monthly minimum sales volume. The sliding-scale bonus is sometimes used in this plan.

4. Salary and bonus. Flat salary plus bonus over quota.
5. Salary, expenses, bonus on sales over quota.
6. Salary and percentage of gross profits.
7. Commission and bonus.
8. Commission and drawing account. As previously described, the amount of the weekly drawing account is stipulated and deducted from commission earnings.
9. Commission plus traveling expense.
10. Commission with sliding-scale drawing account. The amount of the drawing account is raised or lowered according to commission earnings within set periods.
11. Percentage of gross profits.

7. CONTRACTS FOR THE SALE OF MERCHANDISE

What a contract is. We are apt to think of a contract as a formal document, solemnly entered into with strict observance of legal requirements. As a matter of fact, contracts are made every minute of the day—orally, by letter, or by other informal agreement—and these contracts are just as binding upon the parties involved as if they covered many printed pages and were duly signed and executed before a notary. A man boards a streetcar on the way to his office; he has entered into a contract with the transit company. His wife phones the day's food order; she has made a contract with her grocer. A businessman writes for an additional ream of his letterheads; he has contracted with his stationer. What are the elements that make each of these acts contracts? A contract has been defined as an agreement, enforceable at law, between two or more parties to do or not to do a particular thing. In order to be enforceable at law, an agreement must have the following elements:

1. *Offer and acceptance.* An agreement arises from an offer or proposal to do or to refrain from doing a certain thing, and from an acceptance of that same proposal. The offer must be clear and definite; it must be communicated in its exact terms to the party to whom the offer is made, either directly or by some definite act; and it must be accepted unconditionally by the person to whom it is made. If the person to whom an offer is made proposes modifications, those modifications must be accepted by the offeror before

an agreement can result. In other words, in the figurative language frequently used by the courts, there must be a "meeting of the minds" of the parties as to the terms of the agreement. However, an assent to the modifications may be inferred from the fact that the parties thereafter proceeded to carry on the transaction under the conditional acceptance.

2. *Competency of parties.* The parties to the agreement must be legally competent to enter into a contract. The question of competency arises most frequently with respect to infants, insane persons, and drunkards.

Although the laws of some states provide that women become of age at 18, and those of other states provide that marriage removes the infancy status, generally a person is considered to be in his infancy until he reaches the age of 21. An infant is not absolutely incapable of entering into a binding contract. Contracts made by persons under the legal age are not void, but they may generally be avoided or disaffirmed by the infant. In the case of contracts which have not yet been completely carried out—that is, executory contracts—the infant is not bound unless he affirms after coming of age, either by words, by sale of the property, by retaining it after a reasonable time has elapsed, and so forth; failure to affirm implies disaffirmance. In the case of contracts which have been completely carried out—that is, executed contracts—an infant may disaffirm either during infancy or within a reasonable time after he attains his majority; failure to disaffirm within a reasonable time implies affirmance. It is the general rule that an infant may disaffirm even if he cannot return the goods which he has received. Contracts by an infant for articles that are reasonably necessary to his existence, such as food, clothing, shelter, medical care, education, and the like, may be binding upon him in the same manner as if he were an adult.

Like infants, insane persons are not absolutely incapable of making contracts. Their contracts are voidable, not void, and they may be held liable for necessaries.

A person who is so drunk that he is deprived of his reason and does not understand the nature of his acts is in the same position as a mental incompetent, and his contracts may be disaffirmed by him if third persons are not injured thereby, and provided he disaffirms immediately upon restoration of his faculties.

3. *Legality of subject matter.* An agreement that calls for the

performance of an act forbidden by law or inimical to the interest of society is unenforceable. Gambling agreements and usurious contracts, for example, are generally held to be illegal. In some states any contract entered into on a Sunday is illegal.

Under Federal and State laws, contracts that restrain trade, fix prices, or result in unfair trade practices are illegal. For example, under the Federal Robinson-Patman Act a contract that discriminates in price between competing customers of the same seller in the sale of commodities of like grade and quality is invalid, if the effect of the discrimination is to lessen competition or create a monopoly. The Act does permit allowances for differences in the cost of manufacture, sale, or delivery resulting from the different methods or quantities in which such commodities are sold or delivered to the purchasers. For further discussion of anti-price discrimination contracts, see page 362.

4. *Consideration*. Consideration has been defined as something of benefit to the person making a promise, or something of detriment to the person to whom a promise is made. It is the price, motive, or matter inducing the contract and may consist of:

(*a*) Doing some act that one is not obligated to perform.

(*b*) Refraining from doing something that one would otherwise be free to do.

(*c*) Giving some money or property.

(*d*) Giving a promise.

The value of the consideration given to support a promise is generally immaterial.

What a sale is. A sale is an agreement whereby the seller transfers property in goods to the buyer, for a consideration called the price. To be enforceable, a sale must have all the elements necessary to the validity of a contract—namely:

1. Offer and acceptance.
2. Competency of parties.
3. Legality of subject matter.
4. Consideration.

A sale must be distinguished from a bailment and from a consignment. A bailment is a transfer merely of possession of goods under an agreement to return the same goods at some future time. Under a consignment goods are sent by the owner to a commission merchant, to be sold by the latter to third persons, without any transfer of title in the merchandise delivered to the consignee.

Contract of sale and contract to sell. A contract *of* sale should be distinguished from a contract *to* sell goods. In a contract to sell, the seller does not make an immediate transfer of property, but merely agrees to make a transfer at some future time. Under a contract of sale, in the absence of contrary intention, title to the goods sold passes immediately from the seller to the buyer, and the buyer assumes the risk of loss; in a contract to sell, title remains in the seller, and the seller carries the risk of loss, in the absence of contrary agreement, until the time fixed for the sale. The Uniform Sales Act * has formulated certain rules for ascertaining the intention of the parties as to when title is to pass. Goods that are in existence and are owned or possessed by the seller may be the subject of a sale or a contract to sell; goods that are to be subsequently manufactured or acquired by the seller and are to come into existence before the time fixed for delivery (called "future goods") may be the subject of a contract to sell, but not of a contract of sale.

When a sales contract must be in writing; statute of frauds. The general rule, as embodied in the Uniform Sales Act, is that "a contract to sell or a sale may be made in writing (either with or without seal) or by word of mouth, or partly in writing and partly by word of mouth, or may be inferred from the conduct of the parties." However, under a provision of the Act (commonly known as the statute of frauds), a contract to sell or a sale of any goods of the value of $500 or upwards is not enforceable by action unless one of the three following alternatives has been complied with:

1. Some note or memorandum in writing of the contract or sale has been signed by the party to be charged or by his agent in his behalf.

* The Uniform Sales Act, which has been adopted in most of the states, is a codification of the law governing the sale of personal property. Prior to its enactment, a wide conflict of judicial opinion existed in the various jurisdictions with respect to the law governing the sale of merchandise, resulting in much confusion and uncertainty. This conflict has to a large extent been eliminated by the Act, although in some instances differences still exist owing to varying interpretations by the courts of some of the sections of the Act.

2. The buyer has accepted part of the goods and actually received them.

3. The buyer has given something in earnest to bind the contract, or in part payment.

Where goods are to be manufactured by the seller especially for the buyer and are not suitable for sale to others in the ordinary course of the seller's business, the statute of frauds does not apply.

It should be noted that while the Uniform Sales Act fixed $500 as the amount that determines whether or not the statute of frauds applies, some other amount is fixed by statute in some states. Further, the amount is the price fixed in the sale, not the actual value of the merchandise sold. If several articles of merchandise have been sold at one time by one seller, the total purchase determines the amount, even though each article is separately priced.

The memorandum required by the statute of frauds is not necessarily the contract. The contract may be oral; as long as there is some memorandum of it, the statute is satisfied. The memorandum may merely indicate briefly the chief provisions of the contract and may consist of an entry in a book, on a bill head, or in a series of letters. For contract to sell in the form of a letter, see page 343.

Essential provisions of sales contracts. The provisions that may be included in a contract between seller and buyer for the sale of merchandise vary widely with the nature of the business and the individual desires and needs of the parties to the contract. It may be said, however, that such contracts generally include express provisions with respect to the following:

1. *Introduction.* This includes the date and place of making the contract and the names and addresses of both seller and buyer.

2. *Description of merchandise.* The quantity, nature, or quality of the goods should be clearly described, to prevent misunderstanding. Where the quantity is indicated by weight, it should be stated whether the weight is gross or net, and it should be indicated whether allowance is made for shrinkage or for wear and tear. The extent of the details in the description will depend upon how widely the article is known in the trade. Standard products that are extensively advertised may not need detailed description. In sales by sample, the article may be described merely "as per sample." On the

other hand, goods specially manufactured for the buyer should be fully described and accompanied by blueprint and specifications. In the case of specially marked goods, the exact drawing or facsimile of the markings should be furnished by the buyer.

3. *Warranties.* A warranty is a promise of the seller concerning the nature, quality, or durability of the merchandise sold. To prevent dispute as to quality, provision is sometimes made for inspection of the merchandise and the obtaining of an inspection certificate at the time of shipment. A warranty concerning quality or special fitness may be made even in a sale by sample. In addition to the warranties expressed in the contract, the law implies certain warranties of quality, fitness for the purpose for which the goods were sold, and so on.

4. *Shipping instructions.* Definite shipping instructions should be given, including instructions about packing, marking, routing, and time of shipment. To protect the seller in the event that the buyer does not specify the routing, the contract should contain a clause to the effect that, unless specified, routing is at seller's option. If no time of shipment is specified, a reasonable time is implied. As a protection to the seller, the contract may contain a clause limiting his liability in the event of unavoidable delay or impossibility of performance. It may also be provided that each shipment is to be deemed a separate contract and paid for whether or not the balance of an order is filled; this, however, is a disadvantage to the buyer and may be objected to by him.

5. *Time of payment and price.* The contract should definitely state the time of payment. It should also indicate the price of the goods, and whether shipping costs and insurance are included therein. This information is generally covered by the use of certain symbols, such as f.o.b., f.a.s., c. & f., c.i.f. (See page 366 *et seq.* for definitions of these terms.)

If no price is specified, the buyer is liable for the reasonable value of the merchandise. Where the parties makes a sale at a valuation—that is, a sale or contract to sell, providing that the price shall be subsequently fixed by a third party—the value fixed by the third party is binding in the absence of fraud or unfair dealing. The Uniform Sales Act provides that if the third person, without fault of the seller or buyer, fails to fix the price, the contract is thereby avoided; if he is prevented from fixing the price by the seller or buyer, the party not in default is given certain remedies as though the contract had been breached.

6. *Claims.* The contract may provide for the payment of a certain sum as "liquidated damages" in the event of a breach of the contract; or it may provide for adjustment of disputes by arbitration.

7. *Law governing the contract.* Where the parties reside in different states, or where the contract is executed in one state but is to be performed in another, or where the contract is to be performed in various states, the contract may indicate the state, the laws of which shall govern the construction of the contract and the rights and liabilities of the parties.

Legal precautions when selling goods.* When selling goods, take the following legal precautions:

1. Make no misrepresentations to the buyer (oral or written) regarding the goods.
2. Investigate the buyer's financial ability to pay, or sell for cash or upon proper security.
3. Keep the goods insured against fire or other casualty until title passes to the buyer.
4. When performing the contract adhere as strictly as possible to the terms of the sales agreement. Any contemplated variation in performance should be first agreed to by the buyer. Preferably, an agreement varying the terms of the original contract should be in writing.
5. Obtain a receipt for goods delivered.
6. Act quickly upon learning the buyer is insolvent. If the buyer becomes insolvent before he receives the goods, an unpaid seller may be permitted to keep the goods, or if they are in transit, he may stop the transportation of them. Consult counsel for the proper mechanics to use.
7. Consult counsel when a buyer breaches his contract. The seller's rights depend upon the terms of the contract, whether title to the goods has passed to the buyer, and other factors.

---

* *Acknowledgment*: Louis M. Brown, *Preventive Law*. New York: Prentice-Hall, Inc., 1950.

Contract to sell in form of letter of proposal and acceptance.

.st. No. . . . . Office Date: . . . .

. . . . Project: . . . .

Location: . . . .

Architect: . . . .

;entlemen:

. . . . Corporation proposes to furnish you for the ıbove-mentioned project, subject to the terms and conditions herein in- :luded, the materials scheduled herein, all in accordance with our stand- ırd specifications.

SCHEDULE OF MATERIAL: All prices are f.o.b. . . . .

Any tax or other Governmental charge upon the production, sale, ınd/or shipment of the material(s) herein specified, imposed by Federal, State, or Municipal authorities and hereafter becoming effective within the life of this contract, shall be added to the price(s) herein specified, and shall be paid by you.

SHIPMENTS: We reserve right to route shipments.

TERMS: Net cash on or before the 15th of each month for all deliveries made during the preceding month, with privilege of two (2) per cent discount for payment in cash within ten (10) days of delivery.

GENERAL CONDITIONS: 1. We assume no liability for damage to material after delivery, resulting from improper storage and/or handling by you and/or your agents and/or employees.

2. All prices named herein are based upon the present rates of railroad freight. Any increase or decrease in such freight rates effective at the time of shipment shall be added to or deducted from such prices. In the event of your failure to permit us to complete shipment of the material covered by this contract within one (1) year from the date hereof, you shall reimburse us for the expense involved in handling and storing such material at our factory after that date, as well as for any excess of the then-prevailing selling price of our material over the contract price with respect to that portion of the material covered by this contract delivered after such date.

3. Each shipment shall be construed, as regards deliveries and terms of settlement, a separate and independent contract. In case any lot or parcel shall not be accepted and/or paid for in accordance herewith, then we may, without prejudice to other lawful remedy, defer further shipments until settlement is made, terminate this contract, or treat such failure as a breach of the entire contract. If, in our judgment, your financial re-

sponsibility shall at any time become impaired, we may decline to make shipments against this contract and/or any other contract in force with you, except upon receipt of satisfactory security for payment, or of cash before shipment. Our failure to exercise any right under this contract shall not be deemed a waiver thereof.

4. Notice of any claim for defect in the quality of the material delivered hereunder shall be given to us in writing within five (5) days of the date of delivery. Failure to give such notice within such time shall constitute a waiver by you of all claims therefor.

5. If we are prevented from carrying out the herein-contained provisions by reason of any war, revolution, strike, epidemic, fire, cyclone, flood, embargo, weather conditions, car shortage, Providential, Governmental, or other cause, whether of the same or of a different nature, existing or future, beyond our reasonable control, and interfering with the production or delivery of the material as herein contemplated, upon written notice to you, we shall be excused from making deliveries to the extent and for the duration of such interference.

6. Should any dispute or disagreement arise with relation to the matter of payment, allowance or loss, or the interpretation of any one or more of the clauses of this contract, which dispute or disagreement cannot be satisfactorily settled by mutual conference, then the matter shall be settled by arbitration pursuant to the Arbitration Law of the State of New York, by reference to a board of three arbitrators, one to be selected by each of us and the third by the two so selected. In case the selection of any arbitrator is not made within fifteen (15) days of the time either party notifies the other of the name of the arbitrator selected by the notifying party, then the arbitrator or arbitrators not selected shall be appointed pursuant to the New York Arbitration Law. The submission of any dispute or disagreement to arbitration shall not in any way affect or limit our right to file and prosecute a lien under the applicable State law for any and all sums that we claim to be due and owing to us under this contract.

7. This contract is to be construed, and our respective rights are to be determined, according to the laws of the State of New York, and constitutes the full understanding between us with reference to the subject matter hereof, and no statement or agreement, oral or written, made prior to or at the signing hereof, shall vary or modify the written terms hereof. Neither of us shall claim any amendment, modification, or release from any provision hereof by mutual agreement unless such agreement is in writing, signed by the other and specifically stating it is an amendment to this contract.

8. This contract is not assignable or transferable by either party, except to its successors or to the transferee of all or substantially all of its assets,

nd shall be binding upon and inure to the benefit of such successor or ransferee.

This proposal, including all conditions printed or typed on either side hereof, is subject to your prompt acceptance, and to approval by an executive officer of this corporation; and, when so accepted and approved, shall constitute, with the attached schedule, if any, a contract between us, hereinabove sometimes referred to as "this contract." Until so approved by us, prices are subject to change without notice.

Respectfully submitted,

.... Corporation

By ....

ACCEPTED: ...., 19.. APPROVED: ...., 19..

.... Corporation

By .... By ....

Output and requirements contracts. An output contract is one by which a seller agrees to sell his entire output to a single buyer. A requirements contract is one by which a buyer undertakes to buy his entire requirements of a commodity from a single seller.

These two types of contracts are often considered together, for they are governed by the same legal principles. Some conflict of opinion exists, concerning the obligations of the parties under such agreements. Is the seller in the output contract required to produce the same amount as he was producing when the contract was made? Is the buyer in the requirements contract obligated to have substantially the same requirements as when the contract was entered into? According to the view that is supported by the weight of authority, the answer in both cases is "No." Both seller and buyer are required only to act in good faith. The seller in the output contract has performed his undertaking even if he cuts down his manufactures or closes up his plant, provided he does so in good faith; there is no implied agreement in the output contract to continue in business. Similarly, the buyer in the requirements contract does not agree to continue to have requirements. If his requirements taper off or cease because of a change in his needs or because of a sale or discontinuance of his business effected in good faith, he is not in default under the terms of his contract.

The requirements contract has been the subject of considerabl comment from a business standpoint, as well as from a legal poin of view. Large selling organizations often induce purchasers t enter into requirements contracts for their psychological rather tha their legal effect. They are not interested in having a legally draw document upon which suit can ultimately be brought, but they d want the purchaser to feel morally and legally obligated to purchas exclusively from them. The purchaser may even do some of hi buying elsewhere; the seller will not sue, because he is more interested in keeping a substantial part of the buyer's business for a continuous period than he is in recovering damages for breach o the letter of the agreement. The requirements contract often call the purchaser a "dealer," thus making him believe that it is his dut to push the seller's product as well as to use it exclusively.

Sale of merchandise through brokers. In some industries th term "broker" is used interchangeably with "selling agent" or "manufacturer's agent." In a stricter sense, however, a broker is not a selling agent or a manufacturer's agent, but a wholesale middlema whose function it is to bring together a buyer and a seller, and t assist them in consummating a sale. The broker acts for both partie to the sale, but he has no formal contract with either one; he i simply an intermediary. The contract between buyer and seller i generally evidenced by a broker's memorandum of sale or by a standard form of contract, adopted by a trade association of which both buyer and seller are members, in the name of seller and buyer.

Conditional sales contracts. Conditional sales contracts are used frequently in the sale of goods on the installment plan. Under these contracts the seller transfers possession of the goods to the buyer, but retains title thereto until the buyer has paid the entire purchase price and has fully performed his obligations under the contract. If the buyer fails to make the payments as they fall due, or otherwise defaults, the seller has the right to take back his goods. In most states laws have been passed requiring certain formalities in the execution of conditional sales contracts and compelling the seller to file or record the contract with some designated state official if he wishes to protect the reserved title to the goods against third persons. Except in those states that have adopted the Uniform Condi-

›nal Sales Act, these laws are not uniform, and they vary particularly ›ith respect to the following:

1. *Signing of contract.* In some states the signature of the buyer sufficient; in others, the seller's signature is also required. Wit-essing and acknowledgment of the signature may be necessary. ome states require a special affidavit of good faith to be attached.

2. *Copy to be filed or recorded.* In some states the original in-trument must be filed; in others, it is sufficient to file a copy. Some tates require the contract to be spread on the record in full; this is nown as "recording." In some states contracts for certain kinds ›f goods must be filed, while contracts for other goods require no ling.

3. *Time for filing or recording.* In several states filing or record-ng within the period fixed by statute relates back to the date the ontract was executed, giving the seller protection in his reserved itle from the date the contract was entered into. In other states he seller is protected only against those who acquire rights in the ›roperty subsequent to the time of filing or recording.

4. *Period of effectiveness of record.* In some jurisdictions provi-ion is made limiting the effectiveness of the record to a period of ›ears. Generally, renewal may be made by refiling the instrument ›rior to the expiration of the period.

5. *Place of filing or recording.* Most states require the contract o be filed or recorded at the place where the buyer resides. In ome states filing or recording is in a local office, such as the office ›f the town clerk; in others, in a county office. Strict compliance with the governing statute is required to protect the seller in his eservation of title against third persons.

6. *Refiling upon removal of property.* In some states, upon re-moval of the goods by the buyer to another county in the state, or upon removal to another state, the contract must be refiled within a certain time after the seller has received notice of the removal, otherwise the seller loses his reservation of title to the property as against creditors and purchasers.

7. *Risk of loss.* In most states the risk of loss is placed on the buyer, since he is the person who has the use and enjoyment of the property. A few states, however, place the risk on the seller.

The terms of the contract may, of course, determine who shall bea the risk of loss, regardless of statute.

8. *Recording satisfaction of the contract.* Some of the statute provide for entering a release or satisfaction when all the payment have been met.

Form of conditional sales contract. The form of a condition sales contract will vary slightly to conform to the statutory requir ments of a particular state. Most conditional sales contracts, how ever, cover the following details (see the form that begins on pag 349):

1. Names and addresses of buyer and seller.
2. Description of merchandise purchased.
3. Reservation of title in seller.
4. Agreement of buyer to cover merchandise by insurance, to pa taxes and assessments, to make repairs, and so forth.
5. Provision for retaking by seller in event of defaults in paymen of installments, upon removal or encumbrance of merchandise, upo insecurity of buyer, withdrawal of surety, and so on.
6. Assignability of contract.
7. Restriction against oral representations or agreements.

The conditional sales contract is generally accompanied by a promis sory note, signed by the buyer, covering the price of the merchandise

In some respects the conditional sales contract resembles a sal on consignment, a lease, and a bailment. In each of these, as in th conditional sale, possession of the property is given to another, bu title is retained by the owner. The consignment sale differs fron the conditional sale in that the merchandise delivered to the con signee is intended for resale to a third person. A bailment, on th other hand, contemplates no sale whatever, but merely temporar surrender of possession and the performance of some service per taining to the goods, after which they are to be returned to th owner. In a lease of goods, the owner merely grants possession t another for his use and enjoyment over a designated period o payment of a stipulated rental. Contracts that appear to involv consignments, leases, or bailments are generally construed by th courts as conditional sales agreements if the intent is to effect a sale A seller cannot avoid the necessity of giving notice of his reserve title to the goods through filing or recording of the conditional sale ontract by calling the contract a lease or bailment. Under the Jniform Conditional Sales Act, except in Pennsylvania, any contract or the bailment or lease of goods by which the bailee or lessee conracts to pay as compensation a sum substantially equivalent to the alue of the goods, or by which it is agreed that the bailee or lessee s bound to become, or has the option of becoming, the owner of uch goods upon full compliance with the terms of the contract s a conditional sale.

A conditional sales contract must also be distinguished from a hattel mortgage. In transactions involving a chattel mortgage, title s not reserved in the seller, but passes to the buyer, who, in turn, executes a chattel mortgage in favor of the seller. Upon failure to neet the obligations of the mortgage, the seller may regain title hrough foreclosure proceedings. A few states make no distinction between chattel mortgages and conditional sales, but consider all conditional sales as chattel mortgages, subject to the statutes applicable to such mortgages.

The C.O.D. sale, meaning "cash on delivery" or "collect on delivery," is not a conditional sale. Passing of title is not conditional in a C.O.D. sale. Payment is made conditional on delivery, and, vice versa, delivery is made conditional on payment. In the usual C.O.D. sale, title passes upon the making of the contract, and the risk of loss, which is normally an incident of title, falls on the buyer prior to delivery and payment, in the absence of a contrary intention.

Conditional sale contract.

(1) PARTIES: Seller: . . . . Co., a . . . . corporation.
Buyer: . . . .
of . . . .
(City) (County) (State or Province)

(2) SUBJECT OF AGREEMENT: Seller agrees to sell, and buyer agrees to buy, machines under the conditions hereinafter set forth as follows:

Quantity	*Machine and Model*	*Serial No.*	*Price*
. . . .	. . . .	. . . .	. . . .
. . . .	. . . .	. . . .	. . . .
. . . .	. . . .	. . . .	. . . .

(3) TERMS: F. O. B. . . . ., ..., the unpaid price of each machine to be evidenced by a promissory note of even date herewith payable on demand, which notes may be sold or discounted by the seller without waiver of any rights under this contract. Said notes are not payment but merely evidence of the said indebtedness to become due hereunder.

(4) POSSESSION OF PROPERTY: Buyer acknowledges receipt of machines and agrees not to mortgage or encumber same or remove same from the aforesaid state or province or to create or permit any liens or charges thereon, or to part with or to surrender possession of the same or any of the same except on bona fide sale thereof and payment of full purchase price to the seller herein. Buyer agrees to notify seller immediately in the event that machines or any of them are attached, replevined, or levied upon. If a petition in bankruptcy is filed by or against buyer, or if he becomes insolvent or makes an assignment for the benefit of creditors, or takes any action under any law, the operation of which would relieve him from his debts, then, at the option of seller, all of buyer's rights under this contract shall end, and seller shall be entitled to the immediate possession of said machines upon the surrender of buyer's obligations to pay the price thereof.

(5) RESERVATION OF TITLE: Both parties hereto agree that title to said machines shall remain in the seller until the full price thereof is paid, and all of the terms and conditions hereof have been fully complied with. The parties hereto intend a contract of conditional sale and not a chattel mortgage in any sense of the word.

(6) REMEDIES ON DEFAULT: Should buyer make any default in the matter of payments or otherwise, seller, at its option, may either:

(a) Without notice, declare the total amount of the price to be due and payable immediately; or

(b) Immediately repossess said machines, wherever found, with or without process of law (using all necessary force so to do, the buyer hereby waiving all action for trespass or damage thereby), and retain the same, and any and all payments previously made by buyer shall be retained by seller, buyer waiving and relinquishing all rights in any sums paid and in said machines, and seller shall be relieved from all obligations to transfer the same or any of the same; or

(c) Avail itself of the remedies for the enforcement of a seller's rights under a conditional sale agreement provided by the laws of the aforesaid state or province.

(7) STILL EXHIBIT, ETC.: Said machines shall be used only for a still exhibit, shall not be demonstrated or operated, except in necessary moving to or from railroad yards, or warehouse, to or from buyer's place of business, unless seller's written or telegraphic consent is first obtained. Buyer agrees to save seller harmless from all loss or damage of every kind to said machines or to the person or property of the buyer or of any third person, by reason of the use of any of said machines.

(8) No Reimbursement of Advances, etc.: Buyer shall not be entitled to any reimbursement on account of freight, insurance, warehousing, or storage charges, taxes, etc., said machines having been shipped at buyer's request upon the express understanding that said charges shall be paid and discharged by buyer without cost to seller. Buyer agrees to pay and discharge all taxes, liens, charges, and assessments that may be imposed on said machines in the aforesaid state or province.

(9) Attorney's Fees, Costs, etc.: If default is made in the payment of any purchase money note, or if seller shall engage an attorney to enforce collection, or to preserve or enforce its rights under this agreement, buyer agrees to reimburse seller for all reasonable legal expenses, attorney's fees, and court costs and expenses incurred by seller.

(10) Recaption: It is agreed and understood, but not in limitation of the above, that, in the event of the termination of the Agreement subsisting between the parties hereto, seller, at its option, shall, on demand, be entitled to redelivery of the possession of said machines.

(11) Any portion of this contract, including any of the provisions of paragraph 6 hereof, prohibited by law of any state or province, shall, as to said state or province, be ineffective to the extent of such prohibition without invalidating the remaining provisions of the contract.

(12) Interpretation: Both parties intend that the operation and construction of this contract shall be governed by the laws of the State of Illinois.

(13) This agreement is expressly made subject to all and singular the terms and provisions of the Agreement now subsisting between the parties hereto.

(14) Additional Clauses:

(15) Receipt of Copy: Buyer acknowledges receipt of a full, true, and correct copy of this agreement in . . . .
(State or Province)

Dated at . . . ., ..., this . . day of . . . ., 19. . .

Seller: . . . . Co., a corporation

By . . . .

Witness for Buyer: Buyer: . . . .

. . . . By . . . .

Affidavits:

Note to accompany conditional sale contract.

$....... ...., 19..
(City) (State) (Date)

For value received, undersigned promises to pay to the order o .... Corporation, the sum of $......... at the offic of .... Corporation, ..., ..., ir
(City) (State)

.... monthly installments, the first .... installments to be fo $........ each and the final installment to be for $......., with interest after maturity on delinquent installments at the highest legal rate and attorney's fees of ten (10) per cent of the amount thereof if placed with an attorney for collection. The first installment is to become due and payable on the .. day of ...., 19.. and one installment on the .. day of each ensuing month thereafter until all installments are paid.

Default of any payment indicated thereon shall cause the entire balance to become immediately due and payable at the election of the holder hereof without notice. The makers and endorsers hereby severally waive presentment, demand, protest, and notice of protest and nonpayment.

....

By ....
(Owner, Officer, or Firm Member)

....
(Street Address of Maker)

Bills of sale. A bill of sale is a writing evidencing the transfer of personal property from one person to another. The writing contains a direct statement of the transfer of title for a valuable consideration, describes the property transfered, and warrants that the seller owns the property, that it is free from encumbrances, and that he has the right to sell and transfer. A bill of sale is generally not necessary for the transfer of title to personal property, although it is always valuable evidence of the sale and of the identity of the merchandise sold. Some states do, however, require a bill of sale, duly acknowledged and recorded, upon the transfer of certain classes of property, such as motor vehicles, livestock, and so forth. Printed forms are available.

8. CONTRACTS APPOINTING SALES AGENTS

Agency contracts in general. A person who produces, manufac-ures, or otherwise owns or possesses goods for sale, instead of selling lirect to wholesalers, retailers, or consumers, may desire to effect he sale and distribution of his merchandise through agents. These gents may be appointed orally, by letter, or under formal written ontracts, which vary in their essential terms in the following re-pects:

1. *Payment of commissions.* The usual agency arrangement is to hip the goods to the agent on consignment, to be sold by the agent t price schedules fixed by the manufacturer. The manufacturer etains title in the goods until they are actually sold. The agent is ompensated by payment of commission at a rate fixed in the agency ontract, or in some instances by payment of the difference between he value of the sales made through him and the manufacturer's ist prices, less a discount. The agency agreement may specify the ate of commission and periods in which it is to be settled on direct ales and on business reaching the principal through other agents or from customers direct. Or it may provide that commissions hall be paid only on orders which have been accepted by principals, ave been shipped and paid for, less any deductions made by cus-omers, and that no order taken after the expiration of the agreement s to be subject to payment of commissions.

2. *Nature and quantity of product to be distributed.* The lines hat the agent is to sell should be clearly described. An agency ontract may fix the minimum amount of yearly sales that the agent is required to negotiate, or it may fix both the minimum and the maximum amount of his sales.

3. *Extent of territory.* The agent may be limited in respect to the territory in which he is to operate (see the form on page 357), or he may be allowed, under the terms of the contract, to sell anywhere and everywhere. In some instances the manufacturer may find it advisable to grant to the agent the exclusive right to sell and dis-tribute the product within a designated territory, under a so-called "exclusive agency agreement."

4. *Duration of agency.* The term of the agency may be unlimited (see the form on page 357) or it may be fixed. The contract also

generally contains specific provisions for termination prior to ex piration of the term under certain contingencies. If the agenc covers seasonal goods, the seller should fix the date for terminatio so that he can cancel the agreement some time before a new seaso starts, thus avoiding cancellation in the middle of the selling season It is not uncommon to provide that the manufacturer may cancel th agreement, upon written notice to the agent, in the event of:

(*a*) Insolvency, bankruptcy, or other financial difficulty o the agent.

(*b*) Failure of the agent to conduct the business of the agenc in a manner satisfactory to the manufacturer.

(*c*) Failure of the agent to perform the terms and condition of the agreement.

Some agency contracts provide for termination at any time eithe by the manufacturer or by the agent, upon the giving of a desig nated amount of notice of intention to do so, with the proviso tha orders accepted prior thereto shall be filled.

5. *Restriction against representing others.* Many agency agree ments contain a clause providing that the representative shall no represent, or be directly or indirectly in any way interested in th business of competing lines without the principal's knowledge. Th agent is also required to impose the same condition on any subagen whom he may appoint.

6. *Nontransferability of agency.* The agreement may provide tha it is "personal," and that it cannot be transmitted by the agent tc any other party.

7. *Sales assistance by principal.* The principal may be required to furnish advertising matter, information, and samples free. He may also be allowed to send his own salesmen into the agent's territory to promote sales. The agent, however, receives commissions on sales in the territory as provided in the agreement.

8. *Restriction against involving principal in obligations.* The agency agreement may include a provision forbidding the agent to involve the principal in any obligations beyond those fixed in the agreement, or to accept payments from customers for account of the principal, unless specially authorized by the principal.

9. *Disputes.* The agreement may be made subject to arbitration.

Exclusive agency contracts. An exclusive agency contract is an reement by which a manufacturer gives to a distributor, dealer, agent the exclusive right to sell the manufacturer's products in a signated territory, the agent, in turn, agreeing to push sales in at territory but not to sell outside of it. The validity of such ntracts has now been generally established by the decisions of e courts. While the exclusive agency is always based on a definite nderstanding, the agreement need not be a formal one. It may be ral; it may be embodied in a letter; or it may be incorporated in formal written document. The formal contract usually contains rovisions with respect to the following:

1. *Selling rights.* The exclusive agency contract must give the gent a market that is wholly or partly his, exclusively. The manu- icturer may give to the agent either:

(*a*) full exclusive sales rights, agreeing not to sell the article r line to any other jobber in the territory, or to any other dealer in he local market; or

(*b*) limited exclusive sales rights, agreeing not to appoint more han a certain number of agents, or not to sell the article or line to ther dealers within a certain radius of the dealer's place of business.

Metropolitan agents are sometimes given joint exclusive rights; hat is, the agents in the city are limited in number, but they may ell anywhere in the city. The manufacturer may reserve the right o sell direct to special customers, such as the United States Govern- nent, State, County, and Municipal bodies, and to certain classes f trade, such as consumers who purchase for use and not for resale.

2. *Territory.* The boundaries within which the agent is to have exclusive operation are clearly fixed in the agreement. This terri- tory is generally large enough to induce the agent to push the prod- uct. The solicitation of business outside of the fixed territory is prohibited. The agent is specifically enjoined from soliciting business in territory belonging to other agents or assigned to branch offices of the manufacturer.

3. *Minimum quota of purchases.* Some exclusive agency contracts fix a minimum amount that the agent is required to sell within a year in order to retain his exclusive agency. The quota may be based on the population in the territory, on the amount sold by

competitors in the same territory, and so forth, and depends large on the manufacturer's judgment and past experience. The tot amount that the agent is to buy during the year may also be fixe in the exclusvie agency contract.

4. *Maintenance of stock.* The agent generally agrees to maintai a stock of the manufacturer's product which will adequately repre sent the line that he is to sell. Generally the amount of stock is fixed percentage of the quantity that the agent is required to di pose of within a fixed period.

5. *Purchase price from manufacturer.* Some manufacturers se goods to their agents on a consignment basis; others make outrigh sales to the agents. The agency contract may include a price sche ule, fixing the price from the manufacturer to the agent accordin to the quantity of the product purchased, or it may indicate tha the price is determined by a schedule of discounts issued by th manufacturer.

6. *Resale price by agent.* In the case of trade-marked, copy righted, or otherwise identified products, the exclusive agency con tract may include a schedule of prices at which the product is to b resold. In thus seeking to maintain the resale price, the manufac turer should be careful to consider the State and Federal antitrus laws as well as the laws permitting resale price maintenance. Thi subject is treated further on page 359.

7. *Agreement not to sell competing lines.* Under some agenc contracts the agent is required merely to push the product for whic he is granted an exclusive agency. Under other contracts, however the agent agrees to handle the manufacturer's products exclusively The question has been presented to the courts as to whether such a provision violates the Clayton Act, Section 3 of which provide that it shall be unlawful for a person to make a contract for sale of goods on the agreement that the purchaser shall not deal in the goods of a competitor, where the effect is substantially to lessen com- petition or where it tends to create a monopoly. The rule is now fairly well established that an exclusive agency agreement does not necessarily restrain competition or tend to create a monopoly in violation of the antitrust laws. An agreement by the agent not to sell the product of some other manufacturer does not stifle com- petition, for other dealers may sell other products.

8. *Duration of agency.* Many exclusive agency contracts do not

efinitely fix their duration. Where the period is fixed, it usually ns for the term of one year, with privilege on the part of the anufacturer to renew if the agency has proved satisfactory. Some ontracts may provide for terminaton:

(*a*) Upon the expiration of a fixed period of time.
(*b*) By the manufacturer at will upon written notice to the agent.
(*c*) By the manufacturer upon a specified number of days' notice to the agent.
(*d*) Immediately by either party upon violation of the terms of the contract.

Contract appointing exclusive retail dealer for designated territory to sell company's products.

Articles of Agreement, made this .. day of ...., 19.., by and between The .... Company, of ...., ..., Party of the First Part, and ...., of ...., ..., Party of the Second Part.

Witnesseth, That the Party of the First Part, manufacturing .... Stock Office Equipment at ...., ..., hereby appoints Party of the Second Part its Exclusive Retail Dealer for the .... line of Office Equipment, consisting of ....
for the territory of ....

In Addition to Granting This Exclusive Franchise, Party of the First Part agrees:

1. To turn over all orders and inquiries received from the territory involved to the Party of the Second Part, in accordance with the National Policy of the Party of the First Part.

2. To furnish catalogues and all current advertising matter in reasonable quantities, free of charge.

3. To allow the Party of the Second Part the Trade Discounts as shown in the Current Published Trade Discount Sheet for the various divisions of the .... line.

4. To allow the Party of the Second Part to ship orders into other exclusive territory, provided the purchasing power is located in the territory of the Party of the Second Part or in open territory.

5. That, upon its acceptance by the proper authority located at ....,........., this contract will become effective.

6. To allow the Party of the Second Part the privilege to termina this contract by giving the Party of the First Part thirty (30) days' wri ten notice, or without previous notice, upon violation of any of the co ditions set forth herein.

7. The Party of the First Part reserves the right to seek outlets throug other dealers for .... products that the Party of the Secon Part fails aggressively to sell.

In Consideration of the Grant of Its Exclusive Franchise an Other Agreements Made by the Party of the First Part, Party c the Second Part agrees:

1. [*Competing products*] To give the lines of merchandise made avai able on an exclusive basis by the Party of the First Part adequate floc and window display, and not to purchase, display, or offer for sale com peting products, in any grades or styles, offered by other manufacturers

2. [*Terms*] To pay bills for purchases made from the Party of th First Part on the basis of two (2) per cent cash discount if remittance i placed in the mail on or before midnight of the ...... of the mont following the date of the invoices, or on the basis of net payment on th 30th of the month following the date of invoices.

3. [*Restrictions on soliciting business*] Not to solicit business or .... products in territories assigned exclusively to othe dealers, or in cities where Party of the First Part has branch stores or sale offices, it being understood that its branch stores stand in exactly the same relation to exclusive dealers as one exclusive dealer to another.

4. [*Sales by others in territory*] To allow Party of the First Part, or any of its agents or exclusive dealers, to solicit business and accept orders in the territory made a part of this agreement, provided the authority for purchase is located in some other territory.

5. [*Special cases*] To allow the Party of the First Part the privilege to develop and close, through its own representatives, any prospects that require special technical or expert service, apportioning the commission of Party of the Second Part according to the extra expense or special concessions involved. It is understood, however, that before projects of this class are closed, Party of the Second Part will be advised as to the terms of sale and amount of commission that will be received.

6. [*Cancellation of contract*] To allow the Party of the First Part the privilege to terminate this contract by giving the Party of the Second Part thirty (30) days' written notice, or without previous notice, upon violation of any of the conditions set forth herein.

7. [*Government orders*] To allow Party of the First Part, or any branch, or any duly appointed agent or dealer, to accept and execute without obligation or violation of the terms of this Contract orders from the United States Government.

8. [*Termination on sale or consolidation*] To allow the Party of the First Part the option to terminate this contract in the event that there is

sale or consolidation of the business of the Party of the Second Part.

9. [*Notice of changes*] That all of the products, terms, prices, discounts, and conditions specified herein may be changed or discontinued by notice in writing or publication by the Party of the First Part.

10. [*Return of merchandise*] That Party of the First Part will be given the option of taking back all saleable .... merchandise in the possession of the Party of the Second Part in the event of a violation or cancellation of this contract.

This Contract cancels all other previous agreements.

The .... Company,

Retail Dealer ....

By ....

By ....

Accepted ....

Resale price-maintenance agreements. All but a few of the states have enacted laws dealing with resale price maintenance, known as "fair trade" acts. The typical state fair trade law does two things: (1) It permits a manufacturer of branded merchandise to make a contract with a distributor whereby the distributor agrees to sell the product at a fixed price. (2) It provides for the enforcement of prices fixed in this way not only against dealers who sign price-fixing agreements, but also against non-signers.

The state fair trade acts do not permit horizontal price-fixing contracts; that is, such contracts are not permitted between wholesalers and wholesalers, producers and producers, or between retailers and retailers.

To be price-fixed, the article must be (1) identifiable by trademark, copyright, patent, or other means; and (2) in open competition with similar commodities. For example, the Federal Trade Commission, upheld by federal courts, prohibited a film manufacturer from entering into contracts fixing the price of his film because there was no competing product.

There are exceptions under the acts—for example, close-out sales of damaged goods, and sales in which the name, brand, or other identifying marks have been removed. Close-out sales and sales of damaged goods must be clearly described to the public as such.

The laws generally provide that any person injured by a violation of them may bring an action against the price-cutter.

The Miller-Tydings Act, passed in 1937, exempts from the Sherman Anti-Trust Act state-sanctioned contracts or agreements fixing minimum resale prices. The Supreme Court construed this statute a allowing states to enforce "fair trade" agreements only against signer of a price-fixing agreement.* A law passed by Congress in 195 overcomes this decision by providing that minimum resale pric agreements can be enforced against non-signers as well as signers, i the state law applies to non-signers.

Manufacturer—retailer contract form for use under state resale price-maintenance laws.†

AGREEMENT, made in the State of ...., by and between th undersigned, "Manufacturer," and the undersigned, "Retailer,"

WITNESSETH:

WHEREAS, the "Commodities," shown on Schedule A hereto attached as such Schedule shall be constituted from time to time, are, or may here after be, distributed under the trade-mark(s), brand(s), or name o "Manufacturer" in fair, free, and open competition with commodities o the same general class produced by others, and the parties hereto desire to avail themselves of the benefits of the Fair Trade Act of the State o Retailer's address as shown below;

Now, THEREFORE, in consideration of the premises and the mutual obligations herein assumed, the parties hereto agree as follows:

(1) "Retailer" will not (except as specifically permitted by said Fair Trade Act) directly or indirectly advertise, offer for sale, or sell any of such "Commodities" in said state at less than the minimum retail prices stipulated therefor by "Manufacturer."

(2) The minimum retail prices stipulated by "Manufacturer" for the "Commodities" in said state are those now or hereafter designated in Schedule A, plus, in each sale, the amount of all sales and excise taxes applicable to such retail sale in said State.

(3) "Manufacturer," at any time and from time to time, upon ten (10) days' written notice to "Retailer," may eliminate "Commodities" from Schedule A, and/or may add to said Schedule, and stipulate minimum retail prices for, additional "Commodities," and may change the minimum retail price of any one or more of the "Commodities."

(4) (a) The offering or giving of any article of value in connection with the sale by "Retailer" of any of the "Commodities"; (b) the offering or making of any concession of any kind whatsoever (whether by the

---

* Schwegmann Brothers, et al. v. Calvert Distillers Corporation; Schwegmann Brothers, et al. v. Seagram Distillers Corporation (1951), 340 U.S. 928, 71 S. Ct. 941, certiorari denied, 71 S. Ct. 745.

† Form suggested by National Association of Retail Druggists. Reproduced by special permission.

giving of coupons, trading stamps, or otherwise), in connection with any such sale; or (c) the sale or offering for sale of any of the "Commodities" by "Retailer" in combination with any other merchandise shall constitute a breach by "Retailer" of article 1 of this agreement.

(5) "Manufacturer" in good faith will employ all appropriate means, which in the circumstances shall be reasonable, including legal proceedings if such other means fail, to prevent, and to enforce the discontinuance of, any violation of said minimum retail-price stipulations by any competitor of "Retailer," whether the person violating or threatening such violation is or is not a party to a fair-trade contract with "Manufacturer" covering said "Commodities."

(6) "Retailer" will not, where statute or law permits such restriction, sell any of the "Commodities" except to consumers for use.

(7) In addition to any other legal remedy, the parties may have the remedy of injunction to prevent or to enforce the discontinuance of any violation of this agreement.

(8) This agreement may be terminated by either party on ten (10) days' written notice to the other, but termination by "Retailer" shall not affect the rights or obligations of either of the parties hereto under the Fair Trade Act of said State or by reason of any contract made pursuant thereto.

(9) Any notice given under any of the provisions of this agreement shall be well and sufficiently given by delivering the same personally to the party hereto to whom it shall be addressed, or by mailing the same in a sealed postpaid envelope addressed to such party at its address given below.

(10) This agreement shall become effective on the .. day of ...., 19...

IN WITNESS WHEREOF, the parties hereto have executed this agreement on the .. day of ...., 19...

....

Retailer *Manufacturer*

....

(Street) (City) (State) (Street) (City) (State)

(attach store label)

(To be printed at the foot of the contract after the signatures and addresses.)

SCHEDULE A

(If more space needed, add additional page or pages.)

....

....

....

Unfair practices acts. Another group of State laws affecting sales is that prohibiting price discrimination and sales below cost, where the effect is to injure competitors or destroy competition. These acts are frequently referred to as unfair practices acts and fair or unfair sales acts. Some of the laws also prevent discrimination between distributors of commodities of like grade and quality and between purchasers in different communities. Some also prohibit secret payment or allowance of rebates, refunds, commissions, or unearned discounts.

The Federal Robinson-Patman Anti-price Discrimination Act, passed in 1936, amends the Clayton Act to prohibit specific abuses concerning price discrimination that the Clayton Act did not correct. The statute outlaws price-discriminatory practices in the sale and resale of commodities in the United States, including false brokerage, pseudo-advertising and other discriminating service allowances that were found unfairly to favor the large buyer as against the small and independent businessman. It is unlawful under the act for a buyer engaged in interstate commerce knowingly to induce or receive a discrimination in price that is prohibited by the act. The act permits due allowances for differences in the cost of manufacture, sale, or delivery resulting from different measures or quantities in which the commodities are sold or delivered to the purchasers, but allows the Federal Trade Commission to fix quantity limits beyond which no discount will be allowed.

9. CONTRACTS EMPLOYING SALESMEN

Essential provisions of employment contracts. It is the practice in many business houses not to enter into formal contracts in employing salesmen. The contention is that the psychological effect of requiring the employee to sign a formidable-looking paper is bad, and that, so far as the company is concerned, its interests are not furthered by having a legal document in its possession. The company wants good salesmen, not good lawsuits. However, the formal written contract of employment that puts into black and white the arrangements agreed upon between employer and employee still has its staunch adherents. The various provisions that may be included in such contracts are, perhaps, endless, but the following may be listed as those items that it is most essential and most common to cover:

1. The product that the salesman is to sell.
2. The territory that he is to cover.
3. The obligation of the salesman to devote full time to his work.
4. Compensation; whether payment is to be a straight salary, or commissions, or a combination of salary and commissions; whether credit losses may be charged against commissions; whether the salesman is to have a drawing account against commissions, and whether he is to be paid traveling expenses; when commissions are payable.
5. Expenses for which company will be responsible, if any.
6. Furnishing of and responsibility for samples.
7. The making of reports by the salesman.
8. Restrictions on the employee's power to bind the company by orders.
9. Furnishing by the salesman of a fidelity bond for faithful performance of his duties.
10. Restrictions on salesman's activities before and after termination of employment.
11. Duration of contract.
12. Termination of contract—by advance notice, by expiration of fixed period, and so forth.

Agreement for employment of salesman in allotted territory, on commission basis; provision for drawing account and traveling expenses; restriction against representing others during period of employment.

AGREEMENT, made this . . day of . . . ., 19 . ., in the City of . . . ., State of . . . ., between the . . . ., Inc., a corporation organized under the laws of the State of and having its principal office at No. Street, City of . . . ., State of . . . ., party of the first part, and . . . ., of the City of . . . ., State of . . . ., party of the second part, WITNESSETH:

1. [*Nature and period of employment*] The party of the second part agrees to continue in the service of the party of the first part as a salesman of . . . . and other products manufactured by the party of the first part and of such articles as the party of the first part deems

necessary to assist it in the distribution of its products, in .... [*here insert description of salesman's territory*], for a period of .... years from ...., 19..; this contract of employment may, however, be sooner terminated by either party giving .... months written notice of termination thereof to the other party.

2. [*Obligations of employee*] The party of the second part agrees to devote all of his time, attention, and energies to the performance of his duties as such salesman, subject to the control of the party of the first part, to serve the party of the first part diligently and according to the best of his ability in all respects, to make every effort to get orders in all parts of the territory allotted to him as aforesaid, and to straighten out to the best of his ability any complaints that may arise in connection with such orders.

3. [*Restriction against representing others during period of employment*] The party of the second part agrees not to represent, either directly or indirectly, any other person, firm, corporation, or business during said period of employment, unless the consent of the party of the first part is obtained thereto.

4. [*Price of goods and acceptance of orders*] The party of the second part agrees to sell all goods at prices fixed by the party of the first part, which prices shall not materially differ from competitor's prices on similar goods. All orders taken by the party of the second part are subject to acceptance by the party of the first part.

5. [*Payment of commissions*] The party of the first part agrees to pay commissions to the party of the second part, as follows:

(*a*) .... cents per gross on orders for .... [*here insert commodity*] taken by the party of the second part.

(*b*) .... cents per gross on those orders for .... received from customers or others on whom the party of the second part has sent reports to the party of the first part, and called on in person at least once a year.

(*c*) .... cents per gross on orders from jobbers on whom the party of the second part has sent in reports to the party of the first part, and called on in person at least once a year.

(*d*) .... per cent of the selling price on all orders for .... from manufacturers of .... or others on whom the party of the second part has sent in reports to the party of the first part, and called on in person at least once a year.

(*e*) .... on all shipments from contracts taken by the party of the second part before the date of this agreement and paid for after ...., 19.., as follows:

.... per cent per gross on shipments of ....
.... per cent per gross on shipments of ....
.... cents per gross on shipments of .... to jobbers.

Commissions as hereinabove provided shall not become due or payable to the party of the second part until the goods ordered are paid for by the respective customers.

6. [*Drawing account and traveling expenses*] The party of the first part agrees to allow the party of the second part against commissions a drawing account of $........ per week, to be paid to the party of the second part on Thursday of each and every week. Traveling expenses incurred by the party of the second part outside of the cities of ...., ..., and ...., shall be paid by the party of the first part to the party of the second part on Thursday of each and every week for the preceding week.

The party of the first part agrees to pay to the party of the second part, on demand, the amount of commissions in excess of $........ due the party of the second part on ...., ..., ..., and .... of each and every year during the period of his employment under this contract.

7. [*Records and reports*] The party of the first part agrees to keep an accurate account of all orders taken by the party of the second part in, or otherwise received from, the territory allotted to him as aforesaid, and to render to the party of the second part a statement of such account on the first (1st) days of ...., ..., ..., and ....of each year during the period of his employment under this contract.

In Witness Whereof, the parties hereto have hereunto set their hands and affixed their seals the .. day of ...., 19...

.... Corporation

By ....

President

10. FOREIGN TRADE TERMS OF SALE *

It is strongly recommended to manufacturers and exporters that wherever abbreviated forms of export quotations are employed, the forms herein defined be used, so far as possible, to the exclusion of other forms.

I. "ex factory," "ex mill," "ex mine," "ex plantation," "ex warehouse," etc. (named point of origin)

Under this term, the price quoted applies only at the point of origin, and the seller agrees to place the goods at the disposal of the buyer at the agreed place on the date or within the period fixed.

* *Acknowledgment:* "Foreign Trade Definitions," Joint Committee representing the Chamber of Commerce of the United States of America, the National Council of American Importers, Inc., and the National Foreign Trade Council, Inc.

Under this quotation:

Seller must (1) bear all costs and risks of the goods until such time as the buyer is obliged to take delivery thereof; (2) render the buyer, at the buyer's request and expense, assistance in obtaining the documents issued in the country of origin, or of shipment, or of both, which the buyer may require either for purposes of exportation, or of importation at destination.

Buyer must (1) take delivery of the goods as soon as they have been placed at his disposal at the agreed place on the date or within the period fixed; (2) pay export taxes, or other fees or charges, if any, levied because of exportation; (3) bear all costs and risks of the goods from the time when he is obligated to take delivery thereof; (4) pay all costs and charges incurred in obtaining the documents issued in the country of origin, or of shipment, or of both, whch may be required for purposes of exportation, or for purposes of importation at destination.

II. f.o.b. (named inland carrier at named inland point of departure)

[Note:—Seller and buyer should consider not only the definitions but also the "Comments on All F.O.B. Terms" at page 369.]

Under this term, the price quoted applies only at inland shipping point, and the seller arranges for loading of the goods on, or in, railway cars, trucks, lighters, barges, aircraft, or other conveyance furnished for transportation.

Under this quotation:

Seller must (1) place goods on, or in, conveyance, or deliver to inland carrier for loading; (2) provide clean bill of lading or other transportation receipt, freight collect; (3) be responsible for any loss or damage, or both, until goods have been placed in, or on, conveyance at loading point, and clean bill of lading or other transportation receipt has been furnished by the carrier; (4) render the buyer, at the buyer's request and expense, assistance in obtaining the documents issued in the country of origin, or of shipment, or of both, which the buyer may require either for purpose of exportation, or of importation at destination.

Buyer must (1) be responsible for all movement of the goods from inland point of loading, and pay all transportation costs; (2) pay export taxes, or other fees or charges, if any, levied because of exportation; (3) be responsible for any loss or damage, or both, incurred after loading at named inland point of departure; (4) pay all costs and charges incurred in obtaining the documents issued in the country of origin, or of shipment, or both, which may be required either for purposes of exportation, or of importation at destination.

III. f.o.b. (named inland carrier at named inland point of departure) freight prepaid to (named point of exportation)

Under this term, the seller quotes a price including transportation charges to the named point of exportation and prepays freight to named point of exportation, without assuming responsibility for the goods after obtaining a clean bill of lading or other transportation receipt at named inland point of departure.

Under this quotation:

Seller must (1) assume the seller's obligations as under II, except that under (2) he must provide clean bill of lading or other transportation receipt, freight prepaid to named point of exportation.

Buyer must (1) assume the same buyer's obligations as under II, except that he does not pay freight from loading point to named point of exportation.

IV. f.o.b. (named inland carrier at named inland point of departure) freight *allowed to* (named point)

Under this term, the seller quotes a price including the transportation charges to the named point, shipping freight collect and deducting the cost of transportation, without assuming responsibility for the goods after obtaining a clean bill of lading or other transportation receipt at named inland point of departure.

Under this quotation:

Seller must (1) assume the same seller's obligations as under II, but deducts from this invoice the transportation cost to named point.

Buyer must (1) assume the same buyer's obligations as under II, including payment of freight from inland loading point to named point, for which seller has made deduction.

V. f.o.b. (named inland carrier at named point of exportation)

Under this term, the seller quotes a price including the cost of transportation of the goods to named point of exportation, bearing any loss or damage, or both, incurred up to that point.

Under this quotation:

Seller must (1) place goods on, or in, conveyance, or deliver to inland carrier for loading; (2) provide clean bill of lading or other transportation receipt, paying all transportation costs from loading point to named point of exportation; (3) be responsible for any loss or damage, or both, until goods have arrived in, or on, inland conveyance at the named point of exportation; (4) render the buyer, at the buyer's request and expense, assistance in obtaining the documents issued in the country of origin, or of shipment, or of both, which the buyer may require either for purposes of exportation, or of importation at destination.

Buyer must (1) be responsible for all movement of the goods from inland conveyance at named point of exportation; (2) pay export taxes, or other fees or charges, if any, levied because of exportation; (3) be responsible for any loss or damage, or both, incurred after goods have arrived in, or on inland conveyance at the named point of exportation; (4) pay all costs and charges incurred in obtaining the documents issued in the country of origin, or of shipment, or of both, which may be required either for purposes of exportation, or of importation at destination.

VI. f.o.b. vessel (named port of shipment)

Under this term, the seller quotes a price covering all expenses up to, and including, delivery of the goods upon the overseas vessel provided by, or for, the buyer at the named port of shipment.

Under this quotation:

Seller must (1) pay all charges incurred in placing goods actually on board the vessel designated and provided by, or for, the buyer on the date or within the period fixed; (2) provide clean ship's receipt or on-board bill of lading; (3) be responsible for any loss or damage, or both, until goods have been placed on board the vessel on the date or within the period fixed; (4) render the buyer, at the buyer's request and expense, assistance in obtaining the documents issued in the country of origin, or of shipment, or of both, which the buyer may require either for purposes of exportation, or of importation at destination.

Buyer must (1) give seller adequate notice of name, sailing date, loading berth of, and delivery time to, the vessel; (2) bear the additional costs incurred and all risks of the goods from the time when the seller has placed them at his disposal if the vessel named by him fails to arrive or to load within the designated time; (3) handle all subsequent movement of the goods to destination: (a) provide and pay for insurance; (b) provide and pay for ocean and other transportation; (4) pay export taxes, or other fees or charges, if any, levied because of exportation; (5) be responsible for any loss or damage, or both, after goods have been loaded on board the vessel; (6) pay all costs and charges incurred in obtaining the documents, other than clean ship's receipt or bill of lading, issued in the country of origin, or of shipment, or of both, which may be required either for purposes of exportation, or of importation at destination.

VII. f.o.b. (named inland point in country of importation)

Under this term, the seller quotes a price including the cost of the merchandise and all costs of transportation to the named inland point in the country of importation.

Under this quotation:

Seller must (1) provide and pay all transportation to the named inland point in the country of importation; (2) pay export taxes, or other fees or charges, if any, levied because of exportation; (3) provide and pay for marine insurance; (4) provide and pay for war risk insurance, unless otherwise agreed upon between the seller and buyer; (5) be responsible for any loss or damage, or both, until arrival of goods on conveyance at the named inland point in the country of importation; (6) pay the costs of certificates of origin, consular invoices, or any other documents issued in the country of origin, or of shipment, or of both, which the buyer may require for the importation of goods into the country of destination and, where necessary, for their passage in transit through another country; (7) pay all costs of landing, including wharfage, landing charges, and taxes, if any; (8) pay all costs of customs entry in the country of importation; (9) pay customs duties and all taxes applicable to imports, if any, in the country of importation.

Buyer must (1) take prompt delivery of goods from conveyance upon arrival at destination; (2) bear any costs and be responsible for all loss or damage, or both, after arrival at destination.

Comments on All F.O.B. (free on board) Terms

In connection with f.o.b. terms, the following points of caution are recommended:

1. The method of inland transportation, such as trucks, railroad cars, lighters, barges, or aircraft should be specified.

2. If any switching charges are involved during the inland transportation, it should be agreed, in advance, whether these charges are for account of the seller or the buyer.

3. The term "f.o.b. (named port)," without designating the exact point at which the liability of the seller terminates and the liability of the buyer begins, should be avoided. The use of this term gives rise to disputes as to the liability of the seller or the buyer in the event of loss or damage arising while the goods are in port, and before delivery to or on board the ocean carrier. Misunderstandings may be avoided by naming the specific point of delivery.

4. If lighterage or trucking is required in the transfer of goods from the inland conveyance to ship's side, and there is a cost therefor, it should be understood, in advance, whether this cost is for account of the seller or the buyer.

5. The seller should be certain to notify the buyer of the mini-

mum quantity required to obtain a carload, a truck load, or a barge-load freight rate.

6. Under f.o.b. terms, excepting "f.o.b. (named inland point in country of importation)," the obligation to obtain ocean freight space, and marine and war risk insurance, rests with the buyer. Despite this obligation on the part of the buyer, in many trades the seller obtains the ocean freight space, and marine and war risk insurance, and provides for shipment on behalf of the buyer. Hence, seller and buyer must have an understanding as to whether the buyer will obtain the ocean freight space, and marine and war risk insurance, as in his obligation, or whether the seller agrees to do this for the buyer.

7. For the seller's protection, he should provide in his contract of sale that marine insurance obtained by the buyer include standard warehouse to warehouse coverage.

VIII. f.a.s. vessel (named port of shipment)

Under this term, the seller quotes a price including delivery of the goods, along side overseas vessel and within reach of its loading tackle.

Under this quotation:

Seller must (1) place goods along side vessel or on dock designated and provided by, or for, buyer on the date or within the period fixed; pay any heavy lift charges, where necessary, up to this point; (2) provide clean dock or ship's receipt; (3) be responsible for any loss or damage, or both, until goods have been delivered along side the vessel or on the dock; (4) render the buyer, at the buyer's request and expense, assistance in obtaining the documents issued in the country of origin, or of shipment, or of both, which the buyer may require either for purposes of exportation, or of importation at destination.

Buyer must (1) give seller adequate notice of name, sailing date, loading berth of, and delivery time to, the vessel; (2) handle all subsequent movement of the goods from along side the vessel: (a) arrange and pay for demurrage or storage charges, or both, in warehouse or on wharf, where necessary; (b) provide and pay for insurance; (c) provide and pay for ocean and other transportation; (3) pay export taxes, or other fees or charges, if any, levied because of exportation; (4) be responsible for any loss or damage, or both, while the goods are on a lighter or other conveyance along side vessel within reach of its loading tackle, or on the dock awaiting loading, or until actually loaded on board the vessel, and subsequent thereto; (5) pay all costs and charges incurred in obtaining the documents, other than clean dock or ship's receipt, issued in the country of origin, or of shipment, or of both, which may be required either for purposes of exportation, or of importation at destination.

F.A.S. (free along side) Comments

1. Under f.a.s. terms, the obligation to obtain ocean freight space, and marine and war risk insurance, rests with the buyer. Despite this obligation on the part of the buyer, in many trades the seller obtains ocean freight space, and marine and war risk insurance, and provides for shipment on behalf of the buyer. In others, the buyer notifies the seller to make delivery along side a vessel designated by the buyer and the buyer provides his own marine and war risk insurance. Hence, seller and buyer must have an understanding as to whether the buyer will obtain the ocean freight space, and marine and war risk insurance, as is his obligation, or whether the seller agrees to do this for the buyer.

2. For the seller's protection, he should provide in his contract of sale that marine insurance obtained by the buyer include standard warehouse to warehouse coverage.

IX. c. & f. (named point of destination)

Under this term, the seller quotes a price including the cost of transportation to the named point of destination.

Under this quotation:

Seller must (1) provide and pay for transportation to named point of destination; (2) pay export taxes, or other fees or charges, if any, levied because of exportation; (3) obtain and dispatch promptly to buyer, or his agent, clean bill of lading to named point of destination; (4) where received-for-shipment ocean bill of lading may be tendered, be responsible for any loss or damage, or both, until the goods have been delivered into the custody of the ocean carrier; (5) where on-board ocean bill of lading is required, be responsible for any loss or damage, or both, until the goods have been delivered on board the vessel; (6) provide, at the buyer's request and expense, certificates of origin, consular invoices, or any other documents issued in the country of origin, or of shipment, or of both, which the buyer may require for importation of goods into country of destination and, where necessary, for their passage in transit through another country.

Buyer must (1) accept documents when presented; (2) receive goods upon arrival, handle and pay for all subsequent movement of the goods, including taking delivery from vessel in accordance with bill of lading clauses and terms; pay all costs of landing, including any duties, taxes, and other expenses at named point of destination; (3) provide and pay for insurance; (4) be responsible for loss of or damage to goods, or both, from time and place at which seller's obligations under (4) or (5) above have ceased; (5) pay the cost of certificates of origin, consular invoices, or any other documents issued in the country of origin, or of shipment, or of both, which may be required for the importation of goods into the country of destination and, where necessary, for their passage in transit through another country.

C. & F. (cost and freight) Comments

1. For the seller's protection, he should provide in his contract of sale that marine insurance obtained by the buyer include standard warehouse to warehouse coverage.

2. The comments listed under the following c.i.f. terms in many cases apply to c. & f. terms as well, and should be read and understood by the c. & f. seller and buyer.

X. c.i.f. (named point of destination)

Under this term, the seller quotes a price including the cost of the goods, the marine insurance, and all transportation charges to the named point of destination.

Under this quotation:

Seller must (1) provide and pay for transportation to named point of destination; (2) pay export taxes, or other fees or charges, if any, levied because of exportation; (3) provide and pay for marine insurance; (4) provide war risk insurance as obtainable in seller's market at time of shipment at buyer's expense, unless seller has agreed that buyer provide for war risk coverage; (5) obtain and dispatch promptly to buyer, or his agent, clean bill of lading to named point of destination, and also insurance policy or negotiable insurance certificate; (6) where received-for-shipment ocean bill of lading may be tendered, be responsible for any loss or damage, or both, until the goods have been delivered into the custody of the ocean carrier; (7) where on-board ocean bill of lading is required, be responsible for any loss or damage, or both, until the goods have been delivered on board the vessel; (8) provide, at the buyer's request and expense, certificates of origin, consular invoices, or any other documents issued in the country of origin, or of shipment, or both, which the buyer may require for importation of goods into country of destination and, where necessary, for their passage in transit through another country.

Buyer must (1) accept the documents when presented; (2) receive the goods upon arrival, handle and pay for all subsequent movement of the goods, including taking delivery from vessel in accordance with bill of lading clauses and terms; pay all costs of landing, including any duties, taxes, and other expenses at named point of destination; (3) pay for war risk insurance provided by seller; (4) be responsible for loss of or damage to goods, or both, from time and place at which seller's obligations under (6) or (7) above have ceased; (5) pay the cost of certificates of origin, consular invoices, or any other documents issued in the country of origin, or of shipment, or both, which may be required for importation of the goods into the country of destination and, where necessary, for their passage in transit through another country.

C. & F. and C.I.F. Comments

Under c. & f. and c.i.f. contracts the following points on which the seller and the buyer should be in complete agreement at the time the contract is concluded are:

1. It should be agreed upon, in advance, who is to pay for miscellaneous expenses, such as weighing or inspection charges.

2. The quantity to be shipped on any one vessel should be agreed upon, in advance, with a view to the buyer's capacity to take delivery upon arrival and discharge of the vessel, within the free time allowed at the port of importation.

3. Although the terms c. & f. and c.i.f. are generally interpreted to provide that charges for consular invoices and certificates of origin are for the account of the buyer, and are charged separately, in many trades these charges are included by the seller in his price. Hence, seller and buyer should agree, in advance, whether these charges are part of the selling price, or will be invoiced separately.

4. The point of final destination should be definitely known in the event the vessel discharges at a port other than the actual destination of the goods.

5. When ocean freight space is difficult to obtain, or forward freight contracts cannot be made at firm rates, it is advisable that sales contracts, as an exception to regular c. & f. or c.i.f. terms, should provide that shipment within the contract period be subject to ocean freight space being available to the seller, and should also provide that changes in the cost of ocean transportation between the time of sale and the time of shipment be for account of the buyer.

6. Normally, the seller is obligated to prepay the ocean freight. In some instances, shipments are made freight collect and the amount of the freight is deducted from the invoive rendered by the seller. It is necessary to be in agreement on this, in advance, in order to avoid misunderstanding which arises from foreign exchange fluctuations which might affect the actual cost of transportation, and from

interest charges which might accrue under letter of credit financing. Hence, the seller should always prepay the ocean freight unless he has a specific agreement with the buyer, in advance, that goods can be shipped freight collect.

7. The buyer should recognize that he does not have the right to insist on inspection of goods prior to accepting the documents. The buyer should not refuse to take delivery of goods on account of delay in the receipt of documents, provided the seller has used due diligence in their dispatch through the regular channels.

8. Sellers and buyers are advised against including in a c.i.f. contract any indefinite clause at variance with the obligations of a c.i.f. contract as specified in these definitions. There have been numerous court decisions in the United States and other countries invalidating c.i.f. contracts because of the inclusion of indefinite clauses.

9. Interest charges should be included in cost computations and should not be charged as a separate item in c.i.f. contracts, unless otherwise agreed upon, in advance, between the seller and buyer; in this case, however, the term c.i.f. and i. (cost, insurance, freight, and interest) should be used.

10. In connection with insurance under c.i.f. sales, it is necessary that seller and buyer be definitely in accord upon the following points:

(*a*) The character of the marine insurance should be agreed upon in so far as being w.a. (with average) or f.p.a. (free of particular average), as well as any other special risks that are covered in specific trades, or against which the buyer may wish individual protection. Among the special risks that should be considered and agreed upon between seller and buyer are theft, pilferage, leakage, breakage, sweat, contact with other cargoes, and others peculiar to any particular trade. It is important that contingent or collect freight and customs duty should be insured to cover particular average losses, as well as total loss after arrival and entry but before delivery.

(*b*) The seller is obligated to exercise ordinary care and diligence in selecting an underwriter that is in good financial standing. However, the risk of obtaining settlement of insurance claims rests with the buyer.

(*c*) War risk insurance under this term is to be obtained by the seller at the expense and risk of the buyer. It is important that the seller be in definite accord with the buyer on this point, particularly as to the cost. It is desirable that the goods be insured against both marine and war risk with the same underwriter, so that there can be no difficulty arising from the determination of the cause of the loss.

(*d*) Seller should make certain that in his marine or war risk insurance, there be included the standard protection against strikes, riots and civil commotions.

(*e*) Seller and buyer should be in accord as to the insured valuation, bearing in mind that merchandise contributes in general average on certain bases of valuation which differ in various trades. It is desirable that a competent insurance broker be consulted, in order that full value be covered and trouble avoided.

XI. "ex dock" (named port of importation)

Under this term, seller quotes a price including the cost of the goods and all additional costs necessary to place the goods on the dock at the named port of importation, duty paid, if any.

Under this quotation:

Seller must (1) provide and pay for transportation to named port of importation; (2) pay export taxes, or other fees or charges, if any, levied because of exportation; (3) provide and pay for marine insurance; (4) provide and pay for war risk insurance, unless otherwise agreed upon between the buyer and seller; (5) be responsible for any loss or damage, or both, until the expiration of the free time allowed on the dock at the named port of importation; (6) pay the cost of certificates of origin, consular invoices, legalization of bill of lading, or any other documents issued in the country of origin, or of shipment, or of both, which the buyer may require for the importation of goods into the country of destination and, where necessary, for their passage in transit through another country; (7) pay all costs of landing, including wharfage, landing charges, and taxes, if any; (8) pay all costs of customs entry in the country of importation; (9) pay customs duties and all taxes applicable to imports, if any, in the country of importation, unless otherwise agreed upon.

Buyer must (1) take delivery of the goods on the dock at the named port of importation within the free time allowed; (2) bear the cost and risk of the goods if delivery is not taken within the free time allowed.

SECTION 4

Office Management

1. PLANNING AND MAINTAINING THE OFFICE FOR EFFICIENCY

2. EQUIPMENT, FILES, AND APPLIANCES

3. MAKING OFFICE PROCEDURE FUNCTION SMOOTHLY

4. ECONOMIES IN THE USE AND PRINTING OF FORMS

5. HIRING NEW EMPLOYEES

6. TRAINING EMPLOYEES

7. TELEGRAMS AND INTERNATIONAL COMMUNICATIONS

Kinds of Domestic Messages

Special Services of Telegraph Companies

Types of Cable and Radio Messages

8. TELEPHONE SERVICE

Telephone Company "Servicing" Services

9. PRIVATELY-OWNED INTERNAL COMMUNICATION SYSTEMS

10. POSTAL GUIDE FOR EFFICIENT HANDLING OF MAIL

Special Delivery, Special Handling, and Miscellaneous

Bulk Mail

Letters

Printed Matter

Metered Mail

Non-Metered Mail (Printed Indicia)

Precancelled Stamps, Cards, and Envelopes

Stamps

Envelopes

Government Postal Cards

Private Mailing Cards

Business-Reply Cards and Envelopes

Money Orders

SECTION 4
Office Management

Office-management functions. The office-management department is a staff or service department under the direction of an office manager, who is responsible to the treasurer, vice-president, president, general manager, or some other official. The functions of office management generally include direction of matters relating to the building, office appliances, furniture and equipment, stationery and forms, personnel, correspondence, stenography and typing, filing, office methods and routine, and services such as mailing, messenger, and intercommunication.

Qualifications of the office manager. The position of office manager calls for a person with the following four fundamental qualifications: intelligence, imagination, courage, and persistence.

1. *Intelligence*. Obviously anyone in a responsible executive position must have a keen mind that is able to grasp fundamental issues and problems and logically deduce sound conclusions.
2. *Imagination*. An office manager must be able to visualize the merits of plans and methods in order to select the most profitable and practical ones.
3. *Courage*. Courage to introduce, organize, and start a plan is essential if the office manager is to be successful in his work. Without courage, the best intelligence and imagination will not flower into practical results.
4. *Persistence*. Many men having the first three qualifications fail as executives because they do not follow through with their plans. It takes constant effort to bring a plan to a successful conclusion. The general manager, president, or the board of directors must be sold on the plan; employees must be encouraged and stimulated; co-operation from subordinates and department heads must be won.

Besides having the above fundamental qualifications, the office manager must be methodical, have an excellent knowledge of human nature, be able to get along with people, and be able to judge thei capabilities and capacity. In addition, he must be resourceful, hav organizing ability, and possess the attributes that make for leadershir He should come to the position of office manager equipped witl previous general business experience and some accounting training.

1. PLANNING AND MAINTAINING THE OFFICE FOR EFFICIENCY

Physical factors in office planning. Scientific office plannin must take into consideration the physical factors affecting office rou tine. The purpose of office planning is to afford an easy and con venient flow of work and traffic. It is not enough to arrange perfec elevator service to avoid congestion and to neglect some other factor such as location of lockers, which will offset the time saved.

The physical factors to be considered are the following:

1. Elevators.
2. Lockers.
3. Washrooms.
4. Communications.
5. Partitions, railings, doors.
6. Floor covering.
7. Lighting.
8. Air conditioning.
9. Noise reduction.

A brief discussion of the physical factors in office planning is pre sented in the following paragraphs.

Elevators. It is best to have separate elevators for passengers and freight. If the organization is a large one with hundreds of employees, it is wise to stagger the working day and lunch hours so as to avoid congestion. For instance, half of the office force could start the day at 8:30, have lunch hour between 11:30 and 12:30, and leave at 4:30. The other half could come in at 9, have lunch between 12 and 1, and leave at 5.

Locate the departments using the freight elevator, such as the stock room and the mailing department, close to the elevator.

Lockers. Lockers may be centralized in one place, or they may be placed in every department. Having lockers in every depart- ment is preferable if there is sufficient space for them, because it avoids congestion at a central point and allows the employees to be at their desks without loss of time. Metal lockers that accommodate ne belongings of two people and take up very little space are vailable.

Washrooms. If washrooms are to be built into the building, ocate them at convenient locations on every floor. If the wash-ooms are already installed, make sure that the arrangement of the ffices permits easy access to them for every employee.

Communications. Messages to be conveyed may be oral or writ-en. Oral messages are most frequently conveyed by telephone, lthough the use of interoffice communications systems, such as the lictograph, have become popular. Telephone service and interoffice ommunications are treated in another section of this book (pages 471-485). Buzzers, to call in stenographers and department heads, re frequently used. Oral messages to large groups of employees re sometimes conveyed by the use of loudspeakers. Most organi-ations reduce oral messages to a minimum, preferring written mes-ages to oral messages. Written memos are always on record and elp to fix responsibility.

Written messages may be sent by messenger (see paragraph on messenger service on page 423), or they can be sent through the entral transcription department (see page 424). The use of pneu-matic tubes is another method of conveying written messages, par-ticularly in department stores and very large offices.

Partitions, railings, and doors. Many organizations are doing away with private offices, for they take up too much space, obstruct the proper flow of work and ideas, make the problem of office plan-ning and supervision more difficult, and give to the general public an impression of secrecy and inaccessibility. There is a marked tendency to have large open offices with partitions made of wood and glass in instances where privacy is desired.

A few suggestions are given for the use of partitions, railings, and doors.

1. Use railings in offices that are in direct contact with the public, such as employment offices, to prevent people from flocking into the office and disrupting the work.
2. Arrange all partitions and railings so that they do not obstruct the flow of traffic.

3. Have doors and swinging gates at points near the exit to stree or outer office.

4. Have passages wide enough to allow traffic to travel in oppc site directions.

5. Swinging doors should be partly of heavy glass to allow visi bility. If clear plate glass is used, have printing on the door t make it noticeable.

Floor coverings. Floors are made of wood, concrete, or marble The type of covering depends not only on its decorative appeal bu on a consideration of the purchase price, wearing quality, and main tenance cost. Floor coverings reduce the noise in the departmen and help to prevent fatigue and discomfort of employees caused b hard, cold floors. Waxed wooden floors are slippery and dangerous Rugs and carpets are used chiefly in private offices and sometime in foyers and hallways; linoleum, rubber, cork, or composition ar used in other offices.

Lighting. Poor lighting arrangements cause defective eyesight increase fatigue, lower production in the office and factory, and in crease the number of accidents. Any additional expense involvec in improving lighting is usually more than offset by the benefit derived, and in many cases no additional expense is involved.

Lighting troubles are caused by an insufficient amount of light or a poor quality of light. To determine whether there is suffi cient light at a particular spot, measure it with a light meter (an instrument, that can be purchased or borrowed from a local powe company, which measures the intensity of light in foot-candles) and compare it with the standards given below. To check th quality of light, which involves such considerations as color, glare and shadows, follow the suggestions on page 386.

Standards for the quantity of light. While the human eye is able to adapt itself to widely varying amounts of light, ranging all the way from 10,000 foot-candles and more on the beach on a bright summer day, to less than two foot-candles in the average poorly lighted hallway, *it works best in natural daylight.* Artificial illumina tion, therefore, should approach natural daylight as nearly as possible

Many tests have been made to determine the best light for office and factory tasks. The General Electric Company summarizes these as follows:

0–5 Foot-candles: For perceiving larger objects and for casual seeing. Satisfactory for corridors and stairways.

5–10 Foot-candles: For interrupted or casual work in which seeing is important but does not involve discrimination of fine details or low contrasts. Satisfactory for conference and reception rooms, vaults, etc.

10–20 Foot-candles: For ordinary reading when not prolonged, or moderate and prolonged office and factory tasks. Suitable for filing, mail sorting, intermediate reading, and writing at a desk.

20–50 Foot-candles: For moderately critical and prolonged tasks, such as clerical work, benchwork, prolonged reading, rough drawing and sketching, bookkeeping and accounting, and stenographic work.

50–100 Foot-candles: For severe and prolonged tasks, such as proof-reading, drafting, difficult reading, watch repairing, fine machine work, etc.

100 Foot-candles and over: For very severe and prolonged tasks, such as fine engraving and penwork, and discrimination of fine details of low contrast, as in inspection.

Suggestions to increase the quantity of light. If, after testing different locations with the light meter, you find that in some places the light is insufficient, here are ways to increase that light, often at no expense:

1. Clean the lamps and reflectors. A recheck with the light meter will usually then show a higher reading. Arrange for periodic cleaning of lamps and reflectors.

2. Replace blackened bulbs with new ones; blackened bulbs are inefficient, since they do not give out so much light as new ones.

3. Make sure there are no gaps in the lighting due to burned-out bulbs or empty sockets.

4. See that bulbs of the correct voltage are being used. This will insure maximum efficiency. Lamps of too high a voltage will not burn brightly, but will last longer, while lamps of too low a voltage will burn too brightly and burn out much faster.

5. Examine the reflectors to see if the surface has deteriorated, in which case the reflecting parts should be replaced.

6. Insufficient illumination may be due to dark and dingy walls and ceilings. They are important sources of secondary light because they receive and reflect light from the lamps. Walls painted in light colors, such as buff, light-green, and gray tints, will increase illumination a great deal. Ceilings should be painted white.

7. Increase the wattage of the bulbs used. This should not be

done until a check has been made to see that the circuits can stand the increase.

8. Sometimes the overhead lighting will be adequate if supplemented by Illuminating Engineering Society approved-type desk lamps. This will build up the proper amount of light on the desks.

How to improve the quality of light. The quality of light is just as important as the quantity. Too much glare and harsh shadows make office work very tiring, even though the light may be sufficient in amount. The following suggestions are offered to improve the quality of light:

1. If bare lamps are visible, shield them.
2. If globes are objectionably bright, shade them with parchment shades, or replace with (1) oversize globes, (2) semi-indirect fixtures, or (3) indirect fixtures.
3. If illumination is spotty, provide more outlets. Often outlets can be provided by surface wiring connected to one of the outlet circuits that is not loaded to capacity. The distance between ceiling outlets should not exceed the height above the floor.
4. If sharp shadows occur, correct them by changing to fixtures of low brightness. If the shadows are caused by the fact that the light source is too small, conical parchment shades placed around the globes will help.
5. If the lamps are too dim, the reason may be a voltage drop due to inadequate wiring. In this case rewiring is necessary. To determine whether wiring is adequate, have a licensed electrician check with a voltmeter when the maximum load is on.
6. Daylight fluorescent bulbs very closely approach natural daylight and can be used to advantage where form and color must be checked closely, as in certain types of color matching and in inspection. For general office work, they supply cooler light at higher efficiencies. Special starting auxiliaries are built into the lighting fixtures.

Air conditioning. Various studies have been made which show that our thinking and seeing faculties vary with changes in temperature.* Air conditioning corrects the slump periods that studies

* Huntington, Dr. Ellsworth, *Season of Birth*. New York: John Wiley & Sons, Inc.

ndicate occur in the hot summer months by cooling the air and thereby increasing mental activity. By proper control of the air supply in an office, management can greatly reduce the time and work lost due to colds and other illnesses that occur when resistance is low.

Air conditioning is the process of providing, by the use of mechanical equipment, the desired conditions of air temperature, humidity, cleanliness, and motion, and controlling these conditions to provide the atmosphere that is best suited for human health and comfort. The system installed may be either a permanent part of the building or it may be portable, so that the investment need not be lost if the office location is changed.

Most air-conditioning installations at the present time provide: (1) proper ventilation (air supply, air filtering, and air circulation), and (2) air cooling and dehumidification in the summer time. For winter use, air heating and humidification equipment can be added to the large units.

Types of air-conditioning systems available. Several types of air-conditioning equipment are available, the choice depending upon the size of the office or building, the individual needs of the organization, the amount of money to be spent, and the special characteristics of each.

1. A small compact unit can be installed in each room to serve a small area. The smallest ones are placed in the window frame and serve only to ventilate the room or part of it. They keep out dust, dirt, and outside noises, since the windows are kept closed, and supply fresh air from the outdoors by means of intake fans, but do not cool and dehumidify the air. If cooling and dehumidification are desired, the unit just described must be replaced with one that ventilates and in addition cools and dehumidifies the air.

Portable air conditioners that are not connected with the windows can also be purchased. While they do not provide a fresh supply of air from the outdoors as the window units do, they will take care of a larger area.

These small units provide the maximum flexibility; individual offices can be conditioned one at a time, and the occupant of each office has complete control over the operation. Certain disadvantages exist, however. Since each unit requires a separate motor, the combined load of several of them may necessitate extensive rewi ing. The air-intake supply for the window units may be difficult t arrange. The maintenance of a large number of fans, motors, an compressors may be a serious problem.

2. Larger self-contained units to ventilate and cool can be in stalled to handle several rooms at once. These conditioners have refrigerating capacity of from three to ten tons each, dependin upon the size, and can be used in groups to condition an entir floor. A refrigerating capacity of three tons is the ability to mel three tons of ice in twenty-four hours. The five-ton installation will handle an area of about three thousand square feet. They ca be used either without ducts to serve one large space, such as drafting room, or with ducts to serve several small rooms. The will cool and dehumidify the air, as well as provide proper ventila tion. Heating and humidifying equipment can be added for win ter usage to supply warm, moistened air if desired.

3. Air conditioning can also be installed with a central station a a distance from the area to be conditioned. For example, the direct expansion method utilizes a compressor and cooling water and ai supply equipment in the basement. The cooled and filtered air i conveyed in ducts to various parts of the same floor and the floo above. It is not practical for more than two floors, since the duct would have to be too large. Fire-code regulations in some place limit the use of this system to either the basement and first floo or the top two floors of a building.

The indirect-expansion system has the compressor and cooling water tank in the basement. The cool water is pumped to a maxi mum of three or four floors to air-handling equipment on each floor. Here are located the fans, air filters, and supply and return grilles to provide the cooled air. The water, after circulating through the mechanism, returns to the cooling tank to be used over again.

Smaller units are often added to these central systems to air-condition individual offices that are likely to be used at times when it is not necessary to cool the rest of the office or floor, such as an office in which a lot of overtime work is done. Such units are connected by separate water pipes to the central compressor and cooling tank. The use of such units as auxiliaries helps to reduce operating osts, since it is cheaper to operate a small unit to condition an indi-idual office than to run the fans, and so forth, which supply the vhole floor.

Equipment cost factors in air conditioning. No air-condition-ng installation should be made, of course, without a survey to letermine any special conditions that would affect the type of equip-nent to be used. The following factors are important in determin-ng the needs for a particular installation:

1. *Geographical location and exposure.* Places where hot, humid weather exists for long periods require larger equipment. Buildings more exposed to the sun's rays will require larger equipment than those that are for the most part in the shadow.

2. *Size and shape to be conditioned.* Heat passing through the walls and windows is an important factor in the heat load of an area. Irregularly shaped offices, since they have a higher ratio of wall surface to floor area, are more expensive to condition than rectangular offices of the same area.

3. *Type of building construction.* Porous walls or those in which windows are loosely set in the frames are more expensive to condition than others.

4. *Window area.* Heat passes more quickly through glass than through thicker and more resistant wall construction. Therefore, the greater the ratio of window area to wall area, the greater the cost.

5. *Ventilation requirements.* Conditioning an office where a lot of smoking is done, or where unusual odor conditions exist, will be more expensive than otherwise.

6. *Number of people.* A large number of people in an office will make the system more expensive to operate, since more body heat will have to be removed.

7. *Number of lights and office appliances.* A large number of light bulbs and office machines in use will increase the amount of heat to be removed and therefore the cost.

8. *Water characteristics.* The characteristics of the water available to remove from the equipment the heat taken from the room will affect the type of equipment to be installed.

9. *Kind of power.* While electric motors usually drive the condi-

tioning equipment, steam-driven equipment may in some cases b feasible. This type of equipment will affect the costs.

Operating-cost factors in air conditioning. The hours of oper tion will affect the costs of running the air-conditioning system, a will protracted heat spells, type of work, amount of lighting facilities business machines in use, and other factors. Charges for electricit and cooling water will vary with different localities. Maintenanc and repairs will be necessary. The regular operating crew will b able to handle some of these, but outside organizations will occa sionally have to be utilized.

The fixed charges should also be considered. Depreciation migh be based on permanency of occupancy or expected life of the equip ment. The usual maximum is fifteen years. Rental of the spac occupied by the equipment is another element. Insurance and taxe will depend on local conditions.

Noise reduction. Excessive noise in an office increases menta fatigue and is a disturbing factor, hampering efficient production In some cases the ceiling and walls have to be treated with sound-absorbing materials such as felt, porous plaster, Acousti-Celotex, o Akoustolith. If the office or factory is so noisy that it is necessar to sound-proof the walls and ceilings, it is best to consult an acoustical engineer, for the job is highly technical. Usually simple precautions, such as the following, will reduce a large percentage of the noises in the average office:

1. Keep all machines, sliding drawers, doors, and so forth, in good condition and well oiled.
2. If possible, centralize all noisy machines in one department.
3. Use a floor covering of sound-absorbing quality.
4. Place sound-absorbing materials close to noisy machines.
5. Fix all noisy radiators and windows.
6. Shut off noises from hallways with doors.
7. Muffle high-pitched telephone bells or have a lower-pitched bell installed.

Office layout. The aim of office layout is to arrange offices and equipment in such a manner that work and traffic flow in as straight a line or as continuously in one direction as possible. On the surface, such an arrangement seems simple, but the problem is complicated if space is limited, if a number of people have to use the same files, or if there are a number of windows, posts, railings, and doors limiting space available for equipment and machines. Furthermore, offices must be located in relation to other offices; for instance, the credit department should be next to the bookkeeping department, because credit men are always consulting ledger records. Offices dealing with the public should be next to passenger elevators or on the ground floor. Likewise, offices requiring the use of freight elevators should be located conveniently to them.

Steps to be taken in planning office layout. The following steps are recommended in planning office layout:

1. Determine the amount of space needed for every employee, his desk and chair, the files, tables, machines, coat racks, and shelves.
2. Estimate the space required for future expansion, basing the estimate on past growth. The total requirements shown by steps one and two indicate the amount of space needed.
3. Study the usefulness and desirability of the existing equipment and machines and eliminate those that are not needed.
4. Make a rough sketch of the new office, showing all doors, windows, and posts and the approximate location of desks, files, and machines.
5. Cut out templates of cardboard for every piece of equipment in the office. Make them to the scale of ¼ inch to a foot. In making templates of safes, files, and cabinets, be sure to cut them large enough to allow for opening of doors and drawers.
6. Make an exact scaled drawing of the new office, showing all the windows, doors, and posts, and using the same scale of ¼ inch to a foot.
7. Place the templates on the scaled drawing as planned on the rough sketch. The templates will give an exact picture of the new office. If the arrangement is not satisfactory, the templates can be shifted around to another position and yet be in the correct proportion to the room.
8. When the arrangement is satisfactory, take a picture of the plan as a permanent record.

Office maintenance. A clean, well-kept office has an effect upon employee morale. It is short-sighted economy to try to save money by neglecting office maintenance.

Since the office manager is responsible for the maintenance o offices, it is up to him to establish a definite plan and schedule fo the work instead of depending on haphazard methods. A simpl card, filled out by the maintenance men every day, stating the date office cleaned, work done, and the time taken provides a convenien record for the office manager and aids him in checking and controlling the work.

The following suggestions are given to aid the office manager in planning a systematic maintenance schedule:

1. Offices should be swept and dusted every night, and provision should be made for occasional washing or scrubbing of floors.
2. Windows should be cleaned at least once a month, and preferably twice a month; lighting fixtures, at least twice a month.
3. Washrooms and lavatories must be cleaned every night.
4. The condition of chairs and desks should be inspected periodically. If a desk top is badly worn, have the surface refinished or have it covered with a special desk covering of a color that does not reflect light. If chairs have splinters and are causing runs and tears in clothes, have them sanded and refinished.
5. Set aside one day a year for general office cleaning, having the entire office personnel participate.

For maintenance of office equipment, see page 416.

2. EQUIPMENT, FILES, AND APPLIANCES

Office equipment. Office space, especially in large cities, is expensive. Consequently, the maximum utilization of space means money saved. Although economical use of space is primarily an office layout problem, the proper selection and use of office equipment are also important cost-cutting factors.

The standard equipment of an office consists of desks, tables, chairs, and filing cabinets. All of this equipment is made of wood or steel. Chairs are also made of aluminum. Metal has the advantages of durability and indestructibility by fire.

Desks. The desks to be selected depend on their use. Four types are generally used in offices—the clerical desk, the typewriter desk, the secretarial desk, and the executive desk.

The clerical desk is for writing use only. The desk may be single-pedestal, 42 by 30 inches, or double-pedestal, 60 by 34 inches, with five drawers.

The typewriter desk is used for typing. The drop-head type is a double-pedestal desk, 54 by 30 inches, with drawers on each side and a space directly in the center on which the typewriter is placed. When the typewriter is not in use, the center section can be closed, giving the desk a plain-topped writing surface. There is also the fixed platform typewriter desk.

Desks are also designed for use with computing machines.

The secretarial desk is designed for employees who do typing and have need for a clear writing space for clerical work. It is about the same size as the typewriter desk, but the typewriter occupies the space normally occupied by the left-hand or right-hand drawers. When not in use, the typewriter is let down and pushed into the desk under the writing space.

The executive desk is a large desk, usually about 66 by 34 inches, having five or seven drawers.

Where space is a factor, "space-saver" desks that are 50 and 55 inches wide are obtainable in different models.

Shaw Walker Company established the standard height for desks at 29 inches, after studying the correct seating height from the floor. The former standard desk height was 30½ inches, but no one knows why. Obviously, an office equipped with desks 30½ inches from the floor cannot immediately discard them. Only rarely is it possible to cut them down to 29 inches because the change will usually bring the center drawer too close to the worker's legs. The best solution is to make a wooden platform about 1½ inches high to fit under the desk. If the chair permits comfortable good seating posture, the foot rest will permit the worker to keep his feet squarely upon the floor. The latter is an essential of good seating.

Tables. The tables in offices vary in size depending on their use. The usual size is 60 by 36 inches, with the surface about 30 inches from the floor. If rough work is to be done on the table, it is advisable to cover the top with linoleum or some other covering.

Chairs. Office chairs are designed primarily for correct posture, for it is recognized that the posture of an employee has a bearing on fatigue and also on the quality and quantity of his work. The so-called posture chair, designed for such operations as posting, typing, and tabulating, has increased production and lessened fatigue. Its height is easily adjusted to conform to the height of the desk and the size of the worker. The correct seating height from the floor in relation to a desk that is 29 inches high, is 17 inches.

The four types of chairs found in offices are: (1) stenographer chairs, which are adjustable swivel chairs with posture back rests; (2) executive chairs, which are orthopedically designed swivel chairs with arms; (3) swivel chairs without arms; and (4) straight-back non-swivel chairs. All of these chairs, except the straight-back non-swivel chairs, are set on four small, roller-bearing, swivel wheels.

Filing cabinets. Although manufacturers make filing cabinets of various sizes to accommodate letters and forms of standard sizes, the standard filing cabinet is the four-drawer, 8½ by 11, steel cabinet. Where space is limited, a five-drawer cabinet is available.

The features built into the file cabinet are important from the standpoint of efficiency in filing. Equipment now on the market provides file folders that hang and slide easily back and forth on suspension frames. This adds to available filing space and prevents individual folders from sagging.

The type of drawer is also important. The three basic drawer types currently on the market are: (1) rigid—both front and rear ends of the drawer are rigid; (2) drop front—the front of the drawer inclines outward as the drawer is opened, but the back remains rigid; and (3) automatic—both the front and back of the drawer incline outward simultaneously as the drawer is opened. The forward tilting of the drawer provides ample working space; the backward tilting of the rear provides maximum visibility of folders and thus facilitates finding and filing.

Card cabinets for filing job tickets, requisitions, and other small size tickets and record cards are part of the equipment of most offices.

Counter cabinets. Counter cabinets of convenient height, built to be used as counters, and having drawers in the back, are used in offices dealing with individuals who come into the office. The information used by the clerk is filed in the counter cabinets. Cabinet counters are obtainable in various combinations of units, such as letter file drawers, legal files, card files, cash drawer, cupboards with shelves, and an insulated safety cabinet for vital records.

Visible record equipment. Visible-record equipment speeds the location of information and facilitates follow-up. Pertinent facts can be seen at a glance, instead of having to be rooted out of a mass of papers. The following is a description of several types of visible-record equipment:

1. *Board and ticket holders.* This type of visible record is used for housing copies of production orders, job tickets, sales slips, and other individual records. It consists of a board with spring clips that hold a number of papers in place. The last paper filed is almost completely visible since the clip covers only a small part of the filed paper. Some types hold several panels of spring clips. The panels are placed in a swinging position on a stationary or revolving rack.

2. *Visible index equipment for reference and posting.* This equipment provides visibility of an index classification for records to which reference must be made or items posted. The unit consists of (a) the card on which the record is made, (b) the pocket which holds the record card, (c) the tray which holds the pockets in filing position with the index edges exposed, and (d) movable celluloid signals to emphasize particular data. All the forms or cards in each tray or slide are visible at once, thus making the location of a particular card almost instantaneous.

3. *Visible index reference equipment.* This equipment is used where long lists of names with related information must be referred to frequently; for example, customers' lists, or lists of materials and parts used in the planning and production control department. It consists of a frame into which strips are inserted with the name or item in the list. The strips are removed and new names or items are inserted as required. Tube inserts are used if the file gets rough treatment. The frames that hold the strips are housed in various types of holders; for example, rotary stands with single or double tiers, wall brackets, and others.

4. *Looseleaf visible binders.* Accounts and other forms are filed in tiers in a looseleaf binder. The index edge of each account is visible.

Some of the applications of visible-record equipment are described in the following paragraphs.

Visible records in sales management. The cards to be used in sales management must, of course, be well planned, so that the most useful information will be readily seen. The sales-record card might be designed to indicate on the visible margin, by the use of movable colored celluloid signals: (1) the month of the last call by the salesman; (2) the month of the most recent purchase; (3) the percentage of the customer's requirements being filled; and (4) whether or not the customer bought anything in the previous year; in addition, the name and address of the customer are visible. The balance of the card gives details showing individual sales by product and amount, comparisons with other years, what the customer buys and how much, and so forth.

The records are held securely in overlapping kraft pockets, which are mounted on slides to fit into various types of cabinets. The colored signals permit immediate analysis of entire groups of records without the necessity of "drawing off" figures. A positive control over salesmen is provided, making checkups easier.

The cards can be kept up to date very easily, merely by moving the signals when postings are made.

Visible records in accounts receivable. The application of visible records to accounts receivable is particularly useful in installment collections. Here the visible margin shows the name and address of the customer, and the celluloid signal indicates to what date he has paid. A delinquent account is easily spotted because the signal will not have been moved as far as the signals on the nondelinquent accounts.

The pocket behind the name usually contains a ledger card with credit data and details of installments paid. This card can easily be pulled out for posting and can be found very quickly with the eye because the names are visible. If desired, statements can be kept in the same pocket with the ledger cards.

The immediate visibility of the delinquency data greatly aids in keeping up collections, thus strengthening the retailer's cash position, increasing the accounts-receivable turnover rate, and reducing bad-debt losses and collection costs.

Another advantage of visibility in connection with accounts receivable is that the operator will spend a larger proportion of his time in making entries on the cards and a smaller proportion in hunting for the proper sheets, thus increasing his production.

Visible-record equipment aids purchasing. Another application of visible-record installations is in the field of inventory control. The card used is a regular stock card containing the information on orders and requisitions. The visible edge gives the name of the item. The celluloid signal shows how many weeks' supply is on hand. As the supply is used up, the signal is moved over. Thus the stock-record clerk or purchasing agent can tell at a glance how long the supply of each item will last.

The visual signal shows when the ordering point is reached, when the supply is getting dangerously low, and when the item is overstocked. This device saves both clerical and executive time in analyzing and reduces the cost of keeping the record. The progressive signal instantly points out the items needing attention.

Visible panels in the credit department. The panel type of visible-record equipment is extensively used in the authorizing section of the credit department in department and retail stores.

The visible cards on the panels contain the name, address, and credit limit of the customer. Different colored cards indicate whether an account is delinquent or closed. A numbered code is used to indicate various restrictions regarding the account. The panels are arranged alphabetically and have the main alphabetical divisions designated by a celluloid tab fastened to the edge of the panel.

The visible-panel filing system is also used as a master reference file in credit departments that file their accounts numerically. The cards on the panels contain the name, address, and account number of the customer. The clerk can easily find the credit record by first consulting the master file for the account number and then locating the numbered record in the visible file.

Rotary filing device. Office-equipment companies have developed a plastic wheel for rotary filing, to which are attached metal segments holding cards. The whole is enclosed in a cabinet, the top of which is open to reveal the wheel and a section of the cards. A wheel measuring 21 inches in diameter can hold 6,500 cards. By turning the wheel, the clerk can bring the desired card into view.

It is not necessary to make up a special type of card for the machine. Cards already in use can be fitted into the device.

Individual cards can be slipped out if desired. Groups of cards can also be removed, since the metal segments on which they are fastened are detachable. This feature permits easy division of the work on peak-load days, as different clerks can take segments of cards to their own desks.

The unit is portable and can be locked at night. It is desk height, thus enabling hand posting to be done more quickly and more easily and in the most natural writing position.

The device has been used by organizations with large membership lists, because it facilitates looking up the status of persons who are being registered for attendance at conferences and conventions.

Office machines and appliances. Office machines and appliances are introduced into an office in order to save time and money and to increase the quantity and quality of work.

The types of office machines in general use are calculating machines, duplicating machines, addressing machines, time recorders, and dictating machines. These machines are being improved and modernized constantly so that the discussion given on page 399, *et seq.*, is limited to a description of their operation and use.

How to determine the value of an office appliance. Modern office devices often seem expensive when the original cost is examined. A simple way of checking the economy of office appliances is to compare the estimated monthly depreciation with the operator's salary and production. If output is increased as a result of the introduction of the machine, sufficiently to offset the depreciation charge, the machine can be introduced economically.

Considerations in buying office appliances. The following suggestions will aid in the consideration of the purchase of an office appliance:

1. Buy your office equipment from a scientific viewpoint. Standardization of equipment reduces maintenance costs, makes employee transfer easier, and allows quantity discounts. Nevertheless, standardization should not be carried so far that a $200 machine is bought

for each clerk when a $50 machine would be perfectly satisfactory for some.

2. Decide whether it is necessary to perform the task that the machine is designed to do.

3. Test the machine under actual working conditions to check claims for increased production. Do not permit yourself to be biased for or against any equipment, but be sure to get supporting evidence for every claim made about it.

4. If the equipment does increase production, will you be able to utilize the spare time of the operator? If you cannot, there is not much point in getting the machine.

Calculating machines. Adding, billing, and bookkeeping machines are the most common of the calculating machines.

Adding machines. The simplest and most common calculating machine is the adding machine. Its use primarily is to add columns of figures. There are machines that will add, subtract, divide, and multiply, but they are not generally used in smaller offices.

The adding machine may be hand or electrically operated, listing or nonlisting. A listing adding machine records the row of figures on a strip of paper, whereas the nonlisting machine shows the accumulated total on the top or bottom of the machine. The two general types of listing-adding machines are known as full keyboard machines and ten-key machines.

Billing machines. A billing machine is a combination typewriter and calculating machine. There are various types of billing machines adaptable for various uses. The machines are able to do a number of calculating jobs, such as adding, subtracting, dividing, and multiplying. They permit an operator to post entries on ledger accounts at the same time that invoices are being made up. Some of the machines accumulate totals of all postings; others make extensions automatically.

The billing machine is used in large and small organizations to prepare monthly bills. It eliminates the necessity of typing the bills with a typewriter at the end of the month.

Bookkeeping machines. Space does not permit a detailed discussion of the various bookkeeping machines. In principle they are similar to billing machines, and both machines can be used with a little change for similar work. The bookkeeping machine is used in preparing records such as customers' statements, accounts-payable records, cash-received records, cost sheets, stores records, payroll records, and many others.

Punched-card accounting equipment. Punched cards are used for general and cost-accounting work as well as for statistical and analytical research. The cards in many companies comprise the accounts receivable and accounts payable ledgers, stock records, and payrolls. In cost accounting, punched cards can be used to show the cost of direct labor, indirect material and overhead applicable to each job, thus replacing the cost sheets. Examples of statistical and analytical uses are classification of sales by salesmen, by price lines, by territories, by profit lines, and by kinds of merchandise sold. Department stores use the equipment for inventory analyses and classifications, for charge-account analyses, and the like.

Three types of machines are generally necessary to set up a punched-card-accounting process: (1) a key punch, to perforate the tabulating card with the desired holes; (2) a sorter, to separate the punched cards into the desired groups; and (3) the accounting machine, to compute, record, and print the results.

Each card is divided into "fields," in each of which are vertical columns of figures from zero to nine. The figures applicable to each field are recorded by punching out holes in the appropriate columns. The fields are arranged according to the data desired. For example, the accounts-payable card used in a retail store might have fields showing invoice data, vendor's invoice number, vendor's number, department, due date, terms, gross amount, discount, net amount, transportation, total cost, retail price, percentage markup, and posting data.

When punching has been completed, the cards are usually not in any usable order and must be arranged according to the desired classifications. This is the function of the sorter. Since the sorting is done one column at a time, the cards must be passed through the machine as many times as there are columns in the particular field being sorted. This is not a serious drawback, however, as 480 cards can be sorted per minute.

The sorted cards are then run through electric accounting machines, which are so designed as to provide complete flexibility in the arrangement of the data appearing on the forms. As much or as little information as is desired can be printed. The sorted cards can also be run through tabulating machines to give subtotals and grand totals, which are transcribed to report forms by the operator.

Advantages of punched-card accounting. The punched holes are permanent and unalterable, so the cards, once punched and proved, eliminate errors of omission and transposition. Since the operations are entirely automatic, a uniform accuracy for all reports is assured. Reports are available much more quickly than under manual procedures, and many more reports and analyses can be made with punched cards than would be possible if costly manual preparation were necessary.

Many models of machines are available, ranging from very inexpensive to quite elaborate and expensive ones. The manufacturers of the equipment have service bureaus in leading cities that will prepare analyses and reports on a fee basis if desired, thus eliminating part of the outlay for equipment.

Proof machines to speed sorting. Proof machines are available to list, sort, and prove bank checks, sales tickets, vouchers, and other business documents in one operation. The results, ordinarily obtained with three or more separate manual operations, are obtained with but one clerical handling. The items themselves are sorted into different desired classifications; money amounts for each classification are listed and totalled; and all amounts are listed, identified, and totalled on a single proving tape. The automatic proving eliminates the necessity for tedious, time-wasting checking and cross-checking to locate errors.

Keysort for sorting data. Keysort is a system of sorting accounting information by the use of specially printed and punched cards and a selecting needle that resembles an ice pick. An extremely flexible system, it can be used for sales, timekeeping, and payroll records, cost distribution, personnel statistics, and other records.

Description of cards. The information to be sorted is transcribed onto cards, different sizes and styles of which are manufactured to meet varying needs. The four margins are divided into sections according to the classifications desired. Into each section the manufacturer has punched round holes ¼ inch apart, which are used to indicate numbers within the classification. Four holes are required for each digit in the classification and are labelled, respectively, 1, 2, 4, and 7. By using combinations of these four digits, it is possible to notch out in the margin any number from 1 to 9, as indicated by the following table:

1—by notching out 1
2—by notching out 2
3—by notching out 2 and 1
4—by notching out 4
5—by notching out 4 and 1
6—by notching out 4 and 2
7—by notching out 7
8—by notching out 7 and 1
9—by notching out 7 and 2

The indication of the number is made by notching out that portion of the card between the hole and the outer edge of the card. Each group of the four holes 1, 2, 4, and 7 is termed a field. If the classification has three digits in it, three groups of four holes, or three fields, will thus be required for that section.

As an example, the Keysort card illustrated in Figure 35 is being used in connection with labor cost records, one card being used for each operation worked on by each man. The workman's name, order number, clock number, date, starting, ending, and elapsed times, amount applicable to the operation, and other necessary information appear on the body of the card. On the margin of the card appear various classifications: order number, department, employee number, operation number, and others. In this particular case, the workman's number is 213, the order number 12, the opera-

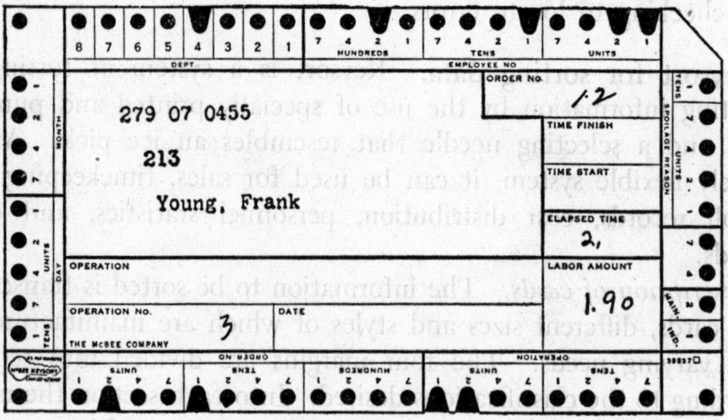

Figure 35. Example of Keysort Card.

tion number 3, and the department number 4, as can be seen by an inspection of the notches made in the illustration.

Types of Keysort cards used. The cards used may in some cases be carbon copies of invoices or other original records. They may be the original records themselves, such as the time cards just described. Again, they may be prepared from some original records as a separate operation, in which case the information to be sorted will be punched on the cards, and the amounts to be tabulated will be written on the face. In most cases only those classifications to be sorted are punched.

The most advantageous use of Keysort cards is obtained when they are used as original records, since such use does not entail transcribing data from the original records to Keysort cards, as the data are written there first.

How notching of Keysort cards is done. Four types of punches to notch the Keysort cards are available from the manufacturer:

1. A hand punch, similar to a railroad conductor's ticket punch.
2. A hand key punch, which has 34 keys arranged in 8 vertical rows.
3. An electric key punch, similar to the hand key punch, but faster in operation, with which an average operator is able to punch the four edges of 600 cards in an hour, each card differently.
4. A gang grooving machine, with which 200 cards in a single position can be punched at one time.

How Keysort cards are classified. The notching is done only for sorting purposes. Tabulation or adding of data on the sorted cards is done on a calculating or adding machine.

The cards to be sorted are placed edgewise on a table, face forward and right side up. One corner of each card has a diagonal cut, to make it possible to tell at a glance whether all the cards are in the right position. The selecting needle is then inserted in the hole for which classification is desired.

As an illustration, assume that from a group of time cards those pertaining to employee number 936 are to be segregated. The needle is first inserted in the 7 hole of the hundreds' field and lifted. All those cards on which the hundreds' digit is 7, 8, or 9 will fall. The needle is then inserted in the 2 hole of the hundreds' field of those cards dropping from the first sort. Cards on which the hundreds' digit is 9 will drop, since the only cards that can drop this time are those in which both 7 and 2 in the hundreds' field have been notched out. The needle is now inserted in the 2 hole of the tens' field. All cards that drop this time will begin 92-, 93-, 96-, or 99-. A sort is now made by inserting the needle in the 1 hole of the tens' classification of the dropped cards, and those cards beginning 93- will drop, since the only cards that can fall are those in which both the 2 and the 1 have been notched out of the tens' field. Two more similar sorts are necessary for the units' field, first by sorting through the 4 hole and then through the 2 hole, thus dropping all cards on which the number 936 has been punched out.

Sorters. Filing time can be greatly reduced by the use of the following types of sorting equipment:

1. *Box or pigeon-hole rack.* Boxes are built in tiers and labeled for alphabetical, numerical, or other groups.

2. *Leaf sorter.* This device consists of fibre leaves hinged to a board. Each leaf has a celluloid tab into which is inserted the letter of the alphabet, name of the state, or other index according to which the papers are to be sorted. The leaves overlap one another so that only the tabs are visible. The sorting clerk lifts the proper tab with her left hand and inserts the paper under the leaf with her right hand.

A similar device has fibre tabs hinged to a circular base that revolves on a ball-bearing spindle at the touch of a finger. Label inserts at the end of the tabs are arranged in alphabetical order, with about ten tabs for each letter of the alphabet. The operator sorts the correspondence by turning the circular tab-wheel to the proper tab, lifting the tab, and inserting the correspondence behind it. Portable, lightweight desk units with from 25 to 100 sorting divisions are also available.

3. *Table and tray sorter.* This is a large sorter consisting of a table for the operator, on each side of which are one to four movable trays, several feet long, each placed on a track. Each tray contains subdividing tabs the width of the papers to be sorted. The tabs are labeled according to the filing system used. The papers to be sorted are placed on the table and are inserted behind the proper subdivision by the operator, who can move the trays back and forth

on the tracks by a push of the finger. The operator thus sits at her work and does not have to reach far to place a paper behind the correct tab.

4. *Needle sort.* The Keysort described at page 401 is an example of a needle sort.

5. *Machine sort.* This is one of the basic units of punched card accounting equipment. (See page 400.)

Use of sorters. With the use of sorters it is not necessary to file material daily in the filing cabinets. The tabs can be used to accumulate material for any desired period, depending upon the capacity of the sorter. Papers are as easily available as in the file cabinets, so that no time is wasted hunting for unfiled material.

One very practical application of a sorting device is in the accounts receivable department of a department store. Here the sales slips are sorted by customers and held until the end of the month. No postings are made during the month to the customer's statement. At the end of the month, the sales checks are totalled, and only the total is entered on the statement. Copies of the sales checks comprising the total are stapled to the statement and mailed to the customer. This practice eliminates the work of posting charges daily and also avoids any chance of error. Each customer gets a copy of the original sales slip just as it was made out at the time of purchase.

Pegboard system to save time and reduce error. The use of the pegboard system makes unnecessary the transcribing of information from several individual records to one summary record. The pegboard system consists of a steel strip, in which pegs are inserted at fixed distances apart, and forms punched across the top margin to correspond with the distance between pegs on the strip. The forms must be carefully printed so that all horizontal lines on the forms will be on the same plane.

The pegboard system used by Continental Baking Company in connection with daily orders for bread taken by the various salesmen illustrates the short cut furnished by this system. Daily each salesman turns in a "salesman's invoice." This form constitutes the order for bread to be delivered the following day. In the center section of the form, under the word "Kind," are printed the names of the different kinds of bread, and in the column headed

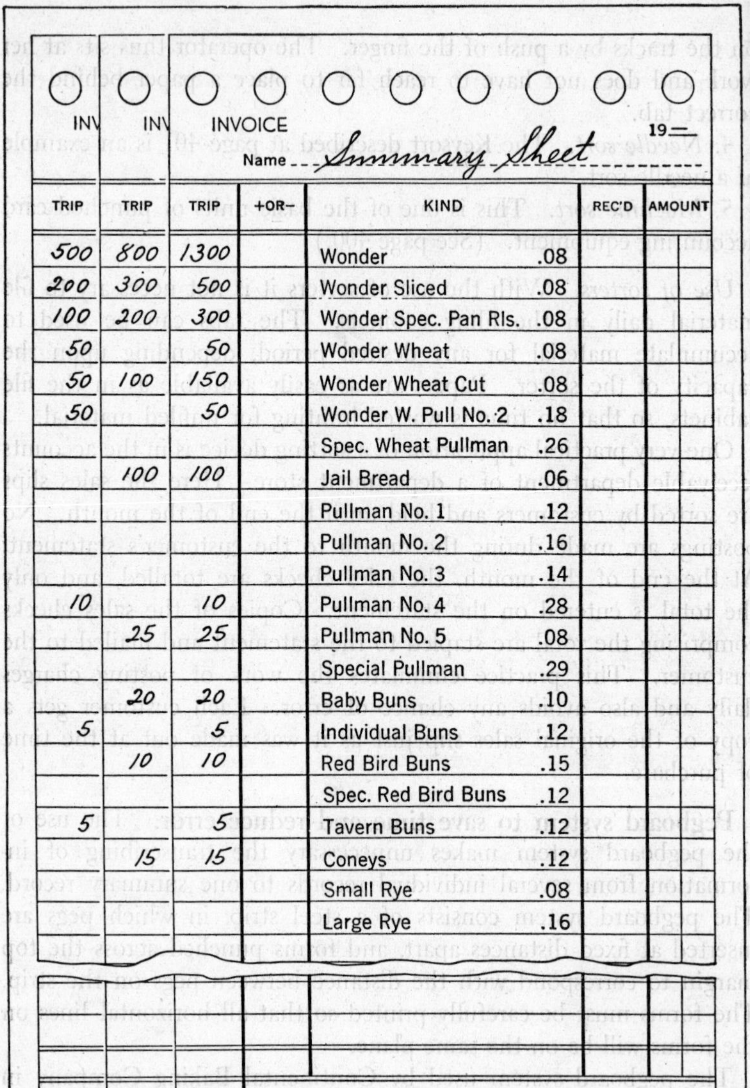

INV INV INVOICE 19—

Name *Summary Sheet*

TRIP	TRIP	TRIP	+OR–	KIND		REC'D	AMOUNT
500	800	1300		Wonder	.08		
200	300	500		Wonder Sliced	.08		
100	200	300		Wonder Spec. Pan Rls.	.08		
50		50		Wonder Wheat	.08		
50	100	150		Wonder Wheat Cut	.08		
50		50		Wonder W. Pull No. 2	.18		
				Spec. Wheat Pullman	.26		
	100	100		Jail Bread	.06		
				Pullman No. 1	.12		
				Pullman No. 2	.16		
				Pullman No. 3	.14		
10		10		Pullman No. 4	.28		
	25	25		Pullman No. 5	.08		
				Special Pullman	.29		
	20	20		Baby Buns	.10		
5		5		Individual Buns	.12		
	10	10		Red Bird Buns	.15		
				Spec. Red Bird Buns	.12		
5		5		Tavern Buns	.12		
	15	15		Coneys	.12		
				Small Rye	.08		
				Large Rye	.16		

Route No. Route No. Route No

Salesman

Figure 36. Peg Board Forms for Determining Day's Orders.

"Trip," the quantity ordered of each. The slips turned in by all the men are then placed on the strip from left to right, as illustrated in Figure 36, so that the "Trip" section of each form is exposed. A blank sheet is then added at the extreme right of the strip, next to the last order. A comptometer operator adds the total of each variety across the sheets and enters the totals on the blank.

The procedure described renders unnecessary the copying of all individual figures from each sheet to a summary record. Time is saved, and errors in transcribing are eliminated.

Duplicating machines. Many instances occur in an office in which numerous copies of a paper are needed. Among the various processes available for obtaining numerous copies are stencil, hectograph, direct and offset printing, and automatic typewriting. These processes are briefly described in the following paragraphs.

Stencil duplication by Mimeograph. Stencil duplication (Mimeograph) provides exact reproduction of typewritten work. The stencil is placed in a typewriter and the ribbon is adjusted or removed, so that the letters, instead of being printed, are cut into the stencil, thus exposing the fibers through which the ink can pass when the stencil is placed on the machine. Illustrations, drawings, and other handwritten matter may also be stencilled by means of a stylus.

The stencil is placed over an ink pad that partially covers a hollow, perforated, revolving cylinder. The ink is applied to the inner surface of the cylinder and passes through the perforations to the pad and then through the letters or designs cut in the stencil, making an impression on the paper as the cylinder revolves. The paper may be fed to the machine either automatically or manually, depending upon the type of machine. With the automatic duplicator, from 1,500 to 7,500 copies can be made per hour. Removable cylinders are available, so that one can be substituted for another when two-color reproduction is desired.

Hectograph method of duplication. Under this method of duplication, impressions are made from an original writing, known as a master copy, to a secondary copy which enables additional copies to be made. The gelatin method and the direct method of hectographing (Ditto) are described below.

(a) Gelatin method. Gelatin duplicators make copies by transferring ink from a typewritten or handwritten master copy to a gelatin duplicating composition that dissolves and holds the ink on its surface until all the copies have been run off. Hard bond paper and special duplicating ink, a duplicating typewriter ribbon, or an indelible pencil are used in preparing the master copy. Different colors may be combined on one original.

The duplicator consists of a flat printing bed over which is stretched a gelatin-covered roll. After one surface has been used, a fresh one may be brought into position by turning a handle.

The original is placed face down on the gelatin copying surface and smoothed with the palm of the hand or a roller. It is then lifted off, having left an impression on the gelatin. The blank sheets are placed one at a time on the gelatin surface and allowed to remain a few seconds until the imprint is made.

(b) Direct method. In this method, a master copy is prepared by writing or typing on a sheet of paper that is backed up by a piece of hectograph carbon paper, with the carbon side against the master sheet. Thus, whatever is written or typed on the master copy appears in reverse on the back of the master. The carbon sheet is removed and destroyed and the master is placed on a drum for rotary reproduction. The master can be re-used a number of times.

Direct printing (Multigraph). Direct printing may be done with a machine such as the Multigraph. The type may be composed by hand or by a keyboard-operated machine that operates at the usual typing speed. In either instance, type is placed directly onto railed segments. The composed segment is then placed on the duplicating machine, and a wide typewriter ribbon is wrapped around the form, or ink is applied by an inking mechanism. As the printing drum of the machine revolves, paper is fed between the ribbon-covered type or the directly inked type and a rubber-covered platen, thus producing a facsimile typewritten letter or an ink-duplicated form at each revolution. Up to 6,000 copies can be produced per hour. Forms may be numbered consecutively with an optional numbering device.

Offset printing (Multilith). Offset printing can be done by the Multilith. The matter to be reproduced is prepared on any one of several metal or paper base duplicatory masters, either directly by typing, by drawing with ink or crayon, by tracing through carbon paper, or by photo-contact process. The prepared plate is placed on a drum of the duplicating machine, and ink and a repellant are fed by rolls to the surface of the plate automatically during revolution of the drum. The drum is in rolling contact with a second drum, which has a smooth rubber blanket wrapped around it and to which the inked image is offset. The paper is fed between the offset blanket drum and impression cylinder or platen, and at each revolution of the drums a complete offset duplicated copy is made on the sheet. Up to 5,800 reproductions can be made per hour.

See page 10 for a description of the super-process—flat-bed process used in preparing letters for quantity distribution.

Automatic typewriter duplication. Automatic typewriters are designed to produce rapidly actual typewritten letters. The machine consists of a standard typewriter operated by an electric mechanism that is controlled by a perforated strip of record paper similar to a player-piano roll. Part of the equipment consists of a perforator with a standard typewriter keyboard, with which the perforations are made.

The typist cuts the material to be produced on the perforator, each perforation representing a character in the typewriter keyboard. When the cutting of the perforations is completed, the perforated paper is cut off and the ends cemented together to form a roll, which is then placed on a drum in front of the automatic typewriter. In the drum are a number of lengthwise slots over which the perforations in the record paper rest. When the machine is started, the drum revolves, carrying the record paper forward under a set of pins. As a perforation passes under a pin, the pin drops into a slot in the drum, actuating a typewriter key as though by hand. After all the perforations have passed over the drum once, the operator removes the finished letter and repeats the process.

The machine may also be used as a standard typewriter, so that at any point the operator may stop the automatic mechanism and typewrite, by hand, information of interest only to the recipient of that particular letter.

Photo-copy machines. Photo-copy machines comprise various types of machines that make facsimiles of documents, papers, signatures, art work, and other material. They are differentiated in the trade from the duplicating machines described above. Three well-known types of photo-copy apparatus (Photostat, Portagraph, and Ozalid) are described below.

Photostat. Photostat Photographic Copying Apparatus provides a simple and practical method for the rapid reproduction of clear, readable copies by means of photography. All models of this apparatus will make copies quickly, accurately, and inexpensively of anything that is written, printed, drawn, typewritten, blueprinted, or photographed. Small objects may also be photographed. These copies may, with few exceptions, be made at same size, or enlarged or reduced as desired.

The various models consist principally of a large camera with a magazine for holding a roll of photographically sensitized paper and compartments for developing and fixing prints within the apparatus. In such models as are mechanically and electrically operated, washing and even drying of the prints is also accomplished.

The magazine and processing compartments are mounted on a stand to the front of which is attached a movable subject-holder of a type suitable to the particular needs of each individual installation. This may be either a Bookholder or an Engineering Board. The Bookholder has a hinged glass top held open by springs while the subject is being inserted. The Engineering Board is made of wood, has no glass cover, and is intended to hold larger subjects than can be placed on the Bookholder. Both subject-holders are charted with lines and numbers to determine the focus and size of copy possible.

The mechanical means for quickly focusing and handling Photostat Photographic Copying Apparatus makes it simple in operation, with no previous knowledge of photography being necessary. Perfect copies are produced with speed, accuracy, and convenience.

The subject matter to be copied is photographed through a lens with a prism attached to the front. The prism provides the means whereby the image, normally reversed by the lens, is again reversed and carried to the sensitized paper in its original position without the need of an intervening negative.

Prints made by this method produce copies in which the original blacks and whites are transposed; that is, white becomes black and black becomes white. If this first print is copied, the black and white will be reversed again to provide black letters on a white background.

Portagraph. The item to be copied is placed on a plate-glass surface at the top of the machine. It is then covered with a piece of ensitized paper, a lid is closed down over the two sheets, an automatic timer is set in motion, and a few seconds later the exposed paper is ready for development. No photographic experience is necessary to operate it, and, since the printing paper used is not sensitive to daylight, no dark room is necessary for either printing or developing. The unit is compact, can be easily carried, and can be used wherever electric current is available. It is particularly useful where facsimiles of art work, maps, signatures, seals, trade-marks, letters, documents, and so forth, are desired.

Ozalid. Copies called Ozaprints are produced by placing a translucent original or master on a sheet or roll of Ozalid sensitized material and feeding it into an Ozalid printmaking machine. In passing through the printmaking machine, the original or translucent master and the sensitized material are exposed to a source of ultra-violet light. The light passes through the translucent material, except where blocked by opaque lines on the original, and changes the chemicals on the sensitized material to a colorless compound. The original is then delivered to a receiving tray on the printmaker and the sensitized material is carried by a moving belt into the developer. Here it is exposed to ammonia fumes which develop the chemicals remaining on the paper; that is, the portions protected by the lines or images on the original. The entire procedure is accomplished in a few seconds and the finished print is ready for immediate use.

Although the Ozalid process has long been used for making copies of engineering drawings and tracings, its versatility is now recognized and demonstrated by a wide variety of other uses. Several large banks use Ozalid machines to produce copies of customers' statements. A nationally known credit rating agency uses Ozalid machines to produce multiple copies of credit reports. Many organizations using Ozalid machines have all their forms, file cards, letterheads, and so forth, printed on translucent material. By this method every letter and record is an Ozalid master, just like an engineering drawing or tracing, and copies can be run off on the Ozalid machine whenever required.

Microfilm equipment. Microfilming is the photographing of records at a high rate of speed and at a high ratio of reduction. The film comes in 16 mm. and 35 mm.; the former is used for ordinary business papers, and the latter for drawings and newspapers. Various types of cabinets are made to house the camera. There is a slot into which the papers are fed and they come to rest in a hopper at the bottom of the cabinet. Some of these machines may be purchased outright; others are rented on a month-to-month basis. A reading machine, which is part of the microfilming equipment, enlarges the documents photographed on the film to original size or larger. Improvements in the design of reader machines enable a clerk to load, adjust, focus and operate the reader while she is seated at a desk.

The film may either be sent back to the manufacturer for processing (and in that case the price of processing is included in the price of the film) or it may be processed in one's own office by means of a special developing machine.

Special cabinets are obtainable from the manufacturers of microfilm equipment for the proper storage of the films. For best preservation of the films, the cabinet should meet the specifications of the United States Bureau of Standards as to humidity and circulation of air among the films. A cabinet that holds 99 100-foot rolls of 16 mm. film will house the equivalent of approximately 2,700,000 letter-size records.

The most essential use of microfilming is to save file space and equipment that would otherwise be used for inactive records. (See page 433.) It is also used to make copies of papers that are to be sent to other locations. For example, some department stores make microfilm records of customers' sales checks and send the checks back to the customer with a statement, but with no description of the items purchased.

Electric typewriters. Electric typewriters have several advantages over nonelectric typewriters. The entire keyboard is electrically powered, including carriage return, backspacer, tabulator, shift and space bar. The touch is a much lighter one, and, since each character receives the same power impulse, the type impression is uniform and even. Fatigue is prevented and production greatly speeded up. As many as twenty clear carbon copies can be printed on some electric typewriters.

Addressing machines. Much time is often lost in typing the name and address of a new customer on the various forms used in the office. This time can be saved by the use of addressing machines, which are of two types: (1) machines that use a fiber stencil ut out with a typewriter, and (2) machines that use an embossed netal plate prepared by a special machine. The plates or stencils re fed into the addressing machine in the order in which they are led. The machine is able to print all the names, but it can be djusted to select any group of names desired. Tabs placed in a ertain position on the plates or slots cut out from the stencil guide he machine automatically to reject or select any plate. Addressing nachines can be used to print the name and address of a customer n various forms. For instance, a group of Chicago insurance companies prepared an Addressograph plate and printed the name and ddress on the following records:

1. Customer's ledger card.
2. Postal acknowledgment of application to the applicant.
3. Identification card.
4. Policy enclosure with instructions for use in case of accident.
5. Two index cards for alphabetical and numerical files.
6. File folder.

An attachment is available for automatically feeding standard marginal punched forms on the Class 1900 Addressograph, directly across the Addressograph table. The flat-folded forms to be imprinted are placed in a loading tray at the front of the writing table, and are fed underneath the impression head of the machine, and finally to a tray at the rear, where they are re-folded into another pack. The strip of forms moves automatically (being propelled by two pin wheels which mesh with the holds along both margins of the forms) a predetermined distance, and stops when the space to be imprinted is correctly positioned under the impression head. After the imprint is made, the strip advances to the position of the next imprint, as long as there are plates in the magazine.

The pin wheels which propel the forms are adjustable to accommodate forms up to 19¼ inches wide. Forms from 3 inches to 11 inches in length can be handled. The rigid action of the impression arm of the Addressograph facilitates preparation of clean carbon copies.

This attachment can be put to the following uses: preparation of installment, dividend, premium, and meeting notices; letters; labels; dividend lists; payroll registers; credit memos; collection devices;

dividend, payroll, pension, and annuity checks; statements; time cards, and many others.

Continuous-form feeding devices of different types are available to meet different requirements.

Dictating and recording equipment. Many mechanical devices are available for recording and transcribing dictation. They are used for letters, memos, and other office dictation. Lightweight models are available for conference recording, hospital research, and countless other purposes. Other models are equipped for the recording of both sides of telephone conversations.

Field organizations have vastly improved their chain of communication through the installation of dictating machines in salesmen's cars. Field men dictate customer reports on the spot and mail the dictated recording to the home office.

The most commonly used dictating and recording equipment may be classified by the medium used for recording the voice—wax cylinder, plastic belt, plastic disc, and wire.

Wax cylinder. This is the oldest type of equipment and therefore is most frequently found in offices, though it is steadily being replaced by the plastic belt machine. The wax cylinder equipment consists of a dictating unit, a transcribing unit, and a shaving machine for preparing the cylinders for re-use. The possibility of breakage of cylinders is its chief disadvantage. About eight one-page letters can be dictated on a cylinder.

Plastic belt. The plastic belt is a flexible, non-breakable medium weighing a fraction of an ounce. Its weight and size make for easy mailing and filing. Because of its inherent shape, it offers exclusive advantages: constant groove speed, uniform back-spacing for the secretary, perfect visibility, and proved economy. Belts for 15 or 30 minutes of recording may be obtained. The system includes a dictating and a transcribing unit; combination dictation-transcribing units are also available.

Plastic disc. The disc recorders are of different sizes. A large-size disc will take about fifteen minutes' dictation on each side. The discs can be mailed in a special envelope since they are light in weight and unbreakable, and can also be filed after transcription. Transcription units are also used with some models; other models are combined dictation-transcription machines.

Wire recorder. Wire recorders magnetically record sound on spools of stainless steel wire. A spool of wire will hold more than an hour of sound. It offers good fidelity of voice and therefore is a good device for "live" messages that are not transcribed but reproduced in sound.

If the dictator wants to make a change or correction, he simply redictates where the change is desired and any error is corrected over the previous dictation on the wire. This feature eliminates the need for correction slips and saves time both in dictating and transcribing. However, a chief disadvantage lies in the secretary's difficulty of place-finding. It takes more time to locate an early portion of the recording for listening-back purposes than on other recording media, such as the belt. The same unit serves for dictating and transcribing.

A buzzer cautions the dictator if the machine is not properly set for dictation, and a bell rings to warn the dictator that he has reached the end of the cylinder.

Time recorders. Small minute wastes grow very rapidly into large money losses. For example, in a factory employing 100 people at 75 cents an hour, the annual loss for 300 working days is over $1,500 if each employee is a minute late in the morning and after lunch and a minute early in leaving for lunch and again at the close of the day. *Attendance time recorders* will eliminate minute losses by revealing the sources and by promoting punctuality. Such clocks are also of particular value today because they provide the kind of record that enables management more easily to comply, and prove compliance, with the various social and labor laws that require accurate accounting for employee time.

The efficiency of any cost system depends partly upon the accuracy with which time records are kept. In the first place, workmen tend to eliminate fractions in filling out job time cards. Moreover, if they wait until the end of the day to fill out their cards, their records are likely to be inaccurate because of hazy memories. This lack of accuracy, of course, upsets the cost determination. *Job time recorders* make it possible for employees to record the time at the exact moment each job is started and finished. Cost determination is thus made more reliable because there is an accurate accounting of the exact amount of time spent on each job or operation. Mechanical job time recorders also help management to determine man and machine efficiency and reveal the amount of time lost between jobs.

Time stamps are used for recording the date and time when mail, documents, rush orders, telegrams, telephone calls, packages, etc. are received. See page 422 for use of time stamps on incoming mail.

Master clocks keep all clocks under control with the accurate time. Each clock in the system is automatically brought into agreement with the master.

Maintaining office appliances. To prolong the life of office appliances, obtain the greatest amount of service, and protect the initial investment in expensive machines, the establishment of a definite maintenance policy is necessary.

Maintenance and repair costs can be kept down by keeping a card index of all the office machines in use. (See Figure 37.) Include on the cards all purchase data, including credit allowed on an old machine, expected life, amount of depreciation to be charged off, and so forth. On the reverse side enter all details of repairs. The record helps to determine whether repair is advisable, or whether the age and condition of the machine warrant replacement instead. Excessive maintenance costs are decreased by making replacements at the proper time.

Record of __________ Card #______
Carriage Length ________ Serial #______
Type ______
Order #______ Date Purchased ______ Guarantee
Expires ______
Purchased from __________
List Price ....$______
Discount ______% ....$
Credit on old machine ....$______ $______
Cash Difference $______
Turned in__________
Date *Department* *Operator*

Figure 37. Record of Office Machines.

Maintenance work can be handled in three ways:

1. *Maintenance contract.* Most appliance manufacturers and their sales distributors provide a maintenance service on a yearly basis. This includes regular inspection, cleaning, adjusting, and oiling. The charges are predetermined and the rates for special service calls are usually indicated in the contract.

2. *Individual service calls.* A call for service is made each time it is required, as well as for regular cleaning and oiling of machines. The cost is likely to be higher than if service is supplied under a maintenance contract.

3. *Company's own repair department.* Large organizations often find it more economical and convenient to train and maintain their own service departments.

Typewriter care. An instruction sheet on how to care for typewriters (Figure 38), distributed among those who use typewriters,

KEEP YOUR TYPEWRITER IN GOOD REPAIR

1. Keep your machine covered when not in use.
2. Move the carriage to extreme right or left when erasing to prevent eraser dust from clogging segment.
3. Oil sparingly—just an occasional drop on the carriage rails is sufficient.
4. Use only light oil—preferably a 3-1 quality, that will not gum; never use Dictaphone oil or motor oil.
5. Never oil any other part of the typewriter—wait for the repairman to oil your machine generally.
6. Clean type with a good quality brush and type cleaning fluid.
7. Wipe off entire machine occasionally with soft cloth, slightly dampened with cleaning fluid; never use alcohol as this will destroy the finish on your typewriter.
8. Use properly-inked ribbons for the style of typeface.
9. Change typewriter ribbons when necessary.
10. Fasten machines to desks for best typing results.

TYPEWRITERS ARE MONEY!
TREAT THEM AS SUCH

Figure 38. Typewriter Care Instruction Sheet.

will help keep the machines in good condition and will reduce repair costs. The instruction sheet shown in Figure 38 has effectively reduced costs in one organization.

Typewriter ribbons. For superior legibility, good appearance of the finished product, and most efficient use of typewriter ribbons, it is best to use special ribbons for special purposes, rather than to make one type of ribbon do all types of work. Below are outlined ribbon characteristics for various kinds of work: *

For the sharpest and cleanest typewritten impressions, as in executive correspondence, use a silk ribbon with a high thread count to the square inch and with a thickness of .003 inches.

When strength, durability, and long ink life are sought, along with a clean-cut, sharp write, use a cotton fabric with a count of 320 to 330 threads per square inch and a body thickness of .0045 inches.

For quality at a lower cost, use a cotton fabric having a count of approximately 304 threads per square inch and a thickness of .005 inches.

For interdepartmental correspondence, where economy, long ink life, durability, and legible impressions are required, rather than an extra sharp write, use a cotton fabric with a count of 260 threads per square inch and a body thickness of .0057 inches.

To meet the stress of unusual mechanical functions as in billing and accounting machines, electrical typewriters, typewriters with hard rubber or brass platens, or flat writing beds, use a reinforced cotton fabric with a count of 260 threads per square inch and a body thickness of .0061 inches.

Old machines (since they are usually more severe in action) and those with hard platens require lightly inked ribbons. Elite type requires a more lightly inked ribbon than do Pica and Gothic types.

Thinner ribbons should be used on noiseless machines than on others. Operators with a light touch also require thin ribbons. The greater the thickness of the letterhead and copy papers, the greater the need for a thin ribbon.

Carbon paper. Carbon paper should be selected on the basis of the type of work to be done. For example, a lighter weight of carbon paper should be used to make fifteen copies than to make three copies. Also, it must be remembered that different finishes of paper will produce different results. If the print is too black, or too dense, use a harder finish carbon. If it is too light or sharp, use a softer finish. Most carbon papers will improve with age, if properly stored.

---

* From *Bankers Monthly*, "There's a Ribbon for Every Job," by Norman D. Stone, October, 1940, p. 578.

The relative durability of two pieces of carbon paper can be tested n an adding machine that has an electric repeat mechanism. Renove the adding machine ribbon and hold a strip of carbon paper n place in front of the tape where the keys strike it. Repeat the ame number over and over again on the machine. Each time it vill strike the carbon in the same place, but the adding-machine ape will move on. Run the number off as many times as a legible print results. Repeat the same process for the other piece of carbon paper. The paper that provides the greater number of legible impressions is the more durable. To make an accurate test, use papers of the same weight and finish.

Improving carbon-copy reproductions. Poor carbon copies may be caused by mishandling the carbon paper, using the wrong grade for the results desired, by faulty carbon paper, or by the faulty condition of the typewriter.

The carbon paper should be kept carefully in the desk to avoid curling and wrinkling; keep it face down, out of the sunlight, and away from steam pipes. Poor interleaving of the carbon paper before insertion in the typewriter will also result in poor copies.

Lack of uniformity in the carbon imprint may be due to lack of rhythm on the part of the operator. It may also be due to defects in the product, such as variations in absorbency of the base paper, even though checked at the factory, and insufficient aging.

Poor carbon copies on a typewriter may be due, not to the carbon paper, but to lack of care in handling the typewriter. The type should be cleaned periodically to prevent its becoming gummy and causing poor impressions. A harder platen is needed if a great many copies are to be made, but if the platen is too hard for the number that are being made, or if it is pitted or slippery, typewriter troubles will occur. If the spools, ribbon guides, and reversing mechanism are out of order, the ribbon will cut, fray, tear, and wear quickly, thus producing streaks on the original and on the copy.

Offset of the carbon coating to the copy will result if the feed rolls are too hard or are improperly adjusted and press too hard on the platen. If the pressure rolls are out of alignment, and force the paper in two or three different directions, the carbon paper will "tree" and cause streaks on the copies.

Binders and saddlebacks for carbon paper. Binders and saddle-backs facilitate the making of carbon copies. Binders are a form o carbon-paper pad that is manufactured by folding over a piece o paper (not carbon paper) about ½ inch from the end and insertin and stitching several sheets of carbon paper into the fold. The cop sheets are inserted between the leaves of the pad. The pad hold carbons and copy sheets together so that no jockeying or aligning i necessary after the setup has been inserted in the typewriter.

When two or three copies are desired, saddleback carbons can b used to advantage. The most common use is in billing operations when the ledger card, the customer's statement, and a duplicate o the customer's statement are all made at once. A saddleback carbon sheet is a piece of carbon paper folded in half, forming four pages The second and fourth sheets are carbonized. The original is placed in front of the first page; the first copy is placed between the second and third pages; and the second copy in back of the last page. Saddleback carbon sheets to make three copies are also available. In this type, an extra fold is made in the sheet, and three carbonized surfaces are provided instead of two.

3. MAKING OFFICE PROCEDURE FUNCTION SMOOTHLY

Reception and information service. Many organizations have found it necessary and beneficial to maintain a reception and information bureau located at a central and convenient point in the building. The need for a reception and information service is two-fold: (1) to greet and direct visitors, and (2) to save employees' time.

The reception office should be spacious and simply and tastefully furnished. The equipment of the office should consist of a desk for the clerk, a telephone, comfortable chairs for visitors, and a table with literature on it, preferably pertaining to the company or its business.

Duties of a reception and information clerk. Organizations are constantly being visited by customers, other individuals who come to transact business, and persons seeking information. It is the duty of the reception clerk to intercept these people, find out what the purpose of their visit is, whom they represent or who sent them, and whom they wish to see. Individuals who come on business, such as salesmen and dealers, should be announced by telephone to the proper party. If the employee is busy, the visitor should be asked to return, or he should be seated. Personal friends of employees should be requested to be seated, and the supervisor should be notified of the nature of the visit. Visitors, such as collectors, insurance salesmen, solicitors, and the like, who attempt to reach employees at their place of business should be tactfully turned away. Undesirable visitors should be reported to the supervisor or to someone capable of handling them. Applicants for employment should be directed to the employment office or told when to call back if definite interviewing hours are maintained.

A capable reception clerk not only creates goodwill for the company but saves the time of busy employees who otherwise would be annoyed and interrupted throughout the day. The reception clerk should report the visit of all important callers on a daily report sheet noting the name, the company they represent and the person they called to see.

Qualifications of a reception clerk. The reception clerk should have the following qualifications:

1. Good appearance.
2. Ability to converse well.
3. Pleasing personality.
4. Tolerance.
5. Courtesy.
6. Ability to make people feel comfortable
7. Ability to think and act quickly.

Value of a well-organized mail department. A well-organized mail department can find many opportunities to be of service. As both the first and the last point of contact between the company and those of its customers with whom business is done by mail, it can expedite the prompt handling of correspondence by early delivery of incoming mail and systematic handling of outgoing mail. In addition, the mail department is in a position to handle and operate the interoffice messenger service.

Mailing-room equipment. Most large organizations have separate mailing rooms in which both incoming and outgoing mail : sorted. Vertical racks with separate pigeonholes for each departmen are set up on tables. One large insurance company has a separat section in which mail that is not addressed to the attention of an particular department is sorted. Similar racks are used to sort outgoing mail.

Hand- or electrically-driven letter openers are available to expedit opening the mail. When such equipment is used, letters of the sam size are gathered together, and their contents jogged down to th bottom of the envelopes by striking the bottom of each envelop on a hard, flat surface. They are then run through the machine on after the other without cutting the enclosures.

In many large organizations envelope-size trays divided into compartments are used by the messenger to transport mail between th different departments and the mailroom.

Procedure for handling incoming mail. The first morning mai as a rule is the largest. It should be placed on a table where i will not get mixed up with other matter, and, until it is sorted, nc one except the sorters should have access to it. A systematic procedure for handling the mail is outlined below:

1. *Sorting.* Separate first-class mail from all the rest and place letters addressed to individuals to one side. Do not open mail addressed to individuals unless it is the company policy to do so.

2. *Opening.* Open special-delivery and air-mail first, then other first-class mail addressed to the firm. Slit the end as well as the flap of the envelopes to make sure that nothing of value is left in the envelope.

3. *Time-stamping.* Time-stamp correspondence and other papers upon arrival to speed up handling by the recipients. The time of the stamp will quickly indicate any undue delay in taking care of the matter.

4. *Money enclosures.* Attach all money enclosures to the letter accompanying each and route at once to the cashier.

5. *Routing the mail.* Route mail to each addressee, whether an individual or department, giving precedence to officers and executives, in the order of their importance.

6. *Damaged mail.* When a letter is received in damaged condi-

ion, note the fact on the envelope and letter and check contents.

7. *Illegible or missing return address.* Where the sender's identification is missing from the letter, be sure to attach the envelope securely to the letter, for even if there is nothing on the envelope to identify the sender, the postmark or handwriting may give a clue to its origin.

Messenger service. In making mail deliveries and pickups the mail department can at the same time deliver and pick up interoffice messages. The following procedure shows how the messenger service can be made to function in conjunction with the mail department:

1. Have incoming and outgoing mail trays placed on every desk.
2. Establish a definite schedule for mail and message pickups and deliveries.
3. Designate one messenger for each floor or section and have him responsible for all pickups and deliveries for that floor.
4. Maintain a central station, preferably in the mail department, and have all mail and messages delivered to the central station. Separate messages from the mail and sort them according to floors.
5. At the scheduled time, have the messengers gather all the mail and messages from the central station, routed for their floors, and make their deliveries, commencing at the same time another pickup.

Handling office supplies. In most organizations the purchasing agent is responsible for the buying of office supplies, but the office manager is responsible for the office-supply room and its operation.

The little sums of money that dribble away every week in wasted paper, pencils, erasers, and the like, amount to a considerable figure at the end of the year if they are uncontrolled. The following suggestions are given to aid in handling and controlling the office stockroom to prevent waste:

1. Provide a central supply room that is adequately lighted and neatly arranged. Be sure that the supply room has sufficient shelf space and is provided with alleys and ladders so that the stock is accessible.
2. Appoint one person who will be held responsible for the appearance of the supply room and the issuance of all supplies.
3. Require everyone to have written stock requisitions before issuing any supplies.

4. Use bin tags that identify the contents of containers to mark the reorder point for supplies.

5. Standardize the shape, size, and quality of forms and paper whenever possible. It will make storage easier and require less space.

6. Eliminate waste wherever possible. Old mimeograph sheets can be cut up and glued into scratch-pads.

Operating a transcription department. Where stenographic work is decentralized or departmentalized, an impartial survey is likely to reveal waste and inefficiencies. Usually more stenographers and typists are employed than are necessary; for example, one department having too much work for one girl but not enough for two will employ two people, and neither will be occupied all the time.

Through the introduction of dictating machines, this difficulty can be eliminated. Where such machines are installed, the usual practice is to supply each dictator with a machine and concentrate the transcription work under the direction of a supervisor in a centralized transcription department.

Centralization is not applied to those in the secretarial classification, since secretaries are valuable to their employers not merely for their stenographic ability but because of their familiarity with the work and detail involved in their employer's duties.

Advantages of a centralized transcription department. A centralized transcription department has the following advantages:

1. Distribution of work is equalized.
2. Uniform standards are promoted.
3. Time is saved.
4. Better training of employees is possible.
5. Job classification is simplified.
6. Distracting noises are reduced in other departments.
7. Greater continuity of work is effected since the absence of one worker does not mean that the work will not be done.
8. Letters are handled more speedily.
9. The quality of work is improved.
10. Equipment is more readily standardized.
11. Less space is used.

Disadvantages of a centralized transcription department. The disadvantages of a centralized transcription department may be summarized as follows:

1. Opposition may develop during organization.
2. Department heads do not have direct control of typists and tend to be more critical of mistakes and delays.
3. Time is spent in sending back inaccurate letters.
4. Delays may result if the transcription department is rushed.
5. Rush letters may disrupt proper handling of work.
6. A supervisor must be employed.

How to make a centralized transcription department function smoothly. A centralized transcription department must function smoothly if it is to give the most efficient service. The following ideas will help it to function smoothly:

1. Give correspondents written instructions on how to use the dictating machine. See below.
2. Have messengers collect recordings every hour from the different machines.
3. Have a separate proofreader to check letters for style, punctuation, and errors. This will save the time of typists. Furthermore, errors are more likely to be caught by the proofreader than by the typist doing the work.
4. Use posture chairs to eliminate fatigue.
5. Supply the typists with letterheads and tissues already stuffed with carbons. It takes less time to insert carbons for a large number of letters all at once than to insert them individually for each letter as it is typed. The carbons can be taken out by the typist after the letter is finished and used over again.

Instructions to correspondents to help transcribers. Speed and accuracy in the centralized transcription department can usually be increased by co-operation of the correspondents. Thus it is well to give instructions on the use of dictating machines and to include the following items:

1. Place a check mark on the indicator strip where any mistake occurs, so that the typist may know ahead of time where corrections have been made.

2. Spell out proper names and unusual words to make certain th typist understands them without having to listen back.

3. While commas and periods may be judged from the inflection of your voice, it is better to dictate them. Paragraphs and unusua punctuations such as parentheses should be dictated.

4. Dictate special instructions at the beginning, or else write then on the indicator strip.

5. Tag rush correspondence with a signal for immediate action This signal can be a red tag inserted into the indicator strip pocke or the correspondence folder.

6. When possible, place correspondence in the correspondence folder. This will save time in dictating and assure accuracy in th

To: .... Date ....

In order that we may serve you efficiently, your co-operation is requested as indicated below:

☐ Please hold mouthpiece touching the upper lip and tilted slightly away from the lower lip.

☐ Please dictate in a higher pitch voice.

☐ Please dictate in a louder tone and enunciate your words more distinctly.

☐ Please dictate more slowly.

☐ Please spell such proper names as do not appear in accompanying files; also spell technical and unusual words.

☐ Please indicate all instructions or corrections on indicator slip; also indicate end of each case or letter on indicator slip.

☐ Please preface corrections, instructions, or interpolations of any nature in your dictation with the word "OPERATOR."

☐ Please dictate periods and paragraphs; also dictate such other punctuation as you do not wish to leave to the judgment of the operator.

☐ When listening back, be sure that control lever is in the extreme upward position; also be sure that the carriage has cleared the previous dictation, i.e., that you have *heard* the last word, before you pull control lever downward to resume dictation.

☐ ....

TRANSCRIPTION DEPARTMENT

Figure 39. Form Used by Transcription Department.

ame and address. If there is no correspondence in the folder, mark no correspondence" on the indicator strip. In the latter case, to ssure accuracy, dictate the name of the person to whom the letter s addressed and write the name and address on the indicator strip.

A company with a centralized transcription department uses the orm on page 426 when letter writers do not use the dictating mahines to best advantage. The form (Figure 39), appropriately hecked, is sent to the dictator by the head of the transcription lepartment.

Daily supply folios for typists. A daily supply folio for each ypist will help to cut stationery losses. From a stationery-supply enter, each typist is provided with a day's supply, according to the umber of letters she is supposed to write. At the end of the day he returns her folio and is credited with the material left over. Each ypist is thus made aware of any waste in letterheads, for she has a fixed number, plus error allowance, to cover estimated needs.

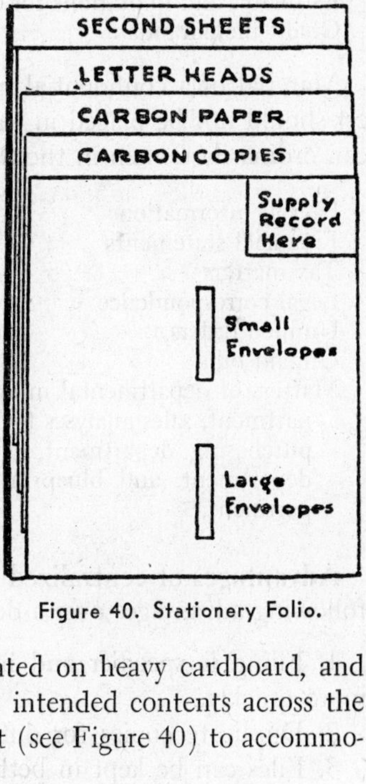

Figure 40. Stationery Folio.

The folio is made with several manila envelopes sufficiently large to hold the size stationery being used. Seal the flaps. Slit open the top and right-hand side of each envelope, trim the under side to the size of the stationery, and the upper side two inches shorter, to allow the typist to see what is in it and to simplify taking the paper from the envelope. Next, glue the envelopes together, so that the top edge of the under side of each envelope is even with the top edge of the upper side of the one beneath it, thus forming a series of pockets, one above the other. The whole can then be mounted on heavy cardboard, and each pocket identified by printing the intended contents across the top. Finally, cut slits in the top pocket (see Figure 40) to accommodate the envelopes.

Operating a central filing system. Filing may be centralized or decentralized. Offices with little correspondence, a small amount of filing, and little need for consulting filed material would find it simpler to file material departmentally. Offices having numerous records, voluminous correspondence, and constant need for consulting filed material would benefit from a central filing system, provided that the central files are easily accessible to all departments, and competent file clerks are available.

The following material can normally be included in the central file:

General correspondence
Interoffice and branch communications
Orders
Invoices
Shipping tickets
Bills of lading
Vouchers
Estimates and quotations for customers
Credit memoranda

Material of a confidential nature or of purely departmental interest should not be placed in the central file. The following material can ordinarily remain in the departmental files:

Payroll information
Financial statements
Tax matters
Legal correspondence
Unfilled orders
Unpaid bills
Matters of departmental interest only, such as tariffs for the traffic department, sales analyses for the sales departments, quotations for the purchasing department, electrotypes and cuts for the advertising department, and blueprints and drawings for the engineering department.

Advantages of centralized filing. A central filing system has the following advantages over a departmental filing system:

1. Filing is speedier and more accurate, and papers are located more quickly.
2. Duplicate copies for different departments can be eliminated.
3. Files can be kept in better condition.

4. Standardization of equipment is promoted.
5. Weeding and transferring can be made more systematic.
6. Greater control can be exercised over material out of the file.

Disadvantages of centralized filing. Certain disadvantages of a central filing system must be considered before such a system is adopted.

1. Department heads often resist the idea.
2. Additional floor space is usually required, and frequently an immediate outlay is required for additional equipment.
3. Full-time file clerks may have to be employed.
4. Selection of material for the central file from the existing department files creates certain problems.

Types of filing systems. Five basic systems of filing are in common use: alphabetical, subject, numerical, geographical, and chronological. Since each system is adapted to certain classes of work, fitness for the work in question is the test that must be met in selecting a system.

The *alphabetical* system is the simplest, oldest, and most common. Since room for expansion must be allowed in each drawer, additional equipment and more room for files are necessary.

Subject filing is a modification of the alphabetical system. It is used when there are a great number of letters from different persons or concerns relating to the same subject. A common example of such a case is in connection with the letting of large contracts. Great care must be exercised in the selection of headings, in order to avoid confusion. It is advisable that one person select all the titles, because two people rarely view a subject in the same light, and each may give the same letter a different title, equally correct.

The *numerical* filing system is an indirect filing method, since it must be used in conjunction with an auxiliary index. Under this system each new correspondent is given a number, the numbers being assigned consecutively. An index card is made out with the correspondent's number and name and is filed alphabetically in a card index. Thereafter, whenever a letter comes from a correspondent, his name is looked up in the index and his number marked on the letter to be filed. Advantages of the system are the rapidity and accuracy of refiling and the opportunity for indefinite expansion.

For most companies, however, these advantages are more than offset by the disadvantage of having to maintain the auxiliary card index and to make two searches, one of the index and the second of the files, every time papers are withdrawn or new material added.

Geographical filing is used principally in sales work and in cases where the country, state, county, or community, rather than the name of a company or individual, is the chief consideration. An auxiliary alphabetical card index is ordinarily used in conjunction with this system.

In *chronological* filing, all letters are filed according to date, either in the order in which they are received, or according to the date upon which they should have attention. This system is often used in collection work. For example, a customer whose account is past due writes that the account will be paid August 6. The letter is filed in the folder for August 6, and on that date is automatically brought to the collection manager's attention. An auxiliary alphabetical index must be used if it is necessary to refer to a letter other than by date. The chronological system is often used in a "tickler" file. See page 431.

Controlling material taken out of the file. A method should be devised for controlling papers taken from the file in order that the file clerk may be able to locate them at any moment. An essential of any method is that no one outside of the filing department be permitted to go to the files to take material.

A simple method of handling requests for filed material is to require a requisition in writing, such as that illustrated in Figure 41, for anything that is to be taken out of the file. In addition, guides of the same size as the folders used in the files should be provided. These guides should preferably be of a different color stock and should have printed on the tab the word "OUT." The guide may provide space on which an entry can be made of the material taken from the file, showing the date, what material was taken, the person requisitioning it, and the date it will be returned. This guide is then placed in the files where the extracted material was located.

Another method, which saves the work of transferring the record from the requisition to the guide, is to have a pocket on the guide into which the requisition may be placed.

A third method, which eliminates the use of guides, is to insert ıe requisition amid the correspondence where the letter was lo-ıted. Under ths method it is advisable to have a separate 3×5 ıch card index identifying alphabeticaly all material out of the les at any time. When any requisition is made, the file clerk first ɔoks in this index to see whether the requested material is already

DATE: ....

TO FILE CLERK:
Please send to ....
Correspondence with ....
Dated .... In re..........
....
....
....

Please send me order for: ....
....
(Name of customer, as billed)
....
(address)
Order Number (s) ....

Miscellaneous material: ....
....
....
....
Signature

Figure 41. Requisition for Filed Material.
[Actual size 6″ x 9″]

ut, and thus does not waste time looking in the files for material hat is not there. When any correspondence is returned to the files, he card pertaining to it in the index is destroyed, and the requisition ; taken out of the place where the correspondence is inserted.

A tickler file system for correspondence wanted in the future. The following procedure for handling material that someone in the organization wants to come up in the future has been in operatic for many years in a large organization and has been found to fun tion smoothly.

The person who will want the correspondence or material in th future fills out the form shown in Figure 42.

	DATE: ....
TO FILE CLERK:	
FROM	
BRING UP THIS MATERIAL:	
JANUARY:	
FEBRUARY:	
MARCH:	
APRIL:	
MAY:	
JUNE:	
JULY:	
AUGUST:	
SEPTEMBER:	
OCTOBER:	
NOVEMBER:	
DECEMBER:	
REMARKS:	
....	

Figure 42. Form Requesting Correspondence Wanted in Future.

The form is attached to the correspondence and sent to the fil clerk, who makes out a 3 × 5 inch card with the name of the com pany or person from whom the correspondence was received, th date it will be wanted, and the name of the person wanting it. Sh files this card alphabetically by name of company in a card inde containing similar cards for all other correspondence that will b wanted in the future. The correspondence itself, together with th follow-up form, is filed chronologically in a separate section of th correspondence files. The separate alphabetical card index is kep to facilitate look-ups. When someone requisitions a certain letter he file clerk first looks in the follow-up card index to see whether : is in the follow-up section.

The first thing each morning, the file clerk takes out of the hronological file all the correspondence which is wanted that day, nd removes the corresponding 3 × 5 inch cards from the file. The orrespondence is distributed by the messengers to the proper people ndicated on the follow-up forms attached to the correspondence. ince this organization uses the "out" control mentioned on page 30, the 3 × 5 inch cards are placed in the card index used for "out" naterial, because the correspondence is now out of the files competely. At the same time, a memorandum is placed in the general iles where the correspondence should be located.

Destruction of records and files. In order to conserve space, a definite procedure for the destruction of accumulated records and correspondence should be established. A schedule should be worked out showing the various kinds of records that accumulate and the period during which they should be kept. In fixing the period, the statute of limitations will serve as a guide in some cases. All states have such statutes limiting the period for bringing legal action. (See table of the statutes on page 1074.)

After the schedule has been worked out, the following diagram may be printed on all carbon second sheets and a hand stamp of the same diagram may be made up to be used in connection with other data. The persons handling correspondence check the proper square before any material is filed. At the end of the year, the file clerk will sort the material to be destroyed. Any questionable matter can be reviewed by the proper person.

FILE RECORD		
1 yr.	Destroy	
	Review	
6 yrs.	Destroy	
	Review	
Permanent		

Microfilming of important records can be undertaken in connection with the program of selective records preservation. It must be applied, however, with discrimination. Microfilming of vital records for security provides protection otherwise unobtainable for all practical purposes.

4. ECONOMIES IN THE USE AND PRINTING OF FORMS

Designing forms. The first consideration in designing forms i the matter of size. It is advisable to use form sizes that can be cu without waste from standard sizes used by printers. The followin table shows sizes and quantities of forms that can be cut fron standard-sized sheets:

Size of Form (in inches)	*Cuts Without Waste from Standard Sheet Measuring*	*Number Obtained from Single Standard-Size Sheet*
2¾ x 4¼	17 x 22	32
2¾ x 8½	17 x 22	16
3½ x 4¼	17 x 28	32
3½ x 8½	17 x 28	16
3½ x 17	17 x 28	8
4¼ x 5½	17 x 22	16
4¼ x 7	17 x 28	16
4¼ x 11	17 x 22	8
4¼ x 14	17 x 28	8
4¼ x 28	17 x 28	4
5½ x 8½	17 x 22	8
5½ x 17	17 x 22	4
7 x 8½	17 x 28	8
7 x 17	17 x 28	4
8½ x 11	17 x 22	4
8½ x 14	17 x 28	4
8½ x 22	17 x 22	2
8½ x 28	17 x 28	2
11 x 17	17 x 22	2
14 x 17	17 x 28	2

The second consideration is the quality of stock to be used. Examine the life and amount of handling of the forms used in your organization to see whether a cheaper stock of paper will serve the purpose. If a form is to be thrown away shortly after it is used, an inexpensive stock should be used. One corporation saved $4,000 in one year as the result of such a study. Its examination revealed that 75 per cent of its forms could be printed on a good grade of sulphite bond, instead of the much higher grade of paper it had been using.

A study of the stock used may also result in greater standardiza-ion of quality, which in turn may result in reduction in price hrough quantity orders. The degree of permanency of the form hould determine the grade of paper to be used. The following able indicates the grades:

Permanency	*Grade of Paper*
1- 3 years	100% sulphite
3- 6 years	75% sulphite, 25% rag
6-10 years	50% sulphite, 50% rag
Over ten years	100% rag

Lastly, the question of how to arrange data on the forms for practical use must be considered. The following suggestions will make the forms more useful:

1. Print the name of the form plainly at the top and provide a place for the date.
2. Give the form an identifying number.
3. Design the form to fit double typewriter spacing. This will speed up work if the typewriter is used and will provide sufficient space for handwriting.
4. Align the printed data that precedes the blank lines on the right-hand side rather than the left-hand side. This will permit the blank spaces to begin one exactly under the other, and the typist can use the tabular key when filling in the form.
5. Where possible, provide boxes in which to enter information, to encourage more economical use of words.
6. Group information by departments, so that each department which uses the form can find the information it needs in one section.
7. Confine information as much as possible to one side of the page.
8. Provide sufficient margin if the form is to be placed in a binder.
9. Make most important items prominent, and place them preferably near the top.
10. Design the form to fit a window envelope.
11. Have everybody who must use the form approve its design.

Ordering forms. When a new form is made up, have a small quantity printed first so that waste will not result if changes have to be made. When the form has proved satisfactory, a quantit sufficient for six or eight months can be ordered.

Order forms of the same size and approximately the same quan tity at the same time, to utilize full capacity of the press. Thi system of ordering will reduce the element of press time in th printer's bill. An additional saving is possible by arranging wit the printer to print some of the forms during his slack period or a his convenience. Under this arrangement he can utilize otherwis unused press space for the forms. This policy will result in lowe quotations from the printer.

Keeping large quantities of forms on hand necessitates storag space which is often expensive. Many printers will make contractua agreements for an annual supply of forms and print them on order Have the type left standing in the case of permanent forms, to re duce composition costs.

Central control of forms. To eliminate waste caused by un necessary forms, facilitate standardization, and bring about greate economy in ordering forms, establish a central control of forms The person responsible can then gather all forms together for a systematic review. The results of central control are likely to be:

1. Elimination of unnecessary forms.
2. Better dovetailing of two or more related forms.
3. A systematic plan of design, classification, and identification.
4. A procedure for introducing new forms.

All proposed forms should be reviewed by the person in control of forms before they are ordered.

5. HIRING NEW EMPLOYEES

Sources of employees. The success of a business organization depends to a great extent on the caliber and capacity of its employees. Furthermore, when the expense of training new employees is considered, it is essential for the employer to know where to get reliable and capable personnel. The sources for new employees upon which an employer can draw are as follows:

1. *Present employees.* Employees frequently know of friends and relatives who are either out of work or who are anxious to change

obs and who are qualified for positions in the company. It is not dvisable to depend heavily on this source, for the maintenance of roper discipline is complicated when the personnel of an office is elated or too friendly. Present employees, especially executives, are good source for employees needed to fill positions such as junior xecutives or supervisors, for an executive usually feels responsible or his candidate and makes recommendations only after careful onsideration.

2. *Applicants coming or writing to the employment department.* A company with a good reputation and sound personnel policies ttracts a great many applicants, who either come in or write to he company for positions. The files of the employment department are an excellent source for new employees.

3. *Employment bureaus.* Nearly all cities have private, commercial employment bureaus that are continually advertising and interviewing individuals seeking positions. Business organizations use he services of these bureaus extensively as a source of employees. These employment bureaus save the employer the time necessary o conduct preliminary interviews by weeding out the obviously nqualified applicants and sending only those who meet the employer's specifications. These bureaus operate on a fee basis, which s usually paid by the applicant. The local State employment service, an affiliate of the Federal employment service, is a free public employment bureau that should not be overlooked as a source of new employees.

4. *Trade journals, trade schools, and competitors.* Industries that require skilled or specialized employees will find good sources by consulting the "position wanted" ads in trade journals and by contacting trade schools. Competitors or businesses that have similar trade problems will sometimes co-operate in finding new employees. Many companies that receive an application from a desirable applicant and cannot hire him at present or in the future will, in many cases, refer the applicant to a competitor.

5. *Colleges, universities, and business schools.* A good many colleges and universities maintain employment bureaus for their undergraduates and graduates. Part-time and temporary positions can be filled by students who are seeking employment while going to school. In many cases large companies send talent scouts to colleges, prior to graduation, to interview the top ten per cent of the graduating

class. Business schools are a good source for secretaries, stenographers, and typists.

6. *Appliance manufacturers.* Office-appliance manufacturers occasionally know of, and recommend, individuals who are skilled in the operation of various office machines.

7. *Customers.* If good customers are told of the need for new employees, they are sometimes in a position to make recommendations.

8. *Associations, welfare organizations, and fraternal societies.* Associations such as the Y.M.C.A. and Y.M.H.A., various welfare organizations, churches, and fraternal societies may be used as source of new employees.

9. *Newspapers.* Newspapers can be used in two ways as a source of employees: (1) by inserting ads in the "help-wanted" column and (2) by watching the "situations-wanted" column. Great care must be exercised in selecting the paper in which to run the advertisement. The choice is determined by the type of personnel wanted and by the class of people reading the paper. There are disadvantages to the use of newspapers. Unless an organization has an employment office capable of handling large numbers of applicants, this method is not recommended. A single advertisement placed in a newspaper, especially during depressions, attracts not only qualified applicants but also those who think they are qualified or those who apply merely because it is another lead. To overcome this drawback, many companies insert blind advertisements in the paper requesting a written outline of the applicant's background and experience, together with a photograph, to be mailed to a post-office box.

Selection of new employees. The call for a new employee originates in the department needing help in the form of an employment requisition. This requisition is sent to the employment department together with information about the position, such as, nature of the position, hours, working conditions, salary, the type of employee required, his duties, age, sex, physical requirement and other information useful for the interviewer. With this information available, the personnel department can make an intelligent selection of the applicants.

The steps in the selection procedure are as follows:

1. *The preliminary interview.* Some companies require a preliminary interview, in which case a simple form, having space for name, address, and position desired, is given the applicants to fill out. A preliminary interviewer quickly interviews the applicants and eliminates those who are obviously not qualified or who do not meet the standards established by the company. An application blank is given to those who pass this preliminary interview.

2. *The application form.* The employment application forms in common use vary in size and design. Basically, all employment applications have space for the following data.

(*a*) *Personal history.* Name, address, telephone number, age, sex, height, weight, date born, and place born.

(*b*) *Education.* Schools, duration of attendance, degrees held.

(*c*) *Previous employment and experience.* The name, address, and line of business of previous employers, applicant's duties, date employed and date left, reasons for leaving and salary.

(*d*) *References,* both personal and business.

(*e*) *Position applied for and minimum salary expected.*

(*f*) *Interests and hobbies.*

(*g*) *Additional information.*

The application form also contains space for interviewer's remarks and rating, results of tests, and applicant's signature. Some applications contain a clause as to the conditions of employment, such as the right of the employer to terminate the employment at any time, the right to inventions, patents, and other conditions deemed necessary. A typical application blank is presented in Figure 43.

3. *The interview.* The applicants who have been given an application form are next interviewed by a more experienced interviewer. The interviewer should attempt to put the applicant at ease and try to encourage him to do most of the talking, asking questions only to draw out information. Specifically, the interviewer attempts to get the following information about the applicant:

(*a*) *What is the applicant's background?* The social and economic environment under which the applicant has lived are important factors influencing his habits, temperament, and outlook on life.

(*b*) *What does he know?* A consideration of the applicant's education and scholastic training largely answers this question. Nevertheless, it is unwise to place too much stress on academic training. Many applicants who never had formal academic training hav a well-rounded cultural background.

(c) *What does he want?* A person with a clear, well-define aim in life has a better chance of success. He is able to mobiliz and concentrate all of his energies and intelligence toward his goa Under normal circumstances, beware of the applicant who appeai ready to do any kind of work or take any position. He apparentl has no well-defined goal.

APPLICATION FOR EMPLOYMENT

SOC. SEC. NO.

Print Name and Address

NAME (First, Middle, Last) DATE

ADDRESS PHONE NO.

POSITION DESIRED SALARY EXPECTED

DATE OF BIRTH

CITIZEN OF U.S.? HEIGHT WEIGHT

SINGLE, MARRIED, DIVORCED, SEPARATED, WIDOW(ER) NUMBER OF DEPENDENTS RELATIONSHIP

LIVE WITH PARENTS, KEEP HOUSE OR BOARD WHO REFERRED YOU TO US

NAMES OF RELATIVES OR FRIENDS EMPLOYED BY THIS COMPANY

EDUCATION

HIGH SCHOOL DATES COURSE

COLLEGE DATES MAJOR COURSE

OTHER SCHOOLS

BUSINESS EXPERIENCE
(LIST MOST RECENT EMPLOYMENT FIRST)

FIRM NAME	NAME OF POSITION	DATES OF EMPLOYMENT	SALARY	REASON FOR LEAVING

PERSONAL REFERENCES
(NOT RELATIVES OR FORMER EMPLOYERS)

NAME	BUSINESS	ADDRESS

PLACE A CHECK MARK TO THE LEFT OF EACH OF THE FOLLOWING KINDS OF WORK WITH WHICH YOU ARE FAMILIAR. IF YOU HAVE HAD MORE THAN ONE YEAR'S EXPERIENCE PLACE A DOUBLE CHECK MARK. IF YOU ARE AN EXPERT PLACE AN "X." ADD ANY NOT LISTED IN BLANK SPACES.

ACCOUNTING	ENGINEERING	STENOGRAPHY	COMPTOMETER	PHOTOSTAT
ACTUARIAL	FILING	SWITCHBOARD	DICTAPHONE	TABULATING
BILLING	MAIL ROOM	TYPING	DUPLICATOR	
CALCULATING	PAY ROLL AUDITING	UNDERWRITING	GRAPHOTYPE	
CLAIM ADJUSTING	PRINTING	ADDING MACHINE	BOOKKEEP. MACH.	
CLERICAL GENERAL	SELLING	ADDRESSOGRAPH	MIMEOGRAPH	
CORRESPONDENCE	SHIPPING	BILLING MACHINE	MULTIGRAPH	
CREDITS	STATISTICAL	CALCULATOR	KEY PUNCH	

SIGNATURE OF APPLICANT

THIS SPACE FOR USE IN PERSONNEL DEPARTMENT

Figure 43. Typical Application Blank Suitable for Positions of Average Responsibility.

SUGGESTED QUESTIONS FOR APPLICATION BLANKS

An analysis of a number of application forms used in the employment of clerical help showed that most forms cover the basic subjects mentioned on page 439. The following is a list of out-of-the-ordinary questions that companies may care to consider in preparing or revising application blanks.

PERSONAL HISTORY

1. How long at present residence? If less than a year, give previous residence and length of stay.
2. Are you a citizen? By birth or naturalization? Give naturalization and immigration details if born in another country.
3. Give birthplace.
4. Do you have any friends or relatives with this company?
5. Names, occupations, and addresses of immediate family.
6. Names of near relatives now living in foreign countries.
7. If you live with parents, do they own home, rent, etc.?
8. Are you the head of a family?
9. In case of emergency, notify . . . .
10. Give details of any injuries and operations.
11. List accidents (driving) you have had that were reported to the police or involved personal injury.
12. How much time have you lost in illness in the past two years?
13. Have you ever worked under any name other than shown above? If so, give full particulars.
14. What are your sports and recreations?
15. Are you sympathetic to Communism?
16. Are you entirely dependent upon your salary? Other sources of income?
17. Name banks where you have had accounts.
18. Do you carry life insurance?
19. What is your total indebtedness? Give details if you wish.
20. Give any unusual details of your financial condition.

EDUCATION

21. Give titles and authors of three texts you studied in college.
22. What did you do during your college vacations?
23. What bookkeeping, accounting, economics, and mathematics courses have you taken?
24. What foreign languages do you speak, read, or write?
25. In what studies were you most interested? Which were most difficult?
26. Where did you rank in your class?
27. What are your present plans for improving your education?
28. What magazines or books have you read recently?

PREVIOUS EMPLOYMENT AND EXPERIENCE

29. Are you right or left handed?
30. Indicate type of position for which you can qualify. (List given.) Why?
31. Of which of your past positions (or what piece of work that you did in them) are you most proud?
32. Ever hired by this company before? When and where?
33. Account for all intervals of unemployment.
34. Give details if ever discharged or requested to resign.
35. If now employed, why would you prefer to work for us rather than present employer?

MISCELLANEOUS

36. For what period do you want employment?
37. Please ask any questions you would like to ask about (name of company).

(*d*) *What are his interests?* A person who is really intereste in a subject usually does a better job than one who has little or r interest.

(*e*) *What is his ability?* The answer to this question depen on the mental and physical qualities of the applicant. The results (the applicant's previous work or scholastic experience or of physica intelligence, and aptitude tests, throw some light on this questio

During the interview the interviewer makes observations as to th applicant's appearance and characteristics. Is the applicant neat dressed, cleanly shaved? Are his nails clean, shoes polished? Doe he sit properly in his chair or does he fidget around? Does h appear excessively nervous? Does he speak well and intelligently These observations not only give a key to the applicant's bac ground, education, and habits but throw some light upon his ten perament.

The applicant also is entitled to information about the compan and the position for which he is applying. The interviewer, durin the interview, should outline briefly the company's business an background, its policies, the nature of the position, duties, hours working conditions, salary, and opportunities for promotion an advancement. The interviewer should at all times be frank an truthful. He should not be too optimistic, or encourage applicant as to the possibilities of getting a position when one is not available or discourage youngsters in their attempt to get their first job. Th interview offers an excellent opportunity to spread goodwill in th community and to establish a sound employee-employer relationship

4. *Tests.* Tests are tools used by employment interviewers t aid them in rating the physical and mental abilities and aptitude of applicants. Some companies have a large variety of tests; other do not have any. It must be remembered that tests do not reveal everything, and too much reliance must not be placed on them. Tests simply give additional information. The usual tests given employment applicants may be classified as (1) intelligence tests, (2) performance tests, (3) personality tests, and (4) interest tests. Special physical tests and medical or physical examinations are also given. Each of these tests will be explained briefly.

Intelligence tests. These tests are sometimes called mental alertness or personnel tests. They seek to measure the reasoning ability the applicant and not his education or knowledge. Dale Yoder * ys of these tests:

"The actual relationship of intelligence to job success in any par- cular situation deserves careful analysis. A principle of major im- ortance here is that they are not always related in a simple and niform manner. In other words, high scores on an intelligence test) not mean success on all jobs. On the contrary, high scores ay be associated with job failure, whereas middle or low scores an be an indicator of job success. Or the relationship of test ores and success on the job may be curvilinear, with poor per- rmance for those who score very low or very high. In part, of ourse, these various relationships reflect differences in job require- ents. In part, also, they reflect the fact that abilities measured y intelligence tests may be complex. Several types of intelligence ay be measured by a single test."

Some well-known intelligence tests are Benge Test of General nowledge, Otis Self-Administering Test of Mental Ability, and e Henmow Nelson Test of Mental Ability.

Performance tests. These tests indicate what the individual can o on specific tasks. They are simple to administer and the results re usually reliable guides for selection of office employees. Clerical ests, typing tests, shorthand tests, tests in operating calculators, add- g machines, bookkeeping machnies, and simple mechanical equip- ent fall into this classification.

The following are examples of clerical performance tests: Benge's lerical Test, Minnesota Vocational Test for Clerical Workers, hurstone Examination in Clerical Work, Form A.

Personality tests. These tests are also sometimes classified as djustment and stability tests. They are designed to appraise the resence or absence of such traits as honesty, reliability, stability, ependability, co-operativeness, loyalty, and persistence.

In this group are Allport's Systematic Questionnaire, Pressey's X-O Test, Humm-Wadsworth Temperament Scale.

Interest tests. Tests of this kind seek to determine the type of vork in which the applicant is genuinely interested. Patterns of

---

* *Personnel Principles and Policies.* New York, Prentice-Hall, Inc., 1952, age 185

interest associated with success in a variety of occupations are th basis of the tests.

Among the interest tests are Strong's Vocational Interest Tes for men and women and the Kuder Preference Record.

Physical tests and examinations. For certain occupations, em ployees may require special physical qualifications, such as stron hands, or sensitivity to sound or touch. There are tests for the purposes.

The most common examination given to applicants is the medic or physical examination. Large companies have their own docto who tends to the medical needs of employees and examines ne applicants. Small companies usually send the applicant to his ow doctor. The purposes of the medical examination are: (1) to dete diseases and defects in order to have the worker correct them; (2 to prevent the spread of contagious diseases; (3) to make the prop placement of workers; (4) to reduce absenteeism; (5) to lessen acc dents; and (6) to reduce the possibility of unjust claims for injurie

Final approval of new employee. After the personnel depar ment has interviewed, tested, and rated the applicants and checke on their references, the top three or four candidates are sent to th department head who sent in the requisition. The departmen head has the authority to accept one of the applicants or reje all of them and request the personnel department to send other Forms sent to former employers and to schools, for reference, a given in Figures 44 and 45. Most organizations hire employees on trial basis, usually three months, and if, within that period, the ne employee has proved satisfactory, he becomes a member of the re ular staff of the company. In cash a rush placement is necessar the applicant is hired pending the check on his references, whic usually do not come in for several days.

Introduction of new employees. The applicant who is accepte is introduced to his fellow workers and is started on his trainin program. (See page 450 for methods of training employees.) Th personnel department furnishes the applicant with an employe manual or other literature concerning the company. (See page 452.

Follow-up of new employees. The personnel department make periodic visits to the new employee for the purpose of checking hi

To ....

....19......

....

The person named below has applied to us for a position as.. We would consider it a favor if you will give us your appraisal. It is perhaps natural to say the best we can for a former employee. But is it not true that a frank, careful and well-weighed opinion concerning applicants for positions will help reduce turnover among employees as well as the expense incident thereto? Indeed, a complete and frank appraisal is fairer to the applicant, for with a knowledge of weaknesses, the new employer can help to overcome them and perhaps prevent failure in the new work. If you will fill out this blank in the same way you would like us to fill it out for you, we shall greatly appreciate your co-operation. We are enclosing a stamped, self-addressed envelope for your reply.

....

..............................New York, N. Y.

Personnel Director.

Name of Applicant

Address

Personal Appraisement	Better Than Average	Average	Below Average	Remarks
1. Is applicant a hard worker?				
2. " " enthusiastic?				
3. " " resourceful?				
4. " " ambitious?				
5. " " honest?				
6. " " courteous?				
7. Has " a good memory?				
8. How is applicant's health?				
9. How about applicant's habits?				

General Analysis	Yes	No	Remarks
10. How long was applicant in your employ?			
11. Were applicant's services satisfactory?			
12. Was applicant a good producer?			
13. Was applicant co-operative with your office?			
14. Was applicant co-operative with customers?			
15. What were applicant's last average yearly earnings?			
16. Would you re-employ applicant?			

17. Why did applicant leave your employ?

18. Please add other pertinent information and sum up your appraisal.

Signed..

Figure 44. Form Sent to Employers for Reference.

progress on the job and his attitude about his position. A simple rating form, filled out by the department head, containing the name of the new employee, the date he started to work, and a series of questions as to his progress, ability to do his work, co-operative spirit, faults, and prospects, provides a good method for following up the progress of a new employee. This information also pro-

Sch.

Address ....

Date ....

A B C COMPANY
300 Main Street,
New York City

ATTENTION OF PERSONNEL DIRECTOR.

Gentlemen:—

In response to your request I give below, in confidence, the school record of .... his
a former student of this school. And also our estimate of her general ability and future possibilities.

I am placing a cross (X) in the appropriate column below.

	Poor	Fair	Good	Exceptional
Record in studies				
Attendance and punctuality				
Conduct				
Sociability				
Estimate of general ability and possibilities				

The student made the best showing in the following subjects: ....

....

The following list of observations may be of service to you: ....

....

Yours truly,

Figure 45. Form Sent to Schools for Reference.

vides a sound promotional record and a good check on the trainin, program. These rating forms should be filled out, if possible, b more than one executive qualified to judge the new employee A consensus of judgment is thus provided, and the danger of persona prejudice on the part of the department head is eliminated. A form of follow-up of new employees, addressed to department heads is given in Figure 46.

Discharge of employees. Employees may leave the services o a company voluntarily; they may be discharged; or they may b laid off because of slackened business activity. Whatever the reasor for the separation of an employee from the company, it is a sounc policy to allow the personnel department to interview all employees about to leave. The reasons for the "exit interview" are as follows:

1. It uncovers weaknesses in the personnel program.
2. It provides data for the study of labor turnover.
3. It suggests improvements in the training program.
4. It promotes goodwill.

It should be a policy of the company never to allow a department head to have the final authority to discharge an employee without

CONFIDENTIAL

Name .... Began ....

The following confidential report is to be made out by you without conferring with the person about whom you are reporting. If, for any reason, any other person is better qualified than you to make the report, return the form immediately with a note to that effect, naming the person who should make out the report.

The purpose is to get a report on each new employee, once a week for four weeks, and thereafter monthly until such time as the employee can surely be trusted to do his work without supervision. Remember, the general purpose is to be as mutually helpful as possible, but at the same time to prevent wasting time on a person who is not likely to prove satisfactory. No action will be taken on your report without personal conference with you and others who may be able to shed some light on the new employee.

(Name of executive)

1. How has he done h work during the past ....?
2. How does he measure up in respect to:

	Good	Fair	Poor
a. Grasping instructions			
b. Following instructions			
c. Initiative			
d. Industry			
e. Accuracy			
f. Clearness			
g. Speed			
h. General cooperative spirit			

3. Any other faults that should be corrected? ....
4. May he be trusted next week to do h work without further supervision? ....
5. What is the prospect that he will work out satisfactorily?
6. Other comments? (over)

Date........................ Signed...............................

Figure 46. Record of Employee's Performance.

the concurrence of the personnel department. In many cases the department head or supervisor may be to blame, and a transfer to another department may save the company the valuable services of an employee.

In many companies a written record of the employee's performance is maintained to help management when faced with the problem of lay-offs. These records are reviewed by the department head and the personnel department to determine which employees are the most valuable. These records determine also the order in whic laid-off employees will be called back to work.

6. TRAINING EMPLOYEES

Purpose of training employees. Training programs are estal lished for the following purposes:

1. To break in new employees in the cheapest and quickes manner.
2. To improve the quality and quantity of the employee's work
3. To equip and develop employees for higher positions and mor responsibility.
4. To improve employee morale.
5. To stimulate interest in the company and for the work.
6. To keep employees alert for new ideas and make them flexibl for changes.

Whom to train. The common practice among a number o companies that have a training program is to train only new em ployees. In most cases this elementary training is very scanty. A good, sound training for all new employees is essential, but it is no by any means a complete training program. Training must be a continuous process, including old employees, supervisors, foremen and executives, in order to obtain maximum results.

Training new employees. The extent to which new employee are trained depends on the work for which they are assigned and the nature of the company's business. In some cases, as with in dustries employing highly skilled or specialized workers, the train ing is extensive and lengthy. In other cases, as with the training of new employees assigned to simple clerical or nonskilled work the training is brief. The point to remember in training new em ployees is to show the best and quickest way to do the job. It is easier to teach a person to do the job in the right way than it is to undo the results of wrong training or of no training at all.

The following suggestions will aid in planning a training pro gram for new employees:

1. Find the best way to do the job and establish that method as a standard. Teach all beginners the standard method of doing the job.

2. Illustrate and develop one point at a time. The average person not capable of grasping more than one fact thoroughly.

3. Develop your training along logical lines and show the relationship between various steps in the job and between other jobs. It is much easier to follow and learn a method if the steps are presented in logical sequence and the job is presented in its proper relation with other jobs.

4. Establish the standard time to do the work and define production standards. Train the worker to develop speed and accuracy to meet standards set for speed and production.

Training old employees. Old employees are trained for the purpose of stimulating greater activity, illustrating newer methods, reviving interest in the work, and preparing the employees for promotions and transfers. Old employees are harder to train and tend to offer more resistance to training programs than new employees. New employees realize that they do not know the business and are anxious to learn and co-operate. Old employees feel that they know all about the business and resent being treated like schoolboys. New employees may be trained in a formal manner, whereas old employees react better to informal training, where they are given an opportunity to plan and participate in the training program.

Training supervisors and foremen. Perhaps the most common weakness of most training programs is the lack of training offered to supervisors and foremen. Supervisors and foremen have a responsible, key position in business and industry. When it is realized that most employees are in closer touch with supervisors and foremen than with any other executives, the importance of training supervisors can be appreciated. A supervisor or foreman not only guides, directs, and supervises the quality and quantity of work produced by his group, but he is also the person who actually puts into practice the personnel policies of the company. A foreman or supervisor capable of getting work done efficiently with the cooperation of the workers and with the minimum amount of friction and antagonism between groups is rapidly replacing the overlording type of foreman of the past.

Supervisors and foremen are usually old employees who thoroughly know the work and have supervisory ability. It is necessary,

nevertheless, to train these men in newer and better methods. Be
sides this training, they should be: (1) fundamentally grounded in
the psychology of handling men; (2) thoroughly familiar with th
personnel policies of the company; and (3) aware of the importanc
of teamwork and co-operation between the various units and de
partments in the company.

Training executives. Executives, more than any other group o
employees, are responsible for the operation and management of a
business enterprise, and it may be truthfully stated that the measure
of success of a business depends to a large extent on the wisdom
of the management group, if not of one individual. For this reason
a training program designed to broaden the outlook of executive
and to develop a reservoir for new executives is a matter of grea
importance. Employees will co-operate and show more interest in
the training program as a whole, if they realize that the manage
ment group feels the need for training.

Suggestions of what to include in executive training, designed to
broaden the outlook of executives, are as follows:

1. A study of the company policies and the aims of such policies
2. A study of methods for evaluating and appraising the work and operations of departments, supervisors, and employees.
3. A study of business history and future social, economic, and political trends.
4. A study of the management's responsibility toward stockholders, customers, and workers.

A careful and comprehensive training program, along with promotions based on merit and along clearly defined promotional channels, creates the best reservoir of future executives. Some companies select college graduates for the purpose of training them for future executives. The candidates receive a thorough training in every department of the company. Still other companies have gone back to the plan of hiring men secretaries to important executives and promoting them to executive positions.

Methods of training. Training may be given to employees by three basic methods: (1) on the job, (2) in a classroom, or (3) by conference.

Training on the job. The most common method of training

mployees is to show them the work under actual working con-
itions and then have them do it. Explanations, suggestions, and orrections are made while the new employees are actually working. Care should be taken to have the work supervised by someone who nows the work thoroughly and who is in a position to watch the new employees and devote some time to them. This method requires no special equipment, is easy, and, if properly done, is the cheapest way to train new employees. The method is used extensively in training routine and nonskilled workers.

Training in a classroom. The classroom method is advisable where large groups of employees are to be trained. This method requires the use of considerable space, classroom equipment such as desks, writing materials, blackboards, slides, books, and formal classroom procedure. The question of who is to train the employees is important. Some companies hire outside professional teachers to do the teaching. The disadvantages of this policy is that such instructors seldom know the particular problems confronting the company. Company executives who are at the same time capable teachers will sometimes devote their time to training employees. The classroom method of training must be considered as a preliminary or background training. The new employees who have successfully completed the classroom training are next placed on the job and closely observed. Those who require further classroom training are requested to attend class until their performance on the job shows a fundamental grasp of its problems.

In some cases companies will send their employees to evening school for specialized training, paying part of the tuition fee. Appliance manufacturers will co-operate in the training program by supplying lecturers and demonstrators to teach employees the use of office machines.

Training by conference method. The conference or meeting method of training is used extensively in the training of old employees, supervisors, and executives. This method differs from the classroom method in that it is informal, depending more on the active participation of the members and less on formal lectures and guidance. The success of a conference depends on the amount of thought given to its planning and the co-operation and participation in the conference given by its members. The program of the meeting should be carefully planned and advance notice given as to the subjects to be discussed. It is advisable to allow the mer bers to have an active part in the planning of the program, therel stimulating interest and co-operation. Such participation is mac possible by sending questionnaires to the conference members as ing their suggestions and opinions, or by discussing, at the meetin, the topic to be dealt with at the next meeting. The conferenc chairman or group leader introduces the subject, encourages activ participation, maintains order, and keeps the discussion within th scope of the subject. Various committees may be appointed t study and report on special problems. Meetings should be hel regularly and on definite dates and as frequently as is though necessary.

Employee manuals. Employee manuals are used as a tool fc training new and old employees. Three broad types of manuals ar prepared for the use of all employees: (1) company manuals, (2 departmental manuals, and (3) procedures manuals.

Company manuals. A company manual may be a simple hand book containing the rules and regulations about practices regardin hours of work, vacation periods, holidays, personal mail, persona telephone calls, and the like. Such a manual may also contain in formation of a general nature to acquaint new employees with th business. In that case it might cover a history of the particula industry; give information about the origin of the particular com- pany and the people who have brought the company to its presen status; tell where the company ranks in the industry; and give othe background information. In addition, a company manual may ex- plain all the different types of employee benefit plans in existence in the company. A section may be devoted to technical terms used in the industry.

Departmental manuals. A departmental manual is generally pre- pared by the department head. It sets down the departmental policies, practices and procedures for the guidance of employees in whatever section of the department they may work. Employees should be able, by referring to the manual, to get the answers to most of the questions that arise in their work. The manual, if properly prepared, becomes an important tool in the training of new employees. The departmental manual is set up in such form that the portions relating to various sections of the department can e given to the employees in those sections. Some department heads refer to give their employees a complete departmental manual in rder that each employee may see how the entire department funcons and how his particular portion of the work fits into the whole.

The departmental manual usually contains procedures that decribe the specific steps involved in carrying out the department's ctivities and operations. Each procedure tells how the work is done nd refers to forms, reports, and other paper work. The cost of eeping a manual up-to-date may be decisive in fixing the amount f detail to be included. Where omission of a single step might esult in error, it is usually advisable to describe the procedure in letail.

Procedures manuals. In some companies all company procedures re set up in a formal way in a procedures manual. Sometimes all tandard practice procedures are issued in a single manual. But his plan may prove too bulky as the number of procedures inreases. More commonly, a series of manuals is issued, each tailored o the needs of selected departments or employees. The procedure nstructions may be written up in narrative form, by the outline method, through the use of charts, or in a combination of all of hese methods.

Manuals for use at the management level. Three broad types of manuals are prepared for use of employees at the management level: (1) policy manuals, (2) organization manuals, and (3) administrative manuals.

Policy manuals. The policies of any company are basic, general, or departmental. *Basic* policies are determined by the board of directors. They establish the principles that management will follow in carrying out its business and tell clearly the company's broad aims as well as its approach to business problems. Since these problems are diversified, the basic policies may be a series of recitals covering a number of fields, such as research, service to the public, free competitive enterprise, human relations, adequate compensation, quality products at fair prices, fair profits, sound advertising, modern selling, realistic accounting, public relations, and high output and lower prices. The *general* policies deal with everyday operations that affect more than one department or division of the company. They are established by the general management group.

The *departmental* policies lay down the guiding principles on whi operations of a particular department are to be based, and are form lated by department heads.

Organization manuals. This manual sets forth the functions, r sponsibilities, authority, and principal relationships of a particul position or a series of positions in the organization. It sometim includes organization charts to show these relationships and job d scriptions. The manual ordinarily affords the answer in any situ tion in which a member of management is unsure of obligation authority. Similarly, the question of what channels to use in ol taining approvals of proposals or decisions on important matte can be determined by consulting the manual. Conflicts betwee individuals over jurisdiction can be immediately resolved by refe ence to it. The manual also provides a certain amount of trainin of employees for the positions covered in it. It aids in the selectio of candidates for positions since it permits individual capabilities t be compared with the requirements of the position.

Administrative procedures. Administrative procedures are genera instructions dealing with matters of policy, organization, and cc ordination. They explain how policies are to be applied and carrie out and clarify organization assignments and relationships affectin several areas of the company. For example, the administrative prc cedures might include (1) the financial, sales, and production aspect of inventories, (2) the research and production relationships in de veloping a new product, and (3) the co-operation between manufac turing and industrial engineering in setting production standards.

A manual of instructions for department heads is a manual o administrative procedures. It enumerates the duties of all depart ment heads and gives detailed instructions to be followed in such areas as personnel, attendance, illness and injury, long-distance calls, and office procedures. Sample forms to be used in the procedures described are included in the manual.

House organs. A house organ is an employee publication, prepared, edited, and published by employees for the purpose of stimulating interest in the company, promoting the feeling of fellowship, and building employee morale. House organs contain interesting news and timely items about the company, hints and suggestions for improving methods of performing tasks, personal news about mployees (such as vacations and promotions), announcements of ontest winners, and stories and jokes pertaining to the company or he employees. The house organ should receive contributions from ll employees, from the president to the office boy. The design of ouse organs varies with each company, but in every case a house rgan should be printed on good paper and in a presentable manner. t should not be too bulky, and its style should be breezy, human, nd interesting.

Company libraries. A company library is a *special library*. A pecial library has been defined simply as a "special collection serving a special clientele and using special methods for the purpose." * More than 2,500 business firms have company libraries. The purposes of a company library may be (1) to serve those in the company who are engaged in research or who have need for information in carrying out their duties, by acquiring and making available sources of information or by knowing where they may be secured, (2) to encourage and enable employees to pursue a program of self-education, and (3) for employee recreation. To serve the purposes for which it is established, the library must be organized and maintained with a view to making it vital and dynamic, rather than static. It calls for proper selection and adequate arrangement of the collection, and for maintenance on a controlled basis by competent personnel to permit the best use of the facilities by the greatest number.

The library should be under the supervision of a competent librarian. The librarian should be responsible to one of the officers of the company, or to a library committee appointed by management. The responsible executive acts as liaison between the library and the organization. The library committee may have such broad functions as determining policies, selecting library material, and reviewing requests for publications by employees. The committee is usually made up of representatives from the major divisions of the company. If the library is exclusively for employee education and recreation, the administration is frequently left to the personnel department or to the training department.

The books should be catalogued, classified, and arranged on shelves in a systematic manner. Some small libraries have found an index

---

* Marian C. Manley, *The Special Library Profession and What It Offers*, pages 181-186. New York: Special Libraries Association, 1938.

system unnecessary; they merely place their books on "general sub-ject" shelves, all economic books in one section, all accounting books in another, and so on. The two prevailing systems of classification and cataloguing are the Library of Congress and the Dewey Decimal systems. The first is highly complex, intended for extremely large (say, over 30,000 volumes) or deeply technical libraries and should be attempted only by one who has had considerable experience in cataloguing.

The Dewey System is flexible enough to meet the needs of small, growing, or large libraries and is easily learned, even by a nonprofessional. Basically, it is divided into ten general areas of knowledge, each with ten subdivisions, which, in turn, have ten subdivisions, and so on, thus making possible the classification of the smallest topics. The numbers and their subjects are listed in one volume.*

7. TELEGRAMS AND INTERNATIONAL COMMUNICATIONS

How to cut telegraph costs. Waste in the use of telegrams and international communications—a few cents here and a few cents there—is costing many business houses a considerable amount of money each year. This waste results from a lack of exact and up-to-date knowledge of the various types of services that telegraph, cable and radio companies offer, and of how they can be used most economically. Western Union is constantly improving its services and is adding new types of services to meet changing business needs. From time to time it issues circulars and advertising pieces which, in terms of dollars and cents, are well worth the few moments that it takes to read them. These circulars and the personal advice of experienced telegraph people are obtainable at any local office of Western Union.

What to consider in trying to economize on telegrams. In trying to make economies in the use of telegraph services, consider three things:

---

* *Dewey Decimal Classification,* Standard 15th ed. Lake Placid Club, Lake Placid, New York: Forest Press, Inc., 1951. (This can be purchased through H. W. Wilson Co.)

1. The urgency of the message. In some cases delivery on the ame day may be essential; in others delivery on the morning of the ollowing day would be satisfactory. The fastest service is, of ourse, the most expensive; it should therefore be used only where he utmost speed is necessary. A description of the various types f domestic messages is given on page 459 *et seq.* An outline of he various types of cable and radio messages is given on page 464 *t seq.*
2. The time difference between cities and countries.
3. Terse wording of the message.

Consider time difference between cities. The difference in ours among the various standard times used throughout the Jnited States must be taken into consideration in sending telegrams. The following list shows what time it is in localities using he various standard times, when it is 12 o'clock noon in places ising Eastern Standard Time:

Eastern Time	12 Noon
Central Time	11 A.M.
Mountain Time	10 A.M.
Pacific Time	9 A.M.

The use of Daylight Saving Time must also be considered. Daylight Saving Time is one hour faster than standard time. Thus, if two cities under consideration are on Daylight Saving Time, the differences indicated above apply. If one of the cities is on Daylight Saving Time, the normal difference indicated is either increased or reduced by one hour. For example, normally it is three hours earlier in San Francisco, which uses Pacific Time, than it is in New York City, which uses Eastern Time. However, if Daylight Saving Time were in effect in New York City, and not in San Francisco, it would be four hours earlier in San Francisco. On the other hand, if San Francisco were on Daylight Saving Time and not New York City, the time difference would be two hours. Daylight Saving Time is in effect in many parts of the country usually between the last Sunday in April and the last Sunday in September.

Saving 78 cents by considering time differences. As an illustration of the loss of money that may result from thoughtlessness in the use of telegrams, consider the case of the Jones Company, located in San Francisco. At 3:30 in the afternoon the Jones Company decides to send to New York the following telegram:

> WIRE CORRECT REFERENCE FOR INFORMATION TO GET STEEL FOR GRAIN BIN PRODUCTION. M14 REFERENCE IN CONTROLS CHECKLIST APPARENTLY INCORRECT.

If the Jones Company merely typed this message, marked it as a full-rate telegram, and dispatched it, it would cost them $1.98. All that it need cost them is $1.20.

The difference, 78 cents, is accounted for as follows:

1. It is 3:30 in San Francisco. Hence it is 6:30 in New York. The people to whom the message is being sent have probably left the office for the day.

2. Since the message will, in any event, probably not be deliverable until the following morning, it should be sent as a night letter. The rate for a night letter of fifty words or less from San Francisco to New York is $1.20. This is all that the Jones Company's message need cost them.

If 78 cents can be saved on a single telegram, the amount saved in a year might be considerable.

Saving through terse wording. Although terse wording of the message should not be carried so far that the person receiving the telegram has difficulty in understanding it, considerable savings can be effected by the exercise of a little care and ingenuity. For example, notice how much more tersely the above message is expressed than the following message:

> WIRE CORRECT REFERENCE FOR INFORMATION NECESSARY TO GET STEEL FOR GRAIN BIN PRODUCTION. YOUR ANALYSIS OF EMERGENCY CONTROLS CHECKLIST FOR GRAIN BINS REFERS TO M14. THIS REFERENCE IS IN ERROR.

The second message contains thirty words, and, if sent from San Francisco to New York City, would cost $2.75. When reduced to nineteen words, as in the first case, it cost $1.98. Seventy-seven cents has been saved by cutting out unnecessary words and expressing the same thought clearly in fewer words.

Kinds of Domestic Messages

Full-rate telegrams. The full-rate telegram is given precedence over all other messages and therefore is faster than any other class of telegraph service. The charge for a full-rate telegram is based on a minimum of fifteen words, an additional charge being made for each word in excess of fifteen. Thus the charge for a full-rate telegram sent from New York City to Detroit is $1.10 for the first fifteen words and 4½ cents for each additional word. Nothing is gained by condensing the message to less than fifteen words. The address and the signature are not counted as words. Code may be used.

Night letters. A night letter is the least expensive message service. Delivery is made on the morning of the next day (morning of next business day in case of business messages). A night letter may be filed with the telegraph company at any time up to 2 A.M. The charge is base on a minimum of fifty words, with an additional charge for each *group* of five words or less in excess of fifty. Nothing is gained by condensing the message to less than fifty words. The cost for a fifty-word night letter is less than the cost of a fifteen-word full-rate or fast telegram. Thus a fast telegram (fifteen words) from Detroit to New York costs $1.10. A night letter (fifty words) between the same cities costs 85 cents. Code may be used.

Day letters. The day letter is a deferred service at reduced rates, the transmission being subordinated to that of full-rate messages. The charge is based on a minimum of fifty words. Nothing is gained by condensing the message to less than fifty words. The charge for a 50-word day letter is approximately 30 per cent more than the initial charge for a full-rate telegram. Thus a full-rate telegram sent from New York City to Detroit costs $1.10 for fifteen words; a day letter of fifty words to the same city costs $1.45. There is an additional charge for each *group* of five words or less in excess of fifty. The address and the signature are not counted as words. Code may be used.

How the charges for a telegram are counted. The following rules are applied in counting the number of chargeable words in telegraphic messages:

1. No charge is made for essential matter in the address and signature.

2. Names of cities, states, and countries that are made up of two or more words—such as New York, South Dakota, and United States—are counted according to the number of words they contain (in these instances two words each).

3. Abbreviations of single words count as one word, provided they do not exceed five characters.

4. Common abbreviations—such as OK, AM, PM, FOB, COD—are counted as one word.

5. Initials, if separated by a space, are counted as separate words but if written together with no spaces, one word for each five characters or fraction thereof. Personal names are counted in accordance with the way they are normally written; for example, Van der Gross is counted as three words; Van Dorne, as two words; and O'Connell, as one word.

6. Mixed Groups of letters and figures, affixes, and the characters $, /, &, %, #, ′ (indicating feet or minutes) and ″ (indicating inches or seconds) are counted at the rate of five characters, or fraction thereof, to the word in messages between points in the United States, and between points in the United States and points in Alaska and Mexico. Thus, "one hundred" is counted as two words, but "100" is counted as one word; "3rd" is counted as one word, the same as "third"; "44B42" (a group of two figures, one letter, a group of two figures) is counted as one word, but "1000th" (composed of six characters) is counted as two words.

7. In messages sent to Canada as well as to other points outside the United States in North America (except Alaska and Mexico), groups of figures, affixes, bars, dashes, and signs are counted as one word each.

8. In messages between points in the United States and points in Alaska, Canada, Labrador, Mexico, Newfoundland and Saint Pierre and Miquelon Islands, punctuation marks are not charged for, but the words "stop," "comma," etc., are counted.

Rates between principal cities. Western Union publishes a table of "Rate-Square Numbers Between Cities." By using this table in conjunction with a "Relationship of Rates" table, also published by Western Union, it is a simple matter to calculate the charge on any class of message, having any number of words, between the principal cities and towns in the United States.

Special Services of Telegraph Companies

Telegraph money orders. Money may be telegraphed to any point in the United States and to almost any country in the world. Money is telegraphed quickly and safely from one point to another in the United States more than 10,000,000 times each year. The rates are the same as a regular telegram of fifteen words plus a small money-order fee. For Night Letter Money Orders, night-letter rates apply, plus the money-order fee.

Commercial news service. Western Union furnishes ticker services that report prices and transactions on the trading floors of all principal exchanges. In addition to continuous quotations by ticker, interval quotations by telegraph from all leading exchanges in the United States and Canada are available via Western Union.

Telemeter service. By use of this service many large companies have direct and instantaneous telegraph connection between their main offices and branches or correspondents. Telegraph usage is measured by meter and the charge is for the number of words a company transmits monthly.

Tie lines: teleprinter; Morse; telephone; Desk-Fax and telefax. Tie lines are direct wires provided without charge by the telegraph company, where the volume of telegraph business justifies their installation, to connect the offices of business houses direct with the operating room of the telegraph company. There are four types of tie-line services:

1. Teleprinter.
2. Morse.
3. Telephone.
4. Desk-Fax and telefax.

A *teleprinter* is operated in much the same way as a typewriter. When a key is struck on a teleprinter located in a business office, the letter so selected is simultaneously recorded on a paper tape on that teleprinter and on the tape of a corresponding machine in the local main operating room of the telegraph company. The message thus typed is at once transferred to a trunk circuit for transmission. In the delivery of messages the procedure is reversed.

Morse tie lines are similarly used for messages sent and received over them by Morse code. Specially trained operators are required.

A *telephone tie line* is a direct telephone connection between a business house and the local main office of the telegraph company. When the telephone is lifted, a telegraph operator is automatically signalled. The message is read to the receiving operator, who transcribes it and releases it for transmission to its destination.

Desk-Fax and *telefax*. The Desk-Fax is a miniature facsimile of a telegraph machine, which takes up less than a square foot of space on the desk of a businessman. It sends and receives telegrams instantly and automatically in picture form, simply by pushing a button. The telegram to be transmitted on the optical Desk-Fax is typed or handwritten on ordinary paper of the proper size. It is placed on the drum and the outgoing button is depressed; nothing further is required of the user. The Western Union office picks up the call with a *Telefax* recorder and by means of a line signal starts transmission. Upon completion of transmission the machine automatically shuts down and returns to the normal stand-by condition.

Receiving a telegram with the Desk-Fax is equally simple. Upon receiving a buzzer call, the user places a Western Union "Teledeltos" receiving blank on the drum, depresses the incoming button and after reception acknowledges receipt by pressing the accept button. If the wrong button is accidentally pressed in either reception or transmission, the machine will not function.

The direct two-way operation of the Desk-Fax machine saves the time formerly required for messenger pickup and delivery. There can be no mistake because the Desk-Fax sends just what it sees, right down to the last period. Telegrams may be sent or received over the machine at any time, day or night. No carbon is necessary since the sender retains his original message after transmission. Telegrams sent and received by Desk-Fax are charged for at regular telegraph rates.

Errand service. Telegraph messengers perform a wide variety of errands; for example:

Business errands. Pickup and delivery of envelopes, documents, blueprints, press releases, advertising cuts, mats and drawings, proofs; carrying of salesmen's samples, and so on.

Personal errands. Pickup and delivery of notes, gifts, and packges of all kinds; securing of forgotten articles from home or office, f garments from tailor, of books from library; taking of prescripons to pharmacist, and so on.

Gift deliveries. Delivery of candy, flowers, cigars, perfume—for irthdays, weddings, anniversaries, and so on.

General errands. Messengers are also available to act as tempoary employees, as guides for visitors, and as intracity couriers.

Errand service is available either on a trip or an hourly basis.

Parcel service. Telegraph messengers are used by retail merhants, drug and department stores, and so on, for scheduled pickup, onsolidation and delivery of merchandise on a deferred basis, or as 'specials." The rates depend on local specifications and volume.

Messenger distribution service. This is an advertising, merhandising, and sales-promotional service offered to national, regional, and local advertisers and agencies. The service includes lelivery, reshipment, and remailing of addressed material of all kinds, distribution of unaddressed samples and printed matter, placement of displays, gathering of market analysis data, making of traffic counts, and a score of other services.

Distribution service rates are established generally on a per unit or per thousand basis, the cost depending upon service specifications and volume.

Actual examples of the use of messenger distribution service. Among the numerous instances in which messenger distribution service was successfully used are the following:

1. The Hudson Motor Car Company used messenger distribution service to announce a new model just being placed on the market.
2. E. R. Squibb & Sons used messenger distribution service as a supplement to its sales campaign when Squibb's Aspirin was placed on the market.
3. The Acacia Mutual Life Insurance Company wrote more than $1,000,000 worth of life insurance in about two months by using messenger distribution service.
4. The *Atlantic City Pictorial Magazine* used messenger distribution service to attract people to Atlantic City as a health and vacation resort.

5. National Oil Products Company used messenger distributio service to introduce a new shampoo.

6. The Southern Cotton Oil Company utilized messenger distr bution facilities to distribute purchase coupons to housewives.

7. Thompson Products, Inc. used messenger distribution servic to deliver 70,000 catalogues directly from the printer to service mar agers of repair shops and garages.

8. F & F Laboratories used messengers to distribute more thai 30,000,000 cough drop samples on busy corners.

9. Procter & Gamble used messenger distribution service to de liver more than 850,000 copper skillets offered as premiums.

Merchandise surveys. The telegraph company conducts fact finding surveys of various kinds among jobbers, retailers, and con sumers. For example, a food concern had a "pantry count" mad from house to house in certain sections to ascertain the names o cereals kept on hand by housewives, the object being to determin how well the company's own product was represented. A sho manufacturer had the telegraph company conduct an inspectior of window displays in retail stores, to ascertain whether his branc was being displayed, and, if so, in the prescribed manner. A drug company utilized the services of the telegraph company to count the number of pedestrians passing certain intersections, the results being used as the basis for determining locations for branch stores.

Operator 25 service. By arrangement with the telegraph com- pany, advertisers may announce through advertising media that the name and address of their nearest dealer or agent may be obtained by calling operator 25 at the local office of the telegraph company. In conjunction with this service, arrangements may be made to have samples and promotional material delivered by messenger to pros- pects calling the telegraph company as a result of the advertisement.

Types of Cable and Radio Messages

International communications. Messages to foreign countries may be sent over either cable or radio facilities, filed directly with any of the international carriers, or at any Western Union telegraph office. If it is desired that a message go by any specific carrier, the name of the desired route should be written or typed on each mes-age immediately after the destination. The services and rates described below are available by all carriers except where otherwise indicated, and are in conformity with the revised telegraph regulations which became effective internationally July 1, 1950.

Full-rate messages (FR). This is the standard fast service for messages in plain or secret (code or cipher) language. The charge per word varies according to the destination of the message and generally does not exceed 30 cents per word. For example, the charge for a full-rate message sent from the United States to England is 19 cents per word and to western European countries is 3 cents per word. There is a minimum charge for five words. Both the address and signature are counted in the charge. See page 467 for the rules for determining charges.

Letter telegrams (LT). Letter telegrams (variously called Cable Letters or Radio Letters) provide a service designed for lengthy messages that are not sufficiently urgent to warrant full-rate dispatch. Letter telegrams may be written only in plain language; however, a registered code address or signature may be used. The charge for a letter-telegram is one-half of the charge per word for a full-rate message; a charge is made for a minimum of twenty-two words. For example, the cost of a full-rate message from the United States to a European country other than England is 23 cents per word; the cost of a night letter to the same country is $2.53 for twenty-two words. A charge is made for the address and the signature.

Letter telegrams are deferred in transmission to all other traffic, but overnight service is generally available in all countries except Australia, New Zealand, the Far East, the Middle East, and in some countries in the Near East. Each country in these areas sets its own limits on delivery of LTs. The following list gives the earliest delivery limits in each country. The times indicated are those *after* which the messages are deliverable.

Country	*"LT" Messages Are Deliverable After:*
Australia	8 AM, Second day
Burma	2 PM, Next day
Ceylon	2 PM, Next day
Continental China	10 AM, Next day, when filed before 12 Noon
	4 PM, Next day, when filed after 12 Noon
Formosa	4 PM, Next day, when filed before 4 PM
	8 AM, Second day, when filed after 4 PM

Country	*"LT" Messages Are Deliverable After:*
Hong Kong	4 PM, Next day
India	2 PM, Next day
Indonesia	2 PM, Next day, when filed before 4 PM 8 AM, Second day, when filed after 4 PM
Japan	4 PM, Next day, when filed before 5 PM 8 AM, Second day, when filed after 5 PM
Macau	2 PM, Next day
Malaya	2 PM, Next day
New Zealand	2 PM, Day of receipt, when received in New Zealand between 12 Midnight and 9 AM (New Zealand Time) 8 AM, Day after receipt, when received in New Zealand between 9 AM and 9 PM (New Zealand Time) 2 PM, Day after receipt, when received in New Zealand between 9 PM and 12 Midnight (New Zealand Time)
Okinawa	4 PM, Next day
Pakistan	2 PM, Next day
Philippine Rep.	4 PM, Next day
Thailand	2 PM, Next day

Shore-to-ship and ship-to-shore messages. This service permits communication by radio with individuals aboard ships at sea. The rates vary according to the place from which they are sent and according to whether they are sent via Atlantic Coast stations, Pacific Coast stations, or Gulf Coast stations.

Radio photo service. This service covers the transmission of photographs by radio. Its principal use is to supply American press associations and newspapers with up-to-the-minute pictures of persons or events abroad. Among the types of material suitable for transmission are financial statements, machine drawings, production curves, fashion designs, architectural designs, typewritten matter, printed matter, affidavits, contracts, signatures, and business and legal papers of all kinds. Photo service is available to the public through Mackay Radio and R.C.A. Communications, Inc.

Direct international services. Recent technical advances in overseas communications are making it possible to obtain direct and private connections for one- or two-way keyboard operation across the oceans. Western Union Cables inaugurated a service of this ype in 1947 known as International Metered Communications providing a direct teleprinter connection between the New York and London offices of the subscriber, over which keyboard conversations are carried on as desired. This service is paid for on a per character basis. Other services of this type are offered on a time basis.

How to save money by using time-difference table. The table on page 469 should always be consulted before a cable or radio message is sent because it enables the sender to determine whether slower transmission at the lower rates will be as effective as faster transmission at the higher rates.

For example, assume that at 2 o'clock you are sending a plain-language message from New York City to a business house in Stockholm, Sweden. By referring to the time chart, you see that at 2 o'clock in New York, it is 8 o'clock in Sweden. The probability is that there will be no one at the office to receive the message. Therefore the low-rate service should be used. Compare the costs of each of the services available. A full-rate message would cost 23 cents per word with a minimum of five words, and a cable letter 11½ cents per word with a minimum charge of twenty-two words. If the message is a long one, it should be sent as a cable letter, and, if possible, advantage taken of the extra words. If the message is less than eleven words, the full-rate would be cheaper that the cable letter.

Daylight Saving Time in the United States and abroad must be taken into consideration in calculating the time differences.

Rules for counting words in international messages. The following rules apply:

1. Each plain-language word containing fifteen letters or less is counted as one word; each word containing more than fifteen letters is counted at the rate of fifteen letters to the word.
2. Secret language words (code or cipher) are counted at the rate of five characters or fraction thereof to the word.
3. Commercial marks and abbreviations, such as FOB, CIF, CAF, SVP, are permitted and are counted at the rate of one word for each five figures or letters or fraction thereof.
4. In addition to the Roman letter alphabet and the Arabic numerals, the following signs may be transmitted in international

American Cable and Radio Corporation International Time Chart

Aleutian Islands Tutuila, Samoa	Hawaiian Island	Tahiti	San Francisco & Pacific Coast	Chicago Central America (except Panama Mexico, Winnipe	Bogota, Havana Lima, Montreal Bermuda New York, Pana	Buenos Aires Santiago Puerto Rico Lapaz, Asuncio	Rio, Santos Sao Paulo	Iceland	Algiers, Lisbon London, Paris Madrid	G. M. T.	Bengasi, Berlin Oslo, Rome, Tu Tripoli, Warsav Stockholm	Cairo, Capetov Istanbul, Mosc	Ethiopia, Iraq Madagascar	Bombay, Ceyl New Delhi	Chungking Chengtu, Kunr	Celebes, Hong Manila, Shang	Korea, Japan Adelaide	Brisbane, Gua Melbourne, N Guinea, Sydn	Solomon Islan New Caledon	Wellington, Auckland
1:00pm	2:00pm	2:00pm	4:00pm	6:00pm	7:00pm	8:00pm	9:00pm	11:00pm	MIDNIGHT	0000	1:00am	2:00am	3:00am	5:30am	7:00am	8:00am	9:00am	10:00am	11:00am	11:30am
2:00pm	3:00pm	3:00pm	5:00pm	7:00pm	8:00pm	9:00pm	10:00pm	MINUIT	1:00am	0100	2:00am	3:00am	4:00am	6:30am	8:00am	9:00am	10:00am	11:00am	MIDI	12:30pm
3:00pm	4:00pm	4:00pm	6:00pm	8:00pm	9:00pm	10:00pm	11:00pm	1:00am	2:00am	0200	3:00am	4:00am	5:00am	7:30am	9:00am	10:00am	11:00am	Mediodía	1:00pm	1:30pm
4:00pm	5:00pm	5:00pm	7:00pm	9:00pm	10:00pm	11:00pm	Medianoche	2:00am	3:00am	0300	4:00am	5:00am	6:00am	8:30am	10:00am	11:00am	NOON	1:00pm	2:00pm	2:30pm
5:00pm	6:00pm	6:00pm	8:00pm	10:00pm	11:00pm	MIDNIGHT	1:00am	3:00am	4:00am	0400	5:00am	6:00am	7:00am	9:30am	11:00am	MIDI	1:00pm	2:00pm	3:00pm	3:30pm
6:00pm	7:00pm	7:00pm	9:00pm	11:00pm	MINUIT	1:00am	2:00am	4:00am	5:00am	0500	6:00am	7:00am	8:00am	10:30am	Mediodía	1:00pm	2:00pm	3:00pm	4:00pm	4:30pm
7:00pm	8:00pm	8:00pm	10:00pm	Medianoche	1:00am	2:00am	3:00am	5:00am	6:00am	0600	7:00am	8:00am	9:00am	11:30am	1:00pm	2:00pm	3:00pm	4:00pm	5:00pm	5:30pm
8:00pm	9:00pm	9:00pm	11:00pm	1:00am	2:00am	3:00am	4:00am	6:00am	7:00am	0700	8:00am	9:00am	10:00am	12:30pm	2:00pm	3:00pm	4:00pm	5:00pm	6:00pm	6:30pm
9:00pm	10:00pm	10:00pm	MIDNIGHT	2:00am	3:00am	4:00am	5:00am	7:00am	8:00am	0800	9:00am	10:00am	11:00am	1:30pm	3:00pm	4:00pm	5:00pm	6:00pm	7:00pm	7:30pm
10:00pm	11:00pm	11:00pm	1:00am	3:00am	4:00am	5:00am	6:00am	8:00am	9:00am	0900	10:00am	11:00am	NOON	2:30pm	4:00pm	5:00pm	6:00pm	7:00pm	8:00pm	8:30pm
11:00pm	Medianoche	MINUIT	2:00am	4:00am	5:00am	6:00am	7:00am	9:00am	10:00am	1000	11:00am	MIDI	1:00pm	3:30pm	5:00pm	6:00pm	7:00pm	8:00pm	9:00pm	9:30pm
MIDNIGHT	1:00am	1:00am	3:00am	5:00am	6:00am	7:00am	8:00am	10:00am	11:00am	1100	Mediodía	1:00pm	2:00pm	4:30pm	6:00pm	7:00pm	8:00pm	9:00pm	10:00pm	10:30pm
1:00am	2:00am	2:00am	4:00am	6:00am	7:00am	8:00am	9:00am	11:00am	NOON	1200	1:00pm	2:00pm	3:00pm	5:30pm	7:00pm	8:00pm	9:00pm	10:00pm	11:00pm	11:30pm
2:00am	3:00am	3:00am	5:00am	7:00am	8:00am	9:00am	10:00am	MIDI	1:00pm	1300	2:00pm	3:00pm	4:00pm	6:30pm	8:00pm	9:00pm	10:00pm	11:00pm	MINUIT	12:30am
3:00am	4:00am	4:00am	6:00am	8:00am	9:00am	10:00am	11:00am	1:00pm	2:00pm	1400	3:00pm	4:00pm	5:00pm	7:30pm	9:00pm	10:00pm	11:00pm	Medianoche	1:00am	1:30am
4:00am	5:00am	5:00am	7:00am	9:00am	10:00am	11:00am	Mediodía	2:00pm	3:00pm	1500	4:00pm	5:00pm	6:00pm	8:30pm	10:00pm	11:00pm	MIDNIGHT	1:00am	2:00am	2:30am
5:00am	6:00am	6:00am	8:00am	10:00am	11:00am	NOON	1:00pm	3:00pm	4:00pm	1600	5:00pm	6:00pm	7:00pm	9:30pm	11:00pm	MINUIT	1:00am	2:00am	3:00am	3:30am
6:00am	7:00am	7:00am	9:00am	11:00am	MIDI	1:00pm	2:00pm	4:00pm	5:00pm	1700	6:00pm	7:00pm	8:00pm	10:30pm	Medianoche	1:00am	2:00am	3:00am	4:00am	4:30am
7:00am	8:00am	8:00am	10:00am	Mediodía	1:00pm	2:00pm	3:00pm	5:00pm	6:00pm	1800	7:00pm	8:00pm	9:00pm	11:30pm	1:00am	2:00am	3:00am	4:00am	5:00am	5:30am
8:00am	9:00am	9:00am	11:00am	1:00pm	2:00pm	3:00pm	4:00pm	6:00pm	7:00pm	1900	8:00pm	9:00pm	10:00pm	12:30am	2:00am	3:00am	4:00am	5:00am	6:00am	6:30am
9:00am	10:00am	10:00am	NOON	2:00pm	3:00pm	4:00pm	5:00pm	7:00pm	8:00pm	2000	9:00pm	10:00pm	11:00pm	1:30am	3:00am	4:00am	5:00am	6:00am	7:00am	7:30am
10:00am	11:00am	11:00am	1:00pm	3:00pm	4:00pm	5:00pm	6:00pm	8:00pm	9:00pm	2100	10:00pm	11:00pm	MIDNIGHT	2:30am	4:00am	5:00am	6:00am	7:00am	8:00am	8:30am
11:00am	Mediodía	MIDI	2:00pm	4:00pm	5:00pm	6:00pm	7:00pm	9:00pm	10:00pm	2200	11:00pm	MINUIT	1:00am	3:30am	5:00am	6:00am	7:00am	8:00am	9:00am	9:30am
NOON	1:00pm	1:00pm	3:00pm	5:00pm	6:00pm	7:00pm	8:00pm	10:00pm	11:00pm	2300	Medianoche	1:00am	2:00am	4:30am	6:00am	7:00am	8:00am	9:00am	10:00am	10:30am
1:00pm	2:00pm	2:00pm	4:00pm	6:00pm	7:00pm	8:00pm	9:00pm	11:00pm	MIDNIGHT	2400	1:00am	2:00am	3:00am	5:30am	7:00am	8:00am	9:00am	10:00am	11:00am	11:30am

When passing the line to the right, add one day. When passing the line to the left, subtract one day.

Courtesy, American Cable and Radio Corporation

messages: Full stop or period (.), comma (,), colon (:), questio mark (?), apostrophe ('), hyphen or dash (-), parenthesis (), frac tion bar (/), and quotation marks (" "). A stroke in a group c figures counts as a figure and not as a separate word. Figures ar classified as cipher and are counted at the rate of five characte or fraction thereof to the word. Punctuation marks, hyphens, an apostrophes are not transmitted except when expressly requested and then they are charged for as one word each. A dollar or cen sign or a pound sterling mark counts as a separate word.

5. In the address, the name of the place of destination, includin the name of the country when it is necessary, is counted as on word regardless of the number of letters it contains, but the name of streets and persons in addresses are counted at fifteen letters o fraction thereof to a word.

6. Each word in the signature is counted.

Registered code addresses. Registered code addresses obviate the expense incurred in using full addresses. The fee is $3 for six months, or $5 per annum. Code addresses may be registered with the Central Bureau of Registered Addresses, 25 Beaver Street, New York City; with international carriers maintaining offices at Washington, D. C. (American Cable & Radio and RCA Communications) and at San Francisco (American Cable & Radio, RCA Communications, and Globe Wireless); and with local Western Union offices. The addresses need be registered with only one carrier, which will supply all other carriers with each new registration.

Reversible code addresses. Reversible code addresses represent a refinement of the code-address principle designed to save tolls that otherwise would be paid for signatures. They involve use of the same code address by the two parties to the correspondence and limitation of the use of that address to correspondence between the parties concerned.

Report of delivery. Advices of the date and time of delivery of messages, by cable or mail, may be arranged by writing the indication "PC" for telegraphic report, or "PCP" for postal card report, immediately before the address. The charge for a telegraph report of delivery is equal to the tolls on six words at full rates between the same points.

Messages repeated back. The repeating of a message back to ne sender may be arranged at the time of filing by writing the hargeable service indication "TC" immediately before the address. charge equal to one and one half the full-rate tolls is made for ne service.

Prepaid replies. The sender of a message may prepay a reply. 'he indication "RP," followed by the amount prepaid, must be inerted immediately before and as part of the address, such indication eing counted and charged for as one word. In addition to the harge for the "RP" indication, the fee for the prepaid reply is harged or collected at the time the message is accepted, since, regardless of whether or not a reply is made, the amount indicated by he "RP" instructions must be remitted by the telegraph company hrough the international accounts to the office of destination.

8. TELEPHONE SERVICE

Long Distance Calls

Station-to-station and person-to-person calls. A station-totation call is made when the caller is willing to talk with anyone who answers the telephone at the called point. A person-to-person call is made when the caller must talk to some one person in particular or to a particular department or P.B.X. telephone. The initial period rates for these calls are somewhat higher than those for station-to-station calls.

Although a station-to-station call is cheaper, in many cases it is more economical to make a person-to-person call. If the person with whom you wish to speak at the called point is likely to be difficult to locate, use person-to-person since the time spent in locating the person may run up the cost of a station-to-station call higher than the cost of a person-to-person call.

Night and Sunday rates. Reduced rates apply daily between 6:00 P.M. and 4:30 A.M., and for all day on Sunday, on calls to most points in the United States, Alaska, Canada, and Cuba, and between 7:00 P.M. and 4:30 A.M., and all day Sunday, on calls to most points in Mexico. Reduced rates do not apply to calls between nearby points. Lower rates are also in effect at night, and all day Sunday on calls to many foreign countries. The time at the calling point governs the application of reduced rates.

Collect calls. Charges may be billed to the called telephone if accepted at the latter (except certain overseas or foreign points).

Special reversed charge service. A subscriber may offer his customers living in specified distant exchanges a special collect call service that enables them to call him without charge and without even requesting that the charges be reversed. A monthly charge, which includes provision of a special directory listing in connection with this service, is made for each exchange from which the subscriber wishes his customers to have this privilege. (The monthly charge, of course, is in addition to the charges for the calls themselves.)

Toll credit card plan. This is a credit arrangement that enables representatives of business firms, and other subscribers who use long distance service frequently while traveling, to have the charges for such calls included in the regular (e.g., "home office") bill for telephone service. The user places his calls in the usual manner except that he also gives the serial number of his credit card, his name and the city and telephone number to which the charges are to be billed.

Appointment calls. At the subscriber's request the telephone company will make arrangements in advance for the establishment of a connection at a specified time. Such calls are charged for at the person-to-person rate.

Messenger calls. If it is necessary to reach someone who does not have a telephone, the operator at the called point may be authorized to send a messenger for the person desired. Whether or not the call is completed, the caller pays the cost of the messenger's service, which is in addition to the regular person-to-person charge for the call.

Conference calls. Conference service makes it possible for a caller to be connected simultaneously with a number of other telephones either in the same city or in several cities. No special equip-nent at the users' telephones is required. (See also the conference services available with private branch exchanges, page 475.)

The uses of conference service are many. Suppose, for example, that a manufacturer in Chicago is about to start a new sales drive. Sales managers in five cities are all waiting for the word "Go." On the morning of the new drive, each sales manager's telephone rings, and each is informed by the conference operator that she has a conference call from Chicago. The voice of the president comes over the wires, giving the sales managers final directions for the new drive; or, the president and the five sales managers can discuss their plans, just as though they were grouped at a conference table.

If he so desired, the president of the company could speak to gatherings of salesmen in each of the five cities, instead of merely to the five sales managers. He could do this by having the telephone company install loud-speaker equipment, appropriate for the number of listeners. A control dial associated with the loud-speaker permits volume adjustment.

When a proposed conference call is to involve a large number of distant calls, it is advisable to discuss the proposed conference with the telephone company well in advance of the time the call is desired.

Overseas and ship-to-shore calls. From any telephone in or connected with the Bell System, it is possible to call practically all important cities in Europe and a great number of other points throughout the world. Information and rates for this service can be obtained from the long distance operator.

It is also possible for the businessman to transact business even when he is at sea—by means of ship-to-shore telephone service—provided that the ship is one of the more than 20 ocean liners equipped for this service and can make effective radio contact with the shore station. Complete information on this service may be obtained from the long distance operator.

Private-line telephone services. Where it is necessary to make numerous calls between two or more points—for instance, between a headquarters office and a factory or warehouse—many business firms contract for private-line service.

The advantages of this private-line service are:

1. The firm has the exclusive use of a direct line of communication to the distant point on a monthly contract basis.

2. Connections are very rapid, although this is not usually a controlling factor in view of the speed of the regular message toll service. Moreover, delays will be encountered when two or more persons wish to use the private line at the same time.

3. A considerable saving in cost per call can be obtained where the volume of calls is heavy.

Service is available on the basis of 24 hours a day, seven days a week, and, where facilities are available, short period private-line service also may be obtained. For such service, rates vary with the time of day. Further details on service periods and rates can be obtained by calling the telephone company business office.

Private Branch Exchange (P.B.X.) Services

Need for a P.B.X. Many business firms need several lines and several stations and, consequently, have a call interconnection problem within their organizations. Numerous situations of this kind are cared for by Private Branch Exchange (P.B.X.) switchboards, although many, particularly where small numbers of lines and stations are involved, are cared for by keys or buttons associated with or built into the telephone instruments.

Essentially, a Private Branch Exchange is, as its name implies, a switchboard located on the subscriber's premises in which are terminated both central office trunks and station lines for the firm's telephone users. Other types of telephone lines—so-called tie lines and paging circuits, for example—are also often terminated therein.

Connections through a P.B.X. Through the medium of a P.B.X. switchboard it is possible to connect

1. Any central office trunk to any station line for the purpose of distributing income calls.

2. Any station line to any central office trunk for the purpose of making outgoing calls.

3. Any telephone within the organization to any other telephone therein without going through the central office at all.

4. In general, other types of circuits terminated within the organization to the foregoing and to each other.

In short, with this ability to complete all manner of interconnecions—inside, outside, and internal—the P.B.X. might well be regarded as the backbone of a business firm's telephone service.

Manual and dial switchboards. In describing Private Branch Exchange systems it is useful to distinguish between manual and dial.

Manual switchboards are those in which all of the switching operaions—e.g., trunk-to-station, station-to-trunk and station-to-station—are performed manually by one or more attendants.

In dial switchboards only the switching of trunks to stations, for the purpose of distributing incoming calls, need be done manually; the other switching operations are done mechanically.

For both the manual and dial varieties there are supplementary facilities which, when circumstances require them, go far to enhance the usefulness of Private Branch Exchange service. Among them are the following:

Loud-speaker paging service through which, by a microphone usually located at the switchboard, people away from their desks or offices can be paged or summoned to the telephone via loud-speakers throughout the premises.

Code calling service through which people can be summoned to the telephone by means of code signals produced automatically via bells, gongs, horns, and the like, throughout the premises.

Conference service through which P.B.X. station users may participate in telephone conferences. One form of P.B.X. conference service is manual, under the control of the P.B.X. attendant; another is dial (in dial P.B.X.'s, of course) under which the parties desiring the telephone conference can be interconnected by dialing a certain code.

Telephone Convenience Aids (Key Telephone Systems)

Aids to efficient office operation. Many convenient telephone arrangements are available for meeting the particular requirements of the professional man or business executive, whether his business is large and has a P.B.X., or is small and has other types of telephone switching equipment. Through the use of various types of keys or buttons—some of them turn-buttons and some push-buttons, built into the telephone instrument itself, if desired—it is possible to perform a number of functions that result in more convenient and efficient business operation. Some of these functions are described below. Either alone or in conjunction with P.B.X. service, their flexibility makes possible a tailor-made service to fit the exact requirements at any location within the establishment. For advice and assistance in planning your internal telephone arrangements, consult the telephone company.

Pick-up. An executive, for example, needing two telephone lines, wants his secretary as well as himself to have access to both. A simple solution to this is to provide both the executive and his secretary with a telephone having a built-in turn button. Turning this button one way connects him (or the secretary) to one line, turning it the other way connects him to the other. This form of access to any one of several lines is called "pick-up" in telephone company parlance.

Holding. The hold feature enables the executive to hold a call on one line and use the same telephone instrument for a call on another line. When he has finished his second conversation he can switch back to the first caller, without the latter having overheard, in the meantime, the second call that was made. This feature is of patricular value where executives have need for obtaining additional information by telephone during the course of a telephone conversation.

Audible signals. For signaling someone else to pick up a call on a telephone, buttons and buzzers are used. The buttons used for this purpose may also be built into the telephone instrument.

Visual signals. This feature indicates which line, among several, is to be answered, and also, by showing the lines already being used, which ones are available for making an outgoing call. The signals may take the form of illuminated buttons in the telephone itself, or a series of lamps mounted on the desk or wall.

Cutoff feature. This feature may be provided on either an automatic or a button-operated basis. It is of value where the same line may be picked up at more than one telephone, insuring privacy and freedom from interruption. Signals, such as telephone bells, may be cut off through key or button operation. An executive, for example, may wish the bell on his telephone silenced during conferences and concurrently to have an extension bell ring at his secretary's desk, where his line can be answered.

Intercommunicating feature. This provides for direct communication between members of an organization. Thus, merely by operating buttons built into his telephone instrument, an executive can communicate directly with any other persons connected with the "intercom" without the call having to be relayed through the switchboard operator. At the same time, the telephones having access to the intercommunicating path are usually connected with the P.B.X. system, so that calls to persons who are not a part of the system can be made through the switchboard operator in the usual way. Intercommunicating equipment is very convenient, for example, for communications between a president and his department heads, or any other group or persons who call one another frequently. Various arrangements of intercommunicating plans are possible.

Conference loud-speaker equipment. Loud-speaker equipment for conference purposes, which consists of a simply operated loud-speaker contained in a small cabinet, can be used with any type of telephone call—inside, local, or long distance. The loud-speaker is connected to the telephone line but can be cut on or off at will, and the volume desired can be regulated much as radio volume is regulated.

With a loud-speaker device associated with his telephone, an executive can have other persons in his office hear a telephone conversation. If a loud-speaker is installed at the other end of the line, the executive can speak to a group of persons, as, for example, a group of salesmen. If a conference call is made, and loud-speakers are attached to each of the telephones, the executive can "broadcast" simultaneously to meetings in distant cities.

Recording of telephone conversations. Equipment for recording telephone conversations may be purchased, for private ownership, from commercial suppliers. However, its connection to telephone lines must be made through the use of telephone company recorder-connector equipment. The recorder-connector produces a distinctive "beep" tone every 15 seconds to let the person at the other end of the line know that the conversation is being recorded.

Automatic telephone answering. By use of equipment available from the telephone company, incoming telephone calls are answered automatically during the subscriber's absence. Before leaving, the subscriber records an appropriate message into the equipment, by speaking into his telephone. Callers, upon hearing it, may record their own messages which may be played back by the subscriber.

In addition, there are privately operated firms—so-called telephone answering services or secretarial bureaus—that make a business of furnishing such a service, using attendants rather than recording apparatus for taking and giving the messages.

Mobile telephone service. This service, now available in many cities, is a radio-telephone extension of wire telephony that interconnects mobile units, such as automobiles, trucks, passenger trains, and switch engines, as well as ships in inland and coastal waters, with the general telephone system. Direct telephone communication with mobile units is used by many lines of business not only to save time and mileage, thus reducing operational costs, but also in order to give faster and better service to customers.

The telephone company will install and maintain the radio-telephone apparatus on the mobile unit on a monthly rental basis, or the subscriber may use equipment that can be purchased through merchandise channels.

Teletypewriter Services

Kinds of teletypewriter service. Teletypewriters will transmit typewritten messages to any part of the country over the facilities of the Bell System. The teletypewriters are specially designed electrical typewriters. Whatever is typed on one machine is simultaneously reproduced in typewritten form on one or more teletypewriters with which it is connected. Two kinds of teletypewriter service are available:

1. Private line.
2. Exchange.

Private-line teletypewriter service. This kind of service involves teletypewriter machines, at two or more locations within the same or different cities, directly connected with one another.

Private-line teletypewriter service may be used not only for intra-organization communication but also for communication with other concerns. For example, two independently owned and operated companies in the same city or different cities may transact so much business with one another that constant communication facilities are necessary. The teletypewriter service, on either a full-time or part-time basis, is an excellent means of linking the two concerns closely together.

Teletypewriter exchange service. This service, commonly called TWX, differs from private-line service in that a subscriber may communicate with any other subscriber to the service. The connections between machines are established through a teletypewriter central office in much the same way that telephone connections are made. If, for example, the John Doe Corporation of Pittsburgh wishes to teletype a message to the James Smith Company of Philadelphia, a John Doe employee types out the number of the Smith Company on her machine. The central-office operator immediately makes the desired connection, the teletypewriter at the Smith Company offices "answers," and the message is then typed. In flexibility, speed, and the advantage of direct connections for two-way communication, the whole teletype-writing process compares favorably with regular telephone service. The permanent character of the record facilitates filing and reference work.

Connections can be established for any length of time that a subscriber wishes. The method of charging is along the same lines as telephone toll rates. The minimum period is three minutes on long distance and five minutes on local connections.

Telephone Company "Servicing" Services

Need for servicing services. The business executive, particularly of a large establishment, should be familiar with and take advantage of the Bell companies' "servicing" services.

There are literally hundreds of telephone and teletypewriter facilities, kinds of equipment, and service usages. Their selection, engineering, and operation are often highly technical matters requiring a degree of "know-how" that subscribers themselves rarely possess. They need the assistance of specialists which, generally speaking, only the telephone companies are equipped to give.

The Bell companies, through servicing and instructional forces aggregating several thousands of people, furnish such assistance without charge as a regular part of their service to their customers. Their representatives are specifically instructed to be as ready to recommend reductions in a subscriber's service where warranted as they are to recommend increases and changes where these are indicated.

Scope of servicing services. The scope of the Bell companies' servicing services may be outlined as follows:

1. Service engineering—advice concerning the type, quantity, layout and usage of facilities and equipment. People on this work are generally called Service Engineers or Servicing Representatives. This work covers all telephone company services—long distance as well as local, key equipment as well as private branch exchange, radiotelephone as well as wire. Directory services are also included. Studies, service observations, interviews with telephone users in the subscriber's establishment, and so forth, are made if necessary, findings appraised, and recommendations formulated and presented to the executives.

2. Training of private branch exchange attendants (who are employees of the subscriber, not the telephone company). This training includes not only classes for initial instruction of beginners and refresher courses for experienced attendants, but also periodic visits to subscribers' premises to observe the switchboard's operation and give the attendants any needed on-the-job coaching. The latter is done by a group of instructresses called P.B.X. Service Advisers.

3. Training of business establishments' personnel (management as well as other employees) in courteous and technically correct telephone usage. Training films on P.B.X. operation and correct telephone usage are available without charge.

4. Training of teletypewriter attendants—the teletypewriter counterpart of the training activity for P.B.X. attendants just described.

5. Placement of private branch exchange attendants. This is an "employment agency" type of service through which the Bell companies recommend capable and well-trained attendants to private branch exchange subscribers, but without charge to either the subscriber or the attendant.

6. Engineering advice to architects, builders and home owners concerning conduits, outlets, and other facilities for telephone wires and cables in home and building construction.

9. PRIVATELY-OWNED INTERNAL COMMUNICATION SYSTEMS

Advantages of an internal communication system. Arrangements for intercommunication between offices in the same company are obtainable at small cost and with considerable saving of time and money in most organizations. This is true regardless of whether the system is a P.B.X., a button arrangement, or a combination of the two subscribed for through the telephone company (see page 477), or one purchased for private ownership. Here are a few of the advantages to be gained with the proper intercommunication system:

1. The executive can speak to an associate instantly.
2. Information can be obtained from any part of the organization while telephoning on outside lines.
3. Intermittent but important dictation can be given to secretaries over the system without waste of time.
4. Throughout the organization, better co-ordination is secured; delays are eliminated; errors are reduced; executive supervision is increased as internal communication is used to weld the organization together; to eliminate walking and visiting; and to encourage instant follow-through on all work.

Factors to be considered in arranging for interoffice communication. An executive interested in buying an intercommunicating system outright should carefully study all service and cost factors involved in each instance. Aside from initial cost considerations, the following should be weighed:

1. *Flexibility.* Can the service or equipment be changed to meet changing communication requirements?
2. *Quality.* Will the standard of communication service be equal to the requirements?
3. *Dependability.* Will the equipment or service fulfill the job continuously for as long a time as required?
4. *Obsolescence.* Will ordinary wear and tear or new developments in the communication field make the equipment depreciate prematurely?
5. *Maintenance.* Can the system be maintained easily, quickly and inexpensively?

6. *Convenience.* Will privately-owned equipment, in addition t the necessary telephone company equipment provide service as co venient to use as a system provided entirely by the telephone con pany?

7. *Continuing costs.* Considering interest, depreciation, mair tenance, taxes and miscellaneous carrying charges, plus charges fc the necessary service provided by the telephone company, will it b economical to buy a communicating system?

8. *Volume of equipment.* Will a privately owned system elim nate a sufficient number of telephone extensions and reduce a suffi cient amount of rented facilities needed at the switchboard to mak the purchase worthwhile?

9. *Busy lines.* Will release of telephone extensions reduce bus signals and the annoyance caused by delays in putting through calls Or will a slow answer from the person talking on the privately-owne system be even more annoying than the busy signal?

Privately owned interoffice communication equipment. There are various makes of interoffice communication equipment on th market that can be purchased outright. Some of the better know are the Executone Intercommunicating System, Dictograph, Web ster Teletalk, and P-A-X.

Executone Intercommunication. Executone Intercommunica tion Systems are available for businesses of various sizes. In its simplest form, it consists of a master station and one staff station, each able to call and converse with the other. With the addition of a station selector, this same master station can enjoy direct two-way conversation with any number of widely separated offices. Should the need arise, several or all of these stations can be called simultaneously. Also available are all-master, fully-intercommunicating systems as well as combined "intercom" and paging systems.

Several different models of Executone equipment have been developed to meet the specialized needs of business and industry. For example, there are models to eliminate background sounds in noisy areas as well as to step up volume for covering in large, noisy areas. There are systems specifically engineered for different fields: audio-visual nurse call systems for hospitals, centralized checking systems for the trucking industry, explosion-proof intercom equipment for hazardous areas, as well as systems for homes, schools, auto service epartments, banks, restaurants, and so on. Models are available ith handsets or earphones for optional confidential use.

Dictograph intercommunication equipment. The Dictograph ystem of intercommunication equipment is purely an internal one; has no connection with the regular telephone system. The instruments used are of two types: (1) executive station; (2) staff station.

Executive station. The little keys on the face of the instrument stablish the connections. One end of the executive station contains microphone, the other a loud-speaker. The executive's messages re transmitted through the microphone. It is not necessary that e be close to the instrument when he speaks, for the microphone s so sensitive that it will pick up a whisper in a large room. Mesages from other persons come to the executive through the loudpeaker. The incoming calls are indicated by white signals.

Conference calls are easily made with the Dictograph system. Simply by pushing the keys indicating the names of the persons with whom he wishes to talk, and a conference key, the executive can establish connection with several persons and can talk to all of them at the same time. Executive calls have priority over all others.

Staff station. This station is smaller than the executive station. It has no loud-speaker or microphone but, instead, has a handset (like a French telephone). The keys are the same. Calls can be made by simply picking up the handset and ringing with the appropriate key; calls are answered when the handset is raised from its cradle.

Paging facilities can be provided to locate roving personnel.

Webster Teletalk. This equipment may be purchased outright or rented from the telephone company. The Teletalk has two basic systems, designated as the "M" and "S" systems, separate from the regular telephone service. In the "M" system, a 12-line key cabinet station and a single-line station may be provided in various combinations. Two-way communication is possible between key cabinet stations and between key cabinet and single line stations. In the "S" system, the 12-line key cabinet stations provide two-way communication; single-line stations may be used as simple loud-speakers for receiving announcements from key cabinets. Although a key station may have access to only 11 other stations this does not limit any one entire system to 12 stations, because it is possible to have more than one unit of 12 stations each. However, the separate units cannc communicate with each other.

Each 12-line key cabinet station contains a loud-speaker-micrc phone, amplifier, talk-listen switch, combined on-off switch and vo ume control, pilot lamp which indicates when the amplifier is turne on, line selector keys for line pick-up and signaling the called statior and buzzer and annunciator signals for indicating incoming calls an identifying the calling station. In addition, the key cabinet statio used in the "S" system has the pilot lamp arranged to indicate whe a busy line has been picked up, and has an earphone to be used fo listening instead of the loud-speaker whenever desired.

Intercommunicating equipment for more than ten connec tions. Where more than ten stations are required and it is desirabl to have a system that is economically adaptable to future growth anc change, an automatic dial telephone system is often the solution Even where less than ten stations are required initially, but standarc telephone service and the convenience of modern "dial" operatio are desired, user-owned automatic dial telephone systems find wid use as a supplement to the conventional rented switchboard.

These automatic interior systems need only two or three wires tc each telephone instead of the multiple wiring required by push button and loud-speaker systems. Each station is connected with a central automatic switchboard, involving no operator, through which connections are automatically made with other telephones. Greater flexibility is provided and lower costs result since additional telephones can be installed merely by connecting them to the switchboard rather than directly to every other phone. This feature also avoids service interruptions when stations have to be moved from one location to another.

Each P-A-X business telephone system consists basically of a central automatic switchboard, made up of the same fundamental units of apparatus as are employed in some public automatic exchanges. It is compact and can be placed in any small room. A variety of phones are offered that are identical in every respect with the ones supplied by Automatic Electric to public telephone companies.

The larger P-A-X systems can be arranged to provide various special communication services to meet the specialized needs of the user. Some of these are:

Code-call. Repeats assigned codes or signals throughout the prem-es under control of any telephone dial. Called party answers from ny P-A-X telephone and obtains direct talking connection.

Conference service. Permits simultaneous connections of several elephones for conference purposes.

Direct line. This is a permanent line between two stations having requent need to call each other. By merely lifting either handset, person signals the other station automatically; dialing is not nec-ssary.

Voice paging. Permits use of public address system by dialing lesignated number from any P-A-X- telephone.

Paging telephone. A special service providing two-way loud-speaker onversation over standard telephone lines by dialing designated umber to reach the area so served.

Message announcer. Provides facilities for the playback of a re-corded message available to any P-A-X telephone by dialing the desig-ated number.

10. POSTAL GUIDE FOR EFFICIENT HANDLING OF MAIL

How to save postage. Every business organization uses mail in some form or another in transacting business. Money can be saved by knowing how and when to use the various types of mail service. A few suggestions are offered here to reduce postage costs:

1. Use business-reply envelopes.
2. Take advantage of third-class bulk mail wherever possible.
3. Reduce labor costs by using metered mail and printed indicia.
4. Be sure that air-mail letters will arrive at the post office in time to meet plane schedules. Unless your mail clerks are familiar with the air-mail schedules, there is a chance that air mail will not arrive any earlier than if sent by ordinary first-class rates. The difference between air-mail postage and ordinary postage is a dead waste unless this precaution is taken.
5. Eliminate special delivery if letters will reach destination in time for the first mail delivery.
6. Economies are possible if you know how and when various classes of mail can be used.

7. Check a day's mail now and then to see whether letters to th same person are going in separate envelopes.

8. Establish a rule that all material addressed to one branch shal be enclosed in one envelope. Saving is obvious; postage is paid o so much per ounce or fraction. Combining fractions saves ounce Saving is also made on envelopes.

9. Have communications to branch offices written on mem paper. This reduces weight of mail going to branch offices.

10. Use lightweight paper for air mail.

11. Give thought to weight of paper and envelopes used for nor mal correspondence. Reduced weight need not mean sacrifice o quality.

12. Do not permit clips to go through the mail. They add t the cost of mailing. To see how much, place a box of clips on th scale.

13. If you are engaged in mailing booklets, catalogues, and othe advertising pieces, your postage cost is a sizable part of the opera tion. Be sure that you are using the most advantageous type o mailing. By all means take it to your post office before you hav the material printed because you may save hundreds or thousand of dollars.

United States Official Postal Guide. For companies that send out large quantities of mail—direct-mail men in particular—the United States Official Postal Guide is an invaluable reference volume. It is divided into two separately bound parts, each of which may be purchased separately from the Superintendent of Documents, United States Government Printing Office, Washington 25, D. C. Part I relates to domestic postal service. It is revised every two years. The textual matter contains information concerning classifications, followed by a State List of Post Offices. The State List of Post Offices serves as a parcel-post guide when used in connection with a *zone key*. Zone keys may be obtained without charge at your local post office. Postage rates, zones, and instructions as to the use of the zone key may be found in Chapter III, Articles 52 to 56, of the Guide.

Part II of the Guide contains postal information and instructions concerning International Postal Service.

Classification of Mail

Classes of mail. There are four classes of mail: first, second, hird, and fourth. Each class may have some special form of handling, air-mail, special delivery, and the like. First-class mail consists of sealed matter and also of certain items that the Post Office Department considers first-class matter whether sealed or not (see the following list). Second-class mail consists of newspapers and periodicals; third-class mail, of unsealed matter weighing less than eight ounces; fourth-class mail, or parcel post, of packages weighing more than eight ounces, but not more than 20 pounds if mailed at a first-class post office (those with annual receipts of $40,000 or more). See page 488 *et seq.* for details about each class.

Mailable items and how to dispatch them. The following list shows the class of mail by which the items mentioned are ordinarily sent.

Item	*How to Send*
Birth announcements	First-class
Bonds	Registered first-class
Books	Third-class
(Special rates apply to books. The book may be autographed. Mark the package Book or Books.)	
Catalogues	Third-class
(Special rates apply to printed catalogues individually addressed, consisting of 24 pages or more and not weighing over 10 pounds. Each piece must be clearly marked "Sec. 34.77, P.L. & R.")	
Checks, filled out	First-class
Cancelled	First-class
Certified	Registered first-class
Endorsed in blank	Registered first-class
Circulars	Third-class
Currency	Registered first-class
Documents	
Signed originals	Registered first-class
Copies	First-class
Drawings	Third-class
Form letters	Third-class
Greeting cards	First-class
In unsealed envelopes	Third-class
(If the greeting cards bear written messages, they must be sent first-class, even though unsealed.)	

Item	*How to Send*
Jewelry	Registered first-class
(If the value is more than $1,000, the package should be insured by a private insurance company.)	
Letters	
Carbon copies	First-class
Duplicate copies	First-class
For delivery to addressee only	Registered first-class
Form (see Form Letters)	
Handwritten or typed	First-class
Magazines	Second-class
Manuscript	Registered first-class
Accompanied by proof-sheets	Third- or fourth-class, depending on weight
(Corrections on proof sheets may include insertion of new matter, as well as marginal notes to the printer. The manuscript of one article may not be enclosed with the proof of another unless the matter is mailed at the first-class rate.)	
Merchandise (see Packages)	
Money orders	First-class
Newspapers	Second-class
Packages	
Not over 8 ounces	Third-class
Over 8 ounces	Parcel post
Containing personal messages	First-class
Periodicals	Second-class
Photographs	Third-class
(Wrap with a cardboard protection and mark the envelope "Photograph—do not bend." Photographs may be autographed.)	
Postal cards	First-class
Post cards	First-class
Plants, seed, cutting, scions, bulbs	Third-class or parcel post depending on weight
Printed matter	
Not over 8 ounces	Third-class
Over 8 ounces	Fourth-class
Sealed matter	First-class
Stock certificates	Registered first-class
Typewritten material (see Manuscript)	First-class

First-class mail. *Rate basis.* The rate is based on the ounce or fraction thereof, without regard to zone.

Preparation for mailing. Seal the matter unless it is a card, and mark oversized or odd-shaped envelopes "First-Class." If the en-elope flap is not gummed, seal with glue or mucilage. Do not seal vith strips of gummed paper or scotch tape.

Weight limit. The weight limit for first-class matter is 70 pounds.

Instructions and postal regulations. Any sealed matter must be ent first-class, except packages bearing *printed* labels authorizing nspection by the postmaster.

When first-class matter is included with second, third, or fourth, t all requires first-class postage, whether sealed or not.

Second-class mail. *Rate basis.* The rate is based on each two ounces or fraction thereof, without regard to zone.

Weight limit. There is no weight limit to second-class matter.

Preparation for mailing when sent unsealed by other than publishers or registered news agent. Address an envelope, slit the ends, and wrap the newspaper or periodical in it. Write "Second-Class Matter" above the address, "To" in front of the address, and "From" in front of the return address.

To call attention to a special passage in the text, mark with symbols, *not words,* in colored pencil. Write "Marked Copy" on the wrapper.

Instructions and postal regulations. Only newspapers and periodicals bearing a printed notice of second-class entry are admissible as second-class matter.

Publications produced by stencil or hectograph methods are not admissible as second-class matter.

The entire newspaper or periodical must be mailed; otherwise, the *higher* third-class rate applies on material weighing up to 8 ounces.

Third-class mail. *Rate basis.* The rate is based on a minimum of two ounces with an increase for each ounce or fraction thereof, without regard to zone. The rate for bulk lots is based on the pound, with a minimum charge per piece.

Weight limit. The weight limit is eight ounces. The same material becomes fourth class or parcel post when mailed in packages weighing over eight ounces. (See "Bulk Mail," page 500, and "Catalogues and books," page 503, for exceptions.)

Preparation for mailing. Do not seal. Wrap so that the postal authorities can examine the contents easily. Designate the contents on the wrapper, such as "Merchandise" or "Printed Matter."

Instructions and postal regulations. This classification includes merchandise, printed matter, and other mailable matter not in the first- or second-class category, and not exceeding eight ounces in weight. Included in the third-class group is a type of mail that is very important to the businessman—the form letter, or circular. (See "Form letters," pages 501-502.)

Writing, except something in the nature of an autograph or inscription, is not permitted on third-class matter.

"Do not open until Christmas," or a similar legend, may be written on the wrapper; other directions or requests may not.

Corrections of typographical errors may be made.

Fourth-class mail (parcel post). *Rate basis.* The rate is by the pound, according to distance or zone. A fraction of a pound is computed as a full pound. To find the zone of the place of destination, telephone the post office, Parcel Post Information, or refer to the zone key for your city.

Weight limit. The minimum weight is more than eight ounces. The maximum weight is 20 pounds if for delivery in zones 3 to 8 and 40 pounds if for delivery in the local, first, or second zone. If the weight is less than eight ounces, third-class postal rates apply.

Size. The size limit is 72 inches in length and girth combined. The length is the distance from one end of the package to the other, not around it, and the girth is the distance around the package at its thickest part. For example, a parcel 35 inches in length, 10 inches in width, and 5 inches in thickness, is 65 inches in length and girth combined (35″ plus 10″ plus 10″ plus 5″ plus 5″). Exceptions to these limitations are (1) parcels containing baby fowl, live plants, trees, shrubs, agricultural commodities, or books; (2) parcels addressed for delivery on a rural route; (3) parcels mailed by air parcel post; (4) parcels mailed to or from second-, third-, or fourth-class post offices; post offices at any military installation, or at any place outside continental United States where domestic mail service is in operation. Parcels covered by the exceptions may weigh as much as 70 pounds and may be 100 inches in length and girth combined.

Preparation for mailing. Pack contents solidly. If they are crushable, pack in an extra heavy cardboard box. Do not seal the package unless it bears a *printed* label that it may be opened for postal inspection.

Instructions and postal regulations. No communications may be nclosed except invoices and customer's orders that relate entirely to ne articles enclosed. When articles are being returned for repair, xchange, or credit, no communication, such as "Please credit my ccount," may be included, but the sales slip may be enclosed.

Seasonal greetings may be enclosed.

A letter may be sent with a parcel by enclosing the letter in an ddressed envelope and attaching it securely to the address side of he package, but not covering the address on the package. Postage nust be paid on the letter at the letter rate and on the package t the parcel-post rate. They will be dispached as fourth-class matter.

Special handling postage entitles fourth-class mail to the same andling as is given to first-class mail, but not to immediate delivery y the office of destination. Nor does special handling insure the afe delivery of the mail.

Domestic Air Mail

Matter mailable by air mail. Any mailable matter except that iable to damage from freezing (cut flowers are acceptable) may be sent by air mail.

Rate basis. The rate on air mail that is not dispatched by air-mail parcel post is based on the ounce or fraction thereof, without regard to distance. The rate on air-mail parcel post is based on the pound or fraction thereof, according to the distance or zone.

Weight and size limit. Air mail may not exceed 70 pounds or 100 inches in length and girth combined (Canadian limit, 60 pounds). Matter exceeding 8 ounces but not weighing more than 70 pounds, nor measuring more than 100 inches in length and girth combined, may be dispatched as air-mail parcel post.

Preparation for mailing. Seal all air mail except parcels weighing over eight ounces that are to be dispatched by air-mail parcel post.

Air mail should be conspicuously marked in the space immediately below the stamps, above the address, "Via Air Mail." Articles for dispatch over seas via Air Mail should bear the blue label "Par Avion —By Air Mail," which may be secured without expense at post offices. Letters or other air mail bearing special-delivery air-mail stamps should be conspicuously marked "Special Delivery—Air Mail."

Instructions and postal regulations. Air mail may be registerec insured, or sent C.O.D. or special delivery if the charges for thes services are paid in addition to the regular air-mail rate. The fee for these services are the same on air mail as on ordinary mail.

For forwarding of air mail, see pages 497, 498; for return of ai mail, pages 499, 500.

Special-delivery air mail. In order to obtain the fullest measur of service for the postage paid at the air-mail rate, air mail shoul be sent special delivery. Matter sent by airplane reaches the offic of address sooner than if sent by train, but when it gets there afte the last regular carrier trip of the day of its arrival, delivery is no made until the following business day, unless it is sent special de livery and the fee therefore is paid in addition to the air-mail postage

Air-mail envelopes. Air-mail envelopes of the distinctive design illustrated, Figure 47, may be used. They should be white, thougl they may be light tints of manila or kraft paper. Such envelope cannot be used for mail that is not carried by airplane. On al designs the words "Via Air Mail" must appear boldly between the postage stamp and the address. The markings on the envelope are blue and red.

The first two designs illustrated in Figure 47 apply particularly to printed envelopes. When ordinary envelopes are used for air mail the mailer may identify the matter for transmission by airplane by placing horizontally across the envelopes two blue lines approximately ¼ inch apart, the upper line to be not less than 1⅛ inches below the top of the envelope. Similar lines may also be placed vertically across the envelope not less than 3½ inches from the right end. (See the third design in Figure 47.)

Registered Mail

Mail that may be registered. All mailable domestic first-, second-, and third-class matter, fourth-class matter if it is sealed and first-class postage is paid, and air mail may be registered. Mailable second- and third-class matter, valued at over $100, on which a registry fee in excess of 85 cents is paid, must be sealed and first-class postage paid. Money, valuable papers and goods, letters to be delivered to the addressee in person ("Deliver to Addressee only"),

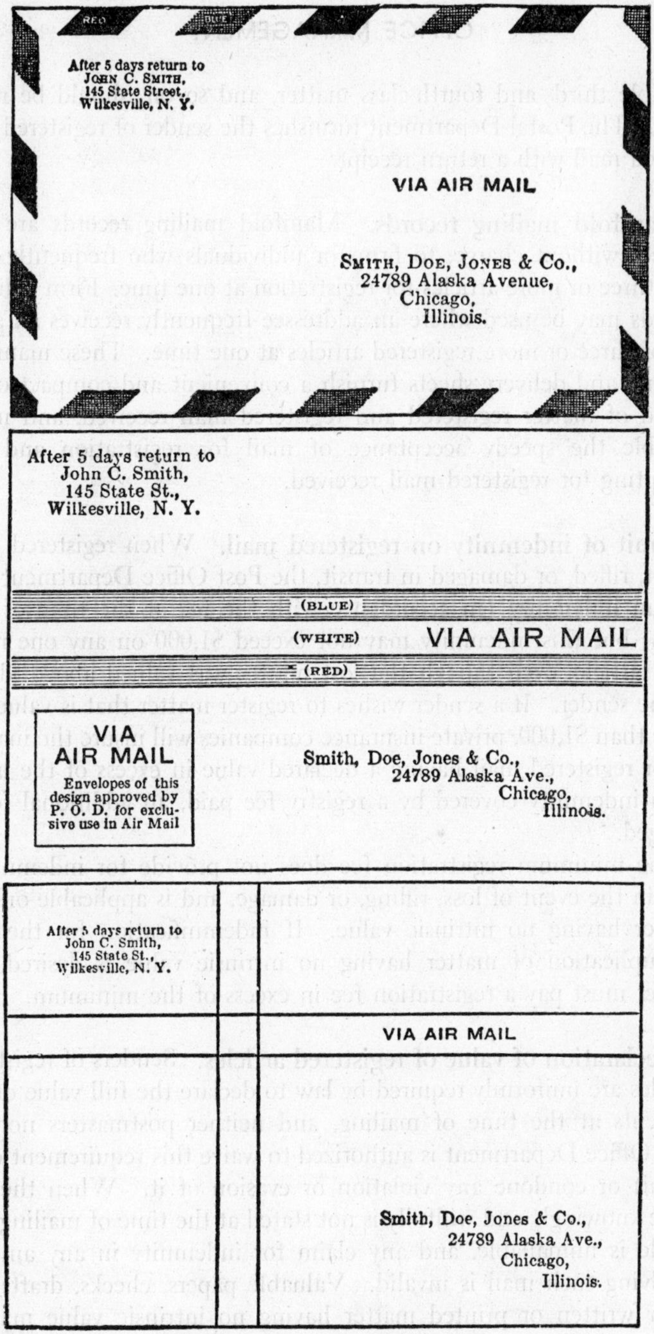

Figure 47. Air Mail Envelopes.

valuable third- and fourth-class matter, and so on, should be registered. The Postal Department furnishes the sender of registered and insured mail with a return receipt.

Manifold mailing records. Manifold mailing records are furnished, without charge, to firms or individuals who frequently present three or more articles for registration at one time. Firm delivery records may be used where an addressee frequently receives an average of three or more registered articles at one time. These manifold mailing and delivery sheets furnish a convenient and compact office record of matter registered and registered mail received, and make possible the speedy acceptance of mail for registration and the receipting for registered mail received.

Limit of indemnity on registered mail. When registered mail is lost, rifled, or damaged in transit, the Post Office Department will pay an indemnity (in accordance with the fee at the time of registry), but this indemnity may not exceed $1,000 on any one registered article, even though the lost matter was valued above $1,000 by the sender. If a sender wishes to register matter that is valued at more than $1,000, private insurance companies will insure the matter.

For registered mail having a declared value in excess of the maximum indemnity covered by a registry fee paid, an additional fee is charged.

The minimum registration fee does not provide for indemnification in the event of loss, rifling, or damage, and is applicable only to matter having no intrinsic value. If indemnification for the cost of duplication of matter having no intrinsic value is desired, the sender must pay a registration fee in excess of the minimum.

Declaration of value of registered articles. Senders of registered articles are uniformly required by law to declare the full value of the contents at the time of mailing, and neither postmasters nor the Post Office Department is authorized to waive this requirement or to permit or condone any violation or evasion of it. When the full value knowingly and willfully is not stated at the time of mailing, the article is unmailable, and any claim for indemnity in any amount involving such mail is invalid. Valuable papers, checks, drafts and other written or printed matter having no intrinsic value may be eclared as "no value." If registry or indemnity is desired, the known r estimated cost of duplication should be declared.

Insured Mail

Mail that may be insured. Domestic third- and fourth-class mail nay be insured for an amount equal to its declared value. First- nd second-class matter may not be insured; such matter should be egistered.

Insured packages may be sent "Special Delivery" or "Special Han- lling" if fees applying to these services are paid in addition to post- ge and insurance charges. The air-mail system handles insured mail f it is sent at the air-mail rate of postage plus insurance fees.

It is suggested that all parcels to be sent as insured (or C.O.D.) nail bear a pledge guaranteeing forwarding and return postage in ddition to the sender's name and address, inasmuch as all such par- els are accepted with that understanding.

Limit of indemnity on insured mail. A single parcel may not be nsured for more than $200. Packages containing articles valued at nore than $200 should be registered (indemnity limit, $1,000).

Fee basis. The insurance fee depends upon the declared value of he insured matter. An extra fee is charged if a return receipt is equested.

C.O.D. Mail

Mail that may be sent C.O.D. Domestic third- and fourth-class nail and sealed domestic unregistered matter of any class bearing postage at the first-class rate may be sent C.O.D. The price of the article and the charges thereon (including, if the sender wishes, the postage and the C.O.D. fee prepaid) will be collected from the addressee. The maximum amount that may be collected on a single C.O.D. parcel is $200. C.O.D. charges are returned to the sender in the form of a money order.

C.O.D. fees. The amount of the C.O.D. charges determines the amount of the C.O.D. fee. Every C.O.D. parcel is *automatically insured* for an amount not exceeding the amount prescribed by the fee paid against nonreceipt of the collectible charges, and against loss, damage, and rifling in an amount equivalent to the value of the package, or the cost of repairs. A small fee is charged for notif ing the sender of inability to deliver a C.O.D. article.

The sender of a C.O.D. parcel must guarantee return and fo warding postage. C.O.D. mail may be sent "Special Delivery" ("Special Handling" if fees applying to these services are paid in add tion to postage and C.O.D. charges. The air-mail system handl C.O.D. mail if it is sent at the air-mail rate of postage, plus C.O.I charges.

Special Delivery, Special Handling, and Miscellaneous

Use of special delivery and special handling. The volume (parcel post is so large that at many busy points packages and othe bulky mail must be consolidated and sent out in carloads at certai times of the day—less frequently than first-class mail is sent ou Special-delivery postage on first-class mail provides immediate d livery at the office of destination. The payment of *special-delive postage* on matter of the second, third, or fourth class entitles suc matter to the most expeditious handling and transportation pra ticable—including special delivery at the office of destination. Pa ment of *special-handling postage* on matter of the fourth class e titles it to the most expeditious handling, transportation, and delive practicable—but not immediate delivery at the office of destinatio Special-delivery service necessarily includes special handling, but on fourth-class mail may be sent special handling without special d livery. Special delivery and special handling do not guarante "safety" for the matter so sent; if the matter is valuable, it shoul be registered or insured. Neither is special-delivery or special-ha dling mail delivered directly to the addressee himself.

Delivery of special-delivery and special-handling mail. Sp cial-delivery mail is delivered from 7 A.M. to 11 P.M. at city delive offices, and from 7 A.M. to 7 P.M. at all other offices (or until aft the last mail, if that is not later than 9 P.M.); at all offices on hol days; and on Sundays at all first- and second-class offices that recei mail on that day. Special-delivery mail is delivered by messeng during the above hours to points within one mile of any post offic points within the limits of the delivery service of cities or village that extend their delivery services more than one mile; and point not more than one-half mile from rural routes.

Fees for special delivery and special handling. The fees ıarged for special-delivery service and for special-handling service thout special delivery are in addition to the regular postage charges. ıe fee is based on the weight and class of the mail.

Special-delivery and special-handling matter may be sent by air ail if the fees applying to these services are paid in addition to e regular air-mail postage charges.

Fee for restricted delivery. There is an extra fee for effecting livery of domestic registered, insured, or C.O.D. mail, when de- ery is restricted to the addressee only, or to the addressee or order.

Sender's receipt or certificate of mailing. Frequently it is de- rable to have some proof that a letter, a package, and so forth, ıs been mailed. The postmaster will furnish the sender of any ass of domestic ordinary mail a receipt or certificate of mailing for ıch article sent. The sender must pay a small fee for each certifi- ıte. Also, the sender of domestic ordinary, registered, insured, or .O.D. mail will be given *additional* receipts or certificates of mail- ıg for each article sent—that is, receipts in addition to the *original* ceipts that are given when mail is registered, insured, and so on— or an additional fee for each receipt.

Forwarding of mail. If an addressee changes from one address o another within the same post-office district, the Post Office De- artment does not regard the delivering of mail to the new address s forwarding, and the delivery is performed without extra charge. Iowever, if the new address is within another post-office district, he following rules apply:

First-class mail. All first-class matter (letters, postal cards, private nailing cards and the like) will be forwarded from one post office o another without additional charge. First-class mail is continued y air.

Second-, third-, and fourth-class mail. Mail of these classes is sub- ect to the payment of additional postage each time it is forwarded rom one post office to another. An Order to Change Address pro- vides a place for the addressee to indicate whether he will guarantee forwarding postage for second-, third-, and fourth-class matter. If forwarding postage is guaranteed, the mail is forwarded rated postage due; otherwise, unless it is of obvious value it is treated as dead mail matter.

Pieces of third- and fourth-class mail matter of obvious value a forwarded without notice if a new address is available, whether not the matter bears a pledge by the sender to pay forwarding po age, or the addressee has guaranteed forwarding postage. If a ne address is not available, such matter is returned promptly to t sender, without regard to any instructions for holding the undeliv able matter a specified period of time.

Senders of third- and fourth-class matter who do not want t matter to be forwarded to the addressee rated postage due, shou indicate that fact on the mailing piece, with instructions as to t disposition to be made of it.

Air parcel-post is forwarded by air unless the matter bears instru tions of the sender to forward by surface mail. Postage is comput at the proper air parcel post zone rate. If the parcel is forward by surface means, the "Air Parcel Post" endorsements are crossed c and the piece is rated for collection of the proper postage accordi to the class involved.

Remailing of first-class mail. Postal regulations explicitly cov the remailing of first-class mail. Prepaid audience or fan mail se to broadcasting stations may, if it has not been opened, be remail to other points in bulk at the third- or fourth-class postage rat according to the weight of the packages. This regulation appli whether such mail is remailed to the headquarters or other statio of the radio-broadcasting systems, or to advertising agencies, or t sponsors or advertisers, irrespective of whether the letters are to l opened finally by the persons or concerns to whom they are remaile in bulk. The same applies to letters prepaid at the first-class ra that were originally sent to feature writers in care of newspapers a remailed unopened in bulk by the latter to the addressees or the agents. This regulation also applies to the advertiser who prepar locally a campaign to be mailed by various dealers or branch offic throughout the country.

If the letters have been opened and are then prepared for remai ing in bulk, they are subject to postage at the first-class rate.

Notice of change of address and reasons for nondelivery. Th Post Office Department provides a service that is of real value t concerns doing a considerable amount of direct-mailing advertisin If such concerns wish to keep their mailing lists up to date, or t ake additional efforts to have mail delivered, the procedure is as llows. On the lower left-hand corner of envelope or wrapper used send third- or fourth-class mail, sender must print "Form 3547 equested." Each piece of mail bearing this inscription must also ow the name and address of the sender in the upper left hand rner of the envelope or wrapper. Notice on form 3547 will be sent the sender only when the addressee has moved and his new ad-ess is known. If the mail is undeliverable and the address of the ldressee is not known, the mail will be returned to the mailer, gibly endorsed to show the reason for nondelivery.

Printing the request for form 3547 on the matter mailed constitutes guarantee on the part of the mailer that he will pay the charge for ie notice, or the return postage in the event it is necessary to return ie mail as undeliverable. Returned mail is rated for collection of turn postage due at the regular third- or fourth-class rate, which-ver is applicable.

Requests for notification on form 3547 apply only to third- and ourth-class matter sent out in the regular course of business for urposes other than obtaining the address of the person to whom the iatter is sent. The facility may not be used on first-class matter, or in connection with mail matter sent out primarily for the pur-ose of collecting past-due accounts.

In addition to this service, the postmaster will check the names on our mailing list if you send them to him on 3″ by 5″ cards. Consult he postmaster about this service and for charges.

Return of mail. *First-class mail.* Undeliverable letters and other rst-class matter with postage of 3 cents or over will be returned to he sender free of charge if his address appears in the upper left orner of the envelope or wrapper.

Single or double postal cards that are undeliverable, as well as ndeliverable single or double post cards, whether they are addressed or local delivery or otherwise, will be returned to the sender only vhen they bear a return address in the upper left corner of the ddress side, together with a guarantee to pay return postage ("Re-urn Postage Guaranteed"). Such post and postal cards will be eturned upon payment of postage, collected upon delivery.

Second-class mail. The rules governing the return of this class of

mail are detailed and exacting; therefore it is best to consult th
postmaster.

Third- and fourth-class mail. Undeliverable mail of these class will be returned to the sender only when his address appears on th upper left-hand corner of the envelope, card, or wrapper, and whe the pledge "Return Postage Guaranteed" appears immediately und the return card. When these requirements are fulfilled, the pos master will return undeliverable mail, and the return postage wi be collected on delivery. If the matter is of obvious value, it is r turned promptly to the sender without regard to instructions fo holding it a specified time. This is done whether or not the matt bears a pledge by the sender to pay return postage. The postage du for returning the mail is computed at the same rate as would b chargeable if the matter were originally mailed at the post offic returning it.

Air parcel post is returned to the sender by surface means unles the piece bears specific instructions that it be returned by air. Th is done whether or not the matter bears a pledge of the sender to pa return postage. When air parcels are returned by surface means th "Air Parcel Post" endorsements are crossed off and the piece is rate for collection of the proper rate of postage according to the class in volved.

Bulk Mail

Advantages of third-class bulk mailing. Bulk mailing cuts dow postal expense, for rates are lower than regular rates, and the work o stamping mail is eliminated; it speeds up mail service, at the busines organization's mail department and at the post office.

Specifications for third-class bulk mail. An annual fee (pe calendar year) must be paid to the postmaster for use of the bulk mailing privilege.

Bulk lots of identical pieces of third-class matter may be mailec in quantities of not less than either 20 pounds or 200 pieces. Postage must be prepaid in money and is supplied in the form of printec indicia, metered stamps, precancelled stamps, or Government pre cancelled envelopes. Uncancelled stamps must not be used.

If there are 10 or more bulk pieces for one post office, these must be tied together and the post office indicated by facing end envelopes ldress side out, or indicating post office on a label. If there are ss than 10 pieces for one post office, but 10 or more for a state, these ust be tied in state bundles; less than 10 for either city or state ust be made up as "miscellaneous" states and labeled. Matter ust be deposited at the proper receiving point at the post office. "Statement of Mailing" must be submitted with each mailing.

Matter mailed at bulk rates cannot be registered, insured, or sent .O.D.; neither can it be mailed to foreign countries.

For particular applications of the bulk-mailing privileges, see Form letters (bulk third class)," "Printed matter (bulk third ass)," and "Catalogues and books (bulk third class)."

Letters

Correspondence letters. Hand- or typewritten letters, or letters produced by automatic typewriter must be mailed first class. Postge may be supplied by affixing stamps, using a postage meter mahine, or using printed nonmetered indicia, for which a special ermit is required. Envelopes should be sealed.

Form letters (regular third class). Printed, multigraphed, and nimeographed letters and letters produced by any other mechanical rocess should generally be sent third class (of course, they may be ent first class). If such letters are to be subject to third-class (or ulk third-class) rates, they must be identical, with certain excepions; they may contain a written, typewritten, hand-stamped, or rinted:

1. Date.
2. Name and address of sender (including hand signature).
3. Name and address of addressee.
4. Corrections of obvious typographical errors.

If changes have to be made in form letters, consult the postmaster efore making them; insertions or changes other than those listed bove subject the letters to the first-class rate.

Further, to be mailable at the third-class rate, form letters that re reproductions or imitations of handwriting or typewriting, whether printed, multigraphed, mimeographed, or reproduced by some mechanical process other than electrical typewriter, must be mailed in quantities of 20 or more, and deposited at a post office window. If they are produced by a mechanical process but are n reproductions of handwriting or typewriting, single pieces may mailed third class in any postal receptacle.

Although printed, multigraphed, and mimeographed letters sent third-class rates must be identical, the copy can change on every pieces, as long as the physical details are identical.

The rate for form letters that meet these requirements is th regular third-class rate.

Postage may be supplied by affixing stamps, affixing precancelle stamps, using a postage meter machine, or using printed nonmetere indicia. However, the last three methods may be used only wit the permission and under the regulation of the Postal Departmen

Envelopes for regular third-class form letters must not be seale the back flap may be tucked in, or postage-saver envelopes may used. Printed return cards or envelopes, order blanks, or othe printed matter may be enclosed in form letters if the weight lim of 8 ounces is not exceeded.

Form letters (bulk third class). If bulk lots of form lette (circulars) that conform to the requirements for regular third-cla mail (identical in terms, no unauthorized changes or additions, an so forth) are mailed in quantities of not less than either 20 pounc or 200 identical pieces, they may be sent at the special bulk rat However, a permit must be obtained from the postmaster for th use of the bulk mailing privilege. The postage must be prepai and supplied in the form of printed indicia, metered stamps, pr cancelled stamps, or Government precancelled envelopes. Uncan celled stamps must not be used on bulk third-class mail.

If meter-machine or printed indicia are used on bulk third-clas mail, the wording "Section 34.66 P. L. & R." must be printed abov or below the meter impression or printed indicia. When precar cancelled stamps are used, the wording must be printed or hanc stamped above or below the stamps.

Envelopes must not be sealed; the flap may be tucked in, c postage-saver envelopes may be used.

Printed Matter

This classification includes folders, printed advertising cards, broac sides, circulars, books, catalogues, and so on.

Printed matter (regular third class). If printed matter is not the nature of personal correspondence, it may be mailed third ss. (There is a special rate for books and catalogues with over pages, including the cover; see "Catalogues and books," below.) e pieces may be mailed singly, preferably at the post office. Mailgs exceeding 8 ounces must be mailed fourth class.

Envelopes must not be sealed; the back flap may be tucked in, or stage-saver envelopes may be used. Also, packages of third-class inted matter must not be sealed.

Postage may be supplied by affixing stamps, affixing precancelled amps, using a postage meter machine, or using printed nonmetered dicia. (See page 507 for specifications if latter method is used.) ecancelled stamps may be used to seal the edges of self-mailers the matter is not sealed against inspection.

Printed matter (bulk third class). The requirements and regulaons applying to "Form letters (bulk third class)" also apply to ilk third-class printed matter, but the following is an additional quirement: If precancelled stamps are used, the wording, "Secon 34.66 P. L. & R." must be printed or hand-stamped in the upper ght-hand corner of the address side, if the printed matter is to be nt by bulk third-class mail.

Catalogues and books. *Fewer than 24 pages.* If catalogues and ooks have fewer than 24 pages, including the cover, conditions and ates set forth in connection with printed matter apply.

Twenty-four or more pages, under 8 ounces. If printed catalogues nd books have 24 or more pages (at least 22 must be printed), ncluding the cover, and do not weigh more than 8 ounces, they nay be mailed at a special rate.

Twenty-four or more pages, over 8 ounces, not over 10 pounds. f printed catalogues and similar printed advertising matter in bound orm have 24 or more pages (22 of which are printed), weigh over ounces but not exceeding 10 pounds, and are individually adressed, they may be mailed at special rates, and must be clearly narked "Sec. 34.77, P. L. & R.," in order to distinguish them from other fourth-class mail. Directories, buyers' guides, calendars, agents' order books, and publications that are sold or show a sales price are not acceptable at catalogue rates.

Publications issued at regular intervals of four or more times a year, circulated free or mainly free. If such publications contain 24 pa[g] or more, 25 per cent or more of which are text or reading mat[ter] and not more than 75 per cent of which are advertising matter, t[hey] may be mailed at a special rate. The maximum weight per pi[ece] acceptable at the special rate is 1.6 ounces. When presented [for] mailing, the pieces must be made up according to states, cities, a[nd] routes. Publications commonly known as "house-organs" are n[ot] accepted in this classification.

Library books. When these consist wholly of reading matter a[nd] contain no advertising other than incidental announcements [of] books, they may be sent by or returned to authorized public librari[es], organizations, or associations not organized for profit, at a spec[ial] rate based on the first pound or fraction thereof with a small incre[ase] for each additional pound or fraction up to and including 70 poun[ds] when addressed to points within the first, second, or third zone [of] the state in which mailed.

Books. Textbooks with incidental blank spaces for students' no[ta]tions; books permanently bound by stitching, stapling, or spiral [or] plastic binding, when covered with paper, cloth, leather, or oth[er] substantial material, and having 24 or more pages, of which at lea[st] 22 are printed; books incidentally containing a few pages of a[n]nouncements of other books, either in display or textual form; boo[ks] in paper jackets; music books in regular bound form; books consisti[ng] largely of pictures, maps, illustrations; Bibles, with space for fam[ily] records may be mailed at a special rate based on the first pound [or] fraction thereof, with an increase for each additional pound.

The following are permissible enclosures with books mailed at t[he] special rates: (a) A single reply envelope or post card, or bot[h]. (b) A single order form. (c) A single loose printed sheet not larg[er] than a page of the book it accompanies, and relating exclusively to [it]. (d) An invoice showing the price of the book.

Incidental announcements of books, whether appearing in t[he] books themselves or in the form of loose circular enclosures n[ot] weighing over one an one-third ounces, are permitted without a[f]fecting the rates. Postage is computed on the full weight of eac[h] parcel. Loose enclosures of this kind weighing over one and on[e]-third ounces and other circulars or printed matter such as folder[s], pamphlets, calendars, catalogues, etc., which would not otherwise b[e] permitted as enclosures, may be enclosed provided a permit is o[b] ained and postage on such enclosures is paid at the third-class rate n addition to the postage on the books themselves. These enclo-ures must in no case exceed 8 ounces. The wrapper of the parcel hould bear a printed or hand-stamped endorsement in the following orm:

Additional Postage at the Third-Class Rate Paid for Enclosure.
(Name of City and State) Permit No.———.

Catalogues enclosed with books under the foregoing arrangement equire postage at the regular third-class rate, and are not acceptable t the special third-class rate, irrespective of the number of pages in he catalogues. The maximum weight of the catalogue is 8 ounces.

Books may be sent as C.O.D. or Insured Mail. They may also be ent as Special Delivery or Special Handling.

Catalogues or books with 24 pages or more may be enclosed in ealed packages if the following words, together with the name and ddress of the sender, appear in the upper left corner on the face of the envelope or wrapper: "CONTENTS, BOOK (or CAT-ALOGUE)—Postmaster: This parcel may be opened for postal in-spection if necessary." This statement must be *printed*; it cannot be written or hand-stamped.

Postage may be supplied by affixing stamps, using a postage meter machine, printed nonmetered indicia, or precancelled stamps—under certain conditions.

Catalogues and books (bulk third class). If catalogues or books that fulfill the above requirements are mailed in quantities of 200 or more, or if the total weight is 20 pounds or more, they may be mailed at the bulk rate, if these requirements are fulfilled:

1. An annual fee per calendar year must be paid for a permit.
2. If there are 10 or more bulk pieces for one post office, the mailings for each must be tied together and labelled correctly. If there are fewer than 10 pieces for one post office, the mailing for each state must be tied together and labelled correctly.
3. Matter sent under the bulk-mailing privilege must be deposited at that department of the post office reserved for such mail.
4. A "Statement of Mailing" (supplied by the Postal Department) must be filled out and submitted with each mailing.

The bulk third-class rate for printed catalogues and books having

24 pages or more (of which at least 22 are printed) is based on th pound or fraction thereof. Matter mailed at the special bulk rate: however, cannot be registered, insured, or sent C.O.D.

Envelopes or wrappers for bulk third-class printed books or cata logues of 24 pages or more may be sealed if the following statement in addition to sender's name and address, is *printed* in the upper lef corner on the face of the package: "CONTENTS, BOOK (o CATALOGUE)—Postmaster: This parcel may be opened for posta inspection if necessary."

Postage may be supplied by affixing precancelled stamps, with a postage meter machine or printed nonmetered indicia. Uncancelle stamps must not be used on bulk third-class mail.

When meter-machine or printed indicia are used on bulk third class mail, the wording "Section 34.66 P. L. & R." must be printec above, below, or on the side of the stamps or printed indicia. When precancelled stamps are used, this wording must be printed or hand stamped.

Metered Mail

Permit required for use of meter. If application is made to the postmaster at the mailing office, permits under Section 35.4 of the postal laws and regulations may be issued to persons or concerns for mailing first-, second-, third-, and fourth-class matter without stamps affixed, provided the mailings are presented in accordance with the regulations. No fee is required for a meter permit.

The person or concern that has obtained the permit takes the meter to the post office and buys a certain amount of postage. The postmaster then sets the meter in accordance with the amount of postage paid for and seals it. When the amount of postage paid for is used up, the meter locks and must be reset by the postmaster after additional money has been paid. It is possible, however, to buy additional postage before the meter locks.

Metered indicia. The meters can be adjusted to imprint the denomination of postage desired. The amount of postage paid must appear on each meter stamp (1 cent, 1½ cents, and so forth). The indicia may be imprinted directly on the envelope, or, with the use of a meter-stamp tape attachment, the indicia may also be imprinted on a gummed strip of paper that can be affixed to bulky envelopes or packages. When used for first- or fourth-class mail, metered indicia ıust show correct date of mailing. Insertion of the wrong date ıakes the mailer liable for a penalty of 10 per cent of the postage. 'he date may not be shown in the meter impressions or stamps on econd- or third-class matter, except when on a separate label or ticker affixed.

Type and quantity of matter that may be metered. Metered .rst-, third-, and fourth-class matter, with the exception of third-class ulk matter mailed under Section 34.66 P. L. & R., may be presented n any quantity and need not be identical as to contents or weight.

Metered bulk third-class matter must be mailed in quantities of ıot less than 20 pounds in weight or 200 identical pieces in number. Vhen metered indicia are used on bulk third-class matter, the wording "Section 34.66 P. L. & R." must be printed adjacent to the ndicia. Metered mail, except packages and irregular overweight natter, must be faced and secured in bundles, each class and deıomination being kept together insofar as practical.

Non-Metered Mail (Printed Indicia)

Permit required for use of printed indicia. It is necessary to btain a permit from the postmaster for the right to use printed ndicia instead of stamps. A fee is charged for the permit.

Printed non-metered mail must be deposited at the post office rom which the permit was obtained. The postage charges for each nailing must be paid in cash, by certified check, or as a charge ıgainst an advance deposit with the post office to cover various mailngs. A Statement of Mailing (Form 3602) that supplies required nformation to the post office must be filled out for each mailing.

Form of printed indicia. The indicia may be printed by a printing press or any other machine that has no locking device. The use of a hand stamp for placing indicia on matter is not permitted. The form for the indicia is regulated by the Postal Department and must be complied with in every case. (Consult the postmaster before printing indicia.) The indicia must appear in the upper right-hand corner of envelopes, cards or wrappers. When the matter mailed is bulk third class, the word-

Sec. 34.66 P. L. & R. U. S. POSTAGE Paid New York, N. Y. Permit No.

Figure 48. Printed Indicia.

ing "Section 34.66 P. L. & R." must appear on the indicia, above th words "U. S. Postage." Also, the amount of postage paid on eac piece need not appear on the indicia used for bulk third-class mai Printed indicia may be of any color that contrasts strongly with th paper on which they are printed.

Type and quantity of matter on which printed indicia ma be used. First-class matter with printed indicia must be presente in quantities of not less than 300 pieces, identical as to weight (first class matter is rarely sent with printed indicia). Second- and thirc class matter, except some bulk mail, must be presented in quantitie of not less than 300 identical pieces, if it bears printed indicia Fourth-class matter bearing printed indicia must comprise not les than 250 identical pieces. Bulk third-class mail may bear printe indicia if the matter is presented in quantities of not less than 2 pounds or 200 identical pieces, and provided the wording "Sectio 34.66 P. L. & R." appears on the indicia, above the words "U. S Postage."

Precancelled Stamps, Cards, and Envelopes

Precancelled stamps. A permit for the use of such stamps mus be obtained from the postmaster; no charge applies. Precancelle stamps are usable on second-class matter (subject to transient second class rates), third-class matter (including bulk third-class), an fourth-class matter. They may not be used on containers that wil be used again.

Precancelled stamps over the 6-cent denomination must bear th printed initials of the permit holder and abbreviations of the mont and year in indelible black ink, as for example:

ABC—JAN 53

NEW YORK
N. Y.

A rubber stamp may be used if printing is not practical, but th stamping must be clear and bold. Indelible black ink must be used

Precancelled cards. Cards may be precancelled by the maile if a permit is obtained.

Precancelled envelopes. Envelopes may be precancelled by the nailer who has a permit to do so, and used to mail first-, second-, hird-, and fourth-class matter, in accordance, of course, with the egulations pertaining to such matter. Bulk third-class matter may e mailed in precancelled envelopes. Precancelled stamped en- elopes, already imprinted with the words "Sec. 34.66 P. L. & R.," re sold by the post office.

Limitation. Precancelled stamps, cards, and envelopes may be nailed only at the post office indicated in the precancellation.

Stamps

Coils of stamps. The following quantities and denominations re available: coils of 500 and 1,000 coiled sidewise or endwise, and coils of 3,000 coiled sidewise—1 cent, 1½ cent, 2 cent, and 3 cent; coils of 500 and 1,000 coiled sidewise—4 cent, 4¼ cent, 5 cent, 6 cent, and 10 cent. The 3,000 coil is designed for special types of stamp-affixing and automatic stamp vending machines. Specific mention of type desired should be made as the core of the coil differs in diameter. For coils of 500 stamps, a charge of 3 cents, in addition to the value of the stamps, is made; for coils of 1,000, a charge of 6 cents; for coils of 3,000, a charge of 18 cents.

Redemption of stamps. Avoid buying stamps in excess. They are not redeemable unless they are sold in damaged condition or are of the wrong denomination. If a purchaser does buy the wrong denomination by mistake, he must return the stamps for exchange to the point of purchase within two days of the date on which they were bought. Cash refunds are not made.

Envelopes

Stamped envelopes. The Postal Department sells stamped en- velopes just as it does postal cards. These envelopes are available in various sizes. The postmaster will supply current prices upon request.

Printed ("special-request") stamped envelopes. The Post Office Department will print a purchaser's return card on stamped envelopes if the latter places at a post office a request for lots of 500 or a multi- ple of 500 of a given size, quality, and denomination. Advertisements will not be printed on the envelopes. The following is a sample of return card that the Post Office will furnish on all special request envelopes:

After 5 days, return to
CITY ELECTRIC DISTRIBUTORS, INC.,
510 West 34 Street,
NEW YORK 1, N. Y.

Privately printed stamped envelopes. Purchasers of stamped envelopes may print their own return cards in particular styles. In using mailing envelopes approximately 6 x 10 inches or larger, it is permissible to use the entire face of the envelope for any decorative design as long as a clear (unprinted) space approximately 6 x 4 inches appears somewhere on the face of the envelope, preferably to the right or center. Smaller envelopes must have at last 3½ inches of space at the right-hand end of the envelope for address and stamps.

Window envelopes. The Post Office Department enforces special requirements for window envelopes. The transparent window must run parallel with the length of the envelope. Further, the window may not occupy any space within 1⅜ inches from the top, or ⅜ of an inch from the bottom or ends of the envelope. The sender's name and complete address must appear in the upper left-hand corner of all window envelopes—it may not appear on the back. The sender's name may be omitted only if his post-office-box number and address are given. The name of a building is not a sufficient address.

Consult the postmaster before buying or printing window envelopes. He will furnish correct specifications.

Window envelopes cost about 50 cents per 1,000 more than other envelopes, but more than seven times that amount is saved by eliminating the typing of the address. For example, a typist can address about three non-window envelopes a minute. If she earns $40 a week for a 35 hour week, the cost of adressing 1,000 envelopes is about $6.35. The saving by using window envelopes is about $5.85 per 1,000. Furthermore, the danger of misaddressing is eliminated with window envelopes.

The claim that window envelopes create an unfavorable impression is true to a certain extent, but consideration must be given to he fact that many business letters are delivered to the addressee's desk without the envelope.

A letter can be folded to fit a window envelope by making the irst crease on a line with the first line of the body of the letter, and then folding from the top one-third the length of the sheet. f this folding is not desirable, two small marks can be printed 1 inch apart on the left edge of the sheet, as a guide for placing he address. An address typed between the marks will permit the sheet to be folded only twice to fit the window envelope.

Stamped window envelopes. These may be purchased from the Post Office Department.

Postage-saver envelopes. This type of envelope is one of the most useful devices of modern business. One end of each envelope is left ungummed, the end flap being merely tucked in. The back flap is sealed. Consequently, postage-saver envelopes have the appearance of first-class mail but are subject to third-class rates. Postage-saver envelopes are very widely used in direct-mail selling.

Government Postal Cards

Sizes of Government postal cards. Government postal cards (not private mailing cards) in single and double form are sold at post offices for the price of the stamp on the face of the cards. The various sizes follow:

No. 5—Domestic single—3 x 5 inches
No. 8—Domestic single—3¼ x 5½ inches.
No. 6—Domestic reply (double)—3¼ x 5½ inches (each half)
No. 4—Domestic air mail single—3¼ x 5½ inches.
No. 7—Foreign single—3¼ x 5½ inches.
No. "F"—Foreign reply—3½ x 5½ inches (each half)
No. 11—Foreign single—3¼ x 5½ inches.
No. 12—Foreign reply—3½ x 5½ inches (each half).

Sheets of Government postal cards. The Government also furnishes postal cards in sheets. Consequently, a business house can readily have matter printed on the cards. Sheets come in the following sizes:

No. 5—Single—4 cards wide—5 cards long (in cases of 5,000).
No. 6—Double—4 cards wide—5 cards long (in cases of 5,000).
No. 8—Single—4 cards wide—10 cards long (in cases of 10,000).

Cards in sheet form cost the same as individual cards. When the sheets are cut up, the cards must conform to the Government specifications.

Messages on Government postal cards. The back and the left-hand third of the front of a Government postal card may contain writing, printing, illustrations, or advertising matter. The right-hand two thirds of the front must be left blank for the address. Government postal cards may not be used for dunning creditors, if the language used is offensive, defamatory, or threatening. However, cards may be used to collect payment, and so forth, if the request is a straightforward and dignified one and contains no reference to balances carried forward, previously billed, or overdue. Consult the postmaster for approval.

Redemption of Government postal cards. If postal cards have been spoiled in the printing and addressing, but have not been cancelled, they may be exchanged for other stamped paper or stamps at the post office for 75 per cent of their face value.

Private Mailing Cards

Specifications for private mailing cards. Post cards manufactured by business concerns must be made of an unfolded piece of cardboard similar in quality and weight to the cardboard used in Government postal cards. The required minimum size is 2¾ by 4 inches; the maximum size, 3⁹⁄₁₆ by 5⁹⁄₁₆ inches.

The right-hand half of the face of such cards must be left blank for the address and stamps. The cards should have in the upper right corner an oblong diagram containing the words, "Place postage stamp here," and at the bottom of the space to the right of the vertical dividing line the words, "This space for the address."

Double (reply) post cards. Double post cards, each half of which meets the above requirements, may also be mailed for the same postge as the single cards. Postage need not be affixed to the reply half t the time the card is originally mailed, but when the reply half is etached and mailed, postage must be affixed. Of course, an arrangenent may be made with the post office whereby the company sending he card will pay the postage as the reply portions are returned. f this is done, the reply halves of the cards must bear printed indicia.

The address of the reply portion must be on the inside when the ard is originally mailed. Stickers may be used to close cards, but netal clips may not be used to seal cards. When the reply portion s used primarily to cover a message on the back of the original porion, postage at the letter rate is required. Dunning cards must be ealed or fastened at the edges.

Folded advertising cards and other matter entirely in print, aranged with a detachable part for use as a post card, are mailable s third-class matter provided (1) the initial portion is not designated as a post card or private mailing card; (2) the initial portion s not within the size prescribed for such cards; and (3) the matter s so folded that the address of the reply portion is on the inside when originally mailed. No inclosures may be made in double cards.

Messages on post cards. The entire back, and the left-hand half of the face of post cards may contain written or printed messages or advertisements and illustrations. The right-hand half of the face must be reserved for the address and stamps.

Postage on post cards. Postage for post cards that meet the requirements set forth above may be supplied by affixing stamps or using a postage meter machine. Printed nonmetered indicia may not be used on cards that bear the words "Post Card" or "Private Mailing Card."

Cards larger than $3\frac{9}{16}$ x $5\frac{9}{16}$ inches. If such cards are entirely in print and do not bear the words "Post Card" or "Private Mailing Card," they may be mailed at the third-class rate for printed matter. If mailed in quantities of 200 or more, they may be sent as bulk third-class printed matter. If they are not entirely in print and contain either the words "Post Card" or "Private Mailing Card," they must be mailed at the first-class rate whether sealed or unsealed.

Postage for these large cards, if they do not bear the words "Post Card" or "Private Mailing Card," may be supplied by affixing stamps, affixing precancelled stamps, using a postage meter machine, or using printed nonmetered indicia.

Business-Reply Cards and Envelopes

Specifications for business-reply cards and envelopes. A permit must be obtained from the postmaster for the use of business-reply cards or envelopes, in accordance with Section 34.9 P. L. & R. The face of the card or envelope must agree with forms suggested by the Post Office Department (consult postmaster before printing cards or envelopes). Dimensions for business-reply cards are as follows:

Minimum dimensions	2¾ x 4 inches.
Maximum dimensions	3⁹⁄₁₆ x 5⁹⁄₁₆ inches.

Cards and envelopes may be printed in one color, or two or more colors may be used, provided that the matter does not resemble air mail.

Postage on business-reply cards and envelopes. Business-reply cards and envelopes that meet all of the above specifications, and that bear the printed name and address of the distributor and also the prescribed indicia (including the permit number) may be returned through the mails without the prepayment of postage. The regular postage plus additional postage on each card or envelope is collected when the cards or envelopes are delivered to the original distributor.

Money Orders

Maximum amount of money orders. The maximum amount for which a money order, domestic or international, may be issued is $100. However, a person who wishes to transmit by money order a sum in excess of $100 may purchase more than one money order.

Payment of money orders. A money order may be paid at its face value if presented by the payee, remitter, or endorsee at any post office within one year from the last day of the month in which it is issued. A money order may be deposited in any bank within this period of validity.

Identification. The applicant for payment must be personally nown by the postmaster or the paying employee to be the owner f the order and must prove his identity. Personal identification by a nancially responsible person may be required. Letters, receipted ills, driver's permits, social security cards, and similar articles can-ot be accepted as conclusive proof of identity, because they are requently stolen with money orders. An identification card to be eld on file at the post office is provided for persons who frequently ash money orders.

SECTION 5

How To Write Effective Business Letters

1. A BETTER-LETTERS PROGRAM

2. GETTING THE RIGHT TONE AND SPIRIT FOR A BUSINESS LETTER

HOW TO WRITE SALES LETTERS

(See Section 1, page 58)

HOW TO WRITE CREDIT LETTERS

(See Section 10, page 1037)

HOW TO WRITE COLLECTION LETTERS

(See Section 10, page 1041)

3. MAKING ANSWERS TO INQUIRIES PRODUCE SALES

4. REVIVING INACTIVE ACCOUNTS THROUGH LETTERS

5. LETTERS THAT BUILD GOODWILL

Holding and Increasing Goodwill of Established Customers

Building Goodwill among New Patrons

Goodwill Through Acknowledgments

General Goodwill Letters

SECTION 5

How To Write Effective Business Letters

Acknowledgment is made to P. T. Ward, "Modern Business English" (New York: Prentice-Hall, Inc.), J. C. McCloskey, "Handbook of Business Correspondence" (New York: Prentice-Hall, Inc.), William H. Butterfield, "Goodwill Letters That Build Business," and L. E. Frailey, "Handbook of Business Letters" (New York: Prentice-Hall, Inc.), for permission to reproduce material from these books in this section.

1. A BETTER-LETTERS PROGRAM

Do your letters lose or win business for you? Under the usual rocedure in many business houses, only occasionally do the files ive up their dead. The so-called routine correspondence of the ales, credit, adjustment, and other departments is handled by minor mployees. The department head is as a rule too busy with his wn work to read every letter that is mailed. Through ignorance r carelessness on the part of his subordinates, curt, vague, and oorly worded letters may be sent out, and the carbon copies may imply disappear into the files. The resultant loss of company prestige and customer goodwill (not to mention actual sales) goes unoticed, since for every customer who will go to the trouble of riticizing the way in which his correspondence is handled, ten will emain silent and place their business elsewhere. Yet one tactless or sarcastic letter, written by a "clever" clerk in reply to a customer's complaint, may destroy the goodwill that has been built up through intensive effort by the sales department. Likewise, the superficial handling of an inquiry may drive away a prospective customer whose business would be worth thousands of dollars a year.

It is not sufficient that letters shall not lose your business; they should actually improve customer relations, build goodwill, and increase sales. How to make letters perform these positive functions is treated in other parts of this section.

A plan to improve letters. To make letters perform the positi functions mentioned above, and to avoid their doing harm, a defin plan or program with regard to the company correspondence desirable. Such a program may provide for two things:

1. Training of employees in the best methods of writing vario types of business letters.
2. Supervision of the company correspondence, so that few letters will be mailed that are not up to the standard set.

In recent years many progressive companies have attacked t problem of improving their correspondence with a seriousness equ to that with which they train their salesmen. Some of these cor panies have established training schools for their employees; othe have engaged expert correspondence supervisors whose duty it is examine the company correspondence and act continuously in a advisory capacity. Programs such as these may entail considerab expense, and for this reason possibly only the larger companies coul afford to support them. Some of the methods used by larger cor panies to "make every letter better" are described below. Howeve a very simple better-letters program, which involves neither expens nor a formal course of study nor the employment of an expert, ca readily be put into effect by any business house. One such progra will be briefly described.

Choosing a correspondence adviser. The first step in a bette letters program is to choose a member of the company to act a correspondence adviser. This individual may be the advertisin manager, the sales manager, a vice president, the secretary, or eve the president. Whoever he is, he should have the following min mum qualifications for the work.

1. He should be one of the best letterwriters in the organizatio and have had considerable experience in writing various types o business letters—sales, credit, collection, adjustment, and others Obviously, to nominate a person who cannot practice what h preaches, and whose letters are inferior to those of some of the peopl whom he is undertaking to advise, is to reduce the whole progran to the level of an office joke.
2. The correspondence adviser must be a person of natural tact Some members of the organization may resent the criticism implie

n the program, and the adviser must therefore be an individual who an overcome this resentment and place the program on a basis of ordiality and mutual helpfulness.

3. The correspondence adviser should have a flair for teaching nd must be the type of person who can distinguish between essential nd nonessential points. For example, the proper tone in letters is question for the adviser to discuss at length; however, he need not ebate controversial points of grammar.

After the correspondence adviser has been chosen, it is important hat it be made clear to the members of the staff that he has the ull support of the executives of the company, and that all employees vill be expected to co-operate and to participate actively.

Telling the staff about the correspondence supervisor. A memorandum signed by the president may be the most effective method of informing the staff of the appointment of a correspondence adviser and of securing its co-operation. The memorandum may ake some such form as the following:

TO ALL MEMBERS OF THE STAFF

There are only two ways in which prospects and customers have any contact with us. The first is through a salesman; the second is by letter. For every call that a salesman makes, possibly three to ten letters are written. It is only natural, then, for us to consider how we can make our etters most effective.

I am going to ask everyone to co-operate in an effort to improve the content, tone, and appearance of the letters written for the company.

We are judged largely by our letters. If they are abrupt, discourteous, badly organized, poorly typed, hard to understand, they will detract from he company prestige rather than add to goodwill. In recent weeks I have seen carbon copies of a number of letters which did not convey the very best impression of our business.

Every letter on the company letterhead should be:

(1) Correct (3) Friendly.
(2) Clear. (4) Courteous.

Every letter should build goodwill, especially in those cases in which we find it necessary to refuse a request, ask for payment of a bill, or adjust a complaint.

It will not be necessary for us to engage in an involved technical study of business correspondence in order to improve our letters. All that we need do is pay particular attention to a few fundamental principles of good letterwriting and make a sincere effort to apply these principles in every letter we write. To help you do this, I have appointed Mr. Clark Correspondence Adviser. Mr. Clark will prepare, every two weeks, bulletin called "Better-Letters Bulletin," copies of which will be sent all members of the organization. These bulletins are intended as a m dium of co-operation; I know that you will accept them in a spirit friendliness and good feeling.

Please participate actively in this program to improve our correspon ence. If you have any comments regarding these bulletins, if you hav any ideas or suggestions for topics to be discussed, if you have any lett problem on which you would like assistance, be sure to communica with Mr. Clark.

Preparing better-letters bulletins. Before the correspondenc adviser begins to issue bulletins, it is advisable for him to draw u a list of the topics that he intends to discuss. He should then con fine himself, in each bulletin, to one particular topic. Moreover, mere outline of general principles is of little value; the applicatio of each principle must be illustrated by specific examples. Thus, the topic treated in Bulletin No. 3 is "Opening and Closing th Letter," examples of how to open and close (and how not to) shoul be cited. Similarly, if Bulletin No. 5 deals with "Replying to Com plaint and Claim Letters," it may be well for the adviser to take a actual complaint letter, prepare a reply to it, and then reproduc both letters in the bulletin, together with explanatory comments Other means of increasing the practical value of the bulletins wil readily suggest themselves.

Topics to be discussed in bulletins. These topics will vary some what according to the nature of the company's business. However the following list may be useful:

1. *Tone and spirit of the letter.* It will probably be found that some members of the staff whose work involves frequent letter writing have a formal, dull, routine style; others may be curt; still others too garrulous. Getting a cordial feeling into the business letter, without becoming undignified, is something of an art, but one that can be acquired through training and practice. This, the tone and spirit of the letter, is perhaps the most important of all the topics that should be dealt with in the bulletins. (For further discussion of the tone and spirit of a letter see page 532, *et seq.*)

2. *Every letter is a sales letter.* This statement is true in the sense

hat any letter, regardless of the subject, can "sell" goodwill and a avorable impression of the company.

3. *Sales opportunities in letter writing.* As an illustration of this oint, suppose that a clerk in the collection department is writing routine collection letter on a small past-due account. He knows hat his company has recently added a new item to its line. In vriting his collection letter there is an opportunity for the clerk to nention this new item and possibly to enclose a catalogue or other nailing piece. Similarly, a reply to a complaint might properly nd with a brief reference to a special offer that the company is naking to its customers for a limited period.

4. *Cutting correspondence costs.* Under this heading suggestions nay be made for greater efficiency in the handling of correspondence. 'or example, some of the company correspondents may be in the abit of dictating names, addresses, and salutations when replying to etters received. A more efficient method is to number each letter o which a reply is being dictated, and to begin the reply by dictating nly the number; as, "Letter No. 6." The transcriber can then btain the name and address by referring to the letter received.

5. *Opening and closing the letter.* The opening and the closing entences or paragraphs of the letter are pitfalls for many correpondents. (For further discussion, see "How to open the letter," age 538, and "How to close the letter," page 540.)

6. *Mechanics of the letter.* A section on this subject will be of nterest chiefly to the company secretaries and stenographers. To dopt a standard style for all letters has many advantages. (For llustrations of various types of letter styles, and also rules governing he form of the inside address, salutation, complimentary close, and o on, see page 615, *et seq.*)

7. *Correctness in grammar and usage.* A periodic review of grammar, sentence structure, and punctuation, with particular attention to common errors, is useful and necessary even in the case of experienced correspondents. (For rules governing correct usage, see "Dictionary of Correct Usage," page 661, *et seq.*)

8. *Special types of letters.* Collection letters, sales letters, answers to inquiries, adjustment letters—each type of business letter gives rise to its own particular problems. After having covered letter writing in general, the correspondence adviser may take up each type separately.

Compiling a correspondence manual. The bulletins may b mimeographed at very slight cost. It is convenient to have them ru off on punched paper and to supply members of the staff with rin binders into which the bulletins may be inserted as they are re ceived. Each correspondent will then have at all times on his des an invaluable reference manual on all matters pertaining to lette writing. Furthermore, when a new employee is engaged, he shoul be given an up-to-date copy of the manual; this will acquaint hir with the company's policy with regard to its correspondence and wi also largely dispense with the need for continuous verbal training b the department head.

In addition to issuing bulletins of advice on topics such as thos suggested above, the correspondence adviser may also distribute fror time to time, for inclusion in the manual, mimeographed copies o actual letters, with comments. Suitable for use are particularly effec tive letters of all kinds, whether received by the company or writte by members of the staff. To include copies of letters prepared b the staff will serve to dispel any idea that the better-letters progran is a form of destructive, and not constructive, criticism. The pro gram must permit praise to be given where praise is due.

Supervising current correspondence. The mere issuance of bul letins, however, is likely to prove only partially effective. Provisio should also be made for supervision of current correspondence, witl the object of bringing to light those aspects of the company letter that could be improved, and also of showing the extent to which the bulletins are being utilized in everyday practice.

One method of supervision is to have a carbon copy of each lette sent through the house mail to the correspondence adviser. The latter can then rapidly glance through the correspondence, select those letters that are deficient in some respect, and return them to the writers with friendly comments and suggestions; letters that are particularly good may be chosen for inclusion in the manual, as previ- ously suggested; letters that are satisfactory, and that call for neithe criticism nor praise, may simply be destroyed.

If the volume of correspondence is heavy and the above procedure would consume too much of the adviser's time, a rotation system may be used. Thus, for a period of one month or longer, the sales de- partment may be asked to send carbon copies to the adviser; the lowing month, the collection department; then the adjustment partment; and so on.

Whatever means is used, it is important that the supervision be ntinuous. If the better-letters program is to produce enduring sults, it must be permanent. The company correspondents need be kept continually "on their toes," just as do the company lesmen.

Getting the staff to participate in the program. If a better-tters program is put into effect, everything possible should be done stimulate the active participation and co-operation of all members the staff. Toward this end the tone of the bulletins should be iendly and informal; the attitude of the adviser one of encourage-ent rather than of criticism or blame. The adviser may inquire ankly whether or not the bulletins are proving helpful, what topics at he has failed to mention should be discussed, and what other embers of the staff think of his ideas. Contributions and com-ents should be solicited, since the more people who participate, e greater the benefits are likely to be. In the final analysis, the bject of a better-letters program is to lift the writing of letters out f the rut of routine into which it is apt to fall. Once interest and nthusiasm have been aroused, improvement in the company cor-espondence will follow. This improvement will result in increased restige for the company, increased goodwill among customers, and, ery probably, as a consequence of these, an advance of a step or wo in sales.

Letter-writing class results in better letters. A letter-writing lass, under the direction of the advertising manager, was formed y Jantzen Knitting Mills. As a result of the instruction given, etter public relations and better personnel relations were created, nd, in addition, the company derived direct profits from increased ales through better selling letters. Here are two examples of the esults of efforts to improve letters through the letter-writing class.

A factory executive decided to return a textile machine that he had urchased on trial. Keeping in mind some of the pointers made in a letter-writing class, the executive wrote the manufacturer explain-ng the firm's efforts to utilize the machine and its reasons for not being able to do so, and offering to prepay the transportation. The maker of the machine was warm in his appreciation of the consideration shown him. If the machine had been returned with a ter explanation such as "cannot use," which situation the manufactur indicated was not an unusual one, the goodwill of the manufactur would have been lost. The machine manufacturer and his fami are potential users of the company's product.

One of the company's salesmen criticized a letter written to retailer in his territory by one of the firm's new corespondents. A a result of the better-letters program, the subsequent correspondenc of this man showed such marked improvement that the same sale man later could not give adequate praise.

Letter-appraisal chart improves correspondence. The lette appraisal chart reproduced in Figure 49 helped develop a high stanc ard of correspondence in the Department of Agriculture under Jame F. Grady. Not only is the chart useful for self-criticism, but, if use in group conferences, it saves time by confining any discussion c the letter to specific reasons for its inadequacy.

A "better letters" booklet. Some companies supply their stenog raphers and typists with a booklet designed to achieve a unifor style, character, and appearance of all letters that are sent out on th letterhead and over the signature of the company.

The 31-page spiral bound booklet of the Caterpillar Tractor Co entitled "Better Letters" is an example of this type of booklet. I measures 8½″ x 11″ and is made up as folows:

Page 1. Arrangement of letters—an explanation of the importance c first impressions created by letters, and a list of pointers for better letter.

Pages 2-3. Reproduction of the recommended style to be followec with instructions as to spacing between the various structural parts of th letter. These pages are reproduced in Figures 50a and 50b.

Page 4. A sample letter to illustrate the style to be used in writing t individuals with whom the writer is well-acquainted.

Page 5. A letter written on the paper to be used for carbon copies c letters.

Page 6. A letter written on the paper to be used when copies are re quired of a letter received from another firm.

Page 7. A letter written on paper to be used for file copies. In th upper right-hand corner is a box spaced off for routing and for indicat ing when the letter can be destroyed by the Files and Record Section Instructions for filling in the box are given in the letter.

Pages 8-9. A letter written on paper to be used for air-mail letters Instructions for writing air-mail letters to export representatives are give in the letter.

LETTER APPRAISAL

This appraisal form is intended to assist you in revising your own letters or in indicating to others the specific weaknesses of the letters that are submitted to you for review.

Before appraising a letter, be sure to determine its exact purpose. What message is it expected to convey? What response is desired from the addressee?

Place a check mark in the column "Yes" or "No" opposite each question which applies to the letter you are appraising.

IS THE LETTER:	Yes	No
1. COMPLETE		
a. Does it give, in the most effective order, all information necessary to accomplish its purpose?		
b. Does it answer fully all the questions, asked or implied, in the incoming letter?		
2. CONCISE		
a. Does the letter include <u>only</u> the essential facts?		
b. Are the ideas expressed <u>in</u> the fewest words consistent with clearness, completeness, and courtesy; have irrelevant details and unnecessary repetition been eliminated?		
3. CLEAR		
a. Is the language adapted to the vocabulary of the addressee?		
b. Do the words exactly express the thought?		
c. Is the sentence structure clear?		
d. Are the paragraphs logical thought units, arranged to promote easy reading?		
4. CORRECT		
a. Is the accuracy of all factual information beyond question?		
b. Are all statements in strict conformity with policies?		
c. Is the letter free from: (1) grammatical errors, (2) spelling errors, (3) misleading punctuation?		
5. APPROPRIATE IN TONE		
a. Is the tone calculated to bring about the desired response?		
b. Is the tone calculated to build or protect good will?		
c. Does the entire letter evidence a desire to cooperate fully?		
d. Is it free from antagonistic words or phrases?		
6. NEAT AND WELL SET UP		
Will a favorable first impression be created by: (1) freedom from strike-overs and obvious erasures; (2) even typing; (3) position of letter on the page?		

HOW EFFECTIVE IS THE LETTER AS A WHOLE?

To what extent is the letter likely to accomplish its purpose, obtain the desired response, and build good will? In other words, how do you rate its <u>general effectiveness?</u> Underline the word which best expresses your rating:

A. OUTSTANDING B. GOOD C. PASSABLE D. UNSATISFACTORY

IN RATING ANOTHER'S LETTER

If the letter is "unsatisfactory," be sure to indicate the specific weaknesses which necessitate revision. Similarly, if the letter is only "passable," indicate clearly the weaknesses to which attention should be given in future letters.

Figure 49. Letter Appraisal Chart.

Page 10. A letter written on paper to be used for copies of air-n letters. The word "Air Mail" is printed on the sheet. The letter gi instructions for indicating who is to receive copies. Routing box is the upper right-hand corner.

Page 11. Reproduction of an inter-office letter on special paper us for the purpose. Instructions are given for use of white tissue copi Routing box is in the upper right-hand corner.

Page 12. File copy of an inter-office letter. Instructions are given use of white tissue copies. Routing box is in the upper right-hand corn

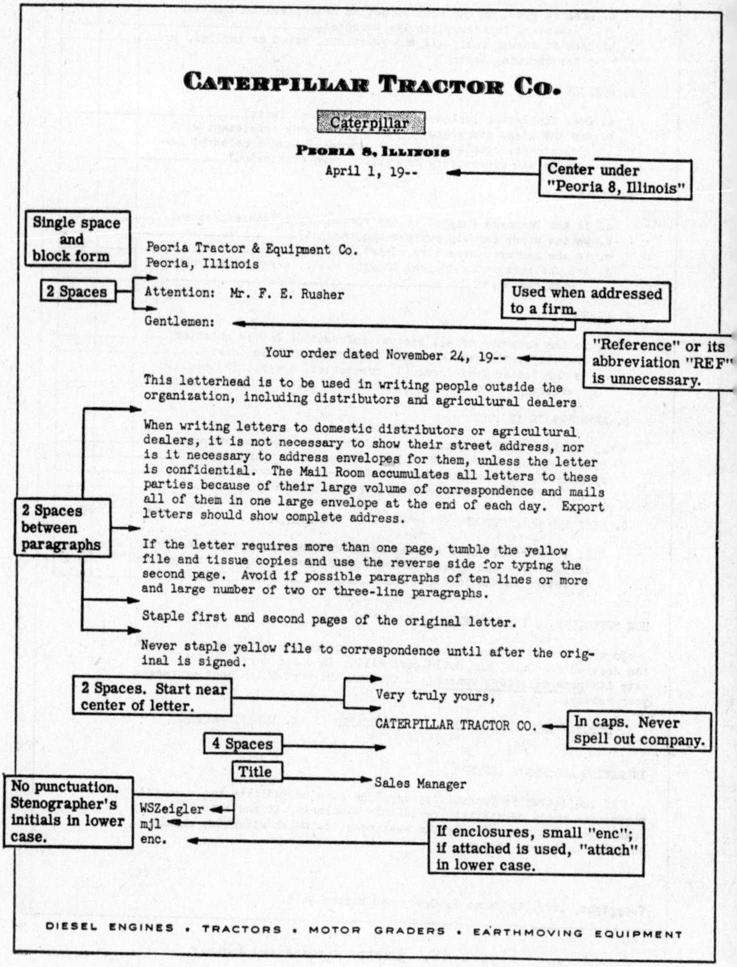

CATERPILLAR TRACTOR CO.

Caterpillar

PEORIA 8, ILLINOIS

April 1, 19--

Peoria Tractor & Equipment Co.
Peoria, Illinois

Attention: Mr. F. E. Rusher

Gentlemen:

Your order dated November 24, 19--

This letterhead is to be used in writing people outside the organization, including distributors and agricultural dealers.

When writing letters to domestic distributors or agricultural dealers, it is not necessary to show their street address, nor is it necessary to address envelopes for them, unless the letter is confidential. The Mail Room accumulates all letters to these parties because of their large volume of correspondence and mails all of them in one large envelope at the end of each day. Export letters should show complete address.

If the letter requires more than one page, tumble the yellow file and tissue copies and use the reverse side for typing the second page. Avoid if possible paragraphs of ten lines or more and large number of two or three-line paragraphs.

Staple first and second pages of the original letter.

Never staple yellow file to correspondence until after the original is signed.

Very truly yours,

CATERPILLAR TRACTOR CO.

Sales Manager

WSZeigler
mjl
enc.

DIESEL ENGINES • TRACTORS • MOTOR GRADERS • EARTHMOVING EQUIPMENT

Figure 50a. Letter with Instructions About Spacing.

Page 13. Instructions for correspondence between offices and em-ɔyees of the company, written on the paper to be used for the purpose. ɔuting box is in the upper right-hand corner.

Page 14. Illustration of proper addressing of a short envelope (3⅝″ 6½″), with instructions for the use of this envelope.

Page 15. Illustration of proper addressing of a long envelope (4¼″ 9½″), with instructions for the use of this envelope.

Page 16. Illustration of airmail envelopes to be used where time is an ıportant factor.

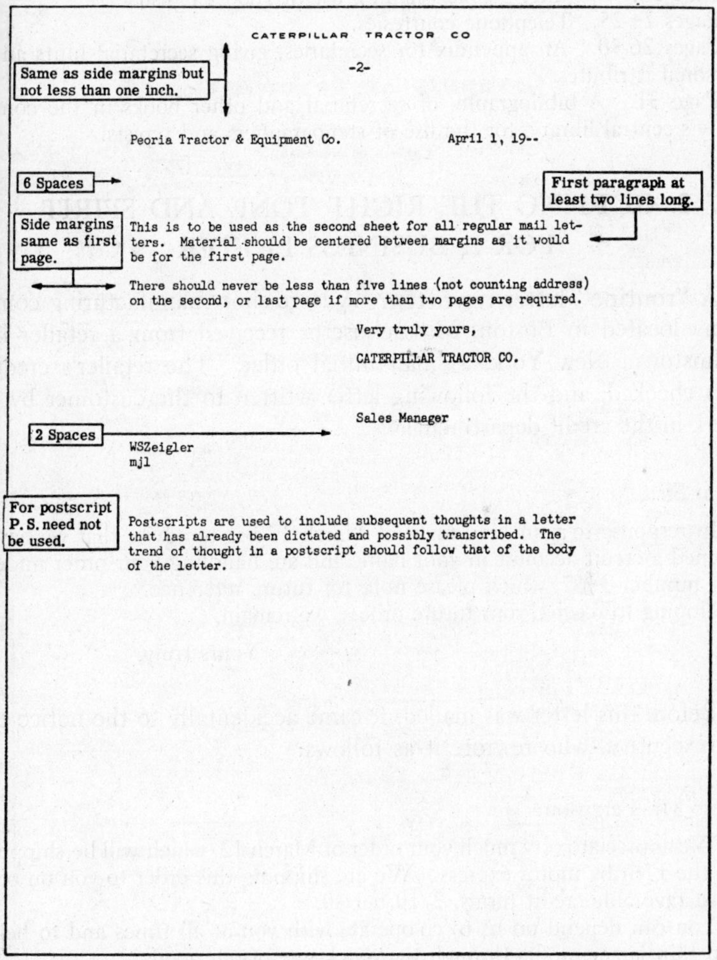

CATERPILLAR TRACTOR CO

-2-

Same as side margins but not less than one inch.

Peoria Tractor & Equipment Co. April 1, 19--

6 Spaces

First paragraph at least two lines long.

Side margins same as first page.

This is to be used as the second sheet for all regular mail letters. Material should be centered between margins as it would be for the first page.

There should never be less than five lines (not counting address) on the second, or last page if more than two pages are required.

Very truly yours,

CATERPILLAR TRACTOR CO.

Sales Manager

2 Spaces

WSZeigler
mjl

For postscript P. S. need not be used.

Postscripts are used to include subsequent thoughts in a letter that has already been dictated and possibly transcribed. The trend of thought in a postscript should follow that of the body of the letter.

Figure 50b. Letter with Instructions About Spacing (page 2).

Page 17. Illustrations of brown Manila inter-office short and long envelopes, with instructions for their use.

Page 18. Illustration of inter-office brown routing envelope, with instructions for its use. The envelope can be used eighteen times.

Pages 19-20. An explanation of how to use the words Caterpillar and Cat.

Page 21. Use of capital letters.

Page 22. Similar sounding words frequently misused; punctuation marks.

Page 23. Spelling; people's names; use of good English.

Pages 24-25. Telephone courtesies.

Pages 26-30. An appendix for secretaries, giving secretarial hints and personal attributes.

Page 31. A bibliography of secretarial and other books in the company's central library, for the use of stenographers and typists.

2. GETTING THE RIGHT TONE AND SPIRIT FOR A BUSINESS LETTER

A "routine" letter rewritten. A large shoe manufacturing company located in Boston, Massachusetts, received from a retailer in Johnstown, New York, a small initial order. The retailer's credit was checked, and the following letter written to the customer by a clerk in the credit department:

Dear Sir:

In response to your kind favor of March 12 beg to advise that we have opened a credit account in your name and are handling your order under our number 3467, which please note for future reference.

Hoping to receive your future orders, we remain,

Yours truly,

Before this letter was mailed, it came accidentally to the notice of an executive, who rewrote it as follows:

Dear Mr. Ferguson:

We appreciate very much your order of March 12, which will be shipped on the 17th by motor express. We are shipping this order to you on our most favorable credit terms, 2/10 net 30.

You can depend on us to co-operate with you at all times and to help you gain larger profits through the quick sale of our goods.

We are packing with your order our latest window display cards, and o a booklet of suggestions for using the cards. Within the next few ys you will hear from our business promotion department, which is nducted exclusively for our customers. Please feel free to make use of is service at any time, without charge or obligation.

We welcome you as a customer, and hope that this order is only the st of many which will prove profitable to you.

Very truly yours,

The difference between the two letters is apparent. The first is ritten in stilted language—*your kind favor of March 12; beg to lvise; hoping to receive your future orders, we remain.* In addi-on, the writer fails to show any real appreciation of the customer's rder and likewise fails to attempt to win reorders by mentioning the indow display cards and the services of the business promotion epartment. In contrast, the second letter is cordial. It is a "sales" etter. It cultivates the customer's goodwill by showing appreciation f his order and expressing an interest in his business. Furthermore, t is specific: the credit terms are stated so that there can be no ubsequent misunderstanding, and the date and method of shpiment re also given.

Avoid stilted phraseology. The primary requisite of good busi-ness writing is the avoidance of stilted or formal phraseology. An examination of the morning mail will supply ample evidence of the fact that many correspondents appear to feel that there is a special language or style for business intercourse. The use of this special style involves the elimination of all friendly feeling from the letter and frequent repetition of such expressions as *same, kind favor, even date, the writer wishes to state, thanking you in advance,* and the like. In reality there is no special language of business correspond-ence. So-called "Business English" is merely everyday English adapted to the needs of business. It is adapted in the sense that it is improved in organization and clarity. There are, however, no rigid conventions with regard to it. If two businessmen were lunching together, one would not say to the other, "I am in receipt of your esteemed favor of March 5, and in reply beg to state . . ." Neither is it necessary or desirable that such language be used through the mails.

Among the expressions that are regarded as stilted, and hence are not good usage in business writing, are the following:

- advise
- and oblige
- as per your instructions
- at hand
- attached please find
- awaiting your further instructions
- beg to state; advise; inform; acknowledge; etc.
- contents duly noted
- enclosed please find
- esteemed favor
- even date; recent date
- for your information wish to state
- hand you herewith
- has come to hand
- hoping to hear from you
- in re
- inst.; prox.; ult.
- kind favor; order, etc.
- oblige
- our Mr. Clark
- permit me to say
- please be advised that
- pursuant to
- regarding your communication
- same
- thanking you in advance
- the writer wishes to say
- this letter is for the purpose inquiring
- trusting you will
- up to this writing
- we are; beg; remain; etc.
- wish to say; advise; inform; a knowledge; etc.
- would ask; state; advise; etc.

To illustrate the improvement that results when stilted phraseolog is eliminated, take the following example of a business letter a originally written and then as rewritten:

(Stilted and Verbose)

Dear Sir:

Replying to your kind favor of the 15th inst. in which you inform u that the enameling sheets ordered by you have not come to hand, beg t advise we have checked up on this shipment and find same left our fac tory March 10 and should have reached you March 13. For your infor mation wish to state that we are now tracing through the express com pany. If the shipment does not arrive by March 19, kindly wire us col lect, and we will duplicate same.

Regretting the inconvenience caused you, we are,

Yours truly,

(Clear and Straightforward)

Dear Mr. Bradley:

Your letter of March 15 reached us this morning.

The shipment of enameling sheets left our factory on March 10, and should have been delivered to you not later than March 13. We have asked the express company to trace the shipment immediately.

If you do not receive the sheets by March 19, please wire us collect, and we will start another shipment at once.

We are sorry this delay occurred and assure you that we will do everything possible to expedite delivery.

Very truly yours,

It will be noted that the second letter contains exactly the same ormation as the first. The improvement in tone is brought about t by the addition of any new material but merely by the elimina-n of stilted phraseology.

Use short sentences and paragraphs. Lack of clarity, the cardi-l sin of business writing, results chiefly from the use of involved iguage and long sentences. The contents of a business letter ould be apparent at a glance. To make the letter easy to read and preclude misunderstanding, use simple words and short sentences, d paragraph wherever a new subject is introduced.

(CONFUSED AND WORDY)

entlemen:

Replying to your letter of October 15, with reference to our carload ipment of September 11, in which you received a five-gallon can of ollodion with a nail driven into the can through the wooden case, which sulted in contents leaking out and running down onto a couple of cases of by 14 Duplitized X-Ray Film Super Speed in six-dozen packages, stain-g fifteen of the boxes; wish to advise that the cartons for the film were ipped to you by parcel post on October 27, which we hope you will ceive without delay. We regret very much the accident of the nail eing driven through the case, and have called it to the attention of the ippers of this material and asked them to be very careful on future ipments.

Very truly yours,

(CLEAR AND STRAIGHTFORWARD)

entlemen:

We regret very much the damage caused by the punctured can of Col-odion, to which you referred in your letter of October 15. On October 7 we sent you by express another can of Collodion and new cartons to place those which were damaged.

We have taken up the matter of the punctured can with our shipping epartment, and also with the carrier, and assure you that every effort vill be made to insure the safe arrival of future shipments.

Very truly yours,

Avoid unnecessary words and phrases. A common fault in letter vriting is to add unnecessary words and phrases to give emphasis or ound out a sentence. For example, letter writers frequently speak of "*final* completion," "*month* of January," or "*close* proximity."

The completion must be final or it is not complete; January must a month; incidents in proximity must be close. Here is a list some padded phrases frequently used in business letters. The *it cized* words are *totally* unnecessary.

It came *at a time* when we were busy.
Leather depreciates *in value* slowly.
During *the year of* 1947.
It will cost *the sum of* one hundred dollars.
At a meeting *held* in Philadelphia.
We will ship these shoes *at a* later *date*.
In about two weeks' *time*.
The mistake *first began* because of a misunderstanding.
A *certain* person by the name of Bill Jones.
It happened at *the hour of noon*.
We see some good in both *of them*.
In *the city of* Columbus.
The body is made *out* of steel.
During the *course of the* campaign.
Perhaps it may be that you are reluctant.
Our uniform *and invariable* rule is.
Somebody *or other* must be responsible.
We are now *engaged in* building a new plant.
By *means of* this device we are able.
The radio sells at *a price of* $200.

Do not use two words with the same meaning for emphasi Some letter writers think that if one word does a job, two words ac emphasis. Actually, the second word makes the thought less effe tive. Here are a few examples of "doubling."

sincere and good wishes
the first and foremost
appraise and determine the worth-while things
deeds and actions
feeling of optimism and encouragement
we refuse and decline
unjust and unfair manner
advised and informed
at once and by return mail
we demand and insist
right and proper consideration
assume obligation or responsibility

Avoid overworking favorite words or expressions. Letter writer frequently overwork their favorite words or expressions. For exam e, a correspondent who habitually uses "records" will say in one ter, "According to our records, the grace period will expire Mony," and in another, "The enclosed is for your records." The way overcome this fault is for the letter writer first to detect his favorite pressions by examining several of his letters, and second, to notice how many cases the expression can be eliminated entirely or reaced by a simple word. In the first illustration, the expression rves no purpose. In the second, it would be better to say, "The nclosed copy is for you."

Do not use big words. Some people think that a large vocabulary f big words makes them seem learned; but simple, short words do ne best job. This statement does not mean that a larger vocabulary not an asset. The more words a writer has, the more clearly and orcibly he can express himself, but he never uses words of many yllables unless there is a reason for it. Why, in a business letter, ay "propertied interests" when you mean "rich people," or "annihiate" when you mean "wipe out," or "transcend" when you mean go beyond?"

A large vocabulary helps one to use different words to express arious shades of meaning. The writer with an adequate vocabulary vrites about the *aroma* of a cigar, the *fragrance* of a flower, the *scent* of perfume, the *odor* of gas, instead of the "smell" of all these things. There is a reason for using words of more than one syllable here.

Avoid words that antagonize. Words that carry uncomplimentary insinuations are not only tactless but they often defeat the purpose of the letter. Never use a word that might humiliate or belittle the reader. Here are some expressions from business letters *to avoid:*

"We do not understand your *failure* to pay this bill." (The insinuation is that the customer cannot be trusted to meet his obligations. Moreover, "failure" is a negative word. We all want our name and actions associated with success.)

"It seems strange that no other customer has mentioned this fault in our product." (You are implying that this one customer is unreasonable.)

"Certainly, you must *know* that we did not offer you any such concession." (He told you that he did not know. He must be a bold-faced liar.")

Use the positive approach. A positive approach is more forcef and effective than a negative one. Usually it is a simple matter change a negative thought to a positive one. The following exa ples show how simply this can be done.

Negative: We cannot quote you a price until we have seen the speci cations.

Positive: We shall be glad to quote you a price just as soon as we ha seen the specifications.

Negative: We cannot ship these goods before August 8.

Positive: We will ship the goods on or shortly after August 8.

How to open the letter. The opening sentence or paragraph the letter should generally go straight to the point, without an beating about the bush. The object is to gain the reader's attentio immediately.

In writing a letter of reply it is unnecessary to give a restatemen of the contents of the letter received. To state that the letter is i reply to one of such-and-such a date is sufficient. Participial oper ings, such as *Referring to your communication of, Answering you letter of, Replying to your letter of, In reply to yours of,* should b avoided. Some examples of poor and good openings follow; fo further examples, see the specimen letters given in each of the late parts of this section.

(POOR OPENING)

Dear Sir:

Replying to your letter of June 9 in which you request that we sen you samples of our new WEAREVER fabrics, we are asking our agent in Cleveland, John Brown & Company, to supply you with the sample requested, and they will be pleased to assist you in carrying out any test that you may wish to make.

(BETTER OPENING)

Dear Sir:

Thank you very much for your request of June 9 for samples of our new WEAREVER fabrics.

We have asked our agents in Cleveland, John Brown & Company, to supply you with a full line of samples. They will be glad to assist you in carrying out any tests you may wish to make.

(Poor Opening)

ear Sir:

In reply to yours of the 15th in which you state that you would be in-ested in receiving more complete information as to our STEADY-EAT OIL BURNER, as you are considering installing a burner in your me, we are enclosing a booklet describing the advantages of the 'EADY-HEAT which we think you will find of value and are also re-esting our local representative in your community, Wallace & Com-ny, to call upon you.

(Better Opening)

ear Sir:

We are glad to respond to your letter of April 15, in which you request ore complete information concerning the STEADY-HEAT OIL URNER.

The enclosed booklet, "Better Heat with STEADY-HEAT," discusses e many advantages of the STEADY-HEAT BURNER. We have also ked our representative in your community, Wallace & Company, to call pon you at your convenience. Wallace & Company will be pleased to ve you full information, without any obligation.

(Poor Opening)

ear Sir:

Answering your letter of April 5 in which you suggest that we take your 0-day note for our March invoice, we note what you say as to poor busi-ess conditions in Harrisburg at the present time due to the closing of everal local plants, but regret that it is not a practice with us to take otes.

(Better Opening)

Dear Sir:

We were very sorry to learn from your letter of April 5 that business onditions in Harrisburg have been poor in recent months. We can eadily appreciate that under the circumstances you will be having diffi-ulty in making collections.

Since it is not a practice with us to take notes, we are sorry that we annot agree to your suggestion. However, we are always glad to co-oper-te with our customers in every possible way and . . . .

A comparison of the "poor" and the "better" openings in the above examples shows the greater effectiveness of a short, clear-cut opening paragraph. The purpose of this opening paragraph is merely to state the subject of the letter, and perhaps to express a word or two of thanks, appreciation, or regret; the subject is then develop in the succeeding paragraphs. The chief fault of the "poor" exa ples is that they attempt to state the subject and to develop it one and the same time; openings such as these leave the reader me tally breathless.

How to close the letter. The closing paragraph or senten should add something to the letter; it need not be a meaningle formality. The better correspondents do not use participial closin such as the following:

Hoping to be favored with an early reply, we are,
Trusting that this will be satisfactory to you, we remain,
Trusting that you will let us hear from you if we can be of furth service,
Thanking you for your order, we remain,
Assuring you of our desire to please you, we are,
Hoping to receive your future orders, we remain,

A more forceful and sincere way of closing the business letter to use a complete sentence or a direct statement. Examples of th type of closing follow; for further examples of effective closings, se the specimen letters given in each of the later parts of this section.

We appreciate your interest and thank you for writing us.
We hope that this initial order is only the beginning of a long busines relationship, which we shall try to make both pleasant and profitable t you.
We are looking forward to pleasant business relations.
We sincerely hope that we may find your name on our active lis within the next thirty days.
Please do not hesitate to write us again if we can be of further servic to you.
We are always eager to make every transaction satisfactory. Please d not hesitate to write us at any time.
We very much regret the delay, and assure you that your future order will be handled promptly.

It is important to suggest only one action in closing a letter. The "divided urge" is one of the most serious faults the closing of a letter can have when the reader is expected to take some action. If he is given a choice of several things to do, he will probably do nothing. Tell the reader the *specific* action that he is to take. Concentrate upon *one* action and do not mention others.

In the following closings, the alternative suggestions tend to con- :e the reader; the specific suggestions are impelling and produce :ion.

Alternative Suggestions	*Specific Suggestions*
Write us a letter, telegraph, or ıd the enclosed card right now.	Send the enclosed card right now.
If it is convenient for you to see :, please drop me a note or call : at AL 4-9200.	When it is convenient for you to see me, please call me at AL 4-9200.
Please mail this payment to ar- 'e at our office within five days. : if you don't feel able to do that ›w, send us a post-dated check : the same amount.	Please mail this payment to arrive at our office within five days, which would be by Saturday.

If you expect the reader to take a certain action in the future, use *ıted action.* That is, tell the reader that you expect the action by given date, or within a certain number of days, not "in the near ıture." Here are two examples of dated action closings:

In order for us to handle this claim promptly for your patient, it will : necessary to have your preliminary report by the *end of this week.*

An *immediate reply by airmail* will enable us to complete the draft of ıe contract by Friday.

Use positive words in closing a letter. "Hope," "may," "if," and trust" tend to defeat the purpose of any business letter. Compare he following negative closings with the positive revisions.

Negative	*Positive*
If you will O.K. the card, we will ladly send you a copy of the bul- etin. *Trusting* you will do this,	Your copy of this interesting bulletin is waiting for you. Just O.K. and mail the card.
Now is the time when our cus- omers are stocking for summer usiness. We *trust* you will join hem, by placing your requirements n the order blank enclosed.	Now is the time when our customers are stocking for summer business. You can join them by placing your requirements on the order blank enclosed.

Methodical habits of dictation. It is not uncommon to see a correspondent pick up a letter, glance at it, and immediately begin to dictate a reply before having formed, either in his own mind or on paper, an outline of what he intends to say. A letter written this way can hardly be other than muddled. The writer probal starts with one thought, passes to a second, and then jumps back the first before going on to the third. The person who receives t letter is confused, perhaps irritated. And it goes without saying th loss of business results, for a person who has written an inquiry a receives a muddled letter in reply will doubtless turn elsewhere f any purchase that he wishes to make.

Methodical habits of dictation consist of gathering all the necessa information and visualizing the letter as a whole before beginning dictate the first paragraph. A simple procedure followed by ma of the best correspondents in handling complaints, inquiries, and forth, is to underscore the main points in the letter received and the to jot down rapidly at the foot of the page an outline of what th reply should contain. For example, suppose that a manufactur of electric irons has received an order for a single iron from a individual; he is compelled to refuse the order because he sells on through retail dealers. The outline of the reply in this case migh be as follows:

1. Thanks.
2. Sell only through dealers.
3. Returning check; visit or telephone dealer.
4. Name, address, and telephone number of dealer.
5. Guarantee.
6. Sales talk.

With this outline as a working basis, the correspondent woul proceed to dictate the letter.

Dear Mrs. Robertson:

Thank you very much for your order of November 5 for one of our new ELECTRA electric irons.

We sincerely appreciate this evidence of interest in the new ELECTRA and wish that we could fill your order. However, as manufacturers, we sell through retail dealers, and our arrangement with the dealers throughout the country does not permit our selling direct from the factory.

We regret, therefore, that we must return your check. May we suggest that you either visit or telephone the ELECTRA dealer in your city, who will be glad to deliver the iron at the price advertised. In buying from the dealer you will have the advantage of choosing from a large stock and will avoid the annoyance of possible delay in shipment.

The name, address, and telephone number of the ELECTRA dealer York is:

Polk Electrical Supply Company, 424 Main Street
Telephone: YORK 3200

Every ELECTRA is guaranteed by us, and also by the dealer, to be in rfect condition.

We hope that you will soon be numbered among the many thousands women who have found that with the new ELECTRA ironing is no nger a drudgery. The ELECTRA is easy to handle. It saves 30 per nt of the time needed when you use any other electric iron now on the arket.

To bring an ELECTRA to your home, simply pick up the telephone ıd call:

YORK 3200

Sincerely yours,

The above letter is a logical, clear reply to the request received. 'isualizing the letter as a whole and, if necessary, making an outline f it, is the work of a moment. It may be the means of saving the riter the embarrassment of realizing, when he is reading over the nished letter, that he has omitted an important point, or the further mbarrassment of receiving from the customer a second letter saying hat the reply is not clear.

Adapt the letter to the reader. Writing good business letters equires imagination. This is obviously true of sales letters but is ılso equally true of any other type. The most successful correspond-ents are those who are able to visualize the person to whom they ıre writing, to reconstruct his or her mode of living and habits of hought, and to adapt their letters to the reader. A letter suitable for ı small retailer in a town in the Middle West would not make a avorable impression on a large retailer in New York; a letter that one would send to a New England farmer would not do for an ıttorney in Chicago; a straight-from-the-shoulder, man-to-man letter would be absolutely wrong for a middle-aged spinster.

The question of adapting the letter to the reader can, of course, be ignored. More often than not it is ignored. By taking a safe middle stand a correspondent can write in exactly the same tone and spirit to anyone with whom his company does business, without giving offense. There is, however, the reverse side of the medal.

Letters written in such a way that they might be intended for anyo often have interest and appeal for no one in particular.

Every letter is a business opportunity. Even though the let may not be a sales letter in the sense that it is an attempt actua to sell goods, it should be a sales letter in the sense that it "sell goodwill and cements a cordial relationship. The question mu then, arise in the mind of the correspondent: "Considering the s tion in life, education, and other circumstances of this particul individual to whom I am about to write, what tone in my letter w be most likely to make for friendship between us—friendship th may, at a later date, result in sales?" If the letter is to a sm retailer, the correspondent may decide that a human, friendly lett showing interest in the retailer's business and perhaps offering hi advice would be most suitable. If the letter is to a large manufa turer, a concise, businesslike style might be most appropriate. If tl letter is to a farmer, a neighborly, gossipy tone may meet with tl best reception.

For most correspondents, of course, adaptation to the reader greatly simplified by the fact that the majority of the people to whor the company writes letters are of one class or type. The probler then resolves itself into experimenting with letters of different tor until the most appropriate one is found. The selection is determi able largely from the nature of the replies received to the lette mailed. When experiments of this kind are being made, persona preference and prejudice must be set aside. The correspondent fc a farm machinery company may be, personally, a man of cultur with an interest in the arts. He himself may prefer the forma well-written business letter. On the other hand, the farmers wh buy the company's machinery may respond more readily to letter beginning, "I was mighty glad, Mr. Hansen, to see from your lette of August 15 that the drought situation in Kansas is now clearing u a bit," rather than, "We are pleased to note from your letter o August 15 that the drought situation in Kansas is now somewha alleviated." The reader's psychology, and not the writer's, is th primary consideration.

Illustration of how to adapt the letter to the reader. To illus trate how the business letter may be adapted to the reader, the following two letters are given. In both cases the situation is the ame: the letters are replies to complaints, written by a correspondent n a large radio manufacturing company. In the first case, however, he complaint was received from a woman whose letter indicated hat she was well educated and had perhaps had business experience; he second was written—in pencil, on ruled paper, and with frequent misspellings—by, obviously, an uneducated customer. The correspondent's replies follow:

TO THE WOMAN

Dear Mrs. Ashton:

We were very sorry to learn from your letter of January 6 that the reception on your TRUETONE RADIO has not been entirely satisfactory.

As manufacturers of this radio we take pride in its reputation for reliable, quality performance. We therefore guarantee every TRUETONE against mechanical defect for a period of one year from the date of purchase.

If you will return the radio to us by parcel post insured or by express insured, we shall be glad to give it a thorough examination and to remedy whatever defect is causing the "fading" mentioned in your letter. The charge for this service will be only $1. This fee covers merely the handling and shipping costs; we make no charge for labor or for any new parts that may be necessary.

To protect the radio against possible damage in transit, please pack it in the original carton, if you still have this, and merely enclose $1. The radio will be returned to you within three days after we receive it.

We appreciate very much your writing us direct and assure you of our desire that you derive full satisfaction from ownership of your TRUETONE.

Very truly yours,

TO THE UNEDUCATED CUSTOMER

Dear Mr. Petersen:

I was mighty sorry to see from your letter of January 6 that your TRUETONE RADIO has been acting up. As you say, it shouldn't do this, being only three months old.

What I wish you would do is pack it up and send it right back to me. Whatever is the matter with it, we'll fix it here in the factory. Every TRUETONE is guaranteed by us for one year from the day you buy it.

When you send the radio, pack it in the box that it was in when you bought it, and put a $1 bill in the box. This $1 is all that you will have to pay, no matter what is wrong with the radio. It covers just the cost of packing the radio and sending it back to you. We pay for the workman's time and for any new parts that have to be put in. That's fair enough, isn't it?

Mail the box by parcel post insured, and we'll send you back the radi three days after we get it.

We want you to know that we're glad you wrote us, and we'll see tha your TRUETONE is fixed right.

Yours truly,

Possibly the foregoing letters are an extreme example of contrast in tone. They may, however, be taken as an illustration of the possibilities in adapting the letter to the reader. The woman would probably be favorably impressed by the courteous tone of the letter written to her; the uneducated customer would doubtless be glad to receive, in reply to his complaint, a letter that he could understand. If the correspondent had written to both parties merely in a standardized tone, two opportunities for creating goodwill would have been lost.

In conclusion, a word of warning may not be out of place. There is danger in generalizing as to which tone to adopt in addressing a particular class. The correspondent must therefore be guided by the character of the letter received from the person to whom he is writing.

3. MAKING ANSWERS TO INQUIRIES PRODUCE SALES

(See "How to Write Sales Letters" beginning at page 58.)

How to answer an inquiry. The following are the chief points to keep in mind in replying to letters of inquiry:

1. Answer inquiries promptly—if possible, within twenty-four hours. To secure the inquirer's business or to make a sale, you must strike while the iron is hot. Should it be necessary to refuse the request, a prompt reply will create goodwill and may result in your name being favorably remembered by the inquirer for future reference. Your business reputation is built upon the small, day-to-day experiences of the people who have contact with you.

2. Every inquiry is a sales opportunity. Your reply should therefore be courteous, helpful, and should show a desire to serve. Because the inquirer's interest is likely to have waned rapidly in the interval before your reply reaches him, it is necessary for you to revive

is interest by reselling him on your product or service. For this urpose, include sales talk in your reply.

3. Although the reply to an inquiry should be a selling letter, it hould first answer specifically and clearly the question that was sked. Nothing is more irritating to an inquirer than to receive a eply which does not answer his question.

4. Most inquiries are incomplete and sketchy. At the time that e is writing, the inquirer probably knows very little about your roduct or service. You should therefore not restrict yourself to nswering the one or two questions that it occurred to him to ask. Try to anticipate other points that may not be clear.

5. Open by thanking the inquirer for his letter and for his interest n your goods. Close by assuring him that you will be glad to be of service to him and to supply him with any additional information hat he may need.

The letter that accompanies booklets. You have already secured the prospect's attention when you have succeeded in getting him to send in a request for booklets. The letter accompanying the booklet is an out-and-out sales letter. Notice how the following etter moves from the direct inquiry to sales material.

Dear Mr. Benson:

Thank you for your request for our new booklets, VARIADEX and TRIPLE CHECK AUTOMATIC. Your copies are being mailed today.

You will find these booklets unusually interesting in their description of Remington Rand's two new filing systems. VARIADEX and TRIPLE CHECK AUTOMATIC are scientifically designed to handle efficiently and economically the complex filing procedure in the modern business office.

You may be concerned with the problem of how to increase speed in file operation, how to eliminate wasteful errors in filing and finding, or how to handle peculiar lists or an unusual volume of correspondence. Whatever your problem, one of these two new filing systems will give you a practical solution.

After you have read these two booklets, you will be interested in seeing an actual demonstration in your office of the system you believe most suited to your purpose. If you wish, a Remington Rand representative will also make an analysis of your filing situation and will recommend the system that can give you the best possible service from your files.

A demonstration of either VARIADEX or TRIPLE CHECK AUTOMATIC will be given you, or an analysis of your files will be made for you, entirely without obligation. Please write or phone the Remingto Rand office at 205 East 42 Street, Murrayhill 4-5000.

Very truly yours,

An answer to a request for more information. Here is an ex ample of an answer to a request for more information about a proc uct. The inquirer asked no specific question; hence the letter is general sales letter. If specific information were called for, this pa ticular letter would not be satisfactory.

Dear Doctor Brown:

Your desire to know more about Anabolic Products is good news to us and we look forward to welcoming you to our ever-growing family c doctors.

You will find no mystery about Anabolic Products—we have no "secret ingredients—and you will find our literature entirely free from sensation alism. The rationale of Anabolic Supplemental Nutrition is far fron difficult.

As a means of acquainting you with our products most in demand, am enclosing a bulletin entitled, "Simplicity Itself." In every case, yo will note that the complete ingredients are given—with Anabolic yo know what you are using. May I suggest that you slip this bulletin unde the blotter on your desk where it will be convenient for quick reference

We feel justified in stressing the quality of Anabolic Products sinc our vegetables are grown in tested soil, fertilized by our own chemica fertilizers, and dehydrated by a method on which we hold exclusive right and patents. Our glandular ingredients are the finest obtainable—neve cold storage—and our vitamin concentrates are standardized by biologica assay.

Your questions are invited, and your orders will be given every attention.

Cordially yours,
ANABOLIC FOODS, Inc.

Giving further information. Some inquiries reveal doubt in the prospect's mind as to some feature of the product. The reply in such cases must convince the reader that the product meets his needs or desires. The following letter stresses quality to convince the reader that the particular product is superior to others:

Dear Mr. Benson:

It is quite true, just as you say, that sheet steel and ARMCO INGOT IRON look alike on the surface. Careful examination under the microscope, however, reveals a vast difference.

In general, when you select articles, you rely upon sight and touch to etermine the quality. Take clothing, for instance: the "feel" of the oth will tell whether the material is all wool as well as a yard wide. Vhen you buy shoes, the "feel" again comes into play and discloses hether the leather is of coarse or fine texture.

With metals, however, sight and touch cannot reveal the true quality. 'he quality of metal is determined by the degree of scientific skill used ı the elimination of impurities.

Here is a simple illustration that brings out the point: you have one efective apple in a barrel of prize winners, and what happens? You ither throw out the decaying apple or lose all.

And so it is with sheet metal. The elements that produce decay, or ust, in ferrous metals are carbon, sulphur, phosphorus, manganese, silion, and the gases—oxygen, hydrogen, and nitrogen. These detrimental lements must be entirely eliminated if possible. If not completely eliminated, they must be reduced to the smallest possible degree.

Here is where ARMCO INGOT IRON excels all other sheet metals. The impurities named are guaranteed not to exceed 16/100 of one per ent. No other sheet manufacturer can give you this guarantee.

It is the pure metal in ARMCO INGOT IRON that will make your oof last longer, because pure iron will resist rust.

Very truly yours,

Letters accompanying catalogues. A request for a catalogue is a step toward a future sale. The tie-up between the enclosure and the letter should be made vital and stimulating. The following letters have a conversational tone that brings the reader close to the vendor:

Dear Mr. Donald:

We were glad to receive your inquiry. The enclosed catalogue of the SUPER ELTO for 19— will give you the information you want on our motor.

But catalogues are funny things—each year we labor intensely to compress between the two covers everything we thing you might want to know about the ELTO—and everything we want you to know, as well. But a catalogue seems never to be more—than a catalogue. It seems always to leave untold a lot of things you'd appreciate knowing.

As you read through it, you'll notice that we strongly emphasize a certain few points about the SUPER ELTO. Quarter-turn starting, as a particular example:

> The plain fact is, we know of nothing more important than this matter of easy starting—easy starting in the genuine, honest sense of the word. Before everything else—before every trip you make, through every year of its use, you must *start* your motor. And on

starting, more than anything else, will depend your satisfaction and pleasure.

But even easy starting should not overshadow other ELTO qualitie For the ELTO has feature after feature far too sound and valuable to b subordinated.

Rudder steering, for instance. One of our users wrote us that "rudde steering *gives brains to the motor!*"

It does seem that way! It's twice as pleasant for the user when he ca sit where he pleases, changing his course with a gentle tug on a vibration less tiller line, letting that rudder do about nine tenths of his steering fo him.

Then there is the Propello-Pump—the huge bearings—the Safet Cushion Drive and . . . .

But it's time to let the catalogue tell its own story. Only, as w pointed out before, a catalogue is just a catalogue. If you find a singl question left unanswered, or want fuller information on any point, pleas write us. We'll answer as fully as we possibly can.

Cordially yours,

* * *

Dear Mr. Muirhead:

You made us feel mighty good when we received your request for our proposition, and we know that you are going to be glad that you wrote, for the rugs that we have for this year's selling are the finest in the field, and the best that we have ever produced.

The catalogue which we are sending you tells our story of weaves, patterns, and profit opportunities in an interesting way, while our prices, as shown on the attached list, are as good as you will find our rugs to be.

But don't forget, in considering the prices, that they are list prices. From these you secure a trade discount of 10-5% off. After deducting this percentage from the lists, you get net prices that are as low as can be secured anywhere. There are none better.

Then, too, we allow the full cost of your freight on all orders that weigh 100 pounds or more (except for Deltone and Tufted Rugs, which are f.o.b. the mill). This policy eliminates the bother of adding freight costs to your merchandise costs after arrival of the goods, which we know you will say is a big help.

Our representative, Mr. Peters, will visit with you within the next thirty days, but if you desire to order before he calls, just drop your specification in the mail box with the assurance that we will give it speedy attention.

With best good wishes,

Sincerely yours,

Answering a letter from a retailer. Where a company distributes its product through a wholesale distributor, it must gently inform the retailer of this fact and at the same time keep in mind the possibility of the retailer becoming a dealer. The following letter covers this situation:

Dear Mr. Stephens:

Immediately upon receipt of your letter of November 8 asking about the CROSLEY LINE, we wrote our wholesale distributor, The Homer King Company, 711 Broadway, Tacoma, Washington, and asked them either to call on you or write you to explain our terms and discounts.

Inasmuch as we have placed wholesale distributors in most of the large centers so that your needs can be more promptly served, we do not sell direct to retailers.

Will you please fill in on the enclosed application blank your name, address, primary business, and the number of sets that you believe will sell in your community? If the wholesale distributor named above does not write you or call upon you within the next five days, please return the application blank direct to us.

We want you to know that we appreciate your interest in the CROSLEY LINE and that we hope your name can be included among the many dealers in your state who are finding CROSLEY their most profitable line.

Very truly yours,

Sending a representative with samples. Sometimes a request is best answered by sending a representative. The following letter shows one large company's method of utilizing a sales possibility in its answer to a request for samples:

Dear Mr. Thompson:

Thank you for your request for samples of our REMCRAFT folder.

We have asked a representative of our branch office, which is listed below, to supply you with samples of REMCRAFT so that you may test them in your own office.

When he delivers these samples, our representative will welcome an opportunity to offer suggestions on any of your filing problems.

Very truly yours,

Letters refusing requests. A letter of this type should be courteous, should explain clearly the reasons for the refusal, and should express regret. It may close with a sales talk about the product.

Dear Sir:

As requested in your letter of January 9, I am glad to send you a cop of the issue of January 2. Please accept it with our compliments.

I also wish to thank you for your kind words for our magazine, bu since our publications are made especially for national advertisers anc advertising agencies, we are prevented from accepting subscriptions out side this field.

In selecting our prospects for subscriptions, we are careful to pick ou only those who are actually advertising in some form. Our experienc has been that readers outside of our field find little of interest in th magazine, and discontinue as soon as their subscriptions are up.

We therefore seek only what we call "logical" subscribers.

I feel quite certain that you will understand our position, but I wan you to know that your interest is very much appreciated.

Very sincerely yours,

* * *

Dear Miss Robson:

Because each woman's search for youth and beauty is an individual problem, it necessarily requires individual attention.

We therefore do not find the use of set formulas suitable for the requirements of our customers. We are sorry that we do not have any of the booklets you requested us to send you.

Why not see your nearest DOROTHY DALE representative for a personal analysis of your beauty problems, and be sure that you are using the course of treatment exactly suited to your type of beauty?

Very truly yours,

* * *

Dear Mr. Ward:

We appreciate very much your order of July 16, but regret that we are unable to accept it because of our established merchandising policy.

Our policy is to grant an exclusive agency for the sale of our products in towns that have a population of 25,000 or less.

This arrangement assures the retailer a very profitable trade. We already have an established agency in your city.

Although no change is contemplated at present, we take pleasure in keeping your name in our files, and assure you that we appreciate your interest in our products.

Very truly yours,

4. REVIVING INACTIVE ACCOUNTS THROUGH LETTERS

Bringing inactive customers back to life. A study * of why customers stop buying at a particular store shows that of every 100 whose accounts are inactive:

68 have drifted away because of store indifference toward them;
14 have stopped buying because of unadjusted grievances;
9 have transferred their patronage to a competitor who offers lower prices or better service;
5 have been influenced by friends to trade elsewhere;
3 have moved, taking their business to more convenient shopping centers, or have made other arrangements more convenient or economical;
1 is dead or unaccounted for.

This record shows that not every inactive account is a lost account. Remove indifference to customers by letters containing words of encouragement and showing individual attention, and many of the inactive accounts will show signs of life. A warm, personal tone is essential in letters to revive inactive accounts. The customer must be made to feel that he has been missed. If his absence is due to dissatisfaction, he must be won over by the expression of a sincere desire on the part of the store to remove the dissatisfaction.

In letters calling attention to the inactive status of the account, it is sometimes effective to mention some special event to stimulate interest. For example, the arrival of new merchandise, price reductions, and the like, may add pulling power to the letter.

A single letter may be effective to regain a substantial part of the inactive accounts. Frequently, however, a series of letters is used. Examples of both kinds are given below.

Series to persons who opened accounts and made no purchases. The following three letters, used by Ovington's, New York, consti-

---

* The findings of this survey, as tabulated above, are listed as authentic by Jules J. Paglin in "The Direct Mail Approach in the Retail Market," *The Reporter Study Course in Direct Mail Advertising* (Henry Hoke, Editor), and by Freida E. Burger, of Namm Store, Brooklyn, New York, in "Reviving Inactive Accounts," *The Credit World*, February, 1937.

tute an effective series to individuals who opened accounts and mad no purchases on credit:

Dear Mr. Johnston:

We had the pleasure of opening an account for you some time ago But you have not made use of it, and so we're sending along this not with the hope that you will do so soon—and often.

We'll be very grateful if you do.

Sincerely,

* * *

Dear Mr. Johnston:

We do not wish to appear persistent with reference to the charge ac count you opened with us, but we are concerned that you have not mad use of it. May I inquire whether, by any chance, this has come abou by some error on our part? I should be very glad to hear from you.

Sincerely,

* * *

Dear Mr. Johnston:

As indicated in a previous letter, it pleased us greatly when you opened a charge account with us. However, you have not used it, and we're won dering whether it is through any fault of ours. If so, we wish that you would frankly tell us.

And, of course, if you simply overlooked it, won't you accept this as a little reminder that we're anxious to serve you?

Sincerely,

Letters to old customers who have not been using their accounts. When a desirable account has been inactive for several months, it may often be brought to life by one or more letters similar to the following:

Dear Mrs. Arnsman:

Your account has not been used for several months, and we are anxious to know the reason. Of course, you may have been away or not had an opportunity to visit the store. However, if your absence is due to any fault of ours, we wish you would give us this opportunity to make it right.

Every one of our Six Sales Floors is teeming with the newest and smartest apparel, things for the home and newest Spring merchandise, at prices which make this indeed a store of moderate price.

We want you to know that your charge account is at your disposal, and we hope you will soon take advantage of its convenience.

We appreciate your past patronage, and want to do all we can to help you enjoy your visits here.

Very truly yours,

* * *

Dear Mrs. Schmuck:

For over 65 years we have enjoyed the patronage of the people of Quincy and many other places in this vicinity. As we grow older, we appreciate more and more the importance of keeping old friends.

We have found that you have not made any purchases through your charge account for some time, and, if it is due to any failure of ours, we wish that you would write us or tell us about it so that we may improve our service to you.

Foremost of all our assets, we place the goodwill and the friendship of our customers, and we sincerely hope that we may have the opportunity to serve you in the very near future.

Very sincerely,

* * *

Dear Mrs. Brown:

Your account has just been placed on my desk, showing that it has not been used for some time. Naturally I am concerned and wonder why you have not used it recently.

Sometimes something happens in our service that displeases a customer. We rarely hear of this in the credit department. Will you take just a minute of your time and tell us if we have failed somewhere along the line? We sincerely miss you as a valuable charge customer, and, now that Easter is so near, I hope to receive a report that you have used your account again.

Speaking of Easter. Have you seen the new Spring things ready for you in our Fashion Centers? This is a special invitation to call. You may use either your monthly charge or our convenient Budget Plan for your purchases. Our merchandise is moderately priced and styled in the usual Brock manner—of course.

I want to take this opportunity to thank you for the privilege of having served you in the past. I hope the Bookkeeping Department will advise me soon that your account is again active. This would please me very much.

Cordially yours,

Letters to find out why good customers have not purchased. Where there is reason to believe that the customer has ceased purchasing because of some dissatisfaction, a letter such as the following may be used:

Dear Mr. Kirk:

If, one of these days, you should discover that a mighty good friend o yours had suddenly stopped visiting you without apparent cause, yo would want to know why, wouldn't you? You can readily understanc then, our concern at not having heard from you for several months.

Although we have always done the very best we could to meet you requirements, being human, we may have fallen down in some particula If this is so, won't you please let us know?

You can rest assured that, whatever the trouble was, we will mak things right. We shall not feel that we are a success until your accoun bears evidence that you are again one of our regular customers.

Very truly yours,

* * *

Dear Mr. Beebe:

In checking through our sales records today, I noticed that you haven' given our salesman an order for merchandise for a considerable time.

Every day our stocks are being augmented with new items that will b of much interest to your customers and profitable for you to handle. hope that it will be convenient for you to give our salesman an order th next time he calls.

We value your business highly, and it occurs to me that we, in som manner, have not served you properly. I would appreciate your usin the enclosed envelope to tell me why our salesman has not been gettin your business.

Sincerely yours,

* * *

Dear Mr. Jones:

Each year we have a sort of "housecleaning" of our office files, and I was surprised when I found that your name was not among our customers for the winter just past.

I wonder, Mr. Jones, if we have fallen down somewhere in our service to you in the past?

Naturally, we like to keep our customers. So if something has happened to cause you to buy elsewhere, we would like to know about it, and to do what we can to make things right.

Give us a ring, Mr. Jones, and let's talk it over.

Sincerely yours,

* * *

Dear Mrs. Allaway:

Just a friendly note to tell you that we have missed you. . . . Your charge account has not been used for several months, and we are wondering why.

This is the time of year when a Forman charge account should serve :s best purposes . . . a season of special opportunities!

You can tell by the calendar that winter is here . . . social festivities ave begun . . . Thanksgiving and Christmas are coming apace! Your harge account fits this program like the proverbial glove!

It is yours to use . . . and it applies to this store and this season with pecial emphasis because Forman's devotes all its thought and energy o the things that make a woman's world!

We want you to have all the advantages that Forman's can offer in he way of fashion and value . . . we want to make your charge account erve you in the most practical and personal way!

So we cordially invite you!

And we invite you also, if our service in the past has been anything ess than completely satisfactory, to tell us frankly. We like to know ur shortcomings . . . so that we can correct them. No postage will be equired when you use the enclosed envelope, and we'll appreciate hearng from you.

Sincerely yours,

* * *

)ear Mr. Smith:

Our records show that it has been some time since you last visited our ervice department. We are wondering whether the service you received vas entirely satisfactory? Whether the work was well done; your car eady when promised? Did you receive courteous attention?

Our service manager is anxious to demonstrate to you what an efficient lepartment he is operating; how he can save you money on your regular pecials. He will tell you how we give fifteen dollars worth of oiling and reasing for ten dollars.

We will be pleased to call for and deliver your car at no additional harge.

We await an opportunity to be of service to you, and add your name o our growing list of satisfied customers.

Yours very truly,

* * *

)ear Mrs. Spellman:

The faint heart that ne'er won the fair lady of old wouldn't do a very hriving grocery business in this day and age.

For we realize it's not enough to supply clean, fresh, dependable foods t the right price. Besides that, a grocer must be willing to render the xtra measure of service to make and keep friends. He must possess the ourage to ask *why* when one whose friendship and business he values tops trading with him.

So we wish you would tell us with the same frankness: What has hap- pened to break our past relationship? If it has been due to any fault of ours, we'd like to know about it and correct it immediately.

Just a few lines on the back of this letter will be enough. The en- closed postage-paid envelope is for your convenience.

With every assurance of our appreciation of this courtesy, let us leav the reminder that your account here is always good—that you will receiv the best telephone-delivery service we can possibly render—and that w will be glad indeed to serve you again.

Hopefully yours,

Old customers return after receiving checkup letter. Busi- nesses selling a product or a service that has a limited life will in- crease sales by writing to customers about the time that renewa should be made. Such a follow-up shows desire to serve, efficiency and progressiveness. Here is a letter that brings repeat busines to the Haskin Optical Company, optometrists and manufacturing opticians of Miami, Florida.

As a vital service to my patients, careful records are kept of all exami- nations, the condition of the eyes, and the date when a checkup should be made.

This is to remind you that an examination of your eyes should be made at this time, as it has been over two years since they were examined.

To safeguard previous work and to insure future good vision and ap- pearance, an appointment is desirable now.

Please telephone 2-5526.

Sincerely yours,

Stunt letters to revive inactive accounts. The stunt letter has been used with considerable success in reviving inactive accounts. A couple of these letters are illustrated in Figures 51 and 52.

Cottrell's Clothing Store of Denver used a "doghouse" letter effec- tively. The first page of the letter, which is of greeting-card size, and is mailed in a plain white envelope, hand-addressed, shows the front of a doghouse. The door of the house is cut out and through it peers a homely but likeable bulldog. Beneath the house is the caption, "Are We in the Doghouse?" The third page shows the same bulldog in between two messages, which read:

"It's Been a Long Time

. . . since you have used your account with us and we're wondering

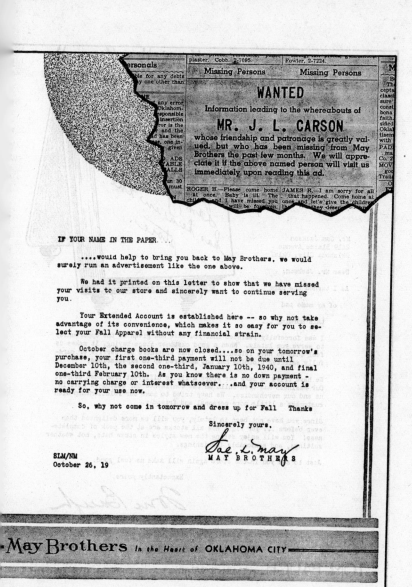

Missing Persons Missing Persons

WANTED

Information leading to the whereabouts of

MR. J. L. CARSON

whose friendship and patronage is greatly valued, but who has been missing from May Brothers the past few months. We will appreciate it if the above named person will visit us immediately upon reading this ad.

ROGER B.—Please come home at once. Baby is ill. The children and I have missed you ... will be forgiven.

JAMES R.—I am sorry for all that happened. Come home at once and let's give the children ...

IF YOUR NAME IN THE PAPER....

....would help to bring you back to May Brothers, we would surely run an advertisement like the one above.

We had it printed on this letter to show that we have missed your visits to our store and sincerely want to continue serving you.

Your Extended Account is established here -- so why not take advantage of its convenience, which makes it so easy for you to select your Fall Apparel without any financial strain.

October charge books are now closed....so on your tomorrow's purchase, your first one-third payment will not be due until December 10th, the second one-third, January 10th, 1940, and final one-third February 10th. As you know there is no down payment - no carrying charge or interest whatsoever....and your account is ready for your use now.

So, why not come in tomorrow and dress up for Fall Thanks

Sincerely yours,

Sae L. May

MAY BROTHERS

SLM/NM
October 26, 19

May Brothers *In the Heart of* OKLAHOMA CITY

Figure 51. A Cleverly Personalized Stunt Letter to Inactive Patrons.

Mr. Sam Jackson
2419 Blaine Avenue
Oklahoma City, Okla.

Dear Mr. Jackson:

As I turned the page

of my memo pad

this morning ...

I was forcefully reminded that you have not given us the opportunity to serve you lately. When a good customer stops buying, it makes us feel that we have fallen down -- that somewhere our service or carefully selected clothing has not measured up to expectations.

We have tried to make our store a little different from most stores. Our business has been built on the confidence our customers have in us and our merchandise. We have tried to make our relationship with customers a little more personal and friendly.

Since you have not been in lately, you will be more delighted than ever before ... for right now all stocks are at the peak of completeness! You will enjoy seeing the new styles in straw hats, hot weather suitings, and seasonable furnishings.

Just to see you in the store again will make us feel good.

Expectantly yours,

TOM BAUGH - Men's Wear

TOM BAUGH • MEN'S WEAR • 117 NORTH ROBINSON PERRINE BUILDING
OKLAHOMA CITY, OKLAHOMA

Figure 52. A Cleverly Personalized Stunt Letter to Inactive Patrons.

if we are 'in the Doghouse' with you. We would appreciate hearing from you."

nd:

Won't You Stop In

. . . and see our new styles in clothing, hats, and furnishings. We have some exceptional values at this time, too."

ollowed by the store's name and address.

5. LETTERS THAT BUILD GOODWILL

Points that help make goodwill letters effective. In the sec-ion on "Tone and Spirit of the Letter" some fundamental prin-ciples of good letter writing were given. In addition to applying hese principles to the letter that aims specifically at creating good-will, the letter writer should give attention to the following points:

1. Give the envelope an individual personality by individually typewriting the address.
2. Send the letter first class so that it arrives sealed.
3. Avoid printed indicia, since these smack of mass mailings and lithographed form letters.
4. Use a good-quality paper to give the letter importance.
5. Have the letter paper and envelope match.
6. Give the letter eye appeal. See the section on "Making the Structural Parts of a Letter Perfect."
7. Be certain that the details of the inside address are absolutely correct. Calling a person by an incorrect name, addressing him as "Mr." when he is a "Dr.," and errors in his address will annoy the reader and hurt the letter as an ambassador of goodwill.
8. Make the letter personal in the salutation by using the expression *Dear Mr. Jones,* instead of the impersonal *Dear Sir, Dear Madam,* and the like.
9. Make the letter radiate warmth, friendship, and sincerity.
10. In closing the letter, use terms that harmonize with a warm personal tone, such as *Very sincerely yours, Yours sincerely, Cordially yours,* and the like.
11. Wherever possible, have the goodwill letter signed by someone in authority. A letter signed by the President, Vice-President,

General Manager, or other ranking officer will create more goodwill than one that is signed by a person holding a modest title or no title at all.

Holding and Increasing Goodwill of Established Customers

Old customers need attention. More and more companies are coming to realize that they have been taking their regular patrons for granted and by so doing have been overlooking opportunities to retain the goodwill of steady customers. They go after the accounts that they have lost with letters to recapture goodwill, but while the account is alive, neglect to write letters that will keep it from becoming inactive. Business affords many opportunities for writing to old customers with the purpose of building goodwill. Some of these opportunities and the letters that have been written for the purpose are given in this section.

Appreciation for patronage. A few words thanking an old customer for his patronage can be written at any time. Such letters should be completely friendly and should express in simple, direct language that "rings" true the sincere appreciation of the sender. They should by no means include any sales talk. Here are some examples:

Dear Mr. Belden:

This is the kind of letter that I am most happy to write, because I am taking this means of thanking you for your constant choice of the Palmer House as your home in Chicago.

Your name ranks high among those of our loyal and distinguished "repeat" clientele who, year after year, give us definite proof that we are setting the pace of hotel leadership in Chicago. It is to friends like you that we owe the success of the Palmer House.

And so I wish to express my sincere appreciation of your patronage and to assure you that we shall continue to do everything within our power to maintain our present standards of service, cuisine, and furnishings.

Thank you again.

Very sincerely yours,

Appreciation for meeting obligations promptly. When a customer has met all his obligations under an installment purchase, a letter thanking him and inviting him to continue to use the credit facilities of the company will help build goodwill.

Dear Mr. Gould:

Your fully paid Accommodation Coupon Book account has just been placed upon my desk, and I am writing to thank you personally for the satisfactory manner in which you cared for this responsibility.

We hope to enjoy the privilege of serving you again within the very near future. Our facilities of credit are always at your disposal.

Very truly yours,

A "thank you" for prompt payment. An occasional word of gratitude for prompt payment will be appreciated and long remembered. A "thank-you" letter is one way of building goodwill. The following letter is an example:

Dear Mrs. Walters:

Time does have a way of passing, doesn't it? And we are apt to forget the part you and many others have contributed to our pleasant relations during the past year. It seems most of us are inclined to remember the less pleasant contacts we have experienced, and often overlook the happy ones.

As we close another year, we again recall that the dependable customer, who pays promptly, many times seems to go unnoticed. You have definitely placed yourself in this class, and if we did not send at least one letter expressing our sincere appreciation, we should doubtless appear ungrateful.

It has been a pleasure and privilege to have your account on our books, and your record sets a high standard for others to attain. We look forward to a mutually pleasant and profitable year during 19—.

Very sincerely yours,

A "thank-you" letter for a large order. This type of goodwill letter falls in the class of acknowledgment of orders and is treated along with other acknowledgments on page 576, *et seq*.

Thanking an old customer for a recommendation. A customer who has recommended your company and brought you a new customer deserves a letter of appreciation. Since such letters are not common in business, they are appreciated and remembered. The following letter shows how simply such a message of gratitude can be expressed:

Dear Mr. Fleming:

This afternoon, when Mr. Walter Pearson purchased a new Standard portable typewriter, he told me that your recommendation had been an important factor in his decision.

I am very glad, Mr. Fleming, that your experience with your Standard portable has been like that of thousands of other Standard owners. The highest compliment you could pay our product was your recommendation of it to a friend.

Mr. Pearson will get a great deal of service and satisfaction from his new Standard, and I am confident he will thank you again and again for recommending this splendid machine. And I want to thank you, too, for your faith in our product and in our organization. We appreciate your friendship and shall always try our best to merit your confidence.

Cordially yours,

Seasonal greetings build goodwill. The holiday season at the end of the year is an ideal opportunity to strengthen friendship through a letter of seasonal greeting. Like the letter of "thank you" for patronage, it should omit any sales message. The letter which best reflects a genuine spirit of friendship is a natural, informal note written with some living person in mind. The following message is an example of a goodwill builder. Such a letter can be written either on plain letterhead or on paper decorated in holiday style.

Dear Mr. Pollack:

Thirty years ago, when this business was founded, I used to enjoy a friendly chat with each of our patrons at this season of the year.

But the rapid growth which has made this a larger, better organization has necessarily deprived me of the opportunity to shake hands with all our friends—to thank them personally for their confidence and goodwill, and to wish them the best of everything at this holiday season.

I am well aware of the substantial part you have played in making 19. . such a successful year for us, and I wish to express my deep gratitude for your friendship and patronage.

And since I have not had a chance to greet you personally and wish you a Merry Christmas, I take this occasion to do so by letter. I sincerely hope that Christmas at your house will prove a fitting climax for 19. ., and that the coming year will bring you more of success and happiness than any which has gone before.

Cordially yours,

Friendly service letters. Goodwill is promoted by offering special, unexpected service to customers. Opportunities present themselves during the year for showing evidence of a desire to serve customers well, and a letter to them will be appreciated. For example, you may want to offer old cash customers a charge account; you may be ready to give the car a customer bought from you a ee inspection; you may want to send customers a free useful gift. . friendly service letter is shown below.

)ear Mrs. Buchanan:

Shopping trips downtown, these hot summer days, are nothing less han hard work. The heat, the crowds, the trip down and home again—ll these consume energy and tire one out.

We can't control either the weather or the crowds, but we *can* offer ou a cool, comfortable place to rest and get your "second wind" in the eat of the day.

Next Monday, June 22, our new air-conditioned lounge will be ready or use. The lounge will occupy the entire north half of the fourth floor. t has been completely equipped with easy chairs, tables, reading lamps, sh stands, and all the other accessories that make for perfect comfort. The latest issues of all the leading magazines will be at your disposal. And most important of all at this time of year, the temperature will al-ways be 72 degrees.

We invite you to make our new lounge your headquarters when you re spending the day downtown. It is an ideal place to meet friends, while away idle moments before an appointment, or "just plain rest." Simply take the elevator to the fourth floor and follow the green neon rrows.

Cordially yours,

Invitation to special events. If you are planning a special event of some kind, invite your customers to attend. They will feel that you appreciate their patronage, and many will welcome the opportunity to attend your special functions. Thus, if your department store is having a special style show, invite old customers to it; if a series of lectures are to be given in the store, ask your customers to come; if it is a special demonstration that is to be given, let your customers know about it. Here is a personal invitation to attend a series of book reviews.

Dear Mrs. Chalmers:

We have good news for you! Beginning next Thursday afternoon, July 18, McIntire's will conduct a series of ten weekly book reviews of the latest outstanding contributions to fiction. You are cordially invited to attend, and an easy chair is being reserved for you.

The book to be reviewed next Thursday is John Jennings' new novel, *Next to Valour*, published by the same house that gave us *Gone With the Wind*. The reviewer will be a well-known Kansas Citian, Miss Elizabeth Larrimore, herself a novelist of established reputation.

This review, and all others in the series, will be given in our air-conditioned lounge on the third floor. All will begin at 2:30 P.M. On Thur day we shall announce the name of next week's reviewer and the tit of the novel to be discussed.

We are sure you will enjoy this Thursday feature during the next te weeks, for we have engaged only persons whose background and exper ence distinguish them as experts in the art of book reviewing.

Please plan to be with us next Thursday afternoon at 2:30.

Cordially yours,

Congratulations to old customers. Especially in small com munities is there opportunity to build goodwill by congratulatin customers upon their accomplishments, or upon the success of thos closely related to them. If you watch the local newspapers, you ca easily find many opportunities for congratulations. Such events a advancement to a better position, election as the officer of a club o lodge, publication of an article or book, graduation of children fron school, the purchase of a home—all are worth a friendly note o congratulation. Here is one such letter sent to a customer who ha been appointed assistant manager of a hotel:

Dear Mr. Sanford:

Davison's wishes to congratulate you on your appointment as Assistan Manager of Hotel Georgian, which we find mentioned in today's press

When we hear of the advancement of one of our young citizens, w are especially interested, because the young people of today are the lead ers of tomorrow. The future of Atlanta depends upon the young peopl of today—and what Atlanta becomes in the future interests Davison' immensely, because we are a substantial part of it and are eager to see i progress.

In your new position we wish for you every success. Our relationshi with you in the past has been a pleasure, and we hope it will continu through the years.

Cordially yours,

Letters of sympathy to customers. Friendly notes that sincerel offer sympathy to a customer who has suffered bereavement, acci dent, or other misfortune can be a welcome surprise. They can, however, be an intrusion if they are not simple and straightforward. The letter of condolence to a customer upon death of a near one should be very brief; it should not philosophize on the meaning of death or quote scripture or poetry. Here are a few examples:

ear Mrs. Griffith:

I learned with deep regret of the recent passing of Mr. Griffith and ish to extend my sincere sympathy in your bereavement.

Very sincerely yours,

* * *

ear Mr. Jurgens:

Upon my return to Topeka this morning, I was grieved to learn of the udden passing of Mrs. Jurgens. You have my deepest sympathy. I nly wish there were some small way in which I could lighten your buren of sorrow.

Sincerely,

* * *

ear Mrs. DeWitt:

I have just read in this morning's paper that your home was damaged y fire last night. I know only too well how discouraging this experience s, for I have been through it myself.

If there is anything I can do to help you, such as providing packing oxes or storing household articles in our storeroom, please let me know. ny service I may be able to render will be a pleasure.

Sincerely yours,

Letters requesting suggestions and criticisms. When you go o old customers for suggestions and criticisms, you usually expect o profit by the replies. This type of letter can at the same time be goodwill builder because: first, it shows the customer that you value is opinion; and, second, it shows that you are trying to offer a better roduct or service. Letters that ask such a favor will bring better esponse if the following points are covered, although not necessarily n the order mentioned:

1. Present a concise statement of what is wanted.
2. Justify the request. If possible, demonstrate the advantage that will accrue to the individual or firm which is asked to supply the nformation.
3. Express appreciation.
4. Make it easy for the person to answer the inquiry. A selfddressed card or envelope, or a suitable blank on which the information may be given, can be included, if appropriate.

The following letter was made easy to answer by phrasing the questions so that only a check was required:

Dear Mr. Stone:

We want to give you a better product. Will you help us?

We are now planning the revision of the Insurance Tax Service. A an old friend, we think that you can give us some mighty fine ideas o how it can be improved. We want this Service to give you in a practica clear, and authoritative way all of the material that will help you pla estates and take advantage of the tax laws to sell more insurance. T achieve this purpose, we are asking you to become an assistant editor, s to speak. All you need do is to answer the few simple questions on th enclosed sheet and return it to us as soon as possible.

The new Insurance Tax Service will be off the press next April—rewri ten and revised from cover to cover, with hundreds of new ideas to hel you sell more insurance. Among the things we would like you to pas on are (1) whether the size of the Service should be increased; (2 whether or not we should enlarge the section on Business Insurance; an (3) whether or not you would like a new section on How to Use th Social Security Act to Sell More Insurance.

We want to help you make 19. . and 19. . banner years. But at th same time we do not want you to pay for material that is of no value t you. With your co-operation we can accomplish both of these aims Will you, therefore, kindly check the enclosed questionnaire, and retur it to us, now, before it slips your mind. It will take only a minute.

No postage is required. Just check the statements that you agree wit and drop it in the mail.

Sincerely yours,

Here are other letters that merely ask for suggestions:

Dear Mr. DeLong:

As you know, we are doing everything possible to assure you of th very best of service at The Star. But something may have occurred t you—either a new service or an improvement in one which we alread offer—that would make The Star more helpful to you.

If you have such a suggestion, we'd certainly appreciate your giving i to us. Won't you write it on the enclosed business reply card, whicl requires no postage, and drop it into the mail?

Thank you.

Sincerely yours,

* * *

Dear Mrs. Howell:

Our organization is greatly interested in serving you satisfactorily.

May we have the pleasure of hearing how we can best meet your re quirements, to enable us to be of service to you more frequently?

For your convenience a stamped, addressed envelope and a correspond ence card are enclosed.

Very truly yours,

Acknowledging criticism or suggestion. Every letter of criti-sm or suggestion should be promptly acknowledged with a friendly hank you" for the writer's interest and help. The acknowledgment ilds goodwill by showing appreciation and eagerness to improve e product and service. Here is one example of a letter acknowl-lging praise and one replying to a criticism:

ear Mrs. Ridgway:

Thank you for your very welcome note of October 2, included with e check in payment of your account.

We certainly appreciate your kind words of approval and encourage-ent. Naturally, we are very glad that you have found our delivery rvice so dependable, and we assure you that every effort will be made maintain this standard.

If ever you think of any additional way in which we can serve you, ease let us know.

Sincerely yours,

* * *

ear Mrs. Sturgis:

Thank you for your helpful letter of June 10. We certainly appreciate customer who stops to do us a good turn, and that is exactly what you ve done.

You are quite right in your suggestion regarding our elevator service, d we are making every effort to remedy the situation as soon as pos-ble. You may have noticed that four of the elevators have not been in eration during the past two weeks. These are being equipped with the west and most efficient automatic floor regulators, which will practi-lly double their speed. As soon as they are ready for operation, the maining four elevators will be similarly equipped.

Within the next month these improvements will be completed, and e feel sure they will enable us to give our customers prompt and effi-ent elevator service.

Meanwhile, we know you will bear with us. We sincerely appreciate ur interest and helpful co-operation, and we shall strive always to serve it.

Cordially yours,

Letters of apology. Goodwill can be retained through prompt nd courteous handling of a customer's complaints. Patronage is ost easily lost through failure to express regret and offer a reason-ble adjustment to a customer who has reported a flaw in merchan-ise or service. This subject is so important that an entire section devoted to it. See page 588, *et seq*.

Welcoming back the old patron. When a customer has turned to the fold, a letter showing that you have missed him a are glad to see him back will please and flatter him. The opport nity to build goodwill in this way should not be missed. Such l ters are usually short and to the point, as is the following one:

Dear Mr. Fuller:

It was good to see you drive in again yesterday, for we haven't had t pleasure of serving you lately.

I hope that you will stop often in the future and give us a chance prove by our actions that we're sincerely glad to have you back.

Cordially yours,

Goodwill letters in times of emergency. When emergenci such as war, reconversion to civilian production, and the like, cau companies to refuse orders, to delay deliveries, to raise prices, or other ways to make drastic changes in regular customer relatior letters may be used to preserve customer goodwill while the critic adjustments are being made. Two such letters follow.

When a direct-mail firm was unable to publish a supplementa catalogue because of constantly advancing prices on its products, met the situation with the letter reproduced on page 571 (Figure 53

In the following letter the company is telling its distributors new policies governing prices, shipping, billing, deliveries, and forth.

To Sylvania Distributors:

The unusual conditions under which the radio industry is operati and the uncertainties of the future call for a redefining of a number our policies governing prices, shipping, billing, etc.

We do not think it necessary to review these conditions in any deta since they are so well known to you. By the same token, it is idle even attempt to prognosticate what may be ahead of us.

We will continue to aggressively promote your business and our ow in the renewal field. We sincerely trust that you will have the resol and foresight to strengthen your position in the field of distribution at time which bids fair to provide unusual opportunities in both prese profits and long range growth and stability.

The following outline of policy has been set up to insure fair an equitable treatment of all of our customers:

1. All orders on hand, placed prior to June 1, for immediate shipmen will be billed at current prices (Distributors' Net Cost Prices, effectiv February 1, 19—).

UNTIL WE HEAR FROM YOU!

Because our 1941 catalog was printed in January of this year and since that time nearly all prices have advanced we have found it necessary to change our prices at this time. We dislike holding your order, but under the circumstances, we feel it necessary to advise you of these changes before completing your order. Will you please check the information below, complete the instructions to us and then mail it back to us in the first mail today. Many thanks for your order.

YOU ORDERED:

Item No.	New Price	DESCRIPTION

NEW TOTAL ______

AS SENT IN ______

DIFFERENCE ______

R-U-S-H

TEAR OFF AND MAIL RIGHT NOW!

NAME ______

STORE NAME ______

CITY ______

STATE ______

Tell us what you want us to do

Return At Once To — **ASH-BRADFORD, Inc.** *South Bend, Indiana*

Figure 53. Goodwill Letter in Time of Emergency.

2. All orders placed on and after June 1 will be accepted subject the following conditions:

(a) Prices in effect on the date orders are received will apply on su portion as shipped within 30 days from date of receipt.

(b) In the event all or any portion of such orders are not shipp within 30 days from date of receipt, prices in effect as of date of sh ment will apply.

(c) Any orders or parts thereof which remain unshipped by us af 30 days from date of receipt, may be cancelled by the customer. (Su cancellation would destroy any seniority which would otherwise be corded.)

(d) Should a revision in prices become necessary, such revision w take effect upon announcement.

May we with all sincerity thank you for the satisfactory relations have had in the past and solicit both your goodwill and your business a future period where mutual understanding and cooperation will be w near a necessity.

Very truly yours,

Building Goodwill Among New Patrons

Letters to new customers. The new patron is forming an opi ion of your firm the moment he enters your place of business a makes his first purchase. If he is satisfied with his purchase a with your service, he may return; but if you give him somethi beyond this minimum, which he has a right to expect, he will more likely to remember your firm favorably and keep coming bac

Appreciation to new charge customers. The opening of a char account creates an opportunity for writing a goodwill letter. Su letters usually thank the customer, welcome him as a user of accou facilities, express desire to serve, and may explain the credit poli of the firm. The following letter is an example:

Dear Mrs. Ormsby:

It was a genuine pleasure to open a charge account for you. Tha you most cordially for this expression of confidence and goodwill.

This is the beginning of what we feel sure will be a lasting friendshi and we want you to be perfectly satisfied in every respect with our me chandise and service.

You can do us no greater favor than to speak frankly if any detail do not "measure up" at any time, so we may make amends immediately.

For our part, we will exert every effort toward making your dealin re so thoroughly pleasant and satisfactory that you'll always look back on the opening of this account as the beginning of a most worthwhile sociation.

Sincerely yours,

Letters of appreciation for initial purchase. Letters of thanks new customers, written after initial purchases, add a personal uch that often results in bringing the customer back more quickly. he examples below build goodwill by a friendly expression of appreation.

hank you, Mr. Hollingsworth . . .

. . . for selecting Freeman's for your purchase yesterday.

We hope you will come back often and give us the chance to prove our service how much we appreciate your patronage. We'll certainly our best to give you satisfaction plus.

Cordially yours,

* * *

ear Mrs. Nicholson:

It is a pleasure to welcome you as a customer of the Home Laundry ad to thank you sincerely for the opportunity to serve you.

As I take a very real and personal interest in your satisfaction, I should eatly appreciate your letting me know—by mail or telephone—how ou liked our handling of your first laundry.

More than that, I want you to know that my interest does not stop ith the first bundle. If at any time our workmanship or service should ot merit your enthusiastic approval, I should consider it a favor if you ould call me at once.

We are ready and eager to serve you in every way possible.

Cordially yours,

Another example of acknowledging the order of a new customer ith a view to building goodwill is given on page 578.

Offering the credit privilege. An offer to reliable cash customers o use the charge-account privilege not only builds goodwill but, hen accepted, frequently results in greater sales to the patron. uch letters should show the advantages of the charge privilege, explain the credit-payment policy, and emphasize the desire to serve. he following letters have a strong service keynote, and are cordial nd convincing. Other examples will be found in "How to Write Credit Letters," page 1037, *et seq.*

Dear Mr. Chandler:

When we cashed a check for you the other day, it occurred to us th you might enjoy a convenient service which makes cash payment unne essary—a charge account.

The charge privilege eliminates the need of paying individually f each purchase and makes it convenient for you to order by telephor It also provides you with an itemized statement of each month's pu chases and brings to you all our announcements of special events a ranged for charge customers.

It will be a pleasure to extend our credit service to you, and we're su you will find an account a real convenience and time saver. Won't yo fill out the enclosed credit card and return it to us in the postage-fr envelope?

Your account will be ready twenty-four hours after we hear from yo It will place all our service facilities at your convenience.

Cordially yours,

* * *

Dear Miss McClellan:

The Auerbach Company has selected your name from a very limite and preferred credit list and is happy to extend to you an invitation t open a charge account.

All that is necessary is simply to sign and return the enclosed card o call at the Department of Accounts whenever convenient and leave yo signature so that we may make up a Charga-plate, the most modern co venience in shopping. This affords you protection, quicker service, an eliminates any possibility of error.

You simply ask to have the merchandise charged—there is no waitin for change or other delay; it is easy to purchase at any time, whether yo are prepared with the cash or not. A charge account also makes it easie to order by telephone or mail.

An itemized statement is mailed each month, and, by charging, yo eliminate the nuisance of sales tax tokens by having the tax included i the bill at the end of the month.

We offer you service and values which will merit your frequent visit to the store, and we sincerely hope that you will enjoy the convenienc of a charge account here.

Very cordially yours,

Checking up on customer satisfaction. A message to a cus tomer some time after he has made a purchase, inquiring as to whether or not he is satisfied with the product or service, will show that you have the customer's interest at heart, that you are depend able, and that you wish to fulfill your service guaranty. Such letter are bound to result in increased respect, confidence, and goodwill or e part of your patrons. Here is how some companies have written their customers along these lines:

st checking up, Mr. Kimball,

. . . because we want to be absolutely sure that you are receiving com-ete satisfaction from the new tuxedo you bought here recently. We all not be content to mark the transaction "closed" until you are satis-d one hundred per cent.

So, if the alteration of any detail would give you more pleasure in earing your new "tux," please let us attend to it for you.

This store is founded upon quality merchandise and efficient service. ur complete lines of leading brands are your guaranty of top-quality oods when you come here to buy wearing apparel. And we want our rvice to measure up to the same high standard.

So please help us see to it that you are always completely satisfied.

Sincerely yours,

* * *

ear Mr. Turner:

It is a pleasure to welcome you to the family of owners of the new hevrolet, and it is a double pleasure because we at Hammond Jones ompany had the privilege of delivering it to you.

Your new Chevrolet is built to give you thousands of miles of depend-ble, economical, and trouble-free motoring, but just as you have insur-nce on your property, so the insurance of that service will be found in egular visits to our Service Department.

We are quite proud of our reputation as an outstanding Chevrolet ervice Department—a reputation that has been built on skilled work-anship and confidence.

Be sure to take advantage of the free inspection and adjustments serv-e which you receive at 500 miles. The purpose of this free service is ot only to protect your car, but also to enable our Service Manager to eet you and advise you about the attention your car should receive. I m sure you will find everyone in his department efficient and eager to ive you the best of attention.

And if I can ever be of service to you, I hope you will call on me.

Cordially yours,

* * *

Dear Mr. Jones:

We wish to thank you for your recent coal order. And we hope you ound the coal satisfactory—and that our men took good care of you in he delivery.

We select our coal with care and try to train our men so that our de-iveries are made promptly and with courtesy.

If your order was not handled perfectly, we want to know about it for we are here for just one purpose—to please you.

And we hope you will like us well enough to remember our pho number the next time you get chilly!

Warmly yours,

Inviting the use of other departments. A letter to patrons wl have confined their purchases to one or two departments, inviti them to visit others, will make better friends and better custome Such a letter should appear as a friendly suggestion rather than a sales solicitation letter. The following examples graciously off to be of service to such customers:

Dear Mr. Sheldon:

I want to send you a personal word of appreciation for opening yo account with this bank. All our facilities are at your disposal, and hope you will utilize the services of any department which can help make your banking a pleasure.

Our trust, title, bond, investment, and safe deposit department are a equipped to render efficient service. Moreover, any of our officers w welcome a visit from you at any time his counsel may be of assistance.

When you opened an account here, this became your bank. Plea let us serve you in any way which will add to your convenience.

Cordially yours,

* * *

Dear Mrs. Reynolds:

Because it is a pleasure to serve you—and we are eager to do it con pletely and well—we'd like to make a suggestion.

All next week, March 12-17, our Kitchen Karnival will be in fu swing. This is an annual feature of our Household Department in th Basement. There will be special displays and demonstrations of the nev est time- and effort-saving devices in kitchenware. In addition, our enti stock of up-to-the-minute kitchen utensils will be on sale at a 10 per cer price reduction.

We are sure you will find a visit to our Household Department nex week both interesting and profitable, so we cordially invite you to come in

Sincerely yours,

Goodwill Through Acknowledgments

Acknowledging the order. Orders can be acknowledged throug personal letters or through routine form letters. The latter, if used should be confined to the usual order. In the following situation knowledgment by personal letter is essential for the maintenance goodwill:

1. Large orders from old customers.
2. First orders from new customers.
3. Orders that are not clear.
4. Delays in shipment.
5. Goods out of stock.

Promptness in acknowledging orders is absolutely necessary, for lay will break down goodwill.

How to acknowledge a large order. Goodwill may be retained y writing a special letter to an old customer who has placed a large rder. Such a letter will accomplish its purpose if it is definite, eerful, and persuasive. Divide the letter as follows to get a good ructure:

1. Thank the customer.
2. Restate the order.
3. Tell how the order is being handled and shipped.
4. Include a paragraph or two of sales talk, concentrating upon e sales points of the goods and the possibilities for profit.

The following letter carries out the usual plan of a good letter cknowledging a large order from an old customer:

ear Mr. Calton:

Thank you for your generous order of March 12, which we take as an ndication of your increased business in our goods.

3 doz. Frocks of Fashion, No. 208, Size 36	$39.00	$117.00
2 doz. Ultra Smart, No. 214, Size 34	35.00	70.00
4 doz. Utility, No. 126, Size 38	19.00	76.00
6 doz. French Inspiration, No. 38, Size 34	49.50	297.00
Total		$560.00

These gowns are being shipped today by American Railway Express nd should reach you on Thursday in time for your week-end trade.

Your customers will find in these smart models just the quality and

design most in vogue among women who pride themselves on their dre
As in the past, we are supplying the unusual, the different, the uncor
mon modes, at lowest prices. To sell our gowns is to convince yo
fashionable trade that you have initiative, and that you are the one wl
first features new styles for those who look for inspiration and indivi
uality in dress.

The styles that we are sending you are authentic, original, and appr
priate.

The most critical buyers will immediately recognize the quality ar
style of these gowns.

We assure you of our personal attention and of our steadfast desire
please you.

Sincerely yours,

Getting the goodwill of a new customer. Here is a workab
outline for constructing the letter to a new customer with a view t
building goodwill:

1. Show appreciation of the order and welcome the customer.
2. Restate the order.
3. State how the order is being handled and shipped.
4. Include one or two paragraphs of sales material creating conf
dence in the house, its goods, and its service.
5. Stress interest in the customer's needs and convince him tha
the firm means to serve him.

The following opening and closing paragraphs make the prece
ing letter suitable for a new customer:

Dear Sir:

Thank you for your order of March 17. I wish to welcome you int
our large family of satisfied customers and to assure you that we shall d
everything in our power to make the sale of our gowns profitable to you
We take a genuine interest in the increased profits of our dealers.

* * *

Your interests are our interests. Quality, style, and price make ou
gowns easy to sell to a discriminating trade. You are situated so that w
can supply you unfailingly and immediately. Gowns shipped you toda
reach you tomorrow morning. This service means that you can carry
representative stock in your store, depending upon us to replenish you
stock within twenty-four hours after you have made sales. The result
for you, is a small investment with large profits, made possible by ou
highly organized and always dependable service.

Sincerely yours,

How to perfect incomplete orders. Occasionally an order is :eived that lacks essential information. The letter sent to the cus- mer for additional information should be developed as follows:

1. Acknowledge the order with thanks.
2. Ask for the additional information without letting the customer el that he is at fault.
3. Present the request as a desire to give prompt and efficient rvice.

A letter such as the following will bring the necessary information ıat was missing in the order.

ear Sir:

Thank you for your order of October 10.

The size that you desire was omitted from your order for M-289, ıede gloves.

Please send us this necessary information, which will enable us to fill ıe order exactly as you want it. As soon as we hear from you, we will :lease the order for immediate shipment.

Very truly yours,

Acknowledgment when shipment is delayed. If the order has een delayed, a letter must be written that will keep the customer ıtisfied. Here are suggestions for the contents of such a letter:

1. Explain what has been done with the order.
2. Express regret.
3. Offer an adjustment.

Gentlemen:

Your order No. 245 was billed out this morning over the Southern Pacific Railroad. I am very sorry that there was a delay, but this was ınavoidable because of a shortage of the quality of coal we know your rade requires.

Ever since the recent labor troubles, we have had a little difficulty in :eeping supplied with this grade. We could, however, have made prompt hipment of an inferior grade, but as I know that your customers demand he best, I waited until we had coal of the quality you usually buy.

I hope this supply reaches you before your present stock is exhausted.

Very truly yours,

Acknowledgment when goods are out of stock. The letter explaining that goods are out of stock will retain goodwill if it includes:

1. An acknowledgment with thanks and an expression of reg that the order cannot be filled.

2. An explanation that the predicament is unusual and will n recur.

3. A substitution, if past experience with the customer warran this procedure.

4. A request for permission to substitute some other item, wi a sales talk to induce acceptance.

5. An offer to be of assistance if no substitution can be made.

Some of the above suggestions are carried out in the followi letter:

Dear Madam:

Thank you for your order of November 10.

We are sending you today, by parcel post insured, the ten yards poplin that you ordered.

Because we realize your immediate need for this material, we ha taken the liberty of sending the poplin in two lengths, 8½ yards an 3 yards, as this is all we have in stock. The new supply will not be ava able until November 18.

We are certain that you will like this poplin, which is of the be quality, and for which we are glad to accept your check in full payme as for ten yards.

Sincerely yours,

How to handle an order that cannot be filled because of polic When an order cannot be filled, the letter of explanation to th customer will build goodwill and leave the way open for future bus ness if it is constructed as follows:

1. Express appreciation for the order.
2. Courteously explain the reasons.
3. If pertinent, show the customer that the refusal is in his ow interests.

The letter on page 542 refuses the order in a straightforward, bus nesslike way. It uses the opportunity to sell the product at the sam time.

How to acknowledge remittances. The routine acknowledg ment of remittances may be covered by a courteous form letter, un less other factors make a special letter advisable. The followin forms are among many that can be used:

ntlemen:

Thank you for your check in payment of your May account.

We wish to express our appreciation of the satisfactory manner in ich you have made your payments.

Very truly yours,

* * *

ntlemen:

We have received your remittance of $. . . . ., for which we thank u. The amount will be placed to your credit.

Very truly yours,

* * *

entlemen:

Thank you for your check for $. . . . . ., which we have placed to your edit. The unpaid balance is now $. . . . . .

Very truly yours,

Building goodwill through acknowledgments of inquiries. Anvers to inquiries about the company's products are really sales tters. These were discussed on page 546, *et seq.*

In the following paragraphs we are concerned with acknowledgents of inquiries not directly related to sales. Every company reeives requests at times for information, help, data to be used in esearch, and the like. The answer affords an opportunity to build oodwill. Below are some suggestions for letters complying with equests and refusing requests.

Retaining goodwill while refusing requests. In a letter refusing grant a request, the following procedure will guard against alienatng goodwill:

1. Be courteous and concise.
2. Refuse the request, state the reason, and express regret.
3. Close with sales material, if pertinent.
4. Offer other assistance, if possible.

Here is a letter that refuses information and at the same time creates goodwill.

Dear Mr. Smith:

Mr. Jones has just turned over to me your letter of February 3, as I am in charge of the correspondence activities of the firm.

Yes, we believe that the people in our organization have written some unusually good letters. Nothing would give me greater pleasure than to

select a portfolio of these and send them to you, but unfortunately I a
not permitted to do so. It has always been against the policy of the fi
to send out our letters for publicity purposes.

If Mr. Sullivan were in town I might try a little salesmanship on hi
and see if he wouldn't be willing to make an exception in this case. Ho
ever, he is in Hawaii, and I would not have time to contact him befc
you will need the letters.

So, under the circumstances, there is nothing that we can do to he
you in the preparation of your manuscript—except give you our be
wishes that it will be completely successful. There is much need f
missionary work in the field of business letter writing, and anyone wh
is undertaking something of this kind deserves the heartiest comme
dation.

Very truly yours,

Getting the maximum goodwill from complying with request The person who receives the material requested will naturally fee kindly disposed toward the company granting it. However, more i gained in goodwill if a letter accompanies the material. Such a lette should cover the following:

1. Cheerfully grant the favor.
2. Offer further assistance.
3. Close with sales material, if pertinent.

Here is a letter that obtains the maximum goodwill.

Dear Mr. Smith:

I consider it a pleasure to be able to assist any way I can in furnishing material for your new manuscript on better business letters.

The letter I mailed to our agents and salesmen last December, a copy of which is enclosed, was intended to stimulate their business-building efforts, and, at the same time, bring to their attention the importance of good public relations. The response to this letter was all that could be expected.

I hope that you will be able to use this in your book.

If I can be of further assistance, please consider me at your service.

Cordially yours,

How to acknowledge letters that praise. Voluntary letters from customers expressing satisfaction with a product may form excellent testimonials for future advertising and sales letters. Such letters require a cheerful, gracious acknowledgment, with a request for permission to quote the comments of the customer in advertising matter.

The acknowledgment may also be used to sell the satisfied cus-

›mer another product, provided the customer has a real or poten-al need for the article offered.

The following letter, asking permission to quote the customer's ›mments, brought the requested "O.K." and an order for the prod-ct offered.

›ear Miss Bell:

Thank you for your letter of the 21st, received today, enclosing remit-ınce of $3.56 to cover our invoice for *The Private Secretary's Manual*, ıd containing your gratifying comment on the material in the book.

If we may have permission to quote your comment, along with that f other alert secretaries, in some of our advertising matter, will you lease return this letter to me with your "O.K." and initials opposite this aragraph.

In the hope of returning the favor, I would like to make a suggestion hat I think would be in line with your ideas of what constitutes a good ecretary.

We have just published a book—*Successful Salesmanship*—that con-ains at least a score of particularly good ideas and "ammunition" for the ales manager of a company like John Morris & Co. A brief description ›f the book is attached.

Since we will gladly send the book on five days' approval, my sugges-ion is that you return the attached card—which is all ready to sign and nail—and let me send you *Successful Salesmanship* with the distinct ınderstanding that if the Sales Manager, after seeing the book, isn't per-ectly willing to O.K. our memo invoice for the price of the book—only $5—then you need only mail it back to us. That will end the matter.

A stamped, addressed envelope is enclosed for the return of this letter with your "O.K." opposite the second paragraph giving permission to quote your comment on the Secretary's Manual.

Yours very truly,

Letters received in absence of addressee. A letter received in the absence of the addressee should be immediately acknowledged by the secretary or assistant of the addressee if it cannot be answered with authority by someone else. The purpose is to build goodwill through courtesy.

Dear Sir:

In the absence of Mr. Van der Beek, I wish to acknowledge your letter of July 25, which is being held for his attention on his return early next week.

Very truly yours,
(signed) Mary Fitts
Secretary to Mr. Van der Beek.

Dear Sir:

Your letter of August 14 arrived the day after Mr. Tauber left on three-week selling trip. Since it does not appear to require an immed ate reply, I will hold it for his attention on his return.

Very truly yours,
(signed) Joan McGregor
Secretary to Mr. Taube

General Goodwill Letters

A letter to disappointed applicants. If applicants for positior are future prospects for the company's product, a letter to those wh are not successful in obtaining employment will help to build gooc will. The following letter of the L. E. Waterman Company sug gests the type of letter suitable under such circumstances:

Dear Mr. Morgan:

Thank you, Mr. Morgan, for the interest you display in Waterman' evidenced by your application for a position on our sales staff.

We regret that our response must be disappointing, as there is n opening at the present time, nor do we anticipate any in the near future However, we are retaining your application in our files, should we hav the occasion to engage a man of your qualifications.

We shall be glad to call on you if the opportunity arises. And mean while, we wish you very early success in attaining a position that will b both profitable and pleasant.

Very truly yours,

Goodwill through letters of introduction. Letters of introduc tion must state the name of the person being introduced, the reasor for the introduction, and sufficient personal or business details tc make the introduction appear appropriate.

When written for delivery by the person being introduced, the letter is left unsealed, and it is properly assumed that it has been read before being presented.

The tone of the letter of introduction depends upon how well the writer knows the principals and the reasons for writing it. Although the letter may actually be conferring a favor on the addressee by bringing him in contact with a person who will be valuable to him, it is usually written in the spirit of asking a favor. For example:

Mr. Harry W. Overbeck,
Winchendon Knitting Mills,
Ware, Massachusetts.

Dear Mr. Overbeck:

This letter will be handed to you by my friend of long standing, Horace Bowes, a well-known writer of articles on business.

Mr. Bowes is engaged in the preparation of a book in which he hopes to outline the development of the textile industry during the last half-century. He believes that through a talk with you he could obtain both information and inspiration that would be valuable to him in this work.

Since you are *the* authority on your particular phase of the industry, he has asked for an introduction to you. I shall appreciate any courtesies you may show him, and I know he will.

Sincerely yours,

The following letter is less formal than that above because it is based on a first-name acquaintanceship:

Dear Harry:

When we had lunch together, I mentioned Jack Hunt, who was doing some big things for one of our lines. Since that time he has decided that he ought to be handling something that will give him a bigger opportunity.

I don't know whether you're interested in getting additional sales right now or not. Maybe you're too far behind in production as it is.

But seriously, talk to this fellow, won't you? Jack Hunt is a good egg. The next lunch is on me.

Sincerely,

The business-pleasure introduction. Sometimes a letter of introduction is written for a business acquaintance who is traveling for pleasure. For example:

My dear McKenna:

John Henry Mainwaring, my good friend and the company's valued client, is on his way to the Pacific Coast. He is accompanied by Mrs. Mainwaring, which means that it is a pleasure trip.

I told him that if his route led through Toledo, he should not fail to look you up, and he said he wouldn't. So if he presents this letter, he has!

Don't let him get away without seeing the factory. And ask him if he'd like to have any checks cashed. Take it from me, they'll be good.

I shall appreciate any courtesies you may show him.

Sincerely,

Introduction on cards. Often an introduction written on a pe sonal or business card adequately fulfills the purpose if there is n necessity for formality or detailed information. Such introductio might read:

Introducing Mr. Samuel A. Leffingwell.
(signed) George D. Twelvetrees.
To introduce Ned Gannon. Treat him right.
(signed) Jack Halliburton.
This is George Rand, the man I spoke to you about.
(signed) H. F. Jones.

Goodwill through thank-you letters. Thank-you letters hel to build goodwill. Opportunities are constantly arising in whic they can be used in business. The letters may be short and shoul not be forced. The following examples illustrate circumstances i which they are useful:

Gentlemen:

Thank you for allowing us the 2% cash discount on our bill after th ten days had elapsed. Basing our belief on your invariable fairnes through all our dealings, we felt sure you would make this allowanc when you understood the circumstances.

Sincerely yours,

* * *

Dear Mr. Fordyce:

I want to express to you my personal appreciation of your courtesy t our salesman, John Titus, when you learned of the disquieting news h had received from home. We are glad to report that his mother passe the crisis and is now resting comfortably.

The help you gave Mr. Titus made us all feel good.

Sincerely yours,

Goodwill through sympathy. A simple but effective way to gai the goodwill of employees is to show concern about them when the are absent because of illness. Here are two illustrative letters:

Dear Mr. Saunders:

I am no doctor, but I know I can help you. Here is how:

Your regular salary check will be sent each week to Mrs. Saunders a long as you are incapacitated. This will relieve your mind of financia worries.

Your work at the office will not get behind, as your good friends here have offered to absorb your duties while you are away. You don't have to worry about your work.

Your job will be waiting for you when you are ready to go on with it -but no sooner.

That leaves you with practically nothing to do except get better.

The boys at the office send you their best.

Sincerely,

* * *

)ear Miss Owens:

I was very sorry to hear of the accident that has laid you up in the ospital. I am told that it was not serious, but I know that it must be ainful, and my sympathies are all with you.

My correspondence is being handled by the three other young women, ut, without wishing to appear too critical, I feel as if I were working vith my right hand tied behind my back.

We shall all be glad to see you when you are well enough to return.

Sincerely,

Goodwill through congratulations. One of the best ways of ostering goodwill in business is to take advantage of opportunities o send congratulatory letters. Such letters presuppose a certain legree of personal relationship. The tone of the letter is governed y the closeness of the relationship. Several examples given below how opportunities for building goodwill in this way.

Mr. Harvey S. Wing,
Boston Store,
Ottumwa, Iowa.

)ear Mr. Wing:

As one department store man to another, I wish to pay homage to our genius for dramatizing your window displays. The way you have vorked out the selling idea for party gowns in your southeast window is nasterly.

Congratulations!

Sincerely,

* * *

Mr. Howard M. Gurney, President,
Wickwire Hosiery Company,
New York City.

)ear Mr. Gurney:

I have just read in today's paper of your election as Mayor of Billings Center, and I hasten to congratulate both you and the community you epresent. I am sure that you will bring to your job the same ability that has made your business such a success.

Sincerely yours,

Mr. Samuel S. Dakin,
Hotel St. Anthony,
San Antonio, Texas.

Dear Sam:

When a salesman breaks his own record for the size of an order, i[illegible] may or may not be something for the sales manager to talk about, but—

When a salesman breaks all the records in his company—*that's news*

You know perfectly well that I am talking about the Wales Compan[illegible] order.

Great work, boy.

Sincerely,

* * *

Mr. A. J. Wortman,
Cooperative Credit Association,
New York City.

Dear Mr. Wortman:

Your talk on "Collection Methods" at yesterday's Rotary Club meet-ing was instructive and interesting to everyone present. I congratulat[illegible] you on your command of the subject and the manner in which you pre-sented it.

Sincerely yours,

6. KEEPING GOODWILL IN ANSWERING COMPLAINTS

How to reply to complaint letters. The following are the chief points to keep in mind in replying to letters of complaint.

1. Answer the complaint or claim letter promptly—if possible, within twenty-four hours. Delay is liable to aggravate the customer's dissatisfaction. If a decision as to whether or not an adjustment should be made cannot be reached immediately, write a brief letter of acknowledgment, expressing regret for the cause of the complaint or claim and assuring the customer that an investigation is being made and that prompt action will be taken.

2. The adjustment letter is a sales letter; it should sell service and satisfaction. The object is to settle the difficulty in a manner satisfactory to both parties, to retain the customer, and to build goodwill.

3. The adjustment letter should assume that the customer is honest in his complaint or claim. Do not try to put the customer in the wrong.

4. Adapt the adjustment letter to the reader and show sincere appreciation of his point of view. Write the letter in a spirit of service and fair treatment.

5. Thank the customer for his letter, and for the opportunity that it gives you to explain your policies or to remedy defects in your goods or service. Take the view that the customer is benefiting you by his criticism. Do not express surprise at the customer's dissatisfaction or tell him that his is the only complaint you have received.

6. Emphasize the positive, constructive side of the adjustment problem. Do not revive the unpleasant aspects by restating the complaint or claim. Do not use offensive words and phrases, such as *you assert, you state, you say, you claim, your claim, your complaint, we cannot understand, we are at a loss, our records show.*

7. If the customer is in the right, explain the cause of the error on your part clearly, concisely, and completely. Express regret, but do not be effusive in apologies.

8. If the customer's letter is sarcastic, angry, or abusive, do not assume that this gives you license to reply in the same tone. Never show irritation, however much the circumstances may seem to justify it. If the customer is in the wrong, do not try to be funny or clever at his expense.

9. If the complaint or claim is the result of a misunderstanding on the part of the customer, do not suggest that he is ignorant or careless. Write a pleasant, friendly letter of explanation; do not adopt a superior tone.

10. Convince the customer of the justness of your decision.

Workable outline for an adjustment letter. The following is a practical outline for the adjustment letter:

1. Get on common ground with the claimant by thanking him for his letter or by expressing regret for the inconvenience caused him. Search out some point on which you can agree with the customer, even though this point be merely an expression of sympathy. An opening of this kind disarms the reader and puts him in a receptive mood.

2. Explain the facts in connection with the claim. However, do not restate the claim in full. Show that you have given the customer's letter careful consideration.

3. State cheerfully the adjustment action that you propose to tak
4. Close by expressing appreciation and a desire to co-operate.

Example of poor adjustment letter. The following letter illu trates the tone that should *not* be used in replying to complaint an claim letters:

Dear Sir:

We were very much surprised to receive your letter of January 27, i which you assert that the ECONOMY OIL BURNER recently installe in your home is not everything that we advertise our burner to be.

If the difficulty of which you complain were caused by faulty design c manufacture, it would certainly seem that we would get complaints fror other people. Yours, however, is the only complaint that we have re ceived, and in the past few months we have sold through our agent more than fifty burners in your state alone.

From what you say about the performance you have been getting, w believe that it is not the fault of the burner that the results are not al you had hoped for. The burner must have been poorly installed.

We advise you to get in touch with whoever installed your ECON OMY for you, and have it put right. We definitely do not advertis anything that is not true.

Very truly yours,

This same letter, rewritten in a better tone, might read as follows:

Dear Mr. Ferguson:

We appreciate very much your writing us direct with regard to the ECONOMY OIL BURNER that you recently purchased. The per formance of every ECONOMY is guaranteed by us, and we welcome any opportunity to show that we are always ready to stand behind our guaranty.

We have mailed a copy of your letter of January 27 to our agents John Brown & Company, who installed the burner for you. We have also instructed John Brown & Company to give the burner a thorough examination—to check the installation in every particular. In the event that any parts are found to be defective, they will be replaced at our expense. It will not be necessary for you to communicate with John Brown & Company; they will call at your home within the next few days.

Since I am anxious to number you among the many enthusiastic users of the ECONOMY, I wish that you would write me personally in, say, two weeks' time, and let me know whether the burner is operating to your entire satisfaction.

Very truly yours,

Letters granting adjustments and acknowledging error. A prompt, complete adjustment is in order when investigation shows that the goods were defective, that there was a delay in shipment, that a mistake was made in filling the order, or that some other error for which the seller is to blame occurred. A frank acknowledgment of the error should be written, and the customer assured that precautions have been taken to avoid similar trouble in the future. The seller should not try to defend himself or offer a lengthy explanation. Such an explanation will merely serve to develop in painful detail the shortcomings of the house. A brief, frank, cheerful letter is most effective.

Gentlemen:

Thank you for writing us on November 10 regarding the platinum setting that you ordered on October 29.

By immediately checking back, we found that a mistake had been made when your order was transcribed in our order department.

We are very sorry that you and your customer have been inconvenienced, but we are at the same time grateful to you for helping us place the blame and prevent similar mistakes in the future.

Although we have never, in the case of expensive settings such as yours, promised delivery in less than two weeks, I am personally taking care of your order and am having it handled so that you will receive the setting not later than Saturday morning.

Please be assured of our desire to co-operate with you, as we have in the past.

Very truly yours,

* * *

Dear Mr. Mitchell:

We are glad you notified us promptly that some of your sheets were damaged in transit.

No doubt the error was made by one of the inspectors in the shipping department. We try to use every safeguard to prevent such an occurrence, but, try as we do, there will be a slip once in a great while. Whenever an error is brought to our attention, we are glad to make things right as quickly as possible.

We have entered a replace order for the fifty sheets. These will be sent not later than Monday of next week.

We are very sorry that you have been inconvenienced, and in the future we shall do everything in our power to see that your shipments reach you in perfect condition.

Very truly yours,

Dear Mr. Gardner:

We were very sorry to learn from your letter of May 3 of the inco venience caused you by the error in your last shipment. Despite th constant and diligent supervision that we give to filling orders correctl it seems that once in a great while a mistake is made.

We are sending you today, by express, the case of canned peaches th you ordered.

With regard to the case of pears sent you in error, we should be oblige if you would hold this in the meantime. Mr. Stark, of our sales depar ment, will visit you on Wednesday of next week. If you are not able t use the pears in your own trade, possibly Mr. Stark can dispose of ther to another customer and save the cost of returning them to us.

We appreciate your writing us promptly concerning the error, an assure you that every care will be taken in filling your future orders.

Very truly yours,

How to handle complaints about service. When a custome complains about the service that he has been receiving, the letter c reply is most effective if it bears the signature of a vice president o other officer of the company. The signature of an officer has conciliatory effect, in that it impresses the customer with the fac that his complaint has received serious attention. The letter ma apologize for the difficulty, sympathize with the customer, and assur him that his business is appreciated and that his unfortunate ex perience has been unusual. It may close with the suggestion tha the customer give the company further opportunity to prove th quality of its service, and that in the future his orders be directed t the personal attention of the writer.

Dear Mr. Lewis:

I very much appreciate your frank letter of August 4.

It was so specific as to details that I was able to take immediate actio toward correcting a situation that obviously had no reason to exist.

I assure you of my regret at your inconvenience. May I suggest tha you communicate with me whenever you find our service not up to th standard of your experiences before this incident.

Sincerely yours,

Vice President

* * *

Dear Mr. Wright:

Your frank letter of May 2 was referred to me, and, despite your re- quest that no apology be made, I am writing you this letter, which, how- ever, is to be a letter of thanks rather than an apology.

Once in a while I read a report in which one of our customers has ıs in this instance) a real, honest-to-goodness reason for thinking that raham & Company do not know how to fill an order correctly. I ques- on whether, if I were you, I should have written as considerately as you id. I sometimes wonder, when such a report comes to me, why some f our customers don't take their business elsewhere without letting us now their grievance. That is why Graham & Company should thank ou for telling us where we have fallen down in connection with your usiness.

Your order was filled on April 23. During that period we received ıore than double our usual amount of business. With the great increase ı volume of orders, coupled with our desire to make immediate ship- ıent of every order, and with a percentage of comparatively inexperi- nced employees, the ordinarily careful supervision and inspection of rders were probably relaxed. The management of a business such as urs, therefore, has to depend to some extent on the letters that come rom customers; and it is for this reason that I welcome yours.

We want an opportunity to prove to you that Graham & Company an and do handle orders correctly; and since you have had so much mis- ortune in connection with your orders, I am going to ask that, in the vent you do decide to give us an opportunity to prove that your recent xperience is not typical, you send your next few orders to me personally, o that I may have them checked and satisfy myself that you are not oing to be caused further inconvenience.

I am doing this because I am sure you are convinced that in buying rom us you do save money, and that your sole reason for discontinuing our dealings with us is that we have made mistakes in recent orders.

Very truly yours,

Vice President

Handling complaints where carrier is at fault. If the carrier is to blame for delay in delivery, the letter should state the date and method of shipment and tell the customer that the goods are being traced at once. It may also ask the customer to write or wire collect if delivery is not made by a certain date, in which event a duplicate shipment will be forwarded.

The seller is usually not legally responsible for damage to goods that he delivered safely into the hands of the carrier, for it is the buyer's responsibility to seek redress from the carrier. However, as a service and a goodwill gesture, many companies make an immediate adjustment to the customer and then take upon themselves the filing of a claim with the carrier, with or without the aid of the customer, as the situation demands. If the goods have been badly damage a duplicate shipment is forwarded immediately. If the damag is slight, the goods may be offered to the customer at a discount.

Dear Mr. Hayes:

Your letter of May 3 reached us this morning.

The shipment of furniture that you ordered on April 18 left our facto on April 23, N.Y.N.H. & H. freight, car #238967, and should certain have been delivered to you not later than April 26. We have asked th railroad to trace the shipment immediately.

If the furniture does not reach you by May 7, please wire us collec and we will forward a duplicate shipment at once, by express.

We very much regret the delay and hope that it will not cause yo serious inconvenience.

Very truly yours,

* * *

Dear Mr. Davidson:

We were very sorry to learn from your letter of March 12 that th mahogany desk which you ordered as a birthday gift for your son arrive so badly damaged that you cannot accept it.

As the Chicago, Milwaukee and St. Paul Railroad gave us a receip acknowledging that the desk was received by them perfectly crated, i must have been damaged in transit. Although our responsibility end when the railroad has accepted the desk, we know how much you are interested in this handsome and useful gift for your son. We are, therefore, sending you today, by prepaid express, another desk exactly like the one you ordered. It should reach you promptly.

If you will please telephone the express company to make a special delivery immediately upon the arrival of the desk at their receiving station, you should have the desk not later than the day of your son's birthday.

Please leave the damaged desk in the hands of the railroad. We shall enter a claim with them so that you will not be troubled further.

We appreciate your writing us promptly and hope that your son will be pleased with the gift that you have chosen for him.

Sincerely yours,

* * *

Dear Mr. Kenney:

We were very sorry to learn from your letter of September 6 that the case of canned tomatoes included with your last order reached you in damaged condition.

As we received from the shipper a receipt showing that the goods as handed over to him were properly crated, the case must have become wet nd the labels soiled in transit. Although our responsibility ended when ve delivered the goods into the hands of the carrier, we realize that you vould have a good deal of difficulty in proving a claim, since the shipnent was signed for before the damage was discovered. Under the circumstances we will be glad to co-operate with you, and suggest that you ccept the tomatoes at a 20% discount.

While it is true that the labels are badly soiled and torn, the contents f the cans will still be in perfect condition, and no doubt you could eadily dispose of the tomatoes by placing them on special sale. The 0% discount will enable you to do this without suffering any loss. It vill also save you the trouble of repacking the goods and trucking them o the freight station.

If this suggestion is agreeable to you, please let us know, and we will redit your account with the 20% discount. We appreciate your writing s promptly and are asking the carrier to be more careful in handling our future shipments.

Very truly yours,

Handling the customer who is at fault. If the customer is in the wrong, but his claim is a small one or his business is valuable, it may be better to grant the claim than run the risk of causing offense. The expense in such cases may be regarded as an investment in advertising and goodwill. A reasonably liberal adjustment policy may make many friends.

Any letter covering this type of situation must be carefully written. The tone must be firm, or the customer may think the company an "easy mark." The fact that an exception is being made must be clearly indicated, and yet not in such a way that the customer will be irritated or humiliated by being made to feel that the adjustment is granted reluctantly or that he is receiving something to which he is not entitled. The object is, on the one hand, to sell service and satisfaction; on the other, to avoid setting up a dangerous precedent.

Dear Mr. Lewis:

Thank you for your letter of September 6. We were very sorry to learn that you have been having trouble with one of the stabilators on your STANDARD car.

A careful examination of the stabilator, as returned to us by your service station in Lynbrook, leads us to believe that the spring did not break because of defective materials or poor workmanship. The adjusting nut appears to have been turned three notches tighter than is necessary on a STANDARD. Each turn of the nut winds the stabilator spring tighter; and, when the spring is too tight, there is excessive strain during the recovery of the car springs after the car has passed a hole or obstruction i the road.

Our guaranty covers only defects in materials and workmanshi However, in view of the fact that you have driven your STANDAR less than three months, we are glad to make an exception and to put new spring in the stabilator without charge.

We are today sending the stabilator to your service station in Lyr brook. It will take the service man less than fifteen minutes to attach i

The enclosed booklet, "The Stabilators on Your STANDARD," ma be of interest. We hope that you will derive full satisfaction from th easy-riding qualities that these stabilators give to thousands of STAND ARD cars.

Very truly yours,

* * *

Dear Mrs. Davies:

We wish to thank you for writing us with regard to your purchase o July 14, and also for returning the shoes for our inspection.

We have examined the shoes, and certainly agree that they are in poo condition, considering the fact that they have been used for only three weeks. However, there seems to have been a misunderstanding between us. The shoes that you purchased were advertised, at a special price, as suitable for indoor wear. Shoes of this type are not strong enough to be worn for tennis.

Although the shoes cannot, of course, be repaired, we wish you to be fully satisfied with every purchase that you make here. Accordingly, we are sending you a shoe that is made of durable canvas and is also unusually light in weight. Many prominent tennis players wear this model, which we now have on sale at the remarkably low price of $2.50.

If you wish to keep the shoes that we are sending, we will be glad to credit you with the full cost of the original pair, $1.50, and to add the balance, $1.00, to your charge account. We are doing this in appreciation of your patronage, and in the hope that you will continue to be one of our valued customers.

Very truly yours,

Letters refusing adjustments. If the claim or complaint is clearly unreasonable or unjust, the letter refusing an adjustment should state the facts in frank, straightforward style. Although the seller must, of course, absolve himself of blame or responsibility, he should be careful to avoid using a tone that seems to accuse the customer. A sincere statement of facts, together with an appeal to the customer's sense of fairness, is most effective. The facts speak for themselves in convincing the customer of the justness of the decision, and the writer's sincerity wins his respect and goodwill. Letters efusing adjustments may properly be long, since the explanation nust be complete.

Dear Mr. Jackson:

The return of merchandise shipped as ordered has become a costly problem, and, insofar as the goods mentioned in your letter of October 3 are concerned, we are asking your co-operation.

These goods were delivered to you some months ago in exact conformity with your order. If they did not please you or were not precisely what you had expected, we feel that in all fairness to us they should have been returned promptly.

Oftentimes, when delay in returning goods occurs, the styles are sold out, and delayed returns then become odd lots for which we have no outlet except at a sacrifice. This is true of the merchandise that you list in your letter.

It is quite embarrassing to us, as I am sure you understand, to offer you any credit less than one hundred cents on the dollar. On the other hand, however, I know that you would not expect us to assume an unwarranted loss.

We are willing to take back the goods and issue credit to you for whatever we can get for them. However, it would undoubtedly be better for you to move the goods through your own store at reduced prices. This, I am sure, would entail a smaller loss.

We leave the decision in your hands.

Cordially yours,

* * *

Dear Mr. Adams:

When a customer writes us for the privilege of returning boots for exchange or credit, the first thought that comes to him is that we have customers scattered all over the United States, and that we can use this returned merchandise by placing it with others.

Naturally, it's embarrassing to us to decline an accommodation, which in itself appears to be only a small item, but, when you consider that over a period of time such requests run into the thousands, you can appreciate that it would be necessary for us to set up a department requiring additional help and resulting in added expense. This expense cannot readily be added into the cost of the goods, becase that would be unfair to those customers who carry large stocks and who do not ask for such privileges. They, therefore, should not be penalized with such costs.

It has been estimated that the cost of handling returned goods ranges from slightly over 50¢ per pair in the case of shoes, lace boots, and cowboy boots to slightly over $1.00 in the case of riding and field boots. This last figure is greater because usually these boots must again be placed on the forms and retread.

All of us realize that a properly balanced stock is the only satisfactor method of fitting a customer. To attempt to fit a customer with a pa of boots, judging from the size of his or her foot, is almost impossibl due to the variation in the types of lasts, etc. There are times when yo feel you cannot afford the risk of keeping a special size in stock, if th boots do not fit, and it is then that you think of an exchange or returi

In our fifty-odd years of dealing with merchants, we have found mos of them to be fair. The trouble, if any, has been that we have not alway understood each other's problems. In this case, if you are willing t reimburse us for the extra handling cost, plus postage both ways, and i the bottoms have not been scratched or soiled, the deal is made. Is thi satisfactory?

Yours very truly,

P. S. Write your reply on the back of this letter and drop it into th mail.

* * *

Gentlemen:

Thank you for your letter of May 4 regarding the shipment of furni ture delivered to you on April 28. We were very glad to hear from you especially since you are one of our new customers, and your letter give us the opportunity to explain our policies.

We regret that we cannot refund the freight charges paid by you, in the amount of $18.35. It has always been our policy to ship f.o.b. Chicago, the home of our factory. By doing this we can give you our merchandise at the lowest possible figure, which just covers the cost of production plus a small competitive profit.

Many firms ship their goods f.o.b. the city in which the retail store is located. However, since someone must pay the freight, and the seller cannot afford to do so, the charges are added to the cost of the merchandise. We do not believe that this policy is fair. What it really means is that the total freight charges are divided among all the customers of the house, regardless of the fact that some are located only a few miles away from the factory while others are in Maine or California.

We endeavor to bring you the high quality of EASYREST FURNITURE at the lowest possible price. We hope that the merchandise recently delivered to you is entirely satisfactory and that we will have many business dealings in the future.

Very truly yours,

* * *

Gentlemen:

The charge of $7.50 for the halftone cut we made for you, to which you refer in your letter of August 3, covers only the actual cost of manufacture.

Your impression that the charge is too high is understandable, for the cost of making such cuts varies greatly. Not only the fineness and clearness of the reproduction, but also the quality of the printing paper, affect materially the labor charge involved in any particular cut.

Our engravers are employees of long standing, who know thoroughly the quality of paper and the type of presses we use. Consequently they are able to do their work with a minimum loss of time and can produce precisely the results required.

After taking these factors into consideration, you will, we are sure, willingly remit the full amount of our statement. You have our assurance that the charge is regular and in accordance with our established rates.

Very truly yours,

* * *

Dear Mr. Hopkins:

We wish that it were possible to grant your request of December 10. Were we to do so, however, we should be compelled in all fairness to do likewise for the several thousand people who purchased STANDARD cars this summer and fall. It would be exceedingly difficult to know where to draw the line.

Styles change in automobiles just as they do in furniture and clothes and hats, and it is impossible to make an adjustment as a result of such changes. For instance, a man would not think of going to his local hat dealer with a hat that he had purchased a month previously to ask that he be given a rebate merely because a new style had just come out.

Your local dealer did not act in bad faith, because no dealer definitely knows just when a model will be changed. When you purchased your STANDARD, you made your selection on the basis of value and assured satisfaction. Only the most modern production methods and our large resources enabled us to manufacture that model to sell at that price.

It is not our policy to stand still. Whenever we find any improvements that have been thoroughly tested, they are embodied at once. Hence, the STANDARD that will come out of the factory six months from now will doubtless have some improvements which are not yet in production. For the same reason the car that we will be building a year hence will differ still further.

You can readily see, therefore, that it is never going to be possible to have the latest model, or perhaps we should say the ultimate model, because our engineers and designers are constantly striving to bring out a better and better automobile.

It may interest you to know that I personally purchased a new STANDARD only eight weeks ago, although by waiting I could have had one of the new models at a saving. We are confident that the car that we manufacture has no superior, and we are sure that you will more and more appreciate your own STANDARD as time goes on.

Very truly yours,

Handling the customer where nothing is really wrong. In many cases a complaint will be made that shows the user of the product needs further education in its use. A proper handling of the situation will save expense, build goodwill, and satisfy the customer.

In the fountain pen industry, for example, the greatest common complaint is so-called "leaking." In almost all cases, the pen itself is absolutely perfect, but its use has been imperfect. To ask people to send their pens in immediately would involve handling expense to the company and a service fee to customers. Furthermore, the impression would be created that the pen is faulty—something to be avoided if the pen is perfect.

The L. E. Waterman Company found the following letter an excellent solution to the problem:

Dear Mrs. Seale:

We're glad you wrote and gave us the opportunity to make any necessary adjustments to your Waterman's gift pen so that it gives you the writing satisfaction millions of other Waterman's users experience.

Rather than inconvenience you immediately by asking you to send your pen to us, may we make this suggestion. Many instances of leaking are caused by improper filling of the pen. When the pen is almost empty, the great amount of air in the barrel will expand and force a few drops of ink out.

Make certain that these "almost empty periods" are kept few and far between, by making certain that your pen is completely full when you fill it. Keep the entire nib under ink for the count of ten, after you snap the filling lever back into place. Give your pen a good big drink of Waterman's ink.

Then, at the first sign of ink flowing heavier again, refill—and you should have no repetition of the trouble. But if these simple instructions do not help, if something is actually wrong with your pen, by all means send it to us at our main office in Newark. We'll be glad to give it our thorough and complete attention.

Very truly yours,

Handling the satisfied customer who asks too much. In many lines of business the owner of a product that has given satisfaction over a period of years will offer the product back to the company in exchange for a new one on the assumption that the company will value the testimonial and possibly use the old product as a relic. The L. E. Waterman Company, for example, receives many letters om people with old fountain pens who offer them in exchange for ew ones. To make the exchange would be unprofitable; to refuse e offer might create ill will. The following letter solves the problem by showing why the offer cannot be accepted and interposing a ir and mutually profitable trade-in for those who do want a new en:

ear Mr. Swanton:

Thank you for the very kind offer of your fountain pen and a letter f testimonial regarding it.

We have never offered to exchange 30-year-old Waterman's for new nes, Mr. Swanton, for a very good reason. Strange as it seems, there re far too many Waterman's pens, 30 years and older, still in active ervice. Then, too, the sentimental and curiosity value of pens that age ill performing perfectly deters owners from returning them.

As we have many of these old veterans in our display cases now, we're ertain your pen would be of far greater service working for you, than nerely reclining on display for us. Should it need some minor adjustnent to restore it to perfect working order, we'd be glad to look it over or you.

Or, if you'd prefer to trade in your old Waterman's for a new one, ve'd accept it as one-third payment for any new pen retailing at up to 5.00, in accordance with our special trade-in plan for the convenience f Waterman's patrons.

Thank you again, Mr. Swanton, for your courtesy and consideration, nd, if we can be of service to you, please don't hesitate to get in touch vith us.

Very truly yours,

7. LEGAL ASPECTS OF BUSINESS LETTERS

Business letters and the law. The law cannot prevent a person from writing anything he pleases, but it can and often does make him responsible for his statements. A letter may involve a person in a contractual obligation; it may subject him to liability for injury to the reputation of another person; it may be used in a lawsuit as evidence of an admission against the writer's interests. The lawbooks are filled with cases in which a letter, thoughtlessly written, has cost the writer endless embarrassment and thousands of dollars. A proper understanding of the legal consequences of a written statement, a moment's consideration of the contents or phraseology of the letter, might have avoided the litigation entirely or changed its outcome.

The dangers of careless letter writing are further increased by the fact that the law may hold a person responsible, not only for th letters which he himself writes, but for those written by his agen and employees. An agent may, by correspondence, bind his prir cipal to contracts entered into within the scope of his authority. principal, or employer, is responsible for libelous letters written b his agent or employee, not only where the agent or employee wa carrying out express directions or acting pursuant to express autho ity, but also where he was acting in the usual course of his emplo ment. Admissions of an agent made in letters within the scope c his authority are allowed as evidence against his principal. A perso is, of course, always liable for letters written by his agent or employe where he ratifies them expressly or by his conduct acquiesces therein

Contracts by Correspondence

What a contract is. A contract has been defined as an agreemen by which two parties mutually promise and engage, or one of then promises or engages to the other, to give some particular thing or t do or abstain from doing some particular act. The contract i created by a proposal or offer by one of the parties and an acceptanc thereof by the other. It may be oral or written, express or implied The following elements are necessary to make the contract valid anc enforceable:

1. The parties must be competent to contract. A person unde 21 years of age is an infant according to law and is not competent tc contract; an insane person cannot enter into a contract, although he may be held liable for necessaries supplied to him.
2. There must be an agreement between the parties—that is, a clear and definite offer on one side, and an unconditional and unqualified acceptance of the offer on the other.
3. The agreement must be supported by a consideration—that is, something of value in the eyes of the law, in the way of price or compensation that may be a benefit to the party promising or a loss to the person to whom the promise is made.
4. The subject matter of the contract must be legal. Gambling and usurious contracts, for example, are illegal.

A letter may constitute a contract. A letter containing a proposal, signed by the person making the proposal, may constitute an ffer, and a reply acquiescing in the proposal, signed by the person) whom the offer was addressed or by his duly authorized agent, ıay constitute an acceptance. The two letters together may result ı a valid and enforceable contract. To establish a contract by corre- ɔondence, the offer must be clear and definite, and the acceptance ıust be without conditions or qualifications. An acceptance upon erms varying from those offered is a rejection of the offer and puts n end to the negotiations unless the party who made the original ffer renews it or properly assents to the modification suggested. 'his does not mean that all the terms of the agreement must appear ı a single letter or even in two letters. The complete contract may e gathered from a series of letters between the parties, determining tep by step the various terms of the contract. It must, however, be lear from the correspondence that the minds of the parties have met vith respect to the material elements of the contract. A circular and rice list announcing goods for sale at specified prices is generally onsidered simply as an invitation for an offer and not an offer itself. 'he final determination of whether or not it is an offer depends upon he intent of the parties as gathered from the correspondence be- ween them.

May oral statements contradict the terms of a contract evi- lenced by letters? Where letters contain a definite and complete :ontract, the law will not permit oral evidence to show what the con- ract between the parties was. This protection against variation or :ontradiction is furnished by the so-called "parol evidence rule." 'he parol evidence rule is a general rule of law which holds that, in he absence of fraud or mistake, extrinsic evidence is not admissible ıpon a trial to show that the real agreement of the parties was lifferent from that expressed in a writing; nor where a writing is ree from ambiguity is parol evidence admissible to explain its mean- ng. If a series of letters does not contain all the terms of the contract, either in the proposition made or in its acceptance, parol evidence may be allowed to prove the exact terms of the contract.

Letters as memoranda satisfying the statute of frauds. The term "statute of frauds" is used to describe the laws in the various states requiring certain contracts and transfers of property to be evidenced by a writing signed by the party who is to be charged therewith, or by his duly authorized agent. The following agrements, among others, are subject to the statute of frauds:

1. An agreement to answer for the debt, default, or miscarriag of another person.

2. Agreements not to be performed within one year from th making thereof.

3. Transfers and contracts for the transfer of real property an interests therein.

4. Contracts for the sale of goods, wares, or merchandise in exces of a certain amount (which varies in the different states), excep where a part of the goods is accepted and received by the buyer c where he gives something in part payment.

No particular form of instrument or language is required for th written memorandum. Any document, written either to evidenc the contract or for any other purpose, is sufficient if it states all th essential elements of the contract with reasonable certainty and i signed by the party to be charged or by his agent. A letter may be a sufficient writing to satisfy the statute of frauds, and several letter may be considered together in supplying the essential elements o such a memorandum as will satisfy the statute. The writing neec not be addressed to the other party to the contract; a letter to hi writer's agent may constitute an adequate memorandum of the contract.

Libelous Letters

What libel is. A libel has been defined as a false and malicious publication that tends to injure the reputation of a living person or the memory of a deceased person, and to expose him to public hatred, contempt, or ridicule. A corporation is a person in this sense, as well as an individual, and a publication that injures the corporation's credit, property, or business is actionable. The libel may be in the form of a writing such as a letter, a printing such as a newspaper, or it may be by signs and pictures. The statutes in some states define a libel, and in such cases the statute governs in determining whether or not a publication constitutes a libel. In Missouri, for example, a libel is defined by law as "the malicious defamation of a person made public by any printing, writing, sign, picture, presentation, or effigy, tending to provoke him to wrath or expose im to public hatred, contempt, or ridicule, or to deprive him of the enefits of public confidence and social intercourse, or any malicious efamation made public as aforesaid, designed to blacken and vilify e memory of one who is dead, and tending to scandalize or provoke is surviving relatives and friends." The fact that a statement which libelous is proved to be true generally frees the person who made e defamation from civil liability therefor.

A libelous letter must be communicated to a third party in rder to be actionable. In order that a suit may be maintained for defamatory writing, it must have been read by someone other than e person defamed. A letter containing a libel that is addressed the person libeled and is not read by anyone else is generally not ctionable. The reader may be a copyist who reproduces a longhand raft. He may be a stenographer who takes the libelous writing by ictation and examines and transcribes the notes, although some ourts have taken the view that publication to a stenographer is rivileged and does not subject the writer to liability unless impelled y actual malice. A private letter between officers of a corporation n the course of a company's business, which is not communicated o others, has been held not to be published, and the corporation has een deemed immune from liability for any damages resulting therefrom. Similarly, a letter written and mailed by one agent of a corporation within the scope of his employment to another agent of the ame corporation does not amount to a publication of such a nature s to constitute a libel against the corporation.

Must pecuniary loss be shown in a suit for libel? The law divides written words charged to be libelous into three classes:

1. Words libelous *per se*.
2. Words libelous *per quod*.
3. Words that cannot possibly bear a defamatory meaning.

The first class includes those words which are injurious upon their face and without the aid of extrinsic proof. The law presumes damage from the mere publication of the libel, and hence calls it libel *per se*—that is, "by itself." To be libelous *per se*, the words must be susceptible of but one meaning and must be of such a nature that the court can presume that they tend to disgrace and degrade a person, to injure him in his business or profession, or to hold him up to public hatred or ridicule and cause him to be shunned and avoided. The second class of libelous words, libel *per quod* (meaning "by which"), includes those words which are reasonably susceptible of a defamatory meaning as well as an innocent one, and may be defamatory by reason of their imputation or of extrinsic facts; such words require proof of pecuniary loss. Words that fall into the third class, and cannot possibly bear a defamatory meaning, cannot be made the basis of an action for libel.

Examples of communications that are libelous. The following kinds of statements have been held in court cases to inflict an injury on a person's business, and to be actionable without proof of pecuniary loss:

1. Imputing insolvency or bankruptcy, or suggesting that a person is in pecuniary difficulties.
2. Imputing to a merchant or tradesman want of credit or responsibility.
3. Charging a merchant with falsifying his scales and selling merchandise to customers by false weight.
4. Charging one with receiving stolen goods.
5. Imputing want of knowledge, skill, or capacity to conduct business; but disparaging the merchandise of another person or the quality of his products, without imputing fraud, is not actionable without proof of pecuniary loss.
6. Imputing to an officer or employee dereliction of duty or lack of due qualification; but a letter to the employer of a person not engaged in a vocation requiring credit, to the effect that the employee refuses to pay his debts, sent for the purpose of obtaining the employer's help in effecting collection, is not actionable without proof of pecuniary loss.

Libelous letters may be privileged. Under certain circumstances communications that ordinarily would be defamatory are deemed by the law to be justified or "privileged." This means that no civil liability for their publication attaches, unless it is proved that the communication was made maliciously. Such privilege occurs where the communication is made by one person in pursuance of a duty—political, judicial, social, or personal—in a matter where his interest concerned, to another person having a corresponding duty or iterest. The court determines in the first instance whether the ccasion exists that justifies the publication of the defamatory statement in the absence of malice, and the person suing must then show ie existence of actual or express malice in order to sustain his action. Malice, in this case, does not necessarily imply hatred, ill will, anger, rath, or vindictiveness; it may mean no more than the antithesis f good faith.

When is the privilege lost? Whether or not a communication is rivileged depends, not only upon the occasion which calls for the ublication, but also upon the character of the communication. If, or example, the defamatory statement goes beyond the plain necesities of the situation, and uses excessive language, the privilege is ost, and the nature of the communication furnishes evidence of xpress malice. If a communication is privileged, the privilege covers ll incidents of the transmission of the communication in accordance with the usual course of business. For example, the communication may be dictated to a stenographer for transmission without oss of the privilege. There is considerable authority for the view hat communications between employer and employee are privileged where the communication relates to matters pertaining to the employment and is made in good faith.

Examples of libelous letters that are privileged. The following letters have been held to be privileged:

1. A letter written in answer to a request for information concerning a former employee.
2. A communication from a mercantile agency to a person having an interest in the particular matter, but not in a report issued for general circulation among its subscribers. A false publication that a person is a criminal, voluntarily made by a credit bureau to subscribers and others, is not privileged.
3. A letter written by a steamship company in the ordinary course of its business to the seller of merchandise to ascertain what it should do with merchandise left in its hands, in which it was stated that the purchaser had filed a petition in bankruptcy.
4. A letter written by an attorney for one creditor to another

creditor, stating that the debtor was insolvent, and requesting a thorization to represent the creditor in bankruptcy proceedings.

5. An answer by a businessman to a confidential inquiry as to th financial standing of some individual, firm, or corporation, when the answer is fairly and honestly made, and the writer has reasonabl and probable cause to believe his statements to be true.

6. A letter from the cashier of a bank to a stockholder regardin the financial standing of a surety on an official bond to the bank.

7. An answer to a request for information concerning the trust worthiness of another who has applied for credit.

Letters as Evidence of Admission Against the Writer

What is an admission that can be used as evidence against the firm? In order that a letter may be offered in evidence as an ad mission against the interest of the firm or person writing, the lette itself must contain an admission of some fact. A letter containing merely an innuendo from which one must conjecture what the writer was referring to cannot be used as evidence of an admission against his interest. A letter containing an admission against in terest, to be allowed as evidence against the writer, need not have been written to the person who is offering it as evidence. It may be written to one who is not a party to the suit. For example, a letter written to a third person telling such person to deal with a designated individual, the writer's agent, and stating that any deal made with him would be satisfactory, was held in a court action to be competent proof of the agent's authority. An anonymous threatening letter, written to frighten a litigant into abandoning a pending suit, was deemed to be in the nature of an admission that a valid cause of action existed and that the writer had no defense thereto. A letter to a third party in which the writer stated that he had entered into a contract with the plaintiff was held admissible in an action on the contract.

When a letter containing an offer of compromise may be admissible as evidence of liability. The law favors the settlement of disputed claims without litigation, and to encourage such settlements the general rule has been laid down that an offer of settlement which has been rejected cannot be used as evidence of the existence or of the amount of liability. This fact is true whether the offer of ompromise is made before or after suit has been begun. Letters ontaining offers of compromise are, however, generally admitted in idence under the following circumstances:

1. Where an offer of settlement is not rejected but is accepted nd agreed upon and thereafter repudiated by the person making e offer; evidence of the offer is allowed in an action on the claim.

2. Where an admission against interest of particular facts, material to the issue before the court, accompanies an offer of compromise ut is independent of it, the admission may be received as evidence ending to establish the facts stated, unless:

(*a*) The admission is so integrated that the offer of compromise inseparable from it.

(*b*) It appears that the admission against interest is made as a oncession to induce a compromise.

(*c*) The admission is stated to be made without prejudice.

3. Where a letter making an offer to pay a certain amount is ritten and received before any controversy is pending as to the mount due, the letter is admissible to show the amount due. imilarly, a letter seeking to determine differences of opinion as to itle to property, written long before suit is brought involving title to he property, is not considered an offer of compromise and is allowed o be introduced as evidence.

May letters be used as evidence against the recipient? A peron to whom a letter is addressed is ordinarily not required to make ny reply, and failure to answer the letter is no evidence of the truth f the facts stated therein. The reason for this general rule is that a erson cannot make evidence for himself by his own "self-serving" leclarations as to the character of his dealings or as to the liability f the person to whom the statement is addressed; a letter from one arty to the other is incompetent to prove the statements therein in avor of the writer. There are, however, exceptions to the general rule. When a letter is written making a claim that in common experience would naturally be denied by the addressee, or where it is his duty to reply, the letter and the failure to reply may be admitted in evidence. Whether or not an unanswered letter is proof of an admission depends upon the circumstances of each case. Want of facility in writing, habitual delay in correspondence, or press of business, may tend to lead to the conclusion that silence is n acquiescence.

A letter may extend or revive an outlawed debt. Statutes hav been enacted in the various states limiting to a fixed period the tim within which suit may be brought on certain causes of action. I New York, for example, an action on a contract, express or implie other than a judgment or a sealed instrument, is barred unless con menced within six years after accrual of the cause of action—that i within six years after the contract has been breached and a right t sue thereon has arisen. These statutes, commonly known as "statute of limitations," are the outgrowth of a legal fiction resting upon th theory that after a long lapse of time during which a claimant ha made no assertion of his rights, the obligation is presumed to hav been paid or discharged. The presumption may, however, be waive by the debtor in any one of the following ways:

1. By an admission or acknowledgment of the existence of th debt, from which a promise to pay may be implied; no expres promise to pay is required, but a mere acknowledgment of a debt i not sufficient unless the acknowledgment is one from which a prom ise to pay is clearly inferable.
2. By an unconditional promise to pay the debt.
3. By a conditional promise to pay the debt, provided the condi tion has been performed.

The acknowledgment or promise may be made either before o after the entire statutory period has expired. If it is made befor the expiration of the limited period, the old debt is vitalized for an other statutory period, dating from the time of the acknowledgmen or promise; if it is made after the statutory period has run, a new cause of action arises. In some states the statutes specifically require that an acknowledgment of indebtedness or promise to pay shall be in writing, signed by the party to be charged therewith, and in such cases signed letters or other signed documents are sufficient to satisfy the requirements. The letter or other document must, however, identify the debt explicitly and certainly; where there are several debts, a general acknowledgment of them is insufficient. Similarly, an acknowledgment is not sufficient if it leaves the amount of the debt in dispute. In some states the statutes requiring acknowledgents or promises to be in writing have been held to apply only to ose acknowledgments or promises made after the statutory period limitations has fully expired.

8. GETTING SALES VALUE OUT OF LETTER LAYOUT

Stationery and letterhead. Rightly or wrongly, people judge any things by appearances. An old-fashioned letterhead, poorly esigned and reproduced on cheap stationery, must inevitably make unfavorable impression. The appearance of the business letter—e design of the letterhead, the quality of the stationery, and the atness and correctness of the typing—has a real sales value; it forms the mind of the reader a subconscious picture of the character of e firm whose name appears at the top of the sheet.

Most business houses use bond stock for their letter paper; ledger, rchment, and many book papers are also suitable. In bond stock e weight most commonly used is twenty-pound, although twenty-ur or twenty-eight pound is sometimes employed. Bond stock of ss than twenty-pound weight is not desirable.

The standard size of letter paper for commercial use is 8½ × 11 ches; other sizes preferred by some firms are 5½ × 8½ inches and ¼ × 10½ inches. Many houses use stationery of note-paper size r business letters addressed to women. The size of the letter paper sed for sales letters varies greatly.

The design of the letterhead should reflect the character of the rm. In general, simplicity and compactness are desirable. The est procedure is to have a specialist submit designs from which a hoice can be made. A number of companies produce letterheads xclusively. Artists, printers, engravers, and lithographers also do xcellent work in designing individual letterheads.

The most usual methods of reproduction are letterpress (printing), thography, offset, engraving, embossing, die-stamping, and plateless ngraving. Each of these methods has its advantages; selection may e made on the basis of taste and expense.

Examples of effective letterheads. A number of effective letter-eads, representative of various lines of business, are reproduced on ages 612-613.

Printed in Black and Blue, on Franconia Bond.

Engraved in Black and Red, on Crane's Japanese Linen Bond.

Engraved in Black, on Howard Bond.

Printed in Black and Orange.

Figure 54. Examples of Effective Letterheads.

NOVO
ENGINE COMPANY
NEW YORK OFFICE 167TH ST. & SEDGWICK AVE.
TELEPHONE 2-1346
CABLE ADDRESS: NOVO · LANSING, MICHIGAN : CODES: BENTLEY'S · GENERAL TELEGRAPH · WESTERN UNION UNIVERSAL EDITION : A.B.C. FIFTH & SIXTH EDITION
LANSING
MICHIGAN
U·S·A

Lithographed in Grey, on Howard Bond.

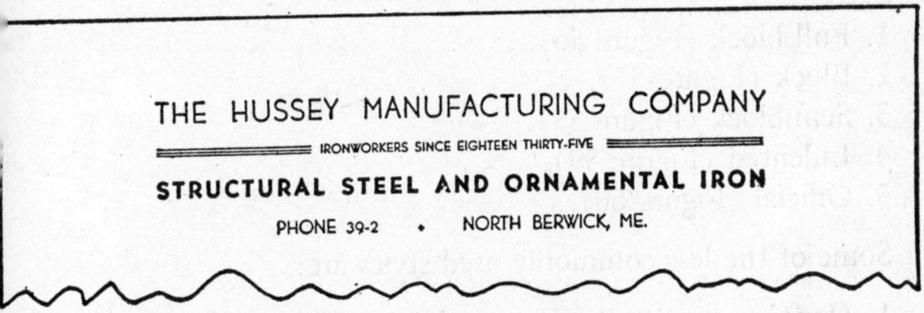

Printed in Blue and Red, on Rockledge Bond.

Telephone
BARCLAY.
7-0993
J. C. SHUTE COMPANY, INC.
WHOLESALE DEALERS & COMMISSION MERCHANTS
•FOREIGN AND DOMESTIC FRUITS•
231 WASHINGTON STREET New York

Designed and engraved by Nahm Photogravure Co., N. Y. C.

Engraved on Adirondack Bond

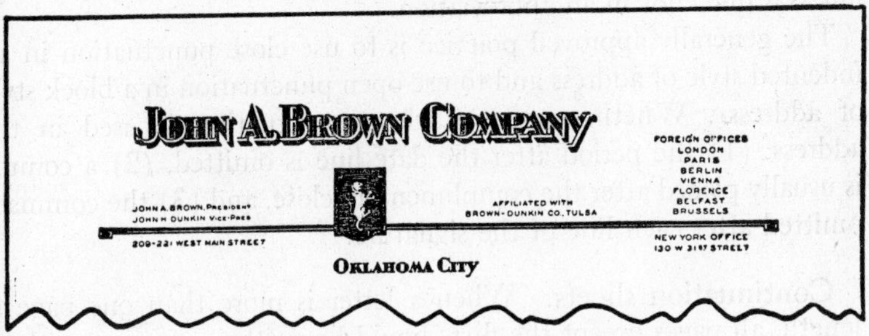

Printed in Black, on Arrowhead Bond.

Figure 55. Examples of Effective Letterheads.

Setup of the letter. The competent secretary or stenograpl gives careful attention to the mechanical setup of the letter—t arrangement on the page, the width of the margins, and the positi of the date, the inside address, the salutation, and the complimenta close. Modern business practice has established certain conventio of good usage and correctness in respect to such matters; observan of these conventions reflects good taste.

The standard styles in which letters are set up are:

1. Full block (Figure 56).
2. Block (Figure 57).
3. Semiblock (Figure 58).
4. Indented (Figure 59).
5. Official (Figure 60).

Some of the less commonly used styles are:

1. Hanging paragraph (Figure 61).
2. Simplified (Figure 62).

Letters written in these styles are reproduced in the followin pages. Read each of the letters for an explanation of its distinguisl ing characteristics.

Punctuation. Either close or open punctuation may be used i the structural parts of a letter. *Close punctuation* means punctua tion marks after the date line, each line of the address, the compli mentary close, and each line of the signature. *Open punctuatio* means the omission of punctuation marks after each of these parts unless a line ends in an abbreviation.

The generally approved practice is to use close punctuation in a indented style of address and to use open punctuation in a block styl of address. Whether open or close punctuation is used in th address, (1) the period after the date line is omitted, (2) a comma is usually placed after the complimentary close, and (3) the comma i omitted after each line of the signature.

Continuation sheets. When a letter is more than one page i length, all pages except the first should be written on paper withou a letterhead. Some firms, however, print their name and address i small type at the top of the continuation sheet, near the left-hand

Prentice-Hall, Inc.

70 Fifth Avenue, New York 11

EXECUTIVE OFFICES

March 25, 19--

In reply refer to 15:1 RTS

Mr. N. D. Edwards, Office Manager
Robertson-Davies Company
35 Fifth Avenue
New York 11, New York

Dear Mr. Edwards:

This is an example of the full block style of letter adopted as standard at Prentice-Hall. We have reproduced this letter in our Employee Manual so that everyone will be familiar with the form and the instructions for its use.

Since Prentice-Hall is a leading exponent of modern business methods, we naturally use the most efficient letter form. This style saves time and energy.

As you can see, there are no indentations. Everything, including the date, the reference, and the complimentary close, begins at the extreme left. This eliminates several mechanical operations in typing letters.

Our dictaphone typists always use this form unless the dictator instructs otherwise. The dictator is at liberty to alter the form if a change is essential for business reasons.

In the reference line we type the department's reference number and the dictator's initials so that the reply can be directed promptly to the proper person. Every department head knows the reference numbers assigned to his department.

As the dictator's name is typed in the signature, we do not consider it necessary to include his initials in the identification line.

Sincerely,

Richard P. Ettinger

Richard P. Ettinger
President

bs

Figure 56. Full Block Style.

The distinguishing feature of the Full Block Style of letter is that all the structural parts of the letter begin flush with the left margin. There are no indentations. The dictator's initials are not included in the identification line, but if the expected reply is to be routed to a person other than the dictator, that person's initials may be typed in the reference line. Open punctuation is used.

HOOVEN LETTERS INCORPORATED

Hooven Individually Typewritten Letters · Multigraphing · Nahmco Process Letters · Addressing · Mimeographing · Offset & Mailing

352 FOURTH AVE · NEW YORK 10, N.Y. · TELEPHONE LEXINGTON 2-6162

HORACE K. NAHM
PRESIDENT

March 25, 19--

In reply please refer to 15:1 MH

The Nahm Photogravure Company
352 Fourth Avenue
New York 10, N. Y.

Attention J. S. Heller

Gentlemen:

This is an example of the block style of letter. Probably more business concerns use it than any other style of letter, because its marginal uniformity saves time for the typist. Many companies are adopting the full block style, however, as it saves even more time than the block.

As you can see, the inside address is blocked and paragraph beginnings are aligned with the left margin, as they are in the full block form. Open punctuation is used in the address.

The date and reference lines are flush with the right margin. The date line is two spaces below the letterhead, and the reference line is two spaces below the date line. The complimentary close begins slightly to the right of the center of the page. Both lines of the signature are aligned with the complimentary close.

I do not advocate including the dictator's initials in the identification line, because his name is typed in the signature.

Sincerely yours,

Mary Haddad

Mary Haddad
Correspondence Chief

Figure 57. Block Style.

The distinguishing feature of the inside Block Style of letter is that the inside address and the paragraphs are blocked, flush with the left-hand margin The salutation and attention line, if any, are aligned with the inside address. The date and reference line are flush with the right-hand margin. The typed signature is aligned with the complimentary close. Open punctuation is used.

D. H. AHREND COMPANY

INCORPORATED

Creative Direct Advertising

325 to 333 EAST 44th STREET • NEW YORK 17 • MURRAY HILL 6-3212

March 25, 19

Mr. N. D. Edwards, Office Manager
Robertson-Davies Company
35 Fifth Avenue
New York 11, New York

Dear Mr. Edwards:

This is an example of the semi-block style of letter. Many companies prefer it to the block style because it combines an attractive appearance with utility. Private secretaries, who are not usually concerned with mass production of correspondence, favor it

This style differs from the block form in only one respect--the first line of each paragraph is indented five or ten spaces. In this example the paragraphs are indented ten spaces. As in all letters, there is a double space between paragraphs.

The date line is flush with the right margin, two or four spaces below the letterhead. The complimentary close begins slightly to the right of the center of the page. All lines of the signature are aligned with the complimentary close. Open punctuation is used in the address.

No identification line is used in this example. As the dictator's name is typed in the signature, his initials are not necessary. The typist's initials are shown on the carbon copy.

Very sincerely yours,

D. H. AHREND COMPANY

Marcia Abbie

MARCIA ABBIE
Assistant to President

Figure 58. Semi-Block Style.

The distinguishing feature of a Semi-Block Style of letter is that all structural parts of the letter begin flush with the left-hand margin, but the first line of each paragraph is indented five or ten spaces. All lines of the typed signature are aligned with the complimentary close. The date is typed in the conventional position. Open punctuation is used.

Large Production Facilities *Day and Night Service*

LENZ & RIECKER

INCORPORATED

Printers

75 VARICK STREET · NEW YORK 13

Holland Plaza Building, *Corner Canal Street*

Telephone, WALKER 5-9395-6-7

March 25, 194-

Mr. N. D. Edwards, Office Manager,
Robertson-Davies Company,
35 Fifth Avenue,
New York 11, New York.

Dear Mr. Edwards:

This is an example of the indented style of letter. I am enclosing three sheets from our Correspondence Manual that describe the other forms in which you are interested.

Many conservative organizations still use the indented style as they prefer it to new forms. The indented style is correct, however, for any type of organization.

Each line of the address is indented five spaces more than the preceding line. The beginning of each paragraph is indented the same as the third line of the address, which is ten spaces. The complimentary close begins a few spaces to the right of the center of the page. Each line of the signature is indented three spaces from the beginning of the complimentary close. Close punctuation is used in the address but not in the signature.

Sincerely yours,

Joseph F. Caradine
Treasurer

Enclosures 3

Figure 59. Indented Style.

The distinguishing feature of the Indented Style of letter is that each line of address is indented five spaces more than the preceding line. The first line of each paragraph is indented ten spaces. Each line of the typed signature is indented three spaces from the beginning of the complimentary close. Close punctuation is used in the address but not in the signature.

GO PLACES AND DO THINGS

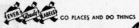

EVER READY *Label* CORPORATION

137 EAST 25th STREET
NEW YORK 10, N. Y.
MURRAY HILL 4-4300

March 25, 19--

Dear Mr Edwards.

This letter is an example of the official style. It is used in many personal letters written by executives and professional men, and looks unusually well on the executive-size letterhead.

The structural parts of the letter differ from the standard arrangement only in the position of the inside address. The salutation is placed two to five spaces below the date line, depending upon the length of the letter. It establishes the left margin of the letter. The inside address is written in block form, flush with the left margin, from two to five spaces below the final line of the signature. Open punctuation is used in the address.

The identification line, if used, should be placed two spaces below the last line of the address, and the enclosure mark two spaces below that. As the dictator's name is typed in the signature, it is not necessary for the letter to carry an identification line. The typist's initials are on the carbon of the letter, but not on the original.

Very truly yours,

Alan Kleiner

Alan Kleiner
Treasurer

Mr. N. E. Edwards, Office Manager
Robertson-Davies Company
35 Fifth Avenue
New York 11, New York

Figure 60. Official Style.

The distinguishing feature of the Official Style of letter is that the inside address is placed below the signature, flush with the left-hand margin, instead of before the salutaton. The identification line and enclosure notations, if any, are typed two spaces below the last line of the address. Open punctuation is used. This style is especially appropriate for personal letters in business.

Mailings incorporated

25 WEST 45TH STREET · NEW YORK 19 NEW YORK · LONGACRE 3-227

March 25, 19--

Mr. N. D. Edwards, Office Manager
Robertson-Davies Company
35 Fifth Avenue
New York 11, New York

Dear Mr. Edwards:

This letter is an example of the hanging paragraph style of letter. It is rarely used as it is more difficult and takes longer to write than the other styles.

The distinctive feature of the hanging paragraph style is that the first line of each paragraph is flush with the left margin and all other lines are indented five spaces. To write this letter it is necessary to use the tabulator after each carriage shift.

The inside address is written in block style. It may be in the standard position or below the signature, to the left, as in the official form. As the address is blocked, open punctuation is used.

Sincerely yours,

Lewis Kleid

Lewis Kleid
President

Figure 61. Hanging Paragraph Style.

The distinguishing feature of the Hanging Paragraph Style is that the first line of each paragraph is flush with the left-hand margin, but all other lines are indented five spaces. It takes longer to write a letter in this style than in other styles, because the tabulator is used after each carriage shift. The inside address and the lines of signature are in block style. Open punctuation is used.

NATIONAL OFFICE MANAGEMENT ASSOCIATION
12 EAST CHELTEN AVENUE
PHILADELPHIA 44, PA.

June 16, 1949

this is a
SIMPLIFIED
letter

Mr. N. D. Edwards
Robertson-Davies Company
35 Fifth Avenue
New York 11, N. Y.

MUCH ADO ABOUT SOMETHING

Your interest in better business letters, Mr. Edwards, makes writing to you a real pleasure. Especially when you give me an opportunity to discuss NOMA's Simplified Letter.

The SL is really just a sensible way of putting a soft collar on business correspondence — a way of combining dignity with informality at a low cost in keystrokes and typewriter manipulation. Yet it incorporates the same sound principles that good letter writers, like you, have demonstrated for years.

Physically, I suppose, the dropping of the meaningless salutation and close, and the use of the left block format will first catch your attention. This letter actually looks as the typewriter was made to make it look.

But, more important, the philosophy behind the SL seeks to reduce slow starting — a long windup and a wobbly pitch. It seeks to combine sincerity and simplification without sacrificing friendliness.

Every letter becomes a challenge. Every letter echoes the sound of the writer's own thinking. As I write to you I'm acutely aware of that sound. I hope you won't think me presumptuous in trying to demonstrate the endless possibilities of this way of letter thinking.

I'd be glad to send you more detailed suggestions on the SL, and to receive your report of experience in trying them out.

Your letter was a happy reminder that letters, too, invite inquiring minds — invite much ado about something simplified.

Vaughn Fry

VAUGHN FRY - PUBLIC RELATIONS

Miss Besse May Miller, Mr. W. H. Evans

there is more to a truly
SIMPLIFIED LETTER
than simply dropping
dear and yours truly

Figure 62. Simplified Letter.

The distinguishing feature of a Simplified Letter is that the saluation and complimentary close are omitted. "Copy to" is also omitted before the names of persons to whom carbon copies of the letter are to be sent. All structural parts of the letter are flush with the left-hand margin. The subject line is placed between the address and the body of the letter. Open punctuation is used.

margin. Continuation sheets should be of the same size and quality as the letterhead. They should be ordered at the same time as the letterhead.

Envelopes. Envelopes should be of the same quality as the letterhead. The most popular sizes for business use are:

No. 5	4½″ by 5⅛″
No. 6¼	3½″ by 6″
No. 6¾	3⅝″ by 6½″
No. 10	4⅛″ by 9½″

No. 6¾ and No. 10 fit the 8½ by 11 letterheads. No. 5, which is the Baronial size, is widely used by business executives for their personal stationery.

9. MAKING THE STRUCTURAL PARTS OF A LETTER PERFECT

Where to type the date line. The standard position of the date line on the page is two to four spaces below the last line of the letterhead, flush with the right-hand margin of the letter. If the letter is very short, you may drop the date line to give a better balance to the page. The date line, however, does not affect the placement of the letter on the page.

The date line is sometimes centered on the page, about two spaces below the letterhead. If this style is used, center the date line *exactly*. Do not use this position unless the date line is easily distinguishable from the letterhead. Figure 63 is an example of a letterhead where the center position is used effectively.

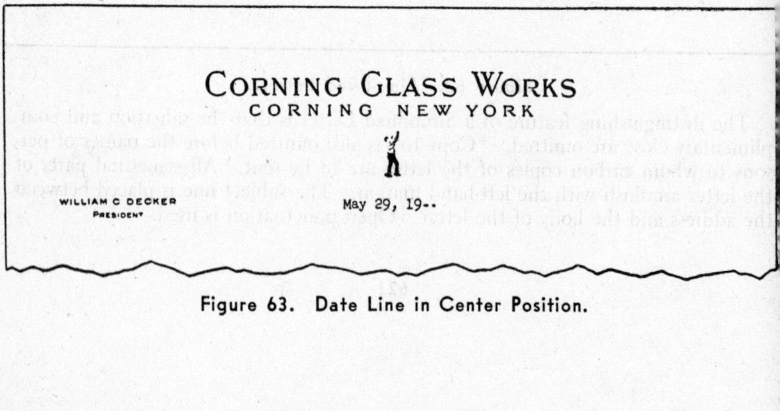

Figure 63. Date Line in Center Position.

With some letterheads, the letter presents a better appearance if e date line is not placed in the standard positions. It is permissible ignore standard practice, but if there is any doubt as to where e date line would be most effective, follow the standard style. gure 64 is a reproduction of a letterhead where the appearance of e letter is improved by placing the date line in a position other an the conventional one.

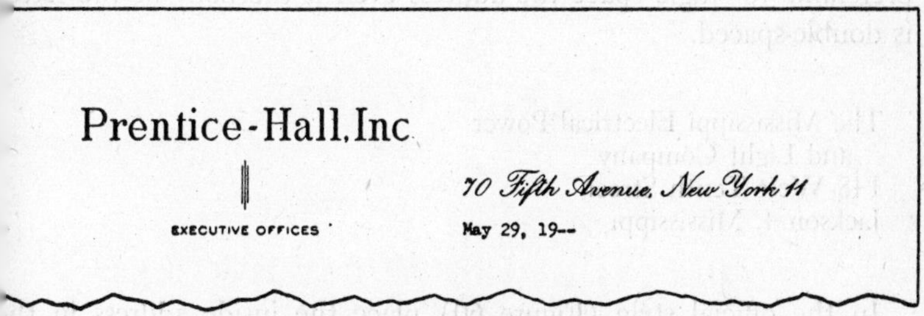
Prentice-Hall, Inc

EXECUTIVE OFFICES

70 Fifth Avenue, New York 11

May 29, 19--

Figure 64. Date Line Aligned with Letterhead.

How to type the date line. 1. Date the letter the day it is dictated, not the day it is typed.

2. Type the date conventionally, all on one line.

3. Do not use *d, nd, rd, st,* or *th* following the day of the month.

4. Do not abbreviate or use figures for the month.

5. Do not spell out the day of the month or the year, except in ery formal letters.

RIGHT	WRONG
eptember 15, 195–	September 15th, 195–
	9/15/5–
	Sept. 15, 195–
	September fifteenth, Nineteen hundred and fifty–

Inside Address

What the inside address contains. The inside address contains the name of the addressee and the address, including the zone number when it is available. In addressing an individual in a company, the inside address contains both the individual's name and that of the company. It may also contain the individual's business title.

Where to type the inside address. Begin the inside address a the left-hand margin of the letter, not less than 2 spaces, nor mo than 12, below the date line. The exact position of the first lin of the address depends on the length of the letter. The insid address should not extend beyond the middle of the page. In th block style of address carry over part of an extremely long lin to a second line. Indent the carry-over line three spaces. It i preferable to single space the address even if the body of the lette is double-spaced.

The Mississippi Electrical Power
   and Light Company
148 West Tenth Street
Jackson 4, Mississippi

In the official style (Figure 60) place the inside address in th lower left-hand corner of the page, even with the left-hand margi of the letter and two spaces below the signature.

How to type the inside address. 1. The inside address shoul correspond exactly with the official name of the company addressed If *Company, Co., The, Inc.,* or *&* is part of the company's officia name, use the form used in the company title.

2. Do not precede the street number with a word or a sign.

RIGHT	WRONG
70 Fifth Avenue	No. 70 Fifth Avenue
	# 70 Fifth Avenue

3. Spell out the numerical names of streets and avenues if the are numbers of 12 or under. When figures are used, do not follow with *d, st,* or *th.* Use figures for all house numbers except *One* Separate the house number from a numerical name of a thorough fare with a space, a hyphen, and a space. Authorities give different rules for writing addresses, but the following are standard, approved forms.

23 East Twelfth Street	2 Fifth Avenue
23 East 13 Street	234 - 72 Street
One Fifth Avenue	

4. Never abbreviate the name of a city. States, territories, and ssessions may be abbreviated, but the better practice is not to breviate them. The following are the approved forms of abbrevia- ns for the state, territories, and possessions:

abama	Ala.	Nebraska	Nebr.
izona	Ariz.	Nevada	Nev.
kansas	Ark.	New Hampshire	N. H.
alifornia	Calif.	New Jersey	N. J.
anal Zone	C. Z.	New Mexico	N. Mex.
olorado	Colo.	New York	N. Y.
onnecticut	Conn.	North Carolina	N. C.
elaware	Del.	North Dakota	N. Dak.
istrict of Columbia	D. C.	Oklahoma	Okla.
orida	Fla.	Oregon	Oreg.
eorgia	Ga.	Pennsylvania	Pa.
awaii	T. H.	Philippine Islands	P. I.
inois	Ill.	Puerto Rico	P. R.
diana	Ind.	Rhode Island	R. I.
ansas	Kans.	South Carolina	S. C.
entucky	Ky.	South Dakota	S. Dak.
ouisiana	La.	Tennessee	Tenn.
aryland	Md.	Texas	Tex.
assachusetts	Mass.	Vermont	Vt.
ichigan	Mich.	Virginia	Va.
innesota	Minn.	Washington	Wash.
ississippi	Miss.	West Virginia	W. Va.
issouri	Mo.	Wisconsin	Wis.
ontana	Mont.	Wyoming	Wyo.

Do not abbreviate the following:

Alaska	Iowa	Samoa
Guam	Maine	Utah
Idaho	Ohio	Virgin Islands

5. The zone number follows the city and is separated from the tate by a comma.

6. If there is no street address, put the city and state on separate nes.

7. Do not abbreviate business titles or positions, such as Presi- ent, Secretary, and Sales Manager. *Mr.* (or *Mrs.* or *Miss*) precedes he individual's name, even when the business title is used.

If a person's business title is short, place it on the first line; if it s long, place it on the second line.

Mr. James E. Lambert, President
Lambert & Woolf Company
1005 Tower Street
Cleveland 3, Ohio

Mr. George F. Moore
Advertising Manager
Price & Patterson
234 Seventh Avenue
New York 5, New York

The modern trend is to omit the business title, particularly if makes the address run over four lines. For example, *Advertisi Manager* would be omitted in the preceding address.

8. In addressing an individual in a firm, corporation, or grou place the individual's name on the first line, and the compan name on the second line.

9. Do not hyphenate a title unless it represents a combinati of two offices.

10. When writing to the officer of a company who holds sever offices, use only the title of the highest office, unless letters from hi are signed differently.

11. If a letter is addressed to a particular department in a cor pany, place the name of the company on the first line and the nan of the department on the second line.

Forms of address. (For the correct forms of addressing men i official or honorary positions see the chart at page 641, *et seq.*)

1. Always precede a name by a title, unless initials indicatin degrees (see 2.) or Esquire (see 4.) follows the name. The use c a business title or position or of Sr. or Jr. after a name does nc take the place of a title.

RIGHT	WRONG
Mr. Ralph P. Edwards, President	Ralph P. Edwards, President

2. Initials or abbreviations indicating degrees and other honor are sometimes placed after the name of the person addressed. Us only the initials of the highest degree; more than one degree ma be used, however, if the degrees are in different fields. A scholasti title is not used in combination with the abbreviation indicatin that degree, but another title may be used in combination witl abbreviations indicating degrees.

Right	Wrong
›bert E. Saunders, Ph.D.	Robert E. Saunders, A.B., A.M., Ph.D.
r. Ralph Jones (*preferred*) *or*	Dr. Ralph Jones, M.D.
ılph Jones, M.D.	Professor Robert E. Saunders, Ph.D.
ıe Reverend Perry E. Moore, D.D., LL.D.	
To a professor	
·ofessor Robert E. Saunders	

3. *Messrs.* may be used in addressing a firm of men, or men and omen, when the names denote individuals. Do not use *Messrs.* a form of address for corporations or other business organizations ıat bear impersonal names.

Right	Wrong
merican Manufacturing Company	Messrs. American Manufacturing Company
lessrs. Marvin, Tobin and Smart	Messrs. James Marshall & Sons
ımes Marshall & Sons	

4. *Esquire* or *Esq.* may be used in addressing prominent attorneys r other high ranking professional men who do not have other titles. *Ir.* does not precede the name when *Esquire* or *Esq.* is used. In ıct, no other title is used with *Esquire* or *Esq.*

Right	Wrong
Ionorable Richard P. Davis	Honorable Richard P. Davis, Esq.
.llison D. Wells, Esquire	Mr. Allison D. Wells, Esquire
Jathan Rogers, Jr., Esq.	Mr. Nathan Rogers, Jr., Esq.

Iote: The title *Esq.* is commonly used in England and in her colonies. There is the proper title to use in addressing the heads of business firms, banking executives, doctors, and the like.

Correct in England

Robert E. Meade, Esq., President
Laurence D. Goode, Esq., M.D.

Forms for addressing women. 1. *Firm composed of women.* In ddressing a firm composed of women either married or unmarried, ıse *Mesdames* or *Mmes.*

2. *Unmarried woman.* Use *Miss* when you are addressing an ınmarried woman or when you do not know whether she is married r unmarried. (A few business concerns now use *Ms.*)

3. *Married woman.* Socially a married woman is addressed by h husband's full name preceded by *Mrs.* In business, she may addressed either by her husband's name or by her given name ar her married name, preceded by *Mrs.* Use the form she prefers if yo know it.

4. *Widow.* Socially a widow is addressed by her husband's fu name preceded by *Mrs.* In business either her husband's full nan or her given name and her married name, preceded by *Mrs.*, is co rect. Use the form that she prefers if you know it.

5. *Divorcee.* If a divorcee retains her married name, the tit *Mrs.* is preferable to *Miss.* If she uses her maiden name, she ma use either *Miss* or *Mrs.* In business she may be addressed by h given name combined with her married name or by both her maide and married names. Follow the form she prefers if you know i Socially she is addressed by her maiden name combined with h married name.

When husband's name is retained		When maiden name is use
Business	*Social*	*Business and Social*
Mrs. Margaret Weeks	Mrs. Barkley Weeks	Mrs. Margaret Barkle
Mrs. Margaret Barkley Weeks		Miss Margaret Barkle

6. *Wife of a titled man.* Do not address a married woman b her husband's title. Adress her as *Mrs. Robert E. Adams* or *Mrs R. E. Adams.* If she is addressed jointly with her husband, th correct form is *Dr. and Mrs. Robert E. Adams, Judge and Mrs Irving Levey.*

7. *Professional women.* Address a woman with a professional titl by her title, followed by her given and last names. A married womar may use her maiden name if she prefers. In social correspondence her title is sometimes dropped in addressing her and her husband.

When you do not know whether an addressee is a man or a woman, use the form of address appropriate for a man. *Women in official or honorary positions are addressed just as men in similar positions, except that Madam, Mrs., or Miss replaces Sir or Mr. See the chart at page 641, et seq.*

8. *Man and woman.* When writing to a man and woman in their individual capacities address them by their respective titles,

ıcing one name under the other. If they are husband and wife, e one line.

Mrs. Jay S. Russell
Mr. Adam L. Matthews
Mr. and Mrs. Harry Smith

Salutations

Where to type the salutation. Type the salutation two spaces elow the inside address, flush with the left-hand margin. If an *tention* line is used, type the salutation two spaces below the atten-on line.

How to type the salutation. 1. Capitalize the first word, the title, nd the name. Do not capitalize *dear* unless it is used as the first ord of the salutation.

2. Use a colon following the salutation. A comma is used only ı social letters, particularly in those written in longhand.

3. *Mr.*, *Mrs.*, and *Dr.* are the only titles that are abbreviated.

Forms of salutation. The form of salutation varies with the tone f the letter and the degree of acquaintanceship between the writer nd the addressee. See the chart at page 632 for salutations of arying degrees of formality, together with the appropriate compliентary close to use with each. See the chart at page 641, *et seq.* or the correct salutation to use in letters to people in official or ıonorary positions.

1. If the letter is addressed to an individual, make the salutation ingular, for example, *Dear Sir*. If the letter is addressed to a com-pany or group, make it plural, for example, *Gentlemen* or *Dear Sirs*.

2. Never use a designation of any kind after a salutation.

RIGHT	WRONG
Dear Mr. Roberts:	Dear Mr. Roberts, C.P.A.:

3. Never use a business title or designation of position in a salutation.

RIGHT	WRONG
Dear Mr. Adams:	Dear Secretary: Dear Secretary Ames:

4. If the letter is addressed to a company to the attention of individual, the salutation is to the company, not to the individual.

5. Follow a title with the surname:

RIGHT	WRONG
Dear Professor Ames:	Dear Professor:

6. The salutation in a letter that is not addressed to any particu person or firm, such as a general letter of recommendation, is *Whom It May Concern.* Note that each word begins with a capit

7. The salutation in a letter addressed to an organization co posed of men and women is *Gentlemen* or *Ladies and Gentleme* to a man and woman, *Dear Sir and Madam;* to a married coup *Dear Mr. and Mrs. Marsh.*

Forms of salutation in letters addressed to women. 1. Do n use Miss as a salutation unless it is followed by a name.

RIGHT	WRONG
Dear Miss Brown: (preferred)	Dear Miss:
Dear Madam:	

2. If the letter is addressed to a firm of women, the salutation *Ladies* or *Mesdames.* Do not use "Dear" or "My dear" with eith of these salutations.

3. The salutation to two women with the same name is:

My dear Mesdames Smith (if married)
My dear Misses Smith (if unmarried)

When in doubt as to whether the addressee is a man or woma use the salutation appropriate for a man. For the correct form salutation in letters addressed to women holding official or honora positions, see the chart at page 641, *et seq.*

Body of the Letter

How to type the body. 1. Single space unless the letter is ve short. Single space a short letter if half-sheet letterheads are use

2. Double space between paragraphs.

3. When the block style is used, begin each line flush with th left-hand margin of the letter.

4. When the indented or semiblock style is used, indent the first e of each paragraph five to ten spaces.
5. Always indent paragraphs when a letter is double-spaced.

How to set up enumerated material in the body of the letter.
1. Indent five spaces from each margin of the letter—more if cessary to center the material.
2. Precede each item with a number, followed by a period. Or e number may be enclosed in parentheses.
3. Begin each line of the indented material two spaces to the ;ht of the number.
4. Single space the material within each item, but double space tween items.

How to write dates. When the day precedes the months, it is rmissible to write the day out or to use the figure with the ordinal breviation. For example, *fifth of March,* or *5th of March.*

Complimentary Close

Where to type the complimentary close. Type the compli- entary close two spaces below the last line of the letter. Begin slightly to the right of the center of the page, except in the full ock style. It should never extend beyond the right margin of e letter.

How to type the complimentary close. 1. Capitalize only the rst word.
2. Follow the complimentary close with a comma. This is the etter practice even when open punctuation is used in the inside ldress.

Forms of complimentary close. The form varies with the tone f the letter and the degree of acquaintanceship between the writer nd the addressee. The degree of formality of the complimentary lose should correspond with the salutation. Notice the following hart, which gives the appropriate complimentary close to use with arious salutations. See the chart at page 641, *et seq.* for the correct omplimentary close to use in letters to people in official or honorary ositions.

VARIOUS SALUTATIONS AND APPROPRIATE COMPLIMENTARY CLOSES

	Salutations	Complimentary Closes
Very Formal	My dear Sir: Sir: My dear Madam: Madam:	Respectfully, Yours respectfully, Respectfully yours, Very respectfully you
Formal	Dear Sir: Dear Madam: Gentlemen: Mesdames:	Very truly yours, Yours very truly Yours truly,
Less Formal (The trend today is to use these forms in business correspondence, rather than the formal forms)	Dear Mr. Satterby: My dear Mr. Satterby: Dear Mrs. Grimshaw: My dear Mrs. Grimshaw: Dear Miss Bylow: My dear Miss Bylow:	Sincerely, Sincerely yours, Yours sincerely, Very sincerely,
Personal (Implying personal acquaintance or previous friendly correspondence)	Dear Mr. Satterby: Dear Mrs. Grimshaw: Dear Miss Bylow:	Yours cordially, Cordially, Cordially yours, Most sincerely,

Signature

What the signature contains. The signature to a business lett usually consists of the typed name of the company, the signatu of the writer, and the typed name of the writer and his business titl Some authorities recommend using the firm name when the pr noun *we* is used throughout the letter and omitting it when *I* is use The modern trend and the approved practice is to omit the fir name, except in a signature to formal documents. The typed nam of the writer can be omitted if it appears on the letterhead.

The inclusion in the signature of the writer's business title o position, indicates that he is writing the letter in his official capacit Thus, if an officer of a company writes a letter on firm statione about a purely person matter, his position is not included in th signature.

Firms of attorneys, certified public accountants, and the like fre ently sign letters manually with the firm name, particularly if the ter expresses a professional opinion or gives professional advice.

Where to type the signature. When the firm name is included the signature, type it two spaces below the complimentary close, writer's name four spaces below the firm name, and the writer's sition either on the same line or on the next line. When the n name is not included, type the writer's name and position four aces below the complimentary close.

When the inside address is typed in block form, align the signa- re with the first letter of the complimentary close. When the dented form is used in the inside address (Figure 59), align the nature with the third or fourth letters of the complimentary close. either case the lines of the signature should be blocked, unless an usually long line makes this arrangement impractical. No line the signature should extend beyond the right-hand margin of e letter.

How to type the signature. 1. Type the firm name in capitals, actly as it appears on the letterhead.

2. Type the signature exactly as the dictator signs his name.

RIGHT	WRONG
Richard P. Miller	*Richard P. Miller*
Richard P. Miller President	R. P. Miller President

3. Business titles and degree letters follow the typed signature. Jo title precedes either the written or typed signature except *Miss* r *Mrs.*

Forms of signature for women. 1. An *unmarried woman* may recede her typed signature with *Miss* in parentheses, or omit it. f no title is included, the implication is that it should be *Miss.*

Eleanor Davis		*Eleanor Davis*
(Miss) Eleanor Davis	*or*	Eleanor Davis

2. A *married woman* should indicate in her signature the title to e used in addressing her. She may precede her typed signature vith *Mrs.* in parentheses, or she may type her married name in

parentheses beneath the pen-written signature. The latter fo
is compulsory for social usage.

Eleanor Davis		*Eleanor Davis*
(Mrs.) Eleanor Davis	*or*	(Mrs. John R. Davis)

3. A *widow* signs her name as she did before her husband's dea

4. Assuming that a divorcee does not use her maiden name, s signs her given name, with or without the initial of her maid name, and her former husband's surname. The typed signatu is the same as the written signature preceded by *Mrs.* in parenthes Or the typed signature may combine her maiden name with h former husband's surname.

RIGHT	WRONG
Eleanor M. Davis	*Eleanor M. Davis*
(Mrs.) Eleanor M. Davis	(Mrs. John R. Davis)
or	
Eleanor M. Davis	
(Mrs. Montgomery Davis)	

Secretary's signature. When a secretary signs her employer name to a letter, she should place her initials immediately below i

Yours very truly,

Hiram R. Jones
m.g.

Hiram R. Jones
President

When she signs a letter in her own name as secretary to he employer, she should not include his initials unless another man i the organization has the same name. Always precede his name b a title.

RIGHT	WRONG
Elizabeth Mason	
Secretary to Mr. Nelson	Secretary to Mr. R. S. Nelson
	Secretary to R. S. Nelson

Miscellaneous Structural Parts of Letters

Attention line. Strictly business letters addressed to a firm are .en directed to the attention of an individual by the use of an *ention line,* in preference to addressing the letter to the individual. ıis practice marks the letter as a business rather than a personal ter and insures that it will be opened in the absence of the indilual to whom it is directed.

Type the attention line two spaces below the address. The word is not necessary. The attention line has no punctuation and is t underscored. When a letter addressed to a firm has an attenon line, the salutation is *Gentlemen* because the salutation is to e firm, not the individual. It is permissible to direct the letter to e attention of an individual wihout including his given name or itials, if they are unknown.

Preferable: Attention Mr. Walter R. Richardson
Permissible: Attention Mr. Richardson

Subject line. Subject lines are a convenience to both the writer ıd the reader. They make it unnecessary for the writer to devote e first paragraph of his letter to a routine explanation of the subct of the letter; they facilitate the distribution of mail to various epartments; they also expedite subject filing.

Center the subject line two spaces beneath the salutation. If the ıll block style of letter (Figure 56) is used, type the subject line ush with the left-hand margin. Never place the subject line before ıe salutation. It is part of the body of the letter, not of the eading.

Sometimes the subject line is preceded by *In re* or *Subject.* The etter practice is to omit these words, except in letters about legal ıatters. In these letters *In re* is customarily used. No punctuation ollows *In re*; a colon follows *Subject.* The important words in a ıbject line are capitalized. The last line may be underlined, but he modern trend is to omit the underlining.

Reference line. If a file reference is given in an incoming letter, nclude a reference line in your reply, whether requested or not. lace your own reference beneath the incoming reference.

When letterheads include a printed reference notation, such as

In reply please refer to, type the reference line after it. Otherwi type the reference line on a line with the salutation in the cen of the letter. If the letter also has a subject line, type the referen line at the right of the letter about four spaces beneath the date.

Your File 3476		April 20, 19. .
Our File 2785	*or*	
		Our Order 846–D

Identification line. The identification line shows who dictat the letter and who typed it. The only purpose of the identificati line is for reference by the business organization *writing* the lett The dictator's name is typed in the signature. Unless company ru require otherwise, the secretary types nothing but her initials in t identification line and does not show them on the original of t letter.

If the company requires the usual identification line, type t initials of the dictator and the stenographer flush with the left-ha margin, on a line with the last line of the signature. If the offic style of letter is used (Figure 60), the identification line is typ two spaces below the address. When the person who signs the lett has not dictated it, type his initials first and follow with those of t dictator and the transcriber.

Forms. In the following illustrations SRD is the dictator ar AM the typist. Lower case instead of capitals may be used for t typist's initials.

SRD:AM	Usual form.
HRL:SRD:AM	When letter is signed by person other than the di tator. (The identification line *must not* appear c the original.)
(AM)	When the letter is composed by the typist.
SRDJr:AM	When father and son with the same name are in th organization.
SRDavis:AM	When the dictator's name is not included in th typed signature. (The identification line should ap pear on the original.)

Enclosure mark. When a letter contains enclosures, type th word *Enclosure* or the abbreviation *Enc.* flush with the left-han margin one or two spaces beneath the identification line. If ther more than one enclosure, indicate the number. If the enclosures e of special importance, identify them. If an enclosure is to be turned, make a notation to that effect.

RPE:ES Enclosure	RPE:ES Enc. 2	RPE:ES Enc. Cert. ck. $2,350 Mtge.—Nelson to Jones

RPE:ES
Enc. Policy 35 4698—M (to be returned)

"Personal" notation. A letter or envelope should not be marked 'ersonal" or "Confidential" as a device to catch the attention of busy man. These words should be used only when no one but e addressee is supposed to see the letter. Type the word *Personal* *Confidential* four spaces above address, which is at the top of the tter. You may underline the notation to catch the eye.

Mailing notation. When a letter is sent by any method other ıan regular mail, type a notation of the exact method on the en- elope, in the space below the stamps and above the address. Make similar notation on the letter two spaces above the address.

Carbon copy distribution notation. When a carbon copy is to e sent to another person, type the distribution notation flush with ıe left-hand margin, below all other notations. If space permits, eparate it from the other notations by two spaces.

SRE:NG
Enclosure
Copy to Mr. S. A. Williams

The abbreviation *c.c.* may be used instead of *Copy to.* In the implified form of letter (Figure 62) neither is used.

Blind copy notation. Type the carbon copy notation in the upper eft-hand portion of the letter *on the carbons only.* This indicates hat the addressee of the letter does not know that a copy was sent to ınyone.

Postscript. When it is necessary to add a postscript to a letter, ype it two spaces below the identification line or the last notation hat is on the letter. The left margin of the postscript should be ndented five spaces from the left margin of the letter itself. You nay include or omit the abbreviation "P.S." Type the dictator's nitials after the postscript.

Heading on second page. If the letter runs to a second pa use a plain sheet, without a letterhead, but of the same size a quality as the letterhead. The heading should contain the nai of the addressee, the number of the page, and the date. Lea spaces between the heading and the body of the letter. (See al "Continuation sheets" on page 614.)

Mr. R. H. Smith 2. September 12, 19—

Envelopes

The items in the envelope address are the same as those in tl inside address (see page 623). The Post Office Department prefe the indented style and that the name of the state be on a separa line from the name of the city. The name of the state must n be abbreviated.

Mr. R. S. Jackson, President,
  Northern Manufacturing Company,
    25 West 79 Street,
      Milwaukee,
        Wisconsin.

Figures 65 and 66 show acceptable and commonly used styles o address on envelopes. They also show the correct placement o the attention line and personal and special delivery notations. Al mailing notations are placed in the position shown by "Special De livery" in Figure 66.

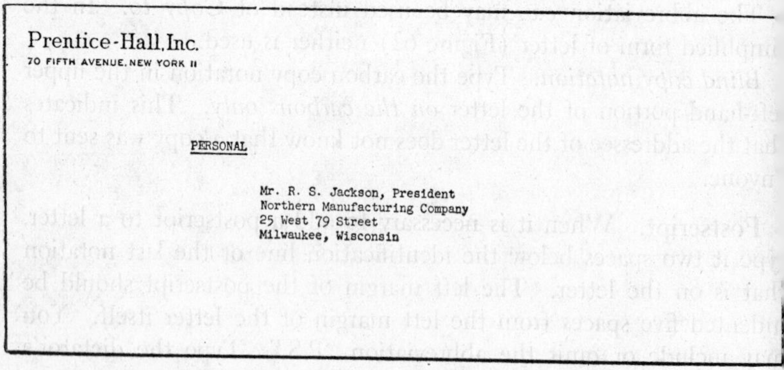
Prentice-Hall, Inc.
70 FIFTH AVENUE, NEW YORK 11

PERSONAL

Mr. R. S. Jackson, President
Northern Manufacturing Company
25 West 79 Street
Milwaukee, Wisconsin

Figure 65. Envelope Showing Correct Placement of Personal Notation.

The name of a foreign country is written in capitals in an address ı the envelope, but usually only initial capitals are used in the inde address.

Prentice-Hall,Inc.
'O FIFTH AVENUE: NEW YORK 11

SPECIAL DELIVERY

Northern Manufacturing Company
25 West 79 Street
Milwaukee, Wisconsin

Attention Mr. R. S Jackson

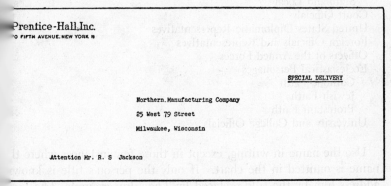

Figure 66. Envelope Showing Correct Placements of Attention Line and Special Delivery Notation.

If the envelope is too large to fit into the typewriter, the address ıould be written by hand, in the same form that is used when the ddress is typed. Since these envelopes are frequently used for mailıg matter other than first-class mail, "First-Class Mail" should be ritten immediately beneath the place for stamps when first-class ıatter is mailed in them. The envelope should be sealed if the mater is first-class mail. (See page 622 for a table of the most popular izes of envelopes.)

10. HOW TO ADDRESS PERSONS HOLDING HONORARY OR OFFICIAL POSITIONS

Every business firm is occasionally called upon to write a letter to person who holds an official or honorary position. The question rises as to the proper form to use.

The chart on page 641 gives the correct forms of written address, saltation, and complimentary close in letters to persons holding official r honorary titles, whether of high or low rank. It also gives the orrect form for referring to those persons in a letter and the correct orm to use in speaking to or informally introducing them. The ecretaries should be trained to refer to this chart.

The chart is broken down into:

Government Officials
- United States
- State and Local

Court Officials
United States Diplomatic Representatives
Foreign Officials and Representatives
Officers of the Armed Forces
Ecclesiastical Personages
- Catholic Faith
- Jewish Faith
- Protestant Faith

University and College Officials

Use the name in writing, except in those few instances where th name is omitted in the chart. If only the person's title is know address him by the title prefaced by *The*. For example, *The Lieu tenant Governor of Iowa*. The salutation would be *Sir* or *My dea Governor*. Every effort should be made, however, to learn the nam of the person addressed.

When a person is acting as an official, the word *acting* precede the title in the address, but not in the salutation or spoken addres For example, *Acting Mayor of Memphis, My dear Mayor Blank*.

Women in official or honorary positions are addressed just as me in similar positions, except that *Madam*, *Mrs.*, or *Miss* replaces S or *Mr.* (See the illustrations in the following chart when a woma is an ambassador or a minister.)

In many cases the name in the address is followed by the ab breviation of a scholastic degree. If the addressee does not hav the degree, do not use the initials. Do not address a person by scholastic title unless he actually possesses the degree that the titl indicates.

Personage	Envelope and Inside Address	Formal Salutation	Informal Salutation	Formal Close	Informal Close	1. Spoken Address 2. Informal Introduction or Reference [1]
The President	The President The White House Washington 25, D. C.[2]	Mr. President	My dear Mr. President:	Respectfully yours,	Faithfully yours, (official) Very respectfully yours (private individual)	1. Mr. President 2. NOT INTRODUCED (The President)
Vice President of the United States	The Vice President United States Senate Washington, D. C. *or* The Honorable John R. Blank Vice President of the United States Washington, D. C.	Sir:	My dear Mr. Vice President:	Very truly yours,	Sincerely yours,	1. Mr. Vice President *or* Mr. Blank 2. The Vice President
Chief Justice of the United States	The Chief Justice The Supreme Court Washington, D. C.	Sir:	My dear Mr. Chief Justice:	Very truly yours,	Sincerely yours,	1. Mr. Chief Justice 2. The Chief Justice
Associate Justice of the United States Supreme Court	Mr. Justice Blank The Supreme Court Washington, D. C.	Sir:	My dear Mr. Justice:	Very truly yours,	Sincerely yours,	1. Mr. Justice *or* Mr. Justice Blank 2. Mr. Justice Blank
Speaker of the House of Representatives	The Honorable John R. Blank Speaker of the House of Representatives Washington, D. C.	Sir:	My dear Mr. Speaker:	Very truly yours,	Sincerely yours,	1. Mr. Speaker *or* Mr. Blank 2. The Speaker, Mr. Blank (The Speaker *or* Mr. Blank)

[1] The form of introduction and the form of reference to a person are usually similar. When they differ, the form of reference is shown here in parentheses.
[2] On the inside address it is permissible to omit "Washington 25, D. C."

UNITED STATES GOVERNMENT OFFICIALS (Continued)

Personage	Envelope and Inside Address	Formal Salutation	Informal Salutation	Formal Close	Informal Close	1. Spoken Address 2. Informal Introduction or Reference
Cabinet Officer (man)	*Formal* The Honorable the Secretary of State Washington, D. C. *Informal* The Honorable John R. Blank Secretary of State Washington, D. C. *If written from abroad* The Honorable John R. Blank Secretary of State of the United States of America Washington, D. C.	Sir:	My dear Mr. Secretary:	Very truly yours,	Sincerely yours,	1. Mr. Secretary *or* Mr. Blank 2. The Secretary of State, Mr. Blank (The Secretary *or* Mr. Blank)
Cabinet Officer (woman)	*Formal* The Honorable the Secretary of Labor Washington, D. C.	Madam:	My dear Madam Secretary:	Very truly yours,	Sincerely yours,	1. Madam Secretary *or* Mrs. (Miss) Blank 2. The Secretary of Labor, Mrs. (Miss) Blank (The Secretary *or* Mrs. (Miss) Blank)
Under Secretary of a Department	The Honorable John R. Blank Under Secretary of the Treasury Washington, D. C.	My dear Mr. Blank:	My dear Mr. Blank:	Very truly yours,	Sincerely yours,	1, 2. Mr. Blank
Assistant Secretary of a Department	The Honorable John R. Blank Assistant Secretary of Agriculture Washington, D. C.	My dear Mr. Blank:	My dear Mr. Blank:	Very truly yours,	Sincerely yours,	1, 2. Mr. Blank

a Division or Bureau	Statistics Department of Labor Washington, D. C.					
United States Senator (man)	The Honorable John R. Blank United States Senate Washington, D. C.	Sir:	My dear Senator Blank:	Very truly yours,	Sincerely yours,	1. Senator Blank *or* Senator 2. Senator Blank
United States Senator (woman)	The Honorable Mary Blank United States Senate Washington, D. C.	Madam:	My dear Senator Blank: *or* My dear Mrs. (Miss) Blank:	Very truly yours,	Sincerely yours,	1. Senator Blank *or* Mrs. (Miss) Blank 2. Senator Blank
United States Representative (man)	The Honorable John R. Blank House of Representatives Washington, D. C.	Sir:	My dear Mr. Blank:	Very truly yours,	Sincerely yours,	1. Mr. Blank 2. Mr. Blank *or* Representative Blank
United States Representative (woman)	The Honorable Mary Blank House of Representatives Washington, D. C.	Madam:	My dear Mrs. (Miss) Blank:	Very truly yours,	Sincerely yours,	1, 2. Mrs. (Miss) Blank
Territorial Delegate	The Honorable John R. Blank Delegate of Alaska House of Representatives Washington, D. C.	Sir:	My dear Mr. Blank:	Very truly yours,	Sincerely yours,	1, 2. Mr. Blank
Resident Commissioner	The Honorable John R. Blank Resident Commissioner of Puerto Rico Washington, D. C.	Sir:	My dear Mr. Blank:	Very truly yours,	Sincerely yours,	1, 2. Mr. Blank
Secretary to the President	The Honorable John R. Blank Secretary to the President The White House Washington 25, D. C.	Sir:	My dear Mr. Blank:	Very truly yours,	Sincerely yours,	1, 2. Mr. Blank
Secretary to the President with military rank	Major General John R. Blank Secretary to the President The White House Washington 25, D. C.	Sir:	My dear General Blank:	Very truly yours,	Sincerely yours,	1, 2. General Blank

UNITED STATES GOVERNMENT OFFICIALS (Continued)

Personage	Envelope and Inside Address	Formal Salutation	Informal Salutation	Formal Close	Informal Close	1. Spoken Address 2. Informal Introduction or Reference
Assistant Secretary to the President	The Honorable John R. Blank Assistant Secretary to the President The White House Washington 25, D. C.	Sir:	My dear Mr. Blank:	Very truly yours,	Sincerely yours,	1, 2. Mr. Blank
High Officials of the United States, in general: Comptroller General, Director of Bureau of the Budget, Librarian of Congress	*Formal* The Comptroller General of the United States Washington, D. C. *Informal* The Honorable John R. Blank Comptroller General of the United States Washington, D. C.	Sir:	My dear Mr. Blank:	Very truly yours,	Sincerely yours,	1, 2. Mr. Blank
Heads of Independent Federal Agencies, Boards, Commissions, Establishments, Organizations, etc.	*Formal* The Chairman of the Board of Governors of the Federal Reserve System Washington, D. C. *Informal* The Honorable John R. Blank Director, Mutual Security Agency Washington, D. C.	Sir:	My dear Mr. Chairman (*or* Mr. Director): *or* My dear Mr. Blank:	Very truly yours,	Sincerely yours,	1, 2. Mr. Blank

Personage	Envelope and Inside Address	Formal Salutation	Informal Salutation	Formal Close	Informal Close	1. Spoken Address 2. Informal Introduction or Reference
Governor of State[3]	*Formal* The Honorable the Governor of Iowa Des Moines *Informal* The Honorable John R. Blank Governor of Iowa Des Moines	Sir:	My dear Governor:	Respectfully yours,	Sincerely yours,	1. Governor Blank *or* Governor 2. Governor Blank *or* The Governor (Outside his own state: The Governor of Iowa)
Lieutenant Governor	The Honorable John R. Blank Lieutenant Governor of Iowa Des Moines	Sir:	My dear Governor Blank:	Respectfully yours, *or* Very truly yours,	Sincerely yours,	1. Governor Blank 2. The Lieutenant Governor of Iowa, Governor Blank (The Lieutenant Governor *or* Governor Blank)
Secretary of State	The Honorable John R. Blank Secretary of State of Iowa Des Moines	Sir:	My dear Mr. Secretary:	Very truly yours,	Sincerely yours,	1, 2. Mr. Blank
Attorney General	The Honorable John R. Blank Attorney General of New York Albany, New York	Sir:	My dear Mr. Attorney General	Very truly yours,	Sincerely yours,	1, 2. Mr. Blank
State Representative or Assemblyman	The Honorable John R. Blank House of Representatives Nashville, Tennessee	Sir:	My dear Mr. Blank:	Very truly yours,	Sincerely yours,	1. Mr. Blank 2. Mr. Blank *or* Representative Blank
Mayor of a city	The Honorable John R. Blank Mayor of Memphis Tennessee	Sir:	My dear Mayor Blank:	Very truly yours,	Sincerely yours,	1. Mayor Blank *or* Mr. Mayor 2. Mayor Blank

[3] The form of addressing Governors varies in the different states. The form given here is that used by the State Department of the United States.

STATE AND LOCAL GOVERNMENT OFFICIALS (Continued)

Personage	Envelope and Inside Address	Formal Salutation	Informal Salutation	Formal Close	Informal Close	1. Spoken Address 2. Informal Introduction or Reference
Commissioners of a city	*Formal* The Commissioners of the City of Buffalo New York	Sirs:	*Always formal*	Very truly yours,	*Always formal*	1. Gentlemen 2. The Commissioners
President of Board of Commissioners	*Formal or Informal* The Honorable John R. Blank President, Board of Commissioners of the City of Buffalo New York	Sir:	My dear Mr. Blank:	Very truly yours,	Sincerely yours,	1, 2. Mr. Blank
District Attorney	The Honorable John R. Blank District Attorney, Sunflower County County Courthouse Indianola, Mississippi	Dear Sir:	Dear Mr. Blank:	Very truly yours,	Sincerely yours,	1, 2. Mr. Blank
City Attorney City Counsel Corporation Counsel	The Honorable John R. Blank City Attorney (City Counsel, Corporation Counsel) Aliceville, Alabama	Dear Sir:	Dear Mr. Blank:	Very truly yours,	Sincerely yours,	1, 2. Mr. Blank
Alderman	Alderman John R. Blank City Hall Aliceville, Alabama	Dear Sir:	Dear Mr. Blank:	Very truly yours,	Sincerely yours,	1, 2. Mr. Blank

COURT OFFICIALS

Personage	Envelope and Inside Address	Formal Salutation	Informal Salutation	Formal Close	Informal Close	1. Spoken Address 2. Informal Introduction or Reference
Chief Justice[4] *of a State Supreme Court*	The Honorable John R. Blank Chief Justice[4] of the Supreme Court of Minnesota Minneapolis, Minnesota	Sir:	My dear Mr.[4a] Chief Justice: *or* My dear Judge Blank:	Very truly yours,	Sincerely yours,	1. Mr. Chief Justice *or* Judge Blank 2. Mr. Chief Justice Blank *or* Judge Blank
Associate Justice *Presiding Justice*	The Honorable John R. Blank Associate (Presiding) Justice, Appellate Division Supreme Court New York, New York	Sir:	My dear Mr. Justice:	Very truly yours,	Sincerely yours,	1, 2. Mr. Justice (*or* Judge) Blank
Judge of a Court[4b]	The Honorable John R. Blank Judge of the United States District Court for the Southern District of California Los Angeles, California	Sir:	My dear Judge Blank:	Very truly yours,	Sincerely yours,	1, 2. Judge Blank
Clerk of a Court	John R. Blank, Esquire Clerk of the Superior Court Boston, Massachusetts	Sir:	My dear Mr. Blank:	Very truly yours,	Sincerely yours,	1, 2. Mr. Blank

[4] If his official title is *Chief Judge,* substitute *Chief Judge* for *Chief Justice.*
[4a] Never use *Mr.* with *Chief Judge* or *Judge.*
[4b] This does not apply to a Justice of the United States Supreme Court.

UNITED STATES DIPLOMATIC REPRESENTATIVES

Personage	Envelope and Inside Address	Formal Salutation	Informal Salutation	Formal Close	Informal Close	1. Spoken Address 2. Informal Introduction or Reference
American Ambassador (man)	The Honorable John R. Blank American Ambassador [6] Paris	Sir:	My dear Mr. Ambassador:	Very truly yours,	Sincerely yours,	1. Mr. Ambassador *or* Mr. Blank 2. The American Ambassador [5] (The Ambassador *or* Mr. Blank)
American Ambassador (woman)	The Honorable Mary L. Blank American Ambassador Paris	Madam:	My dear Madam Ambassador:	Very truly yours,	Sincerely yours,	1. Madam Ambassador *or* Mrs. (Miss) Blank 2. The American Ambassador [5] (The Ambassador *or* Mrs. (Miss) Blank)
American Minister (man)	The Honorable John R. Blank American Minister Helsinki	Sir:	My dear Mr. Minister:	Very truly yours,	Sincerely yours,	1. Mr. Minister *or* Mr. Blank 2. The American Minister,[5] Mr. Blank (The Minister *or* Mr. Blank)
American Minister (woman)	The Honorable Mary Blank American Minister Luxemburg	Madam:	My dear Mrs. (Miss) Blank: *or* My dear Madam Minister:	Very truly yours,	Sincerely yours,	1. Madam Minister *or* Mrs. (Miss) Blank 2. The American Minister,[5] Mrs. (Miss) Blank (The Minister *or* Mrs. (Miss) Blank)

American Chargé d'Affaires ad Interim	John R. Blank, Esquire American Chargé d'Affaires ad Interim Rome	Sir:	My dear Mr. Blank:	Very truly yours,	Sincerely yours,	1, 2. Mr. Blank
American Consul General, Consul, or Vice-Consul	John R. Blank, Esquire American Consul General London, England (The same form for Consul or Vice Consul)	Sir:	My dear Mr. Blank:	Very truly yours,	Sincerely yours,	1, 2. Mr. Blank
High Commissioner	*Formal* The United States High Commissioner to Peru Lima *Informal* The Honorable John R. Blank United States High Commissioner to Peru Lima	Sir:	My dear Mr. Commissioner: *or* My dear Mr. Blank:	Very truly yours,	Sincerely yours,	1, 2. Commissioner Blank *or* Mr. Blank
United States Delegate to the United Nations (with Ambassadorial rank)	The Honorable John R. Blank Chief of the United States Mission to the United Nations New York, New York	My dear Mr. Ambassador: *or* Sir:	My dear Ambassador Blank:	Very truly yours,	Sincerely yours,	1, 2. Mr. Ambassador (The Chief of the United States Mission to the United Nations)

[5] With reference to ambassadors and ministers to Central or South American countries, the phrase is "Ambassador of the United States" or "Minister of the United States."

[6] When an Ambassador or Minister is not at his post, the name of the country to which he is accredited must be added, thus, "The American Ambassador to France."

FOREIGN OFFICIALS AND REPRESENTATIVES

Personage	Envelope and Inside Address	Formal Salutation	Informal Salutation	Formal Close	Informal Close	1. Spoken Address 2. Informal Introduction or Reference
Foreign Ambassador in the United States [7]	His Excellency, John R. Blank Ambassador of Colombia Washington, D. C.	Excellency:	My dear Mr. Ambassador:	Respectfully yours,	Sincerely yours,	1. Mr. Ambassador *or* Mr. Blank 2. The Ambassador of Colombia (The Ambassador *or* Mr. Blank)
Foreign Minister in the United States [7]	The Honorable John R. Blank Minister of Hungary Washington, D. C.	Sir:	My dear Mr. Minister:	Respectfully yours,	Sincerely yours,	1. Mr. Minister *or* Mr. Blank 2. The Minister of Hungary (The Minister *or* Mr. Blank)
Foreign Diplomatic Representative with a Personal Title	His Excellency, Count John Blank [8] Ambassador of Italy Washington, D. C.	Excellency:	My dear Mr. Ambassador:	Respectfully yours,	Sincerely yours,	1. Mr. Ambassador *or* Count Blank 2. The Italian Ambassador (The Ambassador *or* Count Blank)
Secretary General of the United Nations	Mr. John R. Blank Secretary General of the United Nations New York, New York	Sir: *or* My dear Mr. Secretary General:	My dear Mr. Blank:	Respectfully yours,	Sincerely yours,	1. Mr. Blank *or* Sir 2. The Secretary General of the United Nations *or* Mr. Blank

President of a Republic	His Excellency, John R. Blank President of the United States of Brazil	Excellency:	My dear Mr. President:	I remain, with great respect, Very truly yours,	Sincerely yours,	1. Your Excellency 2. NOT INTRODUCED (President Blank *or* The President)
British Prime Minister	The Right Honorable John R. Blank, M. P. Prime Minister London	Sir:	My dear Mr. Prime Minister: *or* My dear Mr. Blank:	Respectfully yours,	Sincerely yours,	1. Mr. Blank 2. Mr. Blank *or* The Prime Minister
Canadian Prime Minister	The Right Honorable John R. Blank, C. M. G. Prime Minister of the Dominion of Canada Ottawa	Sir:	My dear Mr. Blank:	Very truly yours,	Sincerely yours,	1. Mr. Blank 2. Mr. Blank *or* The Prime Minister
Member of the British Cabinet [9]	The Right Honorable John R. Blank, P. C. Secretary of State for Foreign Affairs London	Sir:	My dear Mr. Secretary of State: *or* My dear Mr. Blank:	Respectfully yours,	Sincerely yours,	1, 2. Mr. Blank
Lord Chief Justice	The Right Honorable The Lord Chief Justice of England London [10]	Sir:	My dear Lord Chief Justice:	Respectfully yours,	Sincerely yours,	1. My Lord Chief Justice [10] *or* Sir 2. The Lord Chief Justice

[7] The correct title of all ambassadors and ministers of foreign countries is "Ambassador (Minister) of ...." (name of country) with the exception of Great Britain. The adjective form is used with reference to representatives from Great Britain—British Ambassador, British Minister.

[8] To avoid a long line of address, use this style.

[9] All members of the British Cabinet are members of the Privy Council and as such are entitled to the initials *P.C.* after their names.

[10] If he is a peer in his own right, he is addressed by his title of nobility.

OFFICERS OF THE ARMED FORCES[14]—ARMY

Personage	Envelope and Inside Address	Formal Salutation	Informal Salutation	Formal Close	Informal Close	1. Spoken Address 2. Informal Introduction or Reference
General of the Army	John R. Blank, U.S.A. General of the Army War Department Washington, D. C.	Sir:	My dear General Blank:	Very truly yours,	Sincerely yours,	1, 2. General Blank
General, Lieutenant, Major, or Brigadier General	General (Lieutenant General, Major General, or Brigadier General) John R. Blank, U.S.A.[11] Fort Sam Houston Texas	Sir:	My dear General Blank:	Very truly yours,	Sincerely yours,	1, 2. General Blank
Colonel, Lieutenant Colonel	Colonel (Lieutenant Colonel) John R. Blank, U.S.A. Fort Leavenworth Kansas	My dear Colonel Blank:	My dear Colonel Blank:	Very truly yours,	Sincerely yours,	1, 2. Colonel Blank
Major	Major John R. Blank, U.S.A. Fort Dix New Jersey	My dear Major Blank:	My dear Major Blank:	Very truly yours,	Sincerely yours,	1, 2. Major Blank
Captain	Captain John R. Blank, U.S.A. Fort Schuyler New York	My dear Captain Blank:	My dear Captain Blank:	Very truly yours,	Sincerely yours,	1, 2. Captain Blank
First Lieutenant, Second Lieutenant[12]	Lieutenant John R. Blank, U.S.A. Fort Shelby Mississippi	My dear Lieutenant Blank:	My dear Lieutenant Blank:	Very truly yours,	Sincerely yours,	1, 2. Lieutenant Blank
Chaplain in the United States Army	Chaplain John R. Blank Captain, U.S.A. Fort Dix New Jersey	My dear Chaplain:	My dear Chaplain:	Very truly yours,	Sincerely yours,	1. Chaplain Blank[13] 2. Captain Blank (Chaplain Blank)[13]

[11] *U.S.A.* is changed to *A.U.S.* (Army of the United States) to indicate the Reserve.
[12] Modern usage sanctions the form shown here for unofficial correspondence.
[13] Roman Catholic chaplains and certain Anglican priests are spoken and referred to as "Father Blank," but

Personage	Envelope and Inside Address	Formal Salutation	Informal Salutation	Formal Close	Informal Close	1. Spoken Address 2. Informal Introduction or Reference
Admiral	Admiral John R. Blank, U.S.N.[16] Chief of Naval Operations Department of the Navy Washington, D. C.	Sir:	My dear Admiral Blank:	Very truly yours,	Sincerely yours,	1, 2. Admiral Blank
Fleet Admiral	Fleet Admiral John R. Blank, U.S.N.	Sir:	My dear Admiral Blank:	Very truly yours,	Sincerely yours,	1, 2. Admiral Blank
Rear Admiral	Rear Admiral John R. Blank, U.S.N. United States Naval Academy Annapolis, Maryland	Sir:	My dear Admiral Blank:	Very truly yours,	Sincerely yours,	1, 2. Admiral Blank
Vice Admiral	Vice Admiral John R. Blank, U.S.N. U.S.S. Mississippi San Diego, California	Sir:	My dear Admiral Blank:	Very truly yours,	Sincerely yours,	1, 2. Admiral Blank
Commodore, Captain, Commander	Commodore (Captain, Commander) John R. Blank U.S.S. Texas San Diego, California	My dear Commodore (Captain, Commander) Blank:	My dear Commodore (Captain, Commander) Blank:	Very truly yours,	Sincerely yours,	1, 2. Commodore (Captain, Commander) Blank
Junior Officers (Lieutenant Commander, Lieutenant, Lieutenant, Junior grade, Ensign)	Lieutenant Commander (Lieutenant, etc.) John R. Blank, U.S.N. U.S.S. Missouri Norfolk, Virginia	My dear Mr. Blank:	My dear Mr. Blank:	Very truly yours,	Sincerely yours,	1. Mr. Blank[17] 2. Lieutenant Commander or Lieutenant, etc.) Blank (Mr. Blank[17])
Chaplain	Captain John R. Blank (Ch. C.), U.S.N. Department of the Navy Washington, D. C.	Reverend Sir:	My dear Chaplain:	Very truly yours,	Sincerely yours,	1. Chaplain Blank 2. Captain Blank (Chaplain Blank)

[15] Marine Corps titles are the same as the Army, except that the top rank is *Commandant of the Marine Corps.* *U.S.M.C.* indicates regular service, *U.S.N.R.* indicates the Reserve.
[16] *U.S.N.* indicates regular service, *U.S.N.R.* indicates the Reserve.
[17] Junior officers in the medical or dental corps are spoken to and referred to as "Dr." but are introduced by their rank.

CATHOLIC FAITH

Personage	Envelope and Inside Address	Formal Salutation	Informal Salutation	Formal Close	Informal Close	1. Spoken Address 2. Informal Introduction or Reference
Pope	His Holiness The Pope *or* His Holiness Pope Pius XII Vatican City	Your Holiness:	*Always Formal*	I have the honor to profess myself, with profound respect, the servant of your Holiness.	*Always Formal* *or* Respectfully yours, (permissible)	1. Your Holiness *or* Most Holy Father 2. NOT INTRODUCED (His Holiness *or* The Pope)
Apostolic Delegate	His Excellency, The Most Reverend John Blank The Apostolic Delegate Washington, D. C.	Your Excellency:	My dear [Archbishop]:	I have the honor to be, Excellency, Respectfully yours,	Respectfully, *or* Sincerely yours, (permissible)	1. Your Excellency 2. NOT INTRODUCED (The Apostolic Delegate)
Cardinal in the United States	His Eminence, John Cardinal Blank Archbishop of New York New York, New York	Your Eminence:	My dear Cardinal Blank:	Respectfully yours,	Respectfully, *or* Sincerely yours, (permissible)	1. Your Eminence 2. NOT INTRODUCED (His Eminence *or* Cardinal Blank)
Archbishop in the United States	The Most Reverend John Blank, D.D. [S.T.D.] Archbishop of Boston	Most Reverend Sir: Your Excellency:	My dear Archbishop:	Respectfully yours,	Respectfully, *or* Sincerely yours, (permissible)	1. Your Excellency *or* Archbishop Blank 2. Archbishop Blank
Bishop in the United States	The Most Reverend John Blank Bishop of New Orleans New Orleans, Louisiana	Your Excellency: (ecclesiastical usage) Most Reverend Sir:	My dear Bishop:	Respectfully yours,	Respectfully, *or* Sincerely yours, (permissible)	1. Your Excellency *or* Bishop Blank 2. Bishop Blank
Abbot	The Right Reverend John R. Blank Abbot of Westmoreland Abbey Washington, D. C.	Right Reverend Father Abbot:	Dear Father Abbot: *or* Right Reverend and dear Father Blank:	Respectfully yours,	Respectfully, *or* Sincerely yours, (permissible)	1. Father Abbot 2. Father Blank

Canon	The very Reverend Canon John R. Blank, D.D. [LL.D.] Canon of Washington Cathedral Washington, D. C.	Very Reverend Canon:	Dear Canon Blank:	Respectfully yours,	Respectfully, *or* Sincerely yours,	1, 2. Canon Blank
Monsignor	The Right (or Very) [18] Reverend Msgr. John R. Blank Baltimore, Maryland	Monsignor:	Right (Very) Reverend and dear Monsignor Blank:	Respectfully yours,	Respectfully, *or* Sincerely yours,	1, 2. Monsignor Blank
Brother	Brother Albert Francis, F.S.C. Superior 206 Elm Street Madison, Delaware	My dear Brother:	Dear Brother Francis	Respectfully yours,	Respectfully, *or* Sincerely yours, (permissible)	1, 2. Brother Francis
Superior of a Brotherhood [19] *and Priest*	The Very Reverend John R. Blank, M.M. Director Maryknoll, New York	Very Reverend Father Superior	Dear Father Superior:	Respectfully,	Respectfully,	1. Father Blank
Priest	*With Scholastic Degree:* The Reverend John R. Blank, Ph.D. Notre Dame University Indiana	My dear Dr. Blank:	Dear Dr. Blank:	Very truly yours,	Sincerely yours,	1, 2. Doctor Blank
	Without Scholastic Degree: The Reverend John R. Blank St. Patrick's Church Mobile, Alabama	Reverend Sir:	Reverend and dear Father Blank:	Very truly yours,	Sincerely yours,	1, 2. Father Blank

[18] Dependent upon rank. See the *Official* (Roman) *Catholic Directory.*
[19] The address for the superior of a Brotherhood depends upon whether or not he is a priest or has a title other than Superior. Consult the *Official Catholic Directory.*

CATHOLIC FAITH (Continued)

Personage	Envelope and Inside Address	Formal Salutation	Informal Salutation	Formal Close	Informal Close	1. Spoken Address 2. Informal Introduction or Reference
Sister Superior	The Reverend Sister Superior [20] (order, if used) Convent of the Angels New Orleans, Louisiana	My dear Sister Superior: *or* My dear Reverend Sister:	My dear Sister Superior:	Respectfully,	Respectfully,	1. Sister Blank *or* Sister St. Mary 2. The Sister Superior *or* Sister Blank (Sister St. Mary)
Sister [20a]	Sister Mary Pia, O.P. St. Thomas High School Bayswater, New York	Dear Sister:	My dear Sister Mary Pia:	Respectfully,	Respectfully,	1, 2. Sister Mary Pia
Mother Superior of a Sisterhood (Catholic or Protestant)	The Reverend Mother Superior, O.C.A. [20] Sacred Heart Convent New Orleans, Louisiana *or* Mother Superior, O.C.A. Sacred Heart Convent New Orleans	My dear Reverend Mother *or* My dear Mother Superior:	My dear Reverend Mother: *or* My dear Mother Superior:	Respectfully,	Respectfully, Respectfully,	1, 2. Reverend Mother
Member of Community	Mother Mary Jones, R.S.C.J. Convent of the Sacred Heart	Dear Mother Jones:	My dear Mother Jones:	Respectfully,	Respectfully,	1, 2. Mother Jones

[20] The address of the superior of a Sisterhood depends upon the order to which she belongs. The abbreviation of the order is not always used. Consult the *Official Catholic Directory.*

[20a] A special classification for a ***nun*** is not given here because the exact sense of the word implies a strictly cloistered Religious.

JEWISH FAITH

Personage	Envelope and Inside Address	Formal Salutation	Informal Salutation	Formal Close	Informal Close	1. Spoken Address 2. Informal Introduction or Reference
Rabbi	*With scholastic degree:* Rabbi John R. Blank, Ph.D. *or* Dr. John R. Blank	Sir:	My dear Dr. Blank: *or* My dear Rabbi Blank:	Very truly yours,	Sincerely yours,	1, 2. Dr. Blank
	Without scholastic degree: Rabbi John R. Blank	Sir:	My dear Rabbi Blank:	Very truly yours,	Sincerely yours,	1, 2. Rabbi Blank

PROTESTANT FAITH

Personage	Envelope and Inside Address	Formal Salutation	Informal Salutation	Formal Close	Informal Close	1. Spoken Address 2. Informal Introduction or Reference
Archbishop (Anglican)	To His Grace The Lord Archbishop of Canterbury Canterbury England	Your Grace: *or* My Lord Archbishop:	My dear Archbishop:	Respectfully yours,	Sincerely yours,	1. Your Grace NOT INTRODUCED (His Grace *or* The Archbishop)
Presiding Bishop of the Protestant Episcopal Church in America	The Most Reverend John R. Blank, D.D., LL.D. Presiding Bishop of the Protestant Episcopal Church in America Seabury House Greenwich, Conn.	Most Reverend Sir:	My dear Bishop Blank: *or* My dear Bishop:	Respectfully yours,	Sincerely yours,	1, 2. Bishop Blank
Anglican Bishop	The Right Reverend The Lord Bishop of London London, England	My Lord Bishop:	My dear Bishop:	Respectfully yours,	Sincerely yours,	1. My Lord 2. The Lord Bishop of London
Methodist Bishop	The Reverend Bishop Blank Methodist Bishop Memphis, Tennessee	Reverend Sir:	My dear Bishop Blank:	Respectfully yours,	Sincerely yours,	1, 2. Bishop Blank
Protestant Episcopal Bishop	The Right Reverend the Bishop of Jacksonville *or* The Right Reverend John R. Blank, D.D., LL.D. Bishop of Jacksonville Jacksonville, Florida	Right Reverend Sir:	My dear Bishop: *or* My dear Bishop Blank:	Respectfully yours,	Sincerely yours,	1, 2. Bishop Blank
Anglican Archdeacon	The Venerable John R. Blank The Archdeacon of San Francisco San Francisco, California	Mr. Archdeacon:	My dear Archdeacon:	Very truly yours,	Sincerely yours,	1, 2. Archdeacon Blank

Protestant Episcopal Archdeacon	The Venerable John R. Blank, D.D. The Archdeacon of Baltimore Diocese of Maryland Baltimore, Maryland	Mr. Arch- deacon:	My dear Archdeacon:	Very truly yours,	[illegible]	Blank *or* Dr. Blank
Dean [21]	The Very Reverend John R. Blank, D.D. Dean of St. Luke's Cathedral New York, New York	Very Reverend Sir: *or* My dear Mr. Dean:	My dear Dean Blank:	Very truly yours,	Sincerely yours,	1, 2. Dean Blank *or* Dr. Blank
Protestant Minister	*With Scholastic Degree:* The Reverend John R. Blank, D.D., Litt.D. Starkville, Mississippi	My dear Dr. Blank:	My dear Dr. Blank:	Very truly yours,	Sincerely yours,	1, 2. Dr. Blank
	Without Scholastic Degree: The Reverend John R. Blank Brownsville, Texas	My dear Mr. Blank:	My dear Mr. Blank:	Very truly yours,	Sincerely yours,	1, 2. Mr. Blank
Protestant Priest	*With Scholastic Degree:* The Reverend John R. Blank, D.D. St. Thomas' House Richmond, Virginia	My dear Dr. Blank	My dear Dr. Blank:	Very truly yours,	Sincerely yours,	1, 2. Dr. Blank
	Without Scholastic Degree: The Reverend John R. Blank Richmond, Virginia	My dear Mr. Blank: *or* My dear Father Blank:	My dear Mr. Blank: *or* My dear Father Blank:			1, 2. Mr. Blank *or* Father Blank

[21] Applies only to the head of a Cathedral or of a Theological Seminary.

COLLEGE OFFICIALS

Personage	Envelope and Inside Address	Formal Salutation	Informal Salutation	Formal Close	Informal Close	1. Spoken Address 2. Informal Introduction or Reference
President of a University	John R. Blank, LL.D., Ph.D. *or* Dr. John R. Blank President, Wells College Aurora, New York (Use only highest degree unless degrees are in different fields)	Sir:	My dear Dr. Blank:	Very truly yours,	Sincerely yours,	1, 2. Dr. Blank
	Catholic Priest The Very Reverend John R. Blank, S.J., D.D., Ph.D. President, Fordham University New York 10, New York	Sir:	My dear Father Blank:	Very truly yours,	Sincerely yours,	1, 2. Father Blank
University Chancellor	Dr. John R. Blank Chancellor, University of Alabama University Alabama	Sir:	My dear Dr. Blank:	Very truly yours,	Sincerely yours,	1, 2. Dr. Blank
Professor	Professor John R. Blank *or* (If he holds a doctor's degree) John R. Blank, Ph.D. George Washington University Washington 10, D. C.	My dear Sir: *or* My dear Professor (Doctor) Blank: *or* My dear Dr. Blank:	My dear Professor (Doctor) Blank	Very truly yours,	Sincerely yours,	1, 2. Professor Blank *or* Dr. Blank
Dean or Assistant Dean of a College or Graduate School	Dean John R. Blank School of Commerce *or* (If he holds a doctor's degree) Dr. John R. Blank Dean (Assistant Dean) School of Commerce	My dear Sir: *or* My dear Dean Blank:	My dear Dean Blank:	Very truly yours,	Sincerely yours,	1. Dean Blank 2. Dean Blank *or* Dr. Blank, the Dean (Assistant Dean) of the School of [illegible]

11. DICTIONARY OF CORRECT USAGE

A

ccept, except. ACCEPT means to receive with approval, reply to affirmatively, agree to; EXCEPT means to exclude, make an exception to. *This order will be* ACCEPTED ON [agreed to on] *our usual terms. This order will be* EXCEPTED FROM [made an exception to] *our usual terms.*

ddicted to, subject to. ADDICTED TO means devoted to persistently, as to a bad habit or indulgence; SUBJECT TO means prone to, conditional upon. *Jones is* ADDICTED TO *alcohol. Jones is* SUBJECT TO [prone to] *colds. This arrangement is* SUBJECT TO [conditional upon] *approval by Mr. Jones.*

ffect, effect. These two verbs are totally different in meaning. AFFECT means to have an influence upon, produce an effect upon, effect a change in, concern; EFFECT means to cause, bring about, produce, result in, have as a result. *Passage of this bill would have* AFFECTED [influenced or concerned] *the entire country. Passage of this bill can be* EFFECTED [brought about] *only through the co-operation of both parties.* Note the difference in meaning between the following sentences: *The change of climate may* AFFECT [alter for better or for worse the prospects of] *his recovery. The change of climate may* EFFECT [bring about] *his recovery.* The word AFFECT can never be used as a noun; EFFECT used as a noun, means result. *The* EFFECT [result; not, AFFECT] *of a sarcastic business letter is to antagonize the customer.*

all right. This expression should always be written as two words. There is no such word as ALRIGHT; the forms ALLRIGHT and ALL-RIGHT are also incorrect. *Are you* ALL RIGHT? *It will be* ALL RIGHT *to ship the goods on the tenth.*

all-round. Informal but permissible. Means the same as ALL-AROUND. *Jones is a good* ALL-ROUND [preferable to ALL-AROUND] *salesman.*

almost. See **most.**

already, all ready. ALREADY means beforehand, by or before a particular time; ALL READY means prepared, wholly ready. *I* ALREADY *have all the goods I need. I have the goods* ALL READY [prepared] *for shipment.*

altogether, all together. ALTOGETHER means wholly, completely, entirely; ALL TOGETHER means gathered, assembled. *The story is* ALTOGETHER [entirely] *false. We were* ALL TOGETHER [assembled] *in the room.*

among. See **between.**

an. The use of AN before such words as history, historical, humble, is now regarded as unnecessary; A is the preferred usage, in both written and spoken English [A *history;* A *historical work;* A *humble workman*]. Use A before all consonants except silent *h* [A *history;* but, AN *hour*]. Also, use A before words beginning with the sound of *y* or *w* [A *unit;* A *eulogy;* A *one*].

anyone, any one. Should be written as one word when used to mea anybody. *If we send* ANYONE [anybody], *it should be Jones.* Write two words when the meaning is one particular person or thing fro among a number. *If we send* ANY ONE *of the salesmen, it should b Jones.*

any place, every place, no place, some place. Commonly misuse for ANYWHERE, EVERYWHERE, NOWHERE, SOMEWHERE. *Are you goin* ANYWHERE [not, ANY PLACE] *this afternoon? I have looked* EVERY WHERE [not, EVERY PLACE] *for the missing bill. I have* NOWHERE [no NO PLACE] *to go this afternoon. The book must be* SOMEWHERE [no SOME PLACE] *in the room.*

anywheres, nowheres. Incorrect; use ANYWHERE, NOWHERE. *I can find the letter* ANYWHERE [not, ANYWHERES] *in the files. The lette was* NOWHERE [not, NOWHERES]*to be found.*

apt, liable. These two words are frequently confused. APT usually mean having an unfortunate tendency to; LIABLE usually means exposed t a risk. Correct: *We have found that when we ship by parcel pos delays are* APT [have an unfortunate tendency] *to occur.* Correct: *Thi shipment is* LIABLE *to be* [exposed to the risk of being] *delayed if w ship by parcel post.* Correct: *Businessmen are* APT [have an unfortu nate tendency] *to dictate letters carelessly.* Correct: *A businessma who dictates letters carelessly is* LIABLE *to lose* [exposed to the dange of losing] *his customers.* Where the sense is simple probability, use LIKELY. *The goods are* LIKELY *to* [probably will] *arrive on the tenth*

as . . . as, so . . . as. Use AS . . . AS in affirmative statements; in nega tive statements and in questions implying a negative answer, good usage requires the use of SO . . . AS. Affirmative statement: *This win dow display is* AS *attractive* AS *the last one.* Negative statement *This window display is not* SO *attractive* AS *the last one.* Question implying a negative answer: *Could any businessman be so foolish* AS *to ship such an order?*

as, like. Use AS when a verb follows. *Do* AS *I do. Write this exactly* AS *I dictated it. He tried,* AS *any businessman would* [try], *to get a lower price.* When no verb follows, use LIKE. *His dictation is* LIKE *mine in some respects.*

as, whether. Do not use AS in place of WHETHER or THAT. *I am not sure* WHETHER [not, AS] *I can ship the goods on that date.*

at about. *Omit the* AT. *Jones arrived this morning* ABOUT [not, AT ABOUT] *ten o'clock.*

aught. Means "anything," but in this sense is now obsolete. The name of the symbol 0 is NAUGHT, not AUGHT.

B

back of. Preferable to use BEHIND. *His store is just off Clinton Street,* BEHIND [not, IN BACK OF] *the post office.*

beside, besides. BESIDE means by the side of, close to; BESIDES means additionally, in addition to. *The letter is on my desk,* BESIDE [alongside; not, BESIDES] *the telephone.* BESIDES [in addition to; not, BESIDE] *these two bills, there are several others that should be paid before the fifteenth. We have these two bills, and several others* BESIDES [in addition; not, BESIDE].

tween, among. Use BETWEEN where only two persons or things are referred to; use AMONG where more than two are referred to. *On this point there was a difference of opinion* AMONG [not, BETWEEN] *the directors. On this point there was a difference of opinion* BETWEEN [not, AMONG] *Jones and Smith.*

weekly, bimonthly. BIWEEKLY means once every two weeks; BIMONTHLY means once every two months. SEMIWEEKLY means twice a week; SEMIMONTHLY means twice a month. All four expressions are confusing and should be avoided. It is clearer to use ONCE EVERY TWO WEEKS, ONCE EVERY TWO MONTHS, TWICE A WEEK, TWICE A MONTH.

ıt that, but what. The most common error here is the use of BUT THAT or BUT WHAT after "doubt." Wrong: *There is no doubt* BUT WHAT [or, BUT THAT] *the shipment will reach you promptly.* Correct: *There is no doubt* THAT *the shipment will reach you promptly.*

C

ın, may. CAN denotes ability or power; MAY denotes permission. CAN *you* [will you be able to] *make payment next month?* MAY *we* [will you give us permission to] *ship your order by freight?* CAN *I* [is it possible for me to] *go to Alaska by plane?* MAY *I* [do I have your permission to] *go to Alaska by plane?*

ımpare to, compare with. If the meaning is merely to suggest a similarity, or state that a similarity exists, use TO. If the meaning is to estimate the degree of similarity, or state the details of a similarity, use WITH. *The speaker compared the British law* WITH *the American* [here the meaning is that the speaker made a detailed comparison]. *The speaker compared the new law* TO *a plague* [here the meaning is that the speaker merely suggested a similarity]. In many cases either TO or WITH may be used. *Compared* TO [or, WITH] *him, I am a genius.* After an intransitive verb, only WITH can be used. *Round steak cannot compare* WITH *filet mignon.*

ɔntemplate. Should not be followed by ON, OVER, or any other preposition. *I am* CONTEMPLATING [not, CONTEMPLATING ON, CONTEMPLATING ON MAKING, or CONTEMPLATING OVER] *a trip through the Middle West.*

ɔntemptible, contemptuous. CONTEMPTIBLE means despicable, deserving of being despised; CONTEMPTUOUS means scornful. *He played a* CONTEMPTIBLE [despicable] *trick on Jones. His comments on the new sales plan were very* CONTEMPTUOUS [scornful].

ontinual, continuous. CONTINUAL means occurring in close succession, frequently repeated; CONTINUOUS means without stopping, without interruption. CONTINUAL [frequent] *breakdowns in the factory delayed delivery of the goods. The machinery has been in* CONTINUOUS *operation* [has not been stopped] *for sixty hours. He is* CONTINUAI [frequently] *asking for special favors. He drove* CONTINUOUSLY [wi out stopping] *for six hours.*

could of. See **of.**

credible, credulous, creditable. CREDIBLE means believable; CREDUL means easily imposed upon, believing too easily; CREDITABLE me praiseworthy. *The price quoted seems hardly* CREDIBLE [believab *He is too* CREDULOUS [easily imposed upon] *to make a good purch ing agent. His record as a salesman was highly* CREDITABLE [prai worthy].

D

data. The word DATA is plural; the singular form, now seldom used, DATUM. *We have proved that these* [not, THIS] *data* ARE [not, *reliable.*

different from. This is the correct form, DIFFERENT THAN being inva ably wrong. *My sales plan is* DIFFERENT FROM [not, DIFFERENT THA *the one that you suggested.*

differ from, differ with. DIFFER used in the sense of being differe exhibiting a difference, is followed by FROM, not WITH; in the sense having a difference of opinion, expressing dissent, disputing, it is us ally followed by WITH. *My sales campaign* DIFFERS FROM [is unlik *yours in three ways.* I DIFFER WITH [disagree with] *you as to the val of your sales campaign.*

disinterested, uninterested. DISINTERESTED means unselfish, imparti without thought of personal gain; UNINTERESTED means not intereste not enthusiastic. A *magistrate must perform his duties in a* DISINTE ESTED *manner* [impartial manner, without thought of personal gai *He seems* UNINTERESTED *in his work* [lacking in interest or enthusiasm

E

each other, one another. No differentiation need be made. The ru that EACH OTHER should be used when only two things are referred t and that ONE ANOTHER should be used when more than two are r ferred to, is no longer generally accepted. Hence all the followin forms are correct: *Smith and I see* ONE ANOTHER *quite often. Smit and I see* EACH OTHER *quite often. It will be interesting for the fo of us to see* ONE ANOTHER *again after so many years. It will be inte esting for the four of us to see* EACH OTHER *again after so many year* The possessive of EACH OTHER is EACH OTHER'S, not EACH OTHERS'; th possessive of ONE ANOTHER is ONE ANOTHER'S, not ONE ANOTHERS *They tore* EACH OTHER'S [not, EACH OTHERS'] *clothes. They tore* ON ANOTHER'S [not, ONE ANOTHERS'] *clothes.*

effect. See **affect.**

either. Correct when used to designate one of two persons or thing not correct when used to designate one of three or more. Correct EITHER *of the two men will be suitable.* Wrong: EITHER *of the fou* *men will be suitable.* Correct: ANY [or, ANY ONE] *of the four men will be suitable.* EITHER should be followed by a singular verb. *If* EITHER *Jones or Smith* IS [not, ARE] *going to Chicago, tell* HIM [not, THEM] *to see Brown.*

lse. A common error is to combine ELSE with BUT. Wrong: *It was nothing* ELSE BUT *selfishness on his part.* Correct: *It was nothing* BUT *selfishness on his part.* Correct: *There was no one* BUT [not, ELSE BUT] *him in the room.* For the possessive form, USE SOMEBODY ELSE'S [not, SOMEBODY'S ELSE]. *He took* SOMEBODY ELSE'S [not, SOMEBODY'S ELSE] hat. Similarly: EVERYONE ELSE'S, ANYONE ELSE'S, NO ONE ELSE'S, etc. *I took mine, but he took* EVERYONE ELSE'S [not, EVERYONE'S ELSE].

verybody. Write as one word.

veryone, every one. Write as one word when the meaning is everybody. EVERYONE [everybody] *in the department should attend the weekly sales meetings.* Write as two words when the meaning is each one of a group of persons or things. EVERY ONE [each one] *of the department heads must be present at this meeting. All of the salesmen have done well;* EVERY ONE [each one] *of them deserves a prize.*

very place. See **any place.**

xcept. See **accept.**

F

arther, further. No differentiation need be made. Most writers prefer FURTHER. *I will walk one mile, and no* FURTHER. *The speaker was asked to cite some* FURTHER *examples.*

irstly. When SECONDLY, THIRDLY, etc., follow, begin with FIRSTLY, not FIRST. The choice between FIRSTLY, SECONDLY, THIRDLY, etc., and FIRST, SECOND, THIRD, etc., is a matter of personal preference.

ormer. Correct when used to designate the first of two persons or things; incorrect when used to designate the first of three or more. Correct: *Smith and Jones were at the convention; the* FORMER *gave a very interesting talk.* Wrong: *Smith, Jones, and Brown were at the convention; the* FORMER *gave a very interesting talk.* Correct: *Smith, Jones, and Brown were at the convention; the* FIRST-NAMED *gave a very interesting talk.* However, this construction is awkward; where three or more are mentioned, it is best to repeat the word referred to. Thus: *Smith, Jones, and Brown were at the convention;* SMITH *gave a very interesting talk.*

G

guarantee, guaranty. For the verb, always use GUARANTEE. *We* GUARANTEE [not, GUARANTY] *that the goods will be satisfactory.* For the noun, *business convention has established a specialized use of* GUARANTY, which is illustrated in such expressions as *contract of* GUARANTY, *act of* GUARANTY. However, GUARANTEE is never wrong, even in these connections, and hence a safe rule to follow is: When in doubt, use GUARANTEE.

H

had better, had best. Both good usage. Correct: *You* HAD BETT *not stay in Chicago more than two weeks.* Correct: *It* HAD BEST *done at once.*

had have, had of. Often incorrectly used in place of HAD. Wron *If he* HAD OF [or, HAD HAVE] *tried, he could have done it.* Correc *If he* HAD *tried, he could have done it.*

had ought, hadn't ought. See **ought.**

hardly. This word itself carries a negative idea, and hence should n be followed or preceded by NOT. Wrong: *I* COULDN'T HARDLY *get t table through the door.* Correct: *I* COULD HARDLY *get the tab through the door.*

help. Should not be followed by BUT when used in the sense of avoi Wrong: *I can't* HELP BUT *feel that he really meant to do it.* Correc *I can't* HELP FEELING *that he really meant to do it.*

hopes. Sometimes incorrectly used in place of HOPE. Wrong: W *have no* HOPES *of ever receiving payment.* Correct: *We have no* HOP *of ever receiving payment.*

I

if. Often misused in place of WHETHER. Wrong: *I am not sure* IF *can ship the goods on that date.* Correct: *I am not sure* WHETHER *can ship the goods on that date.*

imply, infer. IMPLY is used to denote something suggested, assume insinuated, or vaguely expressed. *Your letter* IMPLIES *that I have trie to evade payment of the bill.* INFER means to draw from, deduce from gather from, or conclude from. *I* INFER *from your letter that yo cannot grant an extension of time.*

in back of. See **back of.**

inferior, superior. Should always be followed by TO, not THAN. *It i* INFERIOR *from every point of view* TO [not, THAN] *the material pre viously used.*

ingenious, ingenuous. INGENIOUS means clever, skillful; INGENUOU means frank, innocent, trusting. *His suggestion is a very* INGENIOU [clever] *solution of the problem. You would think that a young ma of 22 would not be so* INGENUOUS [trusting, easily imposed upon].

irregardless. There is no such word; the correct form is REGARDLESS Misuse is perhaps caused by confusion with the word IRRESPECTIVE which is somewhat similar in meaning and is correct. *We shoul acknowledge all orders,* REGARDLESS [not, IRREGARDLESS] *of the amount involved.*

K

kind, sort. Write THIS KIND, THAT KIND, not THESE KINDS, THOSE KINDS. Similarly, write THIS SORT, THAT SORT, not THESE SORTS, THOSE SORTS. Wrong: *I don't like* THESE KINDS *of pencils.* Correct: *I don't like* THIS

KIND *of pencil.* Wrong: *I don't like* THOSE SORTS *of pencils.* Correct: *I don't like* THAT SORT *of pencil.*

nd of, sort of. These expressions should not be followed by A or AN. *What* KIND OF [not, KIND OF A] *place is it? It's the* SORT OF [not, SORT OF AN] *account that has to be carefully watched.*

L

tter, last. The word LATTER may be used to designate the second of two persons or things previously mentioned, but should not be used where more than two have been mentioned. Correct: *We are now conducting a special sale of suits and overcoats; the* LATTER *are particularly good value.* But: *We are now conducting a special sale of hats, suits, and overcoats; the* LAST [or, LAST-NAMED; not LATTER] *are particularly good value.* In most cases, as here, the construction with LAST is awkward and may prove ambiguous; it is usually best to repeat the word referred to. Thus: *We are now conducting a special sale of hats, suits, and overcoats; the* OVERCOATS *are particularly good value.*

y, lie. LAY means to put or set down, place, deposit; LIE means to rest, be in a certain position or location. *He likes to* LIE [not, LAY] *down after lunch. The letters are* LYING [not, LAYING] *on your table. He let the pen* LIE [not, LAY] *where it had fallen.* LAY [not, LIE] *the letters on the table.*

arn, teach. Do not use LEARN in the sense of TEACH. *The experience will* TEACH [not, LEARN] *him a lesson. Several years ago I* TAUGHT [not, LEARNED] *him how to check a credit.*

ave go, leave go of. Use LET GO. LET IT GO [not, LEAVE IT GO] *in the meantime. If you* LET GO [not, LEAVE GO OF] *the rope, you'll fall.*

ss. Apply the word LESS only to things that are measured by amount, and not by size, quality, or number. Correct: *He bought* LESS [a smaller amount of] *butter this month than last.* But: *The staff in the New York office is* SMALLER [not, LESS] *than that in the Chicago office.* FEWER [not, LESS] *industrial accidents occurred this year than last.*

able. See **apt.**

ke. See **as, like** and **such as, like.**

kely. See **apt.**

oan, lend. Many authorities object to any use of LOAN as a verb. It is best to use the word only in connection with formal business transactions—as, for example, the placing of a loan by a bank. For general purposes use LEND. *Will you* LEND [not, LOAN] *me ten dollars? He* LENT [not, LOANED] *me ten dollars.* But: *The bank* LOANED *the money at six per cent.*

M

nay. See **can.**

nay of. See **of.**

Messrs. See page 627.

night of. See **of.**

most, almost. Do not use MOST in place of ALMOST. Apart from t fact that MOST is not good usage, in many constructions it changes t meaning. Thus, *I am* MOST *ready to go* [meaning, I am very willi to go] is totally different from, *I am* ALMOST *ready to go.*
must of. See **of.**

N

naught. See **aught.**
nobody. Always write as one word.
no one. Always write as two words.
no place. See **any place.**
nowheres. See **anywheres.**

O

of. COULD OF, SHOULD OF, WOULD OF, MUST OF, MAY OF, MIGHT OF a all incorrect; use COULD HAVE, SHOULD HAVE, WOULD HAVE, MUST HAV MAY HAVE, MIGHT HAVE. *I* COULD HAVE *made a larger profit. I* SHOU HAVE *made a larger profit. I* WOULD HAVE *made a larger profit.* MUST HAVE *made a mistake. I* MAY HAVE *made a mistake. I* MIG HAVE *made a mistake.*
off, from. Do not use OFF in place of FROM. *I bought it* FROM [nc OFF] *Jones.*
off of. Incorrect; omit the OF. *I will give you ten per cent* OFF [nc OFF OF] *the list price.*
one another. See **each other.**
oneself, one's self. The one-word form is preferred. *It is dangero to cut* ONESELF. However, if emphasis is desired, ONE'S SELF may used. *It is wise to know* ONE'S SELF.
only. The meaning that the sentence is intended to convey determin the position of the word ONLY. (1) ONLY *the teacher spoke to Joh* (2) *The teacher* ONLY *spoke to John.* (3) *The teacher spoke* ONLY *John,* or, *The teacher spoke to John* ONLY. Each of these three se tences conveys a different meaning. The first states that the teache and no one else, spoke to John; the second that the teacher did notl ing beyond merely speaking to John; the third that the teacher a dressed John to the exclusion of everyone else. No hard and fast ru can be given. The writer must consider carefully the exact meanir that he wishes to convey, and place the ONLY accordingly. As a fin resort, if there is danger of ambiguity or misunderstanding, the co struction should be changed to eliminate the ONLY entirely. ONL is sometimes erroneously used as a conjunction. Wrong: Your pen the same as mine ONLY that the nib is different. Right: The ON [or ONLY] *difference between your pen and mine is the different nib.*
ought. Do not combine OUGHT with HAD. *I* OUGHT [not, HAD OUGHT *to have waited for the shipment.*
over with. Omit the WITH. *Our annual fall sale is now* OVER [no OVER WITH].

P

air, set. These are the singular, not the plural, forms. Wrong: *Send five* PAIR *of stockings and three* SET *of dishes.* Correct: *Send five* PAIRS *of stockings and three* SETS *of dishes.*

ractícable, practical. PRACTICABLE means feasible, capable of being put into practice; PRACTICAL means useful or successful in actual practice. PRACTICAL may be used with reference to either persons or things. *Jones is a* PRACTICAL *man* [a "doer" rather than a theorist]. *No* PRACTICAL *solution could be found* [no solution that would work]. Note, however, that PRACTICABLE cannot be used with reference to persons, but only with reference to things. Thus, *Jones is a* PRACTICABLE *man* [a man "capable of being put into practice"] is meaningless. The following sentences illustrate the change in meaning that results when one word is substituted for the other: *The scheme is* PRACTICABLE [it can be carried out]. *The scheme is* PRACTICAL [it will be successful when carried out.]

rescribe, proscribe. PRESCRIBE means to lay down definite rules or directions, to dictate, direct, order the use of. PROSCRIBE means to prohibit, condemn. *The sales manager* PRESCRIBED *regular selling hours for the salesmen. The doctor* PRESCRIBED *cod-liver oil. The president* PROSCRIBED [prohibited] *smoking during office hours.*

rincipal, principle. A handy rule to keep in mind when using either of these words is: The word PRINCIPLE is a noun only, and cannot be used as an adjective. Therefore, whenever the form is an adjective, it is always spelled PRINCIPAL. *The New England states have been our* PRINCIPAL *source of business during the past five years.* PRINCIPLE means a fundamental or general truth, a rule. PRINCIPAL, which in the noun form has a variety of meanings, is used in all other cases. *We have always acted on the* PRINCIPLE [fundamental truth] *that honesty is the best policy. The loan, including* PRINCIPAL *and interest, amounted to $158.63. An agent may, by correspondence, bind his* PRINCIPAL *to contracts entered into within the scope of his authority.*

roven. Not good usage; use PROVED. *It was* PROVED [not, PROVEN] *that the carrier was to blame.*

roviding. Not good usage in place of PROVIDED. It is preferable not to use THAT after PROVIDED. *I will give you the order,* PROVIDED [not, PROVIDING] *you agree to make delivery not later than the tenth.*

R

eason. Do not complete a sentence beginning in some such way as THE REASON IS with: (1) a BECAUSE clause; (2) a BECAUSE OF phrase; (3) a DUE TO phrase; or (4) an ON ACCOUNT OF phrase. Complete the sentence with a THAT clause. Wrong: *The reason the goods were delayed was* BECAUSE *an error was made in the shipping department.* Wrong: *The reason the goods were delayed was* BECAUSE OF *an error in the shipping department.* Wrong: *The reason the goods were de-*

layed was DUE TO *an error in the shipping department.* Wrong: *Th reason the goods were delayed was* ON ACCOUNT OF *an error in th shipping department.* Correct: *The reason the goods were delaye was* THAT *an error was made in the shipping department.*

regard. Do not use REGARDS in place of REGARD in the expressions I REGARD TO, WITH REGARD TO. Correct: *With* REGARD [not, REGARDS] *to our past-due accounts, the situation is still unchanged.*

S

same. Not good business usage. Poor: *We will repair the spring an ship* SAME *to you on Wednesday of next week.* Correct: *We will re pair the spring and ship* IT *to you on Wednesday of next week.*

semiweekly, semimonthly. See **biweekly.**

set. See **pair.**

should of. See **of.**

size, sized. Either may be used when preceded by an adjective. A hyphen should connect both these words with a preceding adjective *Different-sized* [or *-size*] *screws . . .*

so . . . as. See **as . . . as.**

someone. Write as one word when SOMEBODY can be substituted; other wise write as two words.

some place. See **any place.**

sort. See **kind.**

sort of. See **kind of.**

such as, like. LIKE is commonly misused in place of SUCH AS, wher the meaning is for example. *In his factory are a number of usefu machines,* SUCH AS [not, LIKE] *cutters and stampers, which are ver seldom idle.*

superior. See **inferior.**

T

teach. See **learn.**

this here, these here, that there, those there. Incorrect; use merely THIS, THESE, THAT, THOSE. *Shipment of* THIS [not, THIS HERE] *orde was supposed to have been made last week.*

W

wait on. Do not use in place of WAIT FOR. *We have been* WAITING FOR [not, WAITING ON] the goods to arrive for three days.

ways. Do not use in place of WAY. *He was a little* WAY [not, WAYS] *ahead. This year's sales are quite a* BIT [not, WAYS] *ahead of last year's,* or, *This year's sales are* CONSIDERABLY *ahead of last year's.*

where. Sometimes misused in place of THAT. *I see in this morning's paper* THAT [not, WHERE] *the Ames Corporation has declared a fifty-cent dividend.*

whether. See **as, whether.**

would of. See **of.**

SECTION 6

Business Protection Through Insurance

1. HOW TO REDUCE THE COST OF AMPLE INSURANCE PROTECTION

2. LAW GOVERNING INSURANCE POLICIES

3. TYPES OF INSURANCE POLICIES

4. FIRE INSURANCE

5. LIABILITY INSURANCE

6. WORKMEN'S COMPENSATION INSURANCE

7. AUTOMOBILE INSURANCE

8. BURGLARY, THEFT, AND ROBBERY INSURANCE

9. FIDELITY AND SURETY BONDS

10. CREDIT INSURANCE

1. MISCELLANEOUS INSURANCE COVERAGES

Fire and Allied Coverages

Other Property Insurance

Floater Policies

Miscellaneous Coverages

12. BUSINESS LIFE INSURANCE

SECTION 6

Business Protection Through Insurance*

1. HOW TO REDUCE THE COST OF AMPLE INSURANCE PROTECTION

Purchase the proper form of insurance. Insurance, like all other mmodities, is placed on the market in various kinds of packages; me packages contain much more protection for a given premium an others.

Purchasing the *most* suitable form of insurance for the situation n keep costs down considerably. For example, any risk may be vered by "specific fire" insurance. If the value of the property risk, however, fluctuates sharply, it will be much cheaper to buy least a part of the coverage as "reporting insurance" if the busiess qualifies for it. The saving arises from the fact that under e reporting form of policy, a premium is charged only on the actual lue of the property at risk; whereas, under the specific form of olicy, the premium must be paid in advance on the full face value f the policy. Since the face value of the policy must be at least qual to the maximum amount that may be at risk at any time, it is pparent that the reporting form of insurance would be cheaper in ich an instance.

Select your broker or agent carefully, and keep him informed. n insurance broker or agent who takes an interest in his client's usiness has been compared to a doctor of medicine. Like a qualified octor the broker or agent can diagnose the needs of the client after careful analysis of all the surrounding circumstances, and can precribe the proper remedy. The agent or broker, on the other hand, who merely "writes up" something when his client informs him that e needs some "burglary insurance," is like the old country "horse

* Acknowledgment is made to Jerome S. Miller, Insurance Consultant, for his ssistance in revising this section.

doctor" who gives out "snake oil" or some similar preparation, every ailment.

A good broker or agent who is interested in the welfare of l policyholders, and who is kept informed by his clients of chang in their circumstances, can do a great deal to point out ways ar means by which the insured can keep down the cost of ample ar proper insurance protection.

Many businessmen make a habit of turning over all policies ar supplementary documents to their insurance broker or agent eve year for examination and analysis. This habit is a good one ar should be cultivated by everyone. In many instances minor chang can be made that will more nearly fit the policy to the needs of tl insured, or that will facilitate the settling of a claim in case of loss. The following example illustrates a condition that is oft found when a lease and a policy of insurance taken out in accor ance with its terms are examined.

Leases usually contain some provision relative to liability for rer and so forth, following a fire. Recently a broker, in examining lease covering the property of his client, found that although tl lessee was paying fire insurance premiums, he was not protecte One provision of the lease provided that the lessee should pay ov to the landlord premiums to effect insurance upon the propert The landlord then took out insurance in his own name. Yet a other clause of the same lease stated that in event of a loss, tl lessee would be liable therefor. As a result of the second clause, i event of a loss, the insurance company would have paid the amour thereof to the landlord, and then would have sued the lessee (wh had actually paid the premiums) for the amount of the loss. Suc a result was prevented in this instance by the addition to the polic of a clause whereby the insurance company agreed not to sue th lessee.

This case illustrates the importance of keeping in close touch wit your insurance agent or broker and informing him of all facts tha may affect the insurance carried.

Read your policy. The importance of reading your policy befor a loss is incurred cannot be overstressed. While most of the state have provided by law for so-called standard policies, the number an variety of permitted endorsements renders it very easy for the insure reduce his liability. Furthermore, in many comparatively new rms, practice has not been standardized, and each company issues olicies conforming to its own ideas of what liability should or should ot be assumed.

Despite the fact that practically every word of the older standard ontracts has long since been interpreted by the courts, almost 4 per ent of all litigation involves insurance or insurance contracts. Mani-estly, the proper time to cure ambiguities, to add endorsements, r to remove unwanted clauses, is before a loss is incurred. But nless the insured will take the time to read his contract (or, better ill, read it in company with his broker or agent), he will never now what changes should be made to adapt the contract to his articular needs.

Some examples of the cost of failure to read a policy. The ost of failure to read a policy before a loss occurs can probably best e illustrated by a number of cases selected at random from among he many court decisions handed down during the past years.

Case 1. The Frisco Frolics Company took out a so-called Theater loater Policy. The form of Theater Floater Policy used covers against ransportation hazards only while the insured's property is being trans-orted by a common carrier. The Frolics Company, however, usually ransported their property and effects in their own trucks. The Frolics Company apparently believed that they were fully protected against loss rom all fire and transportation hazards. A loss was incurred while the rolics Company's property was being transported in the theater com-any's trucks. Subsequently the insurance company refused to pay the laim on the ground that the risk was one which they had not assumed. The Court upheld the contention of the insurance company. Failure f the Frolics Company to have an endorsement attached to the stand-rd policy permitting transportation of property in the company's own rucks voided the insurance when the goods were thus transported. (In-urance Company v. Frolics Company, 65 F.(2d) 928.)

Case 2. The Walsh Construction Company procured a depository ond protecting it against loss of deposits that were made in a designated ank. The Walsh Company believed that it was fully protected. The olicy, however, contained a clause that read: "It is agreed that this bond loes not cover certificates of deposit or any other indebtedness . . . not ubject at all times to immediate withdrawal by the Walsh Construction Company." The Court held that this clause restricted the coverage of he policy to demand deposits, and that, therefore, the Walsh Company ould not recover any part of $200,000 which was deposited in a savings account when the bank failed. (Construction Company v. Insuran Company, 67 F.(2d) 679.)

Case 3. The insured, a lumber dealer, purchased a fire insurance pol that contained a so-called "clear-space clause," whereby the assured agre not to place any lumber within one hundred feet of any manufacturi establishment or dry kiln. The insured, unaware of the clear space pr vision contained in the contract, did not remove certain lumber from t prohibited area. A loss was incurred, and the insurance company refus to indemnify on the ground that the policy was void at the time of t fire, inasmuch as the assured had violated the clear-space provision. T Court upheld the contention of the insurance company, and stated th ignorance that the policy contained the clear-space clause did not excu a violation thereof, even though the agent who had sold the policy kne of the violation. (Insurance Company v. Post, 62 S.W. 140.)

In each of the above cases the insured suffered a loss through fai ure to take the elementary precaution of reading his policy. Suc cases are not infrequent and point to the fact that the time require to read your policy is time well spent.

Budgeting insurance premiums; purchase of long-term policie Insurance contracts, other than life, are ordinarily issued for a singl year. Upon request, however, such policies may be issued for longe than a single year. Such a procedure results in a considerable sav ing in gross premiums. For example, in fire insurance, if the origina premium is the amount shown in the first column of the followin table, the premium for other terms will be the amount shown i the respective columns.

TERM POLICY RATES

One-year Premium	*Three-year Premium*	*Five-year Premium*
.10	.25	.40
.25	.625	1.00
.50	1.25	2.00
1.00	2.50	4.00

The term that will be the most economical in any given instanc can be said to depend upon the rate of interest that could be earned on the prepaid premiums if they were retained in the business.

The disadvantages of paying premiums for terms longer than one year may be largely eliminated by either of the following methods:

1. Budgeting premiums. By properly scheduling the time at which ach policy is to come due, the same amount may be paid each year, et each premium will represent a term longer than one year.

2. Finance companies will advance the portion of the premium pplicable to the term beyond one year, at a charge that will still eave a worth-while saving. See your broker about this service.

Savings resulting from frequent appraisals. Frequent appraisals f insured property may result in considerable savings in premiums. ince, in the event of a loss, only the actual amount thereof is ecoverable, it is folly to carry insurance for an amount in excess f the value of the property insured. But at the same time, coinsur- nce clauses (see page 694 for further explanation) generally compel he policyholder to carry insurance to at least 80 per cent of the alue of the insured property, under penalty of reducing the amount ecoverable in event of a partial loss. The problem is further in- ensified by the fact that values are constantly changing. For exam- le, a prominent engineering concern has estimated that an average uilding which was worth $150,000 in a certain year had increased n value to $200,000 two years later, but was worth only $194,000 the ext year. Consequently, if the insured is to be fully covered, with- ut at the same time paying for unneeded insurance, it is advisable hat expert appraisements be made each year.

Reducing the cost of insurance by means of improvements educing the risk. In many lines of insurance, rates are based on "schedules." From a basic rate certain sums are added for defects below the average, or subtracted for improvements above the aver- age. A comparison of the amount that can be saved over a period of a few years with the cost of making the necessary improvements will often disclose that such improvements form a highly profitable investment.

One outstanding economic justification for agents' and brokers' commissions is the ability of these men to point out to the insured the ways and means by which he can reduce the cost of his insur- ance by improving the risk. The insured, therefore, should not hesi- tate to call upon his broker or agent for information pertaining to specific improvements that he can make, and the savings to be real- ized therefrom; brokers and agents are able and willing to offer this service to their clients.

Savings effected by application of the deductible principl This principle, as indicated in the section on "self-insurance," closely allied with assumption of risk and excess loss insurance (s page 694 for further explanation). Inasmuch as administrative e penses in connection with minor losses are very high, and since greater moral hazard exists where an insurance company assum responsibility for all losses, no matter how trivial, large savings ca often be effected by the application of the deductible principle wit out sacrifice of any essential insurance protection.

The effect of a deductible clause is to limit the liability of the i surance company to large losses, and to render the insured liable f all small losses, as well as a small part of any large loss. For e ample, in automobile collision insurance, in the event of a loss $200 under a policy containing a $50 deductible clause, the compan will be liable for only $150; while if the loss does not exceed $5 the insured will have to assume all liability.

Persons carrying insurance other than fire should ask their broke about the savings that they may effect by application of the d ductible principle.

When purchasing insurance under an experience rating plar do not reveal the fact to persons covered. This principle can b best described by illustration. In the automobile field, many em ployers have found that salesmen who do not know that the em ployer has purchased public liability and property damage insuranc present fewer claims for accidents occurring while they are engage on the business of the employer than do salesmen of other firms (o even of the same firm) who possess such knowledge. Consequentl premiums can be kept lower by not revealing to employees the fac that third parties are protected against loss through negligence o the employee while he is engaged in the business of the employer.

Points to investigate in choosing an insurance company. Be fore insurance is placed with any particular company, the followin points with regard to the company may be investigated.

1. *Financial stability of the company.* If the company is a stoc company, obtain its most recent financial statement. In analyzin the financial statement, compare the income from premiums an investments with the disbursements. Also, study the kind an

uality of the securities composing the assets, the ratio of the total rplus and capital to the liabilities, and the ratio of the total assets the total outstanding insurance.

If the company is a mutual company, follow the same procedure that given for stock companies. In addition, ascertain whether not you will be liable for assessments; whether the company iarges a redundant premium, and operates on the reserve principle; whether it charges a premium that is barely adequate to meet its rdinary losses, and depends on assessments to meet its extraordinary osses.

2. *Record of the company for paying losses promptly.* The mount of time required to investigate and settle a loss depends to great extent upon the type of insurance involved, whether the loss total or partial, and whether the insured kept adequate records. Reliable companies attempt to settle just claims as quickly as possible fter presentation without quibbling over minor details.

3. *Services offered by the company that tend to reduce or elimi-nate the hazard.* Prevention is just as important (and in some lines nore important) as reimbursement for loss. Some companies main-ain adequate, well-trained, and well-equipped inspection staffs; others do little or no prevention work. Inspection services are par-icularly important in compensation insurance, and in the various ines under the general titles of liability and boiler insurance.

4. *Liberality of the contract.* Many clauses may be inserted or omitted that will change either the extent of the coverage granted by any policy, or the amount of reimbursement following any loss, or both. Such clauses naturally have a direct effect upon the cost of the insurance. Should two contracts, apparently the same, be offered at substantially different premiums, the insured should be sure to compare the contracts carefully in order to ascertain if there is any basic difference in the coverage offered.

5. *Cost of the contract.* In property and liability insurance, only the current premium need be considered. However, if the company is a mutual, the possibility of dividends or assessments should not be overlooked.

In life insurance, the usual contract extends over a much longer period than in property insurance. Consequently, the rate of re-turn earned by the company on its investments, the amount of surplus, and the ratio of actual deaths to the number expected may be more important than the quoted premiums for the first ye except in the case of nonparticipating "unchanging cost" contrac

What types of insurance are most important? Although answer to this question that will be applicable to every busin cannot be given, the results of an "Insurance Buying Practices" s vey conducted by the National Association of Credit Men indica that the following lines of insurance, in the order named, are t most important to the average businessman.

INSURANCE BUYING PRACTICES

I *Coverage*	II *Per Cent of Total Businesses Which Need Coverage*	III *Per Cent of Those in Col. II Who Have Coverage*
Fire	100	96
Compensation or Employer's Liability	100	91
Automobile Public Liability and Property Damage	100	74
General Public Liability	100	71
Robbery, Burglary, or Hold-up	100	58
Auto Fire and Theft	100	52
Forgery or Check Alteration	100	50
Windstorm	100	41
Explosion	100	35
Automobile Collision	100	30
Riot, Strike, and Civil Commotion	100	29
Truck Shipment	91	18
Rail Shipment	87	12
Truck Public Liability and Property Damage	76	96
Truck Fire and Theft	76	86
Nonownership Public Liability	76	63
Parcel Post (private, not Government)	76	40
Truck Collision	76	35
Schedule Fidelity Bonds	75	39
Power Plant Insurance	70	66
Salesmen's Samples	63	10
Sprinkler Leakage	58	64
Use and Occupancy	55	39
Individual Fidelity Bonds	48	63
Profits and Commissions	45	25
Rent and Rental Value	45	17

Self-insurance; its advantages and dangers. The term "self-surance" is used in many senses by the insuring public. Depend-g upon the person applying the term, it may mean:

1. No insurance.
2. An attempt to build up certain reserves, which in turn may be ther segregated from, or mixed with, the ordinary assets of the usiness.
3. The scientific application of insurance principles, the main-nance of an adequate segregated reserve, and constant effort to duce losses.

n all cases self-insurance is distinguished from private insurance by ie fact that the insured does not *transfer* the "risk" (that is, the hance of financial loss) to a professional risk-bearer, but assumes l risks himself. The advantages of self-insurance, of course, arise om alleged savings in administration expenses and the elimination f premiums.

The temptation to use self-insurance is often so great that many ersons succumb to its lures and are only awakened when a loss ccurs by the realization that they possess no insurance whatever. he very nature of insurance involves the distribution of risk and he application of the law of averages; unless some basis exists upon hich to distribute the risk and to apply the law of averages, there an be no insurance in the proper sense of the word, regardless of he presence or absence of reserves.

Successful self-insurance. The only form of self-insurance that will rove successful is that of the third type; it must involve more than he mere assumption of risk. Consequently, its proper use is limited o large enterprises that have numerous units to insure. Further-nore, each unit should be located so that the respective units are ot subject to the conflagration hazard (that is, loss of all units by single occurrence of the event insured against). A third requisite of self-insurance is that all units be of approximately equal value. f self-insurance is applied where the units are not of equal value, rivate insurance should be obtained to cover the values in excess of the average; otherwise a single large loss may wipe out the whole nsurance reserve. The fourth requirement for the successful opera-ion of a self-insurance fund is that it be embarked upon slowly; the principal should not attempt in any one year to cover by sel insurance more than 5 per cent to 8 per cent of the total value (the risk; complete assumption of the risk should not take place, ther fore, in less than twelve to twenty years.

In general, there are those who feel that a business enterprise tha owns a minimum of twenty-five widely separated units of approx mately equal value has the minimum requirements to self-insur against the hazards involved in the destruction of the property i self. On the other hand, it is said that no attempt should be mad to self-insure the compensation hazard unless a minimum of 30 employees are regularly employed, inasmuch as a wide divergenc exists between the possible minimum and maximum losses that ma result from an accident.

Points to consider in deciding whether to self-insure. In decidin whether or not to transfer any risk from private carriers to a self insurance fund, the insured should consider the following factors:

1. The maximum possible loss as compared with the amount o loss that the company is prepared to meet readily.
2. Possible legal expenses for the defense of suits that the insur ance companies promise to defend under practically all liabilit (and some property) insurance covers.
3. Whether or not inspection, collection, and other services that the insurance company guarantees under some forms of contracts will be curtailed, extended, or remain unchanged under the self-insurance program. Remember that a curtailment of such services often results in a material increase in losses.
4. The potential cost of:

(*a*) Setting up the fund on a secure and satisfactory basis, which will probably require the services of an insurance expert.

(*b*) Administration expenses.

5. The amount that can be earned by the self-insurance fund if invested in conservative securities that are readily marketable in case of a loss.
6. The nature of the risk and the property to be insured. For example, no greater loss can occur from the collision or theft of an automobile than is involved in the value of the motor vehicle, but the possible loss through liability to third parties for destruction of life and property by the automobile extends into at least six figures.

7. The number of losses that are likely to be incurred within a relatively short period (such as a year).

Very often a business may safely self-insure the common, ordinary losses that may be expected in the normal course of business, and purchase so-called *excess loss insurance* to protect itself against the extraordinary losses. Under such policies the insurance company does not become liable until a loss exceeds a specified amount, and then for the excess only. Application of the same principle is also made under *deductible policies,* of which the automobile deductible collision clause is probably the best example.

2. LAW GOVERNING INSURANCE POLICIES

Conflicts between printed provisions and endorsements. Since standard insurance policies are general contracts, endorsements are frequently added to such policies in order to adapt them to the specific needs of the insured. Very often such endorsements are in conflict with other provisions of the same policy. Where such a difference in meaning exists, the superimposed or endorsed portions of the contract (whether written in longhand, typewritten, stamped, or printed on a separate sheet and attached) control the standard provisions of the contract, and on the theory that they represent the most recent agreement between the parties, only such endorsements are considered in interpreting the policy.

Interpretation of an insurance policy where ambiguities exist. When the wording of any clause or phrase of an insurance contract, whether such clause or phrase is contained in an endorsement or a provision of the contract, lends itself to more than one interpretation, the courts have generally tended to give the benefit of the doubt to the insured, and reject that construction which limits the liability of the insurance company. Moreover, when a literal construction will lead to manifest injustice to the insured, and a liberal but nevertheless reasonable interpretation will prevent injustice by not requiring an impossibility, the courts will adopt the latter construction because the parties are presumed, when the language used by them permits, to have intended a reasonable and not an unreasonable result. And in any event, if the language of an insurance policy is not as clear and unequivocal as it might be, and therefore fairly

susceptible of two meanings, one of which is contended for by t
insured, such language generally will be construed against the ins
ance company, and in favor of the policyholder.

If an ambiguity exists because of two clauses of an insurance poli being so repugnant that they cannot stand together (both claus being provisions, and neither one constituting an endorsement), t courts usually interpret the policy as though the first of such claus (that is, the one that will normally be read first by a person readi the contract from beginning to end) were the only one appeari therein, and as though the second did not exist.

Violation of a policy; is policy again valid when violatio ceases? The answer to this question depends upon the constructio given to insurance contracts by the courts of the state wherein th insured property is located (or, in some cases, in the state wherei the policyholder is domiciled). In general, the courts hold that i after a violation, the conditions of the policy are again complie with, the policy revives, and is in full force and effect, even thoug the insurance company never consented to the violation. Thus th courts of New York and Pennsylvania have held that if a policyholde vacates his building for a period exceeding that permitted by th policy, and without the consent of the insurance company, the polic is void during the period of vacancy, but if afterwards the building i again occupied and a loss occurs, the insurance company would b liable. In a few states, however, a policy once voided remains s until the insurance company consents to its restoration.

If any provision of an insurance policy is violated, the policyholde should consult with his broker or agent as to the advisability o obtaining appropriate endorsements from the insurance company.

Legal status of brokers. A broker is considered the agent of th policyholder, and not of the insurance company. Consequently knowledge on the part of the broker does not constitute knowledg on the part of the insurance company until transmitted by the broke to the company. Likewise, should the broker neglect to turn over a premium to the insurance company, the policy may be void. In many states, however, including New York, the broker is considere the representative of the company for the purpose of premium col lections, and receipt of payment by the broker is considered receipt by the company.

Opinion of agent not binding on insurance company. Insured rsons often inquire of the agent as to the meaning of particular uses of the insurance policy. The courts have generally held that e opinion of the agent as to the legal effect of any provision of a licy is not binding on the insurance company, on the theory that mere opinion does not change old nor create new obligations. nsequently, the insured should consult his agent carefully when doubt as to the meaning of any provision, and thereafter have e insurance company add a clarifying clause to the contract, if cessary.

Oral waiver of policy provisions by agent is not binding. Notthstanding that the standard fire contract, and many other insurce covers, specifically state that "no one shall have power to waive y provision or condition of this policy except as by the terms of is policy may be the subject of agreement added hereto, nor shall y such provision or condition be held to be waived unless such aiver shall be in writing added hereto," many courts have held at an oral waiver by the agent of the insurance company is valid d binding on the company. The courts have been particularly one to uphold such oral waivers where the agent was more than st a soliciting or collecting agent. However, the United States ipreme Court has departed from the rulings formerly so generally cepted by the state courts, and repudiated the doctrine as fundaentally unsound. Many of the states have now repudiated the octrine, and refuse to recognize a waiver unless endorsed on the olicy in writing. Consequently, the insured should protect himlf by sending the policies involved to the agent of the insurance ompany for proper endorsement.

Warranties and representations by the insured. A warranty is a atement which, if subsequently proved false, will void the policy gardless of importance. On the other hand, a representation is a atement that need only be substantially correct, and to avoid the ayment of a claim, the insurance company must prove that the tatement was both false and material. A statement is ordinarily onsidered as material if, had the insurance company been aware f the facts involved, the company would not have issued the policy, r would not have issued it in the existing form or at the existing remium.

Most of the states have now enacted laws that declare warranti to be illegal in insurance policies and class all statements made the insured as representations.

Assignment of an insurance policy. Inasmuch as a policy insurance is a personal contract, the courts have upheld the insu ance companies in their demand that the consent of the compar must be obtained to the transfer by assignment, before a loss, of property insurance contract. Consequently, where the insured a signs his interest in a policy prior to a loss without the consent the insurer, the policy becomes null and void. However, this do not preclude the insured from assigning his right to the *procee* of a policy of insurance *after* a loss has been incurred, since the rig to such proceeds is considered as a chose in action.

Territorial limits on property insurance policies. Practically a insurance contracts written on property which is subject to loss ou side of the territorial limits of the United States and Canada contai a clause that the company is not liable, in the absence of a provisio to the contrary, for a loss occurring outside of the United States an Canada. For example, the usual automobile policy does not protec the insured without special endorsement while he is driving his ca in Mexico.

"Other insurance" on the same property. The standard fire insurance policy, and many other forms of property insurance, stat that unless otherwise provided by an agreement in writing added t the policy, the insurance company will not be liable while any othe insurance (that is, another policy protecting the same interest, in th same property, against the same hazard), whether or not valid, i carried on the same property and interest. This clause has been de clared reasonable and valid by the courts. It is not designed to pre vent the policyholder from obtaining sufficient insurance, or to pre vent him from obtaining insurance with another company, but only to lessen the moral hazard by making it more difficult to obtain insurance for a greater amount than the insured property is worth.

The insured may protect himself against the operation of the "other insurance" clause by either:

1. Obtaining the consent of the insurance company each time that he wishes to take out additional insurance.

2. Securing from the insurance company an endorsement to the ndard policy permitting additional insurance at will. Such en- rsements are issued without extra charge.

Each policy is an independent contract. Every policy of in- rance is regarded as a new and independent contract, the construc- on of which is not dependent upon the terms of any policy that eceded it, unless the policyholder and the insurance company have pressly agreed to the contrary. Where a contract is "renewed," owever, the general rule is that such renewal constitutes a continua- on of all terms and conditions of the original contract, unless herwise specifically provided.

Doctrine of entirety of contract. Frequently several items of roperty, such as several buildings, or the building and contents, or veral automobiles, are insured under one policy, and the premium aid in one sum. In such cases the courts of a majority of the states ave usually held that the contract is to be considered as one and separable, and therefore, if violated as to one item, the entire con- act will be void. Thus, where the building and contents were overed under one policy, and a provision of the policy in regard to ncumbrances was violated as to the building, the court held that he insured could recover for neither the building nor the contents, or the contract was a unit and, if violated as to one item, it was lso violated as to all others. Conversely, where two buildings were nsured under one policy, and the insurance on one became void ecause of violation of the vacancy permit, the court held that if he insurance company admitted liability as to one building, it was lso liable for loss on the other.

However, the courts generally consider the nature of the risk in pplying the doctrine of entirety of the contract. If the several items overed are widely separated and not related to one another so as o be destroyed by a single disaster, and a breach as to one part of the contract cannot affect the other parts, the courts of many of the states have usually considered the contract as divisible. Under this interpretation a breach of a condition affecting only one class of property will not void the policy as to the rest of the property.

Doctrine of insurable interest. Under American law, for a contract of insurance to be valid, the insured must have an "insurable interest" in the subject matter covered. Otherwise, the policy classed as a "wagering policy," and no action can be taken unde in any court of the United States, or in any court of the several stat However, it is usually not necessary for such interest to exist at t time that the policy is issued; if an insurable interest subsists a time during the life of the policy, and again at the time of t loss, it is sufficient. In life insurance, however, the general rule that an insurable interest need exist only at the time that the ins ance is taken out.

Briefly, a person has an insurable interest in the subject matt insured whenever he will directly suffer financial loss by dama thereto, or destruction thereof. Insurable interest in the matter life and health exists to any amount in the insured's own life, a in the lives of others where a relationship arises by reason of ti of marriage, blood, or affinity, and the policyholder expects son benefit from the continuance of the life of the insured. A credit has an insurable interest to the amount of the debt in the life a debtor.

Insurable interest may assume hundreds of forms and may exi under varying conditions. While such an interest must be neith illegal nor immoral, it may be either legal or equitable. Title to th property insured is not necessary. The interest may be either cond tional or contingent; insurable interest does not imply ownershi of property, or even a present or future right to its possession. Th only requisite is that some expectation of profit or benefit must aris from the interest insured and be present at the time of the los Thus an owner or part-owner, one who is in possession of property custodians of property entrusted to their care, creditors in the pro erty of the debtor, debtors in property seized for debt, consignee and consignors of goods, stockholders in corporate property, an tenants for life, have an insurable interest in such property to th extent of the monetary damages that they may sustain by reaso of its destruction.

The standard fire policy, and many other forms of insurance poli cies, specify that the interest of the insured must be that of "uncon ditional and sole ownership." Unless otherwise provided by agree ment in writing added to the contract, the insured should disclos the exact nature of his interest to his broker or agent at the time tha he applies for the insurance in order that such broker or agent ma

:ach the proper endorsements to the policy contract. Similarly, any change takes place in the nature of the policyholder's interest ıring the life of the policy, the broker or agent should be immeately notified.

Protection of beneficiaries of life insurance from claims of editors. Practically all of the states, either by statute or by court :cision, exempt the proceeds of life insurance payable to a specifilly named beneficiary, including the cash-surrender value of the ›licy, from the claims of creditors of the insured. In addition, ost of the states have now enacted a provision exempting all or ırt of the proceeds of life insurance held by an insurance company ınd in some instances by a trustee) from the claims of creditors : the beneficiary, where the insured has provided that such pro:eds are not to be available to creditors of the beneficiary.

For example, the law of Pennsylvania states as follows:

> Whenever under the terms of an annuity or policy of life insurance, r under any written agreement supplemental thereto . . . the proceeds :e retained by such company at maturity or otherwise, no person entled to any part of such proceeds, or any installment or interest due r to become due thereon, shall be permitted to commute, anticipate, ncumber, alienate, or assign the same, or any part thereof, if such perıission is expressly withheld by the terms of such policy or supplemental greement; and if such policy or supplemental agreement so provides, no ayments of interest or of principal shall be in any way subject to such erson's debts, contracts, or engagements, nor to any judicial processes o levy upon or attach the same for payment thereof. . . .

Under such laws as that quoted above, it is possible for the insured o protect his beneficiaries from levy by their creditors against the ›roceeds of or income from the insurance. In short, by proper pro·ision, the insured may insure his insurance. An attorney might e consulted as to the law of any particular jurisdiction, and as to he type of provision that will comply with the terms of the law.

3. TYPES OF INSURANCE POLICIES

Insurance division. Generally speaking, there are two types of nsurance:

1. Insurance that pays the person insured money because of some oss which the insured has suffered.

2. Insurance that prevents the person insured from suffering financial loss because of some circumstance or event, by stepping and paying such money for and in behalf of the insured to a thi party.

The first is usually known as property insurance, and the secor as liability, or third-party, insurance.

Some general forms that property insurance may take are di cussed below. For a detailed discussion of liability insurance an the specific forms that it may take, see page 702.

Adaptability of insurance. Insurance may be adapted to th needs of any particular individual, firm, or corporation by means o

1. Purchase of the basic policy in a *form* that is advantageous t the insured.
2. Endorsements attached to a basic policy.

Endorsements usually limit or extend the risk otherwise assume by the insurance company. The form of the policy detracts or add to the ease with which the insured may:

1. Secure coverage on additional property purchased after th original policy was issued.
2. Cancel insurance on property that the insured no longer owns
3. Adjust the amount of insurance to the value of the property
4. Transfer property from one location to another without affect ing the insurance coverage.

Specific policies. Property insured under a specific policy mus be:

1. Described in the policy in such a manner as to be identifiable from all other property.
2. Located at a definite, fixed location.
3. Insured for a specified sum.

A change cannot be made in any of these three fundamental requirements without the consent of the insurance company. Furthermore, if the policy covers more than one article, each article is insured for a specified sum. For example, under a specific fire insurance policy applying to the building, stock, and fixtures of a retail merchant, the building might be insured for $50,000, the stock or $20,000, and the fixtures for $5,000. The total insurance would therefore be $75,000. Yet, if the actual value of the stock was $30,000 at the time of a loss, and such stock was totally destroyed, if the fixtures were damaged to the extent of $3,000, and the building to $30,000 (total damage, $63,000), the insured could recover a total of only $53,000 ($30,000 on the building, $20,000 on the stock, and $3,000 on the fixtures). Furthermore, such recoverable loss might be further reduced as the result of the operation of a coinsurance clause (for explanation of coinsurance clause, see page 694).

Blanket policies. A blanket policy may cover:

1. The building and its contents, without any definite amount of insurance being assigned to either kind of property. Thus, if in the example given in the preceding paragraph the insured had placed $75,000 of insurance on "building and contents, blanket" and had suffered the same loss, he could have recovered in full, or $63,000.
2. Two or more buildings at definite locations (together with the contents of such buildings), without any definite proportion of the insurance being assigned to any particular location.

General cover contract, or reporting insurance. Essentially, a general cover contract (often called reporting insurance) is not a policy of insurance, but rather an agreement on the part of the insurance company to furnish insurance in such amounts as the insured may need on a month-to-month—sometimes week-to-week or day-to-day basis. The contract is usually an automatic reporting interim binder and provides a convenient method for obtaining adequate protection on fluctuating stocks of goods in stores and warehouses. Most often the contract is issued to cover risks involving more than one location. A limit is usually specified in the policy as to the maximum amount for which the insurance company will be liable at any one location.

The general cover contract is designed to prevent underinsurance or overinsurance by automatically increasing or decreasing the amount of insurance applying at any given location—within the limits specified in the policy—to correspond with fluctuations in the value of the property insured. The premium is computed at the end of each specified period by ascertaining the average amount at risk during the period and applying the standard rate to such amount. Short-rate cancellations, and a great deal of detail w that would otherwise be encountered if specific insurance were be increased or decreased, are thus entirely avoided.

Excess loss insurance. Ordinarily insurance is concurrent—th is, in case of other insurance on the same property, losses are p rated among the various carriers. Excess loss insurance, howev does not apply until all other insurance is exhausted and the lo exceeds a specified sum. If there is no primary insurance, excess lo insurance applies only after the loss exceeds the specified deductib sum. This form of insurance is designed to cover only unusu catastrophic losses, and the premium per $1,000 of insurance is ther fore much lower than that on the ordinary primary forms.

Coinsurance clauses. The insurance companies have added s called coinsurance clauses to most property-insurance contracts a fecting business risks. Such clauses are also sometimes referred as "average clauses," "reduced-rate average clauses," "percentag value clauses," "reduced-rate coinsurance clauses," "contributio clauses," and so forth. Regardless of the name applied to it, or th exact reading of the clause, coinsurance provisions have the sam general effect.

Coinsurance is a basic principle of fairness in business. Too ofte it is misunderstood. Without it no equitable distribution of risk and losses by the insurance companies could exist; schedule ratin would be impossible; and underwriting would be guesswork. If n coinsurance existed, buyers of insurance, knowing that most losse are partial losses, would always buy only a smaller amount of insu ance to take care of these and thus pay a smaller premium. Thi practice would result in the company paying all the small losses an taking the entire risk of any fire (or other event), small or large while receiving a premium only for the losses that happen mos frequently. The result would be either failure of the companie or tremendous increases in the cost of insurance.

Coinsurance is a mutual agreement between the insured and th insurance company that, in consideration for the company's actio in assuming the risk at the premium named, the insured will secur and maintain insurance in an amount at least equal to a specifie percentage of the property's total value. Assuming an 80 per cen coinsurance requirement, for instance, the coinsurance clause be nes an agreement between the company and the insured that the ured, on his $10,000 building, will secure and maintain at least 000 worth of insurance.

f this requirement is completed by the insured, there is no limita- n within the coinsurance clause as to the loss collectible.

f, however, the insured does not maintain enough insurance to ıal the percentage of total value named in the clause, the word- of the clause expresses a penalty on the insured for this failure. e penalty is this: the insured is considered to have assumed the k to the extent of the deficit and, in case of loss, shall bear that portion of the loss himself.

For example, assume that a building worth $100,000 is insured un- r a policy bearing an 80 per cent coinsurance clause. If the owner ries at least $80,000 of insurance (under one or more policies), has satisfied the coinsurance requirements and will be paid the l amount of any loss (up to a limit of the amount of insurance, course). Suppose, however, that he carries only $50,000 of in- rance. He has not lived up to the coinsurance requirement; he ust suffer the penalty and become an insurer in effect for his por- on of the deficit. The company's payment is determined as the oportion of the amount he is carrying ($50,000) to the amount he ould have carried to satisfy the coinsurance requirement ($80,000) five eighths of any loss. His deficit, then, is three eighths, and that the proportion of every loss which he must suffer himself. The llowing table shows the operation of the 80 per cent coinsurance ause where less than the required insurance is carried and loss occurs.

LIABILITY OF COMPANY UNDER 80 PER CENT COINSURANCE CLAUSE

alue of roperty	*Amount of Insurance Carried*	*Amount Required under Coinsurance*	*% of Any Loss Co. Will Pay*	*Loss*	*Amount Company Pays*
100,000	$40,000	$80,000	50%	$6,000	$3,000
100,000	40,000	80,000	50	40,000	20,000
100,000	80,000	80,000	100	2,000	2,000
100,000	80,000	80,000	100	90,000	80,000*
100,000	90,000	80,000	100	90,000	90,000
100,000	60,000	80,000	75	10,000	7,500
100,000	40,000	80,000	50	80,000	40,000
100,000	40,000	80,000	50	85,000	40,000*

* Cannot be more than the amount of insurance in any case.

Floater policies. This type of policy is designed to protect pr erty that is frequently moved about from one location to anotl The insurance applies no matter where the property described the policy may be (except as to places that may be specifically cluded). The wide variety of such property has brought fortl correspondingly wide selection of insurance coverages in floater for

For instance, in the commercial field, a firm may insure the sa ples carried by its force of salesmen against loss by burglary a theft wherever the samples may be—in the salesman's car while is at lunch, in a customer's showroom, in a hotel room, while bei shipped to the salesmen en route, and so forth.

Another example of this type of insurance is a floater policy th protects merchandise owned by a firm while it may be in the han of a processor (and while in transit to and from that place), th while it is sent to a dyer, then while it goes to a dresser, and final while on the way to the owner's premises. All the possibilities loss during the time it is being processed and worked upon a eliminated by means of the policy coverage.

4. FIRE INSURANCE

Protection afforded by the standard fire insurance policy. Tl insuring clause of the standard fire insurance policy of New Yo (which has been adopted without substantial change by nearly a the states) reads as follows:

> The Insurance Company, in consideration of the provisions and stip lations herein named or added hereto and of $——— Dollars premiur does insure Richard Roe and legal representatives, to the extent of tl actual cash value of the property at the time of loss, but not exceedir the amount which it would cost to repair or replace the property, . . against all direct loss by fire, lightning and by removal from premis endangered by the perils insured against, except as herein provided, . . to the described property while located or contained as described herei or pro rata for five days at each proper place to which any of the propert shall necessarily be removed for preservation from the perils insure against. . . .

Meaning of clauses in the standard fire insurance policy Practically every word of the standard fire insurance policy has, a one time or another, been before the courts for interpretation. As result, it has obtained a definite and exact meaning.

1. "*Direct loss by fire.*" The courts have given a very liberal inter-retation to the phrase "direct loss by fire." Practically any loss is overed where fire is the motivating or primary cause. The fire need ot be the cause closest in point of time but it must be possible to race an unbroken connection between the fire that is alleged to be he cause of the loss, and the event that caused the loss, without the ntervention of some new and independent cause. Thus, damage by vater, or by the falling wall of an adjoining building, where fire aused such wall to fall, are covered, even though the fire itself never ame in contact with the insured premises. Again, a midwestern umber concern owned a small locomotive that it used to haul timber rom the forest. A forest fire burned out a bridge and left the loco-notive stranded in the mountains. Although the fire did not injure he locomotive, the court held that inasmuch as the cost of construct-ng a new bridge would be greater than the value of the locomotive, he locomotive was a total loss, the value of which had been proxi-nately destroyed by fire.

To constitute "fire" within the meaning of the policy, there must be actual ignition and flame. Damage from mere heat and smoke without a flame is not covered. Furthermore, the fire must be a hostile fire; that is, not a friendly fire, which is defined as one that has not left the place intended for it, such as a stove or lamp. The company is liable for the smoke damage done by a hostile fire and damage caused by water or other means of extinguishing the fire.

Property "removed from premises endangered by fire" is covered "pro rata for five days" at any location to which the property is re-moved for preservation from fire. After the expiration of five days from the time that the property was removed from the premises described in the policy, however, it must be reinsured at its new location. Such coverage includes loss from mishandling during re-moval but not from theft (the latter being specifically excluded).

Direct loss from fire is further construed to mean only the dam-age to the property itself. Contingent and indirect losses are not covered. Thus a slight fire may cause a business to close down, with a resulting loss in profits many times the value of the property actu-ally destroyed. However, unless an endorsement to the contrary is entered on the policy, only the damage to the tangible property actually destroyed may be recovered. (For covering loss of profits, see "Contingent use and occupancy insurance," page 736.)

2. "*Actual cash value of the property destroyed.*" The fire-insu ance policy is a contract of indemnity; it is not intended that th assured should recover more than he has lost, but that he shall b placed, economically, in the same position as he occupied prior t the fire. To this end, the policy specifies that, regardless of the fac value of the policy, and irrespective of whether the loss is total c partial, the assured may recover only to "the extent of the actual cas value (ascertained with proper deductions for depreciation) of th property at the time of loss or damage," but in any event, "not ex ceeding the amount which it would cost to repair or replace th same with material of like kind or quality within a reasonable tim after such loss or damage, without allowance for any increased cos of repair by reason of any ordnance or law regulating construction." Furthermore, the company reserves the option to "repair, rebuild, o replace the property lost or damaged with other of like kind and quality." The assured, however, may not surrender his proprietary rights to property that has been partially destroyed, and claim a total loss, inasmuch as the policy provides that "there can be no abandonment to this company of the property described."

Since it would be impracticable for insurance companies to make accurate valuations of property at the time that a risk is assumed, and since values fluctuate from year to year, the above provisions of the policy represent a sound application of the true doctrine of insurance. Nevertheless, a number of states, particularly those in the west and south, have passed "valued-policy laws." Generally, such laws provide that in the absence of intentional fraud, the amount recoverable under the policy in case of a total loss is the face value of the policy.

The "actual cash value" of the property destroyed is a question of fact to be determined by appraisal and agreement with the insurance company. As a general rule, the actual cash value is not the cost of the property, nor the cost less depreciation, but the cost of replacement (without allowance for any increased cost by reason of any ordinance or law), less the depreciation. Thus, if a building erected in 1938 at a cost of $75,000 was completely destroyed in 1953, and if, at the time of the loss, the cost of replacing the building (the law regulating construction not having been changed) was $100,000, and the rate of depreciation was 2 per cent per year, the actual cash value of the property destroyed would be $100,000, less depreciation

: $30,000 (2 per cent of $100,000 equals $2,000 per year, times 5 years), or approximately $70,000.

In the case of manufactured goods, it has been stated that the :tual cash value is the "wholesale price, less unincurred expenses ıd unearned profits."

Fire insurance policy is a personal contract. The fire insurance ɔntract states that it "does insure .... and legal repre-:ntatives." It does not "insure the property." It follows, therefore, ıat the fire insurance policy is a personal contract, agreeing to ıdemnify the insured against loss through destruction of the de-:ribed property. The insurance does not follow the property in vent of a change in ownership unless the company gives its consent. uch a rule is necessary since, otherwise, a given property would emain insured even though it passed from an honest and careful wner to a dishonest and careless one, although it is apparent that uch a change would increase the risk tremendously. Consequently, he insurance company, in fairness to itself and other insureds, re-quires that its consent be obtained to any assignment of interest ınder the policy, or to any change of interest, title, or possession of he subject of the insurance. Violation of these requirements voids he policy. As a rule, the company's consent to any change is readily ;iven whenever requested.

Risks excluded in fire insurance policy. The insuring clause ɔf the fire insurance policy states that it protects against direct loss ɔy fire, "except as herein provided." The exceptions are set out in ınother section of the policy as follows:

1. The company is not liable for loss or damage caused directly ɔr indirectly by invasion, insurrection, riot, civil war or commotion, military or usurped power, theft, and neglect of the insured to use ıll reasonable means to save and preserve the property at and after ı fire or when the property is endangered by fire in neighboring premises.

All except the last of these exceptions—neglect of the insured—can be covered by other forms of insurance. See "Riot, and riot attending a strike," page 735.

2. Unless otherwise provided by agreement in writing added to

the policy, the insurance company is not liable for loss or damag occurring under the following circumstances:

(*a*) The insurance company is not liable while the hazard increased by any means within the control or knowledge of th assured. This clause forbids the assured to change the physic structure of the insured building, or to alter the uses for which was employed at the time that the policy was written, in any manne that would increase the hazard of fire, without securing a permi to do so from the insurance company and paying any extra premiur that may be required. An increase in hazard also occurs if an tenant, within the knowledge of the insured, commences to carry o any more hazardous activity after the policy is issued than he wa engaged in at the time of such issuance.

If the insured is in doubt as to whether any particular incident o activity constitutes an increase in hazard, he should consult with hi broker or agent.

(*b*) The insurance company is not liable while a describe building is vacant or unoccupied beyond a period of 60 days. Un occupied buildings are considered poor risks. However, in som instances, an endorsement may be obtained permitting the buildin to remain vacant. Such endorsements are readily issued for period of short duration.

(*c*) The insurance company is not liable for damage caused by explosion or lightning, unless fire ensue, and then for the loss or damage done by fire only. This provision, at times, presents difficul cases for adjustment, since where a fire follows an explosion, it is frequently impossible to ascertain the amount of damaged caused by the explosion, as separate from the loss caused by the fire.

(*d*) The insurance company is not liable for damage to de scribed property while such property is encumbered by a chattel mortgage. However, property not encumbered by a chattel mortgage is not affected. By special agreement with the insurance company, this restriction may be removed.

3. If a building, or any material part thereof, falls, except as the result of fire, all insurance on such building and its contents ceases at once. This provision is inserted on the theory that when the insured building has fallen in part or in whole, it is no longer the original building that burns, but simply the debris. The two most

ommon causes of falling buildings are windstorms and earthquakes. oth of these risks may be covered by separate insurance.

Kinds of property excluded in fire insurance policy. In addi-on to excluding losses due to the risks described in the preceding aragraphs, the standard fire-insurance policy excludes certain kinds f property from coverage.

1. Accounts, bills, currency, deeds, evidences of debt, money, otes, or securities are not covered. Such property is considered to e uninsurable, partly because it affords opportunity for fraud, being ubject to easy concealment, and partly because the determination of he value of such articles is difficult, the company being obliged, in nost cases, to depend upon the statement of the assured. See, how-ver, "Accounts receivable insurance," page 739.
2. Bullion and manuscripts are not covered unless an endorsement s added to the policy.

Endorsements to fire insurance policy. The standard fire in-urance policy was necessarily designed to meet a general situation. It applies to circumstances common to most property owners. How-ever, it often fails to meet the exact needs of the individual policy-holder.

Endorsements have been designed to meet practically any situa-tion imaginable, in order to adapt the standard policy to the specific needs of each policyholder. Such endorsements may:

1. Extend the insurance coverage by providing that risks otherwise excluded are to be assumed by the insurance company.
2. Limit or distribute the indemnity otherwise provided by the contract. Practically all policies covering mercantile or manufacturing risks, in order to establish equity among the various policyholders, are endorsed with 80 per cent—sometimes 90 per cent and 100 per cent—coinsurance clauses (for explanation of coinsurance clauses, see page 694). If the property is situated in different localities, a so-called "distribution" or "pro-rata" clause may be used to limit the amount of insurance applicable to any one location (see "Blanket policies," page 693).
3. Warrant that the insured, in consideration of a reduced premium, will take certain steps to reduce the hazard. Such an endorsement might provide for the proper maintenance of fire-protective

devices, or limit vacancy of a mercantile or manufacturing risk t only one third of the establishment.

4. Permit an increase in the hazard that is not contemplated b the standard policy.

5. LIABILITY INSURANCE

Purpose of liability insurance. The law imposes upon every one the duty of taking reasonable care and precaution to avoi damaging the property, or injuring the person, of others. When th negligence of one party is responsible for a loss suffered by another the injured party is entitled to recover damages from the negligen person, firm, or corporation. Since such damages may amount t many thousands of dollars for a single accident, business concern are greatly in need of some form of protection against such unfore seen financial losses. Such protection may be obtained througl liability insurance (sometimes called third-party insurance).

As a general rule (the exact definition differs from state to state) negligence is the failure to do something that a reasonable and prudent man would do under like conditions, or the commission of an act that a reasonable and prudent man would not do under like circumstances. The question of "what a reasonable and prudent man would do" is usually one for the jury.

The following case illustrates the application of the doctrine. A customer was standing at a counter in a large New York store about eight feet away from a large plate-glass window when the window crashed without warning. The customer was not struck by the flying glass, but, in the excitement, she was pushed down by the crowd and trampled on. The court held that the storekeeper was negligent in allowing a "condition to exist which caused the window to fall," and was therefore liable to the customer for damages, inasmuch as "the rush or stampede was a normal response to the fear or emotional disturbance which the defendant's [storekeeper's] negligent conduct was a substantial factor in creating."

Types of liability. Under the general title of liability insurance a variety of policies are written to protect the policyholder against direct or indirect losses arising out of claims or suits based upon the law of negligence. The most prominent forms of liability insurance are:

1. *Workmen's compensation insurance.* Workmen's compensa-ion insurance covers the employer's liability to his employees under vorkmen's compensation laws. All of the states have enacted such aws. (For detailed discussion see page 706.)

2. *Employer's liability insurance.* Employer's liability insurance s designed to protect the employer from liability under the common aw and statutes to employees not covered by workmen's compensa-ion laws. (For further discussion, see page 709.)

3. *Automobile public liability and automobile property damage iability insurance.* These policies are designed to protect the owner nd operator of an automobile against financial loss from claims for lamages arising out of the ownership, maintenance, or operation of uch automobile. (For further discussion, see page 709.)

4. *Manufacturer's public liability insurance.* This policy protects manufacturers against financial loss from claims for damages brought under the law of negligence, for injuries sustained by any person other than an employee as the result of the alleged negligence of either the manufacturer, his agent, or any of his employees in the conduct of the business.

5. *Contractor's public liability insurance.* This policy is similar to that issued to manufacturers, except that it applies to contractors.

6. *Owners', landlords', and tenants' public liability insurance.* All persons other than manufacturers and contractors may secure protection against damages resulting from legal liability under the law of negligence by purchasing this policy. The policy is similar to that issued to manufacturers.

7. *Elevator public liability insurance.* This policy protects the owner of a building from financial loss as the result of suits brought to obtain damages for injuries suffered in any elevator accident.

8. *Product public liability insurance.* This policy protects manufacturers from loss as the result of their legal liability for damages suffered by the public through the use of their product.

9. *Teams public liability insurance.* This policy protects the owner of teams from loss resulting from suit for damages caused by careless drivers, careless loading or unloading, or frightened and uncontrollable horses.

10. *Theater public liability insurance.* This is a specialized policy for theater owners protecting against financial loss that may arise as

the result of suits brought by the public for injury or alleged injur occurring in the theater.

11. *Garage public liability insurance.* Like the theater policy, thi is a specialized policy designed to meet the many needs of the publi garage operator and owner. (For further discussion, see page 716.

Standard provisions of liability insurance policies. The fol lowing provisions are common to all liability insurance contracts:

1. A promise on the part of the insurance company to pay al judgments assessed against the policyholder.
2. A promise by the insurance company to serve the policyholde by investigating all claims, negotiating for settlements, defending al suits within the scope of the policy and paying all expenses incurrec in connection with such suits, and to reimburse the policyholder fo the expense of necessary immediate surgical aid.
3. A promise by the policyholder to give immediate written notice to the company upon the occurrence of any accident covered by the policy, and to aid the company, when so requested, in securing information, evidence, attendance of witnesses, and to render to the company all the co-operation and assistance within his power.
4. A stipulation that the policyholder shall not voluntarily assume any liability and that the insurance company will not be liable for any settlements or expenditures voluntarily made by the policyholder.
5. A limit of liability that will be assumed by the insurance company of at least:

   (*a*) $5,000 for injuries (or death) to any one individual.

   (*b*) $10,000 for injuries (or death) as the result of any one accident, regardless of the number of persons so injured.

These limits may be increased, for an additional premium, to any figure desired. Thus, limits of $10,000 and $20,000, respectively, can be secured for a premium of 12 to 15 per cent more than the basic premium.

A few forms of property insurance that are primarily intended to cover only direct losses also contain a provision making the insurance applicable to indirect losses. For example, power plant insurance of all kinds includes a provision that protects the insured against loss as the result of suits brought against him after an accident, as well as reimbursement for loss to the power plant itself.

Contingent public liability insurance. Under certain conditions, a contractor may be liable for the negligence of his subcon-
ctor, an owner for the negligence of a contractor employed on his
emises, or a landlord for the negligence of his tenant. To protect
emselves against such risks, contractors may procure contractor's
otective public liability and property damage insurance; the owner
real estate may take out owner's protective liability insurance as a
otection against his contingent liability for the acts of a contractor
igaged on his premises, and landlord's protective liability to protect
gainst loss arising from contingent liability for damages for which a
nant is primarily liable.

Fiduciaries' liability insurance. The law is well settled that
xecutors, administrators, trustees, guardians, and other fiduciaries
e personally liable for negligence that results in a loss to the fidu-
ary's principle, or to the trust estate. In some cases fiduciaries have
ven been held liable for losses that occurred without fault on their
art. Until recently insurance was not available to protect the fidu-
iary against his personal liability for loss to the trust estate, but
asualty companies are now offering such protection.

**Comprehensive public liability and property damage insur-
nce.** In more recent years the insurance companies have developed
form of policy that seeks to provide a new approach to the problem
f insuring against financial loss through liabilities imposed by law.
The previous descriptions of the various liability policies available
xemplify the concept of this form of insurance as it has existed: one
olicy for each hazard or type of hazard, with that policy excluding
overage for all other forms of loss through legal liability.

The comprehensive liability policy, however, insures the policyholder against all liability losses that occur during the policy term,
whether or not such liabilities were existent or apparent at the time
the policy was issued. The premium is determined at the end of
each policy year by making a charge for the determinable avenues
of liability.

This form of all-inclusive insurance should be looked into seriously
by every business firm. It represents the most important advance in
available protection in many years and provides the first means of
protecting against unknown hazards that may appear at any time.

6. WORKMEN'S COMPENSATION INSURANCE

Why workmen's compensation insurance is necessary. Und the common law an employer is liable, subject to certain defense for injuries sustained by his employees through his negligence. B statute, however, every state has abridged or replaced the commo law rule with workmen's compensation laws. Generally these lav provide that every employee is entitled to recover from his employ certain prescribed amounts for injury sustained in the course of h employment. Since the amount of payments that an employer ma be required to make within any one year is subject to wide fluctu tions, most employers prefer to transfer to an insurance company th obligation to compensate injured employees. Such a transfer i effected by the purchase of workmen's compensation insurance.

Methods of meeting the liabilities imposed by workmen' compensation laws. The methods that the employer may use t meet the liabilities imposed by the various workmen's compensatio insurance laws depend upon the law of the state in which the em ployer conducts his business. In a majority of the states, however the employer has a free choice from among several methods; he ma choose one of the following:

1. Insurance in a State fund.
2. Insurance with a private insurance company.
3. Self-insurance.
4. Partial self-insurance.

1. *Insurance in a State fund.* A number of states provide a Stat fund. In some of these states the fund is monopolistic; that is, i operates to the exclusion of private insurance companies. In a few states, certain approved risks may be self-insured, but on conditio that they contribute to the maintenance of the State-fund system. In the other states, insurance in the State fund is voluntary.

Where insurance in a State fund is optional, the employer should carefully investigate the economy and efficiency of such insurance in comparison with insurance with a private insurance company or self-insurance. In several states the experience of some employers has been that insurance in the State fund has not provided prompt claim service, proper treatment of injured workmen, effective acci-ent-prevention service, or an equitable distribution of costs between ifferent industries and the employers included therein; in short, mployers insured in some of the State funds have felt that they did ot receive everything for which they paid. However, the economy nd efficiency of insurance in a State fund naturally varies from state) state. Accordingly, an employer who is contemplating insurance ı a State fund should make inquiry among other concerns within ıe state as to their experience.

2. *Insurance with a private insurance company.* In a majority of ıe states the employer may insure with a private insurance company. 'he standard workmen's compensation policy provides that the in- ırance company will:

(*a*) Pay promptly to any person entitled thereto the benefits rovided by the workmen's compensation law of the state.

(*b*) Indemnify the employer for loss arising from suits for dam- ges in instances where the employee alleges that the compensation ct is not applicable.

(*c*) Protect the worker against loss of benefits resulting from he bankruptcy of the employer.

(*d*) Pay for the benefit of the injured employee the proper cost f medical, surgical, nurse or hospital services, apparatus, appliances, nd medicines; and funeral expenses in the event of death resulting rom injury.

(*e*) Make necessary inspections of the places of work in order o reduce accidents.

(*f*) Investigate all reported claims.

(*g*) Defend, and pay the costs therefor, all suits brought against he employer-policyholder for damages as a result of injuries to em- ›loyees, even though such suits are fraudulent.

3. *Self-insurance of the workmen's compensation risk.* Self-insur- ınce, on proof of solvency, is permitted in most of the states. The equirements of the law vary. In some instances the employer need ›nly demonstrate that he is financially solvent, while in others he nust put up a bond or place a specified amount of cash with the tate as security to meet all losses.

In estimating the savings to be derived from adoption of a self- nsurance plan for workmen's compensation, the employer should ıot overlook:

(*a*) The cost of defending his own lawsuits.
(*b*) First aid, hospitalization, and other medical costs.
(*c*) The cost of investigating and adjusting claims.
(*d*) The cost involved in either maintaining, or failing to mai tain, an adequate accident-prevention program.
(*e*) The stigma that will attach to him personally should h later become bankrupt and be unable to pay just compensatio claims.

4. *Partial self-insurance of the workmen's compensation risk.* Pa tial self-insurance is permitted, of course, in all states that perm self-insurance. Under this system the employer assumes the liabilit for all losses under a specified amount (the limit may be either pe accident or per employee), and the excess risk is placed with a privat insurance company. This system has many advantages for the finan cially responsible employer; it enables him to carry his own norma loss risk without becoming subject to staggering losses that woul impair the financial stability of the business.

Safety devices and employee education. Experience has dem onstrated that a conscious effort to minimize the number and severit of accidents has worth-while results in the form of savings in pre miums. Accident prevention may take either or both of two forms

1. Installation of safety devices.
2. Education of the worker, including observation to discove dangerous practices or habits.

At present, the general consensus is that while safety devices are invaluable, a logical program of education will result in greate savings than are to be gained from the mere installation of safety devices.

As an outstanding example of what may be accomplished by means of efficient and scientific safety work, the record of the Western Clock Company of LaSalle, Illinois, has been cited. Not a single lost-time accident occurred during the three years and 14 days when the record was reported. When it is considered that during this period, 10,029,681 man-hours of labor were involved, and that haz- ardous devices, such as power presses, screw machines, and tool- making machines, were constantly used, the record is remarkable.

Another outstanding example is illustrated in a year's accident fety report of General Motors Corporation. For every million urs worked, there were but 3.43 lost-time accidents among the ore than 200,000 hourly rated workers during that year. In addion to this record, the Fisher Body Division plant at Janesville, 'isconsin, has gone three years without a lost-time accident, and ur other of their plants have gone two years without a lost-time cident.

Most private insurance companies maintain an experienced and ained staff to make inspections of risks. The insurance company serves the right to make inspections or investigations whenever it eems them desirable.

Employer's liability insurance. Although all states have workien's compensation laws, all employees are not covered by those ws. Employers may protect themselves from loss arising from their gal liability to injured employees not covered by workmen's comensation insurance by the purchase of employer's liability insurance. Jnder the common law rule, which still prevails except as modified y statute, employers are not responsible for injury to their employees nless negligence is shown, but the legal definition and interpretaion of negligence are extremely broad.

Employer's liability insurance also forms a part of every contract f workmen's compensation insurance. This provision protects the mployer in the event an employee is injured while in the course of mployment, but is not covered under the regular compensation ontract. Such liability may arise as the result of an accident that ccurs while an employee is engaged in interstate commerce, or as he result of an employee's election (in a few states in which he is ermitted to choose) to forego the benefits of the compensation tatute and to sue the employer under the common law.

7. AUTOMOBILE INSURANCE

Types of automobile coverage. The term "automobile insurance" may refer to protection against:

1. Losses resulting from legal liability for injury (or death) to another person. (No coverage for injury sustained by the insured himself, since this is covered by life and accident insurance.)

2. Losses resulting from legal liability for damage to the proper of another.

3. Losses resulting by reason of damage to the insured's c through collision or upset.

4. Losses caused by theft.

5. Direct damage to the insured's car caused by fire, lightnin tornado, cyclone, windstorm, hail, earthquake, explosion, and oth happenings.

6. Legal liability of an employer for losses for which an employe is primarily responsible.

7. Legal liability of garage keepers, service stations, and autom bile mechanics for negligence resulting in losses to customers.

The first five of the above risks may be covered under separat policies or under a single contract. Generally, the buyer may freel choose which risks he desires to insure.

Automobile public liability insurance. A business firm, as th owner of an automobile, or as the employer of a person operating a automobile, is legally liable to third parties who may be injured b reason of the operation or maintenance of such automobile. Th only limit to a loss of this nature is the aggregate value of all th assets of the business.

The standard automobile public liability policy will indemnify th insured for all loss sustained by reason of legal liability for bodil injury (or death) incurred by any person other than the insure accidentally resulting from the ownership, operation, or maintenanc of the described automobile within the United States and Canada The insurance company also agrees to defend the insured in al suits for damages within the scope of the policy, and to investigate all claims. The basic minimum limit of liability assumed in the standard policy, however, is $5,000 for injury or death to one person, and $10,000 for damages arising from one accident for injury o death to any number of persons. Inasmuch as jury awards are often substantially in excess of these figures, every business should secure an endorsement increasing substantially the limits of liability fo injury to a single person, and also for loss from one accident; the cost of such increased limits is only slightly higher than the charge made for the standard limits. For example, limits of $10,000 and $20,000, respectively, cost only 20 per cent more than the basic limits

$5,000 and $10,000, while the premium for limits of $25,000 and ;0,000 is only 36 per cent higher than basic limits, and the premium ›r $50,000 and $100,000 of limits costs 45 per cent more.

The coverage granted by the liability policy is very broad. In a ›urt case the Supreme Court of Pennsylvania made the following :marks in commenting on the protection afforded by a public lia- ility insurance policy:

'he policy of insurance was unquestionably intended to indemnify the ssured against liability resulting from an accident due to the use or oper- tion of the car. It does not matter under what circumstances the lia- ility might arise. The assured may even be protected against the acts f the driver or his own that may involve a criminal statute; generally ccidents are due to the violation of some law legislatively declared as f criminal aspect, as, for illustration, fast or reckless driving, but insur- nce policies have always been treated as effective and valid under those ircumstances.

Automobile property damage liability insurance. Similarly to iability for bodily injuries to third parties caused by automobile ccidents, a business firm may also be financially responsible for dam- ge to the property of third parties arising from the operation of a notor vehicle.

The protection and services offered under this policy are identical with that of the public liability contract, described above, except that the limit of liability assumed by the insurance company under the standard policy is $5,000 per accident.

Automobile collision insurance. A business firm may incur a substantial loss as the result of accidental collision damage to its own motor vehicles. The collision contract protects against direct loss caused by contact of the insured car with another object.

The cost of full coverage collision insurance has always been high. Consequently, so-called deductible forms are widely used. Under such forms the insured agrees to assume liability for an agreed amount, such as the first $25, $50, $100, of any loss. For example, if a $100 deductible clause was inserted in a policy, and the insured car was damaged to the extent of $500, only $400 would be paid by the insurance company.

The following rates for a new Chrysler sedan in a certain terri- tory bring out the difference in cost for the different coverages:

Full Coverage	$170
$25 deductible	68
$50 deductible	46
$100 deductible	29
$250 deductible	18

By the use of a deductible provision, a business may economical protect itself against the more serious losses; the minor losses, whic to a great extent may be anticipated, can be assumed by the busine by means of an accounting reserve.

The collision policy should be examined to ascertain whether not "upset" is specifically covered. At the present time most of th companies agree to indemnify for loss caused "solely by accident collision with another object or by upset." Whether or not "upset is covered in the absence of a policy provision depends upon th interpretation given to the word "collision" by the courts of th particular state.

Automobile theft insurance. Full-coverage theft insurance pro tects the insured against loss or damage arising from the theft, rob bery, or pilferage of the described automobile. Under the standar policy, theft by an employee, however, is excluded. In addition theft of accessories and tools is not covered unless the entire car i stolen.

Automobile, fire, lightning, and transportation insurance. Th standard automobile fire policy protects against direct loss cause by damage to, or destruction of, the body, machinery, or equipmen of the automobile, arising from fire or lightning, or, while the insure motor vehicle is being conveyed by another vehicle or vessel, agains the perils of transportation. In general, however, the usual exclu sions incident to ordinary fire policies, such as loss attributable to us of the insured car, and loss attributable to personal effects left in th car, are not covered.

Comprehensive damage coverage. The theft and fire insuranc coverage for automobiles may be combined in one policy form tha provides an even broader coverage than the specified perils of theft fire, lightning, and transportation. Called "comprehensive," this coverage protects against loss or damage to the automobile insured from any source. Collision coverage is either included or excluded m the policy, at the choice of the buyer. This policy form has come extremely popular in those states in which it is in existence.

Nonownership automobile liability insurance (contingent liability insurance). The law of agency renders the principal responsible for the acts of his agent. Consequently, in those instances where salesmen, or other employees engaged in the business of the employer, drive their own cars, the employer may be liable to third parties for damages inflicted as a result of the operation of such cars. While the rules established by the courts of the different states vary somewhat in their application to particular circumstances, in general, the employer is liable for the acts of his employee (provided such employee is not an "independent contractor"), if an accident occurs within the scope of, and in the course of, his employment. Whether the employer had knowledge of the use of an automobile by an employee, whether the employee had been forbidden to drive an automobile in the course of his employment, and whether the employee was paid by salary or commission, have been held, by various courts, to be unimportant.

Where the employee-owner carries ample public liability insurance containing the so-called "omnibus clause" (see below), the employer may be protected jointly with the employee. However, even where such insurance is carried by employees, the employer cannot always obtain adequate information as to its validity and sufficiency. A need, therefore, exists for a form of insurance that will protect the nonowner-employer regardless of the circumstances surrounding the use of the automobile by the employee. Such protection is offered by nonownership automobile liability insurance, sometimes called contingent liability insurance. A common form of this policy automatically covers all employees, regardless of their usual duties. Another form covers only employees who are named in the policy.

As indicated above, an employer is not liable for the acts of his employee if such employee is an "independent contractor." Advice of counsel should be obtained, however, as to whether or not a particular set of facts constitute an employee an "independent contractor."

If, after consultation with an attorney, the employer is advised that a court "would" or "might possibly" hold him liable for the acts of his employee-drivers, nonownership liability insurance should be immediately taken out. On the other hand, if in the attorne opinion such "employee-drivers" are "independent contractors," t employer is fairly safe without nonownership liability insurance. I should remember, however, that although it is unlikely that he w be held liable for the acts of his employees, where such employe are independent contractors, he may, nevertheless, be sued for su damages, and will be liable for court costs. Many employers fi that the defense services of the insurance company fully warra the cost of the insurance.

Omnibus clause in automobile insurance. The standard au mobile policy contains a provision, known as the "omnibus claus which in effect makes the insurance follow the car, with certain e ceptions.

Under this clause, the terms of the policy are extended to cover:

1. The legal liability of any other person using the insured aut mobile, or riding in such automobile, with the permission of t named insured. "Permission" for a given purpose, however, do not imply permission for all purposes; the permission must ha been granted or implied for the use of the car in the manner which it was employed at the time of the accident.
2. Any firm or corporation legally responsible for the operatio of such automobile. This provision extends the protection of t policy to an employer, where an employee operates such automobi with the permission of the named insured.

Under no circumstances, however, is the protection granted by th policy available to "a public automobile garage, automobile repa shop, automobile sales agency, automobile service station and th agents or employees thereof." The Supreme Court of Pennsylvani has held that this exception extends to a mechanic or person engage in the business of repairing automobiles, even if the repair work i done at the home of such mechanic.

Automobile fleet insurance. Business firms owning five or mor automobiles of any type may insure them under a single policy o the "fleet plan," which gives them a more flexible form of insuranc than individual specific policies.

The advantages of the fleet plan are:

1. Premiums are based on the actual time each car was in use. eports are made to the company of suspension, disposal, and acquition of automobiles, and a proper premium is retained by the ompany.

2. Automatic coverage for newly acquired car is provided.

3. Fleet discounts in the premium are available. Depending on ie number of cars, the discount ranges from 5 per cent upwards.

Experience rating of large automobile fleets. If the insured esires, he may submit his fleet for special rating, provided at least en automobiles have been insured on a full-time basis for a miniium period of twenty-one consecutive months, or at least five autoiobiles involving an annual basic premium of $1,000 or more have een insured for twenty-one months immediately preceding the appliation for special rating.

Where the previous experience of the company with the policyolder has been satisfactory, a reduction in premium from that pecified in the manual rates may be obtained from the insurance ompany by application for special rating. On the other hand, if he policyholder has had a large number of accidents, and if the xperience of the company with the policyholder has been generally dverse, a special rating may result in rates higher than would othervise be payable.

The policyholder should consult his broker or agent as to the adantages and disadvantages of applying for experience rating.

Which automobile covering is most important? A survey conducted in New Jersey by Yale University and the United States Department of Commerce disclosed that unsatisfied judgments arising out of automobile accidents were either a major or a contributing cause of bankruptcy in at least 4 per cent of all cases. The judgments ranged from $60 to $25,000, and averaged $5,230. In 10 per cent of the cases, practically the only liability of the business was the judgment; in 50 per cent of the cases, the judgment amounted to 75 per cent or more of all liabilities. In addition, a number of other cases were discovered in which payment of an automobile judgment had precipitated the firm into bankruptcy.

When this bankruptcy record is considered in conjunction with the fact that over twice as many persons are killed by the automobile each year as meet death through industrial accidents, the outstanding need for automobile liability insurance is self-evident. If wor men's compensation insurance is a necessity, certainly insuran against a far greater hazard should be considered as indispensabl It therefore follows that the liability lines (that is, automobile publ liability, non-ownership liability, and property damage liability) a the most important automobile coverages from the standpoint of an business.

Self-insurance of automobiles. Under no circumstances shoul self-insurance of the so-called liability lines (see above) be attempte The outstanding reason for insuring such risks with a reliable com pany arises, of course, from the fact that no limit exists to the po sible loss that may be incurred. Furthermore, insurance compani are usually better prepared to defend fraudulent suits than are sma individual business concerns.

On the other hand, the collision and theft hazards offer almos an ideal situation for the application of the principles of self-insu ance where a large number of units are involved. The value c each unit is almost identical; the chance of loss of all units at th same time is practically nil; the amount of any individual loss i limited to the value of the automobile or truck, representing a smal part of the business assets.

Self-insurance of the fire hazard is not quite so satisfactory, inas much as one of the greatest risks is the conflagration hazard—th chance that all machines stored in a single or adjoining buildin will be destroyed by a single catastrophe.

Garage-keeper's insurance. The ordinary automobile insurance contracts are not suitable, by reason of their exclusions, for auto mobile dealers, automobile manufacturers, service stations, an garage-keepers. Consequently, a number of special policies hav been designed to cover the hazards encountered by such concerns

Garage liability insurance may be obtained under any one of the following plans:

1. Payroll basis, under which the premium is based on the total garage payroll. This form is the most liberal, covering both inside and outside hazards, and extending to all automobiles owned or operated at any time by the garage-keeper or any of his employees. Experience rating is available to large risks under this plan.

2. Named-driver basis, covering only accidents occurring while ιy automobile is being driven by the driver named in the policy.
3. Specified-car basis, covering each automobile described in the ›licy. The coverage afforded by this policy is very limited.

Garage collision insurance may be purchased either under a blan-t contract or on the specified car plan.

Various methods have been devised to insure the fire and theft ızards, including specified-car basis, blanket policies, and reporting ›licies. The most advantageous form depends upon the circum-ances of each individual case, such as the number of cars owned ıd the volume of business transacted.

In considering the desirability of taking out insurance, garage-:epers should remember that the rule relative to proof of negligence reversed in most jurisdictions, and that where a customer of a ıblic garage charges negligence, the burden of proof is upon the ırage-keeper to show that he was not negligent. Thus, the Su-·eme Court of Minnesota, in a case involving an automobile that ıd been stolen from a public garage where it had been stored for ıy, said:

> Where a loss occurs under such circumstances as are here disclosed the ırden is upon the bailee [garage-keeper] to show that he was free from ıe negligence; that is, that he exercised such care to keep the property ıfely as a prudent man would ordinarily exercise under such or similar rcumstances.

Nor will a sign placed upon the floor disclaiming liability for re or other losses (or such a provision placed in a storage or other ›ntract) relieve the garage-keeper of liability where he or his em-loyees were negligent. For example, in a suit against a warehouse-ıan for recovery of the value of goods destroyed by fire, the court .eld that failure to supply sufficient hose to reach to all parts of the ›uilding constituted negligence which was the proximate cause of he destruction of goods by fire, and that the warehouseman was iable for damages, regardless of the fact that the contract under vhich the goods were received "expressly provided against liability or loss from such cause." Signs and clauses of such a nature are 'effective to exempt from liability only in the event the loss by fire vas not caused or contributed to by the negligence of the storer."

Comprehensive liability and property damage insuranc Along with the comprehensive form of public liability and proper damage insurance, a comprehensive liability policy for automob hazards has been introduced. This policy protects the insur against any and every liability loss that may occur in connectic with automobiles during the policy period. It makes available single policy by which a business firm can protect itself not on against accidents involving cars that the firm or its employees m own or hire with or without notice to the firm but also against a unknown or unthought-of possibilities of loss that may, and do, cr up unexpectedly. Every business firm should carefully discuss th all-inclusive form with its broker or agent.

8. BURGLARY, THEFT, AND ROBBERY INSURANC

Standard definitions of burglary, theft, and robbery. Und the general designation of burglary, theft, and robbery insurance, variety of policies are issued.

The insurance companies have adopted, and the courts have u held, standard definitions for the offenses against which protectio is offered. The insured should carefully read all such definition inasmuch as they differ from both the commonly accepted meanin of the terms and sometimes from the statutory definitions. How ever, most policies define the crimes of burglary, theft, and robber as follows:

Standard definition of "burglary." Burglary losses are indemnif able when "occasioned by any person making felonious entry int the premises by actual force or violence of which there shall b visible marks made upon the premises at the place of such entry b tools, explosives, electricity, or chemicals." Burglary, therefore, a far as insurance is concerned, does not include loss attributed t sneak thieves or persons who have access to the property.

Standard definition of "theft." Theft and larceny are both use to denote the stealing of property of another where visible mark of illegal entry are not made upon the premises, and the insured i unaware of the theft at the time of the loss; for instance, losse caused by tradesmen, servants, and mechanics working on th premises.

Standard definition of "robbery." Robbery is generally defined as eaning "a felonious and forcible taking of property: (a) by violence flicted upon the person or persons in the actual care and custody the property at the time; (b) by putting such person or persons fear of violence; (c) by any other overt felonious act committed the presence of such person or persons, and of which they were tually cognizant at the time; or (d) from the person or direct care a custodian who, while conveying property insured under the licy, has been killed or rendered unconscious by injuries inflicted aliciously or sustained accidentally."

Types of burglary, theft, and robbery insurance. The principal urglary, theft, and robbery policies commonly used by business oncerns are:

1. Mercantile open-stock burglary insurance.
2. Interior robbery insurance.
3. Outside messenger robbery insurance.
4. Payroll insurance.
5. Mercantile safe burglary insurance.
6. Money and securities insurance.
7. Merchants' protective bonds.
8. Safe deposit box (securities) insurance.

Mercantile open-stock burglary insurance. Huge losses are suffered each year by retailers, wholesalers, jobbers, and manufacturers s the result of burglary of merchandise from storerooms, show indows, lofts, and warehouses. In addition, the ruthless procedure f the thieves, forcible entry to the premises and display cases, and heir haste to "get away" is responsible for the infliction of much amage to goods which are not removed, to the premises, and to he fixtures. To meet these risks, the mercantile open-stock burglary olicy is available.

The policy promises to indemnify the insured for direct loss or amage to furniture, equipment, merchandise, and goods usual to he business, caused by "felonious entry into such premises by actual orce and violence when the premises are not open for business." The protection does not apply, however:

1. If the insured, any associate in interest, servant, or employee s implicated in the burglary.

2. Unless books of account are kept in such manner that the exa amount of loss can be accurately determined.
3. If the loss is caused, or contributed to, by fire.

Certain other less important conditions must also be complied wi before the company is liable. Unless an extra premium is paid, t company is not liable for loss in "an amount in excess of $50.00 account of any one article of jewelry," nor for the burglary of fu from within any show window after the glass therein has be broken from the outside.

Interior robbery. Business organizations that have proper (either money or merchandise) of value within their premises th is exposed during the hours the business is open are in need protection against holdup occurring within the business premises.

The interior robbery policy covers loss of money, securities, ar loss of or damage to merchandise, and damage to the furnitur fixtures, and other such property in the premises. It insures again such loss occasioned by robbery, or an attempt at robbery, con mitted at any time during the day or night. The insured is al protected in case any custodian, after the business has been close is compelled under threat: (1) to return to the premises and adm the thieves, or (2) forcibly detained and made to furnish othe with information or the means of entering the premises.

The stealing of the insured property from within a show windo in the premises while open for business, through the glass havin been broken from the outside, is also covered.

Outside messenger robbery insurance. Banks, hotels, inves ment houses, theaters, jewelry stores, furriers, and other busine concerns that frequently send valuable property other than payrol outside of the premises need suitable insurance coverage. To mee this need, the outside messenger policy has been designed. As th name implies, it is applicable only to the property of the insure that is in transit outside of the insured's premises. Robbery oc curring on the premises is not covered; in this particular the polic is narrower than the payroll policy, which applies at all times whil the payroll is in the hands of the paymaster.

The contract agrees to indemnify the policyholder for all loss c damage by robbery committed at any hour to any property carrie a custodian, including payrolls, provided such robbery occurs side of the insured's premises.

)iscounts from the regular premium are allowed:

. If the custodian travels in a private car, and an additional al-'ance is made if such car is armored.

. If the funds are carried in an approved safe, chest, satchel, wallet.

3. If the custodian is accompanied by a guard at all times.

Payroll insurance. The hazard of loss of payroll by robbery may transferred to an insurance company by means of payroll insur-ce. This type of insurance makes good the insured's loss of payroll oney or checks (and the receptacle in which the money is carried), the loss is occasioned by robbery, or an attempted robbery, from a stodian of the payroll while engaged in any of his regular duties in nnection with such payroll outside or inside the premises. Notice at this policy covers the payroll money whether it is away from or side of the business premises, whereas the robbery insurance dis-ssed in the two previous headings above is limited to coverage her outside or inside the premises.

The policy may also have its coverage extended to include loss of e payroll money from *any* source. This valuable extension costs ry little additional. It arranges protection in case of the disap-earance or destruction or pure loss of the money. Money blowing it of a window, for instance, would be covered under this extension. The stealing of such money or checks by compelling the custodian, hile outside the premises, to admit someone to the premises or rnish him with the means of entrance is also included in the policy overage.

Mercantile safe burglary insurance. By purchasing mercantile afe burglary insurance, merchants, manufacturers, lawyers, doctors, nd private individuals may protect themselves against loss occa-ioned by the felonious abstraction of money, jewelry, securities, or nerchandise from any vault or safe (or part thereof) described in he policy, after entry into such safe or vault has been effected by orce or violence.

The company is not liable:

1. Unless books are accurately kept by the insured so that amount of any loss can be readily determined.

2. If the insured or any employee was implicated in the burgla

3. For the loss of negotiable securities unless the insured attem to prevent their negotiation, payment, or retirement.

4. For loss effected by the opening of any safe or vault by use of any key, or by the manipulation of any lock.

In addition to loss by burglary, this policy form covers the dama caused to the safe or vault itself, equipment, merchandise, and tures in the premises but not in the safe or vault, and damage to t building if the insured is the owner or is liable for it. Of course, t protection applies only when a burglary, or attempted burglary, committed on the safe insured.

Discounts are allowed from the regular premium for:

1. Prepayment of a three-year premium.
2. Employment of watchmen.
3. Excluding money from coverage.
4. Use of underwriter's approved safes, locks, and alarm equ ment.
5. Approved tear-gas systems.
6. Division of insurance, where the same policy covers more tha one safe.

Money and securities insurance. An all-inclusive form of poli insuring against a whole group of losses that may be caused by no employees is called "money and securities" policy. Two divisio of coverage are included. As to money and securities, the insuran is for loss caused by destruction, disappearance, or wrongful abstra tion. As to property other than cash and securities, the insuran is for loss by safe burglary and robbery inside or outside the place business.

Thus, this type of coverage gives comprehensive protection to cas checks, securities, stamps, and those articles of value generally e cluded from the coverage of specific direct damage policies. Remen ber that the fire insurance policy excludes securities and mone This type of policy gives protection against sneak thieves who leav no evidence of their crime.

Destruction is considered in this form to include any kind of occu ıce: explosion, windstorm, fire, and so on that results in the physi- loss of the insured money or securities. Disappearance refers to y loss concerning which there is no physical evidence of burglary, bbery, or theft.

Combining the coverages of inside and outside robbery, safe rglary, and comprehensive loss, this form is attractive to a large mber of business firms.

Merchants' protective bonds. Merchants' protective bonds are combination of burglary insurance, robbery insurance, and fidelity nds, designed to protect for limited amounts the smaller merchant ainst loss arising from most of the miscellaneous hazards to which is subject. A typical "bond" may protect against:

1. Larceny or embezzlement of property or money by any em- oyee.
2. Loss of money or personal property through holdup during siness hours.
3. Loss of money or personal property through robbery while such oney is being transported within a given radius by either the owner any employee.
4. Loss resulting from burglary of safe contents.
5. Loss through damage to doors, windows, locks, and premises used by forcible and felonious entry.
6. Loss or damage to stock or fixtures occasioned by the use of plosives to force entry to a safe.
7. Loss resulting from forgery or alteration of checks.
8. Loss by reason of acceptance of counterfeit money.
9. Loss or damage to cash register, caused by forcible entry.

addition, the contract agrees to pay a reward of $100 to any person ving information leading to the arrest and conviction of a person mmitting burglary, robbery, or murder upon the premises.

Another such grouped policy is known as the "storekeeper's rglary-and-robbery policy" and insures, up to $250 on each item, ainst:

1. Inside robbery.
2. Outside robbery.
3. Kidnapping custodian and forcing opening of the premises.
4. Safe burglary.

5. Burglary from the home of the custodian of funds held ov night, or from the night depository of a bank.

6. Mercantile open-stock burglary.

7. Damage to property merchandise, and so forth, in connecti with any of above.

Securities insurance. An individual business concern that cu tomarily keeps a large amount of valuable securities in a safe-depo box may desire insurance for two reasons:

1. Usually a bank will not reimburse its customers for losses u less it possesses adequate insurance or is legally liable. As a gener rule, a bank is not liable for losses resulting from burglary or the of safe-deposit boxes unless the customer can prove that the ba was negligent. The circumstances that constitute negligence va from state to state, but ordinarily it must be shown that a less degree of care was used by the bank in protecting the property its boxholders than in protecting its own property, or that the oth banks located in the same city commonly exercised greater care tha was exercised by the burglarized bank. Consequently, it is imposs ble for a boxholder to determine in advance whether or not th bank will be legally liable for any loss.

2. Even if the bank has purchased a blanket safe-deposit bo burglary and robbery policy, the individual boxholder cannot b certain of the security that it grants to him, since losses sustaine by the bank itself through burglary or robbery of its own securitie are reimbursed first; recovery for loss arising from any one box limited to 10 per cent of the face of the banker's blanket policy; and as a rule, the amount of valid insurance carried by the bank cann be ascertained.

The bank policy protects only against loss resulting from:

1. Burglary of the contents of the safe-deposit box (burglary i defined as a forcible entry by the use of tools, and so forth).

2. Robbery of the property of the insured from within:

(*a*) The vault containing such safe-deposit box.

(*b*) That part of the bank's premises reserved for the use o customers in its safe-deposit-box department.

(*c*) The banking enclosure reserved for the use of employee the bank, while at least two such persons are regularly at work erein.

(*d*) The bank's premises while the insured or any person au- orized by him is conveying the property between the said vault and e entrance to the bank's premises at any time while two or more the bank's officers or office employees are regularly at work on the emises.

The individual policy, however, protects against *all loss* of securi- s except infidelity and the voluntary giving over of possession or le by the insured (whether through fraud or otherwise).

Securities in safe-deposit vaults are subject to the hazards of bur- ary, robbery, mysterious disappearance, explosion, fire, entry by isrepresentation, and so forth.

9. FIDELITY AND SURETY BONDS

Use of bonds. A bond is a written promise to pay a sum of oney under one or more specified conditions. In this sense it is ke a contract of insurance or indemnity. But, more formally, a ond is a guaranty to the party named in it as the "obligee" (who orresponds to the "insured" named in an insurance policy) that e person or persons named in the bond as the "principal" will erform a certain duty or task, and that, if the principal fails in is, the insurance company, the "surety," will make good the money other damages suffered by the obligee because of this failure of erformance.

The bond is given to facilitate business; its purpose is to guaran- e the responsibility of the principal. The premium charged for e bond, unlike an insurance premium, is not entirely a charge for e risk assumed by the company, but is for the service performed y the company in issuing its bond. In most cases, for instance, e company will not issue its bond until it is completely satisfied s to the responsibility of the principal through investigation and ften through the deposit with it of collateral equal to the financial isk assumed by the company.

In practice, if the principal fails to perform as expected, the surety ompany immediately pays to the obligee the sum involved, and hen proceeds against the principal for reimbursement.

A bond usually provides in substance that:

John Doe . . . ., as Principal, and the Guaranty Comp . . . ., as Surety, are held and firmly bound unto . . . . Rich Roe . . . . as Obligee in the penal sum of . . . . ten thous dollars ($10,000) the condition of the bond being that John Doe, Principal, shall faithfully perform an obligation herein described, that if he does perform such obligation, this bond shall be conside void and fully discharged; otherwise it shall remain in full force effect.

Fidelity bonds. Fidelity bonds cover employees in positions trust, and in substance guarantee the employer against loss shou the person bonded prove to be dishonest. Some bonds also co negligence and incompetency, but such forms are rare.

Four forms of fidelity bonds are in common use:

1. Individual bonds, covering only a specified person in a specifi position.

2. Individual bonds, covering a specified position in the firm, gardless of who may occupy this position.

3. Schedule bonds, covering all employees or positions named an attached schedule. New employees or positions must be added endorsement. Some forms, however, automatically cover new em ployees or positions for a period of ninety days. Discovery form give back protection from date of issue.

4. Blanket bonds, covering all employees at all times, includin employees hired after the bond is issued.

5. Blanket bonds or comprehensive policies giving blanket fideli covering in combination with other coverages such as robbery, bu glary, forgery, etc.

Surety bonds. Surety bonds differ from fidelity bonds in that u der the fidelity bond the surety company guarantees that the princip will *not* do a dishonest or other specified act, while the surety bon guarantees that the principal *will* faithfully perform certain duties o obligations. Surety bonds are issued to cover only persons of exce lent reputation. As a rule, they may not be cancelled, and conse quently are written only after thorough investigation.

As a condition of the issuance of a surety bond, if the surety com pany has any doubt as to the ability of the principal to perform hi obligations, the principal is usually required to place with the surety company securities or other collateral from which the surety company may reimburse itself for any loss that it may suffer under the contract

Contract bonds. Municipalities, states, and private concerns en require as a condition for letting a contract that the contractor bonded for the faithful performance and completion of his con- ct. Bonds guaranteeing such performance are known as contract nds. Surety companies usually issue such bonds with little delay reliable and experienced contractors.

Court or judiciary bonds. Litigants at law are required many nes to file a bond or other security guaranteeing that they will pay the other party, if unsuccessful in the litigation, the monetary mages awarded by the court. Such bonds are known as court or liciary bonds. They are essentially a guaranty of financial strength, d hence surety companies often require that ample security be posited as a condition for the issuance of the bond. Another class court bonds are known as probate bonds. Such bonds are issued executors, administrators, and other fiduciaries to guarantee the ithful performance of their legal duties.

Miscellaneous indemnity bonds. Bonds are used to give "obli- es" all sorts of guaranties involving proper performance of certain oligations and protection against financial loss by the obligee. ome typical bonds may be:

1. Bonds covering the issuance of a duplicate certificate of stock, other security, where the original has been lost.
2. Bonds required by railroads guaranteeing the payment of freight iarges.
3. Bonds to indemnify railroads against loss for delivery of freight ithout first requiring the surrender of the bill of lading.

10. CREDIT INSURANCE

Need for credit insurance. Accounts receivable represent a prime sset of any firm. This asset can depreciate in value without warning nd should be protected to the same extent as the investment in aventory, work-in-process, finished merchandise, and other assets iat become accounts receivable. Credit insurance offers such pro- ection.

Credit insurance is a guarantee to manufacturers, wholesalers, ad- ertising agencies, and certain service organizations that they will be paid for merchandise shipped or for services rendered. It is pro tion against the inability of the debtor to pay his obligations.

Basic forms of credit insurance policies. Two basic forms credit insurance policies are available:

1. *Policies of indemnity.* Under this type of coverage the pol holder is indemnified against losses occurring within the term of policy.

2. *Policies of insurance.* These policies provide protection sales, shipments, and deliveries of merchandise made within the te of the policy. The coverage continues after the sales period has pired and follows the account to a conclusion. If the account is paid by the customer, it is filed with the insurance company as a lc Therefore, while the sales period is usually twelve months, the pol terms may run as long as eighteen months to follow the accounts a definite conclusion.

Losses covered. A credit insurance policy promises indemn against "loss due to insolvency." Insolvency under the policy has much broader meaning than insolvency under the Federal and st laws relating to insolvent debtors. It, in fact, is so broad that t policyholder has a definite control for proving all covered accounts losses, thus guaranteeing a definite value to the entire asset of counts receivable.

Insolvency is defined in two ways:

1. Any account filed with the insurance company for collecti within the time specified in the policy is automatically proved as loss, whether or not insolvency has occurred.

2. Insolvency is deemed to have occurred when:

(*a*) A debtor absconds.

(*b*) A sole debtor dies.

(*c*) A sole debtor is adjudged insane.

(*d*) A receiver is appointed for a debtor.

(*e*) A debtor transfers or sells his stock in trade in bulk.

(*f*) A writ of attachment or execution is levied on a debto stock in trade and said stock sold thereunder, or the writ return unsatisfied.

(*g*) A debtor makes a general offer of compromise to his cre itors for less than his indebtedness.

(*h*) There is a recording of or taking possession under a chattel ·rtgage given by the debtor on his stock in trade.

(*i*) A debtor's business is assigned to or taken over by a com-ttee, appointed by a majority in number as well as of his creditors, amount of the debts owing to them.

(*j*) There is a recording of or taking possession under an assign-ent or a deed of trust made by a debtor for the benefit of his editors.

(*k*) A voluntary or involuntary proceeding is instituted to ad-dge a debtor bankrupt.

(*l*) A proceeding for the relief of a debtor is instituted in a urt of bankruptcy.

Deductions in blanket policy. Under all blankets policies there e two deductions:

1. *Coinsurance deduction.* Blanket policies can be written to ver each account for 80 or 90 per cent of the invoiced price of mer-andise shipped and delivered to the customer.
2. *Primary loss deduction.* In addition to the coinsurance deduc-on, the policyholder assumes a primary loss. This is usually a small action of one per cent of annual sales volume, with a minimum nount expressed in the policy. This figure represents the *usual* or *pected losses* for the line of business being covered.

To the extent of the deductions, the policyholder is a self-insurer. he credit insurance company reimburses for covered losses in excess f the policyholder's participation.

Underwriting basis of credit insurance. Credit insurance poli-ies can be written to cover all risks assumed by the policyholder. Coverage applies on the basis of ratings assigned by a specified mer-antile agency. The best known mercantile agency is Dun & Brad-treet, Inc., although several other agencies, in specialty lines, are lso recognized. The assured may select the credit agency that he esires to be used to govern his coverage under the policy. The redit insurance policy includes a table that shows the maximum mount of coverage on individual accounts in each of the various atings in the rating table of the selected mercantile agency. (The nercantile rating tables are explained at page 983.)

There is one form of policy issued where coverage is not governed by mercantile agency ratings. This policy provides a single limit coverage applying to each debtor and is the broadest form of cov age offered. Because of the nature of the coverage provided, cre insurance companies are more selective in issuing this type of poli Also, the policyholder shares in each account to the extent of 25 p cent, the insurance company assuming 75 per cent of the risk.

In addition to the blanket policies, the insurance companies co individual accounts by separate policies. These are designed to p vide coverage on accounts where large amounts of money are volved. The standard for the coverage is quite high. Consequent the insuring company is somewhat selective for this type of policy.

Limit of coverage in credit insurance. Every credit insuran policy contains a maximum credit limit for each customer of t policyholder. For the most part these limits are established on t basis of mercantile agency ratings. In addition, most policies conta coverage on so-called "inferior ratings." This type of coverage is or limited basis with a maximum liability for losses occurring with del ors whose rating at date of shipment was the so-called "inferio rating."

Loss adjustments. Within twenty days after acquiring knowled of the insolvency as that term was explained at page 728, the insur must file a notification of claim with the insurance company, on form furnished by the company. The filing of the claim places t whole account against the debtor with the insurance company f collection. Certain information about the account must be fil along with the notification of claim, such as the dates of shipmer terms of sale, and the like.

Within sixty days after the claim for excess loss is filed, the insu ance company pays the amount it owes under the policy to t insured. This amount, in general, is equal to the covered loss le (1) the coinsurance deduction and (2) the primary loss.

The insured assigns to the insurance company all claims on whic there has been an adjustment, except those for which a deductio was made in the settlement for agreed salvage. On these, the i sured keeps whatever he can recover on the account from the debt or his estate. On the assigned claims, the insurance company tri to collect from each debtor or his estate as much as it can. Th insured retains an interest in this salvage equal to the amount nsurance deducted on each account entering into the adjustment, ıs its portion of the salvage attributable to the uninsured part of : claim.

Example of loss adjustment. The following are the assumed ts:

1. The primary loss is $5,000.
2. The coinsurance is 10 per cent.
3. The insured files its first claim under the policy. This claim is a default by a customer with an Aa-1 rating, amounting to 5,000.
4. The limit of coverage under the policy for this class of risk is 0,000.
5. The face coverage of the policy is $75,000.
6. The insurance company collects 30 per cent *after* the adjustent. The adjustment would be calculated as follows:

Gross loss proved	$25,000
Single account limit	20,000
Allowable loss	20,000
Coinsurance deduction of 10%	2,000
Net allowance	$18,000
Primary loss deduction	5,000
Payment of adjustment	$13,000

ince the face of the policy exceeds the $13,000, the full adjustment payable. Any subsequent loss will have only deduction for coinsurıce, as the primary loss is deducted only once on losses during the olicy period.

The 30 per cent salvage collected by the insurance company after djustment amounts to $7,500 (30% × $25,000). Of this sum, the ısured's interest amounts to $2,100, determined as follows:

Insured's interest in excess over single limit (30% × $5,000)	$1,500
Insured's interest in covered amount is equal to percentage of coinsurance (30% × $20,000 × 10%)	600
Total	$2,100

Endorsements on credit insurance policy. Any basic credit pol-:y may be modified by riders or attachments to cover situations

peculiar to the insured, or more nearly to fit the policy to the ne[e]
of the insured. Some of the more common endorsements are:

1. *Inferior rating rider.* Attachable to an ordinary policy in or[der] to protect the insured from loss through insolvency of concerns t[hat] are rated lower than first or second by the rating agency specified [in] the policy.

2. *Antedating rider.* If the insured desires to be protected [on] credits extended previous to the date on which the policy was issu[ed,] an antedating rider may be added to the policy at the time that [it] is taken out. The policy then applies, with certain exceptions [set] out in the rider, as though it had been written at the earlier date.

3. *Back sales rider.* A "conditional" back sales rider is usually [at]tached to policies of indemnity in order to include in the policy tho[se] accounts shipped prior to the beginning of the policy term. Thus, [if] losses occur on these prior shipments, such losses are included in t[he] coverage provided by the policy.

4. *Concurrent agency rider.* It is, at times, desirable to have mo[re] than one agency govern coverage. Where the primary agency do[es] not list, or does not rate an account, coverage will still apply if t[he] concurrent agency selected does provide an insurable rating.

5. *Specially purchased and/or processed merchandise rider.* Su[ch] a rider renders the insurance company liable for loss sustain[ed] through insolvency of a firm that had previously placed an order f[or] goods "entailing the purchase of special material, and the manufa[c]ture of goods not usually kept in stock," where such insolvency occu[rs] while the goods are "in process," or before title has been passed b[y] shipment and delivery.

6. *Freight rider.* The credit policy does not cover freight charge[s.] Where the freight charges appear on the customer's account, suc[h] charges may be added to the amount recoverable under the polic[y] through addition of the "freight rider."

7. *Excluded or included sales rider.* Certain classes of risks o[r] types of sales, such as cash transactions, or to a specified compan[y] may be excluded from the policy, thereby reducing the premium, b[y] an "excluded" sales rider. Sales of a subsidiary concern, or sale[s] made by a manufacturer who operates under several trade name[s] may be covered under the regular credit insurance policy by the in[]sertion of an "included" sales rider.

8. *Interim adjustment rider*. Generally, claims are paid only at the 1 of the policy year. If the insured desires more frequent settle-ents, an "interim adjustment rider" may be added to the credit urance contract. An additional premium is charged for such an dorsement.

9. *Consignment rider*. Ordinarily only completed sales are cov-ed by the credit insurance policy. Losses arising from sales made n consignment" may be included within the scope of the policy by e insertion of such a rider.

Collection service of the insurance company. In addition to e protection furnished the policyholder through the indemnifica-on for unusual credit losses, the credit insurance company renders 1 important service, that of investigation and collection. Such col-ction services are fully as important to the insured as are the reim-ursement-for-loss provisions of the policy. The benefits that accrue) the policyholder as the result of such services include:

1. A lower loss ratio, and therefore, over a period of years, a lower remium charge.
2. Inexpensive and capable collection of past-due accounts.
3. Elimination of waste through duplication of effort.
4. Quick payment of collected accounts to the policyholder.
5. The additional profits that normally flow from increased turn-ver of working capital.

How to reduce the cost of adequate credit insurance. To re-luce the cost of adequate credit insurance, it is necessary for the policyholder carefully to define his needs to his insurance broker in order that the policy may conform precisely to the requirements of he insured. Premiums paid for unneeded protection are wasted. On the other hand, the policyholder should be certain that he is fully protected.

A consideration of some of the elements that are considered by the nsurance company in computing the premium will disclose several points at which the cost of credit insurance may be safely reduced.

1. *Single account limits*. The single account limits of coverage required on the different ratings are one of the principal factors en-tering into the computation of the premium. The limits should be high enough to cover fully all the *ordinary* sales. If an occasional

account is larger than the ordinary, it might be excluded from t regular policy (see "excluded sales rider," page 732) and insur under a "specific" credit insurance policy.

2. *Type of policy.* To a considerable extent, the type of poli that the needs of the policyholder require controls the premium. policy covering debtors with inferior ratings costs more than o covering only debtors rated in first and second credits. An approv credit risk policy may possibly be less expensive than a regular polic

3. *Special endorsements.* Special endorsements and riders m either increase or decrease the premium. Endorsements tending decrease the premium include (see page 732 for definitions):

(*a*) Concurrent agency rider.

(*b*) Excluded sales rider.

(*c*) Guarantor rider (whereby the rating of a guarantor is su stituted for that of the debtor).

4. *Primary loss.* The credit insurance policy is designed to cov unusual, unpredictable losses. Consequently, the primary loss, c predictable loss, is deducted from the net loss. Inasmuch as the co of the insurance constitutes total losses plus underwriting expense it is to the advantage of the insured to assume all loss that may b covered by an accounting reserve.

5. *Coinsurance limits.* Under the ordinary policy, the insured i made coinsurer for 10 per cent of all losses. Where this percentag is increased, the liability of the insurance company will be decrease making it possible to insure the weaker risks where the policyholde has a greater interest in these inferior rated accounts.

6. *Past experience of applicant.* Credit insurance makes provisio for merit rating. Hence, if the policyholder carefully investigates al risks before extending credit, over a period of years he may be abl substantially to reduce the cost of his insurance.

7. *Reputation and practices of the policyholder.* Each credit insurance risk is considered on its own basis, and the premium rate computed in accordance with the individual circumstances. As a result, a conference with a reputable insurance expert may disclose other means by which total credit insurance premiums may be reduced.

11. MISCELLANEOUS INSURANCE COVERAGES

Fire and Allied Coverages

Supplemental contract. The fire insurance policy may be en-rsed with the "supplemental contract" at an additional premium cover losses due to windstorm; cyclone, tornado, and hail; explo-on; riot; riot attending a strike; smoke; motor vehicles; and aircraft. he cost of adding these grouped coverages is low and has been idely accepted as a step forward in broadening the protection easily d inexpensively available to business. Each of the coverages is actically self-explanatory. The "contract" becomes part of the fire olicy.

Explosion. This coverage may be purchased separately, and it is sually advisable to do so if the "supplemental coverages" must be urchased in too great an amount because of the coinsurance require-ents of the fire policy. Explosion insurance written separately in a ecific policy can be bought on varying coinsurances.

Riot, and riot attending a strike. Direct loss and damage from illage and looting is covered here, when the loss occurs during and t the place of riot or strike. This coverage can also, in conjunction ith explosion insurance, be bought under a separate policy.

Business interruption (use and occupancy). Fire—and other in-urable hazards, such as lightning, sprinkler leakage, or explosion—ften causes a greater indirect loss through the resulting cessation of usiness operations than arises from the direct loss to the property ctually destroyed. To reimburse the insured for such losses, use and ccupancy insurance (properly called business interruption insur-nce) has been designed. Various forms are in use, but the usual contract promises to indemnify the insured for all loss caused by the orced stoppage of business that results from destruction of, or dam-ge to, the premises, machinery, raw materials, stock, or instruments necessary for the transaction of business. Such indemnifiable loss ncludes estimated net profits, fixed charges, and expenses that con-tinue during enforced idleness (such as interest and salaries paid under contract), and expenses necessarily incurred for the purpose of reducing the loss (for example, cost of moving to a new location until the destroyed premises can be replaced or repaired).

The common items of continuing expense, which are paid und this policy, may include:

1. Rent.
2. Taxes.
3. Telephone charges.
4. Light, heat, power.
5. Advertising previously contracted.
6. Payroll of office staff, important shop employees, and others.
7. Officers' salaries.

The net profits that would have been earned if there had been n interruption in the business are also collectible. This policy has b- come recognized as a primary form of business insurance.

Contingent use and occupancy insurance. The ordinary use an occupancy policy does not reimburse the insured for loss occasione by a cessation of business resulting from an interruption to the co tinuous supply of an article that is absolutely necessary for the opera tion of the business. Contingent use and occupancy insurance ma be purchased to cover this risk. The usual policy promises to inden nify the insured for loss of profits, and expenses incurred, arising ou of damage to or destruction of another business unit upon which th insured is dependent for essential raw materials or parts. The cove age is applicable for the length of time it would take to place th damaged plant in a condition where deliveries could be resumed.

Profits and commissions insurance. One of the indirect losse arising from fire (tornado, riot, explosion, water damage, or othe hazard) that is not covered by the standard policy is deprivation o profits or commissions on stocks of finished goods where delivery i prevented through damage to such goods by the hazard against whicl insurance is taken. Profits and commissions insurance is available fo manufacturers, jobbers, and wholesalers, and for retailers.

Rent insurance. Owners of real property are subject to hug losses through the loss of rent or rental value as the result of th destruction of, or damage to, their property by fire, lightning, wind storm, riot, explosion, earthquake, and so forth. To cover such losses rent and rental value insurance have been designed. In most state the coverage can be effected by merely attaching to any basic direc loss policy a rent insurance endorsement.

Generally, the rent insurance policy promises to indemnify the ›ured for loss of rent or rental value for the period of time that e insured's property is damaged to the extent that it becomes un- nantable. The cover may be issued to owners, lessors, or sublessors ceiving rental income from a residence or other type of building; owners of such property which, although not rented, is apt to be nted at any time; to fiduciaries receiving income from rents; and to vners who occupy their own premises.

Two standard forms are available:

1. Indemnity based upon the rental income or rental value for the eriod estimated to be required to restore the building to a tenant- ble condition. This form is generally the most suitable for small uildings.

2. Indemnity based upon the annual income or rental value of the roperty. This form allows a longer period for restoration and is herefore more suitable for large buildings requiring a long period for eplacement.

Under either form, the entire building, whether occupied or vacant, r only the actual rented or occupied portions of the building, may e covered.

Leasehold insurance. Leasehold insurance, as distinguished from ent insurance, is designed to cover the interest of the tenant or essee. All rights under a lease are usually cancelled when the leased premises are destroyed or rendered unfit for use. The termination of n advantageous lease may result in loss to the holder thereof, arising rom numerous circumstances, including:

1. Should the premises be leased at a figure below current full- ental value, or for less than the lessee would have to pay for other imilar property, a loss amounting to such difference would follow ermination of the lease.

2. If the original lessee subleased the premises at a profit, such profit would be lost.

3. A sublessee may have paid a cash bonus to purchase a valuable long-term lease from the original lessee. Cancellation of the lease would result in a loss of all or part of such bonus.

4. The lessee may have made certain improvements, the value of which he would lose by cancellation of the lease. This interest, how-

ever, is usually covered by improvements and betterments insuranc for which see below.

In addition to the interest represented, leasehold insurance is d tinguished from rent insurance by the manner in which the loss calculated. Under rent insurance indemnity is paid for such peric as is actually required (subject to policy limitations) to restore t building to tenantable condition. Under leasehold insurance, ho ever, a definite calculable loss takes place immediately upon termin tion of the lease. For example, if a building were leased for a peric of ten years at a yearly rental of $15,000, and exactly two years lat a fire resulted in the termination of the lease, and forced the less to rent other premises at a yearly rental of $25,000, the lessee wou have incurred a loss equal to the difference in the yearly renta ($10,000), times the number of years the lease had to run (8), $80,000. But since the whole of such loss is not incurred until tl end of the lease-period, the actual loss is the present value of suc sum, or in this instance, if the policy specified that the present valu was to be obtained by discounting at 4 per cent, the amount payab would be approximately $58,448 (the sum which at 4 per cent con pound interest will equal $80,000 in eight years; see "How to calc late the compound present value," page 1311).

Rates for leasehold insurance are based upon the fire building rat modified for the provisions of the fire-cancellation clause of the leas or, in the absence of such a clause, the statutory provisions of th state wherein the property is located.

Leasehold insurance does not cover loss that arises through othe than a specific contingency insured against, such as fire or eartl quake. Loss resulting from the commission or omission of any ac by the policyholder, or by exercise of an option to terminate the lease is not covered.

Improvements and betterments insurance. The interest of lessee in improvements, additions, betterments, alterations, and re pairs installed as a permanent part of a building, or its fixtures, by the lessee at his expense under the terms of a lease, may be protecte against all direct loss or damage, arising from fire or other specifie contingency, by the purchase of improvements and betterments in surance. The form is not standardized, and care should be take to ascertain that the exact coverage desired is secured.

Accounts receivable insurance. Reputable firms may obtain in-ance to cover loss by reason of destruction by fire or any other ıse of books of accounts. A usual condition is that the accounts stored in a fireproof safe. The basic fire policy specifically ex-des losses from destruction of accounts and evidences of indebted-ss. (For credit insurance, see pages 727-734.)

Other Property Insurance

Sprinkler leakage insurance. The installation of sprinkler sys-ns gives rise to a new hazard arising out of the danger of accidental ease of water from the pipes of the sprinkler system that are placed the ceiling and fitted at intervals with sprinkler heads containing lves held in place by a fusible link. The valves open at a certain gree of heat whether or not such heat is caused by fire, and some-nes as the result of freezing or jarring. The ordinary fire policy vers water damage only when caused by fire; loss from water re-ısed by other causes may be covered by the sprinkler leakage policy.

Power plant insurance. Power plant insurance refers to a number miscellaneous covers that are designed to indemnify the policy-ılder for all direct damage or loss resulting from the accidental ex-osion or breakdown of boilers, wheels, engines, pressure vessels, eam and water turbines, electrical apparatus, and other machinery ed in connection with the generation, distribution, control, or stor-ge of energy for power purposes. In addition, endorsements may be lded to cover indirect damages and consequential loss.

While the forms differ somewhat as to definitions of "explosion," reakdown," and so forth, for the different subjects of power plant ısurance, the standard policy provides indemnity for:

1. Damage to the insured boiler, engine, turbine, machinery, or her described property, caused by internal explosion, or accidental reakdown of such property.

2. Damage to other property of the insured, caused by the explo-on or breakdown of the insured property.

3. Damage to property of others for which the insured is liable, ıused by the hazard or hazards insured against.

4. Liability of the insured arising out of a hazard covered by the olicy for loss of life or injury to members of the public.

5. Defense of suits, even though groundless or fraudulent, brought

against the policyholder because of the occurrence of an accid insured against, including payment of expenses of such defense, terest on any judgment within the limits of the policy, and court co assessed against the insured in such a case.

Among the indirect damage covers which are often added to su contracts by endorsement is that for business interruption (see pa 735).

Power plant inspection service. An important part of all types power plant insurance is the inspection service that is rendered wi the insurance. The insurance company does not promise to ma any designated number of inspections, but usually attempts to mal in the case of steam-boiler insurance, for example, two external a one internal inspection each year.

Experience of insurance companies conducting such inspectio indicates that losses caused by inspected boilers and machinery a 80 to 90 per cent less than similar losses arising from uninspect boilers and machinery. As a result, rates are not only reduced, b many policyholders regard the inspection service as more valuab than the payment of a loss in the event of an explosion or brea down.

Exclusions in power plant insurance policy. The following are t principal exclusions under most plant insurance:

1. Loss or damage caused by fire, or by explosion resulting fro fire, is not covered, inasmuch as this is a risk assumed under t standard fire insurance policy.
2. Damage occurring while any safety device, or regulator of pre sure or speed, is altered, taken out, made ineffective, or set in a ma ner to provide a pressure or speed in excess of that approved by t insurance company.
3. Business-interruption losses, unless covered by an endorsemen
4. The cost of any repairs necessitated by wear and tear, or depr ciation.
5. Boiler insurance usually excludes damage caused by "mere crac ing or fracturing of a cast iron boiler hereby insured unless standa cracking endorsement is attached to the policy."
6. Some forms of power plant insurance exclude damage for brea down of machinery caused by riot, strike, or civil commotion.

Earthquake insurance. Geologists have determined that no sec-n of the United States is entirely free of the earthquake hazard. rthquake insurance, therefore, is needed in sections other than on · Pacific Coast.

The standard earthquake policy covers against all direct loss or mage resulting from earthquake or volcanic eruption, including mage by fire where the fire insurance has been voided by the rthquake (that is, after a material part of the building has fallen). ıe cover may be issued either separately or in conjunction with the e policy. Some companies, however, consider it as an accommoda-ɔn line and issue earthquake policies only when an equivalent nount of fire insurance has been purchased.

Windstorm and tornado insurance. Windstorm and tornado surance promises to indemnify the insured for direct loss or dam-;e resulting from the action of windstorm, cyclone, or tornado. are should be taken to ascertain whether or not losses arising from e after a material part of the building has fallen (thereby voiding ıe fire policy) are covered.

Plate glass insurance. This form indemnifies the insured against ss by reason of breakage of glass. The cost of lettering and orna-ıentation on the glass involved may also be insured. The service erformed by the insurance companies in this field of insurance is ıe prompt replacement of broken glass. A store window which is roken is of no value to the merchant. Speedy replacement so that ıe window may be used for its proper show purposes is important. 'hus, more important than the cost of the glass many times is the rompt replacement service of the insurance company.

Floater Policies

Transportation insurance. Merchandise shipped by business con-erns may suffer loss or damage from many unforeseen causes before t reaches its destination, regardless of the type of carrier used to ransport the merchandise. To protect firms against loss by reason f these unforeseen events, transportation insurance has come trongly to the fore as an important insurance coverage.

Many forms of this policy are written, but all basically insure the nerchandise involved from the time it leaves the premises of the ɔwner until it arrives at and is actually delivered to the destination.

Thus it is insured, for example, while in transit to the freight stati while there awaiting shipment, while en route, while at the unlo: ing shed at the consignee's city, and while in transit to the offi of the consignee.

This insurance may be purchased to cover single shipments or an annual basis to cover all shipments made during the year. A sep rate policy is available if the firm uses its own trucks to ship and ca goods. Still another form is designed to protect the independe motor truckman for loss involving damage to merchandise of l customers while in his trucks during shipment.

Parcel post insurance. Insurance companies issue a liberal "a risk" policy providing indemnity for loss or damage to packages contents while in the custody of the post-office department, or f loss in case of failure to arrive at destination.

Retailers, jobbers, and manufacturers who ship 100 or more pac ages per year will generally find that private parcel post insurance cheaper, more convenient, and entails less clerical detail than Go ernment parcel post insurance.

Registered mail insurance. Banks, trust companies, investme houses, and other concerns making numerous shipments of currenc securities, and other valuables by registered mail (including air mail may protect themselves against loss or damage from practically a risks, except the perils of war and the hazard of theft by employe of either the insured or the addressee. Policies may be issued t cover only a single large shipment, but concerns making numerou shipments during the year will find it advantageous to procure reporting form (see page 693 for description), under which all ship ments made during the policy period are automatically covered. Thi policy may also be endorsed to cover shipments by express.

Garment contractor's insurance. A floater type of policy is use by manufacturers who do not complete all the work in their ow plant that is necessary to turn out completed garments. The articles during their manufacture, may be sent to various types of contrac tors who will perform some work on them and then return them t the owner. The insurance protects the owner while the goods in volved are away from his plant and while they are in transit.

Bailee's customer's insurance. Businesses that are in the position bailee, such as public storers, dyers, cleaners, laundries, ware-)uses, and the like, are ordinarily responsible for the articles en- usted to their care. This form of insurance indemnifies them for image or loss to those articles and not only gives protection to the iilee and to the owner of the goods, but also serves as a goodwill olicy by attracting customers to the obviously responsible bailee id, in times of loss, preventing costly and troublesome arrangements etween the bailee and his customers.

Salesmen's samples insurance. Business concerns that send out ith salesmen valuable merchandise for use as samples may secure rotection with salesmen's samples insurance. The policy is a liberal all-risk" contract. However, the contract should be carefully read efore purchase, inasmuch as the line is not standardized; a few com- anies issue contracts covering only specified hazards.

Jewelers' block insurance. Manufacturers, wholesalers, and re- ailers may protect themselves against practically all types of loss or lamage to jewelry stocks by purchasing a jeweler's block policy. The overage is very broad; only a few specified risks are excluded.

Miscellaneous Coverages

Title insurance. As contrasted with all other forms of insurance, itle insurance does not protect against hazards occurring in the uture; the policy covers only against loss arising from titles that may iave been rendered defective in the past. A large part of every pre- mium is for the service of searching. The usual policy guarantees that, except as otherwise specified, the title is perfect at the time that the insured bought or sold the property to which it attaches.

Rain insurance. Indemnity for loss of income, or reimbursement for expenses incurred where rain, hail, snow, or sleet cause the aban- donment of an enterprise, may be secured through rain insurance. Some contracts specify that $1/10$ or $2/10$ inch of rain must fall before the insured will be entitled to recover for any damage, while under others the company assumes liability if any rain, no matter how little, falls. The premium, of course, is higher on the latter form.

Rain insurance does not cover damage to tangible or real property.

Check alteration and forgery insurance. Although the gener principle of law holds the depositary bank responsible for forger it does not hold the bank responsible for alteration in the body the check. Furthermore, many exceptions to this rule exist, ar there are cases on record where the bank has not been held liable f forgery or alteration. Thus, in addition to the doubt that may exi as to the liability of the bank in any particular transaction, the d positor will have to pay the costs of a legal prosecution and may lo the interest on his money, which is tied up in the meantime. Cons quently, there is a genuine need for check alteration and forge insurance.

Two forms of check alteration and forgery insurance are in con mon use by business concerns other than banks:

1. *Depositors' forgery policy.* This policy may be written to pr tect the checking account of any individual, firm, or corporation oth than a bank. The contract promises to protect the insured, as we as any bank or banks in which he carries a checking account, fro any direct loss, up to the limit of the contract, resulting from forger or alteration of checks or other standard negotiable paper (note drafts, bills of exchange, trade acceptances) issued or ostensib issued by the insured. The policy does not cover instruments draw in lead pencil, unless indelible, or loss encountered by reason of th insured's acceptance of forged or altered checks in the course of hi business.
2. *Commercial forgery policy.* This policy may also be sold to an individual, firm, or corporation other than a bank, but it is peculiarl appropriate for retail concerns and others who daily accept check from strangers in payment for merchandise sold.

The agreement is divided into two sections. Section "A" is iden tical with the coverage offered by the depositors' forgery policy.

Section "B" protects the insured against all loss resulting fron alteration or forgery of incoming bank drafts and checks that th policyholder may take in good faith in the course of his business The agreement, however, does not cover loss arising from instrument drawn in lead pencil, unless indelible, or upon checks returned an marked "no account" or "not sufficient funds."

12. BUSINESS LIFE INSURANCE

Types of organizations that should be interested in business life insurance. Business life insurance is regular life insurance applied to the needs of a business. It protects the business of the insured in the same manner that personal life insurance protects his family.

Although life insurance can be applied to the needs of virtually every form of business organization, it is of particular value to:

1. Sole proprietorships.
2. Partnerships—general and limited.
3. Close corporation.

Uses to which business life insurance can be profitably applied. The various uses to which business life insurance may be profitably applied include:

1. To reimburse the business for loss resulting from the death of a person who has contracted to do some particular or unusual work, or who has undertaken a program of expansion, the fulfillment of which depends upon the personal performance of such person.

2. To protect the business against loss at the death of an employee by:

(*a*) Compensating for the loss of unusual services.

(*b*) Indemnifying for the loss of goodwill attached to the person of an employee or official.

(*c*) Protecting the credit of the business where the extension of credit is dependent upon the business connections or services of an employee or official.

(*d*) Providing a fund to train a successor.

3. To protect the business at the death of a sole or part-owner by:

(*a*) Providing funds for the transfer of the decedent's interest in the business to his heirs in a predetermined manner so that the business itself is not disturbed financially, business-wise, or management-wise.

(*b*) Protecting the credit of the business.

(*c*) Providing a fund to act as a "shock absorber" to tide the business over the difficult period that always follows a sudden change in management.

4. To protect the business against unusual exigencies by:

(*a*) Providing a sinking fund (the cash value of the insurance that may be used in case of emergency.

(*b*) Hedging an ordinary sinking fund designed to retire bonds of the corporation where sale of the bonds is predicated upon the services of certain officers.

Business life insurance trusts. A free choice may ordinarily be made as to whether the proceeds of business life insurance are to be paid to:

1. The partnership or corporation.
2. The proprietor's estate, a creditor, or a named beneficiary.
3. The surviving partners or stockholders.
4. A trustee.

Whenever any policy of business life insurance is placed with a trust company under an agreement whereby the trustee will collect and distribute the proceeds, a business life insurance trust exists.

When the services of a trustee are necessary. Where any part of the proceeds of a policy is to be used for the purchase of the decedent's interest in a partnership, or for the retirement of stock interests in a corporation, it is desirable to arrange for payment of the proceeds to a trustee, preferably a corporate fiduciary. This is true for a number of reasons, chief among which is the difficulty of placing a fair valuation upon the interest of the decedent after his death.

When the services of a trustee are unnecessary. In general, the services of a trustee will represent an unwarranted expense where the only purpose of the insurance is to act as a shock-absorber, to compensate for loss of goodwill, or to reimburse any party for loss suffered through the death of an employee, part-owner or contractor.

Determining factors where use of a trustee's services is optional. Where no part of the insurance is designed for the retirement of business interests, the advantages of having the insurance proceeds paid through a trustee should be compared with the charges made by the trustee.

The outstanding advantages of the insurance trust are:

1. If the trustee is given certain discretionary powers, a single policy may sometimes serve several purposes, thus decreasing the net cost of the business-insurance program.

2. In business-liquidation plans, the trust agreement interposes between the legal representatives of the deceased and the survivors the disinterested services of a fiduciary whose sole aim is to fulfill faithfully the terms of the trust for the benefit of all the parties concerned.

3. In drafting the various agreements involved, the experience of a corporate fiduciary is often invaluable in suggesting the best ways and means of carrying out the desires of the owners of the business.

4. Where insurance is taken out to strengthen or enhance the credit of the enterprise, the services of a trustee render the creditor more secure than if the proceeds were paid directly to the business (since in that event they would be available to all creditors), and protect the interests of the business to a greater extent than if the proceeds were paid to the creditor, himself, in trust.

Charges made by corporate fiduciaries. The charges made by corporate fiduciaries vary in different parts of the country, and sometimes as between different trust companies in the same city. The fees for handling business insurance trusts are quite reasonable and depend upon the duties and responsibilities involved.

Methods used to evaluate the interests of a decedent in a stock-transfer or partnership-liquidation agreement. The following methods are now in general use for the valuation both of stock in a close corporation and of the interest of a decedent in a partnership:

1. *Arbitrary valuation*. A definite price may be specified by agreement between the owners of the business. Inasmuch as values are subject to substantial change within a relatively short period, however, this method, although simple, is highly unsatisfactory, and is usually unjust either to the decedent's estate or to the surviving owners.

2. *Book value*. Another simple method is to specify by agreement that the book value of the decedent's interest as of the date of death shall be used. Although this is an improvement over the first method, injustice still results, since book value seldom represents actual fair market value.

3. *Arbitrary valuation revised at regular intervals.* The parties may specify the value of the interest of each owner at the time that the agreement is entered into, and provide for revision from time to time to conform with changes in value of the various interests. If carefully carried out, and if revisions are made at intervals of approximately six months, this is one of the most desirable and satisfactory methods. In practice, however, the owners frequently fail to certify the proper value of the specified times, with the result that when a death occurs, the last revision in value will be either higher or lower than the fair market value of the decedent's interest in the business.

4. *Arbitration.* Another possible method of valuation is to provide by agreement for arbitration between representatives of the decedent owner and the surviving owners. Provision is also made in most cases for selection of a third, and supposedly neutral, party to represent both interests. If the agreement provides that the determination of the arbitrators is to be binding upon all parties, the only objection that can be raised is the possible delay that may be encountered, and the ill-feeling that may be engendered.

5. *Valuation supervised by the trustee.* The trustee may be directed to conduct an audit of the books of the enterprise as soon as convenient after the death of any owner, and fully to inform all parties in interest as to the results of the audit. If the surviving owners and the decedent's estate can then agree upon a satisfactory valuation for the interest of the decedent, such value will be final. If, after a reasonable time, the parties in interest fail to agree among themselves, the trustee is directed to employ one or more experts to ascertain the fair market value of the decedent's interest. Such experts, after investigation, certify to the trustee the fair market value of the decedent's interest. The certified value is then binding on all parties. The objections to this method arise from the unwillingness of most trustees to assume the added responsibility, and the additional service charges where the responsibility is assumed.

6. *Suggested method.* As indicated above, the third method, if correctly applied, is probably the most satisfactory. Therefore, in order to overcome the objections to this method, it is suggested that the transfer agreement provide:

(*a*) For valuation by the respective owners of their interest in the business at intervals of six months.

(*b*) That if a valuation has been certified to the trustee within seven months of the death of any owner, such valuation is to be final.

(*c*) That in case no certification of value has been made within seven months of the death of an owner, the trustee shall conduct an audit to ascertain the book value of the decedent's interest as of the date of death.

(*d*) That all parties in interest shall be fully informed by the trustee as to the results of the audit.

(*e*) That if the surviving owners and the decedent's executors are then able to agree upon a fair market value for the decedent's interest in the business, such value shall be final and binding on all parties.

(*f*) That if the parties in interest are unable to agree upon a fair value, the trustee shall designate one or more persons who are thoroughly familiar with conditions in the particular industry and locality to make an investigation, and upon the basis of such investigation, to ascertain the fair market value of the decedent's interest, and to certify the same to the trustee.

(*g*) That in such event, the price certified to the trustee shall be final and binding upon all parties.

SECTION 7

Employee Benefit Plans

1. EMPLOYEE BENEFITS AND EMPLOYEE MORALE

2. GROUP INSURANCE

3. GROUP LIFE INSURANCE

4. GROUP HEALTH INSURANCE

5. GROUP ACCIDENT AND SICKNESS INSURANCE (TEMPORARY DISABILITY)

6. PENSION PLANS

Wage-Dividend Plans

Production-Sharing Plans

Other Current Profit-Sharing Plans

SECTION 7

Employee Benefit Plans

. EMPLOYEE BENEFITS AND EMPLOYEE MORALE

What are employee benefits? From the employer's viewpoint, mployee benefits are management's attempts to give substance to he desires that are uppermost in the employee's mind. They help o create a common ground of understanding on which employer nd employee can meet peacefully and cooperatively. Through the chievement of labor-management harmony, and hence greater emloyee morale, they help to make greater productivity possible.

From the employee's viewpoint, employee benefits represent those teps beyond the pay envelope that management takes to insure that ts company will be the best of all possible places to work. In a ense, they implement the promise that management often makes of iner opportunities and better living to be realized from working for he concern.

The objectives of employee benefits. It could be said quite simly that the objective of employee benefit plans is to secure greater mployee morale. Generally, that statement is correct. But specifially, the goal of employee benefits is to get to the roots of employee norale and to insure the presence of the factors that raise its level.

In addition to morale factors, there are other important objectives of employee benefits. Increasingly, individual collective bargaining ontracts call for the installation of one or more benefits, such as penions, insurance, and health provisions. Repeatedly, interest in public-sponsored security measures is stirred up by "planners" within nd without the government. Hence, more and more companies re establishing benefit programs to forestall union demands and dditional government welfare measures.

As employee benefit plans become "musts," those companies that ail to install them will not only place themselves at a disadvantage n the labor market, but must eventually face a deterioration in public elations.

In a recent study of 50 companies, the following aims were men tioned as the reasons for instituting benefits plans:

STATED OBJECTIVES OF COMPANY BENEFIT PLANS *

	Number of Companies
Reduce turnover: to have satisfied, permanent employees; to promote stability	12
Build a sense of security: a sense of security on the part of employees is desirable	12
Build up morale and loyalty: want our employees to be happy; want them to feel this is not just another job (without reference to security or efficiency)	10
Protection for employees: help employees to help themselves; protect employees against loss from sickness and accident	8
Increase efficiency and productivity: to build a happy, efficient working force; better morale increases productivity	5
To attract better class of workers: you can't get men in key jobs without pensions	4
Other answers	4

Desires uppermost in employees' minds. Various attitude sur veys have uncovered many facets of worker opinion, but they are in agreement that most things that employees desire are wanted *in addition* to good wages—that is, wages at least equal to those paid in the same industry or area for a similar job. For industry as a whole, the five fundamental desires of the *average* worker toward which employee benefits should be directed are:

1. Security.
2. The opportunity to "belong."
3. The chance to get ahead.
4. Good supervision.
5. A satisfactory type of work.

The attributes of employee benefit plans. To qualify as an employee benefit all of the following five characteristics should be pres ent in the plan that creates the employees' rights to benefits:

* "Making Employee Benefit Dollars Work Harder," *Public Opinion Index* May, 1950, page 28.

1. It should be sponsored by management, or by employees with ie acquiescence of management. Ideally, the planning should be joint undertaking of management and employees whenever possible.

2. It should offer a tangible or intangible benefit that would not ave accrued to employees without that planned effort.

3. It should cover and appeal to a large number of employees and ot to a selected few.

4. Part, if not all, of the cost should be met by the employer.

5. It should be aimed at satisfying the five fundamental "employee vants" listed above.

On the basis of these attributes, executive bonus arrangements or pecial sales incentive plans are not employee benefits, nor are such vage incentive plans as piecework systems.

Employee benefit plans to be discussed. The following em-loyee benefit plans are explained in the succeeding sections: *

1. Group insurance plans:

   (*a*) Group life—term, paid-up, and level premium.
   (*b*) Group health—hospitalization and medical care.
   (*c*) Group accident and sickness—temporary disability.

2. Pension plans.
3. Deferred profit-sharing plans.
4. Current profit-sharing plans—cash, wage dividend, production-haring.

2. GROUP INSURANCE

Nature of group insurance. Group insurance may be defined as the insurance of a changing group of individuals by means of a single or blanket insurance contract. By its very nature, it lends itself to use by employers who wish to make available to their employees benefits that offer security through insurance. Group insurance in-cludes (1) life insurance of various types, (2) death and dismember-

* For other employee benefit plans (employee stock plans, education and self-mprovement plans, suggestion systems, employee food services, industrial recrea-ion, credt unions, home financing plans, split-dollar insurance, counseling, med-cal and other services), see *Successful Employee Benefit Plans*. New York: Prentice-Hall, Inc., 1952.

ment, (3) hospital expense, (4) medical or surgical expense, and (5 temporary nonoccupational accident and sickness disability.

These features are common to all forms of group insurance:

1. The premiums are collected and the details handled throug some central agency, usually the employer.

2. A general policy is issued to the employer, and a certificate ev dencing the insurance is issued to each employee.

3. The policy is for one year, except for the comparatively ne permanent life policies.

4. Usually one must be employed a certain length of time befor he is eligible for the insurance, except in those states having com pulsory disability insurance laws. This waiting period, or length c service requirement, varies with the employer and with the type c insurance.

5. The premiums may be paid jointly by the employer and em ployee under a contributory plan, or paid entirely by the employe under a noncontributory plan.

6. Rates are based partly on the experience of the particular risk except for hospital and medical and surgical expense insurance tha is underwritten by carriers other than regular insurance companies.

7. The policy must cover a minimum number of lives, and, i contributory plans, does not become effective until 75 per cent of th eligible employees have subscribed. In noncontributory plans, all c the employees must enroll unless they sign a waiver card. Th minimum number varies with the type of insurance and with the state.

8. The policy is issued on a basis which precludes selection of the employees to be covered.

Advantages to employer. Although each type of group insurance has advantages peculiar to it, certain general advantages are commo to group insurance as a whole. Generally, the employer derives the following benefits from a group insurance program:

1. A group insurance program satisfies the employer's sociologica urge to arrange protection against his workers' adversities.

2. Standardization provided under a group insurance contract per mits consistency of treatment of hardship cases. Each case is de

ded on a formula instead of in accordance with bias of superiors r changing management.

3. The traditional "passing of the hat," to which the employer is xpected to contribute generously, is no longer necessary when adersity strikes a fellow-employee or his family.

4. A group insurance program attracts efficient labor and reduces mployee turnover. An employee hesitates to sacrifice protection ffered by insurance by terminating his employment and taking a job hat does not offer equal insurance security.

5. A group insurance program gives the employer desirable publicity and prestige in the community.

As group insurance programs become more and more general, the ast two advantages become less and less important.

What employees shall be eligible? In working out the details of plan, an employer must consider the conditions of eligibility for participation that he wishes to impose, as well as those imposed by he insurance carrier.

When the employer pays the entire cost of the insurance, all employees, or all employees of a particular class, must be allowed to participate after the required waiting period. "Class of employees" neans a group of employees having one or more common characterstics, such as salaried employees, clerical employees, employees in a particular wage bracket, or employees in a particular plant or division. If the employee contributes to the plan, the minimum percentage equired by statutes and the insurance carrier must join. The percentage may be based on the number of employees in a particular class, instead of the total number of employees.

Other factors to consider in determining eligibility are these:

1. *Service.* Under almost all group insurance plans all full-time employees at the time the plan is inaugurated are eligible. New employees usually become eligible after they have completed a certain period of continuous employment. The usual requirement is three months. The waiting period eliminates the paper work that would be involved if floaters were included in the coverage. Companies usually set definite dates at about three-month intervals for bringing into the plan new employees who have become eligible. The length

of service requirement of plans that offer permanent insurance (se
page 764) is usually longer.

2. *Union membership.* Some plans, particularly those admini
tered by the union, or jointly by the union and employer, requi
union membership as a condition of participation.

3. *Income.* Some insurance underwriters impose an income lim
as a condition of eligibility for hospitalization and medical plans.

Shall plans be noncontributory or contributory? Group insu
ance may be written under the noncontributory or contributory pla

1. *Noncontributory plan.* Under a noncontributory plan, the en
ployer pays all premiums, and the employees in the classes eligib
for the insurance are automatically insured upon completion of th
probationary period. The advantages claimed for noncontributor
plans are:

(*a*) Maximum flexibility as to details of plan. The employe
is in a position to modify the plan at any time.

(*b*) Certainty that all employees will come under the plan
Unless employee contributions are compulsory, 100 per cent coverag
is seldom obtained except under noncontributory plans.

(*c*) Avoidance of appearance of dictation or direction by em
ployer in regard to employee's savings.

(*d*) Avoidance of administrative and clerical expense arisin
from payroll deductions.

2. *Contributory plan.* Under a contributory plan, premiums ar
paid by the employer and employees jointly. New employees, other
wise eligible, are not covered until they have signified their intentio
of joining the group and have given the employer permission to mak
the necessary payroll deductions. The principal advantages of con
tributory plans are usually held to be:

(*a*) More liberal coverage is possible if the cost is shared by the
employer and the employees.

(*b*) Employees are encouraged in systematic habits of thrift.

Extent of insurance program. Once an employer has decided
that an insurance program is desirable, he must determine how
extensive the program shall be. Perhaps it is not practical to adopt
a complete insurance program immediately. If not, what coverages

ıall the insurance package include? Each employer must answer ıis question in the light of his own circumstances, tempered by the eeds and demands of his employees. The extent of the financial urden on the employee is particularly important if the plan is to e contributory. Detailed examination of the various group coverges, the costs, and the comparable benefits offered by each assists ıe employer in reaching a decision.

Selecting an insurer. After making a tentative decision about the xtent of the insurance program, the employer might select several rospective insurers. Many employers prefer to deal through their roker in the initiation of an insurance plan. He will place the insurnce with any carrier chosen by the employer, and his services are lso helpful in the subsequent administration of the plan. But some mployers prefer to deal directly with the insurer or through the nsurer's agent. A carrier should be selected only after careful scruiny, especially with reference to (1) low net cost, (2) underwriting ervice, and (3) claims service. The employer can find out from the rospective carrier's clients what kind of service the carrier gives and ts attitude about paying claims.

Getting proposals from insurers. When a few carriers have been elected as having met satisfactorily the required qualifications, the ıext step is to obtain from each a proposal, based on a given set of equirements. For proposal purposes, an employer should ask each nsurer to bid on the same types of coverages and the same basic ımounts and conditions. The information given at pages 764 *et seq.* for each kind of group insurance will be of value in laying out requirements.

To bid intelligently, each insurer will need and request certain facts, in the nature of an employee census. These items of information vary with the type of coverage on which the insurer is bidding, but they usually include the following: (1) date of birth and sex of each employee, (2) date of employment of each employee, (3) percentage of female employees, (4) percentage of married male employees (also female employees with dependent children), and (5) current earnings of each employee.

Placing the contract. When proposals have been received, a careful comparison will indicate the carrier best qualified to provide coverage. It often simplifies administration for the employer to plac his entire insurance program with the same carrier. The norma procedure is to have separate master policies for each type of grou insurance, but to issue only one certificate to the employee. From practical standpoint, an unfavorable experience under one contrac does not affect a favorable experience under another contract. Sup pose an employer's experience under a group life contract has bee extra favorable, whereas his experience under group accident an sickness was not good. The carrier would then ask the employer i he wanted the accounts rated separately or together. It is generall to the advantage of the employer for the carrier to average the experi ence under all accounts.

Employer's application. After an employer selects an insuranc carrier, he submits a preliminary formal application to the company on a standard form. The application is all inclusive for every typ of insurance coverage, containing an insurance schedule that is fille out for the coverages desired. It also contains other provisions tha are later incorporated in the master policy.

Selling the employee on a new plan. After an employer work out all the details of an insurance plan and decides to adopt it, hi first task is to sell the employee on it, whether the plan is contribu tory or noncontributory. He announces the plan to the employee through the media of letters over the president's signature, employe meetings, envelope stuffers, booklets, house organs, reports to em ployees, and the public address system. Material sent to the em ployees' homes is particularly effective. These announcements ex plain the terms and conditions of the plan and the benefits to b derived from it. Underwriters will furnish envelope stuffers, booklets and posters to the employer free of charge. In fact, all carriers re quire that material announcing the plan be approved by them Otherwise, the material might mislead the employee with respect t his rights and privileges, or it might even commit the insurance car rier to the payment of benefits that it did not contemplate.

Selling an employee on a contributory plan means more tha arousing his enthusiasm for it: it means selling him on the idea o joining the plan and contributing to it. This frequently require personal interviewing and solicitation of enrollments. The persona olicitation may be done by representatives of the insurance company, y a team of employees, or by key personnel.

The insurance carrier will send representatives to canvass the employees or to address employee gatherings, show movies, or make alks over a public address system. The objection to this method is hat the insurance plan loses some of its significance as an employer rogram and takes on the aspects of a carrier-promoted plan.

Several employees who have been briefed thoroughly on the plan nay circulate throughout the organization, explaining the plan and nrolling employees. These employees are usually from the personel department. The employer should also designate a representaive to answer questions about the plan after it is installed. In the verage-sized company, this person is usually a junior executive in he personnel department.

Perhaps the most effective selling can be done by key personnel, hat is, department heads, foremen, and supervisors. The customary rocedure is to call a meeting of key personnel and have a company fficial, preferably the president, explain the plan to them. The key ersonnel, in turn, talk to their groups and take applications for the nsurance. It is essential that the key personnel be completely sold n the program.

Keeping the employee sold on the plan. Not only is it necessary o sell employees on a group insurance plan, but it is desirable to eep them fully aware of the benefits afforded by it, if the employer s to gain the greatest advantage from the plan. Employees must be ept sold on a contributory plan in order to keep the percentage of mployees participating in the plan at or above the desired minimum.

Selling the new employee. It is particularly important that a ew employee be given an explanation of the insurance plan and an pportunity to make application for the insurance before he becomes eligible, whether the plan is contributory or noncontributory. If he has not made application for the insurance by the time he becomes eligible, or within the grace period usually allowed, the carrier may require him to submit evidence of insurability to join the plan, especially if the plan has an element of permanent insurance. Should he be uninsurable when he makes his late application, he will not be covered by the group policy.

Although getting a new employee's application for admission to a noncontributory plan is practically a routine matter, selling hi on a contributory plan is not so simple. Every effort should b made to impress upon him the advantages to be derived from th plan. In many companies, the personnel department "sells" eac new employee and secures his application for coverage as soon as h joins the company, although he may not be eligible for participatio for some time. Booklets and other material are also sent to h home.

Taxes. Generally speaking, premiums paid by employers for em ployee group insurance constitute proper deductions under the hea of ordinary and necessary business expenses in computing the ne income of an employer, whether an individual or a corporation. Th premiums are not taxable income to employees and, therefore, ar not subject to the Federal withholding tax. But under the provision of some plans, especially life insurance plans having a feature of per manent life insurance, the premiums might not be deductible from the Federal income tax and, also, might constitute additional incom to the employee.

3. GROUP LIFE INSURANCE

Types of group life insurance policies. Until comparatively re cently, only term, or temporary, life insurance was written under a group policy. Two types of group policies that offer permanent in surance are now available: (1) term insurance, combined with single premium or unit-purchase paid-up insurance, referred to as *paid-up plans,* and (2) permanent insurance on a level premium basis, re ferred to as *level premium plans.* Group term and the two types of permanent insurance are described below.

Nature of group term life insurance. Group term life insurance is similar to individual term life insurance in that it is temporary covering only a specified period, without any paid-up or cash sur render value. Group policies are written on a year-to-year basis They are usually renewable at the option of the employer (the policy holder). The fact that the death risk is assumed on a year-to-year basis means (1) that the amount of risk on each life is a specified amount throughout a given year, and (2) that in each succeeding year the premium cost per $1,000 coverage on a specific life wil crease because the employee is a year older and the probability f death is, therefore, greater. At termination of employment, rough retirement or otherwise, the employee may convert his group rm insurance to an individual life insurance policy at rates applica-le to his age at the time, without furnishing evidence of insurabilty.

Almost all state laws limit to $20,000 the maximum that can be laced on a life under a group policy. The insurance carriers also mit the amount of insurance that they will issue to any one em-loyee. Two factors affect the maximum amount: (1) the total mount of insurance issued for the group at the inception of the overage; (2) the amounts of insurance on the lives of the 50 em-loyees insured for the highest amount. The maximum amount is hen determined from a table.

Nature of a group paid-up plan. Group paid-up life insurance nakes use of the single premium life insurance principle and of the ligibility, coverage, and administrative features of group term life. Each year, a single premium buys for a specific employee a stated unit of life insurance that remains in force during the lifetime of he employee, without payment of further premium. Like an indi-vidual paid-up policy, paid-up insurance purchased under a group policy has a cash surrender value, but the employee is not permitted o cash the policy until his employment terminates.

Under a paid-up plan, the employee is eligible for an aggregate amount of group life insurance, part of which is paid-up and part term. From year to year, an increasing part of the employee's group life insurance becomes paid-up insurance, whereas the amount of term insurance decreases. The proportion that the paid-up insurance bears to the total amount of group life insurance depends upon the percentage fixed in the plan and upon the age of the employee at the time he becomes a member of the plan.

"Money-purchase" and stated value units. The amount of each single unit of paid-up life insurance to be purchased for an employee may be regulated by either of two methods: (1) A predetermined amount is applied to the purchase of as much paid-up insurance as that amount will buy. The contribution remains the same, but the money purchases a smaller unit of paid-up insurance with the ad-vancing age of the employee. (2) Units of paid-up insurance with the same value may be purchased each year. By this method, the

ACCUMULATED AMOUNTS OF PAID-UP INSURANCE PURCHASED *

Years Since Entry	By Employee Contributions of $1.00 Monthly					By Employee Contributions of $1.30 Monthly				
	Age at Entry					Age at Entry				
	20	30	40	50	60	20	30	40	50	60
1	$35.04	$28.68	$23.52	$19.68	$16.80	$45.55	$37.28	$30.58	$25.58	$21.84
2	69.36	56.76	46.68	39.00	33.36	90.17	73.79	60.68	50.70	43.37
3	102.96	84.24	69.36	58.08	49.68	133.85	109.51	90.17	75.50	64.58
4	135.96	111.24	91.68	76.80	65.76	176.75	144.61	119.18	99.84	85.49
5	168.24	137.76	113.52	95.28	81.72	218.71	179.09	147.58	123.86	106.24
10	320.28	262.56	217.32	183.24		416.36	341.33	282.52	238.21	
15	458.04	376.08	312.60	264.96		595.45	488.90	406.38	344.45	
20	582.84	479.88	400.56			757.69	623.84	520.73		
25	696.36	575.16	482.28			905.27	747.71	626.96		
30	800.16	663.12				1,040.21	862.06			
35	895.44	744.84				1,164.07	968.29			
40	983.40					1,278.42				
45	1,065.12					1,384.66				

* This table is based upon the assumption that no change will be made in the premium rates at which employee contributions are applied to purchase paid-up insurance. The Insurance Company reserves the right to change such premium rates for employee contributions made after the first five policy years.

mount applied to the purchase of paid-up insurance increases each ear with the employee's advancing age.

The former method is considered more practical both from the mployee's standpoint and from the standpoint of administration.

Termination of employment. Upon termination of employment, he employee will receive a certificate showing the amount of paid-up nsurance that has been purchased for him. The terminating emloyee may retain the paid-up insurance or surrender it at any time or its cash surrender value. The cash surrender value will at least qual the employee's contributions.

The table opposite shows the amount of paid-up insurance that an be purchased for $1.00 and $1.30 monthly, at present rates.

Nature of a group level premium permanent insurance plan. ike all group insurance, group level premium insurance is issued uner a contract between the insurance company and the employer, for he benefit of the employee and his beneficiary. The contract of nsurance is called a "group permanent contract." It combines the ligibility, coverage, and administrative features of group term life vith the level premium feature of individual life insurance, plus pecial provisions. Level premium merely means that, instead of the remium's increasing with advancing age, the premium on each emloyee's life is the same every year, fixed at a level based on his ttained age at the time the insurance is issued.

A level premium plan answers the demands for a group contract that offers life insurance fully paid up by retirement age and, also, with values available upon termination. The plan may call for whole life or limited payment insurance. A group permanent contract can also be used to fund a pension plan (see page 789).

Whole life and limited payment plans. Under the whole life plan, each employee is insured until death, even if it occurs after retirement, with level premiums payable each year the employee lives. Cash or paid-up values accumulate beginning with the first year and may be made available to the employee upon termination of employment.

Under a limited payment plan (also called life paid-up at a certain age), each employee is insured until death, but premium payments cease at a given age, usually retirement age.

FULL TERMINATION (CASH) VALUES PER $1,000 OF INSURANCE

End of Year	*Whole Life* — *Age on Effective Date of Insurance* 25	40	55
1	$5	$14	$25
5	54	96	148
10	123	203	295
20	277	414	543

End of Year	*Life Paid-up at Age 65 (Limited Payment)* — *Age on Effective Date of Insurance* 25	40	55
1	$7	$19	$60
5	62	124	343
10	140	265	757
20	317	574	842

REDUCED PAID-UP INSURANCE PER $1,000 OF INSURANCE

End of Year	*Whole Life* — *Age on Effective Date of Insurance* 25	40	55
1	$15	$28	$38
5	132	175	209
10	271	338	390
20	503	585	645

End of Year	*Life Paid-up at Age 65 (Limited Payment)* — *Age on Effective Date of Insurance* 25	40	55
1	$19	$38	$91
5	151	226	485
10	309	440	1000
20	577	811	

Termination of employment. Level premium plans fall into hree classifications in respect to terminating employees: (1) noncontributory plans with no vesting; (2) noncontributory plans with some vesting in employees; (3) contributory plans with employee cash values. Under (1), values accumulating from the premium belong to the employer; the terminating employee is generally given a conversion privilege similar to that under group term insurance. Under (2), part of the accumulated values belong to the employer and are treated like values released under (1); part of the values vest in the employee for the purchase of reduced paid-up insurance. Under (3), values arising from the employer's payments sometimes vest in the employee, but under some plans the values are treated as in (1); values arising from the employee's contribution are available to him.

The tables opposite show the cash values and the amount of paid-up insurance that accumulate per $1,000 of insurance under a whole life plan and under a life paid-up at age 65 plan. The amounts vary slightly with the insurance company, and are based on present rates.

Methods of determining amount of insurance. The amount of coverage offered under a group life insurance plan may be a level amount for all employees, or related to salary or wages, occupation, or length of service. Occasionally the amount of insurance varies according to the employee's age when he joins the plan, the older employees being eligible for less insurance than the younger employees. This plan of coverage is rare.

Level amounts. When employees are covered by level amounts, each employee receives the same unit of insuranc. This is the most common coverage in union-negotiated plans, particularly when compensation is not stable and when the plan is noncontributory. This is the simplest coverage plan and the easiest to administer. It involves no changing of certificates or records when an employee's status changes. It produces less fluctuation in total premium and no change in the employee's share.

Salary or wage basis. A predominant factor in the development of group life insurance has been the employer's desire to be relieved of the moral obligation of continuing the payment of wages or salary to the family of a deceased employee. This attitude has brought about a trend toward tying coverage to salary and wages, particularly in contributory plans. There appears to be no criterion for the relation that amount of coverage should bear to earnings. For the purpose of arriving at a schedule of coverage, wage earners are classified according to the standard hourly wage rate or hourly base rate, and salaried employees are classified according to weekly, monthly, or annual earnings exclusive of bonuses and overtime.

The total premium fluctuates with the economic trend. The amount of the insurance automatically goes upward when earnings are high and, theoretically, downward when they are low. Many plans provide that an employee's insurance shall not be decreased if he has a reduction in his basic earnings, but new employees who are hired at the lower scale receive the lower amount of insurance. By tying coverage to earnings, the employer avoids the necessity of amending his plan to keep it in line with economic conditions.

Occupational plan. In plans covering wage earners whose compensation is not stable, coverage is frequently on an occupational basis, with a level amount of insurance to employees in a given class. For example, executives might be allowed $2,500; foremen and salesmen, $2,000; all other employees, $1,000. Occupational classification does not affect the total premium unfavorably, nor does it cause the premium to fluctuate, because the average age and salary in each classification remain within fairly definite brackets. In some cases, it might be difficult to determine in which personnel category a borderline case belongs.

Length-of-service plan. Under length-of-service plans, the amount of coverage available to each employee increases with the years of employment until it reaches a stipulated maximum. For example, an employee's coverage starts at $1,000 and is increased $100 each year until it reaches the maximum. Or the amount of coverage might increase every five years of employment. Some plans call for variable amounts of insurance according to length of service at the time the plan is adopted, with increases for future years of service. Any coverage plan that is tied to length of service results in a relatively large volume of insurance being placed on the lives of older employees, with a corresponding increase in premium. Many employers who have noncontributory plans adopt the length-of-service classification, or a variation of it, as a reward for service and as an additional brake on turnover. Coverage based on length of service is not desirable in contributory plan, because it does not differentiate between the eeds of high-paid and low-paid employees and their ability to pay. 'his disadvantage, however, may be overcome by insuring different ılary groups on different schedules.

Factors that affect the cost. The following factors affect the preıium on group life insurance:

1. Amount of insurance.
2. Plan of coverage. (See types of coverage at page 764.) Level mount and occupational plans of coverage result in the lowest total remium. Coverage tied to wages or salaries has an adverse effect on he cost because the higher-paid employees have a higher age average. Coverage based on length of service increases the premium more than ny other type of coverage.
3. The conversion privilege. This factor may increase the rate because it increases selectivity against the carrier.
4. Ages of the employees.
5. Hazards of occupation and unfavorable climatic conditions.
6. Physical condition of employees. No medical examination is equired for group life insurance, but a carrier will either reject a ubstandard group or load the premium.
7. Experience rating. Both dividends and rate credits depend on (a) the amount of income received from the account, (b) the actual death claim experience of the employee group, and (c) the length of time the policy has been in force.

In addition to the above, the following factors also affect the cost of a level premium plan:

1. Kind of insurance—whether whole life or limited payment life.
2. Vesting feature.

4. GROUP HEALTH INSURANCE

Need for group health insurance. In the United States, the the term "health insurance" generally applies only to hospitalization and medical and surgical costs, whereas disability insurance applies to the cash payments made to an insured for loss of income as a result of accident or illness. In foreign countries, health insurance covers both medical care and disability payments.

The rapid technical advances in medical science, with the accom-panying rise in the cost of medical training, necessary equipment, an expensive drugs, have placed adequate medical care beyond the finan-cial means of the average employee. Many families find it difficul to meet routine medical expenses; many more find it impossible t meet the expenses of a prolonged or severe illness. Voluntary hos-pitalization and medical care insurance, plus disability insurance, i designed to meet this need of the employee. The logical medium fo promotion of voluntary health insurance plans is the employer, indi-vidually and as a group.

What is a hospitalization plan? A hospitalization plan offer employees protection against expenses incurred by reason of hos-pitalization as a result of nonoccupational accident or illness. Thi protection is a vital part of the effort business is making to discourag a compulsory health program. As in other group insurance, insur-ance companies will insure a changing group of individuals agains hospital expense by means of a single or blanket policy. Althoug policies and contracts may be written to provide unlimited benefits the benefits are usually limited and the employee is responsible fo costs in excess of the stipulated maximum benefits.

The cost of group hospitalization insurance, whether underwritten by insurance companies or by Blue Cross or a similar plan (see page 778), is not great for the benefits derived from it, but it is too grea for the low-income worker. As part of an employee benefit program the employer's responsibility is to inaugurate a hospitalization plan and to pay at least part of the cost.

Hospitalization plans may be classified according to the manner in which benefits are received, as follows:

1. *Cash indemnity plans,* which provide benefits by paying cash or making allowances toward the total amount of the hospital bill. Plans underwritten by insurance companies are of this type.
2. *Service plans,* which provide benefits in terms of services rendered by the hospital. The hospital bill is paid by the plan to the extent provided by the plan. The Blue Cross offers this type of benefit.

(See page 773 for a comparison of the features of these types of plans.)

COMPARISON OF FEATURES OF HOSPITALIZATION PLANS

	Cash Indemnity Plans	*Service Plans*
Daily Benefits	Flat daily rate for stipulated number of days.	Semi-private room for stipulated number of days, with partial benefits for additional period. Daily allowance toward charges for private room.
Special Hospital Services	Specific reimbursement for additional hospital charges, usually based upon daily benefit.	Specified extra hospital services, without limit on cost, but only services specified in the contract are allowed.
Choice of hospitals	Any legally recognized hospital in United States or Canada.	Member hospital. Almost all legally recognized hospitals are member hospitals.
Waiting period	No waiting period except for maternity cases and removal of tonsils or adenoids.	No waiting period except for maternity cases, removal of tonsils or adenoids, and preexisting conditons.
Maternity benefits	Daily benefit payments usually limited to 10, 12, or 14 days.	Number of days for which service is available is reduced.
Tonsils and adenoids	Number of days for which benefits payable limited.	Number of days for which service is available limited.
Out patient service	Excluded, except for an allowance for emergency care after accident or an operation in the hospital.	Excluded, except for an allowance for emergency care after accident or an operation in the hospital.
Exclusions	Workmen's compensation cases, military service-connected disabilites, and plastic operations for cosmetic or beautfying purposes.	Workmen's compensation cases, mental or nervous disorders, hospitalization furnished under Federal or state laws; rest cures, admission primarily for diagnosis or physical therapy.
Female employees	Same benefits as male employees at same rate, but large percentage increases employer's premium.	Same benefits as male employees at same rate.
Dependents	Daily benefit frequently less than for the employee.	Same as for employee.
Termination of employment	Insurance automatically ceases.	Subscriber may continue his membership by paying slightly higher rate direct.

What is a medical care plan? Medical care plans provide benefits for surgical expense, medical (nonsurgical) expense, or surgical and nonsurgical expense, arising from nonoccupational accident or illness. Medical care plans may be classified as follows:

1. *Cash indemnity plans,* which provide benefits in cash in accordance with a "schedule of indemnities." Plans underwritten by insurance companies are of this type.
2. *Service plans,* which provide benefits in terms of physicians services when needed, without additional cost to the employee. The National Health Insurance Plan of Greater New York (HIP) is of this type.
3. *Combination service and cash indemnity plans,* which provide the combination of both cash and service benefits in a single contract. Usually the service feature applies only to a specified income group. Blue Shield plans are of this type.

(See pages 776-777 for a comparison of the features of these types of plans.)

Underwriting group health insurance plans. Group hospitalization plans are generally underwritten by insurance companies and by associations similar to Blue Cross. Blue Cross plans are group hospitalization plans sponsored by hospital associations throughout the United States, Puerto Rico, and Canada. The term "Blue Cross" rarely appears in the names of the plans, which vary from locality to locality, but is used colloquially to refer to a plan having the approval of the Blue Cross Commission of the American Hospital Association.

Medical care plans are underwritten by insurance companies; Blue Shield, which is a counterpart of Blue Cross; and organizations that are a liaison between employee groups and medical groups. The last organization is exemplified by Health Insurance Plan of Greater New York, a nonprofit membership organization founded under the Insurance Law of New York State. HIP solicits membership through employers. It contracts with medical groups to provide comprehensive medical and surgical care for its subscribers. The association pays the medical group so much for each subscriber, rather than for the services performed for each member, thus providing complete care without additional cost to the subscriber. Privately owned medical groups, such as Ross-Loos Medical Group, also furnish prepaid medical care on a per capita rather than fee-for-service basis.

There are also numerous plans sponsored by other organizations, for example, industrial plans, which underwrite both hospitalization and medical care plans, or either. Among the better known are the Consolidated Edison Company's Medical Care Plan, which was started in 1902, and the Endicott Johnson Corporation's Medical Care Program, established in 1918.

Shall dependents be allowed to participate? Under many plans financed entirely by the employer, dependents are not eligible. Under others, the employee may secure coverage for his dependents by paying the additional cost. If the employee contributes to the cost of the plan, coverage of dependents is usually optional with him. The current trend, in keeping with the social concept of adequate medical care for everyone, is to include dependents in the coverage, even when the employer pays the entire cost of the program.

What amount of benefits shall be offered? The benefits provided by hospitalization and medical care plans affect the cost materially. The employer must consider carefully the benefits to be derived in relation to the cost of the plan, both to himself and to his employee.

As there is only one Blue Cross plan available for each area, the employer has no decision to make if he decides that the local Blue Cross plan offers more than a group insurance policy. On the other hand, under a group hospital expense insurance policy, premiums are in direct ratio to benefits. If the employer decides that an insurance company offers more than Blue Cross, he must then determine the minimum amount of benefits that are adequate to insure the success of the hospitalization program for his employees.

With reference to a medical care plan, the employer must first decide whether he wants a surgical expense plan only, or a surgical and nonsurgical expense plan. He must then determine whether the nonsurgical care shall cover a physician's visits to the insured's home and visits by the patient to a physician's office, or be limited to in-hospital cases. Of course, the greater the scope of care, the higher the premium.

How should the plan be financed? Group hospitalization and medical care plans are financed entirely by the employer, entirely by

COMPARISON OF FEATURES OF MEDICAL CARE PLANS

	Cash Indemnity Medical Care Plans	*Combination Service and Cash Indemnity Medical Care Plans*	*Service Medical Care Plans*
Income limit	None	Cash benefits applied as credit to total charges for professional services if income exceeds stated amount.	Premium higher for those earning over a stated amount.
Benefits	Reimbursed for surgical fee up to amount listed in a schedule of operations, but not in excess of actual fee. Reimbursed for stated amount for a certain number of visits. Number per week also limited. First two or three visits usually excluded. Limited reimbursement for additional costs, such as X-rays.	Amount listed in schedule of operations allowed. Limits the allowance per daily visit. First two or three visits usually excluded. Patients whose income exceeds certain amount are responsible for higher fees. Participating physicians agree not to charge patients whose income is below a certain amount a higher fee than that specified in contract. Maximum allowance for X-ray, etc.	No limit to benefits. Medical groups participatng in plan are paid on per capita basis.
Exclusions	Workmen's compensation cases, plastic surgical operations for beautifying purposes excluded. Otherwise all-inclusive, covering chronic conditions, alcoholism, heart conditions and nervous breakdown.	Workmen's compensation cases, dental or nursing services; plastic or cosmetic surgery for condition existing at enrollment; alcoholic or drug addiction; congenital anomalies; drugs, appliances, and eye glasses; functional disorders of the mind or nervous system; rest cures.	Workmen's compensation cases, treatment for drug addiction, acute alcoholism, chronic conditions requiring care in institution other than general hospital, prolonged psychiatric treatment, but not psychiatric advice.
Choice of physician	Any legally qualified physician or surgeon.	Any participating physician. Best physicians in community usually participate.	Subscriber selects a participating *group* of physicians.

Waiting period	For maternity cases, tonsils and adenoids, and known pre-existing conditions.	Usually a 10-month waiting period for maternity cases, 6 months for tonsils and adenoids; sometimes for elective operations and pre-existing conditions.	None.
Maternity benefits	Insured reimbursed up to amount listed in schedule of operations.	Schedule of operations includes obstetric delivery, Caesarean section, abdominal operation for ectopic pregnancy, and miscarriage.	Same complete care that any other medical condition is given.
Tonsils and adenoids	Insured reimbursed up to amount listed in schedule of operations.	Schedule of operations includes removal of tonsils and adenoids.	Complete surgical and medical care for treatment and removal of tonsils and adenoids.
Female employees	Same benefits as male. Cost is higher if employees are predominantly female.	Same benefits as male employees, for same premium.	Same benefits as male employees for same premium.
Dependents	Allowance frequently less than for employee.	Same as for employee.	Same as for employee.
Termination of employment	Insurance automatically ceases.	Subscriber may maintain membership by paying slightly higher rate direct.	Subscriber may convert to an individual policy.

the employees, or jointly by the employer and the employees to b covered. Many insurance companies will not write a policy for company that does not contribute. Some organizations' underwr ing plans require the employer to pay a certain percentage, usual 50 per cent. Otherwise, each company bases its contribution upc its ability and willingness to contribute and upon the need of its en ployees for assistance.

Under many contributory plans, the employer pays all the cost f the individual employee, and the employee pays the additional co for dependents. Frequently the employer will pay all the cost group medical insurance if the employee will first subscribe to th hospitalization plan.

Many hospitalization and medical care plans that result from cc lective bargaining are financed entirely by contributions paid by th employer into a union trust fund, the fund providing the benefit The cost may be a flat weekly, monthly, or annual amount for eac covered worker, a stipulated contribution for each hour worked b the employee, a lump sum, or a percentage of the employer's payrol

Factors that affect cost. Blue Cross and Blue Shield plans i each locality have a definite subscription rate. There are no facto that affect the cost to a particular group. The same is true of oth local plans underwritten by medical groups or associations other tha insurance companies. The service benefits provided by these pla are based upon current charges. If those charges are increased c decreased, the benefits change, and the subscription rates fluctua with the changes.

When an insurance company underwrites the plan, the benefi provided have a greater bearing on the cost than any other singl factor. A high percentage of female employees may increase the pr mium. To a lesser extent, the average age of the employees als affects the premium. The premium rate rarely changes when ho pitalization and medical charges decrease or increase, but the cas indemnity benefit constitutes a larger or smaller proportion of th bill. Each group covered by an insurance company is considered in dividually. If the claim experience in that group is favorable, th carrier returns part of the premium to the employer in the form of dividend, or reduces the rate. Occasionally in plans negotiated b a union, the employer passes part of the dividend to the employe surance company premiums rarely increase from year to year, even the claim experience in a particular group is unfavorable.

Features of hospitalization plans compared. The salient fea-res of the two types of hospitalization plans—cash indemnity, ex-nplified by the policies written by insurance companies, and service ›spitalization plans, exemplified by Blue Cross plans—are compared the chart on page 773.

Features of medical care plans compared. The salient features the three types of medical care plans—cash indemnity plans (ex-nplified by policies written by insurance companies), combination ervice and cash indemnity plans (exemplified by Blue Shield plans), nd service plans (exemplified by Health Insurance Plan of Greater ew York [HIP])—are compared in the chart on pages 776-777.

5. GROUP ACCIDENT AND SICKNESS INSURANCE (TEMPORARY DISABILITY)

What are temporary disability benefits? Benefits paid to work-rs incapacitated because of illness or nonoccupational injury are ariously called "disability benefits," "sick benefits," "sickness and ccident benefits," or "health and nonoccupational accident bene-ts." Temporary disability benefits, by whatever name they are alled, are paid as *compensation for wages* to wage earners who are emporarily physically unable to perform their usual or most recent vork without jeopardizing their recovery. Temporary disability im-plies that the worker will sooner or later be able to return to the abor market.

Need for temporary disability benefits. The need for sick bene-its is not seriously disputed. The growing demands for disability protection made by unions in collective bargaining show the impor-ance that the workers place on this phase of employee welfare. Accident and sickness insurance is often the first form of social insur-ance that companies offer their employees.

The need for sick benefits has appeared less urgent for office work-ers than for factory employees, because many companies have fol-lowed the practice of paying their office employees during short periods of illness. However, company sick leave policies vary widely. Few companies continue their sick leave payments for the full period of a protracted illness. Small companies usually have flexible, formal plans that they adapt to the employee, the type of illne and the length of absence from work. The plans, generally speaki grow less liberal as the number of employees increases. Thus, offi employees, as well as factory workers, need assurance that their comes will not cease when they are disabled.

A few states have laws requiring disability protection for employe and other states are considering the adoption of similar laws.

Benefits. The carefully planned temporary disability program pr vides a benefit too low to induce malingering and yet high enou to relieve the employee of excessive anxiety about loss of incon during illness. Two other phases of disability benefits affect t benefits formula: (1) the payments are tax free and thus bear higher ratio to the employee's income than is apparent, and (2) du ing illness an employee has medical expenses and needs a larger i come than normally. If the plan is contributory, and most of the are, the benefits must be large enough to induce the employee participate. Plans show the following trends:

1. Benefits are on a sliding scale, geared to wages and salary, wi minimum and maximum benefits.
2. The maximum benefit is usually 50 per cent of the weekly wag or salary, not to exceed a stated amount.
3. Benefits are usually paid for 13 or 26 weeks for each disabilit The standard maximum is 13 weeks during any one period of di ability. Provision for longer periods of disability is not particularl important from a practical standpoint, because experience has show that disabilities for more than 13 weeks and for more than one pr tracted disability during a year, are rare. Many employees feel, how ever, that they can "get by" during the shorter period and are i greater need of assistance during the protracted period.
4. The majority of plans provide that the benefits shall begin o the eighth consecutive day of disability caused by illness and on th first day of disability caused by accident.
5. Some plans pay full benefits for a specified period and lesse benefits for a longer period.
6. For employees over 60, benefits are normally limited to a tota number of weeks during any consecutive 12 months, instead of fo each disability.

Recurrent illnesses. Almost all group accident and sickness insur-
ice policies limit the number of weeks for which benefits are pay-
ıle for one continuous period of disability. The question of
hether or not an illness is recurrent is sometimes troublesome, when
ore than two weeks elapse between illnesses. A definite interpreta-
on of what is considered a recurrent illness should be had from the
surance carrier. If less than two weeks of work separate illnesses,
ie second illness is considered recurrent, unless it is entirely un-
lated to the previous disability. If an illness is recurrent, the wait-
ıg period does not apply and benefits are available only for the
eeks remaining unpaid from the last illness.

Disabilities not covered. Insured disability benefits plans do not
over absences resulting from sickness or injury compensable under
orkmen's compensation or occupational disease laws, but they some-
mes supplement the benefits payable under those laws. Many
lans exclude maternity cases and self-inflicted injuries. Although
andard insurance policies are usually broader than plans under-
ritten by the employer, some insurance companies offer policies
ıat contain many limitations for a cut-rate premium. The employer
hould examine the exclusions very carefully to avoid adopting a plan
ıat does not offer his employees the protection he anticipated.

How are claims handled? The insurance company handles all
laims. The employer's only obligation is cooperation with the car-
ier by promptly filling in required forms.

The insurance company requires that it be given written notice
f injury or illness within a specified number of days. Forms fur-
ished by the insurance company must be completed by the emloyee, the employer, and the attending physician. The attending
hysician is expected to file an initial statement of disability and, also,
n interim statement if the employee is not able to return to work
s soon as expected. The practice of private insurance companies
s to pay the claim on the day it is received and each week thereafter
luring disability. The policies usually contain a clause giving the
arrier the right to have a physician examine the employee while a
laim is pending.

Not only is the employer relieved of the burden of handling claims,
ut, if any dissatisfaction arises from the manner in which a claim is
andled, the employee cannot reasonably blame the employer.

Factors that affect cost. Factors that affect the cost of a disal ity insurance program are (1) the provisions of the group poli (2) conditions peculiar to the insured group, and (3) the carrie experience with the account.

Provisions of policy. These provisions of the policy have a dire bearing on the premium:

1. Amount of the weekly benefit.
2. Waiting period before benefits are payable.
3. Length of time for which benefits are payable.
4. Payment of benefits during pregnancy. (Careful study shou be given to the advisability of including this provision.)

In states that have a disability benefits law, the employer has r choice of policy provisions, unless he adopts a more liberal plan tha the law requires.

The insured group. The following conditions peculiar to the i sured group materially affect the premium:

1. Number of employees.
2. Percentage of female employees.
3. Percentage of employees in the higher income brackets.
4. Age and racial groups.

Experience rating. Dividends or rate credits ultimately determin the cost of all group insurance, but there is no guarantee of dividend or rate credits. They are based on the carrier's experience with th account. Therefore, the employer who cuts down on his absente rate cuts down his group health and accident premium.

6. PENSION PLANS

Informal and formal pension plans. Before the Federal incom tax law made it possible for businesses to create pension plans a low cost because of tax deductions for contributions to them, pen sion plans were generally of the informal type. An employer gav to some of his employees, usually those on the supervisory staff anc in other responsible positions, a pension based upon recommenda tions of some individual or board within the organization. Since the granting of the pensions was discretionary, there was usually an absence of guiding principles as to who should obtain a pension, how ge it should be, and how the funds required to pay the allowance ould be accumulated.

The pension plan one thinks of today is a formal plan established l maintained by an employer primarily to provide systematically the payment of definitely determinable benefits to his employees er a period of years, usually for life, after retirement. Retirement nefits generally are measured by, and based on, such factors as rs of service and compensation received by the employees. The ermination of the amount of retirement benefits and the contribu- ns to provide such benefits are not dependent upon profits. The ployer takes on a definite commitment to make payments to the irement fund whether or not there are profits. The pension plans t most businesses establish today are qualified under Section 5(a) of the Internal Revenue Code. It is that kind of pension n that is described in this section.

Advantages of a pension plan. A business gains the following vantages by installing a plan for retiring its employees when they ch a specified retirement age:

1. Superannuated employees are eliminated with resulting econo- ies in operation.
2. Labor turnover is decreased.
3. A better class of workers is attracted.
4. Employee efficiency is increased through elimination of financial orries.
5. The social obligation of the employer is discharged.
6. Public goodwill is promoted.
7. Employer and employee are benefited taxwise.

The business advantages correlate with the advantages to the em- oyee. Nevertheless, the latter may be enumerated separately as llows:

1. Fear of dependent or semi-dependent old age is eliminated.
2. A standard of living is provided for employees that will make tirement more attractive than it would be if the employee had to epend only on the subsistence standard afforded by the Social ecurity Act.
3. A fund is established that may be used as a "cushion" in the vent of termination of employment.

4. In effect, additional compensation is given to the employee t may be taxed at a lower surtax rate because of deferment to a ti when his income will be lower.

5. The death benefits provided by many pension plans incre the employee's estate and aid the employee's family.

6. Thrift among employees is encouraged (in contributory plan

The value of pension plans to small businesses. The advanta previously mentioned apply to small corporations as well as lar For the reasons listed below, a pension plan may be even more sirable in the case of a small firm.

1. A small firm cannot absorb the inefficiency resulting from ra labor turnover as well as the large busniess.

2. A pension plan will assist the small business to compete wi the large corporation where the latter's very bigness may be cons ered as an advantage by the person seeking employment.

3. The financial resources of a large firm may enable it to abso pension liabilities as they accrue. A plan permits the small firm acquire the necessary reserve over a period of time.

4. The small firm frequently is passed from father to son. T pension liabilities that turn up because of the advancing age of e ployees who were hired as young men by the father may be unexpected and unbearable burden to the successor. A pensi plan avoids this.

The income tax benefit to the employer. An employer may d duct amounts contributed to a pension plan or trust *in the year t amounts are contributed,* within certain limitations, if the plan trust satisfies the requirements of Sec. 165(a) of the Internal Reven Code. Because of the current deduction that an employer may tak the cost of the plan is considerably reduced. For instance, at t 1952 rates, the cost of a plan to a corporation may be as little as 18 per cent of its contribution. This is a minimum net cost. Sta income taxes bring the actual cost of the contribution lower.

Income tax benefits for the employee. Employees also bene if the plan or trust qualifies under Sec. 165(a). The employer contributions to such a trust do not constitute taxable income t

* This percentage is higher when there are no excess profits taxes and corpor tion rates are lower.

e employee until distributed or made available to him. At that ne, generally, the employee is in a lower surtax bracket with re- ting tax savings. This tax-saving feature is particularly valuable participating executives and key men of a corporation.

Income tax benefits for the trust. The income of a trust form- g part of a pension plan for the exclusive benefit of employees or eir beneficiaries is exempt from tax at all times if the qualifications requirements prescribed by Sec. 165(a) are satisfied. This is an vantage to the corporation in that smaller contributions are re- ired to accumulate the amount needed for the benefits to be paid ider the plan and to the employees.

Requirements for qualification under Sec. 165(a). The follow- g is an outline of the general and specific requirements for qualifi- tion of a pension plan:

General Requirements

Qualification of Plan

Plan is for exclusive benefit of employees.

Sole purpose of plan is to offer employees (or their beneficiaries) either:
(a) share of the profits of the business, or
(b) an income after retirement.

Plan is permanent.

Plan is communicated to employees.

Qualification of Trust

1. Must be impossible under trust instrument for any of corpus or income to be used other than for exclusive benefit of employees (or their beneficiaries).
2. Contributions must be for the purpose of accumulating funds for distribution to employees (or their beneficiaries) according to plan qualified under Sec. 165(a).
3. Certain information to be filed annually.

Specific Requirements for Qualification

. *Coverage requirements:*

(a) 70 per cent or more of all employees; or
(b) 80 per cent or more of all eligible employees, provided 70 per cent of all employees are eligible; or
(c) special classifications of employees, provided (1) classification does not result in discrimination in favor of officers, stockholders, supervisory or highly paid employees; and (2) commissioner approves classification.

In meeting coverage requirements, eligibility requirements for partici- ation must be set forth.

2. *Contribution and benefit requirements:*
   (a) Integration with social security is required if the plan (1) cludes persons earning $3,600 or less, or (2) applies differe rates of contributions or benefits to first $3,600 of earnings th to amounts over $3,600.
   (b) Other requirements affecting contributions and benefits tou the following subjects:
   (1) ceiling on benefits; (2) employee contributions; (3) ba compensation; (4) increase and decrease in compensation; (benefits based on past service credits; (6) funding of past servi benefits.
3. *Requirements as to other features touch the following subjects:*
   (a) Retirement age; (b) death and supplemental benefits; (c) ve ing; (d) discretionary powers; (e) insurance contracts.
4. *Permanency requirement:*
   Plan must be permanent, but employer may retain right to termina plan at will without necessarily disqualifying it. Right to tern nate appears to mean that plan may be withdrawn only for bu ness necessity.
   Commissioner has power to disallow deduction for all "open" tax yea if he determines that abandoned or curtailed plan did not me permanency requirement.
   If employer terminates plan, trustee should notify Commissioner ar await instructions before distributing trust assets.
5. *Limitations to prevent discrimination on early termination:*
   Restrictions must be placed upon benefits payable to 25 top-sala employees (when plan is established) whose pensions exce $1,500. Apply if plan is terminated within ten years. Maximu contributions which can be used for such employees are great than (1) $20,000, or (2) 20 per cent of annual compensatio or $10,000 whichever is less, times number of years since esta lishment of plan.

Pension advisers. A business executive may turn to the followin institutions, organizations, or individuals for help in planning a pe sion program:

1. Life insurance companies.
2. Trust companies and banks doing a trust business.
3. Pension plan consultants.
4. Consulting actuaries.
5. Insurance agents.
6. Industrial relations consultants.

The business will call upon its attorney at some point in planning pension program. The attorney drafts the necessary papers includ- ; the plan and the trust agreement, if any, and makes the applica- n to the Treasury Department for approval of the plan. The nsion adviser usually cooperates with the attorney in preparing ese papers. The attorney also advises his client about the various deral and state laws that must be considered in creating a pension in.

Usually an executive who has to give serious thought to the pen- on problem of his firm will want to learn something about the bject generally before consulting an adviser. The explanation that llows will serve this purpose.

Types of Pension Plans—Methods of Funding

Methods of funding pension plans. When the employer thinks a type of pension plan suitable for his purpose, he thinks in terms the method of accumulating the funds from which the pension owances will be paid. Which of the following methods he uses pends upon which best fits his needs:

1. Group annuities purchased from an insurance company.
2. Individual policies purchased from an insurance company.
3. Group life retirement on a "group permanent" form, purchased om an insurance company.
4. An uninsured or self-administered plan.
5. Deposit administration plan.
6. Combination of self-administered and insured plans.

A brief explanation is given below of how the funds are accumu- ted under each type of plan and the types of benefits usually of- red under each. Additional information about insured and security- vested or self-administered plans is given in the discussion of cost d business factors to be considered in setting up a pension plan.

The advantages of one type of plan over another are not discussed ere for they exist only in relation to the special circumstances and quirements of the employer. For example, a self-administered lan may be ideal for a corporation with 10,000 employees but en- rely inappropriate for a firm with only 100 employees.

Group annuity plans. Under a pension plan funded throu group annuities, the employer enters into a blanket agreement, means of a master contract with an insurance company, where the contributions to the plan are paid over to the insurance compa to purchase annuities representing the pension benefit. The parti pating employees under a group annuity plan receive a certifica merely outlining the arrangement and benefits. Most insurance co panies, in compliance with state laws, will not issue group annuit unless 25 employees are covered, and they impose the additional quirement that a minimum percentage (usually 75 per cent) of eli ble employees participate. Where the employer is unable to me the minimum requirements, the group annuity plan cannot be use

The employer purchases annually, for each employee participati in the plan, a unit of single premium deferred annuity. This u covers the retirement payment attributable to a particular employe service that year. Each year's purchase is a completed transactic only one premium payment is made on the contract. This premiu is based on the employee's sex and age at the time the annuity purchased. Premium rates are usually guaranteed for five-year p riods. Thus, on a single premium basis, even if there were no i creases in the number of participants in the plan or in compensatio the aggregate future service contributions would increase each ye because of the increase in the employee's age. Such a plan, the calls for a low initial contribution with increasing costs until th average age of the group is gradually stabilized. Also, the rate increase will be reduced by severance of employment before retir ment, since the money theretofore contributed will become a cred reducing the company's contributions in the year in which the en ployee leaves.

If required by the plan, additional units of annuity may be pu chased to provide retirement benefits based upon past services re dered by the employee. The group annuity method is sufficientl flexible to permit the employer to purchase these past service annu ties whenever his financial condition permits. Upon retirement each employee, the sum of all the separately purchased units of d ferred annuity will equal the total amount of pension payable to hir

The usual group annuity contract gives only retirement income, s far as employer contributions are concerned.

Individual policy plans. Under the individual retirement annuity ın, the employer purchases a separate contract in the name of each vered employee in an amount that will provide the retirement come contemplated. A minimum number of employees need not covered. This feature commends the individual retirement anity plan to the small employer.

The annual premium retirement annuity is generally used under e individual retirement annuity plan, although the single premium pe is available. Many insurance companies, however, will not issue aight retirement annuities (except in case of uninsurables) but sist that, for a small additional premium, life insurance protection purchased as well. A policy combining these benefits is often lled a "retirement income" or "insurance with income" policy. A pical contract offers about $1,000 to $1,500 of insurance for each 0.00 of monthly retirement income. Such policies provide a sizole death benefit, a feature lacking in the plain annuity.

In the individual policy plan, the level premium deferred annuity ually used provides an income that will begin at a future specified ate, equal to the amount of annuity expected to be due under the an if service is continued to retirement age. The premium, once tablished, is fixed for employees for whom contracts were purased, except for changes because of additional units purchased on count of increase in compensation or reductions due to decrease in ompensation. Payment of premiums continues until the time for ayment of the retirement income arrives. Under such a plan, thereore, the annual cost is constant, not taking into consideration deaths, verance of employment, or retirement. When these events occur, is safe to assume that the new employees hired to take their places ill be younger, and the contributions or premiums will tend to ecline.

Group permanent plans. Group life retirement plans on "group ermanent" form combine group life insurance with group annuities to one contract on a level premium basis, drawn to meet the needs f the employer. Though written on a group basis, this method gives ıbstantially the same type of benefits as individual policies.

A master contract, the Group Policy, is entered into between the mployer and the insurance company, and each employee is given a rinted group certificate containing a summary of the benefits and of the provisions of the group permanent contract. The master c- tract contains all the provisions of the plan. The underlying prin ples of group insurance are applied in group permanent contrac Thus, there are no medical examinations except where the insura exceeds a certain amount, and all employees are covered under same type of contract.

The group permanent plan is available where there are at le 50 eligible employees and at least $250,000 face amount of insuran The plan is available not only on a group income endowment ba but on an ordinary life basis, on a paid-up insurance basis, and other endowment bases.

Contracts are offered on either a contributory or noncontribut basis. The employer is required to pay at least 25 per cent of t cost of the insurance. If employees contribute, at least 75 per ce of those eligible must apply before the insurance can be made eff tive.

The maximum future premium cost of the plan is partially guara teed, since the original rate remains the same for all insurance effect when the plan starts and all that is added during the next fi years. The employer gets back as dividends any savings because low acquisition costs and the actual experience of the insured grou Such dividends must, however, be applied to reduction of that next year's premiums.

The employee cannot select the amount of insurance he wants. must be determined by a formula based upon conditions of emplo ment. The average pension formula meets these conditions. Whe the income endowment form of group permanent contract is use insurance is usually issued at the rate of $1,000 per $10.00 of month retirement income, up to a certain maximum amount of insuranc

Uninsured, security-invested, or self-administered pensio plans. The uninsured, security-invested, or self-administered pensic plan invariably takes the form of a pension trust or pension plan an trust under which the employer makes contributions to the trus These contributions or funds are invested by the trustee as prescribe in the trust agreement. The accumulations of the corpus and th income therefrom are used to make the pension payments called fc by the plan or trust. The payments of benefits are made eithe directly by the trustee, or the accumulated funds are used to pu ase annuities from an insurance company under which payments e made to the retired employees. If annuities are purchased, the igle premium immediate annuity is used. It provides an income at commences immediately. The usual self-administered plan proles only for retirement income for life beginning at the retirement e, though other benefits may be included.

The usual arrangement is to have two instruments: the plan and e trust agreement. The plan contains the eligibility requirements, nefit provisions, rights of participants on termination of employent, and the like. The trust agreement between the employer and e trustee defines the powers and duties of the trustee as to investent and management of the pension funds.

In the security-invested plan, the annual cost of future service enefits can be computed either under the step-up method described r single premium deferred annuities (see page 788) or under the vel contribution method described for individual policy plans. The nount that must be contributed is determined by an independent tuary retained by the employer. In determining the cost, the tuary usually takes into account death rates, interest rates, employee rnover, and similar factors—the same factors considered by the inrance company actuaries. If the actuarial computations fall short providing the benefits contemplated by the plan, the employer ust either make additional payments or scale down the benefits.

Under some self-administered plans arranged through collective argaining, no contributions are made until an employee actually tires. At that time a sum sufficient to pay the retired employee a esignated pension for life is deposited with the trustee. Under ese plans an employee becomes eligible when he reaches retirement ge and has completed the required number of years of service.

Deposit administration plan. The deposit administration plan is n outgrowth of the more commonly used group annuity contract see page 788). The essential difference is that neither employer or employee contributions, if any, are used at the outset to buy eferred annuities. Instead, the contributions are deposited with the isurance company in an undivided account at guaranteed interest tes (usually 2 per cent or 2¼ per cent). The amount of each anual employer deposit is determined by an actuary, just as in a elf-administered trustee plan. When an employee retires, a single premium immediate annuity is bought for him and the cost charged against the deposit account.

The advantages claimed for deposit administration are that it gi the employer the flexibility of a trustee noninsured plan and t characteristic safety of principal and guaranteed earnings of the sured plan.

Combination of self-administered and insured plans. Thou each of the usual types of plans has a degree of flexibility, in so cases a combination of types may best fit the employer's nee Combination plans, however, have been used only to a limited tent. The following combinations are mentioned merely to illustra the variety of combinations that might be worked out in solving company's pension problems: (1) self-administered plan for wa earners and individual annuity contracts for salaried employees; (self-administered plan for earnings of $3,600 or less and individual group annuities for earnings in excess of $3,600; (3) group annui to provide retirement benefits for current and future service and dividual annuities for past service, or *vice versa;* (4) group annui for past service benefits and self-administered for future service; (self-administered to purchase ordinary life insurance for insurab employees and annuities for those who are not insurable, with conv sion of the life policies at retirement age into annuities at rat guaranteed when the policies were first issued.

Business and Cost Considerations

Matters to be considered. Pension plans must be built to fit t company's specific pension problems; they must be adjusted to the siz type, and financial situation of the company, as well as to the nee of the employees. In setting up such a pension plan, the employer concerned with two main points: (1) what is best for the busines and (2) what it will cost. Some of the matters that must be consi ered in creating a plan affect the cost; others do not. The followin points have a relation to cost. Those that do not affect cost a treated at page 802.

1. Should employees contribute to the plan?
2. What eligibility requirements should be set up?
3. What retirement age should be selected?

4. What should be the amount of retirement benefits?
5. Should credit be given for past service?
6. What vesting should be provided—that is, what benefits shall offered on termination of service before retirement?
7. What death benefits should be provided by the plan?
8. What disability benefits should be offered?
9. Should mortality be discounted in advance?
10. Should severance from employment be discounted in advance?
11. How will interest rates affect the cost of the plan?

The consideration of any of the above factors may be influenced what may and may not be done under Sec. 165(a), dealing with alification of plans, and Sec. 23(p), dealing with deduction of con-butions to a plan, of the Internal Revenue Code, and the regula-ns and rulings that interpret the law. The brief explanation that llows of each of the considerations will merely introduce the reader the importance of the factor from the standpoint of costs and mpany policy, for space does not permit an exhaustive explanation.

Contributory versus noncontributory plans. The company may y the entire cost of the plan or the employees may contribute. nployee contributions may be used either to reduce the cost to the nployer or to increase the benefits under the plan.

Before deciding on whether or not a pension plan shall be con-ibutory, factors such as the following must be considered in the ght of the corporation's own problems and policies.

1. What are the advantages of a contributory plan?
2. What are the advantages of a noncontributory plan?
3. How will the employees react?
4. Will employee contributions conflict with any state law or labor nion agreement?
5. If the plan is to be negotiated with a labor union, how will the nployer overcome possible union opposition to contributions by nployees?

Eligibility requirements. The number of employees participat-ng in a plan will affect the cost. To keep the cost within bounds, the lan may provide for the following types of eligibility requirements.

1. *Years of service.* Employees must work for the company a cer-in length of time before they are eligible to participate. The maxi-

mum service period usually required is five years. On the other e of the scale, some noncontributory plans have no service requireme The waiting period may be affected by the type of plan. In insu plans, the tendency is to favor long waiting periods for eligibi because taking employees into the plan and then dropping them cause of termination of employment adds to the cost of the plan. self-administered plans the rate of employee turnover makes less ferference in the cost of the plan. In plans to be negotiated with labor union, many interrelated factors may have to be considered fixing the years of service requirement. For example, if the cost the plan is to be taken into account in settling a wage increase, eli bility provisions may have to be loosened to permit more gene participation in the plan.

2. *Age.* Employees must attain a certain age before they are eli ble. The purpose of this restriction is to avoid including young e ployees among whom turnover is greatest. The most restrictive a requirement is 35. Participation at age 30 or younger is most usu If the age is set too high, the limit may cause discrimination in fav of older and higher-paid employees, thus disqualifying the plan.

Under certain types of plans arranged under collective bargainin the question of age at which an employee becomes eligible to parti pate is relatively unimportant because no employee is eligible befo he reaches retirement age.

3. *Type of work.* For example, the plan may be restricted to cle cal and salaried workers if there is a satisfactory reason for th discrimination, such as heavier turnover among the other worke In the light of the growing interest of unions in negotiated pensio plans, the employer may have to consider whether there should b one plan covering all of his employees, or a plan for nonunion em ployees only, or for union employees only.

4. *Earnings.* For example, eligibility may be limited to those ear ing over $3,600 in order to give them additional benefits not provide by social security. The postwar trend was away from such plans i favor of plans covering all or substantially all of the employees.

Retirement age. The age at which employees are retired varie with industries and conditions. The usual retirement age for bot men and women is 65, but the retirement of women at 60 is no unusual.

In some occupations, age alone is not always a sound basis for irement—years worked must also be considered. This is particuly true in businesses that hire older persons because of required kground and experience, or younger persons either for "steppingne" jobs or to fill jobs that require a physical endurance that cant be maintained until 65.

A plan may provide for any reasonable optional early retirement e, with or without the consent of the employer, and for the paynt of benefits at such early retirement age. The early retirement ovisions usually call for attainment of a certain age, completion of ertain number of years of service, or both.

The cost of a plan is increased when, at the inception of the plan, any of the employees are within a few years of retirement. The oblem of the overage employee can be handled in several ways—rough past service credits, supplemental benefits, exclusion from e plan, and provision on an informal basis.

In pension plans to be negotiated with labor unions, retirement e is one of the factors that will present problems not encountered non-negotiated plans. Unions may require that when an employee aches normal retirement age, he, not the employer, shall decide nether he *must* retire. Many employers will resist such a provion because it tends to defeat one of the objectives of a pension plan to remove overage employees from the payroll without hardship. negotiated plans, therefore, more options may have to be available the employee in determining his retirement date.

Retirement benefits. Most companies approach the question of tirement benefits, which is the heart of any pension plan, with me idea of what the company can afford to spend on a plan and hat it considers adequate retirement benefits. The company may ecide to raise the amount that it expected to spend because it would ot produce sufficient benefits. It may decide upon a particular pe of plan because that will yield more retirement benefits than nother type for the same amount of contributions. Thus, the principal elements to be considered in determining the amount of enefits are the needs of the employees and the amount of contribuons or cost. In addition, the limitations imposed by the tax law ust be considered if the plan is to be qualified. The principal limiation is that the plan must not discriminate as to contributions or benefits in favor of officers, shareholders, supervisory or highly cc pensated employees as against other employees whether within plan or not.

Generally, retirement benefits are paid in the form of a pensi though the entire payment could be made in one lump sum. A lu sum payment is rarely used since it is disadvantageous from a viewpoint and makes possible a squandering of the benefits by t employee.

The plan must set forth a formula under which the employe retirement benefits will be calculated. The choice of a formula pends upon the individual circumstances. The most generally us future service benefit formulae produce benefits based on the e ployee's earnings and years of service, as explained below.

In plans to be negotiated by unions, the employer must be prepa to face a union request for a fixed benefit such as $50, $75, or $1 a month, or a request for benefits that would give employees wi say, 20 years of service the same benefits as those with 40 years service. It must be prepared to answer any demand for minimu benefits if it sees in such a provision a source of contention in su sequent negotiations. Other special problems may arise in negoti ing plans. For example, since benefits are usually based on earnin the method of determining the employee's basic earnings, which complicated by overtime and other factors, must be ironed out.

Pension benefit formulae. The following explanation of bene formulae shows the popularity of each in recent years.

Definite or fixed benefit formula. The employee receives a p centage of each year's compensation while he is a participant in t plan. In recent years, this type of benefit formula has been us most extensively. Most plans accrue benefits ranging from ¾ to per cent on the first $3,000 of annual compensation, and at ra ranging from 1½ per cent to 2 per cent on compensation over $3,0(Under this plan, there is generally a division between past and futu service. If benefits are given for service rendered prior to the cr tion of the plan, a larger percentage for future service may be use or a separate percentage may be used for past service credit. T past service benefit is normally based on compensation at the tin the plan becomes effective.

Example. John Smith joined the company when he was 30. He now 40 and is due to retire in 25 years. If the formula uses a 2 per cent figure for future years and 1 per cent for the past service, ith's pension, based on a salary of $2,000, would be:

$$\begin{aligned} 1\tfrac{1}{2}\% \times \$2{,}000 \times 25 \text{ years} &= \$750 \\ 1\ \% \times \$2{,}000 \times 10 \text{ years} &= 200 \\ \hline & \$950 \text{ annually} \end{aligned}$$

Smith would also be entitled to social security benefits each year. the employer wanted to correlate his plan with social security, a aller annuity would be provided by the plan.

Flat percentage of compensation. The employee receives a retire- ent benefit equal to a fixed percentage of compensation, generally e average compensation for a ten-year period ending at retirement five years prior to retirement. Under such a formula, a higher pen- on benefit may accrue because the last years of service are usually ars of highest compensation. Thus, a 30 per cent pension figured compensation during the years of greatest income might yield gher retirement benefits than a formula of 1½ per cent per year for) years (total 45 per cent) based on average compensation for the tire 30 years.

The flat percentage formula frequently may be unfair inasmuch length of service is not a factor in computing the pension. All nployees earning the same salary, regardless of length of service, ceive the same retirement benefits.

This type of formula has been second in frequency of use in recent ars.

Money purchase plan. Under this type of plan, the employer de- des to contribute a specified or level percentage of the employee's nnual salary. The retirement benefit is the sum that the fixed con- ibutions by the employer and the employee (if it is contributory) ill fund. Recent studies of pension plan provisions indicate that e money purchase plan is on the way out.

Other formulae. Variations and combinations of the formulae ex- lained above are sometimes found in pension plans. Also, benefits ay be based in part on profit-sharing under a supplemental profit- haring retirement plan. Or a plan may provide for a flat dollar ension, without regard to earnings or years of service.

Past service benefits. The main purpose of granting past serv benefits is to enable older employees who were with the company number of years prior to establishment of the plan to obtain bene commensurate with their salary. Obviously, if an employee has n many years to serve before reaching retirement age, contributic made for the comparatively short period of future service will n be adequate to build up a satisfactory pension.

The extent to which benefits will be offered for past service is go erned by two factors: cost and limitations necessary to meet the quirements of the law and regulations.

Cost. The more credit for past service, the more costly the pla Costs may be limited, however, in a number of ways, such as (1) not giving credit for years of service prior to a specified age or da (2) by placing a limit on the number of years for which prior servi credit shall be granted; (3) by applying the pension rate for pa service credit to earnings in excess of a certain amount; (4) by usi graduated rates of credit for past service; for example, 1 per cent the first $3,600 and ¾ per cent of the amount over $3,600 of the e ployee's past annual compensation when the plan went into effec

Meeting requirements of the law. The plan must not result discrimination in favor of officers, shareholders, supervisors, or high compensated employees.

Benefits on termination of employment—vesting. More an more plans are providing that participating employees shall acqui certain rights or interests in the employer's contributions to the pla prior to retirement. These vested rights take the form of severanc benefits and death benefits.

In arriving at the severance benefit provisions, the employer mu decide: (1) whether there shall be immediate or deferred vestin (2) the portion of the employer's contributions that shall vest; (3 the form of vesting.

Time element. Usually vesting is deferred until the employee ha satisfied certain conditions. The most common of these are comple tion of a certain number of years of service, say 5, 10, 15 or more attainment of a certain age; a service and age requirement; a certai numbers of years' participation in the plan; a service and participa tion requirement; an age, service and participation requirement; te mination within a certain number of years of retirement. Occasion y, in plans that have no special provision for disability benefits, e employer's contributions vest when an employee becomes totally sabled.

Extent of vesting. A 100 per cent vesting means that all of the nployer's contributions are vested if the employee has satisfied the e, service, and other requirements. Usually, however, 100 per cent sting occurs only after a certain number of years of service. Thus, per cent of the employer's contributions may vest if severance curs 5 years after service begins, 50 per cent if after 10 years, 75 per nt if after 15 years, and 100 per cent if after 20 years.

Form of vesting. The plan may provide for immediate payment vested rights on severance or for payment only at the normal re-rement age. The type of plan and personnel policies must be con-dered. No employer wants to so liberalize the vesting provisions to encourage termination of employment.

In contributory plans, the employee's contributions are returned to im upon severance of employment, usually with interest.

Death benefits. The provisions to be made in a plan for the pay-ent of death benefits are generally governed by three factors: (1) Whether or not plan is contributory; (2) how benefits paid from em-loyer's contributions will affect cost; (3) what type of plan is used.

Contributory plans. These plans always provide for a return of le employee's contributions if he dies before retirement. Usually, lso, in the event of death after retirement, employee's contributions ss retirement annuity payments already made will be returned to le employee's beneficiaries. These are the minimum provisions in contributory plan. Additional benefits may be provided from the mployer's contributions.

Death benefits from employer's contributions—costs. In the event f death before retirement, all or a portion of the employer's contri-utions may be turned over to the beneficiary of the employee. As o death benefits after retirement, the plan may provide that the re-irement income shall cease entirely or that the balance of the pay-nents may be made to a beneficiary for a specified time. Under ome plans, the employee may have the privilege of taking an option hat permits payment of a lifetime annuity to his wife in the event f his early death after retirement. In that case, the employee gets smaller adjusted monthly income during his retirement. This arrangement makes it especially important for the corporation to co sider the need for death benefits prior to retirement. The followi example illustrates the problem.

Example. Two men were employed about the same time and bo served many years. One retired at age 65, and died 3 months lat His surviving wife receives a substantial pension for the rest of h life. The other died at age 64. His wife receives nothing from t employer's contributions. The unhealthy effect on employee mora of this situation is obvious. Clearly, the more substantial the dea benefits, the more costly the plan.

Type of plan. Some types of plans are more suitable for providi death benefits than others. An individual annuity pension pla which uses retirement income or retirement annuity contracts, aut matically provides for death benefits. The usual group annuity pla provides for no death benefits. The self-administered plan may, b in many cases does not, provide for death benefits. Where dea benefits are not an integral part of the pension plan, the corporatio usually carries group life insurance.

Disability benefits. Disability benefits usually include paymen to employees upon permanent physical disability. Insured plans ge erally do not provide for such benefits. Self-administered plans len themselves to disability benefits. In working out the provisions, tl company must consider such factors as the occupational hazards, tl company's experience with disability cases, the amount of disabili benefits that can be paid, the period of payment, and the costs th will be added by including a suitable disability provision.

The availability of casualty coverages, such as group accident an health and group hospitalization (see page 771), should be consi ered in connection with a study of disability features in a pensio plan.

Discounting for mortality. Contributions to a pension plan a made on one of two bases. (1) The employer may estimate, usin mortality tables, the number of employees who are likely to die b fore reaching retirement age and make contributions on the basis the number of employees who will live to retirement age. This the usual procedure and is known as advance discounting for th effects of mortality. The contributions paid under this basis woul be fully deductible in the year made, subject to actuarial check a the factors used. (2) The employer may assume that all of his ıployees covered by the plan will live to retirement age. If any ıployee dies before retirement age, contributions that were made his behalf and not used as death benefits are deducted from conbutions made thereafter for the surviving employees. Contribuıns made under this basis would not be fully deductible currently, : the part that represents the cost of the "reversionary benefits" ould be disallowed. However, these disallowed excess contribuıns, when released through the death of the employee, would rve to reduce contributions required at future dates, at which time ey would be allowable as extra deductions under the carry-over ovisions of the tax law.

Discounting for severance. Every company that establishes a an loses some of its participants through severance of employment. ı determining the cost of a plan, the company has the option of scounting for severance of employment or not.

If there is a discounting for severance, an estimate is made in lvance of the number of employees who will leave before reaching tirement age. The process involves actuarial computations from me to time, taking into consideration the chances from year to ear of employees continuing in service. The effect of discounting or anticipated separations is to reduce the initial cost of the plan.

If there is no discounting for severance, adjustment is made at the me of actual severance. The adjustment involves deducting from iture contributions the amount of contributions, not otherwise onsumed in severance benefits, previously made on behalf of the mployees who have terminated employment.

Insured plans do not discount for severance; self-administered lans sometimes do.

Interest rates and costs. In a self-administered plan, the trust ınd will earn interest, and those earnings, together with the conributions, will be used to pay the benefits required under the plan. or purposes of arriving at allowable tax deductions, all calculations ıust consider anticipated interest. The higher the rate of interest ssumed, the lower will be the estimated amount of contributions equired to meet the benefits; conversely, the lower the rate of inerest assumed, the higher the contributions. A conservative rate f interest is generally chosen. The Treasury Department is currently allowing the assumption of a rate of interest as low as 2 p cent.

In an insured plan, the employer is not directly concerned wi interest rates. The premiums set by the insurance company ta into consideration the interest factor.

Some non-cost considerations. In addition to the cost facto just discussed, the employer must consider such factors as the follo ing: (1) the appointment of a pension committee; (2) the need f setting up a trust; (3) telling employees about the pension plan.

Pension committee. Most formalized pension plans have a pe sion committee, sometimes called a "retirement committee" or "r tirement board," to administer the operation of the plan. Th committee, which is appointed by the board of directors, usual comprises three to five members, generally officers of the corpor tion. Its duties are set forth in the plan.

The need for a trust. No trust instrument is ordinarily used und the group annuity plan, or a group permanent plan. Under th individual policy plan, a trust is usually used. In self-administere plans, a trust is invariably used.

Telling employees about the pension plan. To qualify, a pla must be communicated to the employees. Most corporations us employee meetings, announcement letters, booklets, and individua conferences to acquaint their employees with the installation of plan and to show how it works. Press releases, particularly in sma towns or where the company is one of the mainstays of the distric may be helpful in making the general public aware of the plan an in gaining public goodwill.

Because the plan benefits are long range and deferred, the em ployee does not forever remain conscious of the fact that the pla really represents a savings account or increase in pay for him. Fo this reason, opportunities for republicizing the plan should not b overlooked.

7. PROFIT-SHARING PLANS WITH DEFERRED BENEFITS

Type of profit-sharing plans to be discussed. This section ex plains profit-sharing plans that meet the requirements of Sectio 165(a) of the Internal Revenue Code. They are known as tax empt profit-sharing trusts. Such a profit-sharing plan is one esolished and maintained by an employer to provide for participan in his profits, by his employees or their beneficiaries, based on a finite predetermined formula for determining the profits to be ared and a definite predetermined formula for *deferred distribution* the benefits. Distribution of the funds accumulated under the an takes place after a fixed number of years, the attainment of a ated age, or upon the prior occurrence of some event such as illss, disability, retirement, death, or severance of employment.

The employer must divest himself of all interest in the profitaring fund. By placing the fund in trust complete divestiture is sured. Therefore, profit-sharing plans usually call for the setting of a trust. The creation of a trust requires the drafting of a trust greement between the employer and the trustee or trustees. This strument is drawn by the employer with the aid of counsel. The ustee may be an individual or a corporate trustee. Because the ontinuous investment process which takes place in all substantial usts is best handled by an organization equipped and staffed to lminister the detailed operations of the trust, a corporate trustee is enerally selected.

Advantages of a deferred profit-sharing plan. A business gains he following advantages by installing a deferred profit-sharing plan:

1. Employee efficiency is increased. Since contributions depend irectly on the profits the employer makes, the employee knows that e will benefit *only* if he exerts himself to help his employer create rofit.
2. Labor turnover is decreased.
3. The employer makes no fixed commitment. The profit-sharing lan continues to exist regardless of amount of profit, but contribuons vary.
4. Profit-sharing serves as a dismissal wage, if distributions are ade at termination of employment.
5. The plan attracts a better class of workers, promotes public oodwill, and fulfills a social obligation of the employer.
6. Employee satisfaction is high.
7. Employer and employee are benefited tax-wise if the plan is pproved.

A deferred profit-sharing plan has a striking appeal to employe
from the outset because:

1. Generally it costs them absolutely nothing; there are no e
ployee contributions and hence no deductions from pay checks.
2. They see in the plan a means of obtaining deferred salary
creases at a time when present increases are subjected to high inco
taxes.
3. They can look forward to receiving some day a much larger su
of money than they would be likely to accumulate by themselves.
4. They like the idea that their shares may be immediately ava
able if they are disabled, retire, or die.

With these advantages so obviously apparent to employees, ev
the youngest person in the company can be enthusiastic about t
plan.

Features of deferred profit-sharing and pension plans co pared. The salient features of each type of plan, in its "pure" sta may be compared as follows:

Profit-sharing plan	*Pension plan*
(1) Provides a share of pre-retirement company profits as additional compensation, payable in whole or in part at retirement.	(1) Provides income after reti ment not based on profits.
(2) Cash disbursements may be made at any predetermined time.	(2) Cash disbursements before tirement generally are ma only for reasons of death, cident, sickness or disability
(3) Employer's contributions are made from profit. The contributions vary in amount depending upon amount of profit and the contribution formula of the plan.	(3) Employer's contributions co stitute an operating expen item. The contributions a not in proportion to profi but may be a fixed amount, such amount as is necessary provide certain benefits.

When distribution is made at retirement, the amount in the fund determines what income or cash will be provided.	(4) Except in the money-purchase type of plan (see page 797), the pension to be paid determines the contribution made.
Employees generally do not contribute.	(5) Employees contribute under approximately 50% of plans.
Where distribution is made on severance of employment, the payment acts as a "cushion" until the employee secures another job.	(6) While distribution on severance of employment may be made, this is not the main purpose of a pension plan. It is only an incidental function.

Income tax benefits for the employer and employee. An em- ɔyer who establishes a profit-sharing plan that meets the require- ːnts of Section 165(a) of the Internal Revenue Code may benefit ː-wise through deductibility of the contributions in arriving at the ːome tax. The law limits the normal deduction to 15 per cent of e payroll of the officers and employees who are members of the ın. However, if any year's contribution is less than 15 per cent of e payroll, the difference may be carried over to years when profits rmit a contribution of more than 15 per cent of the payroll.

Employees also benefit if the profit-sharing plan or trust qualifies ıder Section 165(a). The employer's contributions to the profit- aring trust do not constitute taxable income to the employee until stributed or made available to him. If the distribution is made to m within one taxable year, because of separation from service, it is xable as a gain from the sale or exchange of a capital asset held for ıem than six months. If the distribution is not paid in one year ıt over several years, it is not treated as a long term gain.

The income of the profit-sharing *trust* for the exclusive benefit of nployees or their beneficiaries is exempt from tax at all times if the quirements prescribed by Section 165(a) are satisfied.

Illustration of tax advantages. Any illustration of tax advantages f a profit-sharing plan must necessarily be based on assumptions of a ırticular profit situation and tax rates existing at the time . The lustrations are offered to show a method by which any business can etermine what the tax advantage will be to itself and to any par- cipant in the plan, whether he is an officer, executive, or typical nployee. The higher the income tax rates, the greater the tax

savings. The rates used in the following examples are those wh
were in existence at the time the computation was made.

Example of tax advantages to a corporation. Let us take a ty cal small corporation—call it the X Y Corporation—and its stoc holder-executives. Assume two situations:

Situation 1: The corporation has no profit-sharing trust.
Situation 2: The corporation has a tax-exempt profit-sharing tru

The essential features of this profit-sharing plan are:

1. All officers and employees are members.
2. The corporation agrees to contribute 25 per cent of each yea profits before taxes, but in no event more than the amount deduc ble on its tax return.
3. Individual accounts are set up under the plan for each membe The company contribution each year is allocated to these accounts direct proportion to annual salaries. At the end of each year th trust earnings, which are tax-exempt, are apportioned to the accoun of the members.
4. Members can draw down their entire shares if they retire for ag or disability.* Upon the death of any member while employed, h share is paid over to the beneficiary; or if he has not designated beneficiary, then to his estate.
5. Each year of membership entitles a member to a "vested right in 10 per cent of his account. Thus, if he leaves before 10 years c membership he forfeits part of his account. The forfeited part i then redistributed among the accounts of the remaining member.

The corporation's profits for the year before taxes were $60,00(It had an excess profits credit of $40,000 and a payroll of $85,00(Thus, 25 per cent of profits before taxes was $15,000. However, 1 per cent of payroll was $12,750. Accordingly, the year's contributio to the plan was $12,750, the lesser of the two figures.

The following table shows that it actually cost the corporation onl $2,295 to make the contribution of $12,750:

---

* The example assumes that there are no wage stabilization regulations tha prevent lump-sum distributions.

	No Plan	With a Plan
Profits before taxes	$60,000	$60,000
Contribution to plan	....	12,750
Income subject to tax	$60,000	$47,250
Normal tax and surtax	25,700	19,070
Income after normal tax and surtax	$34,300	$28,180
Excess profits tax	6,000	2,175
Income after taxes	$28,300	$26,005

(The actual cost of the contribution is $28,300 less $26,005, or $2,295)

Example of tax advantages to an executive. Now let's see how ne executives of X Y Corporation fare, first, without the profit-aring plan, and second, with the plan:

J.A., the president, is 40, married, with two children. He owns 50 er cent of the stock. His brother owns the rest.

J.A. draws an annual salary of $12,000 and has additional income f $3,200 from investments. Without the profit-sharing plan his ividends from the company for the year in question would have een $7,150 and with the profit-sharing plan, $6,000. His wife has o income of her own. Living expenses took $11,000 in the particu-ar year. What was left went into common stocks yielding an aver-ge of 5 per cent. His brother's financial picture is much the same.

	No Plan	With a Plan
J.A.'s income for the year before tax	$22,350	$21,200
Income tax (standard deduction)	5,513	5,076
Income after taxes	$16,837	$16,124
Living expenses	11,000	11,000
Available for private investments	$5,837	$5,124
Allocation for year in profit-sharing plan	....	1,800

Thus, the profit-sharing plan cut J.A.'s funds for private investment that year by $713. In return, however, J.A. has $1,800 earning income in a tax-exempt trust. And the trust also has $10,950 in the accounts of the other employees.

Let's see what would happen if tax rates remain the same and t events assumed above repeat themselves year after year:

Investment yield. We assume that J.A.'s private investmer would earn 5 per cent a year. That, however, is before taxes. Ev under a joint return and the income splitting technique, J.A.'s t tax bracket is 38 per cent. He will be in a higher bracket in a ye or so, but for our purposes assume it stays at 38 per cent. So l net return is 3.1 per cent.

And let's assume that the profit-sharing trust funds also yield per cent. However, that is a net return, because the trust is ta exempt. So J.A. gets off to a head start under the trust:

1. He has $1,800 of principal added each year to his profit-sharir fund at an annual cost of $713 in funds for private investment.
2. The trust investments earn a net of 5 per cent instead of a net 3.1 per cent on his own investments.

Forfeitures. However, there is another important factor. In ou example, the employee has to be a member of the plan for ten yea before his rights are fully vested. And if he leaves before 10 years membership are up, he forfeits part of his fund to the other em ployees. Let's assume—very conservatively—that forfeitures swe J.A.'s account each year by only 2 per cent. That brings each year "yield" up to 7 per cent.

Let's trace the two funds ($713 a year in a private investment func as against $1,800 a year in the profit-sharing account) throug twenty-five years, when J.A. becomes 65 years old and plans to retir

Amount After	*Private Fund*	*Profit-sharing Fund*
5 years	$4,000	$11,100
10 years	8,500	26,600
15 years	13,800	48,400
20 years	20,000	78,000
25 years	27,200	121,800

Amount after all taxes. Note that the taxes will have been pai on the private fund. That is not true of the profit-sharing func When J.A. draws down his account at age 65, he presumably ca treat the entire sum as long-term capital gain. That means, at rate in effect in this illustration, that the tax cannot be greater than 2 per cent. Thus, J.A. will have left, *after taxes,* the sum of $90,132–

ıich is $62,932, or 230 per cent *more* than he would have had withıt the profit-sharing plan.

If the corporation had not been subject to excess profits taxes, the fference between the private fund and the profit-sharing fund ɔuld not be so great, of course, but it would still be substantial.

Requirements for qualification under Sec. 165(a). All of the quirements for qualification given at page 785 for pension plans ɔply to profit-sharing plans. In addition, profit-sharing plans must ave a definite formula for (1) profits to be shared, and (2) for disibution of contributions among participants.

Considerations in Creating a Profit-Sharing Plan

Matters to be considered in setting up a profit-sharing plan. 'he following matters must be considered by the employer in setting p a profit-sharing plan:

1. What eligibility requirements shall be set up?
2. What percentage of profits shall be shared with the employee?
3. How shall profits be allocated among employees?
4. What vesting shall be provided? That is, what forfeitures will ɔccur on termination of employment?
5. What provisions shall be made for distribution of participants' hares?
6. Shall participants be informed of the value of their interests in he plan?
7. Shall the employer set up an advisory committee?
8. How shall the trust funds be invested?

The consideration of any of the above factors may be influenced by what may and what may not be done under Section 165(a) of the Internal Revenue Code and Section 23(p), which relates to the deduction allowed for contributions to the fund. The discussion that follows is merely to indicate in a general way how these considerations might be resolved.

Eligibility requirements. The question of which employees shall be eligible to participate in a profit-sharing arrangement is primarily a matter of company policy. The eligibility requirements for pension plans (see page 793) are pertinent. It is important, however, that enough employees participate in a plan to keep it from being di criminatory. Thus, the plan cannot be limited to key employees.

Most profit-sharing plans incorporate a minimum length of servic requirement before the employee becomes a member and begins t build up an interest in profits.

Percentage of profits to be shared. The extent to which profi will be shared with employees depends upon the employer's attitude However, the plan itself must provide a definite formula for dete mining the profits to be shared. The maximum tax deduction c 15 per cent of the annual compensation of employees covered b the plan is usually considered in fixing the profit-sharing formula.

The following are some examples of variations in definite formulae

1. A specified percentage of profits before taxes, but not more tha 15 per cent of annual payroll of participants.
2. A specified percentage of profits before taxes, but not more than the amount deductible on the income-tax return for that year fo contributions to the plan.
3. A specified percentage of annual profits before taxes but afte allowance for the pre-tax amount required for regular dividends o preferred stock and $2 on common stock.
4. A specified percentage of net earnings after taxes.
5. A specified percentage of pre-tax profits in excess of a fixed amount.

Allocation of contributions. A profit-sharing plan must set forth a definite formula for distributing the contributions to the employees or their beneficiaries. The plan may arrange for participation in pro portion to basic compensation. Thus, each participant will share in the year's contribution in the ratio that his basic compensation bears to the total basic compensaion paid all participants. Expressed dif ferently, it may arrange for participation on the basis of a flat percent age of salary, so that if the contribution amounts to 10 per cent of total compensation paid all participants, each individual's share will amount to 10 per cent of *his own* compensation. Or it can allocate units to the participants, giving, let us say, one unit for each $100 of compensation. It is often possible to allocate part of the contribu tion on the basis of years of service or plan membership, in order to reward long service with the company.

Vesting and forfeiture provisions. In setting up a profit-sharing lan, the employer must determine what the participants' rights in he plan are to be in the event of termination of employment before he time fixed for distribution. The plan may provide that all of a articipant's interest in the plan shall be forfeited if he leaves the mploy of the company before a certain number of years of partici-ation. But funds in the profit-sharing plan arising from forfeitures n termination of service, or for other reasons, must not be allocated o the remaining participants in such a manner as to effect discrimi-ation in favor of officers, shareholders, or supervisory or highly com-ensated employees.

Frequently, the severance benefits depend upon the reasons for eaving and the period of service. For example, the entire interest f a participating employee who is discharged for inefficiency may be orfeited regardless of his years of participation in the plan. On oluntary discontinuance of employment, the participant may for-eit 90 per cent of his credit in the trust if he leaves one year from he date on which he becomes a participating employee, 80 per cent f he leaves after two years, 70 per cent after three years, and so on until there are no forfeitures if he leaves after ten years. Also, special provision may be made for payments on discharge other than for cause. Similarly, special provisions may be made for employees who eave to enter the armed forces.

Distribution of participants' shares. The plan must provide for a definite formula for distributing the funds of the trust among em-ployees or their beneficiaries. The various methods of distribution are:

1. Lump sum distribution after a specified number of years have elapsed.
2. Annual distribution after a certain number of years.
3. Distribution when employee attains retirement age.
4. Distribution in event of death, sickness or disability.
5. Distribution on termination of employment.

Informing participants of value of interest. Whether or not participants shall be informed annually of the amounts of annual contribution allocated to them and the amount of net earnings or losses of the trust credited or charged to their accounts, is a matter of business policy. Obviously, if a participant is informed annual of the exact status of his account, the purpose of the plan is bett accomplished.

Advisory committee. Many profit-sharing plans provide for a advisory committee to supervise the management and operation the profit-sharing plan. The committee functions in much the sam way as a pension committee does.

Investment of the profit-sharing fund. The profit-sharing fun held in trust by the trustee may be used or invested in different way Where it is all invested in securities, the portfolio might, for exam ple, consist of about 55 per cent in sound bonds, including Govern ment bonds, 15 per cent in preferred stocks, and 30 per cent in com mon stock. Where the fund is small, diversification can be obtaine by investing in shares of regulated investment companies.

Some trusts purchase life insurance on key employees upon whon profits depend, and name the trust beneficiary. Others invest all o part of each employee's annual share of profits in deferred annuit contracts of the single-premium or annual-premium type.

Provision may be made by some corporations for investment o part of the funds in the corporation's own common stock or othe securities, and, in effect, make the employees part owners of the business through the trust. Still others hold options to buy up the shares of a stockholder at his death, and fund the arrangement through insurance on his life. And there are some trusts which own the corporation's plant and equipment, under a buy-and-lease-back arrangement, to the mutual advantage of employer and employee.

Telling employees about the profit-sharing plan. What was said at page 802 as to telling employees about the pension plan applies with equal force to deferred profit-sharing plans. A definite policy should be formulated by the employer to give effective and repeated publicity to his plan.

8. PROFIT-SHARING PLANS WITH CURRENT BENEFITS

Current and deferred profit-sharing distinguished. If current, profit shares are paid to employees as they are earned, either monthly, quarterly, or annually. If deferred, the amounts intended for the ltimate benefit of employees are paid to a trustee, and the distribution of these amounts and any earnings thereon are delayed until some event occurs, such as a lapse of a fixed period of time, attainment of a stated age, illness, disability, death, or severance of employment. Deferred profit-sharing plans are covered beginning at page 802. Current profit-sharing plans, which comprise about 75 per cent of all plans in operation, are explained in the following paragraphs.

Types of current profit-sharing plans. Current profit-sharing plans, regardless of their individual characteristics, may be classified as:

1. Cash plans.
2. Wage-dividend plans.
3. Production-sharing plans.
4. Other current profit-sharing plans.

Although plans in these categories differ widely in mechanics and formulae, they are all essentially alike in (1) their objectives, (2) prerequisites for success, (3) the process of drawing up the plan, and (4) the means of presenting the plan to employees. These points will be discussed before the types of plans are explained.

Objectives of current profit-sharing plans. The principal reasons for establishing a current profit-sharing plan are:

1. To induce employees to work harder to reduce the spread between profit and break-even point in anticipation of future benefits; to increase production.

2. To create a common interest between employer and worker.

3. To maintain a flexible wage structure; to avoid inordinately high wage rates which in periods of poor business are difficult to reduce without a deterioration in industrial relations.

4. To prevent strikes. (But profit-sharing cannot be considered as a substitute for faulty management policies in the industrial relations sphere; nor can it be used successfully to combat unionism.)

5. To improve public relations.

6. To give employees a stake in the continuation of private enterprise and thus help to preserve capitalism.

7. To promote teamwork, and to insure a fair share of the sales dollar's being returned to employees, in keeping with the progress of the company.

8. To establish confidence and co-operation between labor an management.

Prerequisites of a sound current profit-sharing plan. A curren profit-sharing plan will fail unless the following basic prerequisites fc success are present:

1. Good earnings and a firm financial structure. Too low or to irregular earnings cannot supply a proper incentive.
2. A wage scale at least as high as standard in the industry.
3. Working conditions at least as good as standard in the industry
4. Relatively good basic employer-employee relations.
5. An understanding by employees of (a) the plan and its opera tion, (b) company management, and (c) production problems.
6. Real participation and partnership in the enterprise. The shar of each employee must be sufficient to produce an incentive to fur ther effort.

The process of drawing up the plan. How the plan is drawn up the degree of participation that is allowed to labor, timing, and man ner of introduction are a few of the factors that must be considerec in instituting a plan.

Joint agreement. Once management has decided to adopt profit sharing, the plan should be a written agreement whose terms are de bated and approved by both management and labor.

Plan continuity. A written agreement may insure continuity of the plan, but the employee also wants to be certain that the distribution formula is fixed and not left to the discretion of management.

Provision for stockholder security. Some successful profit-sharing plans provide that a certain percentage of profits, usually 6 to 8 per cent, will be set aside as a return on invested capital before labor's share is determined. Other plans specify that a fixed percentage of profits or a fixed dollar amount of profits will be earmarked for dividends. Such provisions dovetail perfectly into the partnership conception of profit-sharing and often help to strengthen the plan.

Joint administration. In the majority of cases, the committee that administers the plan is composed of employee and employer representatives, and, in more recent plans, management is in the minority.

Drawing up the provisions. A profit-sharing plan commits management to divide profits with employees. Hence, the plan must ontain a contribution formula, an allocation formula, statement of ligibility requirements, a provision for time and form of payment, nd for an administrative body. A statement of employees' rights on ermination should also be included.

Contribution formula. A contribution formula defines the basis pon which shares are computed. The following formulae are used nost frequently:

1. A percentage of profits (commonly 25 to 50 per cent) before rovision for Federal income taxes. A firm that had $1,000,000 in rofits for the year would contribute $500,000 to the profit-sharing und, assuming its agreement called for a 50-50 payment before taxes.
2. A percentage of profits after deduction of income taxes. The irm described above might pay, say, $300,000 in the fund under this ind of provision.
3. A percentage of profits after deduction of taxes and a stipulated mount (usually in dollars) for dividends. If the same firm agreed o set aside $100,000 for dividends, it might then pay $200,000 into he fund.
4. A percentage of the amount that is declared as a dividend. (This formula will be explained more fully in the discussion of wage-dividend plans.)
5. Payments are related to productivity. Profit-sharing plans that use this type of formula differ from firm to firm. They require careful, expert preparation to avoid any semblance of a speed-up plan.

Although some plans incorporate a formula that permits the board of directors to fix the amount of profits to be distributed at their discretion, this is contrary to good profit-sharing practice, which requires a fixed formula to avoid employee suspicion.

Allocation formula. The allocation formula determines how the employee is to participate. In most cases, shares are distributed pro rata on the basis of the employees' annual wages or an average of annual wages for the past five years. In a few instances, the pro rata share is revised by impartial merit rating reports. This latter practice should be avoided because it departs from the fixed-in-advance concept of profit-sharing.

Eligibility. The eligibility provision of a profit-sharing plan outlines who among company employees are entitled to benefits. Usually, all employees are eligible after a qualifying period that may run fro a few months to one or two years of employment. The typical perio is a year. Some plans include detailed requirements to take care re-employed workers, part time employees, employees with long al sence records because of illness, and employees who leave the com pany before the termination of a distribution period.

Termination rights. To avoid the possibility of future misunde standings, the plan should outline specifically a worker's rights o termination of employment. Most plans provide that an employe surrender all rights under the plan if his employment is terminate voluntarily or involuntarily, during the accounting period. For ex ample, if profit-sharing payments are distributed quarterly and th employee leaves during the quarter, he loses whatever share he migh have received for that quarter. But if he leaves during the perio between the declaration of a distribution and the date fixed for th payment, he is entitled to receive his share.

Time and form of payment. Payment of fund shares is usuall made in cash, although a few plans convert the employee's shar into common stock of the company. Distribution is generally mad at the end of the accounting period for which profits are calculated The generally accepted practice is to make payments on an annua basis, but in some instances, to shorten the period between effort an receipt of the profit-sharing bonus, payments are made quarterly o even monthly.

Administration. The plan agreement stipulates who is to admin ister the plan and how members of the administration committe are to be chosen. Administrative duties will naturally hinge upo the nature of the plan. Cash plans require little work, except a payment time. Complicated production plans may demand full-time attention.

Presenting the plan to employees. A plan must be explained and the profit-sharing concept must be sold to employees. They must be informed constantly of company progress under the plan; and, perhaps most important of all, the employee must be made to understand the basic role that *profit-making* plays in the day-to-day business of the company.

A successful launching of a plan depends directly upon the effecveness with which these three methods are used: (1) employee articipation in formulation of the plan, (2) a mass meeting of all nployees to announce the plan, and (3) a booklet to describe the lan as simply as possible. The main point is to convince the emloyees that they are about to gain real participation in *their* company.

Once the plan is announced and put into effect, its durability and ffectiveness depend upon the degree to which employees are kept breast of company and plan developments. Periodic bulletins, comany financial reports, labor-management committees, bulletin board nnouncements, letters from top executives—all of these and more re used in various companies as channels of communication to keep nterest in their plans alive.

Cash Plans

Distinguishing feature of cash profit-sharing plans. Cash profitharing plans usually stipulate that a percentage of profits will be ivided among employees and paid to them at fixed intervals.

Guides in the installation of a cash plan. In working out a cash plan, management must determine, among other things, (1) how o arrive at net profits for purposes of the plan, (2) what the distribuion formulae will be, and (3) how frequently the profit-sharing bonus shall be distributed. Although the answer to each question depends on both management attitudes and the situation within a particular company, the following information, based on a survey of such aspects, may be helpful.

What are "net profits?" Ideally, profits should be defined as accurately as possible to dispel any possibility of employee suspicion. S. C. Johnson & Sons, Inc., Racine, issues the following statement to employees:

Here is the way we go about getting the total share to be distributed. As you know, we use most of the dollars we take in from the sale of our products to pay for:

1. raw materials, containers, and supplies.
2. wages and salaries.
3. freight and shipping costs.
4. maintenance of our property and equipment.
5. depreciation of equipment, buildings, and other property.
6. advertising.

7. property taxes, unemployment taxes, Federal old age benefit tax franchise taxes, sales taxes, transportation and other special taxes.

8. the dozens of other expenses which together add up to the tot cost of making, selling, and distributing our products.

After all these expenditures have been provided for, we have left a su of money which is called "net profit before income taxes." Out of th profit, we first set aside a minimum, reasonable return on the capital i vested in the business. Then, *before* we pay our Federal and state i come taxes, the Board of Directors sets aside a part of the remainir profit as the employees' share of the profit for that fiscal year. This h come to be called "the profit-sharing pool."

What will the distribution formula be? The percentage of profi that is distributed under various plans runs from a low of 8 to 10 pe cent to a high of 50 to 75 per cent (after an amount has been se aside for company needs). A company in an unstable, highly sea sonable industry may feel that it can afford only a low-percentag distribution, since it has to build up a cushion against economi shocks. A well-established company in a relatively stable field may b able to afford a liberal percentage distribution formula in its plan. I addition to business considerations, a management's philosophy play a large part. A company that regards its prosperity as resultin largely from employee efforts may be more liberal than one with different attitude. By and large, plans with large distribution pe centages are found in companies with progressive managements.

How frequently should profits be distributed? The extremes o distribution frequency are represented by annual payments and monthly payments. Experience indicates that the annual perio tends to destroy the incentive of profit-sharing by making the em ployee wait too long for his bonus. If profit-sharing checks are dis tributed monthly, the employee associates the bonus with his wage and thinks of it as part of his earnings to which he is entitled Profit-sharing seems to have its greatest tonic effect on employee morale when payments are made quarterly.

Examples of successful cash-payment plans. The profit-sharing plans of the following companies are of the cash-payment type: W. A. Sheaffer Pen Company (Madison, Iowa), Greenfield-Mills Restaurant Company (Columbus, Ohio), C. A. Norgren Company (Denver), ILG Electric Ventilating Company (Chicago), and Whit

g Corporation (Harvey, Illinois). The plan of the Whiting Cor-
oration is described to illustrate how a cash-payment plan operates.

Whiting Corporation cash-payment plan. Under the plan, 50 er cent of net profits, after an allowance for "rent," is paid monthly) all employees who have been on the payroll for a full quarter. The rent" is an amount reserved for dividends, plant improvements, and ie like. It is a partial return on capital, in that it allows the reten- ion of 5 per cent on net worth, prior to sharing the remaining profits ith employees. The net worth figure is adjusted annually to reflect hanges as determined by outside auditors. Actual payments are iade to employees in accordance with their earnings.

At Whiting, the profit-sharing plan is called the Wage Adjustment 'lan. They speak of it as being such-and-such per cent. It is figured ionthly on the basis of the past three months' operations. For ex- mple, if, during a particular quarter, average monthly net profits o be shared were $10,000 and average monthly payroll for the quar- er averaged $400,000, the wage adjustment would be 2½ per cent. \ worker who earned $350 for the month would receive a bonus at he end of the month of $8.75.

To keep employees informed of the profit-and-loss facts of business ife, Whiting holds "Town Hall Meetings" periodically. Company operations, plans, and profit and loss figures are discussed. At the neetings, simplified income statements are distributed to show ex- ictly how the Wage Adjustment figure was obtained, and any and ll questions are answered. Otherwise, plan administration is con- lucted by management.

Wage-Dividend Plans

Distinguishing feature of wage-dividend plans. Wage-dividend plans fix the percentage of profits allotted to plan participants and listribute shares according to the amount of dividends to stockhold- ers. They tend to emphasize a partnership of stockholder and em- ployee. The stockholder invests capital in the enterprise and, in profitable years, receives dividends as a return on his investment. The worker invests his effort and ingenuity, for which he receives a bonus in addition to his wages or salary. The wage-dividend plan livides profits annually between employees and stockholders according to a fixed relationship formula, so that, whenever a dividend is declared, a wage dividend is paid to employees.

Some well-known wage-dividend plans. Two of the best known of all profit-sharing plans are wage-dividend plans: the Eastman Kodak Wage-Dividend Plan and the Pitney-Bowes Plan. The Eastman Kodak plan is described below to show how such a plan operates. Size or national prominence have no bearing on the successful operation of such plans. The Lincoln Extension Institute, Inc., a Cleveland company with 50 full time and 50 part time workers established a wage-dividend plan in 1946. Many other small companies have also instituted such plans.

Eastman Kodak Company plan. The Kodak wage dividend is paid once a year in March to all employees who joined the company before October 1 of the previous year. Whether or not a wage dividend is paid depends directly upon whether the annual dividend on common stock exceeds 70 cents per share. The formula is a simple one. The wage-dividend rate is one-half of 1 per cent (.005) for each increment of 20 cents over the basic 70 cents. A common stock dividend of 90 cents (70 + 20) fixes the wage dividend rate at one-half of 1 per cent; a dividend of $1.10 (70 + 20 + 20) means a wage-dividend rate of 1 per cent, and so forth. Kodak then multiplies the wage-dividend rate, as declared by the board of directors, by the individual employee's total earnings for the past five years to obtain the wage dividend. Employees who have been with the company less than five years have the rate applied to whatever their total earnings are for the time they have been employed. A premium is thereby placed on length of service. For example:

> . . . if dividends declared on the common stock amounted to $1.40, the wage-dividend rate would be 1¾ per cent (.005 x 3½). In that event, the wage dividend on total earnings of $12,500 would be $218.75, or more than four weeks' average earnings.
>
> If, because of his or her very brief service with the company, an individual's first wage dividend, when figured in the above way, should amount to less than $15, a minimum dividend of $15, less Federal taxes, is paid.*

---

* A *Handbook for Kodak Men & Women,* Eastman Kodak Co., Rochester, N. Y., page 36.

Production-Sharing Plans

Nature of production-sharing plans. Production-sharing plans re essentially hybrid profit-sharing plans. They provide for a bonus, but the distribution is not a direct percentage of company profits. Rather, it is a division of savings resulting from reduced labor costs of production. The purposes and incentives of production-sharing plans are those of profit-sharing, but unlike profit-sharing plans, they dramatize the intimate effect the average worker's efforts can have upon overall company profits. Or, more precisely, they highlight productivity, which is essentially the source of profits. The essence of most production-sharing plans is worker participation in management as a spur to employee morale and, hence, to increased productivity. The principles outlined in the following plans are not an automatic cure-all. They require the desire on the part of both management and labor to work out problems together. Top management must be prepared to accept criticism and act upon it. Employee representatives, whether or not unionized, must make the effort to understand management problems and even to acquire a grasp of competition, marketing, pricing, and the like.

In this general category are the two following well-known plans: (1) the Scanlon plan and (2) the Rucker share-of-production plan. Various other production-sharing plans have been used in individual situations, but the explanation is limited to the two best-known types.*

The Scanlon plan. This type of plan takes its name from Joseph Scanlon, who devised it as a means of saving a steel company from the rocks. The plan worked better than anyone had anticipated.

The basic operating principles of the plan are these: †

> The first task in the application of the Scanlon plan is to find a normal labor cost for the company under consideration, and then to devise a means for giving labor the benefit of *anything* it can save under the norm. In every case, therefore, some kind of link must be found between the worker and overall shop productivity.

---

* For a number of individualized plans, see *Successful Employee Benefit Plans.* New York: Prentice-Hall, Inc., 1952, Ch. 14.

† Russell Davenport, "Enterprise for Everyman." *Fortune Magazine*, January, 1950, p. 57.

The link is nothing more than a way of expressing total output i terms that reduce all operations and all final products to a commo denominator, intelligible to all workers. For example, in a manufa turing plant that makes a variety of products, the number of uni produced of each product has significance only to the employees co cerned with the particular product on which they work. Scanlo therefore, has devised such accounting links as ounces of silver pro essed, pounds of castings produced, tons of merchandise warehouse and the like. Since no two companies are alike, the connecting lin between worker output and overall company production differs fro firm to firm.

In most cases, the workers receive a bonus equal to the entire sav ing effected by reduced labor costs. Management's gain comes fro increased sales without an increase in overhead costs, or, putting i another way, from lower unit costs.

The advantages result from in-plan co-operation and especiall from employee suggestions that increase efficiency of operations an reduce costs. The suggestions are handled first by production com mittees formed from the men on the job. The worker-level commit tee has the power to put in operation any suggestions that do not affect other departments or require substantial outlays of money. It can, therefore, act quickly, and often does. A screening committee, composed of employer (including the boss) and employee representa-tives, which meets monthly, goes over suggestions that have a wider implication. Either the suggestion is accepted and put into effect as rapidly as possible, or a member of the committee is instructed to explain to the worker who made the suggestion exactly why it was not used. There are no prize awards for suggestions that are ac-cepted. The reward lies in the employee's knowledge that he is help-ing to increase productivity and, hence, to augment his bonus.

Example of operation of Scanlon plan. Although no two Scan-lon plan installations are alike, the mechanics of the plan can be understood from viewing the operation of the plan at Lapointe Ma-chine Tool Company, Hudson, Massachusetts.

At Lapointe, the entire amount that workers save through increased productivity is paid to them monthly as a bonus, in addition to their basic wages. The link between productivity and overall output is the ratio of direct labor costs to total production value (sales plus or inus inventory at the end of the month). After exhaustive study past performance, a joint labor-management committee arrived at fair figure. For competitive reasons, Lapointe's management can-ot disclose the exact figure, but the basic idea can be understood om the following simplified example.

Assume that the ratio was established at 40 per cent; that is, over a eriod of time, an average of 40 cents of every sales dollar represented irect labor costs. If total shipments for the month amount to, say, 100,000 and inventory increased $20,000, total production value ould equal $120,000. The "normal" labor cost would be $48,000 $120,000 × 40%). If actual wages paid for the period were $40,000, ie difference, $8,000, would be paid *in full* to *all* workers in propor-on to their basic wages. "All workers" includes the boss.

On a few occasions at Lapointe, productivity has fallen below the orm: to use the figure given in the illustration, actual wages paid ere greater than 40 per cent of sales plus or minus inventory adjust-ients. To provide for this contingency, with full agreement from ibor, Lapointe withholds 7½ per cent of each month's bonus. The ithheld portion is used to compensate for added costs in below-ormal production months. Any balance in the fund is paid to the ien at the end of the year. The establishment of the reserve pro-ects the company against losses and inspires employees to work to rotect the reserve.

Rucker share-of-production plan. This type of plan takes its ame from Allen W. Rucker, president of the Cambridge, Massachu-etts, firm of management consultants, The Eddy-Rucker-Nickels Company. The Rucker Plan, as its author emphasizes, is not a profit-haring plan. Rather, this plan makes it possible for hourly-paid fac-ory workers to increase their monthly and annual earnings in direct roportion to the increase in "production values" that they help to reate. Its principal stimulus for mutual co-operation, as in profit-haring plans, emanates from the creation of an effective partnership etween labor and management. Through participation in the share-of-production committee, employees come to know the problems of nanagement, and by being paid a share of production values, they ome to realize the nature of the effect that their efforts have on the rogress of the company and on themselves. Employees may make added earnings from added productivity, whether or not the co: pany makes a profit.

In every instance in which the Rucker Plan has been established, has been a joint undertaking of employees (whether or not unic ized) and management. A share-of-production committee, with rotating membership representing both employees and manageme is set up to discuss production problems, consider improvements, a explore the possibilities of suggestions to increase productivity.

Basis of the Rucker plan. Although a careful analysis must made of the operating experience of a company before the Ruck Plan can be prepared for installation, the essential formula that for the core of the plan can be applied to most manufacturing firms.

For example: The Jones Company manufactures a line of chi ware. At one end of the production line, clay and coloring mat worth 50 cents are fed into the manufacturing hopper. Five cen worth of heat is added to make the total cost 55 cents. At the otl end of the line, the hopper ejects a colored bowl that sells for $1.(

Along that production line 45 cents has been added to the val of the original materials. That amount is the production val which has been created by the combined efforts of manageme: labor, and the machinery supplied by the stockholder. Who contr uted what and who gets what are determined by a study of the p performance of the company. It may be that 40 per cent of the p duction values is the amount shown by experience to have been p in wages, which means that the remaining share goes to the compa to meet the costs of all other compensation, overhead, taxes, di dends, and business savings for future expansion.

This is the point at which the Rucker Plan enters. Assume, nc that the Jones Company sold $250,000 worth of bowls in the fi quarter of this year, and the material, supplies, and allied co amounted to $150,000. The production values, hence, amount $100,000.

According to the historical experience of the company, 40 per ce or $40,000 of production values is the amount earned by the worke But assume that, during the first quarter, actual regular wages (cluding overtime) amounted to only $35,000, leaving a difference $5,000. This amount then, less a reserve of one-fourth, is distribut pro rata among employees as their share-of-production earnings.

The company's share, $60,000, or 50 per cent of the total produc-n values, goes to pay other compensation, overhead, taxes, and nership obligations. The difference between the total of these ex-nses and $60,000 is profit or loss.

If regular wage earnings (including overtime earnings) exceed the are-of-production credit in any month, the resulting deficit is car-d as a debit to the previously mentioned reserve account. For ex-aple, if the regular payroll at current wage rates in the above illus-ation had amounted to $45,000, when it should have been $40,000, e $5,000 deficit is debited to the reserve account. That deficit is set by credits amounting to one-fourth of share-of-production addi-onal earnings in future months.

At the end of the year, the reserve account is balanced and any edit remaining is paid pro rata to eligible employees, according to e actual regular earnings of each. Should a deficit result in the re-rve account at the year's end, the company always pays out three-urths of any month's additional or share-of-production earnings gardless of the condition of the reserve account.

Other Current Profit-Sharing Plans

Non-classifiable plans. Cash, wage-dividend, and production-shar-g plans are probably the types of profit-sharing plans used most fre-uently. But since each plan must be devised specially for the par-cular company, there are almost as many possibilities for variations 1 types of profit-sharing plans as there are firms willing to install rofit-sharing. The multiplicity of programs, however, does not mean hat a plan is more likely to achieve success because of its uniqueness r the number of nuances that it may contain. On the contrary, the uccess of profit-sharing depends to a large extent on (1) employees' omprehension of the mechanics of the plan and how it ties in with he company operations and (2) the degree to which the plan has een designed to meet special circumstances. The simple, straight-orward, easy-to-understand plan is most likely to achieve results.

Other current-profit-sharing plans include a combination of a cur-ent and deferred plan; a combination of a cash plan and a stock ownership plan; and some unique plans that are devised to meet particular situations and conditions.*

* For a description of several non-classifiable, successful profit-sharing plans, see *Successful Employee Benefit Plans.* New York: Prentice-Hall, Inc., 1952, Ch. 14.

SECTION 8

Accounting for the Business Executive

I. WHAT EVERY BUSINESSMAN SHOULD KNOW ABOUT ACCOUNTING

The Accounting Structure

Accounting Data

Accounting Records

Procedures and Methods

Some Accounting Terminology

2. HOW TO USE ACCOUNTING RESULTS FOR EXECUTIVE CONTROL

Reports for Control of Current Operations

Data for the Planning of Future Operations

3. HOW THE BALANCE SHEET IS CONSTRUCTED

Explanation of Items in the Balance Sheet

Current Assets

SECTION 8

Accounting for the Business Executive

. WHAT EVERY BUSINESSMAN SHOULD KNOW ABOUT ACCOUNTING *

Minimum accounting knowledge required. Most of the infor-ıtion that a businessman needs to direct the operations of his busi-ss intelligently from day to day and to plan for the future comes ›m the accounting records. Although the businessman can usually y on trained accountants for the information on which he must se policy-making decisions, he should have a sufficient knowledge how an accounting system works to understand the extent to ıich he can obtain guidance from the records. As a minimum he ould understand:

1. The general requirements for adequate accounting.
2. The accounting structure.
3. How to use accounting results for executive control.

The first two minimum requirements are explained in this subsec-on. The third requirement is discussed in the next subsection. In ter subsections financial statements are fully explained.

Definition and purposes of accounting. Accounting is the proc-ss of analyzing business transactions and recording them in an or-erly and logical manner in the books of account to show the results f business operations. The accounting records are maintained for ne purposes of: (1) presenting the financial history; (2) supplying urrent information for the control of current operations; (3) supply-ng data for the planning of future operations; and (4) supplying nformation to government agencies, bankers, creditors, investors, and ther outside interests. The first purpose is traditional. Growth of nterprise, increasing complexity of business, rapidity of economic

* Acknowledgment is made to William W. Voorhees, Assistant Controller, ir Associates, Inc., for this subsection.

changes, and the need for prompt reaction to such changes ha however, shifted emphasis from the static or historical aspects of counting to the dynamic aspects expressed in the second and th purposes. The fourth purpose is of ever-increasing importance cause of taxes and other governmental requirements.

General requirements for good accounting. Good accounti can be brought about only through a planned, coordinated effo For adequate accounting there must be:

1. A properly organized system of accounts, backed up by suitab records.
2. A complete layout of methods and procedures to implement t system of accounts.
3. A properly trained and experienced accounting executive wh will insure the adequacy of (1) and (2) and interpret the resul properly. The first two points will be discussed under accountin structure.

The accounting executive. The accounting executive is the ke stone of the accounting structure. Selecting this person is a seriou decision. Obviously, proper accounting education and experienc are requirements of major importance, but there are several other lack of which may cause the most brilliant accountant to be of litt use.

The accounting executive must be approachable, diplomatic, an pleasant, yet firm enough to stand up for what he considers righ Accounting is a service function. As such, it must often sell the valu of its services to other functions. The accounting executive who i liked and respected by the heads of the other departments has ha won his battle.

The accounting executive's background of experience should b broad. Banking, manufacturing, brokerage, insurance, retail trade and many other lines of business have their peculiarities. Specialize experience in a given field is helpful. Experience in several fields i broadening and desirable. Experience in more than one compan in any field is essential. A "one-company" man may have a restricte viewpoint and a tendency to pattern all he does after that one com pany's method.

Experience in activities other than accounting is especially desirɔle. The accounting executive must often put himself in the shoes the sales manager, production manager, purchasing manager, and hers. Practical experience in any of these activities produces a ıller appreciation of the problem at hand and makes for a more fective solution from an accounting standpoint.

Should the businessman need assistance in making the final selecon of an accounting executive, his banker or his auditors are qualied to help him.

The Accounting Structure

The chart of accounts. The chart of accounts provides the frameork within which the accounting records are constructed. It is the ıeans whereby business transactions are *uniformly* classified as to ype, function, object, and responsibility. The nature of the business, he size of the business, the management's need for information, the ost of getting the information—all must be considered in setting up he chart of accounts. For a one-man business, the chart of accounts nay be a simple list of accounts. For a large, complicated business, he chart of accounts may be several pages long, with a code designaion for each account by number, letter, or other symbol to identify t Code identification aids memory of the accounts and saves time.

A simple chart of accounts for a commercial artist's studio is shown n Figure 67. It is an owner-managed corporation, employing several ırtists and retouchers, a photographer, one general office girl and an office boy-messenger. Its quarters are rented, it utilizes a relatively small investment in equipment except in photography, and its principal expenses are labor and supplies. Occasionally, outside services such as typesetting are purchased. The president is principal stockholder, acts as manager and salesman, and sometimes works as an artist on special assignments.

The listing of the accounts follows a pattern that is common in setting up charts of accounts.

Who sets up the chart of accounts. In a one-man business, where accounting requirements are simple, the proprietor or manager himself might set up a chart of accounts adequate for the immediate needs. It is, however, a job that cannot be taken lightly, and is best performed by persons with accounting knowledge. In a larger organization, the accounting executive has this responsibility. Setting up

Assets:
Cash in Bank
Petty Cash
Accounts Receivable
Furniture and Fixtures
Photographic Equipment
Automobile Equipment
Deferred Insurance and Taxes
Liabilities and Capital:
Accounts Payable
Notes Payable
State and Federal Taxes Withheld
Capital Stock Outstanding
Surplus

Sales Accounts:
Sales—Art Work
Sales—Photography
Cost of Sales Accounts:
Professional Salaries
Photo and Art Supplies
Depreciation
Rent
Light and Power
Purchased Services
General and Administrative Expenses:
Office Salaries
Stationery and Postage
Miscellaneous Expense

Figure 67. Simple Chart of Accounts.

the chart of accounts is only part of the job. Once established, i must be continually reviewed. It must be kept in line with curren operations and changed as rapidly as conditions, methods of opera tion, or assignments of responsibility change. If this is not done, ac counting fictions having no relation to the facts will result.

The businessman's interest in the chart of accounts. Whethe or not he is a trained accountant, and whether he is a sole proprieto or chief executive of a large corporation, the businessman has a real though perhaps unrecognized, interest in the accounting framework It is the outline for the maintenance of essential records. From these records are drawn the reports that tell whether the business is pro gressing or retrogressing. The factors responsible for progress or otherwise are spelled out in the figures contained in the books. They can only be brought to light if they have been properly classified and recorded, and this, in turn, can be done only when the proper frame- work has been established.

Accounting data, records, and procedures. The accounting data, records, and procedures, plus the chart of accounts, comprise what is generally referred to as the "accounting system." A short definition of each term will provide an appropriate background for the discus- sion that follows.

Data are the pieces of paper on which the details of transactions appear.

Records, more commonly referred to as "the books," are media herein the data are analyzed, summarized, and recorded.

Procedures are the detailed routines followed in the preparation id summary of the data and in recording them in the books. Each ill be considered in that order.

Accounting Data

Classes of accounting data. The size of the business and its char- cter dictate the simplicity or complexity of the data required for tisfactory accounting results. For clarity of discussion, data may e divided into two general classes, external and internal. A few asic types of each class will be presented to illustrate the nature of counting data and to highlight the importance of the subject to dequate accounting. It must be remembered that there are many pes of specialized data of importance in a particular situation that re not covered here.

External data. These data are the means whereby individual ansactions with those outside the organization are recorded. The rincipal functions that give rise to external data are selling, purchas- ig, and financing.

Selling data. Means must be provided to insure proper recording f each customer's order and acknowledgment of its receipt. An or- er acknowledgment form accomplishes this purpose. It becomes the asis for billing the customer once the goods are shipped.

Copies of sales data become "internal" data for the purposes that vill be outlined under that heading. They may also become "jour- ials" or "ledgers." (See accounting records, page 840.)

Purchasing data. The purchase order, although not actually an ac- counting document, contains important data. It authorizes a sup- plier to ship goods or render services to the business. It establishes he quantity to be supplied and confirms the price to be paid. The nvoices resulting from the purchasing transactions are accounting data.

Purchase requires payment, usually by check. The check serves the dual purposes of eliminating the liability to the supplier and reducing the company's cash account when it is deposited and cleared through the bank.

Financing function data. Banks are agencies outside the business and the specialized papers used in dealings with them are extern accounting data. These are the deposit slips, which are evidence money placed in the bank account, and the bank statement, which a record of all transactions affecting the bank account during th period for which it is prepared.

Other external financial data include promissory notes, which th organization may give to creditors or banks or receive from customer Mortgages, bonds, and other security instruments also fall into th category. In the corporate form of organization, there is the evidenc of ownership known as the stock certificate. Although not solely a accounting document, it has significance in such matters as dividen distribution and establishing the value of capital stock outstanding fo balance sheet preparation (see page 890).

Internal data. These data are the means whereby individual fina cial transactions internal to the organization are recorded. Copies o external data provide the necessary internal data in respect to th selling, purchasing, and financing functions outlined above.

Sales data. Copies of invoices provide the basis for determinin total sales and total sales by type of product, individual customer, an territory, where such analysis is required. They provide the basis fo posting charges to the accounts receivable ledger, or they may becom such a ledger (see page 842).

Purchase data. Copies of purchase orders support a series of inter nal transactions that start when the goods arrive. They authorize th receiving department to accept the goods and tell the accounting de partment what the price is, how much was ordered, and what th terms and conditions of purchase are. They may be used to inform the inspection department as to quality and specifications of good ordered.

Vendors' invoices become the means whereby total liabilities fo goods and services are determined, inventory accounts are charged and unit material costs are determined.

Copies of checks drawn become the data from which total cash dis bursements are ascertained, analyzed, and recorded.

Payroll data. Another class of internal data concerns wages and salaries, commonly referred to as payroll. Pay is generally deter mined either by the passage of time alone or by the results of efforts put forth during a given time. Payments to salaried workers, both

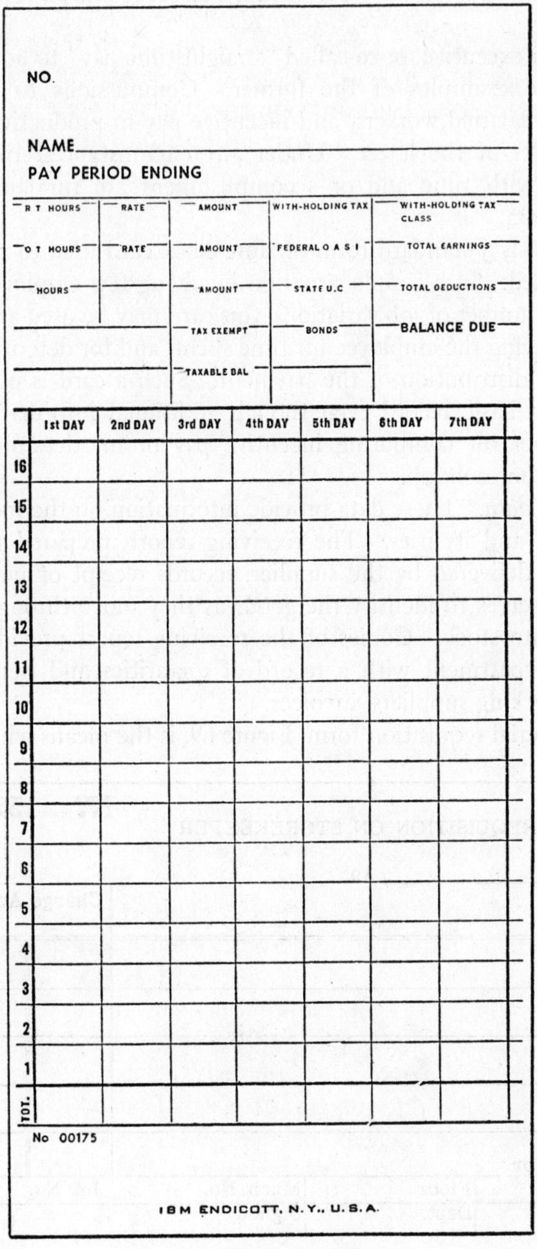
NO.

NAME

PAY PERIOD ENDING

R T HOURS	RATE	AMOUNT	WITH-HOLDING TAX	WITH-HOLDING TAX CLASS
O T HOURS	RATE	AMOUNT	FEDERAL O A S I	TOTAL EARNINGS
HOURS		AMOUNT	STATE U.C	TOTAL DEDUCTIONS
		TAX EXEMPT	BONDS	BALANCE DUE
		TAXABLE BAL		

	1st DAY	2nd DAY	3rd DAY	4th DAY	5th DAY	6th DAY	7th DAY
16							
15							
14							
13							
12							
11							
10							
9							
8							
7							
6							
5							
4							
3							
2							
1							
TOT.							

No 00175

IBM ENDICOTT, N.Y., U.S.A.

Figure 68. Time Clock Card.

clerical and executive, or so-called "straight time pay" to hourly rate workers are examples of the former. Commissions to salesmen bonuses to salaried workers, and incentive pay to productive worker are examples of the latter. Under any circumstances, the record associated with time and/or accomplishment are fundamental accounting data.

Figure 68 is a standard form of time clock card used to record the hours worked. In a simple situation involving few employees and a minimum number of job variations, this card may be used as the basis both for paying the employee for time spent, and for determining the accounting distribution of the payment. Such a card is usually employed as a basic record even though additional information is required either for computing incentive pay or for determining the time spent on each job.

Material data. These data provide information on the movements of material and its uses. The receiving report, prepared when the material is delivered by the supplier, records receipt of material ordered and serves to identify the goods as they move through inspection and into stock. Copies of the receiving report provide the accounting department with a record of quantities and items, to be used in checking suppliers' invoices.

The material requisition form, Figure 69, is the means whereby the

REQUISITION ON STOREKEEPER — No. 15597

Date________________, 19______

Charge Acct. No.

Deliver to

To be used for

Group	Floor	Mach. No.	Job No.
Bldg.	Dept.	Signed	

Figure 69. Requisition on Storekeeper.

MATERIAL REJECTION TICKET № 96967

PART NO.	NAME	QUANTITY ORIG. LOT	QUANTITY REJECTED

DATE	LOCATION	W. O. NUMBER	LAST OPER. COMPLETED

DESCRIPTION OF DEVIATION:

DEFECT DUE TO OPERATION RESPON.	DEFECT DUE TO EMP. NO. RESPON.	QUANTITY REWORK	QUANTITY SCRAP

REASON FOR REJECTION

	√	DEPT. NO.	Acc't. No.		√	DEPT. NO.	Acc't. No.
OPERATOR				ENG. CHANGE			
METHODS				INSPECTION			
TOOLING				OTHER			

MRB DISPOSITION		COST COMPUTATION	UNIT COST	EXT'N
ACCEPT	QTY.	RAW MAT.		
		PCH. PARTS		
REWORK	QTY.	LABOR		
		BURDEN		
SCRAP	QTY.	DEV. TOOLS		
SALVAGE INSP.		DEV. ENG.		
		SUNDRY		
CHIEF INSP.		TOTAL		
FOREMAN		SUPERV. RESP.		

E-1032

DISPOSITION:
1st Stage — FINISHED PARTS STORES
2nd Stage — TABULATING
3rd Stage — PRODUCTION CONTROL

1

Figure 70. Material Rejection Ticket.

material is taken from stock to the point of use or shipment. It r quires approval as a safeguard. It tells where the material is to go ar what it is to be used for. The accounting department prices th requisition and makes entries on the books accordingly.

Material is often spoiled and, if thrown away without a record, re resents a waste that is unaccounted for. Usual procedure calls f the issuance of a scrap ticket, of which Figure 70 is typical. Suc tickets are generally issued by the inspection department when th material is disposed of. The particular form shown serves a dual pu pose. Where the material is thrown away, it becomes a scrap ticke Where the material can be saved with expenditure of addition labor, it also may be used to authorize this expenditure and provid a "charge number" for recording the labor cost.

Accounting Records

Books of account. Accounting records may be generally divide into two classes: (1) journals, referred to as "books of original entry, and (2) ledgers, referred to as "books of final entry." Journals an ledgers, taken together, constitute what is generally referred to as th "books of account."

Journals. An accounting journal is a record wherein the variou data previously described are analyzed and summarized prior to bein recorded in summary form in the ledgers. Journals are either spe cialized or general. Specialized journals, also known as subsidiary journals, are used to record transactions of a like kind that occur fre quently. Transactions not provided for in the specialized journals are recorded in the general journal. (See "adjustment entries" and "closing entries," on pages 845-846.) The most common types of specialized journals are:

The cash journal. All detailed transactions affecting cash are recorded in the cash journal. The details of both receipts and disbursements may be contained under one cover, as is frequently the case in small businesses where a minimum of analysis is required. Generally, however, two separate records, referred to as Cash Receipts Journal and Cash Disbursements Journal are maintained.

The sales journal. This journal contains details of the transactions with customers involving billings for goods or services furnished and credits given to customers for goods returned or other adjustments.

'his record provides the analysis of sales by product class, territory, r in whatever manner is required to suit the individual situation.

The purchase journal. This journal provides the record of detailed ransactions with vendors, the companies or persons from whom the business buys essential goods and services. When a company progresses beyond the "very small" stage, this record is hardly ever found n modern practice. Its place is taken by the "Voucher Register," which is a combination of journal and ledger and which will be described under that heading.

The payroll journal. This is the record of amounts paid to employees. It usually shows hours worked, overtime or other forms of premium compensation, and deductions from gross pay for withholding taxes, social security taxes, unemployment insurance taxes, union dues, or any special deductions that are required to determine "take home pay." Where the requirements for accounting analysis of wage and salary costs are simple, the payroll journal may also provide for such analysis. Relatively complex situations, especially in a manufacturing enterprise, dictate the necessity for a separate analysis which is, in effect, a journal subsidiary to the payroll journal. This record is usually referred to as the "payroll distribution." It analyzes only one of the factors appearing in the payroll journal, "Gross Pay."

Journal forms. Every journal, regardless of its complexity, follows a basic pattern. Provision is made for both the "debits" and "credits" required to round out each transaction under the double entry accounting method now universally employed. In the various specialized journals, provision is made for the analysis required of the record. The journal form itself may be one developed for a given situation, or it may be one of the many standard forms that have been developed by stationery manufacturers and that are available in any office supply store. They are so well catalogued that space limitations make their illustration unnecessary.

Ledgers. These records comprise the accounts to which the data, summarized in journal form, are finally transferred. The transfer process is technically referred to as "posting." Like journals, ledgers are of two general types, general ledger and specialized ledgers, known as subsidiary ledgers.

The general ledger. This is probably the most universal form of record found in business. It is the record in which *all* business data finally come to rest in one way or another. The general ledger i the ultimate financial record of any business, large or small. Every thing—assets, liabilities, income, costs, ownership equity—is recorde here in greater or less detail.

Although this is the ultimate record, not all of the information i recorded in detail. As a business grows, the extent of the essentia details would make the general ledger too voluminous to be practical Consequently, various types of specialized or subsidiary ledgers ar used. The term "subsidiary" is derived from the fact that the special ized ledgers are controlled by the general ledger. Control means tha the sum of the balances in the accounts in a specialized ledger mus agree with the general ledger controlling account for which the sub sidiary ledger provides the details. The implications of control wil become more apparent as the various typical subsidiary ledgers ar discussed.

The accounts receivable ledger. This subsidiary ledger provides th summary of money owed to a company by its customers. Each cus tomer has an account in this ledger. As sales are made, customers' accounts are debited or charged; as remittances are received, custom ers' accounts are credited. Source data are copies of invoices and re mittance advices, as the case may be. The invoice copies may be the same as those used to prepare the sales journal previously described. The remittance advices, which may be on the face of a check or on a separate form, are the basis for the cash receipts journal described above. In some situations it is possible to use invoice copies as the ledger itself.

The accounts payable ledger. This ledger provides a summary of money owed to vendors. Invoices from vendors are credited to their individual accounts; payments are debited to their accounts. The vendors' invoices are the same as those used to prepare the purchase journal. The payment records are the same as those used to prepare the cash disbursements journal. This type of ledger is still found in many companies, but in many others it has been supplanted by the "voucher register."

The voucher register. This record combines the functions of a ledger and a journal and has some of the characteristics of both. A reasonable understanding of its function can be best obtained from a description of how it is operated. The voucher register serves first as a purchase journal. Vendors' invoices are given a voucher number nd are entered in detail and the ultimate accounting classification ecorded, usually in columnar form. This entry provides the several nformation factors otherwise found in a purchase journal. As checks ıre issued in payment, the disbursement is noted in the register ıgainst the invoice or invoices covered by the remittance. Thus, at he end of any given period, a summary of the unpaid invoices (or ouchers) develops a picture of liabilities for purchases (the accounts ›ayable ledger). The successful operation of the voucher register sys-em requires that all expenditures be vouchered and cleared through he register. Where conditions warrant, the operation of the register can be extended to perform the functions of a cash disbursements ournal.

Other subsidiary ledgers. Various other types of subsidiary ledgers are encountered. Some of the more typical are:

1. *The fixed assets ledger.* This is a record describing in detail each piece of property representing the fixed assets. The record may be further broken down between various classes of assets such as buildings, machinery, fixtures, and the like.
2. *The inventory ledger.* This record is often referred to as the "perpetual inventory." It shows, in detail, the quantities of various materials on hand at a given date and their value. Such ledgers may be set up for materials used in production only or, where the volume and variety warrant, may include supplies as well.
3. *The expense ledger.* In large organizations, where the accounting breakdown of expenses is voluminous, it is customary to show details of functional costs in such records. There may be separate ledgers for manufacturing expenses, selling expenses, general administrative expenses, and the like. Moreover, each of these classes of expenses may be broken down to show department responsibility for the various types of expenses.
4. *The stock ledger.* The use of this record is limited to corporations whose capital stock is widely held and frequently traded. The record shows the ownership of capital shares in appropriate detail.

Ledger forms. A ledger form must provide for the following minimum information: date of posting, reference data to show origin of posting, provision for distinguishing debits from credits and, of course, provision for a heading to identify the account. There are many types of ledger forms available commercially and, where the situation warrants, specialized forms are used. As with journals, any good office supply catalog will provide information as necessary.

Procedures and Methods

Importance of procedures and methods. The purpose of accounting has been previously defined as the creation of an orderly financial record for certain uses. Corollary, but equally important are two basic requirements: (1) the information must be made available in time to be of maximum utility; (2) the cost of generating, recording and summarizing the information must be kept at the lowest possible figure consistent with the requirements for that information. These basic considerations indicate the importance of procedures and methods.

Procedures. A procedure may be generally defined as a series of clerical operations that are concerned with the production of accounting data and the summary of that data up to the point of posting in the general ledger. Consideration of procedures includes the routines involving posting of subsidiary ledgers. There are all manner of procedures—sales distribution, sales order, shipment order and billing, timekeeping, and payroll, to name a few.

When the adequacy of accounting procedures is examined, procedures generally must be broken down into considerable detail. Since each has a specialized purpose, it is only possible in this treatment to lay down a few general criteria of suitability. These are:

1. Sufficient copies of data must be made to avoid re-writing.
2. The maximum possible information should be filled in during a single writing to avoid frequent collation, re-insertion into typewriter, and other duplication of effort.
3. Principles of good form design should be followed in arrangement of information to facilitate placing information on the form and taking information from the form.
4. Paper should flow from point to point in orderly fashion.
5. Procedures affecting various parts of the accounting system should be integrated so that the same data required in several different operations are not prepared in more than one place.

Disregard of these criteria usually results in increased clerical cost, delays, and production of inadequate information.

Methods. Methods concern the mechanical devices involved in the production, handling, and storage of data and records. The study of methods requires consideration of adding, calculating and bookkeeping machines and devices, methods of reproduction, summary and sorting equipment and devices, record housing and storage equipment and devices; in short, all of the office devices and machines now available. The selection of the right piece of equipment for the job is just as important in the office as it is in the factory. The wrong selection or inadequate consideration of methods improvement can prove costly.

Some Accounting Terminology

Terms defined. The language of accounting contains many terms that are meaningless to the business executive who has no accounting background. The terms encountered in financial statements are explained in the sections dealing with the balance sheet and the income statement (see pages 854 *et seq.* and 891 *et seq.*) Other terms that the businessman should be familiar with are defined below.

Account. An accounting record maintained in a ledger to which entries are posted from books of original entry in the form of debits (at the left) and credits (at the right). The difference between the totals of both sides of the account is known as the balance. The account assembles all transactions relating to the subject, which is identified in the name of the account.

Accrual accounting. A method of keeping the books of account by which expenses and income are allocated to periods to which they are applicable, regardless of when payment for such expenses and income is made. Adjustment entries are made in the journal to record accrued income, expenses, and other allocations.

Adjustment entries. Journal entries made at the close of a fiscal period to take up income and expense in the proper period and make the profit and loss statement show the net income from operations during a stated period. This involves setting up deferred charges (see page 878) and prepaid expenses (see page 878), deferred income (see page 884), accrued expenses (see page 881) and provisions for bad debts and depreciation. Adjustment entries are also made to correct errors discovered when the books of account are audited at the close of the fiscal period preliminary to preparing an income statement and balance sheet.

Closing entries. Entries made in the general journal at the end o the accounting period to transfer all the balances of the income an expense accounts and the nominal elements of mixed accounts (suc as the profit and loss element in the sales account) to balance shee accounts. The closing entries first transfer the balances to the profi and loss account, which in turn is closed (by closing entries) into th capital account (if it is a sole proprietorship or partnership) and int the earned surplus account (if it is a corporation).

*Double entry bookkeeping.** The method of recording busines financial transactions by equal debits and credits.

In recording financial transactions in the journal, two phases of th transaction (debit and credit) are recorded in each individual entry For instance, the purchase of machinery for cash is recorded by:

Dr. Machinery	$5,000	
Cr. Cash		$5,000

(read "debit machinery; credit cash"). This signifies the two phase of the transaction just made, viz., the acquisition of an asset, machin ery, and the relinquishing of another asset, cash.

As another example, the payment of a non-interest bearing note i recorded:

Dr. Notes Payable	$1,000	
Cr. Cash		$1,000

This signifies the reduction of the liability "notes payable" (by pay ment) and the reduction of the asset, cash.

Since the debits and credits in journal entries must always equal each other, and these balanced entries are, in turn, posted to a ledger, it follows that the aggregate of the debits in all the ledger accounts must be equal to the aggregate of the credits in these accounts. This is the basic concept of double-entry bookkeeping.

It also follows that, since the individual balance in any particular account discloses the same net effect as the aggregate debit and credit totals, the total of all the debit balances in the accounts of a ledger must equal the total of the credit balances. In other words, the ledger should always be in a balance or equilibrium.

Trial balance. A listing of the debit and credit balances of ac-

* Acknowledgment: Tunick and Saxe, *Fundamental Accounting,* page 54. New York: Prentice-Hall, Inc., 1950.

ounts in a ledger (usually the general ledger) for the purpose of eeing that the total debit balances equal the total credit balances, s they should in double entry bookkeeping. It is used as the basis or preparing the balance sheet and income statement.

2. HOW TO USE ACCOUNTING RESULTS FOR EXECUTIVE CONTROL *

Importance of control in business management. Two of the najor purposes of accounting are the furnishing of information for ontrol of current operations and *control of future operations*. Accounting helps management to exercise control of the business through (1) furnishing reports on current operations, and (2) supplying data for the planning of future operations.

Reports for Control of Current Operations

Classification of operating reports. Reports that aid management in the control of current operations can be divided into two general classes:

1. Financial reports.
2. Operating reports.

Each type serves a different purpose and is of major interest to different groups.

Financial reports. The principal types of financial reports are:

1. *Balance sheet.* The balance sheet shows the financial position of a business on a certain day by listing the monetary values of all the assets and the amounts of all the liabilities. The difference between the two represents the net worth of the business on the day as of which the balance sheet is prepared. The balance sheet also shows the proprietary interests in the net worth of the business. The balance sheet amounts are based on the assumption that the company will continue in business indefinitely, and therefore the net worth shown in the statement is in no sense an indication of the amount that might be realized if the company were to be liquidated immediately. Usually the balance sheet presents the condition of the busi-

* Acknowledgment is made to William W. Voorhees, Assistant Controller, Air Associates, Inc., for this subsection.

ness at the beginning of the period as well as at its close. A comple explanation of how the balance sheet is constructed is given begi ning at page 854.

The balance sheet is of great interest to the highest echelons management, such as the board of directors and the president, ar is of even greater interest to outsiders. The latter includes supplie who are asked to extend credit to the business, banks and other len ers to whom applications for loans are made, and those who ha invested capital in the business or who contemplate doing so.

2. *The cash report.* The cash report is usually prepared daily show the interested officers, generally the president and the treasure the cash position of the company each day. Important in this repo are the previous day's balance, the cash receipts for the day, and th day's cash disbursements. This report is usually a summary of eac day's cash receipts and disbursements for a period of a month. form of daily report is shown in Figure 71.

REPORT OF DAILY CASH BALANCE

Month of ____________, 19____

Date	Previous Balance	Received Today	Disbursed Today	Closing Balance
1				
2				
3				

Figure 71. Daily Cash Report.

When conditions are favorable and cash balances are ample, th need for this report is not urgent. However, under unfavorable con ditions, a daily report is important. If the business operates on budget system, weekly cash reports are usually adequate.

3. *Report of daily accounts receivable balances.* The prime func tion of a daily report of accounts receivable balances is to inform management of any lag in receiving collections from customers or their accounts. The report traces the previous day's balance through the current day's billings and the current day's collections on cus tomer accounts, and arrives at the closing balance in accounts receiv

ble daily. A form of daily report of accounts receivable balances is nown in Figure 72.

REPORT of DAILY ACCOUNTS RECEIVABLE BALANCE

Month of__________, 19___

Date	Previous Balance	Billed Today	Collected Today	Closing Balance
1				
2				
3				

Figure 72. Report of Daily Accounts Receivable Balances.

When conditions are favorable and customers pay promptly, the ieed for this report is not urgent. But under unfavorable conditions, vhen payments by customers on their accounts lag, the report of daily ccounts receivable balances becomes important.

4. *Inventory reports.* Through inventory reports, management as vell as those concerned with current inventory operations are kept nformed of changes of the inventory position. For wholesalers, jobers, and other trading companies, the report of inventory balances, ommitments, and inventory turnover is possibly the most important eport for purposes of managerial control and the daily preparation of the report may be warranted. In the case of a manufacturing conern, a statement as to the amount of inventory actually on hand is of real importance only as it is related to the trends in turnover rates and to unfilled orders on hand. Therefore, the rate of turnover, or he number of days' supply, should be shown on the inventory anal-ysis for each major classification of finished goods, and, in many cases, for basic raw materials. Also, inventory reports on work-in-process nay be necessary.

In the finished goods report, comparison is usually made with the figures for the previous month end, beginning of the fiscal year, and at times, for the previous year.

5. *Working capital report.* This report lists the current assets and current liabilities as of the date of the report. This report may be prepared weekly, if the company is suffering from lack of working

capital; otherwise monthly reports are adequate. Comparisons ma be made with the previous month end and in cases where there is regular fluctuation of working capital during the month, it is helpfu to give comparisons with the same date last month.

6. *Other financial reports.* In some companies, such reports as capital expenditures report, a report of fixed assets, an analysis o surplus, and other types of financial reports may be prepared.

Operating reports. Operating reports reveal the use made of th assets and of the manpower of the company, the results of operations and the sources and causes of profits and losses. The principal type of operating reports are explained below.

1. *The income statement.* The income statement is a summary for a definite period, of income received from business operations, al costs and expenses involved in producing the operating income, al income from sources other than direct operations of the business all deductions from income, and the net results of the conduct of the business for the period covered. The income statement may be com bined with a statement of surplus, in which case it will show distri butions of income made during the year to the stockholders, and other changes in the surplus account. In the case of sole proprietor ships and partnerships, the income, profit, and loss statement may be combined with the capital accounts to show changes made in the capital accounts during the year. A complete explanation of how the income statement is constructed is given beginning at page 891.

2. *Analysis of gross profits by product line.* This report is a gauge of sales department effectiveness in price realization. It is essential in a situation where the sales department has a degree of latitude in price quotations. It is, of course, of prime interest to the sales executive. It may be extended to show an analysis of gross profit by salesmen and/or by sales territories. If that is done, the sales executive has an effective tool for controlling his end of the operation. The analysis by product lines reveals the products that are not carrying their share of the load.

3. *Other operating reports for sales.* Other reports that are prepared for control and direction of sales activities include a booking and backlog analysis, a daily report of billings, bookings, and backlog, a lost order report, an analysis of selling or distribution expense, and an analysis of advertising expense by media and by product line.

4. *Operating reports for production.* This group of reports calls for he greatest ingenuity and study. There are an infinite number of eports and analyses that may be used and it is impossible to set forth ny standard types of reports. They include, generally, factory cost eports, departmental cost summaries, reports for control of material, nalyses of direct labor costs, and reports for control of factory overead.

5. *Operating reports for purchasing.* Where materials are an imortant item of cost to the business, reports should be prepared to nable management to see that working capital is not tied up unnecssarily in raw materials. A periodic report of prices of basic materials ogether with charts showing the trends in these prices are helpful to he purchasing department. Frequently this is developed within the urchasing department rather than the accounting department.

General rules for operating reports. Experience has shown that ertain general criteria may be applied to operating reports. These nay be stated as follows:

1. The report must be keyed to the management level for which it s intended. The higher the level, the less detail is required. Thus, report to the foreman of a department contains detailed informaion about that department. The division manager's report on the ame subject would cover all departments in the division in a sumnary form.

2. The report must be timely. Information that is too late to be of use is worse than no information.

3. The report should contain sufficient information to be helpful. It should not contain so much information that it is confusing.

4. The report should contain information only on those factors of the operation about which the supervisor receiving it can do something.

5. The report should be in the best possible form for presentation of the subject matter. Tabulations should not be used where simple charts are clearer, and vice versa.

6. A report should be reviewed periodically to determine the need for change in content or presentation, or even discontinuance.

Solving the problems associated with the development of a report system rests mainly with the accounting executive. If, however, the

businessman has some idea of what he wants, and of when and ho
he should be getting it, his criticisms become constructive.

Data for the Planning of Future Operations

Controls for future operations. Under modern business cond tions the future cannot be left to itself. Any business organizatio from the smallest to the largest, must plan ahead. In the case of th corner grocer the plan may be in the mind of the owner when h says, "I think I'll add a delicatessen counter next year." In the cas of a large corporation, it may be a lavish document resulting fror months of market research, plant site research, engineering studie and the like. It may be something between these extremes, depend ing on the size of the business.

An essential part of any plan is the determination of methods t gauge the results. Reverting again to the example of the corner gro cer, he will install his delicatessen counter only because he feels tha it will produce additional sales income and, hence, more profit. I fact, he will have established in his mind a dollar amount he hope to gain in both sales and profits. Thus, he can measure the degree c realization as time passes after his counter is installed. He can tak appropriate action to get back on his plotted course if actual result measured against his planned goals fall short of what he anticipated When any business organization is in a position comparable to tha of the corner grocer, it can be said to have achieved control.

The principal techniques that are used by large businesses to estab lish controls for future operations are *standard costs* and *budgets* Only a brief description will be given of these techniques since th purpose is merely to show how they tie in with the use of accountin information for control.

Comparison of standard costs and budgets. Standard costs and budgets have similar basic characteristics. Both represent a set o conditions that it is desirable to achieve. In other words, both resul from a conscious effort of predetermination. Both are used as a ref erence point against which results are measured and deviations de rived. Both are considered as devices of "management by exception," which means that variances from predetermined goals are spotlighte and attention focused on the *exceptions* indicated by the variances.

There is one important difference between standard costs and ıdgets. Standard costs, as the name implies, deal only with one pect of the entire operation—cost to manufacture, cost to sell, costs administration. Budgets, on the other hand, are all-inclusive and be properly developed must consider not only costs but sales, ofits, inventories, capital expenditures, cash, and other operations the business. Budgets can be prepared without the use of stand-d costs, but standard costs are extremely helpful in the process.

Tie-in of standard costs with use of accounting information. he term "standard costs" can refer either to the cost of operations nanufacturing, selling, administrative) or to the cost of the prod-cts made and sold. To a great extent, the latter are derived from e former. Standard costs of operations are those having the closest lationship to the accounting information developed in the books.

Two close relationships between standard costs and accounting in-rmation should be noted: (1) The cost standards are based to a eat degree on the past history contained in the accounting records. ast performance is not an absolute criterion of what should happen the future. Conditions will change, material costs will go up and own, and labor costs will rise and fall. Business activity will be igher or lower, having varying effects on the sales and manufacturing ctivities of individual companies. For these reasons what happened one period is not a fair standard in absolute amounts for what hould happen in the next. A study of historical costs will, however, ıdicate certain *relationships* between cost factors and the volume of usiness that can, with experience and judgment, be applied for pro-cting the future. (2) Once the standards have been established, urrent results are measured against those standards to show whether ne plans are being realized.

Tie-in of budgets with the use of accounting information. udgeting is the forecasting of realizable results over a definite period r periods, the planning and coordination of the various operations nd functions of the business to attain the realizable results, and the ontrol of variations from the approved plan in order that the desired esults may be achieved.

First, forecasts are made of probable income and expenditures over relatively long period. Second, approved budgets or plans of opera-ion based in a large measure upon the forecasts are established. The budget period is usually shorter than the forecast period, generally one year, in order to achieve greater accuracy in planning ov the near term and to obviate the necessity for frequent revisions the budgets themselves.) Third, statistics of actual performance a compiled at stated intervals during the budget period and they a compared with the budget allowance. Fourth, variances of actu from budgeted performance are measured and reasons or causes the variances are analyzed. Fifth, the necessary corrective action be taken to reduce or eliminate the cause of the variance is dete mined and the proper persons are authorized to institute the corre tive action. The decisions are followed up to see that the agree upon action is taken and results achieved.

The third step indicates the most direct tie-in of budgets with th use of accounting information. The accounting records become th basis for the preparation of reports for each of the budgets that ha been prepared—the sales budget, the inventory budget, the cost o production budget, the selling expense budget, the administrativ expense budget, and other budgets. Each report compares the actu figures as shown by the accounting records with the budgeted figur and shows the per cent of variance. A study of these reports enabl management to see where the variances have occurred. Armed wit this information, it can seek out the causes of the variances and tak the necessary corrective action.

3. HOW THE BALANCE SHEET IS CONSTRUCTEI

Meaning of descriptive terms in the balance-sheet title. Th statement of financial condition on a certain day is most commonl called a "balance sheet." (See page 847.) The term implies tha the statement has been drawn up from the books of account and tha the figures represent the balances shown in a double-entry ledger afte closing. The following descriptive terms are used to show the natur of the statement:

1. *General balance sheet*. The term "general" has no special sig nificance. It is employed principally by the railroads in presentin their balance sheets.

2. *Condensed balance sheet*. The word "condensed" is used t indicate that the balance sheet is a summary and that details ar omitted. It implies that the balance sheet is supported by schedule

which may or may not accompany the statement. (See page 861.)

3. *Comparative balance sheet.* Any balance sheet so entitled will make comparisons with data for the immediately preceding closing date, or some earlier date or dates. Such statements usually contain columns showing increases or decreases in amounts during the intervening period.

4. *Consolidated balance sheet.* The prefixing of the term "consolidated" indicates that the statement shows the financial condition of a group of companies controlled by the same interests. In other words, the assets and liabilities of the companies whose stocks are owned by the parent company are substituted for the stock of the subsidiary companies, and the financial condition of the group is presented as though the subsidiaries had no separate corporate existence. All intercompany relationships are necessarily eliminated in the preparation of the consolidated balance sheet. For example, if parent Company *A* has loaned subsidiary Company *B* $50,000 and has taken Company *B*'s note therefor, the item would not appear in the consolidated balance sheet, since the note receivable in Company *A*'s accounts is offset by the note payable in Company *B*'s accounts. Another example is the elimination of intercompany profits from the inventories.

No fixed rule is followed by accountants in the determination of the amount of control necessary to justify the inclusion of the subsidiary accounts in the consolidated balance sheet. If the controlling interest is only 51 per cent, it is generally not regarded as sufficient to warrant combining the accounts of the subsidiary with those of the parent company in the consolidated balance sheet. Some accountants consider that a 60 per cent interest is sufficient; others do not combine the accounts of a subsidiary in the consolidated balance sheet unless a 75 or 80 per cent interest is owned by the parent company. On the other hand, some accountants take into consideration the size of the subsidiary company, and if it is so small that a 40 per cent interest is insignificant in comparison with the net worth of the parent company, they will see no objection to consolidating its accounts. Unless a note is appended to the balance sheet to show what principles have been applied in the consolidation, the term "consolidated balance sheet" conveys no accurate idea of what group of companies is covered.

If the accounts of subsidiaries that are not completely owned b the parent company are combined for balance-sheet purposes wit those of the parent company, the interest of the minority stockhol ers must be set forth in the balance sheet as a liability, or, as som accountants call it, an "accountability." This item is further e plained on page 885. The parent company's equity in the aggr gate earnings or losses of the unconsolidated subsidiaries must als appear on the balance sheet.

Combinations of titles. Various combinations of the terms men tioned above are used in entitling balance sheets. Thus it is no uncommon to come upon a "comparative condensed general balanc sheet," or a "condensed consolidated balance sheet," or any othe combination of the terms.

Other titles for balance sheets. Balance sheets are sometime entitled as follows:

1. Statement of financial position.
2. Financial position.
3. Statement of financial condition.
4. Statement of assets and liabilities.
5. Statement of assets, liabilities, and net worth.
6. Statement of ownership.
7. Statement of what the company owned and what it owed.
8. Assets, liabilities, and capital investment.
9. Statement of affairs.

A statement bearing one of the above titles is not necessarily a reflection of balances appearing in the books of account on the date mentioned in the statement. The use of any of the titles in place of "balance sheet" does not attach any particular meaning to the statement except insofar as usage and practice have given them special significance. Statements rendered to banks and others for the purpose of obtaining loans are frequently called "financial statements." The term "statement of condition" is employed in the presentation of the balance sheets of banks. "Statement of affairs" identifies the financial statement of an insolvent company.

How a statement of affairs differs from other balance sheets. A statement of affairs is prepared from the viewpoint of liquidation.

hus it contains two columns for assets, in one of which the going-oncern value is given, and in the other of which the estimated realiz-ole value is noted. It furthermore classifies accounts differently om an ordinary balance sheet in that the assets are grouped to ow those which have been pledged with creditors and those against hich there are no liens, while the liabilities are arranged according priorities, as prior, fully secured, partially secured, and unsecured.

What a pro-forma balance sheet is. A statement that carries e title

Pro-Forma Balance Sheet, ..., 19..

one that gives effect to changes that have not in fact taken place. portrays a financial condition that does not exist, but which it is xpected will exist as a result of certain contemplated transactions. uch balance sheets are prepared, for example, in connection with ew financing, mergers, recapitalizations, reorganizations, and the ke. They are sometimes called "giving-effect" balance sheets. The atement should indicate the transactions to which effect has been iven. Thus, the title would appear as follows:

THE .... COMPANY
Balance Sheet, December 31, 19..
(Giving effect as of that date to the subsequent issuance and sale of $8,500,000 Refunding Mortgage Bonds and the proposed application of the proceeds thereof)

How to entitle the balance sheet. The heading of the balance heet should contain the following three points of information:

1. The name of the person, firm, or corporation whose financial ondition is portrayed.
2. What the statement purports to be.
3. The date as of which the staement is prepared.

The following illustrates a balance-sheet heading:

NTERNATIONAL HARVESTER COMPANY AND AFFILIATED COMPANIES
Consolidated Balance Sheet, December 31, 19..

The date is usually the day on which the books were closed. This s generally the last day of the calendar year or of the fiscal year. The latter term generally means an accounting period of twelve mont ending on the last day of any month other than December. T expression "as of" or "at" before the date is sometimes used; the usu practice, however, is to omit such expressions. If the balance she is a comparative one, showing amounts for the current date and f an earlier date, both dates appear in the heading as follows:

DECEMBER 31, 19. . AND DECEMBER 31, 19. .

Form of the balance sheet. Unless a form of balance sheet is pr scribed by some regulating body, bank, or other outside organizatic calling for a statement of financial condition, the arrangement of tl balance sheet need follow no particular order. The most commc setup of the balance sheet presents the assets on the left-hand side the sheet and the liabilities, capital stock, and surplus on the righ hand side. The balance sheet thus resembles an account.* It is n unusual, however, to list the assets in the upper part of the balan sheet, and to place the liabilities, capital stock, and surplus immec ately below the assets. This form is referred to as the "report" form

The assets and liabilities that appear in the balance sheet vary wit the nature of the business, the accounts maintained in the books c the company, and the purpose for which the financial statement prepared. The items on the asset side can generally be classified intc

1. Current assets.
2. Permanent investments.
3. Sinking funds.
4. Fixed assets.
5. Deferred charges.

The liabilities side of the balance sheet can be divided into:

1. Current liabilities.
2. Fixed liabilities.
3. Deferred credits.
4. Proprietary interests.

An explanation of the groups and the items that comprise them i given on pages 861, *et seq*. No fixed rule exists as to the order i which these groups shall be presented in the balance sheet. A rela tionship should be maintained, however, between the two sides of th balance sheet. If the current assets are presented first on the asse side, the current liabilities should head the liabilities side; if the fixe

* In England, the practice is to use the left-hand side of the balance sheet fo liabilities, capital stock, and surplus, and the right-hand side for the assets.

ets are listed first among the assets, the fixed liabilities or the pro-
etary interests should be stated first among the liabilities.

A balance sheet prepared for submission to a bank, a credit agency, a creditor for purposes of obtaining a loan or credit generally takes e form of an account, with the current assets listed first on the left-nd side and the current liabilities first on the right-hand side.

Methods of clarifying the balance sheet. The following meth-s are commonly used to simplify the reading and understanding of e balance sheet.

1. *Captions above each class of items to indicate their nature.* The ssification given above suggests the captions that may be used. thers will be mentioned as the items are discussed.

2. *Footnotes.* Any item requiring further explanation may be arked with an asterisk or superior figure, and the star or number ay be explained at the foot of the balance sheet. The following an example:

CURRENT ASSETS:		
Cash	$58,667,466.42	*
Marketable securities, at the lower of par or market	49,282,522.00	*
* Amount required for retirement of special stock on April 15, 19.	47,866,368.65	

3. *Notes or comments.* The tendency in recent years has been to arify the balance sheet by appending thereto notes or comments ertaining to the balance sheet as a whole or to particular items. Vith regard to the balance sheet as a whole, if there has been any nange as compared with the preceding period, either in accounting rinciples or in the manner of their application, which has had a aterial effect on the statement, the nature of the change should be dicated. The explanation of items in the balance sheet, beginning n page 861, points out those that require elucidation and indicates ow, by means of explanatory notes, the items can be clarified. See age 866 for an example.

4. *Expansion of items.* The following illustrates an expansion of ne item "Property":

Real Estate and Plants, Raw Sugar Properties, Warehouses, Cooperage, Railroads, Tank Cars, Steamships, Coal Barges,

Wharves and Garages, with their machinery, equipment, etc., and timber and other lands owned in fee or through ownership of the entire capital stock of constituent companies, at cost less depreciation $80,571,809.70

5. *Running comments in the body of the statement.* The follo ing excerpt from an actual balance sheet shows a liberal use comments:

CURRENT ASSETS:

This group comprises cash and items which in the ordinary course of business are convertible into cash in time to meet maturing obligations.

CASH	$ 566,483.22
This item represents money on deposit in banks, in transit, and on hand in the companies' offices.	
INVESTMENTS—At Market Value:	
State, County, and Municipal Bonds ...	530,522.50
Railroad, Industrial, and Public Utility Bonds	104,310.00
Other	3,101.00
The three preceding items represent the temporary investment of excess current funds.	
NOTES, DRAFTS, ACCOUNTS RECEIVABLE, AND ACCRUALS	1,520,738.12
These items at September 30, 19. ., *represent accounts receivable from customers (after deducting reserves of* $111,687.15 *for items which may be uncollectible) and interest receivable from investments,* $21,-274.91, *salesmen's advances,* $7,814.68, *amounts due from employees,* $8,565.25, *and debit balances in accounts payable and sundry accounts receivable,* $55,115.83 *(after deducting reserves of* $17,630.98).	
DUE FROM EMPLOYEES FOR PURCHASES OF CAPITAL STOCK	6,950.92
This amount is receivable from employees on their purchases of shares of stock; the market value of such shares, which are held as collateral, was $11,250.00 *at September* 30, 19. . .	

INVENTORIES	1,243,950.19
This represents the cost of manufactured finished goods, the lower of cost or market of goods purchased for resale, and generally the lower of cost or market of materials and supplies.	
TOTAL CURRENT ASSETS	$3,976,055.95
The sum of the preceding items. (The excess of total current assets over total current liabilities, $3,161,260.73 *at September* 30, 19.., *constitutes "Working Capital.")*	

6. *Schedules.* Since for most purposes a condensed balance sheet is sufficient, it is frequently advisable not to make the statement bulky by including details that can be furnished in the form of schedules. Any item in the balance sheet may be expanded by means of a schedule. The following is a list of schedules commonly prepared in connection with condensed balance sheets:

(*a*) Property account.
(*b*) Securities owned.
(*c*) Investments and advances—affiliated companies.
(*d*) Funds in the hands of trustees.
(*e*) Inventories.
(*f*) Deferred charges.
(*g*) Depletion, depreciation, amortization, and current maintenance reserves.
(*h*) Funded debt.
(*i*) Capital stock.
(*j*) Contingent liabilities.

Explanation of Items in the Balance Sheet

Current Assets

What the current assets of a business are. The current assets of a business are cash and other assets that will be converted into cash during the normal operations of the business, as well as those that can readily and quickly be converted into cash without interfering with the regular operations of the business. The items that ordinarily make up the current assets are discussed below.

Cash. This item includes demand deposits in banks, legal tend checks, bank drafts, and money orders. It may also include pap left at a bank for collection, if the bank has credited the deposito account with the deposit. Cash will be overstated if the compai has, for the purpose of showing a strong cash position, recorded of the last day of the period amounts received after the close of tl period. Post-dated checks, dishonored checks, I.O.U.'s, and postag stamps should not be considered as cash.

Time and special deposits. Time deposits may be shown sep rately among the current assets or may be included with the cas item. In the latter case, the sum representing time deposits shoul be indicated in parentheses, thus:

Cash (including $1,000,000 in time deposits) . .	$1,635,928.00

Special deposits from which predetermined disbursements are to b made, such as dividend accounts, payroll accounts, and the like, ma be included among the current assets.

Marketable securities. This item may include only those securi ties with a ready marketability that are being held during a period o small cash requirements and that will be sold as soon as a need fo cash develops, or it may include as well all securities that are readil marketable and that can be disposed of without undue interferenc with the business. It should not include marketable securities tha will not be sold in the ordinary course of business. For example securities that represent investments made to maintain trade rela tions are not current if by a sale of them the company would inter fere with the purpose for which they were acquired. The item of marketable securities is sometimes divided into "Government securi ties" and "Sundry marketable securities." When listed among the current assets, marketable securities should be included at the lowe of cost or market value. The valuation may be shown in the follow ing manner:

U. S. Government securities at lower of cost or quoted market value (market value $25,419,946)	$24,937,026
Other marketable securities at lower of cost or quoted market value (market value $874,363)	864,210

Accounts receivable. This item should represent the net amount of accounts receivable that will be converted into cash in the regular ourse of business, after accounts ascertained to be worthless have een eliminated. The account should show the amount of reserves or bad debts and the reserves for any other deductions, such as eight to be paid by the customer and deducted from his bills, allow-nces, and discounts. The following illustrates a common method f showing the reserve:

Accounts receivable (less reserves for discounts, freight, and doubtful accounts—$100,754.40)	$235,535.67

In many balance sheets, receivables that will not be converted into ash within a year, such as deferred-payment contracts to the extent which they are not payable within the year, are not included mong the current assets. They may appear as a separate item below he total of current assets, or among the "other assets." See page 79. It is generally considered proper to classify past-due items as urrent receivables, unless collection will be deferred beyond a year.

Accounts receivable should be divided into "trade receivables" and other receivables" in order that the statement may clearly reveal hat portion of the receivables has resulted from trade and what por-ion represents current receivables resulting from other transactions. further division should be made to indicate the amount of receiv-bles arising from sales on regular or installment terms. In the ab-ence of the latter division, the reader of the balance sheet may be led o believe that all of the receivables are collectible within the normal eriod of 30, 60, or 90 days, depending upon the terms of sale in the usiness. The information may be presented thus:

Customers' accounts:	
Regular retail terms	$2,274,074.70
Installment terms	734,802.51

In a consolidated statement, the amount of reciprocal intercom-any receivables and payables is eliminated. (See page 855) Any mounts collectible currently from affiliated companies, not elimi-ated through reciprocal intercompany transactions, should be listed eparately under the accounts receivable as "Affiliated companies' ccounts" to distinguish them from customers' accounts and other ccounts. The item should not be included among the current assets f the debtor company does not have a satisfactory margin of current ssets over current liabilities, including such accounts. Under the latter circumstances, the affiliated companies' accounts would appe under investments or some other title, as the circumstances indicat

Notes receivable. Notes receivable, or bills receivable, as they a sometimes called, are frequently combined with accounts receivabl Whether so combined or entered as a separate item among the cu rent assets, the amount of notes receivable should not include di honored notes—that is, those that have passed their maturity witho being collected. The form of balance sheet contained in the bulleti entitled "Verification of Financial Statements," issued by the Fe eral Reserve Board, includes past-due notes among the current asset but the manner of presenting them, illustrated below, leaves no roo for misunderstanding.

Notes and accounts receivable:
- Notes receivable, customers' (not past-due) . . . .
- Accounts receivable, customers' (not past-due) . . . .
- Notes receivable, customers' (past-due) . . . .
- Accounts receivable, customers' (past-due) . . . .
- Less:
  - Reserve for bad debts . . . .
  - Reserve for discounts, freight, allowances, etc. . . . .

If the reserve for bad debts takes into account possible losses o notes receivable, it should be deducted in the balance sheet fro the total of notes and accounts receivable; if not, the reserve shoul be deducted only from the accounts receivable.

Notes receivable that are not due within a year should be segre gated from the current assets, unless trade practice warrants a diffe ent treatment. (See page 877.) Notes arising from transaction outside of the ordinary business of the company, and notes fro stockholders, directors and employees, should be separated from thos arising from trade accounts. (See page 879.)

What was said of accounts receivable of affiliated companies i equally applicable to notes receivable. Notes of affiliated companie should be listed separately from customers' notes, and should be in cluded among the current assets only if the debtor company has satisfactory margin of current assets over current liabilities, includin such notes.

See page 884 for the manner of noting in the balance sheet th possibility of liability on customers' discounted notes.

Inventories. This item varies in the balance sheet with the nature f the business. A company that purchases finished goods for resale ould have a merchandise inventory; one that manufactures products ould have an inventory of finished goods, goods in process, raw marials, and supplies. Supplies usually denote commodities used in ie operations of a business that are not ingredients of a manufacired product and that are not sold specifically. Since they represent repaid expenses, they may be excluded from the inventory and laced among the deferred charges. Supplies, however, are frequently icluded among the inventories because they involve a physical inentory rather than because they constitute assets of greater currency ian other deferred charges.

Containers, barrels, cartons, bottles, cans, and the like, may repreent materials entering into the production of the product, supplies, r permanent assets. If they constitute materials entering into production, they may be placed among the current assets; if supplies, they iay appear among the deferred charges; and if permanent assets, they iay be included among the fixed properties. (See page 869.)

Included in the inventories may be goods sent out on consignment nd not sold, valued at cost of the goods plus any expenses incurred n sending the merchandise to the consignee. The inventory should iot include merchandise received to be sold on consignment.

What the valuation of inventories in the balance sheet represents. The standard rule for the valuation of inventories is "cost or market, vhichever is lower." Although most balance sheets generally show he basis of valuation by the inclusion of a parenthetical statement mmediately after the item, indicating that the lower of cost or market has been used, that information is not sufficient for a proper unlerstanding of the valuation.

The analyst should know whether costs have been determined by (1) specific identification, (2) average cost, (3) first-in—first-out (Fifo), (4) last-in—first-out (Lifo), or some other method. Also, uch questions as the following are of interest to the analyst:

1. Have the incidental expenditures for freight, drayage, and storage been included in calculation of cost?

2. Have cash discounts been treated as a reduction of cost or as financial income?

3. What method has been used to arrive at the cost where pur-

chases have been made during the year at fluctuating prices an where goods have been manufactured during the year at various costs

4. How have reductions from cost to market been treated in the ac counts, and how are reduced inventories treated in the succeedin period?

In a consolidated statement, the question arises: How have inter company profits on goods included in the inventory been handled The intercompany profits should be eliminated, unless it is imprac ticable to do so, and in that event, a note in the balance sheet should explain that they have not been eliminated. A note in the balance sheet, summarizing in general terms the instructions issued by the company to those charged with the duty of preparing the actual in ventories, would throw some light upon the inventory item. The following two examples of notes, taken from actual balance sheets demonstrate how the inventory item can be clarified. Neither of the notes, to be sure, answers all the questions that arise in an analysi of the asset.

Raw materials and bulk supplies are priced at the lower of cost or mar ket. Miscellaneous supplies, work in process, and finished products are priced at cost or less, a large portion being covered by sales orders a prices in excess of inventory value, the remainder being valued conserva tively, in the opinion of the management, by the provision of reserve considered adequate for losses anticipated from obsolescence.

* * *

The quantities of inventories on hand at the end of the year 19. . were ascertained by employees of the Corporation, by weight, count, or measurement, except in the case of certain raw materials the taking of physical inventories of which was impracticable. As to the latter, the quantities shown by the books were used, the book balances having been adjusted from time to time during the year on the basis of estimates made by such employees.

Inventories, other than contract work in progress, were valued at the lower of cost or market. (Reference is made here to a schedule of inven tories.) In valuing such inventories, interdepartment, interplant, and intercompany profits have not been included.

Contract work in progress was valued at cost, as adjusted by estimated profits or losses on certain work nearing completion or on separate units thereof. Such profits and losses have been taken or provided for, based upon estimates of probable final costs. The income account is charged with such estimated losses and is credited with such estimated profits.

he unbilled portion of the cost of the contract work in progress does ɔt include interdepartment, interplant, or intercompany profits.

Other current assets. A number of other assets may properly be lded under the caption of "current assets," or grouped under a sepa-ıte heading called "other current assets." They include:

1. Agents' balances.
2. Amounts due from employees. This item may be included in other assets." See page 879.
3. Accrued interest and dividends receivable.
4. Bonds and other securities maturing in the near future. The ames of the securities and the maturity dates should be indicated ı the balance sheet.
5. Sight drafts with bills of lading attached, and C.O.D. items.
6. Advances that are returnable within a short period.
7. Good-faith deposits on United States Government contracts.

Fixed Assets or Fixed Capital

What are the fixed assets of a business? All property of a per-nanent nature, whether tangible or intangible, that is used in the peration of the business and that is not intended for sale may be onsidered the fixed assets of an enterprise. Fixed assets appear in he balance sheet under the caption of "fixed assets," "fixed capital," or "capital assets." The use of the latter term is not recommended, ince the assets properly classified as fixed assets do not include all of the assets that represent capital. The items making up this group of assets will be discussed below under the two principal headings of:

1. Tangible fixed assets.
2. Intangible fixed assets.

Tangible Fixed Assets

What the tangible fixed assets are. Tangible fixed assets include and, buildings, machinery and tools, furniture and fixtures, patterns, delivery equipment, containers, and similar property.

How tangible fixed assets are valued. The values of fixed assets set forth in the balance sheet may be:

1. Cost, regardless of upward or downward changes in market value.

2. Increased value on the basis of an appraisal. The latter is justi- fied if the increase has not been credited to the surplus account and if the fact that the books show appraised value has not been over- looked in the determination of depreciation.

3. Decreased value on the basis of appraisal.

The basis of valuation should be indicated for each item, with the year of appraisal noted if appraised value is the basis. The following excerpt from a balance sheet illustrates how the basis is noted:

Land, factory sites, etc., at cost	$ 3,711,960.41
Buildings, docks, etc., at sound values as appraised in 19. ., plus subsequent additions at cost	12,465,553.81
Machinery, equipment, motor trucks, etc., at sound values as appraised in 19. ., plus subsequent additions at cost	14,328,714.54

If the basis of valuation is the same for all the items, it may be noted in the caption as illustrated below:

Fixed Assets, as Revalued by the Company, December 31, 19. ., plus Subsequent Additions at Cost:

The reserve for depletion, depreciation, wear and tear, and obsolescence of the properties included among the fixed assets should appear as a deduction from the values of such properties.

Land. When this item is included among the fixed assets, it should represent land used for plant purposes and not land held for speculation or for future plant use. Nor should it include land held under long-term leases. If cost is the basis, the value may include brokers' commissions, fees for examining and recording title, taxes accrued at the date of purchase, and the cost of such improvements as installing sewers and laying pavements. Interest on installment payments or assessments should not be included in the cost of the land.

The item "real estate" in the balance sheet may represent land and buildings. In the books of account, however, the two assets are ordinarily kept separate, since items of depreciation and insurance may affect one and not the other.

Buildings. Both buildings acquired and buildings constructed are included in this item. In the case of buildings acquired, cost covers the purchase price, the cost of all alterations, improvements, and

·pairs made to restore depreciation that occurred before the property ·as purchased. In the case of buildings constructed, the cost covers ıaterial and labor, or the contract price, and many other incidental ems occurring during the period of construction, such as payments ɔr permits, architects' fees and superintendents' salaries, premiums n workmen's compensation, and taxes and insurance during the onstruction period.

Machinery and tools. The valuation of machinery on the basis f cost includes the purchase price, freight, duty and installation harges, as well as a capitalization of costs of breaking in the machinry and testing it, where these are necessary. It should not include ıny amounts expended in rearranging the machinery after the initial ıstallment. Such expenditures may be carried as a deferred charge. Tools and machinery are generally kept in separate accounts on the ɔooks, since they are subject to different considerations in determinng depreciation.

Furniture and fixtures. The value of furniture and fixtures in the balance sheet indicates the cost of permanent equipment; it should not include amounts expended upon rearrangements and replacements that add no value to the asset. The reserve for depreciation may be given separately or bulked with the general reserve for depreciation of property.

Patterns. If this account is conservatively maintained, the balance will reflect the values of patterns used for regular stock work and will not include the costs of patterns made for special jobs, or patterns, lasts, and so forth, for products that are no longer manufactured. Furthermore, it will show values after substantial reductions have been made from book value.

Delivery equipment. Motor trucks and other delivery equipment are valued at cost less depreciation in the balance sheet. The amount should not include the cost of parts requiring frequent replacements.

Containers. Bottles, boxes, barrels, cans, and the like, that have not been charged to customers, and that are owned by the business, may be included among the fixed property at a valuation that makes liberal allowance for depreciation and for loss through failure of customers to return them. If containers have been billed to customers, the value of any in circulation will be included in the accounts r ceivable (unless, as in the brewery business, the intent is that th containers are charged to customers merely "on memo"), and th property account will not reflect them.

What the balance sheet does not show about the propert items. Information on the following points in regard to fixed tang ble assets is generally not disclosed in a balance sheet unless a not is appended to the statement.

1. Whether the property accounts are charged only with new prop erty or with replacements and improvements as well.
2. Whether the property accounts include any charges, in additio to direct cost, for overhead expense, interest, or other similar expendi tures.
3. Whether cash discounts taken on purchases of fixed assets have been treated as a reduction in the cost of the property, or have been recorded as a financial income.
4. How provision for depreciation has been made—that is, wha classes of property have been considered, what basis has been used and what depreciation rates have been applied.
5. What classes of expenditures, if any, are charged against reserves for depreciation.
6. Upon a sale or abandonment of property, what disposition is made in the accounts of the difference between depreciated value and realized or realizable value.
7. Upon purchasing property from a subsidiary, whether cost to the subsidiary or some other basis is used in charging the property account.

Intangible Fixed Assets

What the intangible fixed assets are. The intangible fixed assets generally include patents, copyrights, trade-marks, formulas and processes, leaseholds, and goodwill. In many balance sheets the intangibles are not valued separately, but are presented as a combined asset and given a value of $1 or some other nominal sum. This does not mean that the intangibles have no greater value than that indicated. It merely indicates that with regard to these items the company has been conservative in not capitalizing them; it furthermore serves to remind the reader of the balance sheet that such assets exist. If the nominal valuation is presented merely for balance-sheet purposes and does not represent the value at which the intangibles are carried on the books, a note such as the following may be inserted after the item:

Intangibles carried on the books at substantial amounts are shown at the nominal amount of $1 for the purposes of the published accounts.

In the following discussion, each of the intangible items will be discussed separately. First, the intangibles that are subject to amortization will be presented—that is, those that should be written off over a definite period of time—patents, copyrights, franchises, leaseholds, and leasehold improvements; then the intangibles that are not subject to amortization—goodwill, trade-marks, and formulas and processes.

Patents. All patents ultimately lose their value, since they are issued for a limited period of seventeen years. They may become valueless long before the expiration of the patent because other patents have superseded them, or because the product manufactured under the patent has lost is marketability, or for other reasons. Deductions must therefore be made from the valuation of patents to allow for the disappearance of the asset. These deductions, known as *amortization*, are generally not set forth in the balance sheet; the value indicated, rather, is a net valuation after the appropriate deductions have been made. Since patents are generally either purchased or applied for, the valuation shown in the balance sheet may represent the following expenditures after deduction for amortization has been made:

1. The cost of the patent, if it was acquired by purchase.
2. The expense involved in obtaining the patent, in providing working models, and in experimenting with them, if the patent is obtained otherwise than by direct purchase.
3. The cost of conducting an experimental department for developing patentable devices. Only so much as may be applied to successful patents granted should be included.
4. The cost of successful litigation that has established the patent.

Copyrights. This item, when more than nominal in value, may indicate that the copyright has been purchased from a previous owner. A conservative treatment of this asset, whether obtained by the company indirectly from the Government or acquired by purchase, would in most cases require it to be written off against the income from the first edition rather than over the life of the copyright, which is twenty-eight years, with the possibility of a renewal for an additional twenty-eight years, since few publications are marketable during the entire life of the copyright. However, in certain instances less drastic treatment may be justifiable.

Franchises. The asset franchises appears usually in the balance sheet of a public-service company and not in that of an industrial enterprise. It represents the cost of obtaining the franchise, less a deduction for amortization, if the franchise has been granted for a limited period. Franchises that are not perpetual and are not limited to a fixed number of years should be written off rapidly.

Leaseholds. The valuation of leaseholds among the intangibles ordinarily represents the advance payment of rent made by the lessee or sublessee on a long-term lease, less the appropriate deduction for amounts written off over the life of the lease. Sometimes the account includes a capitalization of the saving in rent made possible by an advantageous lease. If so, that fact should be evident from the inclusion in the statement of a special surplus account representing the amount added by the capitalization of the saving.

Leasehold improvements. If the lease provides that the lessee shall pay the costs of any alterations or improvements of the leased property, such as new fronts, partitions, and other changes, the improvements become the property of the owner at the expiration of the lease. During the life of the lease, however, the costs of such improvements may be carried in the balance sheet as leasehold improvements, but the cost should be written off during the life of the lease.

Goodwill. The following enumeration of items that frequently make up the goodwill account shows the great difficulty the reader of the balance sheet encounters in understanding the significance of the account.

1. The amount paid for goodwill upon acquisition of a going concern. Many accountants justify a goodwill account only when it is created through the circumstances of a purchase of a going concern.
2. The amount expended in excess of a normal sum, for advertising with the intent of creating goodwill.
3. Valuations arising through the writing-off of the patent account

goodwill instead of to income in cases where the patent has given : owner a monopoly that is expected to continue after the expiran of the patent.

ŧ. Amounts added to the account that in fact are deferred charges expenses, such as organization expenses and costs of establishing ›usiness.

5. Amounts improperly added to the account as arbitrary capitalitions of earnings in excess of a normal return on capital.

The cost of goodwill acquired upon the purchase of a going conrn need not be written off, even though it has declined in value cause of a falling-off of profits. Should the goodwill acquired by ırchase increase in value, any writing-off would result in an underıtement of the net worth and accumulated profits and the creation secret reserves. Additions to the goodwill account arising in ways her than by purchase are generally not justified.

Trade-marks. This item, when it appears in the balance sheet, presents the cost of trade-marks acquired by purchase. Frequently s value does not appear separately in the balance sheet but is inuded with goodwill. Since a trade-mark does not expire as does a atent or copyright, its value is not subject to amortization. Just as is improper to capitalize permanently in the goodwill account mounts expended in creating goodwill through advertising and other ıles-promotion outlays, so it is considered equally unjustifiable to apitalize amounts spent in advertising a trade-mark.

Formulas and processes. Formulas and processes acquired from going concern at a direct cost are generally included in the goodwill nd are not valued as a separate item in the balance sheet. Like rade-marks, formulas and processes have an unlimited life and thereore need not be amortized. They should be written off when they re no longer used.

Investments

How investments appear in the balance sheet. The investment group in the balance sheet embraces permanent investments, temporary investments that cannot be liquidated or that are not intended to be used for current business needs, and advances that will not be collected within the near future. This division of investments, however, is not generally made in the balance sheet. The most comn method of presenting investments is to include a caption "Inv ments," or "Permanent investments," and to show a valuation for

1. Investment in and advances to affiliated companies.
2. Funds.
3. Other investments.

The investments in affiliated companies may be mentioned by nar if they are not too numerous.

If any of the securities have been pledged, or hypothecated, tl fact and the book value of such securities should be stated on the b ance sheet. The following illustrates how the item would appear:

INVESTMENTS:	
Securities of subsidiary and affiliated companies owned (including $31,964,672.66 pledged as collateral to notes payable of this company and to guaranty of notes payable of a subsidiary company) at book value	$256,850,853
Investments in, advances for account of, and account receivable from Deep Rock Oil Corporation (in receivership)—at book value ..	34,149,623
Other Investment Securities (including $6,984,402.32 pledged as collateral to notes payable of this company and to guaranty of notes payable of a subsidiary company)—at book value (market value at December 31, 19. ., $3,216,546.25)	7,056,176

Valuation of permanent investments. The securities held by company may comprise mortgages, bonds, and stocks. Mortgag may be included at their face value, unless it is known that the sec rity behind them has declined in value below the face of the mor gage. Stocks and bonds held for permanent investment are ordinari valued at cost. All minor market fluctuations and all increases i market value should be ignored. If the market value is considerab less than the cost, a reserve should be set up equal to the differenc between the cost and the market value. The reserve is a charg against surplus rather than against profit and loss because it does nc arise from operations. (See page 886.)

In the case of bonds acquired at a premium or at a discount, th valuation reflected in the balance sheet should give effect to adjus ents for amortization of premiums paid and for the accumulation discounts. Such adjustments are made periodically for the purpose bringing the valuation of the securities upon the books to par at aturity.

Investments in controlled subsidiary or affiliated companies. ae valuation in controlled or affiliated companies may reflect one the following:

1. The cost of the securities plus the holding company's proportion the subsidiary's profits (or if the subsidiary's profit and loss statement shows a loss, less the holding company's proportion of the loss), ss the dividends received from the subsidiary.
2. The proportionate share of book value of net assets of controlled mpanies.
3. The cost of the investment to the holding company.

nless the balance sheet indicates how the securities of controlled ad affiliated companies are dealt with, there is no way of determing the true meaning of the valuation.

A consolidated balance sheet will omit from the investment item e stocks of subsidiaries owned by the parent company if the assets ad liabilities of the subsidiaries are included in the consolidated acunts. However, the value of investments in controlled and affilied companies whose accounts are not included in the consolidation ill appear in the balance sheet. (See page 855.)

Other investment securities. This item includes securities of unntrolled companies and holdings of nonaffiliated companies acuired to create and maintain favorable business connections. The aluation indicates the cost of the securities less any reserve that has een set up to reduce the book value from cost to market. The mount of the reserve may be mentioned in parentheses after the em, as:

Other investments, at cost (less reserve, $26,000) . . . $136,020

r the reserve may be shown as a deduction from the value. Frequently the item is presented in the balance sheet at cost, with a parnthetical statement of the value on the basis of market quotations.

Real property. Properties held for speculative purposes or for use a future expansion of the plant should be listed among the permanent investments at cost, irrespective of changes in market val The carrying charges, such as taxes, may be included in the cost.

Investments in the company's own stock. A company that h purchased its own stock with the intention of reissuing it may rega the shares it holds in the same light as it does the securities of oth companies and carry it on the books at the cost or market valu whichever is lower. However, if the stock acquired is regarded retired, but is not actually retired because retirement would invol an amendment of the certificate of incorporation, the par or stat value of the amount held should be shown as a deduction from ou standing capital stock in the capital-stock section of the balance shee (As to shares that are held in the treasury as a result of donatio see page 888. Many accountants hold that treasury stock should any event be reflected in the balance sheet as a deduction from th capital stock.)

Sinking funds. Sinking funds are generally created to meet a co tractual obligation undertaken at the time of the creation of an issu of bonds or notes. The nature of the investments purchased with th funds depends upon the terms of the indenture requiring the creatio and maintenance of the fund. Usually the investments consist bonds of the very issue that the fund is designed to protect. Th value of the sinking fund shown in the balance sheet may represe the total par value of the bonds of the same issue held in the sinkin fund, the cost of other securities purchased with sinking-funds mone if any, uninvested cash, and accrued interest on the securities owne If the company's own bonds have been acquired for the sinking fun and cancelled, they will not appear in the sinking fund as an asse but will be accounted for in the reduction of outstanding obligatio among the liabilities. The item may appear on the balance shee as follows:

Cash resources held by Trustees' account Bond Sinking Funds	$437,652
(Trustees also hold $13,340,000 of redeemed bonds, not included as liabilities in this balance sheet)	

Other funds. Other funds may include:

1. Funds for the retirement of capital stock.
2. Funds to meet some contingent liability; as, for example, a fun

pay damages that may result from an unfavorable decision under
nding litigation.

3. Funds for the payment of future liabilities; as, for example, nds to pay for advertising.

4. Funds representing investments of reserves, such as endowment nds, insurance funds, pension funds, and replacement funds. (See ge 887 for an explanation of funded reserves.)

A separate classification is sometimes made in the balance sheet of nds that represent neither permanent investments nor the usual nds. Amounts held by trustees for the payment of matured and lled bonds would, for example, not represent an investment or a nd.

Securities held as investments of funds are ordinarily valued as ermanent investments. (See page 874.)

Long-term notes receivable. Notes receivable not maturing ithin a year from the date of the balance sheet may be included mong the permanent investments, since they may not be considered ırrent assets.

Temporary investments. When this asset is included among the ıvestments and not in the current assets, it represents securities that ill not be sold in the ordinary course of business and should be alued in the same manner as permanent investments.

Advances. Advances made to subsidiary companies for permanent orking capital constitute, for practical purposes, investments by the arent company in the subsidiary companies, in addition to the investment represented by ownership of the securities of the subsidiary ompanies. The item therefore belongs with the investments. It is rquently combined with the investments in the balance sheet in the ollowing way:

Investments in and advances to affiliated companies	$1,428,333

ɔr included under the caption of investments, as follows:

Notes of and advances to associated companies:	
Controlled companies	$2,333,363
Noncontrolled companies	630,000

Ɔr, the advances may be listed in the balance sheet as a separate tem, without a caption.

Advances to stockholders, officers, and directors may appear unc the investments, under "other assets," or under some other captic except current accounts receivable.

Deferred Charges

What the deferred charges are. Practically every balance she includes a group of items representing deferred charges, for in tl operation of a business there are always certain expenses that are pa in advance. They may be designated in the balance sheet as "d ferred charges," "deferred assets," "deferred charges to future oper tions," "prepaid and deferred charges," "deferred items," "suspen items," or by other names. The items generally include prepaid e penses, unamortized charges, and miscellaneous suspense accounts.

Prepayments. The usual prepayments among the deferred charge are unexpired insurance, prepaid interest, taxes, rent, royalties, an advertising.

Unamortized expenditures. The following deferred charges aris through the application of the amortization process to expenditure that will eventually be entirely charged off to profit and loss:

1. Unamortized bond discount and expense. This item in the bal ance sheet generally represents the difference betwen the face amoun of bonds issued and the consideration received for them that mus still be written off before the entire discount at which the bond were issued by the corporation is wiped out.

2. Unamortized improvements to leased property. Amounts ex pended in erecting buildings upon leased property and in making alterations and improvements to such property must be written of over the life of the lease, for the additions, alterations, and improve ments usually revert to the landlord at the expiration of the lease (See page 871.) The sum shown among the deferred charges as unamortized improvements to leased property reflects the expendi tures that must still be written off. Improvements to leased prop erty are sometimes not included among the deferred charges but are presented as a separate asset, without caption, immediately below the fixed assets. In that case the amortization may be shown as a reserve, in the following way:

ALTERATIONS AND IMPROVEMENTS TO LEASED PROPERTIES:	
At independently appraised reproductive values at December 31, 19.., adjusted for property changes since 19.., including additions at cost	$7,131,149.63
Less Reserve for Amortization	2,875,252.44
	$4,255,897.19

3. Unamortized organization expenses. This item among the de-'red charges indicates the sum expended for organization costs that ıst still be written off.

Miscellaneous suspense items. A variety of items make up this tegory, such as questionable assets, merchandise of doubtful martability, and expenditures that have not finally been classified as sets or expense items.

OTHER ASSETS

What is included among other assets. Many balance sheets do ɔt contain this title, for the assets of the company fit properly under ıe principal categories heretofore discussed. Items that do not fit to the standard groups may be included without caption in the balıce sheet, or may be grouped under the heading of "other assets." he following accounts are frequently placed among the "other ssets:"

1. Stock subscriptions. When there is no immediate intention of ılling upon the subscribers for the unpaid balances of their subscripıons, the unpaid subscriptions may be included in the "other assets" r may be deducted from the capital stock, as explained on page 888. ubscriptions may appear among the current assets when the collecion of the subscriptions is expected in the near future. The item hould not be listed among the assets at all, but as a deduction from apital stock, if there is no probability that the stockholders will be equired to pay the unpaid subscriptions.

2. Deposits as security or guaranties—for example, bonds on deosit with the State Labor Commission; lease deposits.

3. Amounts due from officers and employees.

4. Advances to salesmen and employees.

5. Miscellaneous accounts receivable.

6. Insurance policies. This item is sometimes included among the

investments. The value should represent the cash-surrender va and not a capitalization of premiums paid for the policies. Althou the cash-surrender value of insurance policies is immediately av able, the asset is not a current asset unless there is a definite intenti of surrendering the policies in the near future.

Notes and comments relating to assets. Notes and comme of an informative character may be used freely in the balance sheet clarify the meaning of any item not apparent from its title, to furni information not reflected in the accounts of the company, and supplement the accounts. The following are examples of asset ite that may require notes and comments at the foot of the balance she

Contingent assets. Contingent assets do not appear in the body the balance sheet, since they represent items that are not real ass but that may some day become assets. For example, claims in d pute are contingent until they acquire the status of a collectible ite Contingent liabilities, discussed on page 884, are frequently offs by contingent assets. For example, if the company has endorsed t notes of another company, it has created a contingent liability; shou the original maker of the note default and the company become liab as endorser, it will have a claim against the original maker of the no for reimbursement. That claim is a contingent asset. A footno in the balance sheet may explain the nature of any contingent asset

Sinking-fund arrears. If the sinking fund is in arrears, a note at th foot of the balance sheet should indicate the amount of the arrear The following is an example of such a note:

The Company was in arrears in the amount of $10,000 on Decemb 31, 19.., on sinking-fund contributions required by the trust indentur

Current Liabilities

What the current liabilities are. The current liabilities of a bus ness set forth in the balance sheet should disclose all liabilities fo goods purchased; all liabilities for services rendered; all accrued liabil ties for wages, interest, taxes, bonuses, and the like, and all liabilitie upon due bills, trading stamps, and merchandise coupon books.

Accountants are not in agreement as to the period which deter mines that a liability is current. In some balance sheets the curren liabilities may represent debts that mature within ninety days; i others they may include liabilities payable within a year of the dat the balance sheet. The usual debts included among the current bilities are discussed below.

Accounts payable. This item generally includes obligations on en accounts due trade creditors and amounts due others for expenses. It also includes liabilities for taxes, salaries, and wages, ough these items are frequently listed separately with the current bilities. The advantage of showing separately amounts due trade editors is that this method offers the reader of the balance sheet opportunity to analyze the relationship of the amount due for erchandise and raw materials to purchases for the period. Liabiles to affiliated companies should be shown separately.

Notes and acceptances payable. Sometimes notes and acceptnces payable are divided into trade-notes payable and other notes ayable. As in the case of accounts payable, a separation of tradeotes payable from other notes payable throws light upon the relation f debts for merchandise to goods bought. The balance sheet, or ipporting schedules, should indicate whether the debts are secured r unsecured. Notes payable to affiliated companies should be shown eparately.

Discounted notes, acceptances, and so forth. The sum noted or this item indicates the extent to which the company has become ndebted because of the default of customers whose notes or acceptnces have been discounted.

Accounts and notes due to officers, stockholders, and employees. This debt should appear as a separate item if the amounts re large; if small, they may be included among the accounts payable. n balance sheets that are prepared to be submitted to banks, the mount should be stated as a separate item.

Accrued liabilities. The accrued liabilities may be separated from other current liabilities by a caption. They include amounts that are iabilities at the time the balance sheet is made up, but that are not et due. The usual accruals are for salaries and wages, commissions, axes, interest, rent, gas bills, dues, and other sundry expenses.

Other current liabilities. A number of other items may be included among the current liabilities if they represent debts that must be paid within the near future; among them are:

1. Purchase obligations. This may represent payments that will due currently or during the year on account of purchases of capi assets.

2. Customers' deposits. This debt belongs with the current l bilities whenever there is an obligation to return deposits within a short time or to apply them against sales. Customers' deposits m be carried as a separate item when they are to be held for a lo period. Public-service corporations, for example, usually list cu tomers' deposits as a separate item.

3. Customers' credit balances.

4. Matured interest payable. This item usually refers to sums pa able about the time that the balance sheet is made up. For exampl interest may be due on January 1 and the balance sheet prepare as of December 31. The fund to meet the interest due may be i the hands of the interest-paying agent or in a special bank accou of the company.

5. Dividends declared on certain classes of stock and payable aft the date of the balance sheet.

6. Matured long-term debts unpaid. This class of debt aris through the failure of holders of matured or called bonds to prese their bonds for payment.

7. Unpresented interest coupons and unclaimed dividends.

8. Long-term debts maturing in part or in whole during the yea Some accountants maintain that if the debt is to be refunded—th is, if the sum to meet the maturing obligations is to be raised by th issuance of other long-term obligations—the item should not appea in the current liabilities but should be carried among the fixe liabilities.

9. Reserves representing actual liabilities. (See page 886 for discussion of this class of reserves.)

Fixed Liabilities

What constitute the fixed liabilities? The long-term liabilities or fixed liabilities, generally include all obligations, whether secure or unsecured, maturing in more than one year from the date of th balance sheet. The items that usually make up the fixed liabilitie are discussed below. They appear in the statement, usually, unde the heading of "funded debt."

Mortgages. Any mortgages upon the property of the company ould be listed among the fixed liabilities and should not be prented as a deduction from the property account.

Long-term bonds, debentures, notes, and certificates of indebtlness. Although most balance sheets merely show the par value of ng-term debts outstanding, the statement would be more useful r analytical purposes if it showed:

1. The name of the issue, the rate of interest, and the maturity ate.
2. The par value of bonds outstanding of each issue.
3. The amount of bonds of each issue still unissued.
4. Whether any of the unissued bonds have been pledged.

. schedule of funded indebtedness may be appended to the balance ıeet, giving the above data.

The difference between the par value of bonds outstanding and ıe price received for them should be charged to bond discount, if ıey have been sold for less than par, or credited to the premium on onds account, if they have been sold at a premium. Both of these ccounts are written off periodically. The amount of discount on onds remaining to be amortized will be included among the deerred charges, as explained on page 878. Any premium on bonds ınamortized will be stated among the deferred credits.

In a consolidated balance sheet, the long-term debt may represent he net amount outstanding in the hands of the public if any of the ffiliated companies whose accounts are included in the balance sheet ıold bonds of a related company. In other words, the bonds held as n asset of one company may be offset against the bond liability of he other company.

Deposits. Customers' deposits held for a long period, such as leposits held by public-utility corporations, appear as separate items ımong the liabilities.

Under some circumstances, installment payments received from employees under employee stock-purchase plans are treated like deosits and entered as a liability. The amount is offset by the asset ash. The usual treatment of subscription installment payments, howver, is to show the amount due on subscriptions among the assets and to deduct from the capital stock on the liability side of the bal- ance sheet the amount of uncollected subscriptions. (See page 879

Deferred Credits

What deferred credits represent. The deferred credits in a bal- ance sheet, sometimes called "deferred income" or "miscellaneous un- adjusted credits," represent the opposite of "deferred charges," ex- plained at page 878. They represent an item of gross income that is to be credited to Profit and Loss in a future period, and comprise advance collections of income, unamortized credits, and miscellaneous suspense accounts. The group usually consists of the following items:

1. Advance collections of interest, rent, royalties, dues.
2. Advance collections on contracts or other sales when these are not properly included among the current liabilities.
3. Unamortized premiums on funded debt.
4. Miscellaneous suspense items; that is, receipts that have not definitely been classified as liabilities or income items.

Contingent Liabilities

What are contingent liabilities? Contingent liabilities are not ordinarily incorporated in the balance sheet proper because they do not affect the accounts while they remain contingent. No objection, however, can be found to the practice of including a caption for con- tingent liabilities and entering the items "short"—that is, without carrying the amounts out to the columns that reflect the actual lia- bilities. The more common practice is to indicate the nature and amount of contingent liabilities as footnotes below the balance-sheet totals. The following are examples of contingent liabilities and the manner in which they have been treated in actual balance sheets:

Notes receivable discounted. "Contingent liability on notes dis- counted, $42,980.54."

Obligations of others guaranteed. "The .... Company was contingently liable at December 31, 19.., as guar- antor and indorser of obligations of subsidiary companies, aggregat- ing $6,379,137.61."

Contingent liability as surety. "On December 31, 19.., the .... Company was surety on a bond for $13,112,- 668.94 executed by the .... Co., as principal, pro-ding for the refund by that company to telephone users of sums, any, which may be found to have been collected under rates in xcess of those ultimately held legal. The .... Company was surety on a similar bond of the .... Company in the amount of $3,000,000."

Unsettled tax disputes. "Federal income taxes for certain prior ears are subject to final settlement with the U. S. Treasury Department."

Accounts assigned. "The company was contingently liable on December 31, 19. ., in the amount of $8,500 as guarantor of assigned ccounts receivable."

Lawsuits. "The item of $34,149,623.15, representing the book alue of investments in, advances for account of, and account receivable from Deep Rock Oil Corporation (in receivership), includes a claim of Standard Gas and Electric Company against the Corporation for $9,342,642.37, against which a counterclaim has been sserted. In the opinion of counsel for the Company, the determinaion of the claim and counter-claim should result in a substantial liaility from the Corporation to Standard Gas and Electric Company."

Cumulative dividends in arrears. "No provision has been made in the above statement for cumulative undeclared dividends on the $6 preferred stock, amounting to $6,844,291.12, and on the $5 preferred stock amounting to $7,032,566.25 on September 30, 19. ."

Indemnification of underwriters. "Standard Gas and Electric Company, in connection with the solicitations of deposits of its twenty-year 6 per cent gold notes and 6 per cent convertible gold notes, both of which were originally due October 1, 19. ., agreed under Extension and Deposit Agreement dated June 18, 19. ., to indemnify the underwriters from all loss, liability, or expense incurred or sustained under the Securities Act of 1933, as amended, or at common law or otherwise, arising out of, or based upon, an untrue statement of a material fact, or the omission to state a material fact in the registration statements or the prospectus, subject to certain exceptions as to statements or omissions based entirely on information furnished to the Company by the underwriters."

Minority Interests

Liability to minority stockholders. As indicated on page 856, the interest of minority stockholders in controlled companies must be set up as a liability if the accounts of a subsidiary are taken in the consolidated balance sheet as though the companies were co pletely owned by the parent company. The item is generally stat simply as a liability, under no particular caption, in such terms the following:

Capital stock and surplus of minority interests . . $755,143.49

The portion of surplus of subsidiary companies applicable to th minority interest may be indicated in the item as follows:

Preferred and common stocks of subsidiary companies (consolidated) in hands of public, including $118,483 surplus applicable thereto $1,928,883

In some balance sheets, the minority's interest is shown in the capit stock section of the balance sheet instead of as a separate item amon the liabilities.

Reserves

What reserves are listed among the liabilities? In the discus sion of the assets shown in a balance sheet, such reserves as th reserve for bad debts and reserve for depreciation were mentioned These reserves appear on the assets side of the balance sheet as de ductions from the valuation of the assets to which they pertain be cause they represent reserves against decreases in the value of th assets. All other classes of reserves appear on the liabilities side o the balance sheet. They may be classified as follows:

1. Reserves that represent actual current liabilities. A reserve fo the payment of Federal and state income taxes, for example, shoulc be listed among the current liabilities.

2. Reserves for contingencies. These may be treated in three ways:

(*a*) A reserve for a contingency that is very likely to become a reality should appear as a separate item among the liabilities. Fo example, a reserve for payments to be made under a pending lawsuit for which an unfavorable verdict is expected should be presented as a distinct liability. Companies with investments in Continental Europe during World War II set up contingent reserves among their liabilities as a provision for possible irrecoverable losses in connection with foreign investments.

(*b*) A reserve for a contingency that is likely to become a reality d decrease the value of an asset may be presented as a deduction ɔm the asset. For example, a reserve for declines in the market lue of investments, or a reserve for declines in the market value of erchandise, might appear as deductions from the assets to which ey apply.

(*c*) A reserve for a contingency of loss that is merely possible ıd not definitely probable should appear under the caption of re- rves. An example is a "reserve for unforeseen possibilities."

3. Reserves that represent net worth. Such reserves are either:

(*a*) Appropriation of surplus.
(*b*) Unrealized profit reserves.

reserve that represents an appropriation of surplus may be either quired by contract—as, for example, a reserve for sinking funds— voluntarily set up—as, for example, a reserve for plant extension. ıch reserves should appear under the surplus caption. An unreal- ed profit reserve—as, for example, a reserve for unrealized profit on ɔpraisal of plant—may appear under the caption of reserves; but if ıe asset to which the reserve refers has actually increased in value, ıe item may be included as a separate item under surplus.

Reserves for corresponding funds. When a reserve appears on ıe liabilities side of a balance sheet and a corresponding fund is in- luded among the assets, the conclusion may be drawn that the fund ıown among the assets had been created out of profits of the com- any to the extent indicated in the reserve for the particular fund. uch reserves are temporary appropriations of surplus and belong in he balance sheet under the general heading of surplus. They have he effect of reducing the amount of free surplus available for divi- lends to the extent of the reserve. When the fund is finally dis- ɔursed, the reserve will revert to surplus and be available for dividends.

Capital Stock and Surplus

What the capital stock section should show. The capital stock ection of the balance sheet should indicate the various classes of tock and as to each class the following information should be given:

1. Par value, if any, or the fact that the stock is without par value. In the case of preferred stock, redeemable at or entitled in liquida- tion to an amount in excess of par value, the preferred stock may be carried at its liquidation value.

2. The preferences and other special rights, if any, of each cl of stock.

3. The amount authorized, issued, and outstanding, held in t treasury, and reserved for issuance upon exercise of stock purch warrants.

If part of the purchase price of the stock is still unpaid, and th is no intention of immediately calling the unpaid subscriptions, t uncollected subscriptions should appear as a deduction from the ca tal stock, thus:

Capital stock—authorized, 10,000 shares at $100 par value; issued and outstanding, 800 shares	$800,000
Less uncollected subscriptions	200,000
Paid-in capital	$600,000

(For the inclusion of unpaid subscriptions among the assets, rath than as a deduction from the capital stock, see page 879.)

The premiums on stock that has been sold above par may appe in the capital stock section as a separate item, indicated as "Pr miums on Capital Stock." The amount will remain on the balan sheet indefinitely unless it is eventually transferred to "paid-in su plus" or to "surplus." It will not be transferred to surplus if und the laws of the state in which the company is organized amoun representing premiums on stock may not legally be distributed dividends.

The discount on stock that has been sold below par may appear i the capital stock section of the balance sheet as a deduction therefrom

Treasury stock should appear as a deduction from the capital stoc outstanding to the extent of its par value, since it is not outstandin However, at times it may appear among the assets valued at cos (See page 876.)

Valuing no-par stock in the capital stock section of the balanc sheet. Stock without par value is indicated by that title in the cap tal stock section of the balance sheet and is given a valuation. Tha valuation may represent:

1. The full price received for no-par stock by the corporation.
2. The minimum price that the law of the state in which the cor poration is organized requires to be paid for the stock.
3. The "stated," or "declared," value placed upon the no-par stock

the law of the state in which the corporation is organized provides
hat directors may place a stated or declared value upon no-par stock.

4. An amount arrived at arbitrarily by the board of directors.

Any amount received for no-par stock in excess of the minimum rice or above the stated or declared value becomes surplus or paid-in surplus." If the excess is permitted to be treated as surplus nder the laws of the state in which the corporation is organized, nd is so treated by the corporation, the surplus out of which dividends can be paid is augmented by an amount that has not been arned by the corporation. If the excess is carried as paid-in surplus in the balance sheet, it is clear that the corporation does not egard the amount as a part of its free surplus. However, the mere eparation of the paid-in surplus from the surplus does not signify hat the former will not be used for dividends.

A reader of the balance sheet cannot tell how the sum indicated or no-par stock was determined; he can merely conclude that the amount noted reflects the capital investment behind the outstanding no-par shares.

The capital-stock item in a consolidated balance sheet refers to the capital stock of the parent company. The stock of the subsidiary companies included in the consolidation has been eliminated in the preparation of the consolidated statement. To make this clear, consolidated balance sheets sometimes indicate the name of the parent company in the capital stock item, as follows:

Capital Stock:	
.... Corporation	
Common capital stock:	
Authorized, 2,500,000 shares of no-par value	
Issued, 1,509,556 shares	$52,539,547.11
Less held in treasury, 7,943 shares ...	276,453.22
Outstanding, 1,501,613 shares	$52,263,093.89

Treatment of surplus in the balance sheet. The surplus account is not analyzed in the balance sheet. It is analyzed either in the income statement or in a separate account. If the latter method is used, the balance sheet will show the amount of surplus and will refer to the separate analysis of the surplus account. The explanation of the surplus account, given on page 898, shows how the item included in the balance sheet is generally made up.

How capital and surplus generally appear in the balance shee Various methods of presenting capital stock and surplus are followe in practice, the most common of which are identified and illustrate below.

1. A caption combining capital stock and surplus:

CAPITAL STOCK AND SURPLUS:		
Common Stock—No-par value:		
Authorized	250,000 shares	
Issued and outstanding	189,538 shares	$1,014,000.00
Surplus as per annexed statement		1,588,663.53
		$2,602,663.53

2. A caption combining Capital Stock and Paid-in Surplus, wit earned surplus listed separately:

CAPITAL STOCK AND PAID-IN SURPLUS:		
6% Cumulative Preferred Stock—$100 par value:		
Authorized—	100,000 shares	
Issued—	61,657 shares	$ 6,165,700.00
Common Stock (No-par value):		
Authorized—	2,500,000 shares	
Issued—	2,263,150 shares	
Less in Treasury	7,229 shares	
	2,255,921 shares	
at stated value of $10.00 per share		22,559,210.00
Paid-in Surplus		28,782,600.00
		$ 57,507,510.00
EARNED SURPLUS, as per annexed statement		$ 76,595,940.83
		$154,154,698.44

3. Separate captions for capital stock and surplus:

Preferred 7% cumulative (authorized and outstanding, 20,000 shares of $100.00 each; called for redemption on February 1, 19. .; at redemption value as of December 31, 19. .)	$ 2,500,000.00

Common—without par value (authorized, 1,000,000 shares; issued, 711,000 shares)..	18,486,000.00
Total capital stock	$20,986,000.00
Surplus	3,681,301.12
Total	$25,756,976.49

4. HOW THE INCOME STATEMENT IS CONSTRUCTED

How to head the income statement. The heading of the income statement should contain the following points of information:

1. The name of the person, firm, or organization whose profit and loss statement is being rendered.
2. What the statement purports to be.
3. The period of time covered by the statement.

The terms "condensed," "comparative," and "consolidated" in the title of the income statement have the same significance as they do in the title of the balance sheet. (See page 854.)

The period is generally indicated as "for the year ended ...., 19.."; or "...... months ended ...., 19.."; or "fiscal year ended ...., 19.."

Titles for the income statement. An even greater variety of terms is used for the title of the income statement than is used for the balance sheet. The most common are the following, with the prefix of such terms as "condensed," "comparative," or "consolidated," or combinations of these words:

1. Statement of income.
2. Income statement.
3. Income account.
4. Earnings statement.
5. Statement of earnings.
6. Income and profit and loss statement.
7. Statement of profit and loss.
8. Profit and loss account.
9. Profit and loss statement.
10. Income and earned surplus accounts.

11. Statement of profit and loss and retained earnings (includin variations in earned surplus terminology).
12. Statement of income and retained earnings (including vari tions in earned surplus terminology).
13. Statement of operations (and earned surplus).

If the title does not include a reference to the surplus, a separat statement concerning surplus is generally rendered.

Form of the income statement. The income statement is ger erally presented in "report" or "narrative" form, sometimes als called the "reducing-balance" form or the "running" form. In stat ments so prepared, the items are presented in logical order, on under the other. Even statements that carry the word "account" i their title do not present the items in account form—that is, as debit and credits.

Divisions of the income statement. Every income statement i divisible into two parts:

1. Items dealing with operations of the business.
2. Items relating to nonoperating income and nonoperating charge

Many statements of income contain a third part—namely:

3. Items showing disposition of the net income.

When this section is omitted from the income statement it is usu ally found in a statement of the surplus account.

Grouping of items. Income statements show a greater variet of items and less uniformity of grouping than balance sheets. Manu facturing concerns set up accounts to reflect cost of production; com panies engaged in trading have no such accounts. Organization that are not engaged in manufacturing or trading would emplo accounts suitable for their needs. Whatever the business, and what ever the accounts, the statement is likely to be segregated into th following groups:

1. Sales.
2. Cost of goods sold.
3. Selling expenses.
4. General and administrative expenses.

5. Income other than operating income.
6. Charges other than operating charges.

Io typical order of the groups can be presented. An examination f many published income statements, reflecting the practices of ading accounting firms, reveals a great difference of opinion on the ıbject of placement of the various deductions from and additions) income. In the explanation of items in the income statement nat follows, some of the variations in practice will be indicated.

Methods of clarifying the income statement. The income tatement may be clarified in ways similar to those employed in lucidating items in the balance sheet. They are as follows:

1. By fairly full explanations of the items within the statement roper. For example, the item "Net sales billed" is clearer if preented as follows:

Aggregate net amount billed for products shipped and other classes of usiness (excluding sundry sales, real estate, and certain miscellaneous ervices), less sales commissions, returns, and other allowances.

2. By running comments in the statement. The following is an xample of this form of presentation:

GROSS PROFIT BEFORE DEDUCTING DEPRECIATION	$5,277,070.19
The amount remaining from sales income after deducting manufacturing and purchase costs exclusive of depreciation.	
ADVERTISING, SELLING, DISTRIBUTING, AND ADMINISTRATIVE EXPENSES	4,572,971.74
The cost of marketing the products and administering the business of the companies.	
PROFIT FROM OPERATIONS BEFORE DEDUCTING DEPRECIATION	$ 704,098.45
The amount remaining after deducting the above-described costs and expenses.	
OTHER INCOME	128,963.11
Includes interest on investments, discounts earned for prompt payment of bills for purchases, etc	
GROSS INCOME BEFORE DEDUCTING DEPRECIATION	$ 833,061.56
The sum of the two preceding items.	

OTHER DEDUCTIONS (exclusive of depreciation, interest, and taxes on income)	123,560.13
Includes discounts allowed customers for prompt payment of bills, provision for uncollectible accounts receivable, pensions paid to former employees, net loss on sales of investment securities, etc.	

3. By notes or footnotes appended to the income statement. Fc example:

Gross profit on sales—See Note A	$2,206,800.28

Note A explains the item as follows:

All profit on installment sales is taken into income at the time the sale are recorded on the books, and Federal income taxes are accrued annı ally thereon, even though such taxes are paid only as the installment ac counts receivable are collected.

4. By the use of schedules. Published income statements are sup ported by few schedules, although many are prepared in connectioı with the income statement for the use of the business executives The schedules most commonly made available are those showing de preciation, renewal, maintenance, nonoperating income, and othe charges and credits.

Points in income statements requiring special clarification Income statements do not show upon their face what principles are followed in allocating charges and credits to income account anc surplus account. This can be determined only from a statement prepared especially to disclose this information. As yet business enterprises have not adopted the practice of furnishing such an explanatory statement.

The nature of income from companies controlled but not consolidated is not obvious from the income statement unless the information is especially given.

The company's proportionate share of the undistributed earnings or losses of controlled companies whose accounts are not consolidated for the purposes of the income statement is not apparent from the statement unless a note concerning such income is included in the statement.

Explanation of Items in the Income Statement

Many published income statements are abbreviated or condensed o such an extent that they disclose little information. For example, hey start with gross operating income or merely operating income, nd present no information as to sales or operating costs. The folowing explanation includes items that would appear in a statement vhich reveals all the sources of revenue and all costs and charges.

Sales. The sales, when set forth, are variously termed "gross eceipts," "net sales and billings," "net sales billed," or "net sales." These terms generally reflect the volume of sales, less such deducions as returns, allowances, rebates, allowances made under price uaranties, freight on sales, allowances for the return of containers, nd the like. Provision for doubtful accounts may be deducted from he sales or included among the operating charges. The deductions nay or may not include commissions and cash discounts. Commisions allowed on sales are frequently treated as selling expenses, and ash discounts are sometimes regarded as operating expenses and ncluded under the operating charges.

Operating charges. The components of operating charges are not clearly defined, nor do companies in their published statements undertake to disclose the exact nature and determination of the operating charges. For purposes of this explanation the following are considered the operating charges:

1. Cost of goods sold.
2. Operating expenses.

Many of the items included in the following explanation of these two divisions of operating charges are subject to different treatment. The variations in treatment will be noted.

Cost of goods sold. In a manufacturing concern the cost of goods sold is made up of the total of:

1. Inventory at the beginning of the period,
2. Direct labor,
3. Overhead expenses,

less the inventory at the end of the period. In a trading concern the cost of goods sold is the merchandise cost, which includes buying expenses.

The difference between the cost of goods sold and the sales is termed the "gross profit on sales," or "trading income."

Operating expenses. The operating expenses include:

1. Selling expenses.
2. General expenses.
3. Administrative expenses.
4. Taxes. This item sometimes omits income taxes, which are treated as a deduction from income. Other classes of taxes besides income taxes are also treated as deductions from income in some income statements.
5. Provision for doubtful accounts. This item may be treated as a deduction from the sales, as indicated above.
6. Depreciation and depletion attributable to operations. This item is also sometimes found among the deductions from income.
7. Provision for possible losses. This deduction includes reserves and may be included under the heading of "reserves."

The difference between the "gross profit on sales" and the operating expenses is the "net operating revenue" or "operating income." If all of the items constituting operating expenses have not been deducted, attention may be called to the fact by labeling the difference somewhat as follows: "profit from operations before deducting depreciation"; or if the reserves are separately enumerated, the difference may be termed "operating income before deduction of reserves."

Operating income in a consolidated income statement. In a consolidated income statement, the operating income may omit the profit on intercompany transactions of subsidiaries considered in the consolidation. Or, intercompany profits may be shown as a deduction in some other part of the income statement. The operating income may include dividends received from subsidiaries and affiliated companies not consolidated, as well as the parent company's equity in the undivided profits or losses of subsidiaries and affiliated companies whose accounts are not consolidated in the statement.

Nonoperating income. Additions to income arising from nonoperating sources are included in this group generally under some ading such as "other income," "income from other sources," "non-perating income," or merely under the word "additions." The llowing items are the usual nonoperating sources of revenue:

1. Interest on securities.
2. Interest on bank balances, notes receivable, and the like.
3. Profits realized on sale and on maturity of securities.
4. Dividends.
5. Discounts earned for prompt payment of bills. This item ould not appear here if the discounts were considered in determin-ng cost of goods sold and in the valuation of inventories.
6. Royalties.
7. Losses recovered.

When these items are added to the "net operating income," the total s generally called "total income." Frequently the addition is made on the statement without labeling the total or by merely calling the um "total."

Nonoperating charges. Deductions from income resulting from inancial expenses are subtracted from the total income under the heading of "deductions from income," "interest and other charges," 'other charges," or "deductions." The usual nonoperating charges are:

1. Interest on funded debt.
2. Other interest.
3. Discount on bonds.
4. Depreciation and depletion, not included under operating expenses.
5. Income taxes and other taxes not included among the operating expenses.

The difference between "total income" and the "deductions from income" represents the "net profit" or "net loss" for the period.

The income statement may end with the net profit or net loss and be supplemented by a statement of surplus, or it may be continued to show the changes in the surplus account during the period. In the latter case, the title of the statement will include a reference to the surplus. The presentation of the make-up of the surplus account is practically the same whether it is appended to the income statement or presented in a separate statement. In this discussion th statement of surplus is treated separately, below.

Portion of profits or losses applicable to minority interests. consolidated statement that is prepared as though the parent com pany had a 100 per cent ownership of the stock of subsidiary compa nies, when in fact less than 100 per cent of the stock of the subsidiar is owned, must show the proportion of the income or loss applicab to minority interests. This item usually appears after the "ne profit" or "net loss" item, although in some statements it is place ahead of the figure showing the net profit or loss for the perio

The Statement of Surplus

How to head the statement of surplus. The heading of th statement of surplus, when presented apart from the income state ment, should contain the same three points of information as th income statement—namely:

1. The name of the corporation whose surplus account is presente
2. What the statement purports to be. If the statement analyze earned surplus, as differentiated from capital surplus, the title shoul show it to be a statement of earned surplus; similarly, if the change in the capital-surplus account are being presented, the title shoul convey that information. If the statement covers capital surplus an earned surplus, the general term "surplus" may be used in the title
3. The period of time covered by the statement. The period i indicated in the same way as in the income statement.

What capital surplus is. Capital surplus is that portion of th net worth of a business which is not represented by capital stock o by earned surplus. The most common forms of capital surplus ar "paid-in surplus," "donated surplus," "reduction surplus," and "ap praisal surplus." There is a tendency to replace the term "surplus" as used in "capital surplus" and "paid-in surplus" with terminology to show the source from which the proprietary capital was derived. All surplus accounts are capital surplus except (1) earned surplus, and (2) appropriations of earned surplus.

The following are the usual sources of capital surplus (in other words, the circumstances under which capital surplus is credited). The terms in parentheses show the items commonly designated by terms other than "capital surplus."

1. Premiums upon the sale of par value stock (paid-in surplus).
2. A part of the consideration received from the sale of no-par ɔck, set aside by the directors as paid-in surplus (paid-in surplus). his may also be the capital contributed by stockholders in excess of e stated value of no-par shares.
3. Amounts received upon the resale of treasury stock in excess of e cost of the acquisition.
4. Purchase of assets for less than book value; for example, the ılue of assets acquired from another company in excess of the par ılue of the stock given in payment therefor.
5. Increases in the value of assets beyond the amount paid when ıe property was acquired (appraisal surplus, revaluation surplus, or ɔpreciation surplus).
6. Reductions in capital stock made through redemption at a figre less than the amount originally received for the stock (paid-in ırplus).
7. Conversion of capital stock into another issue of the same comany; for example, the excess of stated value of preferred stock over ar value of common stock into which it was converted.
8. Exchange of capital stock for that of another company; for exmple, excess of issue price over par value for shares issued to acuire the capital stock of a subsidiary company.
9. Restoration of realization of assets previously written off.
10. Merger and consolidation adjustments; for example, undistribıted earnings of a partly-owned company prior to acquisition of the emainder of its stock.
11. Transfer from earned surplus in connection with a stock divilend.
12. Donations of cash, marketable securities, or assets the value of vhich is certain (paid-in surplus).
13. Donations of property or of the company's own stock, which is alled treasury stock (donated surplus). When a non-cash gift is onverted to cash, or marketable securities, the name is changed to aid-in surplus.

Capital surplus is not used for the payment of dividends while the ompany has an accumulation of earned surplus, except under unısual circumstances. Charges are made to the capital surplus acounts under such conditions as the following:

1. On the purchase and sale of the company's issued stock; f example, the excess of cost over the par value of preferred stock a quired for retirement.

2. Transfers to capital, for example, the par value of stock divider shares credited to capital.

3. Write-off of intangibles; for example, the write-down of goo will.

4. Transfers to earned surplus.

5. Adjustments in connection with consolidations, mergers, an recapitalizations; for example, costs and expenses incidental to th liquidation of a subsidiary.

What the statement of surplus should show. The statement surplus should indicate:

1. What the surplus was at the beginning of the period.

2. Additions to profits not resulting from the operation of the bus ness during the period covered by the income statement. These ma be given under the heading of "surplus credits." The following ar examples of such additions to surplus:

(*a*) Increases in the market value of marketable securities.

(*b*) Increase in dollar value of net current assets due to varia tions in foreign-exchange rates.

(*c*) Reinstatement of excess provision made in previous year fo shrinkage in market value of investment securities.

(*d*) Adjustments of reserves where charges to depreciation ir previous years proved to be excessive.

(*e*) Recovery of Federal income taxes for prior years.

3. Deduction of charges not affecting the operations for the perioc covered by the income statement. These may be given under the heading of "surplus charges." The following are examples of such deductions.

(*a*) Obsolete property abandoned.

(*b*) Provision for shrinkage in market value of securities.

(*c*) Taxes applicable to previous years.

(*d*) Net loss on disposal of machinery and equipment.

(*e*) Write-down of marketable securities.

4. The amount of net income added for the year or the amount net loss deducted. This is the sum shown in the income state-ent for the period.

5. The deduction of dividends declared during the year, set forth to each class of stock.

6. The balance of the surplus. This amount is shown on the abilities side of the balance sheet. (See page 890.) It may be di-ided as follows:

(*a*) Appropriations for special purposes; for example, reserves or plant extensions and other reserves representing net worth.
(*b*) Capital surplus.
(*c*) Undivided, or "earned," surplus.

5. HOW TO ANALYZE A FINANCIAL STATEMENT

How to obtain financial statements. Statements of the financial ondition of a business asking for credit can be obtained directly from he firm or indirectly from other sources.

Direct requests. The usual practice is to write a letter asking for financial statement and to enclose a printed form such as that re-roduced in Figure 73. It is advisable to keep on file the postmarked nvelope in which any financial statement is mailed, for following a lebtor's bankruptcy, the statement, if false, is frequently the basis of n indictment charging the use of the United States mail to defraud. The form reproduced on pages 902-903 is a self-mailing form, thus assuring preservation of the evidence of mailing.

Most business firms recognize that it is established practice to supply complete financial information when seeking credit. Some firms, in fact, will even furnish creditors, upon request, with monthly balance sheets and profit and loss statements, after having submitted financial statements that are several months old. However, objections to furnishing statements are sometimes encountered. One-man or family-controlled companies sometimes refuse as a matter of policy or pride. Other companies refuse out of fear that the financial information might fall into hostile hands. If the mailed request is not answered with the desired information, a telephone call to the treasurer or controller of the company, or a personal visit, may bring results. The success of the interview is a matter of salesmanship. Ob-

FOLD IN ON THIS LINE

Form 4E

Date________________195___

FINANCIAL STATEMENT OF____________________________

Kind of Business________________ Address________________

At Close of Business on____________19___ City________________ State________

ISSUED TO________________________ ← { Name of firm asking for statement

[THIS FORM APPROVED AND PUBLISHED BY THE NATIONAL ASSOCIATION OF CREDIT MEN]

For the purpose of obtaining merchandise from you on credit, or for the extension of credit, we make the following statement in writing, intending that you should rely thereon respecting our exact financial condition.

[PLEASE ANSWER ALL QUESTIONS. WHEN NO FIGURES ARE INSERTED, WRITE WORD "NONE"]

ASSETS	Dollars	Cents	LIABILITIES	Dollars	Cents
Cash (In Bank)			**Accounts Payable** (for Merchandise)		
(On Hand)			**Notes & Acceptances Payable**		
Accounts Receivable			**Owe to**________ Bank		
(Amt. Past Due $______)			(When Due______ Secured) (Unsecured)		
(Amt. Sold or Pledged $______)			**Income Taxes,** Accrued		
Notes and Trade Acceptances Receivable			**Other Taxes, Including Sales Taxes,** Accrued		
(Amt. Sold or Pledged $______)			**Interest,** Accrued		
Merchandise Inventory (Do not include Merchandise on Consignment) at Cost or Market, whichever is lower			**Rental, Payrolls, etc.,** Accrued		
(Amount Pledged $______)			**Payables** to Partners, Relatives		
Other Current Assets (Describe)			**Other Current Liabilities** (Describe)		
TOTAL CURRENT ASSETS			TOTAL CURRENT LIABILITIES		
Land and Buildings (Depreciated Value)			**Mortgage on Land and Buildings**		
Machinery, Fixtures and Equipment (Depreciated Value)			**Chattel Mortgage on Mdse. or Equipment**		
			Liens on Mdse. or Equipment		
Due from Officers or Non-Customers			**Other Liabilities,** No Current (Describe)		
Other Assets (Describe)			TOTAL LIABILITIES		
			Net Worth or { **Capital** $______ **Surplus** $______ }		
TOTAL ASSETS			TOTAL NET WORTH AND LIABILITIES		

FOLD IN ON THIS LINE

Surplus (or Net Worth at beginning of period) dated ______ 19__ $______
Add Profit for Period $______ and Adjustments $______ $______
TOTAL $______
Deduct Loss for Period $______ and Dividends (or Withdrawals, if not Incorporated) $______ and Adjustments $______ $______
SURPLUS (or NET WORTH) in Statement Above $______

STATEMENT OF PROFIT AND LOSS FOR PERIOD FROM ______ TO ______

			DETAILS OF EXPENSE OF OPERATIONS		
1. TOTAL SALES FOR PERIOD (Cash $____) (Credit $____)			Salaries, Owners		
2. Inventory at Start of Period $____			Employees		
3. Purchases for Period $____			Rent		
4. Total (Item 2 plus Item 3) $____			Heat, Light, Other Occupancy Expense		
5. Deduct Inventory at Close of Period $____			Advertising		
6. COST OF SALES			Interest		
7. GROSS PROFIT			Taxes, except Income Tax		
8. Less Total Expense			Depreciation, Fixtures, Trucks, Etc.		
9. NET PROFIT			All other Expense		
10. Less Income Taxes					
11. NET PROFIT After Taxes			TOTAL OPERATING EXPENSE		

		INSURANCE CARRIED
Amount you are liable for as endorser, guarantor, surety $	What books of Account do you keep?	Fire Merchandise $
Amount of merchandise held on consignment $	Date of latest inventory	Furn. & Fixt. $
	Date of latest audit	Building $
Amount of machinery or equipment held under lease $	Title to business premises is in name of	Extended Coverage $ U & O $
Amount of machinery or equipment under conditional sale $	If premises leased state annual rental Expiration date of lease	Liability General $
Amount you pay per month on lease or conditional sale contract $	Name of your bank(s) Do you have a Credit Department?	Auto & Truck $ Life for Benefit of Business $

The statement above and on the back of this form has been carefully read by the undersigned (both the printed and written matter), and is, to my knowledg in all respects complete, accurate and truthful. It discloses to you the true state of my (our) financial condition on the ______ day of ______ 195__ Since that time there has been no material unfavorable change in my (our) financial condition, and if any such change takes place I (we) will give you notice. Until such notice is given, you are to regard this as a continuing statement. **The figures submitted are not estimated.** They have been taken from my (our) books and physical inventory taken as on date shown.

Name of Individual or Firm ______

If Partnership, Name Partners } ______ ______
" Corporation, " Officers } ______ ______

How long established ______ Previous business experience ______
______ Where ______

Date of Signing Statement ______ Street ______ City ______ State ______

Witness ______ Signed by ______
Residence Address of Witness ______ Title ______

(Over)

Figure 73. Financial Statement Approved by National Association of Credit Men.

jections can usually be overcome through courtesy and reasonabl ness. If the credit man can create confidence in his company and i himself, and can advance reasons why it is to the advantage of th applicant to furnish the requested information, he will usually su ceed in getting it.

Indirect sources. If the direct request fails, indirect sources ma be tried, such as general and special credit agencies (see page 981) and financial publications. Banks, creditors, suppliers, bonding com panies, and accountants sometimes have the desired financial stat ments, and if they are not honor bound to withhold the information they may supply it.

Extent to which financial statements are used in credit work The policy of business houses in asking for financial statements varies Some stress the importance of putting the customer to as little trou ble as possible and call for a financial statement only when they con sider it necessary. Others make it a practice to request new financia statements from all customers at regular intervals, in order to keep their files up to date. Such factors as the length of time the applican has been in business, its record in the community, the experience o the seller with the account, the amount of credit that is sought, and similar elements, determine whether a financial statement should be required. If a newly established firm is seeking credit, a financial statement is invariably requested. In some lines of industry, most of the firms will ask for financial statements in any case where the order is in excess of $500.

What part of the balance sheet reveals credit strength? The current assets and current liabilities sections of the balance sheet contain the data from which to gauge the bill-paying ability of the customer, for the current assets show the amount of ready funds available with which to meet the current liabilities. The excess of the current assets over the current liabilities is known as the "working capital" of the business.* Since financial statements obtained from an applicant for credit are generally a "window-dressed" portrayal of the financial condition of the company, the reliability of the figures

* The term "working capital" is sometimes applied by businessmen to all the current assets, and the term "net working capital" to the excess of current assets over current liabilities. In this discussion, working capital refers to the difference between the current assets and the current liabilities.

ust be proved. Each item in the current assets and current liabili-es must therefore be examined and analyzed before judgment can passed upon the financial standing of the credit applicant.

Place of fixed assets in credit analysis. The fixed tangible assets id the capital liabilities through which they were secured are of condary importance in the analysis of financial statements for the irpose of determining credit strength alone. The intangible assets, ich as goodwill, patents, and the like, have no place in a credit ialysis.

The attention to be given to fixed tangible assets depends upon the ollowing factors:

1. The nature of the business of the credit applicant. The fixed ssets of a retail establishment may be an inconsequential factor i the determination of credit strength, whereas the fixed assets of a ianufacturing concern may have a direct bearing upon working apital.

2. The prosperity or lack of prosperity experienced in the imme-liate past. The item of fixed assets in a manufacturer's statement hould be given greater attention after a period of low earnings such s is experienced during an economic depression than need be given o it during or immediately after a period of profitable activity. The eason for this is that in many industries, as a result of decreased earn-ngs, the fixed assets are permitted to run down; they become obso-ete and in order to be maintained require greater asset strength. In nany cases a part of the decrease in earnings suffered by the business s due to the fixed overhead cost that must be met while plant and machinery stand idle.

A disproportionate amount of fixed assets would indicate an invest-ment in property beyond the strength of the organization and a need for more working capital than would be required if less were invested in plant and equipment. If a financial statement shows large invest-ment in plant and equipment, greater attention must be given to the earning power and management of the business.

Place of prepaid expenses in credit analysis. Prepaid expenses such as prepaid taxes, insurance, supplies, and the like, are not considered as current assets in an analysis of financial statements for credit purposes. The argument is sometimes raised, however, th the practical effect of excluding them is to show less credit streng than actually exists.

Need for comparative data. An adequate analysis of financi statements requires comparison with previous years; it is therefo highly desirable that the financial statements for several years be avai able. The conclusions reached from an analysis of a single financi statement may be quite different from those drawn from an analys of the same statement in comparison with other years, and ma present a misleading picture of the applicant's affairs.

The comparative statement. Since many business houses as regularly for financial statements from their customers, they are in position to have available comparative figures without asking thei customers for comparative statements. Figure 74 illustrates a com parative statement taken from the files of a large chemical concern. The credit department of a large textile manufacturer uses the forn shown in Figure 75. The comparative statement is made up as soon as comparative figures become available.

In transcribing to the comparative statement the balance shee offered by the customer, no changes are made in the amounts to give effect to the findings upon an analysis of the statement. Thus, if a study of the accounts receivable reveals that many of the account are doubtful and that the reserve for bad debts is insufficient, no indication of this conclusion is made on the comparative statement. The working papers of a particular analysis show the results of the analysis. The comparative statement is used principally to show trends in the customer's business and is referred to whenever the most recent statement is examined.

It will be noticed that in Figure 74 columns are provided to show the percentage that each item in the balance sheet bears to the total. Such percentages are known as "analytical percentages." They are not indispensable in an examination of financial statements and are frequently omitted.

Procedure in analyzing financial statements. A thorough analysis of financial statements cannot be made by merely scanning the statement and drawing conclusions from the impressions gathered.

A procedure of analysis that will yield all the pertinent information with a minimum of effort should be adopted. No method of procedure can be offered as suitable for every examiner of credit risks. Credit men work as individuals; the practice of one efficient individual may be quite different from that of another equally efficient person. One individual may go rather far in making written notes of his analyses of the financial statements submitted; another may leave no written evidence of the analysis. The latter method is subject to criticism if credit decisions are to be reviewed by a superior. The following procedure is suggested as one that will accomplish the purposes of any analysis of financial statements to determine credit strength.

1. Rearrange all data to facilitate the analysis.
2. Reduce the figures to simplify the study.
3. Analyze each current asset and each current liability.
4. Make ratio tests.

Rearrangement of the data in financial statements. Financial statements obtained from customers may be submitted in various forms, with the items grouped in sundry ways. For purposes of analyzing the statement to determine the credit strength of the applicant, the balance-sheet items should be grouped in the order shown in Figure. 75. All assets that are not current should be removed from the current group, and all liabilities that are current should be included in that classification.

The determination of what is current and what is not current depends upon:

1. A general knowledge of accounting (see pages 861 and 880 for an explanation of current assets and current liabilities).
2. An understanding of the credit applicant's business.
3. The answers to questions that have been put to the applicant.
4. Specific inquiry in the absence of information.

Simplification of figures. In the analysis of statements it is sometimes convenient to reduce the figures in the balance sheet to their simplest terms by omitting the minor digits. After such a reduction, the current assets would appear in the working papers as follows:

NAME.. ANALYZED BY..........................
ADDRESS.. DATE..
COMMENT...

Assets	*19—*	*Per Cent*	*19—*	*Per Cent*
Cash..................................	5,679.36	2.78	1,574.98	.89
Accounts Rec. (less Reserve)..........	37,963.17	18.58	31,179.16	17.65
Notes and T. A. Rec....................	11,692.70	5.72	9,753.07	5.52
Mdse. Inventories......................	69,619.03	34.07	54,504.40	30.86
Misc. A/R (claims and agreements) ..	321.48	.16	2,256.50	1.28
Total Current Assets..................	125,275.74	61.31	99,268.11	56.20
Investments (listed)				
Stocks and Bonds.......................			2,932.86	1.66
Real Estate............................	8,000.00	3.91	8,000.00	4.53
Buildings and Machinery (less Dep.)	61,686.83	30.19	56,990.01	32.26
Delivery Equipment (less Dep.)........				
Fur. & Fix. (less Dep.)..............				
Total Fixed Assets....................	69,686.83	34.10	67,922.87	38.45
Goodwill and Org. Exp..............	5,400.00	2.64	5,400.00	3.06
Patents, Formulae, etc..............				
Prepaid Items	3,962.85	1.93	4,049.21	2.29
Total Intangible Assets...............	9,362.85	4.57	9,449.21	5.35
Deficit..................................				
Total Assets..........................	204,325.42	100.00	176,640.19	100.00

Liabilities	*19—*	*Per Cent*	*19—*	*Per Cent*
Taxes and Int. Pay......................	2,594.09	1.27	2,492.36	1.41
Accounts Payable.......................	40,870.98	20.00	34,270.26	19.41
Notes and T. A. Payable...............			4,000.00	2.26
Loans Payable (Bank)..................	6,000.00	2.94	8,000.00	4.53
Total Current Liabilities..............	49,465.07	24.21	48,762.62	27.61
Mortgage Payable......................	12,000.00	5.87	4,000.00	2.26
Bonds Payable..........................				
Total Fixed Liabilities................	12,000.00	5.87	4,000.00	2.26

Figure 74. Form of Comparative Statement.

Liabilities	*19—*	*Per Cent*	*19—*	*Per Cent*
Sinking Funds				
Special Reserves				
Total Reserves				
Capital Stock (Common)	183,000.00	89.56	91,500.00	51.80
Capital Stock (Preferred)			12,000.00	6.79
Surplus and Undivided Profits	40,139.65	19.64	20,377.57	11.54
Total Net Worth	142,860.35	69.92	123,877.57	70.13
Total Liabilities	204,325.42	100.00	176,640.19	100.00
Contingent Liabilities				
Analysis	*19—*	*Per Cent*	*19—*	*Per Cent*
Current Assets	125,275.74		99,268.11	
Current Liabilities	49,465.07		48,762.62	
Working Capital	75,810.67		50,505.49	
Investments			2,932.86	
Available Working Capital	75,810.67		53,438.35	
Equity in Fixed Assets	57,686.83		60,990.01	
Actual Net Worth	133,497.50		114,428.36	
Consisting of Capital Stock	183,000.00		103,500.00	
Surplus (Deficit)	49,502.50		10,928.36	
Ratios	*19—*		*19—*	
Cur. Assets to Cur. Liabilities	2.53 to 1		2.03 to 1	
Fixed Assets to Fixed Liabilities	5.80 to 1		16.98 to 1	
Avail. Working Cap. to Cur. Liabilities	1.53 to 1		1.03 to 1	
Total Assets to Total Liabilities				
Sales to Total Assets				
Net Profits to Total Assets				
Net Profits to Net Worth				
Days Sales Outstanding				
Sales to Net Profits				

Figure 74 Continued.

_______ MILLS INC.

_____ STREET

NEW YORK

CORPORATION | **COMPARISON OF STATEMENTS**

NAME ....

ADDRESS .... BUSINESS ....

ASSETS					
Cash					
Notes Receivable					
Accounts Receivable					
Merchandise, finished					
Merchandise, unfinished					
Raw Material					
Less Reserves					
NET QUICK ASSETS					
Real Estate					
Buildings					
Machinery, Fixtures and Equipment					
Goodwill, Patents, etc.					
Deferred Charges and Misc.					
Less Reserves					
NET FIXED ASSETS					
TOTAL ASSETS					

Bills Payable Merchandise																					
Bills Payable to own Bank																					
Bills Payable otherwise																					
Accounts Payable																					
Deposits																					
Accrued Liabilities																					
Reserve for Taxes																					
TOTAL CURRENT LIABILITIES																					
Bonded Debt																					
Mortgage Loans - due																					
Reserve for Depreciation																					
Other Liabilities																					
Total Liabilities and Reserves																					
Capital Account																					
Preferred Stock Issued																					
Common Stock Issued																					
Surplus and Undivided Profits																					
TOTAL LIABILITIES																					
TOTAL QUICK ASSETS																					
" CURR. LIABILITIES																					
EXCESS QUICK																					
Ratio																					
Sales																					
Net Profit																					
Dividends																					
Depreciation																					
Contingent Liabilities																					
Insurance																					

Figure 75. Form of Comparative Statement Used by a Large Textile Manufacturer.

	(000.00 omitted)	
Current Assets	*19..*	*19..*
Cash	$150	$216
Marketable securities	69	104
Accounts and notes receivable . .	23	29
Inventories	97	91
	$339	$440

Or, the amounts may be set up in the working papers in roun figures, without omitting the digits.

Reducing figures to ratios. In the credit analysis of financial stat ments, certain ratios are helpful in throwing light upon the cred strength of the applicant. A ratio, which is the relationship that or amount bears to another, or the proportion which one amount is (another, is found by dividing the first amount by the second. Thu to find the ratio of current assets to current liabilities, divide the cu rent assets by the current liabilities. Suppose the result obtained 2.73. This would mean that for each dollar of current liabilities ther are $2.73 of current assets.

In noting the ratio on the financial statement or in the workin papers, it may be entered as: (1) 2.73; (2) 273 per cent; or (3) $2.7

Present-day use of ratios in determining credit strength. Mos books on the subject of credit analysis go into a detailed explanatio of analysis of financial statements by means of ratios. They presen perhaps a dozen ratios that may have some significance in determir ing the credit worth of a business organization. The authors recog nize, however, that the ratios have limitations and that too grea reliance cannot be placed upon their efficacy.

Much less importance is attached to ratios today than was the cas several years ago. In certain trades the use of ratios in statemen analysis has been entirely eliminated, while in others they are resorte to sparingly. Where the use of ratios, other than a few fundamenta ones, has not been abandoned, no rigid rule is followed in the appli cation of the ratios; in some analyses many ratios are calculated in arriving at judgment of the financial strength of the credit applicant in others, only a few ratios are calculated. The comparative state ment illustrated in Figure 74 (pages 908-909) shows some of the ratios in use; it will be noticed that in the case presented only three of the ratios were computed.

Among banks the same variation in the use of ratios in statement ılysis exists. Some banks have so little faith in the soundness of io analysis that they never calculate any other than the current ra- and the ratio of quick assets to current liabilities (see page 932); ıile others, in some analyses, calculate many ratios before accepting rejecting an application for a loan. On the whole, it may be said ıt ratios are used more extensively by the banks than in the trade.*

In the following discussion only ratios that are useful in an average edit analysis are explained. They include:

Accounts Receivable to Sales (see page 916).
Sales to Inventories (see page 922).
Accounts Payable to Raw Material Purchases (see page 927).
Current Assets to Current Liabilities (see page 928).
Quick Assets to Current Liabilities (see page 932).
Sales to Working Capital (see page 932).
Sales to Net Worth (see page 932).

---

* Prochnow and Foulke, in *Practical Bank Credit*, published by Prentice-Hall, c., mention the following fourteen comparisons of specific items and groups of ems that should invariably be made in the internal analysis, the objective of ıich is to determine whether the receivables, the inventory, the fixed assets, the ıyables, the sales, and the profits are in satisfactory proportions.

(1) Three important capital ratios
- (a) Fixed assets to tangible net worth (Per Cent)
- (b) Total debt to tangible net worth (Per Cent)
- (c) Net working capital represented by funded debt (Per Cent)

(2) Three important inventory ratios
- (a) Net sales to inventory (Times)
- (b) Net working capital represented by inventory (Per Cent)
- (c) Inventory covered by current debt (Per Cent)

(3) Three important sales ratios
- (a) Average collection period (Days)
- (b) Turnover of tangible net worth (Times)
- (c) Turnover of net working capital (Times)

(4) Three important net profit ratios
- (a) Net profits on net sales (Per Cent)
- (b) Net profits on tangible net worth (Per Cent)
- (c) Net profits on net working capital (Per Cent)

(5) Two important supplementary ratios
- (a) Current assets to current debt (Times)
- (b) Total debt to tangible net worth (Per Cent)

Dun & Bradstreet, Inc., publish tables annually showing the above fourteen aver- ge important ratios over five-year periods for some seventy-two different lines of ndustry and commerce, including manufacturers, wholesalers, and retailers. These atios give a fairly wide basis of comparison in analyzing statements for companies n the lines covered.

Analysis of Working Capital

Scrutinizing the items that make up the current assets. T items that commonly make up the current assets are: cash, accou receivable, trade notes receivable, inventories, and securities rep senting investment of idle cash and not those held for control or lo term investment. Each of these items requires separate analysis determine the correctness and significance of the amounts show Before each item is studied, the following question must be cons ered, for upon its answer depends the conclusions that will be drav in the analysis: Does the statement show the influences of seasor activity or inactivity? The answer is available from general know edge of the conditions in the industry and from the date of the stat ment.

Examination of cash. The correctness of the cash item can l checked by inquiry at the banks in which the company whose stat ment is under consideration keeps its funds; or, if this procedure ca not be followed, by inquiry directly of the applicant for credit determine the following:

1. Whether any I.O.U.'s are included in the cash balance.
2. Whether the balance has been distorted by the addition amounts received after the close of the period for which the balance are shown.
3. Whether any of the cash has been set apart for a specific pu pose; for example, a sinking fund.

The inclusion of foreign bank balances, or any suspicion that th cash includes such balances, should lead to further inquiry as to th exchange rates that have been applied in reducing the balance to do lars and the availability of the funds. Obviously, the state of th foreign-exchange market at the time that the analysis is made shoul be considered in checking the cash.

Since the amount of cash required by a business varies with th nature of the business and the season, no rule can be offered as to th proportion which should exist between cash and other items.

Examination of accounts receivable. The following question arise in the analysis of the accounts receivable:

. Are the accounts receivable as stated all customers' accounts? the answer is not furnished with the statement, it must be ascerned by inquiry.

2. What portion of the accounts receivable represents debts due m subsidiaries, and when are payments generally made by subsidies? The answer to this question must also be determined by direct estioning.

3. Have any of the accounts been pledged or assigned? This quesn is important because any property that is pledged to one creditor not available to others. Furthermore, the pledging of assets may evidence of financial weakness. If the balance sheet does not ow by footnote or other indication that any of the accounts have en pledged, the information must be obtained by direct inquiry. the absence of information in the financial statement, inquiry ould also be made to ascertain whether there is included in the acunts receivable amounts that are not collectible because they have en assigned. In case any of the accounts have been assigned, iniry should be made as to what contingent liability has been asmed through the guaranty of the accounts upon their assignment.

4. Is collection of any part of the accounts receivable likely to be lversely affected by regional or local conditions? To answer this iestion information must be available as to the location of the cusmers of the credit applicant and as to business conditions in various irts of the country.

5. Are the accounts receivable low in amount because the stateient was prepared at the end of a fiscal period that coincides with ie end of the natural business year? Accounts receivable are smallst at that time. Unless this factor is taken into account, the unsually small amount of receivables might give a false impression of ood collections.

6. What is the quality of the accounts receivable? The purpose f looking into the quality of the accounts receivable is to determine hether adequate provision has been made for bad debts. The folowing methods are available for testing the quality of the accounts eceivable:

(*a*) Obtain the names of the accounts receivable outstanding vith amounts in excess of a certain sum. This procedure is, however, iot usual.

(*b*) Ascertain the age of the accounts receivable.

Ascertaining the age of accounts receivable. The firm that h submitted the financial statement is frequently asked for a sta ment showing the age of the accounts receivable outstanding. T following illustrates the form of aging schedule that may be offer in answer to such a request:

	December 31, 19.	
	Amount	*Per Ce*
Less than 30 days old—from date of invoice	$30,000	30.93
31 to 60 days old — " " " "	24,000	24.74
61 to 90 days old — " " " "	16,000	16.50
91 to 120 days old — " " " "	12,000	12.37
Over 120 days old — " " " "	15,000	15.46
	$97,000	100.00

The valuation of the accounts receivable on the basis of their a and in relation to the usual terms of sale will show the amount th should be deducted from the accounts receivable as reported, for pu poses of estimating credit strength. The percentage of value to b applied to each group of accounts depends upon:

1. The nature of the business.
2. The usual credit terms of sale.
3. The collection experience of the company whose statement being analyzed.

Thus, in one business where the credit terms were thirty days, th valuation was made on the following basis: All accounts less tha 30 days old (from date of invoice) were taken at their face valu those in the 31-to-60-days-old class, at 85 per cent of their face valu those in the 61-to-90-days class, at 50 per cent of their face valu and those over 90 days old, at zero.

Determining age of accounts receivable through ratio of ac counts receivable to sales. In the absence of an aging schedule o accounts receivable, the average length of time that accounts are ou standing can be estimated by applying the following formula:

$$\frac{\text{Accounts Receivable Outstanding}}{\text{Net credit sales for the period}} \times \text{days in the period} = \begin{array}{c}\text{Average}\\ \text{collection}\\ \text{period}\end{array}$$

Assume the following facts to be shown by the financial statemen and that the term of credit granted is 30 days.

Net credit sales	$1,383,866.42
Accounts Receivable—customers at end of year	129,665.14
Reserve for Bad Debts	3,780.12

e item of reserve for bad debts is omitted in the computation but tested as to adequacy after the age of the accounts receivable has en determined. If we apply the formula as indicated above, the erage age of the outstanding accounts receivable is 33.73 days, as mpared with 30 days, the term of credit allowed.

$$\frac{\$129,665.14}{\$1,383,866.42} \times 360^{*} = 33.73 \text{ days}$$

e above ratio may also be read as the number of days' sales outnding. With net credit sales for the year of $1,383,866.42, the erage daily sales would be $3,844.07 ($1,383,866.42 ÷ 360), and counts receivable outstanding of $129,665.14 would show 33.73 ys' sales outstanding. If the credit terms are 30 days, the fact that .73 days' sales are outstanding would indicate that a very few of e accounts are overdue.

If the average age of the outstanding accounts greatly exceeds the ormal credit period, the following may be the reasons:

1. The company has been too liberal in extending credit.
2. Its collection department has been too lax in following up slow ustomers.
3. Included in the accounts receivable are amounts due from offiers, directors, salesmen, and others.
4. Collections have slowed up due to general abnormal business onditions. The comparison of average age of accounts outstanding ith the average terms of credit serves as a guide in estimating the mount that should be reserved for bad debts.

Another method of applying the test of accounts receivable is to nultiply the annual sales by the fraction of the year represented by he credit terms. Thus, if the annual sales were $800,000 and the erms of credit were 60 days, the sales would be multiplied by ⅙. The result, $133,333, shows the amount of accounts receivable that vould be outstanding at the end of the month if collections were nade on time. If the accounts receivable outstanding are far in excess of this figure, and the excess is not accounted for by seasonal

* In practice 360 days rather than 365 days is generally used.

conditions, the conclusion may be drawn that many of the accou
are past due.

Weaknesses in test of ratio of accounts receivable to sales. T
calculation made above assumes the following three facts, which,
nonexistent, will render the ratio misleading:

1. That there is an even flow of sales during the year. Suppose t
business is a seasonal one and that a quarter of the year's sales a
made during the month of December. If the ratio is calculated fro
the balance sheet of December 31, the ratio will show a longer peri
for collection of accounts receivable than is actually the case. T
seasonal movements in the business and the date of the balance she
and income statement must therefore be taken into consideration.
2. That there is uniformity of collectibility during the year. Su
pose sales have an even flow during the year but that December c
lections are normally slower than other months. The ratio calculate
from a December 31 balance sheet and income statement would sho
accounts to be older than they would appear if the ratio were calc
lated for any other twelve months' period.
3. That all sales are made on the same terms of credit. The i
come statement ordinarily does not divide the sales into cash sal
and credit sales. If the figure for credit sales is not available and it
known that a large proportion of the sales is made for cash, the rat
calculated by the use of total sales figures will not give a reliab
index of the quality of the accounts receivable.

Comparison of age of accounts shown by ratio with percent ages in the industry. Any specific information on the general su
ject of collections of open-credit accounts in the industry may he
in the judgment of the quality of the accounts receivable in th
particular company under consideration.* A few of the Federal r
serve banks publish in their monthly business reviews current info
mation on the ratio of collections during the month to accounts an
notes receivable outstanding at the close of the preceding month i
one or more industries. This information may be used with grea
advantage.

* The Retail Credit Survey, usually prepared annually by the Federal Reserv
Board and released in June, reports information as to average collection perio
in various fields. The table opposite is from the June 1952 issue.

lmost all of the industries of the country have their own trade ciations. Many of these associations can provide information on rage collection periods and monthly fluctuations.

nother source of information pertaining to average collection iods in various industries is the Dun & Bradstreet, Inc., tables re- ed to on page 913. One of the ratios given in these tables is erage collection period."

Examination of notes receivable. The item of notes receivable ong the current assets raises the following questions:

. Is the presence of notes receivable in the statement unusual? In ny lines of business, sales are made on open account, and notes are en only to close out a past-due account. Notes receivable origi- ing in this way represent an inferior asset and should be excluded m current assets.

Notes received at the time of a sale, in accordance with an estab- ied practice of accepting notes in payment for merchandise, such exists in industries which market high-priced units, represent better ets than open accounts receivable, for the following reasons:

Kind of business	Average collection period for accounts receivable			
	Charge account (In days)		Installment (In months)	
	1951	1950	1951	1950
partment stores	64	62	13	15
en's clothing stores	61	59	8	7
omen's apparel stores	69	67	7	7
rniture stores	64	69	13	15
ousehold appliance stores	56	56	14	16
welry stores	63	63	14	13
ardware stores	52	55	11	12
itomobile dealers	50	47	*	*
itomobile tire and accessory stores	37	49	13	15

* Not computed because the small proportion of installment paper retained automobile dealers gives a collection period not typical of their entire in- allment business.

(*a*) The note receivable is written evidence of a promise to p
(*b*) It can be discounted and converted into cash at lower c
and more readily than the account receivable.
(*c*) It usually bears interest.

2. Do all the notes receivable represent customers' accounts? No received from officers, stockholders, employees, and others for trans tions outside the regular trade should not be considered as curr assets.

3. Are any dishonored or discounted notes included in the tot If any notes receivable include instruments that have been d counted, assigned, or transferred, the contingent liability must taken into account.

Examination of trade acceptances. In evaluating the asset " ceptances receivable," consideration should be given to the followi points:

1. The trade acceptance, when properly used, represents an knowledgment of a debt incurred by the purchase of a particular b of goods.

2. Trade acceptances are sometimes misused in connection wi past-due accounts, loans, or renewals and accommodations, where transfer of goods is immediately involved.

3. It is the practice of some concerns to use the trade acceptan only in transactions with their less reliable customers; those who credit standing is regarded more favorably are sold on open accou Furthermore, strong customers generally prefer to buy on open a count and pay their bills in time to secure a cash discount, if any.

Before the value of the asset "acceptances receivable" can be d termined, therefore, inquiry may have to be made of the compa whose statement is being analyzed, to ascertain:

1. Whether the acceptances originated from current transactio that represent the purchase of goods.

2. Whether, if the first question is answered affirmatively, the co pany follows the procedure of selling on acceptances only to ris considered doubtful.

Trade acceptances arising through a proper use of the instrume in a business which customarily uses the trade acceptance in sellin constitute an asset of ready convertibility, for the acceptances ca discounted or sold in the open market through acceptance dealers. ade acceptances that arise in other ways may have no superiority an asset available to meet current debts and may, in fact, be in-ior to open accounts receivable.

Testing the adequacy of the reserve for bad debts. A minimum serve for bad debts, varying with the line of industry, is generally nsidered necessary, regardless of the condition of the receivables. he two methods by which a provision for doubtful accounts is estab-hed are: (1) as a percentage of sales. Under this plan a relation-ip is established between sales and bad debt losses by analysis of storical data. This percentage is then applied to current sales to termine the current additions to the provision for doubtful ac-unts. (2) By analysis of receivables to determine specific items here losses are likely to be incurred.

The valuation of the accounts, notes, and acceptances receivable on e bases explained above will indicate whether adequate provision is been made in the balance sheet for bad debts.

Examination of inventories. The following are the chief points be considered in appraising the worth of inventories, determining hether too much capital is tied up in them, and detecting misrepre-nsations.

1. How the inventory was determined. The amount of inventories ould represent a valuation of stocks on hand ascertained, where racticable, through an actual count, and not a sum arrived at from cords of perpetual book inventories or an amount estimated by uesswork. Statements prepared by public accountants generally dicate what check the accountants have made to substantiate the ventories shown in the statement. If the statement does not dis-lose whether a physical inventory was taken, and if there is no ccountant's verification thereof, direct inquiry must be made of the pplicant as to how the valuation was made.

2. How the merchandise is valued. One of the purposes of scru-inizing the method of valuing inventories is to discover whether suffi-ient allowance has been made for declines in value due to such auses as changes in styles, deterioration, spoilage, waste, and other osses. (See page 865 for further discussion of this subject.)

3. What part of the inventory represents prepaid expenses that ightfully belong with the deferred charges. Supplies, for example,

that will never become a part of the finished product, eventua to be sold on account and finally converted into cash, should not included with the merchandise inventory.

4. What the nature of the inventories is. The financial stateme of a manufacturer should show what portion of the inventory is ra materials, what part is goods in process, and what amount represer finished goods on hand. Each of these has different values from th standpoint of convertibility into funds for debt-paying purpose In the event of insolvency, raw materials consisting of stable com modities may be disposed of with greater facility than other mercha dise; goods in process are practically valueless in case of forced sal to raise funds; finished goods have a more limited market than ra materials. A division of the inventory into these items is furthe more required to show whether, in view of market conditions an the volume of business done, too much capital is tied up in ra materials.

5. The seasonal influences. In analyzing the inventory item of th balance sheet, the seasonal factor must not be overlooked. A ba ance sheet drawn up at the close of a season should show a reductio in inventories, whereas one prepared at the beginning of a seasor or in the midst of it, may disclose heavier inventories.

6. Whether merchandise has been pledged as collateral. Informa tion should be obtained relative to this question, if the balance shee does not contain the answer.

7. What conclusions can be drawn as to the condition of th stock from information contained in the balance sheet and incom statement. Some light can be thrown upon the valuation of inven tories and the probable salability of the goods by applying certai tests to the inventory.

Determining quality of inventory from ratio of sales to inven tories. An estimate of whether the inventories are out of proportior to the demand being made upon the firm for its products can be determined by applying the following formula:

$$\frac{\text{Sales}}{\text{Average Inventory (at Sales Price of Finished Goods)}} = \begin{array}{l}\text{Number of times}\\ \text{finished stock}\\ \text{turns over}\end{array}$$

The figures shown by an application of this formula indicate how many times the finished goods on hand are turned over during the urse of a year. The figure can be converted to show how much ne is consumed in converting inventories to sales. Thus, if the io of sales to inventories is 3, indicating that inventories turn over ree times in the year, it is clear that 4 months are consumed in nverting inventories to sales. The normal period in which stocks ould be converted into cash or receivables through sales varies th the particular industry and must be known before the signifi-nce of the merchandise turnover becomes clear. In comparison th the normal figure the higher the turnover, the better the inven-ry control and the more favorable generally the condition of the m; the lower the turnover, the poorer the control of inventory and e more costly the price of converting inventories to cash, for the nger it takes to move merchandise, the greater is the financial bur-n of doing so.

A slow turnover of merchandise may indicate that the inventories e overvalued and that they have not been properly depreciated; at they contain unsalable goods; or that the business has over-ought. An unusually rapid turnover might indicate that all pur-ases of material received before the preparation of the statement ad not been included in the balance sheet.

Another method of calculating merchandise turnover is given in e following formula:

$$\frac{\text{Cost of Goods Sold}}{\text{verage Inventory of Finished Goods at Cost}} = \text{Finished goods turnover}$$

The disadvantage of employing this ratio in testing the inventory that usually the financial statement shows the cost of goods sold, ncluding operating expenses; in order to obtain a true turnover, the ost of goods sold before the addition of operating costs should be sed.

Difficulties in applying the merchandise-turnover test. Two ifficulties are encountered in using the ratio of sales to inventories s a test of the inventories:

1. The ratio, in order to be accurate, should make use of average nventories for the year. These are generally not available to one who s analyzing a financial statement for purposes of determining credit trength. An average of the inventories at the beginning and end of

the year, if both figures are available, or only the inventory at the er of the period, must of necessity be substituted.

2. The balance sheet usually shows the inventory at cost (or m ket, whichever is lower). It is therefore necessary to obtain the sal markup and to multiply the inventory value by the appropriate f tor, before applying the formula. Thus, if the markup is 50 per ce the inventory would be multiplied by two. Another method is reduce the sales in the numerator to a cost of sales figure, and divide by the average inventory at cost.

Possible explanations of excessive inventories and slow tur over of merchandise. If the inventory is found to be too larg and the merchandise turnover consequently slow, certain unusu factors such as the following may account for the condition:

1. The inventory may reflect increases in purchases in anticipati of seasonal demand.

2. The trend of prices may be upward, and the large invento may represent a deliberate stocking up in anticipation of a furth rise in prices.

3. The inventory may be high because a larger volume of busine is anticipated.

4. The turnover of merchandise may be slow because the firm e gages in functions that lengthen the period between the acquisiti of inventories and their sale. For example, one manufacturer may engaged largely in assembling parts produced by others; another m undertake the manufacturing of parts as well as their assemblin Obviously, the second firm will have larger inventories than the fir

5. Large inventories may be required because of the distance the firm from the market. Thus a firm located at a great distan from the source of its supplies would require larger inventories th one that can replenish its stock at short notice. Inventories that a excessive because of overbuying, excessive costs, or slow-moving sto are frequently the cause of financial embarrassment.

Examination of marketable securities. In analyzing the item marketable securities, three steps are necessary:

1. Determine whether it is the policy of the company in who statement the item appears to treat marketable securities as availab for meeting current debts. If the company does not follow th

licy, the item should be removed from the current assets and aced among the investments.

2. Secure a list of the stocks and bonds that make up the marketle securities, in order that their current value may be checked ainst that shown in the balance sheet. Stocks and bonds that are t listed on a stock exchange are likely not to be readily convertible to cash and may, with justification, be omitted from the current sets.

3. Inquire whether any of the investments have been pledged.

Examination of current liabilities. Examination of the current bilities is the next step in the analysis of working capital. The view of current liabilities should be made with the following objects view:

1. To see that all of the current debts, including accruals for salaes, wages, and interest, are included among the current liabilities. quiry should be made as to the following:

(*a*) Whether all bills for goods received prior to the preparation f the statement have been included as liabilities.

(*b*) The maturity date of any mortgage outstanding, in order be certain that the debt is included among the current liabilities the mortgage matures in the current year.

(*c*) Whether any dividends are to be paid or withdrawals are to e made that will materially reduce the current assets shown on the atement; if dividends are cumulative, inquiry should be made as the amount in arrears on the statement date. This information ill indicate whether the company's dividend policy is jeopardizing he interests of creditors. Thus, if dividends are being paid while vorking capital is inadequate, or for more than the amount waranted by the current income statement, caution is indicated.

(*d*) The nature of reserves, if that is not clearly indicated in the tatement. Any reserves which represent liabilities that will mature vithin a short period, such as a reserve for taxes, should be included mong the current debts.

2. To determine whether there are any contingent liabilities that nay, upon the happening of the contingency, increase the liabilities. (See page 884.) If the balance sheet gives no evidence of contin-

gent liabilities in footnotes to the balance sheet, direct inquiry shou be made to ascertain if there are any.

3. To discover, through a study of the nature of the liabilities, a implications reflective of the credit standing of the applicant. F example, the item of loans payable to banks, commercial pap houses, or notebrokers implies that the company's credit capacity h been tested by the bank or other institution that has extended cred

4. To ascertain the promptness with which bills are paid.

Examination of accounts payable. The following informatic should be ascertained concerning the accounts payable:

1. What amount of the accounts payable, if any, represents deb due for money borrowed from officers, stockholders, friends, an others? The answer to this question must be learned by direct inquir

2. What are the names and addresses of the firm's principal su pliers? This information is obtained by direct inquiry from the appl cant for the purpose of inquiring of each supplier the line of cred offered to the applicant, how many years the account has been sol the terms of sale, what the applicant owes, and his paying habits.

3. Are the accounts payable unusually large or very small becaus of seasonal influences? Information as to the months in which th accounts payable are at their maximum and minimum, and the total at such times, obtained by direct inquiry, will enable the analyst t make allowances for seasonal factors in analyzing the accounts payable

4. Is the company paying its bills promptly? Information regard ing this question may be obtained in the following ways:

(*a*) A schedule of the age of the accounts payable, similar t that requested for the accounts receivable (see page 916), may b requested of the customer. If obtained, this report will show the volume of past-due accounts and the extent to which the company is failing to take advantage of cash discounts.

(*b*) An estimate of the age of the accounts payable may be made by comparing the number of days' purchases unpaid with the credit terms, as explained below.

(*c*) Credit agencies may be asked to make reports upon the payment record of the credit applicant, in which case it will be un- necessary either to ask for an aging statement of the accounts payable, or to estimate the promptness with which the company is paying its lls. Additional investigation should be made in cases where the edit agency information is obviously not complete.

Estimating the age of accounts payable. In the absence of defi-te information as to the age of outstanding debts incurred in the ırchase of materials, some indication of the promptness with which ıe applicant for credit pays his bills may be obtained by determin-g, through the following formula, the number of days' purchases npaid:

$$\frac{\text{Accounts Payable}}{\text{Raw Material Purchases}} \times 360 = \begin{array}{c}\text{Number of days'}\\ \text{purchases unpaid}\end{array}$$

. comparison of the number of days' purchases unpaid, with the verage terms of credit, which are ascertained by direct inquiry if the ıformation is not available from other sources, may reveal the romptness with which bills are paid. Suppose that the application f the formula to a particular financial statement indicates that 60 ays' purchases remain unpaid and that the average credit terms are 0 days. It would appear that half of the accounts payable are past lue. This conclusion would, of course, be unsound if seasonal pur-hases were reflected in the amount of accounts payable.

The formula should not be applied if bank loans appear in the bal-ınce sheet, for such loans may have decreased the amount of accounts ayable outstanding. If the bank loans were used for the payment of urchases of merchandise, they could be added to the accounts pay-ıble in making the calculation; however, the balance sheet does not eveal to what use the bank loans were put, and direct questioning on this point may be necessary.

Examination of notes, bills, and acceptances payable. Notes pay-able should be broken down into the following classifications to reveal various factors as to the financial standing of the credit applicant.

1. Amounts representing notes given to merchandise creditors. The following inquiries must be made in order to judge the signifi-cance of the total:

(*a*) Is it the custom in the particular line of industry for notes or acceptances to be given in the normal course of trade, or have they been given by the applicant for credit in settlement of overdue accounts? Obviously, if they have been given in settlement of past-du accounts, the credit applicant is a less attractive risk.

(*b*) Do the instruments carry any outside endorsement? If th notes bear outside endorsements, the applicant's name on the not has not been regarded as sufficient and consideration should be give to this fact.

(*c*) Are the obligations past due?

(*d*) Have earlier notes been partly paid when due, and do tho at present outstanding represent notes tendered for the balance?

2. Amounts representing notes discounted by banks. A compar that has discounted its own notes at the bank has passed the bank test for extension of credit. This is clearly a point in favor of th credit applicant, unless the loan has had to be renewed and carrie along by the bank after the borrower completed the season's busines Inquiry should therefore be made to discover the bank's experienc with its loans to the credit applicant.

3. Amounts representing notes sold through notebrokers. Th ability of the company to sell its notes through notebrokers is a sig of strength, for only companies of high credit standing can rais funds in this way.

4. Amounts representing notes given to friends and relatives wh have loaned money to the business. Determine the type of note an conditions of repayment. The fact that the owners of the busines have had to borrow from friends and relatives should be regarded a a signal to move cautiously in granting credit.

Working Capital Ratio

Ratio of current assets to current liabilities. In estimating th ability of the applicant for credit to meet his debts promptly, it i essential to discover from the financial statement how many dollar of current assets there are for each dollar of current liabilities. Thi figure, which is known as the current ratio or working-capital ratio, i found by applying the following formula:

$$\frac{\text{Current Assets}}{\text{Current Liabilities}} = \text{Current ratio.}$$

A company that has the following working capital setup would have a current ratio as indicated below.

	December 31, 19..
CURRENT ASSETS	
Cash on deposit and on hand	$145,141.17
Marketable securities (Less reserve, $16,105; value at market quotations, Dec. 31, 19..)	23,132.91
Accounts and notes receivable	223,996.17
Inventories of raw materials, supplies, work in process, and finished products (Less reserve, $77,334)	478,007.59
Total current assets	$870,277.84
CURRENT LIABILITIES	
Notes payable	$ 18,941.87
Accounts payable	132,327.97
Accrued taxes	20,869.65
Accrued payrolls	23,694.61
Advances received on sales contracts	20,869.65
Total current liabilities	$216,703.75
Working capital	$653,574.09
Current ratio, or dollars of current assets per dollar of current liabilities	4.01

For many years a current ratio of 2 to 1 was taken as the standard, ıd credit men concluded that if there were two dollars of current sets for each dollar of current liabilities, the company had sufficient orking capital. It is now recognized, however, that this rule of ıumb cannot be applied indiscriminately. Current ratios vary con- derably in different lines of trade. They vary also within a particu- ır line for manufacturers, wholesalers, and retailers. And they vary om year to year depending upon whether the country is experiencing rosperity or depression. For the current ratio to have real meaning, ıe credit man must know how it compares with the normal current ıtio for companies similar to the one that he is studying, and with ıe current ratios of the same company in previous periods.*

Importance of current ratio. The relative importance of the cur- ent ratio and of working capital as factors in determining credit trength is clear from the following illustrations of the working capital f a company at two different periods:

* See reference to Dun & Bradstreet tables in footnote on page 913.

FIRST PERIOD

Current Assets	$3,000
Current Liabilities	2,000
Working Capital	$1,000

SECOND PERIOD

Current Assets	$2,000
Current Liabilities	1,000
Working Capital	$1,000

In both periods the working capital is $1,000; but in the second peri the current ratio is 2 to 1, while in the first it is 1.50 to 1. The co pany has a better working-capital position in the second period th in the first, because in the second period it has $2,000 of shrinkab assets with which to pay non-shrinkable liabilities of $1,000, while the first period it had $3,000 of shrinkable assets with which to me $2,000 of non-shrinkable liabilities.

Consideration to be given to the current ratio. The curre ratio can be accepted as an indicator of the credit strength of t firm whose statement is being analyzed only after consideration given to the following factors:

1. An analysis of the nature of the items that are reflected in t current ratio. This is clear from the preceding analysis of curre assets and current liabilities. A strong current ratio, for example, ca ries little weight in favor of the credit applicant if examination of th inventories shows them to be overvalued and if an analysis of th accounts receivable reveals a large volume of doubtful accounts.

2. Seasonal influences. A statement that reflects the financial stat of a company during an inactive period may show a more favorab current ratio than would a statement of the same concern a fe months later when purchases have been made in anticipation of ne seasonal demand and merchandise has not yet been converted int accounts receivable and cash.

3. The proportions which the various items that make up the cu rent assets bear to the total current assets. Since some of the asset are more liquid and more stable than others, it is necessary to stud the current ratio in the light of this consideration. The importanc

the distribution of current assets is discussed further in the next agraph.

. The outlook for expansion or contraction of operations after the e of the balance sheet.

. Changes that are known to have taken place.

. Significance of changes in the company's current assets and cur-t liabilities over a period of time. (See page 933.)

istribution of current assets. A study of the distribution of the rent assets is important in the analysis because certain assets are re liquid than others. A company may have maintained a current io of 2 to 1 for two years, and yet may be considerably weaker in second than in the first year, and vice versa. This can be readily n from the following comparative statements of working capital:

	December 31			
	Second Year	*Per Cent*	*First Year*	*Per Cent*
Current Assets				
Cash	$ 40,000	16⅔	$120,000	50
Receivables	80,000	33⅓	80,000	33⅓
Inventories	120,000	50	40,000	16⅔
Total Current Assets..	$240,000	100	$240,000	100
Current Liabilities	120,000		120,000	
Working capital	$120,000		$120,000	
Current ratio	2 : 1		2 : 1	

both years the company has a current ratio of 2 to 1. In the cond year, however, it is in a less liquid condition than it was in the first year, for in place of $40,000 of inventories and $120,000 cash, it now has $40,000 of cash and $120,000 of inventories. owever, if it is expected that the inventories will be converted into les at a profit and that the eventual value of the current assets will crease as inventories are converted into accounts receivable and timately into cash, the apparent weakness may be no barrier to the tension of credit. Ordinarily, the shift from assets of greater quidity to those of lesser liquidity is regarded unfavorably in analyz-g credit strength.

It is not essential in the analysis of working capital to reduce the istribution of the current assets to percentages of the total if the orrect conclusions can be drawn from a study of the figures as they appear in the statement. Many credit men make their analyses rectly from the figures.

The "acid-test," or "quick," ratio. A test often applied to termine the immediate ability of the applicant to meet current lia ties is to find the ratio of cash, receivables, and marketable securi ("quick-current" assets, "dollar" assets, or "liquid" assets) to curr liabilities. This ratio is called the "acid-test," or "quick," ratio. ventories are omitted on the principle that they are not liquid ass If the marketable securities are stocks that fluctuate violently, t should be omitted from the acid-test ratio. Ordinarily a compa that has its working capital temporarily invested in marketable se rities purchases the highest-grade bonds; such securities may be garded as dollar assets. The analyst determines the generally accep standards for the line of business and compares the applicar "quick" ratio with it.

Other Factors in Financial Analysis

Sales volume as a factor in financial analysis. The relations of the volume of sales to working capital and to net worth must watched for signs of strain due to overtrading. An increasing volu of sales must be accompanied by sufficient working capital and a quate net work.

The first ratio is determined as follows:

$$\frac{\text{Net Sales}}{\text{Working Capital}} = \text{Working capital turnover}$$

The second ratio is determined as follows:

$$\frac{\text{Net Sales}}{\text{Tangible Net Worth}^{*}} = \text{Capital turnover}$$

The ratio tests are useful when compared with the turnovers of t same company for previous periods and with average ratios for

* In a corporation, the net worth is the total of the capital stock, surplus, a reserve accounts that represent surplus. (See page 887.) In a partnership, t net worth is the sum of the partners' capital accounts. In a single proprietorsh the net worth is represented by the proprietor's capital account. For purposes credit analysis, however, the tangible net worth is used; this is found by su tracting from the net worth as above determined the goodwill, copyrights, trad marks, patents, leaseholds, mailing lists, and any other intangible fixed assets.

ıp of companies in the same line of business. Average ratios for ous industries are available from time to time in such publications he *Dun & Bradstreet Monthly Review*.

Vhen the working capital turnover and the capital turnover are ch higher than the average for the same line of business, it may icate a capital insufficient to do the volume of business; when ch smaller, the capital is not active enough.

mportance of the sources of working capital. The sources from ich the credit applicant has acquired its working capital are ex- mely important in analyzing its credit strength, for the following sons:

1. The sources have a direct relation to the control that the firm s over its inventories and other current assets. For example, if all sources for borrowing have been exhausted and among the liabili- s are debts representing loans that are likely to be pressed for pay- ent at maturity, the company will find itself in an awkward position oner than if it had not tapped all the sources of working capital d if its current debts represented only purchases on account.

2. The costs of raising working capital vary with the source. Bor- wing from banks and commercial finance companies is more costly an long-term borrowing; however, the latter involves more perma- ent and rigid obligations.

3. The responsibility for payment varies. A company that has in- eased its working capital through additional investments by owners the business is in a better position than one that has improved its osition by borrowing for the obvious reason that the obligation to ay dividends to investors is not as pressing as the definite responsi- ility to repay on a certain day the loans made at banks or from ther lenders.

4. The shifts made from one method of raising working capital to nother reflect the activity of the firm in maintaining an adequate ıpply of working capital and should be considered.

Determining the sources of the credit applicant's working capi- al. The sources of working capital used by the enterprise whose atement is being analyzed can be learned from:

1. The nature of the liabilities shown in the financial statement.
2. Direct questioning of the credit applicant.

3. The changes in working capital revealed by a study of the co parative statements of the credit applicant. (See page 906.)

By tracing any increase in working capital to the following con tions, the analyst can decide the degree of improvement in working-capital position, for each source has obvious strength weakness.

1. Application to working capital of new contributions of capi by the owners of the business.
2. Application to working capital of funds received upon the sa of long-term obligations.
3. Earnings that have been reinvested in the business and that a reflected in the current assets.
4. Reserves against taxes, contingencies, depreciation, maintenan and sinking funds or amortization of debts that are reflected in t current assets.
5. Writing up of merchandise inventories and marketable securiti

Similarly, by tracing any decrease in working capital to the follo ing causes, the analyst can weigh the seriousness of the decline.

1. Losses incurred.
2. Distribution of earnings, or withdrawal of capital.
3. Use of current funds in the acquisition of fixed and non-curren assets.
4. Use of current funds to fund reserves, to use reserves for mai tenance and other purposes.
5. Marking down of inventory values and marketable securities.

6. FALSE FINANCIAL STATEMENTS

Laws providing punishment for false financial statements. A person or firm that has been defrauded by one who submitted a false financial statement in an effort to obtain credit may look to the fol lowing three classes of laws under which to prosecute the wrongdoer:

1. State larceny laws providing for punishment of persons who obtain money or property by means of false pretenses or misrepre- sentations.
2. State "false statement laws."

3. Federal laws providing punishment for those who use the mails fraudulent purposes.

Prosecution under larceny laws. All of the states have laws ıking it a crime to obtain money or property under false pretenses. osecution under the larceny laws, of persons who obtain credit rough the presentation of false financial statements, has proved satisfactory, for in order to obtain a conviction it is necessary to ove that:

1. The person accused intended to deprive or defraud the true vner of his property.
2. The accused obtained the property.
3. The statement contained fraudulent or false representations or etenses.
4. The defrauded person relied upon the false statement.
5. The money or property was delivered to the person charged ith the crime.

The difficulty of legally proving that the above elements existed as frequently resulted in the acquittal of persons who were unoubtedly recipients of goods obtained from a creditor who relied pon a false financial statement. The court decisions yield many xamples of acquittal handed down because the defrauded creditor ould not supply satisfactory evidence that the merchandise actually as received by the accused, or because he could not prove to the atisfaction of a jury that the purchaser did not intend to pay for he merchandise.

The inadequacy of the larceny laws as a basis for prosecuting the naker of a false statement gave rise to the passage of the falsetatement laws.

Prosecution under the false-statement laws. A majority of the mportant commercial states have enacted a false-statement law, ponsored by the National Association of Credit Men, that overcomes the difficulties encountered in prosecuting the maker of a false statement under the larceny laws. In states that have such a false statement law, all that need be proved against a defendant is:

1. That he made or caused the statement to be made.
2. That the statement is materially false.

3. That the statement was made for the purpose of securing cre
4. That the statement was made with the intent that it shoulc relied upon.

Who can be punished under the false-statement laws? T New York law, which is typical of those enacted in most of states, and is in the form of the model law, provides for the pun ment of any person who commits the following crimes:

1. Makes or causes a false statement regarding financial condi to be made in writing, for the purpose of procuring property credit, and with the intent that it shall be relied upon.
2. Procures property or credit upon the faith of the false st ment, knowing that the statement is false, regardless of whether person procuring the property or credit made the statement.
3. Falsely represents, orally or in writing, that a financial st ment theretofore made continues to be true, and procures prop or credit upon the faith thereof.

Superiority of protection afforded by false-statement la The superiority of the protection afforded by the false-staten laws as compared with the larceny laws may be summarized as follc

1. It is unnecessary to prove that any property was obtained u the strength of the statement; it is unnecessary to prove the phys delivery of the property. In Alabama, Colorado, Florida, Geor Idaho, Nevada, and Virginia, there are special statutory provisi for the punishment of persons who, on the strength of false repc get possession of money, property, credit, or some other valu thing.
2. It is unnecessary to prove any intent to defraud.
3. Whereas under the larceny laws mere extension of time which to pay a debt cannot be made the basis of a charge of larc under the false-statement laws the giving of a false financial st ment for the purpose of obtaining an extension of time is a cri
4. It is not essential that the maker of the false statement the receiver of the credit or property be the same person. Thu partner in a firm who receives credit or property on a false staten rendered by another partner may be liable for punishment; an director who receives credit or property for the benefit of a corp tion may be liable under the statute.

Prosecution under the Federal mail-fraud statute. The Federal laws against using the mails to defraud are a valuable weapon against a debtor who has secured merchandise on credit by mailing a false financial statement. To obtain a conviction under the Federal law, the prosecution must be prepared to prove the following:

1. That the statement is false.
2. That it was made for the purpose of securing money or property.
3. That it was made with the intention that it should be relied upon.
4. That the statement was mailed.
5. That money or property was obtained by means of the false statement.

The punishment provided under the Federal law is more severe than that imposed by the State laws. Furthermore, difficulties sometimes encountered in prosecution under the State laws are overcome by prosecution under the Federal law. For example, under the New York statute, cases must be prosecuted in the county in which the statement was made, regardless of where the statement was delivered, and proof must be furnished that the statement was made in the county in which the prosecution is sought. Under the Federal law, the action may be begun either in the district in which the statement was made, or in that in which the statement was delivered.

The National Association of Credit Men recommends the use of a self-mailing form of financial statement in order to make it easy to prosecute under the Federal mail-fraud statute. The self-mailing form is a combination statement and envelope; when folded, the financial statement is contained within the envelope, and the address of the one to whom it is being sent is on the back of the statement. See Figure 73, pages 902-903.

Some tests in determining whether prosecution should be undertaken. Before deciding to prosecute on an alleged false financial statement, the firm or person contemplating such action must consider whether the statement was materially false. A test to apply is to ask the question: Would credit have been extended if the items that are believed to be false were correctly stated? If the answer is "no," the falsity is probably material.

The difficulty that will be encountered in proving the falsity of a statement must also be considered. Certain items in the balance sheet, such as inventories, machinery, furniture and fixtures, and land and buildings represent estimated values that are subject to fluctuations, different methods of appraisal, and honest difference of opinion. Great difficulty is likely to be experienced in convincing a jury that the valuations set forth in these items are false. However, the valuation of such items as cash, accounts receivable, notes and acceptances receivable, accounts payable, notes and acceptances payable, and mortgages payable are based upon ascertainable facts and falsification of these items can be more readily proved to a jury. It is well to remember that the jury must be convinced beyond a reasonable doubt that the items alleged to be false, are in fact falsely stated.

Can an accountant be held for an incorrect statement? A person or firm that has extended credit, relying upon a financial statement prepared by a public accountant, which later proves to have been erroneous, has no claim against the accountant if the errors are due to ordinary negligence, not fraud, on the part of the accountant or his assistant, even though the accountant is aware that the statement will be used to obtain credit, provided that no contractual relation exists between the accountant and the firm that extended credit.

If the accountant has perpetrated fraud in the preparation of the statement, he can be held liable by persons who extended credit on the strength of the statement, even though there was no contractual relation between the accountant and the third person, and even though the report was not especially prepared for such third person.

Gross negligence in failing to ascertain facts before making a statement, even when not equivalent to fraud, is none the less evidence to sustain an inference of fraud. Thus, where accountants had knowledge that a large amount of accounts receivable of a firm whose accounts they were auditing were dead and that reserves for bad debts were inadequate, and the accountants failed to note this condition on the balance sheet, the accountants were held liable to a trust company which loaned money relying upon the accountants' certified balance sheet. In this case the accountants knew that the statement would be used to obtain credit.

SECTION 9

Raising Capital to Finance Current Needs

SECTION 9

Raising Capital to Finance Current Needs*

Need for regular, cushion, and variable working capital. Every business has need for a minimum amount of liquid capital sufficient to keep up the circulation of the capital from cash to inventories to receivables and back again to cash. This might be termed "regular" working capital. It is the irreducible minimum of capital necessary to keep up the healthy circulation of current assets, or the amount of circulating capital that will always be found in the business.

Every business also needs liquid capital over and above the regular working capital to provide for contingencies that arise at unstated periods. These contingencies are rising prices, business depressions, emergencies, and special operations. Rising prices call for more money to carry inventories and receivables or to increase inventories. Business depressions raise the amount of cash required to ride out unusually stagnant periods. Emergencies such as strikes, fires, and unexpectedly severe competition use up extra supplies of cash. Inauguration of extensive marketing campaigns, experiments with products or with methods of distribution, contracts to supply new businesses, and the like, require additional funds. This excess over regular working capital might be termed "reserve margin" or "cushion" working capital.

Beyond the regular and cushion working capital, a business may require working capital to take care of seasonal needs and expansion of sales. The working capital required for these purposes is called "variable" working capital because it changes with the volume of business.

Regular working capital and reserve margin working capital are

* Acknowledgment is made to Edward F. Gee, "Financing Working Capital Needs," and Theodore H. Silbert and Robert Andrew Klein, "Seeking and Obtaining Short-Term Credit," Chapters 3 and 4, in *Business Finance Handbook*: New York, Prentice-Hall, Inc., 1953.

fixed or permanent requirements and should therefore be supplied by the owner or owners of the business. Variable working capital is needed for temporary periods and therefore may be supplied by the creditors of the business. In other words, the business may borrow for its short-term needs.

Scope of chapter. This chapter covers (1) the qualifications necessary for short-term borrowing, (2) the sources of temporary borrowing, (3) types of short-term loan arrangements and how they work; and (4) how to present the request for a loan. From the explanation of points (2) and (3) the businessman can see which sources are most likely to be available to him and which methods of financing are suitable for his particular situation.

1. QUALIFICATIONS FOR SHORT-TERM BORROWING

Factors affecting qualification for credit. Every lender takes into account the following factors when an application is made for a short-term business loan:

1. *The human element.* The lender wants to know whether the owners and top executives are trustworthy. He therefore looks into the previous record of these individuals, their education, training and experience, and their habits and morals. The efficiency and adequacy of the productive, non-productive, and supervisory personnel are also important to the lender. He wants to be sure that there will be an adequate working force with the skills necessary for efficient operation. He also wants to know whether the employees are contented with their wage rates, working conditions, and labor relations. The provision the business has made for training understudies to fill important managerial posts is also given attention by a lender.

The borrower will not qualify for a loan if the lender is not satisfied with the results of his investigation of the human element.

2. *The financial factor.* The capital invested in the business must be sufficient to assure some protection to the lender. The lender is concerned about the excess of the total assets of the business over its debt. Does it offer enough leeway for shrinkage in the value of assets, the possibility of subsequent operating losses, and hazards to the business? The lender wants to know the nature and quality of the assets, the reliability of the asset valuation, and whether all of the

iabilities have been included. He wants to be sure that the company's physical properties and liquid assets are adequately protected by insurance, and that the company is protected against liability exposures.

To appraise the financial strength of the business, the lender calls for financial statements for a definite period of years. These include the balance sheet, profit and losss statement, surplus or capital statement, and sometimes supplementary details or schedules, such as aging of accounts receivable, breakdown of inventory, and cash budgets for the succeeding fiscal period. Statements certified by a public accountant, known and respected by the lender, carry more weight than those without such evidence of responsibility. The lender, at any rate, wants to be sure that accurate and adequate accounting records have been and are being maintained.

The financial factor in a particular instance may be unsatisfactory to one type of lender and acceptable to another. It may be sufficient to support one method of financing and insufficient to justify another. These statements will become clearer when sources of loans and methods of financing are discussed.

3. *The economic factor.* The ability of a business to repay a loan it is seeking depends upon the economic environment in which the business will operate during the period that the loan is outstanding. Business generally passes through alternate periods of expansion and contraction, known as the business cycle. The lender has to consider whether business generally is headed for prosperity, recession, depression, or recovery, and how the general business outlook will affect the particular business that is applying for a loan. Such economic factors as taxation, government regulation, restrictions, and controls may also have a bearing on the ability of the particular business to operate successfully during the period of the loan. The conditions and prospects within the industry in which the borrower is engaged are also considered by the lender, as well as the stability and economic soundness of the function performed by the particular business. The lender is interested, too, in the use to which the credit will be put and the sources from which the repayment will be made.

Strengthening the qualification for credit. The lender may feel that a loan is justified by the applicant's management record, its capital strength, and the general economic outlook. In that case the borrower may obtain the loan on his simple promise to repay at som future date. On the other hand, the lender may be willing to mak the loan only if he is given additional protection against the borrow er's inability to repay the loan when due. The additional protectio may take the following forms:

1. Collateral.
2. Endorsement and guarantee.
3. Subordination of debts due principals.
4. Restrictive agreement.

Collateral. Assets, or rights to assets, that can be readily sold o turned into cash by the lender are turned over to the lender to pro tect the loan. A loan thus protected is called a collateral loan Stocks and bonds, accounts receivable, life insurance policies, com modities, or inventory items are examples of assets frequently used as collateral. A detailed explanation of the use of these and other assets to secure loans is given in the section beginning at page 957.

By furnishing collateral, the borrower may (1) obtain more credit than the lender would otherwise be ready to extend; (2) obtain credit for a longer period than would otherwise be available; (3) avoid an extensive credit investigation and disclosure of financial details that might otherwise be demanded by the lender; (4) obtain a lower interest rate in some instances.

Endorsement and guarantee. A lender may be willing to make a loan if the officers or stockholders of the borrowing corporation, or some other financially responsible third person will add his personal promise to pay to that of the borrower, by personally endorsing the loan, or becoming a co-maker. The same result can be obtained by having a financially responsible officer, stockholder, or individual guarantee a specific trade accounts payable or other corporate obligation. If the borrower is a weak subsidiary of a strong parent corporation, the guarantee of the parent corporation may be offered or requested to protect the loan. Because the lender may look to the borrower or his endorser or guarantor for payment, the credit risk is reduced.

Subordination of debts. If the applicant for a loan owes money to its officers or stockholders, the debt may stand in the way of obtaining a loan. To overcome this barrier, the officers or stockholders n subordinate their claims against the corporation to the claim of e lender, or to the claims, in general, of all outside creditors. The bordination is effected by an agreement, executed by the corporaon and the individuals to whom the money is owing. The agreeent is filed with each of the creditors concerned.

Restrictive loan agreement. The uncertain credit position of the orrower may cause the lender to ask the borrower to enter into a strictive loan agreement. Such an agreement includes provisions esigned to prevent a dissipation of financial strength. The provions may be promises by the borrower to maintain a certain net orking capital, to keep inventories below a certain amount, to mainain the property in good condition, to keep a required amount of isurance in force, and to render financial statements at fixed interals (monthly, quarterly, or, more rarely, semi-annually). There nay be prohibitions against other borrowing, except for trade credits n the usual course of business. The borrower may be required by the greement to limit salaries, dividends, or investments in fixed assets. The violation of any of the restrictive provisions by the borrower terninates the agreement and makes the entire loan payable immeliately.

Such agreements are most commonly used by banks and insurance companies in arranging revolving credits, term loans, and standby agreements (see page 957). The loans are frequently on an unsecured basis, but they may be secured by collateral.

2. SOURCES OF SHORT-TERM LOANS

Sources, types of loans, and methods of financing. A businessman in need of working capital might first think, "Where shall I go for a loan?" The sources, when listed, may appear numerous, but actually few of them may be available to him. He should know what kinds of businesses make use of a particular source in order to judge whether the source is one he can possibly use. He should know something about the types of loans the different classes of lenders make and how those loans are arranged. Some types of loan arrangements might be entirely suitable to his particular situation; others might not. Also, the type of loan he can obtain may be made by different classes of lenders, but one class might be more ready than another to make it for him.

Thus, sources of loans, types of loans, and methods of short-ter financing are interrelated subjects. However, to clarify the explan tion of short-term borrowing, sources of loans will be discussed sep rately from types of loans and methods by which they are carri out. Although the explanation of the latter subject is reserved f the next section, types of loans made by each source will be in cated in the discussion of the various sources.

Sources of short-term loans. Each of the following sources wi be examined briefly from the standpoint of its use by large and sma businesses:

1. Trade creditors.
2. Commercial banks.
3. Commercial finance companies.
4. Factors.
5. Commercial paper brokers.
6. Acceptance dealers or discount houses.
7. Government institutions.
8. Federal Reserve banks.
9. FHA loans.
10. Industrial banks.
11. Personal finance comp nies.

Trade creditors. No source of current business credit is mor frequently used than trade credit. Most suppliers offer small bus nesses as well as large ones reasonable short-term payment terms a a matter of trade custom. After a good credit relationship has bee established, and conditions warrant it, the business may seek large credit lines or negotiate more liberal terms than those usually offered

A trade creditor must have reasonable assurance of the integrit and ability of business management and of the financial conditio and prospects of the business before he can be expected to part wit his merchandise or services upon the strength of an understandin that payment for such purchases will be made at a later date. A newly established business that is seeking trade credit should there fore contact the principal sources of prospective supply and acquain them with the managers of the business, its financial condition, pros pects, and trade credit requirements. A visit in person, if practicable, is more effective than a letter. The prospective trade creditor should be told something of the background and experience of the princi pals in the business and should be furnished with a complete finan cial statement.

The businessman who extends credit to his own customers has

ıerely to put himself in the place of the firm that asks him for credit) realize the importance of maintaining good relationships with supliers. The best way to do this is to settle all accounts on their terms nd take advantage of cash discounts.

Commercial banks as a source of loans. The commercial bank the first institution the businessman thinks of when he is in need f a short-term loan. All loan transactions are handled by the bank's ɔan department, which is under the direction of loan officers. The ank also has a credit department which obtains and compiles inforıation about borrowers and potential borrowers.

Because a bank's funds are available only for comparatively safe ıort-term loans, banks have developed over the years a set of standrds to guide them. An ideal borrower, from the bank's viewpoint, a concern run by a competent management of sound reputation. t has substantial net worth compared to the amount of the loan ought, has earned profits for a reasonable period of time by hanling a standard product of proved value or by rendering a necesary service, and gives every indication of continuing to operate rofitably in the future. Many companies cannot meet all of these tandards and hence must offer security or an outside guarantor.

The lending officers determine whether the bank's requirements ave been met from a personal interview with the borrower, a study f the financial and operating statements and other written material e submits, and from the credit information independently obtained y the bank's credit department.

A businessman should try to obtain as much information as possiɔle about a bank's lending policy. Some banks are known to specialze in making loans to certain industries. If the concern falls into hese categories, it is likely to find the bank not only willing to xtend funds liberally but also ready to give valuable advice. If a ɔank has had unfavorable experience with a few firms in a particuar industry, it may become reticent about making further loans to uch firms or to other firms in the industry. A small business should ind out whether the bank is interested in making loans to small nterprises.

Types of loans made by a bank. The types of loans generally nade by commercial banks are: (1) unsecured, (2) endorsed or conaker, (3) secured by collateral. Collateral might consist of (a) stocks and bonds, (b) life insurance, (c) bills of lading, warehous receipts, trust receipts, and factors liens for inventory loans, (d accounts receivable, (e) notes and contracts receivable, (f) real es tate mortgage or chattel mortgage on other fixed assets.

The explanation of these types of loans begins at page 957. Not a banks care to make all of the types of loans mentioned or hav facilities for doing so. Sometimes a bank that does not handle th type of loan desired by a customer will be able to make arrange ments for the desired loan with a correspondent bank.

Choosing a bank. The bank a business uses for deposits, check collecting, and other everyday bank services is the one that it wil ordinarily go to for short-term seasonal credit or other business fi nancing requirements. If the company is likely to need large credi lines at certain periods of the year because of seasonal fluctuations it should select a bank whose typical customers receive loans of a size comparable with the company's needs. If the firm is engaged in import and export trade, it should choose a bank that is equipped to handle foreign exchange and letters of credit. If it wants to bor row on field warehousing agreements, or other special credit instru ments, it should select a bank that can and will handle such types of loans. In addition, it should consider the attitudes of the di rectors and officers of the bank. The ultra-conservative bank may have too stringent a credit policy; the bank with an aggressive new-business policy may be lending too close to its limits and thus be unable to help its old customers in times of general business stress.

Such factors as convenient location, facilities for safe deposit boxes, collecting coupons, payroll, and other special services may also have to be given weight.

Commercial finance companies as a source of loans. The commercial finance companies include a group of companies specializing in the extension of secured credit to business firms. They are variously known as commercial credit companies, credit companies, accounts receivable finance companies, factors, and sales finance companies. All are engaged in granting self-liquidating collateralized credit. Through specialized knowledge and techniques, and willingness to take risks, they can supply funds that often cannot be obtained through other channels. They have pioneered in the development of new forms of lending, some of which have been perfected to the point where more conservative lenders, like banks, now employ them. Their ability to take risks lies in thorough screening and detailed supervision of accounts and the charging of somewhat higher rates, to compensate for the overhead arising from multitudinous bookkeeping transactions and for losses.

Types of financing offered by finance companies. The following types of financing are available through commercial finance companies: (1) open accounts receivable financing, (2) factoring, (3) inventory financing, (4) consumer and sales financing, (5) installment financing of income-producing equipment, and (6) import and export financing.

Companies that use the services of commercial finance companies. Commercial finance companies are more tolerant of a borrower's financial position than banks. If the business applying for credit can show that it is well managed and has good prospects for success, commercial finance companies will give the application serious consideration. Of course, it must have sufficient net worth, working capital, and earning power to ensure that it can stay in business and operate successfully. Also, it must be able to offer acceptable collateral. Companies that use the services of commercial finance companies often fall into the following categories:

1. A young undercapitalized company that does not have sufficient working capital at the time of application, but expects in the near future to increase such funds through larger sales volume and retention of earnings.
2. A growing company whose increased sales volume has temporarily overextended its working capital resources.
3. A company whose capital has been reduced through a change in capital structure, such as buying out of a principal.
4. A company whose working capital has been depleted by adverse business, a condition that has since then been corrected.
5. A company whose management lacks experience in its present venture but has high character and ability, and can present sound collateral for secured financing while it improves its management.
6. A company in an industry with large seasonal peaks, such as the bathing suit, winter outerware, and sporting goods industries.
7. A company that for other reasons does not meet the technical

requirements for a bank loan; its progress is retarded by lack of working capital, but it possesses acceptable accounts receivable or other security.

Choosing a commercial finance company. Because of the great variations among finance companies, it is important to choose one that is equipped to handle the type of financing desired. Finance companies are not subject to the statutory restrictions and governmental supervision that apply to banks. For this reason, greater reliance must be placed upon the reputation of the finance company and the integrity of its managers. A well-established company should be selected. In general, the older firms have high standards of conduct. Many of the younger companies, however, are also reliable. The businessman should check into the history of the company and its personnel. He may go to his commercial banker for help in this investigation and to others in the business community, such as credit and trade associations, attorneys, accountants and clients of the finance company. It must be remembered, however, that the opinions of individuals may be biased. The businessman should not hesitate to get acquainted with the executives of the finance company he is considering, for such direct contact is most helpful in forming an opinion about the company.

Since the commercial finance industry is a competitive one, rates of reputable companies tend to be in the same range for similar services and for borrowers of comparable financial strength. Nevertheless, it is advisable to make inquiries of several companies to establish what is a fair rate.

Factors as a source of funds. A factor is a specialized type of commercial finance company. For the most part a factor makes funds available by buying outright the accounts receivable of a company. The seller is then relieved of the risk of loss due to a debtor's insolvency or inability to pay. The factor performs all credit and collection service, leaving the client free to concentrate on other problems of his business.

Factoring companies seek borrowers of good character, relying upon them to assign bona fide sales. The product must be well accepted, for return merchandise wipes out the collateral and forces the factor to rely upon the general financial standing of the client. Factoring companies offer their services to manufacturers, distrib-ors, and jobbers in such lines as textiles, shoes, furniture, equipent and appliance trades, and certain foodstuffs. Progressive ctors who seek to expand into other fields may handle other products as well.

In addition to purchasing accounts receivable, billing, ledgering, llecting the receivables, and guaranteeing the seller against cusmer credit losses, the factor may also extend credit to its clients ainst merchandise on hand or in process of manufacture, against ens on plants or machinery, or on an open note, unsecured basis.

Commercial paper houses as a source of funds. A fairly large, ell-established industrial or mercantile concern might issue shortrm unsecured notes to finance part of its seasonal or temporary orking capital requirements, using commercial paper houses to arket them. The commercial paper house either acts as a broker etween the company issuing the notes and the purchaser of the otes, or it buys the paper from the issuing company and sells it in e open market to banks, insurance companies, and private inestors as prime risk, low-rate, short-term investments. The interest ate to the borrower is usually nominally lower than the prime comercial rate on a direct bank loan.

Only firms in a strong financial position, with good earnings for number of years, ample working capital, and the highest credit tanding can make use of commercial paper brokers.

Commercial paper houses, or note brokers as they are sometimes alled, are usually large financing institutions that also act as secuities dealers, stock brokers, and investment bankers.

Acceptance dealers or discount houses as a source of funds. A usiness that receives bankers' acceptances in payment of such comnodities as cotton, coffee, and other staple goods sold to domestic uyers or importers, may want to convert those bankers' acceptances nto cash rather than hold them until maturity. It may discount he bankers' acceptances at its own bank or sell them to a discount ouse. In either case two charges are involved—the bank's charge or accepting the draft, and the charge for discounting the paper. This latter charge varies with money market conditions and with he maturity. However, bankers' acceptances command the lowest ate of discount because the risk is practically eliminated by the irect responsibility of the accepting bank to make payment at maturity. If the business can borrow on its own notes, it usua prefers to do so and hold the bankers' acceptances until maturi

Like commercial paper houses, discount houses perform other nancing functions. For example, Discount Corporation of New Yo also buys and sells United States Treasury bills, certificates of indel edness, and other government securities.

Government institutions as a source of loans. The princip agency for businesses in need of working capital is the Reconstructic Finance Corporation. Any business enterprise that cannot obta credit through its normal sources, on reasonable terms, can as a la resort apply to the RFC for a loan. Usually a loan application mu have been considered and declined by at least two commercial ban before it will be considered by RFC.

All loans made by RFC must be secured by collateral adequate afford reasonable assurance of repayment when considered with oth factors. These factors include integrity and ability of managemen prospective earning power of the business, whether granting th loan will increase employment or have other favorable effects on th economic life of the community, the soundness of the business an its long range possibilities, and the like. The collateral may consi of (1) a mortgage on fixed assets, (2) a mortgage on chattels, (3) a signment of accounts receivable, (4) a pledge of inventories (prefe ably stored in bonded warehouses), or (5) a pledge of other assets

The Reconstruction Finance Corporation's power to make ne loans terminates June 30, 1954. Congress may order liquidation the RFC before then.

Federal Reserve banks as a source of loans. Under the Bankin Act of 1934, the regional Federal Reserve Banks and their branche are empowered to make loans directly to business firms. Federa Reserve loans can only be made to meet working capital require ments of established firms, and the term cannot be longer than fiv years. Since these powers were granted to the Federal Reserve a an emergency measure to help businesses over the bad spots durin the great depression, the banks today are reluctant to make loan except under unusual circumstances in which a deserving borrowe cannot obtain funds elsewhere. There are no restrictions on the siz of the loan. In the past, however, the banks have tended to favo small and medium-sized businesses.

Generally speaking, all direct loans made by Federal Reserve Banks must be secured. Acceptable security may include: (1) a first mortgage on real estate, plant, and equipment, (2) a pledge of chattels, (3) an assignment of accounts receivable, (4) a pledge of notes receivable, trade acceptances, or warehouse receipts for merchandise stored in acceptable warehouses, (5) an assignment of moneys due or to become due under United States government or other contracts, or (6) such other collateral as may be acceptable to the bank.

FHA loans. The Federal Housing Administration will guarantee, under certain circumstances, the loans made by approved private institutional lenders. Small contractors and others dealing in materials or equipment used for modernization or new constructions may increase their volume of business without increasing their accounts receivable by using the financing offered under the FHA program.

Industrial banks as a source of loans. The industrial banks in this country include Morris Plan banks and other lending institutions that specialize in consumer installment loans. Many of them resemble ordinary commercial banks in that they accept deposits and do a general banking business. However, they are not an integral part of the commercial banking system but rather are collateral to it. The term "industrial" grew out of the emphasis that was originally placed upon loans to industrial workers. Although industrial banks make loans to individuals, some of them make a great many business loans.

The size of the loan that can be made, the terms, and the charges are regulated by state law and vary from state to state. Amounts range from $1,000 to $5,000, depending upon the state law. The term generally is from one to two years. Usually a charge of 6 to 8 per cent of the entire loan is deducted in advance and since the loan is on an installment basis, payable on a regular schedule, the effective annual interest rate is about 12 to 16 per cent. Besides, there may be a charge for cerdit investigation. Inquiry in a particular area may show that because of competition with commercial banks less than the maximum legal rate is charged. Loans from industrial banks may be secured by collateral or made on the guaranty of two or more responsible persons as co-makers.

Since installment loans are a relatively expensive way to obtain business funds, this source would be used by the small businessma only if less costly borrowing from other sources were not availabl

Personal finance companies as a source of loans. As a genera rule, personal finance companies, or small loan companies, as the are commonly called, confine their activities to consumer financin that is, they make loans to individuals payable in monthly instal ments over a ten to twenty-four month period. Most of the loan are character loans, without endorsement and without marketab collateral. Chattel mortgages on household goods are quite com monly taken and foreclosures are rare. Some loans are made fo business purposes.

In most states the small loans companies are regulated by smal loans laws patterned after the Uniform Small Loans Law. Thes loans set the maximum loan that be made by licensed lenders. I most states the maximum loan is $300; in some it is $500; and in few it is $1,000. The laws also set the maximum rate of interes that may be charged on upaid balances. The legal rate varies fron state to state. In some states the rates run from 2 to 3⅓ per cen per month on very small loans, but are graduated downward to 2 o 2½ per cent on loans up to $300. In states that permit loans ove $300, the monthly rates on amounts over $300 run from ½ to ¾ per cent per month. Prepayment without penalty is usually per mitted.

Before utilizing the small loan company as a source of busines funds, the small businessman should carefully consider the cost which, as indicated, are very high.

3. TYPES OF LOAN ARRANGEMENTS AND HOW THEY WORK

Unsecured bank loans. The most desirable and most economic method of financing working capital requirements is through unsecured credit. The business whose management, past operating record, financial condition, and future prospects are sufficiently strong to enable it to borrow from its bank or banks of account on an "open note" or "plain note" basis enjoys a financing advantage that should be carefully protected and maintained.

When credit on this basis is established, borrowings are effected mply by filling in and signing a promissory note in the name of e business entity by a properly authorized representative.

Discount and interest. Discount is interest paid in advance to aturity rather than subsequently paid at intervals or at maturity. n short-term bank loans, discount to maturity at an agreed annual ite negotiated by the borrower is deducted from the face amount f the note and the proceeds are credited to the borrower's account. Vhen such loans, by mutual agreement, are made payable on deand, interest at the agreed annual rate is computed and billed to ie borrower by the bank at stated intervals, perhaps quarterly, and/ r is paid in full to date at the time of the payment in full of the rincipal.

Line of credit established at a bank. Businessmen who anticiate having to finance current operations by bank loans usually ask heir banks for a "line of credit" in order that they may know in dvance how much they can borrow at a particular bank, without ollateral, should the need arise. A bank will establish a line of redit up to the amount it feels it can safely extend to the business, n the basis of its knowledge of the firm's business and strength. line of credit is an advance commitment by the banker to lend up o the indicated amount. While the line is open, the business must eep the bank informed of its operations and financial condition nd must continue its deposit account there. Also, to keep the line pen, the business must make some use of it, for the bank cannot fford to maintain unused loan commitments indefinitely.

The bank generally requires all loans made within the line of redit to be paid off within the period of a year and the borrower o remain free of debt for at least a 30-day period. At or near the nd of the credit year, the business negotiates again with the bank or a line of credit for another year. Many companies are steady orrowers from banks on lines of credits. Total lines exceed the ctual amount borrowed and they rotate their clean-ups with the arious banks throughout the year. The line-of-credit loans are made t interest rates prevailing at the time of the loan.

For example, a business might arrange with its bank in January to btain a line of credit for $200,000 to run for one year. This means hat the business can borrow as many times as necessary during the ear as long as the loan balance due does not exceed the line of credit, that is, $200,000. The company may borrow the full amoun in February, repay it in, say, 90 days, and borrow again, say, $100,00 in May to be paid off in 90 days. In August it could borrow a much as it needs up to $200,000, have that amount paid off befor the period for which the line of credit was arranged expires, an still have a 30-day period during which it will be free of debt to th bank.

Revolving credit arranged by bank. Large corporations fre quently finance their current operations by arranging a revolvin credit for a term of from two to three years. Often several bank participate in the credit arrangement, though the deal is usuall negotiated with one bank. Revolving credits are established unde written loan agreements of the type referred to at page 945. Th agreement stipulates the maximum amount that can be borrowed the interest rate at which all loans under the agreement will be made and the requirements that the borrower must meet. The agreemen binds the bank to make loans to the borrower any time within th period of the agreement that the borrower wants funds, provided of course, that the borrower meets the conditions set forth in th agreement.

To illustrate, a corporation might arrange for a revolving credi of $1,000,000 for 2½ years at 2½ per cent interest. The compan could then borrow as many times as circumstances required durin the 2½ years as long as the total of loans outstanding at any one time does not exceed $1,000,000. All loans will be made at 2½ pe cent as fixed in the agreement, regardless of market changes in interest rates. The bank will, however, require the recipient of the revolving credit to pay a small fee, about ½ of 1 per cent per annum on the unused balance of the credit.

Revolving credit arrangements may provide for either secured o unsecured loans. Four types of collateral are used as security: (1 negotiable bills of lading, covering goods in transit; (2) warehous receipts, covering readily salable staple commodities in warehouses (3) trust receipts; (4) assignments of accounts and notes receivable The procedures for financing with these types of collateral, whethe under a revolving credit or not, will be explained below.

The revolving credit agreement specifies a maximum percentage o the value of the assets offered as security which the bank will lend 'hus, the agreement may fix 80 per cent of the value of pledged acounts receivable, or 75 per cent of the invoice price of goods as the aximum for each of these classes of loans respectively. Each inoice for goods may be a source of a loan. When any of the pledged ssets is withdrawn, the borrower must make repayment of the loan quivalent to the amount withdrawn. Because of this feature, the oan is said to revolve.

Term loans. A term loan is one with a maturity usually of not ess than two and not more than ten years, repayable in monthly, uarterly, semi-annual, or annual installments over the specified period. Before term loans came into common use, the practice was for usinessmen to borrow on short-term notes. The notes were often reewed again and again, and payment frequently was not made until everal years later. Term loans thus are simply a frank recognition of his condition.

Term loans are used for working capital purposes or for any other pecified business purpose, including plant improvements or addiions. They are made by banks and insurance companies, under retrictive loan agreements.

When a business foresees the need of additional funds it may negoiate a term loan to be available under certain contingencies or at a redetermined time. The loan and its agreement do not become perative until the stated time arrives or unless the state event occurs. 'his arrangement is called a *standby commitment,* or *standby credit.*

Loans secured by pledge of stocks and bonds. If the business wns stocks or bonds they may be accepted as collateral for short-term oans by a bank, finance company, or other lender. Securities listed n a national exchange are the most acceptable as loan security. A ank will lend from 60 to 75 per cent of the market value of a listed ecurity, perhaps going as high as 80 to 90 per cent when the security onsists of high-grade bonds or United States Government securities. 'or securities that have a local and more or less active over-theounter market the lender may limit the loan to 50 per cent or less of he last indicated bid price. For securities that are closely owned and or which there is no determinable market, the amount loaned is determined by the lender's appraisal of the financial condition, management, earnings record, and prospects of the firms which issued the ecurities.

In turning over collateral for a loan, the registered owner of stoc endorses it in ink to effect its pledge as collateral. Usually this er dorsement is supplied on a separate power of attorney. Registere bonds are deposited with the lender in a similar way. Coupon bond require nothing more than physical delivery to effect their pledge a collateral. The dividends and interest payments continue to gc when paid, directly to the owner unless otherwise specifically re stricted by the lender.

The borrower signs a collateral note form. This note gives broa powers to the lender, including the right to demand additional co lateral, if in its judgment additional collateral is needed and to hol the collateral for any other debt due the lender. The collateral not provides that in the event of loan payment default, bankruptcy, o failure to deposit additional collateral upon request, the lender ma sell the collateral at public or private sale for the satisfaction of th debt. Upon any such sale, the excess, if any, of the proceeds over th amount of the debt would be returned to the borrower.

Loans secured by assignment of life insurance. A business tha carries life insurance on one or more of its officers or principals ma find that it has, in the cash surrender value of these policies, a highl acceptable form of collateral security. A loan secured by an assign ment of the policy may be obtained from the insurance company, a bank, a loan broker, a finance company, or other lending agency The cash surrender value of the policy, if any, may be computed from a table of values set out in the policy.

The assignment to the lender of all rights, claims, and values of the policy is effected by the use of an instrument of assignment supplied by the insurance company or the lender. The assignment must be properly executed by the owner of the policy and perhaps also, if required, by the insured and the beneficiary, if other than the owner. Physical possession of the policy and of the original of the instrument of assignment is retained by the lender until the loan is paid. A duplicate of the assignment, properly executed, is sent to the insurance company by the lender.

A bank or other lender may be willing to lend close to 100 per cent of the cash surrender value of the policy as set out in its terms.

Loans secured by commodities or inventory items. A bank, finance company, factor, or any other lending agency may arrange loan secured by commodities or inventory items. The instruments sed in such loans include: (a) bill of lading, (b) trade acceptance, c) banker's acceptance, (d) public warehouse receipt, (e) field varehouse receipt, (f) trust receipt, (g) factors lien, (h) chattel nortgage, deed of trust, or conditional sale contract. The nature of hese instruments and how they are used in inventory financing will e brought out in the following paragraphs.

Advances against bill of lading. While goods are in transit, the itle to the goods may be evidenced by a bill of lading. A bill of lading is a receipt given by the railroad or other carrier to the shipper. t serves also as a contract to deliver the goods and as documentary vidence of title to them. When properly endorsed, it may be ledged with a lender as loan security. Upon arrival of the goods, the urchaser may obtain the bill of lading from the lender under trust eceipt, sell the goods, and pay the lender. Or, the purchaser may lace the goods in a public warehouse and return warehouse receipts o the lender to cancel the trust receipt.

A seller may ship merchandise under a negotiable bill of lading nade out in its own name, draw a sight draft on the purchaser for the mount of the sale, endorse the bill of lading in blank and attach it to he draft. It may then either (1) discount the draft with a bank, receiving the cash proceeds immediately, or (2) enter the draft for collection through a bank, receiving the cash proceeds when the draft is aid by the purchaser. The bank is protected, if it discounts the lraft, by recourse on the seller and by a negotiable title, evidenced by he bill of lading, to the goods in transit. The seller is protected, in ither event, by being assured of the payment of the draft by the purchaser before title to the goods is transferred to the purchaser by elease to the purchaser of the bill of lading. If the draft is dishonored, the draft and the attached bill of lading will be returned to the eller and the seller will be able to recall the shipment of goods or to lispose of them elsewhere.

Trade acceptance. A trade acceptance is a draft drawn on the urchaser of a shipment of merchandise by the seller of the merchanlise for the purchase price of the merchandise, payable on a specified uture date or on a determinable future date after delivery of the merhandise and presentation to and acceptance of the draft by the purchaser. By an arrangement with a trade supplier, a business may us such a device to finance inventory purchases.

For example, a purchaser may arrange with a seller to ship an orde of merchandise for $5,000 on a time draft or trade acceptance basis payable sixty days after sight with interest at 6 per cent. The selle ships the merchandise, obtains and endorses a negotiable bill of lad ing, and attaches the bill of lading to a draft drawn on the purchase for $5,000, payable sixty days after sight with interest at 6 per cent He delivers the draft and attached bill of lading to the seller's bank to be forwarded to a bank in the purchaser's city, with instruction to release the bill of lading to the purchaser upon the purchaser' acceptance of the draft. Upon presentation of the draft, the pur chaser writes the word "Accepted" across its face, together with th date, the name of the bank at which payment is to be made, and th purchaser's signature. The bill of lading is then released to the pur chaser, enabling the purchaser to obtain delivery of the merchandis and to have a period of sixty days, from the date the draft was ac cepted, in which to dispose of the merchandise before payment fo the purchase price has to be made.

The accepted draft, or "acceptance," is returned to the seller' bank, and, at the request of the seller, the bank may discount th acceptance (on which both the purchaser and the seller are obli gated) at a mutually satisfactory rate, giving the seller the cash pro ceeds immediately. A few days before the maturity of the accept ance, the bank forwards the acceptance for collection to the bank a which it is payable. On the maturity date, the purchaser, having sol and collected for the merchandise in the meantime, pays the collect ing bank $5,050 (the amount of the original draft plus the agree interest for sixty days at 6 per cent) and receives the cancelled ac ceptance. After deducting its collection charges, the collecting ban remits the proceeds to the seller's bank and the transaction is closed

Banker's acceptance. By negotiation between the seller and th purchaser and between the purchaser and the purchaser's bank, i may be agreed that the draft (with bill of lading attached) for th purchase price of the merchandise will be drawn on (and accepted by the purchaser's bank rather than on (and for acceptance by) the pur chaser. In all such instances, the purchaser must qualify as an accept able credit risk to the bank since, under an acceptance agreemen tween the purchaser and the bank, the bank agrees to accept the aft upon presentation, when accompanied by specified documents f title to specified goods. By the terms of the acceptance agreeent, the title documents are assigned and transferred to the bank, return for the agreement of the purchaser to place funds for the ayment of the acceptance, plus the bank's commission for its service t an agreed rate, in the hands of the bank prior to the maturity date f the acceptance. Since banker's acceptances are prime risks and ave a ready market, the seller will have no difficulty in disposing f the acceptance immediately at a relatively low rate of discount.

Loans secured by warehouse receipts. A warehouse receipt is imply a receipt for goods placed in a warehouse. At one time all oods financed by warehouse receipts had to be stored in independent ublic warehouses. Since these were often not near the borrower's lace of business, inconvenience and extra expense resulted. To void this, a form of service known as "field warehousing" was develped by means of which the warehousing is done on the premises of he borrower. A warehousing company takes a lease of a part of the orrower's premises on which it displays its sign as occupant. The orrower makes written application for storage space therein and a epresentative of the warehousing company signs and issues warehouse receipts to cover the deposited goods and then takes custody of them. Since the agents of the warehousing company are bonded against "any act or acts of fraud, dishonesty, forgery, theft, larceny, embezzlement, wrongful extraction, or willful application or misappropriation or breach of trust," there is little danger of loss through collusion between the operatives of the warehousing company and the agents of the borrower. The types of commodities most commonly field warehoused are: canned food products; miscellaneous groceries; lumber and building supplies; coal and coke; grain, feed, seeds, and other agricultural products; fuel oil and gasoline; wine, liquor, and beer; textiles and clothing; steel and other metals; household appliances; chemicals and drugs; and industrial machinery and equipment.

Procedure. A purchase financed with warehouse receipts as security would be accomplished as follows. The buyer advises his bank that he is ordering goods from the seller and arranges to have the bank pay the draft the seller will forward to the bank with the bill of lading covering the shipment. The seller ships the goods and sen the draft and bill of lading to the buyer's bank. Upon arrival of th shipment, the bank pays the draft, after first having obtained a no from the buyer covering the cost of the goods. To get the goods, th buyer must obtain the bill of lading from the bank. In exchange fo the bill of lading (which represents title to the goods), the buy gives the bank a trust receipt covering the goods. With the bill o lading, the buyer can get the goods and have them stored in a war house, taking the warehouseman's receipt. This warehouse receipt h turns over to the bank, which cancels the trust receipt. The war houseman will release the goods only upon surrender of the war house receipt by the bank, or upon proper notice from the ban ordering partial release. The bank will not give up the warehouse re ceipt or order a partial release of the goods unless the borrowe reduces the loan in proportion to the value of the goods released, o gives the bank a trust receipt covering the goods withdrawn. Whe the goods covered by the trust receipt are sold, the proceeds are use to pay off the loan and the trust receipt is cancelled.

Loans secured by trust receipts. A trust receipt is a financing in strument in the form of an agreement between the lender, called th entruster, and a borrower, called the trustee. It shows that certai goods or property, or evidence of title to these goods or property, having been acquired for financing purposes by the lender, are release by him for a specified purpose under specified conditions to the borrower. While they are in the borrower's possession, the lender retains ownership until the goods or property, or the evidence of title to goods or property, are properly accounted for by the trustee to the entruster. This accounting is through payment or otherwise, as set out in the instrument.

The trust receipt is used most widely in the domestic field to finance the purchase of durable goods such as automobiles, radios, refrigerators, and the like, that are sold to consumers on the installment plan and that are easily identified by a serial number. It is also used extensively for interim financing of staple commodities when it is necessary to release pledged goods from a warehouse in order to sell or process them.

Procedure. The method of arranging a short-term loan with a trust receipt as collateral can best be explained by illustrating how it oper-es in the case of an automobile dealer who does not have the cash acquire the cars from the manufacturer without financial help. he dealer applies to his bank and there arranges a credit for whater amount is needed to pay for the cars. The dealer then places the der with the manufacturer and instructs him to draw on the bank r payment and to forward to the bank the bills of lading to order in the bank's name. When the cars arrive, the bank pays for em. The manufacturer's interest in the transaction ceases when he ceives payment from the bank. The bank gives the dealer the bill lading so that he can get the cars and in exchange has the dealer ecute a trust receipt. Generally, the trust receipt recites that the orrower has received certain goods that are the property of the bank ıd that the borrower will hold them, or the proceeds of their sale, in trust" for the bank. When the dealer makes a sale, the car is reased from trust, the proceeds are used to repay the bank, and the ust receipt for the particular car is cancelled. If the cars are sold n the installment plan, the dealer will obtain the cash with which to epay the bank by selling the installment sales contract either to the ank or to a finance company. The sale of the installment contract a finance company is described at page 966.

Factors lien. A number of states have enacted laws authorizing he creation of factors liens. By complying with these laws, a factor, ank, finance company, or other lending agency may lend to manuacturers (and, in some states, to other forms of business) against the ledge of all raw materials, goods in process, finished goods, and any nd all other materials which the borrower may own in connection vith the operation of its business. The lien is a continuing one and pplies to the entire inventory that may be on hand at the time of the ecessity for enforcing the lien.

The statutory requirements for the creation of a factors lien must e adhered to strictly. These requirements vary from state to state. common requirement is the posting of a sign in a conspicuous locaion in the main place of business of the borrower, or near the pledged nerchandise, giving the name of the factor (and thus notice of the ien). Many states also require filing a notice with the county clerk r other official, giving the names of the borrower and lender, the ype of merchandise subject to the lien, and other information.

Procedure. A written agreement is entered into between the lender and the borrower, establishing a factors lien in favor of t lender as security for advances made or to be made by the lender the borrower upon merchandise. Under this agreement, the bo rower prepares and signs a schedule describing the merchandi pledged and its value. The schedule acknowledges the general li of the lender upon the merchandise in its present form or as it m be manufactured, and also upon the proceeds of the sale of the me chandise. It gives the lender control over the merchandise and records pertaining to it, as well as the right to approve sales merchandise.

The borrower notifies the lender daily of the amount of mercha dise that has been shipped. As the inventory collateral is reduce through shipments, the factors lien attaches to the accounts rece able created by the sale and its proceeds. The lender also requir periodical reports of inventory. It renders monthly statements sho ing the balance of funds advanced to the client, the amount of i ventory collateral held by the lender, changes in these balances occu ring during the month, and the monthly charges. Interest is ge erally charged on the amount of funds advanced.

Financing inventory by means of a factors lien agreement is ofte effected as a supplement to accounts receivable financing and facto ing. It is also used in conjunction with chattel mortgage financin of equipment sales.

Loans secured by accounts receivable. The method of financin accounts receivable used by banks, and generally by finance compa nies, is carried out through a formal agreement, referred to as th *underlying agreement* or *working plan,* which is a continuing arrang ment for advancing funds against open accounts. The accounts re ceivable are assigned to the finance company or purchased by it wit full recourse to the client in the event of non-payment when du The agreement specifies what percentage of the value of the assigne accounts receivable will be available to the borrower (usually fron 75 per cent to 80 per cent, though in some cases the margin runs fron about 65 per cent to 85 per cent). It also sets forth the rights an liabilities of the parties and the over-all conditions by which eac assignment shall operate. Assignments of accounts are made fron time to time as the business needs funds. At such times the com pany prepares a schedule of the assigned accounts, and, in the cas a loan, executes a demand note in the amount of the loan. Dupli-te invoices and shipping receipts are attached to the schedule of counts as further evidence of the assignment. Upon acceptance the schedule, the finance company prepares a pay statement and eck for the amount to be advanced to the client on the accepted counts.

The assignee (lender) usually stamps the assigned accounts in the mpany's accounts receivable ledger, indicating that the account has en assigned. (A few states require this book-marking to validate e assignment.) The manner in which the assigned accounts are llected depends upon whether the accounts are transferred under e notification or non-notification plan.

Notification and non-notification plan. Banks and most finance mpanies use the non-notification type of assignment. Under this an the debtors of the borrower are not notified of the assignment their debts. The borrower collects the accounts and (1) remits e proceeds to the lender in their original form, or (2) deposits them a special agency account, which is subject to withdrawal by the nder only. The borrower prefers the non-notification method be-use it makes for better relationships between it and its customers. he debtor dislikes being told that he is to pay his account to a ird person. He suspects that the company to whom he owes the oney is financially weak and unreliable and he realizes that if his ccount is not paid promptly, a third person, the bank or finance ompany, will know about his delinquency and thus his credit stand-g will be jeopardized.

Under the notification type of plan, which is used by factoring con-erns (see below) and some finance companies, the original invoice r bill is sent to the customer stamped with a notation "Assigned o............" The debtor pays directly to the finance company. he purpose is to protect the finance company from collection and raudulent appropriation by the borrower.

If accounts are not paid promptly, they are usually carried from hirty to sixty days at the stipulated cost. Then, in the case of a sale, he borrower buys back the slow or unpaid accounts; in the case of a ledge, it substitutes other accounts or repays the amount loaned gainst the unpaid account.

Charges for accounts receivable financing. The charges vary not nly from financing agency to financing agency but from customer to customer of the same agency. The agreement stipulates the charg The loan may be made at interest, computed on the average da outstanding balance during a specified period. Or the amount bo rowed may be discounted. Or a service charge may be levied bas upon the total number of accounts and the face amount of t receivables. Some finance companies have both an interest and service charge.

Factoring of accounts receivable. A continuing agreement made between the seller of merchandise and a factoring compa under which the factor contracts to buy all of the accounts receivab as they arise out of sales by the seller. The factor assumes all the ri and has no recourse if the accounts receivable prove uncollectibl The factor, therefore, passes upon the credit standing of the cu tomer to whom the goods are sold. Most factors operate on a no fication basis. In fact, the invoice for the goods is sent to the fact and mailed by it to the customer. The invoice shows that payme is to be made to the factoring company.

The factor is paid a fee of 1 or 2 per cent each month on the fac amount of all accounts bought the previous month. This charge for assuming the credit risk. In addition, the factor charges at t rate of 6 per cent per year. However, this charge is deducted fro the payment for the accounts. For example, if an invoice of goo for $1,000 is sold on 60 days' credit and the seller wants cash imm diately, the factor will give the seller $1,000 less 6 per cent for 6 days, or $990. The following month the fee on the $1,000 will b billed to the seller or deducted from future advances. Although fa toring is an expensive method of raising funds, it eliminates the nee for a credit and collection department by the seller who has his a counts factored.

Sale or discount of notes or contracts receivable. A business en gaged in the sale of goods on the installment basis may convert th notes or contracts it receives from such sales into working capital b selling them to, or discounting them with a bank, finance compan or other lender. This method of financing is appropriate and neces sary when a business sells motor vehicles, household appliances o other consumer goods, or machinery, fixtures and equipment, o other capital goods on an installment plan basis.

A conditional sale contract is concluded between the dealer and hi ustomer. This contract specifies the terms of sale and payment and rovides that the title to the product or products sold is to remain ith the seller until the full purchase price has been paid. The contract is placed on record in a court of proper jurisdiction, and assigned by the seller to the lender (which succeeds to the rights of he seller). The lender notifies the purchaser that his contract is ow held by the lender and that all installment payments should be nade direct to the lender from that point on. A coupon payment ook, showing the amount and maturity of each payment is usually nclosed with the notice.

Instead of using a conditional sale agreement, the sale may be ffected by a series of separate notes payable at specified intervals or single note payable in specified installments, secured by a chattel nortgage or deed of trust on the product or products sold. Whether chattel mortgage or deed of trust is used depends upon which is the referable form of security in the particular state. Either instrument nust be properly recorded. The note or notes are signed by the purchaser, placed on record in a court of proper jurisdiction, and endorsed by the seller to the lender. If a place of payment is specified n each note, the lender must present the note at the place for payment at maturity. Otherwise, the lender may notify the purchaser of he maturity of each note or of the agreed installments, in the latter ase through the use of a coupon payment book similar to that used vith conditional sales contracts.

Recourse arrangements. A business may sell to, or discount with, a ender its notes or contracts receivable on any one of the three bases: (1) with full recourse to the seller; (2) without recourse of any kind on the seller; (3) with limited recourse on the seller. Generally speaking, in the negotiation of arrangements for the sale or discount of notes or contracts receivable, it is desirable for a business to endeavor to consummate an arrangement which calls for no recourse of any kind upon the seller or for recourse to only the minimum extent acceptable to the lender.

Under a full recourse arrangement, upon any default in payments by the maker of the contract, the seller must repurchase the contract from the lender. Under an arrangement without recourse, the seller assumes no responsibility whatsoever for the payment of the instrument. Under a limited recourse arrangement, losses are shared by the seller of the product and the financing agency.

Loans secured by pledge of notes or contracts receivable.
direct loan may be made from a bank, finance company, or oth
lender by a pledge of notes or contracts receivable. Under an a
rangement of this kind, the business will issue its own note to tl
lender, on a collateral note form listing the receivables pledged, pa
able on demand or on some specified or determinable maturity dat
The listing may be made on the collateral note form or on an a
tached schedule. The amount borrowed, as evidenced by the cc
lateral note, may be moderately or substantially less than the unpai
balance, or the aggregate of the unpaid balances, on the receivables c
receivables pledged as security. The extent of the difference depenc
upon the quality of the receivables, the needs of the borrower, or, i
general, upon negotiation between the borrower and the lender. Fc
similar reasons, the interest or discount rate charged by the lende
may be greater or less than the financing rate being charged by th
borrower on the notes or contracts pledged.

Installment financing of income-producing equipment. Ord
narily, a business will use permanent capital to purchase machiner
and equipment needed in the production of its products or for th
services it renders, since the item is a fixed asset. If capital is nc
available for this purpose, the purchase may be made from the manu
facturer on the installment plan, with funds furnished by a comme
cial finance company.

The comercial finance company will either finance the seller of th
equipment or the buyer. The choice of which party to the transac
tion is to be financed is influenced in some states by the statute
Financing the seller has already been explained under loans securec
by pledge of notes or contracts receivable.

In a direct arrangement between the buyer of the equipment anc
the finance company the seller has no part in the financing. Th
buyer signs a note or series of notes calling for regular installmen
payments, and executes a chattel mortgage on the equipment as secu
rity. The mortgage must be recorded as required by the statute. I
provides for foreclosure by the finance company in the event of non
payment of installments due. The charge usually takes the form of
discount deducted in advance.

Liens on fixed assets. In some instances, to supplement othe
security, or in the absence of other acceptable security, a busines

nay give a bank or other lender a lien on the real estate or other fixed ssets of the business as collateral security for a short-term loan for vorking capital purposes. To secure a current loan, for example, a leed or trust or real estate mortgage may be given on a store or plant property, or a chattel mortgage or deed of trust may be given on machinery, equipment, fixtures, motor vehicles, or other capital assets of this kind used in the business. Usually, however, loans against such security are payable over a longer term although they have been obtained for working capital purposes.

4. HOW TO PRESENT THE REQUEST FOR A LOAN

Preparing to apply for a bank loan. The applicant for a bank loan should anticipate that the bank will have certain routine procedures for handling the application, that various data will be required, and that certain questions will have to be answered. The bank, it must be remembered, is always interested in the purpose of the loan, the borrower's plans for repayment, and the sources from which it expects to be able to liquidate the loan. Although applicants are not always asked to fill out a long form of financial statement such as that shown in Figure 76, the form is reproduced here to illustrate the extent of the information that might be called for. Familiarity with this form, plus an understanding of analysis of financial statements (see page 901) will help the applicant present his request intelligently.

Advance preparation by the one who is to negotiate the loan is advisable because incompleteness and lack of clarity in the presentation may result in refusal of the loan. The material should be presented in a way that will give the bank the impression that the borrower knows what facts are important under the circumstances. It should include the following, as far as possible.

1. Balance sheets and profit and loss statements for the past five years, or since the origin of the concern if it has been functioning for a shorter period. If possible, these statements should be certified by a public accountant.
2. Trends in sales, expenses, profits, and so forth.
3. Names of a representative group of customers (debtors).
4. Names of a representative group of suppliers (creditors).

FORM NO. 9

CORPORATION
FINANCIAL STATEMENT
(LONG FORM)

FORM DESIGNED AND APPROVED BY BANK MANAGEMENT COMMISSION AMERICAN BANKERS ASSOCIATION

NAME ______________________________ ______________ (DATE)

BUSINESS ______________________________ ADDRESS ______________________________

TO ______________________________ (NAME OF BANK)

FOR THE PURPOSE OF OBTAINING ADVANCES FROM TIME TO TIME ON BILLS, NOTES AND OTHER COMMERCIAL PAPER SIGNED OR ENDORSED BY THE UNDERSIGNED, AND OF OBTAINING CREDIT GENERALLY, THE UNDERSIGNED MAKES THE FOLLOWING STATEMENT OF ________ FINANCIAL CONDITION AS OF THE CLOSE OF BUSINESS ON THE ______ DAY OF ______________ 19___, AND CERTIFIES TO THE ABOVE-NAMED BANK THAT THE INFORMATION HEREINAFTER SET FORTH IS IN ALL RESPECTS TRUE, ACCURATE AND COMPLETE AND CORRECTLY REFLECTS THE FINANCIAL CONDITION OF THE UNDERSIGNED ON THE DATE AFOREMENTIONED.

(FILL ALL BLANKS, WRITING "NO" OR "NONE" WHERE NECESSARY TO COMPLETE INFORMATION.).

ASSETS				LIABILITIES			
				NOTES PAYABLE			
CASH—ON HAND $______; IN BANK $______				TO BANKS			
NOTES RECEIVABLE OF CUSTOMERS (SEE SCHEDULE)				FOR MERCHANDISE			
ACCOUNTS RECEIVABLE OF CUSTOMERS (SEE SCHEDULE)				FOR MACHINERY, EQUIPMENT, ETC.			
MERCHANDISE—FINISHED (SEE SCHEDULE)				TO OTHERS FOR BORROWED MONEY			
—IN PROCESS				TRADE OR BANK ACCEPTANCES PAYABLE			
—RAW				ACCOUNTS PAYABLE—NOT DUE			
SECURITIES OWNED (OTHER THAN IN SUBSIDIARIES AND AFFILIATES) (SEE SCHEDULE)				—PAST DUE			
OTHER CURRENT ASSETS (ITEMIZE)				DUE TO SUBSIDIARIES AND AFFILIATES			
				DUE TO STOCKHOLDERS, DIRECTORS, OFFICERS, AND EMPLOYEES			
				DIVIDENDS DECLARED BUT UNPAID			
				RESERVED FOR, AND ACCRUED TAXES			
				ACCRUED EXPENSES—WAGES, INTEREST, INSURANCE			
				CHATTEL MORTGAGES } DUE WITHIN 1 YEAR			
				MORTGAGES } DUE WITHIN 1 YEAR			
				BONDED DEBT } DUE WITHIN 1 YEAR			
TOTAL CURRENT ASSETS				OTHER CURRENT LIABILITIES (ITEMIZE)			
INVESTMENTS IN SUBSIDIARIES AND AFFILIATES (EXCLUDING LOANS, ADVANCES, ETC.) (SEE SCHEDULE)							
DUE FROM SUBSIDIARIES AND AFFILIATES (SEE SCHEDULE)							
DUE FROM STOCKHOLDERS, DIRECTORS, OFFICERS, AND EMPLOYEES				TOTAL CURRENT LIABILITIES			
LIFE INSURANCE—CASH SURRENDER VALUE (DO NOT DEDUCT LOANS) (SEE SCHEDULE)				CHATTEL MORTGAGES } DUE AFTER 1 YEAR			
GOODWILL, PATENTS, TRADEMARKS, COPYRIGHTS, DIES, PATTERNS, ETC.				MORTGAGES } DUE AFTER 1 YEAR			
LAND—USED IN BUSINESS (SEE SCHEDULE)				BONDED DEBT (SEE SCHEDULE)			
BUILDINGS—USED IN BUSINESS } BEFORE DEPRECIATION RESERVES				LOANS ON LIFE INSURANCE			
MACHINERY AND EQUIPMENT } BEFORE DEPRECIATION RESERVES				OTHER LIABILITIES (ITEMIZE)			
FURNITURE AND FIXTURES } BEFORE DEPRECIATION RESERVES							
TRUCKS, AUTOS, HORSES, WAGONS, ETC. } BEFORE DEPRECIATION RESERVES							
LAND AND BUILDINGS—NOT USED IN BUSINESS (SEE SCHEDULE)							
PREPAID EXPENSES—INTEREST, INSURANCE, ETC.				TOTAL LIABILITIES			
OTHER ASSETS (ITEMIZE)				RESERVES FOR DEPRECIATION			
				BUILDINGS			
				MACHINERY AND EQUIPMENT			
				FURNITURE AND FIXTURES			
				TRUCKS, AUTOS, ETC.			
				RESERVE FOR CONTINGENCIES			
				OTHER RESERVES (ITEMIZE)			
				TOTAL RESERVES			
				CAPITAL AND SURPLUS			
				PREFERRED STOCK } (SEE SCHEDULE)			
				COMMON STOCK } (SEE SCHEDULE)			
				EARNED SURPLUS			
				CAPITAL SURPLUS			
TOTAL				TOTAL			

(BE SURE ALL SCHEDULES ARE FILLED OUT)

Figure 76. Long Form of Financial Statement (page one).

CONTINGENT LIABILITIES

NOTES RECEIVABLE, TRADE ACCEPTANCES, OR DRAFTS DISCOUNTED OR SOLD		GUARANTOR FOR OTHERS ON NOTES, ACCOUNTS OR CONTRACTS	
NOTES RECEIVABLE OR TRADE ACCEPTANCES PLEDGED OR ASSIGNED		MAXIMUM LIABILITY FOR PROPOSED ADDITIONAL INCOME TAXES	
CUSTOMERS' ACCOUNTS DISCOUNTED OR SOLD		BONDS OR UNFINISHED CONTRACTS	
CUSTOMERS' ACCOUNTS ASSIGNED OR PLEDGED		PURCHASE COMMITMENTS OUTSTANDING	
ACCOMMODATION PAPER, ENDORSEMENTS OR NOTES EXCHANGED WITH OTHERS		LITIGATION IN PROCESS OR THREATENED	
		OTHER CONTINGENT LIABILITIES	

STATEMENT OF PROFIT AND LOSS

FOR THE PERIOD BEGINNING ________ 19____ AND ENDING ________ 19____

GROSS SALES			TOTAL ADMINISTRATIVE, GENERAL AND SELLING EXPENSES		
LESS: RETURNS AND ALLOWANCES			OPERATING PROFIT		
NET SALES			OTHER INCOME		
COST OF GOODS SOLD:			INVESTMENTS		
TOTAL INVENTORIES AT BEGINNING OF PERIOD			CASH DISCOUNTS RECEIVED		
ADD: PURCHASES DURING PERIOD			RECOVERIES FROM NOTES AND ACCOUNTS PREVIOUSLY CHARGED OFF		
FOR MANUFACTURER ONLY — DIRECT LABOR			OTHER		
FOR MANUFACTURER ONLY — DEPRECIATION			TOTAL		
FOR MANUFACTURER ONLY — OTHER FACTORY OVERHEAD					
TOTAL			OTHER EXPENSES		
DEDUCT: TOTAL INVENTORIES AT CLOSE OF PERIOD			INTEREST		
GROSS PROFIT			CASH DISCOUNTS GIVEN		
SELLING EXPENSES			OTHER		
SALARIES			TOTAL		
COMMISSIONS			NET PROFIT OR LOSS BEFORE INCOME TAXES		
TRAVELING			ACCRUED FEDERAL INCOME TAXES		
ADVERTISING			ACCRUED STATE INCOME TAXES		
TOTAL			TOTAL		
ADMINISTRATIVE AND GENERAL EXPENSES					
OFFICERS' SALARIES			NET PROFIT OR LOSS CARRIED TO SURPLUS		
OTHER SALARIES					
RENT					
NOTES AND ACCOUNTS CHARGED OFF					
DEPRECIATION (NOT APPLICABLE ELSEWHERE)			AMOUNT OF DIVIDENDS DECLARED AND/OR PAID SINCE STATEMENT DATE		
TOTAL					

RECONCILIATION OF EARNED SURPLUS			**RECONCILIATION OF CAPITAL SURPLUS**		
EARNED SURPLUS AT CLOSE OF PREVIOUS FISCAL YEAR			CAPITAL SURPLUS AT CLOSE OF PREVIOUS FISCAL YEAR		
ADD: NET PROFITS (FROM PROFIT & LOSS STATEMENT)			ADDITIONS (ITEMIZE)		
OTHER ADDITIONS (ITEMIZE)					
TOTAL ADDITIONS					
			TOTAL ADDITIONS		
LESS: DIVIDENDS PAID			DEDUCTIONS (ITEMIZE)		
CASH—PREFERRED, RATE ____%					
—COMMON, RATE ____%					
STOCK—PREFERRED ____ RATE					
—COMMON ____ RATE					
OTHER DEDUCTIONS (ITEMIZE)					
TOTAL DEDUCTIONS			TOTAL DEDUCTIONS		
EARNED SURPLUS AT END OF PERIOD (SEE BALANCE SHEET)			CAPITAL SURPLUS AT END OF PERIOD (SEE BALANCE SHEET)		

WAS AN AUDIT MADE? ________ NAME OF INDEPENDENT ACCOUNTANTS? ________

THE FISCAL PERIOD OF THIS CORPORATION CLOSES ON THE ________ DAY OF ________

BANK ACCOUNTS

NAME AND LOCATION OF BANKS	CASH BALANCE	CREDIT LINES	AMOUNT OF LOANS	ON WHAT BASIS? (ENDORSEMENTS, RECEIVABLES, COLLATERAL, ETC.)
	$	$	$	

Figure 76. Long Form of Financial Statement (page two).

NOTES AND TRADE ACCEPTANCES RECEIVABLE
—Customers Only (excluding those from affiliates)

NOT DUE
RENEWED
PAST DUE AND PROTESTED
TOTAL NOTES AND TRADE ACCEPTANCES RECEIVABLE
LESS: RESERVE FOR DOUBTFUL
NOTES AND TRADE ACCEPTANCES RECEIVABLE—NET
AMOUNT CONSIDERED OF SLOW COLLECTION
AMOUNT CONSIDERED OF DOUBTFUL COLLECTION

ACCOUNTS RECEIVABLE
—Customers Only (excluding those from affiliates)

ACCOUNTS CHARGED WITHIN:
30 DAYS
31 TO 60 DAYS
61 TO 90 DAYS
3 TO 6 MONTHS
OVER 6 MONTHS
TOTAL ACCOUNTS RECEIVABLE
LESS: RESERVE FOR DOUBTFUL ACCOUNTS
ACCOUNTS RECEIVABLE—NET
AMOUNT OF ACCOUNTS CONSIDERED DOUBTFUL
SELLING TERMS:

MERCHANDISE

MERCHANDISE ON HAND
" CONSIGNED TO OTHERS
" IN TRANSIT
TOTAL
LESS: RESERVES (IF ANY)
TOTAL AS PER STATEMENT

1. AMOUNT OF MERCHANDISE PLEDGED
2. IS MERCHANDISE CONSIGNED TO YOU INCLUDED IN ASSETS?
3. AT WHAT TIME OF YEAR IS INVENTORY HIGHEST? LOWEST?
4. AVERAGE AMOUNT OF INVENTORY
5. DOES INVENTORY REPRESENT PHYSICAL COUNT? WHEN TAKEN?
6. DESCRIBE IN DETAIL THE BASIS OF VALUATION
7. STATE THE EXTENT OF ACCOUNTANTS' VERIFICATION, IF ANY
8. GIVE DATE (OR DATES) ON WHICH INVENTORY IS TAKEN AND BOOKS ARE CLOSED

SECURITIES OWNED

FACE VALUE (BONDS) NUMBER OF SHARES (STOCKS)	PERCENT OF TOTAL ISSUE	DESCRIPTION OF SECURITY	COST	PRESENT BOOK VALUE	MARKET VALUE	INCOME RECEIVED LAST YEAR	TO WHOM PLEDGED
			$	$	$	$	

ARE ALL SECURITIES OWNED REGISTERED IN THE NAME OF THE CORPORATION?

DUE FROM SUBSIDIARIES AND AFFILIATES

NAME OF CONCERN	LOCATION	FOR ADVANCES	WHEN DUE	FOR MERCHANDISE	TERMS
		$		$	

REAL ESTATE

	LOCATION AND DESCRIPTION	AGE	CONDITION	COST WITH IMPROVEMENTS	ASSESSED VALUE
1				$	$
2					
3					
4					
5					

	FIRE INSURANCE	ESTIMATED PRESENT VALUE	MORTGAGE AMOUNT	MORTGAGE MATURITY	MORTGAGEE	USED IN BUSINESS?	YEARLY GROSS RENTAL INCOME
1	$	$	$				$
2							
3							
4							
5							

THE LEGAL AND EQUITABLE TITLE TO ALL THE REAL ESTATE LISTED ABOVE IS SOLELY IN THE CORPORATION'S NAME, EXCEPT AS FOLLOWS:

IF BOOK VALUE (BEFORE DEPRECIATION RESERVES) HAS DECREASED DURING THE YEAR, STATE REASON

LIFE INSURANCE

NAME OF PERSON INSURED	TYPE OF POLICY	FACE AMOUNT OF POLICY	TOTAL CASH SURRENDER VALUE	TOTAL LOANS AGAINST POLICY	TO WHOM POLICY IS ASSIGNED
		$	$	$	

Figure 76. Long Form of Financial Statement (page three).

OND ISSUES (describe each issue separately)

DESCRIPTION OF ASSETS (INCLUDING CURRENT ASSETS, IF ANY) PLEDGED TO SECURE BOND ISSUES:

SUMMARY OF INDENTURE PROVISIONS, INCLUDING SINKING FUND REQUIREMENTS:

THERE ARE NO DEFAULTS IN CONNECTION WITH ANY OF THE PROVISIONS OF THE INDENTURE(S), EXCEPT AS FOLLOWS:

NAME AND ADDRESS OF TRUSTEE(S):

CAPITAL STOCK

PREFERRED ____% PAR VALUE $____ CUMULATIVE?	SUMMARY OF PREFERRED STOCK PROVISIONS:
AUTHORIZED $	
UNISSUED $	
OUTSTANDING $	
COMMON: PAR VALUE $	VOTING POWERS OF PREFERRED STOCKHOLDERS:
AUTHORIZED $	
UNISSUED $	
OUTSTANDING $	AMOUNT OF PREFERRED STOCK DIVIDENDS ACCUMULATED AND UNPAID
COMMON: NO PAR VALUE—SHARES OUTSTANDING	$____, REPRESENTING A PERIOD OF

LIABILITY INSURANCE (automobile, truck, general public liability, etc.)

NAME AND ADDRESS OF INSURANCE COMPANY	TYPE OF POLICY	AMOUNT OF COVERAGE PERSONAL INJURY, ETC.	PROPERTY DAMAGE	EXPIRATION DATE
		$	$	

OTHER INSURANCE

FORM	CARRIED ON	NATURE	ASSIGNEE	AMOUNT
FIRE	MERCHANDISE			$
"	BUILDINGS			
"	MACHINERY AND EQUIPMENT			
"	FURNITURE AND FIXTURES			
"	TRUCKS, AUTOS, WAGONS, ETC.			
CREDIT	ACCOUNTS AND NOTES RECEIVABLE			
USE AND OCCUPANCY				
FIDELITY BONDS				
OTHER				

OFFICERS

	NAMES IN FULL	NUMBER OF SHARES HELD PREFERRED	COMMON	ANNUAL COMPENSATION	ADDRESS
PRESIDENT				$	
VICE-PRES.					
VICE-PRES.					
SECRETARY					
TREASURER					

DIRECTORS

NAMES IN FULL	NUMBER OF SHARES HELD PREFERRED	COMMON	ANNUAL COMPENSATION	ADDRESS
			$	

IN SUBMITTING THE FOREGOING STATEMENT THE UNDERSIGNED GUARANTEES ITS ACCURACY WITH THE INTENT THAT IT BE RELIED UPON BY THE AFORESAID BANK IN EXTENDING CREDIT TO THE UNDERSIGNED AND WARRANTS THAT____HAS NOT KNOWINGLY WITHHELD ANY INFORMATION THAT MIGHT AFFECT CREDIT RISK; AND THE UNDERSIGNED EXPRESSLY AGREES TO NOTIFY IMMEDIATELY SAID BANK IN WRITING OF ANY MATERIAL CHANGE IN____FINANCIAL CONDITION WHETHER APPLICATION FOR FURTHER CREDIT IS MADE OR NOT AND IN THE ABSENCE OF SUCH WRITTEN NOTICE IT IS EXPRESSLY AGREED THAT SAID BANK IN GRANTING NEW OR CONTINUING CREDIT MAY RELY ON THIS STATEMENT AS HAVING THE SAME FORCE AND EFFECT AS IF DELIVERED UPON THE DATE ADDITIONAL CREDIT IS REQUESTED OR EXISTING CREDIT EXTENDED OR CONTINUED.

SIGNATURE OF CORPORATION

SIGNED AT____

OFFICER

THIS____DAY OF____19____

TITLE

Figure 76. Long Form of Financial Statement (page four).

5. Information on working capital, such as aging of accounts receivable, receivables turnover, and inventory turnover.

6. Credit and character references.

7. Evidence of planning for the future, such as (a) budget of estimated sales, expenses, and profits, (b) a cash or working capital budget, and (c) plans for use of the loaned funds.

8. Personal history and history of the business. In composing the history, it is important not to suppress negative information. If there has been a bankruptcy, criminal action, or other blot on the record the borrower should ask a lawyer or prepare a memorandum setting forth the facts objectively. Such a statement presented on the borrower's own initiative will be far less damaging than discovery of the undisclosed facts by the lender.

Advance preparation enables the applicant to analyze the weak spots of his business and to be ready to answer questions and criticisms during the interview with the loan officer.

Interview with the loan officer. Complete frankness should mark the personal interview as the borrower gives the lending officer a bird's-eye view of the business, its achievements, possibilities, and problems. If the banker obtains the impression that facts are being hidden, or that the whole story is not being told, he will be antagonistic toward the borrower's point of view. The bank should be made to feel that it has the borrower's full cooperation in whatever procedures are requested. Offering to show the banker the firm's plant and operations is bound to create a favorable impression. The impression made by the borrower is as important as meeting the technical requirements for obtaining a loan.

Relationship with a bank. Full disclosure is basic in the relationship of a business with its bank. By keeping its bank fully informed of its progress, problems, and plans, a business will find that negotiations for bank credit are materially expedited when and if the need for credit arises. Thus, when a change in operations occurs, such as an addition of a new plant, a major change in personnel, or some other important change develops, a visit or telephone call to the banker is advisable. This is particularly true in the event of any unfavorable development.

Periodical financial statements should be supplied at regular interals, whether or not the business is borrowing. Plans or policies that may lead to a need for bank credit should be discussed with the bank before their adoption and not after the need has become irrevocable. Other needs that arise unexpectedly should be discussed with the bank as soon as they become apparent, without waiting to apply for a loan until the day the funds are needed.

Businessmen should also be aware of the function performed by banks in the interchange of credit information to facilitate business transactions. Banks give credit information to those to whom a firm has given the bank as a credit reference. They also answer credit inquiries received by letter, telephone, telegraph, or in personal interviews, from trade creditors, commercial agencies, or others, and give credit information, upon request, to those to whom a business may sell. A business should guard well its credit standing with its banks. The borrower should make available audited financial statements for a number of years, and other written material relating to the type of financing he seeks. For example, if he is interested in assigning accounts receivable, he should submit an aging statement of his accounts receivable.

During the interview with the finance company executive, the businessman creates a favorable impression by demonstrating knowledge of the affairs of his own company and of the industry. He should have at his fingertips a knowledge of the operational and financial aspects of his business. He should demonstrate readiness to cooperate and give the lender the information he wants. An attitude of frankness is of the utmost importance.

Relationship with finance company. Relations between the borrower and the commercial finance company are conducted informally and with a minimum of official routine. As in the case of relationships with banks, the borrower should inform his financing agency of any major development occurring in the business. If a serious financial crisis should develop, the borrower should let the finance company know about the condition immediately. The finance company may be able to obtain the cooperation of other creditors in working out the problem or under proper circumstances, to advance the necessary funds. The maintenance of good accounting records and the conscientious filling out of necessary forms help to build and sustain cordial dealings.

Applying to finance companies for funds. Before making a r quest for advances from a finance company, the borrower shoul make advance preparations just as he would in applying for a ban loan. He should be prepared to explain the following:

1. Why he needs the amount of funds he seeks.
2. How he expects to use the funds.
3. How the business will benefit by them.
4. How the loan will be repaid.

SECTION 10

Credit and Collections

1. INVESTIGATING TO REDUCE CREDIT RISKS

2. MERCANTILE CREDIT TERMS

3. LAW RELATING TO CHECKS, NOTES AND DRAFTS

Law Relating to Checks

Law Relating to Notes

Law Relating to Drafts or Bills of Exchange

4. HOW TO WRITE CREDIT LETTERS

5. HOW TO WRITE COLLECTION LETTERS

SECTION 10

Credit and Collections

1. INVESTIGATING TO REDUCE CREDIT RISKS

Classification of sources of credit information. The sources to hich a credit man can turn for information concerning an applicant r credit may be classified as follows: (1) general mercantile agency; 2) special or trade agencies; (3) agencies reporting on individuals nd making special investigations; (4) published services; (5) salesen; (6) attorneys; (7) banks; (8) personal interviews. Each of ese sources is discussed in the following pages.

General Mercantile Agency

Information from mercantile agencies. Mercantile agencies have een established to ascertain the credit position of persons and conerns in business and to provide prompt and reliable information for ubscribers to the agency services. Agencies ordinarily try to anticiate inquiry and provide subscribers with either a book of ratings, iving a general capital and credit appraisal, or with a detailed report, r both. Mercantile agencies are both general and special. The genral agency covers a vast field and extends its services to foreign counries. The special agency limits its field to a particular branch of usiness and specializes within an industry.

Dun & Bradstreet, Inc. The general mercantile agency of Dun & Bradstreet, Inc., maintains a central office in New York City and branch offices throughout the country. It has offices and correspondents in foreign countries in which there are trade facilities. Its system of reporting covers the entire country by dividing it into regions, districts, suboffices and reporting stations. An attempt is made to reach every merchant, no matter how remote his location. The agency maintains a nation-wide network of trained reporters and correspondents. The credit reporter interviews the merchant at his place of business, discusses his financial condition and operati trend, and observes his merchandising methods, his stock, his loc tion, and competition. The investigator also calls upon local sourc of credit information, including the banker.

The agency provides subscribers with both Reference Books ar special reports. Because of the nature of its service, Dun & Bra street requires that all reports be held in strict confidence. Moreove it does not sell its books, but lends them as property of the agenc to be returned to the agency for disposal upon the issuance of a ne edition.

The Dun & Bradstreet reference book. Dun & Bradstreet ra ings, which appear on the credit reports, along with other pertinen information, are compiled in the famous "D & B" Reference Book These books, the larger editions of which contain the names of abou 2,800,000 manufacturers, wholesalers, and retailers in the Unite States and Canada, are issued every two months by the Agency to it subscribers. In addition, sectional editions of the Reference Book ar published for sellers with a localized market. The names of the com panies are arranged alphabetically by state and city, and most of th names are followed by a letter and a number which represents Dun & Bradstreet's appraisal of the estimated financial strength and the com posite credit appraisal. The Reference Book, however, does not in clude some service and professional establishments such as stock brokers, beauty and barber shops, and real estate brokers, even though credit reports may have been compiled on those businesses.

As an aid to credit men, to sales managers, and to salesmen, the Reference Book shows population figures, banking and postal facili ties, and county location for trading communities. Also, as a part of each Reference Book listing, a four-digit Standard Industrial Classifi cation number appears before the name and classifies businesses pre cisely as to function and products. Whenever a "C" precedes the code number, the rating of the business has been changed in that par ticular issue of the Reference Book and whenever an "A" precedes the code number, the name is a new one and has been added. A numeral shown immediately preceding the rating represents the last digit of the year, within the past ten years, that the business was started or came under its present ownership.

For convenience of salesmen and traveling executives, the Agency blishes twice a year, in January and July, small or state editions of Reference Book.

Nature of Dun & Bradstreet ratings. A Dun & Bradstreet rating sents condensed conclusions in symbol form and classifies relaely all of the elements of character, capacity, and capital of a busis enterprise, and the trend of its current position. The rating lects, as accurately as possible, the facts and the analysis of the ts given in the credit report. The letter portion of the rating indies the estimated financial strength and the numerical portion of rating reflects the composite credit appraisal in cases where the ter and numeral are used together. In practice, the most comnly used measure for estimated financial strength is the tangible t worth of the business. In some instances, however, the tangible t worth of the business is not the same as the net worth as shown the financial statement due to the elimination of intangible items ch as good will, patents, and the like. There are four degrees of mposite credit appraisal, namely, high, good, fair, and limited.

The blank (—) symbol is assigned when no other symbol applies the circumstances and is used regardless of the size of the business ported. The blank (—) symbol informs the credit man that cirmstances exist which makes it difficult to classify the account thin condensed rating symbols and, as brought out in the Key to atings reproduced in Figure 77, suggests to the subscriber of the gency the advisability of obtaining additional information.

Dun & Bradstreet, as shown in its Key to Ratings, has two addional classifications for subjects of reports, namely, the numeral clasfication and the sales classification. An explanation of both of these assifications and the four brackets or ranges which they cover are own in Figure 77, the Key to Ratings.

A rating, or the absence of a rating, on any concern listed, is not tended to be more, nor should it be inferred to be more, than a reection of the tenor of the information assembled. Nor should it be onstrued as suggesting or intimating that credit should be restricted r withheld, or granted.

How to use Dun & Bradstreet ratings. The Dun & Bradstreet atings may be used as follows:

1. As a means of passing small rush orders that have to be acted on mmediately.

KEY TO RATINGS

	ESTIMATED FINANCIAL STRENGTH			COMPOSITE CREDIT APPRAISAL			
				High	Good	Fair	Limited
AA	Over		$1,000,000	A1	1	1½	2
A+	Over		750,000	A1	1	1½	2
A	$500,000	to	750,000	A1	1	1½	2
B+	300,000	to	500,000	1	1½	2	2½
B	200,000	to	300,000	1	1½	2	2½
C+	125,000	to	200,000	1	1½	2	2½
C	75,000	to	125,000	1½	2	2½	3
D+	50,000	to	75,000	1½	2	2½	3
D	35,000	to	50,000	1½	2	2½	3
E	20,000	to	35,000	2	2½	3	3½
F	10,000	to	20,000	2½	3	3½	4
G	5,000	to	10,000	3	3½	4	4½
H	3,000	to	5,000	3	3½	4	4½
J	2,000	to	3,000	3	3½	4	4½
K	1,000	to	2,000	3	3½	4	4½
L	Up	to	1,000	3½	4	4½	5

CLASSIFICATION AS TO BOTH ESTIMATED FINANCIAL STRENGTH AND CREDIT APPRAISAL

FINANCIAL STRENGTH BRACKET				EXPLANATION
1	$125,000	to	$1,000,000 and Over	When only the numeral (1, 2, 3, or 4) appears, it is an indication that the estimated financial strength, while not definitely classified, is presumed to be within the range of the ($) figures in the corresponding bracket and that a condition is believed to exist which warrants credit in keeping with that assumption.
2	20,000	to	125,000	
3	2,000	to	20,000	
4	Up	to	2,000	

NOT CLASSIFIED OR ABSENCE OF RATING

The absence of a rating, whether as to estimated financial strength or as to credit appraisal, and whether expressed by the hyphen (-), the dash (—), or by the (x) sales listing (see below), or by the omission of any symbol, is not to be construed as unfavorable but signifies circumstances difficult to classify within condensed rating symbols and should suggest to the subscriber the advisability of obtaining additional information.

LISTINGS ONLY AS TO ESTIMATED ANNUAL SALES

When, after investigation has been made, the information obtained regarding concerns listed in the Reference Book is not sufficiently conclusive to permit the assignment of any of the symbols in the above Key to Ratings, in preference to listing these names with no indication of their relative importance, the symbols (1x, 2x, 3x, and 4x) may be used to express, in wide ranges, the stated or estimated annual sales as an index to assist in appraising size. These sales symbols have no other significance; credit appraisal is neither inferred nor implied. The sales bracket ranges are as follows:

ESTIMATED ANNUAL SALES BRACKET

1x	$500,000 and Over Annual Sales	3x	$10,000 to $75,000 Annual Sales
2x	75,000 to $500,000 " "	4x	Up to 10,000 " "

INVESTIGATING

"Inv." in place of the rating is an abbreviation of "investigating." It signifies nothing more than that a pending investigation was incomplete when this book went to press.

Dun & Bradstreet, Inc.

Figure 77. Key to Ratings.

2. As a preliminary sales guide in screening sales prospects.
3. As a check upon other credit information.
4. As a source of information when a periodical revision of the redit file is being made. A change in rating, either up or down, ndicates the possible need to review the credit file.
5. As a guide to determine whether a credit report is necessary.

Limitations in the use of credit ratings. Ratings by Dun & Bradtreet are intended to serve mainly as a summary index to the conent of the reports. As each credit transaction involves not only the ituation of the buyer but also the problems of the seller, the credit nan should not be guided solely by the ratings when he is considerng a risk of any great amount. He wants to know all the details nd to reach his own conclusions in the light of his own particular usiness.

The credit man should recognize that a rating, while representative vhen assigned, may not be representative a month later because of he dynamic nature of business. The Reference Book is subject to onstant revision in many particulars besides ratings. New names re added, old names removed, and addresses kept up to date. About ,000 changes occur daily. Hence, in the case of a fairly large acount, the credit man will need to supplement the rating with more urrent information.

Dun & Bradstreet reports. When a subscriber desires more information than is afforded by the Dun & Bradstreet Reference Book, he may ask the agency to give him a detailed report on the individual or concern. The subscriber may receive a full analysis of an account over the telephone by calling a special number. This analysis includes all information in the report. The subscriber's contract with the agency makes provision for a certain number of reports during the year. Inquiries in excess of the contract figure are charged for additionally.

Reports are sent to subscribers in response to inquiry tickets. The reporting department prepares and edits three types of commercial credit reports, namely, the Analytical Report, the Specialized Report and the Synopsis Report. These three types of reports have the same basic format and are illustrated on subsequent pages of this section.

1. *Analytical Reports.* Analytical Reports are edited by highly trained specialized reporters on the larger and more complicated

business enterprises. These reports are featured by complete metho of operation information and by comparative detailed financial stat ments. They include an analysis of the business based upon thes comparative figures in the light of method of operation, characteri tics, financing methods, and other supplementary data.

The information in the Analytical Report is presented under seve captions, namely, personnel, history, method of operation, subsid aries (where applicable), financial information, trade investigatior and banking relations.

Under the Personnel caption is given a brief description of th background and business career of each officer or partner and th capacity in which he serves the business.

The History of the business from inception down to the presen time is carefully traced under this caption. Each change that ha an important effect on the business is also outlined.

The nature and scope of operations are comprehensively covere under the caption Method of Operation. The products sold o manufactured, the trade to which distribution is made, sales terri tory, number of accounts, selling terms, number of salesmen, sea sonal aspects of the business, number of employees, facilities anc location are all carefully reported under this caption.

The Subsidiary caption is one of the outstanding features of th Analytical report. Under this caption, the name and location of sub sidiaries and the percentage of stock ownership by the parent concer are given. A brief description of the subsidiaries is also given, includ ing a summary of financial condition, nature of operations, and com prehensive coverage of inter-company relations, such as merchandise transactions, loans, advances, endorsements, and guarantees with the parent company and with other related concerns.

Financial Information presents the comparative financial state ments for three years, including operating details such as net sales, net profits, and dividends or withdrawals. Under the analysis portion of Financial Information, the trend of operations and financial position of the business are carefully reviewed in the light of the operational characteristics of the business.

Under the caption Trade Investigation, the paying record of the business is reflected by a tabulation of ledger experiences. The Banking Relations section of the Analytical Report outlines clearly and in detail the nature and scope of the relations of the business with its

ANALYTICAL REPORT — RATING CHANGE
(Dun & Bradstreet, Inc.)

2071
BRISTOL CANDY CORP.

(A) CD 4 AUGUST 18 19--
MANUFACTURER

BRISTOL 3 PA
Bucks County
100 Edgely Road

Chester G. Hoover - Pres.
Henry T. Conroy - Secty & Treas.
F. Charles Young - Vice Pres.

BOARD OF DIRECTORS: The officers and Mrs. Mary S. Lawrence

RATING CHANGE: B I to B+ I

SUMMARY
BUSINESS ESTABLISHED IN 1914. NET SALES AND PROFITS OF RECENT YEARS WERE AT HIGH LEVELS. EXPANSION OF PRODUCTION FACILITIES IN THE LATEST FISCAL PERIOD FINANCED PRIMARILY BY A LONG TERM BANK LOAN. TANGIBLE NET WORTH AT JUNE 30, 19-- $312,817. FINANCIAL POSITION WELL BALANCED. TRADE PAYMENTS ARE DISCOUNT AND PROMPT

PERSONNEL
Management & Control: Mary S. Lawrence, the widow of F. Bradford Lawrence, the founder, owns 50% of the outstanding Capital Stock. The remainder is owned by Chester G. Hoover (25%), Henry T. Conroy (15%), and F. Charles Young (10%). Life insurance of $25,000 is carried on each officer with the corporation as beneficiary.

Chester G. Hoover, born 1884, married. Employed sales department, Federal Biscuit Company, Philadelphia, 1911-1921. Since associated with this business as General Sales Manager to June, 1944, when he was elected President and General Manager.

Henry T. Conroy, born 1901, married. Cashier of Fidelity Trust Company, Baltimore, 1922-1929. Then employed as Office Manager of this business to 1944 when he was elected Secretary and Treasurer.

F. Charles Young, born 1896, married, was employed in the plant from 1921 to 1933 when he became Plant Superintendent. Elected Vice President in charge of production in June, 1944.

Mrs. Mary S. Lawrence takes no active part in the management.

HISTORY
STARTED: October, 1914 by F. Bradford Lawrence, who died in March, 1944. Under the provisions of his will, the three key employees were bequeathed a 50% interest in the business and the subject corporation was formed to carry out this provision.

INCORPORATED: June 29, 1944 under Pennsylvania laws.
Authorized Capital Stock: 250,000 shares Common, $1.00 par value.
Outstanding Capital Stock: 150,000 shares.

METHOD OF OPERATION
Products: Manufactures packaged confections, including chocolates, hard candies and novelty sweets (U.S. Standard Industrial Classification #2071). Seventy-five percent of the volume is in chocolates which retail from $1.25 to $2.50 a pound. Brand names: "Bristols" and "Honey Crunch."
Distribution: To retail candy, (35%), chain, (25%), drug, (20%), grocery, (10%), and department (10%) stores.
Number of Accounts: 2,000 active.
Terms of Sale: 2%-15-Net 30.
Territory: The Eastern Seaboard from Maine to Florida.
Seasons: Sales are highest in November and December (40%).
Salesmen: 10 on salary and commission.
Employees: 125.

Production Facilities-Location: Owns and fully occupies a three-story, brick building, sprinkler equipped, comprising 50,000 square feet of floor space. Also an adjacent two-story, brick building which formerly housed the plant but is now used for warehousing. The buildings, machinery and equipment are in excellent condition.

(CONTINUED)

Figure 78. Dun & Bradstreet Analytical Report (page one).

ANALYTICAL REPORT — RATING CHANGE
(Dun & Bradstreet, Inc.)

BRISTOL CANDY CORP.
Page 2 (A)

BRISTOL 3 PA
August 18, 19--

COMPARATIVE FINANCIAL STATEMENTS

	June 30 19--	June 30 19--	June 30 19--
Cash	$ 78,171	$ 72,913	$ 87,486
U.S. Govt. Bonds	36,710	70,126	---
Accounts Receivable	38,040	29,584	68,640
Inventory	58,053	71,874	138,442
TOTAL CURRENT ASSETS	210,975	244,499	294,570
Fixed Assets	31,232	28,549	253,755
Cash Value Life Insurance	4,154	5,047	6,416
Prepaid Expense	2,036	1,947	6,496
TOTAL ASSETS	248,398	280,043	561,237
Due Banks	---	---	25,000
Accounts Payable	20,179	9,802	10,654
Federal Income Taxes	30,395	38,712	79,131
Accruals	18,049	12,816	8,635
TOTAL CURRENT LIABILITIES	68,624	61,331	123,420
Due Bank-Deferred	---	---	125,000
Common Stock	150,000	150,000	150,000
Earned Surplus	29,774	68,712	162,817
TOTAL LIABILITIES	248,398	280,043	561,237
NET WORKING CAPITAL	142,350	183,168	171,150
CURRENT RATIO	3.07	3.98	2.38
TANGIBLE NET WORTH	179,774	218,712	312,817
Net Sales	735,198	771,035	1,106,165
Net Profit	54,774	68,938	124,105
Dividends	15,000	30,000	30,000

CENTS OMITTED. The foregoing figures were prepared from annual financial reports of the auditors, James Wheaton & Co., C.P.A.'s, Philadelphia, Pennsylvania. Statements were received by mail accompanied by transmittal letters signed by Henry T. Conroy, Treasurer. At June 30, 19--, Accounts Receivable were net of a reserve for bad debts of $3,106. Fixed Assets were net of reserves for depreciation of $31,612. Inventory consisting of finished goods $44,106, in process $14,719 and raw materials $79,612, valued at the lower of cost or market under the "Lifo" method. Fire insurance: Inventory - Maximum coverage $200,000 under a monthly reporting policy; Fixtures and Equipment - $75,000; Buildings - $200,000. Contingent Debt: None.

(CONTINUED)

Figure 78. Dun & Bradstreet Analytical Report (page two).

ANALYTICAL REPORT — RATING CHANGE
(Dun & Bradstreet, Inc.)

BRISTOL CANDY CORP. — BRISTOL 3 PA
Page 3 (A) — August 18, 19--

ANALYSIS
Annual sales volume has been at a high level since formation of the subject corporation. Net profits were correspondingly high and, except for moderate dividends, were retained and invested in Government bonds to finance a plan of plant modernization and expansion. Construction under this plan of fixed asset expansion was started early in the last fiscal year and completed in March. The cost of approximately $250,000 was financed with an unsecured term bank loan of $150,000 and liquidation of Government Bonds. The term bank loan is payable $12,500 semi-annually for five years.

Net Sales were 43% larger in the last fiscal year. This increase in the dollar volume resulted from both a 25% price increase in August following a rise in raw material and labor costs and increased unit sales subsequent to March. Net Profit also was higher as a result of the sales expansion and lower unit production costs subsequent to March, when the plant and manufacturing improvements were completed.

In prior years, seasonal use was made of unsecured bank loans up to $100,000. There has been no recourse to this type of financing during the last three years as inventories were turned rapidly and the collection experience was excellent. Financial position at the last fiscal closing was sound. Compared to Net Sales of that period, inventory comprised primarily of raw materials was equivalent to 45 days sales while accounts receivable were equivalent to 22 days sales.

TRADE INVESTIGATION
Sugar, the basic raw material used, is purchased on a sight draft basis under annual contract with one broker. Such drafts have been honored on presentation. Other raw materials, such as cocoa, flavorings, nut meats, and packaging materials are purchased from seven suppliers. Recent experience of the principal suppliers are included in the following results of a trade survey completed August 12, 19--:

	HIGH CREDIT	OWE	PAST DUE	TERMS OF SALE	PAYMENTS
1.	$ 30,000	3,450	-0-	2%-10-Net 31	Discount
2.	25,000	---	---	2-10-30	Discount
3.	5,555	-0-	---	2-10	Discount
4.	5,399	---	---	2%-10-31	Discount
5.	5,000	---	---	2-10	Discount
6.	4,939	264	---	2-10-30	Discount
7.	3,000	---	---	2-10-Net 30	Discount
8.	659	---	---	2-10	Discount
9.	Requirements	---	---	Sight Draft	Prompt

BANKING RELATIONS
An account is maintained at a local bank. Balances average in medium to high five figures. In 19--, a five-year, unsecured, term loan of $150,000 was granted. Other details of this loan are outlined under "Analysis." A low six-figure line of short term, unsecured, bank credit which is available has not been used in recent years.

8-18-19-- (803 I 29)

Figure 78. Dun & Bradstreet Analytical Report (page three).

depositories. An example of a Dun & Bradstreet "Analytical" repor is illustrated on pages 987-989.

2. *Specialized Reports.* Specialized Reports are written, generall on smaller and less complicated concerns than those covered by Ana lytical Reports, but that are larger and more complicated than th numerous small retail and service enterprises making up the major ity of American business concerns. Specialized Reports are character ized by detailed method of operation information, comparative state ment summaries, and details of the latest statement. They includ a brief interpretation of the financial and operating characteristic and condition of the business. The information in these reports i presented under four general headings entitled: History, Method o Operation, Financial Information, and Payments. A specimen "Spe cialized" report is illustrated on pages 991-992.

3. *Synopsis Reports.* Synopsis Reports, for the most part, are writ ten on retail concerns not covered by Analytical or Specialized Re ports. The outstanding feature of this type of report is the Synopsi section which gives the reader of the report, right at the start, a brie summarization of the highlights of the case. An idea of the age, size, background, financial condition, and paying habits of the business are included in the Synopsis, or lead-off caption of the report. Following captions used to present the remainder of these reports are History, Operation-Location, Financial Information, and Payments, under which are outlined the background of the business and its principals, the products, distribution and operational facilities, the financial position as shown by the latest available balance sheet or financial information, and the manner in which the concern pays its trade obligations. A sample Synopsis report is illustrated on page 993.

Each of the three types of commercial credit reports issued by Dun & Bradstreet, Inc., is designed to give the reader a clear and concise picture of the over-all condition of the business and its management. Each commercial credit report carries a caption "Rating" following which is given the financial strength and the composite credit appraisal symbol, or the (—) symbol which reflects the absence of a specific classification, or a symbol which reflects only the estimated annual sales of the business. The symbol NQ is shown on reports on concerns and business styles not listed in the Reference Book. Financial Information such as balance sheets and related financial state-

SPECIALIZED REPORT — RATING UNCHANGED
(Dun & Bradstreet, Inc.)

5072-5251 (S) CD 8 AUGUST 14 19—
ADAMSON HARDWARE CO. WHOL. & RET. LITCHFIELD, ILL
MONTGOMERY COUNTY
294-300 MAIN STREET

Miss Joan M. Adamson, Genl. Partner Miss Carol T. Adamson, Genl. Partner

RATING: —

SUMMARY

THIS BUSINESS WAS STARTED IN 1895 BY CARL H. ADAMSON, THE FATHER OF THE PRESENT PARTNERS. HE DIED IN 1945, AND IN 1947 HIS TWO DAUGHTERS ASSUMED OWNERSHIP. PROFITS HAVE BEEN EARNED IN RECENT YEARS ON A MATERIALLY INCREASED SALES VOLUME. AT DECEMBER 31, 19—, TANGIBLE NET WORTH WAS $249,540, AND DEBT WAS HEAVY. ASSETS ARE REPRESENTED LARGELY BY INVENTORIES AND THERE IS GENERAL SLOWNESS IN TRADE PAYMENTS. BANK LOANS ARE USED STEADILY.

HISTORY

The business name was registered by the partners on March 15, 1947.

This enterprise was started in 1895 as a hardware jobbing business by the late Carl H. Adamson, who subsequently expanded to include both wholesale and retail sales. On February 13, 1945, Adamson died, and his will bequeathed all his real estate, personal and business assets to his two daughters, Joan M. Adamson and Carol T. Adamson. The Estate continued the business until 1947, when the present partners assumed equal ownership. The partners, born in 1891 and 1893, respectively, are single, and are not active in the management of the business.

The active management of this enterprise has been left in the hands of Robert Casey, born 1898, married. He was formerly employed as Sales Manager by Thomas Hardware & Supply Co., St. Louis, Mo., for a period of twenty years until becoming employed here in 1946.

METHOD OF OPERATION

PRODUCTS: Wholesales (80% of sales) and retails (20%) hardware, paint, sporting goods, electrical appliances, linoleum, fire arms, cement and roofing materials. (U. S. Standard Industrial Classifications: # 5072 and #5251). Sales of hardware alone represent about 65% of the total volume. Merchandise sold is in a medium priced range.

DISTRIBUTION: At wholesale to dealers (50%), lumber yards (30%), factories (10%), and contractors (10%). Retail distribution is to local residents and farmers.
Number of Accounts: About 400 active wholesale accounts are sold.
Territory: Surrounding radius of about 80 miles..
Terms: 2%-10th Prox and cash.
Salesmen: Four salaried salesmen.
Seasons: Peak season around March, with low points around January and February, and again around July and August.
Employees: In addition to the salesmen, there are fifteen store and office employees.

FACILITIES: Store occupies the combined ground floor space of three adjoining buildings, with warehouse space being utilized in buildings to the rear. Four trucks are used for delivery purposes, and a siding connects the property with tracks of the Illinois Central Railroad.

FINANCIAL INFORMATION

	Dec. 31, 19—	Dec. 31, 19—	Dec. 31, 19—
Current Assets	$ 236,967	$ 538,884	$ 494,611
Current Liabilities	31,521	292,808	283,080
Net Working Capital	205,446	246,076	211,531
Tangible Net Worth	206,340	272,629	249,540
Net Sales	250,622	523,408	889,650

(CONTINUED)

Figure 79. Dun & Bradstreet Specialized Report (page one).

SPECIALIZED REPORT — RATING UNCHANGED
(Dun & Bradstreet, Inc.)

(S) CD 8 AUGUST 14 19—

ADAMSON HARDWARE CO. | WHOL. & RET. | LITCHFIELD, ILL. (PAGE # 2)

FINANCIAL INFORMATION (Continued)

From Inventory of December 31, 19— cents omitted:-

ASSETS		LIABILITIES	
Cash on Hand & in Banks	$ 8,519	Accts. Pay.	$ 148,949
Accts Rec. (Whol) (A)	46,622	Notes Pay. Bank	125,000
Accts Rec. (Ret) (B)	14,206	Notes Pay, Trucks	3,365
Merchandise	425,264	Accrued Wages & Tax	5,766
Total Current	494,611	Total Current	283,080
Fixed Assets	36,723		
Prepaid	1,286	Net Worth	249,540
Total Assets	532,620	Total	532,620

(A) Net of bad debt reserve $8,516. (B) Net of bad debt reserve $368.

For the year ended December 31, 19— total sales $889,650; gross profit $179,604; net profit $28,615; Withdrawals $51,704.

Statement furnished direct. Based on audit by William Kearns, CPA, Litchfield, Ill. Inventory was valued at lower of cost or market. No contingent debt reported.

-------0-----

For a number of years, sales of this concern were fairly steady, but increased materially in 19—, and again last year through intensive promotional effort following the death of the former owner. In building sales, however, inventories were considerably increased, a portion of which increase was financed through bank accommodation. The increased inventories also brought about increases in Accounts Payable, and the partnership became predominantly slow in the meeting of trade obligations.

It was stated on August 11, 19— by Robert Casey, General Manager, that steps are being taken to reduce inventories and to put trade payments on a current basis. Purchasing has been curtailed, prices have been reduced, particularly on items subject to reduced customer demand, and several employees have been released. It was stated that sales continue to hold even with last year, and that operations have been profitable. Interim figures were declined.

Accounts are maintained at two local banks where balances average in high four to low five figures. Loans have been granted on own paper and borrowings have been steady since early in 19—.

PAYMENTS

HC	OWE	P.DUE	TERMS	Aug. 12, 19—	
4850			1-10-30	Disc.	Sold 1945 to 19—
2492			2-10-30	Disc.	Sold 1925 to date
7740	2185		2-10-60	Prompt to Slow	Sold years to date
14803	10070	5875	1-10-30	Slow 6-7 mos.	Sold years to date
7550	2650		2-10-60	Slow 30	Sold years
7500	2900	1900	2-10-30	Slow 60-90	Sold years to date
5000	5000	5000	1-10-30	Slow 120	Sold years to date
5000	1588	1588	2-10-30	Slow 150	Sold years to date
5000	1000	1000		Slow 60	Sold years
4475	1642	1642	2-15-30	Slow 18	Sold 1944 to date
4134	2090	525	2-10-30	Slow 60	Sold years
3839			2-10-30	Slow 30-40	Sold years
2258	330		1-10-30	Slow 30-40	Sold years to date
1738	708	708	1-10-EOM	Slow 120	Sold years to date
1663	596	558	1-10-30	Slow 120	Sold years

8-14-50 (744-1 29)

Figure 79. Dun & Bradstreet Specialized Report (page two).

SYNOPSIS REPORT — RATING UNCHANGED
(Dun & Bradstreet, Inc.)

5912 CD I JUNE 26 19--
PENN PINES PHARMACY BROOKLYN 19 N Y
GROSS, MILES, OWNER 1246 HAZEL ROAD

RATING: E 2

SYNOPSIS

BACKGROUND: Business started April, 1946. Owner a pharmacist since 1933.
NET WORTH: $26,865 SALES: $89,232 (Annual)
PAYMENTS: Discount
CONDITION & TREND: Condition sound. Sales increasing and operations profitable.

HISTORY

The style was registered by the owner on April 30, 1946.

Starting capital consisted of $10,500 in savings, a $3,500 bank loan, and a $3,000 loan from members of the owner's family, making a total of $17,000. All loans since repaid.

Miles Gross is 41, and native born. A registered pharmacist, he graduated from Columbia College of Pharmacy in 1933. Employed as a pharmacist by Liggett Drug Co. between 1933 and 1946, and by Ray Drug Co. until this business was started.

OPERATION-LOCATION

Operates a pharmacy with a soda fountain. Drugs and prescriptions afford 50% of sales; balance divided between fountain, sundries, and confectionery. Fixtures are new with a twenty-foot soda fountain. Two clerks employed.

Rents the first floor of a two-story building in good condition. Store measures 20 x 50 feet. Location is in a recently developed residential section.

FINANCIAL INFORMATION

An inventory fiscal year-end statement at April 30, 19---cents omitted:

ASSETS		LIABILITIES	
Cash on Hand	$ 304	Accts Pay	$ 3,724
Cash in Bank	1,872		
Merchandise	14,950		
Total Current	17,126	Total Current	3,724
Fixts & Equip	10,913		
Station Wagon	2,464		
Deposits	86	NET WORTH	26,865
Total Assets	30,589	Total	30,589

Net sales from May 1, 195- to April 30, 19-- $89,232; gross profit $26,181; net profit $10,199; withdrawals $3,732. Monthly rent $150.
Signed: June 26, 19-- PENN PINES PHARMACY By Miles Gross, Owner
Received by mail, No accountant indicated.

------0------

After the war, residential construction stepped up in this section with the result that both sales and profits of this business have mounted steadily. Part of earnings have been re-invested in the business to finance its steady expansion.

PAYMENTS

HC	OWE	P DUE	TERMS	May 20, 19--	
2431	2146		2-10	Disc	Sold 3 yrs. to date
340	230		2-10-N30	Disc	Sold 1946 to 5-5--
250			2-10	Disc	Sold 3 yrs
136	136		2-10Prox	Disc	Sold yrs to date
75			2-10-EOM	Disc	
15			30	Ppt	Sold 1-48 to 5-5--

6-26-- (241 29)

Figure 80. Synopsis Report.

ments are issued immediately upon receipt, as is all other curre information that may have an important effect upon the business.

In addition to the three types of commercial credit reports, th reporting department also investigates and produces Key Accoun and Cost-Plus reports. These reports provide a "made-to-order" re porting service designed to answer specific questions by subscriber about key customers whose orders are large or whose sales, collectio or inventory problems are unusual. This special and expanding serv ice includes personal supervision by a staff analyst at frequent inte vals and always keeps in mind the specific problem of the subscriber

Occasions for use of a Dun & Bradstreet report. Some of th situations in which it is advisable to obtain a report are when:

1. The order is from a new account.
2. The order is of considerable size.
3. A change in rating has occurred.
4. The rating indicates that conditions exist which call for com plete information.
5. Examination of the ledger indicates that unfavorable tendencie in the account are developing.
6. Adverse information is obtained from trade sources.
7. The credit requested is disproportionate to the usual amount.

Special services of Dun & Bradstreet. Besides the Reporting and Reference Book Departments, the activities of which have been previously described, there are six other departments or divisions of the Agency that are devoted to the gathering, preparation, analysis, or dissemination of information pertaining to business and business enterprises. These six departments, all of which contribute to one phase or another of the analysis of risks and the promotion of trade, are as follows:

1. *Business Information Division.* The Business Information Division performs a service which supplies data that help business men to launch a new product or find new markets for existing products. This division helps business (1) to determine the size of a potential market; (2) to establish sales quotas in any market or territory; (3) to determine the best channels of distribution; (4) to gauge the effect of new materials and processes on the lines handled; (5) to test trade or users' acceptance and attitude toward suppliers through representa-

ve sampling of opinion; and (6) to evaluate proposed price levels ıd trade discounts. In addition to these, continuing store audits, esigned to reflect the rate of retail flow of many products and appliıces, are conducted.

2. *Credit Clearing Division.* The special credit information needs f manufacturers and wholesalers of men's and women's apparel and ccessories are serviced by the Credit Clearing Division. Speed and ccuracy in answering credit inquiries are the important factors in ıis highly competitive industry, with its style hazards and rapid turnver in retail outlets.

Subscribers to this service accompany their inquiry with details conerning the specific credit transaction involved, the amount of their rder, selling terms, and ledger experience when previous transactions ave occurred. In response to their inquiry, subscribers receive a ecommendation slip that contains a condensed opinion. Recomıendations furnished by Credit Clearing Division are based on the ıdgment of trained analysts, familiar with the purchasing habits, rade customs, buying seasons, and credit problems in the apparel ıdustry. The details of all inquiries on each account upon which a ecommendation is furnished are recorded on a master card. The ıaster card keeps the analyst informed of the day-to-day buying and aying pattern of accounts. The master card highlights for the anaıyst abnormalities in this pattern. Overactive buying, out of season ourchases, and increasing slow payments are spotted by the analyst vho reviews the master card as inquiries are placed.

The Division also supervises the publication of the Apparel Trades Book, issued four times a year, which covers all buying seasons in the ıpparel line. The volume lists outlets throughout the country with redit ratings and symbols indicating the principal lines of merchanlise handled.

3. *Dun's Review department.* This department publishes "Dun's Review," "Dun's Statistical Review," "Compass Points of Business," "The Weekly Trade Review," and statements about business condiions. Its business conditions staff handles inquiries about business conditions and related statistical data; compiles indexes and baromeers; prepares information, tables, and charts about trade, industrial, ınd economic activity for various company uses. "Dun's Review" each month places before approximately 80,000 heads of American businesses information about the effects on business of significant in-

fluences and developments. The information consists principally (1) summaries of important economic studies, (2) frank statemen of opinion on important and often controversial questions by n tional leaders, and (3) reports of industrial and trade activity.

4. *Foreign department.* Dun & Bradstreet has foreign branche affiliates, and correspondents in important trade centers of the worl Foreign trade analysts familiar with the business customs, languag and local selling conditions in the countries they cover, conduct o the-spot investigations of local exporters, importers, and other com mercial enterprises. These investigations are reflected to a great e tent in the more than 250,000 reports on file at New York on leadin foreign customers for American goods and services. This departmen annually publishes the Latin America Sales Index, which contains th listings with a trade code key of 150,000 industrial, commercial, an professional enterprises in Latin America. It also edits and publishe "International Markets," a monthly bulletin listing hundreds of in quiries received from companies all over the world who seek to bu from, sell to, or get agency connections with American manufacturer

5. *Mercantile claims division.* Commercial credit grantors, throug the Mercantile Claims Division, are offered the following collectio facilities:

(*a*) Reminders, which are attached to invoices and letters be fore accounts are placed for collections.

(*b*) A written demand for payment made by Mercantile Claim Division.

(*c*) A follow-up demand letter.

(*d*) Additional and more persistent efforts, consisting of variou types of demand appropriate to the individual account, including th presentation of accounts by an experienced staff of collection special ists throughout the United States and Canada, whenever practicable

(*e*) On accounts of $500 or more, immediate personal deman when requested, with reports of efforts to collect submitted within 2 hours after receipt of account, whenever practicable.

(*f*) When further action is necessary, reference of accounts, i creditor's behalf, to experienced attorneys or others, the creditor re taining full right of selection. Accounts may be placed for collectio at offices in leading centers of trade throughout the United States an Canada.

6. *Municipal service department.* This department serves the dealer and investor in city, county, and state bonds. A staff of analysts, trained in municipal finance, prepares comprehensive credit surveys based on data obtained through personal investigations and interviews with local officials. Each survey presents a detailed analysis of the economic and social characteristics, management, debt, and current operations of the governmental unit covered. Surveys are prepared on any unit in the United States publicly selling a new general obligation issue of $750,000 or more. At least two surveys are also issued annually on cities of over 50,000 population, counties of over 150,000, thirty-seven of the states, various special districts, and 50 leading revenue situations (such as Port of New York Authority) whose bonds are widely held. This "continuous service" enables investors to appraise their municipal holdings in a systematic manner each year. The surveys are used by commercial and savings banks, trust companies, municipal bond dealers, insurance companies, private estates, fraternal organizations, and individual investors.

Supplementary agency services. The Agency furnishes letters of introduction to its subscribers, upon request, to enable the subscribers' representatives, when traveling, to inquire for information at any of the Agency's branch offices. The Reference Book may be consulted, or a full report read. There is no extra charge for this service.

When a subscriber inquires about a name, the Agency supplies, in addition to the report then in its files or the report prepared as the result of the inquiry, continuous service on the name for a period of a year. This continuous service includes all new and additional information obtained during the year of service. When a new report is issued after the year of continuous service, a renewal notice is sent to the subscriber stating that the year of service has been completed and that a new report has been prepared and may be obtained by returning the renewal notice.

Consulting Reporters, who are top reporters in the business and who are "professional" consultative reporters, work very much on their own responsibility. They work closely with subjects of reports, their banks, and trade suppliers in handling the more complex credit problems and credit reporting situations.

Service Consultants have been set up in the offices of Dun & Bradstreet, Inc., for the purpose of effecting a broadened and more personalized relationship with subscribers to the service. The objective of the Service Consultant is to make certain that each subscriber receives the maximum value from his relationship with the Agency and makes the fullest possible use of the various Agency services.

The Building Trades Division has for its broad purpose the development of a service to meet the unique requirements of suppliers in the building industry.

The Business Library has facilities for the use of service subscribers, business executives, trade associations, banks, and others of the business world in locating published information. A competent staff handles inquiries by telephone and by mail; there is an attractive reference room for those who visit the library. The Business Library collection of standard business and economic literature is supplemented by up-to-date books, pamphlets, releases, reports, and clippings on subjects of special and timely interest. For instance, data are available on various aspects of business management, credit, commodities, industries, prices, statistics, and the like. The library maintains files of trade journals, newspapers, and government releases, as well as collections of current business and trade directories, biographical directories, business histories, operating and financial ratios. The library resources include about 14,000 volumes, 14,000 pamphlets, 200 periodicals, and 200 drawers of vertical files.

Special or Trade Agencies

Two kinds of special agencies. Special agencies are either mutual or privately operated. The former are voluntary associations of manufacturers, jobbers, and wholesalers, organized for the purpose of gathering and disseminating credit information among the members. Credit bureaus are set up, and the members contribute to the support of the agency. The private agencies are maintained for purposes of profit to their proprietors and sell their services to subscribers. Many maintain collection departments as a regular part of the organization.

Special agencies confined to a single industry. Special or trade agencies gather and distribute credit information about persons and firms engaged in a particular line of business, such as furniture, jewelry, lumber, millinery, shoes and leather, textile, and the like. A credit man in a particular line of business usually knows the agency at serves his trade. Although from the standpoint of the agencies emselves, the general agency and the special agency consider each her as competitors, from the viewpoint of the credit man the two ight well be looked upon as complementary.

Services of special agencies. The services and methods of operaon differ in the various special agencies. The more important and ore usual services are as follows:

1. *Special-agency ratings.* Most of the special agencies issue rating ooks, although some of the mutual agencies do not. The ratings ed by special agencies are often somewhat different in form from neral-agency ratings.

2. *Special-agency reports.* The reports supplied by the special gencies follow for the most part the pattern of the general-agency ports. They are likely, however, to contain more complete ledger formation, especially where the co-operation of members is active. ubscribers are permitted a certain number of reports under their ntracts, and they are required to pay an additional fee if they ceed that number.

3. *Special-agency "credit-recommendation" service.* A feature of ie work of some of the special agencies is their so-called "creditecommendation" or "credit-checking" service. Inquiry may be made ither in writing, on a form supplied by the agency, or by telephone. 'he agency responds by making a definite recommendation as to hether or not the order in question should be shipped. The subcriber may request merely the recommendation, or may ask for a eport. Where a report is obtained, a recommendation is appended o it.

4. *Special-agency weekly bulletins.* In addition to the rating books nd reports, the special agencies, in practically every instance, issue veekly bulletins. These are sent to all subscribers and indicate, usully by states, facts such as the following about merchants in the line: hange in firm name; change in rating; change in location; death of n officer; incorporation; robbery; fire; loss by swindle; attachments; ssignments; claims for collection; and bankruptcy. In short, anyhing that would be of interest to a creditor of these merchants is ncluded.

5. *Special-agency tracers.* Another feature of special-agency service s the so-called tracer, or clearing-house report. A creditor in doubt

about a certain account may request the agency to look up the rece
information received from other creditors who have had experien
with the account; the agency may also, from its own observatio
deem it wise to initiate such an inquiry. The agency then circ
larizes its membership for information on the account in questio
offering to furnish all those who supply information with a tabul
tion of the results. In this way there is made available to all who c
operate a complete statement of the status of the particular me
chant's accounts with the trade in general.

6. *Collection service.* A collection department is operated fo
members by some of the special agencies.

Credit Interchange

The use of credit interchange. Credit interchange is the ex
change among business houses of actual ledger experience with re
gard to customers. It is helpful in revising accounts, in eliminatin
undesirable buyers, and in granting or refusing extensions. It aid
in checking special accounts, keeps the credit files alive and up to th
minute, tells whether a customer is overbuying or buying outsid
his legitimate territory, or whether he is paying his new credito
promptly and allowing others to wait. Sometimes ledger credit
interchange reports reveal that a creditor house is mistaken in it
belief that it is the principal creditor.

Credit interchange is also valuable to firms selling a small hous
whose rating is as yet unestablished. It is also useful when a forme
customer requests a reopening of his account.

Credit-interchange bureaus. To facilitate this exchange of credi
information, credit-interchange bureaus have been organized. Som
of the special mercantile agencies offer interchange as one of thei
services. In a number of industries interchange bureaus are operate
by trade associations. The best-known and most widely used system
of interchange of ledger information is that of the National Association of Credit Men.

Credit Interchange Service of the National Association of Credit Men. The National Association of Credit Men is the professional and service organization of the commercial credit managers
and financial executives of the United States. It is a non-profit, co-
operative corporation, founded in 1896, and owned and controlled by

its membership, which is made up of producers, manufacturers, wholesalers, financial institutions, and other firms in the commercial field. Its membership comprises firms in the above categories, locally organized in affiliated units throughout the country. These local credit associations are coordinated to make up the National Association of Credit Men.

Credit Interchange Service, approved and endorsed by the N.A.C.M. as the most practical and efficient medium for the exchange of ledger experience information, is conducted through a National Credit Interchange System. This system consists of fifty-four Bureaus, covering major and minor markets in the country, plus a coordinating unit, the Central Credit Interchange Bureau located in St. Louis, Mo. Each local Bureau participating in the National System is a member-owned-and-controlled institution under the supervision of a local Credit Men's Association or Associations. The principle of member direction and control, and service at cost, prevails. Bureaus serve only as mediums for assembling and disseminating information which is supplied and used by creditors. Each local bureau requires users of the Service to supply a list of the accounts on his ledgers, and to supplement this list with new accounts as they are opened.

How an inquiry is handled. When a member wants to know the experience others have had with a particular account, he makes out an inquiry ticket on a form supplied by the local bureau. On this form he indicates his own experience with the account and sends it to the local bureau of which he is a member. The local bureau knows from its file records who the local creditors of the firm under investigation are, and in what other markets throughout the country the firm is buying. The local bureau next sends out a form to locally known creditors of the firm under investigation. A different form is forwarded to other known affiliated bureaus throughout the country to clear their locally interested members and report their paying account. When the paying record information is received, the local bureau writes a report based on the information given by the interested sources. This report is described below.

What the inquiring member receives. An inquiring member receives, first, a copy of any report, more than one hundred and twenty days old at the time the inquiry is received. Second, it receives one or more preliminary reports containing revised information from local and other markets when available. Finally, it receives a report containing information received from all known creditors, and from re erences supplied by it and other members. This report thus become an up-to-date review of the buying and paying habits of the custome with all creditors throughout the country whose interest it has bee possible to discover.

What a Credit Interchange Report shows. A Credit Interchang Report is a clear, uncolored, impersonal statement of facts as recite by creditors, presented for quick, intelligent appraisal. The repor shows: (1) the business classification of each contributor of informa tion, together with a code date showing when members in that mar ket were canvassed for information; (2) how long the firm reportin has sold to the firm under investigation; (3) date of the last sale; (4) the highest recent credit extended; (5) the amount owing; (6) th amount past due; (7) terms of sale; (8) the paying record; (9) com ments.

The date of last sale is a very important feature on the report, as the value of the information depends on how recent it is.

The comments column provides space for pertinent facts not clear from routine figures as taken from the ledger page. It will show, for example, trends of payment; whether the account is improving or getting slower; unfilled or first orders; whether accounts have been collected by an attorney, or whether the account is in the hands of an attorney; the amount, date placed, and so on.

Trade-group interchange. Another method of direct interchange of ledger experience is the group meeting. Creditors located in the same trading center, who are members of the same credit association and sell to the same line of trade, get together periodically to exchange information on their customers. For example, the credit men representing the wholesale plumbing and heating trade of a large midwestern city meet once a week to exchange information on credit conditions. Each member comes supplied with a quantity of reporting blanks, which are filled out as reports are given. Starting at one end of the table, Mr. Blank reports an order from John Doe, amount $20,000, and gives whatever information he has concerning the customer. Then the man next to him reports the experience of his firm, if any, and so on around the table. The two or three hours' time spent at the meeting each week is more than offset by the time saved during the week.

Other trade groups that have less occasion to meet regularly are "on call" for any time, the secretary of the local association calling the group together on short notice whenever any account requiring immediate attention comes up. In this way doubtful accounts concerning which there have been unfavorable experiences are generally brought to light in time to prevent serious damage.

The members of another bureau go one step further. When the monthly report which the bureau makes up shows that John Doe has bought from different members more than he should have, or that he is getting behind in his payments, he is cordially invited to a luncheon meeting of the association. There his situation is discussed in his presence, and an effort is made to reach some solution that will be agreeable to him. Oftentimes the creditor finds that the credit men have suggestions which are of practical assistance to him, and the informality of the meetings precludes any ill-feeling.

Agencies Reporting on Individuals and Making Special Investigations—Published Services

Difference between mercantile agencies and agencies reporting on individuals. The preceding paragraphs have dealt with sources of credit information regarding companies. The problem of obtaining credit information on individuals is somewhat different. Whereas credit information on a business firm requires an investigation entailing special knowledge of the industry, ability to interpret financial statements, and the like, and covers a period of years, a report on individuals is relatively simple and extends over a much shorter period. A local investigation of the individual is usually sufficient. Banks, loan companies, and installment houses may use these agencies to advantage.

Although there are a number of agencies exclusively in the field of individual reporting, only a few of the leading ones are treated here.

Hooper-Holmes Bureau. The Hooper-Holmes Bureau, Inc., maintains headquarters in Morristown, New Jersey, with branches in 100 cities in the United States and 5 cities in Canada. The agency serves insurance companies principally, although it also serves banks, finance companies, installment houses, and retail stores. The agency not only submits credit information from its files but makes a new, individual outside inspection report on every request for credit information received. Reports are consequently up to date. They ar a great aid to credit men in large cities where individuals move abou frequently.

For the credit man desiring information on individuals, the agenc offers numerous types and styles of reports. These include: (1 Credit report—Individual, (2) Credit report—Farmer, (3) Credit re port—Firm or Corporation, (4) Loan report, (5) Mortgage Loar report, (6) Automobile purchase, (7) Oil Dealer, (8) Standard Fac tual Data report for Federal Housing Administration—Individua Farmer, (9) Petroleum Credit report, (10) Delinquent Debtor report

The individual report is a one-page confidential form report carry ing a series of questions in one column regarding: (1) the contact made in the investigation; (2) the individual's age, lineage, depend ents, reputation, and habits; (3) the individual's occupation; anc (4) his finances. The investigator's answers are in the column to the right of the questions. A space is provided at the bottom of the re port for details of any incomplete or unfavorable answers to the questions.

Derogatory information about an individual coming to the atten- tion of the Agency after a report has been sent to a client is passed on to the subscriber in the form of a supplemental report, for which no charge is made.

Retail Credit Company. This company, established in 1899, fur- nishes personal information on residents of any place in North Amer- ica. The Home Office is in Atlanta, Georgia. The company main- tains 167 branch offices and 912 sub-branches or direct reporting stations throughout the continent.

This investigative and reporting service is used by petroleum com- panies, direct-selling and mail-order houses, automobile finance com- panies, building and loan companies, farm implement distributors, mortgage loan and property improvement agencies, and many others.

The reports furnished by this agency cover typical credit informa- tion and also emphasize character of the subject. Some of the wide variety of reports are:

1. Character Credit Report (Individual): provides character, finan- cial, and credit information on persons other than farmers.
2. Character Credit Report (Farmer): provides character, finan-

ial, and credit information on farmers. Also gives size of farm, type, rop prospects, stability, and other pertinent facts.

3. Delinquent Purchaser Report: provides apparent reason for delinquency, income, and worth to aid in judging collectibility.

4. Personnel Selection Report: covers prior employment record, ducation, health, habits, character, finances of persons being considered for employment.

5. Special Service: exhaustive investigations of unusual situations or transactions beyond scope of regular investigations.

The first three types of reports named above are submitted in question and answer form with some narrative remarks.

A current investigation is the rule. Logical sources of information —persons in position to know necessary facts concerning the subject of a report—are interviewed, usually by full-time investigators. Unfavorable facts are confirmed through records or additional sources. Many reports are further strengthened and broadened by active files, which include previous reports and other recorded data on approximately 24,000,000 persons.

Voluntary follow-up of prior reports is submitted when any significant information comes to hand subsequently.

Proudfoot's Commercial Agency, Inc. Proudfoot's Commercial Agency, Inc., is located in New York City. The agency makes confidential and comprehensive reports, in letter form, on individuals, corporations, partnerships, and associations. The files of the agency contain information and reports on more than seven million names gathered over fifty years of service.

The reports on individuals cover the following data regarding the person under investigation:

1. Age, place of birth, and home life.
2. Extent of education.
3. Complete antecedent history and business activity.
4. Dates of all former connections.
5. Record of suits, judgments, and bankruptcies.
6. Criminal record.
7. Favorable or derogatory comment relative to past record.
8. Financial condition and method of paying bills.
9. Bank and other credit information.

10. Integrity, moral standing.
11. Business reputation.

The reports on partnerships and corporations have three sections (1) the antecedent history and personal background of the principal of the enterprise; (2) a detailed financial picture, including statement analysis, trends over the past several years, as well as a digest of present activity and immediate outlook for the future; and (3) bank and trade investigations and availability of credit.

The agency also reports on professional firms such as law, accounting, engineering, investment counsel, and others.

Although the bulk of the reports serve concerns and individuals in New York City and its environs, they are available to subscribers over a wide area.

Bishop's Service, Inc. Bishop's Service, Inc., established in 1895, is located in New York City and is engaged exclusively in the business of making investigations and credit reports, based on personal character and moral risk, with respect to individuals, firms, and corporations located throughout this country, Canada, Western Europe, and South America.

The reports are narrative in style and rather comprehensive. They emphasize the personal and business records and the habits and associations of the individuals involved, including those charged with the direction and management of firms and corporate activities. The reports include summaries, financial statements, judgment records, litigation, and personality surveys.

Hill's Reports, Inc. Hill's Reports, Inc., of Chicago, serves principally Chicago commercial banks and trust companies, securities houses, mortgage companies, building and loan associations, hotels, and insurance companies. Credit reports are prepared on individuals, partnerships, and corporations by trained reporters and correspondents. These reports are based on individual investigation of each inquiry plus available data from the files of the agency. Although the reports emphasize the character and moral responsibility of the individuals involved, their contents vary according to the requirements of the subscriber. The reports are narrative in style, with no summary or ratings.

Publications. Besides the mercantile and specialized agencies, the credit man may consult various publications issued by publishing companies to aid him in formulating a credit decision. The most important of these services are published by Moody's Investors Service, Inc.; Standard and Poor's Corporation; Fitch Publishing Co., Inc.; and Alfred M. Best Company, Inc.

All of these companies publish yearly manuals, available to subscribers, containing valuable information on nearly every concern in the country that has securities in the hands of the public. Data contained in these manuals cover the financial condition of the company, earnings record, names of officers and directors, and description of obligations and capital securities of the company.

The first three companies serve the investment field, while Alfred M. Best Company operates in the insurance field.

Salesmen as Credit Reporters

Value of salesmen as credit reporters. In the case of smaller accounts, salesmen are frequently a valuable source of credit information. The advantages of using salesmen as credit reporters are the following:

1. The salesman is frequently the only representative of his house who comes in personal contact with the customer.
2. Where salesmen visit customers often and the amount of each sale is small, the expense of obtaining credit data from outside sources may not be warranted.
3. When a salesman's credit report accompanies the order, delivery of the goods is expedited.
4. Extravagant promises to the customer by salesmen are eliminated, such as promises of immediate delivery to customers whose accounts need investigation.
5. Any change affecting the credit risk, financial or otherwise, can be reported immediately, permitting the company to lose little time in reducing or extending the credit limit.
6. Where the account is doubtful, the salesman can advise the customer of ways to improve his business, thereby building a future customer although the credit department will not extend credit on present orders.

Nature of information obtainable through salesmen. In con- nection with new customers, the salesman may consider the followir points:

1. Personal habits and local reputation.
2. Business experience and ability.
3. Location of business.
4. Local conditions.
5. Trade and bank references.
6. Financial statement.
7. Credit recommendation.

Objections to salesmen as credit investigators. Many credi men feel that salesmen as a source of credit information are greatl overestimated, and that such work should be confined to salesme dealing with small firms. The salesman, for instance, is not alway able to inspect all of the merchandise. Nor can he afford to spen too much time on credit work, since his main job is selling. Besides many prospects prefer requests for information, particularly for finan cial statements, to come from credit men. For these reasons man credit departments provide salesmen with forms on which to repor their credit information.

A form of salesmen's reports. The following form of report fo salesmen is sent by one company to salesmen, branch offices, and brokers once a year. The company reports great diversity in the na- ture of the comments, for which space is provided at the bottom of the page. Some salesmen will merely note "O.K."; others write a few lines; some jot down a few paragraphs on the back of the form; and still others will attach a two- or three-page comment.

Our credit records show a credit line of ....

authorized for:

.... of ....

Will you please give us your present comments and recommendations on this line. This is to assure us that:

Your records agree with ours; and that

You believe the line is suitable and proper.

If you believe the line should be revised, either to facilitate the sale of r merchandise, or to conform with the normal requirements of the :ount, please let us know.

Or, if it is unnecessary that a line be continued, we want to suspend :dit and make the file inactive.

Thank you for your co-operation.

Very truly yours,
Company's name
Credit manager's name
Credit Department

ease write your comments below and return this form.

....
....
....
....
....

How to get the salesmen to co-operate. To what extent the ılesman will furnish the information that he can obtain depends to large degree upon the credit man himself. The credit man will ɔon enlist the salesman's active assistance if he is broadminded, if e does his work with the idea of business promotion, and if he :eats customers considerately and thus helps the salesman to retain ıe goodwill of his trade. Among the specific methods used by various ompanies to enlist the salesman's co-operation are the following:

1. *Conferences between salesmen and credit man.* Periodically, he credit man discusses with each salesman, individually, the acounts that he handles. This mutual exchange of information and iewpoint is invaluable to both men. The credit man becomes amiliar with the salesman's problems. Personal contact also enables he credit man to judge to what extent he can rely on information ;iven to him by salesmen. For his part, the salesman learns from onferences with the credit man what constitutes a good credit risk, vhat factors have to be taken into consideration, what the credit ɔolicy of his house is, and, specifically, why some of his accounts have ɔeen turned down.

2. *Payment on n.c.u.p. basis.* Under the n.c.u.p plan ("no commission until paid"), the salesman's personal account on the ledger s credited with the commission at the time the sale is made, but the amount is not paid to him until the customer has settled his bill.

The effect is to make the salesman more discriminating in soliciti accounts.

3. *Collection contests.* Information will be given much more free and accurately by salesmen if they are made wholly, or even or partly, responsible for collections. A number of companies have r ported successful operation of a plan by which a cash prize is award each month to the salesman who leads his district in collection The salesman is less likely to recommend a doubtful account if h knows that he will be expected to assist in collecting it. See pag 1084 for further discussion of collection by salesmen.

4. *Notice of refusal to grant credit.* Salesmen will co-operate be ter with credit departments if they feel that the credit departme does not keep them waiting for information as to the acceptance o rejection of orders. Some credit departments have therefore adopte the practice of sending out a notice to salesmen whenever extensio of credit has been withheld. A simple form giving the reason fo withholding credit is used. The salesmen, knowing that this pra tice is followed, do not wire or write in to the credit department lon before the credit man has completed his investigation to determin whether the order has been accepted.

Attorneys as Credit Reporters

Nature of information obtainable through attorneys. Much o the credit information obtainable through attorneys is similar to tha obtainable through salesmen; it refers to such matters as:

1. Personal habits.
2. Local reputation.
3. Business ability.
4. Location of business.
5. Local trade conditions.
6. Value of real property, and encumbrances thereon.
7. Claims and lawsuits.

Some houses restrict their use of attorneys as credit reporters tc cities with a population of 15,000 or less, because they feel that it is only in such cases that the attorney has sufficient personal knowledge of and contact with the subject to render his report of value. There are, however, numerous individual attorneys and firms that make a ecialty of collection work and the furnishing of credit information; ese attorneys have expert staffs and maintain extensive credit records. It is advisable to ask the firm's attorney to locate an attorney in particular locality who will act as a credit reporter. The company's torney has access to published lists of attorneys' directories that ay be used for this purpose.

Objections to attorneys' reports. In using attorneys' reports, the edit man should bear in mind the following objections that may etract from the value of the report: (1) the attorney is unacquainted ith the credit standards of the inquiring house; (2) he may be a ersonal friend of the credit applicant; and (3) local pride may affect is judgment. In order to be sure that the attorney gives the request or credit information proper attention, he should be compensated or his efforts. Remuneration may be in the form of placing collec-on work with the attorney, or it may be a fee based upon the mount of work done in furnishing the report.

Banks as Credit Reporters

Availability of credit information from banks. In the conduct f their own business, banks maintain complete credit files of their epositors in order to be equipped with full credit information on the asis of which applications for loans can be intelligently considered. This information is for the bank's own use and is kept confidential.

Unless a bank is authorized by a customer to give credit informa-ion to a specific inquirer, or unless the inquiry comes through a orrespondent bank, very little, if any, credit information can be ob-ained other than the fact that the customer has a deposit at the ank, and possibly the age of the account.

Banks are not particularly receptive to inquiry forms sent by non-depositors seeking information about a depositor. These are usually illed out meagerly, if at all. To discourage such promiscuous in-quiries, many state bankers' associations and other organizations of bankers have adopted rules providing that requests for credit infor-mation, unless authorized by the customer, or received through a correspondent bank, must be accompanied by a fee.

Information that may be obtained from banks. The following ist enumerates items of credit information that may be obtainable from a customer's commercial bank, upon authorization, if the customer has ever borrowed from the bank. If he has not, only pa of the items may be covered in the bank's report.

1. Age of the account. Frequent changing of banking connecti is in itself regarded as unfavorable.

2. A general statement of the relationship with respect to loa and deposit balances, including information on how satisfactor the account is conducted.

3. Promptness of the subject in meeting his obligations to t bank.

4. Whether many drafts are presented to the subject through t bank, and, if so, whether these drafts are honored by the subject.

5. Comment on the subject's financial statement, provided that is authorized by the subject.

6. General local reputation of the subject and the bank's opini of him.

7. In the case of some banks, a definite or general expression opinion regarding the risk.

8. A short summary of the history and antecedents of the cor pany.

Information that is not obtainable from banks. The bank ordinarily not in a position to furnish credit men with the followi information:

1. The exact amount of the depositor's account. The bank w give the credit man a general idea of the depositor's responsibilit Such terms as small (three figures), moderate (four figures), or lar (over four figures) are frequently used to describe the amount deposits. The bank however, may, confirm a balance reported by customer on a balance sheet.

2. Details of loans that are outstanding. This information ca be secured only on the proper authorization.

3. Information concerning the customer's financial statement.

Getting information from the credit man's bank. When th credit man is faced with a particularly difficult decision, he may as his own bank to obtain a credit report from the customer's ban Banks in the same city have an accurate credit-interchange syste and can quickly obtain such information. If the customer is out c town, the credit man's bank will communicate with its corresponde nk in the customer's city, which in turn will get in touch with the .stomer's bank.

Generally, more complete information is obtainable if this method used than when the credit man goes direct to the customer's bank. owever, the method is one that can be used only infrequently, and en only if the bank is anxious to please the depositor who makes e request.

The Personal Interview

Value of the personal interview. Through personal interviews, personal calls on customers, the credit man can obtain useful in- ›rmation as well as promote better understanding between the sell- ıg house and its customers. The properly conducted interview ıables the applicant to present his own case most advantageously ıd to receive useful suggestions; it permits the credit man to make ersonal observations and to inquire carefully concerning doubtful oints; and, finally, a free and frank discussion leads to a more satis- ıctory mutual understanding. Wherever a personal contact can be ıstified by the size of the order received or prospects of future busi- ess, and especially where, as a result of the call, the credit man can ıake necessary arrangements to hold worth-while business, the credit ıan should make every attempt to interview the applicant.

A friendly and human attitude on the part of the credit man ccomplishes more than anything else during the personal call. The redit man wants the customer to talk freely. This situation is best ıduced by pleasant and informal discussions in which the credit ıan asks as few direct questions as possible and permits the customer o do the talking. However, the credit man should review the case efore the interview in order that he may direct the conversation long the proper channels. It is preferable to refrain from writing uring the interview. As soon as it is terminated, the results of the ıterview should be put in writing.

Special need for a personal interview. A personal interview or personal call by the credit man is especially useful in the following ases:

1. When an old and valued account is becoming slow in meeting ts obligations. The credit man, through his intimate and wide- pread knowledge of the trade, may be able to suggest to the cus-

tomer means by which the progress of his business can be restor Thus the creditor may suggest a change in the customer's locati (the customer is often the last person to realize that the curre trend of local business is moving away from the street or section which he is located), clearance sales to dispose of old stock, n methods of window display, new methods of advertising, new lin of goods that might be carried to attract patronage, more comple and efficient bookkeeping methods, and so forth.

2. When a new account is under consideration offering unusu opportunity for sales, but involving greater than ordinary risk.

Traveling credit representatives. Some credit men for larg houses spend a considerable part of their time in travel; others ma a tour of their principal customers once or twice a year. Still oth houses employ special credit representatives who spend their enti time visiting customers to inquire into their credit standing. Th advantages of these practices are:

1. The credit man is able to visualize the personality, busine circumstances, and so forth, of each customer. The credit man wh remains always at his desk gains his perspective on credit risks e tirely at second hand.

2. Goodwill between the customer and the selling house is c mented. A call by the credit man establishes a personal relationsh between the customer and the name signed to the credit and colle tion letters.

3. The credit man gains insight into the problems of the sal department, and his judgment may be modified and correcte

4. By visiting references, especially banks, in person, the cred man or representative can usually obtain more definite and reliab information than can be obtained by correspondence.

2. MERCANTILE CREDIT TERMS

Classes of credit terms. The credit terms used in mercanti trade group themselves into six classes: (1) prepayment terms, (2 cash terms, (3) individual-order terms, (4) lumped-order terms, (5 season dating, and (6) consignment terms.

Prepayment terms. Sometimes when a purchaser is in poo credit standing, the seller does not desire to extend any credit, o assume any risk. So much misunderstanding about this very oint has arisen that it seems necessary to explain the meaning of fferent terms where the intention of the seller is to extend no edit, or to demand prepayment.

The so-called prepayment terms are "C.B.D.," cash before de- very; "C.O.D.," cash on delivery; and "S.D.-B.L.," sight draft with gotiable bill of lading attached. In only one of these situations oes the seller assume no risk and extend no credit; that is where e terms are C.B.D. Although the C.O.D. and S.D.-B.L. terms e classed as prepayment terms, the seller, as we shall see from the planation of these terms below, does not have complete assurance payment.

S.D.-B.L. terms. When goods are sold on S.D.-B.L. terms, the ller receives a negotiable or order bill of lading from the carrier. e then draws a draft for the amount of the invoice on the purchaser his bank. After endorsing the bill of lading, he attaches it to e draft and sends both papers, together with the invoice, to a bank the buyer's city. He also notifies the buyer which bank holds the apers. The buyer pays the amount of the invoice to the bank and e shipping papers are then delivered to him so that he can get the oods from the carrier. The bank remits the payment to the seller.

The seller here assumes the risk of having the purchaser refuse accept the goods, in which case the seller would lose the freight harges both ways, unless he were fortunate enough to sell the goods another merchant along the same route. Scheming merchants, to hom the seller will not grant credit, sometimes order goods shipped .D.-B.L. Upon the arrival of the goods, these merchants plead ck of immediate funds and ask the seller to allow them to take the oods and remit in ten days. Thus they hope to compel the seller o extend credit. The seller should be on his guard against such nerchants and should demand a deposit before the goods are hipped to cover the risk involved. The deposit should be sufficient o cover transportation charges and a possible drop in price.

C.O.D. terms. When goods are shipped C.O.D., the buyer pays he carrier the amount of the invoice before the goods are delivered o him. The seller assumes the same risk on C.O.D. terms that he loes on S.D.-B.L. terms, described above. He should consider ask- ng for a deposit to avoid losses in case the goods are not accepted. There is the additional danger that the check the buyer gives to the carrier in payment for the goods will not be honored. The sell therefore, may instruct the carrier to accept only currency or a cer fied check. In this event he should also notify the buyer that t payment must be by currency or certified check.

Cash terms. Many merchants believe that when goods are sc for "cash" no credit is extended. Such is not the case. Wh goods are shipped "cash" there is an expressed or an implied und standing that the purchaser is given ten days' credit. The ten da is allowed him to check the goods received and verify the invoic The bill is due at the end of ten days, and, if not paid, the sell can resort only to the same remedies that are open to any oth credit grantor. The credit standing of one to whom goods are so on "cash" terms should be just as thoroughly examined as that one who is sold on regular terms, for the same risk is involved both cases.

Individual-order terms. These terms are used when shipmen are made to a buyer only once or twice a month. The discou period and the credit period are counted from the date of the in voice. If the terms are 30 days for payment, without discount, the are stated "net 30." If a discount, say 2 per cent, is allowed, th terms are stated "2/10/30" or "2/10 net 30." These two term mean that a discount of 2 per cent is allowed if payment is mad within 10 days from the invoice date; otherwise, the full amount o the bill is due 30 days after date.

R.O.G. or A.O.G. terms. All invoices are dated the day the good are shipped. If a house in New York sells goods throughout th country on "2/10 net 60" terms, it is evident that a house in Jerse City would enjoy a distinct advantage over a house in San Francisco The former would receive its goods within twenty-four hours an have time to check them up before paying within ten days, whil the house in San Francisco would probably have to pay before th goods were received in order to take the cash discount. To over come this disadvantage to distant purchasers some houses date in voices to some of their customers "receipt-of-goods" (R.O.G.) o "arrival of goods" (A.O.G.). This means the time allowed for tak ing discount is measured from the time the goods are received by the purchaser. If the purchaser, however, does not avail himself o the discount within the period allowed, the regular terms are usu ly measured from the date of shipment. The purchaser then ɲjoys the benefit of the R.O.G. or A.O.G. terms only when he kes advantage of the discount. R.O.G. terms may be applied to edit and discount periods on water-borne shipments and other ow freight.

Lumped-order or end-of-month terms. A development that has ad a tendency to lengthen the terms of credit has been the creaon of "lumped-order" terms. These terms originated with merɦants who did a very active business and made purchases almost very day during the month. They found it very inconvenient to ake payments every day during the month; and yet this would be ecessary if they were to avail themselves of the cash discounts. The rger merchants who were active buyers requested the selling houses permit them to pay all their bills once a month and take advanage of the regular discount. The selling houses granted this request, or they wished to keep the goodwill and business of such active ccounts. In this way the custom arose of permitting large houses o pay, on the tenth day of the month, all bills of the previous nonth and deduct the cash discount. Lumped-order terms are now ommon in many lines where buyers give orders twice a month or ftener, or when shipments go out oftener than twice a month.

All deliveries during a monthly period are lumped together, and he credit term for all of them begins at a specified date. For example, goods shipped between January 1 and January 31 on end-ofnonth (E.O.M.) terms are dated February 1. The cash discount nd the 30-day or 60-day credit periods are counted as beginning February 1. Another lumped-order term is the "10 prox." This neans that all credit and discount periods for a calendar month egin the tenth day of the next following (proximate) month. If he credit and discount period begins with the fifteenth day of the ollowing month, the terms are stated M.O.M. (middle of month).

When goods are purchased on E.O.M. terms, many buyers pay heir bills from monthly statements instead of from the invoices. If these statements are prepared and mailed after the close of the nonth, they do not reach the buyers in time for them to take advantage of the cash discount. Even on 10-prox. terms, the buyers ɦave little leeway for making discount payments. Consequently, many lines close the monthly statements on the twenty-fifth day of the month instead of on the last day. The sellers then have t first few days of the month for preparing and mailing statemen Shipments made during those days are included on the statemer of the following month. Customers frequently place orders f goods to be shipped on the twenty-fifth day of the month so as get the maximum credit period.

Season dating. Season dating is used to induce a merchant order goods in advance of production or importation. A merchan for example, may order spring goods the preceding fall. The risl of change in style, bad business conditions, and lack of demand a thus transferred from the manufacturer or importer to the retail or secondary manufacturer. For this reason, the seller is willing compensate the purchaser by extending very favorable terms credit. The terms vary with the different lines of business, som ninety days, some six months, some eight months.

Season dating may work out as follows: In the fall a manufactur receives an order to make a quantity of summer goods. The man facturer immediately begins to make the products. In Decemb or January the goods are delivered with an invoice to the purchase The invoice is given the season dating, say May 1, and the terms ar 2/10/60. The regular terms of discount do not begin to operat until May 1. The purchaser, however, may pay at any time befor May 1 and may deduct interest from the net amount of the bill a the rate of 6 per cent a year.

The distinct advantages to the seller are that advance orders ir duced by season dating transfer the risk of changes in fashion to th purchaser and enable the manufacturer to spread his production On the other hand, the seller must give very long-term credit. Th purchaser enjoys the long-term credit, for it allows him plenty o time to sell the goods. The purchaser, however, must carry mor insurance and provide larger quarters for the stock. Moreover, ther is the danger that the purchaser, encouraged by the long-term seaso dating, may optimistically overestimate the demands of the comin season, overstock with merchandise, and subsequently sustain heav losses through having on hand merchandise that is out-of-style and unsalable except at a loss.

Consignment terms. When a buyer is not a good credit risk and cannot afford to buy goods on C.O.D. terms, a seller sometimes ips goods to him on consignment terms. Under these terms the ller retains title to the goods until they are sold. If the consignee ils, the goods do not belong to the general creditors but to the ller. When the goods are sold, the seller is paid out of the proeds of the sale. If the consignee does not sell the goods, he is ıder no obligation to pay for them, but can return them to the ller.

A consignment contract must follow closely certain legal require-.ents; otherwise, it might be considered a conditional sale contract. he seller would then lose certain valuable rights that a consign-ıent contract gives him. These requirements are: (1) the con-gned goods must be kept apart from the other merchandise, or ıust be marked clearly and distinctly as the property of the con-gnor; (2) the proceeds from the sale of the consigned goods must e kept separate from the consignee's general funds. Because of the :gal technicalities involved, a credit man should have an attorney raw up a form of consignment contract for him and prepare in-tructions to the consignee as to keeping the consigned goods clearly lentified.

. LAW RELATING TO CHECKS, NOTES, AND DRAFTS

Law Relating to Checks

Post-dated check not invalid. A check is not invalid merely ɔecause it bears a date later than that on which it is drawn. For :xample, if on February 1 Tom Downey draws a check to the order ɔf Albert Taylor dated February 20, the check is good. True, Mr. Downey's bank on which the check is drawn will not honor the nstrument until the 20th of the month, but the check is not for :hat reason invalid. Nor is there anything to prevent the holder ɔf the check from transferring it before the date on which it is payable. It has been held by the courts that a person who takes a check which is post-dated is not thereby put upon inquiry as to defects in the payee's right to the proceeds of the check. The Negotiable Instruments Law * specifically provides that an instrument "is not in-

* The Negotiable Instruments Law is a codification of the principal rules of law relating to negotiable instruments as announced in numerous decisions, and was adopted by the various states in response to the general need for uniformity.

valid for the reason only that it is ante-dated or post-dated, provid this is not done for an illegal or fraudulent purpose. The person whom an instrument so dated is delivered acquires the title there as of the date of delivery."

Unsigned check received; how to handle. It is not uncommc in the course of business to receive a check which has not bee signed. Omission of the signature may and generally is merely a oversight on the part of the drawer of the check, but it has bee known to be used as a time-gaining device. As in the case of oth irregularities in the drawing of a check, the instrument may be r turned to the drawer for correction, but a more effective and pe haps safer course is open to the holder of the check. He ma deposit it in his bank for collection with the understanding that th drawer will be requested to sign it upon receipt by the bank o which the check is drawn. Or he may deposit the check in his ban with a sight draft attached, and arrange to have the check and draf forwarded to the bank in which the drawer of the check has his ac count. If omission of the signature was inadvertent, the drawer o the check will be glad to sign it promptly upon request or to hono the sight draft. If it was deliberate, the use is defeated, and little i any loss of time in obtaining payment has been suffered by th payee.

Check received on which amount in writing and amount in figures disagree; how to handle. The Negotiable Instruments Lav provides that where the amount payable is expressed in words anc also in figures, and there is a discrepancy between the two, the sum denoted by the words is the sum payable. While the law furnishe this rule of construction, the banks will generally refuse to accept checks where the amount in writing disagrees with the amount in figures. If a debtor, through inadvertence or in a wily effort to gain time, forwards a check with the amount thus incorrectly indicated, the creditor may, of course, return the check for correction. A much more practical plan is to place an indorsement on the check, guaranteeing it for whichever is the correct amount, and deposit the check for collection. The debtor is then forced to indicate the correct amount of the remittance, and to make immediate payment.

Effect of certification of a check. By certifying a check, a bank undertakes the following:

1. It guarantees the drawer's signature.

2. It represents that it has in its possession funds of the drawer ıfficient to meet the check.

3. It engages that the funds will not be withdrawn from it by ıe drawer to the prejudice of any bona fide holder of the check.

Where the payee of the check has it certified, he, in effect, accepts ıe bank as his debtor, and he thereby releases the drawer of the heck, as well as any person who has indorsed it; should the bank ecome insolvent before the check is paid, the loss falls on the older of the check, not on the drawer. On the other hand, if the rawer of a check has it certified, he remains liable on the check in he event of insolvency of the bank before payment. If a bank has ertified a check by mistake, it may revoke the certification provided : acts promptly and provided no right belonging to the holder of he check has been diminished or lost.

Time within which a check must be presented for payment. The Negotiable Instruments Law provides that a check must be presented for payment within a reasonable time after its issue and that ailure to do so, resulting in loss to the drawer of the check, discharges him from liability thereon to the extent of the loss caused y delay in presentation. The law does not define the period which nay elapse between the giving and presenting of a check, and what s a "reasonable time" must be determined according to the circumstances of each particular case. Ordinarily, if a check is delivered at he same place where the bank is located, it must, in the absence of pecial circumstances, be presented to the bank on which it is drawn during the business hours of the next regular business day after it s received; if the holder fails to present it within that time and the bank on which the check is drawn becomes insolvent so that the drawer loses the amount which he had on deposit to meet the check, he is discharged from liability and the loss must be borne by the one who was lax in presenting the check for payment. The courts have held in some cases that deposit by the payee in his own bank for collection on the day following the receipt of the instrument and presentation by the collecting bank on the day thereafter is a sufficiently prompt demand. The period for presentation of a check is not extended by the fact that the payee indorses it over to a third person.

Check returned marked "insufficient funds;" how to handl Where a check received from a debtor is returned by the ba marked "insufficient funds," it may, of course, be sent back to t drawer. However, the creditor may thus lose entirely his eviden of the debtor's acknowledgment of his obligation, and give him t opportunity of delaying payment indefinitely. Or, if the debtor h merely been slow in making a deposit in his bank sufficient to cov the check, time will be unnecessarily lost while the check trave back and forth between the parties. Rather than return the chec to the drawer, the payee may arrange with the bank on which th check has been drawn to leave the check at the bank until sufficie funds have been deposited to cover it, at which time the bank wi certify the check and return it to the creditor. If the debtor's a count is short by only a small amount, it might be possible in som instances for the holder of the check to deposit to the credit of th maker sufficient funds to raise the account to the necessary amoun and then have the check certified.

In some states, including New York, a person who, with fraudu lent intent, issues a check knowing that he has insufficient funds fo its payment, may be subject to criminal prosecution. A person not subject to criminal prosecution on a post-dated check on th theory that a post-dated check is actually a *promise* to pay. Failur to have sufficient funds to cover the post-dated check is the sam as failure to pay a promissory note when due.

Effect of the death of the drawer of a check. One of the chie points of difference between a check and a bill of exchange is tha the death of the drawer of the check revokes the authority of th bank to pay, while the death of the drawer of a bill of exchange doe not. The reason for this is that a check is a mere order for th payment of money; it does not operate as an assignment of any par of the fund which the drawer of the check may have on deposit i the bank on which the check is drawn. At any time before th check is paid, the drawer may stop payment on it and countermand the authority of the drawee to collect the amount of the check, o the authority of the bank to pay on it. The death of the drawer of the check operates as a revocation of the order to pay. A bank is not, however, presumed to know when the drawer of a check has ied. If, without knowledge of the death of the drawer of a check, ne bank makes payment, it cannot be held liable therefor.

Check given in full settlement of a claim. Ordinarily, if part f a past-due indebtedness is paid, the balance remains due and owng, and an agreement on the part of the creditor to accept part in ischarge of the whole debt is not binding on the creditor unless ome additional consideration is given for his acceptance. Payment f a smaller amount may, however, operate as a full discharge of a ebtor's obligation and bar any further action by him on the orignal claim where:

1. There is a bona fide dispute concerning the claim.
2. A check reciting that it is in full payment of the claim is given o the creditor in settlement.
3. The check is accepted by the creditor or collected by him without objection.

The creditor cannot accept the check and keep alive the debtor's obligation by writing to the debtor advising him that he does not ccept it in full settlement and demands further payment. Nor can person by striking out the words "in full" written on the check void being bound by his acceptance of the check in full payment. Where a check is given in settlement of a disputed claim, therefore, t is important to indicate clearly on the instrument the fact that it epresents payment in full of the claim. And if a check is received n settlement of a claim so marked, it should be returned at once if he amount is not acceptable.

Payment of a forged check by a bank; is the bank liable to the drawer of the check? In disbursing the funds of a depositor, the bank can make payment only in conformity with the depositor's directions. If it pays a check on which the indorsement of the payee's name has been forged, it is not making payment according to the directions of the depositor and may be required to answer to the depositor for the payment. Similarly, the bank is bound to know the signature of its depositor and must account to him if it pays a check on which the depositor's signature has been forged. The bank is from necessity responsible for any omission to discover the original terms and conditions of a check, properly drawn upon it, because at the time of payment it is the only party interested who has the opportunity of inspection. In order to give the bank a fa opportunity to protect its own interests in recovering payment mac on a forged check and prosecuting the forger, the Negotiable Instr ments Law provides that no bank shall be liable to a depositor f the payment by it of a forged or raised check, unless within or year after the return to the depositor of the voucher of such pa ment, such depositor shall notify the bank that the check so pai was forged or raised.

Law Relating to Notes

Note accepted for an old debt. Generally, in order to rend the maker of a note liable therefor, some consideration must hav been given to bind the transaction; that is, something of value i the nature of a benefit to the maker or of a detriment to the paye must have induced the execution of the note. This consideratio need not have a value equal to the amount of the note; its valu may, in fact, be trivial. A debt which is due and owing from th maker of a note to the payee is deemed to be a sufficient consider tion for the note. The Negotiable Instruments Law specificall provides that an antecedent or preexisting debt constitutes value whether the note is payable on demand or at a future time. I Mulligan owes Peters $100, Peters may accept a note from Mulliga which will be binding upon the latter; the old debt is a valid con sideration. Similarly, if Mulligan owes Peters $100, Peters ma accept Casey's note for the debt, provided Peters thereby agrees t forbear from bringing suit against Mulligan. Even if Peters ha previously brought an action against Mulligan and reduced his clain to judgment, he may accept a note from Mulligan to evidence hi claim, and the old debt constitutes a good consideration for the note

Note executed on Sunday is generally invalid. In most states a promissory note executed on Sunday is invalid, so far as the make and the payee are concerned, and will not be enforced by the courts This does not mean that a note may not properly be drawn, signed or dated on a Sunday. These are all preliminaries to "execution," with which the law does not concern itself. A note becomes effec tive on the date of its delivery, and it is the act of delivery which is prohibited on the Sabbath. Even if a note is executed on Sunday, if it appears on its face to have been made on a secular day and is ansferred in good faith, for value, before maturity, to a person ıving no knowledge of the fact that it was executed on Sunday, ıe transferee may enforce the note. A maker of a note which has een executed on Sunday may also be held liable on the note either) the original payee or a subsequent holder if he ratified it on a ecular day by a payment on the note or by any distinct recognition f his obligation.

Note executed by a minor is voidable. A person under 21 years f age is a minor or an "infant" in the eyes of the law, and is al- owed, under certain circumstances, to repudiate his obligations. (In few states the age of majority for females is 18; in others, marriage emoves the infancy status.) A note executed by an infant is gener- lly not void, but voidable; that is, the note is valid, but the infant nay repudiate it before he becomes of age or within a reasonable ime thereafter. Similarly, if an infant indorses a note, he may dis- ffirm his contract of indorsement within the time indicated. What onstitutes a reasonable time depends upon the circumstances of the articular case. If the infant fails to repudiate or disaffirm within reasonable time after arriving at majority, he is deemed to have ffirmed his obligation and is bound thereon. A person, therefore, vho takes a note from an infant does so at his peril, for the infant nay decline to perform his part of the agreement.

The fact that an infant has signed or indorsed a note does not, ıowever, prevent the holder of the note from transferring it, and ıo person liable on the note, other than the infant, may set up the nfant's incapacity in defense of his own obligation. The Negoti- ble Instruments Law specifically provides that the indorsement or ssignment of a note by an infant passes the property therein, not- withstanding that from want of capacity the infant may incur no liability thereon. This means that while an infant who has in- dorsed a note may repudiate his contract of indorsement, the in- dorsee has the right to enforce payment of the note from all parties who executed the instrument prior to the infant indorser, and they cannot plead the incapacity of the minor.

Interest payable on a note. Interest is not payable on the amount of a note prior to its maturity, unless provided for expressly or impliedly, or unless the governing state statute specifies that in- terest shall be payable. Where a note does provide for the payment of interest on the principal, without indicating when the interest to be paid, the interest is not payable until the note matures. If note is not paid at maturity, interest is generally recoverable on th principal of the note from the due date to the date of payment. I the case of a demand note, interest runs from the date of the not since a note payable on demand becomes due immediately. Th interest is in the nature of damages for a detention of payment; does not constitute a distinct claim, and if payment of the princip of the note is accepted, an action cannot afterwards be maintaine to recover the interest.

Note obtained fraudulently; is the maker liable thereon Fraud on the part of the payee of a note in the consideration fo which the note was given or in procuring the note may be set up a a defense by the maker in an action brought against him by th original payee to recover the amount thereof. Where, however, note has been transferred to an innocent holder who acquires it fo value, without any notice or knowledge of the fraud, the maker ca not always avoid liability on the note even if he can prove the frau In some states, the rule is that such an innocent purchaser may hol the maker liable on the note regardless of the nature of the frau practiced by the payee. In other states, a distinction is made by th courts between two kinds of fraud:

1. Ordinary fraud, such as misrepresentation as to the quality c nature of merchandise for which the note was given.
2. Fraud in inducing the signing of the note: as, for exampl where the maker of the note signs the instrument thinking that i is a receipt or an order for goods.

In the first type of fraud, if there is nothing on the face of the in strument to arouse inquiry and no evidence of any suspicious ci cumstances attending the transfer or any proof tending to establis the fact that the purchaser had knowledge or notice of the fraud o the part of the payee, the innocent purchaser may hold the make liable. In the second type of fraud, the maker can avoid liabilit even against the innocent purchaser if he proves that he was no guilty of negligence in signing the instrument. Whether or no the signer of the note was negligent depends upon the circumstance of each case. A person is expected to ascertain what an instrumen ntains before he signs it, either by reading it or by having it read him. If he signs a note without reading it, when he can read and opportunity to do so is furnished, he cannot set up his own nission as a defense to his liability. An illiterate person is generly required to ask someone other than the party seeking his signare to the instrument to read it before he signs, but in the case of ne dealing with an old acquaintance and trusted friend, carelessss might not be imputed if the signer was deceived by relying on e representations of the other party. In any case, in order to avoid ability because of fraud, it must be shown:

1. That a material representation or statement was made intendg that the defrauded person act upon it; the test of materiality is hether, without the representation complained of, the note would ave been executed.
2. That the representation was false.
3. That the person believed it to be true.
4. That he acted thereon to his damage.

Purchase of a note which has been lost or stolen. Ordinarily, he owner of personal property cannot be divested of his right to the roperty without his consent, and if the property is lost or stolen no ne can acquire good title thereto as against the true owner, not ven one who purchases the property in good faith and for value. There is, however, a distinct and universally recognized exception o this rule in the case of negotiable instruments, such as promissory otes, which are payable to bearer or indorsed in blank. To a arge extent negotiable instruments take the place of money and n the ordinary course and transaction of business they are treated ike money or cash, which passes freely from hand to hand without earmarks. Where a person receives a note before maturity, for a air consideration, without any reason for suspecting that the title s in any way defective, he acquires a good title to the note; he can hold the note against the true owner, and may recover on it against he maker and other parties even if the note has been stolen from or lost by the former holder. The former holder retains all his original rights only against the thief or finder, or whoever received he paper from them under suspicious circumstances. A person who takes a note is not bound, at his peril, to inquire into the title of the holder, for his right to the instrument is not dependent upon that of the person from whom the note was obtained. He tak the note free from any imperfections which may attach to it in th hands of the previous holder, provided he is a "holder in du course." A holder in due course is defined in the Negotiable In truments Law as one who has taken the instrument under the fo lowing conditions:

1. That it is complete and regular upon its face.
2. That he became the holder of it before it was overdue, an without notice that it had been previously dishonored, if such wa the fact.
3. That he took it in good faith and for value.
4. That, at the time it was negotiated to him, he had no notice o any infirmity in the instrument or defect in the title of the perso negotiating it.

Effect of alteration of a note. The Negotiable Instrumen Law provides that where a material alteration is made in a not without the assent of all the parties liable thereon, the note avoided except as against the party who has made or authorized o assented to the alteration and subsequent indorsers; where, howeve a note is in the hands of a holder in due course who is not a party t the alteration, he may enforce payment of the note according to it original tenor. A material alteration, as defined by the Negotiabl Instruments Law, includes any alteration which:

1. Changes the date.
2. Changes the sum payable, either for principal or interest.
3. Changes the time or place of payment.
4. Changes the number or the relations of the parties.
5. Changes the medium or currency in which payment is to b made.
6. Adds a place of payment where no place of payment is specified
7. Makes any other change or addition which alters the effect o the instrument in any respect.

Effect of signing a note, leaving blanks to be filled in. Wher a person signs his name to a blank paper and delivers it to anothe person in order that the paper may be converted into a note, th person to whom the paper is delivered is presumed to have author ity to fill it in as a note for any amount. Similarly, where a note i ank in any material particular, the person in possession of the instrument is presumed to have authority to complete it by filling in e blanks. Even if the blanks are filled in contrary to the intent the signer of the note, it is enforceable against him by a third erson who acquires the note in good faith for value, after completion and before maturity, and without notice or knowledge of any efect in the instrument.

Forgery of signature on a note. Where the signature of the aker of a note is forged, he cannot ordinarily be held liable on e note even by one who has purchased the note in good faith and r value, without notice or knowledge of the forgery. The maker ay, however, be precluded from avoiding liability although his signature has been forged, where the forgery has been made possible y his negligence. He may also be prevented from setting up the efense of forgery in a suit brought against him on the note where e has, with full knowledge of the facts affecting his rights, ratified he note after it has been negotiated. The fact that the maker's ignature on a note is forged is not available as a defense to the iability of an indorser of the note, for by his signature the indorser npliedly warrants the validity and genuineness of the instrument to ll subsequent holders in due course. Nor, if an indorser's signature s forged, may indorsers other than the one whose signature is forged, void liability on that account.

Effect of failure to make timely demand for payment of a note. It is not necessary, in order to hold the maker of a note liable hereon, to present a note to him at maturity and to demand payment; his liability attaches automatically upon maturity of the note. To hold an indorser liable, however, the note must be presented for payment to the maker, for the indorser agrees to pay only if the maker has failed to pay after due demand has been made. Due demand means that the note is presented for payment at a proper place on the day it falls due, or in the case of demand note, within a reasonable time after issuance. If the place of payment is specified in the note, the note must be presented at that place. If no place of payment is specified, but the address of the person who is to make payment is given in the note, it should be presented there. If no place of payment is specified and no address is given, the note must be presented at the usual place of business or residence of the maker.

The note must actually be exhibited to the person from whom pa ment is demanded. Presentment of a note to the maker, sufficie to bind the indorser, cannot be made by a telephone demand upc him at his place of business where the note is payable, although l is notified that the note is in the possession of the communicant ar ready for delivery.

To the rule, as indicated above, that timely presentment for pa ment to the maker is necessary to hold the indorser liable, there ar some exceptions. Where a note was made or accepted for the a commodation of the indorser and he has no reason to expect that th instrument will be paid if presented, presentment for payment is nc required in order to charge an indorser with liability. Delay i making presentment for payment is also excused when the delay caused by circumstances beyond the control of the holder and nc imputable to his default, misconduct, or negligence. The followin circumstances are generally deemed to excuse delay:

1. Inevitable accident or overwhelming calamity.
2. Prevalence of a malignant disease which suspends the ordinar operations of business.
3. The presence of political circumstances amounting to virtua interruption and obstruction of ordinary trade negotiations.
4. Breaking out of war between the country of the maker and tha of the holder.
5. Occupation of the country where the parties live, or where th note is payable, by a public enemy, which suspends commercial inter course.
6. Public and positive interdictions and prohibitions of the state which obstruct or suspend commerce and intercourse.
7. Utter impracticability of finding the maker or ascertaining his place of residence.

When the cause of delay ceases to operate, presentment must be made with reasonable diligence. Where the holder of a note has died, and no executor or administrator has qualified to present the note for payment, presentment for payment within a reasonable time after appointment and qualification of the executor or administrator is sufficient.

Effect of failure to give timely notice of non-payment of a note. The general rule is that if an indorser is not given notice of the fact at a note has been dishonored by non-payment, he is discharged om liability. The reason for this rule is that an indorser has a right be put into possession of the material facts on which his liability based, so that he may take the steps necessary for his own protec-on. Notice of non-payment may be given over the telephone, in ersonal conversation, or by writing, and may be conveyed in any rms which sufficiently identify the instrument and indicate that it as been dishonored by non-payment. An indorser may waive notice f non-payment orally or in writing, in which case his liability at-ches although proper notice of non-payment is not given to him. he waiver need not be direct and positive, but may be implied from sage, understanding between the parties, or from any acts or con-uct clearly calculated to mislead the holder and prevent him from reating the note as he otherwise would. To constitute an implied aiver, the acts of the indorser must be such as would warrant the older in not taking the steps necessary to charge the indorser. As n the case of timely presentment of a note for payment, delay in iving notice of dishonor is excused when the delay is caused by cir-umstances beyond the control of the holder and not imputable to is default, misconduct, or negligence; but when the cause of delay eases to operate, notice must be given with reasonable diligence.

Law Relating to Drafts or Bills of Exchange

What is a draft or bill of exchange? The terms "draft" and "bill of exchange" are used interchangeably. A bill of exchange is an in-strument drawn by one person ordering a second person to pay a definite sum of money to a third person on sight or at some definite future time. If payable on sight, the draft is a "sight draft"; if pay-able at some future time, the draft is a "time draft." The person who draws the bill of exchange is the "drawer"; the person who is to pay the bill is the "drawee" or "acceptor"; the person to whom the money is to be paid is the "payee." A person may, and frequently does, draw a draft to his own order upon another.

Difference between a draft and a check. The Negotiable In-struments Law expressly defines a check as "a bill of exchange drawn on a bank payable on demand." A check is, therefore, included in the term "bill of exchange," but it differs from the ordinary draft or bill of exchange in the following important respects:

1. A check is always drawn on a bank, and it is always payable o demand; a draft may or may not be drawn on a bank, and it is ge erally made payable a fixed period of time after sight. A bill of e change, drawn on a bank and payable on demand, is a check.

2. A draft must be presented to the drawee for acceptance; a chec need be presented only for payment.

3. Death of the drawer of a bill of exchange does not revoke th drawee's authority to pay the bill, but death of the drawer of a chec does revoke the bank's authority to honor the instrument.

4. In the case of a draft, delay by the holder in presenting the dra to the drawee for payment may discharge the drawer; in the case c a check, failure to present promptly for payment discharges th maker of the check only if he has sustained injury by the delay.

Difference between a draft and a note. Whereas a bill of ex change involves three parties—the drawer, the drawee, and the paye —a note, before endorsement, involves only two parties—the make and the payee. Prior to his acceptance of the draft, the drawee i not liable, whereas the maker of a promissory note is liable and th note may be collected by suit. Upon acceptance, a bill of exchang becomes, in effect, a promissory note; the acceptor or drawee corre sponds to the maker and is primarily liable, and the drawer corre sponds to the first indorser who is secondarily liable. The Negotia ble Instruments Law provides that "where in a bill the drawer and drawee are the same person, or where the drawee is a fictitious per son, or a person not having capacity to contract, the holder may trea the instrument, at its option, either as a bill of exchange or a promis sory note."

Necessity of presenting a bill of exchange for acceptance. Ac ceptance of a bill of exchange is the signification by the drawee of his assent to the order of the drawer. Where a bill of exchange is pay able at a certain time or on demand, it is not necessary to present it for acceptance in order to hold the drawer or an indorser liable thereon, although it is customary to do so. Where, however, the bil is made payable a designated length of time after sight, it must be presented for acceptance, for otherwise the maturity date of the bill cannot be ascertained. Under the Negotiable Instruments Law, a drawee is allowed twenty-four hours after presentment in which to

:cide whether or not he will accept the bill, but if he does accept, .e maturity date is reckoned from the day of presentation.

Necessity of presenting a bill of exchange for payment. Failure present a bill of exchange to the drawee for payment does not re- ase the acceptor of the bill from liability. But presentment for ayment is necessary in order to charge the drawer. Where the bill f exchange is not payable on demand but at a fixed or ascertainable me, it must be presented on the day it falls due. If it is payable n demand, it may be presented within a reasonable time after the ıst negotiation of the bill. The bill of exchange must be presented or payment at the place specified in the instrument. If not so pecified, it must be presented at the address of the person by whom ayment is to be made, given in the instrument, or if not so given, hen at the usual place of business or residence of such person.

Necessity of protesting an inland bill of exchange, dishonored or non-acceptance or non-payment. An inland bill of exchange is lefined by the Negotiable Instruments Law as "a bill which is, or on ts face purports to be, both drawn and payable within the state." Any other bill is a foreign bill. Unless the contrary appears on the face of the bill, the holder may treat it as an inland bill. It is important to distinguish between a foreign bill of exchange and an inland bill, for a foreign bill which is dishonored by non-acceptance or non-payment is required to be protested * before the drawer of the bill can be held liable, but an inland bill of exchange need not be so protested. All that is necessary in the case of an inland bill is that notice be given to the drawer of the fact of dishonor. The Negotiable Instruments Law specifically provides that where a foreign bill of exchange, appearing on its face to be such, is dishonored by non-acceptance, it must be duly protested for non-acceptance, and where such a bill which has not previously been dishonored by non-acceptance is dishonored by non-payment, it must be duly protested for non-payment. It further provides that if the bill is not so protested, the drawer and indorsers are discharged, but that protest is unnecessary where the bill does not on its face appear to be a foreign bill.

---

* "Protest" is the making of a formal certification, generally by a notary, attesting the refusal to accept or pay a bill of exchange.

If a drawee accepts a forged bill of exchange, has he any r course? It is the duty of the drawee of a bill of exchange to satisf himself that the signature of the drawer is genine before he accep it, for by his acceptance he is deemed to admit the genuineness of th drawer's signature. If he accepts a bill of exchange on which th drawer's signature is forged, he can neither repudiate his acceptanc nor recover any money which he has paid to a bona fide holder c the instrument. The drawee of a bill of exchange is not, howeve bound to know the signature of the payee, and if he pays a bill c exchange containing a forged indorsement, he may recover th amount from the person to whom payment was made. Similarl the drawee is not presumed to know whether or not any part of bill of exchange, other than the drawer's signature, is genuine, and i the bill has been altered, the drawee has a right to recover th amount paid on the bill to an indorser.

4. HOW TO WRITE CREDIT LETTERS

Letters asking customers for credit information. Letters of thi type must be written with great tact, especially if they are to be sen by mercantile houses to small concerns that may not be familiar with customary credit procedure, or by retailers to persons who have prob ably had little business experience. The customer must not be given the impression that the letter is a reflection upon his standing, that his credit is considered doubtful, or that he is being singled out for special investigation. The fact should be made clear that the request for credit references or for a financial statement is merely standard business practice. The tone of the letter should not be negative or formal, but courteous and individual.

New customers. When a letter is received from a new customer requesting credit, or a request is received with an order, or merely an order is received, the letter to the customer requesting credit information will accomplish its purpose if it is constructed as follows:

1. Welcome the customer and thank him for his inquiry or order.
2. Explain or suggest your usual credit procedure or policy.
3. Ask the customer for credit references or for a financial statement. Enclose a printed form for him to fill out and return.
4. Stimulate prompt action by showing the customer that it is to his own interest to supply the necessary information at once, and ex-

ress the hope that his inquiry or order is the beginning of a friendly nd mutually profitable business relationship.

Old customers. In connection with a periodic revision of the redit files, it may be necessary to write to old customers for an up-o-date financial statement. The folowing is a practical outline for letter of this type:

1. Thank the customer for his past business.
2. State that you are revising your credit files and are asking all your customers to supply you with a new financial statement. Make t clear that this request is being made of all your customers.
3. Ask the customer to provide you with the necessary information. Enclose a printed form for him to fill out and return.
4. Assure the customer of your willingness to co-operate with him, as in the past.

Sell the idea to the customer in a persuasive, sympathetic letter with constructive ideas presented cheerfully and considerately.

Reply to customer who refuses credit information. Although most people are familiar with the necessity for giving credit information, a customer occasionally refuses to complete the form sent him. Following is a practical outline for a letter of reply covering this situation.

1. Thank the customer for his letter and for the opportunity it gives you to explain your credit policy. Express regret that your previous letter has given rise to misunderstanding.
2. Explain that request for credit information is merely standard business practice; that no reflection is intended; that the information is treated as strictly confidential; and that you yourself give information concerning your own financial standing to the houses from whom you buy.
3. Assure the customer that his business will be appreciated, and that you will be glad to co-operate with him in every way, and renew your request that he fill out and return the printed form.

Example of letter to customer who refuses to give credit information:

Dear Mr. Clark:

I am glad of the opportunity that your letter of June 6 gives me to explain our request of June 1. I am very sorry that you feel that our asking you to fill out a property statement casts reflection upon your credi standing. No reflection whatsoever was intended.

Our request was merely in line with our usual credit policy. It is a practice with us, as with most established business houses, to ask each new customer to fill out and return a form identical with the one sent you. That we intended no reflection upon you is indicated by the fact that we follow this procedure in opening all new accounts.

We feel that we and our customers are partners in business, and that without a friendly and frank exchange of credit information there cannot be complete co-operation between us. Furthermore, we would always much rather place our confidence in your own statement than in any reports we might obtain from other sources.

We ourselves are glad to supply our creditors with such information about our own standing as we requested from you, because we know that without their co-operation we could not do business on our present scale. We therefore feel that our creditors are entitled to know our financial condition.

Credit is very largely a matter of mutual confidence. We, as the seller, show our confidence in you by accepting your credit. You, as the buyer, show your confidence in us by your willingness to indicate a few essential facts regarding your business.

We hope that you will co-operate with us by supplying the information requested. We assure you that it is intended solely for our files, and that we regard it as strictly confidential. We shall greatly appreciate your business and shall do everything in our power to make our relationship pleasant and profitable to you.

Very truly yours,

Letters of inquiry to customer's credit references. Letters requesting credit information from references supplied by the customer may be brief and concise and should offer to reciprocate when occasion arises. If definite information is desired, ask specific questions or enclose a printed form to be filled out and returned. Letters of this type are usually form letters.

Example of letter to credit references requesting information:

Gentlemen:

The person or firm named below wishes to open an account with us, and has given your name as a credit reference.

Mr. James S. Wilson

....

256 Maple Avenue

....

Newark, N. J.

....

Any information you may furnish us will be treated as strictly confidential.

We shall appreciate an early reply, and assure you of our willingness to reciprocate at any time. A stamped, addressed envelope is enclosed for your convenience.

Very truly yours,

Letters granting credit. A letter granting credit should state clearly the terms of payment, so that there may be no subsequent misunderstanding. It need not, however, be written merely in formal or routine style; it represents an opportunity to capitalize on the customer's interest in the firm and its products. Hence a good letter of this type shows appreciation of the account and ties the customer to the house by creating goodwill and emphasizing service.

Example of letter granting credit:

Dear Mr. Whittemore:

We are very glad to extend to you, in accordance with your request of March 12, our most favorable credit terms, 2/10 net 30.

The information which we have received concerning you is so completely favorable to you personally and as a businessman that we appreciate your choosing us to supply you with merchandise. Your order is going forward today.

We want you to feel that the quality, delivery, and prices which brought us this first order are also to be found in all the other electrical supplies we carry, such as electrical devices manufactured by the Westinghouse Electric & Manufacturing Company and other substantial organizations.

And as our acquaintance ripens, and you become more familiar with our stock, the feeling will grow that for anything and everything electrical, you can depend on Hyland as a sure and constant source of supply.

Please be assured of our appreciation for this initial order. We shall strive to do everything possible to cause it to be but the first of many.

Very truly yours,

Letter to husband of credit applicant. If the applicant for credit is a married woman, in addition to sending a letter to her similar to that described in the preceding paragraphs, one is also sent to the husband. While the purpose of such a letter obviously is to inform the husband that an account has been opened for his wife, the letter is given a sales slant. In the following example, the men's store is introduced to the husband. The letter takes the form of an engraved four-page announcement measuring 5½ x 7 inches. The company seal takes the place of a letterhead. On the third page is a statement of terms. On the last page is a statement of the ideals of th store and a list of addresses at which stores are located.

It is a pleasure to inform you that, as requested by your wife, a charg account has been opened for your joint use.

You will enjoy shopping for your personal needs in .... stores for men, where we hope to have the privilege of serving you often

Letters refusing credit. A letter refusing credit should be courte ous and constructive. It should convince the applicant that the refusal is made with his best interests in mind and that some other form of purchase at present is to his advantage. Such a letter may be constructed as follows:

1. Cheerfully thank the applicant for providing you with credit information.
2. Analyze the applicant's financial condition. Begin with the more favorable aspects and pass tactfully to the less favorable. Explain frankly, but sympathetically, the reasons for your decision not to grant credit. Do not be vague or apologetic.
3. Suggest a definite and practical means by which he can improve his credit standing in order to place himself in a position to receive credit. The suggestion may be that he try to secure addtional capital, that he reduce his inventory by disposing of out-of-date merchandise, that he expand the scope of his business only with caution, and the like. Offer the firm's co-operation.
4. Try to get the customer's business on a cash basis. Retain goodwill by appealing to his sense of sound business policy and thus leave the way open for business relations in the future.

Example of letter refusing credit:

Dear Mr. Benson:

Thank you very much for your business statement of March 1 and also for the references.

We sincerely appreciate this evidence of your interest in our goods. All the references you gave us spoke very highly of you, both personally and as a businessman.

We regret, however, that we feel we are unable—for the present at least—to grant the credit accommodation you ask. From a study of your assets and liabilities it appears to us that you are, frankly, somewhat undercapitalized. In our opinion, however, it is only a matter of time until you will be able to remedy this situation. With your personal ability ıd a favorable location for a hardware store in Westport, there is every ıdication that your future prospects are excellent. As a constructive ıggestion we would advise that you secure $2,500 additional capital if is at all possible for you to do so.

In the meantime, we recommend that you cut your order to us by one-alf and that you advise us to ship to you on a cash basis. You will re-eive a 2% discount for cash, and the balance of your order can be for-varded at a moment's notice if you find that you need it. By cutting our order in half you will lessen the risk of having your shelves over-tocked.

As soon as it appears that accepting your credit will not jeopardize our prospects, we shall be glad to co-operate with you by selling to you n open account. For the present we offer you our most favorable cash erms and assure you of our desire to be of service.

We hope that the arrangement suggested will appeal to you as tem-porarily the most satisfactory from your own standpoint. We are ready o make immediate shipment if you will give us a favorable reply.

Sincerely yours,

Letter referring unacceptable accounts to the Credit Bureau. Frequently the credit man does not wish to undertake an analysis and constructive criticism of the applicant's credit position when his credit cannot be accepted, and prefers instead to refer him to the credit bureau. This is particularly true of retail stores. Should this be the case, the following letter may be used:

Dear Mrs. Smith:

We acknowledge with thanks your application for a charge account, but regret our inability to accommodate you at this time.

The Credit Bureau of Chicago, which is the Clearing House for credit information on individuals purchasing in Chicago, has been unable, from the material on hand, to furnish us with sufficient data to warrant our approval of your application.

May we suggest that you call personally at the office of the Bureau and supply such additional data as may be required to complete its records. The Bureau will then report to us.

Very truly yours,
Director of Accounts

Letters to insistent customers who are not desirable. Instances occur where the credit department does not want the account of a certain customer who has insisted upon credit. The following letter may be used. Notice that it makes no mention of patronizing the store on a cash basis, the reason being that the credit manager felt it would be presumptuous to ask for cash under the circumstances.

Dear Mrs. Doe:

We appreciate your interest in opening a charge account with (nam of store), but regret our inability to complete arrangements for you this time.

It is hoped that there may be other ways in which we can be of servic

Yours very truly,
Director of Accounts

Letter where credit is refused and merchandise is delivered. If customer was permitted to take goods with her at the time the appli cation for credit was made, or if the merchandise was delivered im mediately, and investigation shows the account to be undesirable, letter such as the following may be used:

Dear Mrs. Henry:

We appreciate your interest in opening a charge account with (nam of store), but regret our inability to complete arrangements for you a this time.

However, as an accommodation, we delivered and charged the mer chandise which you selected at the time of making the application. You will receive a bill on the first of the month which will be payable in ful by the tenth.

It is hoped that there may be other ways in which we may be of service to you.

Yours very truly,
Director of Accounts

Letter suspending charge privilege before credit period expires. Frequently the credit department finds it necessary to suspend temporarily the charge privilege before the time for payment expires, because the credit limit has been exceeded. In such a case, the following letter may be used:

Dear Mrs. Smith:

All stores doing a credit business place a limit on each account up to which they will accept charges without question as long as the account is paid promptly. This is done to provide control on the amounts owed by customers.

KIRKMAN'S customers establish their own limits in the sense that the amount of each customer's average monthly payments is considered the limit on that account. We are writing you now because, in approving your recent charge, we noticed that your account exceeds your charge limit, which has been determined according to our established methods.

For this reason we should appreciate your calling at the Credit Depart-ıent before making any further charges. I am sure that satisfactory arıngements can be made at that time. If we have made an error in your harge limit, we shall be glad to discuss the matter with you when you re next in the store.

Thank you for your co-operation, Mrs. Smith.

Very truly yours,

Letters of reply to credit inquiries. In replying to credit inuiries, the credit man should satisfy himself that the inquirer will reat the information confidentially and that the information offered iolates no confidence. The reply should be frank and specific and s helpful to the inquirer as possible. Replies are often so worded hat no express or implied responsibility is assumed by the writer.

Because of the law of libel, caution must be exercised where the eply is unfavorable. Many firms omit any mention of the subject's ıame and address and make their statements as general as possible vhen sending derogatory information.

A standard form for reporting on ledger experience has been preıared by the National Association of Credit Men.

5. HOW TO WRITE COLLECTION LETTERS

Acknowledgment is made to John Whyte and F. R. Otte for permission to reproduce letters from "Letters That Collect" (New York: Prentice-Hall, Inc.)

Two essentials of the effective collection letter. The effective collection letter is one that is written with two purposes in mind:

1. Getting the money.
2. Keeping the customer's goodwill and business.

To accomplish the first purpose without regard to the second is relatively easy, but to accomplish both purposes requires a high degree of skill. The letters reproduced in this section have been selected, on the basis of proved effectiveness, from actual collection correspondence; they represent a cross section of the work of trained and experienced collection men.

Classification of delinquent debtors. From the standpoint of collections, debtors may be classified somewhat as follows:

1. Customers who overlook accounts simply because of negligence or poor business methods.

2. Customers who disregard due dates because of the smallne of the account.
3. Customers who could pay promptly but disregard due dates be cause they think it is more profitable for them to use the creditor money than the bank's.
4. Customers who take unearned discounts because they expect t "get away with it," and because it is profitable for them to take thes discounts.
5. Customers who are temporarily slow, but who usually pay o time. They pay on time when the due dates of the creditor's bil coincide with the seasonal high points in their own business, and the make the creditor wait when these periods do not coincide.
6. Customers who are chronically slow.
7. Customers who are temporarily slow because of local trade con ditions.
8. Customers who are verging on insolvency or who are actuall insolvent.
9. Customers who are crooked or deliberately fraudulent.

Placing the customer in one of the above classes, on the basis o information obtained from the ledger, from the salesman, and pos sibly from interchange reports or trade-group discussions, simplifie the collection problem and indicates the type of treatment that wil be likely to prove most effective.

Fundamental principles for writing collection letters. The fundamental principles that apply to writing any effective business letter apply to collection letters. In addition, observe these three important principles:

1. Be specific—do not hesitate to ask for a check.
2. Use dated action—tell the debtor that the creditor expects certain action by a given date, not "in the near future."
3. Avoid the *divided urge*—concentrate upon one action and do not suggest an alternative.

Here is an extract from a letter that illustrates these principles:

So that you may begin to get your account with us in better shape we must ask for a payment of not less than $100. Please mail this payment to arrive at our office within five days, which means by Saturday.

Suggestions for writing collection letters. The following sugges-ons may be used as a guide in writing collection letters:

1. Be cheerful, optimistic, and constructive in considering the ebtor's predicament.

2. Visualize and individualize the debtor, know his kind of de-inquency, his business, its location and its condition. Consult the redit files, salesmen, and, if necessary, the debtor himself.

3. Adopt the "you" attitude. This does not mean that the per-onal pronoun need be used constantly, but that behind every word here lies sympathetic consideration of the individual case.

4. Beware of brevity. A too-short collection letter becomes curt ınd gives the impression of dunning.

5. When writing to women, avoid the colloquial, breezy style that night be suitable for other debtors.

6. The tone of the strong collection letter should be, wherever possible, one of fairness and goodwill. There should be no hint of exasperation. There are times, however, when a forceful letter be-comes necessary. Before writing one, it is well to obtain legal advice, for certain threats are punishable by law. An uncounseled letter night easily do more harm than good. Many credit men wait until the next day after a forceful letter is written before mailing it.

7. Fix a definite schedule for writing collection letters, preferably in the morning. Correspondents are not interrupted by rush requests for information, and the afternoon is left free for other credit work. Furthermore, letters can be in the mail by the end of the day, which minimizes discrepancies between status of account when the letter is written and when it is mailed.

8. Omit, whenever possible, such words as "enforce," "insist," "de-mand," "compel," "handle," "impossible," "unable," and "annoyed." These are negative words that serve only to irritate the customer.

Stages in collection procedure. Although the circumstances of each individual case necessarily modify the collection procedure, col-lection correspondence is largely based on the cumulative effect of repetition and variety of appeal. The typical unpaid account passes through the following stages of collection correspondence:

1. Reminder.
2. Inquiry.
3. Appeal.
4. Demand.

In this section letters are presented in the following groups: (1 reminders; (2) letters for the early stages of collection; (3) letters fc the middle stages of collection; and (4) letters for the late stages c collection.

Collection Reminders

Forms of reminder. In the first stage it may be assumed that th customer's failure to pay is due to forgetfulness or carelessness. It i therefore necessary to bring the status of the account to the custom er's attention. For this purpose a mild and inoffensive reminde may be used; his reminder may take one of a number of forms.

1. *Duplicate bill or statement and reminder phrase.* A reminde may consist of duplicate bill or statement, on which is prominentl typewritten or rubber-stamped a phrase such as:

> Past due.
> Please remit.
> Account past due. Please remit.
> Please!
> A prompt remittance will be appreciated.
> Please mail us a check.
> May we have check, please?
> Blank days past due. Please remit promptly.
> Please give this your attention.

2. *Stickers.* More forceful than a typewritten or rubber-stampec phrase is a sticker attached to a duplicate bill or statement. Exam ples of stickers are reproduced in Figure 81.

3. *Printed cards.* A reminder may consist of a printed card, with out salutation or signature, on which details as to the standing of the account are filled in. These cards are often preferable to letters for the first reminder since they are impersonal and customers realize that all other delinquents are receiving them under the same circum stances. They should be courteously worded to show fairness, to recall the agreed credit terms, and to impress customers with their impersonal and impartial nature. If the charge privilege is to be tem porarily suspended, the card should warn the customer without giving offense.

Brief reminders that may be used on such a card are the following:

> We respectfully request your immediate attention to the past-due account.

Courtesy, Ever Ready Label Corp.

Figure 81. Collection Stickers.

Just another friendly reminder of our terms which are ordinarily-monthly in full.

You have perhaps allowed this account to escape your notice. Pleas give it your attention.

This statement is sent to you for comparison and as a reminder c mutual understanding as to terms.

Another type of printed card for collection reminder is a simpl notice enclosed with the statement. This eliminates any extra ad dressing and mailing expenses and ties it in immediately with th unpaid account. A different color may be used for each card to pre vent sending of the wrong notice. Notices may be printed on light weight paper, safety bond paper, or card stock of about 3 x 5 inches The seal of a credit organization occasionally embellishes these cards

4. *Combination statement and reminder message.* The reminde correspondence for the first stage of a series of collection letters may be combined with a statement, as illustrated in Figure 82, or ma be a brief form letter as illustrated below:

Gentlemen:

If you have not already done so, won't you mail us a check to cove your due account, $256.34?

We shall be grateful for prompt attention.

Very truly yours,

The Denoyer-Geppert Company, Chicago, through whose courtesy the illustration on page 1047 is reproduced, has used a series of four combination statements and letters. A different color is used for each unit of the series. The statement-letters are folded and enclosed in window envelopes; it is thus necessary to type the customer's name only once—for letter, statement, and envelope.

5. *Age analysis and reminder.* A statement analyzing the overdue balance according to actual monthly purchases has proved an effective way to begin the collection drive against overdue accounts. To many customers, particularly women, a statement sent, for example, in November showing an August balance is more startling than one showing a balance 90 days old. The statement illustrated in Figure 83 is sent 45 days after the bill and is interchanged with card reminders twice a month until the account reaches a six months classification. At that time a series of letters stressing the urgency of payment is started.

6. *Envelope message.* A collection envelope has been used suc-

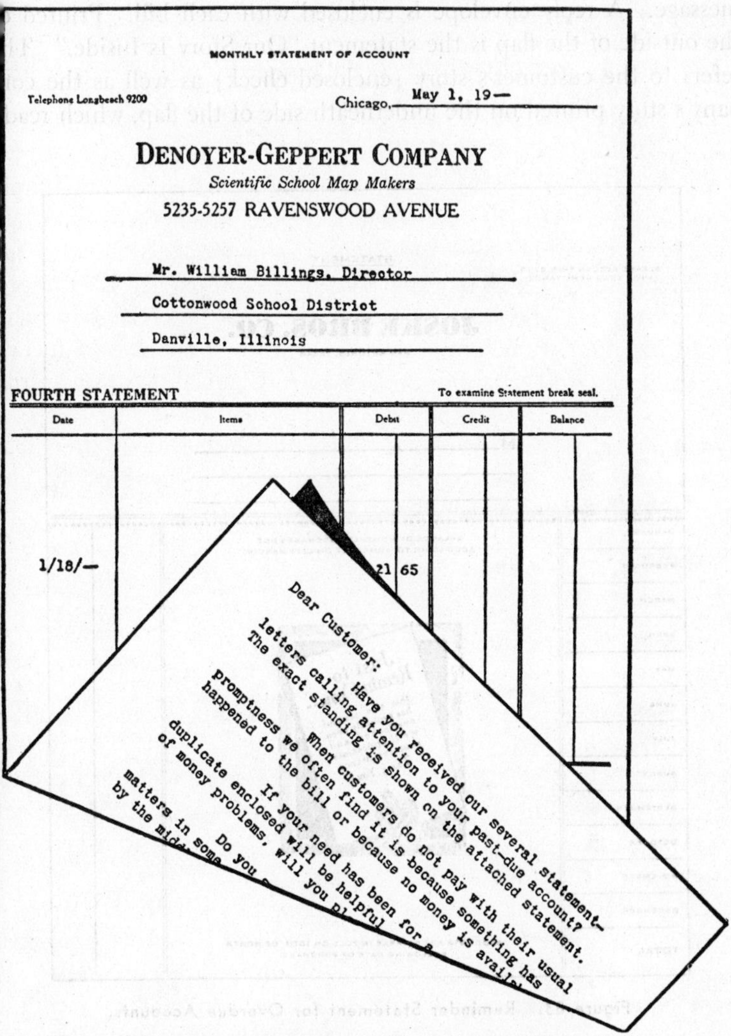
MONTHLY STATEMENT OF ACCOUNT

Telephone Longbeach 9200 Chicago, May 1, 19—

DENOYER-GEPPERT COMPANY
Scientific School Map Makers
5235-5257 RAVENSWOOD AVENUE

Mr. William Billings, Director
Cottonwood School District
Danville, Illinois

FOURTH STATEMENT To examine Statement break seal.

Date	Items	Debit	Credit	Balance
1/18/—		21 65		

Dear Customer:

Have you received our several statement-letters calling attention to your past-due account? The exact standing is shown on the attached statement.

When customers do not pay with their usual promptness we often find it is because something has happened to the bill or because no money is availa...

If your need has been for a ... duplicate enclosed will be helpful ... of money problems, will you pl...

Do you ... matters in some ... by the midd...

Figure 82. A Combination Statement and Letter.

cessfully, especially by firms in the clothing industry. The name and address of the creditor is printed on the envelope, making it ready for mailing.

Another variation of the use of an envelope to hasten collections in the reminder stage is the combination of envelope with collection message. A reply envelope is enclosed with each bill. Printed o the outside of the flap is the statement "Our Story Is Inside." Th refers to the customer's story (enclosed check) as well as the cor pany's story printed on the underneath side of the flap, which read

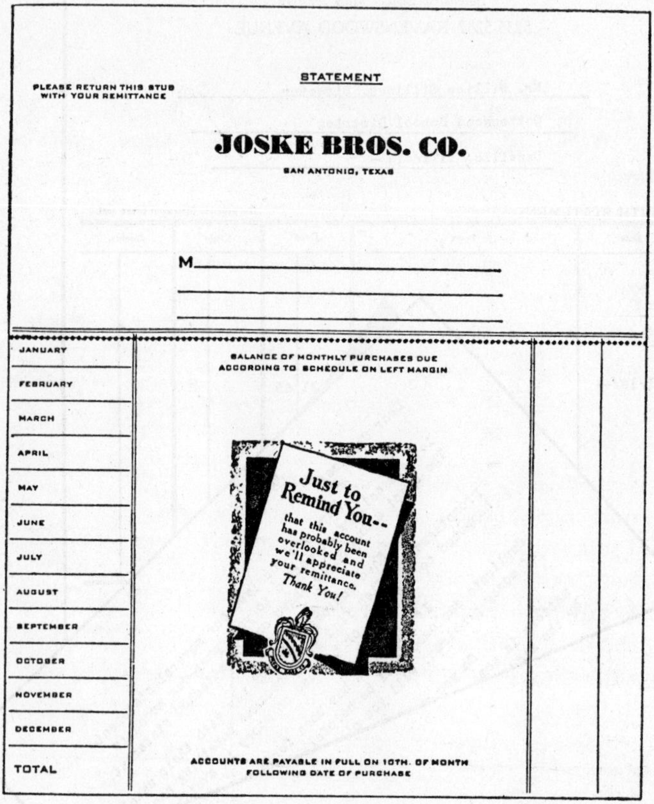
PLEASE RETURN THIS STUB WITH YOUR REMITTANCE

STATEMENT

JOSKE BROS. CO.

SAN ANTONIO, TEXAS

M

JANUARY
FEBRUARY
MARCH
APRIL
MAY
JUNE
JULY
AUGUST
SEPTEMBER
OCTOBER
NOVEMBER
DECEMBER
TOTAL

BALANCE OF MONTHLY PURCHASES DUE ACCORDING TO SCHEDULE ON LEFT MARGIN

ACCOUNTS ARE PAYABLE IN FULL ON 10TH. OF MONTH FOLLOWING DATE OF PURCHASE

Figure 83. Reminder Statement for Overdue Accounts.

OUR INSIDE STORY

One of our ideas about being in business is to be as helpful as we can to our customers. We even help them pay their bills by sending them handy return envelopes like this one.

Won't you slip your check into this envelope to balance your account and help us with our collections? Thank you.

When the flap is opened, there appears a reminder printed on the body of the envelope, which is covered when the flap is sealed. The reminder reads:

MEMO STATEMENT

of Your Account

Balance Due . . . . $. . . . .

THANK YOU

7. *Oversight letter.* Should the collection department desire to use the "oversight" approach for its reminder letter, the following letter may serve as a guide:

Dear Mr. Kirkman:

Your account with us shows a balance of $. . . . ., which is now past due. This is possibly an oversight. We therefore call it to your attention now.

You may overlook this matter again if you put this letter aside, so why not attach a check to it right now and return it in the enclosed envelope.

Very truly yours,

Letters for the Early Stages of Collection

Second stage: Letters of inquiry. In the second stage of the collection series, assuming that one or two reminders have not brought a response, the creditor should make a direct inquiry as to why the bill has not been paid. Is there a legitimate reason for the delay? Or is the debtor just stalling off as long as he can? If the creditor has no traveling representative in the territory, he will have to write and ask the cause. Does it lie with the creditor's goods or services? Are the debtor's collections slow? Are local conditions strained? If the debtor replies with an explanation, the creditor should offer every assistance to help him through his difficulties.

Examples of letters in the second stage. Following are examples of letters that can be used in the second stage in the collection series:

Dear Sir:

It's rather a novelty to have occasion to write you concerning your account for any purpose other than to thank you for a check, for an account such as yours is a boon to a business house.

However, it would appear, unless our records are wrong, that your June account, amounting to $78.50, has not met your customary prompt pa- ment.

Have we made any mistake, or are there any special circumstances th have held up payment of this account?

Very truly yours,

* * *

Gentlemen:

You are one of our new customers, and this is our first credit relatio with you. Our three statements and our letter of March 3 have as y been unanswered. This would indicate that something is wrong.

Did we not come to a satisfactory credit understanding?

Have we made some mistake in the charge?

How do you wish us to handle your account?

By all means be frank in telling us if any mistake has been made, fo you will find us more than willing to correct it.

Very truly yours,

* * *

Gentlemen:

Is there something wrong with the merchandise covered by the abov sum? Do you question the correctness of the charge?

If so, you have only to tell us about it—on the back of this letter, i you wish—and we shall be glad to go into the matter thoroughly wit you.

If everything is satisfactory, but you just haven't got around to sendin in your check, surely you will want to forward it to us now.

Very truly yours,

A sharper tone for a second letter. In certain instances, such as for the poor risk, the second letter of a collection series should assume a slightly sharper tone, as illustrated in the following letter:

Gentlemen:

We have no way of knowing, unless you tell us, why we have not received payment of our invoices of (date—amount) and (date—amount).

We know that you must have a good reason, but that neither settles the account nor enlightens us as to why we should carry it any longer. You cannot expect us to let it drift along without some explanation. It will take you only a moment to write us a letter and put the facts before us. We are sure that our attitude is understandable, for we must have some knowledge of the situation in order to know just where we stand in the matter.

Why not write us about it now?

Very truly yours,

Letters for the Middle Stages of Collection

Third stage: Letters of appeal. The third letter of a collection series will depend largely upon the reply to the second. If the debtor responds with an actual grievance, or if circumstances beyond his control make payment impossible, the creditor's reply will take on an appropriate personal character. If there is no reply, however, the debtor is obviously trying to avoid payment and needs more urgent prodding. Send the poor risk either a draft or a very strong letter. Try to induce payment from the medium or good risk by appealing to such motives as pride, duty, justice and fairness, or self-interest.

An appeal to pride addressed to a new customer. The following letter, sent as the third letter in a collection series to a new customer, appeals to his pride in his reputation among his associates.

Dear Sir:

You will remember that, when you placed an order with us last January, you furnished us with some references to whom we wrote for the purpose of establishing an account in your name. We did not know you ourselves, never having done business with you, and depended entirely upon what these other people and you told us; and when they said you would take care of an account promptly, we trusted you without any hesitation.

However, instead of paying our accounts promptly, you have permitted them to remain unpaid, so that, at this time, we find there are owing two January bills of $24.46 and $35.28, respectively. We have written you about these bills three times, unsuccessfully. Now, of course, there may be some reason why you haven't been able to take care of them, but it would seem that if this is the case you would write us and not permit us to form an erroneous impression of the manner in which you take care of your obligations.

Won't you please let us have your check for $59.74 immediately, so that it will not be necessary to mark your account as slow pay?

Yours very truly,

An appeal to pride, addressed to an old customer:

Dear Mr. Hogan:

We regret very much to find that your account is gradually becoming larger and that your purchases during the current month far exceed your payments.

We have always considered your firm one of our banner customers, and we take it for granted that there is some just reason why you are withholding payment. If that be the case, won't you let us know? Or, bett still, just step into our office and go over the matter with us so that w may adjust it to the satisfaction of both.

We want you to know that we greatly appreciate your account an want you to continue on our books.

This account is now sixty days past due and we know that you do n want that condition to exist.

If it is not convenient for you to come to our office, just call the writ on the telephone, and we may be able to adjust the account.

Very truly yours,

An appeal to co-operation based on mutual interest. A letter tha appeals to co-operation based on mutual interest can be used as th third in a series of collection correspondence.

Dear Mr. Fisk:

We are going to make an extra appeal for payment of your accoun because we must have your full support if our relations with each oth are to be profitable to both of us.

You know that we are interested in your business, and that we ar eager to be of assistance to you. But you place us in a difficult positio when you do not pay our bills—you discourage by just so much our effort to be of most service to you.

We still feel that you want to work with us, so we have hesitated t put our request for payment in the form of a demand. Yet we do thin that we are not unreasonable in asking for and expecting your check a once.

Very truly yours,

An appeal to the customer's sense of honor. The third letter of collection correspondence series appealing to the customer's sense o honor is effective if the customer was fully informed of the credi terms when he received credit. Failure to pay at maturity mean breaking the contract to which he bound himself by accepting th shipment. For this reason the appeal to honor usually stresses th contractual obligation. It will be effective only insofar as credi men conscientiously educate their cusotmers to realize the sanctit of their credit obligation. The following letter makes this appeal:

Gentlemen:

We are unwilling to assume that businessmen of your standing woul intentionally neglect our account or ignore the many letters received fron us concerning it.

We expressed our confidence in you when we delivered, on open terms, e goods covered by our April bill of $43.90, and we are reluctant to ink that that confidence was misplaced. We have been glad to serve ou in the past, and undoubtedly you will want further credit accommoations in the future. If you are to preserve your standing with us, however, you must see to it that immediate provisions are made for settleent of your account.

We know that there are times when the bills seem to pile up faster than e money to pay them. If you have run across some adverse conditions, lease tell us about it. If you are not in a position to remit our entire ill now, please let us have a check for half immediately and a second heck for the balance post-dated a week or ten days.

We believe that you want to adjust matters in a friendly way, and we rust that you will accept our invitation to let us hear from you by return ail.

Yours very truly,

An appeal to the customer's sense of fairness. Another effective ppeal in a collection letter is one to the customer's sense of fairness. mply that he has not been treating the firm fairly; the creditor has elivered satisfactory goods and services; and the debtor should in ustice pay promptly and satisfactorily.

entlemen:

It is necessary for us to call attention to your account for the months f September and October, which is still unpaid. The September acount, under the liberal terms that we are extending to you, should have een paid on or before October 20.

When your account became due, it was not paid, and of course it was atural for you to order your supplies elsewhere. For that reason we ave not received any of your orders for thirty days.

In all fairness, we want to ask whether you think it is right that the eward for carrying your account during the past thirty days should be he loss of your business for that length of time. If we had insisted on ayment, would we not still be able to look upon you as an active cusomer?

We appeal to you to send us a check immediately to cover your acount, thereby re-establishing sound business relations and putting us in position again to receive your orders. We are sure that we will hear from you by return mail.

Very truly yours,

Unique appeal to fair play. The note of sincerity in this unique "50-50" letter appeals to the customer's sense of fairness.

OUR HALF of this letter:

You will see at a glance that this is a real "50-50" letter, because exactly one-half of it belongs to you.

Being human, we can appreciate what hard work it is—and we mean just that—for most of us to sit down and write a letter. Also, we can understand how easily payment of a small bill can be unintentionally overlooked. With these things in mind, we are sending you a reply as your half to our half of this letter. All you have to do is sign your name and address in the space provided and return it to us.

We feel sure you want to pay the amount past due on your account. Please meet us on a "50-50" basis—just tear off and mail back your half, and you will have a better understanding of our earnest desire to meet you half way.

DO IT NOW!

YOUR HALF of this letter:

Dear Mr. Simmons:

Of course I will meet you ha way. You have shown the rig spirit—so will I.

I have overlooked forwarding n remittance for the amount due yc up to this time.

Please accept the enclosed pa ment for $....... as an evidenc of my good intentions.

Name ....

Street ....

City ....

State ....

Mat. No. ....

Course ....

An appeal to the customer's self-interest. An appeal to the customer's self-interest probably brings better results, on the whole, than any other appeal. Show the customer that it is to his own personal advantage to pay now, and that prompt payment improves is credit standing and enables the firm to sell at lower prices. Call his attention to the periodical reporting of delinquents to credit associations, without actually suggesting blacklisting. The latter not only destroys goodwill but may render the creditor liable to legal punishment.

Gentlemen:

When your account was opened with us, we had every reason to believe that you would pay it when it became due.

In making the usual credit investigation, we found that all those with whom you had done business spoke very highly of you in a personal way, and declared that you would meet your obligations promptly.

It is therefore difficult for us to understand why you have not taken care of our account amounting to $193.45.

Before investigating further your manner of making payment to others, in which investigation we should, of course, have to state what our exerience has been with you, we want to give you another opportunity to ay your long past-due account with us.

It would not favorably impress those who have recommended you so ighly to learn that our experience has not fully justified the unqualified ecommendations which they gave to us.

Can we plan—definitely—on hearing from you by return mail?

Very truly yours,

Another appeal to the customer's self-interest:

)ear Mr. Becker:

We are enclosing a statement of your account, which shows a balance lue us of $98.23, and for which remittance in accordance with our terms hould have been received on a net basis last month.

Our friends in the trade very frequently call upon us for information s to the financial responsibility and habits of payment of our customers,)ecause they, too, have you on their books, and they like to get the benefit)f our experience.

We want to be able to tell these firms that you take care of your obligations on a discount basis, or that you pay when due.

You, on the other hand, have sufficient regard for your credit reputation to verify this by taking care of your obligations promptly.

With this in mind, we feel sure that you will not wish to allow your ıccount to become delinquent, and we, in turn, will be gratified to report 'good pay" to inquiries regarding your company. Please give us this opportunity and yourself this advantage by sending your check now.

Very truly yours,

Letters for the Late Stages of Collection

Fourth stage: Letters of demand. If the debtor has not replied to the first three letters sent him, the credit man can assume that he is unduly negligent, irresponsible, or has no intention of paying. Write a fourth letter impressing him with the urgency of the situation and demand payment. Drafts are often used at this stage. If his record is bad, threaten to bring suit or to turn the account over to a collection agency. Even a demand letter can retain customer goodwill by restraint in phrasing and an attitude of fairness, and by showing the debtor that the firm has been patient and considerate. Also, caution should be exercised in threatening to resort to force, for a fifth or sixth letter often brings payment. Many solvent merchants, for instance, feel that they can take their time about paying, since the creditor knows that he will eventually get his money. It is a serious mistake to tell a customer that he is getting his last chance to pay before the account is turned over to an agency or attorney fo collection, and then later to write the customer with the same threat Good companies of established reputation do not try to frighten th customer with one letter after another that merely talks about lega action.

Demand letters, formal in tone. Following are examples of de mand letters, formal in tone, that may be used as the fourth letter in a collection series. Notice how the third illustration, particularly adaptable to retail collections, is firm in demanding payment, bu gives the customer the benefit of the doubt.

Dear Sir:

Your neglect of your overdue account—$56.78, now four months pas due—has obliged us to take measures to protect our interests.

We have therefore scheduled the claim to be placed for collection wit the Mercantile Collection Agency on April 15 if it is still unpaid at tha time.

This notice, however, gives you another chance to settle direct.

We trust that you will take advantage of the extension and thereby avoid mutual unpleasantness and expense.

Yours very truly,

* * *

Gentlemen:

We regret keenly that it is necessary to write again about your account

Many lenient efforts to make an arrangement convenient for you have failed, and the time has now arrived when we must take determined steps for collection.

Unless we hear from you within ten days regarding suitable arrangements for settlement of your debt, we shall not hesitate to turn your account over to our attorney for collection without further notice to you.

Yours very truly,

* * *

Dear Miss Jones:

Thus far in our efforts to collect your account, we have proceeded on the assumption that you have the will to pay and intend to do so.

We shall not change this attitude unless you force us to do so. Although you have ignored the letters we have sent you during recent weeks, we are still not quite convinced that you do not intend to pay this bill.

It would be to your interest to call on our credit manager while we are ill in this frame of mind—say, within the next three days.

Very truly yours,

* * *

ear Mrs. Thompson:

As all ordinary means used for collecting your delinquent balance of .... out of court have failed to bring the desired results, we are otifying you that unless this balance is paid in full or suitable arrangeients are made within seven days, it will be placed with the Adjustment)epartment of the Chicago Credit Bureau with instructions to bring suit t once.

Yours very truly,

A *demand letter, more conciliatory in tone:*

ɜentlemen:

We hope that our co-operation with you, in allowing exceptional time or the payment of your past-due account, has been of help to you.

We have been very considerate in this matter and had sincerely hoped hat you would willingly send us your check before this time.

If you have any reason for withholding payment, you should write us ully and frankly at once. You will find us reasonable and willing to coninue our co-operation. However, when an account such as yours runs o long past the due date, and we do not hear from you, there is no alterıative left for us but to place your account in the hands of our attorneys or collection.

We dislike being forced to take this action, as it is not consistent with ɔur policies, and as it will cause you expense and inconvenience.

We hope that you will send us your remittance at once and not make his step an actual necessity.

Yours very truly,

Action to be taken if the fourth letter brings no response. Should the fourth letter still bring no response, many concerns cite success in sending a letter signed by an officer of the company, such as that reproduced below. Send a fifth, sixth, or seventh letter, decreasing the intervals between them by a day. Express confidence in the debtor, yet, at the same time, point out the seriousness of neglecting bills and appeal to the saving that could have been possible through a discount had the bill been paid on time. Courtesy should be the keynote in announcing legal steps.

On the basis of replies to these letters, the creditor will know whether or not, and, if so, when, to turn the account over to an attorney or collection agency. If these letters are sent by registered mail, especially the one announcing recourse to legal action, or are accompanied by a wire, the effect on the debtor will be heightened.

Letters signed by officials of the company:

Dear Mr. Grant:

I was asked this morning to approve placing your account with our attorneys, but before approving such action, I am writing you this letter.

There is one very important reason why neither you nor I should want this action taken. If we sue you we will get our money, but lawsuits destroy the friendly relationship which we take pride in maintaining with our trade. We value your account and are exceedingly reluctant to take any steps that would interrupt our pleasant business relationship. We wish to keep your goodwill and are confident that you wish to keep our

In selling our line of goods, you are setting a high standard of merchandise and, without doubt, you wish to set an equally high standard of business practice. Believing this, we have tried to be fair and certainly have been patient with you. We have now reached the time when your bills must be paid; therefore, unless you show some disposition to protect your credit, I must authorize the placing of your account with our attorneys.

We trust that you will not force us to take this action by further delaying settlement. Help us to avoid drastic action, please, by mailing us your check immediately.

Very truly yours,
President

Writing for part payment before threatening suit. Before writing a fourth or fifth letter in which immediate suit is threatened, it is often good policy to attempt to secure part payment with other payments arranged at specified intervals. This policy has usually been found to bring some sort of reply. Notice in the letter below that the customer has an "out" by which to save face, although there can be little doubt as to what the consequences will be if this letter, too, is ignored.

Gentlemen:

Ninety per cent of the accounts we collect through attorneys are handled that way because customers will not answer our letters.

We are forced to sue because friendly requests bring neither payment nor explanations.

Your account of $....... is long past due. We assume that the amount is correct, for you have never questioned it.

You have disregarded our letters about it; but in spite of that, we really

.nnot believe that you do not care. There must be some other reason. erhaps you cannot pay it all. But don't you think in fairness to yourlf, as well as to us, that you should mail us a check for all you can and ankly say how you are situated and what you can do about the rest?

We both want to keep away from the lawyers if possible. So, before :nding the account to our attorney, we will wait ten days for your letter ıd check.

Yours very truly,

Notifying debtor to honor a draft. A letter that may be sent to ebtors to whom you are sending a draft follows:

;entlemen:

You have received a number of reminders from us regarding your pastue account, which is now too old to be continued. We are giving you final opportunity to make an adjustment without the aid of more drastic ıeasures.

We have therefore drawn upon you today a draft at five days sight, ırough the State National Bank.

We hope that, upon receipt of this letter, you will promptly arrange) take care of the draft when presented, and thus make unnecessary the npleasantness and expense that will result if the account is placed out f our hands.

Yours very truly,

Stunt collection letters. Most collection correspondents shy way from stunt letters, since they feel that these have no place in letter dealing with a serious business matter. Occasionally, however, a stunt will prove the most effective way of collecting an account, especially with dealers. For example, the following rubber and letter did the trick for a company in the women's garment ndustry. In the spot marked by asterisks was pasted a rubber band. The letter was as follows:

)ear Mr. Jones:

Here is a typical, conventional, normal, common, ordinary, everyday, amiliar variety of rubber band.

* * * *

A certain amount of stretching keeps the rubber lively according to ubber manufacturers, but too much stretching will break it.

Credit terms are a lot like that, aren't they? There's a point beyond which they cannot be stretched.

I hope the rubber band will serve as a reminder. You have stretched sufficiently. Send us a check now.

Very truly yours,

A stunt letter with a timely appeal. The Denoyer-Geppert Cor pany. Chicago, used the following stunt letter effectively by havi it prepared as a facsimile handwritten document on an irregula cut sheet of colored paper, somewhat smaller than letterhead siz Part of the company's seal was stamped in the lower left-hand corne Since the company, which manufactures maps, globes, charts, ar models, has a special type of clientele, it was felt that a special typ of approach was advisable.

Treaties? ?

If both of us were European diplomats, we probably would regard ou contractual obligations as mere scraps of paper. You would then fe free to tell us to forget our account, and we would tell our suppliers o raw materials, and our employees the same thing.

But happily, that isn't the American way. We do pay our debts an our customers do admirably well in paying theirs to us.

Right now WE are faced with a large task, in providing funds to mee Fall purchase bills and repaying our bank for loans during the slack sea son (summer). Anything that can conveniently be done to hurry remi tance on the attached statement will be greatly appreciated and will hel in fulfilling our "non-aggression pacts" with bank and suppliers' Cred Departments.

And—apart from the immediate purpose of this letter—may lastin peace come to a troubled World soon.

Done at Chicago, Illinois this first day of September, in the year 19. . in the full faith of

Denoyer-Geppert Co.

Collection letter resembling legal document. Realizing that lega appearing documents are rarely ignored by customers who have long outstanding debts, a firm multigraphed the following collection lette on a sheet of white paper, stapled it into a blue cover, and folded i to resemble a legal form. The tone of the letter takes the "sting" out of the presentation.

Our Accounting Department does solemnly affirm, maintain, and asse that you owe us $. . . . . . . since December 1, 19. . .

We hate to get excited about so small an amount. We also dislik the usual "collection letter" that bursts into tears in the first paragrap and yells for the law in the second.

Trouble is, though, that when you and 999 other customers owe u small bills like this, the sum total is something to give our Mr. Kimbal headache. He was absent from school the day they taught arithmetic, it even he knows that you can't meet payrolls without cash.

Seriously . . . we have tried to be good-humored and patient about ur account, but it HAS run for more than six months. Won't you ease send it *now—by return mail?* Thank you a lot.

One-word follow-up breaks monotony of series. A series of collecon letters, no matter how well-worded or cleverly composed, may ecome monotonous. The following letter, injected in a series, not nly breaks this monotony but usually jolts the reader into attention.

Dear Smith:
Well?

The Ohio Overcoat Co.,
E. M. Flowers, Credits

6. MISCELLANEOUS COLLECTION PROBLEMS HANDLED BY LETTER

Letters on small past-due accounts. The following illustrate the ype of letter that has proved most successful in collecting small pastue accounts.

A *small-account letter, friendly and courteous:*

Dear Mr. Adams:

Each time we write you about that little balance of $4.64 it costs us, verything included, 35 or 40 cents.

The profit on this item has long since been exhausted.

Won't you save us time, money, and annoyance by writing a check for us now, today, while you think of it?

Very truly yours,

Another friendly small-account letter:

Dear Mr. Benson:

When a man is puzzled over the dozen or so problems that come up in veryday business—buying, selling, advertising, and managing a store—ittle matters such as the enclosed account readily slip his mind.

They do with me, and I like to be reminded of them, so I feel sure hat you will be glad to have this again brought to your attention.

The enclosed stamped, addressed envelope offers a quick, easy way of etting the check back to us.

Very truly yours,

A letter on a small item long past due:

Dear Mr. Breden:

The credit and collection department has called to my attention an c balance on your account, amounting to $80.20. This balance is an amou left over from purchases made by you more than a year ago.

You have been a mighty good customer of ours and, compared wi the business that you have given us, the balance of $80.20 is insigni cant. Still, it takes money, you know, to keep the wheels of progre properly oiled and greased, and in order to do this accounts must be co lected. This particular bill that I am writing about happens to be so ol that it has an accumulation of dust on it.

You have been good enough to send us several payments on accou during the year, but it is now pretty close to the end of the year, and am therefore going to ask you please to write out a check for the fu amount and put it in the enclosed addressed envelope so that we ma balance your account when the next mail arrives.

Your personal attention to this will be much appreciated.

Very truly yours,

Letters educating the customer in the use of discounts. Lette such as the following, pointing out to the customer the advantage of taking the cash discount, are often productive of good results.

A lesson on the advantages of discounts:

Gentlemen:

A notably large percentage of our customers discount their bills, a ver satisfactory procedure from every point of view—theirs and ours. W are hoping that we shall soon include you among them.

We are wondering whether you appreciate how much discounting you bills amounts to, both financially and as a foundation for credit.

Take your case as an illustration. You have been buying from us, o the average, $500 worth of goods a month. Two per cent discount woul net you a saving of $10, and for a period of twelve months you woul earn $120 through your policy of paying promptly. This is certainly nice amount to save on one account alone. If you added the discount that you could save by paying all your bills promptly, you would find tha the figure amounts to a considerable sum.

May we not urge that you give this matter your consideration, anc determine from now on to take advantage of every discount offered.

Yours very truly,

Letters on the taking of unearned discounts. The following letter illustrates methods of handling the problem of deduction of unearned discounts.

An unearned-discount letter requesting check for deduction:

Gentlemen:

We acknowledge your check for $75.25, which is very much appreciated and which we have applied to your account.

With regard to the deduction of 2 per cent cash, we are sorry that we cannot consistently allow it in this instance, as our cash discount terms are 2 per cent 10 days from the date of invoice.

Serving as we do about forty thousand customers, it frequently happens that deductions of this nature are made, and were we to allow them, the aggregate sum involved in the course of a year's business would be large. You will appreciate, also, that it would not be fair for us to allow you the discount in this case when we deny it to other concerns with whom we do business. We feel that it is not fair to the trade, to make special concessions to some that are contrary to our requirements from others.

We are sure that you will agree with us and that you will co-operate with us in the maintenance of our terms. We are enclosing a statement showing a balance of $10.25, and will very much appreciate receiving your check for this sum.

Very truly yours,

A letter refusing a request for longer terms:

Gentlemen:

The request in your letter of October 4, that cash discount be allowed when payment is made between the 10th and the 15th of the month following shipment, has been made to us from time to time by various customers, some of whom buy in very large quantities. We have invariably felt, however, that we were unable to grant the request, for two reasons:

First: Cash discount is a premium offered for prepayment of an invoice, and if the invoice is not paid within 10 days, the extra profit has not been earned. If we have to wait an average of 30 days, our bills are due net, and we are obliged to disallow the discount privilege.

Second: It would obviously be unfair to our many customers who pay in 10 days to permit others to remit in 30 days, as it would be giving the latter a better price than those who pay more promptly. We do not think you would expect us to discriminate in this way.

We want you to know, however, that we fully appreciate your point of view, as we ourselves, with about twenty factories, find it a difficult task to put our discount bills through for payment in 10 days.

We feel confident that, after considering the foregoing, you will agree that our attitude is the only just one to assume, when all the circumstances are taken into account.

Very truly yours,

Letters on time extensions. A debtor should be granted an e tension of time when he advances a good reason, or if it is actual impossible to collect anything on the account at present, althoug there is hope for future payment. The grant should be made gr ciously but should indicate that the procedure is an exception. Th following letter to a retail customer is illustrative.

Dear Madam:

Thank you for your letter of August 24 explaining why you have n paid your account for June. Whenever our customers are in difficultie we appreciate their writing to us frankly.

Since yours is an accommodation account, payable in full by the tent of each month, we usually insist on strict adherence to the terms c credit. However, in view of your explanation, we are glad to grant you request for an extension of time on your account.

We shall, then, expect your check in full payment of your account o September first.

Very truly yours,

Another letter granting an extension of time:

Dear Mr. Johnson:

We have received your letter of May 1, requesting an extension c time on your account.

While we feel, as you no doubt can appreciate, that our usual terms o 90 days are sufficiently long to enable our customers to prepare for an arrange payment of their accounts, we are always glad, in an exceptiona case such as yours, to grant reasonable accommodation.

We are, therefore, extending the due date of your account to June 1 Won't you, however, please bear this date definitely in mind, and mai your remittance promptly. We shall be looking for it not later thar June 3.

Very truly yours,

A letter refusing an extension of time:

Dear Mr. Laswell:

We have your letter of November 10, containing a check for $690.0(in payment of our invoice of October 1. Please accept our thanks.

The following items remain open on our records:

October 15	$460.00
October 31	460.00
	$920.00

The first of the above bills matures tomorrow, and the other on December 1.

You ask that we grant you an additional 30 days on the account that is now due; from this we assume that you refer to the bill of October 15. We are embarrassed by your request, for, if we decline, we risk being thought unappreciative of the business which you have given us, and, if we agree, we are discriminating against others of our customers whom we require to pay promptly in 30 days.

In our opinion, extensions are in reality loans, and we do not think that we should be called upon to usurp the function of the bank in this particular. In addition, the nature of our business is such that close collections are an absolute necessity, and especially at a time when the cost of raw materials has advanced to such an abnormal degree.

We feel confident that you will understand the spirit in which this letter is written, and will withdraw your request.

Yours very truly,

Selling through collections; letters combining collections and sales. The collection letters reproduced up to this point have had as their chief aim the obtaining of payments that are overdue; these letters are illustrative of the more standard types of collection correspondence. The collection letter, however, may also be regarded as partly a sales letter, or as a form of advertising. Many concerns in various lines of business do so regard it, and when writing to a customer with reference to his account, take advantage of the opportunity that the collection letter offers them to:

1. Request additional orders.
2. Emphasize and advertise to the customer the merits of the merchandise sold, and also to suggest to the customer methods by which sales of the merchandise through his own outlets can be increased.
3. Introduce the customer to new lines of goods being sold by the house.
4. Inform the customer of improved service now available.

Some examples of this type of collection letter follow.

A combination collection and sales letter:

Gentlemen:

We notice that your past-due account amounting to $65.43 is still open. Won't you please let us have your check by return mail. It is our policy not to ship additional orders while past-due accounts are outstanding, and at this time of the year you will certainly wish to prepare for the big holiday trade.

Our new line is now ready for your inspection and selection. It is exceptionally strong, and includes complete assortments of broadcloths, silk fibres, shadowynes, poplins, imported madras, and numerous novelty cloths.

All of our shirts are cut very full and made with the greatest care and skill.

We will pack any number per dozen or over in individual Christmas gift boxes, at no additional cost to you.

Delivery December 1 to 10.

Mail us your order now, together with your check for $65.43.

Samples submitted, if desired.

Yours very truly,

Another combination collection and sales letter:

Dear Mr. Miller:

Your account today shows an unpaid balance of $30.16.

Perhaps you had not noticed its maturity, but now that you recall it, we know that you will act promptly.

Cut silks are coming back strong, and the new patterns and shades are the finest we have had for years. If you can use some with which to brighten up, just indicate your requirements on the enclosed order blank and return it with your check for $30.16. Both will be appreciated.

Yours very truly,

A collection letter that also advertises a new product:

Gentlemen:

It is not only because we want to see this account paid that we ask you to send a check today, but it is because we want to do more business with you, and we're afraid that the overdue account, amounting to $36.57, is keeping you away.

The popularity of our new ELECTRA model warrants your stocking this new line. A circular is enclosed. Although introduced only two months ago, the ELECTRA is already demanded in preference to all others. It is advertised in all the leading magazines.

We have not received an order from you for several months, and doubtless you are now in need of some of our line. Just add a number of ELECTRA to your next order, and, at the same time, let us have your check for $36.57 by return mail.

Thank you.

Yours very truly,

7. HOW TO USE FORM COLLECTION LETTERS

Use of form letters. Opinion differs among credit men as to the value of form letters. Some use them almost exclusively; others use them only in the reminder stage of the collection procedure. Many firms, especially department stores, mail-order, and installment houses, handle so many accounts by mail that form letters are the only practical solution, the expense of individually dictated letters being prohibitive. Similarly, either a small or large concern whose business does not necessitate close personal contact with customers, such as wholesalers or jobbers having many small past-due accounts, can use form letters effectively. Manufacturers, wholesalers, and small retailers with a smaller clientele find individual treatment more effective.

Form-paragraph manuals. A number of houses have successfully compromised between the form and the individual letter by creating hundreds of form paragraphs to fit every possible contingency. Each paragraph is given a key number, and each correspondent is provided with a form-paragraph manual. The collection correspondents, by the use of dictating machines, indicate the number of the form paragraphs that are pertinent to the particular case, inserting original material only where special circumstances require it. The records are then transcribed by typists. This system enables a relatively small office staff to handle a heavy volume of collection correspondence and to have each letter individually typed and signed.

Form-letters files and manuals. For effective and easy use, form letters should be numbered and indexed and kept in a form-letter file. When a particular form letter is sent to a debtor, the number of the letter can be marked on the collection or ledger card. This system obviates the necessity for carbon copies of form letters.

In companies where there are many correspondents, a credit and collection correspondence manual has been found a good device for improving the quality of collection letters. Such manuals not only supply the correspondents with form letters and form paragraphs, but they also serve to instruct them in the writing of collection letters that get the money and keep the customer's goodwill. A loose-leaf credit and collection correspondence manual used by the Puget

Sound Power & Light Company, Seattle, Washington, covers the following subjects:

CORRESPONDENCE MATERIAL

Closing sentences or paragraphs	Miscellaneous paragraphs
Letter analyses	Opening sentences or paragraphs
Letterheads and copy sheets	

LETTERS

Appreciation	Merchandise transfer
Auditor's verification	Miscellaneous
Closing bill	Novelty
Deposit	Reminder
Deposit refund	Seriously past due
Discontinuance	Seasonal
Merchandise	Stockholder
Merchandise reclaim	Transfer balance

New letters and other material are added to the manual from time to time by the correspondence committee, which is responsible for the manual. Correspondents are urged to submit copies of outstanding letters to the committee so that they may be considered for inclusion in the manual. Many of the letters may be used verbatim, yet it is not the intention to develop stereotyped or form usage through this medium.

Grouping delinquents to assure applicability of collection procedure. Identical form letters for all delinquents are inadvisable because of the great diversity in the character of the delinquents. Reasonable applicability of form letters can be secured by grouping delinquents and using a special selection of form letters for each group. Delinquents may be grouped according to the following:

1. Causes of delinquency, such as illness, unemployment, dishonesty, negligence, and inability to pay. If groupings are sound and letters are applicable to the group, form letters should be almost as satisfactory as individually written ones.
2. Credit ratings. The groups may be as follows:

(*a*) Poor credit risk, or customer whose ability to pay and habits of paying justify a small credit limit and a short time for payment.

Should he neglect to pay on time, the collection procedure is started immediately.

(*b*) Medium credit risk, or customer whose ability to pay and habits of paying are somewhat better than the poor risk. A longer interval of time is allowed for the operation of the collection system.

(*c*) Good credit risk, or customer who has large financial responsibility even though he may be somewhat slow in paying. Because of his high credit limit he receives the mildest and most lenient collection treatment consistent with the company's policy.

The collector using the credit-rating system must guard against keeping customers in the original classification after their rating has changed. Continual reclassification is an integral part of this grouping system.

Rules governing use of form letters. The following general rules should be observed for an effective collection series:

1. Letters should be revised at periodic intervals, or different series should be alternated every few months. Variety is highly important if effectiveness is to be maintained.
2. The series should be carefully graduated in tone, from perfunctory reminder to threat.
3. The system should be sufficiently elastic to permit of its being adapted to the type of customer. Thus, the habitually slow risk would receive fewer reminders and reach the threat stage sooner than the good risk. Moreover, the time interval between letters may be shorter for the poor risk. Otherwise, the series should be comparatively automatic and mechanical in regard to the particular type of notice or letter to be sent on the definitive date decided upon when the system is devised.
4. Allow for dictation of individual letters when irregularities occur, or when form letters need adaptation to special classes or cases of delinquents. This is tantamount to so arranging the series that the form letters may be dropped as soon as the debtor has replied.

Multigraph letters are generally inadvisable. No debtor's attitude is improved if he gets the impression that he is not worth a personally dictated letter.

Timing collection correspondence. The first letter of a mercantile collection series can be sent the afternoon of the day on which the account is due if the check has not arrived. Successive letter can be spaced anywhere from six to ten days apart. Writing wher the bill is due is, psychologically speaking, the best time, becaus the debtor knows the bill is due and is, in most cases, still enjoyin the goods. The longer the creditor lets the account run, the harde it is to collect without offense. Following is a suggested schedule o letters for the poor and good risk.

	Poor Risk	*Good Risk*
January 15	Purchase made	Purchase made
February 1	Statement	Bill
February 15	Formal reminder	Statement
March 1	First letter	First formal reminder
March 10	Second letter	
March 15		Second formal reminder
March 20	Third letter	
April 1	Threat letter	First letter
April 15		Second letter
May 1		Third letter
May 15		Fourth letter
June 1		Threat letter

Eight-letter sequence. The following sequence illustrates a long series.

NO. 1

Gentlemen:

This letter is being mailed to you just as a reminder of your account with us.

Under the terms of sale, invoice of June 9, amounting to $75.98, is now due for payment.

We shall be pleased to receive your check.

Very truly yours,

NO. 2

Gentlemen:

As you have always been prompt in meeting your obligations, it would appear that our invoice of June 9, carrying terms of 3% 10 days, net 30, to the amount of $75.98, has either gone astray or been misfiled.

We are attaching a duplicate covering the charge in question, and know that you will remit promptly upon having the matter called to your attention.

Very truly yours,

NO. 3

Gentlemen:

Has the mailing of a check to cover a past-due item been overlooked by you? We are sorry not to have received a reply to our letter of July 24.

The item referred to covers merchandise invoiced under date of June 9, to the amount of $75.98.

A reply to this letter in the form of a check will indeed be appreciated.

Very truly yours,

NO. 4

Gentlemen:

Will you please refer to our letter of August 4, in which we brought to your notice an overdue item?

We have received no reply, and our records indicate that you still owe us for shipment of June 9, amounting to $75.98.

The time allowed for payment, based on the terms of sale, has long since expired, and remittance should now be made.

Please give this matter your prompt attention.

Very truly yours,

NO. 5

Gentlemen:

There have been mailed to you a number of reminders of our invoice of June 9, but to none of our letters have we received a reply.

In view of the length of time your account has been appearing as past due, we must insist that the matter of payment now have your attention without further delay.

We shall look forward to receiving, not later than August 29, your check drawn for $75.98.

Very truly yours,

NO. 6

Gentlemen:

The credit department has just called to my attention the fact that you have not responded to its letters dated July 24, August 4, 14, and 24, which were in reference to your past-due account.

You, of course, appreciate that when accounts are neither discounted nor paid promptly when due, it has a tendency to impair your credit standing, particularly so when the creditor's experience is reflected in the trade reports that are from time to time compiled by various agencies.

Perhaps you have some good reason for not responding to the letters that the credit department wrote you. An investigation of our files does not, however, disclose any letters from you complaining about the character or quality of our merchandise, or about the service rendered to you.

In view of this we feel justified in asking that you now give our account your immediate attention.

Yours very truly,
Assistant Treasurer

NO. 7

Gentlemen:

If you were a credit manager and letters written by your assistant and then a letter written by yourself were ignored, particularly when an account was long past due, what would you do?

We have several times requested the payment of your account and have yet to receive a reply telling us either why payment has not been made, or when your check may be expected.

Since we do not appear to be receiving the co-operation to which we believe we are entitled, we feel that more drastic measures will have to be taken.

When your orders were received, they were given our very best attention—and we felt confident that you would meet your bills within a reasonable time. Apparently our confidence has been misplaced.

Our files are being advanced to September 10, at which time we shall expect to receive your check. If it is not received, we shall be obliged to take other steps to protect our interests.

Yours very truly,
Assistant Treasurer

NO. 8

Gentlemen:

Since you will neither reply to the various letters that we have written you, nor remit for your past-due account, there is nothing we can do but refer the matter to an attorney in your city. We are instructing him to proceed with the collection of the account in whatever manner may be deemed necessary to protect our interests.

Within the next few days you will receive a communication from the attorney, advising you of the action that he proposes to take.

Yours very truly,
Assistant Treasurer

8. COLLECTION METHODS

Guide for collection procedure. Remembering always that the creditor has a right to his money, the collection department should follow a technique in its collection procedure that takes into account the following advices:

1. Create a collection program that is systematic, persistent, tactful, and human. In follow-up work, let the attitude be one of friendly co-operation and mutual interest.
2. Make the debtor feel that he is paying voluntarily.

3. Take it for granted that the customer is honest until he proves otherwise.

4. Design all material sent out by the collection department to create the impression that: (a) the bill will be collected when due; (b) there is little doubt in the creditor's mind that the debtor is able to pay; (c) should there be any attempt to defer payment against the creditor's will, all force available will be used, not so much for the recovery of the money as to uphold the principles of good business.

5. Do not accept unusual methods of payment unless unforeseen trouble has made full payment utterly impossible.

6. Use force as a last resort and generally avoid conveying threats.

Effect of statutes of limitations in collection of accounts. Executives responsible for the collection of accounts and contractual payments must familiarize themselves with the provisions and applicability of the statute of limitations of the state wherein the company is operating.

A statute of limitations is a statute limiting the period within which legal action may be brought upon a matured debt. A debt is matured when it is due and payable. All 48 states and the District of Columbia have statutes of limitations. Although the applicability of the statutes is very similar in all jurisdictions, the periods set up the statutes vary from state to state and according to the type of instrument used to evidence the debt.

How the statute of limitations operates. When a debt or claim is matured—that is, due and owing, action for the collection of this debt or claim must be brought within the period required by the local statute, or all future legal action to enforce collection will be barred. However, it is possible to interrupt the running of the statute—that is, to lengthen the limited period—by obtaining from the debtor a payment on account or a promise to pay. For example, suppose an account is payable on October 15, 1952. Assuming it to be a New York account, if the claim is unpaid, legal action must be brought before October 15, 1958, or all legal action will thereafter be barred. However, if, some time before the expiration of the statutory period, let us assume July 7, 1954, the debtor makes a payment on account or makes an acknowledgment of the debt with a promise to pay, the statutory period is renewed and begins to run anew from the date

STATUTES OF LIMITATIONS (In Number of Years)

State	Open Accounts	Notes	Written Contracts	Contracts under Seal
Alabama	3	6	6	10
Arizona	3 See A	6	6	6
Arkansas	3	5	5	5
California	4	4	5	4
Colorado	6	6	6	6
Connecticut	6	6	6	17
Delaware	3	6	3	No Provision
District of Columbia	3	3	3	12
Florida	3	5	5	20
Georgia	4	6	6	20
Idaho	4	5	5	5
Illinois	5	10	10	10
Indiana	6	10	20	20
Iowa	5	10	10	10
Kansas	3	5	5	5
Kentucky	5	15	15	15
Louisiana	3	5	10	10
Maine	6	6	6	20
Maryland	3	3	3	12
Massachusetts	6	6 See B	6	20
Michigan	6	6	6	6
Minnesota	6	6	6	6
Mississippi	6	6	6	6
Missouri	5	10	5	10
Montana	5	8	8	8
Nebraska	4	5	5	5
Nevada	4	6	6	6
New Hampshire	6	6	6	20
New Jersey	6	6	6	16
New Mexico	4	6	6	6
New York	6	6	6	6
North Carolina	3	3	3	10
North Dakota	6	6 See D	6	6 See D
Ohio	6	15	15	15
Oklahoma	3	5	5	5
Oregon	6	6	6	10
Pennsylvania	6	6	6	20
Rhode Island	6	6	6	20
South Carolina	6	6	6	20
South Dakota	6	6	6	20
Tennessee	6	6	6	6
Texas	2	4	4	4
Utah	4	6	6	8
Vermont	6	6 See C	6	8
Virginia	3	5	5	10
Washington	3	6	6	6
West Virginia	5	10	10	10
Wisconsin	6	6	6	20 See E
Wyoming	8	10	10	10

NOTES: A. Executed without the state, 4 years.
B. Witnessed notes, 20 years.
C. Witnessed notes, 14 years.
D. [illegible]

ı which the payment or promise to pay is made. Thus, in our ex-nple, the creditor would have until July 7, 1960 to begin legal action. Alert collection managers, therefore, periodically review old delin-ꞁuent accounts to check on the time remaining in which action may e brought on any particular claim.

Age analysis. An age analysis of accounts affords a complete pic-ıre of the state of collections, helps locate accounts that are becom-ıg habitually slow, and makes possible prompt and appropriate ction.

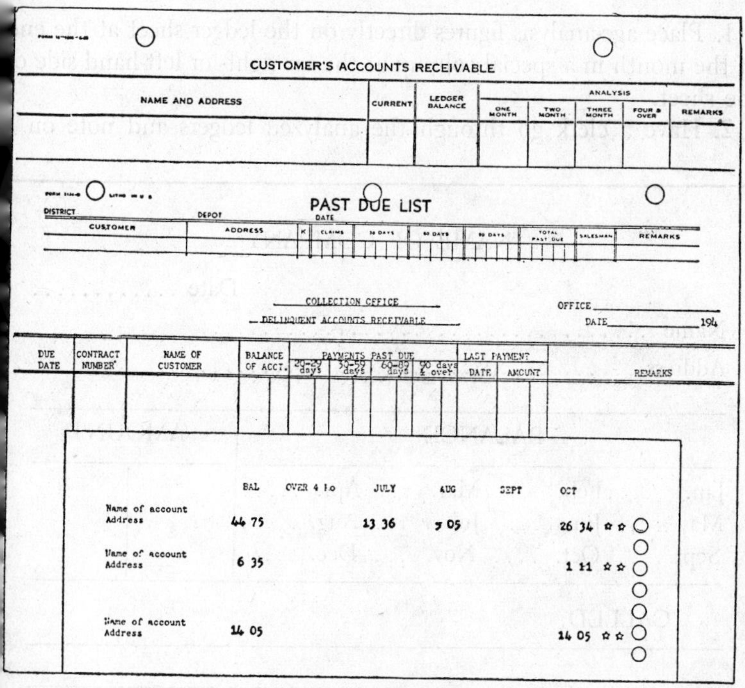
CUSTOMER'S ACCOUNTS RECEIVABLE

NAME AND ADDRESS	CURRENT	LEDGER BALANCE	ANALYSIS: ONE MONTH	TWO MONTH	THREE MONTH	FOUR & OVER	REMARKS

PAST DUE LIST

DISTRICT — DEPOT — DATE

CUSTOMER	ADDRESS	K	CLAIMS	30 DAYS	60 DAYS	90 DAYS	TOTAL PAST DUE	SALESMAN	REMARKS

COLLECTION OFFICE — OFFICE ______

DELINQUENT ACCOUNTS RECEIVABLE — DATE ______ 194

DUE DATE	CONTRACT NUMBER	NAME OF CUSTOMER	BALANCE OF ACCT.	PAYMENTS PAST DUE: 20-29 days	30-59 days	60-89 days	90 days & over	LAST PAYMENT: DATE	AMOUNT	REMARKS

	BAL	OVER 4 Mo	JULY	AUG	SEPT	OCT
Name of account Address	44 75		13 36	5 05		26 34 ☆☆
Name of account Address	6 35					1 11 ☆☆
Name of account Address	14 05					14 05 ☆☆

Figure 84. Age Analyses of Overdue Accounts.

Accounts should be aged periodically. A convenient time is when he monthly accounts receivable trial balance is prepared. Figure 84 hows several examples of age-analysis lists of overdue accounts. Where the account is of questionable collectibility, bad-debt action hould not be delayed. Otherwise, the account can be subjected to the regular collection methods used for the particular group in which it appears.

Follow-up from aging records. Accounts should first be analyzed according to those which are current, less than 30 days old, 30 to 60 days, 60 to 90 days, 90 to 120 days, and older. This is done by analyzing each individual account that is in arrears, removing it from its current classification, and placing it under the proper grouping according to the length of time it is past due.

The following procedure is effective for follow-up from aging records:

1. Place age-analysis figures directly on the ledger sheet at the end of the month in a special column at the far right- or left-hand side of the sheet.
2. Have a clerk go through the analyzed ledgers and note on a

NAME OF COMPANY

Date . . . .

Name . . . .

Address . . . .

BALANCE				AMOUNT
Jan.	Feb.	Mar.	Apr.	
May	Jun.	Jul.	Aug.	
Sept.	Oct.	Nov.	Dec.	

CALLED

Figure 85. Memorandum to Collector.

emorandum, as illustrated in Figure 85, each account having a ast-due balance.

3. For all accounts 60 days past due, make the memorandum in uplicate, the original for the collector and the duplicate for the ollection correspondents. For accounts 30 days delinquent, make nly one copy of the memorandum for the correspondents, since e collectors are not called in until later.

4. Mark the word "File" on the ledger sheet when the first letter written to the customer. This warns the correspondent to consult e file before writing again or taking any other action. Also mark e word "File" on all memoranda made of the account. This arns the collector that correspondence has begun on the account.

Informing customer of age analysis of account. Many collection men think it effective to keep customers informed as to the ge analysis of their accounts. For instance, in one company, whenever any part of a customer's balance is past due, the monthly statement, which is prepared in duplicate, shows an age analysis. The riginal statement is sent to the customer, and the duplicate is retained for use in connection with the collection procedure.

Another company sends its delinquent customers a collection notice on a small card showing the age analysis of the account. The

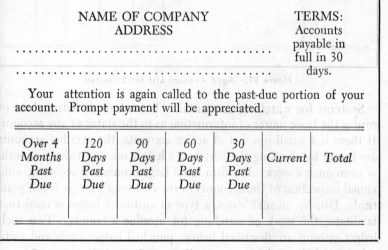

NAME OF COMPANY
ADDRESS

TERMS:
Accounts payable in full in 30 days.

. . . .

. . . .

Your attention is again called to the past-due portion of your account. Prompt payment will be appreciated.

Over 4 Months Past Due	*120 Days Past Due*	*90 Days Past Due*	*60 Days Past Due*	*30 Days Past Due*	*Current*	*Total*

Figure 86. Notice to Customer Showing Age Analysis of Account.

notice, illustrated in Figure 86, shows immediately what portion o the balance has been past due for over four months, 120 days, 9 days, 60 days, and 30 days, the current balance and total. Notice are sent to all accounts 60 days past due or over. After the con pany has sent three aging notices, the account is considered read for the firm's outside collector.

Aging statement sent to salesmen. Some firms follow the prac tice of breaking down each salesman's accounts according to age o outstanding amounts, in order to make salesmen more credit-collec tion-minded, and to gain their co-operation. Figure 87 illustrates an aged-account list for salesmen used by a Midwestern milling company

ACCOUNTS RECEIVABLE

....Office

Entered by ...... Rechecked by ...... Date .... 19..

	DATE	NAME AND ADDRESS	AMOUNT OF INVOICE 1 to 30 days	30 to 60 days	60 to 90 days	over 90 days	Total

Figure 87. Aged Account List for Salesmen.

Systems for watching accounts. The customer's ledger sheet or card is the basic source of information as to the status of any account. If there is a small number of active accounts, the overdue accounts are found by checking the customer's ledger once or twice a month, or even once a week. If a firm has a large number of accounts, individual inspection of the accounts in the customer's ledger is not practical. Usually, in such cases, a type of customer ledger is used that facilitates the work of watching for overdue accounts. Two such ledger systems are described below: punched ledger cards and vertical visible ledger cards.

Punched ledger card. A simple type of ledger card that is espe-
ially adapted for use in collection work has punched holes in the
nargins of the card to facilitate sorting out the past-due accounts.
Letters and numbers near the hole are keys to various types of infor-
nation. All the information needed for sorting the cards for collec-
ion action is placed on the cards by notching out the appropriate
unched holes with an ordinary hand punch. For example, a pay-
nent is transcribed to the card by notching out the hole above the
ign designating the particular month when payment was made. In
he illustrated example, in Figure 88, the information revealed by the
otched-out holes reads as follows: "John Doe's account is of the
ontract type. On the 18th of each month his account is past due.
At the moment he has paid the installments for September, October,
November, and December. January is due. He is not delinquent,
nd the payments are monthly."

Sorting the punched cards for collection action is very simple. The
lerk merely stacks the cards evenly and then runs a selecting needle
hat resembles a skewer or ice pick through the hole that designates
a certain date. The cards that have notched holes for that date—
he accounts that are paid up to date—slide off the selecting needle,
while the delinquent accounts remain on the needle and are lifted
out of the stack of non-delinquent cards.

Vertical visible ledger cards. Each ledger card, in a vertical visible ledger system, is attached to a slotted holding card that fits into
a panel. These panels fit into files or tubs (called trays) adapted
n size and capacity to the requirements of the user. The ledger
card has the debit entries for the charges and the credit entries for
the payments, the same as any customer's ledger. At the top of the
card is a visible strip that shows the name and address of the account
and a scale of weekly or monthly divisions. A colored celluloid signal can be adjusted over these divisions to show the date of the oldest invoice.* Thus, suppose an account makes a purchase of $2,000
on July 1. When the entry is made on the ledger card, the signal is
set over July. It is not moved from that position until all invoices
for the month of July are paid in full. As credits are posted, the

* An alternative procedure is to set the signal at the week or month when payment is due. A glance at the panel of cards shows instantly any signals that have
not been advanced to a due date beyond the current month or week.

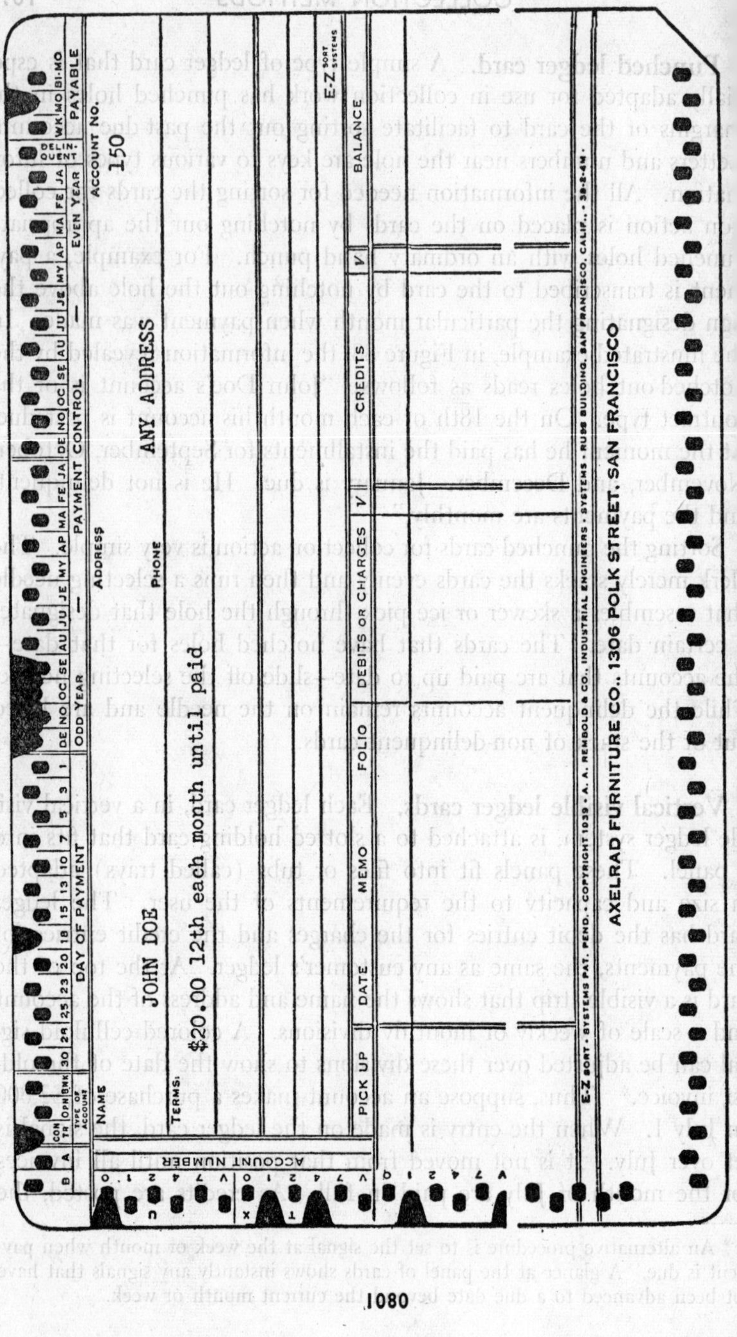
JOHN DOE
ANY ADDRESS
ACCOUNT NO. 150
$20.00 12th each month until paid
NAME
ADDRESS
PHONE
TERMS:
TYPE OF ACCOUNT
CON TR
OPN BNK
B A
DAY OF PAYMENT
30 28 25 23 20 18 15 13 10 7 5 3 1
ODD YEAR
DE NO OC SE AU JU JE MY AP MA FE JA
PAYMENT CONTROL
EVEN YEAR
DE NO OC SE AU JU JE MY AP MA FE JA
DELIN-QUENT
WK MO BI-MO
PAYABLE
ACCOUNT NUMBER
PICK UP
DATE
MEMO
FOLIO
DEBITS OR CHARGES
CREDITS
BALANCE
E-Z SORT SYSTEMS
E-Z SORT · SYSTEMS PAT. PEND. · COPYRIGHT 1939 · A. A. REMBOLD & CO., INDUSTRIAL ENGINEERS · SYSTEMS · RUSS BUILDING, SAN FRANCISCO, CALIF.
AXELRAD FURNITURE CO., 1306 POLK STREET, SAN FRANCISCO

gnal is moved to the right to the position over the month of the st outstanding invoice.

The position of these signals provides an automatic aging of out-anding invoices, calling instant attention to past-due accounts on hich collection activity is required. It is possible, under the verti-al visible ledger system, to have additional movable markers or sig-als on the visible top line. Thus, a marker may be used to show hat steps have been taken in the collection procedure. Another gnal may be used to show that the account needs special watching, r that credit should be stopped.

Collections by telephone. In recent years more and more collec-ion executives are using the telephone to speed up their collection vork. It is an economical and time-saving substitute for the collec-ion interview obtained in a personal visit.

The following advantages recommend the use of the telephone for ollection purposes: (1) A telephone call is personal and direct; it isually affords ready and direct access to the person whom the col-ection executive wishes to reach, and it gets his attention. (2) As t is two-way, the telephone call offers an opportunity to discover easons for nonpayment and to adapt the collection effort to circum-tances disclosed in the interview. (3) The telephone call permits liscussion, during which arrangements for a satisfactory settlement an be made. (4) The telephone call is flexible; it can be a gentle eminder or a forceful demand, as circumstances dictate. (5) This ersonal communication with customers presents opportunities to romote understanding and the goodwill of customers whose con-inuing patronage is desired.

Long-distance calls to speed up overdue payments have been found o be particularly effective because they emphasize the importance and the urgency of the communication.

It is a good idea to keep records of collection calls made and the results obtained just as you keep records of other methods of collec-tion. These will be helpful in recalling conversations, reasons for nonpayment, and so forth, in connection with subsequent calls or letters.

Suggestions as to when the telephone should be used for collec-tions are as follows:

1. Use the telephone only after several form letters have been sen out, except in emergencies.

2. If the present practice is to use statements, reminder notice, an final follow-up by salesmen, try using the telephone after no respons has been received to reminder notice. One company that made th trial found that collections improved, and repeat business was easie to secure.

3. If the present practice is to use a series of leters and to tur over to sales agents accounts not responding, try having the sale agents telephone the accounts. Experience has shown that the are fewer delays if the telephone is used, because sales agents ma not have time to call on accounts for several weeks.

4. Telephone large accounts before expiration of discount perioc

Collections by telegraph. Excellent results are reported from th use of telegrams for collection. A telegram has the advantage o actually reaching the person to whom it is addressed and commanc ing his immediate attention. It is short, and its urgency is direc It bears a certain air of finality. A short wire following several letter to the overdue account asking for a reply is usually effective. If i brings no reply, follow it with another longer one threatening lega action, although the sender must exercise caution in regard to threat of legal action.

Another effective method is to dispatch three wires within on day or over a period of two or three days. A debtor will seldon stand up against the irritation and publicity of such a series. Col lection men and telegraph companies report that telegrams do th trick from 70 to 90 per cent of the time. Western Union has testec forms of collection telegrams that can be procured at its offices.

Examples of collection telegrams. In framing a collection tele gram, care should be taken to avoid threat of bankruptcy or of crimi nal prosecution. In some states such threats constitute the crime o extortion or attempted extortion and are, furthermore, libelous *per se* A list of sample collection telegrams follows.

(1) Cannot understand failure to answer recent letters. Please wir collect.

(2) Closing books for audit. Please oblige with remittance today.

(3) When may we expect remittance covering overdue account Wire collect.

(4) Very important remittance reach us October 3. Ask your co-operation.

(5) Have been very patient. Won't you kindly remit. Urgent.

(6) Must have immediate payment overdue account. Please wire collect.

(7) Please settle overdue account today. Cannot wait longer.

(8) Please assist to continue friendly relationship by mailing check today.

(9) Your promise March 5 not fulfilled. Must have check immediately.

(10) Surprised no reply to frequent letters regarding overdue account now three months in arrears. Extended you credit without hesitation on basis of favorable trade opinions and gave you best service. Please reciprocate by mailing check today. Wire reply collect.

(11) Attention overdue account imperative today. Dislike to take further action.

(12) Make payment noon tomorrow to avoid court action.

Collections by personal call. The personal call by a collector on the debtor has been used advantageously in the following circumstances:

1. When legal processes cannot be used, as in the case of:
   (*a*) Small claims.
   (*b*) State, Federal, or municipal debts.
   (*c*) The honest, but judgment-proof, debtor.

2. For general use by charge-account stores and installment houses for those slow-pay accounts on which mail and telephone have proved unsuccessful.
3. Early in delinquency when the skip risk is believed to be high.
4. For occasional delinquencies where the conditions of risk, size, misunderstanding, or other circumstances demand it.
5. For use in combination with delivery of statements, current or past due, or regular collection of installments.
6. For almost any local account after form letters have been sent out.

This method is, however, expensive. Moreover, many stores prefer to have customers come in to pay their bills, for this means contact with the merchandise. Others object to it because they are afraid of "spoiling" customers.

The outstanding objection to personal collection is the expense entailed. A good collection man should command a good salary and is expected to collect five times his weekly salary. Few concerns ca really afford this. Hence, many stores have adopted the system c remunerating on neither straight-salary nor commission basis, but o a combination of both. Thus, the collector receives a small straigh weekly salary and above this a commission based on the age c accounts, a higher commission being paid for the older accoun This provides both security and incentive.

Where the firm does not need a full-time collector, the group pla may prove economical. The group collector divides his time amon several noncompeting clients. Each client pays him a weekly c monthly fee which, in the aggregate, is enough to hold a really skille man.

Collections by salesmen. The sales and credit department mus determine whether salesmen shall collect overdue accounts. In ce tain lines of business, as, for example, mercantile houses, the majo ity of whose customers are small retailers, salesmen can be use effectively as collectors of overdue accounts. These advantages ar gained by using salesmen as collectors:

1. The salesman is in a better position to keep the customer withi the credit limit.
2. He can obtain prompt action by the credit department in ap proving orders that might otherwise have to be held until he ha corresponded with the customer and secured a check or note.
3. Small businessmen regard it as natural to pay the salesman, sinc to them he represents the selling house.
4. It is harder for the customer to refuse payment to the salesma than to ignore dunning letters.
5. It saves annoyance to the customer from frequent dunning let ters and therefore makes it easier to get repeat orders.

The following plan for having salesmen perform collection wor has been used successfully. Each salesman is sent a weekly item ized statement of the past-due accounts on his next week's itinerary the statement being timed to reach him during the weekend befor he makes the calls. (For discussion of aging statement sent t salesmen, see page 1078.) The salesman is provided with repor forms and is required either to collect the amount of the bill or t send a report to the district office explaining why the customer i unable to make immediate payment. These reports supply mate ial for follow-up letters from the district office. At the end of the month, the results are totalled, and each salesman receives a report showing him the standing of his accounts and his collection-loss record. A prize may be awarded each month to the salesman who leads his district or group in collections.

Aids for the collector. The following ideas have been used successfully to aid in collections by personal collectors:

1. When an account is opened, include a full description of the customer on the ledger card. Give this information to the collector, together with the necessary credit information. The collector can thus "spot" the customer and address him by name. This plan prevents the customer from pretending to be someone else and saying, "Mr. ——— is not at home." It also prevents any mistakes from being made because of similarity in names.

2. Although ordinarily the debtor should be approached in a private place, in the case of the tricky, irresponsible debtor, whose account is not wanted, approach him in public and hand the bill to him in front of others. This can be at his place of employment, at home when he is entertaining, in a store where friends are present, and similar places.

3. If the debtor claims to have just sent a check, ask to see the stub so that it can be traced in the office.

4. If the debtor is always "out" when the collector arrives, leave some evidence of the attempt to collect the bill. For example, slip under the door a printed card bearing a courteous message. Then follow up by telephone. Or, leave the bill with a note penciled thereon that the collector will return again tomorrow.

5. Learn from the debtor's wife his place of business, pay day, and amount to expect, and then await the debtor at his place of business at the right time with the right demand.

6. If the debtor cannot pay the entire amount, secure some payment on account with a promise for the remainder in the future. Make sure to call on the day specified for payment, for the debtor must not secure the impression that the collector is careless or indifferent.

7. If the debtor states that he cannot make a payment, have the collector tell him that the final decision rests with the credit manager. Persuade the debtor to telephone the credit manager to ex-

plain the circumstances and have the debtor telephone in the pre ence of the collector.

8. Test the debtor's attitude before taking action to repossess th merchandise sold under a conditional sales contract with a "repo session" clause. Approach the delinquent customer with the stat ment, "You may lose your (object purchased) if you don't mak your payment." If the customer shows little concern over the po sible loss, or even suggests that the firm repossess the merchandis proceed immediately to repossess the property, since the customer' attitude reveals that he has little interest in settling the account, c finds it impossible to do so. It might also show that he has littl regard for the merchandise and that it may be damaged if left i his possession. On the other hand, if the customer shows that he i anxious to retain possession, he will usually find some means of cor tinuing payments, and in such cases enforcement of the repossessio clause may not be advisable.

Placing an account with a collection agency. The chief advan tages of placing an account with a collection agency rather than wit an attorney are:

1. In many cases the agency is able to effect collection withou instituting legal proceedings. This results from the fact that th average debtor realizes that if he fails to make payment when re quested to do so by an agency, the entire business community wil learn of his delinquency, and his credit will suffer in consequence The usual procedure is for the agency to write the debtor a serie of strong letters, or to send an investigator to his place of business

2. If legal proceedings are necessary, the agency's wide experienc enables it to choose a reputable and conscientious attorney.

3. The agency selects the attorney from a bonded list. The cred itor is thus fully protected against malfeasance.

4. The creditor is relieved of the burden of direct correspondenc with the attorney and supervision of his activities.

5. The agency can be relied upon to see to it that prompt actio is taken and the amount collected promptly remitted.

6. No extra expense is incurred. The agency and the attorney share the fees, which are usually those established by the Commer- cial Law League of America.

The creditor should thoroughly investigate an agency before util-:ing its services, since from time to time various irresponsible gencies have been established. A reputable agency will furnish a ond for the amount of the claim, or for the amount of the cred-or's annual collection business, if requested to do so.

Many companies have found the most satisfactory collection gency to be the collection division of a local association of the Na-ional Association of Credit Men.

House collection agencies. Many firms have set up their own o-called "house" collection agencies, which are in reality dummy oncerns. A name is chosen, stationery printed, and threat letters ent to the debtor. Every effort is made to convey the impression hat the agency is independent of the creditor company. While hese agencies have proved very successful, some credit men doubt he propriety of the procedure.

Placing an account with an attorney. An account should not e placed with an attorney for collection until all other methods of ollection have proved fruitless, and the creditor is prepared to sever usiness relations with the debtor. Many firms have found the nost satisfactory time at which to present an account to an attorney o be sixty days after the maturity date. If allowed to run ninety r one hundred and twenty days, accounts usually become a dead oss. Presentation after sixty days ordinarily results in a fairly siz-ble recovery. A good collection attorney will acknowledge a claim s soon as he receives it and will proceed immediately to attempt to btain payment without going to law. If this is impossible, he will dvise the creditor as to whether a suit is expedient, basing his ad-ice upon such factors as the provability of the claim and the col-ectibility of such judgment as may be obtained.

The creditor usually places his claim in the hands of an attorney n his own city, who will in turn forward it to another attorney in he debtor's city. No extra expense is incurred; the forwarding and he local attorney share the fee, the former usually receiving one hird and the latter two thirds. The use of a forwarding attorney is specially expedient where the amount of the claim is small, because local attorney is likely to be more prompt if the claim is trans-nitted to him by another attorney for whom he acts or expects to act frequently, than if it is forwarded as a single request from commercial house.

The local associations of the National Association of Credit Me are privileged to suggest the names of several good attorneys wh may represent the creditor firm.

The collection fees charged by attorneys vary in different locali ties. The usual fees, however, are those recommended by the Com mercial Law League of America—namely:

18% on the first $500.
15% on the next $500.
10% on the balance.
50% on claims of $30 or less.
$15 on claims of $30 to $83.33.
Suit fees: The Commercial Law League and the American Bar Assc ciation take the position that an attorney is entitled to a reasonabl suit fee commensurate with the work that he has done. They rec ommend a minimum fee of $7.50. Suit fees are not contingent.

Settlement by note. When a debtor offers to pay his past-du account by note, the creditor should consider several questions be fore accepting the note in settlement. There are possibly three argu ments in favor of the note:

1. A note serves as practically conclusive evidence of the debt anc facilitates proof in the event that it subsequently becomes necessary to sue the debtor.

2. The debtor may consider a note a more solemn obligation thar the open account. He realizes, for example, that a note may bc discounted at a bank and presented to him at maturity by the bank For this reason he may be more careful in preparing to meet the note than to pay the open account at any fixed date.

3. A note may be more easily transferred and realized upon by the creditor.

As against the above, the following serious objections to the note may be stated:

1. Failure to pay a note at maturity is by no means uncommon, especially among retailers. Frequently the debtor offers to pay only a part of the note on the due date, tendering another note for the balance.

2. Acceptance of a note serves as a bad precedent. As a rule, a

reditor who has accepted several notes will find it very difficult to btain from the debtor any other form of payment; and, if acceptnce of notes becomes the practice in the creditor's collection effort, ne debtor is buying regularly on greatly extended terms.

3. The creditor, by accepting a note, waives all right to expect or emand payment until the due date of the note, which usually engthens rather than shortens the period of deferred payment. In he event that any immediate action, such as the bringing of a lawuit to enforce payment, were considered desirable, the creditor vould have to postpone such action until after the maturity date f the note.

4. It gives rise to the tendency of accepting a note when a little nore pressure would bring cash.

In view of these disadvantages, it is in many cases advisable tactully to decline the debtor's offer of a note, and to suggest to him ne of the following as an alternative:

1. Part payments on the open account. This procedure extends he time of payment. By not binding himself to a definite extenion, however, the creditor may leave himself free to take whatever ction may be necessary in an emergency.

2. Immediate payment of part of the account, and one or more postdated checks for the balance.

3. In place of a note bearing only the debtor's signature, a note bearing the accommodation endorsement of a third party known by he creditor to be financially sound.

4. In place of an ordinary note, an installment note providing or the payment of small amounts from time to time, on condition, however, that the entire amount shall become due and payable in the event of a default in any installment.

Collections by draft. Important considerations in connection with the use of a draft are the following:

1. In most lines of business the practice of sending a draft is looked upon as a somewhat drastic, if not unfriendly, step, likely to antagonize the debtor. The drawing of a draft should therefore be deferred until it appears that letters are productive of no good results. The draft may be regarded as the last step preliminary to the placing of the account with a collection agency or attorney.

2. Presentation of the draft through the debtor's own bank is in

many cases the most effective procedure, because of the psycholog cal effect upon the debtor. It is worth while to note in the ledg the name of each debtor's bank as ascertained from checks.

3. To insure that the bank will give careful attention to th presentation of the draft, it is advisable for the creditor to enclos a small fee of from twenty-five to fifty cents.

4. The debtor should be notified by letter that he is being draw upon and that he will be expected to honor the draft. See pag 1059 for example of letter of notification.

5. The bank should be instructed as to what to do with the dra if the debtor fails to honor it. The creditor may instruct the ban to return the draft to him with a notation of why the debtor wi not pay it, or may authorize the bank to hand the draft to a ce tain attorney in the debtor's city after a specified number of day has elapsed. In the latter case the letter of notification to th debtor should contain a warning of the consequences of failure t honor.

9. DEALINGS WITH EMBARRASSED DEBTORS *

How should a creditor deal with an embarrassed debtor When a debtor fails to pay his debt at maturity, the claim agains him may be turned over to an attorney and the machinery of th law set in operation against him in an effort to effect collection While this might appear to be the simplest way of disposing of troublesome situation, it may in fact prove to be highly ineffective

When a debtor is insolvent, his assets are virtually a trust fund i which all creditors share alike. In proceeding independently, creditor may find that, even though he may obtain a judgmen against the debtor, other creditors may by appropriate proceeding prevent an unlawful preference. Therefore, in order to obtain th greatest amount for all creditors, some other method of dealing wit the embarrassed debtor may be advisable.

To determine what method shall be used requires familiarity wit debtor and creditor statutes, state insolvency laws, statutes regulat ing assignments for the benefit of creditors, and bankruptcy laws

* Acknowledgment is made to Samuel C. Duberstein, Referee in Bankruptcy Member of New York Bar, Professor Emeritus, St. John's University School o Law.

nder these statutes and the decisions affecting them, which are ›metimes motivated by economic and social expediencies, an emırrassed debtor's business is subject to different forms of treatment. he statutes should be considered with the idea of invoking the law ıat best deals with the problem at hand. The services of an at›rney are usually indispensable in dealing with embarrassed debtors.

Considerations in dealing with embarrassed debtors. Causes f failure, the relation of the debtor to the creditor, and other pracical considerations will enter into the determination of how to deal vith the embarrassed debtor.

A debtor's failure may be due to large overhead expense, cometition, incompetence, lack of capital, high living expenses, gamling, fraudulent schemes, or other causes. In certain instances the usiness should be liquidated; in others efforts should be made to eorganize it. Rehabilitation is the hope of both the creditor and he debtor, but conditions may be such that it would be folly to ave the debtor continue further in business and incur additional osses. The businessman who cannot realize an annual net profit s better off out of business. The constant reverberations which ollow daily failures create a disturbance in the business world that esults in tragedies for the honest merchant with limited capital.

Relation of the debtor to the creditor may be important in a reditor's consideration of the method of dealing with an embarassed debtor. For example, if a debtor is an important outlet for he creditor's merchandise, and the termination of the business vould adversely affect the creditor's volume, he would consider an xtension agreement in an out-of-court adjustment (see page 1095), provided that he is interested in preserving the business and has onfidence in the management. On the other hand, if the debtor's mbarrassed condition is due to faulty management, and it is not proposed under any plan submitted to creditors in an out-of-court djustment to substitute new management, then the creditor should ndeavor to make the best composition settlement that is possible (see page 1098). If a composition settlement cannot be effected, hen the creditor may well join with other creditors in precipitating he debtor into bankruptcy, provided that the debtor is insolvent ınd has committed an act of bankruptcy (see page 1102), on the theory that the first loss in an ill-managed enterprise will ultimatel prove the least costly.

In all cases where dishonesty is one of the causes of the debtor embarrassed position, creditors usually prefer to refuse any settl ment, in order that the illegal, dishonest, or fraudulent acts ma be investigated in bankruptcy proceedings (see page 1101). Whi administrative expenses in bankruptcy may result in a creditor r ceiving a smaller dividend on his claim than would have been rea ized in a voluntary offer of composition, it is always possible tha recoveries may be made by a trustee in bankruptcy against the fo mer management with respect to their acts of dishonesty or frau Furthermore, a vigorous course of action against a dishonest debt acts as a deterrent against other detbors who might otherwise con mit similar acts of dishonesty.

Methods of dealing with embarrassed debtors. The followin methods of dealing with embarrassed debtors are discussed in th section:

1. Collection of claim by suit.
2. Agreements out of court to give the debtor an extension c time to pay or compromise creditors' claims (see page 1095).
3. Assignment of the debtor's assets for the benefit of creditor (see page 1097).
4. Equity receivership proceedings (see page 1100).
5. Bankruptcy liquidation—voluntary or involuntary (see pag 1101).
6. Arrangement proceeding under Chapter XI, Bankruptcy Ac (see page 1108).
7. Corporate reorganization under Chapter X, Bankruptcy Ac (see page 1109).
8. Voluntary wage-earners' plans under Chapter XIII, Bankruptc Act (see page 1112).

Collection of Claim by Suit

Suing to collect an account. When an account has proved un collectible in spite of a methodical collection effort, and legal actio seems advisable, a *final date for payment* should be set, and, if the debtor then fails to pay, the account should be placed with a lawye

:th instructions to take immediate action to protect the rights of e creditor.

The various states have enacted laws that provide not only for ıe maintenance of ordinary suits for the collection of debts but so for "provisional" remedies which may be invoked at the comıencement of a suit or while the suit is pending. Without such :medies the creditor might find himself, at the termination of the ıse, with an uncollectible judgment.

The remedies are: (1) attachment; (2) arrest; (3) receivership; ıd (4) injunction.

1. *Attachment.* In the legal proceeding of attachment, a levy is ıade on property of the debtor. The circumstances under which n attachment proceeding is allowed are fixed by the State statute. ollowing are the principal grounds for obtaining an attachment:

(*a*) The debtor is a nonresident of the state or is a foreign cororation, and attachment is sought against property in the state.

(*b*) The debtor has departed from the state with intent to deraud creditors or avoid process.

(*c*) The debtor keeps himself concealed in the state.

(*d*) The debtor has removed property or is about to remove ıroperty from the state with intent to defraud creditors.

(*e*) The debtor has secured property from a creditor through raudulent representations.

A creditor who obtains a writ of attachment is generally required o furnish a bond to cover the costs of the proceeding and to protect he debtor from any injury that may result to him if the attachment s vacated.

2. *Arrest.* An order of arrest may be obtained where the debtor s a nonresident, or where a resident debtor is about to leave the tate, if the judgment would be ineffectual as a result of the nonesidence or departure.

3. *Receivership.* A receiver may be appointed to take possession of and manage the property which is the subject of the action when t appears that there is danger of fraudulent transfer or removal of he property during the pendency of the action, and if the appointnent of a receiver is necessary to preserve the property before final udgment is entered. While Federal equity receivership proceedings ıre practically obsolete today because of the provisions of Chapter X, dealing with reorganization, and Chapter XI, dealing with ar-

rangements, of the National Bankruptcy Act, explained on pag 1108 *et seq*., ordinary equity receivership proceedings may be mai tained in the several states. This form of action in equity may instituted by a creditor to set aside transfer fraudulently made by debtor in violation of state laws. Generally the creditor must fi obtain a judgment and secure the appointment of a receiver who i stitutes the action to obtain the equitable relief.

The statutes of the various states must be consulted in order avoid objections that may be made by a debtor and his confederat who are seeking to frustrate creditors' rights and remedies by tec nical obstructive measures.

4. *Injunction.* A temporary injunction is obtainable where th creditor seeks to restrain the continuance or commission of an ac that would cause injury to him during the pendency of the actio or where the debtor is doing or threatens to do an act in violatio of the creditor's rights respecting the action that would render eve tual judgment ineffectual; or where the debtor is about to dispos of his property with intent to defraud the creditor.

Rights after recovery of judgment—execution, supplementar proceedings, and garnishment. If ordinary suit is instituted b service of summons and complaint on the debtor, and the debto defaults in answering (or if the creditor wins at the trial), judgme is entered, and an *execution* is issued, which authorizes the sheriff o marshal to seize and sell the property at public auction. Th amount realized upon the sale is applied to satisfy the judgment Should the execution be returned "unsatisfied" by the sheriff o marshal, application should be made to examine the debtor in *sup plementary proceedings*. In such proceedings third parties, such as banks, and the like, may also be examined. Here assets belonging to the debtor may be uncovered and a receiver appointed to take charge. Occasionally the examination discloses that the debtor receives an income from wages, salary, earnings, trust funds, profits, or insurance disability payments, in which event an order of garnishment should be procured. To obtain the order, the creditor is usually required to file with the clerk of the court an affidavit indicating the amount due him and stating his belief that certain designated persons have property belonging to the debtor, or that such persons are indebted to the debtor, and that the process of garnishment is necessary to satisfy his claim. The order is served upon the person having possession of the property of the debtor or indebted to him (known as the garnishee), and from the time of service of such writ the garnishment becomes a continuing levy upon the property in an amount generally not exceeding ten per cent thereof, and continues as a levy until the claim is satisfied. The debtor may, in some states, secure a release of the garnished property by giving a bond in the amount prescribed by the statute.

In some states, after a judgment has been rendered against a debtor, and notwithstanding the provisions for garnishment, the courts may order the judgment debtor to pay to the judgment creditor or apply on the judgment, in installments, such portion of his income as the court may deem proper after taking into consideration the needs of the debtor and his family.

Out-of-Court Agreements

What is an out-of-court agreement? The out-of-court form of settlement agreement is an instrument by which a settlement can be arrived at quickly, economically, and with the least disturbance to the debtor's business. Under this type of settlement the debtor may offer a composition (part payment) in full settlement of the account, or the debtor may request an extension of time to pay the account. This method of out-of-court adjustment does not always prove effective because such a settlement agreement requires the approval of *all* creditors. Sometimes ignorant or obstinate creditors refuse to co-operate with the majority, even though the acceptance of the settlement agreement is in the interests of all creditors. Failure to obtain the necessary consents may lead to the use of one of the other methods of administration described in this section.

How to start an out-of-court adjustment. The signs of weakness in a debtor's business are: his checks or notes are returned unpaid or protested; suits are instituted against him; a chattel mortgage is filed; he is selling merchandise below cost; he is gambling. When any of these conditions appears, the creditor should arrange to confer with his debtor. The creditor should tell the debtor that there are rumors about his condition "on the street"; that it is generally known that suits have been instituted against him. The creditor may indicate his desire to co-operate by giving the debtor the benefit of constructive suggestions in order to facilitate his rehabilitation. He may ask to see the accountant's last report. If it appears that the debtor cannot continue normally, and if he is apparently honest, the creditor may suggest the calling of a meeting of the debtor's largest creditors. As this procedure often leads to an agreement whereby the debtor may continue in business and creditors may obtain the eventual payment of their accounts, it is advisable to consult an experienced attorney to prepare a valid and binding agreement embodying the terms and conditions.

Adjustments through credit bureaus. If the creditors are unwieldy, it may be advisable to have a credit association of which some of the creditors are members call a meeting of all creditors at which the debtor's affairs may be discussed.

Credit bureaus have been organized throughout the country not merely to supply credit data and to collect accounts receivable but also to supervise the administration of a debtor's business affairs. These bureaus are generally organized by credit men so as to minimize credit risks. A meeting of creditors of the debtor is usually called at the bureau either at the instance of the debtor or of the creditors. At such meeting the debtor is required to furnish a statement of his financial condition, showing his list of creditors and the amounts respectively due them, as well as an itemized statement of his assets. Creditors frequently require an audit of the debtor's books in order to ascertain whether or not the debtor has been honest or whether his failure has been due to conditions beyond his control. At the same time the debtor generally makes known his offer of settlement. After the creditors' investigation, if there should appear to be a prospect of the debtor's future success, the creditors may accept a reasonable offer for payment of their obligations. Often, where the debtor's offer is insufficient, the bureau will require the debtor to deliver to it an assignment for the benefit of creditors so that the debtor's assets may be under the direct supervision of the bureau or a creditors' committee that may have been appointed. If the debtor has committed fraud, or has made unlawful preferences, bankruptcy proceedings may be in order.

Ordinarily a committee of creditors should be chosen from the general body of creditors, a custodian placed in charge of the assets, an inventory taken, the debtor's books examined by a certified pubc accountant, the accounts receivable aged, and, if practicable, the ebtor's checks countersigned by a member of the committee. The esults of the investigation should be reported promptly to the cred- tors. As a general rule, it is good policy to follow the recommen- lations of the committee.

When creditors cannot agree. As previously indicated, if all he creditors do not agree, some other method of dealing with em- barrassed debtors must be undertaken. The making of an assign- nent for the benefit of creditors, explained fully below, may be he solution. Unfortunately this plan leads to a cumbersome and xpensive means of liquidation. Another disadvantage of this pro- edure is that it seldom leads to rehabilitation.

If some creditors refuse to co-operate, in the proper case a bank- uptcy "arrangement" proceeding, explained more fully on page 1108, will have the salutary effect of compelling the acceptance of the terms of the settlement by a recalcitrant minority group. There- fore from the point of view of benefits both to the debtor and the creditors, in cases where difficulty is encountered in obtaining the written consent of all creditors to an out-of-court agreement, the ma- chinery provided by the National Bankruptcy Act, either in an "arrangement" proceeding or a "reorganization" proceeding, may be the most effective means of dealing with embarrassed debtors.

Assignment for Benefit of Creditors

What is an assignment for benefit of creditors? An assignment for the benefit of creditors is a transfer by a debtor of his property to an assignee in trust, to apply the property or the proceeds thereof to the payment of his debts, and to return the surplus, if any, to the debtor. In order to operate as an assignment, there must be an absolute transfer of property without retention of any control by the debtor, and the transfer must be made to an assignee. The transfer is generally effected by the execution of a deed of trust or an assignment for the benefit of creditors by the debtor to the as- signee, but no particular form is ordinarily required. The statutes in many states specifically authorize the execution of an assignment for the benefit of creditors under specified conditions; assignments executed pursuant to such statutes are known as "statutory assign- ments." Where these statutory conditions are not met in the execution of an assignment, the assignment may in some states opera as a common law assignment.

Statutory provisions governing assignment for benefit of cred tors. The statutes regulating assignments for the benefit of credito vary in the different states. The following matters are those mo commonly covered:

1. *Form of assignment.* Some statutes specifically require tha the assignment be in writing, signed by assignor and assignee, an duly acknowledged before a notary public.
2. *Property to be included.* The assignment should embrace a of the assignor's property except such as is exempt from executio If all the property is not assigned, a dissenting creditor may set th transfer aside as fraudulent. Omissions of unimportant propert do not generally invalidate the assignment; the property omitte must be of such importance as to show an intention to hinder, de lay, or defraud creditors.
3. *Recording.* Many statutes require that the assignment be file or recorded in the office of a designated public official; in some state failure to file or record makes the assignment invalid.
4. *Filing of inventory.* The assignee is required to file an inven tory of the property and a description thereof within a fixed period
5. *Bond of assignee.* The assignee is required to file a bond to secure the faithful performance of his duties.
6. *Notice to creditors.* Notice of sale and to present claims must be given to creditors either personally by mail or by publication, as prescribed.
7. *Filing of creditors' claims.* Verified claims of creditors must be filed within a designated period with the assignee or his attorney.

Many states have enacted laws forbidding the giving of preferences by insolvent debtors. In any event, if a transfer is made with intent to hinder creditors for the debtor's own advantage, such a conveyance is invalid, and the assignment may be declared fraudulent.

Qualifications and duties of an assignee. The assignee must be a competent person, capable of performing his duties as assignee. Unless the statute provides otherwise, a debtor has a right to choose the assignee without the consent of the creditors, if he does so in ɔod faith. If creditors are consulted before the assignment is made, is advisable to suggest the designation of a major creditor to act ; the assignee.

It is the duty of an assignee for the benefit of creditors to adɪinister the trust to the best advantage and to protect it for the enefit of the creditors and of the debtor. To this end, he may mploy and pay for counsel to advise and assist him in legal matɛrs arising out of the administration of the assigned estate. The ssignee may be held liable for failure to exercise good faith in his ransactions; failure to use reasonable diligence in the management f the trust; willful misapplication of trust funds; and negligence, vant of caution, or misconduct, such as permitting the debtor to etain possession of assigned property. Following are some of the pecific duties of an assignee under an assignment for the benefit of :reditors:

1. File or record the assignment; give notice of the assignment, equesting creditors of the assignor to present their claims, and reɿuesting debtors to make payments to the assignee.
2. Execute a bond for the faithful performance of his duties.
3. Take possession of the property transferred under the assignment.
4. Collect the debts of the assignor.
5. Sell the property transferred under the assignment at public sale, upon due notice to creditors; also advertise at least once before date of sale.
6. Pay all priority claims including taxes; make distribution to creditors out of the proceeds realized upon the sale of the property, and turn over any surplus remaining after such distribution to the assignor.
7. Keep a full and accurate account of the property received and disposed of, and render an account. Generally the account of the assignee must be approved by the court before the assignee may be discharged.

Personal liability of assignee for obligations created by him. The assignee is personally liable for contracts made by him after assumption of his representative capacity. He is also personally liable for any new debts that he creates in the administration of the assignment. The hiring of an attorney, expenses incurred for labor, gas, electricity, and the paying of rental of a house—all these a obligations created by the assignee for which he is personally liab He may, of course, make a claim for reimbursement out of the asse of the assigned estate.

An assignee who receives as an asset of his assignor an unexpir lease has a reasonable time within which to decide whether he w accept the lease and assume the burdens of its covenants on beha of the estate, or whether he will surrender possession of the premis to the landlord. If he does not accept the lease, but continues i possession, he is personally liable for the value of the use and o cupation.

Participation of creditors in assignment. After creditors hav shared in the assets available under a general assignment, they ma unless they have received from the the assignee the face amount c their claims with interest, realize on the remainder of the amoun due on their claims out of any additional property that the debto may acquire. The assignment may not provide that acceptance o the proceeds of the assignment shall operate as a release or dis charge of the claims, since this is the field of the Federal Bankruptc law, by which Congress has superseded the local statute on the sub ject of discharge.

Assignment as an act of bankruptcy. Regardless of whether o not the debtor is insolvent, an assignment for the benefit of creditors is an act of bankruptcy under the Federal bankruptcy laws, if made within four months of the filing of a petion in bankruptcy. An involuntary petition in bankruptcy may not be filed by any creditor who assented in writing to the assignment. If bankruptcy follows, the assignee is required to turn over the property that came into his hands to the trustee in bankruptcy or to account therefor. The assignment need not conform to the technical requirements of the state statutes in order to constitute an act of bankrupcy; it may have been executed in the form of a deed of trust.

Equity Receiverships

Equity receiverships supplanted. Until recently the equity receivership instituted by a creditor's bill was considered the best means of administering insolvent debtors. This form of liquidation, discussed under receivership in connection with provisional

:medies, on page 1093, has been in effect supplanted by the meth-ds of administration provided for under the National Bankruptcy .ct.

Ordinary Voluntary or Involuntary Petition in Bankruptcy (Liquidation)

Policy of the bankruptcy law. The policy of the bankruptcy ıw is to give creditors control of the administration of a debtor's ffairs with reasonable safeguards to creditors in the treatment of he assets and to afford creditors notice of all important steps that ventuate in the final distribution of the assets among creditors on n equitable basis.

Kinds of bankruptcy proceedings. The National Bankruptcy \ct provides for two kinds of bankruptcy proceedings—voluntary .nd involuntary.

Any person, partnership, or corporation (except municipal, bank-ng, insurance, and railroad corporations and building and loan ıssociations) may become a voluntary bankrupt on his or its own ›etition, regardless of the amount owed to creditors.

An involuntary proceeding may be instituted against any natural ›erson (except a farmer or a wage earner) and against any business, :ommercial, or moneyed corporation (except banking, municipal, ailroad, and insurance corporations and building and loan associa-tions), and against any unincorporated company, such as a partner-ship, owing $1,000 or more.

What the petition in bankruptcy alleges. The petition in bank-ruptcy, voluntary or involuntary, must allege that the bankrupt's principal place of business, residence, or domicile was situated within that territorial jurisdiction for the preceding six months, or was situated within that territorial jurisdiction for a longer portion of the preceding six months than in any other jurisdiction.

In an ordinary involuntary petition, where the alleged bankrupt has twelve or more creditors, at least three creditors must sign the petition; where there are less than twelve creditors, one or more creditors must sign. In either event, the aggregate amount of the petitioning creditors' unsecured claims must be $500 or over.

An involuntary petition must allege that the debtor has com-mitted at least one of the acts of bankruptcy as provided by Section

3 of the National Bankruptcy Act, within four months precedin the filing of the petition.

Acts of bankruptcy. The acts of bankruptcy consist of the al leged bankrupt having:

1. Conveyed, transferred, concealed, or removed any part of hi property, with intent to hinder, delay, or defraud his creditors.
2. Transferred, while insolvent, any portion of his property to a creditor, with intent to prefer such creditor over his other creditors.
3. Permitted, while insolvent, any creditor to obtain a lien upon any of his property through legal proceedings, and not having vacated or discharged such lien within thirty days from the date thereof, *or* at least five days before the date set for any sale of such property.
4. Made a general assignment for the benefit of his creditors.
5. While insolvent or unable to pay his debts as they mature, permitted, voluntarily or involuntarily, the appointment of a receiver or trustee to take charge of his property.
6. Admitted in writing his inability to pay his debts and his willingness to be adjudged a bankrupt.

Petition for appointment of receiver. Following the filing of the petition in bankruptcy in triplicate with the Clerk of the Court, to whom is paid the filing fee of $45, the next practical step is to prepare and submit the creditors' petition for the appointment of a receiver. Unless the alleged bankrupt's consent or waiver has been obtained, the application for the appointment of a receiver must be accompanied by a petitioning creditors' bond in the sum of $250 to indemnify the alleged bankrupt for damages in the event that the petition in bankruptcy is dismissed.

The mere filing of the petition in bankruptcy is not a basis for the appointment of a receiver. To justify the appointment of a receiver, the Court must be satisfied that the appointment is necessary to preserve the estate.

Creditor's right to interpose answer to involuntary petition. The right formerly given to a creditor to interpose an answer to an involuntary petition has been taken away in the "ordinary" bankruptcy proceeding. In a corporation reorganization proceeding under Chapter X (see page 1109), a creditor may file an answer.

Adjudication of the bankrupt. If the alleged bankrupt defaults interposing an answer to the involuntary petition, or if the trial the issues results in the upholding of the petition, or if debtor les a voluntary petition, the Court will enter an order or decree of djudication. This means that the alleged bankrupt has been judicially adjudged a bankrupt within the purview of the acts of Conress relating to bankruptcy.

Examination before first meeting. It is not necessary, however, o await the entry of such adjudication in order to enable a creditor, y petition, to examine the bankrupt and others concerning the acts, onduct, and property of the bankrupt. The immediate use of this xamination very often forms the basis for the recovery of assets raudulently or preferentially transferred and the prosecution of dishonest bankrupts and their confederates.

Filing of schedules by the bankrupt. Following the entry of he order of adjudication, and within five days thereafter, the bankupt must file schedules of his assets and liabilities (also unliquidated nd contingent claims), as well as a "Statement of Affairs," on a orm prescribed by the United States Supreme Court. (See page 1106.) If a debtor files a voluntary petition in bankruptcy, he hould accompany it with similar schedules and a statement.

The bankruptcy statute is intended to give the creditors the conrol and administration of a bankrupt estate. It should be recognized that, at the outset of the proceeding, the Court may, on proper petition, without ascertaining the views of the general body of creditors, appoint a receiver. But this "temporary" official must eventually give way to the permanent administrator known as the *trustee in bankruptcy*. The latter is nominated and elected by creditors at the first meeting of creditors.

Sales. Ordinarily sales must be on at least ten days' notice to creditors (less for perishable property) and must realize at least 75 per cent of the appraisal, unless specially confirmed.

Election of trustee in bankruptcy. At the first meeting of creditors usually held before the referee in bankruptcy, a majority in number and amount of creditors' claims is required to elect a trustee. Creditors who have filed their proof of debt may elect one or three trustees. Stockholders, directors, and officers of a corporation that is bankrupt may not participate in the voting for the appointme of a trustee; nor may creditors who are relatives of the bankru participate.

In computing the number of votes for any candidate, the Cou has a right to exclude from voting all claims of $50 or less, insof as number is concerned. However, such claims may be include in the amount. These small claims are excluded to prevent the from creating a deadlock or from controlling an election.

Filing proofs of claims. Creditors are entitled to receive div dends only when they have filed their proofs of claim with the re eree. Proofs of claim must be filed within six months after the dat set for the first meeting of creditors. The Court cannot grant an additional time. Creditors may elect a creditors' committee of no less than three members at the first meeting of creditors, to consul and advise with the trustee in the administration of the bankrupt' estate.

Assets acquired by the trustee. The trustee acquires title to assets of the bankrupt debtor as of the date of the filing of th petition in bankruptcy, as well as title to property passing to th bankrupt by way of devise, inheritance, or bequest within six month from the date of adjudication.

Section 70a of the Bankruptcy Act enumerates the followin classes of the bankrupt's property that pass to the trustee as asset of the bankrupt estate:

1. Documents relating to the bankrupt's property.
2. Patents, copyrights, and trade-marks.
3. Powers that the bankrupt might have exercised for his own benefit.
4. Property transferred by the bankrupt in fraud of creditors.
5. Property, including rights of action, which, prior to the filing of the petition, could by any means have been transferred by him or which might have been levied upon and sold under judicial process against him.
6. Rights of action arising upon contracts or the unlawful taking of or injury to the bankrupt's property.
7. Contingent remainders, executory devises, rights of entry for condition broken, rights of reverter, and like interests in real prop-

ty, which were nonassignable prior to bankruptcy and which, within six months thereafter, become assignable interests or give rise to powers in the bankrupt to acquire assignable interests.

8. Property held by an assignee for the benefit of creditors.

9. Property that vests in the bankrupt within six months after adjudication by bequest, devise, or inheritance.

10. Property in which the bankrupt has at the date of bankruptcy an estate or interest by the entirety, and which within six months after adjudication becomes transferable in whole or in part solely by the bankrupt.

Duties of the trustee. The trustee has the burden of administering a bankrupt estate. He must, by sale, reduce the assets to cash and deposit the funds in a banking institution specially designated by the Court. He is required to examine the bankrupt. He must examine proofs of claim and object to improper ones. He may, without special authorization by creditors, file specifications of objections to the bankrupt's discharge. He must pay dividends to creditors as ordered by the referee. The trustee must file, from time to time, reports showing the condition of the bankruptcy estate. It is his duty to institute appropriate proceedings, suits, and actions against the bankrupt and third parties to "turn over" or account for assets belonging to the estate. The trustee's lot is eased somewhat by the recently enacted law by which, in the absence of the bankrupt's books or records, a presumption now exists that the sales price is the cost price. Of special help to the trustee in recovering assets is Section 67 of the Bankruptcy Act, sometimes referred to as the "Uniform Fraudulent Conveyance Act."

Since the trustee has title to all the assets of the bankrupt estate he represents, he has the power and right to bring any and all such actions as are necessary in order to collect assets which legally belong to the estate, but of which he has not secured possession. Moreover, since he represents all the bankrupt's creditors, he may commence such proceedings as any of the creditors might institute to avoid fraudulent or illegal transactions. Where the trustee fails or refuses to bring such action, the creditors may then petition the court for an order compelling the trustee to bring the suit or apply for his removal.

Referee's duties. The referee in bankruptcy, appointed by the United States judges, presides at the first meeting of creditors and at adjourned hearings, as well as at the examination of the bankrup and other witnesses. He also has other duties related to discharge of the bankrupt and arrangement proceedings mentioned at page 110- Creditors must file their verified proofs of claim in the referee's offic (see page 1104).

Examination of the bankrupt. The bankrupt must attend the first meeting of creditors. The statute requires that the referee shal examine the bankrupt publicly. The bankrupt must also attend the hearings on the objections to his discharge and such other hearings as the Court may direct. He may also be required to file in court in duplicate a sworn inventory giving the cost of merchandise or other property remaining on hand as of the date of bankruptcy.

The "Statement of Affairs" referred to on page 1103, which must be filed by the bankrupt or debtor whether or not he is engaged in business, is in the nature of a questionnaire, wherein the bankrupt furnishes, in effect, a history of his business career within six years preceding the filing of the petition; a statement of his books and records showing by whom they were kept and audited; and also records of his financial statements, inventories, income tax returns, bank accounts, legal proceedings affecting his assets, transfers of property other than in the course of business, losses by fire, theft, or gambling, loans repaid, and so on. This very comprehensive review of the bankrupt's affairs must be filed within five days prior to the holding of the first meeting of creditors and is usually of inestimable help to the Court and examining creditors' counsel.

Discharge of the bankrupt. Where an individual bankrupt, including a partnership and its members, is concerned, his adjudication in bankruptcy acts automatically as a petition for a discharge. The bankrupt corporation, however, is required to file a petition for discharge within six months of the date of adjudication.

The referee is required to mail to creditors a thirty-day notice of the date set for the filing of specifications of objections to a bankrupt's discharge. If no specifications of objections to the discharge are filed, the referee grants the bankrupt's discharge.

Grounds for denial of discharge. The bankrupt will be denied his discharge if he has committed any one of the following acts:

1. An offense punishable by imprisonment as provided by the bankruptcy law.

2. Destroyed, mutilated, falsified, concealed, or failed to keep or preserve books of account or records from which his financial condition and business transactions might be ascertained, unless the Court deems such acts or failure to have been justified.

3. Obtained money or property on credit, or an extension or renewal of credit, by making or publishing or causing to be made or published, in any manner whatever, a materially false statement in writing respecting his financial condition.

4. At any time after the first day of the twelve months immediately preceding the filing of the petition, transferred, removed, destroyed, or concealed or permitted to be removed, destroyed, or concealed any of his property, with intent to hinder, delay, or defraud his creditors.

5. Has, within six years prior to bankruptcy, been granted a discharge, or had a composition or an arrangement by way of composition or a wage earner's plan by way of composition confirmed under the Act.

6. In the course of a proceeding under the Act, refused to obey any lawful order of, or answer any material question approved by, the Court.

7. Failed to explain satisfactorily any losses of assets or deficiency of assets to meet his liabilities.

Investigation of fraud. Creditors may call upon the United States Court through its officers, the referee or trustee, to refer to the United States Attorney the matter of inquiring into the acts, conduct, and property of the bankrupt where it is believed that a criminal offense has been committed in violation of the laws of the United States, such as concealment or fraudulent transfer of assets, using the mails to defraud (for example, mailing a false financial statement), or giving false oaths in bankruptcy proceedings. The United States Attorney will submit the facts to the Federal Grand Jury, which frequently indicts the violators of the law. If necessary in the public interest, the United States Attorney, who now receives notice of hearing on the bankrupt's application for discharge, may file specifications of objections to the bankrupt's discharge.

Voluntary Arrangement Proceedings Under Chapter XI of the Bankruptcy Act (Extension or Modification of Unsecured Debts)

What is an arrangement? The newly created Chapter XI of th Bankruptcy Act is known by the title "Arrangements." In effect, thi chapter supersedes the provisions of the old Bankruptcy Act for com positions and extensions of time for payment of debts.

The word "arrangement" means any *plan* of a debtor for the settle ment, satisfaction, or extension of the time of payment of his un secured debts, upon any terms.

Chapter XI provides only for the treatment of several classes o unsecured creditors and permits the rejection of burdensome execu tory contracts.

Filing a petition. An arrangement proceeding can be filed only as a voluntary proceeding; that is, only a debtor may file a petitio under Chapter XI. It may be instituted by an individual, a partner ship, or a corporation (except banking, municipal, railroad and in surance corporations, and building and loan associations), before o after adjudication in a pending bankruptcy proceeding, but the Dis trcit Court will not stay the old bankruptcy proceeding, except upon terms of indemnity.

The petition for arrangement should be accompanied by the schedules of the debtor's liabilities and assets, including a statement of executory contracts of the debtor. It is imperative that there be attached thereto a "Statement of Affairs" and the debtor's proposed plan of arrangement.

Immediately upon the filing of the arrangement petition, the matter is referred to a referee in bankruptcy, and from that time on the appointed referee exercises complete and original jurisdiction over the matter.

The Court may authorize the debtor to continue and operate the business, but the debtor will be required to indemnify the creditors for any loss resulting from the operation of the business during the time the plan of arrangement is being considered.

Creditors' meeting. The referee calls a meeting of creditors upon at least ten days' notice to consider the plan of arrangement. Such notice to creditors is accompanied by a copy of the plan and a sumıary of schedules of liabilities and assets. At this meeting the debtor ıust be examined. A creditors' committee may be appointed, and tentative trustee may also be nominated at this meeting, at which reditors should file their proofs of claim.

Confirmation of arrangement. The referee will confirm the arangement if he is satisfied that it is for the best interests of creditors; hat the plan is for the best interests of creditors and feasible; that he debtor has not been guilty of any acts which would have barred ıis discharge in bankruptcy; that good faith has been shown on the ›art of the creditors and debtor; and that written acceptances have ›een filed by a majority in number and amount of those creditors vho have filed their claims; and that the consideration to be paid to :reditors and allowances have been deposited.

Termination of proceedings. Upon confirmation of the arrangement, the debtor is discharged from all unsecured debts provided for by the arrangement, except debts that are not dischargeable. A final decree must be entered discharging the debtor or trustee and closing the estate.

If the plan of arrangement is not acted on favorably by creditors or is abandoned by the debtor, the Court enters an order adjudging the debtor a bankrupt and directs that further proceedings be had as in the case of ordinary bankruptcy. If a bankruptcy proceeding was pending when the petition for arrangement was filed, the Court will dismiss the Chapter XI proceeding and direct that the previous bankruptcy proceeding be continued. Where the debtor has perpetrated fraud in the procurement of the confirmation of an arrangement, it will be set aside upon application made within six months of the date of confirmation.

Involuntary or Voluntary Corporate Reorganization Under Chapter X of the Bankruptcy Act (Extension or Modification of Secured and Unsecured Debts)

Corporate reorganizations. Chapter X of the Bankruptcy Act is known as the law pertaining to corporate reorganization. It is an outgrowth of the old Section 77 B. By this method the debtor, stockholders, and creditors seek to avoid the consequences of foreclosures, liquidations, forced sales, and other drastic deflationary effects. This law deals only with the corporate debtor and provides mainly the basis of a modification of secured debts or a change in the corporat capital structure. Chapter X should be invoked only when no ad quate relief can be obtained under Chapter XI, which deals with th modification of unsecured liabilities.

The pendency of the ordinary bankruptcy, either before or afte adjudication, will not prevent the filing of a Chapter X petition.

Another interesting feature is that under Chapter X the proceedin may be voluntary or involuntary, while under Chapter XI only a vol untary proceeding may be filed. The petition under Chapter X ma be filed only in the jurisdiction where the debtor has its principa assets, or its principal place of business, for the period of six month preceding the date of the filing of the petition, or for a longer portior thereof than in any other jurisdiction.

Filing petition in involuntary reorganization. In the involuntary proceeding the petition must allege that the debtor has been adjudged bankrupt in the pending proceeding; or that a receiver in equity has been appointed because of insolvency or inability to pay debts as they mature; or that an indenture trustee is in possession by reason of a default; or that a foreclosure proceeding is pending against the debtor's property; or that the debtor corporation has committed an act of bankruptcy (see page 1102) within four months prior to the filing of the petition.

In contradistinction to the rights of a creditor in the ordinary bankruptcy proceeding, a creditor may interpose an answer to an involuntary reorganization petition. The reorganization petition must be approved by the Court and must be shown to have been filed in good faith. If it is not approved, the petition will be dismissed.

Appointment of trustee. Where the liabilities are over $250,000 in a Chapter X reorganization proceeding, the Court must appoint a disinterested trustee. In cases where the liabilities are less than $250,000, the Court may appoint a trustee or permit the debtor to continue in possession. The trustee must be independent, but there is also provision for the appointment of a co-trustee, who may be drafted from the corporate debtor. He may be a director or an officer. The attorney for the trustee must also be disinterested. The trustee must conduct an examination into the past affairs of the debtor. He is the one who must promulgate the plan of reorganiza-

›n. He calls upon the creditors, debtor, and others for information d data, but the trustee is the one in the first instance to initiate e plan of reorganization. In making his report as to the condition the debtor's affairs as he finds it, the trustee must make that report the judge, the creditors, the stockholders, and also to the Securities ıd Exchange Commission, popularly referred to as the "S.E.C." If in a case involving less than $250,000 in liabilities, the judge de-ınes to appoint a trustee but permits the debtor to continue in the ›eration of its business, the Court may appoint an examiner to con-ıct a disinterested examination into the affairs of the debtor corpo-tion, for the information of the Court and others.

Plan of reorganization. If for any reason the trustee's plan is not ›und satisfactory, then, and not until then, the creditors (and stock-olders where the corporation debtor is solvent) may submit a plan f reorganization. The judge has the right to fix the time for filing ıe claims and to classify creditors.

In cases where the liabilities exceed $3,000,000, the judge must ːfer plans that he regards as worthy of consideration to the Securities nd Exchange Commission for examination and report. In other ases no duty devolves upon the judge to refer the plan to the S.E.C., ut he may do so. The S.E.C.'s report is merely advisory; it is not ›inding on the judge.

Acceptance of plan of reorganization. It is necessary to obtain cceptances of two thirds in number and amount of each class of ːreditors whose claims have been allowed in order to present the mat-er of the application for confirmation of the plan to the Court. In-ofar as stockholders are concerned, where the corporation is solvent, ı majority in number of shares is required to modify their rights. Jsually the judge will confirm any plan of reorganization that has ›een adequately accepted by the creditors and stockholders affected ›y the plan, but he must find, as a prerequisite, that the plan is "fair, ːeasible, and equitable" based upon his informed and independent udgment. Creditors are entitled to priority over stockholders against all of the property of an insolvent corporation, and in such event stockholders are excluded from participation in any plan of reorgani-zation unless they make a reasonable cash contribution.

Voluntary Wage Earners' Plans Under Chapter XIII of the Bankruptcy Act

Dealing with embarrassed wage earners. Frequently wage ear ers incur obligations through the purchase of automobiles, jewelr and furniture on the installment plan and through borrowing fro finance companies. If the debtor happens to be such a wage earne it is advisable to point out to him that if his creditors sue and obta judgments against him, his wages will be garnisheed, and the resul ing annoyance to his employer may lead to his discharge. The debt should be made acquainted with the provisions of Chapter XIII o the Bankruptcy Act, entitled "Wage Earners' Plans," under which h can obtain effective relief and at the same time deal honorably wit his creditors on the basis of an extension or compromise of his obl gations.

Procedure under Chapter XIII. Although no involuntary pet tion in bankruptcy may be filed against a wage-earner debtor unles his earnings exceed $1,500, under this new important provision fo relief, a wage earner who earns from all sources of income a sum nc exceeding $5,000 per year may, at modest expense, invoke this forn of procedure by which he can submit a plan to pay his obligations ou of his future earnings. The debtor's voluntary petition indicatin that he is insolvent or unable to pay his debts as they mature shoul be accompanied by his schedules of assets and liabilities, as well as "Statement of Affairs." Immediately after the filing of the petition the Court issues an order restraining all creditors from proceedin outside of the Federal Court. The referee promptly notifies th creditors to attend a creditors' first meeting, at which the debtor' plan is considered.

Creditors should file with the referee at the first meeting of cred itors their proofs of claim, similar in form to those used in ordinar bankruptcy proceedings. Each creditor filing a claim must state un der oath that such claim is free from usury.

Confirmation of plan. The Court will confirm the wage-earner's plan if accepted in writing by a majority in number and amount of the claims of creditors as filed, and if satisfied that the plan is for the best interests of creditors and feasible. Until the provisions of

e plan are complied with, the Court continues to retain jurisdic-
on of the debtor and his affairs.

Since by this method the debtor submits his future earnings to e control of the Court, the Court may, from time to time, after otaining the views of the debtor and his creditors, increase or reduce ny of the installment payments under the plan or extend or shorten e time for such payments as the circumstances and financial condi- on of the debtor warrant.

SECTION 11

usiness Organizations—Individual Proprietorships, Partnerships, and Corporations

1. SELECTING THE FORM OF ORGANIZATION

2. PARTNERSHIPS

3. DUTIES, POWERS, AND LIABILITIES OF CORPORATE DIRECTORS

4. DUTIES, POWERS, AND LIABILITIES OF CORPORATE OFFICERS

5. STOCKHOLDERS' RIGHTS

6. PREPARING FOR CORPORATE MEETINGS

7. STOCKHOLDERS' MEETINGS

8. DIRECTORS' MEETINGS AND COMMITTEE MEETINGS

9. HOW TO KEEP MINUTES OF MEETINGS

10. DOING BUSINESS IN MORE THAN ONE STATE

SECTION 11

Business Organizations—Individual Proprietorships, Partnerships, and Corporations

1. SELECTING THE FORM OF ORGANIZATION

Choosing a form of organization for a business. In starting a new business or in reorganizing an old one, the first problem to be considered is the form in which the enterprise will be conducted. The choice generally lies among:

1. An individual proprietorship.
2. A general partnership.
3. A corporation.

The individual who expects to conduct a business as sole proprietor will ordinarily choose between the single-proprietorship form and the corporate form. Two or more individuals who propose to enter into a business enterprise together will generally choose between the partnership and the corporation. These forms of business organization are, however, not exclusive. Two or more individuals may carry on an enterprise as:

1. A limited partnership.
2. A joint venture.
3. A joint-stock company.
4. A business trust.

Factors affecting choice of form of organization. Which form of organization shall be chosen in any case will depend upon the relative advantages and disadvantages of each kind of organization to the particular business. The factors as to which advantages and disadvantages should be carefully weighed are:

1. Manner of organization.
2. Taxation; that is, the relative tax burden of doing business under each form.
3. Stability of enterprise; that is, whether or not the organization may be easily disrupted.
4. Extent of risk; that is, extent of liability to creditors of those who have contributed capital to the business.
5. Ease of raising capital.
6. Flexibility of management and control.
7. Power to do business in any state.
8. Definiteness of governing law.

Manner of organization. The *individual proprietorship* is the simplest form of organization. Formalities are unnecessary to establish it. All that the individual need do is to ascertain whether a license is required to conduct the particular business, and whether a license fee or tax must be paid to State or local authorities.

A *general partnership* is also organized with comparative ease. It is usually formed by having the parties interested in the enterprise sign a partnership agreement. A written agreement is not, however, essential to the existence of a partnership. Not only may an oral partnership agreement be effective in establishing the partnership relation, but a partnership may even be implied from the acts and representations of the parties engaged in an enterprise, although no agreement, oral or written, has been made.

When a *limited partnership* is organized, the laws of the state of organization must be complied with strictly; otherwise the enterprise will be deemed to be a general partnership. Organization is effected by filing with some designated State official a contract drawn in accordance with legal requirements.

The chief difference between a general partnership and a limited partnership is that in the latter the liability of one or more of the partners may be limited to the amount agreed to be invested in the business. The limited partnership may have one or more general partners and one or more limited partners. A limited partner must contribute capital to the partnership, and, under the Uniform Limited Partnership Act, the contributions may be cash or other property, but not services. The surname of a limited partner may not appear in the partnership name unless it is also the surname of a eneral partner or unless the partnership had been carried on, be-ore the time the limited partner entered the business, under a name n which his surname appeared.

The limited partnership should not be confused with the *limited-artnership association*, the organization of which is permitted by a ew states. In the state of its organization, the limited-partnership ssociation is treated as a corporation; in other states it is usually reated as a general partnership. Organization of the association is ffected by the filing of a certificate of association with the secretary f state and the county clerk and the payment of an organization tax. nterests in the business are represented by shares which resemble the hares of stock of a corporation but differ from them in that a pur-haser can acquire no rights in the shares until he is elected to mem-ership in the association.

The organization of a *corporation* is not as simple as that of an in-lividual proprietorship or a general partnership. It may be accom-lished only by complying strictly with the laws of the particular state n which the corporation is being organized. These laws provide that certain number of persons, generally three or more, may form a cor-oration by filing in the office of a designated State official a state-nent, known as the articles of incorporation or the certificate of ncorporation, giving certain specified information, and by paying nitial taxes and filing fees. Further, in order to carry out the pur-oses for which the corporation is organized, it is necessary to hold arious organization meetings at which specified details of organiza-tion must be handled.

The *joint venture* (or "*syndicate*," as it is sometimes called) is very much like the partnership and may be organized with equal ease. It is formed merely by agreement between the parties interested in the enterprise. It differs from the partnership in certain technical respects, and in the fact that it is organized for a particular purpose, upon the accomplishment of which its duration terminates.

The *joint-stock company* resembles both the partnership and the corporation. Like the partnership, it is organized under a contract, known as the articles of association, between the parties in interest. Like the corporation, however, it is subject to State laws regulating its organization and the manner of conducting its business, and its capital is divided into transferable shares evidenced by certificates.

The *business trust* (or "Massachusetts trust," or "common law trust," as it is sometimes called) is created by the execution of a dee of trust—an instrument in the nature of a contract between th creator of the trust, certain persons designated as trustees, and one o more beneficiaries. Under the terms of this deed of trust, property i turned over by the creator of the trust to the trustees, to be manage by them for the beneficiaries who are parties to the agreement an any other beneficiaries who may become interested in the trust Interests in the trust are evidenced by certificates resembling th certificates of stock issued by corporations. In some states the stat utes specifically authorize the creation of business trusts and regulat the conduct of their business. In others, such trusts may be organ ized without express statutory authorization. In a few states th organization of a business trust is not permitted.

Taxation. Large businesses are almost obliged to select the corpo rate form of organization because it is the only one under which it i possible to raise large amounts of capital. For such a business, taxa tion is not a determining factor in the choice of a legal business form Where it is practical to operate a business either as an individual pro prietorship, a partnership, or a corporation, taxation usually become an important consideration. Thus, a small business that is to b closely owned would be concerned with this question. Attention i usually given principally to the Federal income tax. The followin provisions are basic in making the comparison between the incorpo rated and the unincorporated forms.

Individual proprietorship and partnership. 1. A business organize as an individual proprietorship or a partnership does not pay ar income tax as a business unit.

2. The sole owner of a business pays an income tax on all of hi income from his business whether it is left in the business, taken out as salary, or withdrawn as profits. He is taxed at the rates applicabl to individuals.

3. In a partnership, each partner pays income tax as an individua on his share of the partnership profits whether it is withdrawn or not The salary paid to each partner is immaterial; it merely enters int the computation of the portion of the profits going to each partner Partnerships must report their net income in order that the authori ies may check on the amount of income reported by the several part ners to whom the income is taxed.

Corporation. 1. A corporation pays income tax as a business unit. The salaries it pays to stockholders are deductible in arriving at its net taxable income. Dividends declared by the corporation are not deductible since they are distributed profits.

2. Salaries paid to stockholders are income to them. Dividends paid by the corporation are income to the stockholders. Dividends, therefore, are taxed twice, once to the corporation (as part of its earnings) and again to the stockholders.

3. The corporation cannot arrange its salary and dividend policies solely to effect a low tax for the stockholders because (a) the corporation can deduct salaries only to the extent that they are reasonable, and (b) earnings that are not needed in the business must be paid out in dividends; otherwise the corporation may be subject to a penalty surtax under Section 102 of the Internal Revenue Code. Thus, a corporation cannot free itself from corporation income tax by paying out all of its income in salaries, nor can it avoid all tax on its stockholders by paying no dividends or salaries.

Although the choice of legal organization on the basis of its effect upon the Federal income tax usually comes up only when the organizers can select the individual proprietorship, general partnership, or the corporate form, mention should be made here of how other forms of organization are treated under the Federal income tax law.

Limited partnerships may be taxed as partnerships or corporations, depending upon their characteristics. *Joint ventures* may be classed as partnerships or corporations, and *joint stock companies* as corporations. A trust that is organized to conduct business and earn income in the same manner as other enterprises is regarded as a corporation.

The Federal income tax does not, of course, cover the whole tax program. There are other Federal taxes to be paid, such as the old age benefits tax, the unemployment insurance tax, and the various excise taxes. These taxes are usually unimportant so far as the choice of a form of organization is concerned. There are also many state taxes to which a business may be subject, such as franchise and license taxes, unemployment insurance taxes, state and local business license taxes, and local property taxes. Some of these would vary with the form of organization; others would not. Then, of course, there are the Federal and state stamp taxes which apply to corporations. Almost every law imposing these taxes gives some official the right to call for books and documents on a moment's notice. For example, state inspectors may call on New York corporations and ask to see the stock transfer books to ascertain whether the proper stamps have been affixed to meet stock transfer requirements.

Guide for determining choice taxwise between partnership and corporation. Sometimes, in a small business, if all profits are to be distributed, it is fairly obvious that the corporate form is disadvantageous because the corporation pays a tax as a business unit and the unincorporated forms do not. Other times it is fairly obvious that the corporate form is better, taxwise, because the firm is expected to make large profits, most of which will be plowed back into the business to meet legitimate needs. Where the tax results are not obvious, to find out which form would be most economical taxwise, facts and estimates must be brought together. Then actual computations must be made of the income taxes to which the business and the owners would be subject if one or another form of organization were used.

Suppose it were practical to operate a business either as a partnership or a corporation, and there were no obvious certainty as to which form would result in lower taxes. To determine the more economical form taxwise, the organizers would do the following:

1. Estimate the anticipated respective net incomes of the partners, if a partnership were formed, and compute the income tax at the prevailing income tax rates applicable to each partner. (An individual includes in his gross income not only his business income, but other income such as rents, royalties, dividends, and interest. Since the individual income tax rates increase as the amount of taxable income increases, each partner's income from sources other than the business may have an important influence on the results of the computation.)
2. Estimate the taxable net income of the corporation. This calls for an estimate of the salaries that would be paid to the stockholders who would presumably be employed by the corporation. Compute the income tax of the corporation at the prevailing corporation rates. For excess profits tax years, estimate the excess profits net income and excess profits credits and compute the excess profits tax.
3. Estimate the income tax of the stockholders from salaries paid by the corporation and dividends received from the corporation and compute the income tax payable by each of the stockholders at the prevailing individual rates. (What was said under point 1 as to income from other sources applies here as well.)

4. Compare the total income taxes of the partners with the sum of the income and excess profits taxes on the corporation and the total income tax on the stockholders. Whichever total is lower would be the more desirable form from the standpoint of the Federal income tax.

The tax factor is usually studied on the basis of the laws as they exist at the time that the question of choice of organization form arises. The laws, it must be remembered, are constantly subject to change. The conclusions reached with regard to the relative income tax burdens on incorporated and unincorporated businesses under a tax law that imposes low rates on individuals and high rates on corporations may not hold under a later tax law that leaves the individual rates unchanged and lowers the corporation tax. Of course, business organizations may be revamped, but the process is always costly.

Stability of enterprise. By stability is meant not the length of time for which the organization may continue but whether or not it may be easily disrupted.

An *individual proprietorship* is not limited in its duration by law. It is not, however, a stable form of organization, for illness of the owner may interupt it, and his death terminates it. A *partnership* is unstable—although it may be organized for a long period of time —for it is terminted by death or withdrawal of any one of the partners. A *coporation,* even though its duration may not always be perpetual, is a stable form of organization, in that it has continuous succession. Death, disability, or bankruptcy of a party interested in the corporation does not terminate it, and the certificates of stock that represent the interests in the enterprise may be transferred from one person to another without interrupting the business. The *joint venture* continues only until the specific purpose for which it was organized is accomplished. The *joint-stock company* is stable, for not only may it have unlimited duration but also it issues transferable certificates of interest. The life of a *business trust* is limited in most states. The trust is nevertheless a comparatively stable form of organization, because the parties interested at the time the trust expires can agree to another trust and, also, because the interests in the enterprise are represented by transferable certificates that give the trust continuous succession.

Extent of liability. The extent to which those who have contributed capital to an enterprise are liable to creditors of the business is a very important factor in the choice of a form of organization. Regardless of the form in which an enterprise is organized, creditors are entitled to be paid out of the assets of the business before capital contributed to the enterprise may be withdrawn. Where, however, those assets are insufficient to satisfy creditors' claims, to what extent may the owners of the business be compelled to pay out of their own property?

A person who acts under an *individual-proprietorship* form of organization is personally liable for all the debts of his business to the full extent of the property that he owns; he cannot limit his liability to creditors to the amount that he puts into the business. Each member of a *general partnership* is fully liable personally for all debts incurred by the partnership, regardless of the amount of his investment in the partnership business. In a *limited partnership*, the limited partners, like stockholders of a corporation, risk only the amount that they have invested in the business. The general partners in a limited partnership, however, are each personally liable for all debts incurred by the enterprise. There must be one or more general partners in any limited partnership.

The *corporation* has a decided advantage over the other types of organizations, in that the creditors of the corporation are limited in the collection of their claims to the assets of the corporation, and if a stockholder has paid for his stock, he cannot ordinarily be compelled to pay creditors out of his own property, even though the corporate assets may be insufficient to pay the creditors' claims.

While the interests of members of a *joint-stock company* are evidenced by certificates of stock, members are personally liable for the company's debts; the statutes of some states, however, permit limitation of liability by inclusion of a provision therefor in the articles of association.

Trustees of a *business trust* are liable to creditors for debts of the trust, unless they obtain exemption from liability by contract with creditors. They may also be liable to the beneficiaries for gross negligence or fraud in the management of the trust property.

Ease of raising capital. Every business enterprise, regardless of the form in which it is organized, may require additional capital from ime to time in the furtherance of its business. Inability to obtain adequate working capital is often the cause of failure of an enterprise. It is important, therefore, before deciding upon the form of organization for a business, to consider what means for raising capital will be available under the various forms of organization.

In an *individual proprietorship,* the owner may raise additional capital needed for his business by borrowing from banks, by purchasing goods on credit, and by himself investing additional amounts in the enterprise. Since he is personally liable for the debts of his business beyond the amount that he has invested in it, banks may be ready to advance funds and merchants may be willing to extend credit to an extent commensurate with the single proprietor's personal means. The amount thus made available will nevertheless always be limited, and a business requiring a large amount of capital to operate successfully should not be organized as an *individual* proprietorship.

A *partnership* may be able to raise capital with greater ease than an individual proprietorship, for the resources of several individuals are combined in one enterprise. As in the case of the single proprietor, the partners assume full personal responsibility for partnership debts, and not only may the partnership be able to borrow on better terms than a corporation, but outsiders may be more willing to extend credit to it because of the security afforded by the partners' full liability.

The *corporation* is generally in a better position to raise large sums of money than are other forms of organizations. It may sell stock and other securities to the public in small amounts that attract many widely scattered investors, for participation in the corporation and ownership of an interest therein will not subject them to any financial risk beyond the amount of their investment.

Flexibility of management and control. In the *individual proprietorship,* management and control are concentrated in one individual. This may operate both as an advantage and as a disadvantage. On the one hand, concentration of control avoids the difficulties often caused under other forms of organization by opposing factions and divided responsibilities. The fact that the person who runs the business has a direct and full interest in its success is conducive to careful management of the enterprise. On the other hand, one individual may not be personally well equipped to perform all the functions of management, and the exclusive management that ties the owner down to his business may become highly burdensome. True the owner may, without formalities, employ assistants and delegate various powers to them, but he will nevertheless have to bear ultimate responsibility for their acts.

In a *general partnership,* each partner usually has an equal right to participate in management, and control is divided among the partners. The fact that the ability and experience of several individuals is thus combined in the furtherance of one enterprise may give the partnership an advantage over the single proprietorship. The division of control among the various partners may, however generate disagreement as to business policies and administration. As compared with the corporate form of organization, the partnership has this advantage—decisions may be arrived at and changes may be effected simply by agreement among the partners, without the formalities necessary under a corporate form of organization.

In a *limited partnership,* a limited partner may not participate in management of the business; if he does, he may be held liable as a general partner. The limited partner is, however, entitled to inspect the books of the partnership and to obtain full information regarding the partnership affairs.

In the *corporation,* those who have contributed to the capital of the business do not necessarily participate in conducting its affairs. Management may be concentrated in the hands of a group of experts who may own but a small portion of the stock of the corporation. The corporation thus avoids the difficulty of the single proprietorship, the business of which may be hampered by the limited ability or experience of one individual. On the other hand, it runs the risk of inefficient management where those who control the business do not have a direct financial interest in it. The corporation also has this advantage over the partnership, that whereas in the partnership each partner has power to act as general agent for the partnership, stockholders cannot bind the corporation by their acts merely because they are stockholders.

From the point of view of management, the *joint venture* resembles the single proprietorship; the syndicate is generally operated by one individual who acts as manager, with the assistance of agents appointed by him. The manager is, of course, answerable to the participants in the syndicate.

The *joint-stock company* resembles the corporation from the point of view of management and control. The articles of association under which the joint-stock company is formed generally provide that management shall be vested in a board of directors or governors elected periodically by the shareholders. These shareholders, like stockholders in a corporation, cannot bind the company by their individual acts, and they participate in the management of the company only by electing the board of governors and by acting at their meetings on matters brought before them by the board.

The *business trust* is managed and controlled by the trustees, whose appointment may be permanent. The powers and duties of the trustees are indicated in the trust agreement. The shareholders or holders of certificates of interest in the trust may not exercise any control; otherwise they will be liable as partners. They cannot elect trustees periodically in the same way that stockholders of a corporation may elect new directors, and they may be given power to elect a new trustee only in the event of death, withdrawal, or removal of the trustee for dishonesty or neglect of duty.

Power to do business in any state. An individual who resides in one state may carry on business in any other state without paying any greater taxes and without incurring any obligations other than those imposed on residents of the state, whether he operates alone as an *individual proprietorship* or with others as a *partnership* or a *joint venture*. His right to do so is guaranteed by the United States Constitution, which provides that the citizens of each state shall be entitled to all the privileges and immunities of citizens of the several states. The state may require the obtaining of a license and the payment of a license fee for carrying on a particular kind of business in the state, but the license will be available to the citizen of any state who meets the uniform conditions imposed, and no greater license fee will be required than is fixed for residents.

Forms of organization that do not create an artificial entity enjoy a freedom of movement in any state that is denied to the *corporation*. The corporation owes its existence to the state in which it is organized, and no other state need recognize its existence. The various states do permit corporations created under the laws of other states to do business within their borders, but only if such corporations comply with certain special state requirements (see discussion on page 1264).

In states that do not recognize the *joint-stock company* as a distinct legal entity, such a company may conduct business in the state without being subject to restrictions imposed upon corporations. However, the statutes of many states governing the right of foreign corporations to do business include joint-stock companies in the definition of foreign corporation.

In doing business outside of the state in which it was organized the *business trust* is now generally subjected to the same restrictions and regulations as a corporation. It was formerly the general rule that trustees of a business trust could carry on business in any state on the same terms as local trustees; the trustees were, however, always subject to local rules governing their relationship to the beneficiaries of the trust and to third persons.

Definiteness of governing law. The legal status of an *individual proprietorship* is well established, and little doubt, if any, exists as to the relationships between the owner, his agents, his creditors, and any other outsider with whom he may come in contact in the course of his business. The same may generally be said of a *partnership*, the laws governing which are fairly uniform and have been codified in many states by the Uniform Partnership Law. *Corporations*, on the other hand, are governed by state statutes that vary from state to state and which, even when similar in wording, are differently interpreted. In the conduct of the corporation's affairs, a familiarity with the corporation laws of several states may be indispensable, for questions may arise in the course of the corporation's business which are governed by the laws of a state other than that in which the corporation was organized. Despite the uncertainty as to the legal effect of corporate acts, however, the corporation is universally recognized as a form of organization, and its essential characteristic, that of limiting liability on the part of stockholders who contribute capital to the enterprise, is uniform in every state. In this respect the corporation has an advantage over the *joint-stock company* and the *business trust*, the legal status of which is not definitely conceded in every state. The business trust is, perhaps, confronted with the greatest difficulties, for not only do the laws vary considerably from state to state, but the law relating to the trust has not been fully established.

A business that is to be carried on in various states may well hesitate to organize as a business trust, for the legal effect of many of its acts will be far from certain. For example, the courts present a great diversity of opinion as to whether the holders of certificates of interest in the trust may appoint and remove trustees, whether a certificate holder has a right to inspect the stock records, and whether he can compel the declaration of a dividend out of surplus profits.

Choosing a name under which to do business. Individual proprietorships are generally conducted under the name of the individual who owns and operates the business. The name of at least one of the partners is also often included in the name under which a partnership operates. Both individual proprietorships and partnerships, however, sometimes find it desirable to carry on business under an assumed or fictitious name. Before using such a name, it is important to ascertain whether or not an assumed or fictitious name must be registered with a state official under the laws of that state. Many states require that every person transacting business under an assumed name, or under any designation, name, or style other than the real name of the individual conducting the business, must file in the office of a designated government official a certificate setting forth the true name and address of the person transacting such business. Penalties are imposed for failure to file such certificates. In some states no suits may be maintained on contracts by individuals who have failed to comply with the statute. Unless the statute refers exclusively to partnerships, regulations governing the use of fictitious names by individuals would also apply to joint ventures and to joint-stock companies, for such organizations are not considered legal entities but are deemed to be conducted by the individuals interested in the enterprise.

Some states impose other restrictions upon the use of fictitious names, as, for example, New York, where the designation "and Company" or "and Co." must represent an actual partner. As far as corporations are concerned, the law in many states requires that the name of the corporation indicate the form of its organization; in some, the use of the word "Company" or "Corporation," followed by "Inc.," is mandatory.

In selecting a name for a business, it is important to choose one that is not already in use by some other organization, for otherwise liability may be incurred for infringement of the goodwill of the older company.

Similarity in corporate names. In most of the states, the secretary of state is directed by statute not to file a certificate of incorporation if the name of the proposed corporation so closely resembles that of an existing corporation that deception or confusion might result. In the absence of statutory provisions, it has been held that the secretary of state is justified in refusing to file a certificate of incorporation where the name selected bears too great a likeness to an existing name. When the state grants a charter to a corporation, it merely authorizes the use of the name selected by the corporation in a legal manner. The state does not adjudge the name to be legal, nor does it decree that its use throughout the state will be lawful.

The corporation's name is an element of its existence. It belongs exclusively to the corporation and will be protected from imitation that constitutes unfair competition. Priority in adoption and use usually confers the superior right to the name. Even aside from statutory provisions, the corporation's right to its name will be protected by an equity court so far as may be necessary to safeguard property rights developed under it and to protect the corporation against fraud, actual or constructive.

Where it is found that there is a similarity in names, the court does not at once grant relief, but proceeds to ascertain whether the facts are such that deception and injury are likely to result. The law will not interfere to restrain a corporation in the use of its name where there exists no conscious intent to injure, no effort to secure for itself the benefit of another's industry, business capacity, and capital outlay, and no harm to the public from imposition through probable confusion. A change of name or the use of an explanatory phrase will be required where deception and injury result from similarity in names.

2. PARTNERSHIPS

Who may become a partner. Any person who is competent to enter into a contract may become a partner.

Alien. An alien may become a partner, provided the nation of which he is a citizen is not at war with the United States. If, after the partnership is organized, war does break out between this country and that of the alien partner, the partnership is suspended and is, in practical effect, dissolved.

Infant. An infant—that is, a person under the age of 21—may enter into a contract of partnership, but he may set aside the agreement if he chooses. During the infant's minority, he may avoid personal liability on partnership transactions. He may also avoid liability after attaining his majority, provided he disaffirms the obligation within a reasonable time after he becomes of age. Neither the adult partner nor third parties may, however, avoid any liabilities on the ground of the infancy of the partner. Nor can the infant prevent the application of the partnership assets to the partnership debts, or recover his original capital contribution to the business.

Incompetent person. An incompetent person who has been adjudicated insane cannot, generally, become a partner; if no judicial declaration of insanity has been made, a partnership agreement although valid may be set aside. If a partner becomes insane during the life of the partnership, the partnership is not thereby dissolved, but the insanity may furnish a ground for dissolution by a court of equity. Until such dissolution, the insane partner's rights and liabilities as a partner continue.

Married woman. A married woman may now generally be a partner, for the statutes in most states have removed the disability to contract imposed upon married women by the common law. In most jurisdictions, a married woman may even become a partner with her husband.

Corporation. A corporation cannot be a partner unless expressly authorized to do so by its charter. It may, however, enter into agreements with others for the purpose of co-operation and joint service.

Partnership. Two or more partnerships may enter into a partnership agreement with each other.

What a partnership agreement should contain. The provisions of the partnership agreement will vary with the needs of the particular enterprise. Every partnership agreement, however, should contain the following:

1. The name under which the partnership is to be conducted.
2. The kind of business to be conducted by the partnership.
3. The principal place of business.
4. The amount of capital to be invested by each partner; a state-

ment of whether the amount is to be paid in cash or in property if any part is in property, a full description thereof, and the amount at which it is to be valued.

5. The amount of interest, if any, which is to be allowed on capital.

6. The amount that each partner is to receive as salary or any other form of compensation or drawing.

7. The amount of interest, if any, that is to be charged against drawings.

8. The manner in which the profits and losses of the business are to be divided among the partners.

9. The powers and duties of each partner.

10. The duration of the partnership.

11. The manner in which the partnership is to be terminated; division of partnership assets among the respective partners.

The partnership agreement may also provide for the keeping of partnership books; the time or times for accounting; the method of settling disputes; the continuation of the partnership business in the event of withdrawal, death, or incompetency of any partner.

Division of profits and losses among the partners.* The partnership agreement often provides for other than an equal distribution of profits and losses. Some of the most common methods of distribution are:

1. On the basis of the ratio of capital invested at organization of the business.
2. On the basis of arbitrary ratios.
3. On the basis of the ratio of the capital accounts at the beginning or at the end of each period.
4. On the basis of the ratio of average investments.
5. Part of the profits may be distributed as salaries or as interest on capital invested, and the remainder in some other ratio.
6. If the investment is less than the amount agreed upon, interest is charged on the shortage; and if the investment is more than the amount agreed upon, interest is credited on the excess; the resulting profit or loss is then distributed in an agreed-upon ratio.

* The material on division of profits is from Curtis and Cooper, *Mathematics of Accounting*. New York: Prentice-Hall, Inc.

Division of profits on basis of arbitrary ratios. The method is ndicated in the following example.

EXAMPLE

A and *B* are partners. *A* has $3,000.00 invested, while *B* has $2,-500.00 invested. *A* is to receive ⅔ of the profits, and *B* is to receive ⅓. The profits for the year are $2,400.00. What is each partner's share?

Solution

Net Profits	$2,400.00
A's share, ⅔ of $2,400.00........	1,600.00
B's share, ⅓ of $2,400.00........	800.00

Division of profits on basis of ratio of capital accounts at beginning or end of each period. The method is indicated in the following example.

EXAMPLE

January 1, *A*'s investment..........	$10,000.00
January 1, *B*'s investment..........	6,000.00
January 1, *C*'s investment..........	4,000.00
Total	$20,000.00
December 31, Profits	$ 4,000.00

Profits are to be shared in the ratio of investments at the beginning of the year.

Solution

	Investment	*Ratio*	*Profits*	*Shares*
A	$10,000.00	10/20	$4,000.00	$2,000.00
B	6,000.00	6/20	4,000.00	1,200.00
C	4,000.00	4/20	4,000.00.	800.00
	$20,000.00	20/20		$4,000.00

Division of profits on basis of ratio of average investments. The procedure under this method is as follows:

1. Multiply each investment by the number of months from the date made until the end of the period; find the sum of the products obtained.

2. Multiply each withdrawal by the number of months from the date withdrawn until the end of the period; find the sum of the products obtained.

3. Deduct the sum of the withdrawal products from the sum of the investment products; the result for each partner is his average investment expressed in month-dollars.

The above three steps are performed for each of the partners' accounts. Then:

4. Add the month-dollars of each of the partners.
5. Multiply the profits by the ratio of each partner's month-dollars to the total month-dollars.

EXAMPLE

A

Debit		*Credit*	
Feb. 1	$1,000.00	Jan. 1	$10,000.00
June 1	1,500.00	May 1	4,000.00
Nov. 1	500.00	July 1	1,000.00

B

Debit		*Credit*	
July 1	$1,000.00	Jan. 1	$ 6,000.00
Dec. 1	1,000.00	Aug. 1	4,000.00
		Oct. 1	2,000.00

Solution

A

Investments Date	Amount	*Time to* End of Year	*Month-Dollars*	
Jan. 1	$10,000 ×	12 months =	$120,000	
May 1	4,000 ×	8 months =	32,000	
July 1	1,000 ×	6 months =	6,000	
				$158,000
Withdrawals				
Feb. 1	$ 1,000 ×	11 months =	$ 11,000	
June 1	1,500 ×	7 months =	10,500	
Nov. 1	500 ×	2 months =	1,000	
				22,500
A's month-dollars				$135,500

B

Investments				
Jan. 1	$ 6,000 ×	12 months =	$ 72,000	
Aug. 1	4,000 ×	5 months =	20,000	
Oct. 1	2,000 ×	3 months =	6,000	
				$ 98,000

Withdrawals

July 1	$ 1,000 × 6 months =	$ 6,000	
Dec. 1	1,000 × 1 month =	1,000	
			7,000
B's month-dollars			$ 91,000

Net profits of the business for the year were $4,530.00 The distribution is as follows:

A's month-dollars	$135,500.00
B's month-dollars	91,000.00
Total month-dollars	$226,500.00

A's share of profits, $\frac{135,500}{226,500}$ of $4,530.00....	2,710.00
B's share of profits, $\frac{91,000}{226,500}$ of $4,530.00....	1,820.00
	$4,530.00

Division of profits in absence of express agreement. If the partners have failed to include in their articles of copartnership an agreement as to the method by which profits are to be distributed, the law provides that the profits shall be divided equally, regardless of the ratio of the partners' respective investments.

Division of losses in absence of express agreement. If losses are incurred and no provision has been made for their distribution, the profit-sharing ratio governs.

States which have adopted the Uniform Partnership Act. The Uniform Partnership Act has been adopted in the states listed below:

Alaska	Maryland	New Jersey	South Dakota
Arkansas	Massachusetts	New Mexico	Tennessee
California	Michigan	New York	Utah
Colorado	Minnesota	North Carolina	Vermont
Delaware	Missouri	Ohio	Virginia
Idaho	Montana	Oregon	Washington
Illinois	Nebraska	Pennsylvania	Wisconsin
Indiana	Nevada	South Carolina	Wyoming

The act in many of its provisions merely codifies general common-law principles governing the relations of partners to persons dealing with the partnership, the relations of the partners to one another and the rights, duties, and obligations arising out of the partnership relation. In some instances, however, as is indicated in the succeeding paragraphs on partnership problems, the law under the Uniform Partnership Act is different from the common law.

Right of partner to receive interest on capital. The partners may agree among themselves whether or not any interest is to be paid on capital contributed by the respective partners to the partnership. In the absence of such an agreement, the partners are not entitled to interest on capital.

Right of partner to receive interest on loans. A partner is entitled to interest on any loans made by him to the partnership, unless it is agreed that he shall receive no interest. The Uniform Partnership Act provides that a partner who, in aid of the partnership, makes any payment or advance beyond the amount of capital that he agreed to contribute shall be paid interest from the date of the payment or advance.

Right of partner to indemnity and contribution. A partner who fails to conform to the partnership agreement or to use the proper skill and diligence in the conduct of the partnership affairs must indemnify his copartners for any losses sustained thereby. Further, if a partner pays more than his just proportion of the firm's debts, he may compel his copartners to contribute their relative shares, unless the partners have agreed among themselves that there shall be no right of contribution or that the amount of contribution shall be limited to a specified amount. The Uniform Partnership Act provides that the partnership must indemnify every partner in respect of payments made and personal liabilities reasonably incurred by him in the ordinary and proper conduct of its business, or for the preservation of its business or property.

A partner is entitled neither to indemnity nor to contribution for payments or losses occasioned by the partner's own negligence, bad faith, or breach of duty.

Liability of a general partner to creditors of the partnership. Each partner is personally liable to creditors for all the debts of the partnership. If the assets of the partnership are insufficient to satisfy the claims of its creditors, the creditors may resort to the personal assets of any one or more of the partners. A partner who is compelled to pay a creditor out of his personal assets is entitled to contribution from each of the other partners. The partners may agree among themselves as to the division of liability among them for partnership debts, but creditors are not bound by such agreements; they may look to any or all of the partners for payment. As between themselves, and in the absence of any contrary arrangement in the partnership agreement, the partners are liable for debts of the partnership in the same proportion that they share in its profits. For liability of an incoming partner, see page 1153. For liability of a limited partner, see page 1128.

Liability of a secret partner; of a dormant, or silent, partner. A secret partner is one who is active in the business, but whose interest in the partnership is not generally known to the public. A dormant or silent partner is one who is neither known to the public as a partner nor engaged actively in the partnership affairs. Both the secret partner and the dormant or silent partner are liable to creditors of the partnership in the same manner as any other partner, regardless of whether or not the creditors knew of their interest in the partnership. In the event of their withdrawal from the partnership, however, no notice need be given creditors to avoid liability for obligations thereafter incurred; since the public did not know of their connection with the partnership, it cannot be misled by lack of notice of termination of the connection. The dormant or silent partner has no voice in the management of the partnership affairs.

Liability of an individual as a partner although he has not entered into a partnership agreement. A partnership relation may be implied from the acts of parties although no agreement of partnership, either written or oral, has been entered into. For example, where two people contribute capital to a joint enterprise and share in the profits and losses of the business, they may be deemed to be partners and subjected to a partner's liability to creditors. Similarly, if one person represents to the public that another person is his partner, and that other person makes no denial of the representation, the second person will not be permitted later to deny that the partnership relation existed, and he may be held liable by creditors as a partner of the business. The rule is that where a person leads other to believe that he is a partner and to act on that belief, he subject himself to a partner's liability.

The Uniform Partnership Act provides that the receipt by a person of a share of the profits of a business is prima-facie evidence tha he is a partner in the business, but no such inference shall be drawn if such profits were received in payment:

1. As a debt by installments or otherwise.
2. As wages of an employee or rent to a landlord.
3. As an annuity to a widow or representative of a deceased partner
4. As interest on a loan, though the amount of payment vary with the profits of the business.
5. As the consideration for the sale of the goodwill of a business or other property by installments or otherwise.

Liability of the members of a partnership for the tort of one partner. A tort is an injury inflicted otherwise than by a mere breach of contract. The members of a partnership are liable for injuries inflicted upon outsiders by one of the partners only where the partner has caused such injury in the course of the partnership affairs. For example, copartners have been held liable in these situations:

1. Where a member of a firm of attorneys gave negligent advice to a client.
2. Where a partner collided with another automobile while driving his car on partnership business.
3. Where a partner made false statements with respect to the financial responsibility of a competitor of the partnership.
4. Where a partner borrowed money for the partnership upon false representations as to the financial ability of the partnership.
5. Where a member of a publishing firm printed a libel in the partnership paper as news.
6. Where a partner in a butcher firm negligently left bad meat about, and a dog that ate it died therefrom.

Copartners have been held *not* liable for damages caused by a partner under the following circumstances:

1. Where a partner maliciously told about a third person untruths which constituted libel, but which were not told in furtherance of the partnership business.

2. Where a partner converted property to his own use.
3. Where a partner, without the consent of his copartners, instituted malicious prosecution against a third person for theft of partnership property.

The Uniform Partnership Act provides that where, by any wrongful act or omission of any partner acting in the ordinary course of the business of the partnership or with the authority of his copartners, loss or injury is caused to any person not a partner in the partnership, or any penalty is incurred, the partnership is liable therefor to the same extent as the partner so acting or omitting to act.

Management of the partnership affairs. In the absence of any contrary arrangement, each partner has an equal right to participate in the management of the partnership affairs, regardless of his proportionate interest in the partnership. The Uniform Partnership Act specifically provides that all partners have equal rights in the management and conduct of the partnership business.

Each partner has inherent power to act as agent for the partnership and to bind it with respect to matters relating to the partnership business. This power, however, may be limited by the terms of the partnership agreement or by any other agreement between the partners, but the limitation is not binding on outsiders who have no knowledge of it. The Uniform Partnership Act provides that an act of a partner that is not apparently for the carrying on of the business of the partnership in the usual way does not bind the partnership unless authorized by the other partners.

Where partners disagree as to how the ordinary affairs of the partnership should be conducted, the opinion of a majority of the partners is generally controlling, provided the majority acts in good faith and for the best interests of the partnership. If a dissenting partner is dissatisfied, he may withdraw from the partnership, or, if the action of the majority is improper, he may apply to the courts for an injunction. The Uniform Partnership Act provides that any difference arising as to ordinary matters connected with the partnership business may be decided by a majority of the partners; but no act in contravention of any agreement between the partners may be done rightfully without the consent of all the partners. It also provides that, unless authorized by the other partners, or unless they have abandoned the business, one or more, but less than all, of the partner have no authority to:

1. Assign the partnership property in trust for creditors or on the assignee's promise to pay the debts of the partnership.
2. Dispose of the goodwill of the business.
3. Do any other act that would make it impossible to carry on the ordinary business of a partnership.
4. Confess a judgment.
5. Submit a partnership claim or liability to arbitration or reference.

The partners may, of course, agree among themselves that certain decisions may be made by one or more of the partners. The partnership agreement may also provide a method for arriving at decisions in case of dissension. If the vote is equally divided and the division of opinion prevents the operation of the partnership business, a dissolution of the partnership becomes necessary.

May one of two partners prevent his copartner from binding him by his acts? Each partner is an agent of the other in effecting transactions within the scope of the partnership business. If, however, one partner objects to certain action taken by his copartner, he may, by giving notice to a third person, prevent his copartner from binding him to any new obligation. For example, each partner has power to issue negotiable paper in behalf of the partnership; but if one of two partners refuses to assent to the issuance of a promissory note and has notified the payee, the payee who accepts the note after such notification cannot enforce the note against the partnership. However, partners cannot impose additional burdens on third persons by objecting to acts of their copartners performed in the course of their implied powers as partners. For example, a partner has implied power to accept payment for partnership debts. A debtor may make payment to a partner even in the face of a notice from his copartner not to pay any sums to him.

Has a partner power to borrow money or to execute negotiable instruments? In considering the power of a partner to borrow money for the partnership, a distinction must be made between trading and nontrading partnerships. A trading partnership is a commercial enterprise in the conduct of which merchandise is bought and ld periodically and continuously. A nontrading partnership is one the conduct of which buying and selling is not involved, incidenlly or otherwise; the business of such a partnership generally relates some employment or occupation. A partner of a trading partnerip has implied power to borrow money to carry on the partnership fairs, and even if he appropriates borrowed funds to his own use, l the partners are liable therefor. As a corollary of the power to orrow, a partner of a trading partnership may make, accept, and idorse negotiable instruments for the partnership, and may pledge rtnership property as security for loans and give chattel mortgages iereof. A partner of a nontrading partnership, however, has no iplied power to borrow money for the partnership, nor has he imied power to execute negotiable instruments or give security for ans. If such a partner borrows money in behalf of the partnership, s copartners are liable only if they authorized the partner to negoate the loan or if they ratified it.

Power of a partner to collect partnership debts. A partner has nplied power to collect partnership debts and to give receipts for ayment. Cash and negotiable paper may be accepted, and, if it is istomary to do so, goods may also be accepted in payment. A parter may compromise debts of the partnership if he acts in good faith id with reasonable care. A corollary of the power to collect debts the power to resort to ordinary legal proceedings for their collecon. The Uniform Partnership Act, however, provides that, unless uthorized by the other partners, or unless they have abandoned the usiness, one or more, but less than all, of the partners have no auiority to confess a judgment or to submit a partnership claim or ability to arbitration or reference.

Power of a partner to lease partnership property. A partner has nplied power to lease both real and personal property in behalf of ie partnership, provided the lease is reasonably necessary to carry on ie partnership business in the ordinary course of its affairs.

Power of a partner to employ assistants. Each partner has imlied power to employ such assistants and to appoint such agents s are reasonably necessary to carry on the partnership business in he ordinary course of its affairs, and to discharge such assistants or agents. A partner may employ counsel to act in behalf of the partnership.

Power of a partner to purchase and sell personal property. A partner has implied power to make purchases for the partnersh on the credit of the firm, of such goods as are reasonably necess to carry on the partnership business in the ordinary course of affa This is true whether the firm is a trading or a nontrading partn ship,* as long as the goods purchased are necessary for the trans tion of business in the ordinary way. For example, a partner in grocery business may purchase a crate of canned goods; a partner o law firm may purchase law books for the partnership. The partn ship is liable for payment even if the partner misappropriates t goods to his own use. A partner also has implied authority in t regular course of business to sell or otherwise dispose of persor property of the partnership, including merchandise, negotiable pap patents, trade-marks, accounts receivable, and, as an incident of t power of sale, to make warranties as to quality and soundness. T extent of a partner's power of sale depends upon the general natu of the partnership business. A partner has no authority, however, use partnership property in payment of his individual debts.

Power of a partner to convey real property belonging to the partnership. Except in the case of partnerships whose business the purchase and sale of real estate, a partner has no implied pow under the common law, to convey real estate of the partnershi The Uniform Partnership Act provides, however, that where title real property stands in the partnership name, a conveyance of re property by any partner is binding as against an innocent holder f value, although the partner had no authority to make the conveyanc Where title to the real property stands in the name of one or mo of the partners, but not all of them, a conveyance by the partne in whose name the title stands is valid as against an innocent hold for value, although the partners had no authority to convey. Whe title is in the name of all the partners, a conveyance executed by a of them passes all their rights in such property.

At common law, title to real property could not be taken in th firm name, nor could real property be conveyed by the partnershi

---

* For difference between a trading and nontrading partnership, see page 114

ıder the Uniform Partnership Act, however, any estate in real ›perty may be acquired or conveyed in the partnership name.

May a partner engage in any other business? A partner may t, without the consent of his copartners, engage in any business, her openly or secretly, which competes with the partnership. If does so, he may be enjoined by a court of equity, and may be reired to account to the partnership for profits made in the compet- ; business. A partner may, however, engage in a noncompetitive ısiness, subject to any provision in the partnership agreement reiring him to devote all of his time and energy to the business of e partnership. In the absence of any express provision, a partner pliedly agrees to devote his time, efforts, and ability to the success the partnership, within reasonable limits. A partner may avail mself of information obtained by him in the course of the partnerip affairs for a purpose outside the scope of the partnership business d not competitive with it.

Is a partner entitled to compensation for his services? It is implied duty of every partner to devote all his time, skill, and ergy for the best interests of the partnership. He is not entitled be paid for his services in carrying on the partnership affairs. he contract of partnership may, however, provide for the com- ›nsation of one or more of the partners for services rendered. This mpensation may take the form of a fixed salary or of an additional are in the partnership profits. Contracts of partnership often ecify an amount that partners may draw at regular intervals out the business; generally, this is not by way of compensation for rvices rendered, but a division of the profits to which the partners e entitled. The Uniform Partnership Act provides that no partner entitled to remuneration for acting in the partnership business, ‹cept that a surviving partner is entitled to reasonable compensaon for his services in winding up the partnership affairs. At comon law, when a partner dies, the surviving partner is held not to entitled to reasonable compensation for his services in winding p the partnership affairs.

Power of a partner to execute instruments in the firm name. 'nder the common law, the power of a partner to bind his copartners by executing instruments in the firm name is subject to the following rules:

1. As to contracts not under seal, a partner has implied pov to sign the partnership name, but only to contracts within the scc of the partnership business; the partnership will not be bound wh a partner signs the firm name to evidence obligations outside of t partnership business.

2. As to instruments under seal, a partner has no implied auth ity, by virtue of the partnership relation alone, to bind the firm other partners by instruments under seal; hence a sealed instrume executed in the name of a firm by one of its members, withc proper authority, where a seal was necessary, is the deed of su member only, and he alone is bound by it.

3. If a partner executes an instrument, which is not by law or the custom of trade required to be under seal, and which wou bind the partners if it were executed as a simple contract, it will bi them, although there may have been an unnecessary seal attache and the seal is regarded as surplusage.

4. An instrument under seal executed by a partner is valid though the partner was not authorized to execute instruments und seal, where the instrument was executed in the presence of the c partners and with their knowledge; it is also valid if it appears th the copartners subsequently ratified the unauthorized act.

5. As an incident of the partner's implied power to collect ai compromise firm debts, it has been held that a partner may execu a general release under seal releasing the firm obligation.

The Uniform Partnership Act makes no distinction betwee sealed and unsealed instruments. Under the Act, every partner an agent of the partnership for the purpose of its business. Tl execution in the partnership name of any instrument pertinent to tl business of the partnership binds the partnership, unless the partn so acting has in fact no authority to act for the partnership in tl particular matter and the person with whom he is dealing has know edge of the fact that he has no such authority.

Instruments executed in a partner's individual name; may partnership be bound thereby? Where a partner signs his ow individual name without signing the partnership name, the partne ip may nevertheless be bound if it is shown that the instrument as intended as a partnership obligation and that the transaction as one entered into for the partnership. The partnership may en be held liable where the other party to the contract was unvare of the existence of the partnership when the contract was ade. The presumption is, however, that where a partner signs his dividual name, it was intended to bind him individually. One artner has no authority to sign the individual name of another artner without his consent.

Partner's right to information and inspection of books. Every artner has the right to full information as to the partnership affairs. furtherance of this right he may at any time inspect any and all artnership books and records and may make extracts therefrom. he books and records must be kept at the firm's place of business, id no partner may remove them from that place without the connt of the other partners. Of course, the right to inspect the books id to make extracts therefrom may not be used by a partner for a audulent purpose.

Under the Uniform Partnership Act, a duty is imposed upon parters to render on demand true and full information of all things ffecting the partnership to any partner or the legal representative of ny deceased partner or partner under disability. The act also reuires that the partnership books be kept, subject to any agreement etween the partners, at the principal place of business of the partership, and that every partner shall at all times have access to the ooks and be permitted to inspect and copy any of them.

When has a partner a right to an accounting? A partner is lways entitled to an accounting upon dissolution of the firm. An ccounting without dissolution will also generally be granted under he following circumstances:

1. If the partner is wrongfully excluded by his copartners from ie partnership business or from possession of partnership property.
2. Where a partner breaches his fiduciary relation and wrongfully erives profits for himself from the business or by use of its property.
3. Where the partners have agreed to a periodical accounting and settlement of distinct transactions upon their completion, without a dissolution.

4. Where the interest of a partner in the partnership has be attached by his individual creditor.

The Uniform Partnership Act provides that any partner sh have the right to a formal account as to partnership affairs:

1. If he is wrongfully excluded from the partnership business possession of its property by his copartners.
2. If the right exists under the terms of any agreement.
3. Where a partner is accountable as a fiduciary.
4. Whenever other circumstances render it just and reasonabl

Ordinarily partners can determine their respective interests in tl partnership by an examination of the books, without a formal a counting, and may settle the firm's affairs in a private accounti without resort to the courts if there is no disagreement betwe them and if the rights of creditors are protected.

Duty of a partner to account for personal benefits. Partne are required to observe the utmost good faith toward one anothe If one partner secures any private advantage from a transaction th concerns the partnership or through any wrongful use of partne ship property, he is required to account to his copartners for tl profits which he derives therefrom. For example, a partner wh secretly and without knowledge of his copartners obtains for himse a renewal of a lease previously held by the partnership violates h duty toward his copartners. Even if the term of the lease to tl partner individually is to begin upon the termination of the partne ship existence, the benefits of the lease belong to the partnershi and the partner must account to the partnership therefor. Th Uniform Partnership Act provides that every partner must accour to the partnership for any benefit, and hold as trustee for it an profits derived by him without the consent of the other partne from any transaction connected with the formation, conduct, liquidation of the partnership or from any use by him of its pro erty. This provision also applies to the representatives of a decease partner engaged in the liquidation of the affairs of the partnershi as personal representatives of the last surviving partner.

May one partner sue another partner? Ordinarily one partne cannot bring an action at law against another partner on a partne ıip claim or liability. Until the affairs of the partnership are wound p, what one partner may owe the partnership is not a debt due to is copartners, but to the partnership. Similarly, if the partnership wes a sum of money to one of the partners, it is not a debt due › him from his copartners, and he cannot bring an action against is copartners on his claim against the partnership. While a parter cannot sue at law to enforce the obligations of his copartners, e may, however, do so by applying to a court of equity for an acounting and settlement of the partnership affairs.

Where there is but a single partnership transaction that is fully osed, one partner may maintain an action at law against the others or his share of the profits of that single transaction without a formal ccounting. Similarly, where the partnership accounts have been ettled, a balance struck, and an agreement made to pay the balance ue, an action at law may be maintained to recover the balance.

Expulsion of a partner from the business. When one or more f the partners ceases to be a member of the firm, the partnership is issolved; that is, the partnership agreement is terminated and if ıe business is to continue, a new agreement must be entered into. ccordingly, a partner cannot be expelled from the business withut dissolution of the partnership. This does not mean that the issolution must be decreed by a court of equity. The partners may e able to arrive at a friendly accounting and determine their reective interests in the business. If, however, an amicable adjustıent is impossible, resort must be had to the courts to compel an ccounting and to decree a dissolution of the partnership. The reıaining partners can then form a new partnership to carry on their nterprise. Partnership agreements sometimes provide for the exulsion of a member under certain circumstances and indicate the ıanner in which the capital contribution of the expelled partner is o be repaid. The expulsion of a partner under such a provision ı the contract of partnership does not prevent the dissolution of the artnership; a new partnership must nevertheless be organized by he remaining partners.

May a partner transfer his entire interest in the partnership? 'he general rule is that the partnership is dissolved if a partner sells is interest in the partnership. Partners may agree in advance under heir partnership contract to accept as a partner an assignee of a partner's interest in the firm, but the partnership is neverthele technically dissolved upon admission of the assignee and a ne partnership is created.

Under the Uniform Partnership Act, a conveyance by a partn of his interest in the partnership does not of itself dissolve the par nership. The assignee is not entitled to interfere in the manag ment of the partnership affairs, nor may he require any informatic or account of partnership transactions, or inspection of the partne ship books; the assignee is merely entitled to receive the profits which the partner who has assigned his interest would have bee entitled.

Withdrawal of a partner. Where no time is fixed in the par nership agreement for the duration of the partnership, a partn may withdraw at any time, provided he does so in good faith ar without injury to his copartners. Even if the term of duration the partnership is fixed by the contract of partnership, a partn may withdraw from the partnership before the expiration of tl period; he may, however, subject himself to liability to the oth partners if the latter are injured by his withdrawal.

The withdrawal of a partner results in dissolution of the partne ship. If the remaining partners desire to continue the business the partnership, they must pay the retiring partner the value of h interest in the partnership, less any damages caused by his prem ture withdrawal. The goodwill of the business is not included arriving at the withdrawing partner's interest. The remaining par ners may agree to assume the liabilities of the partnership, but suc an agreement will not relieve the withdrawing partner from liabili to any creditor of the old partnership who has not consented release him. The withdrawing, or outgoing, partner may also l liable to new creditors of the old partnership who extend credit it without knowledge of his withdrawal. To avoid such liabilit the withdrawing partner must advertise his withdrawal in a new paper of general circulation in the place where the business of th partnership is conducted. Further protection against liability creditors may be afforded the withdrawing partner by an agreemer of indemnification by the remaining partners.

Admission of a new partner into the business. A new partne cannot be brought into the business without the consent of ever ıe of the partners. Further, although all the partners may agree admit the new member, the old contract of partnership is ter- inated, and a new partnership agreement must be entered into. owever, the transaction of the partnership business may continue ithout interruption.

The Uniform Partnership Act specifically provides that no person n become a member of a partnership without the consent of all e partners.

Liability of an incoming partner. Where a person is admitted a partner into an existing partnership, he is not liable, under the ımmon law rule, for partnership debts incurred before he became partner, unless he has assumed such liability.

The Uniform Partnership Act provides that a person admitted as partner into an existing partnership is liable for all the obligations the partnership arising before his admission as though he had een a partner when such obligations were incurred, except that ıis liability shall be satisfied only out of partnership property.

Effect of death of a partner. A partnership is dissolved upon ıe death of a partner. Even if the contract of partnership provides ɔr the continued existence of the partnership after the death of ny partner, the legal representatives of the deceased partner can- ot be compelled to continue the existence of the partnership. The ırviving partners become the representatives of the partnership, and is their duty to pay the firm debts and to distribute the remaining ssets among the surviving partners and the representatives of the eceased partners. They have a right to wind up the affairs of the artnership without interference by the legal representatives of he deceased partner. The surviving partners cannot, however, bind he estate of the deceased partner by new contracts. They must ender an accounting to the legal representatives of the deceased artner and pay them in cash the value of the deceased partner's nterest, including goodwill as a partnership asset. The surviving artners are entitled to a reasonable sum as compensation for wind- ng up the partnership affairs.

Surviving partners and all outsiders are, at common law, deemed o have knowledge of the death of a partner and of the resulting lissolution of the partnership; the power of the partners to act for he partnership automatically ceases upon death of a partner except insofar as it may be necessary to wind up the affairs of the partne ship. Under the Uniform Partnership Act, however, no such know edge of death and notice of the termination of the partner's a thority is imputed. Where a partner, having no knowledge or noti of the death of a partner, acts for the partnership and creates liability, each partner is liable to his copartners for his share of tl liability so created as if the partnership had not been dissolve Further, under the provisions of the Act, the partnership may l bound by the acts of the partner after dissolution as to outsiders wl had no knowledge or notice of the dissolution. Notice of dissol tion should be advertised in a newspaper of general circulation the place where the partnership business is regularly conducted.

Effect of bankruptcy of a partner. If any partner becom bankrupt, the partnership is immediately dissolved, for the bankru loses his right to exercise control over his property, and his intere in the partnership passes to the trustee in bankruptcy. The Un form Partnership Act expressly states that dissolution is caused l the bankruptcy of any partner or of the partnership.

Continuance of a partnership beyond its fixed term. Whe the partnership agreement fixes a definite period for the duration the partnership, but the business is continued after expiration of tl period without any new agreement, the partners are, in effect, doi business as a partnership pursuant to an oral agreement. Wheth or not their rights and duties are the same as under the origin partnership agreement will depend upon the intention of the partie It may be assumed, in the absence of any evidence to the contrar that the partners intended to continue the same relationship th existed prior to the expiration of the original agreement.

The Uniform Partnership Act provides that when a partnershi for a fixed term or particular undertaking is continued after th termination of such term or particular undertaking without an express agreement, the rights and duties of the partners remain th same as they were at such termination, as far as is consistent with partnership at will. It further provides that a continuation of th business by the partners or such of them as habitually acted therei during the term, without any settlement or liquidation of the par nership affairs, is prima-facie evidence of a continuation of the par nership.

Difference between dissolution and liquidation of a partner-ip. A dissolution of a partnership is merely a termination of the iginal partnership agreement, which may be brought about by ath of a partner, admission of a new partner, withdrawal of an d partner, adjudication of a partner as an incompetent person, or nkruptcy of a partner. The remaining partners may continue e business without interruption despite the dissolution, and pro-ed to organize a new partnership. A liquidation, on the other nd, involves not only a dissolution of the partnership, but also a le of the partnership assets, payment of partnership liabilities, and stribution of the balance among the partners in the proportions to hich they are entitled.

The Uniform Partnership Act defines dissolution of a partnership the change in the relation of the partners caused by any partner asing to be associated in the carrying on, as distinguished from e winding up, of the business. It further provides that on dissolu-on the partnership is not terminated, but continues until the wind-g up of partnership affairs is completed.

Incapacity of a partner as ground for dissolution. Where a rtner is temporarily incapacitated from performing his partnership ities, such incapacity does not furnish ground for dissolution. If, owever, his incapacity is permanent, dissolution will be allowed by e courts, since the partner is unable to fulfill one of the essentials f his agreement—that is, to devote his time, effort, and ability to e success of the partnership enterprise.

Failure to make profits as ground for dissolution. Dissolution f a partnership will be allowed by the courts on the ground that it reasonably certain that the business cannot be carried on at a rofit. This is true whether the failure to make profits is the result f misconduct on the part of one of the partners or whether it is ue to the business itself.

Powers of partners after dissolution. Upon dissolution of the artnership, the power of the partners to bind one another generally y their acts ceases. A partner does, however, have power to bind is copartners and the partnership property by such acts as are rea-onably necessary to wind up the partnership affairs. In the absence f any agreement to the contrary, each partner has implied power to take possession of the firm property and to sell, pledge, or oth wise dispose of it in order to wind up the business; to collect del and settle claims; and to complete existing obligations. The partn have no power, however, to incur new obligations by the executi of new contracts, or to make acceptances or renewals of negotial paper, or to make endorsements of negotiable paper other than dorsements without recourse.

The Uniform Partnership Act provides that, except, so far as m be necessary to wind up partnership affairs or to complete tra actions begun but not then finished, dissolution terminates all thority of any partner to act for the partnership.

Who has power to liquidate the business upon voluntary d solution? When dissolution is brought about by the acts of t partners themselves, each partner has, in the absence of any contra agreement, an equal right upon dissolution of the partnership to t possession of its assets, and is under an equal obligation to app the assets to the discharge of the partnership debts. Each partn may collect debts due and may pay off liabilities until the assets a exhausted.

The Uniform Partnership Act provides that, unless otherwi agreed, the partners who have not wrongfully dissolved the partn ship, or the legal representative of the last surviving partner, n bankrupt, have the right to wind up the partnership affairs; provide however, that any partner, his legal representative, or his assigne upon cause shown, may obtain winding up by the court.

Division of profits and losses upon liquidation. If, upon co plete liquidation of the partnership affairs, there are profits or loss they must first be divided in the profit-or-loss ratio—that is, in t proportion in which the partners share profits and losses under t terms of the partnership agreement—and the remaining capit should then be shared by the partners in the capital ratio—that in the proportion in which they are entitled under the terms of t partnership agreement to a return of the capital which they have i vested in the business. Where the partnership is insolvent, t sharing by the partners of losses in the profit-and-loss ratio may sult in a deficit in capital for some one or more of the partne Each partner with a deficit should contribute to the firm the amou of his deficit. If he is unable to pay into the firm any portion s deficit, the remaining partners must pay in, in the profit-and-ss ratio, an amount sufficient to cover this deficit. A partner who is paid in more than his share of the firm's liability has a right to force contribution from the other partners to the extent of the cess.

Distribution of capital upon liquidation * Liquidation may be complished in two ways:

1. All the assets may be converted, all the liabilities paid, the ofits or losss distributed, and all the capital divided at one time.
2. A periodic distribution of the capital may be made before all e assets are converted.

Example of total distribution. The first method of liquidation illustrated below.

EXAMPLE

From the following figures, show the amount of capital distributed to ch partner at dissolution:

	A	B	C
Capital balance before conversion of assets	$10,000	$6,000	$4,000
Profit ratio	40%	40%	20%
Assets converted into cash	$30,000		
Liabilities to be paid	14,000		

Solution

Assets		Liabilities		Net Assets
$30,000	–	$14,000	=	$16,000

Total Investment, $20,000, less Net Assets, $16,000 = Loss, $4,000

	A (40%)	B (40%)	C (20%)	*Total* (100%)
Capital balances before conversion of assets	$10,000	$6,000	$4,000	$20,000
Distribution of loss	1,600	1,600	800	4,000
Balances	$ 8,400	4,400	3,200	16,000
Cash distributed	8,400	4,400	3,200	16,000

Changing a partnership to a corporation. A business that operates under a partnership form of organization may be converted

* The example of the method of total distribution is from Curtis and Cooper, *Mathematics of Accounting*. New York: Prentice-Hall, Inc.

into a corporate form only if all the partners consent. The follo ing steps are generally taken to effect the change:

1. The partners re-evaluate the assets of the partnership in t light of current market conditions, goodwill being entered as an a set on the books.

2. If the value of the assets is thereby increased, the increas value is credited to the partners in the proportion in which they a entitled to share in the profits of the partnership.

3. The partnership sells all its assets to a corporation formed carry on the business, the corporation undertaking to accept all th liabilities of the partnership. Many states have enacted statut known as the Bulk Sales Act for the protection of creditors upc sale, transfer, or assignment in bulk of any part or the whole of stock of merchandise pertaining to the conduct of the busines otherwise than in the ordinary course of trade. These laws diff in the various states, but in general they require that a certain nur ber of days before such sale in bulk, notice thereof be given to cred tors. Strict compliance with Bulk Sales laws may be necessary upo transfer of the partnership assets; otherwise the sale may be deeme fraudulent or void.

4. The corporation issues stock to the partners in payment of th assets so transferred to it. The amount of stock issued by the ne corporation to each partner is generally determined by the amour of capital that he has contributed to the partnership. It should b remembered, however, that while each partner has, in the absenc of a contrary agreement, an equal voice in the management of th partnership affairs and shares equally in its profits, a stockholder i ordinarily entitled to one vote for each share of stock that he hold in the corporation, and dividends are payable to him on each share In order that the individuals may have the same relative interest i the corporation that they had in the partnership, some special ar rangement may be required either in the nature or characteristics o the securities issued by the corporation to represent the respectiv interests, or through the payment of salaries to the individuals. In this respect, the partnership form of organization has greater sim plicity than the corporation, for the contract of partnership may easily provide for any desired division of profits.

3. DUTIES, POWERS, AND LIABILITIES OF CORPORATE DIRECTORS

Who are qualified to act as directors. The statutes in most ates require either that a director be a stockholder of the corpora-on, or that he be a stockholder if the articles of incorporation do not rovide otherwise. Reasonable qualifications for its directors may so be included in the by-laws of the corporation. In the absence f any provision in the statute, charter, or by-laws prohibiting some erson or class of persons from acting as a director, or requiring cer-in qualifications for directors, any person may be a director who is gally competent to contract. In some states one or more directors re required to be residents of the state of incorporation or are re-uired to be citizens of the United States. Even though some of the embers of the board may not have the required qualifications, the cts of the board in behalf of the corporation are binding so far as ne public is concerned.

Number of directors that a corporation is required to have. he statute of the state of incorporation generally fixes the minimum umber of directors that a corporation must have—usually three—nd the maximum number of directors that a corporation may have. he actual number that a corporation decides to have, within the tatutory limitations, is fixed in the charter or in the by-laws. This umber may be increased or decreased in the manner provided by tatute. If the number of directors is fixed by the charter, an amend-nent of the charter is generally required to change the number. If he number is fixed in the by-laws, those who had power in the first nstance to enact the by-law fixing the number of directors may mend the by-law to change the number.

Term of office of directors. The by-laws usually fix the period for vhich directors are to hold office, but even if that period has expired, hey continue to hold office until their successors are elected.

In some states the statutes provide that directors may be divided nto two or more classes whose terms expire at different times. These tatutes generally indicate the number of directors who must be lected annually and the maximum period for which any class of di-ectors may hold office. Even in the absence of such statutes, a corporation may classify its directors, unless its charter or by-laws requir that all directors be elected annually. The chief advantage of cla sifying directors is that there are always some members of the boar who are experienced as directors. For example, suppose a corpora tion is authorized to have nine directors and is permitted to classif them. At its organization, nine directors are elected, three directo to serve for a term of one year, three for a term of two years, an three for a term of three years. At the expiration of the first yea three new directors are elected for a period of three years, to take th place of those three directors whose term has expired; at the expira tion of the second year, three new directors are again elected for term of three years, to take the place of the second group whose terr has now expired. At the end of the third year after organization, th third group of directors is replaced by three new ones elected for period of three years. Each year thereafter, three new directors ar elected to fill the vacancies caused by the expiration of the term c one group of directors; the board will always consist of six old dire tors and three new ones.

Removal of a director with or without cause. A corporation ha an inherent right to remove a director for cause. It may remove director even without cause:

1. If the director was not elected for a fixed term and removal fo cause is not expressly required by statute, charter, or by-laws.
2. If removal without cause is expressly permitted by statute, cha ter, or by-laws.

A director who is elected for a fixed term can be removed only fo cause unless removal without cause is expressly authorizd by statut or charter. The power to remove a director rests with the stockhold ers unless otherwise provided under the laws of the state in whic the corporation is organized; directors cannot remove a director un less expressly authorized to do so. The statutes in most states giv the right of removal to the stockholders in express terms and specif not only what vote is necessary to effect the removal, but also th notice that must be given to the director proposed to be removed an to the stockholders. The corporation's by-laws often contain a provi sion regulating the removal of directors by the stockholders in accord ance with statutory requirements. A director who is to be remove for cause must be given reasonable notice of the intention to remove him, sufficient time to prepare his defense, and a fair hearing.

Resignation of a director. A director may resign at any time, even if he is elected for a fixed period, unless restricted by the corporation's charter or by-laws or by the laws of the state in which the corporation is organized. If a director has entered into a contract with the corporation to act as director for a fixed period, his resignation before the expiration of the period will make him liable to the corporation for damages caused by the breach of his contract.

Where the resignation states that it is to take effect on acceptance, acceptance is necessary to end the tenure of office. Where it states that it is to take effect immediately, no acceptance is necessary unless the statute, charter, or by-laws make it necessary. Any form of resignation, whether written or oral, is sufficient, provided the intention to resign is clear. It is advisable that the resignation be in writing, in order that a record may be made for future use in case of controversy, and that it indicate when the resignation is to take effect. In the absence of such a statement, a resignation takes effect immediately.

Filling of vacancies in the board of directors. The by-laws provide how vacancies in the board of directors shall be filled. These by-laws must be consistent with any provision contained in the charter of the corporation or in the statutes of the state in which the corporation is organized. A usual provision is that a vacancy in the board shall be filled by the board and that the directors so appointed shall hold office until the next annual election. This provision does not give the directors the right to fill newly created directorates. In the absence of any provision in the by-laws, charter, or statute, the power to fill vacancies in the board rests with the stockholders. The board of directors may continue to transact business even though a vacancy has occurred in the board, and even though the remaining number is less than the number of directors required by statute or by the charter, but it cannot transact business if the remaining number of directors does not constitute a quorum.

How to fill vacancies in board where several directors tender resignations at same meeting. The resignations of several directors should not be accepted at one time where the number of directors remaining will constitute less than a quorum, for, in the absence of a quorum, the directors will be unable to fill the vacancies caused by the resignations or transact any business. Each resignation should be accepted separately, and, immediately after each acceptance, the place of the resigned director should be filled. The director filling the vacancy should then assume his duties as director and participate in the acceptance of the resignation of the next director and the election of his successor. The secretary of the meeting should make certain that the directors who are to be elected to fill the vacancies will be present at the meeting so that they can participate in the elections immediately upon their taking office. The necessity for separate acceptance of resignations and separate elections is eliminated where the statute permits resignations to take effect at a future date and vacancies to be filled by the board immediately but to take effect when the resignations take effect.

Are directors entitled to compensation for their services? Directors are not entitled to compenstaion for services rendered within the scope of their duties as directors, unless compensation is authorized in one of the following ways:

1. By charter.
2. By by-law.
3. By resolution of the stockholders.
4. By resolution of the directors before the services were rendered, where the directors have authority to fix their own compensation.
5. By express contract between the director and the corporation.

Nor are directors entitled to compensation for attending meetings, unless payment is expressly authorized. In some jurisdictions, however, directors are entitled to compensation for services rendered outside of their ordinary duties as directors, provided the services are performed at the instance of the corporation and with an understanding that compensation is to be paid. Where, for example, a director devoted practicaly all of his time to the corporation and acted as its manager and superintendent, it was held that he was entitled to be compensated.

Directors cannot, ordinarily, vote themselves compensation unless authorized to do so. Such vote must come from the stockholders. Directors may, however, fix the salary of a corporate officer, who is also a director, for services performed as such officer and outside of his duties as a director, unless expressly prohibited from doing so. If, however, the resolution authorizing payment of compensation is carried only by including the vote of the director who is to receive the compensation, the resolution may be held not to be binding on the corporation. As a general rule, interested directors cannot even be counted in determining whether a quorum is present to vote upon the question of their own salaries. Where the directors fill all or most of the offices of the corporation and it is desired to vote them compensation for their services, the best solution is to have the stockholders either vote the salaries or ratify the action of the directors in voting the salaries. The votes of interested directors who are also stockholders may be counted.

An alternative to the above procedure is to introduce a separate resolution fixing the salary of each officer. The director whose salary as officer is being considered does not vote upon the resolution. This procedure has been held invalid in some cases, principally on the theory that introducing several resolutions is equivalent to breaking the resolution into parts, and all the directors are interested in the common object of getting a salary for each of them.

Power of directors to manage the corporation. The directors, acting as a board, have the power to manage the business of the corporation, to exercise the corporation's powers, and to control its property. This power is exclusive with the directors unless the governing statute, charter, or by-laws provide otherwise. In most states the statutes, in express terms, give to the board of directors entire control over the corporate affairs. In the absence of such statutes, management of the corporate affairs is expressly vested in the board of directors by provision in the charter or by-laws. Stockholders have no right to interfere with the management of the corporation by the directors, except insofar as the consent of stockholders is required by statute, charter, or by-laws, to effect certain transactions, such as an increase in the capital stock, transfer of all the corporate assets, dissolution, and so forth. The fact that the stockholders are holders of substantially all of the outstanding stock, while the directors hold only a few shares necessary to qualify them for office, does not change the general rule. The management is nevertheless vested in the board of directors.

When the courts will interfere with management of the corporation by the directors. The courts will not interfere with the management of the corporation by the board of directors merely because of errors of judgment on its part. Where, for example, the directors honestly and in the exercise of their judgment overexpand the business activities of the corporation to such an extent that the corporation suffers heavy losses, the courts will refuse to oust them from office. Similarly, the courts will not substitute their own judgment for that of the directors who have entered into a lease, in behalf of the corporation, which the directors deem fair and advantageous. Where, however, the directors have acted fraudulently, illegally, oppressively, or beyond their powers, the courts will interfere in order to protect the corporation.

A director cannot agree to relinquish his duty to manage the corporation. The stockholders have a right to expect from every director good faith, reasonable care, and prudence in the consideration of every question that is presented to the board of directors in managing the corporate affairs. A director cannot relieve himself of this obligation by contract. He cannot agree with the stockholders, with his codirectors, or with the corporation that he will act merely as a nominal or "dummy" director. So far as the law is concerned, a director's function is to direct, and no such thing as a "dummy" director exists.

Limitation on power of directors to effect fundamental changes in the corporation. The power of the board of directors to manage the corporate affairs includes the transaction of the ordinary business of the corporation. It does not include the making of fundamental and vital changes in the corporation, such as an increase or reduction in its authorized capital stock, a change in the purposes for which the corporation was organized, a transfer of all the assets of the corporation by sale or lease, a voluntary dissolution of the corporation, and so forth. In most states the statutes contain specific provisions requiring the approval of a certain percentage of the stockholders to enable the directors to effect such basic changes.

What powers may directors delegate to others? The board of directors may delegate to others the performance of ministerial acts and the transaction of the ordinary routine business of the corporation. For example, the board may engage an individual to manage one of its branch stores, with power to hire and fire any and all employees necessary in running the store. It may authorize officers to prepare, execute, and deliver certain documents; to enter into contracts of employment; and to sell securities for the corporation. The directors cannot, however, unless the articles of incorporation specifically authorize them to do so, transfer to others any duties imposed upon them that involve the exercise of judgment and discretion. For example, the board of directors cannot give an employee general power to lease property of the corporation; it cannot delegate to officers the power to determine when calls shall be made for the payment of subscriptions to stock. Nor can the directors delegate powers given to them by the stockholders, which powers they would not otherwise have had. If the stockholders should adopt a resolution granting to the board of directors power to make and adopt all by-laws for the corporation, the board would have no power, in its turn, to adopt a resolution granting to the president the power to make and adopt by-laws.

Is a resolution necessary to effect a delegation of powers by directors? In delegating any of its powers to others, it is advisable that the board of directors, formally, at a duly called meeting, adopt a resolution setting forth clearly the nature and extent of the authority given. A resolution is, however, not essential. The board of directors, by its acquiescence in a course of dealing by the person to whom it has delegated authority informally, is bound by that person's acts performed pursuant to such delegation of authority. The election of a person to an executive office may in itself imply that that person has the usual powers accompanying the office. Even if a resolution delegating authority is adopted, and that resolution specifies the powers granted thereby, the corporation will be bound by the exercise of additional powers not mentioned in the resolution if the board of directors acquiesces therein.

Power of directors to appoint committees. The board of directors may appoint committees to perform various functions for it, the members of which may be directors or others. The power to appoint committees is expressly granted to the board by statute in some states and is confirmed in the by-laws of many corporations. The committee most commonly appointed by the board of directors is the executive committee, which exercises the powers of the board in accordance with the policy of the corporation and under the direction of the board during intervals between directors' meetings. The powers of the executive committee include the transaction of the ordinary business of the corporation; it may be authorized to make loans, to endorse notes in the corporate name, to make purchases for the corporation, to collect debts owing to the corporation. An executive committee that has powers of the board when the board is not in session may not assume sole control of the corporation for an indefinite period, amend by-laws that only the directors are by statute permitted to amend, change the number of members of the committee, remove a member by a majority vote, or appoint or remove officers and fix their salaries. Nor may such an executive committee execute a contract upon which the corporation is about to act. The calling of a meeting of the board may suspend the power of the executive committee to act in place of the board.

Power of directors to employ, compensate, and remove agents and servants. As an incident to its power to manage the corporation, the board of directors has the power to determine who shall carry out its orders, and to appoint such agents and servants for the corporation as it sees fit. This power is generaly confirmed by the charter or by-laws of the corporation. In the absence of fraud, the courts will not interfere with the board of directors in its appointments. It is also within the discretion of the board of directors to fix the amount of compensation of agents and servants appointed by it, and the terms of their employment. The board may provide for payment of compensation in advance; it may authorize payment of commissions in addition to salaries; it may give bonuses to employees.

The power of the board of directors to remove agents and servants follows the power to appoint them. If the length of employment is not fixed by contract, the employee may be removed by the board of directors at any time. If the contract does fix a definite term of employment, a discharge by the directors before the expiration of the time fixed, without proper cause, may subject the corporation to liability in an action by the employee for breach of contract.

May directors appoint agents for a term beyond their own term of office? The board of directors may contract with agents to perform services for the corporation beyond the board's own term of office, provided the contract is reasonable in the light of the surrounding circumstances. The following test of reasonableness has been laid down: Does the power given to the agents appointed beyond the directors' term of office deprive the stockholders of their right to change the management of the corporation at subsequent annual elections? If it does, it is not reasonable, and the contract of employment is invalid. A contract employing an officer for a period as long as the corporation continued in existence was held unreasonable. On the other hand, a contract employing a general manager for a period of ten years was held valid.

May directors ratify unauthorized acts performed by others in behalf of the corporation? The board of directors may ratify unauthorized acts of others only if it could in the first instance have granted authority to perform those acts. For example, the general manager of the corporation, who has no authority to make purchases in behalf of the corporation, buys a carload of merchandise. The board of directors may ratify the purchase, since it could have authorized the general manager to make the purchase in the first place. In order that ratification may be effective, however, it must be made with full knowledge of all the facts. If, for example, the general manager had made a secret profit in the purchase of the merchandise, and the board of directors, unaware of his personal interest in the transaction, had ratified the contract of purchase, the ratification would not be binding upon the corporation, and the directors could subsequently, upon learning the facts, repudiate the transaction.

Is a resolution necessary in order that directors may be deemed to have ratified an unauthorized act? The directors may ratify an agent's unauthorized act by resolution, but such resolution is not essential. Ratification may be implied from acquiescence by the board of directors in the unauthorized act, with full knowledge of the facts. Mere silence on the part of the board of directors does not always mean that the directors have acquiesced.

Power of directors to make contracts for the corporation. As an incident of their power to manage the corporation, the directors have the power to make any contracts in behalf of the corporation necessary, suitable, and proper in carrying out the corporate purposes. In the absence of fraud, their contracts are binding upon the corporation, although they may prove to have been unwise.

The directors may and often do delegate to officers and others their power to contract. Contracts entered into in behalf of the corporation by officers and others without authorization from the board of directors have also been held binding upon the corporation where such unauthorized persons were held out as having had the authority to contract for the corporation, and where the rights of innocent third persons were involved. The directors are not required to sign contracts that they have authorized. Authority to sign in the name of the corporation is generally given to designated officers by statute, charter, by-law, or resolution of the board of directors.

May a director or officer contract with the corporation? A director or officer may enter into a contract with the corporation, provided that he deals openly with the corporation and that the contract is properly authorized. If a director is personally interested in a matter that is being authorized by the board he should not vote upon the question.

Contracts with interested directors are not void merely by reason of the relationship between the parties. A corporation may, however, avoid the contract under the following circumstances:

1. If the interested director or officer participated in authorizing the corporation to enter into the contract, and his vote was necessary to bind the corporation, it is generally held that such a contract may be set aside even if it was fair to the corporation and even if the interested director or officer acted in good faith.
2. If the interested director or officer participated in authorizing the contract, but his vote was *not* necessary to bind the corporation, the courts are in conflict as to the right of the corporation to set aside the contract. Two rules exist:

(*a*) The Federal courts and those of a majority of the American jurisdictions hold that a contract with an interested director or officer who participated in authorizing the contract, but whose vote was not essential to such authorization, is voidable only if unfair to the corporation. These courts examine the contract closely for fraud, and place the burden of proof of fairness upon the officer or director.

(*b*) Some jurisdictions, including New York, hold that a contract with a director or officer may be set aside where the interested director or officer participated in authorizing it, irrespective of whether or not the contract was a fair one, and without any showing that the influence of the interested director or officer determined the action of the corporation. The theory on which this view is based is that a director or officer stands in the relation of a trustee to the corporation, and all contracts made by a trustee or fiduciary in which he is personally interested may be set aside at the election of the party he represents.

3. Whether or not the interested director or officer participated in authorizing the contract, it may always be set aside if it is shown that the contract was not fair to the corporation or that it was not entered into in good faith by the officer or director.

Power of directors to borrow money for the corporation. The power to borrow money rests with the board of directors as an incident of its power to manage the corporation. The directors may, however, delegate the power to borrow to an officer or agent of the corporation expressly by resolution of the board, impliedly by permitting it to appear that the officer or agent has authority to borrow, or by acquiescing in his acts. For example, the board of directors delegates to the vice-president the management of the business. In the course of his duties as manager, the vice-president from time to time borrows money from the bank in order to finance the purchase of merchandise necessary in carrying on the business. The corporation in this case is bound by the loan to the corporation, for the directors have, by entrusting management of the corporate affairs to the vice-president and permitting him to make loans, clothed him with authority to borrow in behalf of the corporation. Even if the vice-president had had no authority to borrow, either express or implied, the directors could not retain the benefits of the loan for the corporation and at the same time disown the acts of its vice-president.

The directors' power to borrow in behalf of the corporation is coextensive with the power of the corporation to borrow. Where the statute or charter limits the amount of indebtedness that the corporation is authorized to incur, the directors are, of course, bound by that limitation. Some statutes impose personal liability upon directors who permit the corporation to incur debts beyond the amount limited by statute.

May the directors give security for loans to the corporation? As an incident of its power to borrow money for the corporation, the board of directors may issue evidences of the corporation's indebtedness in the form of promissory notes, bonds, and so forth, and may give security for the loans to the corporation. This security may be in the form of a mortgage or pledge of specific personal property, a mortgage of specific real property, or a mortgage of all the property owned by the corporation at the time of execution of the mortgage and to be acquired by it in the future. The board of directors may give a mortgage to secure future advances, the mortgage becoming operative when the advances are actually made. It may also give security for a debt that already exists against the corporation, provided the debt is a bona fide one, and the security is given in good faith. The fact that the creditor happens to be a director or stockholder of the corporation does not prevent the giving of security for an antecedent debt, but the courts will scrutinize such transactions closely to determine whether or not they were effected in good faith.

Must the directors obtain the stockholders' consent to mortgage corporate property? The general rule is that the power to mortgage property of the corporation rests with the board of directors as an incident of its power to borrow, subject to contrary provisions in the statute, charter, or by-laws. Officers have no power to mortgage the corporate property unless authorized to do so by the board of directors expressly by resolution, or impliedly by holding out the officer to the public as possessing the power to mortgage. In some states the statutes specifically require the consent of a fixed proportion of the stockholders to the mortgaging of property, and, as a protection to the stockholders, specify the formalities to be followed in obtaining such consent.

May a director or officer lend money to the corporation? A corporation needing funds to carry on its business may borrow them from a director or officer, unless it is specifically prohibited from doing so by statute of the state of its incorporation, or by the provisions of its charter or by-laws. Loans by directors or officers may be made in the form of direct advances of funds or by endorsement of paper executed and negotiated by the corporation. The director or officer may accept interest on the loan at the legal rate, and he may take security for repayment. The entire transaction must, however, be entered into in the utmost good faith, and the courts will subject it to rigid scrutiny. Where a corporation does not need funds, a loan by a director or officer to the corporation is improper, and the director or officer may be compelled to account for any interest received on his loan and to return any security given.

May a director or officer borrow money from the corporation? The statutes in many states prohibit loans by the corporation to directors, officers, or stockholders, and impose upon those authorizing the loan a liability to the corporation for the amount advanced. In other states such loans are permitted provided interest is paid and security given. In the absence of any restrictive statutes, loans may be made to directors, officers, and stockholders provided the transaction is entered into in the utmost good faith. It may be advisable not to lend any funds of the corporation to directors, officers, or stockholders, for such transactions are always regarded by the courts with great suspicion.

Power of directors to make guaranties in the corporate name. In some states the statutes expressly grant to a corporation the power to bind itself as a guarantor; in others the power is expressly forbidden. In the absence of such statutes the general rule is that a corporation has the power to guarantee the obligations of others only where such an act is reasonable and necessary to enable the corporation to carry out the purposes for which it was organized. Where a corporation has power to guarantee the obligations of others, the power to make the guaranty rests with the board of directors. Thus the board of directors of a corporation having power to bind itself as a guarantor may endorse the note of, or guarantee payment of interest and principal on bonds of, a subsidiary corporation. The board of directors may ratify the unauthorized guaranty made by an officer in the corporate name if the corporation has the power to make the guaranty.

Power of directors to purchase and sell property in behalf of the corporation. The power of a corporation to purchase property is exercised by the board of directors. If the directors act in good faith, and the corporation has the power under its charter to acquire the property, the judgment of the directors in acquiring property for the corporation cannot be questioned.

The directors also have power to make sales of property in the course of the corporation's business, and to fix the terms of sale. In the absence of fraud, stockholders cannot object to sales made by the directors on the ground that the price is inadequate. If the directors, for example, in the exercise of their judgment, believe that it is advisible to sell merchandise below market price or below cost, they have a right to do so. Directors may not, however, without the consent of stockholders, sell all the assets of the corporation or so substantial a portion of them that the business of the corporation cannot be continued. The test in determining whether or not the directors may sell property of the corporation without the consent of stockholders may be said to be this: Is the property sought to be sold essentially necessary to enable the corporation to transact its ordinary business? If it is, the property cannot be sold without the consent of stockholders; if it is not, the directors have power in their own discretion to sell it. For example, a corporation engaged in the business of buying and selling real estate and having numerous real estate holdings may have authority to sell any or all of the real estate holdings of the corporation upon the authorization of the directors alone and without action on the part of stockholders. Another corporation organized to own and operate one particular building may not sell that building without the consent of stockholders, for the sale would terminate the business for which the corporation was organized.

Power of directors to lease corporate property. Where a corporation has power to lease its property, that power may be exercised by the board of directors. A lease of corporate property by an officer of the corporation is not binding upon it unless authorized or ratified by the board. Consent of stockholders is not necessary to authorize a lease of property made in carrying on the ordinary business of the corporation unless required by statute, charter, or by-laws. Where, however, it is desired to lease all the property of the corporation, the directors have no power to lease it without the approval of stockholders. The statutes in the various states generally indicate the proportion of stockholders whose consent is necessary to the leasing of all the property of the corporation, and in many instances the statutes define the rights of stockholders who object to the lease. The same authority is necessary to effect a surrender of a lease as was required to make the lease in the first instance.

Corporate property may be leased to directors or stockholders of the corporation, provided the lease is made:

1. In good faith.
2. For the best interests of the corporation.
3. For an adequate consideration.

Power of directors to make gifts of corporate property. Ordinarily the board of directors has no power to give away any property of the corporation. It may, however, donate property in the course of the corporation's business where some benefit accrues to the corporation. For example, the directors may dedicate for public purposes a parcel of the corporation's real estate in order to enhance the value of other parcels of property owned by it and to stimulate their sale. Bonuses may be paid to employees to foster increased effort and efficiency. Donations to charities may be upheld where they are made to further the goodwill of the business. Endowments may be made to a university to carry on research that may benefit the corporation's future productive activities.

Power of directors to elect officers. The officers of the corporation, required by statute, charter, or by-laws, are generally elected annually by the board of directors. In addition to the power to elect these required officers, the by-laws often give to the board of directors the power to appoint such additional officers as it deems necessary in the interests of the corporation. Where the board creates an additional office pursuant to this power, it has the right to abolish that office.

Removal of officers by directors with or without cause. Directors may generally remove an officer for cause, and the courts will not interfere with their action unless it appears that the removal was entirely unwarranted. An officer may be removed without cause only under the following circumstances:

1. If the officer was not appointed for a definite term, and removal for cause is not required by statute, charter, or by-laws.
2. If the statute, charter, or by-laws expressly provide that an officer may be removed without cause.

An officer who is being removed for cause must be given notice of the proposed removal and an opportunity to defend himself.

Power of directors to issue stock. The amount of capital stock that a corporation is authorized to issue is fixed in the articles of incorporation. However, not all of the amount so authorized need be issued at one time. The power to issue stock from time to time rests with the board of directors. Ordinarily action with regard to the issuance of stock must be taken by the board of directors at a meeting, properly called. An issuance of stock is not, however, necessarily invalid because formal action was not taken. If all the stockholders and all the directors are present and concur in the authorization of an issue of stock, the board of directors is presumed to have ratified the issuance even though it did not adopt any formal resolution of issuance. The kind of stock to be issued, the consideration to be received for the stock, and the manner and terms of issuing it, are determined by the board of directors, subject to provisions contained in the laws of the state in which the corporation is organized, its charter, and its by-laws. Directors have no power to issue stock without consideration. As a corollary of the directors' power to issue stock, the by-laws generally give the directors power to issue options to purchase stock.

Directors may incur liability for improper issuance of stock, as, for example, where they issue stock to themselves in order to gain control of the corporation, or where they issue stock to themselves without paying value therefor. For other liabilities of directors in connection with stock issuance, see page 1182.

Power of directors to declare dividends. The power to declare dividends and to determine the manner in which they shall be paid rests with the board of directors. This rule is, however, subject to the following limitations: (1) the directors must act in good faith; (2) a statute may limit or control the action of the board of directors; (3) the charter or by-laws of the corporation or some other governing instrument or contract may place an obligation on the directors to declare a dividend, or may limit its power to do so.

The courts will not interfere with the discretion of the directors in determining whether or not a dividend should be declared unless it appears that the directors have acted fraudulently, oppressively, or unreasonably. Dividends may, however, be declared only out of profits or surplus of the corporation and not out of capital. It is the duty of directors to determine not only whether it is expedient from a business standpoint to distribute profits or surplus to the stockholders but also whether a surplus or profit exists according to the law of the state in which the corporation is organized. These laws vary from state to state.

The by-laws generally give the directors power to close the stock-transfer books of the corporation a certain number of days before a dividend date or to fix a record date to determine which stockholders are entitled to dividends.

Are formalities required in the declaration of dividends by directors? While no formalities are required in declaring a dividend, it is advisable in all instances for the board of directors to adopt a resolution at a duly convened meeting, declaring the dividend and indicating the following:

1. The rate or amount of the dividend.
2. The class of stockholders to whom the dividend is payable.
3. The date set for determination of who is entitled to the dividend.
4. The date when the dividend will be paid.
5. The medium in which the dividend is to be paid.

The minutes of the directors' meeting at which the resolution is adopted should also show the names of those present at the meeting and of those who voted against passage of the resolution declaring the dividend.

May directors revoke a dividend? Ordinarily directors cannot, without the consent of stockholders, revoke a dividend once it has been declared, for a declaration of a dividend creates a debt from the corporation to the stockholders. Revocation of dividends has, however, been upheld by the courts in the following instances:

1. Where the directors illegally declared a dividend that would impair the capital of the corporation, acting under a mistaken belief that there were profits legally available for dividends.
2. Where the action of the board in declaring the dividend had not been made public, and no funds had been set apart for payment.
3. Where, after declaration of the dividend, some event occurred making it inadvisable to pay the dividend; as, for example, where a fire destroyed property of the corporation after declaration of a dividend, and the directors honestly believed it advisable to use the money to restore the property rather than to pay the dividend; or, where war broke out after declaration of a dividend, seriously affecting the corporation's business and making payment of the dividend highly inadvisable.
4. Where the dividend was declared payable in stock, and the stock

out of which the dividend was to be paid had not yet been issued. Where, however, the stock dividend was declared payable out of treasury stock, it was held that the dividend could not be revoked.

Liability of directors for illegal dividends. In most states the statutes specifically provide that directors who declare illegal dividends are liable personally to the corporation and to its creditors. The extent of the liability is determined by the governing statute. The liability may be limited to the amount of debts outstanding when the dividend is declared; it may be extended to debts incurred at any time during continuance of the directors in office; or it may apply to the amount withdrawn from capital, with interest. Penalties in the forms of fines and imprisonment are also imposed in some states. Directors who dissent from the declaration of the illegal dividend or were absent from the meeting at which the illegal dividend was declared may be relieved of liability by statute. The statutes may, however, specify the manner in which such dissent or absence should be indicated or noted in the minutes of the meeting, and these instructions must be followed in order to obtain the exemption from liability. Directors cannot avoid liability for illegal dividends on the ground that they did not know the dividend was illegal, where the facts could have been ascertained with reasonable diligence.

A director who dissents from the declaration of a dividend should, in any event, note his dissent on the minutes of the meeting. A director who was absent from the meeting at which an illegal dividend was declared should inform the board of directors, immediately upon learning of the declaration of the dividend, of his dissent, in order to avoid liability for the acts of his codirectors. See page 1182 for further discussion of director's responsibility for wrongful acts of his associates.

The corporation may recover the illegally paid dividends from stockholders. The fact that the stockholder who received an illegal dividend has transferred his shares does not relieve him of liability for repayment of the dividend.

Power of directors to prosecute and defend suits and to employ counsel. The board of directors has the power to determine whether or not suit should be brought in behalf of the corporation, and, in the absence of fraud, the courts will not interfere with the exercise of the board's discretion. The directors also have the power to employ ounsel to protect the interests of the corporation in instituting, rosecuting, or defending actions, and to incur incidental expenses the conduct of litigation for the corporation. The litigation must, owever, involve the corporation, not the directors personally. Where, or example, stockholders bring suit against the directors personally or mismanagement of the corporation, the directors have no right engage counsel to defend them at the corporation's expense. They nay, however, employ counsel at the corporation's expense where ninority stockholders bring action against the corporation itself, even hough such action is based upon alleged misconduct on the part f the directors or their agents. (See also page 1206.) Actions to nforce the liability of a director to the corporation are also instituted y the board of directors.

Power of directors to compromise claims. The board of direcors has the power to compromise claims against the corporation if, n the honest exercise of their judgment, the directors believe such ompromise to be for the best interests of the corporation. In the bsence of fraud, the courts will not interfere with their action, even hough it appears that better terms could have been secured. Even f the directors have acted fraudulently, the courts may refuse to nterfere if the rights of an innocent third person are involved, and he corporation may be relegated to its remedies against the directors hemselves.

Liability of directors for negligence and neglect of duty. Direcors are personally liable for losses to the corporation resulting from heir negligence in the conduct of the corporation's affairs. This iability exists regardless of whether or not the statutes of the state of incorporation impose liability for acts constituting negligence. They are not liable for mistakes or mere errors of judgment, but they are required to use reasonable care, skill, and prudence in the performance of their duties. Whether or not a director has used reasonable care and diligence is a question of fact, to be determined from the circumstances surrounding each particular case. Gross inattention to the business of the corporation that results in loss to the corporation constitutes negligence for which the directors are liable. A director must devote his time and attention to the affairs of the corporation. The fact that the directors have delegated their powers to others does not relieve them of liability. They cannot completely abandon their duties and have others act for them. (See als page 1164.)

Are directors liable for failure to attend board meetings? It the duty of every director to attend meetings of the board with fair degree of regularity. If a director fails to do so, he may be hel liable for losses that the corporation may sustain because of hi negligence in attending. For example, if one director is continuall absent from board meetings, and his codirectors during his absenc dissipate the assets of the corporation by voting themselves enormou salaries, the absent director as well as his codirectors may be hel liable, even if he knew nothing of their action. Had he been presen at board meetings, he might have been able to prevent the wrongfu action of the other directors. A director is presumed to know every thing concerning the corporate affairs that he could have ascertaine had he used reasonable diligence in performing his functions. Ab sence of a director from a particular board meeting because of press ing business or illness, however, does not constitute actionable negli gence.

If no directors' meetings are held, the whole board may be liabl for losses sustained by the corporation by reason of its failure t manage the corporate affairs. For example, if the president, in th absence of directors' meetings, has assumed entire management o the corporation, using the corporate property for his own purposes the directors may be held liable to the corporation for the value of th property diverted.

Liability of directors for misapplication of assets. Director hold the property of the corporation in trust for the corporation, it stockholders, and its creditors. They must account for all assets tha come into their hands, in the form of cash or otherwise, and are liable for misapplication of any of the assets, whether the misappli cation is innocent or fraudulent. For example, a director may be forced to account for a loan made to him in violation of a State statute; he may be required to return the amount of a gift voted to him by his codirectors; he may be held liable for an amount paid by the corporation as compensation for counsel employed to defend the director personally; he may be compelled to reimburse the cor poration for the use of corporate assets to pay his personal debts. The liability of directors for misapplication or misappropriation of orporate assets applies whether or not a State statute imposing a ability exists. The statutes in many states specifically make the irectors liable for excessive and improper loans to directors or stockolders and for improper issuance of stock.

The directors will not be held liable if no rights of creditors are ffected by their improper acts, and all the stockholders have con- nted thereto.

Liability of directors for acts beyond the corporate powers. cts that are outside the corporation's powers are known as *ultra ires* acts. A director who participates in such acts is liable for any ss resulting therefrom. For example: A corporation is organized manufacture pianos. The directors decide that it would be profitble for the corporation to manufacture and sell sporting goods and ontract to purchase a complete line of bicycles. The purchase and ale of bicycles is clearly not within the scope of the corporation's owers. The directors may be prevented from carrying out the ansaction, or they may be held personally accountable for the full mount expended by the corporation in the *ultra vires* transaction, ogether with interest. Of course, if the stockholders acquiesce in he unlawful transaction, they cannot afterwards hold the directors iable for having entered into it.

Liability of directors for secret profits. Directors are required o act in the utmost good faith in all transactions affecting the cororation. If they secretly profit personally by any transaction either vith the corporation or affecting the corporation, without full dislosure of the facts, the corporation may recover such profits. For xample, where the corporation purchases a parcel of real estate and he seller secretly pays a commission on the sale to one of the direcors of the purchasing corporation who was instrumental in bringing bout the sale, the director can be compelled to account for the secret ommission that he has received. Even if he has given part of the ommission to others, he must account for all of it. The corporation nay also, upon discovery of the facts, rescind the contract, even though the purchase price may have been a fair one and the purchase advantageous to the corporation. A director who enters into a direct transaction with the corporation in which he has an interest must account for any profits made by him in the transaction if he fails to disclose his interest. For example, a director sells to his corporation at a fair price some merchandise that he owns. He fails t disclose that he has bought the merchandise at a very low price wit the express purpose of reselling it to the corporation. The corpor: tion, on learning the facts, may either rescind the sale or hold th director liable for the profit that he made on the transaction. O the other hand, had he disclosed the facts, he would not be con pelled to surrender his profits, for a director may deal with the co: poration provided he does so fairly.

Liability of directors for fraudulent statements and acts. A d rector is personally liable for his fraudulent statements and acts t anyone who was damaged by relying upon them. It is not necessar that the fraudulent statements shall have been made directly to th person injured. For example, a director sends to a credit agency statement of the corporation's affairs that he knows to be false. Th credit agency submits the statement to one of its subscribers wh has applied for information concerning the financial strength of th corporation. Acting upon the false statement, the subscriber extend credit to the corporation, which, as a matter of fact, is hopelessly ir solvent. The subscriber may hold the director personally liable The fact that the director was acting for the corporation and no in his own behalf does not relieve him of liability.

May a director prefer one creditor over others? Although a d rector to whom a corporation is indebted may not obtain an advan tage over other creditors of the corporation by paying off his ow debt in the face of the corporation's insolvency, he incurs no persona liability if he gives a preference to some other creditor in whos claim he has no interest. The preference itself may be illegal, an the creditor who receives it may be held accountable, but the direc tor himself will incur no personal liability to other creditors.

Are directors liable to creditors and stockholders or only t the corporation? Ordinarily directors are liable primarily to the cor poration for their acts of malfeasance, misfeasance, and nonfeasanc in the management of the corporate affairs. Neither the creditor nor the stockholders may sue to enforce such liability except in representative capacity on behalf of the corporation. Where, how ever, the misconduct of a director toward an individual creditor o stockholder has resulted in loss to him, he may hold the directo able in an individual action. The statutes in some states also make irectors liable to creditors under specified circumstances; as, for example, where directors assent to the creation of a debt beyond the mount of indebtedness permitted by statute, or where directors uthorize the declaration of an illegal dividend.

Common law liabilities of directors. In the preceding discusion the liability of directors under the common law were indicated. n summary, they are:

1. For secret profits.
2. For waste of corporation assets.
3. For losses due to negligence.
4. For acts beyond the corporate powers.
5. For fraudulent statements and acts.

Acts for which directors may incur criminal liability under State laws. The following are some of the offenses for which directors are made liable by statute in the various states:

1. Doing business before receiving proper authorization therefor; loing business as a foreign corporation without a license.

2. Conducting the business of a corporation for an unlawful purpose.

3. Issuance of stock certificates before payment of franchise tax.

4. Signing or issuing improper certificates of stock.

5. Exhibiting false records to public officers examining the corporation's affairs.

6. Fraudulent reissuance of cancelled stock certificates.

7. Refusal to exhibit list of stockholders entitled to vote.

8. Signing, issuance, sale, or assignment of notes, bonds, stock, and so forth, fraudulently and without authority.

9. Receiving gratuities for making contracts or transacting business.

10. Sale of position of director of certain classes of corporations, or receipt of consideration for resigning.

11. Failure to notify other directors or officers of service upon director of application for injunction affecting the property or business of the corporation.

12. Refusal or failure to make proper entries in corporate books and records; making of false entries in books, statements, and reports.

13. Failure or refusal to make reports.
14. Illegal authorization of dividends.
15. Misuse of corporate funds.
16. Illegal loans.
17. Making of false statements in advertising for corporation.
18. Engaging in agreements and practices in violation of law against trusts and monopolies.
19. Violation of laws against political contributions by corporations.

Some of these statutes refer expressly to both directors and officers; others merely impose a liability upon officers or upon offenders in general, and directors are liable thereunder by implication. In a few instances, penal statutes refer only to directors and not to officers, as, for example, a New Jersey statute making it a crime to fail to display the corporate name as required by law.

How a director can avoid liability for action taken by his co-directors. The general rule is that, in the absence of a statutory provision, a director is responsible for the wrongful acts of his associates where they have come to his knowledge, and where he acquiesces therein and takes no steps to avert the injurious consequences of the acts when, by due diligence, he might have prevented them from being done. An absent director will not be held liable for acts of his associates if he has not connived at or participated in the acts, or if he was not negligent in failing to act. (See also page 1178.) If he is present at a meeting at which action that he believes to be against the best interests of the corporation is taken, he should have his disapproval noted on the records. A director who fails to do so may be deemed to have concurred in the action taken by the board.

Some statutes specifically require that a director's dissent be noted on the records of the meeting in order that he may avoid liability for action taken at the meeting.

Directors' liabilities under Federal laws. Most of the Federal laws that affect the conduct of business, such as tax laws, anti-trust statutes, fair-trade acts, and laws regulating wages and hours, impose civil or criminal liabilities, or both, for violations of the law. Although all of these statutes do not expressly apply the civil or criminal penalties against directors and officers, there is always the possility that under interpretations of the penalty provisions directors ıd officers of corporations that have violated the law will be subject the penalties. Under certain Federal laws, however, civil and iminal liabilities are imposed directly upon directors and officers for ilure to comply with the provisions of the laws. The Securities ct of 1933, the Securities Exchange Act of 1934, and the Public tilities Holding Company Act of 1935 are examples.

The imposition of heavy penalties against directors and officers by ederal and State laws has tended to make individuals more cautious bout accepting corporate office.

Indemnification of directors and officers. The legislatures of everal states have recognized the justice of indemnifying or reimursing directors and officers for expenses incurred in successfully efending stockholders' suits brought against them. (See page 1206.) The United States Supreme Court has held that such statutes are onstitutional and that they also apply to suits in Federal court if urisdiction is based upon diversity of citizenship. Some of the states ive the right of indemnification not only to past and present direcors and officers, but also to employees.

The statutes that afford protection to the directors and officers re of two types: (1) they give the directors and officers the right to eimbursement whether or not the articles or by-laws of the corporaion make provision for indemnification; or (2) they authorize proviions for indemnification in the articles of incorporation or the by-laws.

Even when there is no specific statutory authority, it is advisable, f permissible, to include an indemnification or reimbursement provision in the articles of incorporation or in the by-laws. Whether this can be done depends upon: (1) policy of state departments in accepting articles of incorporation including the provision; and (2) attitude of the courts in sustaining the provision. Most of the state departments allow articles of incorporation to include an indemnification provision, although the statutes are silent on the subject. Some courts have allowed reimbursement even in the absence of statutory authority, particularly when the successful defense of the suit has preserved corporate property. But the weight of authority, numerically at least, is against such reimbursement where there is no statute authorizing it.

A by-law that permits indemnification of directors and office usually provides:

1. They must not be guilty of negligence or misconduct in the duties.

2. The liability against which they are indemnified includes atto-ney's fees and other expenses.

3. They are indemnified whether or not they are in office at th time the expenses are incurred.

4. Their right to indemnification passes to their heirs, executor and administrators.

6. The indemnification may be against liability incurred for act committed prior, as well as subsequent, to adoption of the by-law

7. The right to indemnification is not exclusive of other rights th directors and officers may have as a matter of law.

4. DUTIES, POWERS, AND LIABILITIES OF CORPORATE OFFICERS

What officers is a corporation required to have? The statutes i most states specify what officers a corporation must have and leav the creation of additional offices to the discretion of the board o directors or of the stockholders. The officers specifically required b statute generally include a president, a secretary, a treasurer, an a resident agent for service of process upon the corporation. In th absence of any statutory requirement as to the number of officers the charter or by-laws may fix the number to meet the needs of th particular corporation. The following are the most usual officers o a corporation:

1. Chairman of the board of directors.
2. President.
3. Assistant to the president.
4. One or more vice presidents.
5. Secretary.
6. Assistant secretary.
7. Treasurer.
8. Assistant treasurer.
9. Controller.
10. General manager.

Who are qualified to act as officers? The statutes in some states prescribe certain qualifications for officers; as, for example, that the president must be a director of the corporation or that some or al of the officers must be stockholders. More frequently, however, the charter or the by-laws specify the qualifications of officers. One person often holds two offices in the same corporation, and the power to do so is confirmed by statute in some states. Two corporations may have the same officers, without impairing transactions between the corporations that have been entered into in good faith. However, in certain classes of corporations that are subject to special legislation, such as banks, public utilities, holding companies, and investment companies, statutory restrictions may prevent an officer or director of one company from holding office in another corporation at the same time.

How officers are chosen. The statutes in most states vest in the board of directors the power to elect or appoint officers. The by-laws also generaly contain a provision, consistent with any statutory requirements, for the election of officers. It is sometimes provided that the officers shall be elected by the board of directors after its election by the stockholders and that a meeting may be held without notice for this purpose immediately after the annual meeting of stockholders and at the same place. Formal acceptance of office is not required, but an individual cannot be forced into an office against his will. The power to fill vacancies in office rests with those who originally had the power to elect or appoint the officers, unless the statute or by-laws give to others the power to fill vacancies in office.

Effect of failure to elect officers. If new officers are not elected, the old officers continue to hold their offices, regardless of whether or not they were elected for a fixed term, until they are removed, until they resign, or until the new officers are elected and qualify. The failure to elect required officers does not ordinarily cause a dissolution of the corporation. Some statutes do, however, provide that a corporation may be dissolved upon a petition to the courts by a creditor, where the corporation has not elected officers or done business within a fixed time.

Term of an officer. The term of office is usually fixed by the statute of the state in which the corporation is organized, or by the corporation's charter or by-laws. The term may be:

1. One or more years.
2. At the pleasure of the board of directors, in which case the board

may not have power to enter into a contract for a definite period of time.

3. For such time as the board of directors may by contract or resolution determine.

4. Until the next annual meeting of directors and until their successors are elected.

If the term of office is not fixed, an officer holds his office at the pleasure of the corporation or until he resigns and his successor is elected. An officer's term of office does not expire merely because the term of the directors who appointed him has expired.

Resignation of an officer. An officer may resign at any time although elected for a fixed period, unless he is restricted by the corporation's charter or by-laws, by the laws of the state in which the corporation is organized, or by the terms of his contract with the corporation. He may resign even if it is provided that officers of the corporation shall hold office until their successors are elected or appointed. A resignation must be tendered in good faith. Where, for example, all the officers resign at one time in order that the corporation may be placed in a receiver's hands, the resignation will not be recognized by the courts, for it will be deemed to be fraudulent.

If a resignation is tendered to take effect on acceptance, it must be accepted before it is effective. If it is tendered to take effect at once, acceptance is not necessary unless made so by statute, charter, or by-laws. The resignation may be written or oral, and no particular form is required.

Removal of an officer with or without cause. A corporation may remove an officer for cause, even if his term of office is fixed. An officer may be removed without cause if his term of office is not fixed, and removal for cause is not required. An officer may also be removed without cause even though his term of office is fixed, if the statute, charter, or by-laws expressly authorize removal without cause. The power to remove an officer rests with the person or persons authorized to elect or appoint him. Generally, this power is given to the board of directors. An officer who is removable at the pleasure of the board need not be given notice of removal or a hearing. Where, however, an officer is being removed for cause, reasonable notice of intention to remove, adequate time to prepare his defense, and a fair hearing are required. An officer who has been removed unlawfully may apply to the courts for reinstatement.

Can the officers bind the corporation by their acts? The officers of a corporation are its agents. They can bind the corporation by their acts only when such acts are within the scope of the authority granted to them. Authority to act may be given to an officer by statute, by the corporation's charter, by its by-laws, and by express resolution of the stockholders or directors granting him authority to act. An officer also has implied authority to do acts that are reasonably necessary to carry into effect the express powers granted. For example, if a corporation gives an officer power to borrow money in its behalf, the officer also has power to arrange the terms of the loan and to agree to give security therefor.

In addition to express and implied powers, officers have so-called "apparent" powers by which they can bind the corporation. For example, where a corporation permits an officer to assume certain powers or holds him out as possessing those powers, the corporation cannot afterwards deny, as against an innocent person who relied upon the officers' apparent authority, that the officer had authority to act. Similarly, if a corporation ratifies an unauthorized act of its officer, that act will be binding upon it. The corporation may not, however, ratify an act of the officer in its behalf that is beyond the powers of the corporation itself. Those who deal with an officer of the corporation are deemed to know the limitations on his authority. Where, however, a limitation is contained in a by-law, an innocent person who knew nothing of the limitation is not bound by it.

Duties performed by officers. Officers have very few inherent powers; that is, powers that exist merely by virtue of their holding a particular office. Such powers as they do have are derived from the State corporation laws, from the corporation's charter and by-laws, and from resolutions of the board of directors and of the committees appointed by the board. The duties performed by persons holding the same office vary widely from one corporation to another. The following lists indicate the detailed duties generally assigned to the chief officers of the corporation. The table on pages 1193-97, compiled from 115 complete replies to a questionnaire, indicates in percentages the number of corporations in which certain administrative functions are supervised by certain officers.

Duties of chairman of the board of directors. The following are the usual duties of the chairman of the board.

1. Acts as senior officer of the corporation.
2. Presides at meetings of the board and of the stockholders.
3. Directs the policy of the corporation.
4. Has primary control over methods and amounts of capital financing.
5. Delegates powers to the president.
6. Acts as ex officio member of all standing committees.
7. Appoints members of all committees not otherwise ordered by the by-laws.

In some corporations, the chairman of the board is not the senior officer, but ranks immediately below the president.

Duties of the president. The following are the usual duties of the president.

1. Calls meetings of stockholders.
2. Signs statements and reports required to be filed with State officials.
3. Makes acknowledgments of instruments.
4. Acts as executive officer and has general management and direction of business.
5. Performs all duties of chairman of board in his absence or in case of his inability to act.
6. Signs certificates of stock with secretary or assistant secretary.
7. Signs and executes in corporate name all deeds, mortgages, bonds, contracts, and so forth.
8. Executes stockholders' consents, and attends and votes at stockholders' meetings of corporations in which the company owns stock.
9. Acts as ex officio member of all committees.
10. Prescribes duties for officers and employees not otherwise defined.
11. Countersigns checks, drafts, and orders for payment of moneys.
12. Appoints officers and employees, except those selected by the board of directors; removes such officers and fills vacancies.
13. Employs and discharges all employees and fixes their salaries.
14. Compensates directors for special services.
15. Appoints his assistants.

16. Sees that all orders and resolutions of the board are carried into effect.

17. Reports to the chairman of the board and consults with him.

See also table on pages 1193-97, indicating that the president often handles real-estate matters, leases, investments, loans, reports to stockholders, budgets, and publicity.

Duties of assistant to the president. The following are the usual duties of the assistant to the president:

1. Relieves a busy president of some of his duties, such as representing him at conferences and meetings.
2. Directs administration of a distinct department of the business, such as production, engineering, sales promotion, merchandising, office management, and so forth.
3. Co-ordinates activities between individual executives or department heads.
4. Serves as member of committees, such as executive committee, management advisory committee, workers' council, pension board, and employee stock-purchase committee.

Duties of the vice president. The following are the usual duties of a vice president:

1. Performs the duties of the president in his absence or in case of his inability to act.
2. Acts as assistant to the president and under his direction.
3. Performs such duties as are assigned to him by the board of directors or by the president.
4. Signs certificates of stock with the secretary.
5. Signs bonds, debentures, and dividend checks.

See also table on pages 1193-97, indicating that the vice president is sometimes charged with budgeting, leases, loans, patents, and real-estate matters.

Duties of the secretary. The following are the usual duties of the secretary:

1. Prepares schedules of meetings and gives notices of meetings.
2. Drafts resolutions, attends and records proceedings of meetings of stockholders and directors; acts as secretary at meetings of executives, branch managers, and department heads.

3. Signs or attests statements and reports filed with State officials published, or submitted to stockholders.

4. Signs acknowledgments of instruments.

5. Maintains the register of stockholders and other stock book and allows inspection by stockholders; prepares stock list and keep it open for inspection.

6. Executes proxies or powers of attorney to vote stock owned by the corporation.

7. Signs certificates of stock with some other designated officer

8. Gives notice of sale of stock forfeited for nonpayment of assessments.

9. Keeps the records and seal of the corporation, and affixes the seal where necessary.

10. Sees that books, reports, and documents are properly prepared, kept, and filed; guides other officers in matters pertaining to corporate procedure and issuance of corporate reports.

11. Maintains a calendar or follow-up record of dates on which various departments are required to take action, and notifies them in advance of the action to be taken.

12. Advises officers and directors of their election.

13. Prepares abstracts of papers belonging to the corporation, and records them.

14. Publishes action in respect to dividends.

15. Registers bonds of the corporation.

16. Transmits to auditor, for recording, copies of contracts providing for payment of money to or by the corporation.

17. Looks after physical care of buildings, real estate, and so forth.

18. Maintains insurance on corporate property.

19. Has charge of correspondence and personal relations with security holders. See also table on pages 1193-97, indicating various administrative functions supervised by the secretary.

Duties of assistant secretary. The following are the usual duties of an assistant secretary.

1. Acts in place of the secretary in his absence or in case of his disability.

2. Performs secretarial duties where the corporation has principal offices in several cities.

3. Where assistant secretary acts for subsidiary, he keeps in com-

munication with secretary of holding company, and sends copies of resolutions, records, documents, and so forth, for filing in main office.

Duties of the treasurer. The following are the usual duties of the treasurer.

1. Files reports of financial condition and tax reports with officials of the State.
2. Prepares reports upon demand of stockholders.
3. Has charge and custody of and is responsible for all funds and securities of the corporation.
4. Deposits funds and maintains bank accounts in banks designated by the board of directors.
5. Keeps books of account of moneys received and paid out in behalf of the corporation.
6. Exhibits books and records to directors during business hours.
7. Receives and gives receipts for moneys due the corporation.
8. Renders a statement of condition of finances at regular meetings of directors and renders full annual report at stockholders' annual meeting.
9. Signs certificates of stock with a designated officer.
10. Arranges for listing of corporation's securities on stock exchange.
11. Signs checks, bills of exchange, and promissory notes.
12. Advises the corporation in regard to financial matters.
13. Handles surety bonds.

Duties of assistant treasurer. The following are the usual duties of an assistant treasurer:

1. Performs all the duties of the treasurer in his absence or in case of his inability to act.
2. Assists treasurer and performs duties assigned to him by the treasurer or by the board of directors.

Duties of the controller. The following are the usual duties of a controller:

1. Acts as principal accounting officer in charge of accounting books and records.
2. Audits payrolls and vouchers and causes them to be properly certified.

3. Initiates, prepares, and issues standard practices relating to al accounting matters and procedures and co-ordinates systems through out the corporation, including clerical and office methods, records reports, and procedures.

4. Obtains from agents and from departments of the corporation reports for recording general operations or for directing accounts.

5. Maintains and enforces classification and other accounting rules prescribed by regulating bodies.

6. Causes to be prepared and filed reports and statistics required by law or prescribed by the president.

7. Prepares balance sheets, income accounts, financial statements and reports.

8. Prepares, as budget director, in conjunction with other officers and department heads, an annual budget covering all activities of the corporation, for submission to the board of directors prior to the beginning of the fiscal year.

9. Approves for payment vouchers, drafts, and other accounts payable, when properly authorized by the president or others designated by the president.

10. Endorses checks, notes, and obligations for collection, deposit, or transfer.

11. Countersigns warrants drawn by the treasurer for depositing securities in safe-deposit boxes or for withdrawing the same.

12. Countersigns checks drawn by the treasurer against funds of the corporation, except as otherwise provided by resolution of the directors.

13. Appoints an auditor and subordinate employees and fixes their compensation.

14. Has charge of records and clerical and office procedure throughout the departments of the corporation and its subsidiaries.

See also table on pages 1193-97, indicating that the controller sometimes handles dividend payments, insurance, leases, and tax matters.

Duties of the general manager. "General manager" is the title given to one who has general direction and control of the corporate affairs. While an officer of the corporation, such as the president, vice president, secretary, or treasurer, may also hold the office of general manager, the latter is ordinarily not an officer of the corporation. He is an agent with power to bind the corporation by contracts necessary in the prosecution of the corporate business. His powers vary with the nature of the business, but usually include the following:

1. Directing and supervising the ordinary details relating to manufacturing, sales, and transportation.
2. Keeping complete records showing all business transacted by him, and all contracts and trade commitments made.
3. Reporting to the president the exact nature, extent, terms, and conditions of all business transacted by him, and contracts and commitments made.
4. Performing such other duties as are prescribed by the board of directors.

TABLE SHOWING DIVISION OF ADMINISTRATIVE FUNCTIONS AMONG OFFICERS

Duty	*Officers Responsible*	*Percentage of Total Replies*
Accounting: supervision of department	Controller	61
	Treasurer	18
	Secretary	8
	Combination of officers	5
	Miscellaneous (including asst. treas., asst. controller, asst. sec., v.p., general auditor, chief accounting officer)	8
Annual report: preparation	Combination of officers	42
	Treasurer	15
	Secretary	11
	President	10
	Controller	10
	Public relations director	4
	Miscellaneous (including asst. treas., asst. to pres., chairman of board, v.p.)	8
Bonds: registration, interest and coupon payments (other than trustee or interest paying agent)	Treasurer	77
	Secretary	13
	Combination of officers	7
	Miscellaneous (including asst. treas., v.p.)	3
Budgeting	Controller	36
	Combination of officers	25
	Treasurer	20
	President	6

TABLE SHOWING DIVISION OF ADMINISTRATIVE FUNCTIONS AMONG OFFICERS (*Continued*)

Duty	*Officers Responsible*	*Percentage of Total Replies*
Budgeting (*Cont.*)	Secretary	3
	Miscellaneous (including asst. treas., asst. to pres., v.p., prod. mgr., dir. of budget, dept. heads)	10
Credits and collections: officer to whom department head is responsible	Treasurer	66
	Controller	15
	Secretary	2
	Combination of officers	2
	Miscellaneous (including pres., v.p., credit mgr., asst. sec., asst. treas., etc.)	15
Dividend payments (other than dividend disbursing agent)	Treasurer	63
	Secretary	23
	Combination of officers	6
	Controller	3
	Miscellaneous (including asst. treas., v.p., chairman of fin. com., fiscal agent)	5
Documents and records: custody of same	Secretary	65
	Combination of officers	18
	Treasurer	11
	Controller	2
	Miscellaneous (including asst. sec., asst. treas., dept. heads, etc.)	4
Filing: supervision of general system	Heads of individual departments	28
	Office manager	24
	Secretary	18
	Combination	11
	Controller	8
	Treasurer	5
	Miscellaneous (including asst. treas., personnel mgr., etc.)	6
Insurance	Treasurer	38
	Secretary	18
	Controller	13
	Combination of officers	12

TABLE SHOWING DIVISION OF ADMINISTRATIVE FUNCTIONS AMONG OFFICERS (*Continued*)

Duty	*Officers Responsible*	*Percentage of Total Replies*
Insurance (*Cont.*)	Vice-president	8
	Insurance manager	6
	Miscellaneous (including pres., asst. treas., legal dept., etc.)	5
Investments	Treasurer	54
	Combination of officers	25
	President	11
	Secretary	1
	Miscellaneous (including chairman of board, v.p., asst. treas., chairman of fin. com.)	9
Leases	Secretary	27
	Combination of officers	16
	Treasurer	14
	Real estate department	13
	Vice-president	12
	President	8
	Controller	1
	Miscellaneous (including asst. treas., asst. sec., legal dept., operating com., etc.)	9
Loans	Treasurer	43
	Combination of officers	29
	President	12
	Vice-president	10
	Controller	1
	Miscellaneous (including chairman of board, asst. treas., asst. to pres., operating com., etc.)	5
Notices of stockholders' and directors' meetings: preparation	Secretary	97
	Treasurer	1
	Combination of officers	1
	Miscellaneous (including asst. sec.)	1
Patents	Legal department	43
	Patent department	25
	Secretary	14

TABLE SHOWING DIVISION OF ADMINISTRATIVE FUNCTIONS AMONG OFFICERS (*Continued*)

Duty	*Officers Responsible*	*Percentage of Total Replies*
Patents (*Cont.*)	Combination of officers	6
	Miscellaneous (including v.p., pres., patent com., etc.)	12
Proxies: preparation	Secretary	86
	Combination of officers	8
	Treasurer	3
	Miscellaneous (including legal dept., asst. sec.)	
Proxies: review after return	Secretary	74
	Combination of officers	18
	Treasurer	2
	Miscellaneous (including proxy com., asst. sec.)	6
Public Relations	Public relations director	35
	President	21
	Combination of officers	18
	Vice-president	12
	Secretary	6
	Miscellaneous (including asst. to pres., adv. mgr., chairman of board, etc.)	8
Real estate matters	Secretary	21
	Real estate department	20
	Combination of officers	20
	Treasurer	12
	Vice-president	11
	President	10
	Miscellaneous (including legal dept., asst. treas., purchasing agent, works manager, chief engineer)	6
Standard practice instructions	Combination of officers	33
	Controller	27
	Department heads	25
	Treasurer	5
	Secretary	3
	Miscellaneous (including personnel director, director of standards, asst. treas., pres., procedure dept.)	7

TABLE SHOWING DIVISION OF ADMINISTRATIVE FUNCTIONS AMONG OFFICERS (*Continued*)

Duty	*Officers Responsible*	*Percentage of Total Replies*
Tax matters	Treasurer	25
	Controller	24
	Combination of officers	24
	Secretary	10
	Legal department	6
	Tax department	6
	Miscellaneous (including v.p., asst. treas., etc.)	5
Transfer of stock (other than transfer agent)	Secretary	72
	Treasurer	23
	Combination of officers	4
	Miscellaneous (including legal dept.)	1

Are officers entitled to compensation for their services? Officers of the corporation who have discretionary control over the managment of the corporation's business are not entitled to compensation for services rendered as an incident of their office unless authorized:

1. By charter.
2. By by-law.
3. By resolution of the board of directors or the stockholders.
4. By agreement between the officer and the corporation, express or implied.

Like directors, however (see page 1162), they may be entitled to compensation for services rendered outside of the ordinary duties of their office. Ministerial officers who are neither directors nor stockholders are entitled to be paid a reasonable amount for their services, unless it was mutually intended that no compensation was to be paid. A ministerial officer may include a secretary, assistant secretary, manager, superintendent, cashier, treasurer, or other officer, depending upon the nature of the officer's duties.

An officer who is guilty of gross misconduct or fraud in management of the corporation's affairs forfeits his right to compensation. He is not however, deprived of compensation because of absence on account of illness, particularly where he had some other officer perform his duties and the corporation suffered no loss.

May an officer lend money to or borrow from the corporation? The principles set forth on pages 1170-71, covering the right of a director to lend money to or borrow money from the corporation, are equally applicable to an officer.

Liability of an officer for mismanagement. An officer occupies a fiduciary relation toward the corporation. By accepting office, he impliedly undertakes to give the corporation the benefit of his best care and judgment and is bound to exercise the utmost good faith in transactions touching his duties to the corporation and its property. He may not profit as an individual by his official position; he is liable for secret profits, even though the corporation suffered no damage. An officer is not, however, personally liable for depletion of the corporate assets unless he was grossly negligent in managing the business entrusted to his care or was guilty of willful destruction. In the absence of positive misfeasance, the courts are reluctant to hold an officer liable for losses suffered by the corporation because of the manner in which the officer discharged his duties. An officer is not chargeable with losses to the corporation caused by mere mistakes or errors in judgment. He is, however, bound by restrictions in the corporation's charter and by-laws and is liable for loss resulting from his failure to observe such restrictions.

Various Federal laws act as a check against the use of inside information by directors and officers for personal gains.

Acts for which officers may incur criminal liability. The liabilities listed on page 1181 *et seq.* for directors are also applicable to officers.

5. STOCKHOLDERS' RIGHTS

Have stockholders a right to participate in management of the corporation? Stockholders have no right to participate in the conduct of the ordinary affairs of the corporation. Management of the corporation is entrusted by the corporation laws of the various states to the board of directors. However, since the board of directors is elected by the stockholders, the stockholders have some measure of control over the conduct of the corporation's affairs. Further, the State statutes or the articles of incorporation may require that the consent of all or of a proportion of the stockholders be obtained before certain action is taken. The following matters are generally subject to approval of the stcokholders:

1. Acceptance of the corporate charter.
2. Amendment of the corporate charter.
3. Adoption of by-laws, unless the power is expressly given to the board of directors by the State laws or by the articles of incorporation.
4. Amendment of the by-laws, if the power to amend is not expressly given to the board of directors.
5. Removal of directors.
6. Merger or consolidation of the corporation with another company.
7. Transfer of all the assets of the corporation by sale or lease.
8. Voluntary dissolution and liquidation of the corporation.
9. Assessments on fully paid stock.

The fact that the consent of stockholders is required for certain action does not mean that the stockholders can take such action without action by the board of directors. Action taken by stockholders without the board of directors will, however, be binding on the corporation if the board of directors ratifies it, or if the corporation acquiesces in the stockholders' action and receives the benefits of the transaction.

Right of stockholders to adopt and amend by-laws. By-laws are simply rules adopted by the corporation for the regulation of its affairs. Since the stockholders constitute the corporation, the power to adopt by-laws rests with them. The board of directors may, however, be authorized to adopt by-laws either by the State statutes or by the provisions of the corporation's articles of incorporation, or the stockholders themselves may by resolution delegate the power to adopt by-laws to the board of directors.

The power to amend by-laws also rests primarily with the stockholders, but the directors may be given the right to effect changes in the by-laws by State statute, by the articles of incorporation, by resolution of the stockholders, or by the by-laws themselves. Directors who are given power to adopt by-laws have no power to amend by-laws adopted by the stockholders, unless the power to amend as well as the power to adopt is expressly given to the directors. Where both stockholders and directors have the power to make and amend by-laws, the by-laws of the directors are subject to the by-laws of the stockholders.

The manner in which the by-laws are amended is prescribed by statute in some states. In the absence of statutory provision therefor, the by-laws themselves may specify the notice and vote necessary to effect an amendment.

Power of stockholders to elect directors. The right to elect directors annually is generally given to the stockholders by statute. The manner in which the election is to be conducted is also regulated in some states. Many statutes require that election shall be by ballot and that it shall be conducted by inspectors or judges of election, appointed as provided in the by-laws. By-laws cannot modify any statutory requirement as to election. If the statute for example, provides that directors may be chosen by a plurality of votes, a by-law cannot require a majority vote for election. The right to fill vacancies in the board for an unexpired term may be taken away from the stockholders by statute and given to the directors. Even under such statutes, however, the stockholders and not the directors generally have the right to elect newly created directors where the number of directors has been increased.

Liability of stockholders to corporation for payment of stock. The stockholder is liable to the corporation for the amount that he has agreed to pay for his stock. This is true even though the certificate of stock issued to him is marked "fully paid and nonassessable." If the stock has a par value, he must generally pay a price not less than the par value. If it is without par value, the price is usually fixed by the directors, under authority granted by the stockholders or the charter.

The time when and the manner in which payment must be made depends upon the terms of the contract between the stockholder and the corporation. If the contract of purchase does not indicate when payments are due, it is implied that they are payable upon call of the directors, made pursuant to statutory provisions. A call is an official declaration that a sum is required to be paid upon a stock subscription. The length of notice of the call that must be given to the stockholders depends upon the provisions of the statute, charter, by-laws, or contract. Failure to respond to a call for payment gives the corporation the right to sue for the amount called for. In addition, the statutes of the various states gives other remedies, including the right to sell the shares and apply the proceeds to the payment of the installment, or to forfeit the shares and all previous payments made thereon.

Liability of stockholders to creditors. The extent of the liability of stockholders to creditors depends upon whether or not the stock has been fully paid. Where a stockholder has paid the full amount due on the stock, the following rules prevail with respect to his liability to creditors:

1. The general rule is that the stockholder is not personally liable for the debts of the corporation beyond the amount paid on his stock, unless the statute of the state where the corporation is organized imposes an additional liability.

2. In some states stockholders of insolvent corporations are made liable for debts due laborers, servants, and other classes of labor, although they have fully paid for their stock. Whether or not a stockholder is relieved of liability for labor debts by a transfer of his shares depends upon the law of the particular state. Generally, the stockholder is not liable for debts contracted after he has made a valid transfer. Some states make both the transferor and the transferee liable for debts contracted prior to the transfer.

Where a stockholder has not fully paid for his stock, the following rules prevail with respect to his liability to creditors:

1. The liability of stockholders to creditors to pay the amount due on their subscriptions arises generally only upon insolvency of the corporation and is governed by constitutional or statutory provisions of the state in which the corporation is organized.

2. The stockholders' liability is limited to the amount which remains unpaid on his stock, unless the statute imposes an additional liability.

3. The stockholders are generally liable to pay to creditors only so much of the amount due on the stock as is necessary to satisfy creditors' claims.

4. Each stockholder is required to bear only his proportionate share of the amount necessary to pay the debts. While each stockholder may be compelled to pay the entire sum remaining unpaid on his shares, if the amount that he has been compelled to pay is more

than his proportionate share of the debts, measured by the proportion which his stock bears to the whole stock, he is entitled to contribution from the other stockholders who have not borne their proportionate share of the debts of the corporation.

Liability of stockholders for assessments on fully paid stock. An assessment is a demand upon stockholders for payment of an amount above the par value or contract price of the stock held by them. A stockholder who has paid for his stock in full cannot be required to pay any additional amount unless an assessment on fully paid stock is authorized by statute or by charter, or unless the stockholder has consented to the making of the assessment.

Issuance of a duplicate certificate of stock upon loss, theft, or destruction of a certificate. A stockholder has a right to the issuance of a duplicate certificate of stock in the event of loss, destruction, or theft of his old certifictae. The statutes in most states confirm this right and indicate the conditions under which the new certificate may be issued. Generally these conditions are also outlined in the corporation's by-laws. The following are the usual requirements:

1. An order from the stockholder upon the corporation, instructing and authorizing the corporation to stop any transfer of the lost certificate.
2. An affidavit from the stockholder, setting forth the facts surrounding the loss of the certificate of stock.
3. Advertisement by the stockholder of the loss of the certificate of stock, and furnishing of evidence of the advertisement to the corporation.
4. A bond of indemnity furnished to the corporation by the stockholder, with surety approved by the board of directors, in the amount required by statute, or by the board of directors if the amount is not fixed by statute. The amount of the bond is usually double the current value of the stock.
5. The lapse of a specified period of time, usually from three to six months, after the stockholder has complied with the requirements, before issuance of the new certificate of stock.

The board of directors may pass a resolution authorizing the issuance of a new certificate of stock in each instance, or it may pass a blanket resolution authorizing a designated officer or its transfer agent and registrar to issue duplicate certificates of stock upon compliance with the required conditions.

The corporation must issue a duplicate certificate of stock when the required conditions have been met; otherwise it will subject itself to liability for damages and may be compelled to issue the new certificate by court procedure. The corporation may be compelled to recognize not only a bona fide holder of the new certificate of stock but also a bona fide holder of the old certificate for the reasons mentioned below. In that event, it is protected by the indemnity bond which it requires the stockholder to furnish as a condition precedent to issuance of the duplicate certificate of stock.

The rights of a purchaser of the old certificate of stock may have to be recognized even though he purchased from a person who found or stole the lost certificate. Under the Uniform Stock Transfer Act, which has been adopted in all the states, a bona fide purchaser of a stock certificate that has been properly endorsed acquires a good title to the stock although he has purchased from a finder or a thief. If, however, the endorsement was forged, the rights of the purchaser, even though he purchased in good faith, may be defeated by the superior claim of the true owner of the certificate.

In some states a corporation is not required to issue a duplicate certificate of stock unless a court order has been obtained. A corporation may, nevertheless, voluntarily issue a new certificate without a court order.

Power of stockholders to increase stock. The power to increase the amount of capital stock that the corporation is authorized to issue rests with the stockholders. It may, however, be conferred upon the directors by express resolution of the stockholders or by charter, unless a statute expressly prohibits such delegation of power. The laws of the state in which the corporation is organized usually indicate the manner in which the increase is to be effected. An amendment of the charter, effected in the following manner, is generally required:

1. The board of directors adopts a resolution, at a meeting properly called and held, recommending an amendment of the charter to increase the amount of the authorized capital stock and calling a meeting of stockholders to pass upon the amendment.

2. The stockholders, at a meeting duly called and held, adopt a resolution authorizing an amendment of the charter to increase the authorized capital stock and instructing the proper officers of the corporation to file the necessary papers required by law to carry out the amendment.

3. The officers execute and file with the State official designated by statute a certificate of amendment or other documents required by law.

In some states, an amendment of the charter is not required to effect an increase in the authorized capital stock. The steps required to be taken to effect an increase are, however, similar to those outlined above; instead of a certificate of amendment of the charter, a certificate of increase is required to be filed.

Stockholders' pre-emptive rights upon issuance of additional stock. The pre-emptive right is the right of each stockholder, upon the issuance of additional shares of stock, to purchase his proportion of the new stock in order to maintain his relative control and interest in the corporation. For example, if A owns $10,000 of the $100,000 worth of stock issued and outstanding, and the corporation increases its authorized capital stock to $200,000, A will have a right to purchase $1/10$ of the new issue, or an additional $10,000 worth of stock, before the stock may be offered to outsiders. The stockholder has a right to purchase the stock at the price fixed by the corporation and, if he fails to take it, it cannot be offered to anyone else upon morc favorable terms. He must be given reasonable notice of his right to subscribe, and a reasonbale opportunity to exercise the right. Stockholders who are not in a position to take and pay for the stock to which they are entitled may sell the rights to anyone who can.

The pre-emptive right of stockholders is governed by statute in many states. These statutes indicate the kind of issues to which the pre-emptive right attaches and in some instances provide that the certificate of incorporation may deny the pre-emptive right to any issue or to any class of stock. Thus statutes may show whether the pre-emptive right applies to issuance of additional stock out of an amount previously authorized; whether it applies only upon an increase in the authorized capital stock; whether it applies upon the issuance of stock for property or for cash; and whether it applies upon the issuance of treasury stock. Frequently the certificate of incorporation will regulate the pre-emptive rights of stockholders pursuant to the governing statute. In the absence of regulating statutes and charter provisions, the court decisions in the particular jurisdiction must be examined to determine under what circumstances the pre-emptive right exists. These decisions, it must be admitted, are in many instances conflicting and confused.

A stockholder may waive his pre-emptive right by agreement with the corporation.

Right of stockholders to reduce capital stock. The right to reduce capital stock rests with the stockholders, as does the right to increase it. The directors have no power to effect a reduction without the approval of the stockholders, unless expressly authorized by statute, by the corporate charter, or by the stockholders themselves. An amendment of the charter is generally required to authorize a reduction in the amount of authorized capital stock. The amendment is effected in the same manner as an amendment to increase the capital stock; that is, by resolution of the directors recommending the amendment and calling a meeting of stockholders, and by resolution of the stockholders approving the amendment. The vote of a majority or two thirds of the stockholders, given at a meeting duly called, is usually required. In addition to the filing of a certificate of amendment with some designated official, some states also require the filing of a statement signed by officers and directors to the effect that the proposed reduction will not reduce the actual value of the assets of the corporation to an amount less than the total amount of its debts and liabilities, plus the amount, as reduced, of its capital stock.

Stockholders' rights to inspect corporate books and records. Stockholders have a right to protect their interest in the corporation by keeping themselves informed as to whether the directors, officers, and agents of the corporation are attending to their duties properly. They may, at reasonable times and for a proper purpose, inspect the books and records of the corporation, including:

1. The corporation's records of its by-laws.
2. Minutes of its meetings.
3. The stock book or register.
4. Account books, ledgers, etc.
5. Minutes of directors' meetings.

A demand for inspection must be made at the office of the corporation in which the books and records are kept or at the principal place of business of the corporation. The inspection need not be made by the stockholder personally; his agent or attorney may inspect and make copies and abstracts of the records. The right of stockholders to inspect the books and to examine the corporate records is confirmed by statute in many states. In some instances, these statutes restrict the right of inspection and examination to designated books and records, such as the list of stockholders, the stock-transfer books, the books of account and financial records, and reports required by law to be filed in some public office. Where the right to inspect is given by statute, it may generally be exercised irrespective of the motive of the stockholder in seeking an inspection. The statutes sometimes impose upon the corporation and its officers or directors penalties for refusing to permit inspection upon proper demand.

Stockholders' rights upon failure of directors to live up to obligations. Should the directors prove to be incompetent to handle the affairs of the corporation, the stockholders' redress is to elect a new board at the next annual election. This remedy may be more apparent than real. If the directors are guilty of fraud or bad faith, the stockholders may take legal action to remove them. Furthermore, they may demand that the corportaion sue the faithless directors for damages. If the board of directors fails to institute an action, any stockholder may sue on behalf of the corporation and any amounts recovered go to the corporation. Such a suit is called a "derivative stockholder action."

Many such suits have been brought in recent years. As a result, there has been a tendency for the legislatures to pass laws that discourage such suits. Under these laws, generally, a complaining stockholder who does not own $50,000 in stock or 5 per cent of the outstanding stock of the company must post a bond covering the costs and attorneys' fees of the corporation and the individual defendants. If the suit is unsuccessful, the defendants have recourse to the security. Such restrictive legislation practically deprives the small individual stockholder of his only effective means of making officers and directors of large corporations account for grievous wrongs.

Another result of the increase in the number of stockholder suits in recent years is the inclusion of a provision in the corporate by-laws to permit a corporation to reimburse directors and officers for costs and expenses incurred in successfully defending a suit brought against them by stockholders on behalf of the corporation. A number of states have passed laws permitting corporations to do this. Of course, if stockholders are successful in a suit, a corporation may not indemnify the recreants. See page 1183.

6. PREPARING FOR CORPORATE MEETINGS

Kinds of corporate meetings. In the conduct of business by a corporation, the following classes of meetings are held:

1. Stockholders' meetings. These are sometimes called "corporate" meetings. They may be regular or special. Regular meetings—which are sometimes called "general" meetings, "stated" meetings, or "annual" meetings—are usually required to be held once a year, for the election of directors. Special meetings—which are sometimes termed "called" meetings or "extraordinary" meetings—are held as the need for them arises.
2. Directors' meetings. Meetings of directors are also regular or special. The regular meetings are those held at regular intervals, as fixed by the by-laws, usually monthly; all other meetings of the board are special meetings.
3. Committee meetings. These meetings are held, for example, by the executive committee, which in large corporations is appointed by the board of directors to exercise during intervals between board meetings all the powers of the board in accordance with the policy of the corporation. The meetings of the executive committee are also usually regular and special.

Who makes preparations for corporate meetings. Preparations for stockholders' meetings are made by the following people, depending upon the division of responsibility in the organization:

1. The secretary.
2. The secretary and the attorney for the corporation.
3. The secretary, the attorney for the corporation, and an organization employed by the attorney to attend to the holding of meetings.

Preparations for directors' meetings and for executive committee meetings are generally made by the secretary of the corporation.

Employment of a service organization to hold annual corporate meetings. The services of an outside organization are employed principally where the holding of meetings is merely a perfunctory matter, and where it is inconvenient for anyone interested in the corporation to attend the meeting. For example, a corporation is organized under the laws of the state of Delaware by a parent corporation, incorporated under the laws of New York and located in New York, to hold title to certain patents. The only stockholder of the Delaware corporation is the New York corporation. The principal office of the Delaware corporation, in Delaware, is in the charge of a resident agent, generally supplied by the service organization. Under the charter of the Delaware corporation, a meeting of stockholders must be held annually for the election of directors. The directors of the New York corporation, who are also the directors of the Delaware corporation, do not want to hold the meeting of the Delaware corporation in New York, for they do not want to do anything that might indicate the Delaware corporation is doing business in New York. Nor do the directors want to journey to Delaware to hold the meeting. The officers of the Delaware corporation, therefore, direct their attorney to advise the service organization, which maintains the principal office of the corporation in Delaware, to hold the annual meeting of the stockholders in Delaware by proxy. The directors of the Delaware corporation will appoint as proxies those who are actually to be present in Delaware at the meeting. The meeting is held by the proxies, and the necessary election takes place. Ordinarily the minutes for such a meeting are prepared by the service organization and examined and approved by the corporation's attorney.

There are several companies offering the type of service described above. The service is available only to attorneys, since such companies are prohibited from practicing law.

Preparations for a stockholders' meeting where responsibility rests with the secretary. A secretary's preparations for a stockholder's meeting can be divided into two parts:

1. Permanent preparations for all meetings.
2. Preparations for a particular meeting.

Permanent preparations for all stockholders' meetings. A permanent-meeting file in which is kept the following material (to be taken by the secretary to every meeting of stockholders) must be maintained:

1. A pamphlet copy of the corporation laws of the state in which the corporation is organized.
2. A copy of the corporation's charter and by-laws and the amendments thereto.
3. A form of check list of preparations for stockholders' meetings (see page 1212).
4. A sheet showing the order of business as usually followed.

Preparations for a particular stockholders' meeting. The following are the steps to be taken in preparing for a particular stockholders' meeting (some of the items refer only to an annual meeting and will, of course, be omitted when preparations are being made for a special meeting):

1. *Send notice of the meeting and proxies to stockholders.* The notice of the meeting may be:

(*a*) A post card, in which case the proxy will be attached to the notice in the form of a business-reply card.

(*b*) An announcement sent in a sealed envelope. The announcement may be accompanied by a "proxy statement" required of corporations that are subject to the Securities Exchange Act of 1934. The proxy in this case may be on a separate business-reply card enclosed with the announcement, or it may be attached to the notice, to be detached and returned in a stamped and self-addressed envelope or in a business-reply envelope that is enclosed with the notice and proxy.

The selection of the style of notice and proxy to be used depends upon such factors as:

(*a*) Cost.

(*b*) The necessity for receiving a large number of proxies.

Experience has proved that a greater number of proxies are returned if the notice and proxy are forwarded by first-class mail than if the post-card method is employed.

Figure 89 shows a single-sheet arrangement of the notice of meeting and the proxy.

2. *Prepare for handling proxies as they are received by the corpora-*

PROXY: The undersigned does hereby constitute and appoint Sewell L. Avery, Silas H. Strawn and Stuart S. Ball, or any one or more of them, with full power of substitution, as my proxy, or proxies, to vote for me and in my name with like effect as if I were personally present and voting at the annual meeting of the shareholders of Montgomery Ward & Co., Incorporated, called to be held on April 25, 1941 and at all adjournments thereof, for the election of directors and upon such other matters as may properly come before the meeting, hereby revoking any proxy or proxies heretofore given.

Executors, Administrators, Trustees, Guardians, etc., will so indicate when signing.

Date

Signed........................Signature........................

Use Pen or Pencil — Whichever You Prefer

No 59526

PLEASE DETACH AND MAIL PROXY CARD

Tear Off on This Line

Annual Shareholders' Meeting

Notice is hereby given that the Annual Meeting of the Shareholders of Montgomery Ward & Co., Incorporated will be held at the office of the Company, 619 West Chicago Avenue, Chicago, Illinois, on the 25th day of April, 1941 at 10:30 o'clock a. m. for the purpose of electing directors for the ensuing year and the transaction of such other business as may properly come before such meeting.

MONTGOMERY WARD & CO., INCORPORATED

STUART S. BALL, Secretary

Shareholders of record March 19, 1941, will be entitled to vote.

IMPORTANT: If you do not expect to attend the annual shareholders' meeting, please sign the attached proxy, detach it from the card, and mail it. No stamp is necessary.

The shareholders of this company number approximately 60,000. The holding of an annual meeting depends on the presence at the meeting in person or by proxy of the holders of more than half the shares. It is therefore vital to the interests of your company that a sufficient number of shareholders attend the meeting or be represented by proxy to make the holding of the meeting possible.

The proxies named are:

SEWELL L. AVERY, Chairman of the Board of Directors
SILAS H. STRAWN, Chairman of the Executive Committee
STUART S. BALL, Secretary

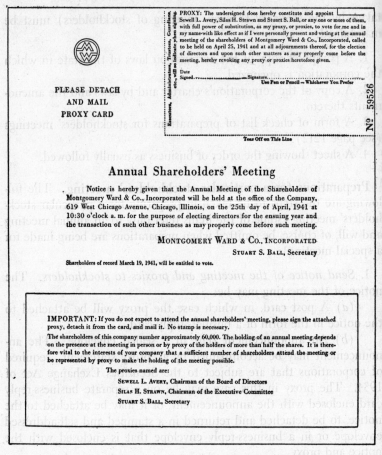

Figure 89. Notice of Annual Meeting and Detachable Proxy.

tion. A plan for handling the proxies upon their return should be worked out in advance and should make provision for:

(*a*) Assignment of responsibility for receiving and checking proxies.

(*b*) Arrangement of the proxies according to class of stock and in numerical order. Proxies should be numbered consecutively before they are sent out, so that when they are returned, they will be in alphabetical order when filed numerically.

(*c*) Inspection of the proxies and acceptance or rejection in accordance with a set of rules furnished to the inspectors by the secretary. See page 1228.

(*d*) Tabulation daily of the number of shares represented by proxies returned, and report to the secretary.

(*e*) Examination of questionable proxies by the secretary or the attorney of the corporation.

3. *Decide, if possible, who shall be nominated as directors.* In most cases the selection of directors depends upon ownership of the controlling interests, relationships with financial institutions, and other factors that make it possible to know in advance who will be the directors for the forthcoming period.

4. *Compile the list of stockholders.* The statutes or by-laws generally require that the corporation prepare a complete alphabetical list of the stockholders a certain number of days before each annual election. In some states it is necessary to file the list for a certain number of days before the meeting at the place where the meeting is to be held. The secretary usually prepares the list as of the date required and has it ready for use at the annual meeting. Where the corporation has an independent transfer agent, the latter prepares the list.

5. *Prepare the ballots.* The preparation of ballots depends upon the method of voting to be employed at the meeting. No particular form of ballot need be used even where a ballot is required, but the ballot for the election of directors should show the name or names of the person or persons voted for, the number of votes cast for each person, and the name of the person casting the vote, with provision for indicating that several stockholders are being represented by one person acting as proxy.

6. *Schedule the order of business.* The business to be transacted at the meeting need not follow any particular order, even though one is prescribed in the by-laws. A logical order of business, however, expedites the business of the meeting. The following is the order generally pursued at an annual meeting of stockholders:

(*a*) Call to order.

(*b*) Election of chairman and appointment of secretary, if necessary.

(*c*) Presentation of proofs of the due calling of the meeting.

(*d*) Presentation and examination of proxies.

(*e*) Announcement of a quorum present.
(*f*) Reading and settlement of minutes of previous meeting.
(*g*) Presentation of list of stockholders.
(*h*) Reports of officers and committees.
(*i*) Appointment of inspectors of election.
(*j*) Opening of polls.
(*k*) Election of directors.
(*l*) Closing of polls.
(*m*) Report of inspectors.
(*n*) Declaration of election of directors.
(*o*) New business.
(*p*) Adjournment.

7. *Decide who shall be nominated as inspectors of election.* See page 1234 for the necessity of this step.

8. *Prepare a tentative draft of the minutes of the meeting and of any resolutions to be presented at the meeting.* This may take any number of forms, including:

(*a*) A synopsis of the minutes.
(*b*) A digest of the topics to be discussed.
(*c*) A skeleton of the minutes, with spaces to be filled in with the missing details as they develop in the meeting.
(*d*) Prepared resolutions.

The form of minutes of meetings given on page 1253 may be used as a guide in preparing tentative minutes.

Check list of preparations for a stockholders' meeting. The following is a form of check list that will aid the secretary in:

1. Preparing for the meeting.
2. Making notes of essential data at the meeting.
3. Writing up the minutes of the meeting.

The check list is filled in as the various matters are attended to and is retained permanently by the secretary, who keeps the list in the file pertaining to a particular meeting.

CHECK LIST OF PREPARATIONS FOR STOCKHOLDERS' MEETING

STOCKHOLDERS' MEETING
OF
(NAME OF COMPANY)

Date	To be held .... as {Regular ..... / Special .....
Adjournments	Adjourned to ....
Notices	Prepared (date) Mailed (to be procured: Published (date) Waiver (date) date ....) Special purposes to be contained in notice ....
Quorum	Shares required for quorum ....
Present	(If a small meeting is held, names may be inserted here; if many attend, the roll may be made up on separate sheets. If these sheets are preserved, they may be "incorporated by reference" into the minutes, and thus space may be saved in the minute book.)
Official Lists	Lists of those entitled to be present: To be prepared by .... (check when in hand) As of (date) .... To be available .... (check when in hand)
Proxies	Name of proxy committee .... Substitute proxies to be given to .... (Check when substitute proxy is given, or check names of committee, first when they have been notified to be present, and again when they have given their word that they will be present. Check proxies; list names of persons to do this, and indicate date when their report is available. Ordinarily a preliminary report will be available a day or two before the meeting, and final checking of proxies tendered by persons at the meeting will have to be done while the meeting is in progress. This, of course, applies only to large meetings and not to those of small companies, or of subsidiaries. Refer-

ence should be made to the rules and regulations of the Securities and Exchange Commission regarding restrictions against solicitation and use of proxies.)

Chairman — Chairman: Notified to be present (date)
(If regular chairman has indicated inability to be present, arrange for substitute and for proper selection at the meeting.)

Reports — (List officers responsible for reports; indicate dates reports are to be ready in manuscript, and if to be printed, dates for submission to printer; indicate date reports are to be available for meeting. Check off dates as each step is taken.)

Action — (List action to be taken. If any matters require resolutions that can be prepared in advance, list them by number, and correspondingly number sheets on which resolutions appear. Prepare resolutions in sufficient number to facilitate discussion and amendment; for latter purpose, it is well to triple-space the typewritten copies of resolutions.)
(The following should follow title of each proposed action:
Proposed by .... Seconded by ....
For: .... shares
Against: .... shares)
(Note: It may be well to omit the action at this place, but to have separate sheets therefor in order that as many items and as many "proposed action sheets" as are necessary may be included.)

Inspectors — Inspectors: (Name them if selected in advance, and check if present; otherwise, write in names as selected, and note how selected.)

Nominations — (Leave space for names of persons nominated.)

Opening and Closing of Polls — How opened ....
How closed ....

Results — (List names of those elected here; above, under nominations, set opposite each nominee's name the number of votes received.)

Certificate Received — (Put down time for receipt of formal certificate of judges or inspectors of election, and note later time when received.)

Publication	(Note any requirements as to publication or filing of reports; this note can be made before the meeting.)
Memoranda of Follow-Up	(A space should be left to note action that must be taken to follow up resolutions that have been passed.)
Adjournment	Hour of adjournment .... (If the meeting is adjourned, a new checkup sheet should be prepared for the adjourned meeting and attached to that for the original meeting.)

Preparations for a stockholders' meeting where secretary and attorney are responsible for meeting. Where the responsibility for holding the stockholders' meeting is delegated to the attorney of the corporation, the secretary has little if any preparation to make. Whatever action he takes will be at the request of the attorney, who will ask the secretary for information needed in making his preparations. Proxies are ordinarily returnable to the corporation, even in instances where the attorney is responsible for the preparation and conduct of the meeting, and the secretary makes all arrangements for handling the proxies as they are returned. Also, the corporation secretary may have to prepare the list of stockholders who have the right to vote (see page 1225).

Preparations for a directors' meeting. The steps in the preparation for a directors' meeting, regular or special, include the following:

1. *Send notice of the meeting to directors.* The notice may be:

(*a*) A printed card with blanks to be filled in by the secretary as to the place, date, and hour.

(*b*) A typewritten notice.

(*c*) A notice with space for the recipient to indicate whether or not he will be present at the meeting.

The last-named form of notice is essential if directors are not actively engaged in the conduct of the business. The secretary can tell from the replies received whether a quorum of directors will be present, and if replies indicate that there will not be a quorum present, he can notify the directors that the meeting will not be held as scheduled. The following is a form of notice of a directors' meeting, illustrating the last type of notice.

NOTICE OF DIRECTORS' MEETING

.... CORPORATION

You are requested to attend a regular meeting of the Board of Directors at the office of the Corporation, No. ...., New York, on Tuesday, ..., at three o'clock P.M.

Please notify me whether or not you will be present.

Respectfully,

....

Secretary

....

I will / will not be present

....

2. *Gather data to be presented at the meeting.* Secretaries usually devise their own systems for accumulating the papers and documents likely to be required at the meeting, for conferring with officers in advance of the meeting, and for notifying officers of reports that are to be ready for the meeting.

3. *Write up the agenda.* The agenda (or "docket," or "order of business," as it is sometimes called) is the outline of action to be taken at the meeting. It is prepared several days in advance of the meeting and has attached to it the papers, reports, and documents that will be required at the meeting as each item of business is taken up. The following order of business may be observed in the agenda:

(*a*) Call to order (by chairman of board, or president, if there is no chairman or if he be absent).

(*b*) Announcement of quorum present.

(*c*) Reading and approval of minutes of previous meeting.

(*d*) Reports of officers and committees.

(*e*) Unfinished business.

(*f*) Election of officers (if there is to be an election).

(*g*) Declaration of dividends (if there is to be one).

(*h*) Other new business.

(*i*) Adjournment.

4. *Prepare material for use of directors at the meeting.* To facilitate the conduct of a meeting, secretaries sometimes furnish the directors, at the time of the meeting, with:

(*a*) Copies of the agenda and reports to which the agenda refers.
(*b*) Copies of the minutes of the previous meeting.
(*c*) Copies of resolution to be voted upon at the current meeting.

If this practice is followed, the secretary must see that the proper number of copies is made ready.

5. *Arrange for the payment of fees.* Directors are frequently paid fees for attendance at meetings in cases where the directors are not employed by the corporation and are not receiving a salary. Where the distribution of fees is delegated to the secretary, he usually requisitions from the treasurer the sum required, in the correct demonminations, and makes whatever preparations are necessary for the distribution either at the meeting or by mail after the meeting.

6. *Make preparations for recording minutes.* These preparations are the same as for meetings of stockholders. See page 1212.

7. STOCKHOLDERS' MEETINGS

Necessity for holding stockholders' meetings. Meetings of stockholders are necessary for the following reasons:

1. The courts generally hold that the stockholders must act concurrently; that is, they cannot bind the corporation if they act individually, even though a majority of them concur and express their consent in writing, unless consent in writing is sufficient under a governing statute.

2. The laws of the state in which the corporation is organized, the charter, and the by-laws give the stockholders certain rights and powers that must, under the law, be exercised at a meeting. Sometimes these powers can be exercised, under the statute, by consent in writing, and a meeting may not be necessary; however, as a matter of expediency, it is wise even in such cases to hold a meeting to obtain the written consents.

3. The corporation is an entity and is entitled to the joint action of its owners, each one of whom has a right to be enlightened by the views of the others. Without a meeting, such interchange of views is impossible.

However, according to the decisions of the courts, the validity of a corporate act does not always depend upon whether or not a meeting of the corporate body has been held in a formal way, even if the act is one of major importance. Irregularities in the holding of the meeting do not necessarily invalidate the proceedings of the meeting; before an objecting stockholder can succeed in nullifying the proceedings at a meeting, he must show that, by the irregularity in the meeting, his rights have been affected.

Calling stockholders' meetings. Stockholders' meetings are called as follows:

1. By the officers empowered by the by-laws of the corporation to call regular and special meetings of the stockholders. Occasionally the certificate of incorporation and in some instances the statute, designates who shall call meetings of stockholders. A statutory provision on the subject must be observed, and if the by-laws conflict with the statute, the latter governs.
2. By the board of directors, in the absence of statutory or by-law provision as to who shall call the meeting.
3. By a certain number of the stockholders, if the power is given to the stockholders by statute, charter, or by-laws. Many of the statutes specifically provide that if an election of directors is not held on the day designated in the by-laws, a meeting for the election of directors may be called by a certain number of the stockholders, if notice has been given as prescribed by the statute. Stockholders may also obtain the power to call a meeting by bringing a suit for mandamus to compel the corporate officers to call a meeting if they have wrongfully refused to do so.

Necessity for notice of stockholders' meetings. The necessity for notice of stockholders' meetings depends upon the kind of meeting that is to be held, as indicated below:

Regular meetings. If the statute, charter, or by-laws do not require notice of regular meetings to be given, and the charter or by-laws fix the time and place at which regular meetings are to be held, the charter or by-laws themselves are sufficient notice to all stockholders, and no further notice is necessary. In all other cases, notice of regular meetings is necessary.

Special meetings. Notice of special meetings must be given to the stockholders in the manner provided in the statute, charter, or by-laws.

Adjourned meetings. Unless otherwise prescribed by the by-laws, notice of an adjourned meeting is unnecessary if the notice of the original meeting was given as prescribed. In order that the notice of the prior meeting shall extend to the adjourned meeting, however, the latter must be held for the same purpose as the original meeting and must be virtually a continuation of it.

Notice need be given only to those stockholders who are entitled to vote, unless the statute expressly provides otherwise. Where the statute does not specifically require the publication of notice, newspaper notices may be omitted.

Length of notice. Great care should be exercised to give the notice in due time. The by-laws or statutes usually indicate how many days before the meeting notice must be given, and such requirements must be strictly observed. Thus, where the by-laws require thirty days' notice, a meeting will be invalid if only twelve days' notice is given. If the statute requires publication of the notice for ten days, it means that the notice is to continue in the publication for a period of ten days. In a daily paper this would require ten different inserts; in a weekly paper, two inserts.

Stockholders' meetings that are valid without required notice. If notice has not been given as required, action taken at a stockholders' meeting will be valid under the following circumstances:

1. If notice is waived by participation in the meeting. A person who is present in person or by proxy, and who participates without dissent in a meeting, thereby waives defects in the notice.

2. If the stockholders waive notice in writing. The signature of a stockholder to a waiver of notice of a meeting should be obtained either before or at the meeting, although waivers signed after the meeting have been held to be effective. The following is a form of waiver of notice of meeting that may be used for any meeting of stockholders.

WAIVER OF NOTICE OF STOCKHOLDERS' MEETING

The undersigned, being all the stockholders of the .... Corporation, a corporation created and organized under the laws of the State of ...., do hereby waive any and all notice as provided by the statutes of ...., or by the Articles of Incorporation or By-laws of the said Corporation, and do hereby consent to the holding of a .... meeting of the stockholders of the said Corporation, to be held on the . . day of . . . ., 19. ., at . . . . o'clock in the . . . . noon, or any adjournment or adjournments thereof, at the office of the Corporation, Room . . . ., No. City of . . . ., State of . . . ., for the following purposes [*insert purposes of meeting*], and do hereby consent to the transaction of any other business that may come before the meeting.

Dated at . . . ., ..., this . . . day of . . . ., 19 . . .

. . . ., holding . . . . shares

. . . ., " . . . . "

. . . ., " . . . . "

(*Signatures of stockholders*)

Contents of notice of stockholders' meeting. The notice of the meeting should contain information as to the following:

1. Time of the meeting, including the hour. The general rule is that a meeting must take place at the time designated in the by-laws or the charter. Generally, where an annual meeting is not held at the time specified in the by-laws, the directors may call a meeting within a reasonable time thereafter.

2. Place of the meeting. Some statutes require meetings to be held within the state; others provide that they may be held either within or without the state. Statutory provisions as to the place of meeting must be followed. If the statute prohibits corporations from meeting outside the state, the proceedings at meetings held without the state will be void, and the board of directors elected at such meetings will have no more power than if no election had been held.

As a matter of practice, if the governing statute requires stockholders' meetings to be held within the state, and a meeting at such place is inconvenient at the time, the meeting may be held at the most convenient place, and all transactions concluded at the meeting may be ratified at a meeting held within the state by dummies acting on stockholders' proxies. If no provision is made in the statute, charter, or by-laws, the stockholders' meetings must be held within the state. However, where all the stockholders participate, a stockholders' meeting held without the state will be valid. Furthermore, if the stockholders waive the invalidity of a meeting convened without the state, or ratify the acts done at the meeting, they cannot later claim that the meeting was invalid.

3. The purpose of the meeting. It is not absolutely essential that the notice of a regular meeting include the purpose of the meeting, unless so required by statute or by-laws. However, if some unusual business is to be transacted at a regular meeting, such as a sale of the corporate property or the amendment of the corporate charter, notice of such unusual business should be given. In the case of special meetings, the notice should include a statement of the matters to be discussed at the meeting.

4. The officer or others who are calling the meeting. This is necessary to indicate that the meeting is called by competent authority.

Time at which stockholders' meeting should start. A meeting is not legal if it is held before the exact time specified in the notice of the meeting, unless all the stockholders are present. It is not essential that the meeting start on the stroke of the hour for which it is called; it is sufficient if it is convened within a reasonable time after the hour fixed in the notice.

Getting a stockholders' meeting started. Several clerks should be appointed to act as ushers, if a large number of stockholders is expected to attend the meeting. The clerks may conduct the stockholders to seats, or they may permit the stockholders to take any seat they wish. Usually the stockholders are permitted to sit where they please. As each person arrives, the clerk asks his name and address, whether he is a stockholder, and whether he has been appointed proxy for a stockholder. The stock records or a list of the stockholders, as well as the filed proxies, should be in the meeting room. The clerk immediately checks the information. If the stockholder has not filed a proxy, he may be asked whether he wishes to do so. If he has filed a proxy, the clerk may inquire whether the stockholder wishes to revoke the proxy or to let it stand. Some corporations discard the proxy if the stockholder is present in person at the meeting.

It is generally advisable to have some executive officer present at the meeting of stockholders, although there is no requirement that the directors or officers attend. In large corporations, general counsel is usually present at the stockholders' meeting to act as adviser to the chairman.

Who presides at a stockholders' meeting. The person who is to preside at the meeting of stockholders is determined in the following ways:

1. The by-laws may designate the officer who is to preside at all stockholders' meetings. By-laws generally give the president or some other officer this right. Occasionally the provision appears in the corporate charter. Provision in the charter or in the by-laws as to who shall preside at the meeting of stockholders must be observed.

2. The stockholders present at the meeting may elect a chairman, if no provision is made in the character or by-laws as to who shall preside. In making the selection the stockholders may vote by a show of hands, a stock vote not being required to give validity to the meeting, in the absence of a statute or by-law providing otherwise. Where the by-law states that "at stockholders' meetings each stockholder shall cast one vote for each share of stock owned by him," the by-law applies to the election of a chairman as well as to the proceedings carried on after the meeting has been regularly organized. Similarly, where the by-law provides that upon demand of a stockholder the vote on any question shall be by stock vote, a stockholder has the right to demand a stock vote for the election of the chairman, and in the absence of such a demand the chairman may be elected by a viva-voce vote.

Selection of a secretary. When a secretary must be selected because the person designated by the by-laws to act as secretary at the stockholders' meetings is not present, the chairman may appoint a secretary. Any stockholder, however, may require an election of a secretary to be held immediately.

Necessity for a quorum to be present at stockholders' meeting. A valid meeting of stockholders cannot be held unless a quorum is present, and if the amount of stock necessary to constitute a quorum is not represented, in person or by proxy, the meeting must adjourn to another time. A quorum, as specified in the statute, charter, or by-laws, must be present not only to begin a meeting but to transact business. Thus, if during the meeting a number of stockholders depart, leaving less than a quorum present, the meeting must be disbanded by adjournment. However, if a meeting is once organized and all the parties have participated, no person or faction can then, by withdrawing capriciously and for the sole purpose of breaking a quorum, render the subsequent proceedings invalid. If stockholders have withdrawn for the purpose of breaking a quorum, because of whim, caprice, or chagrin, the law will consider the action as unavailing and will permit the meeting to proceed.

A quorum is always presumed unless it is questioned at the meeting, or unless the record shows that a quorum in fact is not present.

What constitutes a quorum. The person conducting the meeting should at the outset determine whether or not a quorum is present. The number necessary to constitute a quorum is determined as follows:

1. The by-laws, statute, or charter may fix the amount of stock required to be represented at a meeting. If the by-laws conflict with the statute, the statute must be followed, since the by-law is then void. Thus, if a provision in the by-laws fixes the amount of stock necessary to constitute a quorum at stockholders' meetings, and a provision of the statute specifies that directors shall be elected at an annual meeting of such stockholders as shall attend for that purpose, the directors may be elected by those present, even if the shares represented at the meeting do not constitute a quorum in accordance with the by-law provision.
2. If the statue, charter, or by-laws do not indicate what proportion in interest of the stock outstanding shall constitute a quorum, the persons present at the stockholders' meeting constitute a quorum, no matter how few they are, although there is authority to the effect that at least two persons must be present.

In determining whether or not a quorum is present, only issued stock is counted; stock that has been subscribed and not paid for is not included, unless there is a provision to the contrary in the law or in the certificate of incorporation. Stock that cannot be voted cannot be counted for quorum purposes.

Meaning of terms relating to quorum. If the by-laws or statute does not explicitly define what constitutes a quorum, the following definitions arrived at by the courts may be helpful:

1. *Majority*. The term "majority" used in defining a quorum means more than one half.
2. *Three fifths of the stockholders*. A provision in the by-laws that "three fifths of the stockholders shall constitute a quorum" applies to stockholders per capita, and not to stockholders in interest.

3. *Majority of stock issued and outstanding.* A by-law provision stating that "a majority of the stock issued and outstanding shall constitute a quorum, and all questions shall be decided by a majority of the votes cast" means that quorum members must be voting members.

Who has the right to be present at a stockholders' meeting. Every stockholder who has a right to vote at a meeting has the right to be present at the meeting. Stockholders who have no voting power are not entitled to be present at the meeting. As a matter of policy, however, it may be advisable to permit nonvoting stockholders to attend, unless it is anticipated that nonvoting stockholders will object to action in which they have no voice. An outsider may be permitted to attend a meeting of stockholders even though he has no legal right to do so, but if objection is made to his presence, the matter of whether the outsider is to remain may have to be put to a vote and decided in the same way that other questions are settled.

Conducting a stockholders' meeting. In the absence of express regulation by statute or by-laws, stockholders' meetings, including those for the election of directors, are controlled largely by accepted usage and custom. The fundamental rule is that all who are entitled to take part will be treated with fairness and good faith. While a stockholders' meeting is not of such a formal nature that the rules of parliamentary law must be observed, the ordinary parliamentary usages apply to it.

If the by-laws provide that stockholders' meetings shall be conducted according to the rules prescribed by a manual of parliamentary procedure, the requirement must be enforced.

Who may vote at a stockholders' meeting. Every owner of capital stock has, as an incident of the ownership of shares, the right to vote the stock at all meetings of stockholders, unless such right is denied by some statutory or charter provision, or by an agreement under which he holds his shares. Whoever has the legal title to the stock has the right to vote. Since the officers of a corporation would be placed in an embarrassing position if they had to determine who was the owner of the legal title to stock, it is generally provided in the by-laws that the right to vote rests with the person who appears as the registered owner of the stock on the books of the corporation. In some instances the statute or charter makes this provision.

Holders of record on a certain day to vote. Unless there is some provision to the contrary, a stockholder's right to vote at a meeting is to be determined as of the time when the meeting is held. It is clear that if only the true owners of stock at the time when the meeting is held were permitted to vote stock, just prior to the meeting the corporation would be inundated with demands for transfers of stock in order that the true owner might be present and vote at the meeting. This would mean that until the last minute before the meeting, the corporation could not prepare a list of the stockholders entitled to vote. To avoid this difficulty, there developed the practice, sanctioned by statute, of closing the transfer books a certain number of days before the meeting in order to provide ample time for compiling the necessary list of stockholders. During the period that the books are closed, no transfers can be effected. This expedient, however, proved unsatisfactory and another practice, now used more than that of closing the books, was instituted—namely, that of preparing a list of the stockholders of record on a certain day before the meeting. The list is prima-facie evidence of ownership of the stock and is used to determine who has the right to vote at a stockholders' meeting. The advantage of using the stock list, as against closing the transfer books, is that transfers of stock are not interrupted, but are merely disregarded for purposes of determining the rights of stockholders to vote at a meeting.

In determining who may vote at an adjourned meeting, the chairman may disregard the fact that the meeting is a continuation meeting. Thus new stockholders of record, and stockholders who were not present or represented at the original meeting, but who are present or represented at the adjourned meeting, are permitted to vote.

Disputes as to who may vote. When a dispute arises as to who has the right to vote, the meeting must be guided by the corporate records or the list of corporate stockholders prepared for the meeting. The officers need not look behind the books to ascertain who are the real owners of the shares, although a court of equity will do so in a dispute in which it is seeking to settle the rights between the claimants as such. If one of the stockholders claims that the record is incorrect, he may apply to a court of equity for a writ compelling the acceptance of his vote. This writ must be obtained before the meeting and must be presented to the chairman; in the absence of such writ, the stockholder of record on the books of the corporation should be given the right to vote. The courts have frequently held that a duly qualified stockholder does not lose his right to vote if his name fails to appear on the proper stock-record book or on the list of stockholders because of the negligence, contrivance, or ignorance of the corporation in maintaining its records.

Some instances in which questions as to who may vote arise. Most of the difficult problems as to who has the right to vote arise through the following circumstances:

1. *Sale of stock by the registered holder without transfer on books.* If a stockholder has sold his shares to another, and the transfer has not been registered before the day fixed for determining who has the right to vote at the meeting, the transferee may not vote. The purchaser, however, although not registered as a stockholder, may secure a proxy from the seller and thus obtain the right to vote. If there is no provision in the statute, charter, or by-laws requiring transfer to be made on the books, the purchaser of the stock is entitled to vote if he produces evidence that the stock has been transferred to him.

2. *Pledge of shares by the registered holder.* As between the pledgor and pledgee, the pledgor has the right to vote, since he retains legal title to the stock pledged, If, however, the pledgor permits the pledgee to register the pledgee's name on the books of the corporation as the owner of stock without reservation, the corporation will be justified in recognizing the pledgee as having the right to vote. It has been held that if the pledgor fails to appear at a meeting in person or by proxy, the pledgee has the right to be represented at the meeting.

3. *Stock not fully paid for.* If there is no provision to the contrary, the subscribers to the capital stock of a corporation who are in fact stockholders are entitled to vote at a meeting of stockholders, even if no certificates of stock have been issued. If the subscription to the stock is such that it does not make the subscriber a stock-

holder, as, for example, where the subscription is merely a contract with the corporation to purchase stock, the subscriber is not entitled to vote.

4. *Stock held by a minor.* Where there are no statutory provisions on the subject, the rule seems to be that minors cannot personally vote their shares. The guardian of the minor, or the trustee who holds the shares for a minor, has the voting power.

5. *Death of a registered holder.* When an owner of stock dies, title to the stock passes immediately to the deceased owner's legal representatives. When a representative is able to establish his appointment as administrator or executor he may vote stock of the decedent without causing a change in the corporate records. When the legal title is vested in several executors, they can vote only as co-owners. (See 7, below.) Letters testamentary that are issued by competent authority to an executor are conclusive proof of title to the shares of stock of the corporation and of the right to vote in respect thereof. After delivery of the stock to the heirs, the administrator does not have the right to vote the stock in defiance of the tranferees' wishes even though the transferees fail to transfer the stock out of the name of the administrator to themselves.

6. *Stock registered in the name of a trustee.* The trustee, not the beneficiary, has the voting power. Even if the statute gives to the beneficiary the right to vote, his right will not accrue unless his name appears on the campany's records.

7. *Stock owned in the name of two or more people.* Co-owners of stock must unanimously agree as to the manner in which the stock shall be voted; otherwise their vote will not count. As a matter of practice, one co-owner may present proxies from the other co-owners and exercise the right to vote on that basis. Where stock stands in the name of a partnership, and one partner alone attends the meeting, he may vote the stock in behalf of his partners. If one of the partners dies, any surviving partner may vote the stock standing in the name of the partnership.

8. *Stock registered in the name of a corporation.* Where stock is registered in the name of a corporation, it is voted by proxy properly authorized by the corporation owning the stock. A corporation that has acquired its own stock cannot vote the stock. Nor can the directors of a corporation vote stock of the company held by one of the corporation's subsidiaries.

Voting by proxy. Absent stockholders are generally given the right by statute, charter, or by-laws to vote at a meeting by written proxy. The provisions of the statute, charter, or by-laws must be strictly observed, and proxies that do not meet the requirements should be thrown out. Ordinarily the presiding officer at the meeting is the person who decides whether or not a proxy is acceptable, but in large corporations the power to pass on the validity of proxies is frequently delegated to a special committee of inspectors. These inspectors may be furnished with a set of rules, drawn in the light of the statutory, charter, and by-law requirements of the particular corporation, and with knowledge of the general principles of law relating to proxies. From the following principles relating to various parts of the proxy, a set of rules can be drawn up that will be suitable for a particular corporation.

Acceptance of proxies. The following are the principles forming the basis of rules as to acceptance of proxies.

1. *Compliance with statutory provisions.* While the statutory provisions vary from state to state, the following are the usual provisions:

(*a*) The proxy must be in writing.
(*b*) It is revocable at the pleasure of the person making it.
(*c*) It will expire a certain number of months or years from the date of its execution unless the stockholder signing the proxy indicates the length of time it is to continue in force.
(*d*) The term of the proxy is limited to a definite period.

2. *Form of proxy.* Proxies need not be drawn in any particular form, unless otherwise provided by the statute, charter, or by-laws. Thus, even if a corporation has sent out its own form of proxy with the notice of the meeting, it cannot throw out a proxy simply because some other form has been substituted.

The Securities and Exchange Commission's regulations governing the solicitation of proxies by companies subject to the Securities Exchange Act of 1934 set forth certain requirements as to the form of the proxy. These should be strictly followed. For example, the proxy must contain a space wherein the person solicited may specify how his vote shall be cast on each matter or group of matters described in the proxy statement.

3. *Date.* The proxy need not be dated; hence it should not be thrown out because no date appears on it. The secretary may instruct the examiners of proxies to fill in a date approximating the date of mailing. He may also instruct them that if a proxy is dated prior to the time when it was sent to the stockholder, it may be accepted, provided the stockholder who sends the proxy is actually a stockholder on the date shown on the proxy.

4. *Witnesses.* A witness to the signature of a proxy is not necessary unless the statute, charter, or by-laws provide otherwise. However, witnessing is advisable, for in case the signature is questioned, the witness can assist in proving the signature.

5. *Seal.* The proxy need not be sealed.

6. *Name of person appointed as proxy.* Unless the statute or by-laws otherwise provide, it is not essential that the person to whom the proxy is given should himself be a stockholder. The proxy may be designated as, for example, "any member of the firm of A-B & Co.," without the individual being specifically named. In some of the larger corporations, a proxy committee is selected at the annual meeting of stockholders, which committee, in effect, represents those who control the corporation. The names of members of the proxy committee are placed on what is known as the official proxy, which is sent out with notices of meetings during the course of the year.

7. *Number of shares filled in.* It is not essential that the space provided for the number of shares be filled in. Nor does the filling in of an incorrect amount by the stockholder invalidate the proxy. The inspectors of the proxies may be instructed to insert the correct number of shares owned by the stockholder.

8. *Name of the corporation.* A proxy is not invalid merely because the name of the corporation is incorrectly given, if the name agrees with the name given in the notice of the meeting.

9. *Legibility.* A proxy that is illegible should not be accepted.

10. *Signature of the stockholder.* The most important part of the proxy, with regard to its acceptability, is the signature. The following is a suggested set of rules to be observed by inspectors of proxies in examining signatures:

(*a*) A proxy in which the name of the stockholder is written in the body, but not at the close of the proxy, is void and should not be accepted.

(*b*) The name signed to the proxy should be the same as that in which the certificate is issued. Proxies may be accepted, however, if the initial of the given name, rather than the full name, is given, even though the full name appears in the certificate. If the name is different from that of the registered name, authority for such different signature should accompany the proxy.

(*c*) If the certificate is issued in the name of two or more persons as trustees, the signatures of all the trustees must appear on the proxy, unless the certificate, as issued, specifically empowers one or certain of the trustees to sign.

(*d*) If the certificate is issued to a corporation, authority from the board of directors authorizing the officers to sign the proxy should accompany the proxy. As a matter of practice, however, many corporations accept proxies without the filing of the authority, if the proxy is not challenged.

(*e*) If the certificate is issued to a company that has been succeeded by another corporation, and the proxy is signed and sealed by the successor company, proof of the successorship should be obtained, although the proxy may be accepted if not challenged.

(*f*) If a certificate is signed as an attorney, executor, administrator, or guardian, papers showing the authority should accompany the proxy.

Powers of proxies. The word *proxy* is applied both to the document evidencing the authority of one person to vote for a stockholder and to the person acting as representative. The relationship created by a proxy is governed by the general rules of principal and agent. Proxies may be either general or limited. A general proxy, like a general agent, can represent his principal in all ordinary business, but not in extraordinary business, such as voting on the question of dissolution. Where a proxy is given limited power, or is given instructions as to how to vote, he must act within the limitation and according to instructions. Consequently the secretary should accept a vote only if it is cast in accordance with the instructions; if a proxy attempts to vote otherwise, he acts outside of the scope of his authority, and his vote is not valid. It would seem that the secretary cannot alter the proxy's vote to make it conform to the instructions contained in the proxy, for the vote is given not by the written authorization but by the person. If the administration desires that the vote be in accordance with the instructions, the correct practice would be to adjourn the meeting, notify the stockholder to revoke the proxy, send a new proxy, and get the vote at the adjourned meeting. To save the time of the other stockholders, their proxies could be taken immediately, so that they might be voted at the adjourned meeting in accordance with the administration's desires.

Where a proxy votes for his own personal interests and contrary to the interests of his principal, and the latter promptly repudiates the vote, the action of the proxy may be set aside, unless the interests of third parties would be adversely affected. A proxy may act on questions subsidiary to the principal question on which he is authorized to act; thus he may waive irregularities in a meeting at which he represents a stockholder as proxy, such as a defect in the notice.

Under the regulations issued by the Securities and Exchange Commission, and applicable to a corporation subject to the Securities Exchange Act of 1934, the person to whom the proxy is given may have conferred upon him discretionary authority with respect to matters as to which no specification has been made by the person solicited, with respect to matters not known or determined at the time of the solicitation, and with respect to the election of directors or other officers.

Where several persons are named to act as proxies, and they are not named in the alternative, all those named must agree as to the vote; otherwise their vote will not be received.

Methods of taking the vote at a stockholders' meeting. A vote in an election or upon any question may be taken in the following ways, depending upon the statutory and by-law requirements:

1. By ballot. A ballot must be used if the statute or by-laws so require; otherwise its use is optional.
2. By a show of hands, or by a viva-voce vote; that is, a call for "ayes" and "noes." This method is impractical in stockholders' meetings if there is any dissent, for it shows the per-capita desires of the stockholders and not the per-share determination of the question.
3. By reading the roll of stockholders. Since the roll indicates the number of shares owned by each stockholder, a count of the per-share votes is thus obtained.
4. By written consent of the stockholders. Where written consent to any action is required, a document setting forth the consent should

be prepared and signed by the stockholders, with an indictaion of the shares held by each stockholder.

How many votes is each stockholder entitled to? At common law each member of an incorporated body was entitled to one vote. Today, however, the general rule is that each stockholder is entitled to one vote for each share of stock that he owns, unless the statute, charter, or by-laws provide otherwise.

Sometimes the statutes make special provision regarding the right to vote, as, for example, that stockholders who are in arrears or who are in debt to the corporation may not vote, or that stockholders whose stock has been attached may vote until title is divested. Furthermore, the certificate of incorporation may provide some other method of voting. For example, the holders of a certain class of stock may be given ten votes for the first ten shares and one vote for each ten shares thereafter until a maximum of one hundred shares is reached, whereupon voting rights in respect to shares cease.

Cumulative voting; how conducted. Under the system of cumulative voting each shareholder is entitled to a number of votes equal to the number of shares he owns multiplied by the number of directors to be elected. He may cumulate the votes—that is, cast all the votes for one candidate—or he may distribute his votes among the candidates in any way he sees fit. The majority under this method is always certain to obtain control of the board of directors, and the minority is certain to be represented on the board, if the votes are cast properly.

The corporation laws of some of the states prescribe that directors shall be elected by cumulative voting. In other states, cumulative voting is permitted when the certificate of incorporation or the by-laws so provide. The right to cumulative voting cannot be claimed unless that method of voting is provided for as follows:

1. By statute.
2. By the corporation's charter or by-laws.
3. By contract among all the stockholders, provided the agreement is not otherwise illegal.

To illustrate how cumulative voting operates to give the minority the opportunity to be represented on the board of directors, take as an example the following situation: The corporation has outstanding

100 shares; the majority controls 51 shares and the minority 49 shares. The faction strength is nearly equal. If 5 directors are to be elected, the majority is entitled to 255 votes (51×5) and the minority to 245 votes (49×5). If the majority contents itself with casting this cumulative vote for three out of five directors, it can secure their election by giving each director 85 votes. The minority can elect only 2 directors by giving one of the directors 122 votes and another 123 votes. In this case, if the majority frittered away its strength among the five directors, while the minority concentrated its strength upon four, the minority would gain control of the board.

Determination of shares necessary to control an election under cumulative voting. Often it becomes necessary to determine how many shares one should hold or control under the system of cumulative voting, to insure the election of a certain number of directors. The following method may be used:

1. Multiply the total number of shares entitled to vote by the number of directors it is desired to elect.
2. Divide the figure found in (1) by one more than the total number of directors to be elected.
3. Add one to the figure obtained in (2); the result will be the least number of shares that it will be necessary to hold or control in order to elect the desired number of directors.

Thus, if a company has outstanding 1,000 voting shares, 5 directors are to be elected, and it is desired to elect 2 out of the 5, the least number of shares that it will be necessary to hold or control in order to accomplish this result will be found as follows:

$$\frac{1{,}000 \times 2}{5+1} + 1 = 334\tfrac{1}{3}$$

The desired result, therefore, can be accomplished only if 335 shares are held or controlled (where there is a fraction, it is to be counted as an extra share).

Elections of directors. It is not necessary to elect all of the required number of directors at one meeting. In the election of directors, nominations need not be seconded. A motion to close the nominations may be made and put to a vote at any time. No person has the right thereafter to make nominations, but the closing of the nominations will not prevent the casting of ballots for other persons. Where the election is unanimous, the secretary may cast a ballot for the slate; the ballot is deemed a vote from all voting stock represented at the meeting, and the election is recorded accordingly. The polls may be kept open for a prescribed period during which votes will be taken. After the polls are closed and the vote is announced, they cannot be reopened to receive additional votes. The election is not vitiated, however, if after the polls are closed additional votes are received, provided, of course, that the election results have not been announced. The final results of an election may not be announced until the time has arrived for the closing of the polls, unless a majority of the voting stock has been voted in favor of a slate. Any stockholder may change his vote at any time before the results of the election are announced.

Conduct of election of directors by inspectors. A common regulatory provision of the statutes concerning the election of directors is that the election shall be conducted by inspectors or judges of election appointed in the manner prescribed by the by-laws. It would seem that, in the absence of a statutory requirement, inspectors are not essential. In large corporations it is advisable that inspectors of election be appointed, regardless of whether or not they are required. The function of the inspectors is to distribute and collect the ballots, count the vote, and report, under oath, the result of the election. The inspectors are ministerial officers with some discretionary powers in passing upon the eligibility of the voters. Their decisions, however, are subject to review by the courts. The inspectors may reject votes and may keep the polls open for a reasonable time after the closing hour in order to give stockholders who are ready to vote the opportunity to do so.

Vote necessary to decide an election of directors. The vote necessary to decide an election is determined by:

1. The provisions of the statute, charter, or by-laws.
2. In the absence of any provision, a majority of the votes cast, as distinguished from a majority of those present, will decide the result of an election.

This latter rule applies even if those voting do not constitute a majority of the stockholders, or do not represent a majority of the stock.

A majority of the votes actually cast will determine the election, even if stockholders present who had an opportunity to vote refrained from doing so.

Rules governing tie vote in election of directors. The following illustration explains the effects of a tie vote in an election of directors. Five directors are to be elected by cumulative voting. Six candidates have been nominated. Four hundred votes have been cast. The ballots are tabulated, and the following is shown to be the result of the voting:

A	80 votes
B	80 "
C	60 "
D	60 "
E	60 "
F	60 "

The chairman of the meeting may not declare that no board has been elected and that the old board shall continue in office. A and *B* will be considered elected, and the chairman must permit the stockholders to vote again and again, if necessary, until it is demonstrated that further balloting is futile.

The above rule applies also in the following situation, where straight voting is in effect. 100 shares of stock are to voted. The shares are divided among four stockholders as follows: Jones, 2 shares; Smith, 25 shares; Brown, 40 shares; and Grey, 33 shares. The by-laws require that directors must be elected by a majority of the votes cast. Three directors are to be elected, and there are six candidates. Each stockholder would have as many votes for each of three directors as he has shares. The votes cannot be split among the six candidates. The votes are cast as follows:

A	100 votes
B	100 "
C	2 "
D	25 "
E	40 "
F	33 "

A and *B* are considered elected and the balloting continues for the election of a third director.

Where the votes are divided between two factions, it is inadvisable for either faction to remain silent or to refuse to vote while the other faction votes, for by so doing the voting group is enabled to carry the election.

Results of failure to elect a board of directors. If a majority of the board has been elected, the number is sufficient to constitute a new board of directors, provided the election is valid. The entire old board steps out; the elected majority assumes the duties of the board; and the places of directors not filled at the election are considered vacant. The vacancies are filled in the manner in which vacancies due to causes such as resignation and removal are filled. This procedure has been explained on page 1161.

If less than a majority of the board is elected, those elected cannot be inducted into office, and the old board of directors holds over until its successors are elected.

A similar rule applies in case no election of directors whatever is held on the day designated for the election of directors. The old directors continue to hold office and may discharge their duties until their successors are elected. The statutes generally direct that another meeting for the election of directors be held as soon after the day fixed by the by-laws for the election of directors as may be convenient, or within a certain number of days thereafter.

Vote necessary to decide questions other than election. The vote necessary to decide questions other than an election is determined as follows:

1. By the requirements of the statute, charter, or by-laws.
2. By a majority of the stock represented at the meeting, in the absence of statutory, charter, or by-law requirements. This rule holds even though the majority is less than a majority of the number of stockholders, and less than a majority of the total amount of stock outstanding.

Determining whether vote required by statute is obtained. Where the consent of stockholders is being obtained in accordance with a statutory requirement, care should be exercised to determine just what proportion of the corporate stock is necessary to carry the proposal. Ordinarily the statute specifically states what percentage of the outstanding stock is required. Sometimes the statute is ambiguous and does not state whether the proportion required applies to the individual stockholders or to the number of shares outstanding, irrespective of the number of holders thereof. A provision in the statute or by-laws requiring the approval of "a majority of the stockholders" upon a particular question has been held to mean a majority in interest of the stockholders, and not a majority in number only. But the more general view is that the term "majority of the stockholders," as ordinarily used, means a per-capita majority when the right to vote is per capita, and a stock majority when each share of stock is entitled to vote.

In some cases the statute is so worded that the percentage of consent required is a percentage of the total amount of stock outstanding, irrespective of the classes into which the stock is divided. In other cases certain percentages of each of the several classes of stock are required. Sometimes the statutes require that the consent be obtained from stockholders having the right to vote. In still other cases the statutes provide that the consent be obtained from the stockholders, and the question as to whether stock that is ordinarliy nonvoting has the right to participate in the action is left open. It would seem that nonvoting stock should have the right to vote in any matter specifically affecting the rights of the holders thereof, unless the statute is very clear in indicating that their consent is not required.

Revocation and reconsideration of action by stockholders. The stockholders, while they are still in session, may alter or change any resolution or motion adopted by them at the meeting. They may also reconsider and repeal any vote or resolution after the meeting, unless such action will disturb rights that have become vested as a result of the vote or resolution. Thus, if the stockholders had by resolution authorized the offer of certain shares of stock to an individual at a certain price per share, and the offer was accepted by such individual, the stockholders could not revoke the resolution or alter its terms, without the consent of the individual, for by doing so they would disturb rights that had become fixed under the first resolution.

Adjournment of meeting. In the absence of a provision in the statute, charter, or by-laws to the contrary, a meeting that is regularly convened is not legally adjourned unless the motion to adjourn has been passed by a majority of the stock represented at the meeting, even though it has been passed by a majority of those present at the meeting. The adjournment may take the following forms:

1. To a day certain.
2. *Sine die*; that is, without naming a date. In this case, the adjournment is final.
3. Subject to call of the chair.

If the motion to adjourn indicates no special form, the adjournment is final.

Adjourned meeting; business that can be transacted. At any adjourned meeting at which a quorum is present, unless all the stockholders are present and consent to the transaction of other business only such business may be transacted as might have come before the original meeting, since an adjourned meeting is only a continuation of the original meeting. In regard to voting at an adjourned meeting, see page 1225. In regard to notice of adjourned meetings, see page 1219.

8. DIRECTORS' MEETINGS AND COMMITTEE MEETINGS

Necessity for holding directors' meetings. As a general rule, the directors can bind the corporation by their acts only when they are fully assembled at a meeting. The reason for this rule is that the stockholders have the right to expect the directors to give conscientious consideration to all questions through the interchange of ideas at a formal meeting duly called and noticed, at which all the directors may be heard and their opinions deliberated upon by the other members of the board.

The above rule has the following important exceptions that make it possible for the directors to bind the corporation even though they have not consulted together as a board:

1. If the statute authorizes specific acts to be done by the directors separately, no meeting is necessary.
2. If by usage or custom the directors have managed the affairs of the corporation without formal meetings, and the corporation and its stockholders have by long practice acquiesced in an informal manner of doing business, the acts of the directors, if they are within the scope of their power, are valid; otherwise, great injury may be done to third persons relying on this course of conduct.
3. If the stockholders waive the necessity for directors' meetings,

transactions consummated without any meeting can be attacked only by the state. This right of waiver is based on the fact that the directors derive all their power from the stockholders.

4. Where the directors own all the stock, acts done outside of a formal meeting by all the directors, even though done separately, are valid.

5. If the stockholders, or directors, with knowledge of the facts, acquiesce in informal action by the directors, they are bound thereby, if the acts done or authorized are within the power of the board in the first place. However, it has been held that where the law authorizes an act to be done by the board of directors only at a meeting, validity cannot be given to the acts done by the directors acting severally at different times and places through the signing, by all of the members, of a paper falsely reciting that they were present at a meeting of the board and consented to the acts.

6. Unanimous consent of the directors, even though the consent of each is given separately, may obviate the necessity for a board meeting. However, in some cases, acts of directors have been held invalid even though all of the directors consented thereto.

Calling directors' meetings. Directors' meetings are called as follows:

1. By the officers empowered by the statute or by-laws to call meetings of directors. If the by-laws give the president the power to call special meetings of directors, and provide that, in his absence, the vice president shall take his place and perform his duties, the vice president may call any special meeting that the president could have called had he been present.

2. By a certain number of the directors, if provision is made therefor in the by-laws. Where the by-laws provide that special meetings of the directors shall be called by the president or, at his request, by the secretary, the secretary and another member of the board, even though they constitute a majority of the board, have no authority to call a special meeting.

In the absence of other provisions in the statute or by-laws, the meeting need not be called in any particular manner.

Directors' meetings falling on a Sunday or holiday. If the day set for a regular meeting of directors falls upon a Sunday or a holiday, the following should be done:

1. Follow the by-laws, if provision is made for such a contingency.

2. If no provision is made for holding meetings that fall upon a Sunday or holiday on some other day, give the directors ample notice that the meeting will be held at some other time. The directors should not hold the meeting on the day following the regular day set by the by-laws without notice, for action taken at such a meeting may be invalid. In one instance, a sale of stock sold for failure to pay an assessment levied by directors at a meeting held on the day following the regular day, because the regular day fell on a holiday, was declared invalid.

A statutory provision holding that if the day on which an act of a secular nature, appointed by law or contract to be performed on a particular day, falls on a holiday it may be performed on the next business day, does not apply to meetings of directors, since meetings are held according to by-law regulations, and a by-law is not a contract within the meaning of such statutes. While it would seem therefore, the directors' meetings can be held on a Sunday or holiday, if proper notice is given where necessary, and if there is no prohibiting statute, attention should be given to the laws prohibiting the transacting of business on a Sunday or holiday, if the transactions to be authorized at the meeting are to include the making of contracts. A meeting of directors held on a Sunday is valid if affirmed at a subsequent weekday meeting.

Necessity for notice of directors' meetings. The rules as to the necessity for giving notice of directors' meetings vary, as shown below, with the kind of meeting to be held.

Regular meetings. Unless expressly required by statute, no notice of regular meetings need be given where the by-laws, charter, or resolution of the board of directors specifies the time of the regular meeting.

Special meetings. Notice of a special meeting must be given to every director, unless:

1. There is some express provision in the charter or by-laws, or established usage, to the contrary.

2. It is impractical or impossible to give the notice to each director. For example, failure to give notice is excused where an emergency demands immediate action, and the directors who are no

given notice cannot be notified in time to enable them to attend the meeting.

Where the exceptions are not present, a special meeting held in the absence of some of the directors and without any notice is illegal, and the action of such a meeting, even though affirmed by a majority of the directors, is invalid.

Adjourned meetings. If notice of the original meeting was given, notice of an adjourned meeting need not be given either to directors who were present at the original meeting or to those who were absent, unless otherwise required by the by-laws. An adjournment of a regular meeting at which some directors were absent, without a statement of the hour at which the adjourned meeting will be held, requires notice to be given to the absentees.

When directors' meetings are valid without the required notice. If notice has not been given as required, action taken at the meeting will not be invalid under the following circumstances:

1. If all the directors attend the meeting and do not object to the lack of notice. In many cases the courts have held valid action by the directors in instances where some of the directors did not receive proper notice of the meeting, but where a meeting had been held with a sufficient number of directors present to constitute a quorum, and where the absent directors did not complain or find any fault with what the majority did. In explanation of this leniency, one court has said:

> To hold that in all instances technical conformity to the requirements of the law of corporations is a condition to a valid action by the directors would be to lay down a rule of law which could be used as a trap for the unwary who deal with the corporations, and to permit corporations sometimes to escape liability to which an individual in the same circumstances would be subjected.

2. If the action is ratified at a subsequent meeting. Action taken by the directors at a meeting for which proper notice has not been given may be ratified at a subsequent meeting at which all the directors are present. If the subsequent meeting is called upon proper notice, the business transacted at the improperly called previous meeting may be ratified, even if all the members of the board do not attend the subsequent meeting.

3. If the directors sign a waiver of notice prior to the meeting. Directors who were absent from a meeting, the time and place of which were not fixed, cannot waive the required notice after the meeting has been held. The following is a form of waiver of notice of a directors' meeting.

WAIVER OF NOTICE OF SPECIAL MEETING OF DIRECTORS

We, the undersigned, being all the directors of the .... Corporation, a corporation organized and existing under the laws of the State of ...., do hereby waive any and all notice as provided by the statutes of ...., or by the Articles of Incorporation or By-laws of the said Corporation, and do hereby consent to the holding of a special meeting of the Board of Directors of the said Corporation, to be held on the ... day of ...., 19.., at ...... o'clock in the ......noon, or any adjournment or adjournments thereof, at the office of the Corporation, Room ......, No. ...., City of ...., State of ...., for the following purposes [*insert purposes of meeting*].

We hereby also consent to the transaction of any other business that may come before the meeting.

Dated at ....,.........., this ... day of ...., 19..

....

....

....

(*Signatures of directors*)

Form of notice of directors' meeting. Unless a statute, the charter, or a by-law prescribes a particular form of notice of directors' meetings, any form will be satisfactory. If written ntoice is prescribed, oral notice is not sufficient unless all the directors attend the meeting. The requirement that the notice be in writing does not mean that it must be signed by the person calling the meeting.

If the notice is received by a director or if he attends the meeting, it is immaterial by what means notice was conveyed to him. The manner of serving notice becomes important only when a director is absent from the meeting and a question arises as to whether notice was properly served upon him. If the by-laws are silent regarding the manner in which written notice shall be served, the best practice is to mail notices to directors. There are some cases, however, which hold that when no method of giving notice of directors' meetings is provided for in the by-laws or regulations of a corporation, personal notice must be given to each director.

Contents of notice of directors' meeting. Notice of a meeting of directors should disclose the following information:

1. *Time of the meeting.* In the absence of ny statute, by-law provision, or practice of the corporation fixing the time or method of calling meetings of the board of directors, a reasonable notice is necessary for the validity of the meeting. What is reasonable notice depends upon the circumstances. One day's notice of a meeting that is to be held at a place 24 hours by rail from the place at which notice is served on a director is insufficient.

2. *Place of the meeting.* The statutes of most of the states authorize the holding of directors' meetings, as provided in the by-laws, either within or without the state. If the statute specifies that meetings shall be held within the state, a meeting held ouside the state will not be legal, and the action taken by the directors at such a meeting will not be binding. In the absence of any express provision naming a particular place, the directors may designate any reasonably convenient place within the state. The courts generally agree that the directors may meet outside the state, in the absence of a provision restricting the place of meeting to the state of incorporation, to transact any business in which they act as mere agents of the company or as superintendents of the business. A difference of opinion exists concerning the power of directors to meet outside the state to act upon such matters as the election of officers and the levying of assessments; in other words, to act in a purely corporate capacity. Thus, in one case it was held that the directors may not meet outside the state to make calls upon stock, while in another it was held that a meeting for this purpose may be held outside the state of incorporation.

3. *Purpose of the meeting.* The purpose of a directors' meeting need not necessarily be mentioned in the notice of the meeting, although if the meeting is extraordinary, it is best to state the purpose. The general rule is that at a special meeting called by a general notice any business whatever may be transacted. If the notice of a special meeting states the purpose, the courts are likely to hold that any

extraordinary business outside of that stated in the notice cannot be transacted unless all the directors are present.

Quorum at directors' meeting. A quorum of directors must be present at a meeting to enable the directors to transact business. If there is less than a quorum present, the meeting must necessarily adjourn. A quorum is presumed to be present unless the presumption is questioned, or unless the record discloses that one is not present. A director who is disqualified from voting because of a personal interest in the transaction cannot be included in determining whether or not a quorum is present. A director cannot be tricked into attendance at a meeting against his will in order that a quorum be obtained.

Where there is no provision in the statute, charter, or by-laws, a majority of the required number of directors is the minimum requirement for a quorum, even where there are vacancies in the board. If, by reason of vacancies in the board, the number is reduced to less than the number required for a quorum, the board cannot transact any business until the vacancies are filled. But if the number of directors is reduced below the minimum required by law, business may still be transacted by the board if a quorum still exists and is present.

Vote necessary to authorize action at directors' meeting. Unless expressly provided otherwise in the statute, charter, or by-laws, a majority vote of the directors present at a meeting, as distinguished from a majority of the full board, is sufficient to authorize action. Any director present at a meeting may vote on any subject in which he is not pecuniarily interested. Directors cannot vote by proxy.

Conduct of directors' meeting. In the case of smaller corporations, meetings of the board of directors are usually conducted in an informal manner. Larger corporations, however, generally conduct their directors' meetings with considerable formality.

The chairman of the board sits at the head of the directors' table. The president sits at the right of the chairman, or, if the office of chairman of the board does not exist, the president sits at the head of the table. Usually the secretary sits next to the chairman, often at his left, so that he can be consulted conveniently on any matter in the order of business and hand documents and records to the chairman with a minimum of disturbance. The president generally presides at meetings of directors, unless some other provision is made by the by-laws. Votes are usually taken in an informal way at directors' meetings generally by a call for "yes" or "no" answers. (For the conduct of directors' meetings at which vacancies are to be filled see page 1161. For preparation for a directors' meeting, see page 1215.)

Right of directors to rescind action taken at former meeting. The directors have the right to repeal any resolution passed at a previous meeting, or to rescind any previous action, provided the repeal or rescission does not involve a breach of contract or disturb a vested right. (For right of directors to revoke declared dividends, see page 1175.)

Executive and finance committee meetings. The executive and finance committees are the most active bodies in many large corporations. They are generally created in accordance with the provisions of the by-laws, or by resolution of the board of directors. The by-laws usually prescribe the manner of calling committee meetings, the number of persons necessary to constitute a quorum, the method of filling vacancies, the number of votes necessary to take action, and similar regulations. The by-laws or the resolution creating the committees may provide that the committees shall set up their own rules of procedure. In the absence of special rules governing the conduct of committee meetings, the rules governing meetings of directors apply. Thus the executive or other committee must act as a whole. In the absence of specific requirements, a majority of the committee will constitute a quorum, and a majority of those present at any meeting will have the power to decide questions that come before the meeting. Committee meetings are ordinarily not conducted with as much formality as meetings of the board.

9. HOW TO KEEP MINUTES OF MEETINGS

Necessity for keeping minutes of meetings. Minutes of stockholders', directors', and committee meetings are necessary for the following reasons:

1. The statute, charter, or by-laws may require minutes.
2. A written record of the proceedings eliminates misunderstanding and guides the directors in carrying out their own decisions and those of the stockholders.
3. Minutes are useful if the corporation brings a legal action or

is sued upon a matter that was taken up at a meeting. Ordinarily the minutes are prima-facie evidence of what they purport to show as to the corporate business transacted at the meeting; frequently they are the best evidence. The minutes, however, are subject to contradiction by oral evidence to show what the actual proceedings were, if the minutes do not correctly record them.

From a legal standpoint it is not essential to the validity or binding effect of acts done or authority given by the directors or the stockholders that their votes or decisions be recorded, unless a record is required by the statute, charter, or by-laws. In fact, failure to keep minutes, even when they are expressly required, will not invalidate an act of the board or of the stockholders, if the act is admittedly that of the corporation or if invalidation would injuriously affect the rights of third parties.

Necessity for adopting resolutions. Since, from a legal standpoint, it is not necessary that minutes be kept, it follows that it is not essential that a formal resolution be adopted in order either to bind the corporation or to confer authority to bind the corporation. However, the rule does not diminish the necessity for resolutions from the standpoint of expediency. Resolutions minimize misunderstandings, form a permanent and accurate record of the action agreed upon, and are invaluable as proof of proceedings at a meeting.

When action should be taken by resolution. No hard and fast rules specifying when action should be authorized in the form of a resolution can be drawn. Under the following circumstances resolutions are either required or appropriate:

1. If the matter is one that the statute, charter, or by-laws require to be covered by resolution.
2. If a certificate showing that the authority granted by stockholders or directors to perform a certain act is required to be filed, or likely to be required at some future time.
3. If the matter regulates the management of the corporation and is meant as a permanent rule until changed.
4. If the matter is one of importance.
5. If the matter is one that is likely to be referred to from time to time.
6. If the matter consists of amendments to the charter or by-laws.

Motions and resolutions. Most matters of business that come before a meeting are introduced by a motion recommending that the body assembled express an opinion, take certain action, or order something to be done. A motion, in other words, is a proposal, and the expression "I move" is equivalent to "I propose." A resolution is adopted by a motion, made and seconded, that the resolution be adopted. Every motion need not be followed by a resolution. For example, someone may move that the meeting be adjourned, that a particular discussion be postponed, or that the report of a committee be accepted. Action frequently takes place with neither motion nor resolution. For example, the report of the inspectors of election may be unanimously approved and the secretary directed to file a duplicate in the office of the county court in the state and to attach another to the minutes of the meeting.

When action should be embodied in a by-law rather than made a resolution. In some instances either a resolution or a by-law will accomplish the object desired, and it is a matter of discretion with the directors as to which shall be used. It should be remembered that the by-laws are permanent and continuing rules adopted to govern the corporation, its officers, directors, and stockholders, and that by-laws are less easily changed than is a resolution. It is advisable to embody action in a by-law, rather than in a simple resolution, in the following circumstances:

1. If the subject is to become a fixed policy of the corporation.
2. If notice of the action is to be conveyed to all of the directors and stockholders.

Drafting resolutions. The drafting of resolutions is generally done by the secretary. Frequently resolutions are drafted in advance of a meeting in order to clarify the subject matter and to facilitate discussions. The secretary may submit the draft of the resolution to the officer or department which originated the proposition to make sure that the resolution expresses the wishes of those sponsoring the matter.

The necessity for simple, unambiguous language in recording the minutes of meetings and in drafting resolutions cannot be too strongly emphasized. The courts have repeatedly held that a resolution of the directors or stockholders may constitute a contract. In writing up the minutes, the secretary should use words in their ordinary and general sense. When taking action pursuant to a statute, it is a good plan, in framing the necessary resolution, to follow as nearly as possible the wording of the statute.

Resolutions involving routine matters are usually drafted by the secretary without the aid of counsel. Resolutions relating to matters that involve legal technicalities are generally drafted by counsel. However, the secretary sometimes prepares the initial draft of a resolution requiring legal knowledge, and then refers it to the legal department, with appropriate oral or written explanations. In some organizations the resolutions are submitted to the president for his approval after they have been examined by counsel.

Certain action may require the passage of a resolution in a form satisfactory to some outside person or organization. For example, a resolution to amend the charter may have to be in a form prescribed by the secretary of state; in such case, of course, counsel for the corporation, or the secretary, need only obtain the form and complete it as required. Other resolutions may be prescribed by other outside institutions, as, for example, by the trustee, if the action relates to cancellation of a mortgage; by the transfer agent, if the resolution refers to the appointment of a certain bank or trust company to act as transfer agent; by the bank in which the company is authorizing its officers to deposit funds of the corporation.

Where new topics are brought up unexpectedly at a corporate meeting for discussion, and the secretary has had no opportunity before the meeting to draft a resolution, he may immediately write out the resolution in full and have it approved by the chairman, or he may follow the practice of writing out the resolution after the meeting. The resolution, under the second plan, is accurately worded in the typewritten minutes but is not read until the succeeding meeting. This practice is more suitable for directors' than for stockholders' meetings. At stockholders' meetings it is advisable that adequate time be taken to frame an exact resolution to be voted upon at the meeting.

Recording discussions in the minutes. Generally the argument on particular questions and the discussion that take place at a meeting are not made part of the record, unless some member present specifically requests that his views be made a matter of record. Frequently it is advisable to include an explanatory statement of the resolution or motion in order to clarify the proposal. Where this is necessary, the statement may well become a part of the resolution by being included in the preamble, under the "whereas" clause. The secretary should not hesitate to record in his minutes full details of the transaction; too many secretaries err on the side of brevity.

How to record motions, resolutions, and votes taken. The names of proposers and seconders of motions are generally omitted, although in some cases it may be advisable to show by whom the proposal was introduced. In most cases it is not necessary that the names of those voting for or against a proposition be recorded, unless the statute, charter, or by-laws require this information to be shown. In the case of stockholders' meetings, it is generally sufficient to show the number of shares voting for and against a proposition. Furthermore, by recording the vote in this way, the minutes show that a quorum was present when the business was authorized. Where a special request is made for the recording of dissenting votes by a minority, the entries should be so made by the secretary. It is advisable to indicate in the minutes that a director personally interested in a particular transaction did not vote, or that he left the room.

If no vote is taken on a certain question, and the chairman obtains the consensus of the directors in an informal manner, it is sufficient to note in the minutes that "it was the consensus that," or that "each director present expressed his approval of," or that "doubt was expressed as to," followed by a statement of the facts. This puts on record some evidence of the points covered and the general reaction.

All important written proposals, contracts, or other papers brought before the meeting may be ordered "spread upon the minutes"—that is, written out in full in the minute book.

In certain actions dissenting directors should be particularly careful to have their opposition noted. For example, where the statute places a personal liability upon directors who consent to the issuance of stock for property in excess of the actual value of the property, the minutes should show the names of the directors concurring in the judgment of the value of the property. In connection with the declaration of dividends, recording of dissent may be necessary to save the directors from personal liability for dividends illegally declared.

Arrangement of minutes. The secretary is not required to write the minutes out in his own handwriting. While the minutes can be written in any form, the most usual arrangement is the following:

1. Heading designating whether it is a stockholders', directors', or committee meeting.
2. Time and place of the meeting.
3. Presiding officer and secretary.
4. Proof that notice was given or waived.
5. Statement of amount of stock represented in person or by proxy, with a notation that a quorum was present.
6. Approval of minutes of previous meeting.
7. Report of all business transacted, usually arranged in accordance with the established order of business.
8. Adjournment.

Rules for typewriting minutes of meeting. The following is a suggested set of rules relating to the form to be followed by those who typewrite the minutes in the minute book:

1. The heading designating the meeting should be capitalized and centered.
2. Paragraphs should be indented ten spaces.
3. Names of attending directors and absentees, or similar lists, should be indented fifteen spaces.
4. The text of the minutes should be double-spaced.
5. Double space should be left between paragraphs, and triple space between items in the order of business.
6. Resolutions should be indented fifteen spaces and single-spaced.
7. The words "Board of Directors" and the word "Corporation," when reference is being made to the corporation whose minutes are being written, should be capitalized.
8. Captions in margins should be in capitals or in red type.
9. A margin of an inch and a half or two inches should be left on the left-hand or right-hand side of the page, depending upon whether it is a left-hand or right-hand page, for captions and indexing.
10. The minutes should be summarized in marginal headings.
11. The words "Whereas" and "Resolved" should be capitalized and followed by a comma, and the word "That" after resolved should be capitalized.

12. Sums of money, when mentioned in a resolution, should be written first in words and then in figures in parentheses, as follows: Ten Thousand ($10,000) Dollars.

13. Both sides of the paper should be used.

Examples of minutes. The reproduction of minutes of a regular directors' meeting shown in Figures 90a and 90b indicates the large-size minute page (13 x 8½ inches) adopted by many corpora-

162

REGULAR DIRECTORS MEETING

THE .... CORPORATION
DIRECTORS' MEETING
APRIL 30, 19 ..
---oOo---

APRIL 30, 19 ..

A regular meeting of the Board of Directors of The .... Corporation was held at the office of the Corporation in .... Chicago, Illinois, on Thursday, April 30th, at ten thirty o'clock in the forenoon.

PRESENT

There were present:

F.S. .... Chairman presiding.
C.L. ....
A.R. ....
M.R. ....
P.S. ....
J.M. ....
A.B. ....
M.F. ....

comprising a quorum of the board; also

A.G. .... Secretary.

ABSENT

Absent:

W.I. ....
H.F. ....
A.C. ....
P.H. ....
I.H. ....
H.H. ....
F.B. ....

MINUTES APPROVED

The minutes of the annual directors' meeting held on April 7,19 ..., were read and approved.

On motion duly made, seconded, and carried, the minutes of the Finance Committee meetings of February 12, March 10 and 30, April 16 and 24, 19 ..., were approved.

PRESIDENT'S REPORT

The president reported that results this year slightly exceeded those of last year, both in the number of ...... sold and in the amount of the net profits, which were $1.84 per share on the common stock. Plant operations, which were under curtailment in January and February, were increased to capacity in March. ...... in dealers' stocks and in transit to them, including demonstrators, on April 1st were 46% less than on the same date in 19 .., and 25% less than in 19 ...

The regular dividends on the preferred and common stocks were paid March 1st, which action in the case of the latter stock completed the tenth consecutive year of dividends.

The balance sheet shows substantial increases in cash and decreases in inventories, plant investments, and liabilities.

Eleven plants are now operating at capacity, and production for the second quarter will exceed 4,000 ..... Demand greatly exceeds output, and ... are therefore being distributed among dealers on a pro rata basis. April collections will be about $ .... Generally speaking, conditions with us were never better.

Figure 90a. Minutes of Directors' Meeting, Page 1.

tions. Oblong holes are punched in the sheets so that they may be inserted in the locking binder. The left-hand margin is 1½ inches wide; thus ample room is provided for the use of convenient index captions. Each sheet must be numbered in the upper outside corner.

A set of minutes that may be used as a model for an annual stockholders' meeting is given on page 1253. A set of minutes for an annual meeting of directors is given on page 1255 *et seq*.

183

The treasurer submitted a general profit and loss statement for the first three months of the year 19 .., showing a net profit for that period, after deduction of all interest charges and reserves, of $ .... He also submitted a general balance sheet as of March 31, 19 .., showing a surplus on that date (exclusive of Special Surplus Account) available for dividends of $ ...... These reports were ordered placed on file.

On motion duly made and seconded, the following resolution was unanimously adopted:

WHEREAS, it appears from the report of the treasurer that the net profits of this Corporation for the three months' period ending March 31, 19 .., after deduction of interest charges and reserves, amounted to the sum of .... ($ ....) Dollars, and — 611

WHEREAS, it appears from the report of the treasurer that the surplus (exclusive of Special Surplus Account) available for dividends on March 31, 19 .., was .... ($ ....) Dollars, and the treasurer has reported that the same has not been diminished since that date, it is therefore

PREFERRED STOCK DIVIDEND

<u>RESOLVED</u>, That for the purpose of paying the regular June quarterly dividend of one and three-quarters (1¾%) per cent on ...... Million Two Hundred Thirty-five Thousand ($ ....) Dollars preferred stock of the .... Corporation, there is hereby set apart, out of the surplus, net profits arising from the business of the sum of .... ($ ....) Dollars, and from such sum so set apart, the treasurer is hereby authorized and directed to pay, or cause to be paid, the said regular June quarterly dividend of one and three-quarters (1¾%) per cent on June 1st, 19 .. to the preferred stockholders of record at the close of business on May 9th, 19 ...

The treasurer further reported that the present condition of the Special Surplus Account complied in all respects with the conditions required by the Certificate of Incorporation to exist for the payment of dividends on the common stock, and that the surplus available for dividends on the common stock on March 31st, 19 .., after deduction of the sum of $ .... heretofore at this meeting set apart for the payment of the June quarterly dividend on the preferred stock, is $ .... — 612

On motion duly made and seconded, it was unanimously

COMMON STOCK DIVIDEND — 613

<u>RESOLVED</u>, That for the purpose of paying a quarterly dividend of One ($1.00) Dollar per share on .... (.........) shares of the common stock of The .... Corporation now outstanding, there is hereby set apart, out of the surplus net profits arising from the business of the Corporation, the sum of .... ($ ....) Dollars, and from such sum so set apart the treasurer is authorized and directed to pay, or cause to be paid, the said quarterly dividend of One ($1.00) Dollar per share on June 1st, 19 .. to the common stockholders of record at the close of business on May 9th, 19 ...

REPORT OF V.P.IN CHARGE OF MFG

The vice-president in charge of manufacturing read a written report on manufacturing conditions in the plants, which was ordered received and placed on file.

REPORT ON SALES

In the absence of the vice-president in charge of sales, the president made a report in which he stated that dealers' stocks are very low, and that the demand for ..... is greater than it has ever been. Mechanically the ..... are excellent, and practically no complaints are received in this regard. Report ordered received and placed on file.

On motion duly made and seconded, the meeting adjourned.

....
Secretary   President

Figure 90b. Minutes of Directors' Meeting, Page 2.

MINUTES OF ANNUAL MEETING OF STOCKHOLDERS HELD PURSUANT TO WRITTEN NOTICE OF MEETING

[*Note—The headings in italics ordinarily appear in the minute book as marginal captions.*]

[*Time and place of meeting*] The regular annual meeting of the stockholders of the .... Corporation, a [*give state of incorporation*] corporation, was held at the office of the Corporation, ... Street, in the City of ...., State of ...., on the . . day of ...., 19. ., at ...... o'clock . . M., pursuant to a call made by the President, and written notice given by the Secretary.

[*Presiding officer; Secretary*] Mr. ...., President of the Corporation, presided at the meeting, and Mr. ...., Secretary of the Corporation, was secretary of the meeting, as provided by the By-laws.

The Secretary presented and read the following notice of the meeting:

[*Insert notice of meeting*]

[*Proof of notice*] The Secretary presented an affidavit, duly signed and sworn to by himself, showing that notice of the meeting had been mailed to each stockholder, addressed to such stockholder at the address given by him to the Corporation, postage prepaid, as required by the By-laws of the Corporation. The affidavit was approved and ordered attached to these minutes.

[*List of stockholders; quorum*] A certified alphabetical list of the stockholders of the Corporation was presented, and upon a call of the list and an inspection of proxies, it was found that there were present in person stockholders of the Corporation holding .... shares of stock and represented by proxy, stockholders of the Corporation holding .... shares of stock, being more than a majority of the total number of shares outstanding and entitled to vote.

The proxies were filed with the Secretary.

Thereupon the President announced that legal notice of the meeting had been given, that a quorum was present, and that the meeting was now regularly and lawfully convened and ready to transact business.

[*Inspectors of election*] Upon motion duly made and seconded, ... and .... were unanimously elected Inspectors of Election to count the votes presented to the meeting in person or by proxy. The Inspectors of Election thereupon submitted their oaths as such Inspectors, duly subscribed by them, and the Secretary was directed to attach the same to these minutes.

[*Approval of minutes*] The Secretary then presented the minute of the annual meeting of stockholders held on . . . ., 19. . which were read and approved.

[*Approval of acts of directors and annual report*] Thereupon the President presented to the meeting the following papers and documents all of which were laid upon the table and were publicly declared by the President to be open for inspection by any stockholder:

1. The minutes of the Board of Directors, covering all purchases, contracts, contributions, compensations, acts, proceedings, elections, and appointments by the Board of Directors since the annual meeting held on . . . ., 19. . .

2. The . . . . (insert number)annual report, a copy of which has been mailed to every stockholder of record.

Upon motion duly made and seconded, it was unanimously

Resolved, That all purchases, contracts, contributions, compensations, acts, proceedings, elections, and appointments by the Board of Directors since the Annual Meeting of Stockholders of the Corporation on . . . . , . ., 19. ., and all matters referred to in the Annual Report to Stockholders for the fiscal year ending . . . ., 19. ., be and the same hereby are approved and ratified.

The meeting then proceeded to the election of five directors as successors to the directors whose terms expire with this annual meeting, to hold office for the term of . . . . . . year(s), and until their successors shall be elected and shall qualify.

[*Nomination of directors*] The following were nominated and seconded to be directors:

A	F . . . .
B	G . . . .
C	H . . . .
D	I . . . .
E	J . . . .

There were no other nominations.

Upon motion duly made, seconded, and unanimously carried, the nominations were closed.

Upon motion duly made and seconded, it was unanimously

[*Voting*] Resolved, That the polls remain open for one hour, commencing at . . . . o'clock . . M., and closing at . . . . o'clock . . M.

The President stated that the polls were now open, and would remain open as stated, and that the Inspectors of Election were prepared to receive the votes of the stockholders.

At .... o'clock, the polls having been kept open for one hour, and no others desiring to vote, it was, on motion duly made and seconded, unanimously

RESOLVED, That the polls be closed.

The Inspectors of Election thereupon inspected the proxies and counted the ballots, and submitted their report in writing.

[*Report of Inspectors of Election*] Upon motion duly made and seconded, the report of the Inspectors of Election was unanimously approved, and the Secretary was directed to file the original report and to attach a copy to the minutes of this meeting.

The report of the Inspectors of Election is as follows:

[*Insert report of Inspectors of Election*]

[*Declaration of election*] The Chairman thereupon declared that the five persons receiving the highest number of votes, namely [*insert names*], had been duly elected directors of the Corporation, to serve for the term of .... year(s), and until their successors shall be elected and shall qualify.

[*Adjournment*] No other business having come before the meeting, it was, on motion duly made and seconded, adjourned.

....	....
President	*Secretary*

MINUTES OF ANNUAL MEETING OF DIRECTORS

[*Note—The headings in italics ordinarily appear in the minute book as marginal captions.*]

[*Time and place of meeting*] The .... annual meeting of the Board of Directors of the .... Corporation was held at the office of the Corporation, ..., in the City of ...., State of ...., on the .. day of ...., 19.., at .... o'clock in the ......noon, immediately following the adjournment of the annual meeting of the stockholders.

[*Attendance*] The following directors, being all the directors of the said Corporation, were present:

....
....
....
....
....

[*Chairman; Secretary*] Mr. ...., President of the Corporation, presided, and Mr. .... acted as secretary of the meeting.

[*Quorum*] The Chairman announced that a quorum of the directors was present, and that the meeting, having been duly convened, was ready to proceed with its business.

[*Notice of meeting*] The Secretary presented the notice of the meeting pursuant to which the meeting was held. The same was ordered to be entered in the minutes and is as follows:

[*Insert notice of meeting*]

[*Presentation of minutes of annual stockholders' meeting*] The Chairman laid before the meeting the minutes of the annual meeting of the stockholders of the Corporation, held on the .. day of ...., 19.., showing the election of the following persons as directors of the Corporation, to hold office for the term of ...... year(s), and until their successors shall be elected and shall qualify.

....

....

....

....

....

[*Election of officers*] On motion duly made, seconded, and unanimously carried, the Board of Directors thereupon proceeded to elect the following officers of the Corporation—to wit: President, Vice President, Secretary, and Treasurer.

Mr. .... was nominated for the office of President of the Corporation. No other nominations being made, upon motion duly made, seconded, and unanimously carried, Mr. .... was elected President of the Corporation, and was declared duly elected to the said office.

Mr. .... was nominated for the office of Vice President of the Corporation. No other nominations being made, upon motion duly made, seconded, and unanimously carried, Mr. .... was elected Vice President of the Corporation, and was declared duly elected to the said office.

Mr. .... was nominated for the office of Secretary of the Corporation. No other nominations being made, upon motion duly made, seconded, and unanimously carried, Mr. .... was elected Secretary of the Corporation, and was declared duly elected to the said office.

Mr. .... was nominated for the office of Treasurer of the Corporation. No other nominations being made, upon motion duly made, seconded, and unanimously carried, Mr. .... was elected Treasurer of the Corporation, and was declared duly elected to the said office.

Each of the officers so elected was present and thereupon accepted the office to which he was elected.

Upon motion duly made, seconded, and unanimously carried, the Board of Directors proceeded to fix the salaries to be paid to the President, Vice President, Secretary, and Treasurer for the year 19. . .

[*Compensation of officers*] The Chairman announced that the salary of each officer would be voted upon separately, and that the officer whose salary was under consideration would not participate in the vote.

Mr. . . . ., President, thereupon left the room.

On motion duly made, seconded, and affirmatively voted upon by all the directors then present, it was

[*Salary of President*] RESOLVED, That the salary of Mr. . . . ., President of the Corporation, be fixed at $. . . . . for the year beginning . . . ., 19. ., and ending . . . ., 19. ., payable in semimonthly installments on the fifteenth day and the last day of each calendar month.

The vote having been taken, Mr. . . . . was recalled to the meeting.

The Vice President then left the room.

(*Repeat the minutes given above for each officer*)

[*Adjournment*] There being no further business to come before the meeting, the same was, upon motion, adjourned.

. . . .
President

. . . .
Secretary

How to correct errors in minutes. One of the purposes of reading the minutes of a previous meeting is to offer an opportunity to make corrections of any misstatements or errors that may have crept into the record. The fact that corrections are made after the minutes are prepared is comparatively unimportant, from a legal standpoint, if the entry faithfully shows what was done.

The manner of correcting errors depends upon the importance of the matter to be changed. The chairman may informally direct correction of simple errors such as mistakes in the spelling of names. If a dispute arises as to the correctness of a statement, motion, or resolution reported in the minutes, it may be necessary to put the matter to a vote to determine how the minutes shall read. If the error can be corrected immediately, the correction may be made at the meeting, and the minutes, as changed, offered for approval. If, however, the correction involves a revision of the minutes, the minutes of the current meeting will report the corrections of the minutes of the previous meeting.

Manner of revising minutes. Either of the following methods may be used for revising minutes:

1. Strike out the erroneous matter by drawing a red line through each line of the incorrect material and write in between the red lines the correct minutes. Make a reference in the margin of the minutes to the minutes of the following meeting, showing when the correction was ordered.
2. Strike out the erroneous material in red, and put a note in the margin showing where the revised minutes appear; insert the correct minutes at the end of the original minutes.

Where loose-leaf books are used, it is inadvisable to throw away the pages that were incorrectly written. The better practice is to retain the original pages, to indicate that the minutes are obsolete by reference to the minutes of the meeting at which the errors were discussed, and to insert the corrected minutes in a subsequent page.

If the effect of a resolution adopted at a meeting is to create a contract between the corporation and some other party, the resolution cannot be changed by a memorandum entered on the records after the adjournment of the meeting, without the knowledge or consent of the parties to the agreement. Clerical errors in the writing of minutes are immaterial where the proof is clear that the entry is erroneous. Thus, where it is evident that the directors met on the same day as the stockholders, immediately after the stockholders' meeting adjourned, and that both meetings were held on a certain day, a different date at the head of the minutes of the directors' meeting is simply a clerical error and is immaterial. The fact that corrections are made after the minutes are prepared is comparatively unimportant, from a legal standpoint, if the entry faithfully shows what was done.

Indexing of minutes. Large corporations usually have their minutes carefully indexed so that any business which has been passed upon at a formal meeting, however remote in time, may be referred to and reviewed easily and quickly. Card indexes, loose-leaf binder indexes, or bound books may be used for the purpose.

Rexall, A. G.

Secretary: 411, 463, 536, 667, 735, 767, 805, 843, 884, 922.

Ex Comm.: 412.

Asst. Treas.: 679, 736, 806, 844, 885, 922.

Figure 91. Index Card Used for Indexing Minutes.

Secretary.

Elections: 42, 58, 228, 296, 411, 463, 536, 576, 615, 667,
735, 767, 805, 843, 884, 922.

Resignations: 58.

Figure 92. Index Card Showing Cross-Index of Certain Items in Figure 91.

The making of the index is facilitated by the use of captions in the minutes, as illustrated in Figure 90a-b. The index card contains the subject matter taken from the captions and a reference to the page on which the caption appears. The samples of index cards shown in Figures 91 and 92 illustrate how subjects of resolutions are cross-indexed. If a more detailed index is desired, the captions appearing on the page may bear a number, and the reference on the card may be made to the number rather than to the page. The numbers, of course, should run consecutively through the minute book.

Arrangement of minute books. As a rule, the minutes of the stockholders' meetings and those of the directors' meetings are kept in separate books. Small companies, however, sometimes use one book for both stockholders' and directors' meetings, dividing the book into two distinct parts. Naturally, there are many more pages devoted to directors' meetings than to stockholders' meetings, since the latter usually occur only once a year. An illustration of a standardized type of minute book is shown in Figure 93.

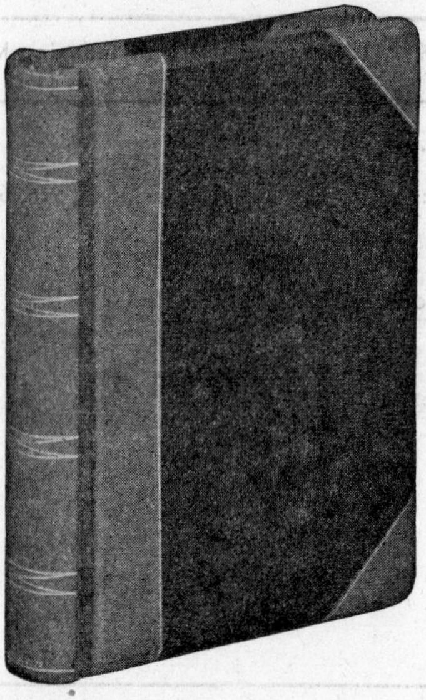

Figure 93. Typical Minute Book.

The minute book of stockholders' meetings (or the single minute book if only one is used) may be arranged as follows: Bind or paste a certified copy of the corporation's charter in the first pages of the book, or merely copy the charter into the book. Leave several blank pages to provide for insertion of amendments. Then, beginning at the top of a right-hand page, copy the by-laws of the corporation, leaving a few blank pages for new by-laws or amendments. After the by-laws, insert the minutes of the first meeting of the stockholders. Continue the minutes of stockholders' meetings after the minutes of the first meeting of stockholders, beginning each set of minutes at the top of a new page.

Resolutions book. Some companies follow the practice of keeping a copy of all resolutions in a separate book, properly indexed. This system avoids the inconvenience of having to leaf through pages of minutes of unrelated matter when reference is made to a particular action authorized by resolution. Furthermore, by keeping the resolutions in a separate place, the minute book is preserved, and perusal of confidential matters contained in the minute book by someone interested only in a particular resolution is prevented.

10. DOING BUSINESS IN MORE THAN ONE STATE

May a corporation do business in any state? A corporation is an artificial entity created by the state in which it is organized, and as such has no inherent right to compel any other state to recognize its existence. In a state other than that in which it was organized, it is known as a foreign corporation. As a matter of comity, the states permit corporations to do business within their borders provided the corporations comply with special terms and conditions imposed. These conditions generall, include:

1. Registration of the presence of the foreign corporation in the state by the filing of certain documents with State officials.
2. Designation of a person in the state to act as agent for the service of process upon the foreign corporation.
3. Payment of certain fees and taxes.

The right of states to regulate the activities of foreign corporations within their borders is subject to various limitations contained in the Federal Constitution. One of these limitations, and by far the most important, is that a state cannot unwarrantably interfere with business carried on by a foreign corporation which is interstate commerce as distinguished from intrastate business. Interstate commerce means shipment from state to state; intrastate business means business done within the state.

What constitutes "doing business" in another state. It is not always easy to determine whether a corporation is engaged in interstate commerce, and is thus free from State regulation, or whether it is doing business within a state. What constitutes "doing business" within a state is determined by the wording of the various state statutes, the interpretation of these statutes by the courts, and the facts and circumstances surrounding each particular case. The following rules are generally accepted in deciding whether or not a foreign corporation is doing business within a state:

1. *Isolated transactions.* Occasional and isolated transactions that do not indicate an intention on the part of the corporation regularly to conduct a substantial part of its business in a state do not constitute doing business in that state. Doing business means a continued activity in carrying out the purposes for which the corporation was organized. For example, a corporation is organized in New York, where it carries on all of its business. A friend of the corporation's president, who lives in Michigan, orders a bill of goods while on a visit to New York. The goods are delivered to the friend in Michigan. The corporation is not doing business in Michigan and need not qualify as a foreign corporation in Michigan. Even where several transactions are effected in the state, the corporation is not necessarily doing business in the state if the transactions are incidental and not in the exercise of the purposes for which the corporation was organized.

2. *Solicitation of business.* A foreign corporation is generally held to be engaged in interstate commerce and not to be doing business in the state when it merely employs salesmen to solicit orders in the state without closing the sale in the state or making shipments from the state. Nor is a corporation engaged in doing business in the state if it merely receives or solicits orders by mail by means of circulars, catalogues, and so forth, but accepts the orders and fills them outside the state. Where, however, the foreign corporation's agent solicits orders from local retailers and turns the orders over to local wholesalers who fill them and receive payment from the retailers, the corporation is doing business in the state. Some courts

hold that while a foreign corporation that merely solicits business in the state may not be required to qualify as a foreign corporation, it may, however, be subject to service of process.

3. *Appointment of agents.* The appointment of an agent in a state does not, in itself, constitute doing business in that state. Whether or not a foreign corporation which has an agent in another state is doing business in that state depends upon the nature of the agent's acts. For example, if all the agent does is solicit orders for goods that are to be shipped into the state, the corporation is not required to qualify as a foreign corporation in the state or to pay taxes on the business solicited. If, however, the agent has the power to bind the corporation by contract, or if he sells goods in the state and makes deliveries from stock on hand, the corporation is deemed to be doing business in the state.

4. *Purchases of goods.* Where a foreign corporation purchases goods in the state through its agents or through the mails, which goods are to be sent to the corporation outside the state in the same condition in which the goods were purchased, the corporation is not doing business in the state. This is the general rule applicable where the question involved is whether or not the corporation is required to qualify as a foreign corporation in the state. Some courts have held, however, that where the question involved is whether or not service of process may be effected upon the foreign corporation, the corporation is doing business in the state if it makes its purchases with regularity and employs agents for the purchase of goods in the state as part of its regular business.

5. *Sales of goods.* A foreign corporation that sells to a resident of another state goods which at the time of sale are outside the state in which the purchaser lives, and which are to be shipped to the purchaser, is not doing business in the state in which the purchaser resides. Even if the goods sold are already in the state in which the purchaser resides, the corporation is not doing business in that state if the transaction is an isolated one.

6. *Ownership of property.* The mere passive ownership of either personal or real property by a foreign corporation in the state does not constitute doing business in that state, and the corporation is not required to qualify as a foreign corporation.

7. *Maintenance of an office.* A foreign corporation is not deemed to be doing business in a state merely because it maintains an office

in the state. The maintenance of any office, however, may be a strong factor in determining the question, and the conclusion drawn depends upon the purpose for which the office is used. For example, where the foreign corporation directs its internal affairs from the office in the state, holds directors' and stockholders' meetings there, keeps its books and records there, it is generally deemed to be doing business in the state. On the other hand, where the corporation maintains an office in the state for the convenience of its salesmen, and the business conducted through the office is entirely in the nature of interstate commerce, the corporation is generally held not to be doing business in the state.

How a foreign corporation qualifies to do business in a state. Each state has its own requirements as to the method of qualification. In most states qualification is effected by the payment of an entrance fee and the filing of the following documents:

1. Application for permission to do business in the state.
2. Copy of the articles of incorporation and all amendments thereto, properly certified.
3. Copy of the by-laws of the corporation, and all amendments thereto, properly attested.
4. Certificate designating a place of business in the state and appointment of an agent for the service of process in the state.
5. Statement of financial condition of the corporation, its capitalization, and the amount of capital and assets to be employed in the state.

Some states also require the filing of a tax report, a certificate of the names and addresses of officers and directors, and an acceptance of the provisions of the state constitution.

In some states, permission to do business is granted for a limited period only and must be renewed upon expiration.

After qualification, is a foreign corporation required to pay any additional taxes or to file any additional reports? Some states require foreign corporations to pay annual taxes based upon the amount of capital employed in the state, and to file the following documents after qualification:

1. Annual tax or information reports.
2. Statement of change in place of business in the state or change

in resident agent appointed for service of process on the corporation in the state.

3. A copy of any amendment to the corporation's articles of incorporation.

Penalties that may be incurred by a foreign corporation which does business in a state without qualifying. The statutes of the various states generally impose one or more of the following penalties for failure of a foreign corporation doing business in a state to comply with the requirements imposed by the state as a condition of doing business:

1. A fine on the corporation.
2. A fine on officers, agents, or employees of the corporation.
3. Imprisonment of officers, agents, or employees of the corporation.
4. Liability of officers, directors, or stockholders for corporate debts or liabilities arising out of transactions within the state.
5. Voiding of contracts entered into by the corporation, or making such contracts unenforceable until compliance with statutory requirements for qualification.
6. Prohibition of the corporation's instituting, maintaining, or defending suits in any State court until compliance with the state's requirements for qualification.
7. Restriction against holding by the corporation of real property in the state, and voiding of conveyances to the corporation.

SECTION 12

Business Mathematics and Short Cuts

8. HOW TO COMPUTE MARKUP AND SELLING PRICE

9. HOW TO CALCULATE COMPOUND INTEREST

10. HOW TO COMPUTE ANNUITIES

11. DEPRECIATION METHODS

12. SHORT CUTS IN BUSINESS MATHEMATICS

Addition

Subtraction

Multiplication

Division

Fractions

13. EXPEDITING CALCULATIONS WITH PREPARED TABLES

14. VERIFICATION OF COMPUTATIONS BY CHECK NUMBERS

15. TABLES OF WEIGHTS, MEASURES, AND VALUES

16. MISCELLANEOUS HANDY TABLES

17. GLOSSARY OF ABBREVIATIONS

SECTION 12

Business Mathematics and Short Cuts

1. HOW TO CALCULATE SIMPLE INTEREST

What interest is. Interest is money paid for the use of money. In interest calculations three factors are involved: (1) principal; (2) time; (3) rate.

The principal is the sum of money upon which the interest is paid—the sum loaned, borrowed, or invested.

The time is the number of periods for which the interest is paid. One year is generally considered as the unit period of time.

The rate is the percentage per period of the principal that is paid as interest. The rate is usually expressed as a certain percentage per year.

There are two kinds of interest:

1. Simple interest.
2. Compound interest.

If the interest is calculated on the original principal only, it is called simple interest. If, however, at the end of the first period of time, the interest for that period is added to the principal and the interest for the second period calculated on this sum, and this process is continued for the given number of periods, the interest is said to be compounded, and the total interest thus realized is called compound interest.

Legal and contract rates of interest in the states of the United States. The rate of interest that may be charged is governed by state statute. The table (page 1272) shows the legal and contract rates in the various states of the United States. The legal rate is the rate of interest charged in the absence of express contract between the parties. The contract rate is the highest rate upon which parties may agree.

LEGAL AND CONTRACT RATES OF INTEREST
IN THE STATES OF THE UNITED STATES

State	*Legal Rate, Per Cent*	*Contract Rate, Per Cent*
Alabama	6	8
Arizona	6	8
Arkansas	6	10
California	7	10
Colorado	6	No limit
Connecticut	6	12
Delaware	6	6 *
District of Columbia	6	8
Florida	6	10
Georgia	7	8
Idaho	6	8
Illinois	5	7
Indiana	6	8
Iowa	5	7
Kansas	6	10
Kentucky	6	6
Louisiana	5	8
Maine	6	No limit
Maryland	6	6
Massachusetts	6	No limit
Michigan	5	7
Minnesota	6	8
Mississippi	6	8
Missouri	6	8
Montana	6	10
Nebraska	6	9
Nevada	7	12
New Hampshire	6	No limit
New Jersey	6	6
New Mexico	6	10; 12 without collateral
New York	6	6 *
North Carolina	6	6
North Dakota	4	7
Ohio	6	8
Oklahoma	6	10
Oregon	6	10
Pennsylvania	6	6
Rhode Island	6	30
South Carolina	6	7
South Dakota	6	8
Tennessee	6	6
Texas	6	10
Utah	6	10
Vermont	6	6
Virginia	6	6
Washington	6	12
West Virginia	6	6
Wisconsin	5	10
Wyoming	7	10

Note.—Rates are subject to change by state statute.
* No limit on certain secured loans repayable on demand.

How to calculate the due date of an obligation. The date of maturity of a loan or other obligation is determined by the wording of the obligation. For example, if, in a transaction on September 5, a debtor agrees to repay a loan in *fourth months,* the money is due on January 5. If, on the other hand, another obligation contracted on September 5 is by agreement to run 120 days, the repayment is due on January 3. In this case the exact number of days is counted in determining the due date because the time was stated in days.

How to calculate the time between dates. There are two methods of calculating the time between dates:

1. Ordinary method. 2. Exact method.

Ordinary method. In the ordinary method (sometimes called the "bond method") the year is considered as having 12 months of 30 days each, or 360 days. The time between dates is then calculated by subtraction, as illustrated in the following example.

EXAMPLE

Find the time between June 15, 1951, and August 3, 1952.

Solution

Years	*Months*	*Days*
1952	8	3
1951	6	15
1	1	18

The time between June 15, 1952, and August 3, 1952, is therefore 1 year, 1 month, 18 days, or 408 days ($360 + 30 + 18 = 408$).

The ordinary or bond method of calculating the time between dates is not commonly used except in interest computations involving long periods of time (usually a period greater than 1 year), and in the calculation of interest on bonds (other than United States Government and some municipal bonds). Where the period of time is short, businessmen and bankers generally use the exact method.

Exact method. In the exact method of calculating the time between dates, the actual number of days in each month is counted. The first day (the day on which the obligation is incurred) is excluded, and the last day (the day on which the obligation terminates) is included.

EXAMPLE

A loan made April 17 is repaid June 26. For how many days should the interest be calculated?

Solution

Exclude the first day, April 17; include the last day, June 26. Then:

Number of days remaining in April	13
Number of days in May	31
Number of days in June to be counted	26
Total number of days	70

The interest should therefore be calculated for 70 days.

Where the exact number of days between dates is counted, it is the general practice of businessmen and bankers to exclude the first day and include the last day, as in the above example. However, in certain sections of the United States (and also in France, Holland, and some other foreign countries), it is customary to include both the first and the last days. If this procedure were followed in the above example, interest would be due for 71 days instead of for 70.

Short method of finding the exact number of days btween dates. The table below may be used as a short cut in finding the exact number of days between dates. The exact number of days between the corresponding dates of any two months is indicated on the line of the month of the beginning date, under the month of the later date. Thus, from any day in January to the same day in August, there are 212 days. In the table this figure is found opposite January, in the column marked *Aug.*

EXACT NUMBER OF DAYS BETWEEN DATES

From Any Day Of	To the Same Day of the Next											
	Jan.	*Feb.*	*Mar.*	*Apr.*	*May*	*June*	*July*	*Aug.*	*Sept.*	*Oct.*	*Nov.*	*Dec.*
January . . .	365	31	59	90	120	151	181	212	243	273	304	334
February . .	334	365	28	59	89	120	150	181	212	242	273	303
March . . .	306	337	365	31	61	92	122	153	184	214	245	275
April	275	306	334	365	30	61	91	122	153	183	214	244
May	245	276	304	335	365	31	61	92	123	153	184	214
June	214	245	273	304	334	365	30	61	92	122	153	183
July	184	215	243	274	304	335	365	31	62	92	123	153
August . . .	153	184	212	243	273	304	334	365	31	61	92	122
September .	122	153	181	212	242	273	303	334	365	30	61	91
October . .	92	123	151	182	212	243	273	304	335	365	31	61
November .	61	92	120	151	181	212	242	273	304	334	365	30
December .	31	62	90	121	151	182	212	243	274	304	335	365

The following examples show how the table is used to measure the exact number of days between any two different dates.

EXAMPLE 1

A loan made June 10 is repaid August 17. For how many days should the interest be calculated?

Solution

From the table, June 10 to August 10	61 days
Add, August 10 to August 17	7 days
Number of days	68 days

EXAMPLE 2

A loan made October 16 is repaid March 13. For how many days should the interest be calculated?

Solution

From the table, October 16 to March 16	151 days
Deduct, March 13 to March 16	3 days
Number of days	148 days

Whenever February 29 of a leap year is included in the period for which the exact number of days is being calculated from the table, add 1 to the result obtained.

Ordinary and exact simple interest. Ordinary interest is simple interest computed on the basis of 360 days to the year. Exact or accurate interest is simple interest computed on the basis of 365 days to the year.

Although ordinary interest is greater than exact interest, owing to the discrepancy of 5 days, the difference is not material except where a large principal and an extended period of time are involved. For example, ordinary simple interest on $500.00 for 90 days at 6% is only 10 cents more than exact simple interest. Since calculations are much easier on the basis of 360 days to the year than of 365, business houses and commercial banks generally compute simple interest on the basis of 360 days to the year, even where the exact number of days for which interest is due is counted.

EXAMPLE 1

Find the simple interest on $2,000.00 from November 16, 1952, to April 8, 1953, at 6%.

Solution

In this case the interest period is short. The usual procedure would therefore be:

(1) Find the exact number of days between the dates.

(2) Compute the interest for this exact number of days on the basis of 360 days to the year.

From the table, the exact number of days between November 16, 1952, and April 8, 1953, is found to be 143. Then:

$$\text{Interest} = \frac{2000}{1} \times \frac{143}{360} \times \frac{6}{100}$$
$$= \$47.67$$

EXAMPLE 2

Find the simple interest on $2,000.00 from December 16, 1951, to February 10, 1953, at 6%.

Solution

In this case the interest period is long. The usual procedure would therefore be:

(1) Find the number of days between the dates by assuming 30 days in each month.

(2) Using this number of days, compute the interest on the basis of 360 days to the year.

Years	*Months*	*Days*
1953	2	10
1951	12	16
1	1	24

At 30 days to each month, 1 year, 1 month, 24 days is 414 days. Then:

$$\text{Interest} = \frac{2000}{1} \times \frac{414}{360} \times \frac{6}{100}$$
$$= \$138.00$$

How to use short methods of calculating ordinary interest at 6%: *Sixty-day method.* At 6% per year:

Interest on $1.00 for 360 days is $.06
" " " 60 " .01 (1/6 of $.06)
" " " 6 " .001 (1/10 of $.01)

It is evident that interest on $1.00 for 6 days at 6% may be computed by moving the decimal point in the principal three places to the left. If this is true of $1.00, it is true of any principal, and a general rule may be stated as follows: Given any principal, to find the interest at 6%:

6 days,	point off	three places to the left
60 "	"	two " "
600 "	"	one place "
6,000 "	the interest is the same as the principal	

Thus:

Interest on $1,280.00	for	6 days	at 6% is $	1.28
" "	"	60 "	"	12.80
" "	"	600 "	"	128.00
" "	"	6,000 "	"	1,280.00

In calculating the interest at 6% on any principal for any number of days, the time, stated in days, may be separated into parts that are multiples or fractions of 6, 60, 600, or 6,000, and the computations are greatly simplified.

EXAMPLE 1

Find the ordinary interest on $760.00 for 15 days at 6%.

Solution

Interest for 60 days = $7.60
" " 15 " = $7.60 ÷ 4
= $1.90

Explanation. Pointing off two places in the principal gives the interest for 60 days. Fifteen days is ¼ of 60 days. Hence divide the interest for 60 days by 4.

EXAMPLE 2

Find the ordinary interest on $842.60 for 124 days at 6%.

Solution

Interest for	60 days =	$8.4260
" "	60 " =	8.4260
" "	4 " =	.5617
" "	124 " =	$17.4137, or $17.41

Explanation. Sixty days plus 60 days plus 4 days equals 124 days. The interest for the 4 days is found by pointing off three places in the principal (which gives the interest for 6 days) and then multiplying this figure by ⅔, since 4 days is ⅔ of 6 days.

EXAMPLE 3

Find the ordinary interest on $754.90 for 137 days at 6%.

Solution

Interest for	60 days	=	$ 7.5490
" "	60 "	=	7.5490
" "	12 "	=	1.5098
" "	5 "	=	.6290
" "	137 "	=	$17.2368, or $17.24

Explanation. Pointing off two decimal places gives the interest for 60 days. Double this to find the interest for 120 days. Twelve days is ⅕ of 60 days; therefore, the interest for 12 days is ⅕ of 60-days' interest, or $1.5098. Five days is 1/12 of 60 days, and the interest is 1/12 of $7.5490, or $0.629. The sum, $17.24, is the interest for 137 days.

One-day or product method. The one-day or product method is convenient where the number of days for which ordinary interest is being calculated cannot be readily divided into fractions or multiples of 6, 60, 600, or 6,000. To find the ordinary interest on any principal at 6% by this method:

1. Point off three decimal places in the principal; this gives the interest for 6 days.
2. Multiply the figure found in (1) by the number of days for which the interest is being calculated; this gives the interest for 6 times the number of days required.
3. Divide the result by 6.

EXAMPLE

Find the ordinary interest on $137.65 for 77 days at 6%.

Solution

```
 $.13765, interest for 6 days
      77
 -------
  .96355
  9.6355
$10.59905, interest for 6 × 77 days
```

$10.59905 ÷ 6 = $1.7665, or $1.77, interest for 77 days

Interchange of principal and number of days. Where the principal is a factor or multiple of 6, the calculation of ordinary interest at 6% can be shortened by interchanging the principal and the number of days. Thus, finding 6% interest on $120.00 for 187 days is the same as finding 6% interest on $187.00 for 120 days. Six per cent interest on $187.00 for 60 days is $1.87, obtained by moving the decimal point two places to the left. Six per cent interest on $187.00 for 120 days is twice $1.87, or $3.74. The interest on $120.00 for 187 days at 6% is, therefore, $3.74.

How to use a short method of calculating ordinary interest at a rate other than 6%. To find the ordinary interest at a rate other than 6%:

1. First find the interest at 6% by one of the methods described in the preceding pages.
2. Adjust the result by adding to or subtracting from the interest computed at 6%, the fractional part thereof that the specified rate is greater or less than 6% rate.

For 3%,	decrease the interest by	½	of the amount computed at 6%
4%,	" " "	⅓	" " " "
4½%,	" " "	¼	" " " "
5%,	" " "	⅙	" " " "
5½%,	" " "	1/12	" " " "
7%,	increase the interest by	⅙	" " " "
7½%,	" " "	¼	" " " "
8%,	" " "	⅓	" " " "
8½%,	" " "	5/12	" " " "
9%,	" " "	½	" " " "

EXAMPLE

Find the ordinary interest on $380.00 for 90 days at 4½%.

Solution

(1) First calculate the interest at 6%.

Interest for 60 days	=	$3.80
" " 30 "	=	1.90
" " 90 "	=	$5.70

(2) The interest at 6% is $5.70. To find the interest at 4½%, deduct ¼ of $5.70. $5.70 ÷ 4 = $1.43. $5.70 − $1.43 = $4.27, the interest on $380.00 for 90 days at 4½%.

The cancellation method. The cancellation method may be used to advantage in many interest calculations, especially in those having odd or fractional rates.

EXAMPLE

Find the ordinary interest on $345.75 for 90 days at 4½%.

Solution

$$\frac{345.75 \times \overset{3}{\cancel{90}} \times .09}{\underset{4}{\cancel{12}} \times \cancel{30} \times 2} = \frac{31.1175}{8}$$

$$= \$3.889, \text{ or } \$3.89$$

Divisors for rates of interest. Find the interest by multiplying the principal by the number of days and diving by the divisor shown in the table for the rate of interest to be applied. When the principal contains cents, point off four places from the right of the result. When the principal contains only dollars point off two places. The use of the divisor saves one operation. Thus, instead of multiplying the product of the principal times the number of days by .06, and dividing by 360, to determine interest at 6%, the product mentioned is divided immediately by 60, the divisor for 6%.

EXAMPLE

Find the interest on $625.24 for 39 days at 4%.

Solution

Multiply the principal by the days: $625.24 × 39 = $2438436. Then divide the product by the general divisor for 4%, and point off four places. 2438436 ÷ 90 = $2.71.

DIVISORS FOR RATES OF INTEREST

For 2%,	divide	by	180
2½%,	"	"	144
3%,	"	"	120
3½%,	"	"	102.86
4%,	"	"	90
5%,	"	"	72
6%,	"	"	60
7%,	"	"	51.43
8%,	"	"	45
9%,	"	"	40
10%,	"	"	36
12%,	"	"	30
15%,	"	"	24

How to use a short method of calculating exact interest. The simplest method of calculating exact interest (that is, interest on the basis of 365 days to the year) is the following:

1. Calculate the ordinary (360-day) interest by one of the short methods described in the preceding pages.
2. Adjust the result to exact interest by deducting from the ordinary interest 1/73 of itself (because the difference of 5 days is 1/73 of 365).

EXAMPLE

Find the exact interest on $60,000.00 for 56 days at 6%.

Solution

(1) The ordinary interest is found to be $560.00.
(2) To find the exact interest, deduct from $560.00 1/73 of $560.00, or $7.67. The exact interest on $60,000.00 for 56 days at 6% is, then, $560.00 – $7.67, or $552.33.

Exact interest table. The table (page 1282) gives the interest on $100 (computed on the basis of 365 days to the year) for 1 day to 100 days at various rates of interest. From the table the interest accruing for other sums and for any other number of days can be easily calculated.

EXAMPLE

Compute the interest on $920 for 22 days at 4%.

Solution

Interest on $100 for 20 days at 4% (from table)	.219179
" " " " 2 " at 4% (from table)	.021918
" " " " 22 "	.241
Multiply by 9.2 ($920 is 9.2 times $100)	9.2
	482
	2169
Interest on $920 for 22 days at 4%	$2.2172, or $2.22

(*Note:* On sums of less than $1,000, the last three digits can be dropped [being careful to increase the last remaining digit by 1 where the digits dropped are more than one-half—thus: .021918 became .022]).

EXACT INTEREST TABLE

Interest on $100 at Various Rates for Various Periods of Time

Days	*2%*	*3%*	*4%*	*5%*	*6%*
1.....	.005479	.008220	.010959	.013699	.016438
2.....	.010959	.016439	.021918	.027397	.032877
3.....	.016438	.024658	.032877	.041096	.049315
4.....	.021918	.032877	.043836	.054795	.065753
5.....	.027397	.041096	.054795	.068493	.082192
6.....	.032877	.049315	.065754	.082192	.098630
7.....	.038356	.057534	.076712	.095890	.115068
8.....	.043836	.065753	.087671	.109589	.131507
9.....	.049315	.073973	.098630	.123288	.147945
10.....	.054795	.082192	.109589	.136986	.164384
20.....	.109589	.164384	.219179	.273973	.328767
30.....	.164384	.246576	.328768	.410959	.493151
40.....	.219178	.328768	.438357	.547945	.657534
50.....	.273973	.410959	.547946	.684932	.821918
60.....	.328767	.493151	.657536	.821918	.986301
70.....	.383562	.575342	.767125	.958904	1.150685
80.....	.438356	.657534	.876714	1.095890	1.315068
90.....	.493151	.739726	.986304	1.232877	1.479452
100.....	.547945	.821918	1.095893	1.369863	1.643836

Use of interest tables. Where calculations in simple interest have to be made very frequently, much time can be saved by the use of a book of interest tables, from which the desired information is obtainable at a glance. In Figure 94 is reproduced a section of one page from the "Delbridge 6% Interest Computer," published by the Delbridge Company, 206 Walnut Street, St. Louis, Missouri. In this volume one page is devoted to each day in the year, and the principal on which interest is computed—on the basis of 360 days to the year—ranges from $0.01 to $200,000.00. Similar tables are available showing simple interest on the basis of 365 days to the year. The same company also publishes volumes of interest tables for rates other than 6% and various small-size books of interest tables.

In the excerpt from one page of the "Delbridge 6% Interest Computer," the numbers in boldface type represent principal, while the numbers in lightface represent the corresponding interest for 287 days at 6%. The following example illustrates the use of these tables.

9 MONTHS AND 17 DAYS. **6 % Interest; on basis of 360 days to a year. 287**

1¢	$0 00	1	05	101	4 83	201	9 61	301	14 40	401	19 18	501	23 96	601	28 75	701	33 53
2¢	00	2	10	102	4 88	202	9 66	302	14 45	402	19 23	502	24 01	602	28 80	702	33 58
3¢	00	3	14	103	4 93	203	9 71	303	14 49	403	19 28	503	24 06	603	28 84	703	33 63
4¢	00	4	19	104	4 97	204	9 76	304	14 54	404	19 32	504	24 11	604	28 89	704	33 67
5¢	00	5	24	105	5 02	205	9 81	305	14 59	405	19 37	505	24 16	605	28 94	705	33 72
6¢	00	6	29	106	5 07	206	9 85	306	14 64	406	19 42	506	24 20	606	28 99	706	33 77
7¢	00	7	33	107	5 12	207	9 90	307	14 68	407	19 47	507	24 25	607	29 03	707	33 82
8¢	00	8	38	108	5 17	208	9 95	308	14 73	408	19 52	508	24 30	608	29 08	708	33 87
9¢	00	9	43	109	5 21	209	10 00	309	14 78	409	19 56	509	24 35	609	29 13	709	33 91
10¢	00	10	48	110	5 26	210	10 04	310	14 83	410	19 61	510	24 39	610	29 18	710	33 96
11¢	01	11	53	111	5 31	211	10 09	311	14 88	411	19 66	511	24 44	611	29 23	711	34 01
12¢	01	12	57	112	5 36	212	10 14	312	14 92	412	19 71	512	24 49	612	29 27	712	34 06
13¢	01	13	62	113	5 41	213	10 19	313	14 97	413	19 76	513	24 54	613	29 32	713	34 11
14¢	01	14	67	114	5 45	214	10 24	314	15 02	414	19 80	514	24 59	614	29 37	714	34 15
15¢	01	15	72	115	5 50	215	10 28	315	15 07	415	19 85	515	24 63	615	29 42	715	34 20
16¢	01	16	77	116	5 55	216	10 33	316	15 12	416	19 90	516	24 68	616	29 47	716	34 25
17¢	01	17	81	117	5 60	217	10 38	317	15 16	417	19 95	517	24 73	617	29 51	717	34 30
18¢	01	18	86	118	5 64	218	10 43	318	15 21	418	19 99	518	24 78	618	29 56	718	34 34
19¢	01	19	91	119	5 69	219	10 48	319	15 26	419	20 04	519	24 83	619	29 61	719	34 39
20¢	01	20	96	120	5 74	220	10 52	320	15 31	420	20 09	520	24 87	620	29 66	720	34 44
21¢	01	21	1 00	121	5 79	221	10 57	321	15 35	421	20 14	521	24 92	621	29 70	721	34 49
22¢	01	22	1 05	122	5 84	222	10 62	322	15 40	422	20 19	522	24 97	622	29 75	722	34 54
23¢	01	23	1 10	123	5 88	223	10 67	323	15 45	423	20 23	523	25 02	623	29 80	723	34 58
24¢	01	24	1 15	124	5 93	224	10 71	324	15 50	424	20 28	524	25 06	624	29 85	724	34 63
25¢	01	25	1 20	125	5 98	225	10 76	325	15 55	425	20 33	525	25 11	625	29 90	725	34 68
26¢	01	26	1 24	126	6 03	226	10 81	326	15 59	426	20 38	526	25 16	626	29 94	726	34 73
27¢	01	27	1 29	127	6 07	227	10 86	327	15 64	427	20 42	527	25 21	627	29 99	727	34 77
28¢	01	28	1 34	128	6 12	228	10 91	328	15 69	428	20 47	528	25 26	628	30 04	728	34 82
29¢	01	29	1 39	129	6 17	229	10 95	329	15 74	429	20 52	529	25 30	629	30 09	729	34 87
30¢	01	30	1 43	130	6 22	230	11 00	330	15 78	430	20 57	530	25 35	630	30 13	730	34 92
31¢	01	31	1 48	131	6 27	231	11 05	331	15 83	431	20 62	531	25 40	631	30 18	731	34 97
32¢	02	32	1 53	132	6 31	232	11 10	332	15 88	432	20 66	532	25 45	632	30 23	732	35 01
33¢	02	33	1 58	133	6 36	233	11 15	333	15 93	433	20 71	533	25 50	633	30 28	733	35 06
34¢	02	34	1 63	134	6 41	234	11 19	334	15 98	434	20 76	534	25 54	634	30 33	734	35 11
35¢	02	35	1 67	135	6 46	235	11 24	335	16 02	435	20 81	535	25 59	635	30 37	735	35 16
36¢	02	36	1 72	136	6 51	236	11 29	336	16 07	436	20 86	536	25 64	636	30 42	736	35 21
37¢	02	37	1 77	137	6 55	237	11 34	337	16 12	437	20 90	537	25 69	637	30 47	737	35 25
38¢	02	38	1 82	138	6 60	238	11 38	338	16 17	438	20 95	538	25 73	638	30 52	738	35 30
39¢	02	39	1 87	139	6 65	239	11 43	339	16 22	439	21 00	539	25 78	639	30 57	739	35 35
40¢	02	40	1 91	140	6 70	240	11 48	340	16 26	440	21 05	540	25 83	640	30 61	740	35 40
41¢	02	41	1 96	141	6 74	241	11 53	341	16 31	441	21 09	541	25 88	641	30 66	741	35 44
42¢	02	42	2 01	142	6 79	242	11 58	342	16 36	442	21 14	542	25 93	642	30 71	742	35 49
43¢	02	43	2 06	143	6 84	243	11 62	343	16 41	443	21 19	543	25 97	643	30 76	743	35 54
44¢	02	44	2 10	144	6 89	244	11 67	344	16 45	444	21 24	544	26 02	644	30 80	744	35 59

Figure 94. Page from the Delbridge 6% Interest Computer.

EXAMPLE

Find the ordinary interest on $328.36 for 287 days at 6%.

Solution

The amount in the table, opposite the boldface number 328, is $15.69. The amount opposite 36¢ is $0.02. The sum of the two amounts, $15.69 and $0.02, or $15.71, is the ordinary interest on $328.36 for 287 days at 6%.

Periodic interest. Periodic interest is simple interest on the principal, plus simple interest on each installment of interest that is not paid when due.

EXAMPLE

Find the periodic interest on a loan of $5,000.00 for 1 year and 6 months at 6%, interest due quarterly; no interest paid until the maturity of the loan.

Solution

Simple interest on $5,000.00 for 3 months			$ 75.00
Multiply by (number of quarterly periods)			6
Total simple interest			$450.00
First quarterly interest is unpaid	15	months	
Last " " " "	0	"	
Average	7½	"	
Multiply by (number of periods)	6		
Total	45	"	
Interest on $75 for 45 months			16.88
Total periodic interest			$466.88

2. PARTIAL PAYMENTS ON DEBTS—RULES FOR COMPUTING INTEREST

Adapted from Curtis and Cooper, "Mathematics of Accounting" New York: Prentice-Hall, Inc.

A debtor who owes a large amount may by agreement make equal or unequal payments on the principal at regular or irregular intervals. The creditor should have interest on the loan, and it is only fair that each payment made should draw interest in favor of the debtor.

There are two methods of applying these payments of principal and interest to the reduction of the debt. The method adopted by the Supreme Court of the United States is termed the "United States Rule"; the other method, which is widely used by businessmen, is termed the "Merchants' Rule."

United States Rule. The United States Rule is now a law in most states, having been made so either by statute or by court decision. The procedure under the United States Rule is as follows:

1. Payments must be applied against accrued interest before any deductions can be made from the principal.

2. Payments that do not equal the accrued interest leave the principal undiminished until other payments are made which are sufficient to cover all accrued interest.

3. Any excess remaining after the payments exceed the accrued interest is applied on the principal.

EXAMPLE

An interest-bearing note for $1,800.00 dated March 1, 1951, had the following indorsements:

September 27, 1951	$500.00
March 15, 1952	25.00
June 1, 1952	700.00

How much was due September 1, 1952?

Solution

	Yr. Mo. Da.	*Yrs.*	*Mos.*	*Days*
Date of note	1951—3—1			
First payment, $500.00 ..	1951—9—27		6	26
Second payment, $25.00 ..	1952—3—15		5	18
Third payment, $700.00 ..	1952—6—1		2	16
Settlement	1952—9—1		3	0
		1	6	0

Explanation. The time is found by successive subtractions of the first date from the second, the second from the third, and so on. The sum of the different times is equal to the time between the date of the note and the date of settlement.

Face of note, March 1, 1951		$1,800.00
Interest on $1,800 at 6% from March 1 to September 27, 6 months and 26 days		61.80
Amount due September 27, 1951		$1,861.80
Deduct payment		500.00
Balance due September 27, 1951		$1,361.80
Interest on $1,361.80 at 6% from September 27 to March 15, 5 months and 18 days, $38.13. As this interest is larger in amount than the payment made at March 15, the interest is not added, and the payment is not deducted.		
Interest on $1,361.80 at 6% from September 27 to June 1, 1952, 8 months and 4 days		55.38
Amount due June 1, 1952		$1,417.18
Deduct sum of payments: March 15	$ 25.00	
June 1	700.00	725.00
Balance due June 1, 1952		$ 692.18
Interest on $692.18 at 6% from June 1 to September 1, 1952, 3 months		10.38
Balance due September 1, 1952		$ 702.56

Merchants' Rule. The procedure under the Merchants' Rule is as follows:

1. The principal draws interest from the date of the loan until the date of final settlement, and such interest is added to the principal.
2. Each payment draws interest from the date of the payment until the date of final settlement.
3. The balance due is the principal plus interest, minus the payments plus interest.

Where the debt runs for more than one year, the principal draws interest from the date of the loan until the end of the first year (one year from the date on which the loan was made). Each payment draws interest from the date of payment until the end of the first year. The balance due at the end of the first year is the principal plus interset for one year, minus the payments plus the interest from the dates on which the payments were made until the end of the first year. The balance due at the end of the second, third, and subsequent years is calculated in a similar manner.

EXAMPLE

For purposes of comparison, the same problem will be used here as was used to illustrate the United States Rule.

Solution

Face of note, March 1, 1951		$1,800.00
Interest, 1 year at 6% to March 1, 1952		108.00
		$1,908.00
Deduct		
First payment, September 27, 1951	$500.00	
Interest at 6% to March 1, 1952, 5 months and 4 days	12.83	512.83
Balance due at beginning of second year ..		$1,395.17
Interest on $1,395.17 at 6%, March 1 to September 1, 1952, 6 months		41.86
		$1,437.03
Deduct:		
Second payment, March 15, 1952	$ 25.00	
Interest at 6% from March 15 to September 1, 1952, 5 months and 16 days ..	.69	
Third payment, June 1, 1952	700.00	
Interest at 6% from June 1 to September 1, 1952, 3 months	10.50	736.19
Balance due		$ 700.84

United States Rule and Merchants' Rule compared. In the examples given in the preceding pages, the difference between the balance as computed by the United States Rule and the balance as computed by the Merchants' Rule is only $1.72, but a much greater difference will occur when the time is long and the amount large.

It is usual to compute the balance due on obligations of one year or less by the Merchants' Rule; the balance due on obligations of more than one year is generally computed by the United States Rule.

3. HOW TO CALCULATE BANK DISCOUNT

What bank discount is. Bank discount is the interest charge made by a bank for converting commercial paper into cash before maturity. Bank discount is computed as simple interest on the amount due at maturity on a note or draft and is deducted in advance. The amount received from the bank—amount due at maturity less the discount and the collection charge—is called the proceeds. The number of days from the date the note is discounted to the date of maturity is called the "term of discount."

How the number of days is counted in bank discount. In bank discount the time is the period from the date of discount to the date of maturity of the instrument. It is the common practice of commercial banks in the United States to charge discount for the actual or exact number of days in the discount period, and to compute the discount on the basis of 360 days to the year. Thus, if a note due May 6 is discounted March 6, the bank counts the actual number of days between these dates, 61, and computes the discount on the basis of 360 days to the year. For the method of calculating the exact number of days between dates, and a useful table, see page 1274; for the method of calculating the date of maturity of an obligation, see page 1272.

How to calculate the bank discount and proceeds on non-interest-bearing paper. The procedure is as follows:

1. The amount due at maturity on non-interest-bearing paper is the amount stated on the face of the instrument.
2. Using the discount rate, compute the bank discount on the face.
3. Compute the collection charge on the face.

4. Deduct from the face the sum of the bank discount and the collection charge; the result is the proceeds.

EXAMPLE

Compute the bank discount and proceeds on a $500.00 non-interest-bearing note, dated June 5, due in 60 days, and discounted June 18 at 6%; collection charge, 1/10%.

Solution

Sixty days from June 5 is August 4, the due date of the note. The exact number of days from June 18, the date of discount, to August 4, the due date, is 47.

Value of note at maturity		$500.00
Bank discount: 6% on $500.00 for 47 days	$3.92	
Collection charge: 1/10% on $500.00	.50	
Total charges		4.42
Proceeds		$495.58

How to calculate the bank discount and proceeds on interest-bearing paper. The procedure is as follows:

1. Compute the value of the instrument at maturity; the value of an interest-bearing instrument is its face plus the interest for the full time of the note.
2. Compute the interest on the value at maturity for the discount period, using the discount rate; the result is the bank discount.
3. Compute the collection charge on the value at maturity.
4. Deduct from the value at maturity the sum of the bank discount and the collection charge; the result is the proceeds.

EXAMPLE

Compute the bank discount and proceeds on a note for $500.00 dated June 5, due in 60 days, and bearing 5% interest; the note is discounted June 18 at 6%, and the collection charge is 1/10%.

Solution

Sixty days from June 5 is August 4, the due date of the note. The exact number of days from June 18, the date of discount, to August 4, the due date, is 47.

Face value of note		$500.00
Interest at 5% for 60 days		4.17
Value of note at maturity		$504.17
Bank discount: 6% on $504.17 for 47 days	$3.95	
Collection charge: 1/10% on $504.17	.50	
Total charges		4.45
Proceeds		$499.72

4. SAVINGS THROUGH CASH DISCOUNT

Cash discount explained. Cash discount is the allowance made by the seller of goods to the buyer on condition that the invoice is paid within a specified time. Assume that goods are sold on terms of "2/10, net 30." This means that if the goods purchased are paid for in cash within ten days from the date of the invoice, the purchaser may subtract 2% from the amount of the invoice. This deduction is called the "cash discount." The goods are supposed, at any rate, to be paid for within 30 days of the date of the invoice. In practice, the debt is usually not paid until 30 days after the first of the month succeeding the month in which the goods are bought. Thus the purchaser gets 2% discount for paying 20 days earlier than the date on which he could be compelled to pay. The discount, therefore, is practically at the rate of 2% for 20 days, or 36% per year.

The following table shows the ordinary discount rates and their equivalent interest rates figured on an annual basis:

CASH DISCOUNT TABLE

½%	10 days	net	30	days	= 9%	per annum
1%	"	"	"	"	= 18%	" "
1½%	"	"	"	"	= 27%	" "
2%	"	"	"	"	= 36%	" "
2%	"	"	60	"	= 14%	" "
2%	30	"	"	"	= 24%	" "
2%	"	"	4	mos.	= 8%	" "
2%	40	"	60	days	= 36%	" "
2%	70	"	90	"	= 36%	" "
3%	10	"	30	"	= 54%	" "
3%	"	"	4	mos.	= 10%	" "
3%	30	"	60	days	= 36%	" "

4% 10 days net 60 days = 29% per annum
4% " " " 4 mos. = 13% " "
5% " " " 30 days = 90% " "
5% " " " 60 " = 36% " "
5% " " " 4 mos. = 16% " "
6% " " " 60 days 43% " "
6% " " " 4 mos. = 20% " "
7% " " " " " = 23% " "
8% " " " " " = 26% " "

5. HOW TO COMPUTE TRADE DISCOUNTS

Uses of trade discounts. Trade discounts are commonly used as a means of adjusting list or catalogue prices to changed market conditions. Manufacturers and jobbers who deal in merchandise that is more or less standardized issue catalogues describing the goods; the prices quoted in the catalogues are the list prices. As the market prices fluctuate, discounts from the list prices are given, these discounts being issued to customers on separate discount sheets to obviate the necessity of frequent reprinting of the catalogues. Successive discounts from the list prices enable the seller to keep in touch with a declining market. If the market turns upward, the seller can raise his prices step by step as desired by canceling successively the discounts previously offered. The seller can allow different discounts to different classes of customers, without naming separate prices, by giving his customers different discount sheets. Trade discounts are also a means of partly concealing the real prices; the catalogue alone, without the appropriate discount sheet, tells nothing as to the real prices of the merchandise.

Chain discounts. Several discounts from the one list price are often given; for example, goods may be priced at $500.00 less discounts of 20%, 10%, and 5%. These are known as "chain discounts," and the several discounts are referred to as a "series of discounts."

How chain discounts are computed. Each discount is deducted from the balance remaining after the deduction of the preceding discount.

EXAMPLE

Goods are priced at $500.00 less discounts of 20%, 10%, and 5%. Find the net price.

Solution

List price	$500.00
20% of $500.00	100.00
	$400.00
10% of $400.00	40.00
	$360.00
5% of $360.00	18.00
Net price	$342.00

Hence the net price is $342.00, and the amount of the discount is $158.00.

Several discounts are *not* equal to the sum of the discounts. Thus, in the above example, the sum of the discounts 20%, 10%, and 5% is 35%; 35% of $500.00 is $175.00. The correct discount is $158.00.

How to find the single trade discount equivalent to a series. Where only two discounts are involved:

1. Add the discounts.
2. Multiply the discounts.
3. Subtract (2) from (1); the result is the single discount equivalent to the two discounts.

EXAMPLE

Find the single trade discount equivalent to discounts of 20% and 10%.

Solution

20% + 10%	30%
20% × 10%	2%
30% − 2%	28%

Hence the single trade discount equivalent to discounts of 20% and 10% is 28%.

An extension of the above method can be used where it is desired to find the single trade discount equivalent to three or more discounts.

EXAMPLE

Find the single trade discount equivalent to discounts of 30%, 10%, and 5%.

Solution

First find the single discount equivalent to the first two discounts—30% and 10%.

30% + 10%	40%
30% × 10%	3%
40% − 3%	37%

Thus the single discount equivalent to discounts of 30% and 10% is 37%. Now find the single discount equivalent to discounts of 37% and 5%.

37% + 5%	42%
37% × 5%	1.85%
42% − 1.85%	40.15%

The single discount equivalent to discounts of 30%, 10%, and 5% is, then, 40.15%.

A second method is:

1. Subtract each single discount from 100%.
2. Find the product of the remainders.
3. Subtract the product from 100%; the remainder is the single discount equivalent to the series.

EXAMPLE

Find the single discount equivalent to the series 30%, 10%, and 5%.

Solution

100%	100%	100%
30%	10%	5%
70%	90%	95%

.70 × .90 × .95 = .5985, or 59.85%

100% − 59.85% = 40.15%, the single discount

A third method is:

1. Subtract the first discount from 100%.
2. Multiply the remainder by the second discount, and deduct the product.

3. Multiply this remainder by the third discount, and deduct the product.

4. Subtract this remainder from 100%; the result is the single discount.

EXAMPLE

Find the single discount equivalent to the series 20%, 10%, and 8⅓%.

Solution

100% − 20%	80%
80% × 10%	8%
80% − 8%	72%
72% × 8⅓%	6%
72% − 6%	66%
100% − 66%	34%

The single discount equivalent to the series 20%, 10%, and 8⅓% is, therefore, 34%.

How to calculate the net price. The procedure is as follows:

1. Reduce the trade discount series to a single discount, by one of the methods described in the preceding pages.

2. Multiply the list price by this single discount; this gives the amount of the discount.

3. Deduct the amount of the discount from the list price; the result is the net price.

EXAMPLE

Find the net price of a gas pump listed at $3,500.00, with discounts of 20%, 12½%, 5%, and 2%.

Solution

100%	100%	100%	100%
20%	12½%	5%	2%
80%	87½%	95%	98%

.80 × .875 × .95 × .98 = .6517, or 65.17%
100% − 65.17% = 34.83%, the single discount
$3,500.00 × 34.83% = $1,219.05, amount of discount
$3,500.00 − $1,219.05 = $2,280.95, the net price

Table of decimal equivalents of chain discounts. The table on pages 1294-95 will be found useful in chain discount computations. Its use is illustrated on page 1296.

DECIMAL EQUIVALENTS OF CHAIN DISCOUNTS

Secondary Discount	Primary Discount 5	7½	10	12½	15	16⅔	20	22½	25	27½	30	32½	33⅓	35	37½
2	.93100	.90650	.88200	.85750	.83300	.81667	.78400	.75950	.73500	.71050	.68600	.66150	.65333	.63100	.61250
2½	.92625	.90188	.8775	.85313	.82875	.8125	.78	.75562	.73125	.70688	.6825	.65813	.65	.63375	.60938
5	.9025	.87875	.855	.83125	.8075	.79166	.76	.73625	.7125	.68875	.665	.64125	.63333	.6175	.59375
5 2½	.87994	.85678	.83363	.81047	.78731	.77187	.741	.71784	.69469	.67153	.64838	.62522	.6175	.60206	.57891
5 5	.85738	.83481	.81225	.78969	.76713	.75208	.722	.69943	.67688	.65431	.63175	.60919	.60167	.58663	.56406
5 5 2½	.83594	.81394	.79194	.76994	.74795	.73328	.70395	.68195	.65995	.63795	.61596	.59396	.58663	.57196	.54996
7½	.87875	.85563	.8325	.80938	.78625	.77083	.74	.71688	.69375	.67063	.6475	.62438	.61667	.60125	.57813
7½ 2½	.85678	.83423	.81169	.78914	.76659	.75156	.7215	.69895	.67641	.65386	.63131	.60877	.60125	.58622	.56367
7½ 5	.83481	.81284	.79088	.76891	.74694	.73229	.703	.68103	.65906	.6371	.61513	.59316	.58583	.57119	.54922
10	.855	.8325	.81	.7875	.765	.75	.72	.6975	.675	.6525	.63	.6075	.60	.585	.5625
10 2½	.83363	.81169	.78975	.76781	.74588	.73125	.702	.68006	.65813	.63619	.61425	.59231	.585	.57038	.54844
10 5	.81225	.79088	.7695	.74811	.72675	.7125	.684	.66263	.64125	.61988	.5985	.57713	.57	.55575	.53438
10 5 2½	.79194	.77111	.75026	.72941	.70858	.69469	.6669	.64606	.62522	.60438	.58354	.5627	.55575	.54186	.52102
10 7½	.79088	.77006	.74925	.72844	.70763	.69375	.666	.64519	.62438	.60356	.58275	.56194	.555	.54113	.52031
10 7½ 5	.75134	.73156	.71179	.69202	.67225	.65906	.6327	.61293	.59316	.57338	.55361	.53384	.52725	.51407	.49429
10 10	.7695	.74925	.729	.70875	.6885	.675	.648	.62775	.6075	.58725	.567	.54675	.54	.5265	.50625
10 10 2½	.75026	.73052	.71078	.69103	.67129	.65812	.6318	.61206	.59231	.57257	.55283	.53308	.5265	.51334	.49359
10 10 5	.73103	.71179	.69255	.67331	.65408	.64124	.6156	.59636	.57713	.55789	.53865	.51941	.513	.50018	.48094
10 10 5 2½	.71276	.694	.67524	.65648	.63772	.62519	.60021	.58145	.5627	.54394	.52518	.50643	.50018	.48767	.46891
10 10 10	.69255	.67433	.6561	.63788	.61965	.6075	.5832	.56498	.54675	.52853	.5103	.49208	.486	.47385	.45563
12½	.83125	.80938	.7875	.76563	.74375	.72923	.70	.67813	.65625	.63438	.6125	.59063	.58334	.56875	.54688
12½ 2½	.81047	.78915	.76781	.74649	.72516	.711	.6825	.66118	.63984	.61852	.59719	.57587	.56876	.55453	.53321
12½ 5	.78969	.76891	.74813	.72735	.70656	.69277	.665	.64422	.62344	.60266	.58188	.5611	.55417	.54031	.51954
12½ 7½	.76891	.74868	.72844	.70821	.68797	.67454	.6475	.62727	.60703	.5868	.5666	.54633	.53904	.52609	.50586
12½ 10	.74813	.72844	.70875	.68907	.66938	.65631	.63	.61032	.59063	.57094	.55125	.53157	.52448	.51188	.49219
12½ 10 5	.71072	.69202	.67331	.65462	.63591	.6235	.5985	.5798	.5611	.54239	.52369	.50499	.49826	.48629	.46758
12½ 10 5 2½	.69295	.67472	.65648	.63826	.62001	.60791	.58354	.56531	.54707	.52883	.51060	.49237	.48580	.47413	.45589
12½ 10 7½	.69202	.67381	.65559	.63739	.61918	.60709	.58275	.56455	.54633	.52812	.50991	.49170	.48514	.47349	.45528
12½ 10 10	.67332	.6556	.63788	.62016	.60244	.59068	.567	.54929	.53157	.51385	.49613	.47841	.47203	.46069	.44297
15	.8075	.78625	.765	.74375	.7225	.70833	.68	.65875	.6375	.61625	.595	.57375	.56667	.5525	.53125
15 2½	.78732	.76660	.74588	.72516	.70444	.69062	.663	.64229	.62157	.60084	.58013	.55941	.55251	.53869	.51797
20	.76	.74	.72	.70	.68	.66667	.64	.62	.60	.58	.56	.54	.53333	.52	.50

Secondary Discount	Primary Discount														
	40	42½	45	47½	50	52½	55	57½	60	62½	65	66 ⅔	70	72½	75
2	.58800	.56350	.53900	.51450	.4900	.46550	.44100	.41650	.39200	.36750	.34300	.32667	.29400	.26950	.24500
2½	.585	.56063	.53625	.51188	.4875	.46313	.43875	.41438	.39	.36563	.34125	.325	.2925	.26813	.24375
5	.57	.54625	.5225	.49875	.475	.45125	.4275	.40375	.38	.35625	.3325	.31667	.285	.26125	.2375
5 2½	.55575	.53259	.50944	.48628	.46313	.43997	.41681	.39366	.3705	.34374	.32419	.30875	.27788	.25472	.23156
5 5	.5415	.51894	.49638	.47381	.45125	.42869	.40613	.38356	.361	.33844	.31588	.30083	.27075	.24819	.22563
5 5 2½	.52796	.50596	.48397	.46194	.43997	.41797	.39597	.37397	.35198	.32998	.30798	.29331	.26398	.24198	.21998
7½	.555	.53188	.50875	.48563	.4625	.43938	.41625	.39313	.37	.34688	.32375	.30833	.2775	.25438	.23125
7½ 2½	.54113	.51858	.49603	.47348	.45094	.42839	.40584	.3833	.36075	.3382	.31566	.30063	.27056	.24802	.22547
7½ 5	.52725	.50529	.48331	.46135	.43938	.41741	.39544	.37347	.3515	.32954	.30756	.29292	.26363	.24166	.21969
10	.54	.5175	.495	.4725	.45	.4275	.405	.3825	.36	.3375	.315	.30	.27	.2475	.225
10 2½	.5265	.50456	.48263	.46069	.43875	.41681	.39488	.37294	.351	.32906	.30713	.2925	.26325	.24131	.21938
10 5	.513	.49163	.47025	.44888	.4275	.40613	.38475	.36338	.342	.32063	.29925	.285	.2565	.23513	.21375
10 5 2½	.50018	.47933	.45849	.43765	.41681	.39597	.37513	.35429	.33345	.31261	.29177	.27788	.25009	.22925	.20841
10 7½	.4995	.47869	.45788	.43706	.41625	.39544	.37463	.35381	.333	.31219	.29138	.2775	.24975	.22894	.20183
10 7½ 5	.47453	.45476	.43499	.41521	.39544	.37567	.3559	.33612	.31635	.29658	.27681	.26363	.23726	.21749	.19772
10 10	.486	.46575	.4455	.42525	.405	.38475	.3645	.34425	.324	.30375	.2835	.27	.243	.22275	.2025
10 10 2½	.47385	.45411	.43436	.41462	.39488	.37514	.35539	.33564	.3159	.29616	.27641	.26325	.23693	.21718	.19744
10 10 5	.4617	.44246	.42323	.40399	.38475	.36551	.34628	.32704	.3078	.28856	.26933	.2565	.23085	.21161	.19238
10 10 5 2½	.45016	.4314	.41264	.39389	.37513	.35637	.33762	.31886	.3001	.28135	.26259	.25009	.22508	.20632	.18757
10 10 10	.4374	.41918	.40095	.38273	.3645	.34628	.32805	.30983	.2916	.27338	.25515	.243	.2187	.20048	.18225
12½	.525	.50313	.48125	.45938	.4375	.41663	.39375	.37188	.35	.32813	.30625	.29138	.2625	.24063	.21875
12½ 2½	.51188	.49055	.46922	.4479	.42656	.40622	.38391	.36258	.34125	.31993	.29859	.2841	.25594	.23462	.21328
12½ 5	.49875	.47797	.45719	.43641	.41563	.3958	.37406	.35329	.3325	.31172	.29094	.27681	.24938	.2286	.20781
12½ 7½	.48563	.4654	.44516	.42493	.40469	.38538	.36422	.34399	.32375	.30352	.28328	.26953	.24281	.22258	.20234
12½ 10	.4725	.45282	.43313	.41344	.39375	.37497	.35438	.33469	.315	.29532	.27563	.26224	.23625	.21657	.19688
12½ 10 5	.44888	.43018	.41147	.39277	.37406	.35622	.33666	.31796	.29925	.28055	.26185	.24913	.22444	.20574	.18704
12½ 10 5 2½	.43766	.41943	.40118	.38295	.36471	.34732	.32824	.31001	.29177	.27354	.2553	.2429	.21883	.2006	.18236
12½ 10 7½	.43706	.41886	.40065	.38243	.36422	.34685	.32780	.30959	.29138	.27317	.25496	.24257	.21853	.20033	.18211
12½ 10 10	.42525	.40754	.38982	.37210	.35438	.33747	.31894	.30122	.2835	.26579	.24807	.23602	.21263	.19491	.17719
15	.51	.48875	.4675	.44625	.425	.40375	.3825	.36125	.34	.31875	.2975	.28333	.255	.23375	.2125
15 2½	.49725	.47653	.45582	.43510	.4144	.39366	.3730	.35222	.3315	.31097	.29007	.27625	.24863	.22791	.20719
20	.48	.46	.44	.42	.40	.38	.36	.34	.32	.30	.28	.26667	.24	.22	.20

Note.—Reproduced by courtesy of Lefax, Inc., Philadelphia, Pa., from "Business Data Sheet No. 5–167."

EXAMPLE

Find the net price of an article listed at $300.00, with discounts of 15%, 10%, and 5%.

Solution

The primary discount is 15%. In the 15% column, on the line for secondary discounts of 10% and 5%, the decimal .72675 is given. Multiply this decimal by the list price. $300.00 × .72675 = $218.03, the net price.

6. HOW TO COMPUTE AVERAGES

Adapted from Curtis and Cooper, "Mathematics of Accounting" New York: Prentice-Hall, Inc.

Simple average. The simple average of a group of items is obtained by adding the items to be averaged and dividing the sum by the number of items added.

EXAMPLE

From the following statistics, find the average rate per kilowatt hour for electrical energy:

New England States	2.88¢
South Atlantic States	2.77¢
Atlantic States	2.19¢
North Central States	1.88¢
Pacific Northwest	1.81¢

Solution

$$2.88 + 2.77 + 2.19 + 1.88 + 1.81 = 11.53$$
$$11.53 \div 5 = 2.306$$

Explanation. The number of items to be added is 5, and the sum is 11.53¢. 11.53 divided by 5 = 2.306, or 2.306¢, the average rate per kilowatt hour.

A not uncommon error in business computations is the use of a simple average where a weighted average is required to give the correct result (for explanation of weighted average, see page 1299).

Moving average. A moving average is a series of simple averages of statistics applicable to groups of an equal number of time units, each successive group excluding the first time unit of the preceding group and including the unit immediately following those of the preceding group. For example, a yearly moving average, by months, may begin with an initial group including the data applicable to the twelve months of 1952. The next group would omit the data applicable to January, 1952, and include the data applicable to the remaining eleven months of 1952 and those applicable to the month of January, 1953.

EXAMPLE

The labor costs in a certain manufacturing plant for the first six months of 1952 were as follows:

January	$3,363.17
February	3,644.15
March	4,472.90
April	3,209.20
May	3,415.40
June	4,152.05

The labor costs for the next two months were:

July	$3,824.06
August	4,015.25

What has been the average labor cost for each six months since January 1, 1952?

Solution

The labor cost for the period from January 1 to June 30 is the sum of the labor costs for each of the six months, or $22,256.87. The average for the period is $22,256.87 ÷ 6, or $3,709.48.

The average for the period from February 1 to July 31 is computed as follows:

Total: January 1 to June 30	$22,256.87
Deduct: January labor cost	3,363.17
	$18,893.70
Add: July labor cost	3,824.06
	$22,717.76

$$\$22,717.76 \div 6 = \$3,786.29$$

The average for the period from March 1 to August 31 is calculated in the same manner:

Total: February 1 to July 31	$22,717.76
Deduct: February labor cost	3,644.15
	$19,073.61
Add: August labor cost	4,015.25
	$23,088.86

$$\$23{,}088.86 \div 6 = \$3{,}848.14$$

Comparison of these averages, $3,709.48, $3,786.29, and $3,848.14 shows an increase for each period.

In permanent records, these averages should be tabulated:

1952	*Labor Cost*	*Moving Average*	*Increase or Decrease*†
January-June	$22,256.87	$3,709.48	$ ...
February-July	22,717.76	3,786.29	76.81
March-August	23,088.86	3,848.14	61.85

† Indicate decreases by means of daggers.

Further comparisons, based on the figures of prior periods, may be made in succeeding years. A column may be annexed to show the increase or decrease of the average of each six-month period compared with the simple average for the preceding year. Another column may be used to show the increase or decrease in the moving average for the current six-month period compared with the moving average for the same period of the preceding year.

Progressive average. The method of progressive average is cumulative. The results of the latest period are added to the total previously computed, and the amount is divided by the previous divisor plus 1.

EXAMPLE

Department A sales were: January, $5,364.00; February, $4,872.00; March, $5,024.00. Department B sales were: January, $2,561.00; February, $2,325.00; March, $2,753.00. Find the progressive monthly averages.

Solution

SALES RECORD

Dept.	*Jan.*	*Feb.*	*Total*	*Aver.*	*March*	*Total*	*Aver.*	*April*
A	5,364	4,872	10,236	5,118	5,024	15,260	5,087	
B	2,561	2,325	4,886	2,443	2,753	7,639	2,546	*etc.*

Explanation. Department A sales for January and February total $10,236.00. $10,236.00 ÷ 2 = $5,118.00, the average for the two months. $10,236.00 + $5,024.00 = $15,260.00, the total sales for the three months. $15,260.00 ÷ 3 = $5,087.00, the average for the three months. The record for the year would be completed in this manner.

The totals and averages of Department B are computed in the same manner.

Periodic average. Periodic average is simple average applied for several periods to statistics applicable to the same unit of time. It may be used to show a variation in expenses, earnings, sales, and so forth.

EXAMPLE

EXPENSES

Month	*1952*	*1951*	*1950*	*1949*	*Total*	*Average*
January ..	$478.60	$392.85	$429.65	$356.00	$1,657.10	$414.28
February .	462.37	529.83	531.33	535.35	2,058.88	514.72
March ...	347.92	629.89	432.45	567.89	1,978.15	494.54

Explanation. The expenses for January for the four years are totaled; the total, $1,657.10, divided by 4, the number of years shown, equals $414.28, the average monthly expense for January. The other averages are calculated in the same manner.

Weighted average. A weighted average should be used where the items entering into the group to be averaged differ from each other in value. The following example illustrates the average-price method of pricing requisitions in cost accounting.

EXAMPLE

A stock record shows the following receipts:

4,800 lbs. @ 20¢
3,000 lbs. @ 18¢
4,000 lbs. @ 21¢

What is the average price per pound for the month?

Solution

4,800 lbs @ 20¢	=	$ 960.00
3,000 lbs. @ 18¢	=	540.00
4,000 lbs. @ 21¢	=	840.00
11,800 lbs.	=	$2,340.00

2,340 ÷ 11,800 = 19.83, or 19.83¢ per pound, average price

A simple average of the three prices paid during the month could be found by adding, 20¢ + 18¢ + 21¢ = 59¢, and dividing by 3, 59¢ ÷ 3 = 19.67¢. This, however, is not the correct average price per pound for the month. If the three prices are to be averaged, each price must be weighted according to the number of pounds bought at that price.

In the averaging of percentages, a simple average is sometimes used where a weighted average is required to give the correct result.

EXAMPLE

A manufactured product is composed of four ingredients, the ratios and costs per pound being as follows:

Material	*Pounds*	*Price per Pound*
A	1	$1.50
B	3	.75
C	4	1.25
D	2	2.00

It was found in the second year that, owing to price fluctuations, the raw material costs had increased as follows:

Material	*Per Cent*
A	50
B	100
C	10
D	25

What was the average percentage of increase in the cost of raw material composing the finished product?

Solution

Material	*Pounds*	*Cost per lb.*	*Total Cost*	*Percentage Price Increase*	*Increased Cost*
A	1	$1.50	$ 1.50	50	$ .75
B	3	.75	2.25	100	2.25
C	4	1.25	5.00	10	.50
D	2	2.00	4.00	25	1.00
			$12.75		$4.50

4.50 ÷ 12.75 = 35.29%, the weighted average percentage

A simple average of the four percentages could be found by adding 50% + 100% + 10% + 25% = 185%, and dividing by 4, 185% ÷ 4 = 46.25%. This, however, is not the correct average percentage of increase in the cost of raw materials composing the finished product. Each of the percentages must be weighted according to the number of pounds of that material in the product. When this is done, as illustrated above, the correct average percentage of increase in cost is found to be 35.29%.

7. HOW TO FIND THE AVERAGE DATE OF AN ACCOUNT

Adapted from Finney, "Principles of Accounting"
New York: Prentice-Hall, Inc.

Average or equated date. The average or equated date of an account is the date on which the balance of the account can be paid without loss of interest to either party. The average date may be desired for several purposes, among which are:

1. To determine the date on which settlement is to be made.
2. To determine the date that should be given to an interest-bearing note issued in settlement of the account.
3. To determine the amount of interest to be added to the balance of the account in making settlement. For instance, if the balance of the account is $500.00, the average date June 5, and the settlement date July 16, interest should be paid on $500.00 for 41 days.

George Smith has the following account with William Dawson:

WILLIAM DAWSON

June	1	Terms 30 days. .	100.00	
"	11	Terms 30 days. .	100.00	

One bill is due on July 1, the other on July 11. The average date is July 6, because the payment of the first $100.00 five days after it is due is exactly offset by the payment of the second $100.00 five days before it is due.

This account might be settled by the payment of $200.00 on July 6. If it is paid on July 16, interest on $200.00 for 10 days should be included in the payment. If an interest-bearing note is given on July 16, it should be dated July 6, or interest from July 6 to July 16 should be included in its face.

How to find the average date of a one-sided account. When an account contains debits only or credits only, the procedure in determining the average date is as follows:

1. Assume that all items in the account are paid at a date prior to the maturity of any item in the account. This assumed date is called the focal date. (Any date can be used as the focal date, but the most convenient focal date is the last day of the month preceding the first date on which any item is due.)
2. Determine the number of months and the number of days between the focal date and the maturity of each item.
3. Multiply each item in the account by the number of months and by the number of days between the focal date and the maturity date of the item.
4. Add the products of months, and reduce to a basis of days by multiplying by 30.
5. Add the products of days, including those obtained by reducing months to days.
6. Divide this total number of days by the balance of the account.
7. Reduce the days, determined in step (6), to months and days on the basis of 30 days to the month. Count forward from the focal date this number of months and days; the result is the average date of the account.

EXAMPLE

Find the average date of the following account.

JAMES WHITE

Aug.	3	Terms cash	600.00	
"	12	Terms 2/10; n/30	500.00	
Sept.	7	Terms 2/10; n/30	400.00	

Solution

The focal date is July 31, the last day of the month preceding the first date on which any item is due.

			Time from Focal Date		Products	
Date	*Debits*	*Date Due*	*Months*	*Days*	*Months*	*Days*
Aug. 3	600.00	Aug. 3	0	3	0	1,800.00
Aug. 12	500.00	Sept. 11	1	11	500.00	5,500.00
Sept. 7	400.00	Oct. 7	2	7	800.00	2,800.00
					30 × 1,300 =	39,000.00
	1,500.00					49,100.00

$49{,}100 \div 1{,}500 = 32\frac{10}{15}$, or 33 days, or 1 month and 3 days

The average date is 1 month and 3 days forward from July 31, or September 3.

Dates used in averaging. The dates to be used in the averaging should be the dates on which the items have a cash value equal to their face.

1. Sales on cash terms take the date of sale.
2. Sales on credit terms take the date on which the credit term expires.
3. Returns and allowances take the date that applies to the invoice on which the return or allowance is being made.
4. An interest-bearing note takes the date of the note, because the note is worth face value on that date.
5. A non-interest-bearing note takes the date of maturity, because it is not worth face value until maturity.

How to find the average date of a compound account. When an account contains both debits and credits, the process of determining the average date is called compound average. Compound averaging is performed as follows:

Steps (1), (2), (3), (4), and (5) are taken as in the averaging of a one-sided account, for both debits and credits.

6. Compute the balance of the account.
7. Determine the difference between the sum of the debit products and the sum of the credit products.
8. Divide this difference by the balance of the account, and reduce the quotient to months and days.
9. If the balance of the account and the balance of the products are both debits or both credits the average date is forward from the

focal date. If either is a debit and the other a credit, the average date is backward from the focal date.

Two examples of compound averaging are given below. In the first the average date is forward from the focal date; in the second, backward from the focal date.

EXAMPLE 1

Find the average date of the following compound account:

D. L. BURTON

May 7	Terms cash . . .	750.00	June 2	Int.-bearing note 1 month	1,500.00
" 19	2/30; n/30 . . .	1,200.00	" 10	Cash	100.00

Solution

The focal date is April 30, the last day of the month preceding the first date on which any item is due.

			Time from Focal Date		Products	
Date	*Amount*	*Date in Average*	*Months*	*Days*	*Months*	*Days*
Debits:						
May 7	750.00	May 7	0	7	0	5,250.00
May 19	1,200.00	June 18	1	18	1,200	21,600.00
					30 × 1,200 =	36,000.00
	1,950.00					62,850.00
Credits:						
June 2	1,500.00	June 2	1	2	1,500	3,500.00
June 10	100.00	June 10	1	10	100	1,000.00
					30 × 1,600 =	48,000.00
	1,600.00					52,000.00
Balances	350.00					10,850.00

10,850 ÷ 350 = 31, or 1 month and 1 day

Since the balance of the account and the balance of the products are both debits, the average date is 1 month and 1 day forward from April 30, or June 1.

EXAMPLE

For purposes of this example, assume the same account, except that the note does not bear interest.

Solution

			Time from Focal Date		Products	
Date	*Amount*	*Date in Average*	*Months*	*Days*	*Months*	*Days*
Debits (Totals as above):						
	1,950.00					62,850.00
Credits:						
June 2	1,500.00	July 2	2	2	3,000	3,000.00
June 10	100.00	June 10	1	10	100	1,000.00
					$30 \times 3{,}100 =$	93,000.00
	1,600.00					97,000.00
Balances	Dr. 350.00					Cr. 34,150.00

$34{,}150 \div 350 = 97\frac{20}{35}$, or 98, or 3 months and 8 days

In this case the balance of the account is a debit, while the balance of the products is a credit. The average date is therefore 3 months and 8 days backward from the focal date, or January 22 (still considering 30 days to the month).

How can the average date of an account be prior to any date in the account? In the first example the $1,500.00 note bore interest, and the average date of the account was June 1; the $350.00 balance in the account bore interest from that date. In the second example the $1,500.00 note, due in one month, bore no interest; as an offset, the $350.00 balance of the account should bear interest for approximately $4\frac{1}{3}$ additional months, or from January 22.

8. HOW TO COMPUTE MARKUP AND SELLING PRICE

Difference between figuring percentage of profit on cost price and on selling price. The difference between figuring the percentage of profit on the cost price and on the selling price is indicated in the following examples.

EXAMPLE 1

The cost price of an article is \$3.00. The selling price is to be computed as cost plus 25%. What is the selling price?

Solution

$$\frac{3}{1} \times \frac{25}{100} = \$0.75$$

$$\$3.00 + \$0.75 = \$3.75, \text{ the selling price}$$

EXAMPLE 2

The cost price of an article is \$3.00. The selling price is to be computed so that a profit of 25% will be made on the selling price. What is the selling price?

Solution

$$\begin{aligned} \text{Let } 100\% &= \text{selling price} \\ 25\% &= \text{margin} \\ 75\% &= \text{cost price, or } \$3.00 \\ 100\% &= \frac{300}{75}, \text{ or } \$4.00, \text{ the selling price} \end{aligned}$$

From these two examples it is apparent that a merchant who sold this \$3.00 article for \$3.75, with the idea of making a profit of 25%, would be acting on an illusion. He would have to sell the \$3.00 article for \$4.00 in order to make a profit of 25%, because the cost is only a part of the selling price. Actually, a margin of 25% on the cost price is equivalent to a margin of only 20% on the selling price; this can be shown from the figures used in Example 1, above:

$$\begin{aligned} \text{Cost price} &= \$3.00 \\ \text{Addition to cost price} &= .75 \\ \text{Selling price} &= 3.75 \end{aligned}$$

$$\text{Percentage profit on selling price} = \frac{0.75}{3.75} \times \frac{100}{1} = 20\%$$

The table below shows the percentage that has to be added to the cost in order to make a given percentage on the selling price.

PROFIT PERCENTAGE TABLE

Add to Cost (%)	*To Make on Selling Price* (%)	*Add to Cost* (%)	*To Make on Selling Price* (%)
5	4¾	31.58	24
7½	7	33⅓	25
10.00	9	35.00	26
11.11	10	37½	27¼
12.36	11	40.00	28½
12½	11⅛	42.86	30
13.63	12	45.00	31
14.94	13	47.00	32
16.28	14	50.00	33⅓
16.43	14¼	53.85	35
17.65	15	55.00	35½
19.05	16	60.00	37½
20.00	16⅔	65.00	39½
20.49	17	66⅔	40
21.96	18	70.00	41
23.46	19	75.00	42¾
25.00	20	80.00	44½
26.58	21	85.00	46
28.21	22	90.00	47½
29.88	23	100.00	50

How to calculate the markup and the selling price when cost of doing business and percentage of profit are based on selling price. Markup is that component which is added to cost in order to arrive at a selling price. The table on page 1308 shows the markup percentage on cost necessary to meet the total percentage deductions from selling price.

EXAMPLE

What should be the markup and the selling price of an article if the cost price is $15.00, the discount is 2% of the selling price, the commission allowed salesmen is 5% of the selling price, the overhead cost of doing business is 15% of the selling price, and the profit desired on the selling price is 7%?

Solution

The "total deductions from selling price" equal 29% (2% + 5% + 15% + 7%). In the table on page 1308, the figure opposite 29% is

MARKUP TABLE

Total Deductions from Selling Price	*Markup Percentage on Cost*	*Total Deductions from Selling Price*	*Markup Percentage on Cost*
1%	1.0101%	26%	35.1351%
2	2.0408	27	36.9863
3	3.0928	28	38.8889
4	4.1667	29	40.8451
5	5.2632	30	42.8571
6	6.383	31	44.9275
7	7.5269	32	47.0588
8	8.6957	33	49.2537
9	9.8901	34	51.5151
10	11.1111	35	53.8461
11	12.3595	36	56.25
12	13.6364	37	58.7301
13	14.9425	38	61.2903
14	16.2791	39	63.9344
15	17.647	40	66.6667
16	19.0476	41	69.4915
17	20.4819	42	72.4138
18	21.9512	43	75.4386
19	23.4568	44	78.5714
20	25.	45	81.8181
21	26.5823	46	85.1851
22	28.2051	47	88.6792
23	29.8701	48	92.3076
24	31.5789	49	96.0784
25	33.3333	50	100.

40.8451%. To find the markup, multiply the cost price, $15.00 by 40.8451; the result is $6.13. The selling price is $15.00 plus $6.13, or $21.13.

To find the markup without the use of the table, the procedure would be as follows:

1. Let 100% represent the selling price.
2. Deduct from 100% the sum of the percentage deductions from selling price.
3. Divide the total deductions from the selling price by the figure found in (2).

$$100\% = \text{selling price}$$
$$100\% - (2\% + 5\% + 15\% + 7\%) = 71\%$$
$$29\% \div 71\% = 40.8451\%$$

To find the selling price without the use of the table, the procedure would be as follows:

1. Let 100% represent the selling price.
2. Deduct from 100% the total deductions from the selling price and the percentage of net profit desired.
3. Divide the cost price by the figure found in (2).

Solution

$$100\% = \text{selling price}$$
$$100\% - (2\% + 5\% + 15\% + 7\%) = 71\%$$
$$\$15.00 \div 71\% = \frac{15}{1} \times \frac{100}{71} = \$21.13, \text{ the selling price}$$

9. HOW TO CALCULATE COMPOUND INTEREST

Adapted from Moore, "Handbook of Financial Mathematics"
New York: Prentice-Hall, Inc.

How to calculate the compound amount. The compound amount of any sum is the amount to which that sum accumulates in a specified time and at a specified rate of compound interest. Thus the compound amount is the original investment, or principal, plus the compound interest. The compound amount minus the original principal is the compound interest.

Table of compound amount of 1. The table (pages 1313-16) shows the compound amount of 1 ($1, £1, 1 peso, or any other monetary unit) for different numbers of periods and at different rates of interest per period. In calculating, by the use of the table, the amount to which any sum accumulates at compound interest, the procedure is as follows:

1. Find in the table the compound amount of 1 for the given number of periods and at the given rate of interest per period.
2. Multiply this figure by the original principal.

How to calculate the number of periods and the rate of interest per period. The rate of interest is usually expressed as a certain percent per year. The interest at this stated percent per year may, however, be compounded more often than once a year; as, semi-annually, quarterly, monthly.

1. The number of periods is the number of years.
2. The rate of interest per period is the stated rate.

If the interest is compounded more often than once a year:

1. The number of periods is the number of years multiplied by the times per year that the interest is compounded. Thus, if the number of years is 5 and the interest is compounded quarterly, the number of periods is $5 \times 4 = 20$. If the number of years is 3 years and 6 months and the interest is compounded semiannually, the number of periods is $3\frac{1}{2} \times 2 = 7$.

2. The rate of interest per period is the stated rate divided by the times per year that the interest is compounded. Thus, if the stated rate is 4% per year compounded quarterly, the rate of interest per period is $4\% \div 4 = 1\%$.

EXAMPLE 1

What will $1,000.00 amount to in 10 years at 4% per year compounded annually?

Solution

Since the interest is compounded annually, the number of periods is the number of years, 10, and the rate of interest per period is the stated rate, 4%. Then:

(1) In the table (page 1315) the figure given in the 4% column opposite 10 is 1.48024428. This is the amount to which $1.00 will accumulate in 10 years at 4% per year compounded annually.

(2) To find what $1,000.00 will amount to, multiply 1.48024428 by 1,000. The result is $1,480.24.

EXAMPLE 2

What will $1,000.00 amount to in 10 years at 4% per year compounded quarterly?

Solution

Since the interest is compounded more often than once a year, the number of periods is the number of years multiplied by the times per year that the interest is compounded; $10 \times 4 = 40$. The rate of interest per period is the stated rate divided by the times per year that the interest is compounded; $4\% \div 4 = 1\%$. Then:

(1) In the table (page 1313) the figure given in the 1% column opposite 40 is 1.48886373. This is the amount to which $1.00 will accumulate in 10 years at 4% per year compounded quarterly.

(2) To find what $1,000.00 will amount to, multiply 1.48886373 by 1,000. The result is $1,488.86.

Formula for compound amount.—The compound amount may also be calculated by the use of the formula

$$P(1+i)^n$$

where

P = original principal
i = rate of interest per period
n = number of periods

How to calculate the compound present value. The compound present value (or present worth) of a sum of money due at a fixed future date is that sum which, at compound interest, will increase in the given time to the sum due. Thus, if $10,000.00 is due 4 years hence, and money is worth 4% per year compounded semiannually, the compound present value is that principal which, placed at interest now at 4% per year compounded semiannually, will accumulate in 4 years to $10,000.00.

Table of compound present value of 1. The table (pages 1317-20) shows the compound present value of 1 ($1, £1, 1 peso, or any other monetary unit) for different numbers of periods and at different rates of interest per period. In calculating, by the use of the table, the compound present value of any sum, the procedure is as follows:

1. Find in the table the compound present value of 1 for the given number of periods and at the given rate of interest per period.
2. Multiply this figure by the sum whose present value is to be ascertained.

For method of determining number of periods and rate of interest per period, see page 1309, "How to calculate the number of periods and the rate of interest per period."

EXAMPLE

The Maryland Finance Company signs an agreement to sell a piece of real estate 2 years and 3 months hence for $33,500.00. If money is worth 4% per year compounded quarterly, what is the present value of the contract?

Solution

Since the interest is compounded quarterly, the number of periods is $2\frac{1}{4} \times 4 = 9$. The rate of interest per period is $4\% \div 4 = 1\%$. Then:

(1) In the table (page 1317) the figure given in the 1% column opposite 9 is 0.91433982. This is the compound present value of $1.00 for 2 years and 3 months at 4% per year compounded quarterly.

(2) To find the compound present value of $33,500.00, multiply 0.91433982 by 33,500. The result, $30,630.38, is the present value of the contract.

Formula for compound present value. The compound present value may also be calculated by the use of the formula

$$P\left(\frac{1}{(1+i)^n}\right)$$

where

P = sum whose present value is to be ascertained
i = rate of interest per period
n = number of periods

How to calculate the compound present value of an interest-bearing debt. To find the compound present value of a debt bearing compound interest, two steps are necessary.

1. Calculate the compound amount of the debt; that is, the face plus the compound interest to maturity.
2. Calculate the compound present value of the result found in 1.

EXAMPLE

The Brockton Machine Tool Company is put into a receiver's hands. Among the assets is a 5-year obligation of $9,500.00 bearing interest at 5½% per year compounded annually. What is the present value of the asset if money is worth 6% per year compounded annually?

Solution

(1) Calculation of compound amount: The number of periods is 5. The rate of interest per period is 5½%. The table (page 1316) shows the compound amount of 1 for 5 periods at 5½% per period to be 1.30696001. Hence the compound amount of $9,500.00 is 1.30696001 × 9,500 = $12,416.12.

(2) Calculation of compound present value: The number of periods is 5. The rate of interest per period is 6%. The table (page 1320) shows the compound present value of 1 for 5 periods at 6% per period to be 0.74725817. Hence the compound present value of $12,416.12 (the result found in the preceding step) is 0.74725817 × 12,416.12 = $9,278.05. Thus the receiver of the Brockton Machine Tool Company holds an asset whose present value is $9,278.05.

COMPOUND AMOUNT OF 1

	½%	⅝%	¾%	⅞%	1%	1⅛%
1	1.0050 0000	1.0062 5000	1.0075 0000	1.0087 5000	1.0100 0000	1.0112 5000
2	1.0100 2500	1.0125 3906	1.0150 5625	1.0175 7656	1.0201 0000	1.0226 2656
3	1.0150 7513	1.0188 6743	1.0226 6917	1.0264 8036	1.0303 0100	1.0341 3111
4	1.0201 5050	1.0252 3535	1.0303 3919	1.0354 6206	1.0406 0401	1.0457 6509
5	1.0252 5125	1.0316 4307	1.0380 6673	1.0445 2235	1.0510 1005	1.0575 2994
6	1.0303 7751	1.0380 9084	1.0458 5224	1.0536 6192	1.0615 2015	1.0694 2716
7	1.0355 2940	1.0445 7891	1.0536 9613	1.0628 8147	1.0721 3535	1.0814 5821
8	1.0407 0704	1.0511 0753	1.0615 9885	1.0721 8168	1.0828 5671	1.0936 2462
9	1.0459 1058	1.0576 7695	1.0695 6084	1.0815 6327	1.0936 8527	1.1059 2789
10	1.0511 4013	1.0642 8743	1.0775 8255	1.0910 2695	1.1046 2213	1 1183 6958
11	1.0563 9583	1.0709 3923	1.0856 6441	1.1005 7343	1.1156 6835	1.1309 5124
12	1.0616 7781	1.0776 3260	1.0938 0690	1.1102 0345	1.1268 2503	1.1436 7444
13	1.0669 8620	1.0843 6780	1.1020 1045	1.1199 1773	1.1380 9328	1.1565 4078
14	1.0723 2113	1.0911 4510	1.1102 7553	1.1297 1701	1.1494 7421	1.1695 5186
15	1.0776 8274	1.0979 6476	1.1186 0259	1.1396 0203	1.1609 6896	1.1827 0932
16	1.0830 7115	1.1048 2704	1.1269 9211	1.1495 7355	1.1725 7864	1.1960 1480
17	1.0884 8651	1.1117 3221	1.1354 4455	1.1596 3232	1.1843 0443	1.2094 6997
18	1.0939 2894	1.1186 8053	1.1439 6039	1.1697 7910	1.1961 4748	1.2230 7650
19	1.0993 9858	1.1256 7229	1.1525 4009	1.1800 1467	1.2081 0895	1.2368 3611
20	1.1048 9558	1.1327 0774	1.1611 8414	1.1903 3980	1.2201 9004	1.2507 5052
21	1.1104 2006	1.1397 8716	1.1698 9302	1.2007 5527	1.2323 9194	1.2648 2146
22	1.1159 7216	1.1469 1083	1.1786 6722	1.2112 6188	1.2447 1586	1.2790 5071
23	1.1215 5202	1.1540 7902	1.1875 0723	1.2218 6042	1.2571 6302	1.2934 4003
24	1.1271 5978	1.1612 9202	1.1964 1353	1.2325 5170	1.2697 3465	1.3079 9123
25	1.1327 9558	1 1685 5009	1.2053 8663	1.2433 3653	1.2824 3200	1.3227 0613
26	1.1384 5955	1.1758 5353	1.2144 2703	1.2542 1572	1.2952 5631	1.3375 8657
27	1.1441 5185	1.1832 0262	1.2235 3523	1.2651 9011	1.3082 0888	1.3526 3442
28	1.1498 7261	1.1905 9763	1.2327 1175	1.2762 6052	1.3212 9097	1.3678 5156
29	1.1556 2197	1.1980 3887	1.2419 5709	1.2874 2780	1.3345 0388	1.3832 3989
30	1.1614 0008	1.2055 2661	1.2512 7176	1.2986 9280	1.3478 4892	1.3988 0134
31	1.1672 0708	1.2130 6115	1.2606 5630	1.3100 5636	1.3613 2740	1.4145 3785
32	1.1730 4312	1.2206 4278	1.2701 1122	1.3215 1935	1.3749 4068	1.4304 5140
33	1.1789 0833	1.2282 7180	1.2796 3706	1.3330 8265	1.3886 9009	1.4465 4398
34	1.1848 0288	1.2359 4850	1.2892 3434	1.3447 4712	1.4025 7699	1.4628 1760
35	1.1907 2689	1.2436 7318	1.2989 0359	1.3565 1366	1.4166 0276	1.4792 7430
36	1.1966 8052	1.2514 4614	1.3086 4537	1.3683 8315	1.4307 6878	1.4959 1613
37	1.2026 6393	1.2592 6767	1.3184 6021	1.3803 5650	1.4450 7647	1.5127 4519
38	1.2086 7725	1.2671 3810	1.3283 4866	1.3924 3462	1.4595 2724	1.5297 6357
39	1.2147 2063	1.2750 5771	1.3383 1128	1.4046 1843	1.4741 2251	1.5469 7341
40	1.2207 9424	1.2830 2682	1.3483 4861	1.4169 0884	1.4888 6373	1.5643 7687
41	1.2268 9821	1.2910 4574	1.3584 6123	1.4293 0679	1.5037 5237	1.5819 7611
42	1.2330 3270	1.2991 1477	1.3686 4969	1.4418 1322	1.5187 8989	1.5997 7334
43	1.2391 9786	1.3072 3424	1.3789 1456	1.4544 2909	1.5339 7779	1.6177 7079
44	1.2453 9385	1.3154 0446	1.3892 5642	1.4671 5534	1.5493 1757	1.6359 7071
45	1.2516 2082	1.3236 2573	1.3996 7584	1.4799 9295	1.5648 1075	1.6543 7538
46	1.2578 7892	1.3318 9839	1.4101 7341	1.4929 4289	1.5804 5885	1.6729 8710
47	1.2641 6832	1.3402 2276	1.4207 4971	1.5060 0614	1.5962 6344	1.6918 0821
48	1.2704 8916	1.3485 9915	1.4314 0533	1.5191 8370	1.6122 2608	1.7108 4105
49	1.2768 4161	1.3570 2790	1.4421 4087	1.5324 7655	1.6283 4834	1.7300 8801
50	1.2832 2581	1.3655 0932	1.4529 5693	1.5458 8572	1.6446 3182	1.7495 5150
51	1.2896 4194	1.3740 4375	1.4638 5411	1.5594 1222	1.6610 7814	1.7692 3395
52	1.2960 9015	1.3826 3153	1.4748 3301	1.5730 5708	1.6776 8892	1.7891 3784
53	1.3025 7060	1.3912 7297	1.4858 9426	1.5868 2133	1.6944 6581	1.8092 6564
54	1.3090 8346	1.3999 6843	1.4970 3847	1.6007 0602	1.7114 1047	1.8296 1988
55	1.3156 2887	1.4087 1823	1.5082 6626	1.6147 1219	1.7285 2457	1.8502 0310
56	1.3222 0702	1.4175 2272	1.5195 7825	1.6288 4093	1.7458 0982	1.8710 1788
57	1.3288 1805	1.4263 8224	1.5309 7509	1.6430 9328	1.7632 6792	1.8920 6684
58	1.3354 6214	1.4352 9713	1.5424 5740	1.6574 7035	1.7809 0060	1.9133 5259
59	1.3421 3946	1.4442 6773	1.5540 2583	1.6719 7322	1.7987 0960	1.9348 7780
60	1.3488 5015	1.4532 9441	1.5656 8103	1.6866 0298	1.8166 9670	1.9566 4518

From J. W. Glover, "Tables of Applied Math. in Finance, Insurance, Statistics." George Wahr, publisher, Ann Arbor, Michigan.

COMPOUND AMOUNT OF 1 (*Cont.*)

	1¼%	1⅜%	1½%	1¾%	2%	2¼%
1	1.0125 0000	1.0137 5000	1.0150 0000	1.0175 0000	1.0200 0000	1.0225 0000
2	1.0251 5625	1.0276 8906	1.0302 2500	1.0353 0625	1.0404 0000	1.0455 0625
3	1.0379 7070	1.0418 1979	1.0456 7838	1.0534 2411	1.0612 0800	1.0690 3014
4	1.0509 4534	1.0561 4481	1.0613 6355	1.0718 5903	1.0824 3216	1.0930 8332
5	1.0640 8215	1.0706 6680	1.0772 8400	1.0906 1656	1.1040 8080	1.1176 7769
6	1.0773 8318	1.0853 8847	1.0934 4326	1.1097 0235	1.1261 6242	1.1428 2544
7	1.0908 5047	1.1003 1256	1.1098 4491	1.1291 2215	1.1486 8567	1.1685 3901
8	1.1044 8610	1.1154 4186	1.1264 9259	1.1488 8178	1.1716 5938	1.1948 3114
9	1.1182 9218	1.1307 7918	1.1433 8998	1.1689 8721	1.1950 9257	1.2217 1484
10	1.1322 7083	1.1463 2740	1.1605 4083	1.1894 4449	1.2189 9442	1.2492 0343
11	1.1464 2422	1.1620 8940	1.1779 4894	1.2102 5977	1.2433 7431	1.2773 1050
12	1.1607 5452	1.1780 6813	1.1956 1817	1.2314 3931	1.2682 4179	1.3060 4999
13	1.1752 6395	1.1942 6656	1.2135 5244	1.2529 8950	1.2936 0663	1.3354 3611
14	1.1899 5475	1.2106 8773	1.2317 5573	1.2749 1682	1.3194 7876	1.3654 8343
15	1.2048 2918	1.2273 3469	1.2502 3207	1.2972 2786	1.3458 6834	1.3962 0680
16	1.2198 8955	1.2442 1054	1.2689 8555	1.3199 2935	1.3727 8571	1.4276 2146
17	1.2351 3817	1.2613 1843	1.2880 2033	1.3430 2811	1.4002 4142	1.4597 4294
18	1.2505 7739	1.2786 6156	1.3073 4064	1.3665 3111	1.4282 4625	1.4925 8716
19	1.2662 0961	1.2962 4316	1.3269 5075	1.3904 4540	1.4568 1117	1.5261 7037
20	1.2820 3723	1.3140 6650	1.3468 5501	1.4147 7820	1.4859 4740	1.5605 0920
21	1.2980 6270	1.3321 3492	1.3670 5783	1.4395 3681	1.5156 6634	1.5956 2066
22	1.3142 8848	1.3504 5177	1.3875 6370	1.4647 2871	1.5459 7967	1.6315 2212
23	1.3307 1709	1.3690 2048	1.4083 7715	1.4903 6146	1.5768 9926	1.6682 3137
24	1.3473 5105	1.3878 4451	1.4295 0281	1.5164 4279	1.6084 3725	1.7057 6658
25	1.3641 9294	1.4069 2738	1.4509 4535	1.5429 8054	1.6406 0599	1.7441 4632
26	1.3812 4535	1.4262 7263	1.4727 0953	1.5699 8269	1.6734 1811	1.7833 8962
27	1.3985 1092	1.4458 8388	1.4948 0018	1.5974 5739	1.7068 8648	1.8235 1588
28	1.4159 9230	1.4657 6478	1.5172 2218	1.6254 1290	1.7410 2421	1.8645 4499
29	1.4336 9221	1.4859 1905	1.5399 8051	1.6538 5762	1.7758 4469	1.9064 9725
30	1.4516 1336	1.5063 5043	1.5630 8022	1.6828 0013	1.8113 6158	1.9493 9344
31	1.4697 5853	1.5270 6275	1.5865 2642	1.7122 4913	1.8475 8882	1.9932 5479
32	1.4881 3051	1.5480 5986	1.6103 2432	1.7422 1349	1.8845 4059	2.0381 0303
33	1.5067 3214	1.5693 4569	1.6344 7918	1.7727 0223	1.9222 3140	2.0839 6034
34	1.5255 6629	1.5909 2419	1.6589 9637	1.8037 2452	1.9606 7603	2.1308 4945
35	1.5446 3587	1.6127 9940	1.6838 8132	1.8352 8970	1.9998 8955	2.1787 9356
36	1.5639 4382	1.6349 7539	1.7091 3954	1.8674 0727	2.0398 8734	2.2278 1642
37	1.5834 9312	1.6574 5630	1.7347 7663	1.9000 8689	2.0806 8509	2.2779 4229
38	1.6032 8678	1.6802 4633	1.7607 9828	1.9333 3841	2.1222 9879	2.3291 9599
39	1.6233 2787	1.7033 4971	1.7872 1025	1.9671 7184	2.1647 4477	2.3816 0290
40	1.6436 1946	1.7267 7077	1.8140 1841	2.0015 9734	2.2080 3966	2.4351 8897
41	1.6641 6471	1.7505 1387	1.8412 2868	2.0366 2530	2.2522 0046	2.4899 8072
42	1.6849 6677	1.7745 8343	1.8688 4712	2.0722 6624	2.2972 4447	2.5460 0528
43	1.7060 2885	1.7989 8396	1.8968 7982	2.1085 3090	2.3431 8936	2.6032 9040
44	1.7273 5421	1.8237 1999	1.9253 3302	2.1454 3019	2.3900 5314	2.6618 6444
45	1.7489 4614	1.8487 9614	1.9542 1301	2.1829 7522	2.4378 5421	2.7217 5639
46	1.7708 0797	1.8742 1708	1.9835 2621	2.2211 7728	2.4866 1129	2.7829 9590
47	1.7929 4306	1.8999 8757	2.0132 7910	2.2600 4789	2.5363 4351	2.8456 1331
48	1.8153 5485	1.9261 1240	2.0434 7829	2.2995 9872	2.5870 7039	2.9096 3961
49	1.8380 4679	1.9525 9644	2.0741 3046	2.3398 4170	2.6388 1179	2.9751 0650
50	1.8610 2237	1.9794 4464	2.1052 4242	2.3807 8893	2.6915 8803	3.0420 4640
51	1.8842 8515	2.0066 6201	2.1368 2106	2.4224 5274	2.7454 1979	3.1104 9244
52	1.9078 3872	2.0342 5361	2.1688 7337	2.4648 4566	2.8003 2819	3.1804 7852
53	1.9316 8670	2.0622 2460	2.2014 0647	2.5079 8046	2.8563 3475	3.2520 3929
54	1.9558 3279	2.0905 8019	2.2344 2757	2.5518 7012	2.9134 6144	3.3252 1017
55	1.9802 8070	2.1193 2566	2.2679 4398	2.5965 2785	2.9717 3067	3.4000 2740
56	2.0050 3420	2.1484 6639	2.3019 6314	2.6419 6708	3.0311 6529	3.4765 2802
57	2.0300 9713	2.1780 0780	2.3364 9259	2.6882 0151	3.0917 8859	3.5547 4990
58	2.0554 7335	2.2079 5541	2.3715 3998	2.7352 4503	3.1536 2436	3.6347 3177
59	2.0811 6676	2.2383 1480	2.4071 1308	2.7831 1182	3.2166 9685	3.7165 1324
60	2.1071 8135	2.2690 9163	2.4432 1978	2.8318 1628	3.2810 3079	3.8001 3479

COMPOUND AMOUNT OF 1 (*Cont.*)

	2½%	2¾%	3%	3½%	4%	4½%
1	1.0250 0000	1.0275 0000	1.0300 0000	1.0350 0000	1.0400 0000	1.0450 0000
2	1.0506 2500	1.0557 5625	1.0609 0000	1.0712 2500	1.0816 0000	1.0920 2500
3	1.0768 9063	1.0847 8955	1.0927 2700	1.1087 1788	1.1248 6400	1.1411 6613
4	1.1038 1289	1.1146 2126	1.1255 0881	1.1475 2300	1.1698 5856	1.1925 1860
5	1.1314 0821	1.1452 7334	1.1592 7407	1.1876 8631	1.2166 5290	1.2461 8194
6	1.1596 9342	1.1767 6836	1.1940 5230	1.2292 5533	1.2653 1902	1.3022 6012
7	1.1886 8575	1.2091 2949	1.2298 7387	1.2722 7926	1.3159 3178	1.3608 6183
8	1.2184 0290	1.2423 8055	1.2667 7008	1.3168 0904	1.3685 6905	1.4221 0061
9	1.2488 6297	1.2765 4602	1.3047 7318	1.3628 9735	1.4233 1181	1.4860 9514
10	1.2800 8454	1.3116 5103	1.3439 1638	1.4105 9876	1.4802 4428	1.5529 6942
11	1.3120 8666	1.3477 2144	1.3842 3387	1.4599 6972	1.5394 5406	1.6228 5305
12	1.3448 8882	1.3847 8378	1.4257 6089	1.5110 6866	1.6010 3222	1.6958 8143
13	1.3785 1104	1.4228 6533	1.4685 3371	1.5639 5606	1.6650 7351	1.7721 9610
14	1.4129 7382	1.4619 9413	1.5125 8972	1.6186 9452	1.7316 7645	1.8519 4492
15	1.4482 9817	1.5021 9896	1.5579 6742	1.6753 4883	1.8009 4351	1.9352 8244
16	1.4845 0562	1.5435 0944	1.6047 0644	1.7339 8604	1.8729 8125	2.0223 7015
17	1.5216 1826	1.5859 5595	1.6528 4763	1.7946 7555	1.9479 0050	2.1133 7681
18	1.5596 5872	1.6295 6973	1.7024 3306	1.8574 8920	2.0258 1652	2.2084 7877
19	1.5986 5019	1.6743 8290	1.7535 0605	1.9225 0132	2.1068 4918	2.3078 6031
20	1.6386 1644	1.7204 2843	1.8061 1123	1.9897 8886	2.1911 2314	2.4117 1402
21	1.6795 8185	1.7677 4021	1.8602 9457	2.0594 3147	2.2787 6807	2.5202 4116
22	1.7215 7140	1.8163 5307	1.9161 0341	2.1315 1158	2.3699 1879	2.6336 5201
23	1.7646 1068	1.8663 0278	1.9735 8651	2.2061 1448	2.4647 1554	2.7521 6635
24	1.8087 2595	1.9176 2610	2.0327 9411	2.2833 2849	2.5633 0416	2.8760 1383
25	1.8539 4410	1.9703 6082	2.0937 7793	2.3632 4498	2.6658 3633	3.0054 3446
26	1.9002 9270	2.0245 4575	2.1565 9127	2.4459 5856	2.7724 6978	3.1406 7901
27	1.9478 0002	2.0802 2075	2.2212 8901	2.5315 6711	2.8833 6858	3.2820 0956
28	1.9964 9502	2.1374 2682	2.2879 2768	2.6201 7196	2.9987 0332	3.4296 9999
29	2.0464 0739	2.1962 0606	2.3565 6551	2.7118 7798	3.1186 5145	3.5840 3649
30	2.0975 6758	2.2566 0173	2.4272 6247	2.8067 9370	3.2433 9751	3.7453 1813
31	2.1500 0677	2.3186 5828	2.5000 8035	2.9050 3148	3.3731 3341	3.9138 5745
32	2.2037 5694	2.3824 2138	2.5750 8276	3.0067 0759	3.5080 5875	4.0899 8104
33	2.2588 5086	2.4479 3797	2.6523 3524	3.1119 4235	3.6483 8110	4.2740 3018
34	2.3153 2213	2.5152 5626	2.7319 0530	3.2208 6033	3.7943 1634	4.4663 6154
35	2.3732 0519	2.5844 2581	2.8138 6245	3.3335 9045	3.9460 8899	4.6673 4781
36	2.4325 3532	2.6554 9752	2.8982 7833	3.4502 6611	4.1039 3255	4.8773 7846
37	2.4933 4870	2.7285 2370	2.9852 2668	3.5710 2543	4.2680 8986	5.0968 6049
38	2.5556 8242	2.8035 5810	3.0747 8348	3.6960 1132	4.4388 1345	5.3262 1921
39	2.6195 7448	2.8806 5595	3.1670 2698	3.8253 7171	4.6163 6599	5.5658 9908
40	2.6850 6384	2.9598 7399	3.2620 3779	3.9592 5972	4.8010 2063	5.8163 6454
41	2.7521 9043	3.0412 7052	3.3598 9893	4.0978 3381	4.9930 6145	6.0781 0094
42	2.8209 9520	3.1249 0546	3.4606 9589	4.2412 5799	5.1927 8391	6.3516 1548
43	2.8915 2008	3.2108 4036	3.5645 1677	4.3897 0202	5.4004 9527	6.6374 3818
44	2.9638 0808	3.2991 3847	3.6714 5227	4.5433 4160	5.6165 1508	6.9361 2290
45	3.0379 0328	3.3898 6478	3.7815 9584	4.7023 5855	5.8411 7568	7.2482 4843
46	3.1138 5086	3.4830 8606	3.8950 4372	4.8669 4110	6.0748 2271	7.5744 1961
47	3.1916 9713	3.5788 7093	4.0118 9503	5.0372 8404	6.3178 1562	7.9152 6849
48	3.2714 8956	3.6772 8988	4.1322 5188	5.2135 8898	6.5705 2824	8.2714 5557
49	3.3532 7680	3.7784 1535	4.2562 1944	5.3960 6459	6.8333 4937	8.6436 7107
50	3.4371 0872	3.8823 2177	4.3839 0602	5.5849 2686	7.1066 8335	9.0326 3627
51	3.5230 3644	3.9890 8562	4.5154 2320	5.7803 9930	7.3909 5068	9.4391 0490
52	3.6111 1235	4.0987 8547	4.6508 8590	5.9827 1327	7.6865 8871	9.8638 6463
53	3.7013 9016	4.2115 0208	4.7904 1247	6.1921 0824	7.9940 5226	10.3077 3853
54	3.7939 2491	4.3273 1838	4.9341 2485	6.4088 3202	8.3138 1435	10.7715 8677
55	3.8887 7303	4.4463 1964	5.0821 4859	6.6331 4114	8.6463 6692	11.2563 0817
56	3.9859 9236	4.5685 9343	5.2346 1305	6.8653 0108	8.9922 2160	11.7628 4204
57	4.0856 4217	4.6942 2975	5.3916 5144	7.1055 8662	9.3519 1046	12.2921 6993
58	4.1877 8322	4.8233 2107	5.5534 0098	7.3542 8215	9.7259 8688	12.8453 1758
59	4.2924 7780	4.9559 6239	5.7200 0301	7.6116 8203	10.1150 2635	13.4233 5687
60	4.3997 8975	5.0922 5136	5.8916 0310	7.8780 9090	10.5196 2741	14.0274 0793

	5%	5½%	6%	6½%	7%	8%
1	1.0500 0000	1.0550 0000	1.0600 0000	1.0650 0000	1.0700 0000	1.0800 0000
2	1.1025 0000	1.1130 2500	1.1236 0000	1.1342 2500	1.1449 0000	1.1664 0000
3	1.1576 2500	1.1742 4138	1.1910 1600	1.2079 4963	1.2250 4300	1.2597 1200
4	1.2155 0625	1.2388 2465	1.2624 7696	1.2864 6635	1.3107 9601	1.3604 8896
5	1.2762 8156	1.3069 6001	1.3382 2558	1.3700 8666	1.4025 5173	1.4693 2808
6	1.3400 9564	1.3788 4281	1.4185 1911	1.4591 4230	1.5007 3035	1.5868 7432
7	1.4071 0042	1.4546 7916	1.5036 3026	1.5539 8655	1.6057 8148	1.7138 2427
8	1.4774 5544	1.5346 8651	1.5938 4807	1.6549 9567	1.7181 8618	1.8509 3021
9	1.5513 2822	1.6190 9427	1.6894 7896	1.7625 7039	1.8384 5921	1.9990 0463
0	1.6288 9463	1.7081 4446	1.7908 4770	1.8771 3747	1.9671 5136	2.1589 2500
11	1.7103 3936	1.8020 9240	1.8982 9856	1.9991 5140	2.1048 5195	2.3316 3900
12	1.7958 5633	1.9012 0749	2.0121 9647	2.1290 9624	2.2521 9159	2.5181 7012
13	1.8856 4914	2.0057 7390	2.1329 2826	2.2674 8750	2.4098 4500	2.7196 2373
14	1.9799 3160	2.1160 9146	2.2609 0396	2.4148 7418	2.5785 3415	2.9371 9362
15	2.0789 2818	2.2324 7649	2.3965 5819	2.5718 4101	2.7590 3154	3.1721 6911
16	2.1828 7459	2.3552 6270	2.5403 5168	2.7390 1067	2.9521 6375	3.4259 4264
17	2.2920 1832	2.4848 0215	2.6927 7279	2.9170 4637	3.1588 1521	3.7000 1805
18	2.4066 1923	2.6214 6627	2.8543 3915	3.1066 5438	3.3799 3228	3.9960 1950
19	2.5269 5020	2.7656 4691	3.0255 9950	3.3085 8691	3.6165 2754	4.3157 0106
20	2.6532 9771	2.9177 5749	3.2071 3547	3.5236 4506	3.8696 8446	4.6609 5714
21	2.7859 6259	3.0782 3415	3.3995 6360	3.7526 8199	4.1405 6237	5.0338 3372
22	2.9252 6072	3.2475 3703	3.6035 3742	3.9966 0632	4.4304 0174	5.4365 4041
23	3.0715 2376	3.4261 5157	3.8197 4966	4.2563 8573	4.7405 2986	5.8714 6365
24	3.2250 9994	3.6145 8990	4.0489 3464	4.5330 5081	5.0723 6695	6.3411 8074
25	3.3863 5494	3.8133 9235	4.2918 7072	4.8276 9911	5.4274 3264	6.8484 7520
26	3.5556 7269	4.0231 2893	4.5493 8296	5.1414 9955	5.8073 5292	7.3963 5321
27	3.7334 5632	4.2444 0102	4.8223 4594	5.4756 9702	6.2138 6763	7.9880 6147
28	3.9201 2914	4.4778 4307	5.1116 8670	5.8316 1733	6.6488 3836	8.6271 0639
29	4.1161 3560	4.7241 2444	5.4183 8790	6.2106 7245	7.1142 5705	9.3172 7490
30	4.3219 4238	4.9839 5129	5.7434 9117	6.6143 6616	7.6122 5504	10.0626 5689
31	4.5380 3949	5.2580 6861	6.0881 0064	7.0442 9996	8.1451 1290	10.8676 6944
32	4.7649 4147	5.5472 6238	6.4533 8668	7.5021 7946	8.7152 7080	11.7370 8300
33	5.0031 8854	5.8523 6181	6.8405 8988	7.9898 2113	9.3253 3975	12.6760 4964
34	5.2533 4797	6.1742 4171	7.2510 2528	8.5091 5950	9.9781 1354	13.6901 3361
35	5.5160 1537	6.5138 2501	7.6860 8679	9.0622 5487	10.6765 8148	14.7853 4429
36	5.7918 1614	6.8720 8538	8.1472 5200	9.6513 0143	11.4239 4219	15.9681 7184
37	6.0814 0694	7.2500 5008	8.6360 8712	10.2786 3603	12.2236 1814	17.2456 2558
38	6.3854 7729	7.6488 0283	9.1542 5235	10.9467 4737	13.0792 7141	18.6252 7563
39	6.7047 5115	8.0694 8699	9.7035 0749	11.6582 8595	13.9948 2041	20.1152 9768
40	7.0399 8871	8.5133 0877	10.2857 1794	12.4160 7453	14.9744 5784	21.7245 2150
41	7.3919 8815	8.9815 4076	10.9028 6101	13.2231 1938	16.0226 6989	23.4624 8322
42	7.7615 8756	9.4755 2550	11.5570 3267	14.0826 2214	17.1442 5678	25.3394 8187
43	8.1496 6693	9.9966 7940	12.2504 5463	14.9979 9258	18.3443 5475	27.3666 4042
44	8.5571 5028	10.5464 9677	12.9854 8191	15.9728 6209	19.6284 5959	29.5559 7166
45	8.9850 0779	11.1265 5409	13.7646 1083	17.0110 9813	21.0024 5176	31.9204 4939
46	9.4342 5818	11.7385 1456	14.5904 8748	18.1168 1951	22.4726 2338	34.4740 8534
47	9.9059 7109	12.3841 3287	15.4659 1673	19.2944 1278	24.0457 0702	37.2320 1217
48	10.4012 6965	13.0652 6017	16.3938 7173	20.5485 4961	25.7289 0651	40.2105 7314
49	10.9213 3313	13.7838 4948	17.3775 0403	21.8842 0533	27.5299 2997	43.4274 1899
50	11.4673 9979	14.5419 6120	18.4201 5427	23.3066 7868	29.4570 2506	46.9016 1251
51	12.0407 6978	15.3417 6907	19.5253 6353	24.8216 1279	31.5190 1682	50.6537 4151
52	12.6428 0826	16.1855 6637	20.6968 8534	26.4350 1762	33.7253 4799	54.7060 4084
53	13.2749 4868	17.0757 7252	21.9386 9846	28.1532 9377	36.0861 2235	59.0825 2410
54	13.9386 9611	18.0149 4001	23.2550 2037	29.9832 5786	38.6121 5092	63.8091 2603
55	14.6356 3092	19.0057 6171	24.6503 2159	31.9321 6963	41.3150 0148	68.9138 5611
56	15.3674 1246	20.0510 7860	26.1293 4089	34.0077 6065	44.2070 5159	74.4269 6460
57	16.1357 8309	21.1538 8793	27.6971 0134	36.2182 6509	47.3015 4520	80.3811 2177
58	16.9425 7224	22.3173 5176	29.3589 2742	38.5724 5233	50.6126 5336	86.8116 1151
59	17.7897 0085	23.5448 0611	31.1204 6307	41.0796 6173	54.1555 3910	93.7565 4043
60	18.6791 8589	24.8397 7045	32.9876 9085	43.7498 3974	57.9464 2683	101.2570 6367

COMPOUND PRESENT VALUE OF 1

n	½%	⅝%	¾%	⅞%	1%	1⅛%
1	0.9950 2488	0.9937 8882	0.9925 5583	0.9913 2590	0.9900 9901	0.9888 7515
2	0.9900 7450	0.9876 1622	0.9851 6708	0.9827 2704	0.9802 9605	0.9778 7407
3	0.9851 4876	0.9814 8196	0.9778 3333	0.9742 0276	0.9705 9015	0.9669 9537
4	0.9802 4752	0.9753 8580	0.9705 5417	0.9657 5243	0.9609 8034	0.9562 3770
5	0.9753 7067	0.9693 2750	0.9633 2920	0.9573 7539	0.9514 6569	0.9455 9970
6	0.9705 1808	0.9633 0683	0.9561 5802	0.9490 7102	0.9420 4524	0.9350 8005
7	0.9656 8963	0.9573 2356	0.9490 4022	0.9408 3868	0.9327 1805	0.9246 7743
8	0.9608 8520	0.9513 7745	0.941 7540	0.9326 7775	0.9234 8322	0.9143 9054
9	0.9561 0468	0.9454 6827	0.9349 6318	0.9245 8761	0.9143 3982	0.9042 1808
10	0.9513 4794	0.9395 9580	0.9280 0315	0.9165 6765	0.9052 8695	0.8941 5881
11	0.9466 1489	0.9337 5980	0.9210 9494	0.9086 1724	0.8963 2372	0.8842 1142
12	0.9419 0534	0.9279 6005	0.9142 3815	0.9007 3581	0.8874 4923	0.8743 7470
13	0.9372 1924	0.9221 9632	0.9074 3241	0.8929 2273	0.8786 6260	0.8646 4742
14	0.9325 5646	0.9164 6840	0.9006 7733	0.8851 7743	0.8699 6297	0.8550 2835
15	0.9279 1688	0.9107 7604	0.8939 7254	0.8774 9931	0.8613 4947	0.8455 1629
16	0.9233 0037	0.9051 1905	0.8873 1766	0.8698 8779	0.8528 2126	0.8361 1005
17	0.9187 0684	0.8994 9719	0.8807 1231	0.8623 4230	0.8443 7749	0.8268 0846
18	0.9141 3616	0.8939 1025	0.8741 5614	0.8548 6225	0.8360 1731	0.8176 1034
19	0.9095 8822	0.8883 5802	0.8676 4878	0.8474 4709	0.8277 3992	0.8085 1455
20	0.9050 6290	0.8828 4027	0.8611 8985	0.8400 9624	0.8195 4447	0.7995 1995
21	0.9005 6010	0.8773 5679	0.8547 7901	0.8328 0917	0.8114 3017	0.7906 2542
22	0.8960 7971	0.8719 0736	0.8484 1589	0.8255 8530	0.8033 9621	0.7818 2983
23	0.8916 2160	0.8664 9179	0.8421 0014	0.8184 2409	0.7954 4179	0.7731 3210
24	0.8871 8567	0.8611 0985	0.8358 3140	0.8113 2499	0.7875 6613	0.7645 3112
25	0.8827 7181	0.8557 6135	0.8296 0933	0.8042 8748	0.7797 6844	0.7560 2583
26	0.8783 7991	0.8504 4606	0.8234 3358	0.7973 1101	0.7720 4796	0.7476 1516
27	0.8740 0986	0.8451 6378	0.8173 0380	0.7903 9505	0.7644 0392	0.7392 9806
28	0.8696 6155	0.8399 1432	0.8112 1966	0.7835 3908	0.7568 3557	0.7310 7348
29	0.8653 3488	0.8346 9746	0.8051 8080	0.7767 4258	0.7493 4215	0.7229 4040
30	0.8610 2973	0.8295 1300	0.7991 8690	0.7700 0504	0.7419 2292	0.7148 9780
31	0.8567 4600	0.8243 6075	0.7932 3762	0.7633 2594	0.7345 7715	0.7069 4467
32	0.8524 8358	0.8192 4050	0.7873 3262	0.7567 0477	0.7273 0411	0.6990 8002
33	0.8482 4237	0.8141 5205	0.7814 7158	0.7501 4104	0.7201 0307	0.6913 0287
34	0.8440 2226	0.8090 9520	0.7756 5418	0.7436 3424	0.7129 7334	0.6836 1223
35	0.8398 2314	0.8040 6976	0.7698 8008	0.7371 8388	0.7059 1420	0.6760 0715
36	0.8356 4492	0.7990 7554	0.7641 4896	0.7307 8947	0.6989 2495	0.6684 8667
37	0.8314 8748	0.7941 1234	0.7584 6051	0.7244 5053	0.6920 0490	0.6610 4986
38	0.8273 5073	0.7891 7997	0.7528 1440	0.7181 6657	0.6851 5337	0.6536 9578
39	0.8232 3455	0.7842 7823	0.7472 1032	0.7119 3712	0.6783 6967	0.6464 2352
40	0.8191 3886	0.7794 0693	0.7416 4796	0.7057 6171	0.6716 5314	0.6392 3216
41	0.8150 6354	0.7745 6590	0.7361 2701	0.6996 3986	0.6650 0311	0.6321 2080
42	0.8110 0850	0.7697 5493	0.7306 4716	0.6935 7111	0.6584 1892	0.6250 8855
43	0.8069 7363	0.7649 7384	0.7252 0809	0.6875 5500	0.6518 9992	0.6181 3454
44	0.8029 5884	0.7602 2245	0.7198 0952	0.6815 9108	0.6454 4546	0.6112 5789
45	0.7989 6402	0.7555 0057	0.7144 5114	0.6756 7889	0.6390 5492	0.6044 5774
46	0.7949 8907	0.7508 0802	0.7091 3264	0.6698 1798	0.6327 2764	0.5977 3324
47	0.7910 3390	0.7461 4462	0.7038 5374	0.6640 0792	0.6264 6301	0.5910 8355
48	0.7870 9841	0.7415 1018	0.6986 1414	0.6582 4824	0.6202 6041	0.5845 0784
49	0.7831 8250	0.7369 0453	0.6934 1353	0.6525 3853	0.6141 1921	0.5780 0528
50	0.7792 8607	0.7323 2748	0.6882 5165	0.6468 7835	0.6080 3882	0.5715 7506
51	0.7754 0902	0.7277 7886	0.6831 2819	0.6412 6726	0.6020 1864	0.5652 1637
52	0.7715 5127	0.7232 5849	0.6780 4286	0.6357 0484	0.5960 5806	0.5589 2843
53	0.7677 1270	0.7187 6620	0.6729 9540	0.6301 9067	0.5901 5649	0.5527 1044
54	0.7638 9324	0.7143 0182	0.6679 8551	0.6247 2433	0.5843 1336	0.5465 6162
55	0.7600 9277	0.7098 6516	0.6630 1291	0.6193 0541	0.5785 2808	0.5404 8120
56	0.7563 1122	0.7054 5606	0.6580 7733	0.6139 3349	0.5728 0008	0.5344 6843
57	0.7525 4847	0.7010 7434	0.6531 7849	0.6086 0817	0.5671 2879	0.5285 2256
58	0.7488 0445	0.6967 1985	0.6483 1612	0.6033 2904	0.5615 1365	0.5226 4282
59	0.7450 7906	0.6923 9239	0.6434 8995	0.5980 9571	0.5559 5411	0.5168 2850
60	0.7413 7220	0.6880 9182	0.6386 9970	0.5929 0776	0.5504 4962	0.5110 7887

From J. W. Glover, "Tables of Applied Math. in Finance, Insurance, Statistics." George Wahr, publisher, Ann Arbor, Michigan.

COMPOUND PRESENT VALUE OF 1 (*Cont.*)

	1¼%	1⅜%	1½%	1¾%	2%	2¼%
1	0.9876 5432	0.9864 3650	0.9852 2167	0.9828 0098	0.9803 9216	0.9779 9511
2	0.9754 6106	0.9730 5696	0.9706 6175	0.9658 9777	0.9611 6878	0.9564 7444
3	0.9634 1833	0.9598 5890	0.9563 1699	0.9492 8528	0.9423 2233	0.9354 2732
4	0.9515 2428	0.9468 3986	0.9421 8423	0.9329 5851	0.9238 4543	0.9148 4335
5	0.9397 7706	0.9339 9739	0.9282 6033	0.9169 1254	0.9057 3081	0.8947 1232
6	0.9281 7488	0.9213 2912	0.9145 4219	0.9011 4254	0.8879 7138	0.8750 2427
7	0.9167 1593	0.9088 3267	0.9010 2679	0.8856 4378	0.8705 6018	0.8557 6946
8	0.9053 9845	0.8965 0571	0.8877 1112	0.8704 1157	0.8534 9037	0.8369 3835
9	0.8942 2069	0.8843 4596	0.8745 9224	0.8554 4135	0.8367 5527	0.8185 2161
10	0.8831 8093	0.8723 5113	0.8616 6723	0.8407 2860	0.8203 4830	0.8005 1013
11	0.8722 7746	0.8605 1899	0.8489 3323	0.8262 6889	0.8042 6304	0.7828 9499
12	0.8615 0860	0.8488 4734	0.8363 8742	0.8120 5788	0.7884 9318	0.7656 6748
13	0.8508 7269	0.8373 3400	0.8240 2702	0.7980 9128	0.7730 3253	0.7488 1905
14	0.8403 6809	0.8259 7682	0.8118 4928	0.7843 6490	0.7578 7502	0.7323 4137
15	0.8299 9318	0.8147 7368	0.7998 5150	0.7708 7459	0.7430 1473	0.7162 2628
16	0.8197 4635	0.8037 2250	0.7880 3104	0.7576 1631	0.7284 4581	0.7004 6580
17	0.8096 2602	0.7928 2120	0.7763 8526	0.7445 8605	0.7141 6256	0.6850 5212
18	0.7996 3064	0.7820 6777	0.7649 1159	0.7317 7990	0.7001 5937	0.6699 7763
19	0.7897 5866	0.7714 6020	0.7536 0747	0.7191 9401	0.6864 3076	0.6552 3484
20	0.7800 0855	0.7609 9649	0.7424 7042	0.7068 2458	0.6729 7133	0.6408 1647
21	0.7703 7881	0.7506 7472	0.7314 9795	0.6946 6789	0.6597 7582	0.6267 1538
22	0.7608 6796	0.7404 9294	0.7206 8763	0.6827 2028	0.6468 3904	0.6129 2457
23	0.7514 7453	0.7304 4926	0.7100 3708	0.6709 7817	0.6341 5592	0.5994 3724
24	0.7421 9707	0.7205 4181	0.6995 4392	0.6594 3800	0.6217 2149	0.5862 4668
25	0.7330 3414	0.7107 6874	0.6892 0583	0.6480 9632	0.6095 3087	0.5733 4639
26	0.7239 8434	0.7011 2823	0.6790 2052	0.6369 4970	0.5975 7928	0.5607 2997
27	0.7150 4626	0.6916 1847	0.6689 8574	0.6259 9479	0.5858 6204	0.5483 9117
28	0.7062 1853	0.6822 3771	0.6590 9925	0.6152 2829	0.5743 7455	0.5363 2388
29	0.6974 9978	0.6729 8417	0.6493 5887	0.6046 4697	0.5631 1231	0.5245 2213
30	0.6888 8867	0.6638 5615	0.6397 6243	0.5942 4764	0.5520 7089	0.5129 8008
31	0.6803 8387	0.6548 5194	0.6303 0781	0.5840 2716	0.5412 4597	0.5016 9201
32	0.6719 8407	0.6459 6985	0.6209 9292	0.5739 8247	0.5306 3330	0.4906 5233
33	0.6636 8797	0.6372 0824	0.6118 1568	0.5641 1053	0.5202 2873	0.4798 5558
34	0.6554 9429	0.6285 6546	0.6027 7407	0.5544 0839	0.5100 2817	0.4692 9641
35	0.6474 0177	0.6200 3991	0.5938 6608	0.5448 7311	0.5000 2761	0.4589 6960
36	0.6394 0916	0.6116 3000	0.5850 8974	0.5355 0183	0.4902 2315	0.4488 7002
37	0.6315 1522	0.6033 3416	0.5764 4309	0.5262 9172	0.4806 1093	0.4389 9268
38	0.6237 1873	0.5951 5083	0.5679 2423	0.5172 4002	0.4711 8719	0.4293 3270
39	0.6160 1850	0.5870 7850	0.5595 3126	0.5083 4400	0.4619 4822	0.4198 8528
40	0.6084 1334	0.5791 1566	0.5512 6232	0.4996 0098	0.4528 9042	0.4106 4575
41	0.6009 0206	0.5712 6083	0.5431 1559	0.4910 0834	0.4440 1021	0.4016 0954
42	0.5934 8352	0.5635 1253	0.5350 8925	0.4825 6348	0.4353 0413	0.3927 7216
43	0.5861 5656	0.5558 6933	0.5271 8153	0.4742 6386	0.4267 6875	0.3841 2925
44	0.5789 2006	0.5483 2979	0.5193 9067	0.4661 0699	0.4184 0074	0.3756 7653
45	0.5717 7290	0.5408 9252	0.5117 1494	0.4580 9040	0.4101 9680	0.3674 0981
46	0.5647 1397	0.5335 5612	0.5041 5265	0.4502 1170	0.4021 5373	0.3593 2500
47	0.5577 4219	0.5263 1923	0.4967 0212	0.4424 6850	0.3942 6836	0.3514 1809
48	0.5508 5649	0.5191 8050	0.4893 6170	0.4348 5848	0.3865 3761	0.3436 8518
49	0.5440 5579	0.5121 3860	0.4821 2975	0.4273 7934	0.3789 5844	0.3361 2242
50	0.5373 3905	0.5051 9220	0.4750 0468	0.4200 2883	0.3715 2788	0.3287 2608
51	0.5307 0524	0.4983 4003	0.4679 8491	0.4128 0475	0.3642 4302	0.3214 9250
52	0.5241 5332	0.4915 8079	0.4610 6887	0.4057 0492	0.3571 0100	0.3144 1810
53	0.5176 8229	0.4849 1323	0.4542 5505	0.3987 2719	0.3500 9902	0.3074 9936
54	0.5112 9115	0.4783 3611	0.4475 4192	0.3918 6947	0.3432 3433	0.3007 3287
55	0.5049 7892	0.4718 4820	0.4409 2800	0.3851 2970	0.3365 0425	0.2941 1528
56	0.4987 4461	0.4654 4829	0.4344 1182	0.3785 0585	0.3299 0613	0.2876 4330
57	0.4925 8727	0.4591 3518	0.4279 9194	0.3719 9592	0.3234 3738	0.2813 1374
58	0.4865 0594	0.4529 0770	0.4216 6694	0.3655 9796	0.3170 9547	0.2751 2347
59	0.4804 9970	0.4467 6468	0.4154 3541	0.3593 1003	0.3108 7791	0.2690 6940
60	0.4745 6760	0.4407 0499	0.4092 9597	0.3531 3025	0.3047 8227	0.2631 4856

n	2½%	2¾%	3%	3½%	4%	4½%
1	0.9756 0976	0.9732 3601	0.9708 7379	0.9661 8357	0.9615 3846	0.9569 3780
2	0.9518 1440	0.9471 8833	0.9425 9591	0.9335 1070	0.9245 5621	0.9157 2995
3	0.9285 9941	0.9218 3779	0.9151 4166	0.9019 4271	0.8889 9636	0.8762 9660
4	0.9059 5064	0.8971 6573	0.8884 8705	0.8714 4223	0.8548 0419	0.8385 6134
5	0.8838 5429	0.8731 5400	0.8626 0878	0.8419 7317	0.8219 2711	0.8024 5103
6	0.8622 9687	0.8497 8491	0.8374 8426	0.8135 0064	0.7903 1453	0.7678 9574
7	0.8412 6524	0.8270 4128	0.8130 9151	0.7859 9096	0.7599 1781	0.7348 2846
8	0.8207 4657	0.8049 0635	0.7894 0923	0.7594 1156	0.7306 9021	0.7031 8513
9	0.8007 2836	0.7833 6385	0.7664 1673	0.7337 3097	0.7025 8674	0.6729 0443
10	0.7811 9840	0.7623 9791	0.7440 9391	0.7089 1881	0.6755 6417	0.6439 2768
11	0.7621 4478	0.7419 9310	0.7224 2128	0.6849 4571	0.6495 8093	0.6161 9874
12	0.7435 5589	0.7221 3440	0.7013 7988	0.6617 8330	0.6245 9705	0.5896 6386
13	0.7254 2038	0.7028 0720	0.6809 5134	0.6394 0415	0.6005 7409	0.5642 7164
14	0.7077 2720	0.6839 9728	0.6611 1781	0.6177 8179	0.5774 7508	0.5399 7286
15	0.6904 6556	0.6656 9078	0.6418 6195	0.5968 9062	0.5552 6450	0.5167 2044
16	0.6736 2493	0.6478 7424	0.6231 6694	0.5767 0591	0.5339 0818	0.4944 6932
17	0.6571 9506	0.6305 3454	0.6050 1645	0.5572 0378	0.5133 7325	0.4731 7639
18	0.6411 6591	0.6136 5892	0.5873 9461	0.5383 6114	0.4936 2812	0.4528 0037
19	0.6255 2772	0.5972 3496	0.5702 8603	0.5201 5569	0.4746 4242	0.4333 0179
20	0.6102 7094	0.5812 5057	0.5536 7575	0.5025 6588	0.4563 8695	0.4146 4286
21	0.5953 8629	0.5656 9398	0.5375 4928	0.4855 7090	0.4388 3360	0.3967 8743
22	0.5808 6467	0.5505 5375	0.5218 9250	0.4691 5063	0.4219 5539	0.3797 0089
23	0.5666 9724	0.5358 1874	0.5066 9175	0.4532 8563	0.4057 2633	0.3633 5013
24	0.5528 7535	0.5214 7809	0.4919 3374	0.4379 5713	0.3901 2147	0.3477 0347
25	0.5393 9059	0.5075 2126	0.4776 0557	0.4231 4699	0.3751 1680	0.3327 3060
26	0.5262 3472	0.4939 3796	0.4636 9473	0.4088 3767	0.3606 8923	0.3184 0248
27	0.5133 9973	0.4807 1821	0.4501 8906	0.3950 1224	0.3468 1657	0.3046 9137
28	0.5008 7778	0.4678 5227	0.4370 7675	0.3816 5434	0.3334 7747	0.2915 7069
29	0.4886 6125	0.4553 3068	0.4243 4636	0.3687 4815	0.3206 5141	0.2790 1502
30	0.4767 4269	0.4431 4421	0.4119 8676	0.3562 7841	0.3083 1867	0.2670 0002
31	0.4651 1481	0.4312 8391	0.3999 8715	0.3442 3035	0.2964 6026	0.2555 0241
32	0.4537 7055	0.4197 4103	0.3883 3703	0.3325 8971	0.2850 5794	0.2444 9991
33	0.4427 0298	0.4085 0708	0.3770 2625	0.3213 4271	0.2740 9417	0.2339 7121
34	0.4319 0534	0.3975 7380	0.3660 4490	0.3104 7605	0.2635 5209	0.2238 9589
35	0.4213 7107	0.3869 3314	0.3553 8340	0.2999 7686	0.2534 1547	0.2142 5444
36	0.4110 9372	0.3765 7727	0.3450 3243	0.2898 3272	0.2436 6872	0.2050 2817
37	0.4010 6705	0.3664 9856	0.3349 8294	0.2800 3161	0.2342 9685	0.1961 9921
38	0.3912 8492	0.3566 8959	0.3252 2615	0.2705 6194	0.2252 8543	0.1877 5044
39	0.3817 4139	0.3471 4316	0.3157 5355	0.2614 1250	0.2166 2061	0.1796 6549
40	0.3724 3062	0.3378 5222	0.3065 5684	0.2525 7247	0.2082 8904	0.1719 2870
41	0.3633 4695	0.3288 0995	0.2976 2800	0.2440 3137	0.2002 7793	0.1645 2507
42	0.3544 8483	0.3200 0968	0.2889 5922	0.2357 7910	0.1925 7493	0.1574 4026
43	0.3458 3886	0.3114 4495	0.2805 4294	0.2278 0590	0.1851 6820	0.1506 6054
44	0.3374 0376	0.3031 0944	0.2723 7178	0.2201 0231	0.1780 4635	0.1441 7276
45	0.3291 7440	0.2949 9702	0.2644 3862	0.2126 5924	0.1711 9841	0.1379 6437
46	0.3211 4576	0.2871 0172	0.2567 3653	0.2054 6787	0.1646 1386	0.1320 2332
47	0.3133 1294	0.2794 1773	0.2492 5876	0.1985 1968	0.1582 8256	0.1263 3810
48	0.3056 7116	0.2719 3940	0.2419 9880	0.1918 0645	0.1521 9476	0.1208 9771
49	0.2982 1576	0.2646 6122	0.2349 5029	0.1853 2024	0.1463 4112	0.1156 9158
50	0.2909 4221	0.2575 7783	0.2281 0708	0.1790 5337	0.1407 1262	0.1107 0965
51	0.2838 4606	0.2506 8402	0.2214 6318	0.1729 9843	0.1353 0059	0.1059 4225
52	0.2769 2298	0.2439 7471	0.2150 1280	0.1671 4824	0.1300 9672	0.1013 8014
53	0.2701 6876	0.2374 4497	0.2087 5029	0.1614 9589	0.1250 9300	0.0970 1449
54	0.2635 7928	0.2310 9000	0.2026 7019	0.1560 3467	0.1202 8173	0.0928 3683
55	0.2571 5052	0.2249 0511	0.1967 6717	0.1507 5814	0.1156 5551	0.0888 3907
56	0.2508 7855	0.2188 8575	0.1910 3609	0.1456 6004	0.1112 0722	0.0850 1347
57	0.2447 5956	0.2130 2749	0.1854 7193	0.1407 3433	0.1069 3002	0.0813 5260
58	0.2387 8982	0.2073 2603	0.1800 6984	0.1359 7520	0.1028 1733	0.0778 4938
59	0.2329 6568	0.2017 7716	0.1748 2508	0.1313 7701	0.0988 6282	0.0744 9701
60	0.2272 8359	0.1963 7679	0.1697 3309	0.1269 3431	0.0950 6040	0.0712 8901

COMPOUND PRESENT VALUE OF 1 (*Cont.*)

	5%	5½%	6%	6½%	7%	8%
1	0.9523 8095	0.9478 6730	0.9433 9623	0.9389 6714	0.9345 7944	0.9259 2593
2	0.9070 2948	0.8984 5242	0.8899 9644	0.8816 5928	0.8734 3873	0.8573 3882
3	0.8638 3760	0.8516 1366	0.8396 1928	0.8278 4909	0.8162 9788	0.7938 3224
4	0.8227 0247	0.8072 1674	0.7920 9366	0.7773 2309	0.7628 9521	0.7350 2985
5	0.7835 2617	0.7651 3435	0.7472 5817	0.7298 8084	0.7129 8618	0.6805 8320
6	0.7462 1540	0.7252 4583	0.7049 6054	0.6853 3412	0.6663 4222	0.6301 6963
7	0.7106 8133	0.6874 3681	0.6650 5711	0.6435 0621	0.6227 4974	0.5834 9040
8	0.6768 3936	0.6515 9887	0.6274 1237	0.6042 3119	0.5820 0910	0.5402 6888
9	0.6446 0892	0.6176 2926	0.5918 9846	0.5673 5323	0.5439 3374	0.5002 4897
10	0.6139 1325	0.5854 3058	0.5583 9478	0.5327 2604	0.5083 4929	0.4631 9349
11	0.5846 7929	0.5549 1050	0.5267 8753	0.5002 1224	0.4750 9280	0.4288 8286
12	0.5568 3742	0.5259 8152	0.4969 6936	0.4696 8285	0.4440 1196	0.3971 1376
13	0.5303 2135	0.4985 6068	0.4688 3902	0.4410 1676	0.4149 6445	0.3676 9792
14	0.5050 6795	0.4725 6937	0.4423 0096	0.4141 0025	0.3878 1724	0.3404 6104
15	0.4810 1710	0.4479 3305	0.4172 6506	0.3888 2652	0.3624 4602	0.3152 4170
16	0.4581 1152	0.4245 8109	0.3936 4628	0.3650 9533	0.3387 3460	0.2918 9047
17	0.4362 9669	0.4024 4653	0.3713 6442	0.3428 1251	0.3165 7439	0.2702 6895
18	0.4155 2065	0.3814 6590	0.3503 4379	0.3218 8969	0.2958 6392	0.2502 4903
19	0.3957 3396	0.3615 7906	0.3305 1301	0.3022 4384	0.2765 0832	0.2317 1206
20	0.3768 8948	0.3427 2896	0.3118 0473	0.2837 9703	0.2584 1900	0.2145 4821
21	0.3589 4236	0.3248 6158	0.2941 5540	0.2664 7608	0.2415 1309	0.1986 5575
22	0.3418 4987	0.3079 2567	0.2775 0510	0.2502 1228	0.2257 1317	0.1839 4051
23	0.3255 7131	0.2918 7267	0.2617 9726	0.2349 4111	0.2109 4688	0.1703 1528
24	0.3100 6791	0.2766 5656	0.2469 7855	0.2206 0198	0.1971 4662	0.1576 9934
25	0.2953 0277	0.2622 3370	0.2329 9863	0.2071 3801	0.1842 4918	0.1460 1790
26	0.2812 4073	0.2485 6275	0.2198 1003	0.1944 9579	0.1721 9549	0.1352 0176
27	0.2678 4832	0.2356 0450	0.2073 6795	0.1826 2515	0.1609 3037	0.1251 8682
28	0.2550 9364	0.2233 2181	0.1956 3014	0.1714 7902	0.1504 0221	0.1159 1372
29	0.2429 4632	0.2116 7944	0.1845 5674	0.1610 1316	0.1405 6282	0.1073 2752
30	0.2313 7745	0.2006 4402	0.1741 1013	0.1511 8607	0.1313 6712	0.0993 7733
31	0.2203 5947	0.1901 8390	0.1642 5484	0.1419 5875	0.1227 7301	0.0920 1605
32	0.2098 6617	0.1802 6910	0.1549 5740	0.1332 9460	0.1147 4113	0.0852 0005
33	0.1998 7254	0.1708 7119	0.1461 8622	0.1251 5925	0.1072 3470	0.0788 8893
34	0.1903 5480	0.1619 6321	0.1379 1153	0.1175 2042	0.1002 1934	0.0730 4531
35	0.1812 9029	0.1535 1963	0.1301 0522	0.1103 4781	0.0936 6294	0.0676 3454
36	0.1726 5741	0.1455 1624	0.1227 4077	0.1036 1297	0.0875 3546	0.0626 2458
37	0.1644 3563	0.1379 3008	0.1157 9318	0.0972 8917	0.0818 0884	0.0579 8572
38	0.1566 0536	0.1307 3941	0.1092 3885	0.0913 5134	0.0764 5686	0.0536 9048
39	0.1491 4797	0.1239 2362	0.1030 5552	0.0857 7590	0.0714 5501	0.0497 1341
40	0.1420 4568	0.1174 6314	0.0972 2219	0.0805 4075	0.0667 8038	0.0460 3093
41	0.1352 8160	0.1113 3947	0.0917 1905	0.0756 2512	0.0624 1157	0.0426 2123
42	0.1288 3962	0.1055 3504	0.0865 2740	0.0710 0950	0.0583 2857	0.0394 6411
43	0.1227 0440	0.1000 3322	0.0816 2962	0.0666 7559	0.0545 1268	0.0365 4084
44	0.1168 6133	0.0948 1822	0.0770 0908	0.0626 0619	0.0509 4643	0.0338 3411
45	0.1112 9651	0.0898 7509	0.0726 5007	0.0587 8515	0.0476 1349	0.0313 2788
46	0.1059 9668	0.0851 8965	0.0685 3781	0.0551 9733	0.0444 9859	0.0290 0730
47	0.1009 4921	0.0807 4849	0.0646 5831	0.0518 2848	0.0415 8747	0.0268 5861
48	0.0961 4211	0.0765 3885	0.0609 9840	0.0486 6524	0.0388 6679	0.0248 6908
49	0.0915 6391	0.0725 4867	0.0575 4566	0.0456 9506	0.0363 2410	0.0230 2693
50	0.0872 0373	0.0687 6652	0.0542 8836	0.0429 0616	0.0339 4776	0.0213 2123
51	0.0830 5117	0.0651 8153	0.0512 1544	0.0402 8747	0.0317 2688	0.0197 4188
52	0.0790 9635	0.0617 8344	0.0483 1645	0.0378 2861	0.0296 5129	0.0182 7952
53	0.0753 2986	0.0585 6250	0.0455 8156	0.0355 1982	0.0277 1148	0.0169 2548
54	0.0717 4272	0.0555 0948	0.0430 0147	0.0333 5195	0.0258 9858	0.0156 7174
55	0.0683 2640	0.0526 1562	0.0405 6742	0.0313 1638	0.0242 0428	0.0145 1087
56	0.0650 7276	0.0498 7263	0.0382 7115	0.0294 0505	0.0226 2083	0.0134 3599
57	0.0619 7406	0.0472 7263	0.0361 0486	0.0276 1038	0.0211 4096	0.0124 4073
58	0.0590 2291	0.0448 0818	0.0340 6119	0.0259 2524	0.0197 5791	0.0115 1920
59	0.0562 1230	0.0424 7221	0.0321 3320	0.0243 4295	0.0184 6533	0.0106 6592
60	0.0535 3552	0.0402 5802	0.0303 1434	0.0228 5723	0.0172 5732	0.0098 7585

How to calculate the compound discount. The compound discount on a sum due in the future is the difference between that sum and its compound present value.

EXAMPLE

What is the compound discount, at 6% per year compounded annually, on a loan of $8,200.00 due in 7 years?

Solution

(1) The table (page 1320) shows the compound present value of 1 for 7 periods at 6% to be 0.66505711. The compound present value of $8,200.00 is, therefore, $0.66505711 \times 8{,}200 = \$5{,}453.47$.

(2) The compound discount is the difference between the sum due and its compound present value, or $\$8{,}200.00 - \$5{,}453.47 = \$2{,}746.53$.

10. HOW TO COMPUTE ANNUITIES

Adapted from Moore, "Handbook of Financial Mathematics"
New York: Prentice-Hall, Inc.

What an annuity is. An annuity is a series of equal payments made or due at equal intervals of time. Examples of annuities are: bond coupons, regular preferred stock dividends, periodic contributions to sinking funds and depreciation funds, insurance premiums, periodic payments to beneficiaries by insurance companies, income from trust funds, rent on land or buildings, and installment payments. Although the word annuity suggests annual payments, it applies to any series of equal payments made at equal intervals of time, whether the payments be made annually, semiannually, quarterly, monthly, or otherwise.

Ordinary annuities and annuities due. Annuities are of two principal types:

1. Ordinary annuities.
2. Annuities due.

An ordinary annuity is one in which the payments are made at the end of each period; payments to sinking funds and to depreciation funds are usually made at the end of each period. An annuity due is one in which the payments are made at the beginning of each period; insurance premiums and rent payments on land or buildings are usually made at the beginning of each period.

It is necessary to distinguish between these two classes of annuities because the method of computation used in connection with ordinary annuities is slightly different from that used in connection with annuities due. The distinction can best be visualized by means of a diagram. As an example, take two annuities payable at annual intervals for a term of 6 years. In Figure 95, the arrows in the upper half (pointing downward) indicate the time of the six payments in an ordinary annuity; the arrows in the lower half (pointing upward) indicate the time of the payments in an annuity due. It is important to note that the straight line in the center of the diagram indicates the length of the term, and that this length is the same for both these annuities.

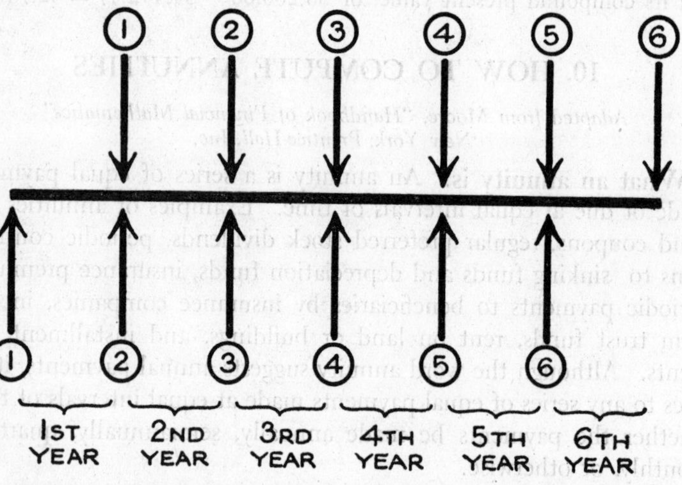

Figure 95. Comparison of an Ordinary Annuity with an Annuity Due.

How to calculate the amount of an ordinary annuity. The amount of an annuity is the sum of the invested rents (periodic payments) and the compound interest thereon to the end of the term of the annuity.

Table of amount of annuity of 1 per period. The table on pages 1330-33 shows the amount of an annuity of 1 per period ($1, £1, 1 peso, or any other monetary unit) for different numbers of periods and at different rates of interest per period. The procedure in calculating the amount of an ordinary annuity is as follows, provided the interest is compounded the same number of times a year as the rent payments are made (which is generally the case):

1. Find in the table the amount of an annuity of 1 per period for the given number of periods and at the given rate of interest per period.
2. Multiply this figure by the periodic rent.

EXAMPLE

To redeem a bond issue of $2,000,000.00 in 20 years, the Eastport Oil Corporation placed $30,000.00 in a sinking fund at the end of each six months. The sinking fund earned 5% per year compounded semiannually. What was the amount in the fund at the end of 10 years?

Solution

Since the payments are made at the end of each six months, the number of periods is $10 \times 2 = 20$. The rate of interest per period is $5\% \div 2 = 2\frac{1}{2}\%$. Then:

(1) In the table (page 1332) the figure given in the 2½% column opposite 20 is 25.54465761. This is the amount of an annuity of 1 for 20 periods at 2½% per period.

(2) To find the amount of an annuity of $30,000.00, multiply 25.54465761 by 30,000. The result, $766,339.73, is the amount in the sinking fund at the end of 10 years, if payments of $30,000.00 are made at the end of each six months and interest at 5% per year is compounded semiannually.

Formula for amount of an ordinary annuity. The amount of an ordinary annuity may also be calculated by the use of the formula

$$R\left[\frac{(1+i)^n - 1}{i}\right]$$

where

R = periodic rent
i = rate of interest per period
n = number of periods

How to calculate the amount of an annuity due. In an annuity due the periodic rent payments are made at the beginning of each period, while in an ordinary annuity the periodic rent payments are made at the end of each period.

In the diagram (page 1322) it is seen that the ordinary annuity of six rents earns no interest after the date of the sixth payment; the annuity due of six rents earns interest for one full period after the date of the sixth payment. Consequently, the amount of the annuity due of six rents is equal to:

1. The amount of the ordinary annuity of six rents; *plus*
2. Interest on the amount of the ordinary annuity of six rents for one period.

This is equivalent to saying that the amount of the annuity due of six rents is equal to:

1. The amount of an ordinary annuity of seven rents; *minus*
2. One rent.

The procedure in calculating the amount of an annuity due is, therefore, as follows:

1. Calculate the amount of an ordinary annuity for one more than the given number of periods.
2. Deduct from the figure found in (1), one periodic rent; the result is the amount of the annuity due.

EXAMPLE

At the beginning of each six-month period, the Donahue Construction Company places $40,000.00 in a depreciation fund for its machinery. To what amount will the fund have accumulated at the end of 7 years, if interest at 5% per year compounded semiannually is earned?

Solution

Since the payments are made semiannually, the given number of periods is $7 \times 2 = 14$. The rate of interest per period is $5\% \div 2 = 2\frac{1}{2}\%$. Then:

(1) Adding 1 to the given number of periods makes the number of periods 15. In the table (page 1332) the figure in the 2½% column opposite 15 is 17.93192666. This is the amount of an annuity of 1 for 15 periods at 2½% per period. To find the amount of an annuity of $40,000.00, multiply 17.93192666 by 40,000. $17.93192666 \times 40{,}000 =$ $717,277.07.

(2) Deducting one rent, $40,000.00, from $717,277.07 gives $717,277.07 − $40,000.00 = $677,277.07. This is the amount to which the depreciation fund will have accumulated at the end of 7 years, if payments of $40,000.00 are made at the beginning of each six-month period and interest at 5% per year compounded semiannually is earned.

Formula for amount of an annuity due. The amount of an annuity due may also be calculated by the use of the formula

$$R\left[\frac{(1+i)^{n+1}-1}{i}-1\right]$$

where

$$R = \text{periodic rent}$$
$$i = \text{rate of interest per period}$$
$$n = \text{number of periods}$$

How to calculate the present value of an ordinary annuity. The present value (or present worth) of an annuity is that sum which, invested at compound interest, will provide for the withdrawal of a stated number of equal rents at equal intervals of time. The interest earning increases the investment, and the rent withdrawals decrease it. The withdrawal of the last rent should exhaust the inevstment.

If the rents are withdrawn at the end of each period, the annuity is an ordinary annuity. If the rents are withdrawn at the beginning of each period, the annuity is an annuity due.

The present value of an annuity is also sometimes referred to as the "cash equivalent" of the annuity.

Table of present value of annuity of 1 per period. The table on pages 1334-37 shows the present value of an annuity of 1 per period ($1, £1, 1 peso, or any other monetary unit) for different numbers of periods and at different rates of interest per period. The procedure in calculating the present value of an ordinary annuity is as follows, provided the interest is compounded the same number of times a year as the rent withdrawals are made (which is generally the case):

1. Find in the table the present value of an annuity of 1 for the given number of periods and at the given rate of interest per period.
2. Multiply this figure by the periodic rent.

EXAMPLE

Under the terms of a contract the Dubois Celluloid Novelty Company is obligated to make payments of $2,500.00 at the end of each quarter for 8 years. To provide for these payments the Dubois Company decides to set up a fund out of which the quarterly payments will be made. What amount must be invested in the fund, if interest at 5% per year compounded quarterly is earned?

Solution

Since the payments are to be made quarterly, the number of periods is $8 \times 4 = 32$. The rate of interest per period is $5\% \div 4 = 1\frac{1}{4}\%$. Then:

(1) In the table (page 1335) the figure in the $1\frac{1}{4}\%$ column opposite 32 is 26.24127418. This is the present value of an annuity of 1 for 32 periods at $1\frac{1}{4}\%$ per period.

(2) To find the present value of an annuity of $2,500.00, multiply 26.24127418 by 2,500. 26.24127418 × 2,500 = $65,603.19. This is the amount which must be invested in the fund, at 5% per year compounded quarterly, to provide for payments of $2,500.00 at the end of each quarter for 8 years.

Formula for present value of an ordinary annuity. The present value of an ordinary annuity may also be calculated by the use of the formula

$$R\left[\frac{1-\dfrac{1}{(1+i)^n}}{i}\right]$$

where

R = periodic rent
i = rate of interest per period
n = number of periods

How to calculate the present value of an annuity due. In an annuity due the periodic rents are due at the beginning of each period, while in an ordinary annuity the periodic rents are due at the end of each period.

Referring to the diagram (page 1322), if the present value of the ordinary annuity of six rents is to be calculated, it is apparent that, since the first rent is due at the end of the first period, this first rent will be subject to discount; in the annuity due of six rents, however, the first rent is due at the beginning of the first period, and hence this first rent will not be subject to discount. Consequently, the present value of the annuity due of six rents is equal to:

1. The present value of the ordinary annuity of six rents; *minus*
2. The discount on one rent (the first).

This is equivalent to saying that the present value of the annuity due of six rents is equal to:

1. The present value of an ordinary annuity of five rents; *plus*
2. One rent (that is, the first rent, which is not subject to discount).

The procedure in calculating the present value of an annuity due is, therefore, as follows:

1. Calculate the present value of an ordinary annuity for one less than the given number of periods.

2. Add to the figure found in 1, one periodic rent; the result is the present value of the annuity due.

EXAMPLE

A building is leased for 15 years at an annual rental of $7,000.00, payable in installments of $1,750.00 at the beginning of each quarter. What is the cash value of the lease if money is worth 4% per year compounded quarterly?

Solution

Since the payments are due quarterly, the number of periods is 15 × 4 = 60. The rate of interest per period is 4% ÷ 4 = 1%. Then:

(1) Deducting 1 from the given number of periods makes the number of periods 59. In the table (page 1334) the figure in the 1% column opposite 59 is 44.40458879. This is the present value of an annuity of 1 for 59 periods at 1% per period. To find the present value of an annuity of $1,750.00, multiply 44.40458879 by 1,750. 44.40458879 × 1,750 = $77,708.03.

(2) Adding one periodic rent, $1,750.00, gives $77,708.03 + $1,750.00 = $79,458.03.

The cash value of the lease is, therefore, $79,458.03.

Formula for present value of an annuity due. The present value of an annuity due may also be calculated by the use of the formula

$$R\left[\frac{1-\dfrac{1}{(1+i)^{n-1}}}{i}+1\right]$$

where

R = periodic rent
i = rate of interest per period
n = number of periods

Deferred annuities. A deferred annuity is an annuity in which a number of periods are to elapse before the periodic payments or rents are to begin. Since, when the payments do begin, they may occur either at the end or at the beginning of each period, there are two kinds of deferred annuities:

1. Deferred ordinary annuities.
2. Deferred annuities due.

A deferred ordinary annuity is a deferred annuity in which the payments are to be made at the end of each period after the interval of deferment has expired. A deferred annuity due is a deferred annuity in which the payments are to be made at the beginning of each period after the interval of deferment has expired.

How to calculate the amount of a deferred annuity. The amount of a deferred annuity is the same as the amount of an annuity that is not deferred. No interest is earned during the deferment interval, because no payments have been made during this interval. Therefore, if it is desired to find the amount of a deferred ordinary annuity, the procedure described on page 1322, "How to calculate the amount of an ordinary annuity," may be followed without modification; to find the amount of a deferred annuity due, the procedure described on page 1323, "How to calculate the amount of an annuity due," may be followed. The deferment interval is disregarded in the calculation of the amount of a deferred annuity.

How to calculate the present value of a deferred ordinary annuity. The present value of a deferred annuity is the value of the annuity as of the beginning of the interval of deferment. Hence the present value of a deferred annuity is not the same as the present value of an annuity that is not deferred.

The procedure in calculating the present value of a deferred ordinary annuity is as follows:

1. Eliminate the number of periods in the interval of deferment, and calculate the present value, at the given rate of interest per period, of an ordinary annuity for a number of periods corresponding to the number of rents.

2. Multiply the figure found in 1 by the present value of 1, at the given rate of interest per period, for the number of deferred periods; the result is the present value of the deferred ordinary annuity.

EXAMPLE

The Broadfield Bituminous Company has a mine estimated to yield $75,000.00 net per year for 16 years, but it is not deemed advisable to start production until 3 years from now. What is the present value of the output, if money is worth 5½% per year compounded annually?

Solution

(1) The number of periods corresponding to the number of rents is 16; the rate of interest per period is 5½%. In the table (page 1337), the

present value of an ordinary annuity of 1 for 16 periods at 5½% is found to be 10.46216203. The present value of an annuity of $75,000.00 is, therefore, 10.46216203 × 75,000 = $784,662.15225.

(2) The number of periods in the interval of deferment is 3; the rate of interest per period is 5½%. In the table on page 1320, the present value of 1 for 3 periods at 5½% is shown to be 0.85161366. Then, $784,662.15225 × 0.85161366 = $668,229.01.

Thus the present value of the output of the mine is $668,229.01.

How to calculate the present value of a deferred annuity due. The procedure in calculating the present value of a deferred annuity due is as follows:

1. Eliminate the number of periods in the interval of deferment, and calculate the present value, at the given rate of interest per period, of an annuity due for a number of periods corresponding to the number of rents.
2. Multiply the figure found in 1 by the present value of 1, at the given rate of interest per period, for the number of deferred periods; the result is the present value of the deferred annuity due.

EXAMPLE

The Thorndike Engineering Corporation is at present devoting its entire resources to subway construction, but expects to complete this work by the end of 3 years. At that time it will be able to undertake some survey work in the Andes which, it is estimated, will take 6 years, and for which work the company will receive a fee of $150,000.00 a year, payable in advance. If money is worth 5% per year compounded annually, what is the present value of this contract?

Solution

(1) The first step is to calculate the present value of an annuity due of $150,000.00 for 6 periods at 5% per period. This is equivalent to finding the present value of an ordinary annuity of $150,000.00 for 5 periods at 5% per period, and adding one rent (for method of calculating present value of an annuity due, see page 1326). In the table on page 1337, the present value of an ordinary annuity of 1 for 5 periods at 5% is found to be 4.32947667. The present value of an ordinary annuity of $150,000.00 is, therefore, 4.32947667 × 150,000 = $649,421.50. Adding one rent gives $649,421.50 + $150,000.00 = $799,421.50. This is the present value of an annuity due of $150,000.00 for 6 periods at 5%.

(2) The number of periods in the interval of deferment is 3; the rate of interest per period is 5%. In the table on page 1320, the present value of 1 for 3 periods at 5% is shown to be 0.86383760. Then, $799,421.50 × 0.86383760 = $690,570.35.

Thus the present value of the contract is $690,570.35.

AMOUNT OF ANNUITY OF 1

	½%	⅝%	¾%	⅞%	1%	1⅛%
1	1.0000 0000	1.0000 0000	1.0000 0000	1.0000 0000	1.0000 0000	1.0000 0000
2	2.0050 0000	2.0062 5000	2.0075 0000	2.0087 5000	2.0100 0000	2.0112 5000
3	3.0150 2500	3.1087 8906	3.0225 5625	3.0263 2656	3.0301 0000	3.0338 7656
4	4.0301 0013	4.0376 5649	4.0452 2542	4.0528 0692	4.0604 0100	4.0680 0767
5	5.0502 5063	5.0628 9185	5.0755 6461	5.0882 6898	5.1010 0501	5.1137 7276
6	6.0755 0188	6.0945 3492	6.1136 3135	6.1327 9133	6.1520 1506	6.1713 0270
7	7.1058 7939	7.1326 2576	7.1594 8358	7.1864 5326	7.2135 3521	7.2407 2986
8	8.1414 0879	8.1772 0468	8.2131 7971	8.2493 3472	8.2856 7056	8.3221 8807
9	9.1821 1583	9.2283 1220	9.2747 7856	9.3215 1640	9.3685 2727	9.4158 1269
10	10.2280 2641	10.2859 8916	10.3443 3940	10.4030 7967	10.4622 1254	10.5217 4058
11	11.2791 6654	11.3502 7659	11.4219 2194	11.4941 0662	11.5668 3467	11.6401 1016
12	12.3355 6237	12.4212 1582	12.5075 8636	12.5946 8005	12.6825 0301	12.7710 6140
13	13.3972 4018	13.4988 4842	13.6013 9325	13.7048 8350	13.8093 2804	13.9147 3584
14	14.4642 2639	14.5832 1622	14.7034 0370	14.8248 0123	14.9474 2132	15.0712 7662
15	15.5365 4752	15.6743 6132	15.8136 7923	15.9545 1824	16.0968 9554	16.2408 2848
16	16.6142 3026	16.7723 2608	16.9322 8183	17.0941 2028	17.2578 6449	17.4235 3780
17	17.6973 0141	17.8771 5312	18.0592 7394	18.2436 9383	18.4304 4314	18.6195 5260
18	18.7857 8791	18.9888 8532	19.1947 1849	19.4033 2615	19.6147 4757	19.8290 2257
19	19.8797 1685	20.1075 6586	20.3386 7888	20.5731 0526	20.8108 9504	21.0520 9907
20	20.9791 1544	21.2332 3814	21.4912 1897	21.7531 1993	22.0190 0399	22.2889 3519
21	22.0840 1101	22.3659 4588	22.6524 0312	22.9434 5973	23.2391 9403	23.5396 8571
22	23.1944 3107	23.5057 3304	23.8222 9614	24.1442 1500	24.4715 8598	24.8045 0717
23	24.3104 0322	24.6526 4387	25.0009 6336	25.3554 7688	25.7163 0183	26.0835 5788
24	25.4319 5524	25.8067 2290	26.1884 7059	26.5773 3730	26.9734 6485	27.3769 9790
25	26.5591 1502	26.9680 1492	27.3848 8412	27.8098 8900	28.2431 9950	28.6849 8913
26	27.6919 1059	28.1365 6501	28.5902 7075	29.0532 2553	29.5256 3150	30.0076 9526
27	28.8303 7015	29.3124 1854	29.8046 9778	30.3074 4126	30.8208 8781	31.3452 8183
28	29.9745 2200	30.4956 2116	31.0282 3301	31.5726 3137	32.1290 9669	32.6979 1625
29	31.1243 9461	31.6862 1879	32.2609 4476	32.8488 9189	33.4503 8766	34.0657 6781
30	32.2800 1658	32.8842 5766	33.5029 0184	34.1363 1970	34.7848 9153	35.4490 0769
31	33.4414 1666	34.0897 8427	34.7541 7361	35.4350 1249	36.1327 4045	36.8478 0903
32	34.6086 2375	35.3028 4542	36.0148 2991	36.7450 6885	37.4940 6785	38.2623 4688
33	35.7816 6686	36.5234 8820	37.2849 4113	38.0665 8820	38.8690 0853	39.6927 9829
34	36.9605 7520	37.7517 6000	38.5645 7819	39.3996 7085	40.2576 9862	41.1393 4227
35	38.1453 7807	38.9877 0850	39.8538 1253	40.7444 1797	41.6602 7560	42.6021 5987
36	39.3361 0496	40.2313 8168	41.1527 1612	42.1009 3163	43.0768 7836	44.0814 3417
37	40.5327 8549	41.4828 2782	42.4613 6149	43.4693 1478	44.5076 4714	45.5773 5030
38	41.7354 4942	42.7420 9549	43.7798 2170	44.8496 7128	45.9527 2361	47.0900 9549
39	42.9441 2666	44.0092 3359	45.1081 7037	46.2421 0591	47.4122 5085	48.6198 5906
40	44.1588 4730	45.2842 9130	46.4464 8164	47.6467 2433	48.8863 7336	50.1668 3248
41	45.3796 4153	46.5673 1812	47.7948 3026	49.0636 3317	50.3752 3709	51.7312 0934
42	46.6065 3974	47.8583 6386	49.1532 9148	50.4929 3996	51.8789 8946	53.3131 8545
43	47.8395 7244	49.1574 7863	50.5219 4117	51.9347 5319	53.3977 7936	54.9129 5879
44	49.0787 7030	50.4647 1287	51.9008 5573	53.3891 8228	54.9317 5715	56.5307 2957
45	50.3241 6415	51.7801 1733	53.2901 1215	54.8563 3762	56.4810 7472	58.1667 0028
46	51.5757 8497	53.1037 4306	54.6897 8799	56.3363 3058	58.0458 8547	59.8210 7566
47	52.8336 6390	54.4356 4146	56.0999 6140	57.8292 7347	59.6263 4432	61.4940 6276
48	54.0978 3222	55.7758 6421	57.5207 1111	59.3352 7961	61.2226 0777	63.1858 7097
49	55.3683 2138	57.1244 6337	58.9521 1644	60.8544 6331	62.8348 3385	64.8967 1201
50	56.6451 6299	58.4814 9126	60.3942 5732	62.3869 3986	64.4631 8218	66.6268 0002
51	57.9283 8880	59.8470 0058	61.8472 1424	63.9328 2559	66.1078 1401	68.3763 5152
52	59.2180 3075	61.2210 4434	63.3110 6835	65.4922 3781	67.7688 9215	70.1455 8548
53	60.5141 2090	62.6036 7586	64.7859 0136	67.0652 9489	69.4465 8107	71.9347 2332
54	61.8166 9150	63.9949 4884	66.2717 9562	68.6521 1622	71.1410 4688	73.7439 8895
55	63.1257 7496	65.3949 1727	67.7688 3409	70.2528 2224	72.8524 5735	75.5736 0883
56	64.4414 0384	66.8036 3550	69.2771 0035	71.8675 3443	74.5809 8192	77.4238 1193
57	65.7636 1086	68.2211 5822	70.7966 7860	73.4963 7536	76.3267 9174	79.2948 2981
58	67.0924 2891	69.6475 4046	72.3276 5369	75.1394 6864	78.0900 5966	81.1868 9665
59	68.4278 9105	71.0828 3759	73.8701 1109	76.7969 3900	79.8709 6025	83.1002 4923
60	69.7700 3051	72.5271 0532	75.4241 3693	78.4689 1221	81.6696 6986	85.0351 2704

From J. W. Glover, "*Tables of Applied Math. in Finance, Insurance, Statistics.*" George Wahr, publisher, Ann Arbor, Michigan.

AMOUNT OF ANNUITY OF 1 (*Cont.*)

	1¼%	1⅜%	1½%	1¾%	2%	2¼%
1	1.0000 0000	1.0000 0000	1.0000 0000	1.0000 0000	1.0000 0000	1.0000 0000
2	2.0125 0000	2.0137 5000	2.0150 0000	2.0175 0000	2.0200 0000	2.0225 0000
3	3.0376 5625	3.0414 3906	3.0452 2500	3.0528 0625	3.0604 0000	3.0680 0625
4	4.0756 2695	4.0832 5885	4.0909 0338	4.1062 3036	4.1216 0800	4.1370 3639
5	5.1265 7229	5.1394 0366	5.1522 6693	5.1780 8938	5.2040 4016	5.2301 1971
6	6.1906 5444	6.2100 7046	6.2295 5093	6.2687 0596	6.3081 2096	6 3477 9740
7	7.2680 3762	7.2954 5893	7.3229 9419	7.3784 0831	7.4342 8338	7.4906 2284
8	8.3588 8809	8.3957 7149	8.4328 3911	8.5075 3045	8.5829 6905	8.6591 6186
9	9.4633 7420	9.5112 1335	9.5593 3169	9.6564 1224	9.7546 2843	9.8539 9300
10	10.5816 6637	10.6419 9253	10.7027 2167	10.8253 9945	10.9497 2100	11.0757 0784
11	11.7139 3720	11.7883 1993	11.8632 6249	12.0148 4394	12.1687 1542	12.3249 1127
12	12.8603 6142	12.9504 0933	13.0412 1143	13.2251 0371	13.4120 8973	13.6022 2177
13	14.0211 1594	14.1284 7745	14.2368 2960	14.4565 4303	14.6803 3152	14.9082 7176
14	15.1963 7988	15.3227 4402	15.4503 8205	15.7095 3253	15.9739 3815	16.2437 0788
15	16.3863 3463	16.5334 3175	16.6821 3778	16.9844 4935	17.2934 1692	17.6091 9130
16	17.5911 6382	17.7607 6644	17.9323 6984	18.2816 7721	18.6392 8525	19.0053 9811
17	18.8110 5336	19.0049 7697	19.2013 5539	19.6016 0656	20.0120 7096	20.4330 1957
18	20.0461 9153	20.2662 9541	20.4893 7572	20.9446 3468	21.4123 1238	21.8927 6251
19	21.2967 6893	21.5449 5697	21.7967 1636	22.3111 6578	22.8405 5863	23.3853 4966
20	22.5629 7854	22.8412 0013	23.1236 6710	23.7016 1119	24.2973 6980	24.9115 2003
21	23.8450 1577	24.1552 6663	24.4705 2211	25.1163 8938	25.7833 1719	26.4720 2923
22	25.1430 7847	25.4874 0155	25.8375 7994	26.5559 2620	27.2989 8354	28.0676 4989
23	26.4573 6695	26.8378 5332	27.2251 4364	28.0206 5490	28.8449 6321	29.6991 7201
24	27.7880 8403	28.2068 7380	28.6335 2080	29.5110 1637	30.4218 6247	31.3674 0338
25	29.1354 3508	29.5947 1832	30.0630 2361	31.0274 5915	32.0302 9972	33.0731 6996
26	30.4996 2802	31.0016 4569	31.5139 6896	32.5704 3969	33.6709 0572	34.8173 1628
27	31.8808 7337	32.4279 1832	32.9866 7850	34.1404 2238	35.3443 2383	36.6007 0590
28	33.2793 8429	33.8738 0220	34.4814 7867	35.7378 7977	37.0512 1031	38.4242 2178
29	34.6953 7659	35.3395 6698	35.9987 0085	37.3632 9267	38.7922 3451	40.2887 6677
30	36.1290 6880	36.8254 8602	37.5386 8137	39.0171 5029	40.5680 7921	42.1952 6402
31	37.5806 8216	38.3318 3646	39.1017 6159	40.6999 5042	42.3794 4079	44.1446 5746
32	39.0504 4069	39.8588 9921	40.6882 8801	42.4121 9955	44.2270 2961	46.1379 1226
33	40.5385 7120	41.4069 5907	42.2986 1233	44.1544 1305	46.1115 7020	48.1760 1528
34	42.0453 0334	42.9763 0476	43.9330 9152	45.9271 1527	48.0338 0160	50.2599 7563
35	43.5708 6963	44.5672 2895	45.5920 8789	47.7308 3979	49.9944 7763	52.3908 2508
36	45.1155 0550	46.1800 2835	47.2759 6921	49.5661 2949	51.9943 6719	54.5696 1864
37	46.6794 4932	47.8150 0374	48.9851 0874	51.4335 3675	54.0342 5453	56.7974 3506
38	48.2926 4243	49.4724 6004	50.7198 8538	53.3336 2365	56.1149 3962	59.0753 7735
39	49.8862 2921	51.1527 0636	52.4806 8366	55.2669 6206	58.2372 3841	61.4045 7334
40	51.4895 5708	52.8560 5608	54.2678 9391	57.2341 3390	60.4019 8318	63.7861 7624
41	53.1331 7654	54.5828 2685	56.0819 1232	59.2357 3124	62.6100 2284	66.2213 6521
42	54.7973 4125	56.3333 4072	57.9231 4100	61.2723 5654	64.8622 2330	68.7113 4592
43	56.4823 0801	58.1079 2415	59.7919 8812	63.3446 2278	67.1594 6777	71.2573 5121
44	58.1883 3687	59.9069 0811	61.6888 6794	65.4531 5367	69.5026 5712	73.8606 4161
45	59.9156 9108	61.7306 2810	63.6142 0096	67.5985 8386	71.8927 1027	76.5225 0605
46	61.6646 3721	63.5794 2423	65.5684 1398	69.7815 5908	74.3305 6447	79.2442 6243
47	63.4354 4518	65.4536 4131	67.5519 4018	72.0027 3637	76.8171 7576	82.0272 5834
48	65.2283 8824	67.3536 2888	69.5652 1929	74.2627 8425	79.3535 1927	84.8728 7165
49	67.0437 4310	69.2797 4128	71.6086 9758	76.5623 8298	81.9405 8966	87.7825 1126
50	68.8817 8989	71.2323 3772	73.6828 2804	78.9022 2468	84.5794 0145	90.7576 1776
51	70.7428 1226	73.2117 8237	75.7880 7046	81.2830 1361	87.2709 8948	93.7996 6416
52	72.6270 9741	75.2184 4437	77.9248 9152	83.7054 6635	90.0164 0927	96.9101 5661
53	74.5349 3613	77.2526 9798	80.0937 6489	86.1703 1201	92.8167 3746	100.0906 3513
54	76.4666 2283	79.3149 2258	82.2951 7136	88.6782 9247	95.6730 7221	103.3426 7442
55	78.4224 5562	81.4055 0277	84.5295 9893	91.2301 6259	98.5865 3365	106.6678 8460
56	80.4027 3631	83.5248 2843	86.7975 4292	93.8266 9043	101.5582 6432	110.0679 1200
57	82.4077 7052	85.6732 9482	89.0995 0606	96.4686 5752	104.5894 2961	113.5444 4002
58	84.4378 6765	87.8513 0262	91.4359 9865	99.1568 5902	107.6812 1820	117.0991 8992
59	86.4933 4099	90.0592 5804	93.8075 3863	101.8921 0405	110.8348 4257	120.7339 2169
60	88.5745 0776	92.2975 7283	96.2146 5171	104.6752 1588	114.0515 3942	124.4504 3493

AMOUNT OF ANNUITY OF 1 (*Cont.*)

	2½%	2¾%	3%	3½%	4%	4½%
1	1.0000 0000	1.0000 0000	1.0000 0000	1.0000 0000	1.0000 0000	1.0000 0000
2	2.0250 0000	2.0275 0000	2.0300 0000	2.0350 0000	2.0400 0000	2.0450 0000
3	3.0756 2500	3.0832 5625	3.0909 0000	3.1062 2500	3.1216 0000	3.1370 2500
4	4.1525 1563	4.1680 4580	4.1836 2700	4.2149 4288	4.2464 6400	4.2781 9113
5	5.2563 2852	5.2826 6706	5.3091 3581	5.3624 6588	5.4163 2256	5.4707 0973
6	6.3877 3673	6.4279 4040	6.4684 0988	6.5501 5218	6.6329 7546	6.7168 9166
7	7.5474 3015	7.6047 0876	7.6624 6218	7.7794 0751	7.8982 9448	8.0191 5179
8	8.7361 1590	8.8138 3825	8.8923 3605	9.0516 8677	9.2142 2626	9.3800 1362
9	9.9545 1880	10.0562 1880	10.1591 0613	10.3684 9581	10.5827 9531	10.8021 1423
10	11.2033 8177	11.3327 6482	11.4638 7931	11.7313 9316	12.0061 0712	12.2882 0937
11	12.4834 6631	12.6444 1585	12.8077 9569	13.1419 9192	13.4863 5141	13.8411 7879
12	13.7955 5297	13.9921 3729	14.1920 2956	14.6019 6164	15.0258 0546	15.4640 3184
13	15.1404 4179	15.3769 2107	15.6177 9045	16.1130 3030	16.6268 3768	17.1599 1327
14	16.5189 5284	16.7997 8639	17.0863 2416	17.6769 8636	18.2919 1119	18.9321 0937
15	17.9319 2666	18.2617 8052	18.5989 1389	19.2956 8088	20.0235 8764	20.7840 5429
16	19.3802 2483	19.7639 7948	20.1568 8130	20.9710 2971	21.8245 3114	22.7193 3673
17	20.8647 3045	21.3074 8892	21.7615 8774	22.7050 1575	23.6975 1239	24.7417 0689
18	22.3863 4871	22.8934 4487	23.4144 3537	24.4996 9130	25.6454 1288	26.8550 8370
19	23.9460 0743	24.5230 1460	25.1168 6844	26.3571 8050	27.6712 2940	29.0635 6246
20	25.5446 5761	26.1973 9750	26.8703 7449	28.2796 8181	29.7780 7858	31.3714 2277
21	27.1832 7405	27.9178 2593	28.6764 8572	30.2694 7068	31.9692 0172	33.7831 3680
22	28.8628 5590	29.6855 6615	30.5367 8030	32.3289 0215	34.2479 6979	36.3033 7795
23	30.5844 2730	31.5019 1921	32.4528 8370	34.4604 1373	36.6178 8858	38.9370 2996
24	32.3490 3798	33.3682 2199	34.4264 7022	36.6665 2821	39.0826 0412	41.6891 9631
25	34.1577 6393	35.2858 4810	36.4592 6432	38.9498 5669	41.6459 0829	44.5652 1015
26	36.0117 0803	37.2562 0892	38.5530 4225	41.3131 0168	44.3117 4462	47.5706 4460
27	37.9120 0073	39.2807 5467	40.7096 3352	43.7590 6024	47.0842 1440	50.7113 2361
28	39.8598 0075	41.3609 7542	42.9309 2252	46.2906 2734	49.9675 8298	53.9933 3317
29	41.8562 9577	43.4984 0224	45.2188 5020	48.9107 9930	52.9662 8630	57.4230 3316
30	43.9027 0316	45.6946 0830	47.5754 1571	51.6226 7728	56.0849 3775	61.0070 6966
31	46.0002 7074	47.9512 1003	50.0026 7818	54.4294 7098	59.3283 3526	64.7523 8779
32	48.1502 7751	50.2698 6831	52.5027 5852	57.3345 0247	62.7014 6867	68.6662 4524
33	50.3540 3445	52.6522 8969	55.0778 4128	60.3412 1005	66.2095 2742	72.7562 2628
34	52.6128 8531	55.1002 2765	57.7301 7652	63.4531 5240	69.8579 0851	77.0302 5646
35	54.9282 0744	57.6154 8391	60.4620 8181	66.6740 1274	73.6522 2486	81.4966 1800
36	57.3014 1263	60.1999 0972	63.2759 4427	70.0076 0318	77.5983 1385	86.1639 6581
37	59.7339 4794	62.8554 0724	66.1742 2259	73.4578 6930	81.7022 4640	91.0413 4427
38	62.2272 9664	65.5839 3094	69.1594 4927	77.0288 9472	85.9703 3626	96.1382 0476
39	64.7829 7906	68.3874 8904	72.2342 3275	80.7249 0604	90.4091 4971	101.4644 2398
40	67.4025 5354	71.2681 4499	75.4012 5973	84.5502 7775	95.0255 1570	107.0303 2306
41	70.0876 1737	74.2280 1898	78.6632 9753	88.5095 3747	99.8265 3633	112.8466 8760
42	72.8398 0781	77.2692 8950	82.0231 9645	92.6073 7128	104.8195 9778	118.9247 8854
43	75.6608 0300	80.3941 9496	85.4838 9234	96.8486 2928	110.0123 8169	125.2764 0402
44	78.5523 2308	83.6050 3532	89.0484 0911	101.2383 3130	115.4128 7696	131.9138 4220
45	81.5161 3116	86.9041 7379	92.7198 6139	105.7816 7290	121.0293 9204	138.8499 6510
46	84.5540 3443	90.2940 3857	96.5014 5723	110.4840 3145	126.8705 6772	146.0982 1353
47	87.6678 8530	93.7771 2463	100.3965 0095	115.3509 7255	132.9453 9043	153.6726 3314
48	90.8595 8243	97.3559 9556	104.4083 9598	120.3882 5659	139.2632 0604	161.5879 0163
49	94.1310 7199	101.0332 8544	108.5406 4785	125.6018 4557	145.8337 3429	169.8593 5720
50	97.4843 4879	104.8117 0079	112.7968 6729	130.9979 1016	152.6670 8366	178.5030 2828
51	100.9214 5751	108.6940 2256	117.1807 7331	136.5828 3702	159.7737 6700	187.5356 6455
52	104.4444 9395	112.6831 0818	121.6961 9651	142.3632 3631	167.1647 1768	196.9747 6946
53	108.0556 0629	116.7818 9365	126.3470 8240	148.3459 4958	174.8513 0639	206.8386 3408
54	111.7569 9645	120.9933 9573	131.1374 9488	154.5380 5782	182.8453 5865	217.1463 7262
55	115.5509 2136	125.3207 1411	136.0716 1972	160.9468 8984	191.1591 7299	227.9179 5938
56	119.4396 9440	129.7670 3375	141.1537 6831	167.5800 3099	199.8055 3991	239.1742 6756
57	123.4256 8676	134.3356 2718	146.3883 8136	174.4453 3207	208.7977 6151	250.9371 0960
58	127.5113 2893	139.0298 5692	151.7800 3280	181.5509 1869	218.1496 7197	263.2292 7953
59	131.6991 1215	143.8531 7799	157.3334 3379	188.9052 0085	227.8756 5885	276.0745 9711
60	135.9915 8995	148.8091 4038	163.0534 3680	196.5168 8288	237.9906 8520	289.4979 5398

AMOUNT OF ANNUITY OF 1 (*Cont.*)

	5%	5½%	6%	6½%	7%	8%
1	1.0000 0000	1.0000 0000	1.0000 0000	1.0000 0000	1.0000 0000	1.0000 0000
2	2.0500 0000	2.0550 0000	2.0600 0000	2.0650 0000	2.0700 0000	2.0800 0000
3	3.1525 0000	3.1680 2500	3.1836 0000	3.1992 2500	3.2149 0000	3.2464 0000
4	4.3101 2500	4.3422 6638	4.3746 1600	4.4071 7463	4.4399 4300	4.5061 1200
5	5.5256 3125	5.5810 9103	5.6370 9296	5.6936 4098	5.7507 3901	5.8666 0096
6	6.8019 1281	6.8880 5103	6.9753 1854	7.0637 2764	7.1532 9074	7.3359 2904
7	8.1420 0845	8.2668 9384	8.3938 3765	8.5228 6994	8.6540 2109	8.9228 0336
8	9.5491 0888	9.7215 7300	9.8974 6791	10.0768 5648	10.2598 0257	10.6366 2763
9	11.0265 6432	11.2562 5951	11.4913 1598	11.7318 5215	11.9779 8875	12.4875 5784
10	12.5778 9254	12.8753 5379	13.1807 9494	13.4944 2254	13.8164 4796	14.4865 6247
11	14.2067 8716	14.5834 9825	14.9716 4264	15.3715 6001	15.7835 9932	16.6454 8746
12	15.9171 2652	16.3855 9065	16.8699 4120	17.3707 1141	17.8884 5127	18.9771 2646
13	17.7129 8285	18.2867 9814	18.8821 3767	19.4998 0765	20.1406 4286	21.4952 9658
14	19.5986 3199	20.2925 7203	21.0150 6593	21.7672 9515	22.5504 8786	24.2149 2030
15	21.5785 6359	22.4086 6350	23.2759 6988	24.1821 6933	25.1290 2201	27.1521 1393
16	23.6574 9177	24.6411 3999	25.6725 2808	26.7540 1034	27.8880 5355	30.3242 8304
17	25.8403 6636	26.9964 0269	28.2128 7976	29.4930 2101	30.8402 1730	33.7502 2569
18	28.1323 8467	29.4812 0483	30.9056 5255	32.4100 6738	33.9990 3251	37.4502 4374
19	30.5390 0391	32.1026 7110	33.7599 9170	35.5167 2176	37.3789 6479	41.4462 6324
20	33.0659 5410	34.8683 1801	36.7855 9120	38.8253 0867	40.9954 9232	45.7619 6430
21	35.7192 5181	37.7860 7550	39.9927 2668	42.3489 5373	44.8651 7678	50.4229 2144
22	38.5052 1440	40.8643 0965	43.3922 9028	46.1016 3573	49.0057 3916	55.4567 5516
23	41.4304 7512	44.1118 4669	46.9958 2769	50.0982 4205	53.4361 4090	60.8932 9557
24	44.5019 9887	47.5379 9825	50.8155 7735	54.3546 2778	58.1766 7076	66.7647 5922
25	47.7270 9882	51.1525 8816	54.8645 1200	58.8876 7859	63.2490 3772	73.1059 3995
26	51.1134 5376	54.9659 8051	59.1563 8272	63.7153 7769	68.6764 7036	79.9544 1515
27	54.6691 2645	58.9891 0943	63.7057 6568	68.8568 7725	74.4838 2328	87.3507 6836
28	58.4025 8277	63.2335 1045	68.5281 1162	74.3325 7427	80.6976 9091	95.3388 2983
29	62.3227 1191	67.7113 5353	73.6397 9832	80.1641 9159	87.3465 2927	103.9659 3622
30	66.4388 4750	72.4354 7797	79.0581 8622	86.3748 6405	94.4607 8632	113.2832 1111
31	70.7607 8988	77.4194 2926	84.8016 7739	92.9892 3021	102.0730 4137	123.3458 6800
32	75.2988 2937	82.6774 9787	90.8897 7803	100.0335 3017	110.2181 5426	134.2135 3744
33	80.0637 7084	88.2247 6025	97.3431 6471	107.5357 0963	118.9334 2506	145.9506 2044
34	85.0669 5938	94.0771 2207	104.1837 5460	115.5255 3076	128.2587 6481	158.6266 7007
35	90.3203 0735	100.2513 6378	111.4347 7987	124.0346 9026	138.2368 7835	172.3168 0368
36	95.8363 2272	106.7651 8879	119.1208 6666	133.0969 4513	148.9134 5984	187.1021 4797
37	101.6281 3886	113.6372 7417	127.2681 1866	142.7482 4656	160.3374 0202	203.0703 1981
38	107.7095 4580	120.8873 2425	135.9042 0578	153.0268 8259	172.5610 2017	220.3159 4540
39	114.0950 2309	128.5361 2708	145.0584 5813	163.9736 2995	185.6402 9158	238.9412 2103
40	120.7997 7424	136.6056 1407	154.7619 6562	175.6319 1590	199.6351 1199	259.0565 1871
41	127.8397 6295	145.1189 2285	165.0476 8356	188.0479 9044	214.6095 6983	280.7810 4021
42	135.2317 5110	154.1004 6360	175.9505 4457	201.2711 0981	230.6322 3972	304.2435 2342
43	142.9933 3866	163.5759 8910	187.5075 7724	215.3537 3195	247.7764 9650	329.5830 0530
44	151.1430 0559	173.5726 6850	199.7580 3188	230.3517 2453	266.1208 5125	356.9496 4572
45	159.7001 5587	184.1191 6527	212.7435 1379	246.3245 8662	285.7493 1084	386.5056 1738
46	168.6851 6366	195.2457 1936	226.5081 2462	263.3356 8475	306.7517 6260	418.4260 6677
47	178.1194 2185	206.9842 3392	241.0986 1210	281.4525 0426	329.2243 8598	452.9001 5211
48	188.0253 9294	219.3683 6679	256.5645 2882	300.7469 1704	353.2700 9300	490.1321 6428
49	198.4266 6259	232.4336 2696	272.9584 0055	321.2954 6665	378.9989 9951	530.3427 3742
50	209.3479 9572	246.2174 7645	290.3359 0458	343.1796 7198	406.5289 2947	573.7701 5642
51	220.8153 9550	260.7594 3765	308.7560 5886	366.4863 5066	435.9859 5454	620.6717 6893
52	232.8561 6528	276.1012 0672	328.2814 2239	391.3079 6345	467.5049 7135	671.3255 1044
53	245.4989 7354	292.2867 7309	348.9783 0773	417.7429 8108	501.2303 1935	726.0315 5128
54	258.7739 2222	309.3625 4561	370.9170 0620	445.8962 7485	537.3164 4170	785.1140 7538
55	272.7126 1833	327.3774 8562	394.1720 2657	475.8795 3271	575.9285 9262	848.9232 0141
56	287.3482 4924	346.3832 4733	418.8223 4816	507.8117 0234	617.2435 9410	917.8370 5752
57	302.7156 6171	366.4343 2593	444.9516 8905	541.8194 6299	661.4506 4569	992.2640 2213
58	318.8514 4479	387.5882 1386	472.6487 9040	578.0377 2808	708.7521 9089	1072.6451 4390
59	335.7940 1703	409.9055 6562	502.0077 1782	616.6101 8041	759.3648 4425	1159.4567 5541
60	353.5837 1788	433.4503 7173	533.1281 8089	657.6898 4214	813.5203 8335	1253.2132 9584

PRESENT VALUE OF ANNUITY OF 1

	½%	⅝%	¾%	⅞%	1%	1⅛%
1	0.9950 2488	0.9937 8882	0.9925 5583	0.9913 2590	0.9900 9901	0.9888 7515
2	1.9850 9938	1.9814 0504	1.9777 2291	1.9740 5294	1.9703 9506	1.9667 4923
3	2.9702 4814	2.9628 8699	2.9555 5624	2.9482 5570	2.9409 8521	2.9337 4460
4	3.9504 9566	3.9382 7279	3.9261 1041	3.9140 0813	3.9019 6555	3.8899 8230
5	4.9258 6633	4.9076 0029	4.8894 3961	4.8713 8352	4.8534 3124	4.8355 8200
6	5.8963 8441	5.8709 0712	5.8455 9763	5.8204 5454	5.7954 7647	5.7706 6205
7	6.8620 7404	6.8282 3068	6.7946 3785	6.7612 9323	6.7281 9453	6.6953 3948
8	7.8229 5924	7.7796 0813	7.7366 1325	7.6939 7098	7.6516 7775	7.6097 3002
9	8.7790 6392	8.7250 7640	8.6715 7642	8.6185 5859	8.5660 1758	8.5139 4810
10	9.7304 1186	9.6646 7220	9.5995 7958	9.5351 2624	9.4713 0453	9.4081 0690
11	10.6770 2673	10.5984 3200	10.5206 7452	10.4437 4348	10.3676 2825	10.2923 1832
12	11.6189 3207	11.5263 9205	11.4349 1267	11.3444 7929	11.2550 7747	11.1666 9302
13	12.5561 5131	12.4485 8837	12.3423 4508	12.2374 0202	12.1337 4007	12.0313 4044
14	13.4887 0777	13.3650 5676	13.2430 2242	13.1225 7945	13.0037 0304	12.8863 6880
15	14.4166 2465	14.2758 3281	14.1369 9495	14.0000 7876	13.8650 5252	13.7318 8509
16	15.3399 2502	15.1809 5186	15.0243 1261	14.8699 6656	14.7178 7378	14.5679 9514
17	16.2586 3186	16.0804 4905	15.9050 2492	15.7323 0885	15.5622 5127	15.3948 0360
18	17.1727 6802	16.9743 5931	16.7791 8107	16.5871 7111	16.3982 6858	16.2124 1395
19	18.0823 5624	17.8627 1733	17.6468 2984	17.4346 1820	17.2260 0850	17.0209 2850
20	18.9874 1915	18.7455 5759	18.5080 1969	18.2747 1445	18.0455 5297	17.8204 4845
21	19.8879 7925	19.6229 1438	19.3627 9870	19.1075 2361	18.8569 8313	18.6110 7387
22	20.7840 5896	20.4948 2174	20.2112 1459	19.9331 0891	19.6603 7934	19.3929 0371
23	21.6756 8055	21.3613 1353	21.0533 1473	20.7515 3300	20.4558 2113	20.1660 3580
24	22.5628 6622	22.2224 2338	21.8891 4614	21.5628 5799	21.2433 8726	20.9305 6693
25	23.4456 3803	23.0781 8473	22.7187 5547	22.3671 4547	22.0231 5570	21.6865 9276
26	24.3240 1794	23.9286 3079	23.5421 8905	23.1644 5647	22.7952 0366	22.4342 0792
27	25.1980 2780	24.7737 9457	24.3594 9286	23.9548 5152	23.5596 0759	23.1735 0598
28	26.0676 8936	25.6137 0889	25.1707 1251	24.7383 9060	24.3164 4316	23.9045 7946
29	26.9330 2423	26.4484 0635	25.9758 9331	25.5151 3319	25.0657 8530	24.6275 1986
30	27.7940 5397	27.2779 1935	26.7750 8021	26.2851 3823	25.8077 0822	25.3424 1766
31	28.6507 9997	28.1022 8010	27.5683 1783	27.0484 6417	26.5422 8537	26.0493 6233
32	29.5032 8355	28.9215 2060	28.3556 5045	27.8051 6894	27.2695 8947	26.7484 4236
33	30.3515 2592	29.7356 7265	29.1371 2203	28.5553 0998	27.9896 9255	27.4397 4522
34	31.1955 4818	30.5447 6785	29.9127 7621	29.2989 4422	28.7026 6589	28.1233 5745
35	32.0353 7132	31.3488 3761	30.6826 5629	30.0361 2809	29.4085 8009	28.7993 6460
36	32.8710 1624	32.1479 1315	31.4468 0525	30.7669 1757	30.1075 0504	29.4678 5127
37	33.7025 0372	32.9420 2550	32.2052 6576	31.4913 6810	30.7995 0994	30.1289 0114
38	34.5298 5445	33.7312 0546	32.9580 8016	32.2095 3467	31.4846 6330	30.7825 9692
39	35.3530 8900	34.5154 8369	33.7052 9048	32.9214 7179	32.1630 3298	31.4290 2044
40	36.1722 2786	35.2948 9062	34.4469 3844	33.6272 3350	32.8346 8611	32.0682 5260
41	36.9872 9141	36.0694 5652	35.1830 6545	34.3268 7335	33.4996 8922	32.7903 7340
42	37.7982 9991	36.8392 1145	35.9137 1260	35.0204 4446	34.1581 0814	33.3254 6195
43	38.6052 7354	37.6041 8529	36.6389 2070	35.7079 9947	34.8100 0806	33.9435 9649
44	39.4082 3238	38.3644 0774	37.3587 3022	36.3895 9055	35.4554 5352	34.5548 5438
45	40.2071 9640	39.1199 0831	38.0731 8136	37.0652 6944	36.0945 0844	35.1593 1212
46	41.0021 8547	39.8707 1634	38.7823 1401	37.7350 8743	36.7272 3608	35.7570 4536
47	41.7932 1937	40.6168 6096	39.4861 6774	38.3990 9535	37.3536 9909	36.3481 2891
48	42.5803 1778	41.3583 7114	40.1847 8189	39.0573 4359	37.9739 5949	36.9326 3674
49	43.3635 0028	42.0952 7566	40.8781 9542	39.7098 8212	38.5880 7871	37.5106 4202
50	44.1427 8635	42.8276 0314	41.5664 4707	40.3567 6047	39.1961 1753	38.0822 1708
51	44.9181 9537	43.5553 8201	42.2495 7525	40.9980 2772	39.7981 3617	38.6474 3345
52	45.6897 4664	44.2786 4050	42.9276 1812	41.6337 3256	40.3941 9423	39.2063 6188
53	46.4574 5934	44.9974 0671	43.6006 1351	42.2639 2324	40.9843 5072	39.7590 7232
54	47.2213 5258	45.7117 0853	44.2685 9902	42.8886 4757	41.5686 6408	40.3056 3394
55	47.9814 4535	46.4215 7370	44.9316 1193	43.5079 5298	42.1471 9216	40.8461 1514
56	48.7377 5657	47.1270 2976	45.5896 8926	44.1218 8647	42.7199 9224	41.3805 8358
57	49.4903 0505	47.8281 0410	46.2428 6776	44.7304 9465	43.2871 2102	41.9091 0613
58	50.2391 0950	48.5248 2396	46.8911 8388	45.3338 2369	43.8486 3468	42.4317 4896
59	50.9841 8855	49.2172 1636	47.5346 7382	45.9319 1939	44.4045 8879	42.9485 7746
60	51.7255 6075	49.9053 0818	48.1733 7352	46.5248 2716	44.9550 3841	43.4596 5633

From J. W. Glover, "Tables of Applied Math. in Finance, Insurance, Statistics." George Wahr, publisher, Ann Arbor, Michigan.

	1¼%	1⅜%	1½%	1¾%	2%	2¼%
1	0.9876 5432	0.9864 3650	0.9852 2167	0.9828 0098	0.9803 9216	0.9779 9511
2	1.9631 1538	1.9594 9346	1.9558 8342	1.9486 9875	1.9415 6094	1.9344 6955
3	2.9265 3371	2.9193 5237	2.9122 0042	2.8979 8403	2.8838 8327	2.8698 9687
4	3.8780 5798	3.8661 9222	3.8543 8465	3.8309 4254	3.8077 2870	3.7847 4021
5	4.8178 3504	4.8001 8962	4.7826 4497	4.7478 5508	4.7134 5951	4.6794 5253
6	5.7460 0992	5.7215 1874	5.6971 8717	5.6489 9762	5.6014 3089	5.5544 7680
7	6.6627 2585	6.6303 5140	6.5982 1396	6.5346 4139	6.4719 9107	6.4102 4626
8	7.5681 2429	7.5268 5712	7.4859 2508	7.4050 5297	7.3254 8144	7.2471 8461
9	8.4623 4498	8.4112 0308	8.3605 1732	8.2604 9432	8.1622 3671	8.0657 0622
10	9.3455 2591	9.2835 5421	9.2221 8455	9.1012 2291	8.9825 8501	8.8662 1635
11	10.2178 0337	10.1440 7320	10.0711 1779	9.9274 9181	9.7868 4805	9.6491 1134
12	11.0793 1197	10.9929 2054	10.9075 0521	10.7395 4969	10.5753 4122	10.4147 7882
13	11.9301 8466	11.8302 5454	11.7315 3222	11.5376 4097	11.3483 7375	11.1635 9787
14	12.7705 5275	12.6562 3136	12.5433 8150	12.3220 0587	12.1062 4877	11.8959 3924
15	13.6005 4592	13.4710 0504	13.3432 3301	13.0928 8046	12.8492 6350	12.6121 6551
16	14.4202 9227	14.2747 2754	14.1312 6405	13.8504 9677	13.5777 0931	13.3126 3131
17	15.2299 1829	15.0675 4874	14.9076 4931	14.5950 8282	14.2918 7188	13.9976 8343
18	16.0295 4893	15.8496 1651	15.6725 6089	15.3268 6272	14.9920 3125	14.6676 6106
19	16.8193 0759	16.6210 7671	16.4261 6837	16.0460 5673	15.6784 6201	15.3228 9590
20	17.5993 1613	17.3820 7320	17.1686 3879	16.7528 8130	16.3514 3334	15.9637 1237
21	18.3696 9495	18.1327 4792	17.9001 3673	17.4475 4919	17.0112 0916	16.5904 2775
22	19.1305 6291	18.8732 4086	18.6208 2437	18.1302 6948	17.6580 4820	17.2033 5232
23	19.8820 3744	19.6036 9012	19.3308 6145	18.8012 4764	18.2922 0412	17.8027 8955
24	20.6242 3451	20.3242 3193	20.0304 0537	19.4606 8565	18.9139 2560	18.3890 3624
25	21.3572 6865	21.0350 0067	20.7196 1120	20.1087 8196	19.5234 5647	18.9623 8263
26	22.0812 5299	21.7361 2890	21.3986 3172	20.7457 3166	20.1210 3576	19.5231 1260
27	22.7962 9925	22.4277 4737	22.0676 1746	21.3717 2644	20.7068 9780	20.0715 0376
28	23.5025 1778	23.1099 8508	22.7267 1671	21.9869 5474	21.2812 7236	20.6078 2764
29	24.2000 1756	23.7829 6925	23.3760 7558	22.5916 0171	21.8443 8466	21.1323 4977
30	24.8889 0623	24.4468 2540	24.0158 3801	23.1858 4934	22.3964 5555	21.6453 2985
31	25.5692 9010	25.1016 7734	24.6461 4582	23.7698 7650	22.9377 0152	22.1470 2186
32	26.2412 7418	25.7476 4719	25.2671 3874	24.3438 5897	23.4683 3482	22.6376 7419
33	26.9049 6215	26.3848 5543	25.8789 5442	24.9079 6951	23.9885 6355	23.1175 2977
34	27.5604 5644	27.0134 2089	26.4817 2849	25.4623 7789	24.4985 9172	23.5868 2618
35	28.2078 5822	27.6334 6080	27.0755 9458	26.0072 5100	24.9986 1933	24.0457 9577
36	28.8472 6737	28.2450 9080	27.6606 8431	26.5427 5283	25.4888 4248	24.4946 6579
37	29.4787 8259	28.8484 2496	28.2371 2740	27.0690 4455	25.9694 5341	24.9336 5848
38	30.1025 0133	29.4435 7579	28.8050 5163	27.5862 8457	26.4406 4060	25.3629 9118
39	30.7185 1983	30.0306 5430	29.3645 8288	28.0946 2857	26.9025 8883	25.7828 7646
40	31.3269 3316	30.6097 6996	29.9158 4520	28.5942 2955	27.3554 7924	26.1935 2221
41	31.9278 3522	31.1810 3079	30.4589 6079	29.0852 3789	27.7994 8945	26.5951 3174
42	32.5213 1874	31.7445 4332	30.9940 5004	29.5678 0135	28.2347 9358	26.9879 0390
53	33.1074 7530	32.3004 1264	31.5212 3157	30.0420 6522	28.6615 6233	27.3720 3316
44	33.6863 9536	32.8487 4243	32.0406 2223	30.5081 7221	29.0799 6307	27.7477 0969
45	34.2581 6825	33.3896 3495	32.5523 3718	30.9662 6261	29.4901 5987	28.1151 1950
46	34.8228 8222	33.9231 9108	33.0564 8983	31.4164 7431	29.8923 1360	28.4744 4450
47	35.3806 2442	34.4495 1031	33.5531 9195	31.8589 4281	30.2865 8196	28.8258 6259
48	35.9314 8091	34.9686 9081	34.0425 5365	32.2938 0129	30.6731 1957	29.1695 4777
49	36.4755 3670	35.4808 2941	34.5246 8339	32.7211 8063	31.0520 7801	29.5056 7019
50	37.0128 7574	35.9860 2161	34.9996 8807	33.1412 0946	31.4236 0589	29.8343 9627
51	37.5435 8099	36.4843 6164	35.4676 7298	33.5540 1421	31.7878 4892	30.1558 8877
52	38.0677 3431	36.9759 4243	35.9287 4185	33.9597 1913	32.1449 4992	30.4703 0687
53	38.5854 1660	37.4608 5566	36.3829 9690	34.3584 4633	32.4950 4894	30.7778 0623
54	39.0967 0776	37.9391 9178	36.8305 3882	34.7503 1579	32.8382 8327	31.0785 3910
55	39.6016 8667	38.4110 3998	37.2714 6681	35.1354 4550	33.1747 8752	31.3726 5438
56	40.1004 3128	38.8764 8826	37.7058 7863	35.5139 5135	33.5046 9365	31.6602 9768
57	40.5930 1855	39.3356 2344	38.1338 7058	35.8859 4727	33.8281 3103	31.9416 1142
58	41.0795 2449	39.7885 3114	38.5555 3751	36.2515 4523	34.1452 2650	32.2167 3489
59	41.5600 2419	40.2352 9582	38.9709 7292	36.6108 5526	34.4561 0441	32.4858 0429
60	42.0345 9179	40.6760 0081	39.3802 6889	36.9639 8552	34.7608 8668	32.7489 5285

PRESENT VALUE OF ANNUITY OF 1 (*Cont.*)

	2½%	2¾%	3%	3½%	4%	4½%
1	0.9756 0976	0.9732 3601	0.9708 7379	0.9661 8357	0.9615 3846	0.9569 3780
2	1.9274 2415	1.9204 2434	1.9134 6970	1.8996 9428	1.8860 9467	1.8726 6775
3	2.8560 2356	2.8422 6213	2.8286 1135	2.8016 3698	2.7750 9103	2.7489 6435
4	3.7619 7421	3.7394 2787	3.7170 9840	3.6730 7921	3.6298 9522	3.5875 2570
5	4.6458 2850	4.6125 8186	4.5797 0719	4.5150 5238	4.4518 2233	4.3899 7674
6	5.5081 2536	5.4623 6678	5.4171 9144	5.3285 5302	5.2421 3686	5.1578 7248
7	6.3493 9060	6.2894 0806	6.2302 8296	6.1145 4398	6.0020 5467	5.8927 0094
8	7.1701 3717	7.0943 1441	7.0196 9219	6.8739 5554	6.7327 4487	6.5958 8607
9	7.9708 6553	7.8776 7826	7.7861 0892	7.6076 8651	7.4353 3161	7.2687 9050
10	8.7520 6393	8.6400 7616	8.5302 0284	8.3166 0532	8.1108 9578	7.9127 1818
11	9.5142 0871	9.3820 6926	9.2526 2411	9.0015 5104	8.7604 7671	8.5289 1692
12	10.2577 6460	10.1042 0366	9.9540 0399	9.6633 3433	9.3850 7376	9.1185 8078
13	10.9831 8497	10.8070 1086	10.6349 5533	10.3027 3849	9.9856 4785	9.6828 5242
14	11.6909 1217	11.4910 0814	11.2960 7314	10.9205 2028	10.5631 2293	10.2228 2528
15	12.3813 7773	12.1566 9892	11.9379 3509	11.5174 1090	11.1183 8743	10.7395 4573
16	13.0550 0266	12.8045 7315	12.5611 0203	12.0941 1681	11.6522 9561	11.2340 1505
17	13.7121 9772	13.4351 0769	13.1661 1847	12.6513 2059	12.1656 6885	11.7071 9143
18	14.3533 6363	14.0487 6661	13.7535 1308	13.1896 8173	12.6592 9697	12.1599 9180
19	14.9788 9134	14.6460 0157	14.3237 9911	13.7098 3742	13.1339 3940	12.5932 9359
20	15.5891 6229	15.2272 5213	14.8774 7486	14.2124 0330	13.5903 2634	13.0079 3645
21	16.1845 4857	15.7929 4612	15.4150 2414	14.6979 7420	14.0291 5995	13.4047 2388
22	16.7654 1324	16,3434 9987	15.9369 1664	15.1671 2484	14.4511 1533	13.7844 2476
23	17.3321 1048	16.8793 1861	16.4436 0839	15.6204 1047	14.8568 4167	14.1477 7489
24	17.8849 8583	17.4007 9670	16.9355 4212	16.0583 6760	15.2469 6314	14.4954 7837
25	18.4243 7642	17.9083 1795	17.4131 4769	16.4815 1459	15.6220 7994	14.8282 0896
26	18.9506 1114	18.4022 5592	17.8768 4242	16.8903 5226	15.9827 6918	15.1466 1145
27	19.4640 1087	18.8829 7413	18.3270 3147	17.2853 6451	16.3295 8575	15.4513 0282
28	19.9648 8866	19.3508 2640	18.7641 0823	17.6670 1885	16.6630 6322	15.7428 7351
29	20.4535 4991	19.8061 5708	19.1884 5459	18.0357 6700	16.9837 1463	16.0218 8853
30	20.9302 9259	20.2493 0130	19.6004 4135	18.3920 4541	17.2920 3330	16.2888 8854
31	21.3954 0741	20.6805 8520	20.0004 2849	18.7362 7576	17.5884 9356	16.5443 9095
32	21.8491 7796	21.1003 2623	20.3887 6553	19.0688 6547	17.8735 5150	16.7888 9086
33	22.2918 8094	21.5088 3332	20.7657 9178	19.3902 0818	18.1476 4567	17.0228 6207
34	22.7237 8628	21.9064 0712	21.1318 3668	19.7006 8423	18.4111 9776	17.2467 5796
35	23.1451 5734	22.2933 4026	21.4872 2007	20.0006 6110	18.6646 1323	17.4610 1240
36	23.5562 5107	22.6699 1753	21.8322 5250	20.2904 9381	18.9082 8195	17.6660 4058
37	23.9573 1812	23.0364 1609	22.1672 3544	20.5705 2542	19.1425 7880	17.8622 3979
38	24.3486 0304	23.3931 0568	22.4924 6159	20.8410 8736	19.3678 6423	18.0499 9023
39	24.7303 4443	23.7402 4884	22.8082 1513	21.1024 9987	19.5844 8484	18.2296 5572
40	25.1027 7505	24.0781 0106	23.1147 7197	21.3550 7234	19.7927 7388	18.4015 8442
41	25.4661 2200	24.4069 1101	23.4123 9997	21.5991 0371	19.9930 5181	18.5661 0949
42	25.8206 0683	24.7269 2069	23.7013 5920	21.8348 8281	20.1856 2674	18.7235 4975
43	26.1664 4569	25.0383 6563	23.9819 0213	22.0626 8870	20.3707 9494	18.8742 1029
44	26.5038 4945	25.3414 7507	24.2542 7392	22.2827 9102	20.5488 4129	19.0183 8305
45	26.8330 2386	25.6364 7209	24.5187 1254	22.4954 5026	20.7200 3970	19.1563 4742
46	27.1541 6962	25.9235 7381	24.7754 4907	22.7009 1813	20.8846 5356	19.2883 7074
47	27.4674 8255	26.2029 9154	25.0247 0783	22.8994 3780	21.0429 3612	19.4147 0884
48	27.7731 5371	26.4749 3094	25.2667 0664	23.0912 4425	21.1951 3088	19.5356 0654
49	28.0713 6947	26.7395 9215	25.5016 5693	23.2765 6450	21.3414 7200	19.6512 9813
50	28.3623 1168	26.9971 6998	25.7297 6401	23.4556 1787	21.4821 8462	19.7620 0778
51	28.6461 5774	27.2478 5400	25.9512 2719	23.6286 1630	21.6174 8521	19.8679 5003
52	28.9230 8072	27.4918 2871	26.1662 3999	23.7957 6454	21.7475 8193	19.9693 3017
53	29.1932 4948	27.7292 7368	26.3749 9028	23.9572 6043	21.8726 7493	20.0663 4466
54	29.4568 2876	27.9603 6368	26.5776 6047	24.1132 9510	21.9929 5667	20.1591 8149
55	29.7139 7928	28.1852 6879	26.7744 2764	24.2640 5323	22.1086 1218	20.2480 2057
56	29.9648 5784	28.4041 5454	26.9654 6373	24.4097 1327	22.2189 1940	20.3330 3404
57	30.2096 1740	28.6171 8203	27.1509 3566	24.5504 4760	22.3267 4943	20.4143 8664
58	30.4484 0722	28.8245 0806	27.3310 0549	24.6864 2281	22.4295 6676	20.4922 3602
59	30.6813 7290	29.0262 8522	27.5058 3058	24.8177 9981	22.5284 2957	20.5667 3303
60	30.9086 5649	29.2226 6201	27.6755 6367	24.9447 3412	22.6234 8997	20.6380 2204

PRESENT VALUE OF ANNUITY OF 1 (*Cont.*)

	5%	5½%	6%	6½%	7%	8%
1	0.9523 8095	0.9478 6730	0.9433 9623	0.9389 6714	0.9345 7944	0.9259 2593
2	1.8594 1043	1.8463 1971	1.8333 9267	1.8206 2642	1.8080 1817	1.7832 6475
3	2.7232 4803	2.6979 3338	2.6730 1195	2.6484 7551	2.6243 1604	2.5770 9699
4	3.5459 5050	3.5051 5012	3.4651 0561	3.4257 9860	3.3872 1126	3.3121 2684
5	4.3294 7667	4.2702 8448	4.2123 6379	4.1556 7944	4.1001 9744	3.9927 1004
6	5.0756 9206	4.9955 3031	4.9173 2433	4.8410 1356	4.7665 3966	4.6228 7966
7	5.7863 7340	5.6829 6712	5.5823 8144	5.4845 1977	5.3892 8940	5.2063 7006
8	6.4632 1276	6.3345 6599	6.2097 9381	6.0887 5096	5.9712 9851	5.7466 3894
9	7.1078 2168	6.9521 9525	6.8016 9227	6.6561 0419	6.5152 3225	6.2468 8791
10	7.7217 3493	7.5376 2583	7.3600 8705	7.1888 3022	7.0235 8154	6.7100 8140
11	8.3064 1422	8.0925 3633	7.8868 7458	7.6890 4246	7.4986 7434	7.1389 6426
12	8.8632 5164	8.6185 1785	8.3838 4394	8.1587 2532	7.9426 8630	7.5360 7802
13	9.3935 7299	9.1170 7853	8.8526 8296	8.5997 4208	8.3576 5074	7.9037 7594
14	9.8986 4094	9.5896 4790	9.2949 8393	9.0138 4233	8.7454 6799	8.2442 3698
15	10.3796 5804	10.0375 8094	9.7122 4899	9.4026 6885	9.1079 1401	8 5594 7869
16	10.8377 6956	10.4621 6203	10.1058 9527	9.7677 6418	9.4466 4860	8.8513 6916
17	11.2740 6625	10.8646 0856	10.4772 5969	10.1105 7670	9.7632 2299	9.1216 3811
18	11.6895 8690	11.2460 7447	10.8276 0348	10.4324 6638	10.0590 8691	9.3718 8714
19	12.0853 2086	11.6076 5352	11.1581 1649	10.7347 1022	10.3355 9524	9.6035 9920
20	12.4622 1034	11.9503 8249	11.4699 2122	11.0185 0725	10.5940 1425	9.8181 4741
21	12.8211 5271	12.2752 4406	11.7640 7662	11.2849 8333	10.8355 2733	10.0168 0316
22	13.1630 0258	12.5831 6973	12.0415 8172	11.5351 9562	11.0612 4050	10.2007 4366
23	13.4885 7388	12.8750 4240	12.3033 7898	11.7701 3673	11.2721 8738	10.3710 5895
24	13.7986 4179	13.1516 9895	12.5503 5753	11.9907 3871	11.4693 3400	10.5287 5828
25	14.0939 4457	13.4139 3266	12.7833 5616	12.1978 7672	11.6535 8318	10.6747 7619
26	14.3751 8530	13.6624 9541	13.0031 6619	12.3923 7251	11.8257 7867	10.8099 7795
27	14.6430 3362	13.8980 9991	13.2105 3414	12.5749 9766	11.9867 0904	10.9351 6477
28	14.8981 2726	14.1214 2172	13.4061 6428	12.7464 7668	12.1371 1125	11.0510 7849
29	15.1410 7358	14.3331 0116	13.5907 2102	12.9074 8984	12.2776 7407	11.1584 0601
30	15.3724 5103	14.5337 4517	13.7648 3115	13.0586 7591	12.4090 4118	11.2577 8334
31	15.5928 1050	14.7239 2907	13.9290 8599	13.2006 3465	12.5318 1419	11.3497 9939
32	15.8026 7667	14.9041 9817	14.0840 4339	13.3339 2925	12.6465 5532	11.4349 9944
33	16.0025 4921	15.0750 6936	14.2302 2961	13.4590 8850	12.7537 9002	11.5138 8837
34	16.1929 0401	15.2370 3257	14.3681 4114	13.5766 0892	12.8540 0936	11.5869 3367
35	16.3741 9429	15.3905 5220	14.4982 4636	13.6869 5673	12.9476 7230	11.6545 6822
36	16.5468 5171	15.5360 6843	14.6209 8713	13.7905 6970	13.0352 0776	11.7171 9279
37	16.7112 8734	15.6739 9851	14.7367 8031	13.8878 5887	13.1170 1660	11.7751 7851
38	16.8678 9271	15.8047 3793	14.8460 1916	13.9792 1021	13.1934 7345	11.8288 6899
39	17.0170 4067	15.9286 6154	14.9490 7468	14.0649 8611	13.2649 2846	11.8785 8240
40	17.1590 8635	16.0461 2469	15.0462 9687	14.1455 2687	13.3317 0884	11.9246 1333
41	17.2943 6796	16.1574 6416	15.1380 1592	14.2211 5199	13.3941 2041	11.9672 3457
42	17.4232 0758	16.2629 9920	15.2245 4332	14.2921 6149	13.4524 4898	12.0066 9867
43	17.5459 1198	16.3630 3242	15.3061 7294	14.3588 3708	13.5069 6167	12.0432 3951
44	17.6627 7331	16.4578 5063	15.3831 8202	14.4214 4327	13.5579 0810	12.0770 7362
45	17.7740 6982	16.5477 2572	15.4558 3209	14.4802 2842	13.6055 2159	12.1084 0150
46	17.8800 6650	16.6329 1537	15.5243 6990	14.5354 2575	13.6500 2018	12.1374 0880
47	17.9810 1571	16.7136 6386	15.5890 2821	14.5872 5422	13.6916 0764	12.1642 6741
48	18.0771 5782	16.7902 0271	15.6500 2661	14.6359 1946	13.7304 7443	12.1891 3649
49	18.1687 2173	16.8627 5139	15.7075 7227	14.6816 1451	13.7667 9853	12.2121 6341
50	18.2559 2546	16.9315 1790	15.7618 6064	14.7245 2067	13.8007 4629	12.2334 8464
51	18.3389 7663	16.9966 9943	15.8130 7607	14.7648 0814	13.8324 7317	12.2532 2652
52	18.4180 7298	17.0584 8287	15.8613 9252	14.8026 3675	13.8621 2446	12.2715 0604
53	18.4934 0284	17.1170 4538	15.9069 7408	14.8381 5658	13.8898 3594	12.2884 3152
54	18.5651 4556	17.1725 5486	15.9499 7554	14.8715 0852	13.9157 3453	12.3041 0326
55	18.6334 7196	17.2251 7048	15.9905 4297	14.9028 2490	13.9399 3881	12.3186 1413
56	18.6985 4473	17.2750 4311	16.0288 1412	14.9322 2996	13.9625 5964	12.3320 5012
57	18.7605 1879	17.3223 1575	16.0649 1898	14.9598 4033	13.9837 0059	12.3444 9085
58	18.8195 4170	17.3671 2393	16.0989 8017	14.9857 6557	14.0034 5850	12.3560 1005
59	18.8757 5400	17.4095 9614	16.1311 1337	15.0101 0852	14.0219 2383	12.3666 7597
60	18.9292 8952	17.4498 5416	16.1614 2771	15.0329 6574	14.0391 8115	12.3765 5182

ANNUITY WHICH AMOUNTS TO 1

	½%	⅝%	¾%	⅞%	1%	1⅛%
1	1.0000 0000	1.0000 0000	1.0000 0000	1.0000 0000	1.0000 0000	1.0000 0000
2	0.4987 5312	0.4984 4237	0.4981 3200	0.4978 2203	0.4975 1244	0.4972 0323
3	0.3316 7221	0.3312 5865	0.3308 4579	0.3304 3361	0.3300 2211	0.3296 1130
4	0.2481 3279	0.2476 6842	0.2472 0501	0.2467 4257	0.2462 8109	0.2458 2058
5	0.1980 0997	0.1975 1558	0.1970 2242	0.1965 3049	0.1960 3980	0.1955 5034
6	0.1645 9546	0.1640 8143	0.1635 6891	0.1630 5789	0.1625 4837	0.1620 4034
7	0.1407 2854	0.1402 0082	0.1396 7488	0.1391 5070	0.1386 2828	0.1381 0762
8	0.1228 2886	0.1222 9118	0.1217 5552	0.1212 2190	0.1206 9029	0.1201 6071
9	0.1089 0736	0.1083 6218	0.1078 1929	0.1072 7868	0.1067 4036	0.1062 0432
10	0.0977 7057	0.0972 1962	0.0966 7123	0.0961 2538	0.0955 8208	0.0950 4131
11	0.0886 5903	0.0881 0358	0.0875 5094	0.0870 0111	0.0864 5408	0.0859 0984
12	0.0810 6643	0.0805 0742	0.0799 5148	0.0793 9860	0.0788 4879	0.0783 0203
13	0.0746 4224	0.0740 8039	0.0735 2188	0.0729 6669	0.0724 1482	0.0718 6626
14	0.0691 3609	0.0685 7198	0.0680 1146	0.0674 5453	0.0669 0117	0.0663 5138
15	0.0643 6436	0.0637 9845	0.0632 3639	0.0626 7817	0.0621 2378	0.0615 7321
16	0.0601 8937	0.0596 2202	0.0590 5879	0.0584 9965	0.0579 4460	0.0573 9363
17	0.0565 0579	0.0559 3732	0.0553 7321	0.0548 1346	0.0542 5806	0.0537 0698
18	0.0532 3173	0.0526 6239	0.0520 9766	0.0515 3756	0.0509 8205	0.0504 3113
19	0.0503 0253	0.0497 3252	0.0491 6740	0.0486 0715	0.0480 5175	0.0475 0120
20	0.0476 6645	0.0470 9597	0.0465 3063	0.0459 7042	0.0454 1531	0.0448 6531
21	0.0452 8163	0.0447 1083	0.0441 4543	0.0435 8541	0.0430 3075	0.0424 8145
22	0.0431 1380	0.0425 4281	0.0419 7748	0.0414 1779	0.0408 6372	0.0403 1525
23	0.0411 3465	0.0405 6360	0.0399 9846	0.0394 3921	0.0388 8584	0.0383 3833
24	0.0393 2061	0.0387 4959	0.0381 8474	0.0376 2604	0.0370 7347	0.0365 2701
25	0.0376 5186	0.0370 8096	0.0365 1650	0.0359 5843	0.0354 0675	0.0348 6144
26	0.0361 1163	0.0355 4094	0.0349 7693	0.0344 1959	0.0338 6888	0.0333 2479
27	0.0346 8565	0.0341 1523	0.0335 5176	0.0329 9520	0.0324 4553	0.0319 0273
28	0.0333 6167	0.0327 9159	0.0322 2871	0.0316 7300	0.0311 2444	0.0305 8299
29	0.0321 2914	0.0315 5946	0.0309 9723	0.0304 4243	0.0298 9502	0.0293 5498
30	0.0309 7892	0.0304 0969	0.0298 4816	0.0292 9434	0.0287 4811	0.0282 0953
31	0.0299 0304	0.0293 3430	0.0287 7352	0.0282 2068	0.0276 7573	0.0271 3866
32	0.0288 9453	0.0283 2633	0.0277 6634	0.0272 1454	0.0266 7089	0.0261 3535
33	0.0279 4727	0.0273 7964	0.0268 2048	0.0262 6976	0.0257 2744	0.0251 9349
34	0.0270 5586	0.0264 8883	0.0259 3053	0.0253 8092	0.0248 3997	0.0243 0763
35	0.0262 1550	0.0256 4911	0.0250 9170	0.0245 4324	0.0240 0368	0.0234 7299
36	0.0254 2194	0.0248 5622	0.0242 9973	0.0237 5244	0.0232 1431	0.0226 8529
37	0.0246 7139	0.0241 0636	0.0235 5082	0.0230 0473	0.0224 6805	0.0219 4072
38	0.0239 6045	0.0233 9614	0.0228 4157	0.0222 9671	0.0217 6150	0.0212 3589
39	0.0232 8607	0.0227 2250	0.0221 6893	0.0216 2531	0.0210 9160	0.0205 6773
40	0.0226 4552	0.0220 8271	0.0215 3016	0.0209 8780	0.0204 5560	0.0199 3349
41	0.0220 3631	0.0214 7429	0.0209 2276	0.0203 8169	0.0198 5102	0.0193 3069
42	0.0214 5622	0.0208 9499	0.0203 4452	0.0198 0475	0.0192 7563	0.0187 5709
43	0.0209 0320	0.0203 4278	0.0197 9338	0.0192 5493	0.0187 2737	0.0182 1064
44	0.0203 7541	0.0198 1583	0.0192 6751	0.0187 3039	0.0182 0441	0.0176 8949
45	0.0198 7117	0.0193 1243	0.0187 6521	0.0182 2943	0.0177 0505	0.0171 9197
46	0.0193 8894	0.0188 3106	0.0182 8495	0.0177 5053	0.0172 2775	0.0167 1652
47	0.0189 2733	0.0183 7032	0.0178 2532	0.0172 9228	0.0167 7111	0.0162 6173
48	0.0184 8503	0.0179 2890	0.0173 8504	0.0168 5338	0.0163 3384	0.0158 2632
49	0.0180 6087	0.0175 0563	0.0169 6292	0.0164 3265	0.0159 1474	0.0154 0910
50	0.0176 5376	0.0170 9943	0.0165 5787	0.0160 2900	0.0155 1273	0.0150 0898
51	0.0172 6269	0.0167 0928	0.0161 6888	0.0156 4142	0.0151 2680	0.0146 2494
52	0.0168 8675	0.0163 3425	0.0157 9503	0.0152 6899	0.0147 5603	0.0142 5606
53	0.0165 2507	0.0159 7350	0.0154 3546	0.0149 1084	0.0143 9956	0.0139 0149
54	0.0161 7686	0.0156 2623	0.0150 8938	0.0145 6619	0.0140 5658	0.0135 6043
55	0.0158 4139	0.0152 9171	0.0147 5605	0.0142 3430	0.0137 2637	0.0132 3213
56	0.0155 1797	0.0149 6925	0.0144 3478	0.0139 1449	0.0134 0824	0.0129 1592
57	0.0152 0598	0.0146 5821	0.0141 2496	0.0136 0611	0.0131 0156	0.0126 1116
58	0.0149 0481	0.0143 5801	0.0138 2597	0.0133 0858	0.0128 0573	0.0123 1726
59	0.0146 1392	0.0140 6809	0.0135 3727	0.0130 2135	0.0125 2020	0.0120 3366
60	0.0143 3280	0.0137 8795	0.0132 5836	0.0127 4390	0.0122 4445	0.0117 5985

From J. W. Glover, "Tables of Applied Math. in Finance, Insurance, Statistics." George Wahr, publisher, Ann Arbor, Michigan.

	1¼%	1⅜%	1½%	1¾%	2%	2¼%
1	1.0000 0000	1.0000 0000	1.0000 0000	1.0000 0000	1.0000 0000	1.0000 0000
2	0.4968 9441	0.4965 8597	0.4962 7792	0.4956 6295	0.4950 4950	0.4944 3758
3	0.3292 0117	0.3287 9173	0.3283 8296	0.3275 6746	0.3267 5467	0.3259 4458
4	0.2453 6102	0.2449 0243	0.2444 4478	0.2435 3237	0.2426 2375	0.2417 1893
5	0.1950 6211	0.1945 7510	0.1940 8932	0.1931 2142	0.1921 5839	0.1912 0021
6	0.1615 3381	0.1610 2877	0.1605 2521	0.1595 2256	0.1585 2581	0.1575 3496
7	0.1375 8872	0.1370 7157	0.1365 5616	0.1355 3059	0.1345 1196	0.1335 0025
8	0.1196 3314	0.1191 0758	0.1185 8402	0.1175 4292	0.1165 0980	0.1154 8462
9	0.1056 7055	0.1051 3906	0.1046 0982	0.1035 5813	0.1025 1544	0.1014 8170
10	0.0945 0307	0.0939 6737	0.0934 3418	0.0923 7534	0.0913 2653	0.0902 8768
11	0.0853 6839	0.0848 2973	0.0842 9384	0.0832 3038	0.0821 7794	0.0811 3649
12	0.0777 5831	0.0772 1764	0.0766 7999	0.0756 1377	0.0745 5960	0.0735 1740
13	0.0713 2100	0.0707 7903	0.0702 4036	0.0691 7283	0.0681 1835	0.0670 7686
14	0.0658 0515	0.0652 6246	0.0647 2332	0.0636 5562	0.0626 0197	0.0615 6230
15	0.0610 2646	0.0604 8351	0.0599 4436	0.0588 7739	0.0578 2547	0.0567 8852
16	0.0568 4672	0.0563 0388	0.0557 6508	0.0546 9958	0.0536 5013	0.0526 1663
17	0.0531 6023	0.0526 1780	0.0520 7966	0.0510 1623	0.0499 6984	0.0489 4039
18	0.0498 8479	0.0493 4301	0.0488 0578	0.0477 4492	0.0467 0210	0.0456 7720
19	0.0469 5548	0.0464 1457	0.0458 7847	0.0448 2061	0.0437 8177	0.0427 6182
20	0.0443 2039	0.0437 8054	0.0432 4574	0.0421 9122	0.0411 5672	0.0401 4207
21	0.0419 3748	0.0413 9884	0.0408 6550	0.0398 1464	0.0387 8477	0.0377 7572
22	0.0397 7238	0.0392 3507	0.0387 0331	0.0376 5638	0.0366 3140	0.0356 2821
23	0.0377 9666	0.0372 6080	0.0367 3075	0.0356 8796	0.0346 6810	0.0336 7097
24	0.0359 8665	0.0354 5235	0.0349 2410	0.0338 8565	0.0328 7110	0.0318 8023
25	0.0343 2247	0.0337 8981	0.0332 6345	0.0322 2952	0.0312 2044	0.0302 3599
26	0.0327 8729	0.0322 5635	0.0317 3196	0.0307 0269	0.0296 9923	0.0287 2134
27	0.0313 6677	0.0308 3763	0.0303 1527	0.0292 9079	0.0282 9309	0.0273 2188
28	0.0300 4863	0.0295 2134	0.0290 0108	0.0279 8151	0.0269 8967	0.0260 2525
29	0.0288 2228	0.0282 9689	0.0277 7878	0.0267 6424	0.0257 7836	0.0248 2081
30	0.0276 7854	0.0261 5511	0.0266 3919	0.0256 2975	0.0246 4992	0.0236 9934
31	0.0266 0942	0.0260 8798	0.0255 7430	0.0245 7005	0.0235 9635	0.0226 5280
32	0.0256 0791	0.0250 8850	0.0245 7710	0.0235 7812	0.0226 1061	0.0216 7415
33	0.0246 6786	0.0241 5053	0.0236 4144	0.0226 4779	0.0216 8653	0.0207 5722
34	0.0237 8387	0.0232 6864	0.0227 6189	0.0217 7363	0.0208 1867	0.0198 9655
35	0.0229 5111	0.0224 3801	0.0219 3363	0.0209 5082	0.0200 0221	0.0190 8731
36	0.0221 6533	0.0216 5438	0.0211 5240	0.0201 7507	0.0192 3285	0.0183 2522
37	0.0214 2270	0.0209 1394	0.0204 1437	0.0194 4257	0.0185 0678	0.0176 0643
38	0.0207 1983	0.0202 1327	0.0197 1613	0.0187 4990	0.0178 2057	0.0169 2753
39	0.0200 5365	0.0195 4931	0.0190 5463	0.0180 9399	0.0171 7114	0.0162 8543
40	0.0194 2141	0.0189 1931	0.0184 2710	0.0174 7209	0.0165 5575	0.0156 7738
41	0.0188 2063	0.0183 2078	0.0178 3106	0.0168 8170	0.0159 7188	0.0151 0087
42	0.0182 4906	0.0177 5148	0.0172 6426	0.0163 2057	0.0154 1729	0.0145 5364
43	0.0177 0466	0.0172 0936	0.0167 2465	0.0157 8666	0.0148 8993	0.0140 3364
44	0.0171 8557	0.0166 9257	0.0162 1038	0.0152 7810	0.0143 8794	0.0135 3901
45	0.0166 9012	0.0161 9941	0.0157 1976	0.0147 9321	0.0139 0962	0.0130 6805
46	0.0162 1675	0.0157 2836	0.0152 5125	0.0143 3043	0.0134 5342	0.0126 1921
47	0.0157 6406	0.0152 7799	0.0148 0342	0.0138 8836	0.0130 1792	0.0121 9107
48	0.0153 3075	0.0148 4701	0.0143 7500	0.0134 6569	0.0126 0184	0.0117 8233
49	0.0149 1563	0.0144 3424	0.0139 6478	0.0130 6124	0.0122 0396	0.0113 9179
50	0.0145 1763	0.0140 3857	0.0135 7168	0.0126 7391	0.0118 2321	0.0110 1836
51	0.0141 3571	0.0136 5900	0.0131 9469	0.0123 0269	0.0114 5856	0.0106 6102
52	0.0137 6897	0.0132 9461	0.0128 3287	0.0119 4665	0.0111 0909	0.0103 1884
53	0.0134 1653	0.0128 4453	0.0124 8537	0.0116 0492	0.0107 7392	0.0099 9094
54	0.0130 7760	0.0126 0797	0.0121 5138	0.0112 7672	0.0104 5226	0.0096 7654
55	0.0127 5145	0.0122 8418	0.0118 3018	0.0109 6129	0.0101 4337	0.0093 7489
56	0.0124 3739	0.0119 7249	0.0115 2106	0.0106 5795	0.0098 4656	0.0090 8530
57	0.0121 3478	0.0116 7225	0.0112 2341	0.0103 6606	0.0095 6120	0.0088 0712
58	0.0118 4303	0.0113 8287	0.0109 3661	0.0100 8503	0.0092 8667	0.0085 3977
59	0.0115 6158	0.0111 0380	0.0106 6012	0.0098 1430	0.0090 2243	0.0082 8268
60	0.0112 8993	0.0108 3452	0.0103 9343	0.0095 5336	0.0087 6797	0.0080 3533

	2½%	2¾%	3%	3½%	4%	4½%
1	1.0000 0000	1.0000 0000	1.0000 0000	1.0000 0000	1.0000 0000	1.0000 0000
2	0.4938 2716	0.4932 1825	0.4926 1084	0.4914 0049	0.4901 9608	0.4889 9756
3	0.3251 3717	0.3243 3243	0.3235 3036	0.3219 3418	0.3203 4854	0.3187 7336
4	0.2408 1788	0.2399 2059	0.2390 2705	0.2372 5114	0.2354 9005	0.2337 4365
5	0.1902 4686	0.1892 9832	0.1883 5457	0.1864 8137	0.1846 2711	0.1827 9164
6	0.1565 4997	0.1555 7083	0.1545 9750	0.1526 6821	0.1507 6190	0.1488 7839
7	0.1324 9543	0.1314 9747	0.1305 0635	0.1285 4449	0.1266 0961	0.1247 0147
8	0.1144 6735	0.1134 5795	0.1124 5639	0.1104 7665	0.1085 2783	0.1066 0965
9	0.1004 5689	0.0994 4095	0.0984 3386	0.0964 4601	0.0944 9299	0.0925 7447
10	0.0892 5876	0.0882 3972	0.0872 3051	0.0852 4137	0.0832 9094	0.0813 7882
11	0.0801 0596	0.0790 8629	0.0780 7745	0.0760 9197	0.0741 4904	0.0722 4818
12	0.0724 8713	0.0714 6871	0.0704 6209	0.0684 8395	0.0665 5217	0.0646 6619
13	0.0660 4827	0.0650 3252	0.0640 2954	0.0620 6157	0.0601 4373	0.0582 7535
14	0.0605 3653	0.0595 2457	0.0585 2634	0.0565 7073	0.0546 6897	0.0528 2032
15	0.0557 6646	0.0547 5917	0.0537 6658	0.0518 2507	0.0499 4110	0.0481 1381
16	0.0515 9899	0.0505 9710	0.0496 1085	0.0476 8483	0.0458 2000	0.0440 1537
17	0.0479 2777	0.0469 3186	0.0459 5253	0.0440 4313	0.0421 9852	0.0404 1758
18	0.0446 7008	0.0436 8063	0.0427 0870	0.0408 1684	0.0389 9333	0.0372 3690
19	0.0417 6062	0.0407 7802	0.0398 1388	0.0379 4033	0.0361 3862	0.0344 0734
20	0.0391 4713	0.0381 7173	0.0372 1571	0.0353 6108	0.0335 8175	0.0318 7614
21	0.0367 8733	0.0358 1941	0.0348 7178	0.0330 3659	0.0312 8011	0.0296 0057
22	0.0346 4661	0.0336 8640	0.0327 4739	0.0399 3207	0.0291 9881	0.0275 4565
23	0.0326 9638	0.0317 4410	0.0308 1390	0.0290 1880	0.0273 0906	0.0256 8249
24	0.0309 1282	0.0299 6863	0.0290 4742	0.0272 7283	0.0255 8683	0.0239 8703
25	0.0292 7592	0.0283 3997	0.0274 2787	0.0256 7404	0.0240 1196	0.0224 3903
26	0.0277 6875	0.0268 4116	0.0259 3829	0.0242 0540	0.0225 6738	0.0210 2137
27	0.0263 7687	0.0254 5776	0.0245 6421	0.0228 5241	0.0212 3854	0.0197 1946
28	0.0250 8793	0.0241 7738	0.0232 9323	0.0216 0265	0.0200 1298	0.0185 2081
29	0.0238 9127	0.0229 8935	0.0221 1467	0.0204 4538	0.0188 7993	0.0174 1461
30	0.0227 7764	0.0218 8442	0.0210 1926	0.0193 7133	0.0178 3010	0.0163 9154
31	0.0217 3900	0.0208 5453	0.0199 9893	0.0183 7240	0.0168 5535	0.0154 4345
32	0.0207 6831	0.0198 9263	0.0190 4662	0.0174 4150	0.0159 4859	0.0145 6320
33	0.0198 5938	0.0189 9253	0.0181 5612	0.0165 7242	0.0151 0357	0.0137 4453
34	0.0190 0675	0.0181 4875	0.0173 2196	0.0157 5966	0.0143 1477	0.0129 8191
35	0.0182 0558	0.0173 5645	0.0165 3929	0.0149 9835	0.0135 7732	0.0122 7045
36	0.0174 5158	0.0166 1132	0.0158 0379	0.0142 8416	0.0128 8688	0.0116 0578
37	0.0167 4090	0.0159 0953	0.0151 1162	0.0136 1325	0.0122 3957	0.0109 8402
38	0.0160 7012	0.0152 4764	0.0144 5934	0.0129 8214	0.0116 3192	0.0104 0169
39	0.0154 3615	0.0146 2256	0.0138 4385	0.0123 8775	0.0110 6083	0.0098 5567
40	0.0148 3623	0.0140 3151	0.0132 6238	0.0118 2728	0.0105 2349	0.0093 4315
41	0.0142 6786	0.0134 7200	0.0127 1241	0.0112 9822	0.0100 1738	0.0088 6158
42	0.0137 2876	0.0129 4175	0.0121 9167	0.0107 9828	0.0095 4020	0.0084 0868
43	0.0132 1688	0.0124 3871	0.0116 9811	0.0103 2539	0.0090 8989	0.0079 8235
44	0.0127 3037	0.0119 6100	0.0112 2985	0.0098 7768	0.0086 6454	0.0075 8071
45	0.0122 6752	0.0115 0693	0.0107 8518	0.0094 5343	0.0082 6246	0.0072 0202
46	0.0118 2676	0.0110 7493	0.0103 6254	0.0090 5108	0.0078 8205	0.0068 4471
47	0.0114 0669	0.0106 6358	0.0099 6051	0.0086 6919	0.0075 2189	0.0065 0734
48	0.0110 0599	0.0102 7158	0.0095 7777	0.0083 0646	0.0071 8065	0.0061 8858
49	0.0106 2348	0.0098 9773	0.0092 1314	0.0079 6167	0.0068 5712	0.0058 8722
50	0.0102 5806	0.0095 4092	0.0088 6550	0.0076 3371	0.0065 5020	0.0056 0215
51	0.0099 0870	0.0092 0014	0.0085 3382	0.0073 2156	0.0062 5885	0.0053 3232
52	0.0095 7446	0.0088 7444	0.0082 1718	0.0070 2429	0.0059 8212	0.0050 7679
53	0.0092 5449	0.0085 6297	0.0079 1471	0.0067 4100	0.0057 1915	0.0048 3469
54	0.0089 4799	0.0082 6491	0.0076 2558	0.0064 7090	0.0054 6910	0.0046 0519
55	0.0086 5419	0.0079 7953	0.0073 4907	0.0062 1323	0.0052 3124	0.0043 8754
56	0.0083 7243	0.0077 0612	0.0070 8447	0.0059 6730	0.0050 0487	0.0041 8105
57	0.0081 0204	0.0074 4404	0.0068 3114	0.0057 3245	0.0047 8932	0.0039 8506
58	0.0078 4244	0.0071 9270	0.0065 8848	0.0055 0810	0.0045 8401	0.0037 9897
59	0.0075 9307	0.0069 5153	0.0063 5593	0.0052 9366	0.0043 8836	0.0036 2221
60	0.0073 5340	0.0067 2002	0.0061 3296	0.0050 8862	0.0042 0185	0.0034 5426

ANNUITY WHICH AMOUNTS TO 1 (*Cont.*)

	5%	5½%	6%	6½%	7%	8%
1	1.0000 0000	1.0000 0000	1.0000 0000	1.0000 0000	1.0000 0000	1.0000 0000
2	0.4878 0488	0.4866 1800	0.4854 3689	0.4842 6150	0.4830 9179	0.4807 6923
3	0.3172 0856	0.3156 5407	0.3141 0981	0.3125 7570	0.3110 5166	0.3080 3351
4	0.2320 1183	0.2302 9449	0.2285 9149	0.2269 0274	0.2252 2812	0.2219 2080
5	0.1809 7480	0.1791 7644	0.1773 9640	0.1756 3454	0.1738 9069	0.1704 5645
6	0.1470 1747	0.1451 7895	0.1433 6263	0.1415 6831	0.1397 9580	0.1363 1539
7	0.1228 1982	0.1209 6442	0.1191 3502	0.1173 3137	0.1155 5322	0.1120 7240
8	0.1047 2181	0.1028 6401	0.1010 3594	0.0992 3730	0.0974 6776	0.0940 1476
9	0.0906 9008	0.0888 3946	0.0870 2224	0.0852 3803	0.0834 8647	0.0800 7971
10	0.0795 0458	0.0776 6777	0.0758 6796	0.0741 0469	0.0723 7750	0.0690 2949
11	0.0703 8889	0.0685 7065	0.0667 9294	0.0650 5521	0.0633 5690	0.0600 7634
12	0.0628 2541	0.0610 2923	0.0592 7703	0.0575 6817	0.0559 0199	0.0526 9502
13	0.0564 5577	0.0546 8426	0.0529 6011	0.0512 8256	0.0496 5085	0.0465 2181
14	0.0510 2397	0.0492 7912	0.0475 8491	0.0459 4048	0.0443 4494	0.0412 9685
15	0.0463 4229	0.0446 2560	0.0429 6276	0.0413 5278	0.0397 9462	0.0368 2954
16	0.0422 6991	0.0405 8254	0.0389 5214	0.0373 7757	0.0358 5765	0.0329 7687
17	0.0386 9914	0.0370 4197	0.0354 4480	0.0339 0633	0.0324 2519	0.0296 2943
18	0.0355 4622	0.0339 1992	0.0323 5654	0.0308 5461	0.0294 1260	0.0267 0210
19	0.0327 4501	0.0311 5006	0.0296 2086	0.0281 5575	0.0267 5301	0.0241 2763
20	0.0302 4259	0.0286 7933	0.0271 8456	0.0257 5640	0.0243 9293	0.0218 5221
21	0.0279 9611	0.0264 6478	0.0250 0455	0.0236 1333	0.0222 8900	0.0198 3225
22	0.0259 7051	0.0244 7123	0.0230 4557	0.0216 9120	0.0204 0577	0.0180 3207
23	0.0241 3682	0.0226 6965	0.0212 7848	0.0199 6078	0.0187 1393	0.0164 2217
24	0.0224 7090	0.0210 3580	0.0196 7900	0.0183 9770	0.0171 8902	0.0149 7796
25	0.0209 5246	0.0195 4935	0.0182 2672	0.0169 8148	0.0158 1052	0.0136 7878
26	0.0195 6432	0.0181 9307	0.0169 0435	0.0156 9480	0.0145 6103	0.0125 0713
27	0.0182 9186	0.0169 5228	0.0156 9717	0.0145 2288	0.0134 2573	0.0114 4809
28	0.0171 2253	0.0158 1440	0.0145 9255	0.0134 5305	0.0123 9193	0.0104 8891
29	0.0160 4551	0.0147 6857	0.0135 7961	0.0124 7440	0.0114 4865	0.0096 1854
30	0.0150 5144	0.0138 0539	0.0126 4891	0.0115 7744	0.0105 8640	0.0088 2743
31	0.0141 3212	0.0129 1665	0.0117 9222	0.0107 5393	0.0097 9691	0.0081 0728
32	0.0132 8042	0.0120 9519	0.0110 0234	0.0099 9665	0.0090 7292	0.0074 5081
33	0.0124 9004	0.0113 3469	0.0102 7293	0.0092 9924	0.0084 0807	0.0068 5163
34	0.0117 5545	0.0106 2958	0.0095 9843	0.0086 5610	0.0077 9674	0.0063 0411
35	0.0110 7171	0.0099 7493	0.0089 7386	0.0080 6226	0.0072 3396	0.0058 0326
36	0.0104 3446	0.0093 6635	0.0083 9483	0.0075 1332	0.0067 1531	0.0053 4467
37	0.0098 3979	0.0087 9993	0.0078 5743	0.0070 0534	0.0062 3685	0.0049 2440
38	0.0092 8423	0.0082 7217	0.0073 5812	0.0065 3480	0.0057 9505	0.0045 3894
39	0.0087 6462	0.0077 7991	0.0068 9377	0.0060 9854	0.0053 8676	0.0041 8513
40	0.0082 7816	0.0073 2034	0.0064 6154	0.0056 9373	0.0050 0914	0.0038 6016
41	0.0078 2229	0.0068 9090	0.0060 5886	0.0053 1779	0.0046 5962	0.0035 6149
42	0.0073 9471	0.0064 8927	0.0056 8342	0.0049 6842	0.0043 3591	0.0032 8684
43	0.0069 9333	0.0061 1337	0.0053 3312	0.0046 4352	0.0040 3590	0.0030 3414
44	0.0066 1625	0.0057 6128	0.0050 0606	0.0043 4119	0.0037 5769	0.0028 0152
45	0.0062 6173	0.0054 3127	0.0047 0050	0.0040 5968	0.0034 9957	0.0025 8728
46	0.0059 2820	0.0051 2175	0.0044 1485	0.0037 9743	0.0032 5996	0.0023 8991
47	0.0056 1421	0.0048 3129	0.0041 4768	0.0035 5300	0.0030 3744	0.0022 0799
48	0.0053 1843	0.0045 5854	0.0038 9766	0.0033 2506	0.0028 3070	0.0020 4027
49	0.0050 3965	0.0043 0230	0.0036 6356	0.0031 1240	0.0026 3853	0.0018 8557
50	0.0047 7674	0.0040 6145	0.0034 4429	0.0029 1393	0.0024 5985	0.0017 4286
51	0.0045 2867	0.0038 3495	0.0032 3880	0.0027 2861	0.0022 9365	0.0016 1116
52	0.0042 9450	0.0036 2185	0.0030 4617	0.0025 5553	0.0021 3901	0.0014 8959
53	0.0040 7334	0.0034 2130	0.0028 6551	0.0023 9382	0.0019 9509	0.0013 7735
54	0.0038 6438	0.0032 3245	0.0026 9602	0.0022 4267	0.0018 6110	0.0012 7370
55	0.0036 6686	0.0030 5458	0.0025 3696	0.0021 0137	0.0017 3633	0.0011 7796
56	0.0034 8010	0.0028 8698	0.0023 8765	0.0019 6923	0.0016 2011	0.0010 8952
57	0.0033 0343	0.0027 2900	0.0022 4744	0.0018 4563	0.0015 1183	0.0010 0780
58	0.0031 3626	0.0025 8006	0.0021 1574	0.0017 2999	0.0014 1093	0.0009 3227
59	0.0029 7802	0.0024 3959	0.0019 9200	0.0016 2177	0.0013 1689	0.0008 6247
60	0.0028 2818	0.0023 0707	0.0018 7572	0.0015 2047	0.0012 2923	0.0007 9795

ANNUITY WHICH 1 WILL BUY

	½%	⅝%	¾%	⅞%	1%	1⅛%
1	1.0050 0000	1.0062 5000	1.0075 0000	1.0087 5000	1.0100 0000	1.0112 5000
2	0.5037 5312	0.5046 9237	0.5056 3200	0.5065 7203	0.5075 1244	0.5084 5323
3	0.3366 7221	0.3375 0865	0.3383 4579	0.3391 8361	0.3400 2211	0.3408 6130
4	0.2531 3279	0.2539 1842	0.2547 0501	0.2554 9257	0.2562 8109	0.2570 7058
5	0.2030 0997	0.2037 6558	0.2045 2242	0.2052 8049	0.2060 3980	0.2068 0034
6	0.1695 9546	0.1703 3143	0.1710 6891	0.1718 0789	0.1725 4837	0.1732 9034
7	0.1457 2854	0.1464 5082	0.1471 7488	0.1479 0070	0.1486 2828	0.1493 5762
8	0.1278 2886	0.1285 4118	0.1292 5552	0.1299 7190	0.1306 9029	0.1314 1071
9	0.1139 0736	0.1146 1218	0.1153 1929	0.1160 2868	0.1167 4037	0.1174 5432
10	0.1027 7057	0.1034 6963	0.1041 7123	0.1048 7538	0.1055 8208	0.1062 9131
11	0.0936 5903	0.0943 5358	0.0950 5094	0.0957 5111	0.0964 5408	0.0971 5984
12	0.0860 6643	0.0867 5742	0.0874 5148	0.0881 4860	0.0888 4879	0.0895 5203
13	0.0796 4224	0.0803 3039	0.0810 2188	0.0817 1669	0.0824 1482	0.0831 1626
14	0.0741 3609	0.0748 2198	0.0755 1146	0.0762 0453	0.0769 0117	0.0776 0138
15	0.0693 6436	0.0700 4845	0.0707 3639	0.0714 2817	0.0721 2378	0.0728 2321
16	0.0651 8937	0.0658 7202	0.0665 5879	0.0672 4965	0.0679 4460	0.0686 4363
17	0.0615 0579	0.0621 8732	0.0628 7321	0.0635 6346	0.0642 5806	0.0649 5698
18	0.0582 3173	0.0589 1239	0.0595 9766	0.0602 8756	0.0609 8205	0.0616 8113
19	0.0553 0253	0.0559 8252	0.0566 6740	0.0573 5715	0.0580 5175	0.0587 5120
20	0.0526 6645	0.0533 4597	0.0540 3063	0.0547 2042	0.0554 1532	0.0561 1531
21	0.0502 8163	0.0509 6083	0.0516 4543	0.0523 3541	0.0530 3075	0.0537 3145
22	0.0481 1380	0.0487 9281	0.0494 7748	0.0501 6779	0.0508 6371	0.0515 6525
23	0.0461 3465	0.0468 1360	0.0474 9846	0.0481 8921	0.0488 8584	0.0495 8833
24	0.0443 2061	0.0449 9959	0.0456 8474	0.0463 7604	0.0470 7347	0.0477 7701
25	0.0426 5186	0.0433 3096	0.0440 1650	0.0447 0843	0.0454 0675	0.0461 1144
26	0.0411 1163	0.0417 9094	0.0424 7693	0.0431 6959	0.0438 6888	0.0445 7479
27	0.0396 8565	0.0403 6523	0.0410 5176	0.0417 4520	0.0424 4553	0.0431 5273
28	0.0383 6167	0.0390 4159	0.0397 2871	0.0404 2300	0.0411 2444	0.0418 3299
29	0.0371 2914	0.0378 0946	0.0384 9723	0.0391 9243	0.0398 9502	0.0406 0498
30	0.0359 7892	0.0366 5969	0.0373 4816	0.0380 4431	0.0387 4811	0.0394 5953
31	0.0349 0304	0.0355 8430	0.0362 7352	0.0369 7068	0.0376 7573	0.0383 8866
32	0.0338 9453	0.0345 7633	0.0352 6634	0.0359 6454	0.0366 7089	0.0373 8535
33	0.0329 4727	0.0336 2964	0.0343 2048	0.0350 1976	0.0357 2744	0.0364 4349
34	0.0320 5586	0.0327 3883	0.0334 3053	0.0341 3092	0.0348 3997	0.0355 5763
35	0.0312 1550	0.0318 9911	0.0325 9170	0.0332 9324	0.0340 0368	0.0347 2299
36	0.0304 2194	0.0311 0622	0.0317 9973	0.0325 0244	0.0332 1431	0.0339 3529
37	0.0296 7139	0.0303 5636	0.0310 5082	0.0317 5473	0.0324 6805	0.0331 9072
38	0.0289 6045	0.0296 4614	0.0303 4157	0.0310 4671	0.0317 6150	0.0324 8589
39	0.0282 8607	0.0289 7250	0.0296 6893	0.0303 7531	0.0310 9160	0.0318 1773
40	0.0276 4552	0.0283 3271	0.0290 3016	0.0297 3780	0.0304 5560	0.0311 8349
41	0.0270 3631	0.0277 2429	0.0284 2276	0.0291 3169	0.0298 5102	0.0305 8069
42	0.0264 5622	0.0271 4499	0.0278 4452	0.0285 5475	0.0292 7563	0.0300 0709
43	0.0259 0320	0.0265 9278	0.0272 9338	0.0280 0493	0.0287 2737	0.0294 6064
44	0.0253 7541	0.0260 6583	0.0267 6751	0.0274 8039	0.0282 0441	0.0289 3949
45	0.0248 7117	0.0255 6243	0.0262 6521	0.0269 7943	0.0277 0505	0.0284 4197
46	0.0243 8894	0.0250 8106	0.0257 8495	0.0265 0053	0.0272 2775	0.0279 6652
47	0.0239 2733	0.0246 2032	0.0253 2532	0.0260 4228	0.0267 7111	0.0275 1173
48	0.0234 8503	0.0241 7890	0.0248 8504	0.0256 0338	0.0263 3384	0.0270 7632
49	0.0230 6087	0.0237 5563	0.0244 6292	0.0251 8265	0.0259 1474	0.0266 5910
50	0.0226 5376	0.0233 4943	0.0240 5787	0.0247 7900	0.0255 1273	0.0262 5898
51	0.0222 6269	0.0229 5928	0.0236 6888	0.0243 9142	0.0251 2680	0.0258 7494
52	0.0218 8675	0.0225 8425	0.0232 9503	0.0240 1899	0.0247 5603	0.0255 0606
53	0.0215 2507	0.0222 2350	0.0229 3546	0.0236 6084	0.0243 9956	0.0251 5149
54	0.0211 7686	0.0218 7623	0.0225 8938	0.0233 1619	0.0240 5658	0.0248 1043
55	0.0208 4139	0.0215 4171	0.0222 5605	0.0229 8430	0.0237 2637	0.0244 8213
56	0.0205 1797	0.0212 1925	0.0219 3478	0.0226 6449	0.0234 0823	0.0241 6592
57	0.0202 0598	0.0209 0821	0.0216 2496	0.0223 5611	0.0231 0156	0.0238 6116
58	0.0199 0481	0.0206 0801	0.0213 2597	0.0220 5858	0.0228 0573	0.0235 6726
59	0.0196 1392	0.0203 1809	0.0210 3727	0.0217 7135	0.0225 2020	0.0232 8366
60	0.0193 3280	0.0200 3795	0.0207 5836	0.0214 9390	0.0222 4445	0.0230 0985

From J. W. Glover, "Tables of Applied Math. in Finance, Insurance, Statistics." George Wahr, publisher, Ann Arbor, Michigan.

ANNUITY WHICH 1 WILL BUY (*Cont.*)

	1¼%	1⅜%	1½%	1¾%	2%	2¼%
1	1.0125 0000	1.0137 5000	1.0150 0000	1.0175 0000	1.0200 0000	1.0225 0000
2	0.5093 9441	0.5103 3597	0.5112 7792	0.5131 6295	0.5150 4950	0.5169 3758
3	0.3417 0117	0.3425 4173	0.3433 8296	0.3450 6746	0.3467 5467	0.3484 4458
4	0.2578 6102	0.2586 5243	0.2594 4478	0.2610 3237	0.2626 2375	0.2642 1893
5	0.2075 6211	0.2083 2510	0.2090 8932	0.2106 2142	0.2121 5839	0.2137 0021
6	0.1740 3381	0.1747 7877	0.1755 2521	0.1770 2256	0.1785 2581	0.1800 3496
7	0.1500 8872	0.1508 2157	0.1515 5616	0.1530 3059	0.1545 1196	0.1560 0025
8	0.1321 3314	0.1328 5758	0.1335 8402	0.1350 4292	0.1365 0980	0.1379 8462
9	0.1181 7055	0.1188 8906	0.1196 0982	0.1210 5813	0.1225 1544	0.1239 8170
10	0.1070 0307	0.1077 1737	0.1084 3418	0.1098 7534	0.1113 2653	0.1127 8768
11	0.0978 6839	0.0985 7973	0.0992 9384	0.1007 3038	0.1021 7794	0.1036 3649
12	0.0902 5831	0.0909 6764	0.0916 7999	0.0931 1377	0.0945 5960	0.0960 1740
13	0.0838 2100	0.0845 2903	0.0852 4036	0.0866 7283	0.0881 1835	0.0895 7686
14	0.0783 0515	0.0790 1246	0.0797 2332	0.0811 5562	0.0826 0197	0.0840 6230
15	0.0735 2646	0.0742 3351	0.0749 4436	0.0763 7739	0.0778 2547	0.0792 8852
16	0.0693 4672	0.0700 5388	0.0707 6508	0.0721 9958	0.0736 5013	0.0751 1663
17	0.0656 6023	0.0663 6780	0.0670 7966	0.0685 1623	0.0699 6984	0.0714 4039
18	0.0623 8479	0.0630 9301	0.0638 0578	0.0652 4492	0.0667 0210	0.0681 7720
19	0.0594 5548	0.0601 6457	0.0608 7847	0.0623 2061	0.0637 8177	0.0652 6182
20	0.0568 2039	0.0575 3054	0.0582 4574	0.0596 9122	0.0611 5672	0.0626 4207
21	0.0544 3748	0.0551 4884	0.0558 6550	0.0573 1464	0.0587 8477	0.0602 7572
22	0.0522 7238	0.0529 8507	0.0537 0331	0.0551 5638	0.0566 3140	0.0581 2821
23	0.0502 9666	0.0510 1080	0.0517 3075	0.0531 8796	0.0546 6810	0.0561 7097
24	0.0484 8665	0.0492 0235	0.0499 2410	0.0513 8565	0.0528 7110	0.0543 8023
25	0.0468 2247	0.0475 3981	0.0482 6345	0.0497 2952	0.0512 2044	0.0527 3599
26	0.0452 8729	0.0460 0635	0.0467 3196	0.0482 0269	0.0496 9923	0.0512 2134
27	0.0438 6677	0.0445 8763	0.0453 1527	0.0467 9079	0.0482 9309	0.0498 2188
28	0.0425 4863	0.0432 7134	0.0440 0108	0.0454 8151	0.0469 8967	0.0485 2525
29	0.0413 2228	0.0420 4689	0.0427 7878	0.0442 6424	0 0457 7836	0.0473 2081
30	0.0401 7854	0.0409 0511	0.0416 3919	0.0431 2975	0.0446 4992	0.0461 9934
31	0.0391 0942	0.0398 3798	0.0405 7430	0.0420 7005	0.0435 9635	0.0451 5280
32	0.0381 0791	0.0388 3850	0.0395 7710	0.0410 7812	0.0426 1061	0.0441 7415
33	0.0371 6786	0.0379 0053	0.0386 4144	0.0401 4779	0.0416 8653	0.0432 5722
34	0.0362 8387	0.0370 1864	0.0377 6189	0.0392 7363	0.0408 1867	0.0423 9655
35	0.0354 5111	0.0361 8801	0.0369 3363	0.0384 5082	0.0400 0221	0.0415 8731
36	0.0346 6533	0.0354 0438	0.0361 5240	0.0376 7507	0.0392 3285	0.0408 2522
37	0.0339 2270	0.0346 6394	0.0354 1437	0.0369 4257	0.0385 0678	0.0401 0643
38	0.0332 1983	0.0339 6327	0.0347 1613	0.0362 4990	0.0378 2057	0.0394 2753
39	0.0325 5365	0.0332 9931	0.0340 5463	0.0355 9399	0.0371 7114	0.0387 8543
40	0.0319 2141	0.0326 6931	0.0334 2710	0.0349 7209	0.0365 5575	0.0381 7738
41	0.0313 2063	0.0320 7078	0.0328 3106	0.0343 8170	0.0359 7188	0.0376 0087
42	0.0307 4906	0.0315 0148	0.0322 6426	0.0338 2057	0.0354 1729	0.0370 5364
43	0.0302 0466	0.0309 5936	0.0317 2465	0.0332 8666	0.0348 8993	0.0365 3364
44	0.0296 8557	9.0304 4257	0.0312 1038	0.0327 7810	0.0343 8794	0.0360 3901
45	0.0291 9012	0.0299 4941	0.0307 1976	0.0322 9321	0.0339 0962	0.0355 6805
46	0.0287 1675	0.0294 7836	0.0302 5125	0.0318 3043	0.0334 5342	0.0351 1921
47	0.0282 6406	0.0290 2799	0.0298 0342	0.0313 8836	0.0330 1792	0.0346 9107
48	0.0278 3075	0.0285 9701	0.0293 7500	0.0309 6569	0.0326 0184	0.0342 8233
49	0.0274 1563	0.0281 8424	0.0289 6478	0.0305 6124	0.0322 0396	0.0338 9179
50	0.0270 1763	0.0277 8857	0.0285 7168	0.0301 7391	0.0318 2321	0.0335 1836
51	0.0266 3571	0.0274 0900	0.0281 9469	0.0298 0269	0.0314 5856	0.0331 6102
52	0.0262 6897	0.0270 4461	0.0278 3287	0.0294 4665	0.0311 0909	0.0328 1884
53	0.0259 1653	0.0266 9453	0.0274 8537	0.0291 0492	0.0307 7392	0.0324 9094
54	0.0255 7760	0.0263 5797	0.0271 5138	0.0287 7672	0.0304 5226	0.0321 7654
55	0.0252 5145	0.0260 3418	0.0268 3018	0.0284 6129	0.0301 4337	0.0318 7489
56	0.0249 3739	0.0257 2249	0.0265 2106	0.0281 5795	0.0298 4656	0.0315 8530
57	0.0246 3478	0.0254 2225	0.0262 2341	0.0278 6606	0.0295 6120	0.0313 0712
58	0.0243 4303	0.0251 3287	0.0259 3661	0.0275 8503	0.0292 8667	0.0310 3977
59	0.0240 6158	0.0248 5380	0.0256 6012	0.0273 1430	0.0290 2243	0.0307 8268
60	0.0237 8993	0.0245 8452	0.0253 9343	0.0270 5336	0.0287 6797	0.0305 3533

	2½%	2¾%	3%	3½%	4%	4½%
1	1.0250 0000	1.0275 0000	1.0300 0000	1.0350 0000	1.0400 0000	1.0450 0000
2	0.5188 2716	0.5207 1825	0.5226 1084	0.5264 0049	0.5301 9608	0.5339 9756
3	0.3501 3717	0.3518 3243	0.3535 3036	0.3569 3418	0.3603 4854	0.3637 7336
4	0.2658 1788	0.2674 2059	0.2690 2705	0.2722 5114	0.2754 9005	0.2787 4365
5	0.2152 4686	0.2167 9832	0.2183 5457	0.2214 8137	0.2246 2711	0.2277 9164
6	0.1815 4997	0.1830 7083	0.1845 9750	0.1876 6821	0.1907 6190	0.1938 7839
7	0.1574 9543	0.1589 9747	0.1605 0635	0.1635 4449	0.1666 0961	0.1697 0147
8	0.1394 6735	0.1409 5795	0.1424 5639	0.1454 7665	0.1485 2783	0.1516 0965
9	0.1254 5689	0.1269 4095	0.1284 3386	0.1314 4601	0.1344 9299	0.1375 7447
10	0.1142 5876	0.1157 3972	0.1172 3051	0.1202 4137	0.1232 9094	0.1263 7882
11	0.1051 0596	0.1065 8629	0.1080 7745	0.1110 9197	0.1141 4904	0.1172 4818
12	0.0974 8713	0.0989 6871	0.1004 6209	0.1034 8395	0.1065 5217	0.1096 6619
13	0.0910 4827	0.0925 3252	0.0940 2954	0.0970 6157	0.1001 4373	0.1032 7535
14	0.0855 3653	0.0870 2457	0.0885 2634	0.0915 7073	0.0946 6897	0.0978 2032
15	0.0807 6646	0.0822 5917	0.0837 6658	0.0868 2507	0.0899 4110	0.0931 1381
16	0.0765 9899	0.0780 9710	0.0796 1085	0.0826 8483	0.0858 2000	0.0890 1537
17	0.0729 2777	0.0744 3186	0.0759 5253	0.0790 4313	0.0821 9852	0.0854 1758
18	0.0696 7008	0.0711 8063	0.0727 0870	0.0758 1684	0.0789 9333	0.0822 3690
19	0.0667 6062	0.0682 7802	0.0698 1388	0.0729 4033	0.0761 3862	0.0794 0734
20	0.0641 4713	0.0656 7173	0.0672 1571	0.0703 6108	0.0735 8175	0.0768 7614
21	0.0617 8733	0.0633 1941	0.0648 7178	0.0680 3659	0.0712 8011	0.0746 0057
22	0.0596 4661	0.0611 8640	0.0627 4739	0.0659 3207	0.0691 9881	0.0725 4565
23	0.0576 9638	0.0592 4410	0.0608 1390	0.0640 1880	0.0673 0906	0.0706 8249
24	0.0559 1282	0.0574 6863	0.0590 4742	0.0622 7283	0.0655 8683	0.0689 8703
25	0.0542 7592	0.0558 3997	0.0574 2787	0.0606 7404	0.0640 1196	0.0674 3903
26	0.0527 6875	0.0543 4116	0.0559 3829	0.0592 0540	0.0625 6738	0.0660 2137
27	0.0513 7687	0.0529 5776	0.0545 6421	0.0578 5241	0.0612 3854	0.0647 1946
28	0.0500 8793	0.0516 7738	0.0532 9323	0.0566 0265	0.0600 1298	0.0635 2081
29	0.0488 9127	0.0504 8935	0.0521 1467	0.0554 4538	0.0588 7993	0.0624 1461
30	0.0477 7764	0.0493 8442	0.0510 1926	0.0543 7133	0.0578 3010	0.0613 9154
31	0.0467 3900	0.0483 5453	0.0499 9893	0.0533 7240	0.0568 5535	0.0604 4345
32	0.0457 6831	0.0473 9263	0.0490 4662	0.0524 4150	0.0559 4859	0.0595 6320
33	0.0448 5938	0.0464 9253	0.0481 5612	0.0515 7242	0.0551 0357	0.0587 4453
34	0.0440 0675	0.0456 4875	0.0473 2196	0.0507 5966	0.0543 1477	0.0579 8191
35	0.0432 0558	0.0448 5645	0.0465 3929	0.0499 9835	0.0535 7732	0.0572 7045
36	0.0424 5158	0.0441 1132	0.0458 0379	0.0492 8416	0.0528 8688	0.0566 0578
37	0.0417 4090	0.0434 0953	0.0451 1162	0.0486 1325	0.0522 3957	0.0559 8402
38	0.0410 7012	0.0427 4764	0.0444 5934	0.0479 8214	0.0516 3192	0.0554 0169
39	0.0404 3615	0.0421 2256	0.0438 4385	0.0473 8775	0.0510 6083	0.0548 5567
40	0.0398 3623	0.0415 3151	0.0432 6238	0.0468 2728	0.0505 2349	0.0543 4315
41	0.0392 6786	0.0409 7200	0.0427 1241	0.0462 9822	0.0500 1738	0.0538 6158
42	0.0387 2876	0.0404 4175	0.0421 9167	0.0457 9828	0.0495 4020	0.0534 0868
43	0.0382 1688	0.0399 3871	0.0416 9811	0.0453 2539	0.0490 8989	0.0529 8235
44	0.0377 3037	0.0394 6100	0.0412 2985	0.0448 7768	0.0486 6454	0.0525 8071
45	0.0372 6752	0.0390 0693	0.0407 8518	0.0444 5343	0.0482 6246	0.0522 0202
46	0.0368 2676	0.0385 7493	0.0403 6254	0.0440 5108	0.0478 8205	0.0518 4471
47	0.0364 0669	0.0381 6358	0.0399 6051	0.0436 6919	0.0475 2189	0.0515 0734
48	0.0360 0599	0.0377 7158	0.0395 7777	0.0433 0646	0.0471 8065	0.0511 8858
49	0.0356 2348	0.0373 9773	0.0392 1314	0.0429 6167	0.0468 5712	0.0508 8722
50	0.0352 5806	0.0370 4092	0.0388 6550	0.0426 3371	0.0465 5020	0.0506 0215
51	0.0349 0870	0.0367 0014	0.0385 3382	0.0423 2156	0.0462 5885	0.0503 3232
52	0.0345 7446	0.0363 7444	0.0382 1718	0.0420 2429	0.0459 8212	0.0500 7679
53	0.0342 5449	0.0360 6297	0.0379 1471	0.0417 4100	0.0457 1915	0.0498 3469
54	0.0339 4799	0.0357 6491	0.0376 2558	0.0414 7090	0.0454 6910	0.0496 0519
55	0.0336 5419	0.0354 7953	0.0373 4907	0.0412 1323	0.0452 3124	0.0493 8754
56	0.0333 7243	0.0352 0612	0.0370 8[illegible]47	0.0409 6730	0.0450 0487	0.0491 8105
57	0.0331 0204	0.0349 4404	0.0368 3114	0.0407 3245	0.0447 8932	0.0489 8506
58	0.0328 4244	0.0346 9270	0.0365 8848	0.0405 0810	0.0445 8401	0.0487 9897
59	0.0325 9307	0.0344 5153	0.0363 5593	0.0402 9366	0.0443 8836	0.0486 2221
60	0.0323 5340	0.0342 2002	0.0361 3296	0.0400 8862	0.0442 0185	0.0484 5426

ANNUITY WHICH 1 WILL BUY (*Cont.*)

	5%	5½%	6%	6½%	7%	8%
1	1.0500 0000	1.0550 0000	1.0600 0000	1.0650 0000	1.0700 0000	1.0800 0000
2	0.5378 0488	0.5416 1800	0.5454 3689	0.5492 6150	0.5530 9179	0.5607 6923
3	0.3672 0856	0.3706 5407	0.3741 0981	0.3775 7570	0.3810 5166	0.3880 3351
4	0.2820 1183	0.2852 9449	0.2885 9149	0.2919 0274	0.2952 2812	0.3019 2080
5	0.2309 7480	0.2341 7644	0.2373 9640	0.2406 3454	0.2438 9069	0.2504 5645
6	0.1970 1747	0.2001 7895	0.2033 6263	0.2065 6831	0.2097 9580	0.2163 1539
7	0.1728 1982	0.1759 6442	0.1791 3502	0.1823 3137	0.1855 5322	0.1920 7240
8	0.1547 2181	0.1578 6401	0.1610 3594	0.1642 3730	0.1674 6776	0.1740 1476
9	0.1406 9008	0.1438 3946	0.1470 2224	0.1502 3803	0.1534 8647	0.1600 7971
10	0.1295 0458	0.1326 6777	0.1358 6796	0.1391 0469	0.1423 7750	0.1490 2949
11	0.1203 8889	0.1235 7065	0.1267 9294	0.1300 5521	0.1333 5690	0.1400 7634
12	0.1128 2541	0.1160 2923	0.1192 7703	0.1225 6817	0.1259 0199	0.1326 9502
13	0.1064 5577	0.1096 8426	0.1129 6011	0.1162 8256	0.1196 5085	0.1265 2181
14	0.1010 2397	0.1042 7912	0.1075 8491	0.1109 4048	0.1143 4494	0.1212 9685
15	0.0963 4229	0.0996 2560	0.1029 6276	0.1063 5278	0.1097 9462	0.1168 2954
16	0.0922 6991	0.0955 8254	0.0989 5214	0.1023 7757	0.1058 5765	0.1129 7687
17	0.0886 9914	0.0920 4197	0.0954 4480	0.0989 0633	0.1024 2519	0.1096 2943
18	0.0855 4622	0.0889 1992	0.0923 5654	0.0958 5461	0.0994 1260	0.1067 0210
19	0.0827 4501	0.0861 5006	0.0896 2086	0.0931 5575	0.0967 5301	0.1041 2763
20	0.0802 4259	0.0836 7933	0.0871 8456	0.0907 5640	0.0943 9293	0.1018 5221
21	0.0779 9611	0.0814 6478	0.0850 0455	0.0886 1333	0.0922 8900	0.0998 3225
22	0.0759 7051	0.0794 7123	0.0830 4557	0.0866 9120	0.0904 0577	0.0980 3207
23	0.0741 3682	0.0776 6965	0.0812 7848	0.0849 6078	0.0887 1393	0.0964 2217
24	0.0724 7090	0.0760 3580	0.0796 7900	0.0833 9770	0.0871 8902	0.0949 7796
25	0.0709 5246	0.0745 4935	0.0782 2672	0.0819 8148	0.0858 1052	0.0936 7878
26	0.0695 6432	0.0731 9307	0.0769 0435	0.0806 9480	0.0845 6103	0.0925 0713
27	0.0682 9186	0.0719 5228	0.0756 9717	0.0795 2288	0.0834 2573	0.0914 4809
28	0.0671 2253	0.0708 1440	0.0745 9255	0.0784 5305	0.0823 9193	0.0904 8891
29	0.0660 4551	0.0697 6857	0.0735 7961	0.0774 7440	0.0814 4865	0.0896 1854
30	0.0650 5144	0.0688 0539	0.0726 4891	0.0765 7744	0.0805 8640	0.0888 2743
31	0.0641 3212	0.0679 1665	0.0717 9222	0.0757 5393	0.0797 9691	0.0881 0728
32	0.0632 8042	0.0670 9519	0.0710 0234	0.0749 9665	0.0790 7292	0.0874 5081
33	0.0624 9004	0.0663 3469	0.0702 7293	0.0742 9924	0.0784 0807	0.0868 5163
34	0.0617 5545	0.0656 2958	0.0695 9843	0.0736 5610	0.0777 9674	0.0863 0411
35	0.0610 7171	0.0649 7493	0.0689 7386	0.0730 6226	0.0772 3396	0.0858 0326
36	0.0604 3446	0.0643 6635	0.0683 9483	0.0725 1332	0.0767 1531	0.0853 4467
37	0.0598 3979	0.0637 9993	0.0678 5743	0.0720 0534	0.0762 3685	0.0849 2440
38	0.0592 8423	0.0632 7217	0.0673 5812	0.0715 3480	0.0757 9505	0.0845 3894
39	0.0587 6462	0.0627 7991	0.0668 9377	0.0710 9854	0.0753 8676	0.0841 8513
40	0.0582 7816	0.0623 2034	0.0664 6154	0.0706 9373	0.0750 0914	0.0838 6016
41	0.0578 2229	0.0618 9090	0.0660 5886	0.0703 1779	0.0746 5962	0.0835 6149
42	0.0573 9471	0.0614 8927	0.0656 8342	0.0699 6842	0.0743 3591	0.0832 8684
43	0.0569 9333	0.0611 1337	0.0653 3312	0.0696 4352	0.0740 3590	0.0830 3414
44	0.0566 1625	0.0607 6128	0.0650 0606	0.0693 4119	0.0737 5769	0.0828 0152
45	0.0562 6173	0.0604 3127	0.0647 0050	0.0690 5968	0.0734 9957	0.0825 8728
46	0.0559 2820	0.0601 2175	0.0644 1485	0.0687 9743	0.0732 5996	0.0823 8991
47	0.0556 1421	0.0598 3129	0.0641 4768	0.0685 5300	0.0730 3744	0.0822 0799
48	0.0553 1843	0.0595 5854	0.0638 9766	0.0683 2506	0.0728 3070	0.0820 4027
49	0.0550 3965	0.0593 0230	0.0636 6356	0.0681 1240	0.0726 3853	0.0818 8557
50	0.0547 7674	0.0590 6145	0.0634 4429	0.0679 1393	0.0724 5985	0.0817 4286
51	0.0545 2867	0.0588 3495	0.0632 3880	0.0677 2861	0.0722 9365	0.0816 1116
52	0.0542 9450	0.0586 2186	0.0630 4617	0.0675 5553	0.0721 3901	0.0814 8959
53	0.0540 7334	0.0584 2130	0.0628 6551	0.0673 9382	0.0719 9509	0.0813 7735
54	0.0538 6438	0.0582 3245	0.0626 9602	0.0672 4267	0.0718 6110	0.0812 7370
55	0.0536 6686	0.0580 5458	0.0625 3696	0.0671 0137	0.0717 3633	0.0811 7796
56	0.0534 8010	0.0578 8698	0.0623 8765	0.0669 6923	0.0716 2011	0.0810 8952
57	0.0533 0343	0.0577 2900	0.0622 4744	0.0668 4563	0.0715 1183	0.0810 0780
58	0.0531 3626	0.0575 8006	0.0621 1574	0.0667 2999	0.0714 1093	0.0809 3227
59	0.0529 7802	0.0574 3959	0.0619 9200	0.0666 2177	0.0713 1689	0.0808 6247
60	0.0528 2818	0.0573 0707	0.0618 7572	0.0665 2047	0.0712 2923	0.0807 9795

11. DEPRECIATION METHODS

Adapted from Finney, "Principles of Accounting," and Curtis and Cooper, "Mathematics of Accounting" New York: Prentice-Hall, Inc.

Factors to be taken into account in calculating depreciation. The factors that must be taken into consideration in estimating depreciation are:

1. Cost, which includes installation and other incidental expenditures.
2. Scrap or residual value, which is the estimated value that may be recovered from the asset after it is taken out of service. This scrap value should be net after estimated costs of dismantling are deducted.
3. Estimated life. This will, of course, be affected by the policy concerning repairs, and this policy should be taken into consideration in estimating the life.

These factors determine the total depreciation to be provided and the estimated life over which the total depreciation is to be spread. The portion of the total depreciation to be charged to each period of the total life depends upon the depreciation method used.

Straight-line method of depreciation. This is the simplest and most common method. It results in spreading the total depreciation equally over all periods of life. The procedure under the straight-line method is as follows:

1. Find the difference between the cost and the scrap value.
2. Divide the figure found in 1 by the number of periods that the asset is expected to be of service. The result is the depreciation charge per period.

EXAMPLE

What will be the depreciation charge and the asset valuation at the end of each year for an asset costing $1,000.00, and having an estimated life of 10 years and an estimated scrap value of $100.00?

Formula

Cost − Scrap = Depreciation
Depreciation ÷ Number of years = Annual charge

Arithmetical Substitution

$1,000.00 − $100.00 = $900.00
$900.00 ÷ 10 = $90.00

TABLE OF DEPRECIATION

Years	*Periodic Depreciation Charge*	*Accumulated Depreciation Reserve*	*Asset Value*
			$1,000.00
1	$90.00	$ 90.00	910.00
2	90.00	180.00	820.00
3	90.00	270.00	730.00
4	90.00	360.00	640.00
5	90.00	450.00	550.00
6	90.00	540.00	460.00
7	90.00	630.00	370.00
8	90.00	720.00	280.00
9	90.00	810.00	190.00
10	90.00	900.00	100.00

Working-hours method of depreciation. This method recognizes the fact that property, particularly machinery, depreciates more rapidly if it is run full time or overtime than if it is run part time. Not only is the wear and tear greater, but there is less opportunity for making repairs. Moreover, the full-time and overtime years get more benefit from the asset than do the part-time years. The procedure under the working-hours method is as follows:

1. Find the difference between the cost and the scrap value.
2. Divide the figure found in 1 by the total number of hours that the asset is expected to be of service; this gives the depreciation charge per hour.
3. Multiply the figure found in 2 by the number of working hours per period. The result is the depreciation charge per period.

EXAMPLE

A machine costing $7,400.00 will have a scrap value of $200.00. Machines of this class have a working-hour average life of 24,000 hours. What will be the depreciation charge and the asset valuation at the end of each year, if the machine is run as follows:

First year	2,000 hours	Sixth year	2,000 hours
Second year	2,000 "	Seventh year	3,000 "
Third year	1,800 "	Eighth year	3,000 "
Fourth year	2,600 "	Ninth year	3,000 "
Fifth year	2,800 "	Tenth year	1,800 "

Formula

Cost − Scrap = Depreciation
Depreciation ÷ Total number of hours = Charge per hour

Arithmetical Substitution

$7,400.00 − $200.00 = $7,200.00
$7,200.00 ÷ 24,000 = $0.30

TABLE OF DEPRECIATION

Years	*Number of Hours*	*Periodic Depreciation Charge*	*Accumulated Depreciation Reserve*	*Asset Value*
				$7,400.00
1......	2,000	$600.00	$ 600.00	6,800.00
2......	2,000	600.00	1,200.00	6,200.00
3......	1,800	540.00	1,740.00	5,660.00
4......	2,600	780.00	2,520.00	4,880.00
5......	2,800	840.00	3,360.00	4,040.00
6......	2,000	600.00	3,960.00	3,440.00
7......	3,000	900.00	4,860.00	2,540.00
8......	3,000	900.00	5,760.00	1,640.00
9......	3,000	900.00	6,660.00	740.00
10......	1,800	540.00	7,200.00	200.00

Unit-production method of depreciation. This method is similar to the working-hours method in that it distributes the depreciation among the periods in proportion to the use made of the asset during each period. The estimated life is stated in units of product which can be produced by the asset before it is worn out, and the rate of depreciation is a rate per unit of product. The procedure under the unit-production method is as follows:

1. Find the difference between the cost and the scrap value.
2. Divide the figure found in 1 by the total number of units of product that it is expected the asset will produce during its life; this gives the depreciation charge per unit of product.
3. Multiply the figure found in 2 by the number of units produced per period. The result is the depreciation charge per period.

EXAMPLE

A certain one-purpose machine that costs $1,000.00, and has no scrap value, has been installed in a factory. A machine of this class produces 10,000 units of product during its life. Assuming that the annual production is as given below, set up a table showing the depreciation to be written off each year.

First year	1,000 units	Fifth year	1,000 units
Second year ..	2,000 "	Sixth year	1,200 "
Third year ...	1,800 "	Seventh year ..	1,200 "
Fourth year ..	1,000 "	Eighth year ...	800 "

Formula

Cost − Scrap = Depreciation
Depreciation ÷ Total number of units = Charge per unit

Arithmetical Substitution

$1,000.00 − $0.00 = $1,000.00
$1,000.00 ÷ 10,000 = $0.10

TABLE OF DEPRECIATION

Years	*Units Produced*	*Periodic Depreciation Charge*	*Accumulated Depreciation Reserve*	*Asset Value*
				$1,000.00
1.......	1,000	$100.00	$ 100.00	900.00
2.......	2,000	200.00	300.00	700.00
3.......	1,800	180.00	480.00	520.00
4.......	1,000	100.00	580.00	420.00
5.......	1,000	100.00	680.00	320.00
6.......	1,200	120.00	800.00	200.00
7.......	1,200	120.00	920.00	80.00
8.......	800	80.00	1,000.00	0.00

Reducing-charge methods of depreciation. Although actual depreciation is usually small during the early periods of life, and large during the later periods, it is sometimes contended that theoretical depreciation should be provided in an opposite manner; that is, by making large charges during the early periods and small charges during the later periods. This procedure is advocated on the theory that the cost of the use of an asset is composed of two elements—repairs and depreciation—and that the sum of these two charges should be a fairly uniform amount year by year. Since repairs tend to increase with the age of the asset, it is contended that the depreciation charge should decrease, in order that the increasing repair charges and the decreasing depreciation charges will tend to equalize each other and produce a uniform total charge.

This method is excellent theory, but the plan of making decreasing depreciation charges assumes that repairs will increase in the same proportion that depreciation decreases. Perhaps they will, but it is likely to be a matter of luck. If it is desirable to equalize the total repair and depreciation charges, it would seem better to create two reserves: one for depreciation on the straight-line method, and another for repairs. By estimating the total repair charges to be made during the life of the asset, and by providing a reserve for repairs by equal periodical charges, an equality is maintained as between periods. Such a plan is subject to the objection that it may be difficult to estimate accurately the total future repair cost, but with statistics showing past experience it should be no more difficult to do this than to estimate depreciation.

Three methods of providing a diminishing depreciation charge are:

1. Fixed-percentage-of-diminishing-value method.
2. Sum-of-digits method.
3. Diminishing-rates-on-cost method.

Fixed-percentage-of-diminishing-value method. The difficulty encountered in this method is that of finding the rate percent to be used in the calculation of the charge. The procedure is as follows:

1. Divide the scrap value by the cost.
2. Extract the root, corresponding to the number of periods of depreciation to be taken on the life of the asset, of the figure found in 1.
3. Deduct from 1 the result obtained in 2, to find the rate percent to be used.
4. Multiply the net asset or the carrying value of the asset at the beginning of each period by the rate found in 3, to obtain the depreciation charge for each period.

EXAMPLE

What will be the depreciation charges for an asset valued at $1,000.00, with a scrap value of $100.00, which is to be written off in 10 years by the fixed-percentage-of-diminishing-value method?

The following are the formula and solution for the calculation of the rate:

Formula	*Arithmetical Substitution*
$1-\sqrt[n]{\dfrac{\text{Scrap value}}{\text{Cost value}}}=r$	$1-\sqrt[10]{\dfrac{100}{1{,}000}}=20.5672\%$

Solution, Part 1

$$100 \div 1{,}000 = .1$$
$$\log .1 = \bar{1}.000000$$
$$\text{Changed, } \bar{1}.000000 = 9.000000 - 10$$
$$9.000000 - 10 \div 10 = .900000 - 1$$
$$\text{Changed} = \bar{1}.900000$$
$$\text{The antilog of } \bar{1}.900000 = .794328$$
$$1 - .794328 = 205672, \text{ or } 20.567\%$$

Solution, Part 2

$1,000.00 × 20.567% = $205.67, first depreciation charge
$1,000.00 − $205.67 = $794.33, new asset value
$794.33 × 20.567% = $163.37, second depreciation charge

This process is continued for each of the 10 years.

TABLE OF DEPRECIATION
(Rate, 20.567%)

Year	*Periodic Depreciation Charge*	*Accumulated Depreciation Reserve*	*Asset Value*
			$1,000.00
1..........	$205.67	$205.67	794.33
2..........	163.37	369.04	630.96
3..........	129.77	498.81	501.19
4..........	103.08	601.89	398.11
5..........	81.88	683.77	316.23
6..........	65.04	748.81	251.19
7..........	51.66	800.47	199.53
8..........	41.04	841.51	158.49
9..........	32.60	874.11	125.89
10..........	25.89	900.00	100.00

It should be clearly understood that the rate to be used in the fixed-percentage-of-diminishing-value method cannot be computed by dividing 100% by the years of life. If this were done in the above example, a rate of 10% would be obtained. Since the correct rate is 20.567%, it is evident that the use of a 10% rate would leave a large balance undepreciated at the end of 10 years.

Sum-of-digits method. The procedure under this method is as follows:

1. Find the sum of the digits, or numbers representing the periods of useful life of the asset. Use this sum as the denominator of certain fractions.
2. Use the same digits or numbers in inverse order as the numerators of these fractions.
3. Compute the periodic depreciation by multiplying the total depreciation by the fractions obtained in 1 and 2.

EXAMPLE

An asset is valued at $1,000.00, and has a scrap value of $100.00. What should be the depreciation charges if the asset is to be written down in 9 years by the sum-of-digits method?

Solution

TABLE OF DEPRECIATION

Year	*Fractional Part*	*Periodic Depreciation Charge*	*Accumulated Depreciation Reserve*	*Asset Value*
				$1,000.00
1.......	9/45	$180.00	$180.00	820.00
2.......	8/45	160.00	340.00	660.00
3.......	7/45	140.00	480.00	520.00
4.......	6/45	120.00	600.00	400.00
5.......	5/45	100.00	700.00	300.00
6.......	4/45	80.00	780.00	220.00
7.......	3/45	60.00	840.00	160.00
8.......	2/45	40.00	880.00	120.00
9.......	1/45	20.00	900.00	100.00
45.......	45/45	$900.00		

The denominator of the fractions used in the second column is found by adding the first column. The numerators are the same numbers taken in inverse order.

Diminishing-rates-on-cost method. The procedure under this method is as follows:

1. Choose a depreciation rate for each year. No formula is used in determining the rates, which are chosen arbitrarily and diminish from year to year.

2. Multiply the cost by the rate chosen for the year. The result is the depreciation charge.

EXAMPLE

What will be the depreciation charge each year on an asset the cost of which is $6,000.00, scrap value $400.00, and estimated life 8 years?

Solution

DEPRECIATION TABLE

Year	*Rate*	*Periodic Depreciation Charge*	*Accumulated Depreciation Reserve*	*Asset Value*
				$6,000.00
1........	15⅔%	$ 940.00	$ 940.00	5,060.00
2........	14⅔	880.00	1,820.00	4,180.00
3........	13	780.00	2,600.00	3,400.00
4........	12	720.00	3,320.00	2,680.00
5........	11	660.00	3,980.00	2,020.00
6........	10	600.00	4,580.00	1,420.00
7........	9	540.00	5,120.00	880.00
8........	8	480.00	5,600.00	400.00
	93⅓%	$5,600.00		

Annuity method of depreciation. The theory applied in this method is that the depreciation charge should include, in addition to the amount credited to the reserve, interest on the carrying value of the asset.

The investment in property is regarded, first, as the amount of scrap value that draws interest, and second, as an investment in an annuity to be reduced by equal periodic amounts. The interest on the scrap value plus the equal periodic reduction of the investment is the charge to depreciation, offset by a credit to interest computed on the diminishing value of the property, and a credit to the reserve account for the balance. This charge to depreciation is the same each period during the life of the property. The theory of an investment in an annuity is that the annuity is to be reduced by equal periodic payments, and as the credits to interest will decrease, the credits to the reserve must correspondingly increase.

The procedure under the annuity method is as follows:

1. Find the difference between the cost and the scrap value.
2. Divide the figure found in 1 by the present value of an annuity of 1.
3. Calculate the interest on the scrap value for one period at the given rate percentage.
4. Determine the sum of 2 and 3. The result is the periodic charge to depreciation.

EXAMPLE

Calculate by the annuity method the annual charge to depreciation for an asset valued at $1,000.00, with a scrap value of $100.00, which is to be written off in 10 years on a 6% basis.

Formula

$$\left[\frac{\text{Cost} - \text{Scrap}}{\dfrac{1 - \dfrac{1}{(1+i)^n}}{i}}\right] + (\text{Scrap} \times i) = \text{Periodic charge}$$

Arithmetical Substitution

$$\left[\frac{1{,}000 - 100}{\dfrac{1 - \dfrac{1}{(1.06)^{10}}}{.06}}\right] + (100 \times .06) = \$128.28$$

Solution

(1) The difference between the cost and the scrap value is $1,000.00 − $100.00 = $900.00.

(2) The present value of an annuity of 1 for 10 years at 6% is 7.36008705 (from the table on page 1337). Then, $900.00 ÷ 7.36008705 = $122.28.

(3) The interest on the scrap value for one period is $100.00 × .06 = $6.00.

(4) The sum of (2) and (3) is $122.28 + $6.00 = $128.28. This is the periodic charge to depreciation.

In the above example, the $900.00 represents the present value of the sum to be spread over the life of the asset, and the $100.00 represents the scrap value. In the following tables, the fifth column always contains the carrying value of the annuity, plus $100.00 The two tables are given to show the similarity between an annuity in which an investment was made and equal annual rents withdrawn, and the annuity method of depreciation.

TABLE OF REDUCTION OF AN ANNUITY

End of Period	*Rents Withdrawn*	*Credits to Interest*	*Amortization of Investment*	*Present Value of Annuity, Plus $100*
				$1,000.00
1......	$ 128.28	$ 60.00	$ 68.28	931.72
2......	128.28	55.90	72.38	859.34
3......	128.28	51.56	76.72	782.62
4......	128.28	46.96	81.32	701.50
5......	128.28	42.08	86.20	615.10
6......	128.28	36.91	91.37	523.73
7......	128.28	31.42	96.86	426.87
8......	128.28	25.61	102.67	324.20
9......	128.28	19.45	108.83	215.37
10......	128.29	12.92	115.37	100.00
	$1,282.81	$382.81	$900.00	

TABLE OF REDUCTION OF THE VALUE OF AN ASSET

End of Period	*Depreciation Charge*	*Credits to Interest*	*Credits to Reserve*	*Value of Asset*
				$1,000.00
1......	$ 128.28	$ 60.00	$ 68.28	931.72
2......	128.28	55.90	72.38	859.34
3......	128.28	51.56	76.72	782.62
4......	128.28	46.96	81.32	701.50
5......	128.28	42.08	86.20	615.10
6......	128.28	36.91	91.37	523.73
7......	128.28	31.42	96.86	426.87
8......	128.28	25.61	102.67	324.20
9......	128.28	19.45	108.83	215.37
10......	128.29	12.92	115.37	100.00
	$1,282.81	$382.81	$900.00	

Two objections may be raised to the annuity method. First, it results in the addition of interest to the cost of production, a procedure of more than doubtful propriety. Second, it throws the interest charge into operations under the name of depreciation. Even if interest were a proper element of cost, it would seem that the charge should be clearly stated as interest and should not be confused with depreciation.

Sinking-fund method of depreciation. The theory of the sinking-fund method is that the money set aside in a fund should draw interest, this interest to be added to the fund at the end of each year. The total accumulation of the fund should be equal to the depreciation charged during the life of the asset. While in theory a fund equal to the total accumulation is set aside, usually in practice no such fund exists.

The procedure under the sinking-fund method is as follows:

1. Find the amount of the total depreciation of the asset by deducting the scrap value from the cost.

2. Divide the figure found in 1 by the amount of an ordinary annuity of 1 at the sinking-fund interest rate, for the number of periods of the life of the asset. This will give the periodic sum to be placed in the sinking fund.

3. To the periodic sum found in 2, add a sum equal to the interest on the sinking fund for the period. This gives the periodic charge to depreciation and the credit to reserve for depreciation.

EXAMPLE

An asset costs $1,000.00, and has a scrap value of $100.00 at the end of 10 years. Determine the periodic depreciation charge by the sinking-fund method, on a 6% interest basis.

Formula

$$\frac{\text{Cost} - \text{Scrap}}{\frac{(1+i)^n - 1}{i}} = \text{Periodic deposit in sinking fund}$$

Arithmetical Substitution

$$\frac{1{,}000 - 100}{\frac{(1.06)^{10} - 1}{.06}} = \$68.28$$

Solution

(1) The difference between the cost and the scrap value is $1,000.00 – $100.00 = $900.00.

(2) The amount of an ordinary annuity of 1 for 10 years at 6% is 13.18079494 (from the table on page 1333). Then, $900.00 ÷ 13.18079494 = $68.28.

The formula and solution just shown give only the first periodic charge to depreciation. Each periodic charge is an amount equal to the sum of the first periodic payment and the interest on the accumulated depreciation reserve. Table B, below, shows the periodic charges to depreciation and the credits to the reserve account for each of the 10 years.

It is not necessary to accumulate a sinking fund in order to use the sinking-fund method of depreciation. The depreciation entries are independent of the fund entries. If a sinking fund were accumulated for the above example, the entries would be as shown in Table A.

TABLE A.—ENTRIES TO THE SINKING FUND

Year	*Debit to Sinking Fund*	*Credit to Cash*	*Credit to Interest*	*Accumulation of Fund*
1........	$ 68.28	$ 68.28	$	$ 68.28
2........	72.38	68.28	4.10	140.66
3........	76.72	68.28	8.44	217.38
4........	81.32	68.28	13.04	298.70
5........	86.20	68.28	17.92	384.90
6........	91.37	68.28	23.09	476.27
7........	96.86	68.28	28.58	573.13
8........	102.67	68.28	34.39	675.80
9........	108.83	68.28	40.55	784.63
10........	115.37	68.29	47.08	900.00
	$900.00	$682.81	$217.19	

TABLE B.—DEPRECIATION ENTRIES BY THE SINKING-FUND METHOD OF DEPRECIATION

End of Year	*Depreciation Charge and Reserve Credit*	*Accumulated Depreciation Reserve*	*Asset Value*
			$1,000.00
1..........	$ 68.28	$ 68.28	931.72
2..........	72.38	140.66	859.34
3..........	76.72	217.38	782.62
4..........	81.32	298.70	701.30
5..........	86.20	384.90	615.10
6..........	91.37	476.27	523.73
7..........	96.86	573.13	426.87
8..........	102.67	675.80	324.20
9..........	108.83	784.63	215.37
10..........	115.37	900.00	100.00

The sinking-fund method is sometimes used by public utilities in order to determine what amount must be taken out of income to provide a fund for the replacement of the assets. Having determined this amount, the utility is allowed to charge a rate for its service sufficient to provide for depreciation as well as for the other expenses. The cash provided by the income is put into the fund, and the charges to depreciation are made in accordance with the accumulation of the fund. Thus, as the investment in, or carrying value of, the fixed assets is diminished, the fund is increased, and the capital is kept intact.

Appraisal method of depreciation. This method consists merely of estimating the value of the asset at the end of each period and writing off as depreciation the difference between the balance of the asset account and the appraised value. The appraisal method is likely to result in burdening some periods with heavy charges and relieving other periods, for if the depreciation charges correspond with actual depreciation, the charges will be light during the early years and heavy during the later ones. On the other hand, the burden may be reversed by charging the early periods with large amounts, on the theory that the property loses value rapidly in the early part of its life, because its value is quickly reduced to a secondhand basis. This practice improperly introduces the element of realizable values, when only going-concern values should be considered.

When the appraisal method is used, care should be taken to ignore upward or downward fluctuations in market value.

Composite-life method of depreciation. The composite life of a plant as a whole, sometimes called the average or mean life, may be computed as in the following illustration:

Asset	*Cost*	*Residual Value*	*Total Depreciation*	*Estimated Life*	*Annual Depreciation (Straight-Line)*
A	$20,000.00	$5,000.00	$15,000.00	20 years	$ 750.00
B	12,000.00	2,000.00	10,000.00	10 years	1,000.00
C	8,000.00	2,000.00	6,000.00	8 years	750.00
D	500.00	100.00	400.00	2 years	200.00
			$31,400.00		$2,700.00

$31.400.00 ÷ $2,700.00 = $11\frac{17}{27}$, the composite, or average, life.

This computation indicates that $31,400.00 depreciation should be provided to cover one exhaustion of the plant as a whole. On the straight-line method, $2,700.00 depreciation will be provided annually. At this rate it will take $11\frac{17}{27}$ years to provide $31,400.00 depreciation. Hence $11\frac{17}{27}$ years is the composite life of the plant.

Federal income tax; deduction for depreciation. In computing the Federal income tax, a reasonable allowance is made for the exhaustion, wear, and tear of property used in the trade or business. While the straight-line method is generally used, the income tax regulations provide that the deduction need not necessarily be at a uniform rate. According to an early ruling, any recognized trade practice is permissible, provided it results in an annual charge over the useful life of the property according to some reasonably consistent plan. The unit-production method, the diminishing-value method, and the sinking-fund method are specifically mentioned in a pamphlet, issued by the Treasury Department, known as "Bulletin 'F'—Income Tax Depreciation and Obsolescence Estimated Useful Lives and Depreciation Rates."

It should be remembered, however, that the depreciation deduction under the Federal income tax law is highly technical and hedged about by numerous rules and regulations. For example, the basis upon

TABLE SHOWING DEPRECIATION RATE FOR VARIOUS ASSETS

(Page from a table contained in the pamphlet "Bulletin 'F'," issued by the Bureau of Internal Revenue.)

MOTOR AND OTHER VEHICLES

	Years		*Years*
Automobiles:		Trucks:	
Passenger	5	Outside use—	
Salesman	3	Electric	10
Horse-drawn vehicles	8	Gas, light	4
Motorcycles	4	Medium	6
Tractors	6	Heavy	8
Trailers	6	Inside use	15

OFFICE EQUIPMENT

	Average useful life (years)		*Average useful life (years)*
Adding machines	10	Call system and annunciators	14
Addressing and mailing machines	15	Cases:	
Billing machines	8	Book	20
Binders, loose-leaf	20	Display	20
Blue-printing machines	15	Chairs:	
Bookkeeping machines	8	Bentwood	5
Cabinets and files	15	Heavy	16
Calculators	10	Check perforators	10

	Average useful life (years)		*Average useful life (years)*
Check writers	8	Lockers	25
Cleaners, electric vacuum	6	Lunch-room equipment	15
Clocks:		Mirrors	20
Time	15	Money machines	10
Time-stamping	10	Numbering machines	10
Wall	20	Photographing machines	16
Coolers, water	10	Pneumatic-tube systems	20
Desks	20	Racks and stands	15
Dictation machines	6	Rugs, carpets, and mats	10
Duplicating machines	10	Safes and vaults	50
Fans, electric	10	Scales, counter and mail	10
Folding and sealing machines	10	Settees	13
		Shades, window	10
Helmets, rescue	6	Signs, board	10
Hospital equipment	15	Tables	15
Lamps, desk and floor	10	Typewriters	5
Linoleum	8	Wardrobes	20

which depreciation is computed is the same as that for computing the gain from a sale, which may be entirely different from book value.

The rate of depreciation, under the Federal income tax law, depends in every instance upon the estimated useful life of the property. In Bulletin "F," revised January 1942, the probable useful life of several hundred items is set forth.* The table above is reproduced from this source. Since that date, the courts and Board of Tax Appeals have handed down numerous decisions approving a certain rate for various assets. While the rates given in the Bureau's table and in the decisions of the courts and Board of Tax Appeals are entitled to great weight, they may not be used arbitrarily, but are a useful guide or starting-point from which the correct rate may be determined. The question in every case is one of fact to be determined in the light of the experience of the property under consideration and all other pertinent evidence. A page from a table compiled from court and Board decisions is illustrated below.

---

* The 1950 Revenue Act allows a depreciation period of five years for any "emergency facility." An emergency facility is defined as ". . . any facility, land, building, machinery or equipment, or any part thereof, the construction, reconstruction, erection, installation, or acquisition of which was completed after December 31, 1949, and with respect to which a certificate . . . has been made." The certificate, known as a Necessity Certificate, is obtained from the National Security Resources Board.

ANOTHER TABLE SHOWING DEPRECIATION RATE FOR VARIOUS ASSETS

(Page from a table compiled from decisions of the courts and the Board of Tax Appeals.)

Asset	*Useful Life (Yrs.)*	*Rate (%)*	*Authority*
Plumbing	33⅓	3	Union Co., 14 B.T.A. 1310
	20	5	Lord & Bushnell Co., 7 B.T.A. 86
Plank roads	10	10	Lord & Bushnell Co., 7 B.T.A. 86
Plows	5	20	Louis Titus, 2 B.T.A. 754
Power plants	20	5	Art. Metal Const. Co., 4 B.T.A. 493
			Chicago Ry. Equipment Co., B.T.A. 471
	15	6⅔	Frost Manufacturing Co., 13 B.T.A. 802
	14²⁄₇	7	Lassen Lumber & Box Co., 6 B.T.A. 241
	10	10	Atlas Tack Co., 9 B.T.A. 1322
Power transmission lines	15⁵⁄₁₃	6½	Quito Electric Light & Power Co., 10 B.T.A. 538
	10	10	Lord & Bushnell Co., 7 B.T.A. 86
Rafting gear	2	50	J. S. Hoskins Lumber Co., 3 B.T.A. 846
Railroads	25	4	Great Northern Railway Co., 30 B.T.A. 691
	6⅔	15	Fort Orange Paper Co., 1 B.T.A. 1230
	3	33⅓	Lytle Const. Co., 21 B.T.A. 1423 †
. bridges and trestles	10	10	Richmond Belt Railway Co., 13 B.T.A. 1291
. grading	33⅓	3	Richmond Belt Railway Co., 13 B.T.A. 1291
. rails	20	5	Richmond Belt Railway Co., 13 B.T.A. 1291
. ties	8	12½	Richmond Belt Railway Co., 13 B.T.A. 1291
Raisin Stemmers .	10	10	Lloyd H. Wilbur, 5 B.T.A. 597
Refrigerators	5	20	Strauss Market, Inc., 2 B.T.A. 1264
Refrigerator cars .	20	5	American Refrigerator Transit Co., 31 B.T.A. 465 (No. 96) (nonacquiescence, C.B. June 1935, p. 23)
Sawmill	20	5	Woods Lumber Co., 44 B.T.A. 88
Scales	10	10	Hickory Spinning Co., 2 B.T.A. 439
			Lord & Bushnell Co., 7 B.T.A. 86
	4	25	David T. Long, 17 B.T.A. 584
Scows	30	3⅓	Morris & Cummings Dredging Co., 10 B.T.A. 351
	20	5	Bartley Scow Co., 1 B.T.A. 1165
Sewing machines .	10	10	Pinkus Happ, 7 B.T.A. 865
Signs	20	5	Cooperative Publishing Co., 5 B.T.A. 340
	10	10	Lord & Bushnell Co., 7 B.T.A. 86
	6⅔	15	When Clothing Co., 1 B.T.A. 973

† Construction work only.

Asset	*Useful Life (Yrs.)*	*Rate (%)*	*Authority*
Slot machines ...	5	20	E. J. Roberts, Memo T. C.
Smoke stack	4	25	Magdalen Doerfler, Beneficiary, 13 B.T.A. 921
Sprinkler systems.	40	2½	Oliver Finnie Co., 2 B.T.A. 134
	20	5	H. Sheldon Mfg. Co., 13 B.T.A. 1299
	10	10	Atlas Plywood Co., 17 B.T.A. 156
	16	6¼	Long Island Drug Co., 35 B.T.A. 328
	15	6⅔	Elberta Crate & Box Co. (Memo B.T.A. 3-3-40)
Steam shovels ...	5	20	Parker Gravel Co., Inc., 21 B.T.A. 51
	3	33⅓	Nichols Contracting Co., 15 B.T.A. 102
Steamships, freight	33⅓	3	Kinsman Transit Co., 1 B.T.A. 552 **
			Valley Steamship Co., 1 B.T.A. 1107 **
. Great Lakes ..	33⅓	3	A.R.R. 27, C.B. June 1920, p. 139
. lumber trade .	20	5	A.R.R. 279, C.B. Dec. 1920, p. 168
. ocean-going ..	20	5	A.R.R. 4822, C.B. June 1924, p. 159
	12	8⅓	Seas Shipping Co., Inc., 16 B.T.A. 841 (nonacquiescence, C.B. June 1930, p. 75)
	28⁴⁄₇	3½	American So. African Line, 30 B.T.A. 753 *
	25	4	American So. African Line, 30 B.T.A. 753 *

* Includes obsolescence allowance.
** Great Lakes.

12. SHORT CUTS IN BUSINESS MATHEMATICS

Adapted from Curtis and Cooper, "Mathematics of Accounting" New York: Prentice-Hall, Inc.

Addition

Addition of columns. Add each column separately, setting the sums one place to the left each time. After the last column has been added, add the individual sums in regular order—that is, from right to left. (See Example 1.)

To check, repeat the process beginning at the left.

or

Add each column separately, and, as each sum is set one place to the left, add the number carried from the column at the right. The answer is the total of the last column and the outer figures. (See

Example 2.) The second method saves a little time but is not checked as in Example 1.

Example 1	*Example 2*
4572	4572
3986	3986
2173	2173
5911	5911
2765	2765
4937	4937
24	24
32	34
40	43
20	24
24344	

Savings accomplished.

1. Time required to readd a column of figures for the purpose of picking up the carrying figure is saved.

2. Saves time in checking for errors. For example, if, in the final summary of additions, there is an error of \$100.00, the hundreds' columns of the subtotals may be verified quickly without the necessity of readding all the columns.

Subtraction

Subtraction by addition. Instead of subtracting in the usual way, add to the subtrahend the number required to make the subtrahend equal to the minuend.

Thus, in the following example, instead of thinking 7 from 16 is 9, think $7 + 9 = 16$. Write the 9. Add 1, the digit carried over, to the 8, making 9. $9 + 8 = 17$. Write 8 and add 1, the digit carried over, to 1, making 2. $2 + 0 = 2$. Write 0. $3 + 5 = 8$. Write 5. Answer: 5,089.

EXAMPLE

Minuend	8276
Subtrahend	3187
Difference	5089

Purpose. The common error in subtraction caused by overlooking the fact that borrowing from the next higher order has taken place is avoided by changing the process of subtraction to that of addition.

Balancing an account. In most cases inspection will tell which side of the account is the greater in amount. Add the larger side, and put the same footing on the smaller side, leaving space for the balance; then add from the top downward, supplying the figures necessary to make the column total equal to the footing previously placed there.

EXAMPLE

Debits		*Credits*
$ 1,956.18		$ 134.26
3,452.75		258.19
289.34		764.83
5,726.31		2,375.94
	Balance,	7,891.36
$11,424.58		$11,424.58

Explanation. The balance, $7,891.36, was found as follows: Inspection showed the debit side to be the larger in amount. It was therefore added, and the footing of the account, $11,424.58, was placed under both debit and credit columns. The first order of the credits—that is, the cents—adds to 22. Insert 6 to make 28. With 2, the digit carried over, the second order, the dimes, adds to 22. Insert 3 to make 25. The third order, the dollars, with the digit carried over, adds to 23. Insert 1 to make 24. The fourth order, the tens of dollars, with the digit carried over, adds to 23. Insert 9 to make 32. The fifth order, the hundreds of dollars, with the digit carried over, adds to 16. Insert 8 to make 24. The sixth order, the thousands of dollars, with the digit carried over, adds to 4. Insert 7 to make 11.

Multiplication

TABLE OF SHORT CUTS IN MULTIPLICATION

To multiply by						To multiply by					
1¼	add	0	and divide	by	8	25	add	00	and divide	by	4
1⅔	"	0	"	"	6	31¼	"	000	"	"	32
2½	"	0	"	"	4	33⅓	"	00	"	"	3
3⅓	"	0	"	"	3	50	"	00	"	"	2
5	"	0	"	"	2	66⅔	"	000	"	"	15
6¼	"	00	"	"	16	83⅓	"	000	"	"	12
6⅔	"	00	"	"	15	125	"	000	"	"	8
8⅓	"	00	"	"	12	166⅔	"	000	"	"	6
12½	"	00	"	"	8	250	"	000	"	"	4
14²⁄₇	"	00	"	"	7	333⅓	"	000	"	"	3
16⅔	"	00	"	"	6						

Using factors as a short cut in multiplication. When factors of the multiplier are used, there are only two multiplications, whereas in the ordinary method there is an addition as well.

EXAMPLE

Multiply 439 by 24.

Solution

Ordinary Method	*Shorter Method*
439	439 $24 = 6 \times 4$
24	6
1756	2634
878	4
10536	10536

Multiplication by 11. Put down the units' digit (right-hand figure) as the units' digit of the product. Then add the tens' digit (second figure) to the units' digit and put down the sum. If it is over 10, put down the right-hand figure and carry 1. Then add the hundreds' digit (third figure) to the tens' digit, adding the 1 if there was a carry-over. If it is over 10, put down the right-hand figure and carry 1, as before. Continue in the same way with each digit to the left. Then put down the first figure and carry 1 if there is a carry-over.

EXAMPLE

Multiply 5,846 by 11.

Solution

Put down 6, the units' digit. Add 4 and 6, put down 0, and carry 1. Add 8 and 4 and 1 carried over, and put down 3 and carry 1. Add 5 and 8 and 1 carried over, and put down 4 and carry 1. Put down 5 plus 1 carried over, 6. The answer is 64306.

Multiplication by 15. Annex a cipher to the multiplicand, and increase the result by one half of the multiplicand.

EXAMPLE

Multiply 8,435 by 15.

Solution

$$\begin{array}{r} 84350 \\ 42175 \\ \hline 126525 \end{array}$$

Multiplication by 75. Annex two ciphers, then divide by 4, and subtract this quotient from the product.

EXAMPLE

Multiply 4,728 by 75.

Solution

```
472800
118200
------
354600
```

Multiplication of numbers ending with ciphers. Multiply the significant figures and annex as many ciphers as there are final ciphers in both the multiplier and the multiplicand.

EXAMPLE

Multiply 756,000 by 4,200.

Solution

```
  756
   42
-----
31752
```

Annex five ciphers. Answer: 3,175,200,000.

Multiplication by 9, 99, 999, etc. Multiply by 10, 100, or 1,000, etc., and subtract the original number from the result.

EXAMPLE

Multiply 8,356 by 99.

Solution

```
          835,600
          - 8,356
          -------
Answer:   827,244
```

Multiplication by numbers near 100, as 98, 97, 96, etc., and by numbers near 1,000, as 997, 996, etc. This method is of value in finding the net proceeds of some amount less 2%, 3%, etc., and also in many other situations.

Multiply the number by 100 (or 1,000) and subtract the product of the multiplicand and the difference between 100 (or 1,000) and the exact multiplier.

EXAMPLE

Multiply 3,247 by 97.

Solution

Multiply the number by 100, and subtract 3 times the number.

$$\begin{array}{r} 324{,}700 = 3{,}247 \times 100 \\ \underline{9{,}741} = 3{,}247 \times 3 \\ 314{,}959 = 3{,}247 \times 97 \end{array}$$

Multiplication of two numbers, each near 100, 1,000, etc. Products of numbers in this class may be calculated mentally.

EXAMPLE 1

Multiply 96 by 98.

Explanation. Step 1. Multiply the complements of the two numbers, and, if the product occupies units' place only, prefix a cipher. Result, 08.

Step 2. Subtract the complement of one number from the other number, and write the result at the left of the result in Step 1. The complement of either number subtracted from the other number leaves the same remainder; as, 96 – 2 or 98 – 4 each equal 94. Answer: 9,408.

Solution

	Complement
96	4
98	2
9408	

EXAMPLE 2

Multiply 996 by 988.

Solution

	Complement
996	4
988	12
984,048	

Explanation. When numbers near 1,000 are multiplied, ciphers are prefixed to the product of the complements, so that the product occupies three places.

Multiplying by numbers a little larger than 100, as 101, 102, etc. Annex two ciphers to the multiplicand, and to this add the product of the multiplicand and the units' figure of the multiplier. Annex three ciphers for multipliers over 1,000.

EXAMPLE

Multiply 3,475 by 104.

Solution

$$\begin{array}{rl} 347{,}500 & \\ 13{,}900 & (4 \times 3{,}475) \\ \hline 361{,}400 & \end{array}$$

Multiplication of two numbers, each a little more than 100. To the sum of the numbers (omitting one digit in the hundreds' column), annex two ciphers, and add the product of the supplements (excess over 100).

EXAMPLE

Multiply 112 by 113.

Solution

$$\begin{array}{rl} 112 & \\ 113 & \\ \hline 12500 & \text{(sum of numbers, with one digit in the hundreds' column omitted)} \\ 156 & \text{(product of supplements, } 12 \times 13) \\ \hline 12656 & \end{array}$$

Explanation. In instances similar to the foregoing, a knowledge of the multiplication tables to 20 × 20 makes mental results possible, and is invaluable in inventory and other extensions.

Mental multiplication by a single method. Instead of using the various methods of rapid multiplication for different multipliers explained in the preceding pages, it is possible to use one method for all two- and three-digit multipliers. The following explanation is adapted from *Mental Multiplication, How to Figure Mentally*, by Charles Lipkin, C.P.A.

Mental multiplication with two-digit multipliers. The multiplying is done downward. In multiplying by the units' digit of the multiplier, put the answer down, but only in one digit, and carry the rest. Thus, in multiplying 6 by 7, answer 42, put down 2 and carry 4. In multiplying by any other digit of the multiplier except the units' digit, do not put the answer down, but carry, except at the end.

EXAMPLES

	439
	× 11
$9 \times 11 = 99$, carry 9	9
$9 + (3 \times 11) = 42$, carry 4	29
$4 + (4 \times 11) = 48$	4829

	439
	× 75
$9 \times 75 = 675$, carry 67	5
$67 + (3 \times 75) = 292$, carry 29	25
$29 + (4 \times 75) = 329$	32925

In the above examples knowledge of the multiplication tables was assumed. Assuming now that no multiplication table is known above 9×9, the process is as follows: Multiply downward as above. Set down the partial product's *units'* digit when multiplying by the *units'* figure of the multiplier; always carry the *entire* partial product when multiplying by the *tens'* figure of the two-digit multiplier.

EXAMPLES

	439
	× 11
$9 \times 1 =$	9
$9 \times 1 = 9$, carry 9	
$9 + (3 \times 1) = 12$, carry 1	29
$1 + (3 \times 1) = 4$, carry 4	
$4 + (4 \times 1) = 8$	829
$4 \times 1 = 4$	4829

	439
	× 75
$9 \times 5 = 45$, carry 4	5
$4 + (9 \times 7) = 67$, carry 67	
$67 + (3 \times 5) = 82$, carry 8	25
$8 + (3 \times 7) = 29$, carry 29	
$29 + (4 \times 5) = 49$, carry 4	925
$4 + (4 \times 7) = 32$	32925

Mental multiplication with three-digit multipliers. In multiplying by a number of three digits, consider such multiplier as consisting of *two* figures: a *tens'* figure of *one* digit (the hundreds' digit of the multiplier), and a *units'* figure of *two* digits (the tens' and units' digits of the multiplier); thus, 119 is seen as 1 19, 223 as 2 23, etc.

EXAMPLES

	439
	× 119
9 × 19 = 171, carry 17	1
17 + (3 × 19) + 90 (9 of 439 × 10) = 164, carry 16 ...	41
16 + (4 × 19) + 30 (3 of 439 × 10) = 122, carry 12 ...	241
12 + 40 (4 of 439 × 10) = 52	52241

	439
	× 327
9 × 27 = 243, carry 24	3
24 + (3 × 27) + 270 (9 of 439 × 30) = 375, carry 37 ..	53
37 + (4 × 27) + 90 (3 of 439 × 30) = 235, carry 23 ..	533
23 + 120 (4 of 439 × 30) = 143	143553

How to abbreviate decimal multiplication when a given number of decimal places is required. It is a waste of time to carry out decimal multiplication to a denomination smaller than that in which the data are expressed; often it is unnecessary to carry it beyond the third or fourth decimal.

EXAMPLE

Multiply 4.7892 by 3.1765, and obtain the answer correct to four decimal places.

Solution

4.7892		= multiplicand
56713		= multiplier reversed
14.3676		= 4.7892 × 3.
.4789	2	= 4.789~~2~~ × .1
.3325	4 ~~4~~	= 4.78~~92~~ × .07
. 287	3 ~~5~~ ~~2~~	= 4.7~~892~~ × .006
. 23	9 ~~4~~ ~~6~~ ~~0~~	= 4.~~7892~~ × .0005
15.2128	~~0~~ ~~3~~ ~~8~~ ~~0~~	

Explanation. The multiplier, 3.1765, is written in the reverse order, 56713, the units' digit being placed under the lowest order of the multiplicand that is desired in the product—ten thousandths. Multiply by each digit of the reversed multiplier, beginning with that digit of the multiplicand which stands directly above the digit of the multiplier used, taking care to include the digit carried over from the multiplication of the one (or two) rejected digits at the right.

Multiplication by use of a table of multiples. It is not uncommon to have to use the same number many times in making calculations, especially in cost accounting. A saving of time and increased accuracy in the work are achieved if a table of multiples of the number is constructed. Suppose that you have to perform a number of multiplications in which 326,834 is one of the factors. A table of multiples may be constructed with an adding machine by locking the repeat key. Subtotal after each pull of the handle. The subtotals should check with the product column shown below. If the table is prepared by repeated additions, and not with an adding machine, the 10th product should be computed, as it will verify all, unless there are compensating errors in the work.

TABLE OF MULTIPLES

Multiplier	*Product*
1	326,834
2 (326,834 + 326,834)	653,668
3 (653,668 + 326,834)	980,502
4 (980,502 + 326,834)	1,307,336
5 (1,307,336 + 326,834)	1,634,170
6 (1,634,170 + 326,834)	1,961,004
7 (1,961,004 + 326,834)	2,287,838
8 (2,287,838 + 326,834)	2,614,672
9 (2,614,672 + 326,834)	2,941,506

Verification

10 (2,941,506 + 326,834)	3,268,340

EXAMPLE

Multiply 326,834 by 5,249.

Solution

2941506	= 9 times 326,834
1307336	= 4 times 326,834
653668	= 2 times 326,834
1634170	= 5 times 326,834
1715551666	= product

HANDY MULTIPLICATION AND DIVISION TABLE

1	**2**	**3**	**4**	**5**	**6**	**7**	**8**	**9**	**10**	**11**	**12**	**13**	**14**	**15**	**16**	**17**	**18**	**19**	**20**	**21**	**22**	**23**	**24**	**25**	
2	**4**	6	8	10	12	14	16	18	20	22	24	26	28	30	32	34	36	38	40	42	44	46	48	50	**2**
3	6	**9**	12	15	18	21	24	27	30	33	36	39	42	45	48	51	54	57	60	63	66	69	72	75	**3**
4	8	12	**16**	20	24	28	32	36	40	44	48	52	56	60	64	68	72	76	80	84	88	92	96	100	**4**
5	10	15	20	**25**	30	35	40	45	50	55	60	65	70	75	80	85	90	95	100	105	110	115	120	125	**5**
6	12	18	24	30	**36**	42	48	54	60	66	72	78	84	90	96	102	108	114	120	126	132	138	144	150	**6**
7	14	21	28	35	42	**49**	56	63	70	77	84	91	98	105	112	119	126	133	140	147	154	161	168	175	**7**
8	16	24	32	40	48	56	**64**	72	80	88	96	104	112	120	128	136	144	152	160	168	176	184	192	200	**8**
9	18	27	36	45	54	63	72	**81**	90	99	108	117	126	135	144	153	162	171	180	189	198	207	216	225	**9**
10	20	30	40	50	60	70	80	90	**100**	110	120	130	140	150	160	170	180	190	200	210	220	230	240	250	**10**
11	22	33	44	55	66	77	88	99	110	**121**	132	143	154	165	176	187	198	209	220	231	242	253	264	275	**11**
12	24	36	48	60	72	84	96	108	120	132	**144**	156	168	180	192	204	216	228	240	252	264	276	288	300	**12**
13	26	39	52	65	78	91	104	117	130	143	156	**169**	182	195	208	221	234	247	260	273	286	299	312	325	**13**
14	28	42	56	70	84	98	112	126	140	154	168	182	**196**	210	224	238	252	266	280	294	308	322	336	350	**14**
15	30	45	60	75	90	105	120	135	150	165	180	195	210	**225**	240	255	270	285	300	315	330	345	360	375	**15**
16	32	48	64	80	96	112	128	144	160	176	192	208	224	240	**256**	272	288	304	320	336	352	368	384	400	**16**
17	34	51	68	85	102	119	136	153	170	187	204	221	238	255	272	**289**	306	323	340	357	374	391	408	425	**17**
18	36	54	72	90	108	126	144	162	180	198	216	234	252	270	288	306	**324**	342	360	378	396	414	432	450	**18**
19	38	57	76	95	114	133	152	171	190	209	228	247	266	285	304	323	342	**361**	380	399	418	437	456	475	**19**
20	40	60	80	100	120	140	160	180	200	220	240	260	280	300	320	340	360	380	**400**	420	440	460	480	500	**20**
21	42	63	84	105	126	147	168	189	210	231	252	273	294	315	336	357	378	399	420	**441**	462	483	504	525	**21**
22	44	66	88	110	132	154	176	198	220	242	264	286	308	330	352	374	396	418	440	462	**484**	506	528	550	**22**
23	46	69	92	115	138	161	184	207	230	253	276	299	322	345	368	391	414	437	460	483	506	**529**	552	575	**23**
24	48	72	96	120	144	168	192	216	240	264	288	312	336	360	384	408	432	456	480	504	528	552	**576**	600	**24**
25	50	75	100	125	150	175	200	225	250	275	300	325	350	375	400	425	450	475	500	525	550	575	600	**625**	**25**
	2	**3**	**4**	**5**	**6**	**7**	**8**	**9**	**10**	**11**	**12**	**13**	**14**	**15**	**16**	**17**	**18**	**19**	**20**	**21**	**22**	**23**	**24**	**25**	

Multiplication.—A number in the top line multiplied by a number in the column at the extreme left produces the number shown where the top line and the side line meet. *Example:* $17 \times 14 = 238$.

Division.—A number in the table divided by the number at the top of that column produces the number shown in the column at the extreme left. Also, a number in the table divided by the number in the column at the extreme left produces the number shown at the top of that column. *Example:* $266 \div 14 = 19$.

Division

TABLE OF SHORT CUTS IN DIVISION

To divide by				
1¼	multiply by	8	and divide by	10
1⅔	"	6	" "	10
2½	"	4	" "	10
3⅓	"	3	" "	10
3¾	"	8	" "	30
6¼	"	16	" "	100
7½	"	4	" "	30
8⅓	"	12	" "	100
9 1/11	"	11	" "	100
11⅑	"	9	" "	100
12½	"	8	" "	100
14 2/7	"	7	" "	100
16⅔	"	6	" "	100
25	"	4	" "	100
31¼	"	16	" "	500
33⅓	"	3	" "	100
75	"	4	" "	300
125	"	8	" "	1,000
175	"	4	" "	700
275	"	4	" "	1,100
375	"	8	" "	3,000
625	"	8	" "	5,000
875	"	8	" "	7,000

Division by use of a table of multiples. If a number of divisions are to be made with the same divisor, it is advantageous to set up a table of multiples of the divisor.

EXAMPLE

Assume that 328 is to be used a number of times as a divisor, and that one of the dividends is 587,954.

TABLE OF MULTIPLES

Multiplier	*Product*
1	328
2	656
3	984
4	1,312
5	1,640
6	1,968
7	2,296
8	2,624
9	2,952

Explanation. Inspection shows the first digit in the quotient to be 1. The second partial dividend is 2,599. The table of multiples shows the largest product contained therein to be 2,296, opposite 7. The third partial dividend is 3,035, and the table of multiples shows the largest product contained therein to be 2,952, opposite 9. The fourth partial dividend is 834, and the largest product contained therein is 656, opposite 2. The remainder is 178. The fraction 178/328 may be reduced to 89/164, or it may be changed to a decimal.

Solution

```
328)587954(1792 89/164
    328
    2599
    2296
     3035
     2952
      834
      656
      178
```

$$\frac{178}{328} = \frac{89}{164}$$

Division in this manner is rapid, as no time is lost through selection of a quotient so large that when the product is found it exceeds the dividend, necessitating another trial.

Reciprocals in division. The reciprocal of any number is found by dividing 1 by the number. The reciprocal of 5 is 1 ÷ 5, or .2, and the reciprocal of 25 is 1 ÷ 25, or .04.

The quotient in a division may be found by multiplying the dividend by the reciprocal of the divisor. Hence, in instances in which it is necessary to find what percent each item is of the total of the items, the use of the reciprocal of the divisor will save time and provide a check on these computations.

Procedure: To find what percent each item is of the total of the items:

1. Divide 1 by the total of the items to obtain the reciprocal of the total.

2. Using the result obtained in 1 as a fixed multiplier, multiply each of the individual items, and the respective results obtained will be the percentages that the individual items are of the total sum.

EXAMPLE

Find the percentage that each department's monthly expense is of the total monthly expense.

Department	*Expense*
A	$ 600.00
B	500.00
C	1,200.00
D	700.00
E	1,000.00
Total	$4,000.00

Solution

Divide 1 by 4,000 to obtain the reciprocal, .00025. Multiply the expense of each department by this reciprocal, and the product will be the percentage that the department's expense is of the total expense.

Department	*Expense*		*Reciprocal*		*Per Cent*
A	$ 600.00	×	.00025	=	15 %
B	500.00	×	.00025	=	12½%
C	1,200.00	×	.00025	=	30 %
D	700.00	×	.00025	=	17½%
E	1,000.00	×	.00025	=	25 %
Total	$4,000.00				100 %

Division of decimals. Division of decimals may often be abbreviated, especially when the divisor is given to a greater number of decimal places than are contained in the dividend, and when only three or four decimals are essential in the quotient.

EXAMPLE

Divide 4.39876 by 2.4871934, and obtain the quotient correct to three decimal places.

Solution

Ordinary Method

```
2.4871934)4.398 7600 (1.768
          2 487 1934
          1 911 56660
          1 741 03538
            170 531220
            149 231604
             21 2996160
             19 8975472
              1 4020688
```

Abbreviated Method

```
2.487 1934)4.398 7(1.768
      (1934 struck out)
           2 487 2
           1 911 5
           1 741 0
             170 5
             149 2
              21 3
              19 9
               1 4
```

Explanation. Observation of the ordinary method shows that the third decimal place in the quotient is not affected by the digit in the third decimal place in the divisor (except through the digits carried).

Since the units' digit of the divisor is contained in the units' digit of the dividend, the first digit in the quotient is in the units' place, and, as three decimal places are required, the quotient will contain four digits. Therefore, the last four digits of the divisor will not affect the quotient, except through the digits carried over.

The first four digits of the divisor, 2.487, are contained once in 4.398. Multiplication of that part of the divisor used, by the quotient digit (including the digit carried over from the one or two following digits—in this case considering the 9 as a unit and adding it to the 1, making 2) gives 24872, and this result deducted from the previous dividend leaves 1911 5 for the new dividend.

Cancel the right-hand digit, 7, of the divisor, and divide 1911 by 248, obtaining the quotient 7. Multiplying the divisor by 7 (and including the carrying digit) gives 1741 0, and subtracting leaves a new dividend of 170 5.

Cancel another digit, 8, of the divisor, and divide by 24. This is contained 6 times in 170. The product (including the digit carried over) is 149 2, and this product subtracted leaves a new dividend of 21 3.

Cancel another digit, 4, of the divisor. Divide 21 by 2, using the carried digit; the result is 8. The new product is 19 9, and this product subtracted from 21 3 leaves a remainder of 1 4.

Fractions

Kinds of fractions. There are two ways of writing fractions: ¾ is a common fraction; .75, or 0.75, is a decimal fraction.

A proper fraction is a fraction that has a numerator smaller than its denominator; for example, ¾.

An improper fraction is a fraction that has a numerator greater than its denominator; for example, 4/3.

A mixed number is a whole number and a fraction; for example, 23⅖.

Multiplication of any two mixed numbers ending in ½.

1. *When the sum of the whole numbers is an even number.* To the product of the whole numbers, add one half of their sum, and annex ¼.

EXAMPLE

Multiply 24½ by 8½.

Solution

```
 24½
  8½
-----
192     (8 × 24)
 16     (½ of the sum of 24 and 8)
-----
208¼    (¼ annexed)
```

2. *When the sum of the whole numbers is an odd number.* To the product of the whole numbers, add one half of their sum, less 1, and annex ¾.

EXAMPLE

Multiply 15½ by 6½.

Solution

```
 15½
  6½
-----
 90     (6 × 15)
 10     (½ of 15 + 6 − 1)
-----
100¾    (¾ annexed)
```

Multiplication of a mixed number by a mixed number.

EXAMPLE

Multiply 524½ by 27⅓.

Solution

```
  524½
   27⅓
-------
 14148   6    = common denominator of fractions
             -
  174⅔   4  )
   13½   3  }  = numerators of changed fractions
    ⅙    1  )
-------  -
14336⅓   8/6  = 1⅓
```

Explanation. Multiply 524 by 27, obtaining the first part of the answer, 14,148. Next, take ⅓ of 524, obtaining 174⅔. Then take ½ of 27, obtaining 13½. Finally, take ⅓ of ½, obtaining ⅙. Add the four partial products, and the complete product is 14,336⅓.

How to use aliquot parts. An aliquot part of any number is a part which will be contained in that number without leaving a re-

ALIQUOT PARTS AND DECIMAL EQUIVALENTS

Explanation: If you have to multiply or divide by any of the numbers appearing under "decimal equivalent," you can use their corresponding aliquot parts. For instance, if you have to divide by 14 2/7 (or .14 2/7), the chart shows its aliquot part to be 1/7.

← Aliquot Parts →														Decimal Equivalent
1/2's	3rd's	4th's	5th's	6th's	7th's	8th's	9th's	10th's	12th's	16th's	24th's	32nd's	64th's	
													1/64	.01 9/16
												1/32		.03 1/8
											1/24			.04 1/6
													3/64	.04 1/8
										1/16				.06 1/4
													5/64	.07 13/16
									1/12					.08 1/3
												3/32		.09 5/8
								1/10						.10
													7/64	.10 15/16
							1/9							.11 1/9
						1/8								.12 1/2
													9/64	.14 1/16
					1/7									.14 2/7
												5/32		.15 5/8
				1/6										.16 2/3
													11/64	.17 3/16
										3/16				.18 3/4
			1/5											.20
													13/64	.20 5/16
											5/24			.20 5/6
												7/32		.21 7/8
							2/9							.22 2/9
													15/64	.23 7/16
		1/4												.25
													17/64	.26 9/16
												9/32		.28 1/8
					2/7									.28 4/7
											7/24			.29 1/6
													19/64	.29 11/16

Aliquot Parts														
1/2's	3rd's	4th's	5th's	6th's	7th's	8th's	9th's	10th's	12th's	16th's	24th's	32nd's	64th's	Decimal Equivalent
								3/10	.....	.....	.....	.....	.....	.30
										5/16	.....	.....	.....	.31 1/4
													21/64	.32 13/16
	1/3	.....	.....	.....	.....	.....	.....	.....	.....	.....	.....	.....	.....	.33 1/3
												11/32	.....	.34 3/8
													23/64	.35 15/16
						3/8	.....	.....	.....	.....	.....	.....	.....	.37 1/2
													25/64	.39 1/16
			2/5	.....	.....	.....	.....	.....	.....	.....	.....	.....	.....	.40
												13/32	.....	.40 5/8
									5/12	.....	.....	.....	.....	.41 2/3
													27/64	.42 3/16
					3/7	.....	.....	.....	.....	.....	.....	.....	.....	.42 6/7
										7/16	.....	.....	.....	.43 3/4
							4/9	.....	.....	.....	.....	.....	.....	.44 4/9
													29/64	.45 5/16
											11/24	.....	.....	.45 5/6
												15/32	.....	.46 7/8
1/2	.....	.....	.....	.....	.....	.....	.....	.....	.....	.....	.....	.....	.....	.50
													33/64	.51 9/16
												17/32	.....	.53 1/8
											13/24	.....	.....	.54 1/6
													35/64	.54 11/16
							5/9	.....	.....	.....	.....	.....	.....	.55 5/9
										9/16	.....	.....	.....	.56 1/4
					4/7	.....	.....	.....	.....	.....	.....	.....	.....	.57 1/7
													37/64	.57 13/16
									7/12	.....	.....	.....	.....	.58 1/3
												19/32	.....	.59 3/8
			3/5	.....	.....	.....	.....	.....	.....	.....	.....	.....	.....	.60
													39/64	.60 15/16
						5/8	.....	.....	.....	.....	.....	.....	.....	.62 1/2
													41/64	.64 1/16
												21/32	.....	.65 5/8

ALIQUOT PARTS AND DECIMAL EQUIVALENTS (*Cont.*)

Aliquot Parts														Decimal Equivalent
1⁄2's	3rd's	4th's	5th's	6th's	7th's	8th's	9th's	10th's	12th's	16th's	24th's	32nd's	64th's	
	2⁄3													.66 2⁄3
													43⁄64	.67 3⁄16
										11⁄16				.68 3⁄4
								7⁄10						.70
													45⁄64	.70 5⁄16
											17⁄24			.70 5⁄6
					5⁄7									.71 3⁄7
												23⁄32		.71 7⁄8
													47⁄64	.73 7⁄16
		3⁄4												.75
													49⁄64	.76 9⁄16
							7⁄9							.77 7⁄9
												25⁄32		.78 1⁄8
											19⁄24			.79 1⁄16
													51⁄64	.79 11⁄16
			4⁄5											.80
													53⁄64	.82 13⁄16
				5⁄6										.83 1⁄3
												27⁄32		.84 3⁄8
					6⁄7									.85 5⁄7
													55⁄64	.85 15⁄16
						7⁄8								.87 1⁄2
							8⁄9							.88 8⁄9
													57⁄64	.89 1⁄16
								9⁄10						.90
												29⁄32		.90 5⁄8
									11⁄12					.91 2⁄3
													59⁄64	.92 3⁄16
										15⁄16				.93 3⁄4
													61⁄64	.95 5⁄16
											23⁄24			.95 5⁄6
												31⁄32		.96 7⁄8
													63⁄64	.98 7⁄16

mainder. Thus, 5, 10, 20, and 50 are aliquot parts of 100; that is, $5 = 1/20$ of 100, $10 = 1/10$ of 100, etc.

As a means of saving time in multiplication and in division, it is convenient to know the decimal equivalent of a common fraction, or, conversely, to know the common fraction equivalent to a decimal fraction. The table on pages 1378-80 will be useful in this connection.

Multiplication by aliquot parts.

EXAMPLE

Find 16⅔% of 475.34.

Solution

$$6\overline{)\$475.34}$$
$$\$79.22$$

Explanation. Since .16⅔ equals ⅙, find ⅙ of $475.34.

EXAMPLE

Find the cost of 256 units at 37½¢ each.

Solution

$$256 \times 3/8 \times \$1 = \$96$$

Explanation. 37½¢ is ⅜ of $1. Therefore, $256 \times 3/8 \times \$1 = \$96$.

Division by aliquot parts. It is difficult to divide a number by a mixed number. If the divisor is an aliquot part, the quotient may be found by multiplication, as follows:

EXAMPLE

Divide 4,875 by 16⅔.

Solution

$$\begin{array}{r} 48.75 \\ 6 \\ \hline 292.50 \end{array}$$

Explanation. Since 16⅔ is ⅙ of 100, divide 4,875 by ⅙ of 100, or 100/6. This is the same as multiplying by 6/100. Therefore, divide by 100 by pointing off two decimal places from the right, and multiply the result by 6. The answer is 292.50, or 292½.

EXAMPLE

The production cost of 1,250 units is $3,170. Find the cost per unit.

Solution

$$\begin{array}{r} .3170 \\ 8 \\ \hline \$2.5360 \end{array}$$

Explanation. 1,250 is ⅛ of 10,000. Divide $3,170 by 10,000 by pointing off 4 decimal places from the right; then multiply the result by 8. The cost per unit is found to be $2.536.

13. EXPEDITING CALCULATIONS WITH PREPARED TABLES

Specially prepared tables. Companies that have to make frequent calculations of various types can have special tables prepared to insure accuracy and speed, or they can purchase prepared tables that meet their needs. Two examples of such tables are given on pages 1383 and 1385.

Prorating of insurance premiums expedited by charts. Prorating of insurance premiums, which occurs through changes in car coverages during the policy period, has been expedited for the State Farm Insurance Companies, Illinois, by the use of calculators prepared by Meilicke Systems, Inc., Chicago, Illinois.

The calculators consist of 180 cards, one for each day of a six-month period. Each card, which is 8 × 5¼ inches, carries the pro-rata unearned premium for a particular period for the amounts of $1 to $15, with 5-cent divisions. For instance, suppose the unearned premium is wanted on a policy that has run 4 months 6 days. The card for this period is examined, and the unearned premium under $12 is noted. Reference to the card reproduced in Figure 96 shows that it is $3.60. If the premium were $12.20, the unearned premium would be $3.66. The earned premium is easily found by subtracting the unearned premium from the full premium.

The cards are kept on a small metal container for easy handling. The cost of these calculators is about 7% of the cost of electrically operating calculating machines. This cost included making 54,000 necessary calculations, for which the accuracy was guaranteed by Meilicke Systems, Inc.

4 MO. **6**

			1		2		3		4		5		6		7		8		9		10		11		12		13		14
			30		60		90		120		150		180		210		240		270		300		330		360		390		420
5	02	*5*	32	*5*	62	*5*	92	*5*	122	*5*	152	*5*	182	*5*	212	*5*	242	*5*	272	*5*	302	*5*	332	*5*	362	*5*	392	*5*	422
10	03	*10*	33	*10*	63	*10*	93	*10*	123	*10*	153	*10*	183	*10*	213	*10*	243	*10*	273	*10*	303	*10*	333	*10*	363	*10*	393	*10*	423
15	05	*15*	35	*15*	65	*15*	95	*15*	125	*15*	155	*15*	185	*15*	215	*15*	245	*15*	275	*15*	305	*15*	335	*15*	365	*15*	395	*15*	425
20	06	*20*	36	*20*	66	*20*	96	*20*	126	*20*	156	*20*	186	*20*	216	*20*	246	*20*	276	*20*	306	*20*	336	*20*	366	*20*	396	*20*	426
25	08	*25*	38	*25*	68	*25*	98	*25*	128	*25*	158	*25*	188	*25*	218	*25*	248	*25*	278	*25*	308	*25*	338	*25*	368	*25*	398	*25*	428
30	09	*30*	39	*30*	69	*30*	99	*30*	129	*30*	159	*30*	189	*30*	219	*30*	249	*30*	279	*30*	309	*30*	339	*30*	369	*30*	399	*30*	429
35	11	*35*	41	*35*	71	*35*	101	*35*	131	*35*	161	*35*	191	*35*	221	*35*	251	*35*	281	*35*	311	*35*	341	*35*	371	*35*	401	*35*	431
40	12	*40*	42	*40*	72	*40*	102	*40*	132	*40*	162	*40*	192	*40*	222	*40*	252	*40*	282	*40*	312	*40*	342	*40*	372	*40*	402	*40*	432
45	14	*45*	44	*45*	74	*45*	104	*45*	134	*45*	164	*45*	194	*45*	224	*45*	254	*45*	284	*45*	314	*45*	344	*45*	374	*45*	404	*45*	434
50	15	*50*	45	*50*	75	*50*	105	*50*	135	*50*	165	*50*	195	*50*	225	*50*	255	*50*	285	*50*	315	*50*	345	*50*	375	*50*	405	*50*	435
55	17	*55*	47	*55*	77	*55*	107	*55*	137	*55*	167	*55*	197	*55*	227	*55*	257	*55*	287	*55*	317	*55*	347	*55*	377	*55*	407	*55*	437
60	18	*60*	48	*60*	78	*60*	108	*60*	138	*60*	168	*60*	198	*60*	228	*60*	258	*60*	288	*60*	318	*60*	348	*60*	378	*60*	408	*60*	438
65	20	*65*	50	*65*	80	*65*	110	*65*	140	*65*	170	*65*	200	*65*	230	*65*	260	*65*	290	*65*	320	*65*	350	*65*	380	*65*	410	*65*	440
70	21	*70*	51	*70*	81	*70*	111	*70*	141	*70*	171	*70*	201	*70*	231	*70*	261	*70*	291	*70*	321	*70*	351	*70*	381	*70*	411	*70*	441
75	23	*75*	53	*75*	83	*75*	113	*75*	143	*75*	173	*75*	203	*75*	233	*75*	263	*75*	293	*75*	323	*75*	353	*75*	383	*75*	413	*75*	443
80	24	*80*	54	*80*	84	*80*	114	*80*	144	*80*	174	*80*	204	*80*	234	*80*	264	*80*	294	*80*	324	*80*	354	*80*	384	*80*	414	*80*	444
85	26	*85*	56	*85*	86	*85*	116	*85*	146	*85*	176	*85*	206	*85*	236	*85*	266	*85*	296	*85*	326	*85*	356	*85*	386	*85*	416	*85*	446
90	27	*90*	57	*90*	87	*90*	117	*90*	147	*90*	177	*90*	207	*90*	237	*90*	267	*90*	297	*90*	327	*90*	357	*90*	387	*90*	417	*90*	447
95	29	*95*	59	*95*	89	*95*	119	*95*	149	*95*	179	*95*	209	*95*	239	*95*	269	*95*	299	*95*	329	*95*	359	*95*	389	*95*	419	*95*	449
																												1500	450

MEILICKE SYSTEMS, Inc.
3466 N. Clark St., Chicago, Ill.
Pat. Aug 10, 1915—Feb. 19, 1929

Figure 96. Calculator for Prorating Insurance Premiums.

[actual size 8″ x 5¼″]

The user of this system points out these additional advantages: (1) the life of the calculators will be at least as long as the average calculating machine; (2) no maintenance is required; (3) calculators are conveniently kept on the desk of the individuals using them, and occupy less space than the average calculating machine.

Freight-rate calculator with prefigured totals improves calculation efficiency. Freight-rate calculation efficiency increased 50%, auditing efficiency 200%, and labor cost decreased 75% in a trucking company after it had purchased two sets of prefigured freight-charge computations. Each set consists of loose-leaf sheets in a binder, each sheet consisting of two banks of figures, the upper bank showing totals in units from 1 to 100, and the lower bank totals in hundreds from 100 to 10,000. A supplementary row at the bottom shows totals in steps of 10,000 up to 70,000 (see Figure 97, opposite, which shows these calculations for a multiplier of 68). The freight-rate calculator gives immediate and accurate totals with no mental disposition of fractions or shifting of decimals and is simple to operate.

To compute the freight charges for an LCL shipment of 3280 lbs. at 68 cents per 100 lbs., first refer to the figure opposite 32 in the lower bank ($21.76) and then to the figure opposite 80 in the upper bank ($.54), the total being the freight charge ($22.30) for the shipment.

Another use of the calculator is in the determination of freight-charge proration between two or more carriers, as in a joint haul. Thus, "A" Line gets 37% of the rate and "B" Line 63%. Reference to the lower bank would show that "A" gets 25.16 cents of each 68 cents, and "B" 42.84 cents, or a total of 68 cents for the through rate.

The calculator can also be used for computing payroll earnings. Thus, an employee works 39¾ (39.75) hours at 68 cents per hour. Reference to 39 in the lower bank gives $26.52 as his pay for 39 hours' work, and reference to 75 in the upper bank gives 51 cents as his pay for ¾ hour, making his total paycheck $27.03.

Other applications include inventory and billing extensions.

68
168

FREIGHT CHARGES IN CENTS

Lbs.		Lbs.		Lbs.		Lbs.		Lbs.		Lbs.		Lbs.		Lbs.		Lbs.		Lbs.	
1	01	11	07	21	14	31	21	41	28	51	35	61	41	71	48	81	55	91	62
2	01	12	08	22	15	32	22	42	29	52	35	62	42	72	49	82	56	92	63
3	02	13	09	23	16	33	22	43	29	53	36	63	43	73	50	83	56	93	63
4	03	14	10	24	16	34	23	44	30	54	37	64	44	74	50	84	57	94	64
5	03	15	10	25	17	35	24	45	31	55	37	65	44	75	51	85	58	95	65
6	04	16	11	26	18	36	24	46	31	56	38	66	45	76	52	86	58	96	65
7	05	17	12	27	18	37	25	47	32	57	39	67	46	77	52	87	59	97	66
8	05	18	12	28	19	38	26	48	33	58	39	68	46	78	53	88	60	98	67
9	06	19	13	29	20	39	27	49	33	59	40	69	47	79	54	89	61	99	67
10	07	20	14	30	20	40	27	50	34	60	41	70	48	80	54	90	61	100	68

Lbs.		Lbs.		Lbs.		Lbs.		Lbs.		Lbs.		Lbs.		Lbs.		Lbs.		Lbs.	
1C	68	11C	748	21C	1428	31C	2108	41C	2788	51C	3468	61C	4148	71C	4828	81C	5508	91C	6188
2	136	12	816	22	1496	32	2176	42	2856	52	3536	62	4216	72	4896	82	5576	92	6256
3	204	13	884	23	1564	33	2244	43	2924	53	3604	63	4284	73	4964	83	5644	93	6324
4	272	14	952	24	1632	34	2312	44	2992	54	3672	64	4352	74	5032	84	5712	94	6392
5	340	15	1020	25	1700	35	2380	45	3060	55	3740	65	4420	75	5100	85	5780	95	6460
6	408	16	1088	26	1768	36	2448	46	3128	56	3808	66	4488	76	5168	86	5848	96	6528
7	476	17	1156	27	1836	37	2516	47	3196	57	3876	67	4556	77	5236	87	5916	97	6596
8	544	18	1224	28	1904	38	2584	48	3264	58	3944	68	4624	78	5304	88	5984	98	6664
9	612	19	1292	29	1972	39	2652	49	3332	59	4012	69	4692	79	5372	89	6052	99	6732
10	680	20	1360	30	2040	40	2720	50	3400	60	4080	70	4760	80	5440	90	6120	100	6800
20M 136.00				30M 204.00		40M 272.00						50M 340.00		60M 408.00				70M 476.00	

1-64 Copyrighted-1924-1938 By John LaBonte

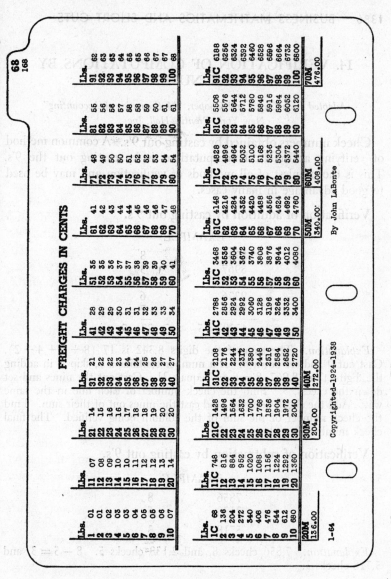

Figure 97. Freight Rate Calculator.

(68 refers to multiplier on the side shown, and 168 refers to the multiplier on the reverse side.)

Obtainable from Systems, Inc., 4856 North Hoyne Ave., Chicago 25, Ill.

14. VERIFICATION OF COMPUTATIONS BY CHECK NUMBERS

Adapted from Curtis and Cooper, "Mathematics of Accounting" New York: Prentice-Hall, Inc.

Check numbers obtained by casting out 9's. A common method of verifying arithmetical computations is by casting out the 9's. This is the simplest of all methods of verification and may be used to good advantage in many cases.

Verification of addition by casting out 9's.

EXAMPLE

8342	8
8967	3
8378	8
9276	6
8431	7
43394—5	32—5

Explanation. The sum of the digits 8,342 is 17 $(8 + 3 + 4 + 2)$. Cast out 9 and set down 8. If a number contains a 9, skip it in adding the digits; thus, 8,967, $8 + 6 + 7$ equals 21. Cast out the nines and set down the excess, 3. Find the check number of each line in the same way. Add the check numbers, and cast the nines out of their sum. Find the check number of the sum of the column being verified. The final check number in each case is 5.

Verification of subtraction by casting out 9's.

EXAMPLE

7856	8
2138	5
5718	3

Explanation. 7,856 checks 8, and 2,138 checks 5. $8 - 5 = 3$, and 5,718 checks 3.

Verification of multiplication by casting out 9's.

EXAMPLE

482	5
376	7
181232—8	35—8

Explanation. 482 checks 5, and 376 checks 7. $7 \times 5 = 35$. 35 checks 8, and the product, 181,232, also checks 8.

Verification of division by casting out 9's. Division may be verified by multiplication; that is, the product of the quotient and the divisor should equal the dividend. Apply the same principle in verifying with check numbers.

EXAMPLE

```
13)76492(5884
   65
   114
   104
    109
    104
      52
      52
```

Explanation. 76,492 checks 1. 13 checks 4. 5,884 checks 7. $4 \times 7 = 28$, and 28 checks 1, which is also the check number of the dividend.

Verification of division where there is a remainder by casting out 9's. The check number of the remainder added to the product of the check number of the quotient and the check number of the divisor should equal the check number of the dividend.

EXAMPLE

```
32)75892(2371
   64
   118
    96
    229
    224
      52
      32
```

Explanation. Step 1: The remainder, 20, checks 2. The quotient, 2,371, checks 4. The divisor, 32, checks 5. $2 + (4 \times 5) = 22$, and 22 checks 4.

Step 2: The dividend, 75,892, checks 4.

Step 1 and Step 2 should produce the same check number.

Check figure "11" verifies posting as made. The check figure "11" for inventory and cost-record posting verifies every posting immediately. Somewhat like the method of casting out 9's, it can be used for arithmetic processes other than posting.

EXAMPLE

Check the following addition:

951.63	....	2
615.38	....	4
2,397.43	....	9
3,964.44	....	4

Explanation. Starting with the last digit to the right, add the alternate (odd) figures. Then add the in-between (even) figures. If the former sum is less than the latter, add sufficient multiples of 11 to make it larger. Then subtract the sum of the even from the sum of the odds. If the remainder is 11 or over, subtract the largest multiple of 11 less than the remainder. The result is the check figure. Thus, in 951.63, $3 + 1 + 9 = 13$, and $6 + 5 = 11$, $13 - 11 = 2$, the check figure.

In 615.38, $8 + 5 + 6 = 19$, and $3 + 1 = 4$, $19 - 4 = 15$. Since 15 is larger than 11, 11 is subtracted to give the check figure 4.

In 2,397.43, $3 + 7 + 3 = 13$, and $4 + 9 + 2 = 15$. Here 11 must be added to 13 (giving 24) in order to make the odds larger than the evens, and $24 - 15 = 9$.

The total is similarly checked, and the sum of the check figures less the largest possible multiple of 11 gives the check figure for the column total.

This check figure will catch the common error of transposition of adjacent figures, such as posting 2,317.43 as 2,317.34, which the figure 9 will not catch. The check figure 11, however, will not catch the transposition of alternate figures, such as posting 2,317.43 as 2,713.43. Multiplication, division, and subtraction can be verified with the check figure 11 in a manner similar to that described for the check figure 9.

Another method of using check figures in posting. To use the check figure 11 or other check figures in proving the accuracy of postings from one source to another, determine the check figure for the entry in the ledger (or other record to which the posting is being made), and place that check figure in the check column for the entry in the journal (or other source of the posting), without computing the check figure for the journal entry. If you fail to balance out, determine the check figures for the original data (in this case, the journal entries) and compare with the check figures entered from the ledger sheets. For example, $43,668.94 is posted from journal to ledger as $43,686.94. The check figure for the ledger amount (using the method described in the preceding paragraph) is 0, and is entered opposite $43,668.94 in the check column of the journal. When the figures do not balance out, the journal entry check figures are determined, whereupon the check figure for $43,668.94 is found to be 4, while a 0 appears in the check column, thus indicating the source of error.

This method is more rapid than that of determining both check figures in the beginning.

15. TABLES OF WEIGHTS, MEASURES, AND VALUES

LONG MEASURE

United States Standard

12 inches	1 foot
3 feet	1 yard
5½ yards, or 16½ feet	1 rod
320 rods, or 5,280 feet	1 mile
1,760 yards	1 mile
40 rods	1 furlong
8 furlongs	1 statute mile
3 miles	1 league

Metric System

10 millimeters	1 centimeter
10 centimeters	1 decimeter
10 decimeters	1 meter
10 meters	1 dekameter
10 dekameters	1 hektometer
10 hektometers	1 kilometer
10 kilometers	1 myriameter

Comparisons of Long Measures

1 inch	25.4001 millimeters	1 centimeter	.3937 inch
1 foot	.304801 meter	1 meter	39.37 inches
1 yard	.914402 meter	1 meter	3.28083 feet
1 rod	5.029 meters	1 meter	1.093611 yards
1 mile	1.60935 kilometers	1 kilometer	.62137 mile

SQUARE MEASURE

United States Standard

144 square inches	1 square foot
9 square feet	1 square yard
30¼ square yards	1 square rod
272¼ square feet	1 square rod
40 square rods	1 rood
4 roods	1 acre
160 square rods	1 acre
640 acres	1 square mile
43,560 square feet	1 acre
4,840 square yards	1 acre

Metric System

100 square millimeters	1 square centimeter
100 square centimeters	1 square decimeter
100 square decimeters	1 square meter
100 square meters	1 square dekameter
100 square dekameters	1 square hektometer
100 square hektometers	1 square kilometer
100 square kilometers	1 square myriameter

Comparisons of Square Measures

1 square inch	6.452 square centimeters
1 square foot	.0929 square meter
1 square yard	.8361 square meter
1 square rod	25.293 square meters
1 acre	.40467 hectare
1 square mile	2.59 square kilometers
1 square millimeter	.00155 square inch
1 square centimeter	.155 square inch
1 square meter	10.764 square feet
1 square meter	1.196 square yards
1 square kilometer	.3861 square mile
1 square kilometer	247.11 acres
1 square dekameter, or 1 are	1,076.41 square feet
100 acres = 1 hectare	2.4711 acres

SOLID OR CUBIC MEASURE (VOLUME)

United States Standard

1,728 cubic inches	1 cubic foot
27 cubic feet	1 cubic yard
128 cubic feet	1 cord of wood
24¾ cubic feet	1 perch of stone
2,150.42 cubic inches	1 standard bushel
231 cubic inches	1 standard gallon
40 cubic feet	1 ton (shipping)

Metric System

1,000 cubic millimeters	1 cubic centimeter
1,000 cubic centimeters	1 cubic decimeter
1,000 cubic decimeters	1 cubic meter
1,000 cubic meters	1 cubic dekameter
1,000 cubic dekameters	1 cubic hektometer
1,000 cubic hektometers	1 cubic kilometer
1,000 cubic kilometers	1 cubic myriameter

Comparisons of Solid or Cubic Measures (*Volume*)

1 cubic inch	16.3872 cubic centimeters
1 cubic foot	.02832 cubic meter
1 cubic yard	.7646 cubic meter
1 cubic centimeter	.061 cubic inch
1 cubic meter	35.314 cubic feet
1 cubic meter	1.3079 cubic yards
1 cubic decimeter = 1 liter	61.023 cubic inches
1 liter	1.05671 liquid quarts
1 liter	.9081 dry quart
1 hectoliter or decistere	3.5314 cubic feet or 2.8375 bushels
1 stere, kiloliter, or cubic meter	1.3079 cubic yards or 28.37 bushels

LIQUID MEASURE (CAPACITY)

United States Standard

4 gills	1 pint
2 pints	1 quart
4 quarts	1 gallon
31½ gallons	1 barrel
2 barrels	1 hogshead
1 gallon	231 cubic inches
7.4805 gallons	1 cubic foot
16 fluid ounces	1 pint
1 fluid ounce	1.805 cubic inches
1 fluid ounce	29.59 cubic centimeters

Metric System

10 milliliters	1 centiliter
10 centiliters	1 deciliter
10 deciliters	1 liter
10 liters	1 dekaliter
10 dekaliters	1 hektoliter
10 hektoliters	1 kiloliter
10 kiloliters	1 myrialiter

DRY MEASURE

United States Standard

2 pints	1 quart
8 quarts	1 peck
4 pecks	1 bushel
2,150.42 cubic inches	1 bushel
1.2445 cubic feet	1 bushel

Metric System

In the metric system the same table is used for both Liquid Measure and Dry Measure.

Comparisons of Liquid and Dry Measure

1 liquid quart	.94636 liter
1 liquid gallon	3.78543 liters
1 dry quart	1.1012 liters
1 peck	8.80982 liters
1 bushel	.35239 hektoliter
1 milliliter	.03381 liquid ounce, or .2705 apothecaries' dram
1 liter = 1 cubic decimeter	61.023 cubic inches .03531 cubic foot .2642 gallon 2.202 pounds of water at 62° F.
28.317 liters	1 cubic foot
3.785 liters	1 gallon

AVOIRDUPOIS MEASURE (WEIGHT)

(Used for weighing all ordinary substances except precious metals, jewels, and drugs)

United States Standard

$27\frac{11}{32}$ grains	1 dram
16 drams	1 ounce
16 ounces	1 pound
25 pounds	1 quarter
4 quarters	1 hundredweight
100 pounds	1 hundredweight
20 hundredweight	1 ton
2,000 pounds	1 short ton
2,240 pounds	1 long ton

Metric System

10 milligrams	1 centigram
10 centigrams	1 decigram
10 decigrams	1 gram
10 grams	1 dekagram
10 dekagrams	1 hektogram
10 hektograms	1 kilogram
10 kilograms	1 myriagram
1,000 kilograms	1 metric ton

TROY MEASURE WEIGHT)

(Used for weighing gold, silver, and jewels)

24 grains	1 pennyweight
20 pennyweights	1 ounce
12 ounces	1 pound

Comparison of Avoirdupois and Troy Measures

1 pound troy	5,760 grains
1 pound avoirdupois	7,000 grains
1 ounce troy	437½ grains
1 ounce avoirdupois	480 grains
1 karat, or carat	3.2 troy grains
24 karats	pure gold

Comparison of Avoirdupois and Troy Measures with Metric Weights

1 grain .0648 gram 1 ounce (avoir.) 28.3495 grams 1 ounce (troy) 31.10348 grams	1 gram	15,4324 grains .03527 ounce (avoir.) .03215 ounce (troy)
1 pound (avoir.) .45359 kilogram 1 pound (troy) .37324 kilogram	1 kilogram	2.20462 pounds (avoir.) 2.67923 pounds (troy)
	1 tonne, or metric ton	.9842 ton of 2,240 pounds, or 19.68 hundredweight 1.1023 tons of 2,000 pounds

1,000 kilograms ...	2,204.6 pounds
1.016 metric tons, or 1,016 kilograms	1 ton of 2,240 pounds
.9072 metric ton ..	1 ton of 2,000 pounds

APOTHECARIES' MEASURE (WEIGHT)

(Used for weighing drugs)

20 grains	1 scruple
3 scruples	1 dram
8 drams	1 ounce
12 ounces	1 pound

APOTHECARIES' FLUID MEASURE (CAPACITY)

60 minims	1 fluid dram
8 fluid drams	1 fluid ounce
16 fluid ounces	1 pint
8 pints	1 gallon

Comparisons (Approximate Liquid Measure)

Apothecaries'	*Common*	*Metric*
1 minim	1 to 2 drops	0.06 cu. cm.
60 minims, or 1 fluid dram	1 teaspoonful	3.75 cu. cm.
2 fluid drams	1 dessertspoonful	7.50 cu. cm.
4 fluid drams	1 tablespoonful	15.00 cu. cm.
8 fluid drams	1 fluid ounce	28.39 cu. cm.
2 fluid ounces	1 wineglassful	59.20 cu. cm.
4 fluid ounces	1 teacupful	118.40 cu. cm.
16 fluid ounces	1 pint	473.11 cu. cm.

Note: Drops are not accurate measures, but for practical purposes it may be considered that one minim equals one drop of watery liquids and fixed oils, but two drops of volatile oils and alcoholic liquids, such as tinctures and fluid extracts.

SURVEYORS' LONG MEASURE

7.92 inches	1 link
25 links	1 rod
4 rods, or 100 links	1 chain
80 chains	1 mile

SURVEYORS' SQUARE MEASURE

625 square links	1 square rod
16 square rods	1 square chain
10 square chains	1 acre
640 acres	1 square mile
36 square miles	1 township

MARINERS' MEASURE

6 feet	1 fathom
100 fathoms	1 cable's length as applied to distances or intervals between ships
120 fathoms	1 cable's length as applied to marine wire cable
7½ cable lengths	1 mile
5,280 feet	1 statute mile
6,080 feet	1 nautical mile
1.152⅔ statute miles	1 nautical or geographical mile
3 geographical miles	1 league
60 geographical miles, or 69.16 statute miles	1 degree of longitude on the equator, or 1 degree of meridian
360 degrees	1 circumference

Note: A knot is not a measure of distance but a measure of speed. Current usage makes a knot equivalent to a marine mile per hour (properly it is 1/120 of a marine mile). Hence, when the speed of vessels at sea is being measured, a knot is equal to a nautical mile, or 6,080 feet, or 2,026.66 yards, *per hour.*

CIRCULAR OR ANGULAR MEASURE

60 seconds (60″)	1 minute (1′)
60 minutes (60′)	1 degree (1°)
30 degrees	1 sign
90 degrees	1 right angle or quadrant
360 degrees	1 circumference

Note: One degree at the equator is approximately 60 nautical miles.

COUNTING

12 units or things	1 dozen
12 dozen, or 144 units	1 gross
12 gross	1 great gross
20 units	1 score

PAPER MEASURE

24 sheets	1 quire
20 quires	1 ream
2 reams	1 bundle
5 bundles	1 bale

Note: Although a ream contains 480 sheets, 500 sheets are usually sold as a ream.

UNITED STATES AND BRITISH WEIGHTS AND MEASURES COMPARED

1 British Imperial bushel	1.03205 United States (Winchester) bushels
1 United States bushel	.96895 British Imperial bushel
1 British quart	1.03205 United States dry quarts
1 United States dry quart	.96895 British quart
1 British quart (or gallon)	1.20094 United States liquid quarts (or gallons)
1 United States liquid quart (or gallon)	.83268 British quart (or gallon)

METRIC SYSTEM EXPLAINED

(For metric tables of weights and measures see page 1389ff.)

The fundamental units of the metric system are the meter—the unit of length, and the kilogram—the unit of mass.

The liter is defined as the volume of a kilogram of water at the temperature of its maximum density, 4° centigrade. All other units are the decimal subdivisions or multiples of these. These three units are simply related. For example, for all practical purposes 1 cubic decimeter equals 1 liter and 1 liter of water weighs 1 kilogram.

The metric tables are formed by combining the words "meter," "gram," and "liter" with the six numerical prefixes, as in the following:

Prefixes *Meaning*		*Units*
milli- = *one-thousandth*	.001	
centi- = *one-hundredth*	.01	"meter" *for length*
deci- = *one-tenth*	.1	"gram" *for weight or mass*
..... *Unit = one*	1.	
deka- = *ten*	10	"liter" *for capacity.*
hecto = *one hundred*	100	
kilo- = *one thousand*	1000	

UNITED STATES MONEY

10 mills	1 cent
10 cents	1 dime
10 dimes	1 dollar
10 dollars	1 eagle

ROMAN NUMERALS

I	1	IX	9	XVII	17	LXX	70	D	500
II	2	X	10	XVIII	18	LXXX		DC	600
III	3	XI	11	XIX	19	or XXC	80	DCC	700
IV	4	XII	12	XX	20	XC	90	DCCC	800
V	5	XIII	13	XXX	30	C	100	CM	900
VI	6	XIV	14	XL	40	CC	200	M or	
VII	7	XV	15	L	50	CCC	300	cIc	1000
VIII	8	XVI	16	LX	60	CCCC	400	MM	2000

Note. A dash line over a numeral multiplies the value by 1,000. Thus, $\overline{\mathrm{X}}$ = 10,000; $\overline{\mathrm{L}}$ = 50,000; $\overline{\mathrm{C}}$ = 100,000; $\overline{\mathrm{D}}$ = 500,000; $\overline{\mathrm{M}}$ = 1,000,000; $\overline{\mathrm{CLIX}}$ = 159,000; $\overline{\mathrm{DLIX}}$ = 559,000.

GENERAL RULES IN ROMAN NUMERALS

(1) Repeating a letter repeats its value: XX = 20; CCC = 300.

(2) A letter placed after one of greater value adds thereto: VIII = 8; DC = 600.

(3) A letter placed before one of greater value subtracts therefrom: IX = 9; CM = 900.

ARABIC NUMERALS

Trillions	Billions	Millions	Thousands	Hundreds
7,	256,	423,	896,	384

Note: In the United States and France a billion is a thousand millions (1,000,000,000). In Britain and Germany a billion is a million millions (1,000,000,000,000).

FOREIGN WEIGHTS AND MEASURES

Denominations	*Where Used*	*American Equivalents*
Almude	Portugal	4,422 gals.
Ardeb	Egypt	5.6188 bu.
Are	Metric	0.02471 acre.
Arratel or libra	Portugal	1.0119 lbs.
Arroba	Argentine Republic	25.32 lbs.
"	Brazil	32.38 lbs.
"	Cuba	25.36 lbs.
"	Paraguay	25.32 lbs.
"	Venezuela	25.40 lbs.
" (liquid)	Cuba, Spain, and Venezuela	4.263 gals.
Arshine	Russia	28 in.
" (sq.)	"	5.44 sq. ft.
Artel	Morocco	1.12 lbs.
Baril	Argentine Republic	20.077 gals.
	and Mexico	20.0787 gals.
Barrel	Malta (customs)	11.2 gals.
Berkovets	Russia	361.128 lbs.
Bongkal	Fed. Malay States	832 grains.
Bouw	Sumatra	7,096.5 sq. metrs.
Bu	Japan	0.12 inch.
Bushel	British Empire	1.03205 U. S. bu.
Caffiso	Malta	5.40 gals.
Candy	India (Bombay)	569 lbs.
"	India (Madras)	500 lbs.
Cantar	Egypt	99.05 lbs.
"	Morocco	112 lbs.
"	Turkey	124.45 lbs.
Cantaro	Malta	175 lbs.
Carat, metric	World	3.086 grains.
Catty	China	1.333$\frac{2}{3}$ lbs.
"	Japan	1.32 lbs.
"	Java, Malacca	1.36 lbs.
"	Siam	2$\frac{1}{3}$ lbs.
" (stand.)	Siam	1.32 lbs.
"	Sumatra	2.12 lbs.
Centaro	Central America	4.2631 gals.
Centner	Brunswick	117.5 lbs.
"	Bremen	127.5 lbs.
"	Denmark, Norway	110.23 lbs.
"	Prussia	113.44 lbs.
"	Sweden	93.7 lbs.
"	Double or metric	220.46 lbs.
Chetvert	Russia	5.957 bu.

Denominations	*Where Used*	*American Equivalents*
Ch'ih	China	12.60 inches.
" (metric)	China	1 meter.
Cho	Japan	2.451 acres.
Comb	England	4.1282 bu.
Coyan	Siam	2,645.5 lbs.
Cuadra	Argentine Republic	4.2 acres.
"	Paraguay	94.70 yds.
" (sq.)	Paraguay	1.85 acres.
"	Uruguay	1.82 acres.
Cubic meter	Metric	35.3 cu. ft.
Cwt. (hundredweight)	British	112 lbs.
Dessiatine	Russia	2.6997 acres.
Drachma (new)	Greece	15.43 gr., or 1 grm.
Fanega (dry)	Ecuador, Salvador	1.5745 bu.
"	Chile	2.75268 bu.
"	Guatemala, Spain	1.53 bu.
"	Mexico	2.57716 bu.
" (double)	Uruguay	7.776 bu.
" (single)	Uruguay	3.888 bu.
"	Venezuela	3.334 bu.
" (liquid)	Spain	16 gals.
Feddan	Egypt	1.04 acres.
Frail (raisins)	Spain	50 lbs.
Frasco	Argentine Republic	2.5098 liq. qts.
"	Mexico	2.5 liq. qts.
Frasila	Zanzibar	35 lbs.
Fuder	Luxemburg	264.18 gals.
Funt	Russia	0.9028 lb.
Gallon	British Empire	1.20094 U. S. gal.
Garnice	Poland	1.0567 gal.
Gram	Metric	15.432 grains.
Hectare	"	2.471 acres.
Hectoliter: Dry	"	2.838 bu.
" Liquid	"	26.418 gals.
Jarib	Persia (New)	2.471 acres.
Joch	Austria	1.422 acres.
"	Hungary	1.067 acres.
Ken	Japan	5.97 feet.
Kilogram (kilo)	Metric	2.2046 lbs.
Kilometer	"	0.62137 mile
Klafter	Austria	2.074 yds.
Koku	Japan	5.119 bu.
Kwamme	Japan	8.2673 lbs.
Last	Belgium, Holland	85.134 bu.

Denominations	Where Used	American Equivalents
Last	England	82.56 bu.
Last	Germany	2 metric tons. (4,409 + lbs.)
"	Prussia	112.29 bu.
"	Scotland, Ireland	82.564 bu.
League (land)	Paraguay	4,633 acres.
Li	China	1,890 ft.
Libra (lb.)	Argentine Republic	1.0128 lbs.
"	Central America	1.014 lbs.
"	Chile	1.014 lbs.
"	Cuba	1.0143 lbs.
"	Mexico	1.01467 lbs.
"	Peru	1.0143 lbs.
"	Uruguay	1.0143 lbs.
"	Venezuela	1.0143 lbs.
Litre	Metric	1.0567 liq. qts.
"	Metric	0.90810 dry qts.
Livre (lb.)	Greece	1.1 lbs.
"	Guiana (Dutch)	1.089 lbs.
Load (timber)	England	50 cu. ft.
Lumber (std.)	in Europe	165 cu. ft., or 1,980 ft. b. m.
Manzana	Nicaragua	1.742 acres.
"	Costa Rica, Salvador	1.727 acres.
Marc	Bolivia	0.507 lb.
Maund	India	$82\frac{2}{7}$ lbs.
Metre	Metric	39.37 inches.
Mil	Denmark	4.68 miles.
" (geographic)	Denmark	4.61 miles.
Milla	Nicaragua	1.1594 miles.
"	Honduras	1.1493 miles.
Mina (old)	Greece	2.202 lbs.
Morgen	Prussia	0.63 acre.
Oke	Egypt	2.8052 lbs.
" (Ocque)	Greece	2.82 lbs.
"	Turkey	2.828 lbs.
Pic	Egypt	22.83 inches.
Picul	Borneo and Celebes	135.64 lbs.
"	China	$133\frac{1}{3}$ lbs.
"	Java	136.16 lbs.
"	Philippine Islands	139.44 lbs.
Pie	Argentine Republic	0.94708 foot.
"	Spain	0.91416 foot.
Pik	Turkey	27.9 inches.
Pood	Russia	36.113 lbs.

Denominations	Where Used	American Equivalents
Pund (lb.)	Denmark	1.102 lbs.
Quart	British Empire	1.20094 liq. qt.
"	" "	1.03205 dry qt.
Quarter	Great Britain	8.256 bu.
Quintal	Argentine Republic	101.28 lbs.
"	Brazil	129.54 lbs.
"	Castile, Peru	101.43 lbs.
"	Chile	101.41 lbs.
"	Mexico	101.47 lbs.
"	Metric	220.46 lbs.
Rottle	Palestine (south)	6.35 lbs.
Sack (flour)	England	280 lbs.
Sagene	Russia	7 feet.
Salm	Malta	8.2 bu.
Se	Japan	0.02451 acre.
Seer	India	2 2-35 lbs.
Shaku	Japan	11.9303 inches.
Sho	"	1.91 liq. quarts.
Skalpund	Sweden	0.937 lbs.
Stone	British	14 lbs.
Sun	Japan	1.193 inches.
Tael (Kuping)	China	575.64 grs. (troy)
Tan	Japan	0.25 acre.
Tchetvert	Russia	5.96 bu.
To	Japan	2.05 pecks.
Ton	Space measure	40 cu. ft.
Tonde (cereals)	Denmark	3.9480 bu.
Tonde Land	"	1.36 acres.
Tonne	France	2204.62 lbs.
Tsubo	Japan	35.58 sq. ft.
Tsun	China	1.26 inches.
Tunna (wheat)	Sweden	4.5 bu.
Tunnland	"	1.22 acres.
Vara	Argentine Republic	34.0944 inches.
"	Costa Rica, Salvador	32.913 inches.
"	Guatemala	32.909 inches.
"	Honduras	32.953 inches.
"	Nicaragua	33.057 inches.
"	Chile and Peru	32.913 inches.
"	Cuba	33.386 inches.
"	Mexico	32.992 inches.
Vedro	Russia	2.707 gals.
Verst	"	0.663 mile.
Vloka	Poland	41.50 acres.
Wey	Scotland and Ireland	41.282 bu.

The *metric carat* of 200 milligrams is now very generally in use. The word also is used to denote the proportion of alloy in a metal. Thus, pure gold is 24 carats fine.

FOREIGN MONEY

The principal source of this compilation is the United States Government Printing Office Style Manual.

Country	Basic monetary unit [1]			Principal fractional unit [1]	
	Name [2]	*Abbreviation*	*Symbol*	*Name* [2]	*Abbreviation*
Argentina	Peso [3]	P	$	Centavo	Ctvo.
Australia	Pound [4]	L., st(l)g	£	Shilling Penny (pence)	s. d.
Austria	Schilling	S		Groschen	
Belgium	Franc [5]	F., fr		Centime	c.
Bolivia	Boliviano	B		Centavo	Ctvo.
Brazil	Cruzeiro (=1 milreis) [6]		1$000	Real (reis)	Rs.
British Honduras	Dollar	Dol	$	Cent	
Bulgaria	Lev (leva, lew)	L		Stotinka (stotinki)	
Canada [7]	Dollar	Dol	$	Cent	c., ct., cts.
Ceylon. (See India, British.)					
Chile	Peso	P	$	Centavo	Ctvo.
China	Yuan (yuan, yuans)		$	Fen (fens, fen)	
Colombia	Peso	P	$	Centavo	Ctvo.
Costa Rica	Colon (colones)		₡	Centimo	Ctmo.
Cuba	Peso	P	$	Centavo	Ctvo.
Czechoslovakia	Koruna (koruny, korun)	Kč., cr		Heller (heller), haler (haleru)	Ha.
Danzig	Gulden	G., dg		Pfennig (pfennings, pfennige)	pf.
Denmark	Krone (kroner)	Kr., cr		Öre (öre), øre (øre)	
Dominican Republic	Dollar	Dol	$	Cent	
Ecuador	Sucre	S/		Centavo	Ctvo.
Egypt	Pound	LE	£E	Piaster	Pi., pias.
El Salvador	Colon (colones)		₡	Centavo	Ctvo.
Estonia	Kroon (kroons, krooni)	Kr., cr., Ekr.		Sent (senti)	
Finland	Markka, (markkaa), mark (marks)	MK, FMK.		Penni (pennia)	Pia.
France	Franc	F., fr		Centime	
Germany	Reichsmark (reichsmarks, reichsmark)	RM		Reichspfennig (reichspfennigs, reichspfennige)	Rpf.
Great Britain [8]	Pound	L., L. st(l)g.	£	Shilling Penny (pence)	s. d.
Greece	Drachma (drachmas, drachmae, drachmai)	Dr., D		Lepton (lepta)	
Guatemala	Quetzal (quetsales)	Q		Centavo	Ctvo.
Haiti	Gourde	Gde, G		Centime	
Honduras	Lempira	L	$	Centavo	Ctvo.
Hong Kong	Dollar	D., dol	HK$	Cent	
Hungary	Pengö (pengö, pengös)	P		Fillér (fillér, fillérs)	
India, British [9]	Rupee	R		Anna	
Indochina	Piaster	P		Centime	
Iran [10]	Rial			Dinar	
Ireland	Pound	L., L. st(l)g.	£	Shilling Penny (pence)	s. d.
Italy	Lira, lire	L		Centesimo (centesimi)	Ctmo.
Japan	Yen (yen)		¥	Sen (sen)	
Latvia	Lat (lats, latu, lati)	L		Santims (santimi)	
Liberia	Dollar	Dol			
Lithuania	Lit (lits), litas (litai, litu)	L		Cent (cents), centas (centai)	
Malaya, British	Straits dollar		$, S$	Cent	
Mexico	Peso	P	$	Centavo	Ctvo.
Netherlands [11]	Florin (florins), guilder (gulden)	Fl., G		Cent	
Newfoundland	Dollar	Dol	$	Cent	

FOREIGN MONEY (*Cont.*)

Country	Basic monetary unit [1]			Principal fractional unit [1]	
	Name [2]	*Abbreviation*	*Symbol*	*Name* [2]	*Abbreviation*
New Zealand ...	Pound	L., L. st(1)g.	£	Shilling .... / Penny (pence) ...	s. / d.
Nicaragua	Cordoba	C	C$	Centavo	Ctvo.
Norway	Krone (kroner)	Kr	......	Öre (öre), øre (øre)	
Panama	Balboa	B	......	Centesimo	Ctmo.
Paraguay	Guarani	....	......	....	
Peru	Sol (sols, soles)	S/	......	Centavo	Ctvo.
Philippines	Peso	P	P	Centavo	Ctvo.
Poland	Zloty (zlotys, zloty, zlote)	Zl	......	Grosz (groszy, grosze)	
Portugal	Escudo	....	$ [12]	Centavo	Ctvo.
Rumania	Leu (lei), ley (leys)..	L	......	Ban (bani)	
Salvalor. (See El Salvador.)					
Spain	Peseta	P., Pta .	......	Centimo, céntimo..	Ctmo.
Straits Settlements	Dollar	Dol	$	Cent	
Sweden	Krona (kronor)	Kr	......	Öre (öre)	
Switzerland	Franc	....	......	Centime	
Thailand	Baht (bahts), bat (bat)	....	......	Satang (satang) ..	
Turkey	Pound	LT	£T	Piaster	
U. S. S. R. (Russia).	Ruble [13]	R	......	Kopeck, kopek	
Union of South Africa.	Pound	....	£	....	
Uruguay	Peso	P	$	Centesimo	Ctmo.
Venezuela	Bolivar (bolivars, bolivares).	B	......	Centimo	Ctmo.
Yugoslavia	Dinar (dinars, dinari).	Din	......	Para	

[1] The conventions for writing sums of money in foreign countries are similar on the whole to that in the United States; i. e., the symbol or abbreviation of the basic unit is placed before the sum and a period, a comma, or simply a space before the fractional part, e. g., RM. 1.225,50 means 1,225 reichsmarks 50 reichspfennigs. For some other conventions, see footnotes below.

[2] Unless otherwise indicated in parentheses, the plural of these terms are formed regularly (by addition of "s"). When more than one plural form are given, the first is the one preferred.

[3] Gold peso (oro sellado) is abbreviated o/s or o$s; paper money (moneda nacional) is abbreviated m/n, e. g., $939,976,290 (m/n).

[4] Sums are written as in Great Britain. (See footnote 8.)

[5] The belga (B.) is used only in exchange transactions, and its value is $0.1695.

[6] The conto is 1,000 milreis. Sums are written: 25.376:125$320 (read 25,376 contos 125 milreis 320 reis).

[7] Including Newfoundland.

[8] Sums of money are written as follows: £5 4s. 6d. or £5:4:6 or £5.4.6 or 5/4/6. The pound is also the unit in all the British colonies and territories except where a local currency exists. In a number of the African possessions the local shilling is the principal unit, and it has the same value as the English shilling. In the British West Indies the local dollar of 100 cents is used in most cases, the pound sterling being the equivalent of 4.80 local currency ($4.80).

[9] The rupee is also used in Ceylon and some of the African territories.

[10] The pahlavi (100 rials) has the same value as the British pound sterling.

[11] Including Netherland India.

[12] The symbol ($) is used between the escudo and the centavo; the colon (:) used between the conto (= 1,000 centavos) and the escudo, e. g., 125.750:350$50 (read 125,750 contos 350 escudos 50 centavos).

[13] The chervonets (chervontsi, chervontsy) is the equivalent of 10 rubles. Quotations are usually in rubles.

16. MISCELLANEOUS HANDY TABLES

PRORATION OF TAXES

(Compiled by Walter C. Clark, for the San Francisco Real Estate Yearbook)

The following table is for computing the pro rata of taxes for six months. For example, you are prorating taxes as of October 22, so there is to be charged against the seller of the property 3 months and 22 days. Refer to the table, and you will find 3 months .50, and 22 days .1221, making a total of .6221, which is the amount to be charged against the seller, per $1.00 of taxes.

MONTHS

1	.1666	4	.6666
2	.3333	5	.8333
3	.50	6	1.000

DAYS

1	.0055	16	.0888
2	.0111	17	.0944
3	.0166	18	.0999
4	.0222	19	.1055
5	.0277	20	.1111
6	.0333	21	.1166
7	.0388	22	.1221
8	.0444	23	.1277
9	.05	24	.1333
10	.0555	25	.1389
11	.0611	26	.1444
12	.0666	27	.15
13	.0722	28	.1555
14	.0777	29	.1611
15	.0833	30	.1666

RENTAL READY RECKONER

(Cushman & Wakefield, Inc., New York)

Rent per Year	*Rent per Month*	*Rent per Day* (30 *days*)	*Rent per Day* (31 *days*)	*Rent per Year*	*Rent per Month*	*Rent per Day* (30 *days*)	*Rent per Day* (31 *days*)
$1	$.09	....	....	1,025	85.42	2.847	2.756
2	.17	....	....	1,050	87.50	2.917	2.823
3	.25	....	....	1,075	89.59	2.986	2.890
4	.34	....	....	1,100	91.67	3.056	2.958
5	.42	....	....	1,125	93.75	3.125	3.025
6	.50	....	....	1,150	95.84	3.195	3.092
7	.59	....	....	1,175	97.92	3.264	3.159
8	.67	....	....	1,200	100	3.334	3.226
9	.75	....	....	1,225	102.09	3.403	3.293
10	.84	.028	.027	1,250	104.17	3.472	3.36
20	1.67	.056	.054	1,275	106.25	3.541	3.428
25	2.09	.070	.068	1,300	108.34	3.611	3.495
30	2.50	.084	.081	1,325	110.42	3.681	3.562
40	3.34	.111	.108	1,350	112.50	3.75	3.629
50	4.17	.139	.134	1,375	114.59	3.82	3.697
60	5	.166	.161	1,400	116.67	3.889	3.764
70	5.84	.195	.189	1,425	118.75	3.958	3.831
75	6.25	.208	.202	1,450	120.84	4.028	3.898
80	6.67	.222	.215	1,475	122.92	4.098	3.965
90	7.50	.25	.242	1,500	125	4.167	4.033
100	8.34	.278	.269	1,525	127.09	4.236	4.10
125	10.42	.347	.336	1,550	129.17	4.306	4.167
150	12.50	.417	.403	1,575	131.25	4.375	4.234
175	14.59	.486	.470	1,600	133.34	4.445	4.301
200	16.67	.556	.538	1,625	135.42	4.514	4.369
225	18.75	.625	.605	1,650	137.50	4.584	4.436
250	20.84	.695	.672	1,675	139.59	4.653	4.503
275	22.92	.764	.740	1,700	141.67	4.723	4.570
300	25	.834	.807	1,725	143.75	4.792	4.638
325	27.09	.903	.874	1,750	145.84	4.861	4.705
350	29.17	.972	.941	1,775	147.92	4.931	4.772
375	31.25	1.042	1.009	1,800	150	5	4.84
400	33.34	1.112	1.076	1,825	152.09	5.07	4.906
425	35.42	1.181	1 143	1,850	154.17	5.139	4.973
450	37.50	1.25	1.21	1,875	156.25	5.209	5.04
475	39.59	1.32	1.277	1,900	158.34	5.278	5.108
500	41.67	1.389	1.344	1,925	160.42	5.347	5.175
525	43.75	1.458	1.412	1,950	162.50	5.417	5.242
550	45.84	1.528	1.479	1,975	164.59	5.487	5.31
575	47.92	1.598	1.546	2,000	166.67	5.56	5.377
600	50	1.667	1.613	3,000	250	8.334	8.065
625	52.09	1.737	1.68	4,000	333.34	11.111	10.753
650	54.17	1.806	1.748	5,000	416.67	13.889	13.441
675	56.25	1.875	1.815	6,000	500	16.667	16.13
700	58.34	1.945	1.882	7,000	583.34	19.445	18.818
725	60.42	2.01	1.950	8,000	666.67	22.223	21.506
750	62.50	2.084	2.017	9,000	750	25	24.194
775	64.59	2.153	2.084	10,000	833.34	27.778	26.882
800	66.67	2.223	2.151	11,000	916.67	30.556	29.57
825	68.75	2.292	2.218	12,000	1,000	33.34	32.259
850	70.84	2.361	2.286	13,000	1,083.34	36.111	34.947
875	72.92	2.431	2.352	14,000	1,166.67	38.889	37.635
900	75	2.50	2.420	15,000	1,250	41.667	40.323
925	77.09	2.57	2.487	16,000	1,333.34	44.445	43.011
950	79.17	2.639	2.554	17,000	1,416.67	47.223	45.699
975	81.25	2.708	2.621	18,000	1,500	50	48.388
1,000	83.34	2.778	2.689	19,000	1,583.34	52.778	51.076

MONTHLY, SEMIANNUAL, AND ANNUAL PAYMENTS TO PRINCIPAL AND INTEREST PER $1,000 AT VARYING RATES OF INTEREST

The following table shows the amount that must be repaid to principal and interest per thousand dollars (where payments are made monthly, semiannually, or annually) on loan terms from five to twenty-five years and at interest rates varying from 5% to 3½%. Suppose you borrow $5,000 at 4% interest, interest and principal to be paid monthly over a term of 10 years, at which time the loan will be completely amortized. How much will you have to pay per month? Consulting the table, you see that the loan will cost $10.13 per thousand. Your total cost will be five times this amount, or $50.65.

Amortization Period in Years	For Loans Amortized Monthly						For Loans Amortized Semiannually					For Loans Amortized Annually				
	No. of Payments	At 5% Interest	At 4½% Interest	At 4¼% Interest	At 4% Interest	At 3½% Interest	No. of Payments	At 5% Interest	At 4½% Interest	At 4% Interest	At 3½% Interest	No. of Payments	At 5% Interest	At 4½% Interest	At 4% Interest	At 3½% Interest
5	60	18.88	18.65	18.53	18.42	18.20	10	114.26	112.79	111.33	109.88	5	230.98	227.80	224.63	221.49
8	96	12.66	12.43	12.31	12.19	11.96										
10	120	10.61	10.37	10.25	10.13	9.89	20	64.15	62.65	61.16	59.70	10	129.51	126.38	123.30	120.25
12	144	9.25	9.01	8.88	8.76	8.52										
15	180	7.91	7.65	7.53	7.40	7.15	30	47.78	46.20	44.65	43.13	15	96.35	93.12	89.95	86.83
17	204	7.29	7.03	6.90	6.77	6.52										
19	228	6.81	6.54	....	6.27	6.02	38	41.08	39.43	37.83	36.25	19	82.75	79.41	76.14	72.95
20	240	6.60	6.33	6.20	6.06	5.80	40	39.84	38.18	36.56	34.98	20	80.25	76.88	73.59	70.37
24	288	5.97	5.69	....	5.41	5.14	48	36.01	34.29	32.61	30.97	24	72.48	68.99	65.59	62.28
25	300	5.85	5.56	5.42	5.28	5.01	50	35.26	33.52	31.83	30.18	25	70.90	67.44	64.02	60.68

Annual	Monthly (12 mo. to yr.)	Weekly* (52 weeks to yr.)	Daily† (6 days to week)	Annual	Monthly (12 mo. to yr.)	Weekly* (52 weeks to yr.)	Daily† (6 days to week)
$1000.00	$ 83.33	$19.23	$3.20	$ 2340.00	$195.00	$ 45.00	$ 7.50
1040.00	86.67	20.00	3.33	2392.00	199.33	46.00	7.67
1080.00	90.00	20.77	3.45	2400.00	200.00	46.15	7.69
1092.00	91.00	21.00	3.50	2444.00	203.67	47.00	7.83
1100.00	91.67	21.15	3.52	2496.00	208.00	48.00	8.00
1144.00	95.33	22.00	3.67	2500.00	208.33	48.08	8.01
1196.00	99.67	23.00	3.83	2520.00	210.00	48.46	8.08
1200.00	100.00	23.08	3.85	2548.00	212.33	49.00	8.17
1248.00	104.00	24.00	4.00	2600.00	216.67	50.00	8.33
1300.00	108.33	25.00	4.17	2640.00	220.00	50.77	8.46
1320.00	110.00	25.38	4.23	2700.00	225.00	51.92	8.65
1352.00	112.67	26.00	4.33	2760.00	230.00	53.08	8.85
1380.00	115.00	26.54	4.42	2800.00	233.33	53.85	8.97
1400.00	116.67	26.92	4.49	2860.00	238.33	55.00	9.17
1404.00	117.00	27.00	4.50	2880.00	240.00	55.38	9.23
1440.00	120.00	27.69	4.61	2900.00	241.67	55.77	9.29
1456.00	121.33	28.00	4.67	3000.00	250.00	57.69	9.61
1500.00	125.00	28.85	4.81	3120.00	260.00	60.00	10.00
1508.00	125.67	29.00	4.83	3240.00	270.00	62.31	10.38
1560.00	130.00	30.00	5.00	3360.00	280.00	64.62	10.77
1600.00	133.33	30.77	5.13	3380.00	281.67	65.00	10.83
1612.00	134.33	31.00	5.17	3480.00	290.00	66.92	11.15
1620.00	135.00	31.15	5.19	3500.00	291.67	67.31	11.22
1664.00	138.67	32.00	5.33	3600.00	300.00	69.23	11.54
1680.00	140.00	32.31	5.38	3640.00	303.33	70.00	11.67
1700.00	141.67	32.68	5.45	3900.00	325.00	75.00	12.50
1716.00	143.00	33.00	5.50	4160.00	346.67	80.00	13.33
1740.00	145.00	33.46	5.57	4200.00	350.00	80.77	13.46
1768.00	147.33	34.00	5.67	4420.00	368.33	85.00	14.17
1800.00	150.00	34.61	5.77	4500.00	375.00	86.54	14.42
1820.00	151.67	35.00	5.83	4680.00	390.00	90.00	15.00
1860.00	155.00	35.77	5.96	4800.00	400.00	92.31	15.38
1872.00	156.00	36.00	6.00	4940.00	411.67	95.00	15.83
1900.00	158.33	36.54	6.09	5000.00	416.67	96.15	16.02
1920.00	160.00	36.92	6.15	5100.00	425.00	98.08	16.35
1924.00	160.33	37.00	6.17	5200.00	433.33	100.00	16.67
1976.00	164.67	38.00	6.33	5400.00	450.00	103.85	17.31
1980.00	165.00	38.08	6.35	5500.00	458.33	105.77	17.63
2000.00	166.67	38.46	6.41	5700.00	475.00	109.62	18.27
2028.00	169.00	39.00	6.50	6000.00	500.00	115.38	19.23
2040.00	170.00	39.23	6.54	6300.00	525.00	121.15	20.19
2080.00	173.33	40.00	6.67	6500.00	541.67	125.00	20.83
2100.00	175.00	40.38	6.73	6600.00	550.00	126.92	21.15
2132.00	177.67	41.00	6.83	6900.00	575.00	132.69	22.11
2160.00	180.00	41.54	6.92	7000.00	583.33	134.62	22.44
2184.00	182.00	42.00	7.00	7200.00	600.00	138.46	23.08
2200.00	183.33	42.31	7.05	7500.00	625.00	144.23	24.04
2220.00	185.00	42.69	7.11	8000.00	666.67	153.85	25.64
2236.00	186.33	43.00	7.17	8500.00	708.33	163.46	27.24
2280.00	190.00	43.85	7.31	9000.00	750.00	173.08	28.85
2288.00	190.67	44.00	7.33	9500.00	791.67	182.69	30.45
2300.00	191.67	44.23	7.37	10000.00	833.33	192.31	32.05

* Fifty-two weeks to the year instead of $52\frac{1}{6}$ weeks.
† Weekly rate on the basis of six days to the week.

TIME IN WHICH MONEY DOUBLES ITSELF AT INTEREST

Rate per cent	*Simple Interest*	*Compound Interest*
2	50 years	35 years 1 day
2½	40 "	28 " 26 days
3	33 " 4 months	23 " 164 "
3½	28 " 208 days	20 " 54 "
4	25 "	17 " 246 "
4½	22 " 81 days	15 " 273 "
5	20 "	14 " 75 "
6	16 " 8 months	11 " 327 "
7	14 " 104 days	10 " 89 "
8	12 " 6 months	9 " 2 "
9	11 " 40 days	8 " 16 "
10	10 "	7 " 100 "

TABLE SHOWING PRICE OF FRACTIONAL PART OF A DOZEN

The following table shows the cost of any fractional part of a dozen ranging from 50 cents to $5.00, in steps of 5 cents each. With proper placement of ciphers and decimals, the table can range from $5.00 to $50.00 per dozen, or from 5 cents to 50 cents per dozen. Fractions have been dropped, and the nearest even cent prices are given.

Cost Per Doz.	COST OF ANY FRACTIONAL PART OF A DOZEN — NUMBER OF ARTICLES 1	2	3	4	5	6	7	8	9	10	11	12
50	4	8	13	17	21	25	29	33	38	42	46	50
55	5	9	14	18	23	28	32	37	41	46	50	55
60	5	10	15	20	25	30	35	40	45	50	55	60
65	5	11	16	22	27	33	38	43	49	54	60	65
70	6	12	18	23	29	35	41	47	53	58	64	70
75	6	13	19	25	31	38	44	50	56	63	69	75
80	7	13	20	27	33	40	47	53	60	67	73	80
85	7	14	21	28	35	43	50	57	64	71	78	85
90	8	15	23	30	38	45	53	60	68	75	83	90
95	8	16	24	32	40	48	55	63	71	79	87	95

COST OF ANY FRACTIONAL PART OF A DOZEN

Cost Per Doz.	Number of Articles 1	2	3	4	5	6	7	8	9	10	11	12
100	8	17	25	33	42	50	58	67	75	83	92	100
105	9	18	26	35	44	53	61	70	79	88	96	105
110	9	18	28	37	46	55	64	73	83	92	101	110
115	10	19	29	38	48	58	67	77	86	96	105	115
120	10	20	30	40	50	60	70	80	90	100	110	120
125	10	21	31	42	52	63	73	83	94	104	115	125
130	11	22	33	43	54	65	76	87	98	108	119	130
135	11	23	34	45	56	68	79	90	101	113	124	135
140	12	23	35	47	58	70	82	93	105	117	128	140
145	12	24	36	48	60	73	85	97	109	121	133	145
150	13	25	38	50	63	75	88	100	113	125	138	150
155	13	26	39	52	65	78	90	103	116	129	142	155
160	13	27	40	53	67	80	93	107	120	133	147	160
165	14	28	41	55	69	83	96	110	124	138	151	165
170	14	28	42	57	71	85	99	113	127	142	156	170
175	15	29	44	58	73	88	102	117	131	146	160	175
180	15	30	45	60	75	90	105	120	135	150	165	180
185	15	31	46	62	77	93	108	123	139	154	170	185
190	16	32	48	63	79	95	111	127	143	158	174	190
195	16	33	49	65	81	98	114	130	146	163	179	195
200	17	33	50	67	83	100	117	133	150	167	183	200
205	17	34	51	68	85	103	120	137	154	171	188	205
210	18	35	53	70	88	105	123	140	158	175	193	210
215	18	36	54	72	90	108	125	143	161	179	197	215
220	18	37	55	73	92	110	128	147	165	183	202	220
225	19	38	56	75	94	113	131	150	169	188	206	225
230	19	38	58	77	96	115	134	153	173	192	211	230
235	20	39	59	78	98	118	137	157	176	196	215	235
240	20	40	60	80	100	120	140	160	180	200	220	240
245	20	41	61	82	102	123	143	163	184	204	225	245
250	21	42	63	83	104	125	146	167	188	208	229	250
255	21	43	64	85	106	128	149	170	191	213	234	255
260	22	43	65	87	108	130	152	173	195	217	238	260
265	22	44	66	88	110	133	155	177	199	221	243	265
270	23	45	68	90	113	135	158	180	201	225	248	270

COST OF ANY FRACTIONAL PART OF A DOZEN

Cost Per Doz.	Number of Articles 1	2	3	4	5	6	7	8	9	10	11	12
275	23	46	69	92	115	138	160	183	206	229	252	275
280	23	47	70	93	117	140	163	187	210	233	257	280
285	24	48	71	95	119	143	166	190	214	238	261	285
290	24	48	73	97	121	145	169	193	218	242	266	290
295	25	49	74	98	123	148	172	197	221	246	270	295
300	25	50	75	100	125	150	175	200	225	250	275	300
305	25	51	76	102	127	153	178	203	229	254	280	305
310	26	52	78	103	129	155	181	207	233	258	284	310
315	26	53	78	105	131	158	184	210	236	263	289	315
320	27	53	80	107	133	160	187	213	240	267	293	320
325	27	54	81	108	135	163	190	217	244	271	298	325
330	28	55	83	110	138	165	193	220	248	275	303	330
335	28	56	84	112	140	168	195	223	251	279	307	335
340	28	57	85	113	142	170	198	227	255	283	312	340
345	29	58	86	115	144	173	201	230	259	288	316	345
350	29	58	88	117	146	175	204	233	263	292	321	350
355	30	60	89	118	148	178	207	237	266	296	325	355
360	30	60	90	120	150	180	210	240	270	300	330	360
365	30	61	91	122	152	183	213	243	274	304	335	365
370	31	62	93	123	154	185	216	247	278	308	339	370
375	31	63	94	125	156	188	219	250	281	313	344	375
380	32	63	95	127	158	190	222	253	285	317	348	380
385	32	64	96	128	160	193	225	257	289	321	353	385
390	33	65	98	130	163	195	228	260	293	325	358	390
395	33	66	99	132	165	198	230	263	296	329	362	395
400	33	67	100	133	167	200	233	267	300	333	367	400
405	34	68	101	135	169	203	236	270	304	338	371	405
410	34	68	103	137	171	205	239	273	308	342	376	410
415	35	69	104	138	173	208	242	277	311	346	380	415
420	35	70	105	140	175	210	245	280	315	350	385	420
425	35	71	106	142	177	213	248	283	319	354	390	425
430	36	72	108	143	179	215	251	287	323	358	394	430
435	36	73	109	145	181	218	254	290	326	363	399	435
440	37	73	110	147	183	220	257	293	330	367	403	440
445	37	74	111	148	185	223	260	297	334	371	408	445

COST OF ANY FRACTIONAL PART OF A DOZEN

Cost Per Doz.	Number of Articles 1	2	3	4	5	6	7	8	9	10	11	12
450	38	75	113	150	188	225	263	300	338	375	413	450
455	38	76	114	152	190	227	265	303	341	379	417	455
460	38	77	115	153	192	230	268	307	345	383	422	460
465	39	78	116	155	194	233	271	310	349	388	426	465
470	39	78	118	157	196	235	274	313	353	392	431	470
475	40	79	119	158	198	238	277	317	356	396	435	475
480	40	80	120	160	200	240	280	320	360	400	440	480
485	40	81	121	162	202	243	283	323	364	404	445	485
490	41	82	123	163	204	245	286	327	368	408	449	490
500	42	83	125	167	208	250	292	333	375	417	458	500

MATHEMATICAL SIGNS AND SYMBOLS

$+$ .... Plus, the sign of addition.

$-$ .... Minus, the sign of subtraction.

$\times$ .... The sign of multiplication.

$\div$ .... The sign of division.

$:$ .... Is to, $::$ .... As, $:$ .... Is to — The signs of proportion. Thus $3 : 6 :: 4 : 8$.

$\because$ .... Because.

$\therefore$ .... Therefore.

$=$ .... Equals, the sign of equality.

$>$ .... Greater than.

$<$ .... Less than.

$\sqrt{}$ .... Square Root.

$\sqrt[3]{}$ .... Cube Root. $\sqrt[4]{}$ Fourth Root. $\sqrt[5]{}$ Fifth Root, etc.

() [] { } .. Indicate that the figures enclosed are to be taken together Thus $10 \times (7 + 4)$; $8 - [9 \div 3]$; $30 \left\{\frac{7+3}{4-2}\right\}$.

° ′ ″ ..... Degrees, minutes, seconds. Thus 25° 15′ 10″ represents 25 degrees, 15 minutes, 10 seconds.

′ ″ ...... Feet, inches. Thus 9′ 10″ = 9 feet 10 inches.

∞ ...... Infinity.

$\perp$ ...... Perpendicular to.

$\parallel$ ...... Parallel to.

...... Number; numbered.

° ...... Degree.

○ ...... Circle.

$\angle$ ...... Angle.

∟ ...... Right-angle.

□ ...... Square.

▭ ...... Rectangle.

Δ ...... Triangle.

0 ...... The cipher, zero.

% ...... Per cent.

‰ ...... Per thousand.

℈ Scruple., ʒ Drachm., ℥ Ounce. — Apothecaries' weight.

COMPARISON OF CENTIGRADE AND FAHRENHEIT TEMPERATURES

To convert from ° F to ° C, subtract 32 from ° F and divide by 1.8.
To convert from ° C to ° F, multiply ° C by 1.8 and add 32.
Water freezes at 0°C and 32°F. Water boils (at sea level) at 100° C and 212° F.

C	F	C	F	C	F	C	F
−40	−40	8	46.4	56	132.8	104	219.2
−39	−38.2	9	48.2	57	134.6	105	221.
−38	−36.4	10	50.	58	136.4	106	222.8
−37	−34.6	11	51.8	59	138.2	107	224.6
−36	−32.8	12	53.6	60	140.	108	226.4
−35	−31.	13	55.4	61	141.8	109	228.2
−34	−29.2	14	57.2	62	143.6	110	230.
−33	−27.4	15	59.	63	145.4	111	231.8
−32	−25.6	16	60.8	64	147.2	112	233.6
−31	−23.8	17	62.6	65	149.	113	235.4
−30	−22.	18	64.4	66	150.8	114	237.2
−29	−20.2	19	66.2	67	152.6	115	239.
−28	−18.4	20	68.	68	154.4	116	240.8
−27	−16.6	21	69.8	69	156.2	117	242.6
−26	−14.8	22	71.6	70	158.	118	244.4
−25	−13	23	73.4	71	159.8	119	246.2
−24	−11.2	24	75.2	72	161.6	120	248.
−23	− 9.4	25	77.	73	163.4	121	249.8
−22	− 7.6	26	78.8	74	165.2	122	251.6
−21	− 5.8	27	80.6	75	167.	123	253.4
−20	− 4.	28	82.4	76	168.8	124	255.2
−19	− 2.2	29	84.2	77	170.6	125	257.
−18	− 0.4	30	86.	78	172.4	126	258.8
−17	+ 1.4	31	87.8	79	174.2	127	260.6
−16	3.2	32	89.6	80	176.	128	262.4
−15	5.	33	91.4	81	177.8	129	264.2
−14	6.8	34	93.2	82	179.6	130	266.
−13	8.6	35	95.	83	181.4	131	267.
−12	10.4	36	96.8	84	183.2	132	269.6
−11	12.2	37	98.6	85	185.	133	271.4
−10	14.	38	100.4	86	186.8	134	273.2
− 9	15.8	39	102.2	87	188.6	135	275.
− 8	17.6	40	104.	88	190.4	136	276.8
− 7	19.4	41	105.8	89	192.2	137	278.6
− 6	21.2	42	107.6	90	194.	138	280.4
− 5	23.	43	109.4	91	195.8	139	282.2
− 4	24.8	44	111.2	92	197.6	140	284.
− 3	26.6	45	113.	93	199.4	141	285.8
− 2	28.4	46	114.8	94	201.2	142	287.6
− 1	30.2	47	116.6	95	203.	143	289.4
0	32.	48	118.4	96	204.8	144	291.2
+ 1	33.8	49	120.2	97	206.6	145	293.
2	35.6	50	122.	98	208.4	146	294.8
3	37.4	51	123.8	99	210.2	147	296.6
4	39.2	52	125.6	100	212.	148	298.4
5	41.	53	127.4	101	213.8	149	300.2
6	42.8	54	129.2	102	215.6		
7	44.6	55	131.	103	217.4		

SQUARES, SQUARE ROOTS, CUBES, AND CUBE ROOTS OF NUMBERS 1–100

No.	Sq.	Cube	Square Root	Cube Root	No.	Sq.	Cube	Square Root	Cube Root	No.	Sq.	Cube	Square Root	Cube Root
1	1.000	1.000	1.000	1.000	35	1225	42875	5.916	3.271	68	4624	314432	8.246	4.081
2	4	8	1.414	1.259	36	1296	46656	6.000	3.301	69	4761	328509	8.306	4.101
3	9	27	1.732	1.442	37	1369	50653	6.082	3.332	70	4900	343000	8.366	4.121
4	16	64	2.000	1.587	38	1444	54872	6.164	3.362	71	5041	357911	8.426	4.140
5	25	125	2.236	1.710	39	1521	59319	6.245	3.391	72	5184	373248	8.485	4.160
6	36	216	2.449	1.817	40	1600	64000	6.324	3.420	73	5329	389017	8.544	4.179
7	49	343	2.645	1.913	41	1681	68921	6.403	3.448	74	5476	405224	8.602	4.198
8	64	512	2.828	2.000	42	1764	74088	6.480	3.476	75	5625	421875	8.660	4.217
9	81	729	3.000	2.080	43	1849	79507	6.557	3.503	76	5776	438976	8.717	4.235
10	100	1000	3.162	2.154	44	1936	85184	6.633	3.530	77	5929	456533	8.775	4.254
11	121	1331	3.316	2.224	45	2025	91125	6.708	3.556	78	6084	474552	8.831	4.272
12	144	1728	3.464	2.289	46	2116	97336	6.782	3.583	79	6241	493039	8.888	4.290
13	169	2197	3.605	2.351	47	2209	103823	6.855	3.608	80	6400	512000	8.944	4.308
14	196	2744	3.741	2.410	48	2304	110592	6.928	3.634	81	6561	531441	9.000	4.326
15	225	3375	3.873	2.466	49	2401	117649	7.000	3.659	82	6724	551368	9.055	4.344
16	256	4096	4.000	2.519	50	2500	125000	7.071	3.684	83	6889	571787	9.110	4.362
17	289	4913	4.123	2.571	51	2601	132651	7.141	3.708	84	7056	592704	9.165	4.379
18	324	5832	4.242	2.620	52	2704	140608	7.211	3.732	85	7225	614125	9.219	4.396
19	361	6859	4.358	2.668	53	2809	148877	7.280	3.756	86	7396	636056	9.273	4.414
20	400	8000	4.472	2.714	54	2916	157464	7.348	3.779	87	7569	658303	9.327	4.431
21	441	9261	4.582	2.758	55	3025	166375	7.416	3.803	88	7744	681472	9.380	4.448
22	484	10648	4.690	2.802	56	3136	175616	7.483	3.825	89	7921	704969	9.434	4.464
23	529	12167	4.795	2.843	57	3249	185193	7.549	3.848	90	8100	729000	9.486	4.481
24	576	13824	4.899	2.884	58	3364	195112	7.615	3.870	91	8281	753571	9.539	4.497
25	625	15625	5.000	2.924	59	3481	205379	7.681	3.893	92	8464	778688	9.591	4.514
26	676	17576	5.099	2.962	60	3600	216000	7.746	3.914	93	8649	804357	9.643	4.530
27	729	19683	5.196	3.000	61	3721	226981	7.810	3.936	94	8836	830584	9.695	4.546
28	784	21952	5.291	3.036	62	3844	238328	7.874	3.957	95	9025	857375	9.746	4.562
29	841	24389	5.385	3.072	63	3969	250047	7.937	3.979	96	9216	884736	9.798	4.578
30	900	27000	5.477	3.107	64	4096	262144	8.000	4.000	97	9409	912673	9.848	4.594
31	961	29791	5.567	3.141	65	4225	274625	8.062	4.020	98	9604	941192	9.899	4.610
32	1024	32768	5.656	3.174	66	4356	287496	8.124	4.041	99	9801	970299	9.944	4.626
33	1089	35937	5.744	3.207	67	4489	300763	8.185	4.061	100	10000	1000000	10.000	4.641
34	1156	39304	5.831	3.239										

PERPETUAL CALENDAR[1]

For Ascertaining the Day of the Week for Any Given Date

YEARS

C'ter	1700		1800				1900				2000			
0	53	81		27	55	83	**00**	*	*	*	01	29	57	85
1	54	82		**28**	**56**	**84**	1	29	57	85	2	30	58	86
2	55	83	**00**	*	*	*	2	30	58	86	3	31	59	87
3	**56**	**84**	1	29	57	85	3	31	59	87	**4**	**32**	**60**	**88**
4	*	*	2	30	58	86	**4**	**32**	**60**	**88**	*	*	*	*
5	57	85	3	31	59	87	*	*	*	*	5	33	61	89
6	58	86	**4**	**32**	**60**	**88**	5	33	61	89	6	34	62	90
0	59	87	*	*	*	*	6	34	62	90	7	35	63	91
1	**60**	**88**	5	33	61	89	7	35	63	91	**8**	**36**	**64**	**92**
2	*	*	6	34	62	90	**8**	**36**	**64**	**92**	*	*	*	*
3	61	89	7	35	63	91	*	*	*	*	9	37	65	93
4	62	90	**8**	**36**	**64**	**92**	9	37	65	93	10	38	66	94
5	63	91	*	*	*	*	10	38	66	94	11	39	67	95
6	**64**	**92**	9	37	65	93	11	39	67	95	12	40	68	**96**
0	*	*	10	38	66	94	**12**	**40**	**68**	**96**	*	*	*	*
1	65	93	11	39	67	95	*	*	*	*	13	41	69	97
2	66	94	**12**	**40**	**68**	**96**	13	41	69	97	14	42	70	98
3	67	95	*	*	*	*	14	42	70	98	15	43	71	99
4	**68**	**96**	13	41	69	97	15	43	71	99	**16**	**44**	**72**	
5	*	*	14	42	70	98	**16**	**44**	**72**	00	*	*	*	
6	69	97	15	43	71	99	*	*	*	*	17	45	73	
0	70	98	**16**	**44**	**72**		17	45	73		18	46	74	
1	71	99	*	*	*		18	46	74		19	47	75	
2	**72**		17	45	73		19	47	75		**20**	**48**	**76**	
3	*		18	46	74		**20**	**48**	**76**		*	*	*	
4	73		19	47	75		*	*	*		21	49	77	
5	74		**20**	**48**	**76**		21	49	77		22	50	78	
6	75		*	*	*		22	50	78		23	51	79	
0	**76**		21	49	77		23	51	79		**24**	**52**	**80**	
1	*		22	50	78		**24**	**52**	**80**		*	*	*	
2	77		23	51	79		*	*	*		25	53	81	
3	78		**24**	**52**	**80**		25	53	81		26	54	82	
4	79		*	*	*		26	54	82		27	55	83	
5	**80**		25	53	81		27	55	83		**28**	**56**	**84**	
6	*		26	54	82		**28**	**56**	**84**		*	*	*	

DAY OF MONTH

J	F	M	A	M	J	J	A	S	O	N	D	Days
1									1			**M**
2				1					2			**T**
3				2			1		3			**W**
4	1	1		3			2		4	1		**T**
5	2	2		4	1		3		5	2		**F**
6	3	3		5	2		4	1	6	3	1	**S**
7	4	4	1	6	3	1	5	2	7	4	2	**S**
8	5	5	2	7	4	2	6	3	8	5	3	**M**
9	6	6	3	8	5	3	7	4	9	6	4	**T**
10	7	7	4	9	6	4	8	5	10	7	5	**W**
11	8	8	5	10	7	5	9	6	11	8	6	**T**
12	9	9	6	11	8	6	10	7	12	9	7	**F**
13	10	10	7	12	9	7	11	8	13	10	8	**S**
14	11	11	8	13	10	8	12	9	14	11	9	**S**
15	12	12	9	14	11	9	13	10	15	12	10	**M**
16	13	13	10	15	12	10	14	11	16	13	11	**T**
17	14	14	11	16	13	11	15	12	17	14	12	**W**
18	15	15	12	17	14	12	16	13	18	15	13	**T**
19	16	16	13	18	15	13	17	14	19	16	14	**F**
20	17	17	14	19	16	14	18	15	20	17	15	**S**
21	18	18	15	20	17	15	19	16	21	18	16	**S**
22	19	19	16	21	18	16	20	17	22	19	17	**M**
23	20	20	17	22	19	17	21	18	23	20	18	**T**
24	21	21	18	23	20	18	22	19	24	21	19	**W**
25	22	22	19	24	21	19	23	20	25	22	20	**T**
26	23	23	20	25	22	20	24	21	26	23	21	**F**
27	24	24	21	26	23	21	25	22	27	24	22	**S**
28	25	25	22	27	24	22	26	23	28	25	23	**S**
29	26	26	23	28	25	23	27	24	29	26	24	**M**
30	27	27	24	29	26	24	28	25	30	27	25	**T**
31	28	28	25	30	27	25	29	26	31	28	26	**W**
	29	29	26	31	28	26	30	27		29	27	**T**
		30	27		29	27	31	28		30	28	**F**
		31	28		30	28		29			29	**S**
			29			29		30			30	**S**
			30			30					31	**M**
						31						**T**
												W
												T

[1] *Devised by Charles W. Gerstenberg.*

Directions

Step 1. Locate year on this page, and "counter" opposite thereto at extreme left.

Step 2. Locate day of month; carry over to day column at extreme right and count down number of days indicated by "counter" in Step 1. For leap years (those in **bold face** type preceding asterisk*), the counter should be increased by one for days after February 29.

Example. What day of the week was June 13, 1938?

Solution:

Step 1. The "counter" opposite 38 is observed to be **5.**

Step 2. The letter opposite the number 13 (on extreme right, under **J** for June) is **W.** Counting down 5, it is found that June 13, 1938, was a Monday.

Example. What day of the week was August 8, 1912 (a leap year)?

Solution:

Step 1. Under column headed **1900,** find the number 12. Opposite it, on the extreme left, the "counter" is observed to be **0.** Since 1912 was a leap year (indicated by **bold face** type), and since August 8 is after February 28, increase the counter by 1. The "counter" is $(0 + 1 = 1)$.

Step 2. Under column headed **A** for August locate the day of the month, which in this instance is 8. Follow over to the letter **W** in column headed **Days;** count down 1 (number of counter) to the letter **T** (for Thursday). August 8, 1912, was a Thursday.

AMERICAN EXPERIENCE TABLE OF MORTALITY

Age	No. Living	Deaths Each Year	Death-Rate Per 1,000	Expect. of Life	Age	No. Living	Deaths Each Year	Death-Rate Per 1,000	Expect. of Life	Age	No. Living	Deaths Each Year	Death-Rate Per 1,000	Expect. of Life
10....	100.000	749	7.49	48.72	39....	78.862	756	9.59	28.90	68....	43.133	2.243	52.00	9.47
11....	99.251	746	7.52	48.08	40....	78.106	765	9.79	28.18	69....	40.890	2.321	56.76	8.97
12....	98.505	743	7.54	47.45	41....	77.341	774	10.01	27.45	70....	38.569	2.391	61.99	8.48
13....	97.762	740	7.57	46.80	42....	76.567	785	10.25	26.72	71....	36.178	2.448	67.66	8.00
14....	97.022	737	7.60	46.16	43....	75.782	797	10.52	26.00	72....	33.730	2.487	73.73	7.55
15....	96.285	735	7.63	45.50	44....	74.985	812	10.83	25.27	73....	31.243	2.505	80.18	7.11
16....	95.550	732	7.66	44.85	45....	74.173	828	11.16	24.54	74....	28.738	2.501	87.03	6.68
17....	94.818	729	7.69	44.19	46....	73.345	848	11.56	23.81	75....	26.237	2.476	94.37	6.27
18....	94.089	727	7.73	43.53	47....	72.497	870	12.00	23.08	76....	23.761	2.431	102.31	5.88
19....	93.362	725	7.76	42.87	48....	71.627	896	12.51	22.36	77....	21.330	2.369	111.06	5.49
20....	92.637	723	7.80	42.20	49....	70.731	927	13.11	21.63	78....	18.961	2.291	120.83	5.11
21....	91.914	722	7.85	41.53	50....	69.804	962	13.78	20.91	79....	16.670	2.196	131.73	4.74
22....	91.192	721	7.91	40.85	51....	68.842	1.001	14.54	20.20	80....	14.474	2.091	144.47	4.39
23....	90.471	720	7.96	40.17	52....	67.841	1.044	15.39	19.49	81....	12.383	1.964	158.60	4.05
24....	89.751	719	8.01	39.49	53....	66.797	1.091	16.33	18.79	82....	10.419	1.816	174.30	3.71
25....	89.032	718	8.06	38.81	54....	65.706	1.143	17.40	18.09	83....	8.603	1.648	191.56	3.39
26....	88.314	718	8.13	38.12	55....	64.563	1.199	18.57	17.40	84....	6.955	1.470	211.36	3.08
27....	87.596	718	8.20	37.43	56....	63.364	1.260	19.88	16.72	85....	5.485	1.292	235.55	2.77
28....	86.878	718	8.26	36.73	57....	62.104	1.325	21.33	16.05	86....	4.193	1.114	265.68	2.47
29....	86.160	719	8.34	36.03	58....	60.779	1.394	22.94	15.39	87....	3.079	933	303.02	2.18
30....	85.441	720	8.43	35.33	59....	59.385	1.468	24.72	14.74	88....	2.146	744	346.69	1.91
31....	84.721	721	8.51	34.63	60....	57.917	1.546	26.69	14.10	89....	1.402	555	395.86	1.66
32....	84.000	723	8.61	33.93	61....	56.371	1.628	28.88	13.47	90....	847	385	454.54	1.42
33....	83.277	726	8.72	33.21	62....	54.743	1.713	31.29	12.86	91....	462	246	532.47	1.19
34....	82.551	729	8.83	32.50	63....	53.030	1.800	33.94	12.26	92....	216	137	634.26	.98
35....	81.822	732	8.95	31.78	64....	51.230	1.889	36.87	11.67	93....	79	58	734.18	.80
36....	81.090	737	9.09	31.07	65....	49.341	1.980	40.13	11.10	94....	21	18	857.14	.64
37....	80.353	742	9.23	30.35	66....	47.361	2.070	43.71	10.54	95....	3	3	1000.00	.50
38....	79.611	749	9.41	29.62	67....	45.291	2.158	47.65	10.00					

17. GLOSSARY OF ABBREVIATIONS

In addition to the following list, other lists of abbreviations are given as indicated.

Abbreviations of months and days (page 1430).
Abbreviations of foreign currencies (pages 1400-1401).

General Abbreviations

A

@ .... at (referring to price)
a, A. .... acre(s)
A. .... Atlantic Reporter
A.(2d) .... Atlantic Reporter (second series)
A-1 .... first class
a.a. .... always afloat
A.A.E. .... American Association of Engineers
a.a.r. .... against all risks
A.A.S. .... Fellow of the American Academy
A.B.A. .... American Bankers Association
abbr. .... abbreviated, -ion
abr. .... abridged
abt. .... about
a.c. .... alternate current
a/c .... account
A/C .... account current
acc. .... acceptance; accepted
acct. .... account
A.C.A. .... Associate of the Institute of Chartered Accountants
A/cs Pay .... accounts payable
A/cs Rec. .... accounts receivable
A.C.S. .... American College of Surgeons
a/d .... after date
ad .... advertisement (*pl.* ads)
ad lib., ad libit. .... at one's pleasure; freely; to the quantity or amount desired
ad loc. .... to, *or* at, the place
admr., adms., admstr. .... administrator
admrx., admx. .... administratrix
ad. val. .... according to value (*ad valorem*)
AEC .... Atomic Energy Commission
A.E.F. .... American Expeditionary Forces
A.E.S. .... American Electrochemical Society
A. & F. .... August and February
affd. aff'd .... affirmed
afft. .... affidavit
AFL.; A.F. of L. .... American Federation of Labor
A.G. .... Adjutant General
a.g.b. .... a good brand
A.G.F.A. .... Assistant General Freight Agent
agst. .... against
agt. .... agent; against; agreement
a.h. .... after hatch; ampere-hour(s)
A.H.Q. .... Army headquarters
A.I.B. .... American Institute of Banking
A.I.C.E. .... American Institute of Chemical Engineers
A.I.E. .... American Institute of Engineers
A.I.E.E. .... American Institute of Electrical Engineers
A.I.M.E. .... American Institute

of Mining & Metallurgical Engineers
A.J.O.J. .... April, July, October, January
a.m. .... before noon (*ante meridian*)
A.M.A. .... American Medical Association
amp. .... ampere(s)
amt. .... amount
a.n. .... arrival notice (shipping)
A.N.F.M. .... August, November, February, May
anon. .... anonymous
ans. .... answer; answered
a/o .... account of
A. & O. .... April and October
A. to O.C. .... attached to other correspondence
AP .... Associated Press
A/P .... additional premium; authority to pay
Apd. .... assessment paid
app. .... appeal (legal)
appd. .... approved
approx. .... approximately
A/R .... all risks; against all risks (marine ins.)
ARC .... American (National) Red Cross
art. .... article
A/S .. after sight; account sales; alongside (chartering)
A.S. .... Academy of Science
a.s. .... at sight
ASA .... American Standards Association
A.S.A. .... American Statistical Association
A.S.C.E. .... American Society of Civil Engineers
A.S.E. .... Amalgamated Society of Engineers
A.S.M.E. .... American Society of Mechanical Engineers
assigt. .... assignment
assmt. .... assessment
assn. *or* **ass'n** .... association
asst. .... assistant
A.S.T. .... Atlantic standard time
ASTA .... American Society of Travel Agents, Inc.
A.S.T.M. .... American Society for Testing Materials
A/T .... American terms (grain trade)
at. no. .... atomic number
A. to O.C. .... attached to other correspondence
ats. .... at suit of (law)
atty. .... attorney
at. vol. .... atomic volume
at. wt. .... atomic weight
AUS .... Army of the United States
A.V. .... Authorized Version
A/V .... according to value (ad valorem)
av., avdp. .... avoirdupois
av. *or* **age.** .... average
Ave. .... Avenue
A/W .... actual weight; all water (transp.)
A.W.G. .... American wire gauge

B

b7d, b10d, b15d .... buyer 7 days to take up, etc. (stock market)
bal. .... balance
bar. .... barometer
b.b. .... bail bond; bill book; break bulk
bbl. .... barrel(s)
B/C .... bill of collection
B/D .... bank draft; bar draft (grain trade)
Bd. of Rev. .... Board of Review
bd.ft. .... board feet
bdl. .... bundle
B/E .... bill of exchange; bill of entry

B/F .... brought forward (bookkeeping)
B/G .... bonded goods
B/H .... bill of health
b.h.p. .... brake horsepower
bibliog. .... bibliography, -er, -ical
biog. .... biography, -er, -ical
biol. .... biology, -ical, -ist
bk. .... bank; book
bkpt. .... bankrupt
bkt., bsk. .... basket(s)
B/L .... bill of lading
bl. .... bale(s)
Bldg. .... Building
B.L.E. .... Brotherhood of Locomotive Engineers
Blvd. .... Boulevard
b. m. .... board measure (timber)
b.o. .... buyer's option; back order
b/o .... brought over
B.O. .... branch office
B/P .... bills payable; bill of parcels
B. Pay. .... bills payable
b.p.b. .... bank post bill
B/R .... bills receivable; builders' risks
B. Rec. .... bills receivable
Brig. Gen. .... Brigadier General
Bro. .... Brother
Bros. .... Brothers
B/S .... bill of sale; bill of store
Bs/L .... bills of lading
B/St .... bill of sight
b.t. .... berth terms
b.t.u. .... British thermal unit(s)
bu. .... bushel(s)
bul., bull. .... bulletin
bus. .... business; bushels
Bus. Mgr. .... business manager
B/v .... book value
B.W.G. .... Birmingham wire gauge
bx .... box

C

c. .... cent(s); carat; chapter(s)
c/- .... case(s)
C.A. .... Chartered Accountant
CAA .... Civil Aeronautics Administration
C/A .... capital account; credit account; current account; commercial agent; close annealed
ca. .... centare(s)
CAB .... Civil Aeronautics Board
C a/c .... current account
c.a.f. .... cost, assurance, and freight
Cantab. .... of Cambridge (*Cantabrigiensis*)
cap. .... capital
caps .... capital letters
Capt. .... Captain
cart. .... cartage
C.A. .... Chartered accountant
C/B .... cash book
C.B.D. .... cash before delivery
C.B.S. OR **CBS** .... Columbia Broadcasting System
cc. .... cubic centimeter
CCC .... Commodity Credit Corporation
C.C. .... continuation clause (marine ins.)
ccm. .... centimeter(s)
c/d .... carried down (bookkeeping)
C/D .... commercial dock; consular declaration; certificate of deposit
c. & d. .... collection and delivery
CDE .... Code (Western Union cable)
cf. .... compare
c/f .... carried forward (bookkeeping)
c. & f. .... cost and freight

c.f.i. .... cost, freight, and insurance
c.f.o. .... cost for orders
cg. .... centigram(s)
C.G.A. .... cargo's proportion of general average
cge.pd. .... carriage paid
cgm. .... centigram(s)
ch.(s) .... chapter(s)
C.I. .... consular invoice
C.I.E. .... captain's imperfect entry (Customs)
c.i.f. .... cost, insurance, and freight
c.i.f. & c. .... cost, insurance, freight, and charges
c.i.f. & e. .... cost, insurance, freight, and exchange
c.i.f. & i. .... cost, insurance, freight, and interest
c.i.f.i. & e. .... cost, insurance, freight, interest, and exchange
c.i.f.L.t. .... cost, insurance, and freight, London terms
C.I.O. .... Committee on Industrial Organization
CIR .... Commissioner of Internal Revenue
civ. civil
ck. .... cask(s); check
C/L .... cash letter
cl. .... centiliter(s)
c.l. .... carload
c/l .... craft loss
cld. .... cleared
cm. .... centimeter's
cm.pf. .... cumulative preferred (stocks)
C/N .... credit note; consignment note; circular note
cn. .... consolidated (bonds)
C/O .... cash order; certificate of origin; case oil
Co. .... company; county
c/o .... carried over (bookkeeping); in care of
c.o.d. .... certificates of deposit (securities)
C.O.D., c.o.d. .... cash, or collect, on delivery
col. .... column
Col. .... Colonel
coll.tr., clt. .... collateral trust (bonds)
Coll. .... Collector (internal revenue)
Comm. .... Committee; Commission
Com'r, Comm. .... Commissioner
consgt. .... consignment
Const. .... Constitution
co-op. .... co-operative
corp. .... corporation, corporal
c.o.s. .... cash on shipment
c-p. .... candle power
C/P .... charter party; custom of port (grain trade)
C.P.A. .... Certified Public Accountant
C.P.D. .... charterers pay dues
C.R. .... class rate; current rate; company's risk; carrier's risk
cr. .... credit; creditor
c/s .... cases
C/S .... colliery screened (coal trade)
CSC .... Civil Service Commission
C.S.T. .... Central Standard Time
C/T .... cable transfer; California terms (grain trade)
C.T. .... Central Time
ct. .... cent(s)
ctge. .... cartage
c.t.l. .... constructive total loss (marine ins.)
c.t.l.o. .... constructive total loss only (marine ins.)
c. to. s. .... carting to shipside
cu. .... cubic

cu. cm. .... cubic centimeter(s)
cu. ft. .... cubic feet
cu. in. .... cubic inch(es)
cu. mi. .... cubic mile(s)
cum. .... with; cumulative
cum. pref., cu. pf. .... cumulative preferred (stocks)
cur. .... current
c.v. .... chief value
C.W. .... commercial weight
c.w.o. .... cash with order
cwt. .... hundredweight(s)

D

d. .... pence
d/a .... days after acceptance
D/A .... deposit account; documents against acceptance; discharge afloat
dal. .... decaliter(s)
d. & w.t.f. .... daily and weekly till forbidden
D.B. .... day book; deals and battens (timber trade)
D.B.B. .... deals, battens, and boards (timber trade)
d.b.h. .... diameter at breast height
dbk. .... drawback
db. rts. .... debenture rights (securities)
d.c. .... direct current
D/C .... deviation clause
D/D .... demand draft; delivered at docks; delivered at destination; dock dues
D/d .... Days after date
dd. .... delivered
dd/s .... delivered sound (grain trade)
deb., deben. .... debenture
dec. .... decision
decim. .... decimeter(s)
def. .... deferred (securities)
deft. .... defendant
Dem. .... Democrat
dep.ctfs. .... deposit certificates
dept., dpt. .... department
depr. .... depreciation
d.f. .... dead freight
D.F.A. .... Division Freight Agent
dft. .... draft
dg. .... decigram(s)
dia., diam. .... diameter
dir. .... director
dis. .... discount
dist. .... district
div. .... dividend; division
D. & J. .... December and June
dkg. .... dekagram(s)
dkl. .... dekaliter(s)
dkt. .... docket
dkm. .... dekamater(s)
dks. .... decastere(s)
D/L .... demand loan
dl. .... decileter(s)
DL .... day letter (telegraph)
dld. .... delivered
d.l.o. .... dispatch loading only
D.L.O. .... Dead Letter Office
D/N .... debit note
D/O .... delivery order
do. .... ditto (the same)
dom. .... dominion
doz. .... dozen
d.p. .... direct port
D/P .... documents against payment
D/R .... deposit receipt
dr. .... debit; debtor; drawer
Dr. .... Doctor
dr. ap. .... apothecaries' dram(s)
dr. av. .... dram(s) avoirdupois
D/s .... days after sight
ds. .... decistere(s)
D/W .... dock warrant
d.w. .... dead weight
d.w.c. .... dead weight capacity
dwt. .... pennyweight(s)
d. & w.t.f. .... daily and weekly till forbidden

D/y .... delivery
dz. .... dozen

E

ea. .... each
E.A.O.N. .... except as otherwise noted
ed. .... editor; edition(s); education
E.D.T. .... Eastern daylight saving time
e.e. .... errors excepted
eff. .... effective
e.g. .... for example, (*exempli gratia*)
elec. .... electric
Encyc. .... Encyclopedia
enc. .... enclose
end. .... endorse, endorsement
eng. .... engine; engineer; engraved
Env.-Ext. .... Envoy Extraordinary
E. & O.E. .... errors and omissions excepted
e.o. .... ex officio
e.o.h.p. .... except as otherwise herein provided
e.o.m. .... end of month (payments)
equip. .... equipment
Esq. .... Esquire
est. .... estate; estimated
E.S.T. .... Eastern standard time
estab. .... established
et al. .... and others (*et alii*)
etc. .... and the others; and so forth (*et cetera*)
et seq. .... and the following (*et sequens*)
et ux .... and wife (*et uxor*)
et vir .... and husband
Ex. B.L. .... exchange bill of lading
ex. cp *or* **x/cp** .... ex coupon
ex d. *or* **ex div.** .... ex dividend
exd. .... examined
exec. .... executive
ex int. .... ex interest
ex n. .... ex new
exp. .... express; expenses; export
ex r. .... ex rights
exr. .... executor
exrx. .... executrix
ex ship .... delivered out of ship

F

f. .... following (after a numeral)
F., Fahr. .... Fahrenheit
f.a. .... free alongside
F. & A. .... February and August
f.a.a. .... free of all average (marine ins.)
fac. .... facsimile
f.a.c. .... fast as can
F.A.C.P. .... Fellow of the American College of Physicians
f.a.q. .... fair average quality; free at quay
f.a.q.s. .... fair average quality of season
f.a.s. .... free alongside ship; firsts and seconds (lumber)
F.A.M. *or* **F. and A.M.** .... Free and Accepted Mason
f.b. .... freight bill
fbm .... feet board measure
FCA .... Farm Credit Administration
FCC .... Federal Communications Commission
f.c. & s. .... free of capture and seizure (transp.)
f.c.s.r.c.c. .... free of capture, seizure, riots and civil commotions
f.d. .... free discharge; free delivery; free dispatch
f. & d. .... freight and demurrage
FDIC .... Federal Deposit Insurance Corporation

ff. .... following (after a numeral); folios
f.f.a. .... free from alongside; free foreign agency
F.G.A. .... foreign general average (marine ins.)
F.H.A. .... Federal Housing Administration
f.i.a. .... full interest admitted
f.i.b. .... free into bunkers; free into barge
fig.(s) .... figure(s)
f.i.o. .... free in and out
f.i.t. .... free of income tax; free in truck
f.i.w. .... free in wagon
F.L.N. .... following landing numbers
fl. oz. .... fluid ounce(s)
fm. .... fathom(s)
F.M. .... frequency modulation
F.M.A.N. .... February, May; August, November
FMCS .... Federal Mediation and Conciliation Service
F.O. .... firm offer; free overside
f.o. .... for orders; firm offer; full out terms (grain trade)
F.O.B., f.o.b. .... free on board
f.o.c. .... free on car; free of charge
f.o.d. .... free of damage
f.o.f. .... free on field (air mail)
fol. .... folio; following
f.o.q. .... free on quay
f.o.r. .... free on rail
f.o.r.t. .... free out rye terms (grain trade)
f.o.s. .... free on steamer
f.o.t. .... free on truck
f.o.w. .... free on wagon; first open water
F.P. .... floating (or open) policy; fully paid
F.P.A. .... free of particular average (marine ins.)
F.P.A.A.C. .... free of particular average, American Conditions (marine ins.)
F.P.A.E.C. .... free of particular average, English Conditions (marine ins.)
FPC .... Federal Power Commission
f.p.m. .... feet per minute
f.p.s. .... feet per second
F/R .... freight release
F.R.B. .... Federal Reserve Board (or Bank)
f.r.o.f. .... fire risk on freight
F.R.S. .... Federal Reserve System
frt. .... freight
FSA .... Federal Security Agency
ft. .... foot *or* feet
f.t. .... full terms
FTC .... Federal Trade Commission
F.T.W. .... free trade wharf
f.v. .... on the back of the page (*folio verso*)
fwd. .... forward
f.w.d. .... fresh water damage
F.X. .... foreign exchange
F.Y.I. .... for your information (interoffice use)

G

g .... gram (metric)
G/A .... general average (marine ins.)
G/A con. .... general average contribution (marine ins.)
G/A dep. .... general average deposit (marine ins.)
gal. .... gallon(s)
G.A.R. .... Grand Army of the Republic
g.f.a. .... good fair average
G.F.A. .... General Freight Agent
g. gr. .... great gross

GHQ . . . . General Headquarters (Army)
gi. . . . . gill(s)
gm. . . . . gram(s)
Gov. . . . . Governor
govt. . . . . government
G.P.A. . . . . General Passenger Agent
g.p.m. . . . . gallons per minute
gr. . . . . gram(s); grain; gross
gro. . . . . gross
gr. wt. . . . . gross weight
G.T.C. . . . . good till canceled, *or* countermanded
G.T.M. . . . . good this month
G.T.W. . . . . good this week, becomes void on Saturday
guar. . . . . guaranteed

H

ha. . . . . hectare(s)
H.C. . . . . held covered (insurance); House of Commons
hd. . . . . head
hdqrs. . . . . headquarters
hdwr. . . . . hardware
H.F.M. . . . . hold for money
hg. . . . . hectogram(s)
hhd. . . . . hogshead(s)
hist. . . . . historic, -ian, -ical
hl. . . . . hectoliter(s)
hm. . . . . hectometer(s)
Hon. . . . . Honorable
H.P. *or* **hp.** . . . . horsepower
H.P.N. . . . . horsepower nominal
hq. . . . . headquarters
hr. . . . . hour(s)
H.W. . . . . high water
H.W.M. . . . . high-water mark
H.W.O.S.T. . . . . high-water ordinary spring tide
hyp. . . . . hypothesis

I

I.B. . . . . invoice book; in bond
I.B.I. . . . . invoice book, inwards
ibid. . . . . in the same place (*ibidem*)
I.B.O. . . . . invoice book, outwards
ICC . . . . Interstate Commerce Commission
I.C.&C. . . . . invoice cost and charges
id. . . . . the same (*idem*)
i.e. . . . . that is (*id est*)
I.E.E. . . . . Institute of Electrical Engineers
I.F.T.U. . . . . International Federation of Trade Unions
IGD . . . . Inspector General's Department
I.H.P. . . . . indicated horsepower
I.L.O. . . . . International Labor Organization
I.L.P. . . . . Independent Labour Party (Brit.)
imp. gal. . . . . imperial gallon(s)
in. . . . . inch(es)
Inc. . . . . incorporated
incog. . . . . incognito
I.N.P. . . . . International News Photos
I.N.S. . . . . International News Service
inst. . . . . in the present month (*instant*)
Inst. . . . . Institute, -ion
int. . . . . interest
I.O.O.F. . . . . Independent Order of Odd Fellows
inv. . . . . invoice
I.P.A. . . . . including particular average
I.Q. . . . . intelligence quotient
IRC . . . . Internal Revenue Code
ital. . . . . italics
i.v. . . . . invoice value; increased value
I.W.W. . . . . Industrial Workers of the World

J

J. .... Judge, Justice
J/A .... joint account
J.A.J.O. .... January, April, July, October
J. & D. .... June and December
J. & J. .... January and July
jnt. stk. .... joint stock
J.O.J.A. .... July, October, January, April
jour. .... journal
J.P. .... Justice of the Peace
Jr. .... junior
J.S.D.M. .... June, September, December, March

K

k. .... carat; knot
kc. .... kilocycle(s)
K.C. .... Knights of Columbus
K.D. .... knocked down
K.D.C.L. .... knocked down, in carloads
K.D.L.C.L. .... knocked down, in less than carloads
kg. *or* **kgm.** .... kilogram(s)
kilo. .... kilometer(s)
K.K.K. .... Ku Klux Klan
kl. .... kiloliter(s)
km. .... kilometer(s)
kn. .... kronen
K.P. .... Knights of Pythias
kv. .... kilovolts
kw. .... kilowatt(s)
kwi-hr. .... kilowatt-hour(s)

L

l. .... line; liter(s)
L .... listed (securities)
L/A .... letter of authority; landing account; Lloyd's agent
lang. .... language
lat. .... latitude
lb. .... pound(s)
lb. ap. .... apothecaries' pound(s)
l.c. .... lower case; in the place cited
LC .... Deferreds (cable messages)
L/C .... letter of credit
l.c.l. .... less than carload lot
ldg. .... loading
ldg. & dely. .... landing and delivery
lds. .... loads
lge. .... large
lg. tn. .... long ton(s)
L.I.P. .... life insurance policy
lkg. & bkg. .... leakage and breakage
Ll. & Co.'s .... Lloyd's and Companies
L.M.C. .... Lloyd's machinery certificate
l.m.c. .... low middling clause (cotton trade)
L.M.S.C. .... let me see correspondence
loc. cit. .... in the place cited (*loco citato*)
log. .... logarithm
long. .... longitude
lr. .... lire
L.R.M.C. .... Lloyd's refrigerating machinery certificate
L.S. .... place of the seal (*locus sigilli*)
l.t. .... long ton
Ltd. .... limited (British)
ltge. .... lighterage
Lt.-V. .... light vessel
lv. .... leave
L.W. .... low water
L.W.M. .... low-water mark

M

m. .... married; masculine; meter(s)
M .... thousand
M. .... Monsieur (plu. MM); Noon (*meredies*)

m/a .... my account
Maj. .... Major
M.A.N.F. .... May, August, November, February
math. .... mathematics, -ical
max. .... maximum
max. cap. .... maximum capacity
M.B.C. *or* **MBC** .... Mutual Broadcasting Company
M.B.M. .... thousands (of feet) board measure
m.c. .... marked capacity (freight cars)
M.C. .... Master of ceremonies, Member of Congress
M/C .... metalling clause (marine ins.); marginal credit
m/d .... months after date
M/D .... memorandum of deposit
mdse .... merchandise
M.E. .... Methodist Episcopal
med. .... medium; medicine; medical
memo .... memorandum(s)
m.e.p. .... mean effective pressure
Messrs. .... Misters (Messieurs)
mfg. .... manufacturing
mfr. .... manufacturer
m. *or* **mgm** .... milligram(s)
Mgr. .... Monsignor; Monseigneur
Mgr. .... Manager
M.H. .... main hatch; Medal of Honor
mi. .... mile(s)
min. .... minute(s)
min. B/L .... minimum bill of lading
M.I.P. .... Marine insurance policy
misc. .... miscellaneous
m.i.t. .... milled in transit
M.J.S.D. .... March, June, September, December
ml. .... milliter(s)
Mlle. .... Mademoiselle
mm. .... millimeter(s)
MM. .... Messieurs
Mme. .... Madam
Mmes. .... Mesdames
M. & N. .... May and November
mo. .... month(s)
M.O. .... money order
M.O.H. .... medical officer of health
M.P. .... Member of Parliament; mounted police; military police
m.p.h. .... miles per hour
Mr. .... Mister (not to be written out)
ms.(s) .... manuscript(s)
M.S. .... motor ship
M/s .... months after sight
M. & S. .... March and September
Msgr. .... Monsignor; Monseigneur
mst. .... measurement
M.S.T. .... Mountain standard time
mt. .... empty
Mt., mt. .... mountain
M.T. .... metric tone
mt.ct.cp. .... mortgage, certificate coupon (securities)
mtg. .... mortgage
m.v. .... market value
M.V. .... motor vessel

N

N. .... north
n/a .... no account (banking)
N/A .... no advice (banking)
n.a.a .... not always afloat (shipping)
NACA .... National Advisory Committee for Aeronautics
N.A.M. .... National Association of Manufacturers
N.A.S. .... National Academy of Science

natl. .... national
naut. .... nautical
n.b. *or* **N.B.** .... note well (*nota bene*)
N.B.C. *or* **NBC** .... National Broadcasting Company
N/C .... new charter; new crop
N.C.O. .... noncommissioned officer
n.c.u.p. .... no commission until paid
N.C.V. .... no commercial value
N.D., n.d. .... no date
n.e. .... not exceeding
N/E .... no effects (banking)
NEA .... Newspaper Enterprise Association
N.E.A. .... National Education Association; National Editorial Association
N.E.P. .... New Economic Policy (Russia)
n.e.s. .... not elsewhere specified
n/f .... no funds (banking)
N.F.M.A. .... November, February, May, August
N.G., ng. .... no good
N.H.P. .... nominal horsepower
N.L. .... night letter (telegraph)
NLRB .... National Labor Relations Board
N.L.T. .... night letter cable
N.M. .... night message
n/m .... no mark
N. & M. .... November and May
NMB .... National Mediation Board
NOMA .... National Office Management Association
No. .... number
N/O .... no orders (banking)
N.O.E. .... not otherwise enumerated
N.O.H.P. .... not otherwise herein provided
nom. std. .... nominal standard
non seq. .... does not follow (*non sequitur*)
N.O.S. .... not otherwise specified
N.P. .... no protest (banking)
n/p .... net proceeds
N.P.L. .... nonpersonal liability
n.r. .... no risk; net register
n.r.a.d. .... no risk after discharge
NS *or* **N.S.F.** .... not sufficient funds (banking)
n.s.p.f. .... not specially provided for
n.t. .... net ton; new terms (grain trade)
nv .... nonvoting (stocks)
nt.wt. .... net weight

O

o/a .... on account of
O. & A. .... October and April
ob. .... died (*obit*)
O.B./L, ob/l .... order bill of lading
obs. .... obsolete
o/c .... open charter; old charter; old crop; open cover; overcharge
o/d .... on demand
o.e. .... omissions excepted
OE .... Old English
O.J.A.J. .... October, January, April, July
O/o .... order of
o.p. .... out of print
O.P. .... open, *or* floating, policy
op. .... opinion
op. cit. .... in the work cited (*opere citato*)
o. & r. .... ocean and rail (transp.)
o.r. .... owners' risk (transportation)
o.r.b. .... owner's risk of breakage (transp.)
o.r.c. .... owner's risk of chafing (transp.)

ORC .... Officers' Reserve Corps
o.r.d. .... owner's risk of damage (transp.)
o.r.det. .... owner's risk of deterioration (transp.)
o.r.f. .... owner's risk of fire, *or* freezing (transp.)
o.r.l. .... owner's risk of leakage (transp.)
o.r.s. .... owner's risk of shifting (transp.)
o.r.w. .... owner's risk of becoming wet (transp.)
o/s .... out of stock
O/S .... on sample; on sale or return
o.s. & d. .... over, short, and damaged (transp.)
o/t .... old terms (grain trade); on truck
Oxon. .... of Oxford (*Oxoniensis*)
oz. .... ounce(s)

P

p. .... page
p.a. .... by the year (*per annum*)
P/A .... particular average; power of attorney; private account; Purchasing Agent
P.a.C. .... put and call (stock market)
pam. .... pamphlet
part. .... participating (securities)
pat. .... patent
Pat. Off. .... Patent Office
P/Av. .... particular average
P.B. .... permanent bunkers
P.B.X. .... private branch exchange (telephone)
p.c. .... per cent; post card
P/C .... price current; petty cash; per cent
P.D. .... port dues
pd. .... passed; paid
pfd. .... preferred
Pi. .... piaster(s)
p. & i. .... protection and indemnity
pk. .... peck(s)
pkg. .... package
p.l. .... partial loss
P. & L. .... profit and loss
plf. *or* **plff.** .... plaintiff
p.m. .... afternoon (*post meridiem*)
P.M. .... postmaster; Provost Marshall
pm. .... premium
P/N .... promissory note
P.O.D. .... pay on delivery
P.O.R. .... payable on receipt; payable on reorder
p.p. .... picked ports; on behalf of (*per procurationem*)
P.P. .... parcel post
pp. .... pages
ppd. .... prepaid
p.p.i. .... policy proof of interest (marine ins.)
ppt. .... prompt loading
pr. .... pair; price
pref. .... preface
Pres. .... President
prin. .... principal
Prof. .... Professor
pro tem. .... for the time being (*pro tempore*)
prox. .... proximate
P.S. .... postscript
P.S.T. .... Pacific standard time
P/S .... public sale
pt. .... pint(s)
P.T. .... Pacific time
p.t. .... private terms (grain trade)
p.w. .... packed weight (transp.)
Pvt. .... Private (Army)
pwt. .... pennyweight
P.X. .... please exchange; Post Exchange

Q

Q. .... question; query
q.d.a. .... quantity discount agreement
Q.E.D. .... which was to be proved or demonstrated (*quod erat demonstrandum*)
qlty. .... quality
QMGO .... Quartermaster General's Office
qn. .... quotation
QQ. .... questions; queries
qr. .... quarter
qt. .... quart(s)
q.v. .... which see (*quod vide*)

R

R/A .... refer to acceptor
RAR .... Regular Army Reserve
R/C .... reconsigned
r. & c. .... rail and canal (transp.)
r.c. & l. .... rail, canal, and lake (transp.)
rcd. .... received
R/D .... refer to drawer
r.d. .... running days
r.d.c. .... running down clause (marine ins.)
re .... in regard to
R.E. .... real estate
recd .... received
ref. .... referee
reg. .... registered; regulation(s)
rep. .... report
Rep. .... Republican
res. .... residue
retd. .... returned
Rev. .... Reverend
rev. A/C .... revenue account
revd., rev'd .... reversed
revg., rev'g .... reversing
rf., rfg. .... refunding (bonds)
r.f. .... radio frequency
RFC .... Reconstruction Finance Corporation
R.F.D. .... Rural Free Delivery
rfg. .... refunding
R.I. .... reinsurance
r. & l. .... rail and lake (transp.)
r.l. & r. .... rail, lake, and rail (transp.)
rm. .... ream (paper); room(s)
r. & o. .... rail and ocean (transp.)
R.O.G. .... receipt of goods
r.o.m. .... run of mine (coal)
ROTC .... Reserve Officers' Training Corps
rotn. no. .... rotation number
R.P. .... return premium
R/p .... return of post for orders
r.p.m. .... revolutions per minute
r.p.s. .... revolutions per second
R.R. .... railroad
RRB .... Railroad Retirement Board
R.S.V.P. .... please reply (*Répondez, s'il vous plait*)
R.V.S.V.P. .... please reply at once
r. & w. .... rail and water (transp.)
Rt. .... right(s) (stock)
Ry. .... Railway

S

s7d, s10d, s15d .... seller 7 days to deliver, etc. (stock market)
s/a .... subject to approval; safe arrival
S.A.E. .... Society of Automotive Engineers
s.a.n.r. .... subject to approval no risk (no risk until insurance is confirmed)
S/B .... statement of billing (transp.)
s.c. .... small capital letters; same case (legal)
sc., scil. .... namely, to wit (*scilicet*)

S.C. . . . . salvage charges
s. & c. . . . . shipper and carrier
s.c. & s. . . . . strapped, corded, and sealed (transp.)
s.d. . . . . without a day being named (*sine die*)
S/D . . . . sea-damaged (grain trade); sight draft
S.D.B.L. . . . . sight, draft, bill of lading attached
S.D.M.J. . . . . September, December, March, June
sec., secy. . . . . secretary
sec.(s) . . . . section(s)
SEC . . . . Securities and Exchange Commission
Sen. . . . . senate; senator
ser. . . . . series
S.F. . . . . sinking fund
sgd. . . . . signed
S. & F.A. . . . . shipping and forwarding
sh. . . . . share agent
sh.p. . . . . shaft horsepower
shpt. . . . . shipment
sh. tn. . . . . short ton
sic . . . . so; thus (to confirm a word that might be questioned)
s.i.t. . . . . stopping in transit (transp.)
sk. . . . . sack(s)
s.l. . . . . salvage loss
S. & M. September and March
S/N . . . . shipping note
S.O. . . . . seller's option; shipping order; ship's option
soc. . . . . society
S.O.L. . . . . Shipowner's liability
S.O.S. . . . . distress signal of ships
S.P. . . . . supra protest
s.p.a. . . . . subject to partial average (marine ins.)
s.p.d. . . . . steamer pays dues
sq. ft. . . . . square feet
sq. in. . . . . square inch(es)
sq. mi. . . . . square mile(s)
sq. rd. . . . . square rod(s)
sq. yd. . . . . square yard(s)
Sr. . . . . Senior; Señor
S.S. . . . . steamship; screw steamer
SSE . . . . south-southeast
SSW . . . . south-southwest
sta. . . . . station; stamped (securities)
stat. . . . . statute(s)
std. . . . . standard (timber trade)
stg. . . . . sterling
stk. . . . . stock
str. . . . . steamer
S.S. . . . . Steamship
S. to S. . . . . station to station
S.U.C.L. . . . . set up in carloads (transp.)
S.U.L.C.L. . . . . set up in less than carloads (transp.)
supp. . . . . supplement
supt. . . . . superintendent
s.v. . . . . sailing vessel
S.W. . . . . shipper's weights; southwest
S.W.G. . . . . standard wire gauge
syn. . . . . synonymous

T

t. . . . . metric ton(s)
T.A. . . . . Traffic Agent
t.b. . . . . trial balance
T/C . . . . until countermanded
T/D . . . . time deposit
T.E. . . . . trade expenses
tel. . . . . telegram; telegraph; telephone
tf. *or* t.f. . . . . till forbidden (advtg.)
T. & G. . . . . tongued and grooved (timber trade)
T.G.B. . . . . tongued, grooved, and beaded
T/L . . . . time loan
t.l.o. . . . . total loss only (marine ins.)
tn. . . . . ton

TNT .... trinitrotoluene
T/O .... transfer order
T/R .... trust receipt
tr. .... transpose
trans. .... transitive; translated; transportation
transp. .... transportation
treas. .... treasurer
T. R. .... tons registered (shipping)
T. T. .... telegraphic transfer
TVA .... Tennessee Valley Authority
TWP .... township
TWS .... timed wire service (telegraph)
ty., ter. .... territory

U

U. .... University
U/A .... underwriting account (marine ins.)
UGT .... urgent (cable)
ult. .... of the last month (*ultimo*)
U.N. .... United Nations
UNESCO .... United Nations Educational, Social, and Cultural Organization
univ. .... university
u.p. .... under proof
U.P., UP .... United Press
U/w .... underwriter

V

v. .... volt; versus
VA .... Veterans Administration
V.C. .... valuation clause
vid. .... see (*vide*)
viz. .... namely (*videlicet*)
vol. .... volume
v.o.p. .... value as in original policy
vs. .... verse; versus
vt. .... voting (stock)
v.v. .... vice versa

W

w. .... watt (elec.)
W. .... West
W.A. .... with average (marine ins.)
W.B. .... water ballast; warehouse book; way bill
w.b.s. .... without benefit of salvage (marine ins.)
w/d .... warranted
w.g. .... weight guaranteed
whsle. .... wholesale
w.i. .... when issued (stock exch.)
wk. .... week
w.l. .... wave length
W/M .... weight and/or measurement
WNW. .... west-northwest
W.O.L. wharfowners' liability
w.p. .... without prejudice; weather permitting
W.P.A. .... with particular average (marine ins.)
w.p.p. .... waterproof paper packing
W.R. .... warehouse receipt
w. & r. .... water and rail (transp.)
w.r.o. .... war risk only
wt. .... weight
W.W. ww. .... with warrants (securities)
W/W .... warehouse warrant

X

x-c. ***or*** **x-cp.** .... ex coupon
x-d. ***or*** **x-div.** .... ex dividend
x-i, ***or*** **x-in.** ***or*** **x-int.** .... ex interest
x-n. .... ex new
x-pr. .... ex privileges
x-rts. .... ex rights
xw .... ex warrants

Y

yb. .... yearbook
yd. .... yard
yr. .... year

Z

z. .... zone; zero

Abbreviations of Months and Days

Jan. .... January
Feb. .... February
Mar. .... March
Apr. .... April
May .... May
June .... June
July .... July
Aug. .... August
Sept. .... September
Oct. .... October
Nov. .... November
Dec. .... December

Sun. *or* S. .... Sunday
Mon. *or* M. .... Monday
Tues. *or* Tu. .... Tuesday
Wed. *or* W. .... Wednesday
Thurs. *or* Th. .... Thursday
Fri. *or* F. .... Friday
Sat. .... Saturday

Index

C

D

E

H

M

O

T

V

W

Y

Z

[illegible]